July 2003 through March 2004 Exams

Dalton Review *for the* CFP® *Certification Examination*

Volume I - Outlines and Study Guides

BISYS®

Your Vision • Our Solutions™

BISYS®
Your Vision • Our Solutions™

BISYS EDUCATION SERVICES

Formerly Dalton Publications
143 Mallard Street, Suite E
Saint Rose, Louisiana 70087
www.bisyseducation.com
www.daltonpublications.com

ISBN 1-890260-50-9 **Dalton Review for the CFP® Certification Examination: Volume I: Outlines and Study Guides**
2003 – 2004 Edition

ISBN 1-890260-51-7 Dalton Review for the CFP® Certification Examination: Volume II: Problems and Solutions
2003 – 2004 Edition

ISBN 1-890260-52-5 Dalton Review for the CFP® Certification Examination: Volume III: Case Exam Book
2003 – 2004 Edition

ISBN 1-890260-53-3 Dalton Review for the CFP® Certification Examination: 3-Volume Set
2003 – 2004 Edition

This publication is designed to provide accurate and authoritative information with regard to the subject matter covered. It is sold with the understanding that the publisher is not engaged in rendering legal, accounting, financial planning, or other professional services. If legal advice or other professional assistance is required, the services of a competent professional should be sought.

Certified Financial Planner Board of Standards, Inc. owns the marks CFP®, CERTIFIED FINANCIAL PLANNER™, and CFP (with flame logo)®, which it awards to individuals who successfully complete initial and ongoing certification requirements.

If found, please notify the following:

Name of CFP® Candidate:______________________________

Address:______________________________

City, State, Zip:______________________________

Phone:______________________________

E-mail: ______________________________

Additional information on review materials and live instructional review courses near you is available from:

www.bisyseducation.com
www.daltonpublications.com

Please visit our website regularly for updates to this and other products!

PRODUCTS AND SERVICES FOR THE CFP® CERTIFICATION EXAMINATION

LIVE INSTRUCTIONAL REVIEWS FOR THE CFP® CERTIFICATION EXAMINATION

Courses are offered in various cities around the country four to eight weeks prior to each CFP® Certification Examination (the exam) date. The program is designed to allow you to pass the exam while being both *effective and efficient*. The review is taught in two weekends (Friday, Saturday, and Sunday) for a total of six days. Exam specialists teach two four-hour sessions each day. Sessions cover Fundamentals of Financial Planning; Insurance Planning; Investment Planning; Income Tax Planning; Pensions, Employee Benefits, and Retirement Planning; Estate Planning; and Case Analysis.

Our instructors lecture on each topic in a concise manner and provide selected readings and problems from the Dalton Review for the CFP® Certification Examination texts. Instruction for the review course consists mainly of teaching substantive material and mastering both knowledge and application. The course includes working problems to assure that the substantive materials taught can be applied to the exam-like questions, as well as actual exam management techniques.

The following are tentative locations for our live instructional reviews:

VOLUME I: OUTLINES AND STUDY GUIDES, 7TH EDITION

The first volume of the three-volume set provides you with a complete reference outline in over 1,000 pages. Volume I includes detailed coverage of the six topics and is presented in an outline format. Each section contains examples, example questions, illustrations, and an index. The text is updated to reflect law and inflation adjustments through February 2003.

The introduction in *Volume I* presents helpful tips on what to expect when taking the exam, tips for studying, sample study plans, and a forecast of the number of questions expected in each area of the exam.

VOLUME II: PROBLEMS AND SOLUTIONS, 7TH EDITION

This second volume of the three-volume set offers over 1,500 multiple-choice problems, including 39 item sets to prepare you for the exam. The text is updated to reflect law and inflation adjustments through February 2003.

The answers to the multiple-choice problems and item sets in *Volume II* are identified by topical categories to assist you in focusing your study efforts. The introduction includes tips for solving both straight and combination-type multiple-choice problems.

VOLUME III: CASE EXAM BOOK, 7TH EDITION

Volume III completes the three-volume set and provides the exam candidate with 12 comprehensive cases (each with 15-26 multiple-choice questions in each case) updated to reflect law and inflation adjustments through February 2003. The answers and explanations for each multiple-choice question are provided. This text will prepare you for the three comprehensive cases given on the exam. Your preparation in this area is extremely important since case-type questions are weighted more heavily than the general multiple-choice questions.

Our students who have used the *Case Exam Book* have said that this book is a <u>must</u> if you want to be prepared for the exam!

MOCK EXAMS: SERIES A, EXAMS 1 AND 2

These supplements to the three-volume set simulate a session of the comprehensive exam. Each mock exam contains multiple-choice questions, item sets, a comprehensive case and will assist you in evaluating your performance prior to the actual exam.

The mock exams are diagnostic tools that you can use to assess your progress. They are useful in identifying areas of strengths and weakness and are excellent tools for creating a study program to meet your individual needs. The texts are updated to reflect law and inflation adjustments through February 2003.

UNDERSTANDING YOUR FINANCIAL CALCULATOR, 3RD EDITION

This text is designed to assist you in gaining proficiency in using and understanding your financial calculator. In addition to helping master the keystrokes for the financial calculator, it is also designed to assist students with the underlying financial theory-type problems given on the exam. Being familiar with the financial calculations is critical, since mastering these problems is an important step to passing the exam.

All calculations are worked out **step-by-step** showing keystrokes and displays for five of the most popular financial calculators. These include: HP 17B II, HP 12C, HP 10BII, TI BAII Plus, and Sharp EL-733A.

Understanding Your Financial Calculator covers the basic operations of the calculators, basic TVM calculations, fundamental problems (such as mortgages, education needs analysis, and retirement needs analysis), investment planning concepts, calculations (such as IRR, YTM, YTC, Sharpe, Treynor, Jensen, and standard deviation), and more. This text also includes a student workbook with over 200 basic, intermediate, and advanced practice problems and calculations. This text is a great reference for the exam and for practitioners.

FINANCIAL PLANNING FLASHCARDS, 5TH EDITION

Dalton Publications' Financial Planning Flashcards were created as a study supplement to the three-volume set. The set includes over 1,000 flashcards covering topics in each of the areas on the exam and can help you learn basic concepts and definitions. Flashcards provide an excellent way to learn the material by prompting you to recall facts and information quickly. Their portability makes them a valuable study tool for those on the go!

TEST BANK SOFTWARE

Our computerized test bank is an interactive software product including over 1,800 questions taken from *Volume II, Mock Exam A-1, Mock Exam A-2, Released Cases and Questions*, and additional practice questions written by our authors. The software will allow you to keep score, track your time and progress, and break down your score by sections.

FROM THE AUTHORS

This text is intended as the basis for preparation for the CFP® Certification Examination (the exam), either as self-study materials or as part of a review course. The materials in this volume are organized according to the six functional areas tested on the exam and are presented in an outline format that includes examples with questions and illustrations to help candidates quickly comprehend the material.

We have structured *Volume I* and *Volume II* into six manageable study units:

1. Fundamentals of Financial Planning
2. Insurance Planning
3. Investment Planning
4. Income Tax Planning
5. Retirement and Employee Benefit Planning
6. Estate Planning

The multiple-choice problems and item sets in *Volume II* have been grouped into primary categories that correspond to the major topic headings in the outlines from *Volume I.* In addition, the answers also identify more specific topical categories within each study unit.

We are indebted to Certified Financial Planner Board of Standards, Inc. for permission to reproduce and adapt their publications and other materials.

We welcome any comments concerning materials contained in or omitted from this text. Please send your written comments to BISYS Education Services, 143 Mallard Street, Suite E, St. Rose, Louisiana 70087, or fax your comments to us at (504) 461-9860.

Wishing you success on the exam.

Michael A. Dalton, Ph.D., JD, CPA, CLU, ChFC, CFP®

James F. Dalton, MBA, MS, CPA/PFS, CFA, CFP®

Cassie F. Bradley, Ph.D., CFP®

CHANGES FOR THE 2003 - 2004 EDITION

The 2003 - 2004 Edition of the Review texts for the CFP® Certification Examination includes several changes:

- Updated the materials to reflect law and inflation adjustments through February 2003.
- The Retirement Planning section in Volume I was revamped for better understanding.
- A new section in Volume II was added called "Cognitive Connections." This section contains questions that test the integration of at least 2 topics.
- One comprehensive case was added to each of the Mock Exams.
- Volumes I and II were streamlined and enhanced based on customer comments.

ACKNOWLEDGMENTS AND SPECIAL THANKS

We are most appreciative for the tremendous support and encouragement we have received from everyone throughout this project. We are extremely grateful to the users of out texts who were gracious enough to provide us with valuable comments concerning our first six editions.

We very much appreciate the continued support of the many registered programs who have adopted our Review Materials. We understand that our success is a direct result of that support.

We greatly appreciate the assistance of the following individuals who reviewed the outlines and problems and solutions for technical accuracy: Tim Bellows, JD, CFP®; Peter Blackwell, MBA, CFP®; Kevin Fink, CFP®; Randy Gardner, LLM, MBA, CPA, CFP®; Kathy Hartin, CPA, CFP®; and Randy Martinez, CPA, CFP®.

We have received so much help from so many people, it is possible that we inadvertently overlooked thanking someone. If so, it is our shortcoming, and we apologize in advance. Please let us know if you are that someone, and we will correct it in our next printing.

We deeply appreciate the cooperation of CFP Board for granting us permission to reproduce and adapt their publications and other materials. The following item copyrighted by CFP Board is reprinted (or adapted) with permission: CFP Board's Standards of Professional Conduct.

Thanks to John J. Dardis for granting us permission to use material from "Estate & Benefit Planning Symposium" in the Estate Planning outline of *Volume I.*

FUNDAMENTALS OF FINANCIAL PLANNING

INSURANCE PLANNING

INVESTMENT PLANNING

INCOME TAX PLANNING

RETIREMENT PLANNING

ESTATE PLANNING

INTRODUCTION

Introduction

Purpose of Volume I

This text is intended as the basis for preparation for the CFP® Certification Examination (the exam) either as self-study materials or as part of a review course. The materials in this volume are organized by the six topic areas tested on the exam and are presented in outline format using examples, questions, and exhibits to help candidates quickly comprehend the material.

Volume I contains information on the following areas:

- Fundamentals of Financial Planning
- Insurance Planning
- Investment Planning
- Income Tax Planning
- Retirement and Employee Benefit Planning
- Estate Planning

Before you begin your study, review the table of contents in both *Volume I* and *Volume II* to familiarize yourself with the topics related to the exam.

ABOUT THE CFP® CERTIFICATION EXAMINATION (THE EXAM)

EXAMINATION PROCEDURES

Read carefully the procedures outlined in the *Guide to CFP® Certification*. The section entitled "CFP® Certification Examination" covers:

- Dates of examinations
- Alternate test dates and test facilities
- Fees for the examination
- Scheduling confirmations
- Withdrawal from the exam
- Medical emergencies
- Items to bring to the examination
- Examination misconduct
- Examination scoring
- Score reports
- Pass score
- Reexamination procedures
- Review and appeals

A copy of the *Guide to CFP® Certification* may be obtained from:

Certified Financial Planner Board of Standards, Inc.
1700 Broadway, Suite 2100
Denver, CO 80290-2101
Telephone: (800) 487-1497
(303) 830-7500
Fax: (303) 860-7388
Website: www.CFP-Board.org
E-mail: initialcert@CFP-Board.org

DATE GIVEN

The exam is generally given on the third Friday and Saturday of March, July, and November each year.

Friday (1 session - afternoon)	4 hours
Saturday (2 sessions)	6 hours
Total	**10 hours**

Exam Dates	Application Deadline
July 18-19, 2003	June 4, 2003
November 21-22, 2003	October 8, 2003
March 19-20, 2004	February 4, 2004

For future exam dates, contact CFP Board at www.CFP-Board.org or call (303) 830-7543.

QUESTION TYPES

The examination consists of approximately 285 multiple-choice questions. The majority of these are stand-alone questions that contain all relevant information within the body of a problem. Also included are item set questions where one fact pattern will be used to answer several questions. A portion of the exam is in the form of case analysis. Each session of the exam contains one case with 15-20 questions. The information needed to answer these questions is generally found within the body of the case. These cases can be several pages long, making it difficult to efficiently organize the information to answer the questions.

The stand-alone questions, item sets, and case questions may test only one particular area of financial planning, such as investments. However, many of the questions are integrated questions, meaning that more than one topic is covered in the question. For example, a question might integrate investments and taxation. These integrated questions are designed to test your ability to analyze fact situations involving many planning considerations.

DISTRIBUTION OF TOPICS

The topics on the exam are targeted as follows:

Topic Covered	Percent of the Exam
Fundamentals	13%
Insurance	10%
Investments	19%
Income Tax	17%
Employee Benefits	8%
Retirement	18%
Estates	15%
Total	**100%**

* The majority of topics within the employee benefits section are discussed in the retirement section. The remaining topics in employee benefits are discussed in the tax and insurance sections. For an in-depth breakdown of all topics, please refer to the updated topic list, located in the *Guide to CFP® Certification.*

Cognitive Levels Tested (Target)	Percent of the Exam
Knowledge Level	5%
Comprehension/Application	35%
Analysis/Synthesis/Evaluation	60%
Total	**100%**

Scoring Method	Point Value per Question	Approximate Number	Points	Percent
Stand-alone questions and item sets	2 points	235	470	76%
Case questions	3 points	50	150	24%
Total		**285**	**620**	**100%**

The examination division of the CFP Board assigns the value weights to questions according to type, cognitive level, and level of difficulty.

TIME AND TIME ANALYSIS

There are 10 hours of examination time.

1. Friday (4 hours) – 1 case, item sets, and multiple choice.
2. Saturday (morning session – 3 hours) – 1 case, item sets, and multiple choice.
3. Saturday (afternoon session – 3 hours) – 1 case, item sets, and multiple choice.
4. Approximately 285 questions overall.
5. Case questions 15-20 per case.

	Time (minutes)	Approximate Number of Multiple-Choice Questions	Average Time
Average indicated time per stand-alone and item set question	400	235	1.5 - 1.7 minutes each (Friday and Saturday)
Average indicated time per case question	200	50	4.0 minutes each (Friday and Saturday)
Average indicated time per question	600	285	2.1 minutes each (Overall)

The authors suggest that you strive to average 1.5 minutes per question throughout your study in *Volume II.* The cases and case analyses presented in *Volume III: Case Exam Book* should provide you with a realistic approximation of exam conditions regarding cases. The case multiple-choice questions should take about 75-90 minutes per set, including reading the case.

PASS RATES

The pass rates have ranged from 42% to 66% on recent exams. This exam is a pass/fail professional exam with no partial credit. Therefore, it is vitally important that you be thoroughly prepared for all the topics covered on this examination.

DALTON'S PASS RATES

Dalton's Live Instructional Reviews have consistently averaged a 70% to 80% first-time pass rate. In fact, of the students who use Dalton Publications' study materials and attend Dalton Live Reviews, 90% to 95% are successful in their pursuit of CFP® certification.

PLAN YOUR STUDY TIME

BE PREPARED TO SPEND THE TIME

- The CFP® Certification Examination (the exam) will demand a great deal of your time and effort. Make passing a priority in your life. If it is not in your top three or four priorities at this time, perhaps you should wait until it is.
- A comprehensive review will take you approximately 300 hours including any time spent in or out of class. This time will vary depending on your level of knowledge in the base material and your experience in the practice or simulated practice of financial planning. Whether or not you attend a live review will also impact the amount of study time necessary to pass. The Dalton Live Review will focus you on what you need to know to pass the exam and will streamline your study efforts.
- Do not fool yourself! This exam is comparable to other professional exams, such as the CPA exam, CFA exams, or Bar exam, and is extremely rigorous.

KNOW YOUR FINANCIAL CALCULATOR

- You need a very thorough knowledge of your financial calculator. It is imperative that you are familiar with the time-value-of-money calculations, as well as the underlying financial theory. If you are deficient in this area, you should take the time (approximately 6-8 hours) to learn the calculator before beginning your study program.
- Work problems 71-118 in the fundamentals section of *Volume II* as practice. Also, work thoroughly through *Understanding Your Financial Calculator* book.
- It is especially helpful to learn the keystrokes. Pay close attention to where the cash flows occur in time. Mastering these problems is an important step in passing the exam.
- We recommend the HP 12C, HP 10B, HP 10BII, or an equivalent.

DEVELOP A STUDY PLAN

- The exam is comprehensive and encompasses an enormous amount of material and information. Studying on a regular basis will be a great asset in accomplishing your goal of passing the exam. With work, family, eating, and sleeping, much of the day is already gone. For this reason, it is important to develop a study plan and keep study materials with you at all times.
- Get organized. Make a preliminary study plan keeping all specifics (such as date, number of problems attempted, number correct, total time (hours), etc.). Your study plan should be divided into the six subject areas for more manageable use of your study time. You may want to use the sample study plan at the end of this section to track your progress.
- You will need self-discipline to adhere to your plan.

SAMPLE YOUR KNOWLEDGE

- It is crucial to begin your study program by first evaluating your current knowledge. Once you have an idea of what you currently know, you must then determine the areas in which you are deficient. Basically, you must determine where your strengths and weaknesses lie.
- We recommend that you sample your knowledge by taking a random sample of 20 multiple-choice questions in each of the six major areas from *Volume II*. Be sure to mark the time that you start and the time that you finish. Put a (G) by any questions where you had to guess the answer.
- If you score above 70% in any area, take another sample and continue with this method as long as your percentage correct stays above 70%. Continue until you have answered all the questions. Anytime you score less than 70%, you should carefully read the entire outline in *Volume I* that relates to the material you have been testing, then, take another sample.
- Note the questions you answer incorrectly and the topics they cover. Go over those questions and allow time to devote more study time to the areas to which they pertain.
- Most candidates will need practice in some topical areas in each of the above. Don't be discouraged.
- We recommend that you write down your progress in your study plan. Try to get each topic to 65%-70% correct with one or more above 80%. You are almost certain to pass.
- Evaluation:
    - 80% or more correct and 1.7 minutes or less per question = extremely well prepared.
    - 70% or more correct and 1.7 minutes or less per question = well prepared.
    - 50-60% or more correct and 2.0 minutes or less per question = marginally prepared (risk).
    - Less than 50% and/or over 2.0 minutes per question = need serious review (serious risk).

TIME MANAGEMENT

- After you determine your areas of strength and weakness, you should be able to estimate the number of hours you will need to study in order to pass the exam. At this point, you should take out your calendar, and count the number of weeks you have remaining to study prior to the exam. Divide the number of hours you need to study by the number of weeks until the exam. This will allow you to determine the number of hours you must study per week. This figure can then be further refined into hours to study per weekday and per weekend, etc.
- For example, Paul is taking the exam in November. It is now the middle of July, and he has just received his Dalton materials. He purchased the full set, *Volumes I, II, and III, Understanding Your Financial Calculator, Mock A-1, Mock A-2,* the *Financial Planning Flashcards,* and the *Test Bank.* He has registered for and plans to attend a Dalton Live Instructional Review. He has 17 weeks until the exam and has decided that he needs to study a full 350 hours to pass. Based on this information, he will need to study 20 hours per week. To accomplish this goal, Paul decided to study 2 hours each weekday and 10 hours on the weekend (except for the weeks he attends the Live Review). He will always carry at least one section of the flashcards with him so that he can make the best use of any "downtime" he encounters. Using this information (along with Paul's knowledge of his own areas of strength and weakness), Paul decided the following schedule would be appropriate:

Week	Topics to Cover	Hours
1	*Understanding Your Financial Calculator*	20
2	Fundamentals *Volume I* (all) and Fundamentals *Volume II* (half)	20
3	Fundamentals *Volume II* (half) and Insurance *Volume I* (all)	20
4	Insurance *Volume II* (all) and Investments *Volume I* (half)	20
5	Investments *Volume I* (half) and Investments *Volume II* (all)	20
6	Estates *Volume I* (all) and Estates *Volume II* (half)	20
7	Estates *Volume II* (half) and Retirement *Volume I* (all)	20
8	Retirement *Volume II* (all) and Tax *Volume I* (half)	20
9	Tax *Volume I* (half) and Tax *Volume II* (all)	20
10	Item Sets, Cognitive Connections and catch-up	20
11	Test Bank and attend Live Review	34
12	Test Bank and attend Live Review	34
13	*Volume III* (half)	20
14	*Volume III* (half)	20
15	*Mock A-1* and *Mock A-2* and review	12
16	Review weak topics and catch-up	20
17	Review weak topics	10

MONTHLY CALENDAR

- You might find it beneficial to invest in a large monthly calendar and hang it where you will see it every day. Be sure to mark all of your upcoming commitments with regard to work, family, outside activities, etc., on your calendar. This will help you plan and anticipate any time constraints that may lead to obstacles in your study program. For example, during Week 3 of Paul's schedule, he knows that he must attend an out-of-town wedding and will only have time to study the two hours he is on the plane. Even though he will make good use of his flashcards during that time, he still must adjust his schedule to spend more time studying during Weekend 2 and on the weekdays during Weeks 2 and 3 in order to compensate for the fluctuation in his study program. You may find that you will need to cancel commitments or turn down new commitments you would otherwise accept in order to maintain your focus. Remember, your study time for the CFP® Certification Examination is limited and must be one of your top priorities!
- You will also want to indicate on your calendar the subject areas on which you plan to focus your study time each week. This will help you plan which commitments you will and will not be able to accept as weeks go by. For example, in Week 8 Paul's brother calls and wants to schedule dinner for Week 9. Paul knows that he will be studying tax (his hardest subject) and that this area might require more study time than other areas. Thus, Paul decides that he should not schedule any additional events for Week 9, and declines.
- Make the most of your travel time to and from the Live Review. For example, because Paul will be traveling to and from the Live Review by train, he can study the remaining sections of his flashcards.

WEEKLY CALENDAR

- Before you begin your first week of study, list all of the activities in which you participate. Determine how long each activity takes to complete and whether or not this activity is performed at a specific time each day, week, month, etc.
- Make sure to include your work hours, drive time, family time, meals, sleep, and any other miscellaneous activities you might do that take up your time. You may want to use the sample schedule at the end of this section to track your activities.
- Once you have logged your activities in your weekly and monthly calendars, review your schedule, and decide which time slots are full and which are open. Using this information, you should be able to develop a realistic study plan for each day. If you find that your current activities do not leave you enough free time to study, you will need to eliminate enough activities so that you will have adequate study time to prepare for the exam. If you discover that you do not have the appropriate amount of time for exam preparation, it would be to your benefit to postpone taking the exam until it is a higher priority or until you have fewer commitments. Before each week begins, review your weekly schedule and update it for any new commitments. Although you will need to be flexible with your scheduled study time, it is important to stick with your scheduled study time as much as possible. Try to anticipate missed study time and be sure to reschedule the missed time for another day.

MAKE A DAILY TO-DO LIST

- Before you begin each study session, make a tentative list of what you want to accomplish during your study time. You may also want to keep a spiral notebook or binder so you will be able to continuously evaluate and reevaluate your progress. Write down the number of pages that you plan to read and/or the number of problems that you plan to work during your study session. Be realistic when you write this list and work very hard to stick to your study plan.

PREPARE TO STUDY

There are many ways you can maximize the benefits of your study time. The following are some of our suggestions to most efficiently and effectively study:

CREATE A SUITABLE STUDY ENVIRONMENT

The most important thing you can do to help facilitate your studying is to create a suitable study environment. Your study area should be:

1. Quiet. You want to find a place that is free from all extraneous noise (including the television and disruptive people).
2. Away from distractions. Stay away from areas where there are a lot of distractions. For example, try not to study close to a telephone, since you might be tempted to answer it and talk. You might also want to try to avoid studying at work or at home if coworkers or family members will interrupt you.
3. Study in a well lit location. You will want to study in an area where you will be able to see the information as well as stay awake and alert.
4. Be comfortable, but not too comfortable. You want to be relaxed so that you see studying as a beneficial activity and not a punishment. You should not, however, let yourself get so comfortable that you will be tempted to fall asleep.
5. Have all of your materials readily available. Gather everything you will need during your study session beforehand. This includes pencils, pens, books, highlighters, a calculator, and paper. Try to sit at a desk or table so that you have a firm writing surface and room for all of your materials.

USE THE MULTIPLE-CHOICE QUESTIONS TO DIRECT YOUR STUDY

- Keep in mind that you should not spend the majority of your study time on material you've already learned. There is a natural tendency to do so, as it is a lot more fun and certainly more comforting, but unfortunately, counter-productive. The subject in which you scored the lowest should be studied the most. The multiple-choice questions can be used as a monitoring tool if you keep thorough records. We recommend that you study the multiple-choice questions and the outlines as needed. You should use the three volumes to complement your comprehensive study plan.

BECOME THOROUGHLY KNOWLEDGEABLE WITH THE MATERIAL

- The exam is professionally rigorous and tests across Bloom's Taxonomy of Cognitive Learning. You can expect a small percentage of problems to test at the knowledge level and a much larger percentage to test at the application, synthesis, and evaluation levels.
- The difference in passing and failing is the difference between being thoroughly prepared and proactive, versus being casually acquainted and reactive. For example, when you think of IRAs, your mind should create a picture of the following topics that relate to IRAs:
  - Eligibility
  - Deductible/nondeductible
  - Allocation between spouses
  - Transferability
  - Rollover
  - Assignment/pledging
  - Investments
  - Penalties
  - Distribution prior to 70½
  - Minimum distributions
  - Roth IRAs and Coverdell Education Savings Accounts
  - Death
  - Inclusion in Gross Estate
  - QDRO
  - Active participation in a pension plan
  - Joint life distribution
- You should be immediately prepared and ready to answer any question about any subtopic in IRAs. If the mentioning of IRAs does not bring anything to mind, or if only a few of the listed topics come to mind, you are not thoroughly knowledgeable.
- The problem with being only casually acquainted with the material is twofold: (1) you take too much time thinking of an answer, and (2) you let the exam lead you to incorrect answers. You must discipline yourself to aggressively answer the questions and you must monitor the time it takes you to answer the average multiple-choice question. Remember, when you are thoroughly knowledgeable, the questions are fairly easy. When you are only casually acquainted, the questions are much harder and take longer to answer.

TEXTBOOK PREVIEWING

As you are reviewing *Volume I*, there are two things you should do:

- Be sure to study the title of each section. Not only will this preview what you are about to read, it will also help you to narrow your scope of study.
- Look for relationships. By looking for relationships between current information and subjects you have read about previously, you can learn to group concepts together and increase memory retention.

THINGS TO MARK

- Definitions. Often knowing a word's definition can help you to distinguish terms that might otherwise prove confusing. On the exam, knowing the definition of key words and concepts can often help you eliminate possible answers on multiple-choice questions.
- Signal words. Words such as, "and," "or," "except," "not," and "also," indicate the relationships between concepts.
- Key words and phrases. Key words are words or phrases that should instantly bring to mind a number of questions, issues, or ideas relating to the topics identified by the key words or phrases. For example, the phrase "substantial and reoccurring" is a key phrase that relates to the funding of profit-sharing plans. Keywords and phrases are the foundation on which you should build your basis of knowledge.

NOTE-TAKING METHODS

- Flashcards or note cards. Notes taken on note cards can also be used as valuable tools for review. You can use them as flashcards, which are much more portable than textbooks or notebooks, and force memory recall, which is a requirement of the exam. You can create your own flashcards or use Dalton's Financial Planning Flashcards which number over 1,000, to enhance your studying on the go.
- Study notes. Traditional study notes allow you to trigger key concepts that you have read about. This is crucial for review purposes. Study notes should be rewritten within 48 hours of taking them to clarify any areas that seem ambiguous.

STUDY METHODS

SQ3R Study System

- Survey. Glance through material and get a general idea about the key information within the text.
- Question. Think about questions that could be asked about the material. If the section title is "Key Concepts of Estate Planning," a possible question might be, "*What are the key concepts of estate planning?*"
- Read. Read through the material carefully, marking the text and taking notes as you go.
- Recite. After each section, pretend that you are lecturing to a friend or colleague on the material. Are you able to retain the information?
- Review. Be sure to go over each section and review information that you might be confused about.

SOAR Study Formula

- Survey the book. Skim over the outline topics. Review the table of contents to see the major categories of information. Review the index for important topics and keywords. Also look at each individual section and review the topics, major points, and information contained within each section.
- Organize. Organize the information that you have read and taken notes on. Some ways to facilitate this are to:
    - Underline books.
    - Make notes for books (charts, note cards, etc.)
- Anticipate. Anticipate the information that you think will be tested. Formulate possible test questions, and evaluate your ability to answer these questions correctly in a testing environment.
- Recite and Review. Just as with the SQ3R method, the SOAR method places final emphasis on being able to recite information as if lecturing on its key points and reviewing any areas where you have deficiencies.

MNEMONICS

- Mnemonics literally translates to, "to help the memory." These are techniques that can be incorporated into your study plan in order to increase your retention of information. The most common use of mnemonics is to create an acronym or a sentence with the first letter of each keyword. For instance, "PRIME" is an acronym used to help students remember systematic risks. P-R-I-M-E stands for Purchasing Power Risk, Reinvestment Rate Risk, Interest Rate Risk, Market Risk, and Exchange Rate Risk.

DALTON'S FINAL TIPS

- Avoid whining. Avoid whining about your having to know or learn some area of financial planning that is technical and that most planners have to look up. One purpose of the exam is to serve as gatekeeper to the profession; another is to help you develop a healthy sense of professional humility about what you know. Also, clients will expect you to know everything.
- Study what you don't know. Your lowest-scoring subject should be the subject you study the most.
- Think positively. It will help you pass.
- Find a way to make it fun. Don't fight the problem.

STUDY PLAN

Date	# Attempted	# Correct	% Correct	Average Time per Question	Study Outline	Total Time	Notes

WEEKLY ACTIVITIES/COMMITMENTS

Time	Monday	Tuesday	Wednesday	Thursday	Friday	Saturday	Sunday
12 am							
1							
2							
3							
4							
5							
6							
7							
8							
9							
10							
11							
12 pm							
1							
2							
3							
4							
5							
6							
7							
8							
9							
10							
11							

EXPECTED QUESTION DISTRIBUTION

The authors have prepared an analysis of the likely topics and frequency of expected questions as indicated in this section.

FUNDAMENTALS OF FINANCIAL PLANNING EXAM ANALYSIS

	Number of Expected Questions	Percent of Exam
The Financial Planning Process	3 questions	
Financial Statements	2 questions	
Budgeting	1 question	
Internal Analysis	2 questions	
Personal Use -- Assets and Liabilities	2 questions	
Economics	2 questions	
Financial Institutions	2 questions	
Time Value of Money	8 questions	
Educational Funding	3 questions	
Business Organizations	2 questions	
Property	2 questions	
Consumer Protection	2 questions	
Bankruptcy and Reorganization	2 questions	
Regulatory Requirements	2 questions	
Ethics	2 questions	
Expected on Exam	***37 questions***	***13%***

INSURANCE PLANNING EXAM ANALYSIS

	Number of Expected Questions	Percent of Exam
Principles of Insurance	2 questions	
Risk Exposure	3 questions	
Legal Aspects	2 questions	
Property and Liability	4 questions	
Life Insurance	4 questions	
Health Insurance and Long-Term Care	4 questions	
Disability Insurance	3 questions	
Employee Benefits	2 questions	
Social Insurance	2 questions	
Other (including tax and business use)	2 questions	
Expected on Exam	*28 questions*	*10%*

INVESTMENT PLANNING EXAM ANALYSIS

	Number of Expected Questions	Percent of Exam
Basic Investment Concepts	5 questions	
Securities	12 questions	
Security Markets	3 questions	
Securities Law	3 questions	
Security Market Indexes	1 questions	
Investment Concepts	8 questions	
Security Analysis	6 questions	
Performance Measurements	7 questions	
Investment Strategies	4 questions	
Client Assessment	5 questions	
Expected on Exam	*54 questions*	*19%*

INCOME TAX PLANNING EXAM ANALYSIS

	Number of Expected Questions	Percent of Exam
Fundamentals/Compliance	4 questions	
Tax Computation and Concepts	14 questions	
Accounting Methods	3 questions	
Business Entities	3 questions	
Trusts and Estates	3 questions	
Basis	4 questions	
Depreciation	2 questions	
Like-Kind Exchanges	2 questions	
Property	5 questions	
AMT	3 questions	
Passive Activity Rules	2 questions	
Charitable Contributions	3 questions	
Expected on Exam	*48 questions*	*17%*

RETIREMENT PLANNING EXAM ANALYSIS

	Number of Expected Questions	Percent of Exam
Retirement Needs Analysis	2 questions	
Social Security plus Medicare	7 questions	
Retirement Plans	9 questions	
Qualified Plan Rules	8 questions	
Distributions	5 questions	
Other Tax-Advantaged Plans	7 questions	
Analysis of Factors	8 questions	
Regulatory Requirements	2 questions	
Invested Consideration	3 questions	
Expected on Exam	*51 questions*	*18%*

EMPLOYEE BENEFITS PLANNING EXAM ANALYSIS

	Number of Expected Questions	**Percent of Exam**
Group Insurance, Tax Implications	2 questions	
Group Disability	3 questions	
Group Medical, including COBRA	2 questions	
Cafeteria Plans, Flexible Spending	3 questions	
Stock Options (ISOs, NQSOs)	4 questions	
Nonqualified Plans	6 questions	
Stock Plans	3 questions	
Expected on Exam	*23 questions*	*8%*

ESTATE PLANNING EXAM ANALYSIS

	Number of Expected Questions	**Percent of Exam**
Basic Concepts	1 question	
Basic Documents	3 questions	
Property Ownership Interest	2 questions	
Probate Process	2 questions	
Federal Gift & Estate Tax	7 questions	
Valuation of Assets	2 questions	
Marital Deduction	2 questions	
Trusts	3 questions	
Other Lifetime Transfers	5 questions	
Life Insurance in Estate Planning	2 questions	
GSTT	2 questions	
Special Provisions	3 questions	
Postmortem Planning	3 questions	
Estate Tax Reduction Techniques	4 questions	
Common Estate Planning Mistakes	2 questions	
Expected on Exam	*43 questions*	*15%*

YOUR COMMENTS FOR VOLUME I: OUTLINES AND STUDY GUIDES

Our goal is to provide a high-quality product to you and other CFP® candidates. With this goal in mind, we hope to significantly improve our texts with each new edition. We welcome your written suggestions, corrections, and other general comments. Please be as detailed as possible and send your written comments to:

BISYS Education Services
143 Mallard Street, Suite E
St. Rose, Louisiana 70087
(504) 461-9860 Fax

	Page	Question	Comments for Volume I (please be as specific as possible)
1.	______	______	______
2.	______	______	______
3.	______	______	______
4.	______	______	______
5.	______	______	______
6.	______	______	______
7.	______	______	______
8.	______	______	______
9.	______	______	______
10.	______	______	______
11.	______	______	______
12.	______	______	______
13.	______	______	______
14.	______	______	______
15.	______	______	______

Name ______________________

Address ______________________

Phone __________ (Work) __________ (Home) __________ (Fax)

E-mail ______________ **Do you require a response?** ________ **Yes** ________ **No**

Fundamentals of Financial Planning

Outlines and Study Guides

TABLE OF CONTENTS

TABLE OF EXHIBITS

Fundamentals

I. THE FINANCIAL PLANNING PROCESS

The financial planning process is an excerpt from the "Topic List for CFP® Certification Examination" and has been reprinted with permission of the CFP Board.

A. Establishing Client-Planner Relationships.

1. Explain issues and concepts related to the overall financial planning process, as appropriate to the client.
2. Explain services provided, the process of planning, documentation required.
3. Clarify client's and CFP® practitioner's responsibilities.

B. Gathering Client Data and Determining Goals and Expectations.

1. Obtain information from client through interview/questionnaire about financial resources and obligations.
2. Determine client's personal and financial goals, needs, and priorities.
3. Assess client's values, attitudes, and expectations.
4. Determine client's time horizons.
5. Determine client's risk tolerance level.
6. Collect applicable client records and documents.

C. Determining the Client's Financial Status by Analyzing and Evaluating General Financial Status, Special Needs, Insurance and Risk Management, Investments, Taxation, Employee Benefits, Retirement, and/or Estate Planning.

1. General.
    a. Current financial status (e.g., assets, liabilities, cash flow, debt management).
    b. Capital needs.
    c. Attitudes and expectations.
    d. Risk tolerance.
    e. Risk management.
    f. Risk exposure.
2. Special needs.
    a. Divorce/remarriage considerations.
    b. Charitable planning.
    c. Adult dependent needs.
    d. Disabled child needs.
    e. Education needs.
    f. Terminal illness planning.
    g. Closely held business planning.

3. Risk management.
    a. Life insurance needs and current coverage.
    b. Disability insurance needs and current coverage.
    c. Health insurance needs and current coverage.
    d. Long-term care insurance needs and current coverage.
    e. Homeowners insurance needs and current coverage.
    f. Auto insurance needs and current coverage.
    g. Other liability insurance needs and current coverage (e.g., umbrella, professional, errors and omissions, directors and officers).
    h. Commercial insurance needs and current coverage.
4. Investments.
    a. Current investments.
    b. Current investment strategies and policies.
5. Taxation.
    a. Tax returns.
    b. Current tax strategies.
    c. Tax compliance status (e.g., estimated tax).
    d. Current tax liabilities.
6. Employee benefits.
    a. Available employee benefits.
    b. Current participation in employee benefits.
7. Retirement.
    a. Current retirement plan tax exposures (e.g., excise tax, premature distribution tax).
    b. Current retirement plans.
    c. Social Security benefits.
    d. Retirement strategies.
8. Estate planning.
    a. Estate planning documents.
    b. Estate planning strategies.
    c. Estate tax exposures.

D. DEVELOPING AND PRESENTING THE FINANCIAL PLAN.

1. Developing and preparing a client-specific financial plan tailored to meet the goals and objectives of the client, commensurate with client's values, temperament, and risk tolerance, covering:
   a. Financial position.
      i. Current statement.
      ii. Projected statement.
      iii. Projected statement with recommendations.
   b. Cash flow.
      i. Projections.
      ii. Recommendations.
      iii. Projection with recommendations.
   c. Estate tax.
      i. Projections.
      ii. Recommendations.
      iii. Projection with recommendations.
   d. Capital needs at retirement.
      i. Projections.
      ii. Recommendations.
      iii. Projection with recommendations.
   e. Capital needs projections at death.
      i. Recommendations.
      ii. Projection with recommendations.
   f. Capital needs: disability.
      i. Recommendations.
      ii. Projection with recommendations.
   g. Capital needs: special needs.
      i. Recommendations.
      ii. Projection with recommendations.
   h. Income tax.
      i. Projections.
      ii. Recommendations.
      iii. Projection with strategy recommendations.
   i. Employee benefits.
      i. Projections.

j. Asset allocation.
   i. Statement.
   ii. Strategy recommendations.
   iii. Statement with recommendations.

k. Investment.
   i. Recommendations.
   ii. Policy statement.
   iii. Policy recommendations.
   iv. Policy statement with recommendations.

l. Risk.
   i. Assessment.
   ii. Recommendations.

m. List of prioritized action items.

2. Presenting and reviewing the plan with the client.
3. Collaborating with the client to ensure that plan meets the goals and objectives of the client, revising as appropriate.

E. IMPLEMENTING THE FINANCIAL PLAN.

1. Assist the client in implementing the recommendations.
2. Coordinate as necessary with other professionals, such as accountants, attorneys, real estate agents, investment advisers, stockbrokers, and insurance agents.

F. MONITORING THE FINANCIAL PLAN.

1. Monitor and evaluate soundness of recommendations.
2. Review the progress of the plan with the client.
3. Discuss and evaluate changes in client's personal circumstances (e.g., birth/death, age, illness, divorce, and retirement).
4. Review and evaluate changing tax laws and economic circumstances.
5. Make recommendations to accommodate new or changing circumstances.

Note: See section, "CFP Board's Financial Planning Practice Standards" on page 183 for additional information

II. PERSONAL FINANCIAL STATEMENTS

A. STATEMENT OF FINANCIAL POSITION (BALANCE SHEET).

See Exhibit 1 at the end of this section.

1. Assets and liabilities should be presented at fair market value (FMV).
2. Statement needs to be appropriately dated.
3. Net worth should be indicated.
4. Footnotes should be utilized to describe details of both assets and liabilities.
5. Property should be identified with owner (e.g., JTWROS, or H for husband, W for wife, etc.).
6. Categories of assets - Depends on type and use of asset.
    a. Cash and cash equivalents.
    b. Invested assets (investment portfolio).
    c. Use assets (residence, furniture, and autos).
    d. Assets should be listed in order of liquidity (the ability to convert to cash quickly).
7. Liabilities should be categorized according to maturity date.
    a. Current liabilities - due within one year.
    b. Long-term liabilities - generally mortgages and notes.
8. Net Worth = Assets - Liabilities.

B. STATEMENT OF RECURRING CASH FLOWS (FOR PAST YEAR AND PRO FORMA FOR NEXT YEAR).

See Exhibit 2 at the end of this section.

1. Indicate period covered.
2. Inflows:
    a. Gross salaries.
    b. Interest income.
    c. Dividend income.
    d. Rental income.
    e. Refunds due (tax).
    f. Other incoming cash flows.
    g. Alimony received.
3. Outflows:
    a. Savings and investment - by item.
    b. Fixed outflows - nondiscretionary.
        i. House payments.
        ii. Auto payments.
        iii. Taxes.

   c. Fixed outflows - discretionary.
      i. Club dues.
      ii. Utilities (a portion may be a variable outflow).
   d. Variable outflows - nondiscretionary.
      i. Food.
   e. Variable outflows - discretionary.
      i. Vacations.
      ii. Entertainment.
4. Net discretionary cash flow = inflows - outflows.
5. Footnotes should be used to explain details of income and expenses.

EXHIBIT 1: STATEMENT OF FINANCIAL POSITION EXAMPLE

Dennis and Denise Smith
Statement of Financial Position
As of January 1, 2003

ASSETS[1]			LIABILITIES AND NET WORTH[2]		
Cash/Cash Equivalents			**Liabilities**		
JT	Cash (Money Market)	$40,000	Current:		
			H	Bank Credit Card 1	$5,000
	Total Cash/Cash Equivalents	$40,000	W	Bank Credit Card 2	7,000
			W	Bank Credit Card 3	8,000
Invested Assets			H	$Auto_1$ Note Balance	10,000
W	Publications, Inc.	$300,000	W	$Auto_2$ Note Balance	10,000
W	Denise's Bakery	100,000		Current Liabilities	$40,000
W	Denise's Investment Portfolio	90,000			
H	SPDA	110,801	Long-Term:		
H	Dennis' Investment Portfolio (IRA)	200,000	Mortgage - Primary Residence		$150,000
H	Defined Benefit Plan (Vested)	400,000	Mortgage - Vacation Home		120,000
	Total Investments	$1,200,801		Long-Term Liabilities	$270,000
Personal Use Assets				Total Liabilities	$310,000
JT	Primary Residence	$300,000			
JT	Vacation Home	180,000		**Net Worth**	$1,552,801
JT	Personal Property & Furniture	100,000			
H	Auto1	20,000			
W	Auto2	22,000			
	Total Personal Use	$622,000			
	Total Assets	**$1,862,801**		**Total Liabilities & Net Worth**	**$1,862,801**

Notes to financial statements:

[1] All assets are stated at fair market value.

[2] Liabilities are stated at principal only.

Titles and Ownership Information

H = Husband

W = Wife

JT = Joint husband and wife (with survivorship rights) - JTWROS

EXHIBIT 2: STATEMENT OF CASH FLOW EXAMPLE

Charles and Vicki Jones
Statement of Cash Flow
January 1, 2003 to December 31, 2003

Inflows - Annual		
Charles' Schedule C Net Income	$42,000	
Vicki's Salary	55,000	
Dividend Income	1,220	
Interest Income	1,110	
		$99,330
Outflows - Annual		
Savings and Investments		
IRAs	$4,000	
Dividends	1,220	
Interest	1,110	
		$6,330
Fixed Outflows - Annual		
Mortgage (P&I)	$11,592	
Property Taxes	3,000	
Home Owners Insurance	720	
Utilities	1,200	
Telephone	1,200	
Auto (P&I) Payment	9,000	
Auto Insurance	1,800	
Gas/Oil/Maintenance	3,600	
Credit Card Payments	7,200	
		$39,312
Variable Outflows		
Taxes[1]	$26,142	
Food	8,490	
Medical/Dental	2,400	
Clothing/Personal Care	3,600	
Child Care	3,000	
Entertainment/Vacation	3,000	
Discretionary	6,564	
		$53,688
		$99,330
[1]Notes on taxes		
FICA - Charles	$5,935	
FICA - Vicki	4,208	
Est. Pmts - Charles	5,000	
Fed. W/H - Vicki	11,000	
	$26,142	

III. ANALYSIS OF FINANCIAL STATEMENTS AND IDENTIFICATION OF STRENGTHS AND WEAKNESSES

A. DESCRIBED.

1. Information on financial statements provides useful information to financial planners.

Examples

1. For a given asset, there may be a corresponding liability and a payment, which should be shown or is shown on the cash flow statement.
2. For any given liability, there should be a corresponding asset.

B. RATIO ANALYSIS.

1. Ratio analysis will give the planner a good idea or starting point in analyzing the client's financial situation.
   a. Liquidity Ratio = Liquid assets ÷ monthly expenses. Most planners suggest 3 - 6 months coverage of fixed and variable outflows.
   b. Housing Payment Ratio = All monthly nonexecutory housing costs* ÷ monthly gross income ≤ 28%.

      *Includes principal, interest, taxes, insurance, and any condominium fee (if a renter, then the ratio is: rent + insurance ÷ monthly gross income ≤ 28%).
   c. Total Payments Ratio = (All monthly payments and housing costs from above) ÷ gross monthly income ≤ 36%. The 28% and 36% are common mortgage lender standards and are healthy targets for most clients.
   d. Solvency Ratio = Total assets ÷ total debt ≥ 1.1.
   e. Savings Ratio = Savings per year ÷ gross income. The savings ratio should be 8% - 25% depending on age. For example, a savings ratio of 8% or more for a younger individual.
   f. Debt to Income Ratio = Annual debt payment ÷ gross income ≤ 30%.
2. The cash flow statement should be analyzed using a month-to-month comparison, calculating each outflow as a percent of total income. The objective is to develop a predictive model for each expenditure (e.g., savings is 10% of gross income).

3. Typical strengths and weaknesses:

STRENGTHS	WEAKNESSES
• Adequate savings.	• Inadequate savings.
• Appropriate investments.	• Inappropriate investments.
• Appropriate risk coverage.	• Uncovered catastrophic risks:
• Appropriate net worth.	*Life, Health, Disability, Property,*
• Appropriate emergency fund.	*Liability, Umbrella.*
• Valid and appropriate will and transfer plan.	• Inadequate net worth.
• Well-articulated goals.	• Inadequate emergency fund.
• Excellent cash flow management.	• No will or invalid will.
• Knowledge about investments.	• Inadequately defined financial goals.
	• Poor budget - improper use of cash flow.
	• Lack of knowledge about investments.

IV. BUDGETING

A. DESCRIBED.

1. Planners and clients should remember that good budgeting is a learned phenomenon, and, as such, there is a learning curve (the more you do it, the better you get at it).
2. Budgeting requires planning for the expected, the recurring, and supposedly nonexpected (every month it's something).
3. Budgeting is a process of projecting, monitoring, adjusting, and controlling future income and expenditures.
4. Budgeting may be used to determine the Wage Replacement Ratio for capital needs analysis for retirement where the client is sufficiently close to retirement to be able to estimate the retirement budget.

B. STEPS.

1. Start with a year of bank statements, checks, and check stubs. Create a spreadsheet of all expenditures by month by category. If needed, retrieve a year's copies of credit card expenditure information to assist in determining the amounts and categories of expenditures.
2. Once the dollar amounts are determined per category per month, calculate these as a percentage of gross income. Analyze each category looking for consistent percentage expenditures to develop a predictive model for that particular expenditure.
3. Identify which costs are sensitive to general inflation and which are fixed (e.g., home mortgage).
4. Forecast next year's income on a monthly basis.
5. Determine how much expenditures will amount to and in which months the expenditure will occur. Often insurance bills are paid annually or semiannually. If they arrive at the wrong time, they can play havoc with cash flows.
6. Project the budget for the next 12 months.
7. Compare actual expenditures for the month to expected expenditures. Adjust the next 11 months accordingly.
8. Continue to analyze, picking out specific expenditure categories that you can control. Utilities are an example of a cost that can be managed. Long distance telephone bills may be reduced by changing carriers.

C. SAVING AND CONSUMPTION HABITS.

1. Information about a client's saving and consumption habits assists the planner in developing a successful strategic financial plan for the client.
2. If the client does not have a history of saving money consistently, it is wise to develop a strategy in which money is directed into savings prior to the client receiving a check from their employer. Similarly, if the client has a history of making large dollar purchases impulsively, it would be wise to encourage investments in assets with early withdrawal penalties and/or those where withdrawal is difficult.
3. Withdrawal penalties or delays may discourage the client from making such impulse purchases. Historical behavior is the best indicator of future behavior. Therefore, a good way to collect information about the client's saving and consumption habits is by asking the client about their previous saving and consumption habits.

V. INTERNAL ANALYSIS

A. LIFE CYCLE POSITIONING.

Life cycle positioning information is needed because it plays a significant role in affecting the goals and behaviors of individuals. It also suggests which financial risks currently exist. In order to identify the client's life cycle positioning, the planner needs to have information about the client's age, marital status, dependants, income level, and net worth.

1. Age.
   a. Age is one of the most important factors in financial planning. Generally, youth gives little thought or consideration to retirement goals or wealth-transfer goals. As people age, they become aware that adequate retirement income requires funding. At some time, they begin to seriously plan for this financial goal.
   b. In the recent past, it was common for persons to become conscious about their "retirement reality" as late as age 40, or even age 50. Today, it seems that clients are beginning to become more aware of this issue at a much younger age. Perhaps this phenomenon is due primarily to the increased amount of readily available information on the cost of retirement and the necessity to plan early.
2. Marital Status.
   a. The second factor that affects goal determination is marital status. The desire to provide for one's dependents creates a host of goals to achieve and risks to avoid. For example, it is common for married persons to combine their future economic resources to jointly purchase assets like a house by jointly committing to indebtedness. The purchase of a personal residence through indebtedness, which can only be afforded by combining both incomes, creates an interdependency of one spouse to the other.
   b. In the event one spouse was to suffer unemployment, untimely death, disability, or some other catastrophic event, the commitment to the repayment of the debt may not be met. Marital status is a signal to the financial planner that the client has someone other than himself to protect, and therefore, needs to protect his income stream.
3. Dependents.
   a. The third factor affecting the creation of goals is dependents and their ages. Dependents may be children, grandchildren, or elderly parents. Persons with children quite commonly have goals of providing education for their children. Education is an expensive goal that requires substantial expenditures made over a finite period.
   b. Grandchildren may also be considered as a factor of dependency. A person may have grandchildren as early as in their 30's but more commonly in their 50's or older. The significance of grandchildren as a factor is not that they are actual dependents, but rather that grandchildren may signal the initial phase of wealth transfer. Grandparents may find themselves with more assets and income than they feel is necessary. They then begin to help provide financially for their grandchildren.
   c. Other examples of dependencies that affect goals are caring for an aging parent or providing special care to a handicapped person. It is important for the planner to realize that not only married persons with children have dependents. Single childless persons may have financial dependents by taking on the obligations of aging parents or other loved ones.

4. Income and net worth.

   a. Income and net worth are the last two factors concerning life cycle positioning. Substantial income suggests an opportunity to achieve financial goals as long as the goals are realistic relative to the income.

   b. Lower income presents greater challenges in achieving financial security and financial independence. Persons with a low income and low net worth generally have a more difficult time overcoming financial setbacks.

   c. A person with substantial net worth is generally less likely to suffer catastrophic consequences as a result of a single financial setback. However, substantial net worth also implies a need for increased management of assets and planning, and an increasing emphasis and concern about the avoidance of all taxes.

B. FINANCIAL PLANNING FOR SPECIAL CIRCUMSTANCES.

1. There are certain instances where a careful analysis of internal factors should be reviewed and closely monitored. These special circumstances include, but are not limited to: divorce (remarriage), disabilities (of the client or the client's dependants), terminal illness (of the client or the client's dependants), unexpected death of a family member (of the client's spouse or the client's dependents), nontraditional families, and job change or job loss.

2. The financial planner should always tactfully inquire about these topics. The planner must use extreme caution when initiating this discussion with the client. If the client does not want to discuss any of these topics, the planner should be sensitive not to push the issue. However, the planner must be cognizant of these issues at all times.

C. LIFE CYCLE PHASES AND CHARACTERISTICS.

1. As people progress through the life cycle, there is a tendency to move subtly but surely among financial objectives due to changes in personal financial circumstances. We have identified and labeled these life cycle phases and characteristics as the Asset Accumulation Phase of life, the Conservation/Protection Phase of life, and the Distribution/Gifting Phase of life.

2. While not all people move through these phases at the same rate, a sufficient percent of people do, so that financial planners can gain valuable insight into their client's objectives and concerns by identifying which phase or phases their client is in at a particular point in time. Exhibit 3 illustrates the life cycle phases and the typical characteristics of each.

EXHIBIT 3: LIFE CYCLE PHASES AND CHARACTERISTICS

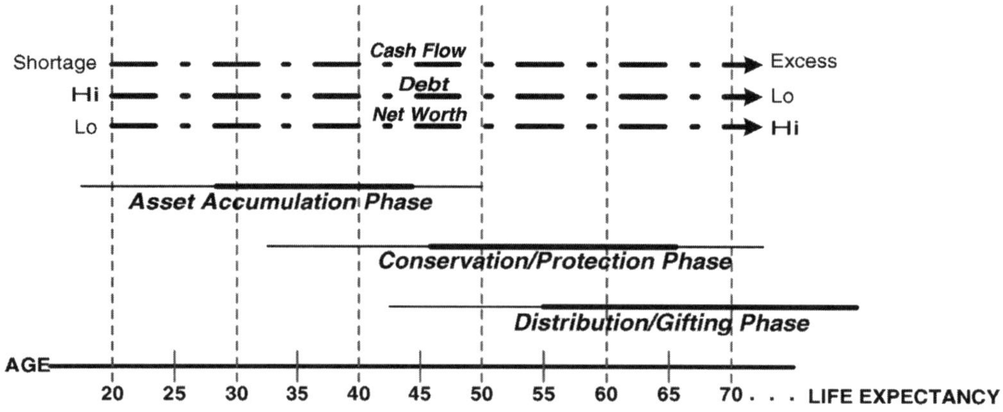

a. Asset Accumulation.

   i. The Asset Accumulation Phase is described as beginning somewhere between the ages of 20 and 25 and lasting until somewhere around age 50 for many persons. The beginning of the phase is characterized by limited excess funds for investing, high degree of debt to net worth, and low net worth.

   ii. At the beginning of the phase, there generally is a low appreciation for the risks that exist. As the person moves through the Asset Accumulation Phase, cash for investments generally increases, there is less use of debt as a percent of total assets, and there is an increase in net worth.

b. Conservation/Protection.

   i. The Conservation/Protection Phase begins when one has acquired some assets, usually in late 30s or 40s and may last throughout the work life expectancy, and depending on the nature of the person, may last all the way to life expectancy. It is also characterized by an increase in cash flow, assets, and net worth with some decrease in the proportional use of debt.

   ii. People generally become more risk averse as more assets are acquired. Therefore, from an investments viewpoint, they are more concerned about losing what they have acquired than acquiring more. They become aware and concerned with many of the risks they ignored at the beginning of the Asset Accumulation Phase, including an increased awareness of life's risks (untimely death, unemployment, disability, etc.).

c. Distribution/Gifting.

   i. The Distribution/Gifting Phase begins subtly when the person realizes that they can afford to spend on things they never believed possible. The Asset Accumulation and Conservation/Protection Phases make this phase possible. It is quite common that at the beginning of this phase the person remains in both the Asset Accumulation and Conservation/Protection Phases. (Yes, there is a period for many people when they are being influenced by all three phases simultaneously, although not necessarily to the same degree.)

   ii. When parents purchase new cars for adult children, pay for a grandchild's private school tuition, or treat themselves to expensive vacations relative to their tradition, they are likely to be in the Distribution/Gifting Phase.

D. RISK TOLERANCE LEVELS.

1. Knowledge of risk tolerance levels is needed to assist the financial planner in determining the types of investments and the style of risk management best suited for the client. The style of risk management refers to the issue of self-insuring reasonable risks versus over-insuring in an attempt to mitigate even small losses.

2. Essentially, it is the choice of balancing lower premiums with self-reliance for smaller losses, or alternatively, higher premiums with less loss exposure. However, risk tolerance levels are subject to misinterpretation because they are so subjective. The statement, "I am not very risk tolerant," may mean something different to each client. Therefore, additional questioning is needed to ensure understanding.

VI. PERSONAL USE - ASSETS AND LIABILITIES

A. FINANCING STRATEGIES.

1. Buying vs. leasing.

   a. The effect on cash flow when buying a home.

      i. Income – Expenses = Discretionary Cash Flow.

      ii. Down payment, closing costs, mortgage insurance, property insurance and taxes, maintenance, and operating expenses are all costs associated with purchasing a home. Families also purchase more life insurance when they own a home, in the event of one of the spouse's deaths.

      iii. Upfront charges place a heavy burden on the homeowner.

      iv. Interest on mortgage is deductible.

      v. There are different types of mortgage payments to choose from (variable rate, fixed rate, balloon payment) that can change both short-term and long-term cash flow.

   b. The effect on cash flow when renting living quarters.

      i. Cost is fixed and there is no long-term commitment.

      ii. There is no property tax associated with renting.

      iii. Maintenance and repair costs are usually grouped with the rental fee.

      iv. Insurance is substantially lower than a homeowner's.

      v. It is a good time to start saving toward the purchase of a house.

   c. The following two statements of cash flows compare and contrast what a homeowner's and a renter's cash flows might look like.

Statement of Cash Flow (Renter)		Statement of Cash Flow (Homeowner)	
Gross Salary	$55,500	Gross Salary	$55,500
Interest/Dividend Income	$1,000	Interest/Dividend Income	$1,000
Total Inflows	**$56,500**	**Total Inflows**	**$56,500**
After-Tax Savings Investment	$5,250	After-Tax Savings Investment	$1,750
Renters Insurance	$150	Residential Insurance	$350
Term Life Insurance	$200	Term Life Insurance	$350
Taxes (Federal, State, Soc. Sec.)	$10,000	Taxes (Federal, State, Soc. Sec)	$12,000
401(k) Contribution	$2,350	401(k) Contribution	$2,350
Annual Rent	$8,400	Mortgage Principal and Interest	$7,200
Total Financial Outflows	**$26,350**	**Total Financial Outflows**	**$24,000**
Food	$4,000	Food	$3,200
Transportation with Insurance	$4,500	Transportation with Insurance	$4,000
Utilities	$2,400	Home Maintenance	$3,700
Medical	$1,200	Utilities	$3,700
Vacation	$5,000	Medical	$1,200
Clothing	$5,000	Vacation	$4,200
Miscellaneous	$8,050	Clothing	$4,900
		Miscellaneous	$7,600
Total Living-Expense Outflows	**$30,150**	**Total Living-Expense Outflows**	**$32,500**

B. DEBT.

1. Debt is appropriate when matched properly with the economic life of the asset and the ability to repay.

Example

The purchase of an automobile that is expected to be used for three years (36 months) has a maximum realistic economic life of five years (60 months). It should probably be financed over 36 months but certainly no longer than 60 months.

2. The issues:

   a. Risk - There are a number of risks to consider. The risks include:

      i. A shortened economic life.

      ii. Increasing cash outflows for repairs as the asset ages.

      iii. The changing of the initial utility curves of the purchaser during the holding period unexpectedly reducing the overall utility of the asset.

b. Matching debt repayment cash flows to economic life - Generally, the considered cash flows are not just the principal and interest to retire the debt. Also included are the cash flows associated with the increase in repairs and maintenance due to asset aging (both real and personal property) as well as the prospect of higher executory costs (insurance and taxes).

c. Cost of replacement - The cost of the replacement asset will have to either be borne entirely by future cash flows, or the current asset value will help to offset replacement costs. One question is whether the cost of the new asset is increasing in price faster than the old asset. Another question is whether the value of the old asset (exchange value to another buyer) is diminishing faster than the debt is being extinguished. If so, the purchasers of such an asset may find that they are in a negative equity position. This is the primary reason that lenders insist on down payments and generally establish a repayment schedule to ensure that the borrower will always be in a positive equity position. Such a position will reduce the likelihood that the borrower will abandon the property.

C. HOME MORTGAGES.

1. Types.
   a. 30-year fixed mortgage.
   b. 15-year fixed mortgage.
   c. Variable mortgage.
   d. Balloon mortgage.
2. Issues in the selection of mortgages.
   a. Length of time expected to stay in the house.
   b. Cash flow capacity.
   c. Tolerance for risk.
   d. The spread between yields after a quantitative analysis comparison of fixed-to-fixed rates and fixed-to-variable rates.
   e. If the time expected to be in the house is short, the more likely that an adjustable rate mortgage (ARM) is the mortgage of choice. This is simply because most ARMs have a 2 - 3% lower interest rate than a 30-year fixed rate mortgage and have 2/6 caps (2% maximum interest rate increase per year, 6% life of loan).
   f. The downside risk to an ARM is the prospect of the interest rate increasing periodically causing the payment to increase proportionally.
   g. Another advantage of an ARM is that, due to the low initial interest rate, the principal and interest (P&I) payments are low relative to a 30-year fixed rate mortgage. It is easier to qualify for a mortgage using the traditional lender hurdle rates of 28%/36%.
   h. When comparing a 15-year to a 30-year fixed rate mortgage, the interest rates will usually be about 0.5% different assuming the same down payment. The cash flows will differ depending on the interest rate and the size of the mortgage.

Example.

	Sales Price	Down Payment	Paid Closing Costs	Mortgage Amount	Term Months	Interest Rate	P & I Payment
Fixed 30 Year	$180,000	$36,000	$5,760	$144,000	360	8.5%	$1,107
Fixed 15 Year	$180,000	$36,000	$5,760	$144,000	180	8.0%	$1,376
ARM 30 Year	$180,000	$36,000	$5,760	$144,000	360	6.0%	$863

i. While the ARM has the current lowest payment, the risk is that at some point in the life of the ARM the maximum interest rate is 12.0% assuming a 2%/6% cap at which time the monthly P&I payment could be $1,481.20 over a 30-year period. It should be pointed out that in this particular example, loan qualifying would be easier using the ARM because the initial payment is lower (assuming $200 per month taxes and $75 per month insurance):

   i. 30-year fixed rate - Total monthly housing costs = $1,107 + $200 + $75 = $1,382; monthly gross income needed to qualify for loan = $1,382 ÷ 0.28 = $4,935.71.

   ii. 15-year fixed rate - Total monthly housing costs = $1,376 + $200 + $75 = $1,651; monthly gross income needed to qualify for loan = $1,651 ÷ 0.28 = $5,896.43.

   iii. ARM - Total monthly housing costs = $863 + $200 + $75 = $1,138; monthly gross income needed to qualify for loan = $1,138 ÷ 0.28 = $4,064.28.

3. Tolerance for risk.

   a. If a client has a low tolerance for fluctuating payments, a fixed mortgage should be selected. Assuming a higher risk tolerance, the planner will have to consider the length of expected ownership (shorter term will mitigate risk) and the opportunity cost of alternative investments. The client may consider an ARM.

   b. It is generally not appropriate to select an ARM (using the first year teaser rate) simply to qualify for a loan and hope that cash flows will be sufficient to pay for any interest increases.

4. Savings due to mortgage selection.

   a. The savings is a result of (1) the 15-year mortgage causing earlier retirement of the principal indebtedness, and (2) the slightly lower interest rate. However, many 30-year loans are selected simply as a necessity to meet lender qualification requirements. If no prepayment penalties exist, most of the savings can be achieved by paying a 30-year loan according to a 15-year amortization schedule.

Example (See previous example).

	Number of Payments	Monthly Payment	Total Payment	Loan	Interest Paid
30-Year Fixed	360	$1,107	$398,604.75	$144,000	$254,604.75
15-Year Fixed	180	$1,376	$247,705.02	$144,000	$103,705.02
Savings			$150,899.73	$0	$150,899.73

b. The total interest paid is determined by multiplying the amount of the payment by the number of payments and then subtracting the principal borrowed.

5. Calculating mortgage payments.

   a. Mortgages can be calculated using the time value of money concepts discussed later in this section.

Example

Sara purchased a house for $200,000. She made a $10,000 down payment and took out a 30-year loan for the remainder at 8%. Sara's monthly loan payment will be $1,394.15. It can be calculated using the following keystrokes on your financial calculator.

PV	=	190,000 (200,000 – 10,000)
FV	=	0
N	=	360 (30 x 12)
i	=	0.6666 (8 ÷ 12)
PMT_{OA}	=	**$1,394.15**

Note: This is discussed in more depth later in this section. Also, the payment is an ordinary annuity because the payments are in arrears.

VII. ECONOMIC ENVIRONMENT - BASIC CONCEPTS

A. DEMAND.

1. The amount of a commodity people buy depends on its price.
2. The relationship between price and quantity bought is called the demand curve.
   a. Downward sloping demand - If the price of a commodity is raised (all other things equal), buyers tend to buy less of the commodity.
   b. The demand curve (see Exhibit 4) measures price on the vertical axis and quantities demanded on the horizontal axis.

EXHIBIT 4: THE DEMAND CURVE

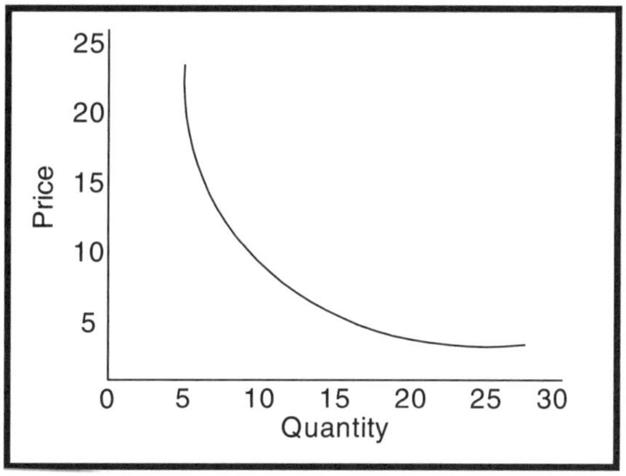

   c. When the price is lowered (all other things equal), quantity demanded increases.
3. Quantity demanded tends to fall as price rises for two reasons:
   a. Substitution effect - When the price of a good rises, consumers substitute other similar goods for it.
   b. Income effect - When the price rises, consumers curb consumption.
4. The average income of consumers is a key determinant of demand. As incomes rise, individuals tend to buy more.
5. The size of the market clearly affects the market demand.
6. The prices and availability of related goods influence the demand for a commodity.
7. Special influences affect demand. Expectations about future economic conditions, particularly prices, may affect demand.
8. Factors affecting demand:
   a. The price of the good.
   b. Average income.
   c. Population.
   d. The prices of related goods.
   e. Tastes.
   f. Special influences.
9. Demand curve shift - Influences, other than the price of the good, change.

B. SUPPLY.

1. Supply means the quantity of a good that businesses willingly produce and sell.
2. The supply curve for a commodity shows the relationship between its market price and the amount of that commodity producers are willing to produce and sell. The supply curve (see Exhibit 5) measures price on the vertical axis and quantities supplied on the horizontal axis.

EXHIBIT 5: THE SUPPLY CURVE

3. Behind the supply curve - The force operating on supply is the fact that producers supply commodities for profit. A key element affecting supply decisions is the cost of production.
4. Another element influencing supply is the price of related goods. Related goods are goods that can be readily substituted for one another in the production process. If the price of one production substitute rises, the supply of another substitute is likely to decrease.
5. A reduction in tariffs and quotas on foreign goods will open the market to foreign producers and will tend to increase supply. If a market becomes monopolized, the price at each level of output will increase.
6. Factors affecting supply:
   a. The price of the good. It affect the quantity supplied.
   b. Technology.
   c. Input prices.
   d. Prices of related goods.
   e. Target organization.
   f. Special influences.
7. Competition:
   a. Pure competition exists when there are many competitors selling a product or service with very little difference.
   b. An oligopoly occurs when you have a small number of companies that control the market for a given type of product or service.
   c. A monopoly occurs when a single company owns all or nearly all of the market for a given type of product or service.

C. SUPPLY AND DEMAND INTERACTION.

1. The market equilibrium comes at the price and quantity where the supply and demand forces are in balance.
2. Supply and demand can do more than tell us about the equilibrium price and quantity. They can be used to predict the impact of changes in economic conditions on prices and quantities.
3. When factors underlying demand or supply change, these lead to shifts in demand or supply and to changes in the market equilibrium of price and quantity.
4. Care must be taken not to confuse a change in demand, denoted by a shift of the demand (supply) curve, with a change in the quantity demanded (supplied), denoted by movement to a different point on the same demand curve after a price change.
5. Rationing by prices - By determining the equilibrium prices and quantities of all inputs and outputs, the market allocates (rations) the scarce goods of the society among the possible uses.

D. PRICE ELASTICITY OF DEMAND.

1. The price elasticity is the responsiveness of the quantity demanded of a good to changes in the good's price, other things held constant.
2. The percentage change in quantity demanded is divided by the percentage change in price.
3. Elastic and inelastic demand - Goods differ in their elasticities. Demand for necessities (e.g., food) responds little to price changes, while luxuries are generally highly price-sensitive.
4. A good is elastic when its quantity demanded responds greatly to price changes and is inelastic when its quantity demanded responds little to price changes.
5. Unit-elastic demand occurs when the percentage change in quantity is exactly the same size as the percentage change in price.
6. The slope is not the same as the elasticity because the demand curve's slope depends on the changes in price and quantity, whereas the elasticity depends on the percentage changes in price and quantity.
7. Elasticity and revenue - Elasticity helps to clarify the impact of price changes on the total revenue of producers.
8. Total revenue.
   a. When demand is price inelastic, a price decrease reduces total revenue.
   b. When demand is price elastic, a price decrease increases total revenue.
   c. In the case of unit-elastic demand, a price decrease leads to no change in total revenue.
9. Economic factors determine: the magnitude of price elasticities for individual goods; the degree that a good is a necessity or a luxury; the extent to which substitutes are available; the time available for response; and the relative importance of a commodity in the consumer's budget.
10. The price elasticity of supply measures the percentage change in quantity supplied in response to a 1% change in the good's price.

E. INFLATION.

1. Inflation denotes a rise in the general level of prices. The rate of inflation is the rate of change in the general price level and is measured as follows:

$$\text{Rate of inflation (year t)} = \left[\frac{\text{Price level (year t)} - \text{Price level (year t - 1)}}{\text{Price level (year t - 1)}}\right] \times 100$$

2. The opposite of inflation is deflation, which is a decline in general price levels, often caused by a reduction in the supply of money.
3. Disinflation denotes a decline in the rate of inflation (a reduction in the rate at which prices rise).
4. Moderate inflation is characterized by slowly rising prices.
5. Galloping inflation occurs when money loses its value very quickly and real interest rates can be minus 50% or 100% per year. People hold only the bare minimum amount of money needed for daily transactions. Financial markets wither away, and funds are generally allocated by rationing rather than by interest rates. People hoard goods, buy houses, and never lend money at the low, nominal interest rate.
6. Impact of inflation - During periods of inflation, all prices and wages do not move at the same rate.
7. Effects of inflation.
   a. A redistribution of income and wealth occurs among different classes.
   b. Changes are created in the relative prices and outputs of different goods, or sometimes in output and employment for the economy as a whole.
8. Real interest rate adjustment - Inflation persists for a long time, and markets begin to adapt. An allowance for inflation is generally built into the market interest rate.
9. The major redistributive impact of inflation occurs through its effect on the real value of people's wealth. In general, unanticipated inflation redistributes wealth from creditors to debtors (that is, unanticipated or unforeseen inflation helps those who have borrowed money and hurts those who have lent money). An unanticipated decline in inflation has the opposite effect.
10. Inflation affects the real economy in two specific areas: total output and economic efficiency.
11. There is no necessary relationship between prices and output.
12. Inflation may be associated with either a higher or a lower level of output and employment.
13. Generally, the higher the inflation rate, the greater are the changes in relative prices.
14. Distortions occur when prices get out of line relative to costs and demands.

F. MEASURES OF INFLATION.

1. A price index is a weighted average of the prices of numerous goods and services. The most well known price indexes are the Consumer Price Index (CPI), the Gross Domestic Product (GDP) deflator, and the Producer Price Index (PPI).

   a. The Consumer Price Index (CPI) - Measures the cost of a market basket of consumer goods and services, including prices of food, clothing, shelter, fuels, transportation, medical care, college tuition, and other commodities purchased for day-to-day living.

      i. A price index is constructed by weighting each price according to the economic importance of the commodity in question.

      ii. Each item is assigned a fixed weight proportional to its relative importance in consumer expenditure budgets as determined by a survey of expenditures in the 1982-1984 period.

   b. GDP deflator - Is a broader price index than the CPI. It is designed to measure the change in the average price of the market basket of goods included in GDP. In addition to consumer goods, the GDP deflator includes prices for capital goods and other goods and services purchased by businesses and governments.

   c. The Producer Price Index (PPI) - Is the oldest continuous statistical series published by the Labor Department. It measures the level of prices at the wholesale or producer stage. It is based on approximately 3,400 commodity prices including prices of foods, manufactured products, and mining products.

   d. Index-number problems - The cost of living is overestimated compared to the situation where consumers substitute relatively inexpensive for relatively expensive goods. The CPI does not accurately capture changes in the quality of goods. Although the CPI is modified from time to time, the CPI is not corrected for quality improvements.

VIII. MONETARY AND FISCAL POLICY

A. MONETARY POLICY.

1. The Federal Reserve Bank (Fed) controls the supply of money enabling it to significantly impact interest rates. The Fed will follow a loose, or easy, monetary policy when it wants to increase the money supply to expand the level of income and employment. In times of inflation and when it wants to constrict the supply of money, the Fed will follow a tight monetary policy.

   a. Easy monetary policy - The supply of money increases resulting in the circulation of more money. This leads to more funds available for banks to lend and ultimately to a decline in interest rates.

   b. Tight monetary policy - The supply of money is restricted resulting in less money available for banks to lend. This leads to an increase in interest rates.

2. The Fed has several methods of controlling the money supply.

   a. Reserve requirements - The reserve requirement for a member bank of the Federal Reserve Bank is the percent of deposit liabilities that must be held in reserve. As this requirement is increased, less money is available to be loaned to customers, resulting in a restriction of the money supply.

   b. Federal Reserve discount rate.

      i. This is the rate at which member banks can borrow funds from the Federal Reserve to meet reserve requirements.

      ii. When the Fed raises the discount rate, it increases the borrowing cost and discourages member banks from borrowing funds. This results in a contraction of the money supply.

      iii. The Fed will lower the discount rate when it wants to increase the money supply. Banks are able to borrow funds at lower rates and lend more money, which increases the supply.

> **Note:** The discount rate is the borrowing rate from the Federal Reserve and the Fed Funds Rate is the overnight lending rate between member banks.

   c. Open market operations.

      i. This is the process that the Federal Reserve follows to purchase and sell government securities in the open market.

      ii. The Fed will buy government securities to cause more money to circulate, therefore, increasing lending and lowering interest rates.

      iii. The Fed will sell government securities to restrict the money supply. As investors purchase government securities, more money leaves circulation, which decreases lending and increases interest rates.

      iv. It is important to note that the Federal Open Market Committee (FOMC) is in charge of open market operations.

B. Fiscal Policy.

1. Taxation, expenditures, and debt management of the federal government is called fiscal policy. Economic growth, price stability, and full employment are other goals that may be pursued by changes in fiscal policy.
   a. Expansionary fiscal policy - When the government increases purchases of good and services while holding its revenues constant, it creates a budget deficit and stimulates aggregate demand.
   b. Restrictive fiscal policy - When the government either reduces its expenditures of goods and services or raises taxes, which causes a reduction in the budget deficit or a budget surplus.
2. Changes in taxation will affect corporate earnings, disposable earnings, and the overall economy.
   a. As tax rates increase, corporations' after-tax income declines, which reduces their ability to pay dividends. This may cause the price for equities to decrease.
   b. Tax increases also reduce individuals' disposable income and limit the amount of money entering the economy.
   c. The demand for tax-free investments is also influenced by changes in taxation levels. As increases in taxes occur, the attractiveness of tax-free instruments also increases.
3. Government expenditures - Corporate earnings benefit from increases in government expenditures.
4. Deficit spending - Deficit spending occurs when expenditures exceed revenues of the government. By selling securities to the public to finance deficits, Treasuries compete with other securities. This drives the prices down. The decrease in price causes the yields to rise.

C. The Nature of Interest Rates.

1. The price of money is the interest rate.
2. The discount rate is the interest rate charged by the Fed on a loan that it makes to a member bank.
3. The nominal interest rate measures the yield in dollars per year per dollar invested.
4. The return on investments in terms of real goods and services is a real interest rate measure. The return in terms of dollars is an absolute measure. The real interest rate measures the quantity of goods we get tomorrow for goods forgone today. The real interest rate is obtained by correcting nominal, or dollar, interest rates for the rate of inflation.

$$\frac{1 + \text{nominal rate}}{1 + \text{inflation rate}} - 1 \times 100 = \text{real rate}$$

IX. BUSINESS CYCLE THEORIES

A. DESCRIBED.

1. Business cycles consist of swings in total national output, income, and employment marked by widespread expansion or contraction in many sectors of the economy.
2. Business cycles generally occur as a result of shifts in aggregate demand. The cycle consists of two phases, expansion and contraction, and two points, peak and trough.
   a. The expansion phase comes to an end and goes into the contraction phase at the upper turning point, or peak.
   b. Similarly, the contraction phase gives way to that expansion at the lower turning point, or trough. The emphasis here is not so much on high or low business activity as on the dynamic aspects of rising or falling business activity.

EXHIBIT 6: BUSINESS CYCLES (GENERAL)

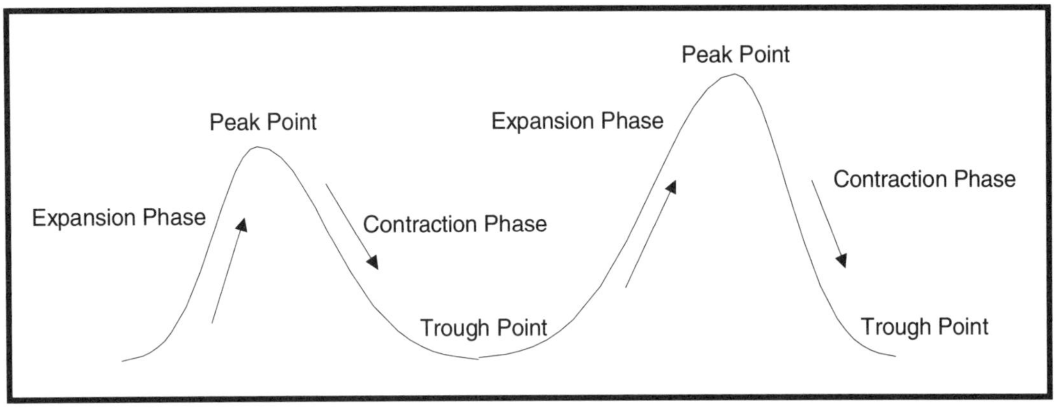

3. Definitions.
   a. Peak point – that point at the end of the expansion phase when most businesses are operating at capacity and gross domestic product (GDP) is increasing rapidly. The peak is the point at which GDP is at its highest point and exceeds the long-run average GDP. Usually employment peaks here.
   b. Trough point – that point at the end of the contraction phase where businesses are operating at their lowest capacity levels. Unemployment is rapidly increasing and peaks because sales fall rapidly. GDP growth is at its lowest or negative.
   c. Contraction phase – leads to trough. Business sales fall. Unemployment increases. GDP growth falls.
   d. Expansion phase – leads to peak. Business sales rise. GDP grows. Unemployment declines.

e. Recession – a decline in real GDP for two or more successive quarters characterized by:
   i. Consumer purchases decline.
   ii. Business inventories expand.
   iii. GDP falls.
   iv. Capital investment falls.
   v. Demand for labor falls.
   vi. Unemployment is high.
   vii. Commodity prices fall.
   viii. Business profits fall.
   ix. Interest rates fall due to demand for money.

f. Depression – persistent recession and a severe decline in economic activity.

EXHIBIT 7: HYPOTHETICAL BUSINESS CYCLE

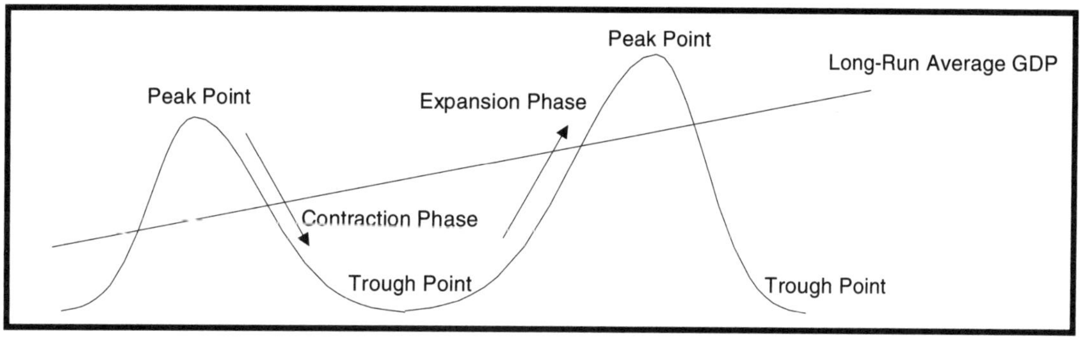

GDP trend line assumes expansion at 3% annually.

Note: The business cycle is not symmetrical as drawn. The pattern of the business cycle is irregular and unpredictable.

4. Each phase of the cycle passes into the next. Each is characterized by different economic conditions.
5. Capital formation - Certain economic variables always show greater fluctuations than others do in the business cycle.
6. Durable goods (leader) are subject to violently erratic patterns of demand. It is the durable or capital goods sector of the economy that shows, by far, the greatest cyclical fluctuations.
7. Consumption movements (laggy) seem to be the effect rather than the cause of the business cycle. There is good reason to believe that the movements of durable goods represent key causes in a more fundamental sense.

8. External and internal factors.

   a. The external theories find the root of the business cycle in the fluctuations of something outside the economic system such as wars, revolutions, political events, rates of growth of population and migrations, discoveries of new lands and resources, scientific and technological discoveries, and innovations.

   b. The internal theories look for mechanisms within the economic system itself that give rise to self-generating business cycles. Thus, every expansion will breed recession and contraction, and every contraction will in turn breed revival and expansion in a quasi-regular, repeating, never-ending chain. However, each peak and valley is higher than the last, leading to growth in the economy over the long-term, despite the business cycle.

EXHIBIT 8: ACTUAL BUSINESS CYCLE

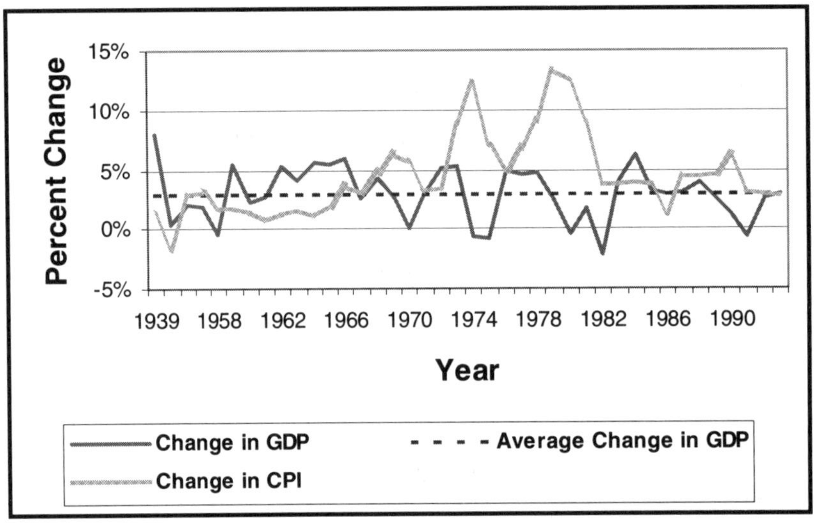

9. Actual business cycle.

   a. The actual business cycle has averaged growth of approximately 2.9% per year.

   b. The business cycle will exceed the average in some years while in other years the growth will be less than the average.

   c. Decreases in interest rates are often accompanied by economic expansions while increases in interest rates are accompanied by economic contractions.

X. FINANCIAL INSTITUTIONS

A. DESCRIBED.

Providers of financial services include banks, money market mutual funds, financial services companies, financial planners, brokerage firms, and insurance companies. The primary providers of cash management services are banks and similar institutions, money market mutual funds, stock brokerage firms, and financial services companies.

B. BANKS AND SIMILAR INSTITUTIONS.

1. There are several financial institutions that offer various forms of checking and savings accounts:
   a. Commercial banks.
   b. Mutual savings banks.
   c. Savings and loan associations.
   d. Credit unions.
2. Commercial banks.
   a. Commercial banks are chartered under federal and state regulations. Commercial banks offer numerous consumer services such as checking, savings, loans, safe-deposit boxes, investment services, financial counseling, and automatic payment of bills.
   b. Approximately 14,000 commercial banks exist nationwide with over 50,000 branch offices.
   c. Each account in a federally chartered bank is insured against loss up to $100,000 in principal and interest per account by the Bank Insurance Fund (BIF) of the Federal Deposit Insurance Corporation (FDIC), an agency of the federal government, subject to an aggregate limit of $100,000 for each person's accounts at that bank titled similarly (see discussion below).
3. Mutual savings banks.
   a. A mutual savings bank (MSB) is quite similar to a savings and loan association (S&L). Historically, MSBs accepted deposits in order to make housing loans.
   b. Technically, the depositors of savings are the owners of the institution.
   c. MSBs are state chartered and have either FDIC's BIF insurance or a state-approved insurance program up to $100,000 per account.
   d. MSBs are not permitted in all states. Most are located throughout the Northeast.
   e. Similar to S&Ls, MSBs compete for consumer loans and offer interest-bearing negotiable order of withdrawal (NOW) accounts.
4. Savings and loan associations.
   a. The purpose of S&Ls is to accept savings and provide home loans. S&Ls are also called thrift institutions.
   b. Approximately 2,400 S&Ls exist nationwide with over 15,000 branches.
   c. S&Ls also make installment loans for consumer products (e.g., automobiles and appliances).
   d. S&Ls are not permitted to provide demand deposits (such as checking accounts with a commercial bank); however, they can offer interest-bearing NOW accounts, which are similar to demand deposit accounts.

e. The FDIC insures accounts in all federally chartered S&Ls up to $100,000 in principal and interest per account through its Savings Association Insurance Fund (SAIF) as well as some state-chartered institutions.

f. S&Ls are either mutual or corporate. The mutual savings and loans, which are more common, have the depositors as the actual owners of the association (shareowners). Corporate savings and loans operate as corporations and issue common and preferred stock to denote ownership.

5. Credit unions.

    a. Credit unions are not-for-profit cooperative ventures that are largely run by volunteers. They are developed to pool the deposits of members that are then used to invest or lend to members/owners.

    b. Members are usually joined by a common bond such as work, union, or fraternal association.

    c. Regulations make it possible for people to remain members of a credit union after the common bond has been severed.

    d. Credit unions with federal charters have their accounts insured up to $100,000 through the National Credit Union Share Insurance Fund (NCUSIF), administered by the National Credit Union Administration (NCUA), that provides the same safety as deposits insured by the FDIC.

    e. Credit unions accept deposits and make loans for consumer products. They also make home loans.

    f. Employment-related credit unions typically make use of payroll deductions for deposits and loan repayments, often offer free term life insurance up to certain limits, and usually offer free credit life insurance.

C. FDIC INSURANCE.

1. Any person or entity can have FDIC insurance on a deposit. A depositor does not have to be a United States citizen, or even a resident of the United States.

2. The FDIC insures deposits in some, but not all, banks and savings associations.

3. Federal deposit insurance protects deposits that are payable in the United States. Deposits that are only payable overseas are not insured.

4. Securities, mutual funds, and similar types of investments are not covered by FDIC insurance. Creditors (other than depositors) and shareholders of a failed bank or savings association are not protected by federal deposit insurance. Treasury securities (bills, notes, and bonds) purchased by an insured depository institution on a customer's behalf are not FDIC insured.

5. All types of deposits received by a qualifying financial institution in its usual course of business are insured. For example, savings deposits, checking deposits, deposits in NOW accounts, Christmas Club accounts, and time deposits (including certificates of deposit, or CDs), are all FDIC insured deposits. Cashiers' checks, money orders, officers' checks, and outstanding drafts are also insured. Certified checks, letters of credit, and travelers' checks for which an insured depository institution is primarily liable are also insured, when issued in exchange for money or its equivalent, or for a charge against a deposit account.

6. Deposits in different qualified institutions are insured separately. If an institution has one or more branches, however, the main office and all branch offices are considered to be one institution. Thus, deposits at the main office and at branch offices of the same institution are added together when calculating deposit insurance coverage. Financial institutions owned by the same holding company but separately chartered are separately insured.

7. The FDIC presumes that funds are owned as shown on the "deposit account records" of the insured depository institution.

8. The basic FDIC insured amount of a depositor is $100,000. Accrued interest is included when calculating insurance coverage. Deposits maintained in different categories of legal ownership are separately insured. Accordingly, a depositor can have more than $100,000 insurance coverage in a single institution if the funds are owned and deposited in different ownership categories. The most common categories of ownership are single (or individual) ownership, joint ownership, and testamentary accounts. Separate insurance is also available for funds held for retirement purposes.

9. Federal deposit insurance is not determined on a per-account basis. A depositor cannot increase FDIC insurance by dividing funds owned in the same ownership category among different accounts within the same institutions. The type of account (whether checking, savings, certificate of deposit, outstanding official checks, or other form of deposit) has no bearing on the amount of insurance coverage.

10. Single ownership accounts.

    a. A single (or individual) ownership account is an account owned by one person. Single ownership accounts include accounts in the owner's name, accounts established for the benefit of the owner by agents, nominees, guardians, custodians, or conservators, and accounts established by a business that is a sole proprietorship.

    b. All single ownership accounts established by, or for the benefit of, the same person are added together and the total is insured up to a maximum of $100,000.

    c. If an individual owns and deposits funds in his or her own name but then gives another person the right to withdraw funds from the account, the account will generally be insured as a joint ownership account.

    d. Example of insurance for single ownership accounts.

Depositor	Type of Deposit	Amount Deposited
A	Savings Account	$25,000
A	CD	100,000
A	NOW Account	25,000
A's Restaurant (A Sole Proprietorship)	Checking	25,000
Total Deposited		$175,000
Maximum Amount of Insurance Available		(100,000)
Uninsured Amount		$75,000

e. The Uniform Gifts to Minors Act is a state law that allows an adult to make an irrevocable gift to a minor. Funds given to a minor under the Uniform Gifts to Minors Act are held in the name of a custodian for the minor's benefit. The funds are added to any other single ownership accounts of the minor, and the total is insured up to a maximum of $100,000.

11. Joint accounts.

a. A joint account is an account owned by two or more individuals.

b. Joint accounts are insured separately from single ownership account if each of the following conditions are met:

i. All co-owners must be natural persons. This means that legal entities such as corporations or partnerships are not eligible for joint account deposit insurance coverage.

ii. Each of the co-owners must have a right of withdrawal on the same basis as the other co-owners. For example, if one co-owner can withdraw funds on his or her signature alone, but the other co-owner can withdraw funds only on the signature of both co-owners, then this requirement has not been satisfied; the co-owners do not have equal withdrawal rights. Likewise, if a co-owner's right to withdraw funds is limited to a specified dollar amount, the funds in the account will be allocated between the co-owners according to their withdrawal rights and insured as single ownership funds. So, for example, if $100,000 is deposited in the names of A and B, but A has the right to withdraw only up to $5,000 from the account, $5,000 is allocated to A and the remainder is allocated to B. The funds, as allocated, are then added to any other single ownership funds of A or B, respectively.

iii. Each of the co-owners must have personally signed a deposit account signature card. The execution of an account signature card is not required for certificates of deposit, deposit obligations evidenced by a negotiable instrument, or accounts maintained by an agent, nominee, guardian, custodian, or conservator, but the deposit must in fact be jointly owned.

c. The interests of each individual in all joint accounts he or she owns at the same FDIC-insured depository institution are added together and insured up to $100,000 maximum. Each person's interest (or share) in a joint account is deemed equal unless otherwise stated on the deposit account records.

d. Example of insurance for joint ownership accounts.

Account	Owners	Balance
#1	A and B	$100,000
#2	B and A	25,000
#3	A, B, and C	75,000
#4	D and A	80,000

A's Ownership Interest	
Account #1 (A and B)	$50,000
Account #2 (B and A)	12,500
Account #3 (A, B, and C)	25,000
Account #4 (D and A)	40,000
Total deposited:	$127,500
A's ownership interest in the joint account category is limited to $100,000, so $27,500 is uninsured.	
B's Ownership Interest	
Account #1 (A and B)	$50,000
Account #2 (B and A)	12,500
Account #3 (A, B, and C)	25,000
Total deposited:	$87,500
B's ownership interest in the joint account category is $87,500. That amount is less than the $100,000 maximum, so it is fully insured.	
C's Ownership Interest	
Account #3 (A, B, and C)	25,000
Total deposited:	$25,000
C's ownership interest in the joint account category is $25,000. That amount is less than the $100,000 maximum, so it is fully insured.	
D's Ownership Interest	
Account #4 (D and A)	40,000
Total deposited:	$40,000
D's ownership interest in the joint account category is $40,000. That amount is less than the $100,000 maximum, so it is fully insured.	

e. Community property laws do not affect deposit insurance coverage. In states recognizing this form of ownership, an account in the sole name of one spouse will be insured as the single ownership account of that spouse. Separately, a qualifying joint account in the names of both spouses will be insured as a joint account.

f. A deposit account held in two or more names that does not qualify for joint account deposit insurance coverage is treated as being owned by each named owner as an individual, corporation, partnership, or unincorporated association, as the case may be, according to each co-owner's actual ownership interest. As such, each owner's interest is added to any other single ownership accounts or, in the case of a corporation, partnership, or unincorporated association, to other accounts of such entity, and the total is insured up to $100,000.

12. Business accounts.

    a. Funds deposited by a corporation, partnership, or unincorporated association, are FDIC insured up to a maximum of $100,000. Funds deposited by a corporation, partnership, or unincorporated association, are insured separately from the personal accounts of the stockholders, partners, or members. To qualify for this coverage, the entity must be engaged in an independent activity. "Independent activity" means that the entity is operated primarily for some purpose other than to increase deposit insurance.

    b. Funds owned by a business that is a sole proprietorship are treated as the individually owned funds of the person who is the sole proprietor. Consequently, funds deposited in the name of the sole proprietorship are added to any other single ownership accounts of the sole proprietor and the total is insured to a maximum of $100,000.

D. MONEY MARKET MUTUAL FUNDS.

1. A mutual fund is an investment company that raises money by selling shares to the public and investing the money in a diversified portfolio of securities. The investments are professionally managed with securities purchased and sold at the discretion of the fund manager.
2. Many mutual fund companies have created money market mutual funds (MMMF) that serve as money market accounts. The accounts can be used for purposes of cash management.
3. A MMMF is a mutual fund that pools the cash of many investors and specializes in earning a relatively safe and high return by buying securities that have short-term maturities (always less than one year).
4. The average maturity for the portfolio cannot exceed 120 days. This reduces price swings so that the money funds maintain a constant share value.
5. Securities are bought and sold almost daily in money markets that result in payment of the highest daily rates available to small investors.
6. Money deposited in mutual funds is not insured by the federal government; however, MMMFs are considered extremely safe due to the high quality of the securities.
7. Accounts in money market mutual funds provide a convenient and safe place to keep money while awaiting alternative investment opportunities.

E. STOCK BROKERAGE FIRMS.

1. A stock brokerage firm is a licensed financial institution that specializes in selling and buying investment securities.
2. Such firms usually receive a commission for the advice and assistance they provide. Commissions are based on the buy/sell orders they execute.
3. Stock brokerage firms usually offer money market fund accounts where clients may place money while waiting to make investments in stocks and bonds.
4. Money held in a money market mutual fund at a stock brokerage firm is not insured against loss by any government agency; however, most brokerage firms purchase private insurance against such losses.

F. FINANCIAL SERVICES COMPANIES.

1. Financial services companies are national or regional corporations that offer a number of financial services to consumers, including traditional checking, savings, lending, credit card accounts, and MMMFs as well as advice on investments, insurance, real estate, and general financial planning.
2. Financial services companies are also referred to as nonbank banks because they provide limited traditional banking services, either accepting deposits or making commercial loans, but not both.

XI. TIME VALUE OF MONEY

A. TIME VALUE OF MONEY CONCEPTS.

1. Time value of money (TVM) is one of the most useful and important concepts in finance and personal financial planning. Essentially, the concept of time value of money is that money received today is worth more than the same amount of money received sometime in the future. A dollar received today is worth more than a dollar received one year from today because the dollar received today can be invested and will be worth more in one year. Alternatively, a dollar to be received a year from now is currently worth less than a dollar today.

2. There are two time periods and two values for time value of money analysis: future and future value and present and present value. Future value is the future dollar amount to which a sum certain today will increase compounded at a defined interest rate and a period of time. Present value is the current dollar value of a future sum discounted at a defined interest rate and a period of time.

B. FUTURE VALUE OF A SINGLE SUM DEPOSIT.

1. A dollar in hand today is worth more than a dollar to be received next year. If you had one dollar now, you could invest, earn interest, and end up next year with more than one dollar.

Example

Calculation 1:

Connie has an account of $100 that pays 10% interest compounded annually. At the end of year 1, Connie would have:

PV = $100 = Present value of her account, or the beginning amount.

i = 10% = Interest rate per period. Expressed as a decimal, i = 0.10.

FV_n = Future value, or ending amount, of Connie's account at the end of n years.

Whereas, PV is the value now, at the present time, FV_n is the value n years into the future, after compound interest has been earned. Note also that FV_0 is the future value zero years into the future, which is the present, so $FV_0 = PV$.

n = Number of periods, often years, involved in the transaction.

n = 1, so $FV_n = FV_1$, is calculated as follows:

This means that the future value, FV, at the end of 1 period is the present value multiplied by 1 plus the interest rate. The equation can now be used to find how much Connie's $100 will be worth at the end of 1 year at a 10% interest rate:

$FV_1 = \$100(1 + 0.10) = \$100(1.10) = \$110$

Connie's account will earn $10 of interest; therefore, she will have $110 at the end of the year.

Example

Calculation 2:

Another way to look at this problem is with a timeline. On a timeline, Time 0 is today; Time 1 is 1 period from today, or the end of 1 period; Time 2 is 2 periods from today, or the end of 2 periods; and so on. Thus, the values on timelines represent end-of-period values. At Time 0 (today), when Connie opens her bank account, she has $100. The timeline below shows $100 at Year 0. She would like to know how much she would have at the end of the year (Year 1 on the timeline) if the account pays an interest rate of 10%. The interest rate of 10% is shown above the timeline to indicate how much her deposit will increase. The equation shows that the account will grow to $110 at the end of the year, so she could replace the first question mark with $110.

Year 0		Year 1		Year 2		Year 3		Year 4		Year 5
	10%		10%		10%		10%		10%	
$100		?		?		?		?		?

Now suppose Connie leaves her funds on deposit for 5 years. How much will she have at the end of the fifth year? The answer is n = 5; i = 10; PV = $100; FV = $161.05.

Year	Beginning Amount	Interest Factor	Ending Amount	Interest (Annual)
1	$100.00	1.10	$110.00	$10.00
2	110.00	1.10	121.00	11.00
3	121.00	1.10	133.10	12.10
4	133.10	1.10	146.41	13.31
5	146.41	1.10	161.05	14.64
				$61.05

EXHIBIT 9: FUTURE VALUE TABLE

Periods	Interest Rates (i)									
(n)	1%	2%	3%	4%	5%	6%	7%	8%	9%	10%
1	1.0100	1.0200	1.0300	1.0400	1.0500	1.0600	1.0700	1.0800	1.0900	1.1000
2	1.0201	1.0404	1.0609	1.0816	1.1025	1.1236	1.1449	1.1664	1.1881	1.2100
3	1.0303	1.0612	1.0927	1.1249	1.1576	1.1910	1.2250	1.2597	1.2950	1.3310
4	1.0406	1.0824	1.1255	1.1699	1.2155	1.2625	1.3108	1.3605	1.4116	1.4641
5	1.0510	1.1041	1.1593	1.2167	1.2763	1.3382	1.4026	1.4693	1.5386	1.6105
6	1.0615	1.1262	1.1941	1.2653	1.3401	1.4185	1.5007	1.5869	1.6771	1.7716
7	1.0721	1.1487	1.2299	1.3159	1.4071	1.5036	1.6058	1.7138	1.8280	1.9487
8	1.0829	1.1717	1.2668	1.3686	1.4775	1.5938	1.7182	1.8509	1.9926	2.1436
9	1.0937	1.1951	1.3048	1.4233	1.5513	1.6895	1.8385	1.9990	2.1719	2.3579
10	1.1046	1.2190	1.3439	1.4802	1.6289	1.7908	1.9672	2.1589	2.3674	2.5937

2. Solve future value problems in one of three ways:

   a. Regular calculator - Use a regular calculator, either by multiplying (1+i) by itself n - 1 times or by using the exponential function to raise (1+ i) to the *n*th power.

   b. Compound interest tables - There are many appropriate interest tables available to find the proper interest factor. For example, find the correct interest factor for the 5-year, 10% problem addressed in the previous example. Look down the first column to Period 5 and across the row to the 10% column to find the interest factor, 1.6105. Using this interest factor, multiply it by the $100 initial investment.

      $FV_5 = PV\ (FV_{10\%,\ 5\ years}) = \$100\ (1.6105) = \$161.05.$

   c. Financial calculator - Financial calculators are programmed to solve most discounted cash flow problems. The calculators generate the $FVIF_{i,n}$ factors for a specified pair of i and n values, then multiply the computed factor by the PV to produce the FV. In the illustrative problem, enter PV = 100, i = 10, and n = 5, and press the FV key. The answer, $161.05, rounded to two decimal places, is displayed. The FV will appear with a minus sign on some calculators. The logic behind the negative value is that the initial amount is an investment (the PV) and the ending amount is a disinvestment (the FV), so one is an inflow and the other is an outflow. Some calculators may require pressing the Compute key before pressing the FV button. Financial calculators permit you to specify the number of decimal places. Use at least two places for problems where the answer is in dollars or percentages and four if the answer is an interest rate in decimal form.

Note: The most efficient way to solve most problems is to use a financial calculator. However, it is important to understand how the tables are developed and used, and to understand the logic and the math that underlie all types of financial analyses. Otherwise, you will not understand stock and bond valuation, lease analysis, capital budgeting, and other important TVM topics.

C. PRESENT VALUE.

1. This calculation is used to determine what a sum of money to be received in a future year is worth in today's dollars based on a specific discount rate.

   a. Calculation 1.

   The example above shows that an initial amount of $100 growing at 10% a year would be worth $161.05 at the end of 5 years. One should be indifferent to the choice between $100 today and $161.05 at the end of 5 years, assuming that the opportunity cost was 10% per year. The $100 is defined as the present value, or PV, of $161.05 due in 5 years when the opportunity cost is 10%. Therefore, if X is anything less than $100, one should prefer the promise of $161.05 in 5 years to X dollars today; if X were greater than $100, one should prefer X.

   The concept of present values can also be illustrated using a timeline. The following timeline shows the future value amount of $161.05 at Year 5. A question mark appears at Year 0 - this is the value of interest - and the interest rate of 10% appears above the timeline, indicating opportunity cost.

0	10%	1	10%	2	10%	3	10%	4	10%	5
?										$161.05

   The present value of a sum due n years in the future is the amount that, if it were on hand today, would grow to equal the future sum. Since $100 would grow to $161.05 in 5 years at a 10% interest rate, $100 is the present value of $161.05 due 5 years in the future when the appropriate interest rate is 10%.

   Finding present value, or discounting, is simply the reverse of compounding;

   $FV_n = PV(1+i)^n$, can be transformed into a present value formula by solving for PV:

$$PV = \frac{FV_n}{(1+i)^n} = FV_n(1+i)^{-n} = FV_n\left(\frac{1}{1+i}\right)^n$$

   Tables have been constructed for the last term in parentheses for various values of i and n; Exhibit 10 is an example. For our illustrative case, look down the 10% column in Exhibit 10 to the fifth row. The figure shown there, 0.6209, is the present value interest factor ($PV_{i,n}$) used to determine the present value of $161.05 payable in 5 years, discounted at 10%:

   $PV = FV_5(PV_{10\%,\ 5\ years})$

   $= (\$161.05)(0.6209)$

   $= \$100$

   b. Calculation 2.

   A financial calculator could be used to find the PV of the $161.05. Just enter n = 5, i = 10, and FV = $161.05, and press the PV button to find PV = $100. On some calculators, the PV will be given as -$100, and, on some calculators, you must press the Compute key before pressing the PV key.

EXHIBIT 10: PRESENT VALUE OF $1 DUE AT THE END OF N PERIODS

$$PV_{k,n} = \frac{1}{(1+i)^n} = \left(\frac{1}{1+i}\right)^n$$

Periods	Interest Rates (i)									
(n)	1%	2%	3%	4%	5%	6%	7%	8%	9%	10%
1	.9901	.9804	.9709	.9615	.9524	.9434	.9646	.9259	.9174	.9091
2	.9803	.9612	.9426	.9246	.9070	.8900	.8734	.8573	.8417	.8264
3	.9706	.9423	.9151	.8890	.8638	.8396	.8163	.7938	.7722	.7513
4	.9610	.9238	.8885	.8548	.8227	.7921	.7629	.7350	.7084	.6830
5	.9515	.9057	.8626	.8219	.7835	.7473	.7130	.6806	.6499	.6209
6	.9420	.8880	.8375	.7903	.7462	.7050	.6663	.6302	.5963	.5645
7	.9327	.8706	.8131	.7599	.7107	.6651	.6227	.5835	.5470	.5132
8	.9235	.8535	.7894	.7307	.6768	.6274	.5820	.5403	.5019	.4665
9	.9143	.8368	.7664	.7026	.6446	.5919	.5439	.5002	.4604	.4241
10	.9053	.8203	.7441	.6756	.6139	.5584	.5083	.4632	.4224	.3855

Example

- A client invested $10,000 in an interest-bearing promissory note earning an 11% annual rate compounded monthly. At the end of 7 years, the note will be worth $21,522.04, assuming all interest is reinvested at the 11% rate.

  PV = $10,000
  i = 0.91666 (11÷12)
  n = 84 (7 x 12)
  FV = $21,522.04

- Bill Barnett purchased $60,000 worth of silver coins 8 years ago. The coins have appreciated 7.5% compounded annually over the last 8 years. Today, the coins are worth $107,008.67.

  PV = $60,000
  i = 7.5
  n = 8
  FV = $107,008.67

D. SOLVING FOR TIME AND INTEREST RATES.

1. So far, only one equation has been used, Equation 1, and its transformed version, Equation 2:

$$(1)\quad FV_n = PV(1+i)^n = PV(FV_{i,n})$$

$$(2)\quad PV = \frac{FV_n}{(1+i)^n} = FV_n(PV_{i,n})$$

2. There are four variables in the equations:
   a. PV = present value = \$100 in the examples.
   b. FV = future value = \$161.05 after 5 years at 10%.
   c. i = interest (or discount) rate = 10% in the examples.
   d. n = number of years = 5 in the examples.
3. If the values of three of the variables are known, the fourth can be determined. Thus far, the interest rate (i) and the number of years (n) as well as either the PV or the FV have been given. In many situations, however, the unknown will be either n or i.
4. Periods (n) – Example.
   a. Calculation 1.

   Assume the following: PV = \$100, FV = \$161.05 and i = 10%. Determine the number of periods, n, involved.

$$\begin{aligned} FV_n &= PV(FV_{i,n}) \\ \$161.05 &= \$100\ (FV_{10\%,n}) \\ FV_{10\%,n} &= \$161.05 \div \$100 \\ FV_{10\%,n} &= \$1.6105 \end{aligned}$$

   The interest rate of 10% is given, and the future value interest factor is the unknown (refer to Exhibit 9). In Exhibit 9, the 10% column is used to find the future value interest factor of \$1.6105 (row 5). The number of time periods for \$100 to accumulate to \$161.05 is equal to 5.

   b. Calculation 2.

   The problem could also be solved using Equation 2, solving for the length of time it takes \$100 to grow to \$161.05 at a 10% interest rate:

$$\begin{aligned} PV_n &= FV(PV_{i,n}) \\ \$100 &= \$161.05\ (PV_{10\%,n}) \\ PV_{10\%,n} &= \$100 \div \$161.05 \\ PV_{10\%,n} &= \$0.6209 \end{aligned}$$

   The interest rate of 10% is given, and the present value interest factor is the unknown (refer to Exhibit 10). In Exhibit 10, the 10% column is used to find the present value interest factor of 0.6209 (row 5). Thus, the number of time periods for \$100 to accumulate to \$161.05 is equal to 5.

c. Calculation 3.

The easiest way to solve the problem is by using a financial calculator. Input i = 10, PV = 100, FV = \$161.05 (or - \$161.05), and then press the n key to find n = 5 years.

> **Note:** Be cautious when solving for term (n) because some financial calculators (i.e., HP 12C) treat (n) as a whole number; therefore, your answer is not always precise when calculating for term. Anytime you calculate for (n), you may need to find the answer by trial and error. Recalculate one of the other known factors (i.e., FV or PV) using the whole numbers (n). The recalculated known factor will likely be too high or low using the whole number (n). You will then have to continue using different values for (n) until you have correctly recalculated the known factor.

Pay close attention to this example.

Example			Correct Calculation		
FV	=	\$400	FV	=	\$400
i	=	4.5	i	=	4.5
PV	=	\$250	PV	=	\$250
n	=	11	n	=	10.678

Once you have finished the calculation using a financial calculator, reenter the n and calculate the FV to assure yourself that the n calculated is correct to the precise degree that you require (e.g., two decimal places).

5. Interest Rate – Example.

a. Calculation 1.

Assume the following: PV = \$100, FV, = \$161.05, and n = 5. The interest rate that \$100 would grow to \$161.05 over 5 periods must be determined.

$$FV_5 = PV\,(FV_{i,n})$$
$$\$161.05 = \$100\,(FV_{i,5})$$
$$FV_{i,5} = \$1.6105$$

The number of time periods, 5, is given; the future value interest factor is the unknown (refer to Exhibit 9). Period 5 row is used to find the future value interest factor of \$1.6105 (10% column). Thus, \$100 accumulates to \$161.05 at an interest rate equal to 10%.

b. Calculation 2.

Alternatively, the equation could be set up as follows:

$$PV = FV_5(PV_{i,5})$$
$$\$100 = \$161.05\,(PV_{i,5})$$
$$PV_{i,10\%} = \$0.6209$$

The number of time periods, 5, is given; the present value interest factor is the unknown (refer to Exhibit 10). The Period 5 row is used to find the present value interest factor of 0.6209 (10% column). Thus, \$100 accumulates to \$161.05 at an interest rate equal to 10%.

c. Calculation 3.

The easiest way to solve the problem is with a financial calculator. Input PV = 100, FV = \$161.05 (or - \$161.05), and n = 5. Press the i key to find i = 10%.

Example

- Joe purchased 10 shares of an aggressive growth mutual fund at \$90 per share 7 years ago. Today, he sold all 10 shares for \$4,500. His average annual compound rate of return on this investment before tax was 25.8499%.

PV = \$900
FV = \$4,500
n = 7
i = 25.8499

- John borrowed \$800 from his father to purchase a mountain bike. John paid back \$1,200 to his father at the end of 5 years. The average annual compound rate of interest on John's loan from his father was 8.4472%.

PV = \$800
FV = \$1,200
n = 5
i = 8.4472

E. FUTURE VALUE OF AN ANNUITY.

An annuity is a series of equal payments at fixed intervals for a specified number of periods. Payments are given the symbol PMT. If the payments occur at the end of each period, they are referred to as an ordinary annuity, sometimes called a deferred annuity. If the payments are made at the beginning of each period, they are referred to as an annuity due (e.g., lease or rent payment). Both ordinary annuities and annuities due are common in financial planning.

1. Future Value of an Ordinary Annuity - Example.

A promise to pay \$1,000 a year for 3 years is a 3-year annuity. If each payment is made at the end of the year, it is an ordinary annuity. Patty receives such an annuity and deposits each annual payment into a savings account that pays 10% interest. How much will Patty have at the end of 3 years?

a. Calculation 1.

The answer is shown graphically as a timeline (Exhibit 11). The first payment is made at the end of Year 1, the second at the end of Year 2, and the third at the end of Year 3. The first payment is compounded for 2 years, and the last payment is not compounded at all. When the future values of each of the payments are summed, the total is the future value of the annuity. Patty's total is \$3,310.00.

EXHIBIT 11: TIMELINE FOR AN ORDINARY ANNUITY

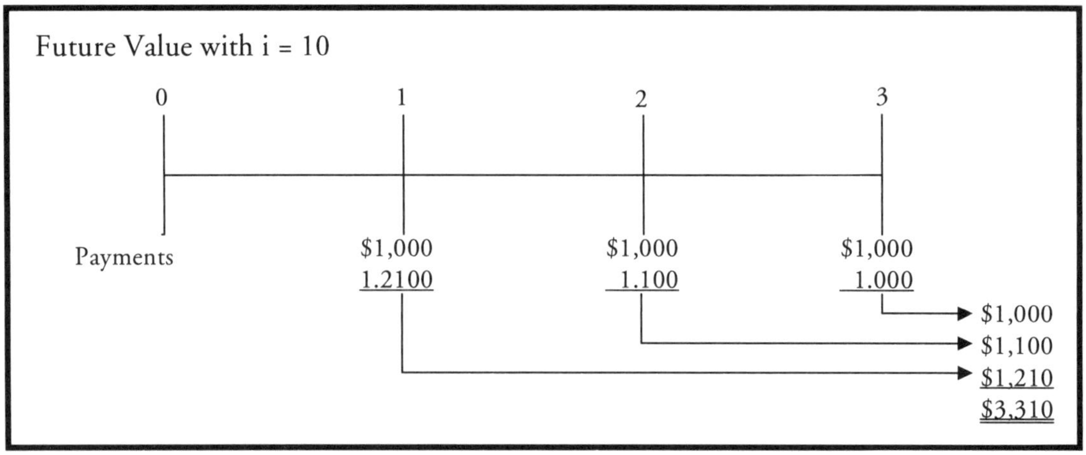

EXHIBIT 12: FUTURE VALUE OF AN ORDINARY ANNUITY

$$FVOA_{i,n} = \frac{(1 + i)^n - 1}{i}$$

Periods	Interest Rates (i)									
(n)	1%	2%	3%	4%	5%	6%	7%	8%	9%	10%
1	1.0000	1.0000	1.0000	1.0000	1.0000	1.0000	1.0000	1.0000	1.0000	1.0000
2	2.0100	2.0200	2.0300	2.0400	2.0500	2.0600	2.0700	2.0800	2.0900	2.1000
3	3.0301	3.0604	3.0909	3.1216	3.1525	3.1836	3.2149	3.2464	3.2781	3.3100
4	4.0604	4.1216	4.1836	4.2465	4.3101	4.3746	4.4399	4.5061	4.5731	4.6410
5	5.1010	5.2040	5.3091	5.4163	5.5256	5.6371	5.7507	5.8666	5.9847	6.1051
6	6.1520	6.3081	6.4684	6.6330	6.8019	6.9753	7.1533	7.3359	7.5233	7.7156
7	7.2135	7.4343	7.6625	7.8983	8.1420	8.3938	8.6540	8.9228	9.2004	9.4872
8	8.2857	8.5830	8.8923	9.2142	9.5491	9.8975	10.2598	10.6366	11.0285	11.4359
9	9.3685	9.7546	10.1591	10.5828	11.0266	11.4913	11.9780	12.4876	13.0210	13.5795
10	10.4622	10.9497	11.4639	12.0061	12.5779	13.1808	13.8164	14.4866	15.1929	15.9374

b. Calculation 2.

Annuity problems can also be solved using a financial calculator. To solve Patty's problem, key in n = 3, i = 10 and PMT = 1,000, and then press the FV key to produce the correct answer, $3,310.00.

2. Future Value of an Annuity Due - Example.

   Had Patty's three $1,000 payments in the above example been made at the beginning of each year, the annuity would have been an annuity due.

   a. Calculation 1.

      In terms of the timeline, each payment would have been shifted one period to the left, so there would have been $1,000 under Period 0 and a zero under Period 3; thus, each payment would be compounded for one extra year. The equation is modified to handle annuities due as follows:

      FVA_n (Annuity due) = $PMT(FV_{i,n})(1+i)$

      Since payment is compounded for one extra year, multiplying the term $PMT(FVA_{i,n})$ by (1+i) solves the extra compounding. Applying this equation to the previous example:

      FVA_n (Annuity due) = $1,000(3.3100)(1.10) = $3,641.00

      $3,641.00 is the future value for the annuity due versus $3,310.00 for the ordinary annuity. Since the payments are received faster, the annuity due is more valuable at the end of 3 years.

   b. Calculation 2.

      i. Annuity due problems can also be solved with financial calculators, most of which have a switch or key marked Due or Beg that permits conversion from ordinary annuities to annuities due.

Example

Christine Mastbo has been dollar cost averaging into a mutual fund by investing $2,000 at the end of every quarter for the past 7 years. She has been earning an average annual compound return of 11% compounded quarterly on this investment. Today, the fund is worth $82,721.95.

PMT_0 = $2,000
i = 2.75 (11 ÷ 4)
n = 28 (7 x 4)
FV_{OA} = $82,721.95

F. PRESENT VALUE OF AN ANNUITY.

1. The difference between the present value of an annuity due and the present value of an ordinary annuity is that the annuity due's payments are made at the beginning of each period rather than at the end, as for an ordinary annuity. This makes the present value of an annuity due always larger than the present value of an ordinary annuity with the same payments. This calculation is quite common in financial planning and is most often used for educational funding and for retirement capital needs analysis.

Example

Amanda is offered the following alternatives: (1) a 3-year annuity with payments of $1,000 at the end of each year, or (2) a lump-sum payment today. She has no current need for the money during the next 3 years, and if she accepts the annuity, she would deposit the receipts in a savings account that pays 10% interest. Similarly, the lump-sum receipts would be deposited in an account paying 10%. How large must the lump-sum payment be to make it equivalent to the annuity?

Calculation 1:

The present value of the first payment is PMT$[1 \div (1 + i)]$, the PV of the second is PMT$[1 \div (1 + i)]^2$, and so on. The PV of annuity due will always be greater than the PV of an ordinary annuity. To equate the two calculations, multiply the PV of the ordinary annuity by $(1 + i)$:

PVA_n(Annuity due) = PMT($PVA_{i,n}$)(1+i).

If payments were made at the end of each year, Amanda's 10%, 3-year annuity has a present value of $2,486.85.

PVA = $1,000 (2.48685)

= $2,486.85

Calculation 2:

Again, a financial calculator can be used to solve the problem.

Ordinary Annuity

n = 3

i = 10

PMT_{OA} = $1,000

PV_{OA} = $2,486.85

Therefore, the lump-sum payment must be equal to or greater than $2,486.85 if the $1,000 is paid at the end of each year.

Example

Tim, injured in an automobile accident, won a judgment that provides him $1,500 at the end of each 6-month period over the next 6 years. If the escrow account that holds Tim's settlement award earns an average annual rate of 11% compounded semiannually, the defendant would initially be required to pay Tim $12,927.78 to compensate for his injuries.

PMT_{OA} = $1,500

i = 5.5 (11 ÷ 2)

n = 12 (6 x 2)

PV_{OA} = $12,927.78

Example

Jane wants to withdraw $4,000 at the beginning of each year for the next 7 years. She expects to earn 10.5% compounded annually on her investment. The lump sum Jane should deposit today is $21,168.72.

PMT_{AD} = $4,000

i = 10.5

n = 7

PV_{AD} = $21,168.72

G. SERIAL PAYMENTS.

1. A serial payment is a term of art. It means a payment that increases at some constant rate (usually inflation) on an annual (ordinarily) basis. There are many situations where it is more affordable to increase payments on an annual basis since the payor expects to have increases in cash flows or earnings to make those increasing payments (e.g., life insurance, educational needs, retirement needs).
2. Serial payments differ from fixed annuity payments (both ordinary and annuity due payments) in that serial payments are not a fixed amount per year. The result is that the initial serial payment is less than its respective annuity due or ordinary annuity payment. The last serial payment will obviously be greater than the last respective fixed annuity payment, but will have the same purchasing power as the first serial payment.

AMORTIZATION SCHEDULE 1

Schedule of Equal Annuity Payments (Annuity Due)

	Deposit (Beginning of Year)	Account Balance (Year-End)	Target	
1	$18,462.43	$20,493.29	$100,000.00	Today 1/1/02
2	18,462.43	43,240.84	105,000.00	1/1/03
3	18,462.43	68,490.63	110,250.00	1/1/04
4	18,462.43	96,517.89	115,762.50	1/1/05
5	18,462.43	127,628.15	121,550.63	1/1/06
6	0	127,628.15	127,628.16	1/1/07

Off 0.01

AMORTIZATION SCHEDULE 2

Schedule of Equal Ordinary Annuity Payments

	Payment (End of Year)	Account Balance (Year-End)		Target	
1	$0	$20,493.29		$100,000.00	Today 1/1/02
2	20,493.29	22,747.55		105,000.00	1/1/03
3	20,493.29	47,997.33		110,250.00	1/1/04
4	20,493.29	76,024.59		115,762.50	1/1/05
5	20,493.29	107,134.85		121,550.63	1/1/06
6	20,493.29	127,628.14	Beg. of Yr.	127,628.16	1/1/07

After last deposit

Off 0.02

N	= 5	N	= 5
i	= 11	i	= 5
FV	= $127,628.16	PV	= $100,000
PMT_{OA}	= $20,493.29	FV	= $127,628.16

The calculation of the initial serial payment will depend on when it is to be made (today or 1 year from today at the first year-end). If it is to be made today and the payment is an annuity due, the calculation is as follows:

FV = $100,000
N = 5
i = 5.7142857 [[(1.11 ÷ 1.05) -1] x 100]
PMT_{AD} = $16,876.75

Each successive period serial payment will increase by 5% (the inflation rate). An amortization table is provided (Amortization Schedule 3) to demonstrate the deposits, account balance, and the target account balance. The future value is stated in real terms ($100,000) for purposes of the calculation.

AMORTIZATION SCHEDULE 3

Schedule of Annuity Due Serial Payments

	Deposit (Beginning of Year)	Account Balance (Year-End)	Target Balance (Beginning of Year)
1	$16,876.75	$18,733.19	$100,000.00
2	17,720.58	40,463.69	105,000.00
3	18,606.61	65,568.03	110,250.00
4	19,536.94	94,466.52	115,762.50
5	20,513.79	127,628.14	121,550.63
6	0		127,628.16

Off 0.02

FV = $100,000 (real dollars)
i = 5.7142857 (real rate of earnings)
N = 5
PMT_{AD} = $16,876.75

The calculation of the serial payment made in arrears (Amortization Schedule 4) is a little odd. Because the payment is to be made at year-end, the calculated ordinary annuity payment must be inflated by the appropriate inflation rate to determine the first payment to be made at the end of year one. This is consistent with the year-end value in year one for Amortization Schedule 3.

N = 5
i = 5.7142857
FV = $100,000
PMT = $17,841.13 today
x 1.05
$18,733.19 at year-end

AMORTIZATION SCHEDULE 4

Deposits Made in Arrears (OA)

	Deposit (End of Year)	Interest	Account Balance (Year-End)	Target Balance	
1	$0	$0	$18,733.19	$100,000.00	2002
2	18,733.19	2,060.65	20,793.84	105,000.00	2001
3	19,669.85	4,451.01	44,914.70	110,250.00	2002
4	20,653.34	7,212.48	72,780.52	115,762.50	2003
5	21,686.01	10,391.32	104,857.85	121,550.63	2004
6	22,770.31	0	127,628.16	127,628.16	2005

Exactly Equal

FV = $100,000
N = 5
i = 5.7142857
PMT_{OA} = $17,841.13 (today)

3. One difficulty in using serial payments is determining exactly how much to deposit and when to make those deposits. The second difficulty is having confidence that the calculation is accurate. These two problems arise due to the nature of changing prices (inflation rate) and the earnings rate growing at different rates. The proof is the ability to present an amortization table, such as Amortization Schedules 3 and 4, to assure that the payments and timing are correct.

H. NET PRESENT VALUE.

1. Net present value (NPV) analysis is a common technique employed by businesses and investors to evaluate capital projects and capital expenditures, generally in the capital budgeting area.
2. The model assumes:
   a. Information is known about the future (cash flows, life, etc.).
   b. All reinvestments in nonlike life assets are made at the weighted average cost of capital of the firm. (This is a more conservative assumption than the internal rate of return (IRR) method, which assumes the reinvestment rate is the IRR calculated.)
3. NPV is considered a superior model to IRR, when comparing investment projects of unequal lives, as it helps answer the question of whether a company should buy a particular piece of equipment or make a particular investment.
4. The resultant of the analysis is in dollars.
5. NPV equals the difference between the initial cash outflow (investment) and the present value of discounted cash inflows.

If: NPV > 0; then IRR > required rate of return.

If: NPV = 0; then IRR = required rate of return.

If: NPV < 0; then IRR < required rate of return.

Example

If the present value of a series of cash flows is $200 and the initial outflow is $150, then the NPV equals $50 ($200 - $150). An NPV, which is greater than zero, implies that the IRR of the cash flows is greater than the discount rate used to discount the future cash flows. An NPV of zero implies that the discount rate used is equal to the IRR for the cash flows. An NPV that is negative implies that the discount rate used is greater than the true IRR of the cash flows. As a general rule, you should look for investments that have a positive NPV.

XII. EDUCATIONAL FUNDING

A. INTRODUCTION

1. One of the most common financial planning goals of parents is to provide an education for their children.
2. Over the past fifteen years, tuition at colleges and universities throughout the country has increased at an annual rate of seven percent, while the Consumer Price Index (CPI) has only averaged three percent.
3. There are many ways an individual can save for future education costs or pay for current ones.
    a. The most significant consideration is how much time exists before the student enters college.
    b. There are many funding options available for parents of very young children who are years away from entering college.
    c. Those parents with children nearing college age or currently entering college, or individuals paying for their own education, do not have as many options and savings methods.

B. NEEDS ANALYSIS

1. Before creating an educational funding plan, individuals should first determine the estimated needs.
2. Examples of needs include the following:
    a. Tuition and tuition-related expenses.
    b. Books, school supplies, and equipment (calculator, computer).
    c. Lodging.
    d. Meals.
    e. Transportation.
    f. Entertainment (school sporting events) and leisure (health club).
    g. Travel expenses.
    h. Tutoring (if necessary).
    i. Extra-curricular (fraternity/sorority dues).
    j. Clothing and attire.
    k. Other considerations particular to the student or family.

C. EDUCATIONAL SAVINGS CALCULATION

See the Educational Funding section in *Understanding Your Financial Calculator, 3rd Edition*, Dalton, James F., published by Dalton Publications.

D. TAX CREDITS AND DEDUCTIONS

1. General.
   a. The credits include:
      i. The HOPE scholarship credit.
      ii. The lifetime learning credit.
   b. The deductions include:
      i. Employer Educational Assistance Program Deduction.
      ii. Qualified Higher Education Expense Deduction.
2. The HOPE scholarship credit.
   a. The HOPE scholarship credit is a by-product of the Taxpayer Relief Act of 1997.
   b. Benefits.
      i. The HOPE scholarship credit equals 100 percent of the first $1,000 of qualified expenses paid in the tax year, plus 50 percent of the next $1,000.
      ii. The maximum credit allowed in a given year is $1,500 per student.
   c. Requirements.
      i. This tax credit is available for qualified tuition and related expenses incurred and paid after 1997 in the first two years of post-secondary education for the taxpayer, spouse, or dependent.
      ii. A student must be enrolled no less than half time to be eligible.
      iii. The credit is subject to a phaseout based on the taxpayer's adjusted gross income as follows:
         A) Married filing jointly: $83,000 - $103,000 for 2003.
         B) All other taxpayers: $41,000 - $51,000 for 2003.

> **Note:** AGI, for purposes of this credit, includes AGI and foreign earned income exclusions and United States possessions and Puerto Rico income inclusions.

3. The lifetime learning credit.
   a. The lifetime learning credit is another by-product of the Taxpayer Relief Act of 1997.
   b. Benefits.
      i. The lifetime learning credit provides annual per taxpayer reimbursement for qualified tuition and related expenses per family in the amount of $2,000 per year in the year 2003.
      ii. The taxpayer must spend $10,000 annually on qualified expenses in 2003 in order to qualify for the <u>full</u> credit. However, a partial credit can be obtained with lower levels of education expense.
      iii. This credit is based on a 20 percent factor of the qualified expenses. In other words, to obtain the full $2,000 credit in 2003, there must be qualified education expenses of at least $10,000.

c. Requirements.

i. This tax credit is available for tuition and enrollment fees for undergraduate, graduate, or professional degree programs paid after June 30, 1998.

ii. Half-time enrollment or more is required. If, however, the courses taken are geared towards the acquisition or improvement of job skills, the student may be enrolled less than half time.

iii. The lifetime learning credit can be claimed for an unlimited number of years.

iv. The credit is subject to a phaseout based on the taxpayer's adjusted gross income as follows:

A) Married filing jointly: $83,000 - $103,000 (for 2003).

B) All other taxpayers: $41,000 - $51,000 (for 2003).

d. Coordination of the HOPE scholarship credit and the lifetime learning credit.

i. If two or more children in the same household incur qualified expenses in the same year, the parents may claim a lifetime learning credit for the family, a HOPE Scholarship Credit for each child, or a lifetime learning credit for one child and a HOPE Scholarship Credit for the other.

ii. Only one credit is allowed per child per year.

4. Employer's Educational Assistance Program.

a. Under the Employer's Educational Assistance Program, an employer can pay for an employee's tuition (both graduate and undergraduate), enrollment fees, books, supplies, and equipment while these employer benefits are excluded from the employee's income up to $5,250 per year (for 2003).

b. The employer or employee cannot, however, also claim an educational credit (HOPE scholarship or lifetime learning credit) for the same expenses. If the employee has expenses greater than $5,250 then the employee will be permitted to claim an educational credit for the expenses over $5,250 (assuming the employee also meets the requirements for the educational credits).

c. TRA 2001 has made the exclusion permanent.

5. Deduction for qualified higher education expenses.

a. Benefits.

i. In 2003, taxpayers with adjusted gross income that does not exceed $65,000 ($130,000 in the case of married couples filing joint returns) are entitled to a maximum deduction of $3,000 per year for qualified education expenses. Taxpayers with adjusted gross income above these thresholds would not be entitled to a deduction.

ii. In 2004 and 2005, taxpayers with adjusted gross income that does not exceed $65,000 ($130,000 in the case of married taxpayers filing joint returns) are entitled to a maximum deduction of $4,000 for qualified education expenses. Taxpayers with adjusted gross income that does not exceed $80,000 ($160,000 in the case of married taxpayers filing joint returns) are entitled to a maximum deduction of $2,000.

b. Requirements.

i. TRA 2001 permits taxpayers an above-the-line (for AGI) deduction for qualified higher education expenses paid by the taxpayer during a taxable year.

ii. Qualified higher education expenses are defined in the same manner as for purposes of the HOPE Scholarship Credit (qualified tuition and enrollment fees).

c. Coordination with other tax benefits.

i. Taxpayers are not eligible to claim the deduction and a HOPE scholarship credit or lifetime learning credit in the same year with respect to the same student.

ii. A taxpayer may not claim a deduction for amounts taken into account in determining the amount excludable due to a distribution (i.e., the earnings and the contribution portion of a distribution) from a Coverdell ESA or the amount of interest excludable with respect to education savings bonds (Series E, EE, or I bonds).

d. The provision is effective for payments made in taxable years beginning after December 31, 2001, and before January 1, 2006.

E. QUALIFIED TUITION PROGRAM (SECTION 529 PLANS FORMERLY KNOWN AS QUALIFIED STATE TUITION PROGRAMS)

1. Introduction.

In 1996, Congress enacted Section 529 of the Internal Revenue Code (IRC) through the Small Business Job Protection Act of 1996. Section 529 was modified by the Taxpayer Relief Acts of 1997 and 2001.

2. Plan sponsors.

a. States are allowed to enact these plans in accordance with the IRC Section 529.

i. Each state can use its own statutory language but the plan must be in conformity with Section 529 to be an eligible plan.

ii. Although state plans may differ, they must all contain the required provisions under IRC Section 529.

b. For years after 2001, eligible educational institutions can also create plans.

i. An eligible educational institution is generally an accredited post-secondary educational institution.

ii. To be an eligible educational institution the plan must receive a ruling of determination from the IRS.

iii. Distributions from an eligible educational institution are not excluded from income until taxable years after 2003.

Note: Distributions from qualified state tuition plans are excluded in 2003.

3. Types of plans.
   a. There are two versions of the Section 529 plan.
      i. Prepaid tuition plans.
         A) Allow the contributor to prepay tuition today at a particular school for an individual in the future.
         B) The plan will lock in today's prices, but subjects the participant to many risks.
         C) The main risks are that the beneficiary may choose a school different from the one named in the plan, or the beneficiary is not accepted into the school named in the plan.
         D) Before investing in this type of plan, the participant will want to investigate the details of the particular plan as they relate to the above factors.
      ii. Savings Plan.
         A) This plan allows an individual to make contributions today into a savings fund.
         B) The earnings grow tax deferred.
         C) If the proceeds are used for higher educational expenses after 2001 for a state-sponsored plan, the distributions are tax free. If the proceeds are used for higher educational expenses after 2003 for an eligible educational institution-sponsored plan, the distributions are tax free.
4. Qualified Tuition Program (QTP) Rules.
   a. Contributions must be made in cash.
      i. Cash, check, money order, credit cards, etc., are acceptable.
      ii. Property is not an allowed contribution.
   b. Plans must use separate accounting for each beneficiary.
   c. Direction of investments.
      i. A plan can permit the contributor to select among different investment strategies designed exclusively for the program when the initial contribution is made to establish the account.
      ii. The IRC states that neither the contributor nor the beneficiary can direct the investment. However, Notice 2001-55, issued September 7, 2001, announced that the final regulations area expected to state that the individual can change the investments one time per year. Until the final regulations are issued, taxpayers can rely on this notice.
   d. No pledging of interest as security.

5. Plan advantages.
   a. Tax-deferred growth.
   b. Tax-free distributions (after 2001 for state-sponsored plans and after 2003 for eligible educational institutions) for qualified education expenses (taxed to beneficiary for years prior to 2002).
   c. Generally, removes assets from taxable estate.
   d. Generally, low commission and management fees.
   e. Many states offer state income tax deductions for contributions (i.e., NY allows an annual state income tax deduction of up to $5,000 for contributions).
   f. The contributor can change the beneficiary at any time.
   g. The contributor decides when and how expenses are paid.
   h. The amount deposited varies by state, but can be as much as is reasonable to fund educational costs. Some states have maximum contributions as high as $250,000.
   i. For gift tax purposes, contributions can be treated as though they were made ratably over a five-year period.
   j. Contributions are not phased out, even at higher AGI levels.
   k. Can be coordinated with other educational plans, but no "double dipping" (i.e., if the beneficiaries claim the lifetime learning credit or HOPE scholarship credit, then no tax advantages are allowed for the <u>same</u> expenses).
6. Qualified expenses.
   a. Tuition.
   b. Fees.
   c. Books.
   d. Supplies.
   e. Equipment.
   f. Certain room and board expenses (requires at least half-time status).
      i. Normally assessed fee, if school lodging.
      ii. School determines reasonable amount for other locations.
7. Estate and gift tax consequences.
   a. The contributions are removed from the contributor's gross estate (even though he/she still has the power to change the beneficiary).
   b. Contribution can be a split gift (i.e., half made by the donor, and half by the donor's spouse as available under IRC Section 2513).
   c. Contribution is considered a completed gift of a present interest, allowing it to qualify for the annual exclusion.
   d. Favorable gift tax rules at contribution – Five-year averaging can be elected, allowing an individual to use five year's worth of annual exclusions on an initial contribution.

Example

In Year 1, when the annual exclusion is $11,000, Patti makes a contribution of $65,000 to a QTP for the benefit of her child, Cindi. Patti elects under Section 529(c)(2)(B) to account for the gift ratably over a five-year period beginning with the calendar year of contribution. Patti is treated as making an excludible gift of $11,000 in each of Years 1 through 5 and a taxable gift of $10,000 in Year 1.

In Year 3, when the annual exclusion is increased to $12,000, Patti makes an additional contribution for the benefit of Cindi in the amount of $7,000. Patti is treated as making an excludible gift of $1,000 under Section 2503(b); the remaining $6,000 is a taxable gift in Year 3.

e. If contributor dies within the five-year period, then the deferred portion for calendar years after the date of death is included in the gross estate.

Example

In Year 1, when the annual exclusion is $11,000, Patti makes a contribution of $55,000 to a QTP for the benefit of her child, Cindi. Patti elects under Section 529(c)(2)(B) to account for the gift ratably over a five-year period beginning with the calendar year of contribution.

Assume Patti dies in Year 2. The gross estate will include $33,000 of the deferred portion (Years 3, 4, and 5).

Assume, instead, Patti only made a $20,000 contribution in Year 1 and again elected to account for the gift ratably over the five-year period. Patti is treated as making an excludable gift of $4,000 in each of Years 1 through 5, because the 5-year averaging, if elected, must be ratable over the 5-year period. Under the assumption that Patti dies in Year 2, the gross estate will include $12,000 of the deferred portion (Years 3, 4, and 5).

f. Generation-Skipping Transfer Tax (GSTT) does not apply on the gift as long as it does not exceed the exclusion amount.

8. Change of beneficiary.
   a. Allowed at any time.
   b. Rollovers will not be considered a taxable distribution if the funds are transferred to one of the following within 60 days of the distribution:
      i. To another qualified tuition program for the benefit of the designated beneficiary (as long as a previous transfer to a qualified tuition program for the benefit of the designated beneficiary has not occurred within the last 12 months).
      ii. To the credit of another designated beneficiary under a qualified tuition program who is a member of the family of the designated beneficiary with respect to which the distribution was made.
   c. Any change in the designated beneficiary of an interest in a qualified tuition program will not be a taxable distribution if the new beneficiary is a member of the family of the old beneficiary.

d. A transfer that occurs by reason of a change in the designated beneficiary, or a rollover of credits or account balances from the account of one beneficiary to the account of another beneficiary, will be treated as a taxable gift by the old beneficiary to the new beneficiary if the new beneficiary is assigned to a lower generation than the old beneficiary, as defined in IRC Section 2651, regardless of whether the new beneficiary is a member of the family of the old beneficiary. The transfer will be subject to the generation-skipping transfer tax if the new beneficiary is assigned to a generation two or more levels lower than the generation assignment of the old beneficiary.

Example

In Year 1, Parent makes a contribution to a QTP on behalf of Child. In Year 4, Parent directs that a distribution from the account for the benefit of Child be made to an account for the benefit of Grandchild. The rollover distribution is treated as a taxable gift by Child to Grandchild, because, under IRC Section 2651, Grandchild is assigned to a generation below the generation assignment of Child.

---

9. Funds used for nonqualified expenses.
   a. The distribution is included in the gross income of the distributee.
   b. Form 1099-G must be filed by payor.
10. Ten percent penalty.
   a. A 10 percent additional tax will be applied to any distribution that is includible in gross income based on the above rules.
   b. The penalty is waived if the distribution is:
      i. Made to a beneficiary (or to the estate of the designed beneficiary) on or after the death of the designated beneficiary.
      ii. Attributable to the designed beneficiary's being disabled.
      iii. Made on account of a scholarship, allowance, or payment received by the account holder to the extent the amount of the payment or distribution does not exceed the amount of the scholarship, allowance, or payment.
11. Distribution of funds.
   a. Distributions are prorated between contributions and earnings.

Example

Assume the contributor deposits $100, has $10 of earnings, and has a distribution of $11. The $11 distribution will be comprised of $10 return of contribution and $1 earnings.

---

12. Limits to amounts contributed.
   a. State sets limit.
   b. Contributions cannot exceed reasonable cost.

F. COVERDELL EDUCATION SAVINGS ACCOUNTS (FORMERLY EDUCATION IRAS)

1. Introduction.
   a. Educational IRAs were authorized by the Taxpayer Relief Act of 1997.
   b. They were renamed Coverdell Education Savings Accounts (Coverdell ESA) in 2001.
   c. Coverdell ESAs are designed to offer tax benefits to those individuals who wish to save money for a child/grandchild's qualified education expenses.
   d. A Coverdell ESA is an investment account established with contributions of cash. These contributions are not deductible.
   e. Contributions can be made for the benefit of children that are under 18 years of age.
2. Benefits.
   a. The contributions grow tax free within the account.
   b. Money withdrawn from the account is free from tax or penalty if the funds are used for qualified educational expenses.
   c. If the funds are used for anything other than higher education expenses, the earnings are generally subject to income tax and a 10 percent penalty.
   d. Generally, the parent (responsible individual) maintains the right to change the beneficiary to another family member at any time.
3. Requirements.
   a. A Coverdell ESA can be established for any child under the age of 18 by a parent, grandparent, other family members or friends, or even by the child, as long as the contributor who establishes the account does not have income over $220,000 if filing married or $110,000 if filing single.

PHASEOUTS FOR 2003

Single	Married
$95,000 - $110,000	$190,000 - $220,000

   b. Beginning in 2002, annual contributions can be made up to $2,000 (TRA 2001) for each beneficiary. This includes contributions from all sources, including parents, grandparents, etc.
   c. TRA 2001 expands the definition of qualified education expenses (beyond undergraduate or graduate level courses) that may be paid tax free from a Coverdell ESA to include qualified elementary and secondary school expenses. Expenses include:
      i. Tuition, fees, academic tutoring, special need services, books, supplies, and other equipment incurred in connection with the enrollment or attendance of the beneficiary at a public, private, or religious school providing elementary or secondary education (kindergarten through grade 12) as determined under state law,
      ii. Room and board, uniforms, transportation, and supplementary items or services (including extended-day programs) required or provided by such a school in connection with such enrollment or attendance of the beneficiary, and
      iii. The purchase of any computer technology or equipment or Internet access and related services, if such technology, equipment, or services are to be used by the beneficiary and the beneficiary's family during any of the years the beneficiary is in school.

d. When the beneficiary attains age 30 (unless the beneficiary has special needs or dies), the account must be distributed to the beneficiary within 30 days. The distribution will be subject to income tax and the 10 percent penalty as discussed within this section.

i. The Coverdell ESA may be rolled over (tax and penalty free) into a Coverdell ESA for a family member of the original beneficiary.

ii. If the new beneficiary is a generation below the generation of the original beneficiary the distribution is treated as a taxable gift.

iii. If the beneficiary dies and the account has not been distributed during the 30-day period, the remaining balance is considered distributed to the beneficiary and included in the beneficiary's estate.

e. No contributions can be made to the account once the beneficiary turns 18 years of age.

4. Estate and gift tax consequences.

a. The contributions are removed from the contributor's gross estate (even though he/she still generally has the power to change the beneficiary).

b. Contribution can be a split gift (i.e., half made by the donor, and half by the donor's spouse as available under IRC Section 2513).

c. Contribution is considered a completed gift of a present interest, allowing it to qualify for the annual exclusion.

d. Favorable gift tax rules at contribution – Five-year averaging can be elected, allowing an individual to use five year's worth of annual exclusions on an initial contribution.

5. Distributions and withdrawals.

a. Distributions or withdrawals from Coverdell ESAs are comprised of principal and earnings.

b. The designated beneficiary of a Coverdell ESA can take withdrawals at any time. Distributions are always paid to the beneficiary (or beneficiary's estate) and will not be repaid to the contributor.

c. The principal is always excluded from taxation, whereas earnings are excluded if used to pay for qualified educational expenses.

d. Withdrawals are tax free whether the student is enrolled full time, half time, or less than half time as long as the withdrawals do not exceed the student's qualified educational expenses.

6. Ten percent penalty.

a. A 10 percent additional tax will be applied to any distribution that is includible in gross income based on the above rules.

b. The penalty is waived if the distribution is:

i. Made to a beneficiary (or to the estate of the designed beneficiary) on or after the death of the designated beneficiary.

ii. Attributable to the designed beneficiary's being disabled.

iii. Made on account of a scholarship, allowance, or payment received by the account holder to the extent the amount of the payment or distribution does not exceed the amount of the scholarship, allowance, or payment.

7. Coordination with other tax benefits.

   a. TRA 2001 allows a taxpayer to claim a HOPE scholarship credit or lifetime learning credit for a taxable year and to exclude from gross income amounts distributed (both the contributions and the earnings portions) from a Coverdell ESA on behalf of the same student as long as the distribution is not used for the same educational expenses for which a credit was claimed for years after 2001.

G. SAVINGS BONDS

1. Series EE United States savings bonds ("EE bonds").

   a. The face values of EE bonds start as low as $50 and increase up to $10,000.

   b. EE bonds are purchased at one-half of their face value.

   c. EE bonds have varying interest rates, but face value must be reached within 17 years.

   d. If used to pay for qualified higher education expenses at an eligible institution or state tuition plan, EE bonds bestow significant tax savings, that is, no federal income tax on the interest.

   e. Qualified higher education expenses include rolling over proceeds from the savings bonds into a Qualified Tuition Program (IRC Section 529 Plan) or a Coverdell ESA (formerly known as an Education IRA).

   f. To attain tax-free status, EE bonds must be purchased in the name of one or both parents of the student/child.

   g. The parent(s) are considered the owners of the bond, and must be at least 24 years old before the first day of the month of the issue date of the bond.

   h. Also, the owners must redeem the bonds in the same year that the student/child's qualified higher education expenses are paid.

   i. The exclusion is subject to a phaseout in the years in which the bonds are cashed and the tuition is paid. The phaseouts for 2003 are $87,750-$117,750 for joint returns and $58,500-$73,500 for other returns.

   j. Series I bonds have the same tax benefits as EE bonds for purposes of qualified higher education expenses. (See Investment Planning section of this text for more discussion.)

H. GOVERNMENT GRANTS AND LOANS (FINANCIAL AID)

1. Determining financial need.

   a. Financial Need, also known as Demonstrated Financial Need, refers to "the difference between what it costs to attend a particular college and the amount that a student and the student's family can afford to pay towards those expenses." This need is determined through the use of standardized formulas. Although a student is usually eligible for all of the student's demonstrated financial need, colleges are not necessarily able to meet the full need.

   b. The amount of money that students and parents can be expected to contribute toward a college education is referred to as the Estimated Family Contribution (EFC).

c. The EFC is composed of two parts:

   i. The parents' contribution.

   ii. The student's contribution.

   Both of these are determined by using federal and/or alternate guidelines.

d. Federal guidelines, or Federal Methodology, are formulas that are used to determine the demonstrated financial need of a student. The Federal Methodology is used by the government and takes into consideration income, some assets, expenses, and family size.

e. The alternate methodology is called Institutional Methodology. It is used to determine a student's need for nonfederal financial aid. Although it is similar to the Federal Methodology, it assumes a minimum expected contribution from the student and takes home equity into consideration. Furthermore, it allows a more generous treatment of some expenses.

f. The amount of aid for which students are eligible can be influenced by their dependency status. Students are either considered dependent on their parents for financial support or independent of financial support. For federal aid, dependency status is determined according to federal guidelines. Colleges may have different definitions of independence when it comes to distributing college funds.

2. Applying for financial aid.

   a. In order to apply for federal financial aid, students and their parents must fill out the Free Application for Federal Student Aid (FAFSA). This form, distributed by the Department of Education, is used to determine a student's need according to the Federal Methodology.

   b. When a student reapplies for federal financial aid, a partially preprinted form called the Renewal FAFSA is used.

   c. To be eligible, certain requirements must be met. For example, you must:

      i. Be a U.S. citizen or eligible noncitizen.

      ii. Be registered with Selective Service (if required).

      iii. Attend a college that participates in the following programs:

         A) Federal Pell Grants (Pell Grants).

         B) Federal Supplemental Educational Opportunity Grants (FSEOG).

         C) Federal Subsidized and Unsubsidized Stafford Loans.

         D) Stafford/Ford Federal Direct Subsidized and Unsubsidized Loans.

         E) Federal Perkins Loans.

         F) Federal Work-Study (FWS).

      iv. Be working toward a degree or certificate.

      v. Be making satisfactory academic progress.

      vi. Not owe a refund on a federal grant or be in default on a federal educational loan.

      vii. Have "financial need" as determined in part by the Free Application for Federal Student Aid (except for some loan programs).

d. Additional financial aid information.

i. Federal student loans must be repaid.

ii. Less-than-half-time students may be eligible for Federal Pell Grants and some other federal student aid programs.

iii. Students who have received a bachelor's degree are not eligible for Federal Pell Grants or FSEOG, but may be eligible for other federal student aid programs.

iv. Students attending two schools in the same enrollment period must inform both Financial Aid Administrators (FAAs). Students cannot receive Pell Grants at both schools.

v. Conviction of drug distribution or possession may make a student ineligible.

e. The U.S. Department of Education also has a toll-free number to answer questions about federal student aid programs. This number is 1-800-4 FED AID.

3. Types of financial aid.

a. Federal Pell Grants.

i. Federal Pell Grants are outright gifts from the government based on the student's need and the cost of attending the chosen school.

ii. Only undergraduate students who have not previously received a bachelor's degree are eligible for the grants.

iii. The maximum amount of award ranges each year depending on program funding. The maximum award was $3,300 for the 2001-2002 school year.

iv. The Federal Pell Grant Program is the largest need-based student aid program.

b. Federal Supplemental Educational Opportunity Grant (SEOG) Program.

i. The Federal Supplemental Educational Opportunity Grant (SEOG) Program is another grant program for undergraduates with exceptional financial need.

ii. This program is managed by colleges instead of the federal government.

iii. The SEOG Program awards grants of up to $4,000.

iv. Students are automatically considered when they submit a FAFSA form.

c. Federal Perkins Loan Program.

i. The Federal Perkins Loan Program is a federally funded program administered by colleges.

ii. This program provides loans of up to $4,000 per year for an undergraduate program (up to a total of $20,000 per student if student completes two years of undergraduate work; otherwise, the total a student can borrow is $8,000).

iii. Graduate students and professional study students may borrow up to $6,000 per year.

iv. The total loan amount may reach $40,000 if a student pursues graduate and professional studies (the total includes any loans as an undergraduate).

v. Characteristics of a Perkins Loan include a 5% fixed interest rate, deferred repayment, a nine-month grace period, and a maximum of ten years to repay the loan. Students are automatically considered if they complete a FAFSA.

d. Federal College Work-Study Program.

   i. Although the Federal College Work-Study Program is sponsored by the government, it is administered through colleges.

   ii. Students work ten to fifteen hours per week at a job that is typically on campus in order to earn a portion of their financial aid package.

e. Federal PLUS Loans.

   i. Federal PLUS Loans allow the parents of undergraduate students to borrow up to the total costs of education minus other financial aid awards.

   ii. The interest rate is variable, based on the 91-day T-Bill rate plus 3.1%, and is capped at 9%.

   iii. Loans are not made based on financial need, but borrowers must show that they do not have unsatisfactory credit history.

   iv. Repayment of the loan must begin within 60 days of disbursement.

   v. Graduate and independent undergraduate students may defer the principal, but must pay the interest on the loan immediately.

f. Subsidized Federal Stafford Loans.

   i. Subsidized Federal Stafford Loans are based on financial need.

   ii. The interest is variable, based on the 91-day T-bill rate plus 2.3%, capped at 8.25%.

   iii. The government pays the interest while the student is enrolled in college.

   iv. Repayment of the loan may take up to ten years and is deferred until six months after the student graduates, leaves school, or drops below half-time status.

   v. Borrowers are charged a 3% origination fee and a guaranty fee of up to 1%. Both are deducted from the face value of the loan before disbursement.

g. Unsubsidized Federal Stafford Loans.

   i. Unsubsidized Federal Stafford Loans are available for students who do not qualify for subsidized loans or require additional funds.

   ii. The major differences between unsubsidized and subsidized loans are that the government does not pay the interest during the college years and repayment begins almost immediately after disbursement.

   iii. The interest while the student is in school, in deferment, or in a grace period, is variable based on the 91-day T-bill rate plus 1.7%, capped at 8.25%.

   iv. The interest during repayment or forbearance is the same as the subsidized Federal Stafford Loan (91-day T-bill rate plus 2.3%, capped at 8.25%).

   v. Both types of Stafford loans are available to undergraduate and graduate students.

I. OTHER SOURCES

1. Aid directly from the institution.
   a. Each school has its own method of providing aid through loans, scholarships, discounts, and campus jobs.
   b. The school's financial aid advisor should adequately explain to the student the school's available options and programs.
   c. Some schools will allow a student to pay tuition on a monthly installment plan, which may provide more flexibility to the student and parents.
   d. Other schools may offer discounts or scholarships for superior athletic or academic performance either prior to or after enrollment. The school has an incentive to entice superior athletes and academic students in order to increase their level of top students and to better compete with other schools, which in turn enhances the school's image.
2. Aid from Armed Forces.
   a. The U.S. Armed Forces have numerous programs and scholarships that may pay for tuition, fees, and books for those who enlist or enroll in the military.
   b. The student may also receive monthly payments for other expenses.
   c. Information regarding the many programs available through the U.S. Armed Forces can be obtained from the college attended or from the Administrative Office of the desired branch of military.
3. Other scholarships.
   a. There are many forms of scholarships that are awarded by groups that are separate and apart from the school and state, or federal government.
   b. Numerous civic organizations award scholarships based on need, merit, and/or the student's or parents' affiliation with that civic organization.
   c. There are various types of scholarships available to students who have high grades and high standardized (entrance) test scores, including National Merit Scholarships.
   d. Scholarships can also be provided through a particular church or religious organization.
4. Traditional IRA.
   a. Generally speaking, if a taxpayer withdraws funds from his or her traditional IRA prior to age 59½, the taxpayer is required to pay a 10 percent early withdrawal penalty on all or part of the amount withdrawn.
   b. The 10 percent penalty does not apply if a taxpayer withdraws funds from a traditional (or Roth) IRA to pay for qualified higher educational expenses for the taxpayer, the taxpayer's spouse, or the child or grandchild of the taxpayer or taxpayer's spouse.
   c. Unlike a Coverdell Education Savings account, the taxpayer will owe federal income tax on the amount withdrawn.

5. Roth IRA.
   a. The Roth IRA was also created by the Taxpayer Relief Act of 1997.
   b. Contributions.
      i. The Roth IRA does not provide for tax-deductible contributions.
      ii. Contributions grow tax free within the IRA.
      iii. As a result of TRA 2001, contributions to Roth and traditional IRAs have increased to $3,000 for years 2003-2004; $4,000 for years, 2005 through 2007; and $5,000 in 2008 and thereafter.
      iv. Contributions to Roth IRAs are limited to the lesser of the annual limit or earned income in 2002.
      v. Contributions can be made as late as the due date of the individual's tax return for the previous tax year.
      vi. Contributions to a Roth IRA can be made for years beyond the age of 70½, whereas traditional IRAs prevent contributions after the attainment of age 70½.
      vii. Allowed contributions to Roth IRAs are phased out for joint filers with an adjusted gross income between $150,000 and $160,000, and for single taxpayers with an adjusted gross income between $95,000 and $110,000.
   c. Distributions.
      i. A distribution from a Roth IRA is not includible in the owner's gross income if it is a "qualified distribution," or to the extent that it is a return of the owner's contributions to the Roth IRA.
      ii. Qualified distributions are distributions that occur after a five-year holding period and on account of one of the following four reasons:
         A) Death.
         B) Disability.
         C) Attainment of age 59½.
         D) First-time house purchase (limit of $10,000).
      iii. If a distribution is not a qualified distribution and it exceeds contribution (and conversions) to Roth IRAs, then the distribution will be subject to income tax and may be subject to the 10 percent penalty.
      iv. Excess distributions can avoid the 10 percent penalty if the proceeds are used for qualified higher education costs.
      v. The taxpayer is always able to withdraw amounts up to their total contribution without income tax or penalty.
   d. Requirements.
      i. Qualified higher educational expenses are tuition, fees, and room and board.

e. Benefits.

i. In short, Roth IRAs may be an even more attractive vehicle for education savings than Educational IRAs because the age of the student is irrelevant (versus the 30-year-old requirement) and because contributions are higher.

ii. Funds in a Roth IRA not used for education can be used for retirement of the parent (contributor).

6. Equity lines of credit.

a. A home equity loan or line of credit is yet another vehicle that can be used to fund college-related expenses.

b. Because home equity loans are secured by a house, the interest rate on a home equity loan may be lower than rates for an unsecured student loan.

c. Many state schools do not consider the value of the home when determining eligibility for financial aid, but numerous private colleges take equity in the home into account.

d. If equity in the home is considered in the financial aid equation, a home equity loan could decrease home equity and possibly improve one's eligibility for financial aid.

e. Further, the interest on home equity loans is normally deductible as an itemized deduction.

f. As a general rule, using home equity loans and lines of credit to pay for higher education expenses should be a last resort, or at least done after researching all other options, rates and conditions for alternative funding.

g. Borrowing too much against the home could result in foreclosure or other difficult situations.

7. Uniform Gift to Minor's Act.

a. The Uniform Gift to Minor's Act ("UGMA") allows parents the option to put assets in a custodial account for a child.

b. If the child is below 14 years of age, the child's unearned income (i.e., interest, dividends) may be taxed at the income tax rate of the parents.

c. If the child is 14 years or older, the child's unearned income (i.e., interest, dividends) is taxed at the tax rate for the child.

d. Custodial account assets are considered an asset of the child and considered in determining financial aid.

8. Interest on educational loans.

a. Interest paid on student loans for undergraduate and graduate education may be deducted as an adjustment to the taxpayer's AGI.

b. The deduction for years 2001 and beyond is $2,500.

c. The loaned funds must have been spent on tuition and enrollment fees, books, supplies, equipment, room and board, transportation, or other necessary expenses.

d. For years after 2001, there is a phaseout of this deduction for taxpayers filing jointly with an AGI from $100,000 to $130,000 and for single filers with an AGI from $50,000 to $65,000.

9. Highlights of tax benefits for higher education.

The following exhibit provides a glance at the highlights and attributes of the various vehicles covered in this section.

EXHIBIT 13: HIGHLIGHTS OF TAX BENEFITS FOR HIGHER EDUCATION FOR 2003

	Hope Credit	**Lifetime Learning Credit**	**Coverdell Education Savings Account[1]**	**Traditional, Roth, SEP & SIMPLE IRAs[1]**	**Student Loan Interest**	**State Tuition Programs[2] (Section 529 Plans)**	**Education Savings Bond Program[1]**	**Employer's Educational Assistance Program[1]**	**Qualified Higher Education Expenses[4]**
What is your benefit?	Credits can reduce the amount of tax you must pay		Earnings are not taxed	No 10% additional tax on early withdrawal	You can deduct the interest	Earnings are not taxed	Interest is not taxed	Employer benefits are not taxed	Deduction of expenses "for AGI"
What is the annual limit?	Up to $1,500 per student	Up to $2,000 per family	$2,000 contribution per beneficiary	Amount of qualifying expenses	$2,500	None	Amount of qualifying expenses	$5,250	Maximum: 2002-2003 $3,000 2004-2005 $4,000
What expenses qualify besides tuition and required enrollment fees?	None		Books Supplies Equipment Room & board if at least a half-time student Payments to state tuition program	Books Supplies Equipment Room & board if at least a half-time student	Books Supplies Equipment Room & board Trans-portation Other necessary expenses	Books Supplies Equipment Room & board if at least a half-time student	Payments to Coverdell ESAs Payments to state tuition program	Books Supplies Equipment	None
What education qualifies?	1st 2 years of under-graduate	All undergraduate and graduate[3]							Qualified higher education expenses
What are some of the other conditions that apply?	Can be claimed only for 2 years Must be enrolled at least half-time in a degree program		Can contribute to Coverdell Education Savings Accounts and state tuition program in the same year Must withdraw assets by age 30		No longer a 60 month limit Must have been at least half-time student in a degree program	Distribution is excluded from gross income Hope and Lifetime Learning Credit are permitted in the same year but not for the same expenses	Applies only to qualified series EE bonds issued after 1989 or series I bonds	Does not expire after December 31, 2001	Cannot claim Hope or Lifetime Learning Credit in same year for the same student
In what income range do benefits phase out?	2003: $41,000 - $51,000; $83,000 - $103,000 for joint returns		$95,000 - $110,000; $190,000 - $220,000 for joint returns	No phaseout	$50,000 – $65,000 $100,000 – $130,000 for joint returns	No phaseout	2003: $58,500 - $73,500; $87,750 - $117,750 for joint returns	No phaseout	2002-2003 Single < $65,000 MFJ < $130,000 2004-2005 Single $65,000-80,000 MFJ $130,000 – 160,000

[1] Any nontaxable withdrawal is limited to the amount that does not exceed qualifying educational expenses.

[2] Exclusion is extended to distributions from Qualified Tuition programs established by an entity other than a State after December 31, 2003.

[3] For Coverdell Education Savings Accounts, qualified elementary and secondary school expenses are also permitted (Grades K-12).

[4] For years 2004 – 2005 AGI less than $65,000 ($130,000 married) can take a maximum deduction of $4,000 and taxpayers with AGI between $65,000 and $80,000 ($130,000 and $160,000 married) can take a maximum deduction of $2,000. This deduction expires for years after 2005.

XIII. BUSINESS ORGANIZATIONS

> **Note:** Only a basic understanding of these concepts is usually tested on the exam.

A. LEGAL FORMS OF BUSINESS ORGANIZATIONS.

1. Sole proprietorship - A business owned by an individual, who is personally liable for the obligations of the business.
2. General partnership - An association of two or more persons, who jointly control and carry on a business as co-owners for the purpose of making a profit. Generally, the partners are personally liable for the obligations of the business (both jointly and severally).
3. Limited partnership - A partnership in which at least one partner is a general partner and at least one other is a limited partner, who does not participate in management and has limited liability.
4. Limited liability partnership (LLP) – Usually a professional partnership (CPAs, attorneys) wherein the partners have limited liability to the extent of investment except where personally liable through malpractice. This form protects the individual assets of the nonmalpracticing partners.
5. Limited liability company (LLC) – An entity where the owners (members) have limited liability for debts and claims of the business even while participating in management. The governing document is called an operating agreement. Some states prohibit single member LLCs.
6. Corporation - A separate legal entity that is created by state law and operates under a common name through its elected management. Owners (shareholders) have limited liability.
7. S corporation - A corporation with ≤ 75 shareholders, all individuals other than resident aliens, certain estates or trusts, and no more than one class of stock.
8. Other forms of business organizations.
   a. Joint venture - An association formed to carry out a single transaction or a series of similar transactions that, for tax purposes, is treated the same as a partnership (although no partnership tax return is filed).
   b. Syndicate or investment group - A number of persons who pool their resources in order to finance a business venture.
   c. Business trust - A number of people turn over management and legal title to property to one or more trustees, who distribute the profits to the participants (the beneficiaries of the trust).
   d. Cooperative - An association (may be incorporated) organized in order to provide an economic service to its members (or shareholders).

B. SOLE PROPRIETORSHIPS.

A business owned and controlled by one person who is personally liable for all debts and claims against the business. A sole proprietorship is taxed directly to the individual, who must include a Schedule C in his or her individual tax return (Form 1040).

C. GENERAL PARTNERSHIPS.

1. Characteristics of a general partnership are found in partnership law (the law of agency).
    a. The elements of a general partnership:
        i. A common ownership interest in an ongoing business.
        ii. A sharing of profits and losses of the business.
        iii. A right to participate in the management and operation of the business.
    b. A partnership is treated as an entity, separate and apart from its individual members for limited purposes:
        i. The partnership has the capacity to sue and be sued in the name of the partnership (state laws vary).
        ii. Judgments can be entered against a partnership in its partnership name.
        iii. The partnership is subject to liquidation proceedings under Federal Bankruptcy Laws.
        iv. The partnership can participate in transfers and ownership of personal and real property (state laws vary).
    c. A partnership may be treated as an aggregate under federal laws and some state laws.
2. Formation of a partnership.
    a. No special formality is ordinarily necessary to create a partnership.
    b. A partnership may be expressly created by contract.
        i. Partnership agreement may be either a verbal contract or a written contract.
            A) A partnership agreement must be in writing in order to be enforceable, under the Statute of Frauds, if it authorizes partners to deal in transfers of real property.
            B) If a partnership is formed for a term of more than one year under a verbal agreement, it is treated as a partnership at will, which may be terminated by any party without liability. A partnership for term requires the assent of all partners for dissolution.
            C) Usual contents of articles of partnership:
                1) Name - State law may restrict use of certain names and/or words.
                2) Nature of business and duration.
                3) Contributions to be made by individual partners.
                4) Manner of dividing profits and losses - Unless otherwise specified, partners share profits equally. If no provision is made for the manner of sharing losses, losses are shared in the same proportion, as are profits.
                5) Salaries and drawing accounts, if any.
                6) Restrictions on the authority of any partners.
                7) Conditions for withdrawal from partnership and provisions for the continuation of the business if the partnership is dissolved (partnership buy and sell agreement).

ii. Capacity of partners.

A) Minors - Partnership agreement is voidable by a partner who is a minor. However, if rights of creditors are involved, the minor cannot withdraw his or her original investment in the partnership.

B) If a partner is adjudicated to be mentally incompetent or insane after the partnership is formed, the partnership is not automatically dissolved.

C) Corporations - State laws vary.

1) Traditionally, a corporation could not be a partner.

2) If that corporation's charter (certificate or articles of incorporation) so provides, it may be a partner.

iii. Consent to formation of partnership by all partners is necessary.

c. Partnership may be implied if parties intended to be co-owners of a business.

i. Factors to be considered:

A) Joint ownership of business property.

B) Sharing management responsibilities.

C) Contributing capital or investing jointly.

D) Sharing profits or losses.

ii. It does not, however, necessarily mean that a group of people has formed a partnership if they are co-owners of property or share gross income (Universal Partnership Act (UPA) Sec. 7).

iii. A person will not be treated as a partner merely because he or she receives a share of profits in payment of a debt, wages, interest on a loan, annuity to a widow or representative of a deceased partner, or consideration for the sale of goodwill or other property.

d. Partner by estoppel.

i. A party, although not a partner, may be estopped from denying that the party is a partner and, therefore, may be held liable as a partner to third persons who reasonably relied and dealt with or advanced credit to the partnership if such nonpartner:

A) Held themselves out as being a member of a partnership, or

B) Consented to a misrepresentation of an alleged partnership relationship by another.

ii. The purported partner does not become a partner but may be liable as one to third persons.

3. Partnership property includes:

a. Real and personal property contributed by individual partners at the time of formation of the partnership or subsequently for the permanent use of the partnership.

b. Property subsequently acquired with partnership funds on account of the partnership.

c. Any realized appreciation in the value of partnership property.

4. Rights and duties of partners.
    a. Each partner has a right and a duty to share in the management of the partnership. Unless otherwise provided in the partnership agreement:
        i. Each partner has one vote, regardless of his or her interest in the firm.
        ii. In connection with ordinary business decisions, majority vote controls.
        iii. Unanimous consent is required for changing the partnership agreement, for altering the scope of the business or the capital structure, and in matters significantly affecting the nature, liability, or existence of the partnership.
        iv. Each partner is expected to devote full time and exclusive service to the partnership absent of a contrary agreement.
        v. Unless otherwise agreed, partners do not receive remuneration for their partnership services, except that surviving partners are entitled to reasonable compensation for services rendered in winding up the affairs of the dissolved partnership.
        vi. Each partner has the right to examine the books and records of the partnership, which should be maintained at the place of business of the firm, and has the right to information concerning the partnership's business from co-partners.
    b. Accounting.
        i. The purpose of accounting is to determine the value of each partner's proportionate share in the partnership.
        ii. An accounting may be rendered voluntarily.
        iii. A partner may bring an equitable action for an accounting.
            A) Usually, accounting occurs in connection with dissolution proceedings.
            B) Accounting is available if:
                1) The partnership agreement so provides.
                2) A partner has been wrongfully excluded from the business.
                3) A partner is wrongfully withholding profits in violation of fiduciary duty.
                4) Other circumstances "render it just and reasonable."
    c. Property rights.
        i. Rights with respect to specific partnership property.
            A) Partners are tenants in partnership, which means they are co-owners of partnership property with the right to possession for partnership purposes.
            B) Upon the death of a partner, rights in specific partnership property vest in the remaining partners.
            C) A partner may not assign rights to specific partnership property nor subject it to marital rights, attachment or execution by the partner's individual creditors, etc.

ii. Rights to an interest in the partnership.

A) Each partner has a right to a share of the profits and surplus (considered to be personal property).

B) A partner's interest in the partnership is subject to assignment, attachment, and other charging orders. An assignment does not dissolve the partnership or permit an assignee to interfere with management.

d. Fiduciary duties.

i. Each partner is an agent for co-partners and is, therefore, accountable as a fiduciary.

ii. A partner must act in good faith with loyalty and honesty for the benefit of the partnership and make full disclosure to co-partners of matters relating to the partnership.

iii. A partner will be liable for any personal gain or profits derived from using the partnership property or the exercise of power as a partner.

5. Relationship between partners and third persons.

a. In dealing with third persons on behalf of the partnership, each partner acts as an agent for the partnership and its members.

b. A partner's authority to bind the partnership contractually may be based upon:

i. Express actual authority provided for in the partnership agreement.

ii. Implied actual authority.

A) Necessary for the conduct of the ordinary business of the partnership.

B) Usually, partners have broad implied authority, which will vary with the nature of the particular business of each partnership, unless limited by agreement.

iii. Apparent authority.

A) A third person who deals with a partner may assume that the partner has authority to bind the firm in a transaction relating to the usual business of the firm.

B) Unless the third person knows that the partner lacks authority, the partnership and co-partners will be liable to the third party for any damage.

iv. Partners may ratify unauthorized acts of a partner.

c. Admissions and representations concerning partnership affairs made by an authorized partner bind the partnership if they are made while conducting the ordinary business of the partnership.

d. Knowledge of or notice to a partner of facts concerning matters relevant to the partnership's affairs will be imputed to the partnership and other partners.

e. The partnership and the co-partners are liable for breaches of trust and for torts committed by a partner or employee while acting within the scope of his or her authority in the ordinary course of business of the partnership.

f. Liability of partners to third persons - Partners are jointly liable in contract. In most states, actions based upon contract must be brought against all the partners jointly (together).

6. Termination of partnership - Occurs following the dissolution and winding up (liquidation) of a partnership.

   a. Dissolution - Occurs when a partner ceases to be associated with the partnership business, resulting in a change in the relation of the partners.

      i. By acts of the partners:

         A) If the partnership agreement provided for a partnership for term and the term has elapsed or the purpose for which it was formed has been accomplished, the partnership is dissolved.

         B) Partners may mutually agree to dissolution.

         C) If the partnership is a partnership at will, a partner's good faith withdrawal or expulsion dissolves the partnership without liability.

         D) If the partnership was for a specified term, withdrawal of a partner without cause will subject the withdrawing partner to liability; expulsion without cause subjects other partners to liability.

         E) Admission of a new partner results in dissolution of the former partnership and the creation of a new one. The new partnership is liable for the obligations of the old partnership.

         F) Voluntary or involuntary transfer of a partner's interest for the benefit of creditors does not automatically dissolve a partnership.

      ii. Dissolution by operation of law:

         A) Death of a partner.

         B) Bankruptcy of the partnership or a partner (in most cases).

         C) Illegality, which makes it unlawful to continue the business or continue with one of the partners.

      iii. Dissolution by judicial decree:

         A) Upon application of a partner.

            1) A partner has been judicially declared mentally incompetent.

            2) A partner is permanently incapable of participating in management.

            3) The business of the partnership can only be operated at a loss.

            4) Improper conduct of a partner.

            5) Serious personal dissension among partners.

         B) Upon application of a third party.

            1) Assignee of a partner if it was a partnership at will.

            2) Judgment creditor of a partner who obtained a charge on the interest of the partner's debtor in the partnership.

b. Notice of dissolution - Failure to give required notice results in liability.

   i. A withdrawing partner must give notice to co-partners.

   ii. Personal notice must be given to those who extended credit to the partnership, and public notice must be given to those who dealt with the firm on a cash basis if dissolution occurs because of acts of the parties or by operation of law, except for illegality or bankruptcy.

c. Winding up.

   i. Dissolution terminates the authority of partners, except the authority to complete unfinished business. Unfinished business is that which is necessary for winding up, including collecting, preserving, and selling partnership assets, discharging liabilities, collecting debts owed to the partnership, allocating current income, and accounting to each other for the value of their interests in the partnership.

   ii. Distribution of assets.

      A) Distribution is made out of partnership assets and any additional contributions by partners necessary to pay liabilities of the partnership.

      B) Order of payment:

         1) Payment to outside creditors.

         2) Payment to partners who have made advances or incurred liabilities on behalf of the partnership.

         3) Return of capital contributions to partners.

         4) Payment of any surplus to partners in accordance with ratios fixed by agreement or, if none, equally.

      C) Concept of marshaling of assets arises when the partnership and/or an individual partner is insolvent.

         1) If the partnership is insolvent, partnership's creditors have priority over individual's creditors with respect to partnership assets. The partnership's creditors may then look to partners' assets.

         2) If a partner is insolvent, the order of payment is:

            a) Partner's creditors.

            b) Partnership creditors.

   iii. Taxation at Dissolution.

      A) In General.

         1) When dissolution occurs, the partnerships taxable year closes with respect to all its partners.

         2) If partners use different taxable years than the partnership, a bunching of income may occur.

B) Liquidating Distributions.

1) When a partnership liquidates, the liquidating distributions made to a partner usually consist of an interest of several partnership assets.

2) The partner may be required to recognize gain on the distribution. The calculation of gain is based on a set of distribution ordering rules.

a) Cash is considered distributed first. The partner will recognize gain to the extent the cash received exceeds his or her basis in the partnership interest.

b) The partner's remaining basis is then allocated to inventory and receivables.

c) Any additional basis is then allocated to the other assets received by the partner.

3) If the partner received only money, receivables, or inventory, the partner will be allowed to recognize a loss if the partner's basis in the partnership interest exceeds the partner's basis in the assets distributed.

4) The partnership itself typically does not recognize gain or loss on liquidating distributions.

7. Taxation of partnerships.

a. Partnerships are flow-through entities for purposes of federal income taxation.

b. Items of income and deduction, which occur at the partnership level, will not be taxed to the partnership. Instead, those items of income and deduction will be reported to the partner on his or her individual federal income tax return (Form 1040).

c. Income and deductions will flow-through to the partner and retain their character. Items which flow-through separately and retain their character include the following:

i. Income and loss items (such as ordinary income, rental income, capital gain income, etc.).

ii. Deductions (such as charitable contributions, Section 179 expense, etc.).

iii. Credits (such as low-income housing, rental real estate, etc.).

iv. Investment interest.

v. Self-employment.

vi. Adjustments and tax preference items (such as depreciation, depletion, etc.).

vii. Foreign taxes.

viii. Other (such as tax-exempt interest income, distributions of property or money, nondeductible expenses, etc.).

d. These items of income and deduction are reported on Schedule K of the Federal Partnership Return (Form 1065) and will be reported to the partners on Schedule K-1. Each partner will receive a Schedule K-1 that includes his share or allocation of each item of income and deduction. The sum of all Schedule K-1's will equal the amount reported on Schedule K.

e. Each of the separately stated items on Schedule K-1 will be reported in the appropriate place on the partner's individual federal income tax return (Form 1040). For example, interest and dividends are reported on Schedule B.

EXHIBIT 14: SCHEDULE K-1 (FORM 1065)

SCHEDULE K-1 (Form 1065)
Department of the Treasury
Internal Revenue Service

Partner's Share of Income, Credits, Deductions, etc.

▶ See separate instructions.

For calendar year 2002 or tax year beginning , 2002, and ending , 20

OMB No. 1545-0099

2002

Partner's identifying number ▶	Partnership's identifying number ▶
Partner's name, address, and ZIP code	Partnership's name, address, and ZIP code

A This partner is a ☐ general partner ☐ limited partner ☐ limited liability company member
B What type of entity is this partner? ▶ ....
C Is this partner a ☐ domestic or a ☐ foreign partner?

D Enter partner's percentage of:

	(i) Before change or termination	(ii) End of year
Profit sharing	.... %	.... %
Loss sharing	.... %	.... %
Ownership of capital	.... %	.... %

E IRS Center where partnership filed return:

F Partner's share of liabilities (see instructions):

Nonrecourse	$ ....
Qualified nonrecourse financing	$ ....
Other	$ ....

G Tax shelter registration number ▶ ....

H Check here if this partnership is a publicly traded partnership as defined in section 469(k)(2) ☐

I Check applicable boxes: (1) ☐ Final K-1 (2) ☐ Amended K-1

J Analysis of partner's capital account:

(a) Capital account at beginning of year	(b) Capital contributed during year	(c) Partner's share of lines 3, 4, and 7, Form 1065, Schedule M-2	(d) Withdrawals and distributions	(e) Capital account at end of year (combine columns (a) through (d))
			( )	

		(a) Distributive share item		(b) Amount	(c) 1040 filers enter the amount in column (b) on:
Income (Loss)	1	Ordinary income (loss) from trade or business activities	1		See page 6 of Partner's Instructions for Schedule K-1 (Form 1065).
	2	Net income (loss) from rental real estate activities	2		
	3	Net income (loss) from other rental activities	3		
	4	Portfolio income (loss):			
	a	Interest	4a		Sch. B, Part I, line 1
	b	Ordinary dividends	4b		Sch. B, Part II, line 5
	c	Royalties	4c		Sch. E, Part I, line 4
	d	Net short-term capital gain (loss)	4d		Sch. D, line 5, col. (f)
	e	(1) Net long-term capital gain (loss)	4e(1)		Sch. D, line 12, col. (f)
		(2) 28% rate gain (loss)	4e(2)		Sch. D, line 12, col. (g)
		(3) Qualified 5-year gain	4e(3)		Line 5 of worksheet for Sch. D, line 29
	f	Other portfolio income (loss) (attach schedule)	4f		Enter on applicable line of your return.
	5	Guaranteed payments to partner	5		See page 6 of Partner's Instructions for Schedule K-1 (Form 1065).
	6	Net section 1231 gain (loss) (other than due to casualty or theft)	6		
	7	Other income (loss) (attach schedule)	7		Enter on applicable line of your return.
Deductions	8	Charitable contributions (see instructions) (attach schedule)	8		Sch. A, line 15 or 16
	9	Section 179 expense deduction	9		See pages 7 and 8 of Partner's Instructions for Schedule K-1 (Form 1065).
	10	Deductions related to portfolio income (attach schedule)	10		
	11	Other deductions (attach schedule)	11		
Credits	12a	Low-income housing credit:			
		(1) From section 42(j)(5) partnerships	12a(1)		Form 8586, line 5
		(2) Other than on line 12a(1)	12a(2)		
	b	Qualified rehabilitation expenditures related to rental real estate activities	12b		See page 8 of Partner's Instructions for Schedule K-1 (Form 1065).
	c	Credits (other than credits shown on lines 12a and 12b) related to rental real estate activities	12c		
	d	Credits related to other rental activities	12d		
	13	Other credits	13		

For Paperwork Reduction Act Notice, see Instructions for Form 1065. Cat. No. 11394R Schedule K-1 (Form 1065) 2002

Schedule K-1 (Form 1065) 2002 — Page 2

		(a) Distributive share item		(b) Amount	(c) 1040 filers enter the amount in column (b) on:
Investment Interest	14a	Interest expense on investment debts	14a		Form 4952, line 1
	b	(1) Investment income included on lines 4a, 4b, 4c, and 4f	14b(1)		See page 9 of Partner's Instructions for Schedule K-1 (Form 1065).
		(2) Investment expenses included on line 10	14b(2)		
Self-employment	15a	Net earnings (loss) from self-employment	15a		Sch. SE, Section A or B
	b	Gross farming or fishing income	15b		See page 9 of Partner's Instructions for Schedule K-1 (Form 1065).
	c	Gross nonfarm income	15c		
Adjustments and Tax Preference Items	16a	Depreciation adjustment on property placed in service after 1986	16a		See page 9 of Partner's Instructions for Schedule K-1 (Form 1065) and Instructions for Form 6251.
	b	Adjusted gain or loss	16b		
	c	Depletion (other than oil and gas)	16c		
	d	(1) Gross income from oil, gas, and geothermal properties	16d(1)		
		(2) Deductions allocable to oil, gas, and geothermal properties	16d(2)		
	e	Other adjustments and tax preference items (attach schedule)	16e		
Foreign Taxes	17a	Name of foreign country or U.S. possession ▶			Form 1116, Part I
	b	Gross income from all sources	17b		
	c	Gross income sourced at partner level	17c		
	d	Foreign gross income sourced at partnership level:			
		(1) Passive	17d(1)		
		(2) Listed categories (attach schedule)	17d(2)		
		(3) General limitation	17d(3)		
	e	Deductions allocated and apportioned at partner level:			
		(1) Interest expense	17e(1)		
		(2) Other	17e(2)		
	f	Deductions allocated and apportioned at partnership level to foreign source income:			
		(1) Passive	17f(1)		
		(2) Listed categories (attach schedule)	17f(2)		
		(3) General limitation	17f(3)		
	g	Total foreign taxes (check one): ▶ ☐ Paid ☐ Accrued	17g		Form 1116, Part II
	h	Reduction in taxes available for credit (attach schedule)	17h		Form 1116, line 12
Other	18	Section 59(e)(2) expenditures: a Type ▶			See page 9 of Partner's Instructions for Schedule K-1 (Form 1065).
	b	Amount	18b		
	19	Tax-exempt interest income	19		Form 1040, line 8b
	20	Other tax-exempt income	20		See pages 9 and 10 of Partner's Instructions for Schedule K-1 (Form 1065).
	21	Nondeductible expenses	21		
	22	Distributions of money (cash and marketable securities)	22		
	23	Distributions of property other than money	23		
	24	Recapture of low-income housing credit:			
	a	From section 42(j)(5) partnerships	24a		Form 8611, line 8
	b	Other than on line 24a	24b		

Supplemental Information

25 Supplemental information required to be reported separately to each partner (attach additional schedules if more space is needed):

Schedule K-1 (Form 1065) 2002

D. LIMITED PARTNERSHIPS.

1. Formation.
   a. The partners sign a certificate that sets forth the firm name, nature and duration of business, location of principal place of business, names and addresses of members, capital contributions of limited partners, share of profits or other compensation that limited partners are entitled to receive, methods for changes in membership, and subsequent continuation of the business.
   b. The certificate is filed with the designated state or local official.
2. Liability of partners to creditors.
   a. A limited partner is liable to creditors only to the extent of that partner's contributed or promised capital.
   b. A limited partner will be liable as a general partner if:
      i. The surname of the limited partner is included in the partnership name.
      ii. The limited partner participates in management.
      iii. The limited partner learns that the firm is defectively formed and fails to withdraw from the partnership.
   c. A general partner is liable to creditors in the way of unlimited personal liability.
3. Rights of a partner.
   a. A limited partner (member) has no authority to bind the partnership; however, a general partner has such authority.
   b. A limited partner and general partner have the same rights as partners in a general partnership with respect to suing, examining books, accounting, the return of partner's capital contribution, the assignments of rights to partner's interest, etc.
4. Dissolution.
   a. By acts of parties.
      i. Expiration of term in which the partnership was formed.
      ii. If the partnership is not formed for a specified term, the will of a general partner.
      iii. Withdrawal or expulsion of a general partner unless otherwise provided in the certificate or unless members consent to continuation.
   b. By operation of law.
      i. Death or insanity of a general partner if the business cannot be continued in accordance with certificate or consent of other members.
      ii. Illegality.
      iii. Bankruptcy of firm or a general partner.
   c. Limited partner's withdrawal, death, assignment of interest or bankruptcy (unless it causes the bankruptcy of the firm) does not result in the dissolution of the firm.

d. Winding up and liquidation procedure, following dissolution, is the same as that for a general partnership except for the priorities in distribution.

   i. The Uniform Limited Partnership Act specifies the following order for distribution of the partnership's assets:

      A) Outside creditors.

      B) Limited partners' shares of profit and any other compensation.

      C) Limited partners' return of capital contributions.

      D) Advances, loans, etc. made by general partners.

      E) General partners' shares of profits.

      F) General partners' return of capital contributions.

   ii. The Revised Uniform Limited Partnership Act changes the order by including claims of partners, who are creditors, with outside creditors and combining limited and general partners together.

5. Taxation of limited partnerships.

   a. Limited partnerships are taxed under the same concepts as a partnership.

   b. See Taxation of Partnerships.

E. FAMILY LIMITED PARTNERSHIP (FLP).

1. Introduction.

   a. A Family Limited Partnership ("FLP") is a partnership with a general partner and at least one limited partner. FLPs are generally designed to address several purposes: convenient administration of investments, while retaining control, as a vehicle for annual gifts for transfer tax planning purposes. In addition, FLPs provide for creditor protection for limited partners.

   b. A typical FLP is instituted by a senior family member who transfers business or investment assets to the partnership. The general partner has significant control over the business activities of the partnership, makes investment and management decisions, and determines when distributions should be made to the limited partners. This determination is based upon the general partner's evaluation of the needs of the partnership operations. Often, the senior family member serves as general partner.

   c. The partnership agreement will govern how partnership income is divided among the partners. Generally, both general and limited partners share income and cash flow based on their percentage interest in the partnership. The taxable income of the FLP is reported annually and allocated to each partner on the basis of that partner's percentage interest. The allocation is noted on the Schedule K-1 issued to each partner. Usually, the general partner annually distributes at least enough cash to pay the income tax liability attributable to each partner.

   d. Distributions are not taxable to the extent the partner has basis in the partnership interest. The partnership itself (unlike a corporation) is not subject to tax, because it passes through all items of income and deduction to the partners. Limited partners also have restrictions on their ability to transfer their partnership units to others, so that the general partners can prevent the units from being transferred outside of the family.

2. Advantages.

   a. The principal benefit of an FLP is its significant impact in reducing a transferor's gift and estate tax. By using an FLP, the owner can take advantage of gift and estate tax valuation rules relating to "minority interests" and "marketability" that can reduce transfer taxes. Due to the significant restrictions imposed on the limited partnership units, the partnership units typically will have a value that is approximately 30 percent less than the value of the assets that originally were transferred to the partnership. Actual discounts can range from 25% to 60%. Besides reduced asset values for estate and gift tax purposes through significant valuation discounts, other benefits include:

      i. Ability of the general partners to make substantial gifts yet maintain control of the partnership assets.

      ii. Continuing control of income from transferred assets since distributions from an FLP must be authorized by general partners.

      iii. Identification of partnership assets as separate assets and not marital assets. This would be important in the event of a divorce.

      iv. Control the future investment of family assets and retain a critical mass to enhance future investment opportunities.

      v. Reduced probate costs with respect to real estate located in other states. No ancillary administration is required.

      vi. Institutionalization and enhancement of family communication on family business and investment matters.

F. CORPORATIONS.

1. Nature of corporations.

   a. Business corporations are artificial, legal entities whose creation and operations are controlled by state statutes.

   b. A corporation is regarded as a person who is separate from the shareholders. The owners of interests in corporations, for most purposes under federal and state constitutions and statutes, are not restricted to natural persons.

      i. The capacity of a corporation to sue and be sued in the name of the corporation.

      ii. The protection against self-incrimination (restricted to natural persons).

      iii. Criminal liability.

      iv. Licensing statutes.

   c. Shareholders.

      i. Shareholders are generally the holders of ownership interests in the corporation. Their interests are freely transferable.

      ii. Death of a shareholder does not dissolve or otherwise affect the corporation.

      iii. Shareholders enjoy limited liability (amount of their investment) and are not personally liable for the debts of the corporation.

      iv. Shareholders have equitable interests in, but not legal title to, corporate property.

      v. Shareholders do not represent the corporation but vote for the board of directors which determines corporate policy and appoints officers. The officers represent the corporation.

      vi. Shareholders may sue and be sued by the corporation, and they may deal with the corporation in an "arm's length" transaction.

d. Tax considerations (double taxation of profits).

i. The profits of a corporation are taxed to the corporation at special corporate rates.

ii. Distributions of profits, in the form of dividends, are treated as taxable income to the recipients.

iii. If shareholders sell their shares, they are taxed on any gains, but perhaps at a rate lower than the rate imposed on ordinary income.

2. Classifications of corporations.

a. Based upon location.

i. Domestic corporation - Conducts business in the state of its incorporation.

ii. Foreign corporation - Conducts business outside of the state of its incorporation.

iii. Alien corporation - Incorporated in a country other than the United States.

b. Based upon sources of funds (or revenue), function and ownership arrangements.

i. Public corporation - Formed by legislative bodies for governmental purposes.

ii. Private corporation - Created for private benefit.

A) Issues shares of stock.

B) May be a closely held corporation - Shares of stock are held by one individual or by a small group.

iii. Nonprofit corporation - Organized for charitable, religious, educational, social, etc., purpose under special state statute.

iv. Professional corporation - A private corporation, the members of which engage in a profession, organized in order to gain advantages relating to taxes, pension, and insurance plans, etc.

c. Subchapter S corporation - A corporation that meets certain qualifications, provided for in Subchapter S of the Internal Revenue Code, may elect to be treated in a manner similar to a partnership for federal tax purposes. Corporate income is not taxed but is allocated among the shareholders for income tax purposes.

3. Formation of a corporation.

a. Promoter's activities before a corporation comes into existence: analyze economic feasibility, find investors, assemble necessary personnel, property and capital, and take preliminary steps for organization and incorporation.

b. Promoters are generally personally liable on preincorporation agreements.

i. Liability during the promotion period.

A) A promoter is a party to a contract and, therefore, bound as a party.

B) The corporation is not in existence, therefore, is not liable as a party to a contract.

ii. Liability after incorporation.

A) A promoter remains liable to other contracting party, unless:

1) Released by the contracting party.

2) The contracting parties clearly indicated that the promoter would not be personally liable.

3) The corporation is substituted as a party to the contract in a novation.

B) Corporation becomes liable after incorporation if:

1) It enters a novation.

2) It adopts or becomes an assignee of the rights of the promoter, who remains secondarily liable.

4. Incorporation procedure.

a. The corporation's charter, articles of incorporation, or certificate of incorporation generally must contain:

i. A corporate name.

A) Must use the word "corporation" or "incorporated" or an abbreviation, such as "corp." or "inc."

B) The name cannot be misleading or subject to confusion with the name of another organization.

ii. General nature and purpose.

iii. Duration - Usually perpetual.

iv. Capital structure.

v. Internal organization - May be described in articles of incorporation or in bylaws.

vi. Location of registered office and agent to receive service of process within the state.

vii. Names, addresses, and signatures of incorporators.

A) Usually, incorporators need not have any interest in the corporation, nor must they be subscribers.

B) The number of incorporators varies from one to three; statute may provide that incorporators need not be natural persons.

b. Articles of incorporation are filed with the appropriate state official (typically the secretary of state), necessary fees are paid, and notice of the filing is given.

c. Organizational meetings.

i. Incorporators elect the board of directors, adopt bylaws, authorize the board to issue stock, etc.

ii. The board of directors adopts minutes of meetings of incorporators (if required), preincorporation contracts, a seal, and a form for stock certificates, accepts subscriptions, etc.

iii. Bylaws are internal rules for governing and regulating the conduct of corporate affairs. Bylaws cannot conflict with articles of incorporation or statutes.

5. Improper incorporation.
   a. De jure corporation - The corporation was organized in accordance with required mandatory conditions precedent to incorporation. The corporate status or existence cannot be attacked.
   b. De facto corporation - The corporation operates as a corporation but fails to comply with some statutory mandate. Thus the state may challenge its existence.
   c. Corporation by estoppel - The corporation has neither de jure nor de facto status. Associates (alleged shareholders, directors) who participated in holding the association out as a corporation are precluded from denying that it was a corporation against third parties, who, in reliance upon the holding out, changed their positions and were, therefore, injured.
6. Disregarding the corporate entity.
   a. In unusual situations, a court may ignore the legal fiction of the corporation as an entity (pierce the corporate veil) when the corporation has been used to perpetuate fraud, circumvent law, accomplish an illegal purpose, or otherwise evade law.
   b. Courts will disregard the corporate entity, even though technically a corporation exists, and hold directors, officers, or shareholders personally liable for the transactions conducted in the corporate name.
   c. Courts will disregard the corporate entity if a corporation is not maintained as an entity, separate from its shareholders, in order to prevent abuse of the corporate privilege for personal benefit.
      i. Records and funds have been commingled, and the enterprise has not been established on an adequate financial basis (e.g., thin capitalization).
      ii. This arises occasionally in the case of a close corporation with only one or a few shareholders or in the case of parent-subsidiary corporations.
7. Corporate financing.
   a. Debt securities.
      i. In general, bonds are evidences of obligations to pay money. The term "bond" is often used; although, technically, this particular obligation may be a debenture.
         A) Bonds are secured by a lien or other security interest in assets.
         B) Debentures are secured by the general credit of the borrower rather than by specific property.
         C) Bonds are issued by business firms, governments, and others to investors with a designated maturity date when the principal, or face amount, is to be paid.
         D) Bonds provide fixed income because interest is paid at specified times and at specified rates.
         E) Discount - Bonds may be sold for less than their face value.
         F) Premium - Bonds may be sold for more than their face value.
      ii. Corporate bonds - Agreement is termed the bond indenture. Bondholders do not participate in corporate affairs.

A) Debentures are unsecured obligations - If the issuing corporation defaults, holders of debentures can look only to assets in which other creditors or bondholders have no security interests.

B) Mortgage bonds - Secured by real property.

C) Equipment trust bonds - Secured by equipment, legal title is vested in a trustee.

D) Collateral trust bonds - Secured by intangible corporate property such as shares of stock in other corporations or accounts receivable.

E) Convertible bonds - Bonds that may be exchanged for other bonds or stock at a specified rate.

F) Callable bonds - The issuing corporation has the right to repay the principal prior to maturity.

b. Equity securities - Every corporation issues common stock and may be authorized to issue preferred stock.

i. Authorized shares - Stock which the corporation is empowered by its charter to issue.

ii. Issued shares - Authorized shares that have been sold.

A) Outstanding shares - Shares that have been issued and are in the hands of shareholders.

B) Treasury shares - Issued shares that have been reacquired by the corporation.

iii. Par value shares - Shares that have been assigned a stated dollar value.

A) May be originally issued for an amount greater than par (premium).

B) In most states, par value shares cannot be originally issued for less than par value (discounted).

iv. No par shares - Shares that are not assigned any specific fixed price. No par shares are usually issued for a price that is fixed by the board of directors.

v. Stated capital.

A) Sum of par value of all issued par value shares and consideration received for all no par value shares.

B) Includes outstanding and treasury shares.

c. Classifications.

i. Common stock.

A) The owners of common stock are entitled to a pro rata share of properly declared dividends out of corporate profits without any preferences (e.g., after payment of taxes and interest to lenders and bondholders). They are entitled to any specified dividends required to be paid to preferred shareholders, if any preferred stock has been issued.

B) Common stock shareholders have a right to vote.

C) Common stock shareholders have rights to ultimate distribution of assets of corporation upon dissolution.

ii. Preferred stock - Holders of preferred stock have a preference that usually entails rights to receive dividends or distribution upon liquidation of the corporation. Corporations may issue different classes and/or series of preferred stock.

A) Cumulative preferred - If the corporation fails to pay a dividend, the dividend is carried over and paid in a subsequent year before the holders of common stock receive dividends.

B) Participating preferred - Preferred shareholders share in distribution of additional dividends after payment of dividends to holders of preferred and common stock if there are additional distributions of corporate profits.

C) Convertible preferred - Preferred shares may be exchanged for common stock or other preferred stock at a specified rate.

D) Redeemable (callable) preferred - The corporation has the right to purchase, reacquire and cancel shares at a specified price.

8. Corporate purpose - Defines the nature of the business in which the corporation engages.

a. The purpose must be legal and may be broadly stated in the charter.

b. Every corporation "has the purpose of engaging in any lawful business unless a more limited purpose is set forth in its articles of incorporation."

9. Corporate powers - Necessary to accomplish purpose for which the corporation is formed.

a. Statutory, general powers apply to all corporations organized under a state business corporation law. General powers usually include the power to have perpetual existence, to enter into a contract, to sue and be sued, to lend and borrow money, to buy, hold, lease, receive, dispose of and sell real and personal property, etc.

b. Express powers are those specifically enumerated in the corporate charter.

c. Implied powers are those that are incidental or necessary in order to carry out the corporation's purpose and express powers.

d. Ultra vires acts - Corporate exercise of power that it does not possess. These include:

i. While acting as an agent of the corporation, corporate director(s) or officer(s) participate in something that the corporation is not authorized to do because it is not in furtherance of the corporation's purpose.

ii. Illegal acts.

iii. Acts that are ratified by the shareholders.

A) The act was one that could have been authorized by the shareholders when it was originally done.

B) Unanimous ratification is necessary if there has been a gift or wasting of corporate assets.

e. Corporate liability for wrongful acts.

i. Torts - A corporation is liable for torts committed by its officers, directors, agents, and employees acting within the scope of their employment in furtherance of the corporation's business.

ii. Crimes - A corporation may be liable for a crime that carries an imposed fine as punishment.

10. Corporate management - Shareholders.
    a. Shareholders' position in the corporation - Shareholders have limited powers.
        i. The shareholders' approval is necessary in order to make fundamental changes that affect the corporation (i.e., amending the charter, merging with another corporation or dissolving).
        ii. The shareholders have power to elect and remove members of the board of directors for cause.
        iii. With some limitations, the shareholders have the right to inspect books, records, and shareholders' lists.
        iv. The shareholders do not participate in the management of the corporation.
    b. Meetings of the shareholders.
        i. Annual meeting.
            A) Usually, the date and place are fixed in the bylaws.
            B) Written notice must be given within the specified statutory period of time, but may be waived.
        ii. Special meetings may be called.
        iii. Quorum (minimum number of shares that must be represented at a meeting) - Fixed in the corporate charter within specified statutory range.
        iv. Voting.
            A) The corporation prepares a list of record owners of shares at a certain cutoff date.
            B) Unless otherwise specified by statute or charter, the usual vote required for shareholder action is as follows:
                1) Election of members of board of directors - Plurality of those shares represented at meeting.
                2) Other nonextraordinary matters - Majority of those shares represented at meeting.
                3) Extraordinary matters.
                    a) Statute or charter may require a specified proportion of all shares.
                    b) Usually, a greater than majority vote is required.
                    c) Methods of voting.
                        i) Straight voting - One vote per share standing in the name of a record holder.
                            A) Cumulative voting for election of directors.
                            B) May be provided for in charter.
                            C) In some states, cumulative voting is mandatory.
                            D) A shareholder's vote is equal to the number of shares that he or she owns multiplied by the number of directors to be elected.

ii) Proxy voting.

A) Shareholder may vote in person or by proxy.

B) A proxy is a written, revocable authorization to an agent to cast the vote of the shareholder.

iii) Voting agreements - Shareholders may agree to pool votes by casting them in a prescribed manner.

iv) Voting trusts - Legal title to shares is transferred to a trustee who votes the shares for the benefit of shareholders. The shareholders retain the rights to receive dividends and receive voting trust certificates.

11. Corporate management - Directors.

a. Qualifications, election, and tenure.

i. There are few statutory requirements for qualification as a director.

ii. The number of directors is specified in the charter or bylaws.

iii. The initial board of directors is named in the charter or elected by the incorporators. Subsequent directors are elected by the shareholders.

iv. The term of a director is usually one year but may be longer; directors may be divided into classes with staggered terms.

v. Provisions in the charter and/or statute determine the method of filling vacancies.

vi. Shareholders have power to remove directors, with or without cause, in accordance with the charter or bylaws. Directors may have power to remove a director for cause.

b. Functions of board of directors - Responsible for the management of the corporation.

i. The board must act as a body at a meeting. The Model Business Corporation Act (MBCA) does, however, provide for signed, written unanimous consent in lieu of a meeting.

A) Regular meetings are provided for in the bylaws. Notice is not necessary.

B) Special meetings may be called, but notice is required.

C) Quorum requirements vary from state to state (usually a majority) and are established by the bylaws.

D) Directors may not vote by proxy.

E) Ordinarily, a majority vote is necessary for board action.

F) Directors may participate in meeting through conference telephone communications.

ii. Corporate powers are exercised by the board of directors. Management responsibilities are:

A) Declare dividends.

B) Make policy decisions concerning the scope of business, initiate major changes in corporate financing, structure, etc.

C) Appoint, supervise, and remove officers.

D) Fix compensation of officers and directors.

iii. Delegation of powers of board of directors.

A) Functions relating to ordinary, interim managerial decisions may be delegated to an executive committee.

B) Functions relating to daily operations are normally delegated to officers, who as agents carry out the transactions on behalf of the corporation.

12. Role of directors and officers.

a. Directors manage the corporation and establish general policies and the scope of the business within the purposes and powers stated in the corporate charter.

i. Directors may not act individually; they must act convened as a board.

ii. The board of directors has power to authorize actions that are legal exercises of the corporation's powers.

iii. The board supervises and selects officers, defines their duties and authority, and fixes their compensation if not otherwise provided for in the bylaws.

iv. Dividends are declared by the board of directors.

b. The business judgment rule.

i. Directors are normally not liable for poor business judgment or honest mistakes if they act in good faith in what they consider to be the best interests of the corporation, and with the care that an ordinarily prudent person would exercise under similar circumstances.

ii. The directors are not insurers of business success.

c. Duties of directors.

i. If there is a breach of these duties, directors are liable to the corporation. The corporation may sue in its own name, or a derivative suit may be brought by shareholders or a representative, such as a trustee in bankruptcy.

ii. Standards of conduct for directors are owed to the corporation.

iii. Fiduciary duties of directors are owed to the corporation. As fiduciaries, directors are required to perform their duties in good faith, acting in the best interests of the corporation. Directors must use the same amount of care as an ordinary prudent person in a like position under similar circumstances.

A) Directors should supervise officers to whom they have delegated responsibilities.

B) Directors should not use their positions to secure personal advantages.

C) Directors who deal with the corporation must make full disclosure.

iv. Directors are liable to the corporation if they:

A) Compete with the corporation.

B) Usurp a corporate opportunity.

C) Fail to disclose an interest conflicting with that of the corporation.

D) Engage in insider trading in buying or selling shares by using confidential information that they possess because of their position.

E) Improperly issue a dividend or other distribution.

F) Make an improper stock issue.

G) Fail to comply with provisions of law, the corporate charter, or bylaws of the corporation.

v. Contracts between a corporation and a director of a corporation that has one or more common directors may be scrutinized by the courts.

d. Rights of directors.

i. Participate in meetings of the board of directors; notice of special meetings must be given.

ii. Inspect the books and records of the corporation.

iii. Indemnification for expenses, judgments, fines, costs, etc., incurred in corporate-related criminal or civil actions, other than actions brought by or on behalf of the corporation.

iv. Compensation may be fixed in the charter or by the board of directors.

e. Rights and duties of corporate officers and managers who deal with third persons as agents of, and on behalf of the corporation.

i. Usually, officers include a president, one or more vice presidents, a secretary, and a treasurer selected by the board of directors.

ii. The board may also select other officers and agents.

iii. Law of agency and employment applies. The authority of officers, other agents, and employees may be expressed (in the charter, bylaws, or resolutions of the board of directors) or implied (customary and incidental power of such officers); actual authority or apparent authority (because the corporation holds out that its officers have the usual power of similar officers of other corporations); or the board may ratify acts of its officers.

iv. Officers have fiduciary duties similar to those of directors.

13. Shareholder rights.

a. Right to have a stock certificate evidencing rights of an owner of a proportionate interest in the corporation according to the total number of shares issued.

i. Intangible personal property.

ii. A shareholder whose ownership interest is recorded has the right to:

A) Receive notice of meetings and participate in meetings.

B) Dividends when declared.

C) Participate in the distribution of assets upon dissolution.

D) Receive operational and financial reports.

iii. Certifies that the named person is the owner of the stated number of fully paid and nonassessable shares.

iv. In some states shares of stock may be issued with certificates.

b. Right to transfer shares (may be restricted).

i. A stock certificate is usually transferred by negotiation.

A) It has physical delivery and an endorsement on the certificate itself so that a good faith purchaser for value is the owner of the shares represented by the certificate, free of adverse claims. The purchaser is entitled to be registered as a shareholder and receive a new certificate.

B) Until the corporation is notified of the transfer, it recognizes the record holder (transferor) as entitled to all shareholder rights.

ii. Restrictions on transferability are enforceable if noted on the certificate. Such limitations are usually provided for in the case of a small closely held corporation, in order to maintain ownership within the group.

A) Consent of the group is necessary in order to transfer shares, or

B) The corporation or shareholders have the right of first refusal.

iii. A provision has been made for transfers of uncertificated securities in the 1977 revisions of Article 8 of the Uniform Commercial Code (UCC), which has been adopted in a few states.

c. Preemptive rights.

i. The right of current shareholders to purchase or subscribe to newly issued stock in proportion to the amount of stock currently owned before it is offered to the public.

ii. Preserve prior relative power of each shareholder.

iii. Statutes vary.

iv. Stock warrants are issued to the shareholders of record so that they can purchase the shares in accordance with their preemptive rights.

d. Right to dividends and other distributions.

i. Dividends are distributions of cash or other property, including shares of stock, to shareholders in proportion to their respective number of shares or interests in the corporation.

ii. Dividends are payable to record holders on a specified record date.

iii. Shareholders do not have rights to dividends (distributions of profits) until declared by the board of directors.

iv. Cash dividends - Once declared, dividends are corporate debts and cannot be rescinded.

v. Stock dividends - May be revoked before actually issued to shareholders.

vi. Statutes impose restrictions on issuance of dividends that will result in the corporation's insolvency or in impairment of its capital.

A) Dividends may only be paid out of legally available funds of a corporation, in accordance with state law.

B) Dividends cannot be declared if it will result in insolvency of the corporation or impair its capital. Directors may be liable to the corporation and/or shareholders for improper issuance of dividends, especially if they acted in bad faith.

vii. Directors must act diligently, prudently, and in good faith and may be liable civilly and criminally for improperly or illegally declaring dividends.

viii. Ordinarily, directors are not required to declare dividends unless a refusal to do so is an abuse of discretion.

e. Right to vote. Normally common and preferred stockholders have the right to vote, unless the right is denied in the charter.

i. Usually, preferred shareholders are denied the right to vote.

ii. Treasury shares cannot be voted.

f. Inspection right. A shareholder (for more than six months or of more than five percent of the outstanding shares) has a right to obtain information and examine a copy of relevant books, records and minutes for proper purposes in person or by an agent, attorney, etc.

14. Shareholder liabilities - Shareholders are not normally personally liable to creditors of the corporation. They may, however, be liable in the following situations:

    a. In some cases, majority shareholders are treated as also owing a fiduciary duty to the corporation and minority shareholders.

    b. A shareholder is liable for illegally or improperly paid dividends if he or she had knowledge that the dividends were improper.

    c. A shareholder is liable if he or she received shares that were issued for no consideration or consideration that did not satisfy the statutory requirements (water stock).

    d. A shareholder is liable for any unpaid stock subscriptions.

15. Special taxes applicable to C corporations.

    a. In general.

        i. C corporations may be required to pay one of the following taxes, in addition to their regular federal income tax liability:

            A) Personal holding company tax.

            B) Accumulated earnings tax.

        ii. These taxes are paid by the C corporation.

    b. Personal holding company tax.

        i. The objective of the personal holding company tax is to discourage individual taxpayers from using the corporate entity solely for tax avoidance.

        ii. The personal holding company tax applies only if the corporation is considered a personal holding company, and the corporation has undistributed personal holding company income.

            A) A corporation will be considered a personal holding company if it meets both of the following tests:

                1) Ownership test – During the last half of the taxable year, greater than 50% of the value of the outstanding stock of the corporation is owned by five or fewer individuals, and

                2) Passive income test – At least 60% of the corporation's adjusted ordinary gross income consists of personal holding company income.

                    a) Adjusted ordinary gross income is the company's gross income, with several adjustments. Adjustments include reductions for property taxes, depreciation, and interest expense.

                    b) Personal holding company income is generally defined as passive income and certain income from services.

            B) Undistributed personal holding company income is the corporation's adjusted taxable income, less the dividends paid deduction.

1) Adjusted taxable income is the corporation's taxable income, adjusted by the following:

   a) Additions to taxable income:

      i) Dividends-received deduction.

      ii) Net Operating Loss (NOL) deduction.

      iii) Rental property adjustment.

   b) Subtractions from taxable income:

      i) Federal income taxes.

      ii) Charitable contributions in excess of the deductible amount.

      iii) Net capital gain reduced by applicable taxes.

2) The dividends paid deduction is the sum of the following:

   a) Dividends paid during the year.

   b) Dividends paid within 2½ months of the close of the taxable year.

   c) Consent dividends.

   d) Liquidating distributions.

   e) Deficiency dividends.

iii. The tax is computed by multiplying the undistributed personal holding company income by the highest individual income tax rate (currently 38.6% for 2003).

   A) The tax is calculated on Form 1120-PH. This form must be filed with the corporation's annual tax return, Form 1120.

   B) The personal holding company tax is levied in addition to the regular tax.

   C) S corporations are not subject to the personal holding company tax.

c. Accumulated earnings tax.

   i. The objective of the accumulated earnings tax is to discourage individual taxpayers from using the corporate entity solely for tax avoidance.

   ii. The tax applies whenever a corporation accumulates earnings beyond its reasonable needs, unless the corporation can prove to the contrary by a preponderance of evidence.

16. Taxation at liquidation.

   a. In general.

      i. For tax purposes, a liquidation occurs when a corporation is no longer a going-concern.

      ii. A complete liquidation is taxed as a sale or exchange to the shareholder. This treatment is similar, but not identical, to the tax treatment of a qualified stock redemption.

b. Effect on shareholder.

i. In general, the shareholders are treated as having sold their stock to the liquidating corporation. As a result, the shareholders may recognize gain or loss.

ii. The gain or loss recognized is calculated as the difference between the fair market value of the property received from the corporation and the adjusted basis of the shareholder's stock.

c. Effect on corporation.

i. A liquidating corporation may or may not be required to recognize gain or loss, depending on the nature of the transaction.

ii. Generally, the corporation is required to recognize gain or loss upon complete liquidation.

A) The gain or loss is calculated as if the corporation's assets were sold at fair market value.

B) Losses may be disallowed in certain circumstances.

1) If the distribution is made to certain related parties, the loss may be disallowed.

2) If the distribution is made with certain built-in loss property, the loss may be disallowed.

G. S CORPORATIONS.

1. Taxation of S corporation shareholders.

a. In general, the IRS treats S corporation shareholders as partners. Shareholders of S corporations are required to report pro rata shares of corporate items that flow through.

b. It should be noted that while partnerships have great flexibility in the allocation of income and deductions, this advantage is not available to S corporations. All items of income are reported based on the ownership percentage of each shareholder.

c. The principal advantage of S corporation status is the avoidance of the double taxation scheme associated with C corporation status.

d. The S corporation must file an annual return on Form 1120S due 3 months and 15 days after the close of the tax year. However, an extension of up to six months may be granted.

e. Generally an S corporation must be a calendar year taxpayer unless they can establish a business purpose to the satisfaction of the IRS for the deviation.

f. For purposes of the Code's fringe benefit provisions, an S corporation is treated as a partnership, and a shareholder-employee who owns more than two percent of its stock is treated as a partner. Thus, the value of benefits provided to a more-than-two-percent shareholder-employee must be included in that shareholder's gross income unless the Code specifically allows exclusion of the benefit by a partner.

g. Accident and health insurance premiums paid by an S corporation for a more-than-two-percent shareholder-employee are deductible by the corporation and are included in the shareholder's gross income. For 2003, 100 percent of the amount included in income may be deducted by the shareholder-employee.

2. Election.

   a. Requirements for S corporation election – Must be deemed a "small business corporation."

      i. The entity must be organized under the laws of any U.S. state or territory.

      ii. Shareholders may be individuals, estates, certain trusts or certain tax-exempt organizations. Partnerships and corporations <u>may not</u> be shareholders.

         A) A grantor, voting trust, or a testamentary trust may be an eligible shareholder for two years after the deemed owner's death.

         B) Exempt organizations such as qualified pension plans, profit-sharing plans, stock bonus plans, and charitable organizations may be shareholders.

      iii. Only citizens or residents of the U.S. may be shareholders.

      iv. The entity may only have one class of stock issued and outstanding.

         A) The rights of the holders must be identical with regards to profits and assets of the corporation.

         B) However, two classes are permitted if the only difference is voting rights.

      v. The entity may have no more than 75 shareholders.

         A) A husband and wife (and their estates) are considered one shareholder regardless of how they hold their shares.

   b. How to make the election.

      i. S corporation status is elected by having all shareholders consent and file Form 2553 by the 15th day of the 3rd month of the tax year in which the shareholders wish the election to take effect.

      ii. The corporation must meet all of the eligibility requirements in the preelection period of the tax year in which the shareholders want the election to take effect.

      iii. A late filing may be treated by the IRS as timely if the corporation can show reasonable cause for the late filing and it files the election by the earlier of twelve months after the original due date of the election or the unextended due date of the tax return for the first year the corporation intends to be an S corporation.

3. Special taxes applicable to S corporations.

   a. In general.

      i. Although S corporations are flow-through entities, they may be required to pay one of the following taxes:

         A) Built-in gains tax.

         B) LIFO recapture tax.

         C) Excess net passive income tax.

      ii. These taxes are paid by the S corporation, not by the shareholders.

b. Built-in gains tax.

i. The built-in gains tax applies to S corporations that used to be C corporations.

ii. The tax is imposed on any unrealized built-in gain that is recognized on the disposition of any asset by the S corporation.

A) The unrealized built-in gain is the difference between the fair market value and the basis of an asset, as of the date the C corporation converts to an S corporation (conversion date).

B) The recognized built-in gain is any gain recognized from the sale of an asset within the 10-year period following the S election.

C) Any assets acquired by the S corporation after the conversion date are not subject to the built-in gains tax.

D) Any appreciation of the asset after the date of conversion is not subject to the built-in gains tax.

Example

Parrish Industries, a former C corporation, elected S corporation status last year (conversion date). On the conversion date, Parrish owned land with a fair market value of $75,000 and an adjusted basis of $50,000. Therefore, the unrealized built-in gain is $25,000 ($75,000 - $50,000). In the current year, Parrish sells the land for $80,000, resulting in a $30,000 gain on sale. Parrish will be subject to built-in gains tax on $25,000, the unrealized built-in gain as of the conversion date.

iii. The tax is computed by applying the highest corporate income tax rate (currently 35%) to the S corporation's net recognized built-in gain for the tax year.

iv. The amount of recognized built-in gain passed through and taxed to shareholders is reduced by the built-in gain tax paid by the S corporation.

c. LIFO recapture tax.

i. The LIFO recapture tax applies to S corporations that used to be C corporations.

ii. A C corporation that uses the LIFO (last-in, first-out) method of inventory valuation in its last taxable year before making an S corporation election must include in income a LIFO recapture amount.

A) The LIFO recapture amount is the excess of the inventory valuation under the FIFO (first-in, first-out) method over the inventory valuation under the LIFO method.

B) The recapture amount is reported in the taxable income of the C corporation in its last tax year.

C) The inventory's basis is increased by the LIFO recapture amount.

Example

StaceCo converted from a C corporation to an S corporation. On the date of the conversion, StaceCo had inventory with a LIFO basis of $90,000. The FIFO value of the inventory was $140,000. StaceCo must add the $50,000 ($140,000-$90,000) LIFO recapture amount to its last C corporation tax return.

iii. The LIFO recapture tax is the tax on the LIFO recapture amount.

A) The tax is calculated based on the corporation's ordinary income tax rate.

B) The tax is payable by the corporation in four installments.

1) The first installment is due with the C corporation's final income tax return (Form 1120).

2) The remaining three installments are due with the S corporation's income tax returns (Form 1120S) for the three subsequent tax years.

Example

Assume the same facts as in the previous example. If StaceCo is taxed at the 35% corporate income tax rate, its last C corporation tax return tax liability will increase by $17,500 (35% x $50,000 LIFO recapture amount). StaceCo must pay $4,375 (one-fourth of $17,500) of the LIFO recapture tax with its last C corporation income tax return (Form 1120). The remaining three installments of $4,375 must be paid with StaceCo's next three tax returns (Form 1120S).'

C) No interest is due if the required installments are paid on a timely basis.

D) There is no requirement that estimated tax payments be made with respect to any LIFO recapture tax due.

E) Any additional appreciation attributable to the inventory (over its FIFO basis) will be subject to the built-in gains tax as the inventory is sold.

d. Excess net passive income tax.

i. The excess net passive income tax applies to S corporations that used to be C corporations.

ii. The S corporation must pay a tax on its excess net passive income if passive investment income exceeds 25% of its gross receipts during the year.

A) Passive investment income is generally gross receipts derived from royalties, rents, dividends, interest, annuities, and gains from sales of securities.

B) Net passive income is passive investment income reduced by any allowable deduction directly connected with the production of such income.

C) The tax is imposed on the excess net passive income (ENPI). ENPI is calculated as follows:

$$\text{ENPI} = \text{Net passive income} \times \frac{\text{Passive investment income less 25\% of gross receipts}}{\text{Passive investment income}}$$

D) The tax only applies if the S corporation has accumulated earnings and profits at the end of its taxable year.

iii. Tax on excess passive income.

A) The tax is based on the maximum corporate income tax rate (currently 35%).

Example

In the current year, SAP Company, an S corporation that was formerly a C corporation, had gross receipts of \$200,000. Gross receipts included \$75,000 of passive rental income. Rental expenses were \$30,000 for the year. Therefore, SAP Company has excess net passive income (ENPI) of \$15,000 for the taxable year. The ENPI is calculated as follows:

$$\$15,000 = \$45,000 \times \frac{[\$75,000 - (25\% \times \$200,000)]}{\$75,000}$$

The excess net passive income tax is \$5,250 (35% x \$15,000).

B) The tax on excess net passive income paid by the S corporation reduces the amount of each item of passive investment income that flows through to the shareholders.

4. Revocation and termination of S corporation status.

a. This election may be revoked by the consent of more than half of the corporate shareholders (including nonvoting) and may specify a particular date; but if not, revocation is effective the first of the following tax year unless made effective in the first 15 days of tax year, in which case, it relates back to the beginning of the tax year.

b. S corporation status is terminated on the day a terminating event occurs (any event which causes the S corporation to no longer meet the requirements of S corporation status).

i. If a corporation has accumulated earnings and profits as well as passive investment income that exceeds 25% of gross receipts for three consecutive years, its election will be terminated beginning with the following year.

c. Taxation at Liquidation.

i. S corporations are subject to many of the same liquidation rules applicable to C corporations.

ii. In general, the distribution of property to shareholders in complete liquidation is treated as if the property was sold to the shareholders.

iii. The S corporation incurs no tax on liquidation gains.

H. LIMITED LIABILITY COMPANIES (LLCS).

1. LLCs are one of the most versatile types of entities. An LLC provides limited liability to its members and allows great flexibility regarding the taxation of the entity.

2. Taxation of LLCs.

   a. Under the IRS "Check the Box" regulations, an LLC can be taxed as any of the following:

      i. Sole proprietorship – Only available for single-owned LLCs. The owner will disregard the LLC for tax purposes and simply file a Schedule C on the individual return (Form 1040) to report the activity of the LLC.

      ii. Partnership – Available for LLCs with 2 or more owners (members). A partnership return (Form 1065) will be filed to report the income of the LLC. The members will each receive a Schedule K-1 with their apportioned income and will report this income on the appropriate schedule on their individual federal income tax returns (Form 1040).

      iii. Corporation – Available for any LLC. A corporate return (Form 1120) will be filed to report income of the LLC. Just as a corporation, the LLC will have two levels of taxation.

      iv. S corporation – Available for those LLCs that elect to be treated as a corporation (association) and file Form 2553 to elect small business treatment. This form must be filed by the 15th day of the third month after the beginning of the LLC. As with shareholders of S corporations, members will report income on their individual federal tax returns based on the Schedule K-1 they receive from the S corporation return (Form 1120S).

EXHIBIT 15: DIFFERENCES BETWEEN TYPES OF BUSINESS ORGANIZATIONS

	Type of Business Organization					
	Sole Proprietor	**Partnership***	**LLP**	**LLC****	**S-Corp**	**Corporation**
What type of liability do the owners have?	Unlimited	General Partnership – Unlimited; Limited Partnership – Limited	Limited	Limited	Limited	Limited
What federal tax form is required to be filed for the organization?	Form 1040, Schedule C	Form 1065	Form 1065	Form 1040, Schedule C, or Form 1065, or Form 1120, or Form 1120S	Form 1120S	Form 1120
Under what concept is the organization taxed?	Individual level	Flow-through	Flow-through	LLCs can be taxed as sole proprietorships, partnerships, corporations, or S-corporations	Flow-through	Entity level
On what tax form is the owner's compensation reported?	Form 1040, Schedule C	Schedule K-1	Schedule K-1	Form 1040, Schedule C, or Schedule K-1, or Form W-2 and Schedule K-1, or W-2	W-2 and Schedule K-1	W-2 (dividends are reported on Form 1099-div)
What is the nature of the owner's income from the organization?	Self-employment income	Self-employment income*	Self-employment income	Self-employment income, or W-2 income and ordinary income, W-2 income	W-2 income and ordinary income	W-2 income and dividend income
What is the basis for determining tax- advantaged retirement plan contributions?	Net Schedule C income (less 1/2 SE tax)	Self-employment income* (less 1/2 SE tax)	Self-employment income (less 1/2 SE tax)	Self-employment income (less 1/2 SE tax) or W-2 income	W-2 income	W-2 income

Flow-through: All items of income will flow from the entity to the individual partners/owners/members return while retaining the character of the income at the entity level.

* Limited Partners will generally not have self-employment income.

** The LLC will have the same tax characteristics and attributes as the type of entity it has elected to be taxed as.

Note: Family Limited Partnerships (FLPs) have the same treatment for general partners as general partnerships and for limited partners the same treatment as limited partnerships.

EXHIBIT 16: SUMMARY OF TAXATION ALTERNATIVES FOR VARIOUS BUSINESS ENTITIES

Taxation Theory	Proprietorship	Partnership	LLP	LLC	S Corporation	C Corporation
Aggregate Theory	Schedule C			Single owner LLC can file as proprietorship		
Hybrid Theory		Form 1065	Form 1065	Form 1065		
Entity Theory				1120 or 1120S by election		Form 1120
Other Notes					Property distribution, stock redemption, and liquidation are like Subchapter C	

Aggregate Theory – The entity is not a separate taxable entity from the owners. Contributions to and distributions from are not taxable events.

Hybrid Theory – The income is taxed under an aggregate concept, but the entity must file and report the taxable income (Subchapter K).

Entity Theory – The entity is a separate taxable entity, and must determine its tax liability and file on an annual basis. Contributions to and distributions from are generally taxable events (Subchapter C).

XIV. CONTRACTS

Note: Only a basic understanding of these concepts is usually tested on the exam.

A. NATURE AND TYPES OF CONTRACTS.

1. A contract is an agreement made by two or more parties that contains a promise or set of promises to perform or refrain from performing some act or acts that can be enforced by a court.
2. Elements of a contract.

   In order to have a contract, certain elements must be present.

   a. Agreement - The mutual assent and agreement of the parties must be evidenced by an offer and an acceptance.

   b. Consideration - Legally sufficient and bargained-for consideration must be exchanged for contractual promises.

   c. Contractual capacity - There must be two or more parties who have contractual capacity.

   d. Legality - The purpose and subject matter of the contract must not be contrary to law or public policy.

   e. Genuineness of assent - The assent of the parties must be real, genuine, and voluntarily given.

   f. Form - The agreement must be in the form that is required by law, if one is prescribed. If real estate is involved, then the Statute of Frauds requires that the agreement be in writing.
3. Types of contracts and distinctions between them.

   a. Based upon the manner in which the assent of the parties is given.

      i. Express contract - The terms of the agreement are stated in words used by the parties.

      ii. Implied - The terms of the agreement are inferred from the conduct of the parties even though nothing is said.

      iii. The parties must objectively have the intention of entering into a contract.

Note: A quasi contract (sometimes called contract implied in law) is not a contract. Equity imposes a duty to pay the reasonable value for a benefit received in order to avoid unjust enrichment. It is an equitable principle.

   b. Based upon the nature of the promises made.

      i. Bilateral contract - Reciprocal promises are exchanged by the parties (i.e., the promise of one party is exchanged for the promise of the other).

      ii. Unilateral contract - One party makes a promise in exchange for the other party's actually performing some act (performance) or refraining from performing some act (forbearance).

c. Based upon compliance with a statute requiring a special formality.

   i. Formal contract - Some formality is prescribed for their creation.

      A) Contract under seal or notarial act.

      B) Recognizances.

      C) Negotiable instruments and letters of credit.

   ii. Informal contract - Simple contracts for which no special form or formality is required.

d. Based upon the stage of performance of the contractual promises.

   i. Executed contract - Contract that has been completely performed by all parties.

   ii. Executory contract - Contract that has been partly performed or totally unperformed by all parties.

e. Based upon legal validity and enforceability.

   i. Valid and enforceable contract - All elements of a contract are present.

   ii. Void contract - Agreement has no legal effect (it was not really a contract).

   iii. Voidable contract - One of the parties has the option of avoiding contractual obligations.

   iv. Unenforceable contract - Contract that cannot be proven in the manner required by law, and/or fails to meet a procedural or formal requirement.

B. AGREEMENT.

1. An agreement must have the manifestation of apparent mutual assent by parties to the agreement. Only present, objective intent of the parties, which they have manifested by such words or conduct as would indicate to a reasonable person an intention to be bound by the same terms, is recognized in law. This concept is referred to as objective assent.

2. Terms.

   a. Material, essential terms include identification of the parties, the subject matter, the consideration or price to be paid, and the quantity (if appropriate).

   b. Incidental terms.

3. The offer - The offeror shows assent when he or she communicates a proposal (the offer) to the offeree that sets forth with reasonable clarity, definiteness, and certainty, the material terms under which he or she is presently, objectively agreeing and intending to be bound.

   a. Objective intent manifested by offeror.

      i. The words and/or conduct used by the offeror must be such that a reasonable person would be warranted, under the circumstances, in believing that a real agreement was intended by the offeror.

      ii. It is necessary to distinguish offers from:

         A) Expressions of opinions.

         B) Preliminary negotiations and invitations soliciting offers.

         C) Statements of intention.

         D) Advertisements, catalogues, circulars, price lists.

         E) Offers that are made in jest or under emotional stress.

F) Other nonoffer situations.

1) Requests for bids.

2) Requests of auctioneer for bids at auctions.

3) Social invitations.

4) Agreements to agree.

5) Sham transactions.

b. Definiteness and clarity of material terms - All of the material, essential terms must be indicated in the offer with clarity, definiteness, and certainty or a method stated by which the terms will be made certain.

i. The offeror may provide that one or more of the terms be more definite by reference to an outside standard or third person.

ii. Material terms.

A) The subject matter of the contract.

B) The price.

C) The quantity.

c. Communication of offer - The terms of the offer must be received by the offeree.

i. Offeree must have knowledge of all the material terms of the offer.

ii. An offer may be made to a specific offeree to whom it is communicated.

iii. A public offer, such as an offer for a reward, is treated as communicated to those people who have knowledge of it.

d. Termination of offer.

i. By actions of the parties.

A) Revocation by the offeror.

1) Revocation must be communicated to offeree. It must, therefore, be received by the offeree prior to acceptance.

2) An offer to a specific offeree is effectively terminated when the revocation of the offer is received by the offeree.

3) A public offer is effectively terminated when revocation is given in the same manner and for the same period of time as had been used in order to make the offer.

4) Irrevocable offers (common law option contract, statutory "firm offer").

5) Offer to enter into a unilateral contract.

a) Traditional view - Offer to enter into a unilateral contract may be revoked even though the offeree has begun performance.

b) Modern view applies doctrine of promissory estoppel. The offeror is barred (estopped) from revoking the offer when the offeree has changed position in justifiable reliance on the offer.

B) Rejection by offeree.

1) Offeree demonstrates his or her intention not to accept the offer.

2) Rejection must be communicated to the offeror.

3) A counteroffer constitutes a rejection.

4) An inquiry by the offeree is distinguishable from a rejection.

ii. Because of lapse of time.

A) If a duration is stated in the offer, the offer terminates after expiration of the stated period of time.

B) If a duration is not stated in the offer, the offer lapses after a reasonable period of time.

iii. By operation of law.

A) Destruction of the subject matter.

B) Death or insanity of an offeror or offeree.

C) Supervening illegality.

4. Acceptance - The offeree accepts the offer when he or she unequivocally manifests his, her, or its assent to the terms of the offer.

a. Requisites.

i. Offeree has knowledge of the terms of the offer.

ii. Offeree's overt conduct manifests willingness and intention to be bound.

iii. Offeree complies with conditions, if any, stated in the offer (acceptance must be in the proper manner, at the proper place, and at the proper time).

iv. Acceptance must be made by the party to whom the offer was directed.

v. Acceptance must positively, unequivocally accord to the terms of the offer.

b. Manner of acceptance.

i. If a bilateral contract is contemplated, the offeree makes a promise.

ii. If a unilateral contract is contemplated, the offeree performs required act or forbears from acting.

iii. Silence, generally, will not be considered to be an acceptance unless:

A) There was a similar, prior course of dealings, or

B) The offeree accepted the benefits, or

C) The offeree exercised dominion over the subject matter.

c. Effective moment of acceptance.

i. If a unilateral contract is contemplated, acceptance is effective when the performance or forbearance is completed.

ii. If a bilateral contract is contemplated, acceptance is effective when the offeree gives the requisite promise (usually, when the acceptance is sent so that it is out of the offeree's control, even if the acceptance is not received by the offeror).

iii. The offeror may include a condition in the offer that acceptance will not be effective until it is received by the offeror.

iv. A contract is created at the moment that the acceptance is effective.

C. CONSIDERATION.

1. The concept of legally sufficient consideration.

   a. Parties to a contract.

      i. Promisor - The party who makes a promise to do or refrain from doing something.

      ii. Promisee - The party who receives a promise.

      iii. Unilateral contract - Only one party (A) is the promisor. The other party (B) is the promisee.

      A ——— promise made by A ———▶ B

      iv. Bilateral contract - Promises are exchanged by the parties. Each party is, therefore, a promisor as to the promise that he or she makes and a promisee as to the promise he or she receives. Each promise must be supported by consideration.

      A ——— promise made by A ———▶ B

      A ◀——— promise made by B ——— B

   b. There must be a presently bargained-for exchange between the parties. Consideration may be thought of as the "price" paid by the promisee for a promise so that mutual obligations are present.

      A ——— promise made by A ———▶ B

      A ◀——————————————— B
      bargained for "price" = consideration

   c. Legally sufficient consideration exists when either the promisee incurs a legal detriment or the promisor receives a legal benefit, or both.

      i. A legal detriment is incurred by a promisee if the promisee does one of the following:

         A) Actually gives up something that he or she has a legal right to keep in the case of a unilateral contract.

         B) Actually refrains or forbears from doing something that he or she has a legal right to do in the case of a unilateral contract.

         C) Promises to surrender something that he or she has a right to retain as in a bilateral contract.

         D) Promises to forbear from doing something that he or she has a right to do as in a bilateral contract.

      ii. A legal benefit is received by a promisor if the promisor receives something to which he or she is not entitled, but for the contract.

      iii. It is not necessary that an economic or material loss be incurred by the promisee or benefit received by the promisor. All that is necessary is a surrender or receipt of a legal right.

2. Adequacy of consideration.
   a. The consideration received by one party was grossly inadequate (equitable principle).
   b. No consideration was given.
      i. Past or moral consideration, love, and affection.
      ii. Performance of a preexisting duty that is imposed by law or owed because of an existing contract.
      iii. Performance of an illegal act.
      iv. Illusory promise - A promise that appears to be a promise but is not really an undertaking to do anything.
3. Problem areas in business concerning consideration.
   a. Methods for dealing with uncertainty as to future market conditions.
      i. Requirements contracts.
         A) Consideration is given if a buyer agrees to purchase and a seller agrees to sell all or up to a specified amount that the buyer needs or requires.
         B) Contract is illusory if a buyer agrees to purchase only the goods that he or she may wish, want, or desire.
      ii. Output contracts.
         A) A seller agrees to sell and a buyer agrees to purchase all or up to a specified amount of the seller's output.
         B) A contract is illusory if its terms permit a seller to sell to other purchasers or if a seller's obligation to produce is based upon the seller's wish, want, or desire.
      iii. Exclusive dealings contract.
         A) One party has the sole or exclusive right to deal in or with the products or property of the other.
         B) Parties have obligations to use their best efforts to promote subsequent sale, supply sufficient quantity, etc.
      iv. Option to cancel clauses.
         A) If the right to cancel is absolute and unconditional, the contract is illusory.
         B) If the right to cancel is conditioned upon the happening of some event, the contract is enforceable.
   b. Settlement of claims or debts.
      i. A promise to pay or actual payment of part of a mature, liquidated, undisputed debt is not consideration for creditor's release of debtor's obligation to pay the remaining balance.

ii. Parties may settle by entering into an accord (new agreement) and satisfaction (performance of new terms) if:

A) The obligation to pay or the amount of the debt is disputed.

B) The obligation to pay is not yet due; the debt is not a mature one.

C) The amount owed is not liquidated; the amount is not a definite, certain, or exact sum of money or a sum that is capable of being made definite by computation.

D) Other or additional consideration is given.

E) Creditor's promise to release debtor is in a signed writing.

iii. Release and/or covenant not to sue.

A) A release is a relinquishment of a right or discharge of an obligation or claim that one has against another person. It must be supported by consideration.

B) A covenant not to sue is a promise by one who has a right to bring an action that he, she, or it will not sue in order to enforce such right of action. It must be supported by consideration.

4. Promises enforceable without consideration.

a. New promise to pay debt barred by the statute of limitations.

b. New written promise or reaffirmation of promise to pay debt that will otherwise be barred by discharge in bankruptcy.

c. Doctrine of promissory estoppel or detrimental reliance - In those states where the doctrine has been adopted, the promisor will not be able to plead lack of consideration if:

i. A promise is made to induce a promisee to act in a particular way.

ii. The promisor can foresee that the promisee will justifiably rely upon the promise.

iii. The promisee substantially changes his or her position in the foreseeable manner and incurs damage because of reasonably relying upon the promise.

iv. It is grossly unfair not to enforce the promise.

d. Charitable subscriptions.

D. CAPACITY.

1. Contractual capacity.

a. Minors.

i. Statutes prescribe the age of majority. In most states, age 18 is the age of majority.

ii. Minors' rights to disaffirm.

A) Minors may disaffirm contracts during minority and for a reasonable period of time after attaining the age of majority.

B) Minors may not disaffirm if a contract has been approved by a court or, in some states because of statute, if the contract is for:

1) Life or medical insurance.

2) Educational loan.

3) Medical care.

4) Marriage.

5) Enlistment in armed forces.

6) Transportation by common carrier.

C) Conveyances of real property cannot be disaffirmed until the minor reaches the age of majority.

D) The contract is voidable by the minor but not by the adult. If the minor disaffirms, each party must make restitution by returning consideration received from the other party.

E) Executory contracts.

1) Minor may disaffirm contract - Because the minor received nothing from the other party, there is no need to make restitution.

2) Majority rule - Continued silence after reaching majority is treated as disaffirmance of an executory contract.

F) Executed contracts - Minor may disaffirm contract.

1) The adult with whom a minor has contracted must make restitution (return any consideration received from minor).

2) If personal property was sold by a minor to an adult, who resold it to an innocent good faith purchaser, the purchaser will not be required to return the property to the minor.

3) The minor must return consideration received from the adult.

a) The majority rule is that the minor must make restitution only if the minor is able to do so.

b) In some states:

i) By statute, a deduction is made for deterioration, depreciation, and damage.

ii) Minor must pay reasonable value for any benefit conferred.

G) Contracts for necessaries.

1) Necessaries include food, clothing, shelter, and services rendered for the minor's protection.

2) A minor may disaffirm a contract for necessaries, not provided by a parent or guardian, but is liable in quasi contract for the reasonable value of necessaries that were furnished to the minor.

iii. Ratification.

A) A contract will be enforceable if the minor indicates an intention to be bound (ratification) after reaching the age of majority.

B) Express written or oral ratification.

C) Implied ratification by conduct indicating satisfaction with the contract (retaining consideration or accepting benefits).

b. Intoxicated persons.

   i. Contracts made by one who is so intoxicated that his or her judgment is impaired and cannot comprehend the legal consequences of entering into a contract are voidable.

   ii. Contracts may be disaffirmed while intoxicated or within a reasonable time after becoming sober.

      A) Restitution must be made.

      B) Intoxicated persons cannot disaffirm if a third person would be injured.

      C) Intoxicated persons must pay the reasonable value for necessaries that were furnished.

c. Mentally incompetent persons.

   i. One is considered mentally incompetent or insane if his or her judgment is impaired and that person cannot understand or comprehend the nature and effect of a particular transaction.

   ii. If a person is declared judicially incompetent, his or her contracts are void.

   iii. A contract that is made by a person who is mentally incompetent but has not been so adjudicated is voidable by the mentally incompetent person while he or she is mentally incompetent, or within a reasonable time after regaining sanity, or by his or her guardian or other representative.

   iv. Contracts for necessaries may be disaffirmed, but the mentally incompetent party is liable for reasonable value of necessaries furnished.

d. Others who may be treated as lacking capacity.

   i. Convicts - In some states, those who have been convicted of major felonies do not have full capacity to make contracts.

   ii. Aliens.

      A) Citizens of other countries who are legally in the United States generally have contractual capacity, and their contracts are valid.

      B) Enemy aliens and illegal aliens have limited contractual capacity.

2. Genuineness of assent.

   a. Mistake.

      i. A mistake is an error or unconscious ignorance or forgetfulness of a past or present fact that is material, very important, or essential to the contract.

      ii. Mistakes as to material facts should be distinguished from mistakes of judgment as to value or quality.

      iii. Unilateral mistake - In general, if only one party to a contract has made a mistake, the party cannot avoid the contract unless the other party was responsible for the mistake being made, knew of the mistake, or should have known of the mistake and failed to correct it.

      iv. Mutual or bilateral mistakes concerning material facts - In general, if both parties have made a mistake as to a material fact, the contract is voidable at the option of either party (i.e., existence, nature, or identity of subject matter).

b. Fraudulent misrepresentation.

   i. Fraud in the execution - If a party has been led to believe that an act that he or she is performing is something other than executing a contract, his or her assent is not real, and any contract that appears to have been formed is void.

   ii. Fraud in the inducement - A contract is voidable if a party was damaged by being induced to enter the contract while reasonably relying upon a false representation of a material fact.

      A) Elements of fraud in the inducement.

         1) A misrepresentation of material fact was made via representation, other words, or conduct.

         2) A misrepresentation of law.

         3) A misrepresentation was made by one who had knowledge that it was false or acted with reckless disregard.

         4) A misrepresentation was made with intent to deceive. The evidence that the representation was made to induce the deceived party to enter into the contract is the fact that the contract was actually formed.

         5) Reliance on the representation. Reliance must have been such that a reasonable person would have been justified in relying on the representation.

         6) Injury to the deceived innocent party. The contract would not have been formed or would have been more valuable if the representation had been true.

      B) Fraud because of silence or concealment.

         1) There is no duty to inform a contracting party of facts.

         2) Exceptions.

            a) A seller must disclose latent defects which are not ordinarily discoverable but which cause an object to be dangerous.

            b) A seller with superior knowledge may not conceal facts, knowing that the other party lacks knowledge.

            c) When a party has previously misstated a material fact and later realizes that he or she made a misstatement, that party is then required to make a correction.

            d) When parties have a fiduciary or confidential relationship, the party with knowledge of relevant facts has an obligation to disclose them to the other party.

            e) Statutes, such as the Truth in Lending Act, require disclosure of certain relevant facts.

         3) Innocent misrepresentation - If a party unintentionally makes a representation without knowledge of its falsity, the other party, who relied upon the representation and was damaged, may rescind the contract.

C) Undue influence.

1) When a party who is in a dominant position because of a confidential relationship secures an unfair advantage in a contract with a weaker, dominated party, the contract is voidable and may be disaffirmed by the dominated party.

2) There is a rebuttable presumption of undue influence when:

a) The parties are in a familial or fiduciary relationship based upon trust and confidence.

b) The contract is extremely unfair to the dominated party.

3) A presumption may be rebutted by showing:

a) Full disclosure was made.

b) Consideration received was adequate.

c) Independent advice was received by the weaker party.

D) Duress.

1) If a party is coerced into entering a contract because of the wrongful use of force or a threat of force, the contract is voidable.

2) Assent may have been induced by fear of:

a) Bodily injury to a party or relative.

b) Criminal (but not civil) prosecution of a party or relative.

c) Harm to property or business under unusual circumstances.

E) Adhesion contract and unconscionability.

1) An adhesion contract arises when one party with overwhelming bargaining power takes such unfair advantage of the other party that the latter has no choice but to adhere to dictated terms or do without a particular good or service.

2) The resulting contract may be held to be unenforceable because of unconscionability.

E. THE STATUTE OF FRAUDS.

1. In order to be enforceable, some contractual promises must be evidenced by a writing that is signed by the parties against whom they are being enforced.

2. Contracts that must be in writing:

   a. Contracts for sales of interests in real property.

   b. Contracts that cannot be performed within one year.

   c. Collateral, or secondary, promises to answer for obligations of others.

   d. A promise is within the Statute of Frauds and must be in a signed writing if:

      i. The promise is made to the obligee (rather than the principal obligor) by one who is not presently liable for the debt or who does not have a present duty to perform.

      ii. The liability of the guarantor is secondary, or collateral, to that of the principal obligor.

      iii. If the main purpose or primary object of the secondary promisor is to protect his or her own interest or to obtain a material benefit, an oral promise will be enforced.

      iv. Promises are made by executors or administrators to personally pay the debts of the decedents' estates.

e. Unilateral promises made in consideration of marriage and prenuptial agreements.

f. Contracts for the sale of goods and other personal property (covered by UCC).

i. Contract for the sale of goods for a price of $500 or more. Exceptions:

A) Partial performance - Buyer pays for or receives and accepts goods.

B) Goods (not ordinarily suitable for resale) to be specially manufactured for the buyer by the seller who has begun production of the goods.

C) Sales between merchants when either party, within a reasonable period of time, sends a written confirmation to which the other party fails to object within ten days.

D) Admissions, in pleadings or in court, that the contract existed.

ii. Other code provisions.

A) The Statute of Frauds is satisfied by payment or delivery and acceptance of securities.

B) Security agreements.

C) Contract for sale of miscellaneous personal property when price is more than $5,000.

3. Sufficiency of writing - Memorandum evidencing the contract need only contain basic, essential terms of the contract.

4. Parol evidence rule.

a. If a written instrument is regarded by the parties as their complete integrated agreement, other oral or written evidence is inadmissible for purposes of changing, altering, or contradicting the effect of the writing.

b. Parol evidence is admitted to show:

i. A modification of the writing.

ii. The contract was void or voidable.

iii. The meaning of ambiguous or vague language.

iv. The writing was incomplete.

v. A prior course of dealings or a trade usage.

vi. Gross typographical or clerical errors.

vii. Another separate contract with a different subject matter.

5. Interpretation of contracts.

a. The plain meaning rule - When the words used in a writing are plain, clear, unequivocal, and unambiguous, their meaning will be determined from the face of the written document alone.

b. If the words used in a writing are ambiguous or not clear:

i. The interpretation that results in a reasonable, effective, and legal contract is preferred over one that results in an unreasonable, ineffective, or illegal agreement.

ii. A writing will be interpreted as a whole. All writings that are part of the same transaction will be interpreted together, and words will not be taken out of the context in which they are used.

iii. A word will be given its ordinary, commonly accepted meaning, and a technical term will be given its technical meaning.

iv. Specific terms will be given greater consideration than general language.

v. Handwritten words prevail over typewritten words, and typewritten words prevail over preprinted words.

vi. When multiple meanings of language are possible, the language will be interpreted most strongly against the party who chose the words.

vii. The court will admit evidence of usage in trade, prior dealings, and course of performance.

F. DISCHARGE AND PERFORMANCE.

1. Conditions.

   a. A condition is an operative event, the occurrence or nonoccurrence of which changes, limits, precludes, gives rise to, or terminates a contractual obligation.

   b. Types of conditions.

      i. Condition precedent - A conditioning event must occur before performance by the promisor is required. Until then, the promisee has no right to receive performance.

      ii. Condition subsequent - The occurrence of the conditioning event extinguishes an existing contractual duty.

      iii. Concurrent condition - The performance of each party is conditioned on the performance of the other party.

   c. How conditions arise.

      i. Express - Condition clearly stated by parties.

      ii. Implied in fact - Condition that is understood or implied.

      iii. Implied in law (constructive) - Imposed by court in order to achieve justice or fairness.

2. Discharge by performance.

   a. Full, complete performance in a manner prescribed by the contract discharges the performing party.

   b. Tender of complete performance - An unconditional offer to perform by one ready, willing, and able to do so, discharges the party if his or her tender is not accepted.

   c. Time for performance.

      i. If time for performance is not stated, performance is to be rendered within a reasonable period of time.

      ii. If parties stipulate that time is of the essence (vital), the time requirement must be followed.

      iii. If time for performance is stipulated, but not vital, performance prior to or within a few days of the stated time satisfies contract.

   d. Part performance.

i. If partial performance is accepted, the performing party can recover the value of performance.

ii. If performance is substantial (i.e., minor, trivial deviation from contractual obligation) and deviation is not the result of bad faith, the performing party is discharged but is liable for his or her failure to render complete performance.

iii. Partial performance that is something less than substantial performance is a breach of contract. It results in the discharge of the party entitled to receive performance but not the discharge of the partially performing party.

e. Effect of contractual conditions on discharge by performance.

i. Strict compliance with express conditions is necessary.

ii. Substantial performance of constructive conditions is necessary.

iii. Express personal satisfaction condition - The promise of one party to pay may be conditioned on that party's satisfaction with the other party's performance.

A) If personal taste, preferences, aesthetics, fancy, or comfort is involved, payment is excused if dissatisfaction is honest and in good faith, even though a reasonable person would have been satisfied.

B) If satisfaction relates to operative fitness, merchantability, or mechanical utility, payment is excused when dissatisfaction is honest and a reasonable person would have been dissatisfied.

3. Discharge by breach of contact.

a. A breach of contract is the nonperformance of a contractual duty.

b. A party, who totally fails to perform, is not discharged and is liable for damages for breach of contract. The other party is, however, discharged and need not hold himself or herself ready to perform.

c. If a party performs in part, but his or her performance does not amount to substantial part performance, there is a material breach of contract.

i. The partially performing party is not discharged and is liable for the material breach of contract.

ii. The other party is discharged and need not hold himself or herself ready to perform.

d. If there is a minor, nonmaterial breach of contract, the breaching party is liable for damages if the breach is not cured. The nonbreaching party is not discharged and is required to perform.

e. Anticipatory breach of contract.

i. If a party repudiates a contract before he or she is required to perform, the other party may sue immediately and does not have to remain ready to perform.

ii. The doctrine of anticipatory breach does not apply to a promise to pay a stated sum of money, a unilateral contract, or a bilateral contract that is executory on one side only.

f. Privity of contract.

i. The connection or relationship between two parties each having a legally recognized interest in the same subject matter.

ii. When you are talking of a privity of contract it is the relationship between the parties of a contract that allows them to sue each other but prevents a third party to sue based on the contract.

Example

Assume City A contracted with Water Company B to provide water to the city's fire hydrants. Person C's house catches on fire and burns down because there is no water in the hydrant. Person C could not sue Water Company B based on the fact that Water Company B breached its contract with City A because it is not a party to the contract, but City A could sue Water Company B under the contract.

g. Surety.

i. A surety is a person who has pledged as part of the contract to pay back money or perform a certain action if the principal to a contract fails, similar to collateral or similar to a guarantor.

4. Discharge by agreement of the parties.

a. Provision in original contract.

b. New, subsequent, valid, enforceable contract.

i. Elements of contract, including consideration, must be present.

ii. Mutual rescission - Parties agree to discharge and relieve each other of their obligations.

A) If the original bilateral contract was executory, consideration is present because each party gives up existing rights.

B) If the original contract was either a unilateral or a bilateral contract executed by one party, new consideration must be given to the party who performed in exchange for his or her promise to relieve the nonperforming party of his or her contractual duty to render the originally promised performance.

c. Release - A statement by one party that relieves the other party of a contractual duty. A release often includes a promise not to sue for breach of contract.

d. Accord and satisfaction.

i. Accord - Parties agree that a different (substitute) performance will be rendered by one party in satisfaction of his or her original obligation.

ii. Satisfaction - The substitute performance is actually rendered and accepted.

iii. Until substitute performance is rendered, the original contractual obligations are merely suspended.

e. Substituted agreement - Parties agree to enter a new agreement with different terms as a substitute for an original contract that is expressly or impliedly discharged.

f. Novation - Parties agree with a third person that the contractual duties of one of the original parties will be assumed by the third person. The third person is substituted for one of the original parties with the consent of the party entitled to receive the performance.

5. Discharge by operation of law.

a. Material alteration of a written contract without consent.

b. Running of the statute of limitations, which operates to bar access to judicial remedies.

c. Discharge (decree) in bankruptcy.

d. Impossibility - The occurrence of a supervening, unforeseen event makes it impossible to perform.

   i. Object of contract becomes illegal.

   ii. Death or serious illness or incapacitation of a party who was to perform personal services.

   iii. Destruction of specific subject matter of the contract.

   iv. Economic frustration - An unforeseen event occurs that frustrates the purpose for which one of the parties entered the contract. Therefore, the value of the expected performance he or she is to receive is destroyed.

   v. Commercial impracticability - An extreme change in conditions makes performance impracticable because it will be extremely difficult, burdensome, or costly to render.

   vi. Temporary impossibility - When performance is temporarily suspended because of unexpected occurrences and subsequent circumstances make performance very difficult, parties may be discharged.

G. REMEDIES.

1. Remedies at law - money damages.

   a. Compensatory damages - Awarded to a nonbreaching party in order to compensate for the actual harm or loss caused by the breach.

   b. Consequential or special damages - Speculative, unforeseeable, remote, indirect or unexpected damages, which do not ordinarily flow from a breach of contract, are not recoverable unless contemplated by the nonperforming party since he or she was given notice thereof.

   c. Punitive or exemplary damages - An unusual award by a court to punish for willful, wanton, or malicious (tortious) harm caused to a nonbreaching party.

   d. Nominal damages - An inconsequential sum that establishes that the plaintiff had a cause of action but suffered no measurable pecuniary loss.

   e. Mitigation of damages - A party who suffers damages has a duty to reduce actual damages if he or she is able to do so.

   f. Liquidated damages - The parties may provide in their contract that a stated sum of money or property will be paid, or, if previously deposited, forfeited, if one of the parties fails to perform in accordance with the contract. Such provisions will be enforced unless they are unreasonable and, therefore, are penalties.

2. Equitable remedies.

   a. Not available if:

      i. Remedy at law (usually money damages) is adequate, determinable, and available.

      ii. Aggrieved party has shown bad faith, fraud, etc.

      iii. Aggrieved party has unnecessarily delayed in bringing an action (laches).

      iv. A court will have to supervise execution of remedy.

b. Rescission and restitution.

   i. Rescission means cancellation or abrogation of a contract. It may be mutually agreed to by parties to a contract or awarded as a remedy by a court.

   ii. Usually, restitution is also given by a court so that previously rendered consideration, or its value, is returned.

c. Specific performance - An order by a court to render a contractually promised performance.

   i. Specified performance will be granted when:

      A) Contract involves unique personal property or real property that is always considered to be unique.

      B) Performance that is to be rendered is clear and unambiguous.

   ii. Specified performance will not be granted when performance to be rendered involves personal services.

d. Injunction - An order enjoining or restraining a person from doing some act.

e. Reformation - A court may correct an agreement so that it will conform to the intentions of the parties.

f. Quasi contract - A court may require one who has received a benefit to pay for the benefit conferred in order to prevent unjust enrichment.

XV. AGENCY RELATIONSHIPS

A. THE NATURE OF AGENCY.

1. By using a representative or agent, one person may conduct multiple business operations.
2. A corporation can function by using agents exclusively.

B. AGENCY DISTINGUISHED FROM OTHER RELATIONSHIPS.

1. Principal - agent relationship.
   a. An agent acts on behalf of and instead of a principal to engage in business transactions.
   b. An agent may bind his or her principal in contract with a third person.
   c. An agent has a degree of independent discretion.
2. Employer (master) - employee (servant) relationship.
   a. In order to determine if a relationship is one of employment, one must examine the surrounding circumstances.
      i. An employer controls, or has the right to control, the employee in the performance of physical tasks.
      ii. Employees have little or no independent discretion.
      iii. Employees are paid for time rather than results.
   b. The rights and duties of an employee differ from those of an agent. Today, the distinction is important for purposes of applicability of legislation such as tax, Social Security, unemployment, workplace safety, and workers compensation statutes.
3. Independent contractor.
   a. An independent contractor engages to bring about some specified end result and is normally paid at the completion of performance.
   b. The person employing an independent contractor does not exercise control over the details of the performance.
   c. An independent contractor cannot bind the person employing him in a contract with a third party.
   d. An independent contractor usually uses his or her own material, equipment, and employees.

C. FORMATION OF AGENCY RELATIONSHIP.

1. In general.
   a. An agency may be formed for any legal purpose.
   b. An agency is a consensual relationship but not necessarily a contractual one. Consideration need not be given by a principal.
   c. Generally, no special formalities are required in order to create an agency.
      i. Unless required by the Statute of Frauds or other statute, a writing is not necessary.
      ii. If the appointment of an agent is in a writing, the writing is called a power of attorney.

d. Capacity.

i. A principal must have legal (contractual) capacity because contracts entered into by his or her agent are treated as contracts of the principal. If a principal lacks capacity, such contracts are voidable by the principal but not the third party.

ii. An agent need not have legal (contractual) capacity in order to act as an agent, but the contract of agency may be avoided by the agent, who lacks capacity (but not the principal).

2. Agency created by agreement.

a. The agent and principal affirmatively indicate that they consent to the formation of the agency.

b. The agreement may be expressed or implied based upon the conduct of the parties.

3. Agency created by ratification.

a. The principal's consent to the agency is given after the purported agent acted on behalf of the principal.

b. Ratification may be expressed or implied.

c. Ratification relates back to the time that the agent acted without authorization.

4. Agency created by estoppel - A person may be estopped to deny the existence of an agency if he or she caused a third party to reasonably believe that a person was his or her agent because it appeared that an agency relationship existed (apparent authority).

D. AGENT'S DUTIES TO PRINCIPAL.

1. Duty to perform - An agent is required to follow instructions, use reasonable skill and diligence in carrying out agency obligations, and use special skills, which the agent possesses, if they are applicable.

2. Duty to notify - An agent has the duty to notify a principal of material information that relates to the subject matter of the agency.

3. Duty of loyalty.

a. An agent may neither compete with his or her principal nor act for another principal unless full disclosure is made to the principal, and the principal consents.

b. After termination of an agency, the agent may not disclose trade secrets, confidential information, customer lists, etc., acquired in the course of his or her employment as an agent.

c. Conflicts of interest - Any secret profits or benefits received by an agent, acting adversely to his or her principal, belong to the principal who may recover them from the agent.

4. Duty to account - An agent must account to his or her principal for any monies or property rightfully belonging to the principal that have come into the agent's hands. An agent should not commingle such property with his or her own property or that of others.

5. Remedies available to principal for breach of duties by agent.

   a. Principal's right to indemnification - If a principal is required to pay damages to an injured party for an agent's tortious conduct or, as a result of an agent's violation of the principal's instructions, incurs a loss, the principal may recover the resulting damages from the agent.

   b. A principal may seek remedies based upon breach of contractual duties or in tort based upon a breach of the fiduciary duty.

   c. Transactions by an agent that violate the agent's fiduciary duty to the principal are voidable by the principal.

   d. A court will impose a constructive trust on property received by an agent who has used his or her agency position in conflict with those of his or her principal. The property (or the proceeds of its sale) is treated as held for the benefit of the principal.

E. PRINCIPAL'S DUTIES TO AGENT.

1. A principal has an obligation to perform in accordance with his/her contract with an agent.

2. Duty to compensate, indemnify, and reimburse agent.

   a. A principal is required to pay any agreed compensation to his or her agent.

   b. If no compensation is specified, a principal is required to pay expenses, losses and reasonable compensation for services rendered by the agent. An exception exists when the agency is a gratuitous one or there are circumstances, such as a family relationship, that indicate compensation was not intended.

   c. There is no duty to pay compensation to an agent who has failed to perform his or her duties.

3. Duty of cooperation - A principal is required to assist an agent in performing his or her duties and to do nothing to prevent such performance.

4. Duty to provide safe working conditions.

5. Remedies available to an agent for breach of duties by a principal.

   a. Indemnification - A principal may be required to indemnify an agent for payments or liabilities incurred in executing his or her obligations and for losses caused by the failure of the principal to perform his or her duties.

   b. An agent may obtain a lien against the principal's property.

   c. An agent may sue for breach of contract or file a counterclaim if sued by the principal.

   d. An agent may bring an action for an accounting.

   e. An agent may withhold further performance.

F. TERMINATION OF AGENCY RELATIONSHIP.

1. Termination by act of the parties.

   a. Lapse of time.

      i. An agency expires at the end of a specified time if one is stated.

      ii. An agency terminates after the expiration of a reasonable period of time if no term has been specified.

b. Purpose accomplished - An agency is terminated when the objective for which it was created has been achieved.

c. Occurrence of specific event - An agency ends upon the happening of a particular event if its formation had been so conditioned.

d. Mutual agreement - The parties may consent to the termination of an agency.

e. Termination by one party.

i. A principal may revoke the authority of an agent, or an agent may renounce his or her appointment as an agent.

ii. Either party may have the power, but not necessarily the right, to terminate an agency.

A) If an agency is an agency at will (not for a stated term or for a particular purpose), either party has the power and right to terminate the agency.

B) If an agency is not an agency at will, a party may not have the power and right to terminate the agency and is, therefore, liable to the other party for the wrongful termination (breach of contract).

iii. An agency may be terminated for cause.

iv. A principal has neither the power nor the right to terminate an agency coupled with an interest (which is also referred to as a power coupled with an interest or a power given as security).

A) The agency is said to be irrevocable.

B) This is distinguished from situations in which an agent merely derives proceeds or profits from transactions.

2. Termination by operation of law.

a. Death or insanity terminates an agency.

i. Knowledge of the death or insanity is not required.

ii. An agency coupled with an interest is not automatically terminated.

iii. Statutory exceptions exist.

b. Bankruptcy of the principal terminates the agency.

i. Insolvency does not terminate the relationship.

ii. Bankruptcy of the agent does not necessarily terminate the agency relationship.

c. Impossibility.

i. Destruction of the subject matter of the agency.

ii. Outbreak of war.

iii. Change in law making further conduct of the agency illegal.

d. Unforeseen change in circumstances.

3. Notice required for termination.
    a. If termination is by the act of a party, the agency continues between the principal and the agent until notice is given by the principal who is revoking the agency or by the agent who is renouncing authority.
    b. Notice must be given to third persons.
        i. Actual notice must be given to third persons who dealt with the agent.
        ii. Constructive notice must be given to those who knew of the agency by publication in a newspaper, posting of a sign, etc.
    c. The party terminating the agency or another person may give the notice.
    d. Notice generally is not required if the agency is terminated by operation of law.

XVI.NEGOTIABLE INSTRUMENTS

A. DESCRIBED.

1. Two important functions:
    a. Extension of credit.
    b. Substitute for money.
2. If an instrument is negotiable, Article 3 of the UCC applies.
3. If an instrument is nonnegotiable, ordinary contract law applies. Assignees of contractual rights can get only the rights given by the assignor and, therefore, are burdened by any defenses between prior parties.
4. Whether or not an instrument is negotiable is determined by analyzing its form and content on the face of the instrument.
    a. Individuals accepting such instruments can determine whether they are negotiable.
    b. If a holder of a negotiable instrument is a holder in due course, that holder may collect on the instrument despite most contractual defenses.

B. TYPES OF COMMERCIAL PAPER.

1. A draft has three parties in which one person or entity (drawer) orders another (drawee) to pay a third party (payee) a sum of money.

Example

The following example is a draft in which Donna Jones is the drawer, Acme Publications is the drawee, and Allison is the payee.

August 29, 2002

On August 29, 2003, pay to the order of Allison $1,000 plus 6% annual interest from August 29, 2002.

To: Acme Publications, Inc.

(signed) **Donna Jones**

2. A check is a special type of draft that is payable on demand, and the drawee must be a bank. The check writer is the drawer.
3. A promissory note is a two-party instrument.
    a. Party A (the maker) promises to pay a specified sum of money to Party B (the payee).

b. The following example is a promissory note in which Jean Smith is the maker and Kristin Fourroux is the payee.

August 29, 2002

I promise to pay to the order of Kristin Fourroux $1,000 plus 6% annual interest on August 29, 2003.

To: Acme Publications, Inc.

(*signed*) **Jean Smith**

c. May be payable on demand or at a definite time.

4. A certificate of deposit is an acknowledgment by a financial institution of receipt of money and a promise to repay it. It is actually a special type of promissory note in which the maker is the financial institution.

C. REQUIREMENTS.

In order for an instrument to be negotiable, it must have all of the following requirements on the face of the instrument:

1. In writing.
2. Signed by maker or drawer.
3. Contain an unconditional promise or order to pay.
4. State a fixed amount in money.
5. Payable on demand or at a definite time.
6. Payable to order or to bearer, unless it is a check.

D. AMBIGUITIES.

1. Words control over figures.
2. Handwritten terms control over typewritten and printed terms.
3. Typewritten terms control over printed terms.
4. Omission of a date does not destroy negotiability, unless the date is necessary to determine when it is payable.
5. Omission of the interest rate is allowed because the judicial interest rate (rate used on court judgment) is automatically used.
6. Statement of consideration or where the instrument is drawn or payable is not required.
7. The instrument may be postdated or antedated and remain negotiable. For example, a bank may pay a postdated check before the date on the check unless the drawer notifies the bank to defer the payment.
8. The instrument may have a provision that by endorsing or cashing it, the payee acknowledges full satisfaction of debt, and the instrument remains negotiable.

9. If an instrument is payable to the order of more than one person, either payee may negotiate or enforce it. If payable to him and her, all payees must negotiate or enforce it.

Example

- If the instrument states, "Pay to the order of H. Fetzer <u>or</u> J. Becknell," then only one signature is required to negotiate or enforce it.

- If the instrument states "Pay to the order of H. Fetzer <u>and</u> J. Becknell," then both signatures are required to negotiate or enforce it.

10. If it is not clear whether the instrument is a draft or a note, the holder may treat it as either.

E. NEGOTIATION.

1. Two methods of transferring commercial paper:
   a. Negotiation.
      i. One who receives a negotiable instrument by negotiation is called a holder.
      ii. If the holder further qualifies as a holder in due course, he or she can obtain more rights than the transferor had.
      iii. There are two methods of negotiation.
         A) Negotiating order paper requires both endorsement by the transferor and delivery of the instrument. Order paper includes negotiable instruments made payable to the order of A.
         B) Negotiating bearer paper is accomplished by delivery alone; endorsement is not necessary.
            1) Subsequent parties may require endorsements for identification.
            2) The holder may endorse the bearer paper if he or she so chooses.
   b. Assignment.
      i. An assignment occurs when a transfer does not meet all requirements of negotiation.
      ii. The assignee can obtain only the same rights that the assignor had.
2. Endorsements.
   a. Blank endorsement - It converts order paper into bearer paper and the bearer paper may be negotiated by mere delivery.
   b. Special endorsement - Indicates the specific person that the endorsee wishes to negotiate the instrument.
      i. The words "pay to the order" of are not required on the back as an endorsement. The back of the instrument needs to be payable to the order or to the bearer on the front only.
      ii. If the instrument is not payable to order or to bearer on its face, it cannot be turned into a negotiable instrument by using these words in an endorsement on the back.

iii. The bearer paper may be converted into order paper by the use of a special endorsement. For example, a check made out to "cash" is delivered to Julie. Julie writes on the back "payable to Keri," and Julie signs the back. It was bearer paper until this special endorsement.

iv. If last (or only) endorsement on the instrument is a blank endorsement, any holder may convert that bearer paper into order paper by writing "Pay to A" above that blank endorsement.

c. Restrictive endorsement - Requires endorsees to comply with certain conditions (e.g., "for deposit only").

d. Qualified endorsement - Disclaims the liability normally imposed on the endorser. Normally, by signing the check, the endorser promises, automatically, to pay the holder or any subsequent endorser the amount of the instrument if it is later dishonored. Qualified endorsements, otherwise, have the same effects as other endorsements.

3. If the payee's name is misspelled, the payee may endorse it with the proper spelling, the misspelling, or both. The endorsee may require both.

4. If an order instrument is transferred for value without being endorsed, the transferee may require endorsement from the transferor. Upon obtaining the endorsement, the transferee will become a holder.

5. Federal law recently standardized endorsements on checks. The endorser should turn the check over and sign in the top portion of the check next to the short edge. The purpose is to avoid interference with bank's endorsements. The endorsements placed outside of this area do not destroy the negotiability but may delay the clearing process.

6. If a check has a statement that it is nonnegotiable (i.e., it is not governed by Article 3, etc.), the check is still negotiable. This is not true of other negotiable instruments, whereby such statements destroy negotiability.

F. HOLDER IN DUE COURSE.

1. A holder in due course is entitled to payment on a negotiable instrument despite most defenses that the maker or the drawer of the instrument may have:

   a. An assignee of contractual rights receives only the rights that the assignor had. (Assignee takes these rights subject to all defenses that could have been asserted against assignor.)

   b. An ordinary holder of a negotiable instrument has the same rights as the assignee.

2. To be a holder in due course, a taker of an instrument must:

   a. Be a holder of a properly negotiated negotiable instrument.

   b. Give value for the instrument.

   c. Take in good faith.

   d. Take without notice that it is overdue, that it has been dishonored, or that any person has a defense or claim to it.

3. Rights of a holder in due course.
   a. A transfer of a negotiable instrument to a holder in due course cuts off all personal defenses against a holder in due course. Personal defenses are assertable against ordinary holders and assignees of contractual rights to avoid payment. An exception is if the holder in due course takes subject to all personal defenses of a person with whom the holder in due course directly dealt.
   b. Some defenses are assertable against any party including a holder in due course. These defenses are called real (or universal) defenses.
   c. Types of personal defenses.
      i. Breach of contract.
      ii. Lack or failure of consideration.
      iii. Prior payment.
      iv. Unauthorized completion.
      v. Fraud in the inducement.
      vi. Nondelivery.
      vii. Ordinary duress or undue influence.
      viii. Mental incapacity.
      ix. Illegality.
   d. Real defenses.
      i. Forgery.
      ii. Bankruptcy.
      iii. Fraud in the execution.
      iv. Minority (or infancy).
      v. Mental incapacity, illegality, or extreme duress.
      vi. Material alteration of instrument.
   e. Holder through a holder in due course.
      i. A party who does not qualify as a holder in due course but obtains a negotiable instrument from a holder in due course is called a holder through a holder in due course.
      ii. Obtains all rights of a holder in due course.
      iii. A holder in due course washes an instrument so that any holder thereafter can be a holder through a holder in due course.
   f. Exceptions.
      i. If a party reacquires an instrument, his or her status remains unchanged.
      ii. One who was involved in fraud or illegality affecting the instrument may not become a holder through a holder in due course.

g. Federal Trade Commission (FTC) holder in due course rules.

   i. Applies when a seller of consumer goods or services receives a note from a consumer or arranges a loan with a bank, etc., for that consumer.

   ii. Requires a seller or lender to put a notice on these negotiable instruments that all holders take subject to any defenses that the debtor could assert against the seller.

   iii. The rule does not apply to any nonconsumer transactions and does not apply to any consumer noncredit transactions.

G. LIABILITY OF PARTIES.

1. Two general types of warranties on negotiable instruments:

   a. Contractual liability.

   b. Warranty liability.

2. Contractual liability.

   a. Refers to liability of any party who signs a negotiable instrument as a maker, drawer, drawee, or endorser.

   b. A maker of a note has that primary liability. This means that the maker has absolute liability to pay according to the note's terms until it is paid or until the statute of limitations has run.

   c. No party of a draft (or check) initially has primary liability because the drawee has only been ordered to pay by the drawer.

   d. Drawer has secondary liability on draft and is liable only if the drawee fails to pay.

   e. Endorsers of the note or draft have secondary liability. The holder can hold the endorser liable if the primary parties obligated to make payment fail to pay.

   f. Drawers and endorsers may avoid secondary liability by signing without recourse.

   g. Upon certification of the check, the drawer and all previous endorsers are discharged from liability because the bank has accepted the check and agreed to pay it.

3. Warranty liability.

   a. Two types under which holder can seek payment from secondary parties:

      i. Transfer warranties.

      ii. Presentment warranties.

   b. Transfer warranties - The transferor gives these transfer warranties whenever a negotiable instrument is transferred for consideration:

      i. Transferor has good title.

      ii. All signatures are genuine or authorized.

      iii. Instrument has not been materially altered.

      iv. No defense of any party is good against the transferor.

      v. Transferor has no notice of insolvency of the maker, drawer, or the acceptor.

c. Transfer warranties generally give the loss to the parties who dealt face to face with the wrongdoer and were in the best position to prevent or avoid forged, altered, or stolen instruments.

d. If not endorsed by the transferor, the transferor makes all five warranties only to the immediate transferee. If endorsed by the transferor, the transferor makes them to all subsequent holders taking in good faith.

e. To recover under warranty liabilities (either transfer or presentment warranties), a party does not have to meet conditions of proper presentment, dishonor, or timely notice of dishonor that are required under contractual liability against endorsers.

4. Signatures by authorized agents - An agent may sign on behalf of another person (or principal) and that principal is liable, not the agent, if the signature indicates that the principal is liable.

5. An accommodation party is liable on the instrument in the capacity in which he or she has signed, even if the taker knows of his or her accommodation status.

   a. Notice of default need not be given to an accommodation party.

   b. The accommodation party has the right of recourse against the accommodated party if the accommodation party is held liable.

6. If there are multiple endorsers, each is liable in full to subsequent endorsers or holders.

7. Once the primary party pays, all endorsers are discharged from liability. Cancellation of a prior party's endorsement discharges that party from liability. Intentional destruction of an instrument by a holder discharges prior parties to the instrument.

8. Persons whose signature was forged on an instrument are not liable on that instrument. The forged signature operates as the signature of the forger. Therefore, if the signature of the maker or drawer is forged, the instrument can still be negotiated between the parties, and a holder can therefore acquire good title. However, a forged endorsement does not transfer title. Accordingly, persons receiving it after forgery cannot collect on it.

H. BANKS.

1. Banks include savings and loan associations, credit unions, and trust companies.

2. The relationship between bank and depositor is debtor-creditor.

3. Checks.

   a. Banks are not obligated to pay on a check presented more than 6 months after the date, but they may pay in good faith and charge the customer's account.

   b. Even if a check creates an overdraft, a bank may charge the customer's account.

   c. Banks are liable to the drawer for damages caused by wrongful dishonor of a check. Wrongful dishonor may occur if the bank, in error, believes that funds are insufficient when, actually, they are sufficient.

d. Payment of bad checks, such as forged or altered checks.

   i. A bank liable to the drawer for payment on bad checks, unless the drawer's negligence contributed, since the bank is presumed to know the signatures of its drawers.

   ii. A bank cannot recover from a holder in due course to whom the bank paid on a bad check.

   iii. If the drawer fails to notify the bank of a forgery or an alteration within 30 days of the bank statement, the drawer is held liable on subsequent forgeries or alterations done in the same way by the same person.

e. An oral stop payment order is good for 14 days. A written stop payment order is good for six months and is renewable.

   i. The stop payment order must be given so as to give the bank reasonable opportunity to act on it.

   ii. A bank is liable to the drawer if the bank pays after an effective stop payment order only when the drawer can prove that the bank's failure to obey the order caused the drawer's loss. If the drawer has no valid defense to justify dishonoring instruments, the bank has no liability for failure to obey the stop payment order.

   iii. If the drawer stops payment on the check, the drawer is still liable to the holder of the check unless the drawer has a valid defense.

XVII.PROPERTY

A. PERSONAL PROPERTY.

1. Introduction - Personal property (personalty) includes rights and interests associated with ownership in things, other than real property, capable of being possessed and movable. Personal property may be tangible or intangible.
    a. Tangible personal property - Rights in movable property, subject to physical possession.
    b. Intangible personal property - Rights in a thing that lacks physical substance (e.g., patents, copyrights, and royalties).
    c. Fixtures - Personal property attached to real property.
2. Property rights.
    a. Right to possession and enjoyment.
    b. Right to make disposition by sale, gift, or conveyance.
3. Title to property may be held.
    a. Fee simple - The total collection of ownership rights held by one person.
    b. Concurrent ownership by two or more persons.
        i. Tenancy in common - Two or more persons own an undivided share, which may be unequal, in property that is transferable during their lifetimes and by inheritance, without rights of survivorship among the co-tenants.
        ii. Joint tenancy with right of survivorship.
            A) Two or more persons own equal undivided interests, acquired simultaneously, and have equal rights to use, enjoy, etc., and rights of survivorship.
            B) The transferor must have clearly indicated an intention to create a joint tenancy.
            C) A joint tenant may sever and transfer his or her interest during his or her lifetime (right of partition).
        iii. There is a presumption that a co-tenancy is a tenancy in common.
        iv. Tenancy by the entirety - A joint tenancy existing between spouses cannot be transferred by either spouse without the consent of the other (survivorship rights).
        v. Community property - Undivided interests held by spouses in property acquired during the course of marriage in Arizona, California, Idaho, Louisiana, Nevada, New Mexico, Texas, Washington, and Wisconsin.
4. Acquisition and transfer of ownership of personal property.
    a. Possession with intent to control and exclude others gives one rights with respect to personal property.
    b. One may take possession of unwanted property, such as personal property, that has been voluntarily abandoned.
    c. Purchase.
    d. Gift - Voluntary transfer of ownership rights without receipt of adequate consideration.
        i. Requirements for an effective gift:

A) Delivery by donor.

1) Actual, physical transfer of possession to donee.

2) Constructive delivery, such as keys to an automobile, given to a donee without retention of control or dominion.

3) Constructive delivery to a third person with unconditional and absolute instructions to deliver to donee. Gifts to minors by delivery to a custodian are covered by a Uniform Act.

B) Donative intent - Donor intends to presently transfer rights of ownership and relinquishes dominion and control.

C) Acceptance by donee.

ii. Types of gifts.

A) Inter vivos - Absolute, present transfer during donor's lifetime (irrevocable).

B) Mortis causa - Transfer given in contemplation of imminent death as a result of illness or peril (revocable).

1) Expressly revocable by donor while living.

2) Revocable, if and when, donor recovers or survives peril.

3) Revocable upon death of donee before donor.

e. Misplaced, lost, and abandoned property.

i. Misplaced - The owner intentionally left property at a location that was inadvertently forgotten. The owner of the premises where property is found is entrusted with holding property as a bailee for the owner.

ii. Lost - Property is accidentally, involuntarily left by owner.

A) Finder's right of possession is good against all but the true owner.

B) In many states, if found on private property by one who is trespassing, the owner of the premises holds lost property as a bailee for true owners.

C) If found by an employee, the employer holds lost property as a bailee.

iii. Abandoned - The owner discarded property without intending to reclaim it. Property belongs to the first person who takes possession with the intention of owning it.

f. Inheritance.

g. Creation or production - Property created through mental or physical labor belongs to the producer or creator.

i. Patents - Federal statute gives inventors monopolies or exclusive rights to use their inventions for 17 years in exchange for full disclosure.

ii. Trademarks - (Federal Statute) - Perpetual protection from infringement is given to one who first adopts and uses a distinctive symbol, design, or mark.

iii. Copyright - Federal statute prohibits reproduction of literary or other creative works, without permission, for the life of the creator plus fifty years. This is subject to some exceptions, such as "fair use," library reproduction, and works created prior to 1978.

h. Blind trusts.

   i. A blind trust can be used to hold assets where ownership of the assets may give rise to conflict of interest issues.

   ii. These trusts are commonly used by government officials.

   iii. The official, his/her spouse, or dependent child has a beneficial interest which is certified by the Director of the Office of Government Ethics.

   iv. The official has no knowledge or control of the management of the trust assets and only receives the income from the assets.

i. Uniform Transfers to Minors Act (UTMA) and Uniform Gifts to Minors Act (UGMA).

   i. The Uniform Gift to Minors Act allows parents the option to put assets in a custodial account for a child. If the child is below 14 years of age, all income earned by the assets (above the kiddie tax threshold) are taxed at the income tax rate of the parents. If the child is 14 years of age or older, the income earned by the assets is taxed at the rate for the child. Notably, this is considered an asset of the child and is considered in determining financial aid.

   ii. Starting in the mid 1980's, states started adopting the Uniform Transfers to Minors Act, which is similar to the UGMA, except it expanded the types of properties legally transferable to a minor. Nearly all states have adopted the UTMA, but many people still refer to it as UGMA.

B. REAL PROPERTY.

1. Introduction.

   a. Real property refers to rights associated with ownership or possessory interests in land and things of a permanent nature on or affixed to land or contained above or below the surface.

   b. If there is an interference with the use and enjoyment of real property, action may be brought based upon trespass. If one has acquired title to real property by conveyance and there is a defect in the title, the transferee may sue the transferor for breach of a covenant or a warranty contained in the deed.

2. Nature of real property.

   a. The land or soil itself, bodies of water contained on the land, natural and artificial structures attached to it, and plant life and vegetation growing on the land.

   b. Subsurface and air rights.

      i. One has rights to the air immediately above the land sufficient to have a cause of action, based upon trespass, for a direct interference with the use and enjoyment of the land.

      ii. A property owner has the exclusive right to minerals, oil, and other matter found beneath the surface, and may transfer this right to another (i.e., it may be partitioned from the land).

   c. Plant life and vegetation - Includes trees, natural vegetation, and cultivated crops.

d. Fixtures - Personal property affixed to real property.

i. Fixtures that are attached or affixed to real property are included in the sale of realty unless the contract for sale provides otherwise.

ii. The objective intention of the party who placed the item determines whether or not the item is a fixture.

3. Ownership interest in real property.

a. Freehold estates - Estates for indefinite time (possessory interest in land) are transferable during the owner's lifetime or as an inheritance.

i. Fee simple absolute - The owner possesses all the rights that one may possess, convey, or inherit in land.

ii. Life estates - Duration is measured by the life of one or more persons.

A) Measured by the life of a person to whom the estate is given or the life of another person.

B) It may not be inherited but may be conveyed during the lifetime of the person by whose life it is measured.

C) A life tenant has the right to possess, use, and convey specific interest in the property. The life tenant also has an obligation to pay taxes, make repairs, and not commit waste.

D) May be created by voluntary acts of the parties or by operation of law.

b. Estates less than freehold - Leaseholds for a determinable period of time in accordance with a contract of lease.

i. Tenancy for a specified term.

A) Generally, a lease is for a specified number of years.

B) No notice of termination at the end of the term is needed.

C) Upon the death of the tenant, the rights under the lease become part of the decedent's estate or personal property.

D) Statutes may require that the lease be in writing in order to be enforceable (Statute of Frauds or State Laws).

ii. Periodic tenancy.

A) Created by contracting to pay rent periodically without stating the duration of the lease or by tenant holding over after expiration of a lease for a specified term (month to month).

B) Terminated after giving one period's notice or as provided by statute.

iii. Tenancy at will - Terminated upon death or, at common law, the will of either party, or after giving such notice as required by statute.

4. Concurrent ownership - Property may be held by two or more people simultaneously rather than individually.
   a. Tenancy in common.
      i. Two or more persons own undivided shares (which may be equal or unequal) in property.
      ii. Each tenant may transfer his or her interest during his or her lifetime, by will or by inheritance, without rights of survivorship among the other co-tenants.
   b. Joint tenancy with right of survivorship.
      i. Two or more persons own equal, undivided shares of an entire estate that they acquire simultaneously, have equal rights of enjoyment, and rights of survivorship.
      ii. The transferor must have clearly indicated an intention to create a joint tenancy.
      iii. A joint tenant may sever and transfer interest during lifetime.
      iv. There is a presumption that a co-tenancy is a tenancy in common unless there is a clear intention to create a joint tenancy.
   c. Tenancy by the entirety - A joint tenancy existing between spouses cannot be severed by either spouse without the consent of the other.
   d. Community property - In some states, spouses own undivided half interests in property acquired during the period of their marriage (other than by gift or inheritance).
   e. Condominium ownership - Each owner owns the unit that he or she occupies and is a tenant in common with others with respect to common areas.
5. Transfer of ownership.
   a. A conveyance by deed (sale or gift).
   b. Will or inheritance.
   c. Eminent domain - Government takes property for public use and compensates the owner by paying the fair value of the property taken.
   d. Adverse possession - One in actual, open, exclusive, continuous, hostile possession of real property for a statutory period of time acquires title to the property.
6. Future interests - A present, existing right to have possession of real property after the termination of a preceding estate.
   a. Reversionary interests and powers of termination.
      i. Arise when a grantor makes a conveyance of less than all interests without disposing of the residue.
      ii. The owner of the reversionary interest may transfer the future interest during lifetime.
      iii. Upon the death of the owner of the reversionary interest, the interest vests in owning heirs or devisees.
      iv. Reversion.
         A) The interest retained by a grantor who transfers a life estate to another without making a disposition of the interest remaining after the death of the person who is the measuring life.
         B) A vested, future interest.

v. Possibility of reverter.

A) It is the interest retained by a grantor who has conveyed a fee simple determinable.

B) It is contingent upon the happening of the event specified in the conveyance, which terminates the grantee's interest automatically.

vi. Power of termination.

A) The interest retained by a grantor, who has conveyed a fee simple subject to a condition subsequent is not automatically terminated upon the happening of the condition.

B) The grantor (or heirs) must affirmatively exercise right of entry.

b. Remainders and executory interests.

i. Created by the same instrument that conveyed a present possessory interest.

ii. May be conveyed and inherited.

iii. Vested remainder - An absolute right to possession that exists at the end of a prior life estate or leasehold.

iv. Contingent remainder - The right to possession depends upon the termination of a preceding estate and the occurrence of a contingency or the existence and identification of some person.

v. Executory interest - The right to possession takes effect either before the natural termination of a preceding estate, upon the occurrence of some contingency (a shifting executory interest), or after the termination of the preceding estate (a springing executory interest).

XVIII.CONSUMER PROTECTION

A. INTRODUCTION.

1. There is a trend away from caveat emptor (let the buyer beware). The emphasis of protective legislation and regulation has been preventing deceptive practices and assuring full disclosure of material information that relates to sales of personal property, real property, services, and credit transactions.
2. A consumer is usually considered to be an actual person who obtains or tries to obtain personal property, real property, services, money, or credit for personal, household, or family use. Small businesses and farmers or farm units may also be afforded protection under legislation and regulation dealing with consumers.

B. PUBLIC POLICY ISSUES.

1. The potential benefits and costs of consumer protection judicial decisions, statutes, and regulations must be balanced.
2. Existing and potential costs of compliance may include increases in prices for consumer goods and services and a decrease in competition due to costs of compliance.

C. ADVERTISING.

1. The Federal Trade Commission (FTC) administers a number of federal consumer protection statutes and is authorized to prevent unfair or deceptive acts or practices in commerce (deceptive advertising).
2. Procedures are followed when the FTC believes that a deceptive advertisement is being used.
   a. The FTC conducts an investigation of a possible deceptive advertisement on its own initiative or following a consumer or competitor's complaint.
   b. A hearing may be conducted by an administrative law judge whose ruling may be appealed by the advertiser to the FTC.
   c. If the FTC upholds the decision against the advertiser, its decision can be appealed to a U.S. Court of Appeals.
3. The FTC may issue a cease and desist order that requires that an unfair or deceptive advertisement be discontinued and may initiate a consumer redress action for rescission or reformation of contracts that were entered into by consumers with the advertiser as a result of the misleading advertisement.
4. Counter-advertising - The FTC may require that an advertiser correct misinformation in an advertisement.
5. Unfair or deceptive acts or practices.
   a. Deceptive advertising refers to intentional misrepresentations of facts that are material or relevant factors included in a purchaser's decisions to buy the advertised products or services.
   b. Statements made in an advertisement are deceptive if they are scientifically untrue or contain false product differentiation.
   c. An advertisement is deceptive if a reasonable consumer would be misled. In general, puffing is not considered to be deceptive.

6. Bait-and-switch advertising.

    a. The advertisement relates to one item, which is offered for sale at a low price. When a consumer tries to purchase that item, a salesperson tries to get the consumer to buy a more expensive item.

    b. FTC guidelines are designed to prevent practices such as refusal to sell an advertised item, failure to have an adequate quantity of an advertised item available, failure to supply the advertised item within a reasonable time, and discouragement of employees from selling an advertised item.

D. CREDIT PROTECTION.

1. Federal Truth-in-Lending Act (Consumer Credit Protection Act) is administered by the Federal Reserve Board.

    a. The Act applies when a debtor is a natural person; the creditor in the ordinary course of its business is a lender, seller, or provider of services; and the amount being financed is less than $25,000.

    b. Regulation Z uniform disclosure requirements provide consumers with means of comparing the terms and costs of credit.

        i. Financing charges (including interest; charges for loans and insurance; and finders, credit report, appraisal, financing, and service fees) must be stated in an annual percentage rate (APR).

        ii. The consumer must be informed of the number of payments, the dollar amount of each payment, the dates that payments are due, and prepayment provisions including prepayment penalties.

2. Credit card.

    a. Fair Credit Billing Act amends the Truth-in-Lending Act.

    b. A credit cardholder is given limited right to withhold payment, if there is a dispute concerning goods that were purchased with a credit card.

    c. Billing disputes - If a credit cardholder believes that an error has been made by the issuer:

        i. The cardholder may suspend payment, but must notify and give an explanation to the card issuer concerning an error within 60 days of receipt of the bill (in writing).

        ii. The issuer of the credit card must acknowledge receipt of notification within 30 days and has 90 days to resolve the dispute.

    d. A credit cardholder will not be liable for more than $50 (per card) if there was an unauthorized use of the card and notice thereof was given to the card issuer.

    e. A credit card issuer may not bill a cardholder for unauthorized charges if a credit card is improperly issued.

3. Fair Credit Reporting Act.
   a. Upon request, one who is refused credit or employment because of information in a credit bureau report must be supplied with a summary of the information in the report including the sources and recipients of the information. The individual must be given an opportunity to correct errors.
   b. Consumers have the right to be informed as to the nature and scope of a credit investigation, the kind of information that is being compiled, and the names of people who will receive a credit report.
   c. The compiler of a credit report must exercise reasonable care in preparing a credit report.
   d. Inaccurate or misleading data must be removed from a credit report, and the consumer has the right to add a statement regarding a disputed matter not to exceed 100 words.
4. Equal Credit Opportunity Act - Prohibits discrimination based upon race, religion, national origin, color, sex, marital status, age, or receipt of certain types of income.

E. DEBT COLLECTION.

1. The Fair Debt Collection Practices Act prohibits debt collectors from engaging in certain practices:
   a. Contacting a debtor at his or her place of employment if the employer objects.
   b. Contacting a debtor at unusual or inconvenient times, or, if the debtor is represented by an attorney, at any time.
   c. Contacting third parties about the payment of the debt without court authorization.
   d. Harassing or intimidating debtor or using false and misleading approaches.
   e. Communicating with the debtor after receipt of notice that the debtor is refusing to pay the debt except to advise the debtor of action to be taken by the collection agency.
2. Garnishment.
   a. A state court may issue an order for garnishment of a portion of a debtor's wages in order to satisfy a legal judgment that was obtained by a creditor.
   b. The Truth in Lending Act and Federal Bankruptcy Law provide that a certain minimum income and no more than 25 percent of a judgment debtor's after-tax earnings can be garnished.

F. STATE LAWS.

1. Statutes, which vary from state to state, have codified, simplified, and otherwise expanded the protection afforded by the common law (lemon laws, right of redhibition).
2. State consumer protection legislation may be stricter than comparable federal law.

XIX.BANKRUPTCY AND REORGANIZATION

A. THE BANKRUPTCY REFORM ACT OF 1978, AS AMENDED (U.S.C., TITLE 11).

1. Establishes Bankruptcy Courts with jurisdiction over all controversies affecting the debtor or the debtor's estate.
2. Provides procedures for:
   a. Voluntary and involuntary liquidation (bankruptcy) of bankruptcy estates of natural persons, firms, partnerships, corporations, unincorporated companies, and associations (Chapter 7).
   b. Reorganization of persons, firms, and corporations (Chapter 11).
   c. Adjustment of debts of individuals with regular income (Chapter 13).

B. LIQUIDATION - ORDINARY OR STRAIGHT BANKRUPTCY (CHAPTER 7).

1. Voluntary liquidation.
   a. Commenced by any natural person, firm, association, or corporation (except certain organizations under other chapters).
   b. Petitioning debtor need not be insolvent unless it is a partnership.
   c. The debtor will be granted an order for relief if the petition is proper and if the debtor has not been discharged in bankruptcy within the past six years.
2. Involuntary liquidation.
   a. Commenced against any debtor, except railroad, banking, insurance, or municipal corporations, building or savings and loan associations, credit unions, nonprofit organizations, ranchers, or farmers.
   b. Creditors who have noncontingent, unsecured claims in the amount of $5,000 or more file a petition with the Bankruptcy Court.
      i. If there are 12 or more creditors, three of them must join in the petition.
      ii. If there are less than 12 creditors, one must file the petition.
      iii. If a party so requests, a temporary trustee may be appointed to take possession of the debtor's property in order to prevent a loss.
   c. The court will grant an order for relief if the debtor fails to file an answer or, if debtor files an answer, but creditors prove that:
      i. The debtor is not paying debts as they become due, or
      ii. A general receiver, assignee, or other custodian was appointed or took possession of the debtor's property within 120 days preceding the filing of the petition.
3. Automatic stay.
   a. The filing of a voluntary or involuntary petition stays or suspends most litigation or other action that might be taken by creditors against the debtor or the debtor's property.
   b. Secured creditors may, however, apply for relief from the automatic stay if they are not adequately protected.

4. The debtor must file documents with the Bankruptcy Court. These documents include:
   a. A list of secured and unsecured creditors with their addresses and the amounts owed.
   b. A schedule of assets.
   c. A statement of financial affairs.
   d. A list of current income and expenses.
   e. A schedule of exempt property if the debtor wishes to claim exemptions. The debtor has the option of taking exemptions provided by either the law of the state where the debtor is domiciled or the Federal Bankruptcy Act that provides for the following exemptions:
      i. Equity in a home and burial plot not exceeding $7,500.
      ii. Interest in one motor vehicle up to $1,200.
      iii. Interest in personal household goods, clothing, books, animals, etc., up to $200 for any single item, but not exceeding a total of $4,000.
      iv. Interest in jewelry up to $500.
      v. Other property worth up to $400 plus up to $3,750 of the unused part of the $7,500 exemption for equity in a home and/or burial plot.
      vi. Items used in a trade or business up to $750.
      vii. Interests in life insurance policies.
      viii. Professionally prescribed health aids.
      ix. Federal and state benefits such as Social Security, veterans' disability, and unemployment benefits.
      x. Alimony and child support, pensions, and annuities.
         A) The U.S. Supreme court decided in Patterson v. Shumate that assets in qualified plans were outside the reach of creditors with regards to bankruptcy proceedings.
      xi. Rights to receive certain personal injury and other awards.
5. An order for relief is entered, and an interim or provisional trustee is appointed.
6. Bankruptcy estate - All tangible and intangible property, wherever located, in which the debtor had legal and/or equitable interests at the time that the petition was filed, including:
   a. Property that may be exempt.
   b. Community property; property that the debtor transferred but that the trustee can reach because the transfer is voidable; causes of action; and proceeds, rents, and profits generated by property in the estate.
   c. Property that was received by the debtor as a gift and/or inheritance, and property acquired in a settlement with a spouse or as a beneficiary of life insurance within 180 days after filing of the petition.
7. First meeting of creditors - Within ten to thirty days after the order for relief is entered, the court calls the meeting of creditors which is attended by the debtor. A trustee is elected or an interim (provisional) trustee becomes the permanent trustee at that meeting.

8. Claims of creditors.
   a. Filed within six months of the first meeting of creditors.
   b. Claims that arose before the filing of the petition are allowed unless objected to or unenforceable or excluded:
      i. Claims for interest accruing after the petition was filed.
      ii. Claims of landlords or employees based upon breach of a lease or contract for no more than one year's rent or wages.
9. The trustee.
   a. The trustee takes title to property that is included in the debtor's bankruptcy estate.
   b. Duties and powers of trustee - Trustee administers the estate of the debtor by collecting assets, reducing them to cash, and approving claims.
      i. Trustee may assume or reject executory contracts.
      ii. Trustee may bring actions to avoid transfers of the debtor's assets that the debtor or a judgment, lien, or unsecured creditor would have had a right to avoid under state law or the Bankruptcy Act.
      iii. Trustee is empowered to avoid transfers of property interests that were not perfected when the petition was filed.
      iv. Trustee may avoid preferential transfers, which are transfers of property or payments that favor one creditor over other creditors. With some exceptions, a preferential transfer includes those made:
         A) When the debtor was insolvent.
         B) To or for the benefit of a creditor for, or on account of, an antecedent debt.
         C) During the 90 days before the petition was filed.
         D) Resulting in the receipt by the creditor of a greater percentage of payment than would be made under the provisions of the bankruptcy law.
      v. Fraudulent transfers are voidable by the trustee - Transfer made in order to hinder, delay, or defraud creditors or for less than reasonable consideration when the debtor was insolvent or, as a result of the transfer, becomes insolvent.
10. Priority of payment of claims.
   a. Secured creditors that have valid liens or security interests in property are entitled to exercise their security interests.
      i. A secured creditor can accept the collateral in full satisfaction of the debt.
      ii. A secured creditor has the option of foreclosing on the collateral and using proceeds in order to pay off the debt.
         A) If proceeds exceed debt:
            1) Excess may be used to cover reasonable costs incurred by a secured creditor because of the debtor's default.
            2) Trust gets any remaining balance.
         B) If there is a deficiency, a secured creditor becomes an unsecured creditor as to the balance.

b. Priorities of payment of claims of unsecured creditors - Each class of debts must be fully paid before the next class is entitled to share in the remaining proceeds. If there are insufficient proceeds to fully pay a particular class of creditors, proceeds are distributed pro rata, and the remaining classes receive nothing.

11. Discharge of debtor from debts.

a. Nondischargeable debts.

i. Back taxes (three years).

ii. Those based upon fraud, embezzlement, misappropriation, or defalcation against the debtor acting in a fiduciary capacity.

iii. Alimony and child support.

iv. Intentional tort claims.

v. Property or money obtained by the debtor under false pretenses or fraudulent representations.

vi. All student loans are nondischargable, unless paying the loan will impose an undue hardship on the debtor and the debtor's dependents.

vii. Unscheduled claims (not listed).

viii. Claims from prior bankruptcy action in which the debtor was denied a discharge for a reason other than the 6-year limitation.

ix. Consumer debts of more than $500 for luxury goods or services owed to a single creditor within 40 days of the order for relief.

x. Cash advances aggregating more than $1,000 as extensions of open-end consumer credit obtained by the debtor within 20 days of the order for relief.

xi. Judgments or consent decrees awarded against the debtor for liability incurred as a result of the debtor's operation of a motor vehicle while intoxicated.

b. Denial of discharge of a debtor - Assets are distributed, but the debtor remains liable for unpaid portion of the claims.

C. REORGANIZATION (CHAPTER 11).

1. Any individual, business firm, or corporate debtor who is eligible for Chapter 7 liquidation (except stockbrokers, commodities brokers, and railroads) is eligible for Chapter 11 reorganization.

2. A voluntary or involuntary petition may be filed. The automatic stay and entry or order for relief provisions apply.

3. The debtor remains in possession and may continue to operate the debtor's business.

4. Fair and equitable plans for settling claims and/or extending time for payment in order to avoid liquidation are approved by the court.

5. The debtor may file a plan for reorganization within 120 days after the order for relief. If debtor does not do so or if the plan is not approved, the trustee, creditors, or shareholders' committee appointed by the court, or any party in interest, may file a plan within 180 days after the order for relief.

6. The plan must be approved by a majority in number and two-thirds in amount of each class of creditors and shareholders, whose claims and interests will be impaired.
7. If the court finds that the plan is fair and confirms it, the plan is binding on all parties, although not accepted by a class of creditors or shareholders.
8. Provisions are made for the conversion of a reorganization into a liquidation proceeding.
9. Creditors may prefer private, negotiated adjustments of creditor-debtor relations (out-of-court workouts).
10. A debtor can reject an existing collective bargaining agreement if the debtor has proposed modifications and the union has rejected the modifications without good cause.

D. ADJUSTMENT OF DEBTS OF AN INDIVIDUAL WITH REGULAR INCOME (CHAPTER 13).

1. An individual debtor, who is a wage earner or engaged in business, may voluntarily file a petition for adjustment of debts.
   a. The debtor's noncontingent, liquidated, unsecured debts amount to less than $100,000 and secured debts amount to less than $350,000.
   b. The debtor remains in possession.
   c. Automatic stay provisions apply.
   d. The debtor submits a plan that may provide for a reduction in the amount of obligations and/ or for additional time within which to pay debts.
2. A reasonable plan which provides for timely payments and is made in good faith will be confirmed by the court. In most instances, the plan will have to be approved by all secured creditors. Approval by unsecured creditors is not necessary.
3. Most plans call for payments of all or a portion of future income or earnings to be made to a trustee for a three-year period (may be extended for up to five years).
4. A Chapter 13 may be converted into a Chapter 7 liquidation or Chapter 11 reorganization.

XX. TORTS

A. INTRODUCTION.

1. Tort law is concerned with wrongs committed against the person or property of another. In other words, a tort is a private wrong, whereas a crime is a public wrong.
2. Unreasonable, wrongful conduct by one individual resulting in injury to the person or property of another for which the wrongdoer (tortfeasor) should compensate the injured party.
3. Remedies for torts are obtained in civil actions. If a defendant's conduct is also criminally wrong, he or she may be prosecuted by the state for a crime as well.
4. As a result of the defendant's breach of duty not to harm the plaintiff, the plaintiff is injured.
5. Elements of a tort:
   a. A duty was owed by the defendant.
      i. A private obligation other than an obligation arising out of contract.
      ii. Defendant owed duty of not unreasonably causing harm to the person or property of the plaintiff.
      iii. Plaintiff has a reciprocal right not to be wrongfully injured.

   b. Breach of duty - Defendant violated the duty owed to plaintiff because of some act or omission that was intentional, careless, or abnormally dangerous.

   c. Injury to plaintiff - Plaintiff incurred some loss, harm, wrong to or invasion of a protected interest. It is not necessary that plaintiff be financially or physically harmed.

   d. Proximate causation - Plaintiff's injury was caused by defendant's breach of duty.
      i. Factual cause.
         A) Injury would not have occurred without the defendant's wrongful act or omission.
         B) Defendant's conduct was a substantial factor in causing the injury.

      ii. Proximate or legal cause - Defendant's conduct was the immediate, foreseeable, direct cause, (rather than remote cause) of plaintiff's injury.

B. INTENTIONAL TORTS.

1. Defendant consciously desired (intended) to perform an act that resulted in harm to the plaintiff or the plaintiff's property. Additionally, if the defendant's actions were substantially certain to cause harm to the plaintiff or the plaintiff's property, the defendant's actions may be deemed intentional.
2. Wrongs against the person.
   a. Battery.
      i. Intentional infliction of a harmful or offensive touching of the person, or what is usually close enough to be considered to be part of the person, which brings about harmful or offensive contact.
      ii. Defenses.
         A) Privilege or consent.
         B) Reasonable force to defend oneself, other persons, or one's property.

b. Assault.

   i. Threat by defendant to inflict immediate bodily harm to plaintiff that intentionally creates reasonable apprehension of imminent harmful or offensive contact.

   ii. Defenses.

      A) Privilege.

      B) Self-defense of others.

      C) Defense of property.

c. False imprisonment (false arrest).

   i. Unreasonable, intentional confinement of a plaintiff without justification (there must be confinement).

   ii. Present interference with the freedom to move without restraint.

   iii. Merchant protection statutes permit reasonable detention of a suspected shoplifter if there is justified or probable cause to believe that the suspect has taken or interfered with the merchant's property.

   iv. Injury may include harm to one's reputation and mental distress.

   v. Defense - consent.

d. Infliction of mental distress - Extreme and outrageous conduct that intentionally or recklessly results in severe emotional stress to another.

e. Defamation - Harm to reputation and good name.

   i. Publication of statement to or within hearing of others that holds plaintiff up to contempt, ridicule, or hatred.

   ii. Slander - False oral statement.

   iii. Libel - False written statement.

   iv. Defenses - Truth or privilege.

f. Misrepresentation (fraud or deceit).

   i. False representation of fact made by the defendant with knowledge of its falsity or reckless disregard for the truth.

   ii. The defendant intended to induce the plaintiff to change his or her position. Fraud or deceit may result from silence or inaction.

   iii. The plaintiff reasonably relied on the representation.

   iv. As a result of the misrepresentation, the plaintiff was damaged.

   v. In a commercial setting, a seller's puffing is distinguishable from actionable misrepresentation.

3. Wrongs against property.

   a. Trespass to land - Wrongful interference with another person's real property rights even though there is no actual harm to the land. This includes direct or indirect breach of borders.

   b. Trespass to personal property - Defendant unlawfully injures or interferes with plaintiff's right to exclusive possession and enjoyment of personal property.

   c. Conversion - A wrongful taking and keeping of chattel to which one has no right, so serious as to constitute remedy as sale.

C. NEGLIGENCE.

1. Unintentional failure to exercise reasonable care under the circumstances so that a foreseeable risk to another person is created. An injury to the plaintiff results.
2. Elements.
   a. The defendant owed a duty to exercise reasonable care.
   b. The defendant breached that duty.
   c. The plaintiff suffered actual damages.
   d. The plaintiff's injury was caused by the defendant's failure to exercise reasonable care.
      i. Causation in fact. A "but for" analysis or substantial factor in bringing about the harm.
      ii. Proximate cause/legal cause.
3. Defenses.
   a. Contributory and comparative negligence - Plaintiff's own negligence contributed to his or her own injury.
      i. Common law doctrine of contributory negligence - Plaintiff cannot recover from defendant at all.
      ii. Comparative negligence - The amount of damages is apportioned between the plaintiff and defendant, based upon the relative percentage of fault for each of the parties.
      iii. A negligent plaintiff may be able to recover if a negligent defendant had the last clear chance to prevent injury to a helpless plaintiff.
   b. Implied or expressed assumption of the risk - Plaintiff, expressly or impliedly, knowingly and voluntarily placed self in a situation involving risk.

D. STRICT LIABILITY.

Liability without fault and without regard to defendant's intent or exercise of reasonable care.

1. Abnormally dangerous activities.
   a. The activity involves a high degree of risk that cannot be completely guarded against even with the exercise of reasonable or extraordinary care (blasting or crop dusting).
   b. The risk is one that involves potentially serious harm.
   c. The activity is one that is not commonly performed in the geographic area.
2. Employers are strictly liable to their employees for injuries sustained in the ordinary course of their employment under the workers compensation statutes.
3. Employers and principals are strictly liable for torts committed by employees and agents, acting within the ordinary course of their employment.
4. Manufacturers of products are held strictly liable for damages caused by their products in many states.
5. Strict liability is liability without the need to prove negligence. In other words, strict liability has the same elements of negligence except it is immaterial whether the strictly liable defendant knew or should have known of the injury-causing defect.

XXI.PROFESSIONAL LIABILITY - FINANCIAL PLANNERS

A. INTRODUCTION.

As members of a profession, financial planners are expected to comply with standards of ethics and to perform their services in accordance with accepted principles and standards. Those financial planners who fail to carry out these duties may be civilly liable to their clients, for whom they have agreed to provide services and to third persons who may have relied upon statements, prepared by them. In addition, sometimes civil and criminal liability may be imposed upon financial planners because of statutes, such as the federal securities laws.

B. POTENTIAL COMMON LAW LIABILITY TO CLIENTS.

1. Liability based upon breach of contract.
    a. The failure to perform one's contractual duties is a breach of contract for which one is liable to the party to whom the performance was to be rendered.
    b. Thus, if a financial planner has agreed to perform certain services for a client and fails to honestly, properly, and completely carry out those contractual duties, the financial planner will be civilly liable to the client for breach of contract.
    c. In most cases, if there has been a breach of contract by a financial planner, courts will award compensatory damages as a remedy to the client.
        i. The measure of damages will be equal to the foreseeable losses that the client incurs as a result of the breach.
        ii. Damages may include expenses that are incurred by a client in order to secure the services of another financial planner and penalties that are imposed upon the client who failed to meet statutory deadlines.
    d. In an action that is based upon breach of contract, liability is not imposed because of the breach of a duty that existed as a result of tort law. It is, therefore, not a defense where:
        i. The financial planner exercised reasonable care and conformed to accepted principles and standards.
        ii. The client's own negligence contributed to the client's injury.
2. Liability based upon the tort of negligence.
    a. A financial planner has a duty to exercise the same standard of care that a reasonably prudent and skillful financial planner in the community would exercise under the same or similar circumstances.
    b. A violation of generally accepted principles and standards is prima facie evidence (i.e., evidence good and sufficient on its face) of negligence.
    c. Although a financial planner may have complied with principles and standards, he or she may still be considered as not having acted with reasonable care.
    d. A financial planner is not liable for errors of judgment.
    e. A financial planner is liable for his or her negligence.
    f. If a financial planner is found to be liable for negligence, damages may be awarded in order to compensate the client for any reasonable, foreseeable injuries that were incurred.

g. Defenses that may be asserted by a financial planner in an action that is based upon negligence:

i. Lack of negligence.

ii. Lack of proximate cause between the breach of the duty that was owed by the financial planner and the injury that was incurred by the client.

iii. The client's own negligence (or intentional acts), or the fault of a third party, contributed to the client's loss.

3. Financial planner's liability based upon fraud. In an action based upon fraud, the client must establish that:

a. The financial planner made a false representation of a material fact.

b. The representation was made by the financial planner with knowledge that it was false (actual fraud) or with reckless disregard for its truth or falsity (constructive fraud).

c. The financial planner intentionally made the misrepresentation in order to induce the client to act or not act.

d. The client was injured as a result of the client's reasonable reliance on the misrepresentation.

C. POTENTIAL COMMON LAW LIABILITY TO THIRD PERSONS.

Third persons are people who were not clients of the financial planner but had knowledge of documents that were prepared by the financial planner.

1. Contract liability.

a. Traditionally, in common law, a financial planner does not owe contractual duties to third persons unless they are direct parties to or third party beneficiaries of a contract for the services of the financial planner.

b. This is so because there is lack of privity of contract between the financial planner and the other person.

2. Tort liability.

a. Tort liability is based upon negligence in failing to exercise ordinary, reasonable care.

b. Restatement of Torts (Second) position - A financial planner may be liable to a third person who has no privity of contract, but who reasonably and foreseeably relied upon the documents prepared by the financial planner.

D. POTENTIAL STATUTORY LIABILITY.

1. Liability under Section 11 of the Securities Act of 1933.

a. Securities Act of 1933 relates to new issues of investment securities (i.e., going public).

b. Registration statements, including financial statements, must be filed with the Securities and Exchange Commission (SEC) before investment securities can be offered for sale by issuer.

2. Liability under the Securities Exchange Act of 1934.

   a. The Securities Exchange Act of 1934 relates to the purchase and sale of investment securities in the market (i.e., being public).

   b. Section 18 - A financial planner is liable for false and/or misleading statements of material facts that are made in applications, reports, documents, and registration statements, which are prepared by the financial planner and filed with the SEC.

   c. Section 10(b) and SEC Rule 10b-5.

      i. Liability is imposed upon those (including financial planners) who, because of their inside positions, have access to material information (which is not available to the public and which may affect the value of securities) and trade in the securities without making a disclosure.

      ii. Section 10(b) provides that it is unlawful to use any manipulative or deceptive device in connection with the sale or purchase of securities.

      iii. Rule 10b-5 provides that, "in connection with the purchase or sale of any security," it is unlawful:

         A) To "employ any device, scheme, or artifice to defraud."

         B) To "make any untrue statement of a material fact or to omit to state a material fact necessary in order to make the statements made, in the light of the circumstances under which they were made, not misleading."

         C) To "engage in any act, practice, or course of business which operates or would operate as a fraud or deceit upon any person."

      iv. A financial planner may be liable to a person who purchased or sold securities when it can be established that:

         A) The statement or omission was material.

         B) The financial planner intended to deceive or defraud others.

         C) As a result of his or her reasonable reliance upon the misrepresentation, the purchaser or seller incurred a loss.

3. Criminal liability for willful conduct is imposed by the Securities Act of 1933, the Securities Exchange Act of 1934, the Internal Revenue Act, and other federal statutes as well as state criminal codes.

XXII.REGULATORY REQUIREMENTS

A. INTRODUCTION.

The issuance and sale of corporate securities are extensively regulated by the Securities and Exchange Commission (SEC), a federal agency that administers the Securities Act of 1933, the Securities Exchange Act of 1934, and other federal statutes. A major objective of securities regulation is to protect the investing public by requiring full and correct disclosure of relevant information. Both the federal and state governments require a substantial amount of regulation; however, most is from the federal government because the majority of trading is across state borders.

B. FEDERAL SECURITIES REGULATION.

This legislation is based on the power of Congress to regulate interstate commerce.

1. Federal regulatory statutes are administered by the SEC.
2. Securities Act of 1933.
   a. This securities act is primarily concerned with new issues of securities or issues in the primary market.
   b. The term investment security is broadly defined:
      i. "Any note, stock, treasury stock, bond, debenture, evidence of indebtedness, certificate of interest or participation in any profit-sharing agreement ... investment contract ... or, in general, any interest or instrument commonly known as a 'security' or any certificate of interest or participation in ... receipt for ... or right to subscribe to or purchase, any of the foregoing."
      ii. Includes those transactions in which:
         A) A person invests money or property in a common enterprise or venture.
         B) An investor reasonably expects to make a profit primarily or substantially as a result of the managerial efforts of others.
   c. The 1933 Act requires full disclosure of material information that is relevant to investment decisions, and prohibits fraud and misstatements when securities are offered to the public through the mail and/or interstate commerce.
   d. A registration statement contains a thorough description of the securities, the financial structure, condition and management personnel of the issuing corporation, and a description of material pending litigation against the issuing corporation. This statement is filed with the SEC.
   e. The 1933 Act also requires that a prospectus, based upon the information in the registration statement, be given to any prospective investor or purchaser.
   f. After registration, there is a 20-day waiting period.
      i. During the waiting period, an issuer can obtain underwriters and distributes a red herring prospectus.
      ii. The issuer may solicit revocable offers from prospective purchasers after filing the registration statement, but may not sell securities until the effective date of the statement.
   g. After the waiting period, the registered securities can be bought and sold, and tombstone advertisements placed in newspapers and other publications.

h. Securities that are exempt from registration requirements include:

   i. Intrastate offerings where all offerees and issuers are residents of the state in which issuer performs substantially all of its operations.

   ii. The issuer is a governmental body or nonprofit organization.

   iii. The issuer is a bank, savings institution, common carrier, or farmers' cooperative and is subject to other regulatory legislation.

   iv. Commercial paper having a maturity date of less than 9 months (270 days).

   v. Stock dividends, stock splits, and securities issued in connection with corporate reorganizations.

   vi. Insurance, endowment, and annuity contracts.

i. Regulation A requires less demanding disclosures and registration for small issues of less than $1,500,000.

j. Transactions that are exempt from registration requirement (Regulation D):

   i. Private, noninvestment company sales of less than $500,000 worth of securities in a twelve-month period to investors who will not resell the securities within two years.

   ii. Private, noninvestment company sales of less than $5,000,000 worth of securities in a twelve-month period to:

      A) Accredited investors.

         1) Anyone whose individual net worth, or joint net worth with spouse, is greater than $1,000,000 at the time of investment; or

         2) Anyone whose individual income was greater than $200,000, or joint income with spouse was greater than $300,000, in each of the two most recent years; AND can expect to reach that same level of income in the current year; or

         3) Any trust with total assets in excess of $5,000,000, not formed for the specific purpose of acquiring the securities offered, whose purchase of the securities is directed by a person who has such knowledge and experience in financial and business matters that he is capable of evaluating the merits and risks of the prospective investment; or

         4) Any organization that was not formed for the purpose of acquiring the securities being sold, with total assets in excess of $5,000,000; or

         5) Any entity in which all of the equity owners are Accredited Investors.

      B) Investors who are furnished with purchaser representatives who are knowledgeable and experienced regarding finance and business, or

      C) Up to 35 unaccredited investors that have financial and business knowledge and experience, who are furnished with the same information as would be contained in a full registration statement prospectus.

   iii. Sales of any amount of securities to accredited investors or those furnished with independent purchaser representatives (private placement).

k. Civil liability for failure to register and for misstatements and omissions in a registration statement.

    i. Imposed upon the issuing corporation, its directors and anyone who signed or provided information that was incorporated in the registration statement, and underwriters.

    ii. Liable to persons acquiring shares.

3. Securities Exchange Act of 1934.

    a. While the Securities Act of 1933 was limited to new issues, the 1934 Securities Act extended the regulation to securities sold in the secondary markets. The Act provided the following provisions:

        i. Establishment of the SEC - The SEC's primary function is to regulate the securities markets.

        ii. Disclosure requirements for Secondary Market - Annual reports and other financial reports are required to be filed with the SEC prior to listing on the organized exchanges. These reports include the annual 10K Report, which must be audited, and the quarterly 10Q Report, which is not required to be audited.

        iii. Registration of organized exchanges - All organized exchanges must register with the SEC and provide copies of their rules and bylaws.

        iv. Credit regulation - Congress gave the Federal Reserve Board the power to set margin requirements for credit purchases of securities. Securities dealers' indebtedness was also limited to 20 times their owners' equity capital by this Act.

        v. Proxy solicitation - Specific rules governing solicitation of proxies were established.

        vi. Exemptions - Securities of federal, state, and local governments; securities that are not traded across state lines; and any other securities specified by the SEC are exempt from registering with the SEC. This includes Treasury bonds and municipal bonds.

        vii. Insider activities - A public report, called an insider report, must be filed with the SEC every month in which a change in the holding of a firm's securities occurs for an officer, director, or 10% or more shareholder. The 1934 Act forbids insiders profiting from securities held less than 6 months and requires these profits be returned to the organization. In addition, short sales are not permitted by individuals considered to be insiders.

        viii. Price manipulation - The Securities Exchange Act of 1934 forbids price manipulation schemes such as wash sales, pools, circulation of manipulative information, and false and misleading statements about securities.

b. Liability under the Securities Exchange Act of 1934.

   i. Insider trading (Sec. 10(b) and SEC Rule 10b-5).

      A) Liability is imposed upon directors and others (tippees) who, because of their positions, have access to information not available to the public that may affect the future market value of the corporation's securities.

      B) Liability is imposed when misleading or deceptive omissions or misrepresentations of material facts are given in connection with the purchase or sale of securities.

      C) SEC, purchaser, or seller of securities who has been damaged may bring action.

      D) An outsider who comes into possession of nonpublic market information does not have a duty to make a Rule 10b-5 disclosure.

   ii. Rule 10b-5 applies when the facilities of a stock exchange, the U.S. mail, or an instrumentality of interstate commerce are used.

   iii. Insider reporting and trading - Officers, directors, and large shareholders are required to file reports with the SEC and may be liable to the corporation for gains made in trading in securities.

   iv. The Insider Trading Sanctions Act of 1984 authorizes the SEC to bring a civil suit against a person who, while in possession of material nonpublic information, violates or aids in the violation of the 1934 Act or SEC rules.

   v. Proxy statements (Sec. 14(a)) - Full disclosure is required of those soliciting proxies from shareholders.

   vi. A financial planner may be held liable to a person who purchased or sold securities when it can be established that:

      A) The statement or omission was material.

      B) The financial planner intended to deceive others.

      C) As a result of his or her reasonable reliance upon the misrepresentation, the purchaser or seller incurred a loss.

4. Investment Company Act of 1940 requires registration with the SEC and restricts activities of investment companies (including mutual funds).

5. State regulation of securities (Blue Sky Laws) - State securities laws also regulate the offering and sale of securities in intrastate commerce.

   a. Anti-fraud provisions similar to federal laws.

   b. Regulation of brokers and dealers in securities.

   c. Registration and disclosure are required before securities can be offered for sale.

   d. Some state statutes impose standards of fairness.

   e. Some state statutes are more restrictive than the federal statute and SEC rules.

C. NASD.

> **Note:** The following excerpts from "An Explanation of the NASD Regulations and Qualification Requirements – February 1998" have been reprinted with the permission of the NASD.

1. The National Association of Securities Dealers, Inc. (NASD) is a self-regulatory organization of the securities industry that was established under the 1938 Maloney Act Amendments and is subject to oversight by the Securities and Exchange Commission. The NASD is responsible for the regulation of the NASDAQ Stock Market as well as the over-the-counter securities market. Through its subsidiaries, NASD Regulation Inc. and the NASDAQ Stock Market, Inc., the NASD develops rules and regulations, conducts regulatory reviews of members' business activities, and designs and operates marketplace services and facilities. The NASD helps establish and coordinate the policies for its two subsidiaries and oversees their effectiveness.

2. NASD Regulation, Inc. (NASDR) was established in 1996 as a separate, independent subsidiary of the National Association of Securities Dealers, Inc. to separate the regulation of the broker/dealer professional from the operation of the NASDAQ Stock Market. The purpose of NASDR is to regulate the securities markets for the benefit and protection of investors.

3. Membership in the NASD entitles a firm to participate in the investment banking and over-the-counter securities business, to distribute new issues underwritten by NASD members and to distribute shares of investment companies sponsored by NASD members.

4. Every securities professional associated with a member firm who will engage in securities transactions must register with the NASD as a registered representative or principal. Each applicant must be thoroughly investigated to determine that he has not violated any federal or state law or any NASD or exchange rule that would prohibit him from entering the securities business. He must then pass a qualification examination to demonstrate that he is knowledgeable and has a thorough understanding of securities products; SEC, NASD and exchange rules and regulations; the operation and interrelation of financial markets; economic theory; kinds of risk; balance sheet analysis; portfolio analysis; types of customer accounts; and tax treatment of various investments.

5. Generally, you must score at least 70% to pass an NASD examination. Proctor automatically truncates the scores to whole numbers.

EXHIBIT 17: QUALIFICATIONS/REGISTRATION REQUIREMENT CHART FOR REGISTERED REPRESENTATIVES		
Securities Transaction/Activity	**Qualification**	**Registration Requirement**
Mutual funds (closed-end funds on the initial offering only); variable annuities; variable life insurance; unit investment trusts (initial offering only)	Investment Company Products/Variable Contracts Limited Representative	Series 6
Corporate securities (stocks and bonds); rights; warrants; mutual funds; money market funds; unit investment trusts; REITs; asset-backed securities; mortgage-backed securities; options; options on mortgage-backed securities; municipal securities; government securities; repos, and certificates of accrual on government securities; direct participation programs; securities traders; mergers and acquisitions; venture capital; corporate financing	General Securities Representative	Series 7
Direct participation programs (real estate; oil and gas; equipment leasing; and other limited partnerships)	Direct Participation Programs Limited Representative	Series 22
Municipal securities	Municipal Securities Representative	Series 52
Equity Traders	Equity Traders Limited Representative	Series 55
Corporate securities (stocks and bonds); rights; warrants; closed–ends funds; unit investment trusts; money market funds; REITs; repos and certificates of accrual on corporate securities; securities traders; mergers and acquisitions; venture capital; corporate financing	Corporate Securities Limited Representative	Series 62
Accept unsolicited securities orders (all securities except municipal securities and direct participation programs) only from the firm's clients	Assistant Representative - Order Processing	Series 11
Government securities; government agency securities; mortgage-backed securities	Government Securities Representative	Series 72
Both the Series 65 and Series 66 exams were developed by the North American Securities Administrators Association (NASAA) and administered by NASD Regulation. Unlike NASD exams, such as the Series 6 and 7, you do not need to be sponsored by a broker-dealer.	Investment Advisor Representative	Series 65/66

XXIII.INVESTMENT ADVISERS' REGULATION AND REGISTRATION

A. INTRODUCTION.

The Securities and Exchange Commission (SEC) regulates investment advisers and their activities under the Investment Advisers Act of 1940. Unless exempt under specific provisions of the Act, a person covered by the Act must register with the SEC as an investment adviser.

B. REGULATION.

1. Definition - An investment adviser is a person who:
   a. Provides advice or issues reports or analyses regarding securities.
   b. Is in the business of providing such services.
   c. Provides such services for compensation.
      i. Compensation is the receipt of any economic benefit that includes commissions on the sale of products.
      ii. Certain organizations and individuals are excluded, including:
         A) Banks and bank holding companies (except as amended by the Gramm-Leach-Bliley Act of 1999).
         B) Lawyers, accountants, engineers, or teachers, if their performance of advisory services is solely incidental to their professions.
         C) Brokers or dealers, if their performance of advisory services is solely incidental to the conduct of their business as brokers or dealers, and they do not receive any special compensation for their advisory services.
         D) Publishers of bona fide newspapers, newsmagazines, or business or financial publications of general and regular circulation.
         E) Those persons whose advice is related only to securities that are direct obligations of or guaranteed by the United States.
         F) Incidental practice exception is not available to individuals who hold themselves out to the public as providing financial planning, pension consulting, or other financial advisory services.
2. Exceptions - The Act provides limited exemptions. Investment advisers who, during the course of the preceding 12 months, had fewer than 15 clients and do not hold themselves out generally to the public as investment advisers. Also those whose only clients are insurance companies.
3. Disclosure - The Act generally requires investment advisers entering into an advisory contract with a client to deliver a written disclosure statement on their background and business practices. Form ADV Part II must be given to a client under Rule 204-3, known as the "brochure" rule.
   a. In accordance with the Investment Adviser Brochure Rule, an investment adviser shall furnish each advisory client and prospective client with a written disclosure statement which may be a copy of Part II of Form ADV, or written documents containing at least the information then so required by Part II of Form ADV, or such other information as the administrator may require.

   b. Disclosure should be delivered not less than 48 hours prior to entering into any investment advisory contract with such client or prospective client, or at the time of entering into any contract, if the advisory client has a right to terminate the contract without penalty within five business days after entering into the contract.

   c. If an investment adviser renders substantially different types of investment advisory services to different advisory clients, any information required by Part II of Form ADV may be omitted from the statement furnished to an advisory client or prospective advisory client if such information is applicable only to a type of investment advisory service or fee which is not rendered or charged, or proposed to be rendered or charged, to that client or prospective client.

4. Inspections - The 1940 Advisor's Act and the SEC's rules require that advisers maintain and preserve specified books and records and are made available for inspection.

5. Restriction on the use of the term, Investment Counsel - A registered investment adviser may not use the term investment counsel unless its principal business is acting as an investment adviser and a substantial portion of its business is providing "investment supervisory services."

6. Anti-Fraud Provisions - Section 206 of the Act, Section 17 of the Securities Act of 1933, Section 10(b) of the Securities Exchange Act of 1934, and Rule 10b-5 prohibit misstatements or misleading omissions of material facts, fraudulent acts, and practices in connection with the purchase or sale of securities or the conduct of an investment advisory business. An investment adviser owes his or her clients undivided loyalty and may not engage in activity that conflicts with a client's interest.

7. Registration - Form ADV is kept current by filing periodic amendments. Form ADV-W is used to withdraw as an investment adviser.

8. Filing Requirements.

   a. Forms - ADV and ADV-W can be obtained from the SEC's Office of Consumer Affairs and Information Services in Washington, DC, or from the Commission office in your area (www.sec.gov/offices/invmgmt/advinst.htm).

   b. Copies - All advisers' filings must be submitted in triplicate and typewritten. Copies can be filed, but each must be signed manually.

   c. Fees - Must include a registration fee of $150, by check or money order payable to the Securities and Exchange Commission, with your initial application of Form ADV. No part of this fee can be refunded.

   d. Name and Signatures - Full names are required. Each copy of an execution page must contain an original manual signature.

9. Prohibition on commission registration.

   a. In the Fall of 1996, Congress amended the Advisers Act to reallocate regulatory responsibility for investment advisers between the SEC and state authorities. Congress did this by prohibiting certain advisers from registering with the SEC. As a result, for the most part, larger advisers will be regulated by the SEC, and smaller advisers will be regulated by state securities authorities.

b. Only certain types of advisers are permitted to register with the SEC (and, therefore, must register with the SEC, unless exempt under a specific rule). Following is a list of advisers who are permitted to register with the SEC:

   i. Advisers having "assets under management" of $25 million or more. The $25 million threshold has been increased to $30 million. However, advisers with assets under management between $25 million and $30 million may still register with the SEC.

   ii. Advisers to registered investment companies.

   iii. Advisers who have their principal office and place of business in a state that has not enacted an investment adviser statute or that have their principal office and place of business outside the United States.

10. Advisers are required to report their eligibility for SEC registration on Schedule I to Form ADV upon initial registration. Schedule I must be filed every year to establish and report their continuing eligibility for SEC registrations.

C. REFORM OF PREVIOUS ACTS.

1. The Glass-Steagall Act (1933) prohibited commercial banks from acting as investment bankers, established the Federal Deposit Insurance Corporation (FDIC), and prohibited commercial banks from paying interest on demand deposits. This was one of the first of many securities regulation laws that has impacted the investment markets. However, the Gramm-Leach-Bliley Act, passed by Congress in November 1999, eliminates many of the restrictions against affiliations among banks, securities firms, and insurance companies:

   a. The Act repeals the affiliation sections of the Glass-Steagall Act that prohibit a bank holding company and a securities firm that underwrites and deals in ineligible securities from owning and controlling each other.

   b. It also amends the Bank Holding Company Act (1956) to permit cross-ownership and control among bank holding companies, securities firms and insurance companies, provided that such cross-ownership and control is effected through a financial holding company that engages in activities that conform to the Act.

   c. A bank must register as an investment advisor if it provides investment advice to a registered investment company, provided that, if the bank provides such advice through a "separately identified department or division," that department or division shall be deemed to be the investment advisor.

D. INVESTMENT ADVISER REGISTRATION DEPOSITORY.

1. The Investment Adviser Registration Depository (IARD) is an electronic filing system for Investment Advisers sponsored by the Securities and Exchange Commission (SEC) and North American Securities Administrators Association (NASAA), with NASD Regulation, Inc. serving as the developer and operator of the system.

2. The IARD system collects and maintains the registration and disclosure information for Investment Advisers and their associated persons. The new IARD system supports electronic filing of the revised Forms ADV and ADV-W, centralized fee and form processing, regulatory review, the annual registration renewal process, and public disclosure of Investment Adviser information.

3. IARD provides regulators with the ability to monitor and process Investment Adviser information via a single, centralized system (www.iard.com).

EXHIBIT 18: ADV FORM (PART II – PAGE 1)

OMB APPROVAL	
OMB Number:	3235-0049
Expires:	February 28, 2001
Estimated average burden hours per response.	9.01

FORM ADV
Part II - Page 1

Uniform Application for Investment Adviser Registration

Name of Investment Adviser:					
Address:	(Number and Street)	(City)	(State)	(Zip Code)	Area Code: ( ) Telephone Number:

This part of Form ADV gives information about the investment adviser and its business for the use of clients.
The information has not been approved or verified by any governmental authority.

Table of Contents

(Schedules A, B, C, D, and E are included with Part I of this Form, for the use of regulatory bodies, and are not distributed to clients.)

Potential persons who are to respond to the collection of information contained in this form are not required to respond unless the form displays a currently valid OMB control number.

XXIV.CODE OF ETHICS AND PROFESSIONAL RESPONSIBILITY

Note: Content taken directly from the CFP Board's Standards of Professional Conduct Code of Ethics - as of 2001.

Part I—PRINCIPLES.

Preamble and Applicability.

The Code of Ethics and Professional Responsibility (Code of Ethics) has been adopted by the Certified Financial Planner Board of Standards, Inc. (CFP Board) to provide principles and rules to all persons whom it has recognized and certified to use the CFP®, CERTIFIED FINANCIAL PLANNER™ and certification marks (collectively "the marks"). The CFP Board determines who is certified and thus authorized to use the marks. Implicit in the acceptance of this authorization is an obligation not only to comply with the mandates and requirements of all applicable laws and regulations but also to take responsibility to act in an ethical and professionally responsible manner in all professional services and activities. For purposes of this Code of Ethics, a person recognized and certified by the CFP Board to use the marks is called a CFP Board designee. This Code of Ethics applies to CFP Board designees actively involved in the practice of personal financial planning, in other areas of financial services, in industry, in related professions, in government, in education or in any other professional activity in which the marks are used in the performance of professional responsibilities. This Code of Ethics also applies to candidates for the CFP certification who are registered as such with the CFP Board. For purposes of this Code of Ethics, the term CFP Board designee shall be deemed to include current certificants, candidates and individuals who have been certified in the past and retain the right to reinstate their CFP certification without passing the current CFP® Certification Examination.

Composition and Scope.

The Code of Ethics consists of two parts: Part I — Principles and Part II — Rules. The Principles are statements expressing in general terms the ethical and professional ideals that CFP Board designees are expected to display in their professional activities. As such, the Principles are aspirational in character but are intended to provide a source of guidance for CFP Board designees. The comments following each Principle further explain the meaning of the Principle. The Rules in Part II provide practical guidelines derived from the tenets embodied in the Principles. As such, the Rules describe the standards of ethical and professionally responsible conduct expected of CFP Board designees in particular situations. This Code of Ethics does not undertake to define standards of professional conduct of CFP Board designees for purposes of civil liability.

Due to the nature of a CFP Board designee's particular field of endeavor, certain Rules may not be applicable to that CFP Board designee's activities. For example, a CFP Board designee who is engaged solely in the sale of securities as a registered representative is not subject to the written disclosure requirements of Rule 402 (applicable to CFP Board designees engaged in personal financial planning) although he or she may have disclosure responsibilities under Rule 401. A CFP Board designee is obligated to determine what responsibilities he or she has in each professional relationship including, for example, duties that arise in particular circumstances from a position of trust or confidence that a CFP Board designee may have. The CFP Board designee is obligated to meet those responsibilities. The Code of Ethics is structured so that the presentation of the Rules parallels the presentation of the Principles. For example, the Rules which relate to Principle 1 - Integrity are numbered in the 100 to 199 series, while those Rules relating to Principle 2 - Objectivity are numbered in the 200 to 299 series.

Compliance.

The CFP Board requires adherence to this Code of Ethics by all CFP Board designees. Compliance with the Code of Ethics, individually and by the profession as a whole, depends on each CFP Board designee's knowledge of and voluntary compliance with the Principles and applicable Rules, on the influence of fellow professionals and public opinion, and on disciplinary proceedings, when necessary, involving CFP Board designees who fail to comply with the applicable provisions of the Code of Ethics.

Terminology In This Code of Ethics.

"**Client**" denotes a person, persons, or entity who engages a practitioner and for whom professional services are rendered. For purposes of this definition, a practitioner is engaged when an individual, based upon the relevant facts and circumstances, reasonably relies upon information or service provided by that practitioner. Where the services of the practitioner are provided to an entity (corporation, trust, partnership, estate, etc.), the client is the entity acting through its legally authorized representative.

"**CFP Board designee**" denotes current certificants, candidates for certification, and individuals that have any entitlement, direct or indirect, to the CFP certification marks.

"**Commission**" denotes the compensation received by an agent or broker when the same is calculated as a percentage on the amount of his or her sales or purchase transactions.

"**Conflict(s) of interest(s)**" denotes circumstances, relationships or other facts about the CFP Board designee's own financial, business, property and/or personal interests which will or reasonably may impair the CFP Board designee's rendering of disinterested advice, recommendations or services.

"**Fee-only**" denotes a method of compensation in which compensation is received solely from a client with neither the personal financial planning practitioner nor any related party receiving compensation which is contingent upon the purchase or sale of any financial product. A "related party" for this purpose shall mean an individual or entity from whom any direct or indirect economic benefit is derived by the personal financial planning practitioner as a result of implementing a recommendation made by the personal financial planning practitioner.

"**Personal financial planning**" or "**financial planning**" denotes the process of determining whether and how an individual can meet life goals through the proper management of financial resources.

"**Personal financial planning process**" or "**financial planning process**" denotes the process which typically includes, but is not limited to, these six elements: establishing and defining the client-planner relationship, gathering client data including goals, analyzing and evaluating the client's financial status, developing and presenting financial planning recommendations and/or alternatives, implementing the financial planning recommendations and monitoring the financial planning recommendations.

"**Personal financial planning subject areas**" or "**financial planning subject areas**" denotes the basic subject fields covered in the financial planning process which typically include, but are not limited to, financial statement preparation and analysis (including cash flow analysis/planning and budgeting), investment planning (including portfolio design, i.e., asset allocation, and portfolio management), income tax planning, education planning, risk management, retirement planning, and estate planning.

"Personal financial planning professional" or **"financial planning professional"** denotes a person who is capable and qualified to offer objective, integrated, and comprehensive financial advice to or for the benefit of individuals to help them achieve their financial objectives. A financial planning professional must have the ability to provide financial planning services to clients, using the financial planning process covering the basic financial planning subjects.

"Personal financial planning practitioner" or **"financial planning practitioner"** denotes a person who is capable and qualified to offer objective, integrated, and comprehensive financial advice to or for the benefit of clients to help them achieve their financial objectives and who engages in financial planning using the financial planning process in working with clients.

Part 1: Principles.

Introduction.

These Principles of the Code of Ethics express the professions recognition of its responsibilities to the public, to clients, to colleagues, and to employers. They apply to all CFP Board designees and provide guidance to them in the performance of their professional services.

Principle 1 – Integrity.

A CFP Board designee shall offer and provide professional services with integrity.

As discussed in Composition and Scope, CFP Board designees may be placed by clients in positions of trust and confidence. The ultimate source of such public trust is the CFP Board designee's personal integrity. In deciding what is right and just, a CFP Board designee should rely on his or her integrity as the appropriate touchstone. Integrity demands honesty and candor which must not be subordinated to personal gain and advantage. Within the characteristic of integrity, allowance can be made for innocent error and legitimate difference of opinion; but integrity cannot co-exist with deceit or subordination of one's principles. Integrity requires a CFP Board designee to observe not only the letter but also the spirit of this Code of Ethics.

Principle 2 – Objectivity.

A CFP Board designee shall be objective in providing professional services to clients.

Objectivity requires intellectual honesty and impartiality. It is an essential quality for any professional. Regardless of the particular service rendered or the capacity in which a CFP Board designee functions, a CFP Board designee should protect the integrity of his or her work, maintain objectivity, and avoid subordination of his or her judgment that would be in violation of this Code of Ethics.

Principle 3 – Competence.

A CFP Board designee shall provide services to clients competently and maintain the necessary knowledge and skill to continue to do so in those areas in which the designee is engaged.

One is competent only when he or she has attained and maintained an adequate level of knowledge and skill, and applies that knowledge effectively in providing services to clients. Competence also includes the wisdom to recognize the limitations of that knowledge and when consultation or client referral is appropriate. A CFP Board designee, by virtue of having earned the CFP certification, is deemed to be qualified to practice financial planning. However, in addition to assimilating the common body of knowledge required and acquiring the necessary experience for certification, a CFP Board designee shall make a continuing commitment to learning and professional improvement.

Principle 4 – Fairness.

A CFP Board designee shall perform professional services in a manner that is fair and reasonable to clients, principals, partners, and employers and shall disclose conflict(s) of interest(s) in providing such services.

Fairness requires impartiality, intellectual honesty, and disclosure of conflict(s) of interest(s). It involves a subordination of one's own feelings, prejudices, and desires so as to achieve a proper balance of conflicting interests. Fairness is treating others in the same fashion that you would want to be treated and is an essential trait of any professional.

Principle 5 – Confidentiality.

A CFP Board designee shall not disclose any confidential client information without the specific consent of the client unless in response to proper legal process, to defend against charges of wrongdoing by the CFP Board designee or in connection with a civil dispute between the CFP Board designee and client.

A client, by seeking the services of a CFP Board designee, may be interested in creating a relationship of personal trust and confidence with the CFP Board designee. This type of relationship can only be built upon the understanding that information supplied to the CFP Board designee or other information will be confidential. In order to provide the contemplated services effectively and to protect the client's privacy, the CFP Board designee shall safeguard the confidentiality of such information.

Principle 6 – Professionalism.

A CFP Board designee's conduct in all matters shall reflect credit upon the profession.

Because of the importance of the professional services rendered by CFP Board designees, there are attendant responsibilities to behave with dignity and courtesy to all those who use those services, fellow professionals, and those in related professions. A CFP Board designee also has an obligation to cooperate with fellow CFP Board designees to enhance and maintain the profession's public image and to work jointly with other CFP Board designees to improve the quality of services. It is only through the combined efforts of all CFP Board designees in cooperation with other professionals, that this vision can be realized.

Principle 7 – Diligence.

A CFP Board designee shall act diligently in providing professional services.

Diligence is the provision of services in a reasonably prompt and thorough manner. Diligence also includes proper planning for and supervision of the rendering of professional services.

Part II – Rules.

Introduction.

As stated in **Part I -- Principles,** the Principles apply to all CFP Board designees. However, due to the nature of a CFP Board designee's particular field of endeavor, certain Rules may not be applicable to that CFP Board designee's activities. The universe of activities by CFP Board designees is indeed diverse and a particular CFP Board designee may be performing all, some or none of the typical services provided by financial planning professionals. As a result, in considering the Rules in Part II, a CFP Board designee must first recognize what specific services he or she is rendering and then determine whether or not a specific Rule is applicable to those services. To assist the CFP Board designee in making these determinations, this Code of Ethics includes a series of definitions of terminology used throughout the Code of Ethics. Based upon these definitions, a CFP Board designee should be able to determine which services he or she provides and, therefore, which Rules are applicable to those services.

Rules that Relate to the Principle of Integrity.

Rule 101.

A CFP Board designee shall not solicit clients through false or misleading communications or advertisements:

a. Misleading Advertising: A CFP Board designee shall not make a false or misleading communication about the size, scope or areas of competence of the CFP Board designee's practice or of any organization with which the CFP Board designee is associated; and

b. Promotional Activities: In promotional activities, a CFP Board designee shall not make materially false or misleading communications to the public or create unjustified expectations regarding matters relating to financial planning or the professional activities and competence of the CFP Board designee. The term "promotional activities" includes, but is not limited to, speeches, interviews, books and/or printed publications, seminars, radio and television shows, and video cassettes; and

c. Representation of Authority: A CFP Board designee shall not give the impression that a CFP Board designee is representing the views of the CFP Board or any other group unless the CFP Board designee has been authorized to do so. Personal opinions shall be clearly identified as such.

Rule 102.

In the course of professional activities, a CFP Board designee shall not engage in conduct involving dishonesty, fraud, deceit or misrepresentation, or knowingly make a false or misleading statement to a client, employer, employee, professional colleague, governmental or other regulatory body or official, or any other person or entity.

Rule 103.

A CFP Board designee has the following responsibilities regarding funds and/or other property of clients:

a. In exercising custody of or discretionary authority over client funds or other property, a CFP Board designee shall act only in accordance with the authority set forth in the governing legal instrument (e.g., special power of attorney, trust, letters testamentary, etc.); and

b. A CFP Board designee shall identify and keep complete records of all funds or other property of a client in the custody of or under the discretionary authority of the CFP Board designee; and

c. Upon receiving funds or other property of a client, a CFP Board designee shall promptly or as otherwise permitted by law or provided by agreement with the client, deliver to the client or third party any funds or other property which the client or third party is entitled to receive and, upon request by the client, render a full accounting regarding such funds or other property; and

d. A CFP Board designee shall not commingle client funds or other property with a CFP Board designee's personal funds and/or other property or the funds and/or other property of a CFP Board designee's firm. Commingling one or more clients' funds or other property together is permitted, subject to compliance with applicable legal requirements and provided accurate records are maintained for each client's funds or other property; and

e. A CFP Board designee who takes custody of all or any part of a client's assets for investment purposes shall do so with the care required of a fiduciary.

Rules that Relate to the Principle of Objectivity.

Rule 201.

A CFP Board designee shall exercise reasonable and prudent professional judgment in providing professional services.

Rule 202.

A financial planning practitioner shall act in the interest of the client.

Rules that Relate to the Principle of Competence.

Rule 301.

A CFP Board designee shall keep informed of developments in the field of financial planning and participate in continuing education throughout the CFP Board designee's professional career in order to improve professional competence in all areas in which the CFP Board designee is engaged. As a distinct part of this requirement, a CFP Board designee shall satisfy all minimum continuing education requirements established for CFP Board designees by the CFP Board. (**Note from the authors:** To gain more information on the continuing education requirements, visit the CFP Board web site at www.CFP-Board.org and select CFP Certificants, then Continuing Education Requirements.)

Rule 302.

A CFP Board designee shall offer advice only in those areas in which the CFP Board designee has competence. In areas where the CFP Board designee is not professionally competent, the CFP Board designee shall seek the counsel of qualified individuals and/or refer clients to such parties.

Rules that Relate to the Principle of Fairness.

Rule 401.

In rendering professional services, a CFP Board designee shall disclose to the client:

a. Material information relevant to the professional relationship, including but not limited to conflict(s) of interest(s), changes in the CFP Board designee's business affiliation, address, telephone number, credentials, qualifications, licenses, compensation structure and any agency relationships, and the scope of the CFP Board designee's authority in that capacity.

b. The information required by all laws applicable to the relationship in a manner complying with such laws.

Rule 402.

A financial planning practitioner shall make timely written disclosure of all material information relative to the professional relationship. In all circumstances such disclosure shall include conflict(s) of interest(s) and sources of compensation. Written disclosures that include the following information are considered to be in compliance with this Rule:

a. A statement of the basic philosophy of the CFP Board designee (or firm) in working with clients. The disclosure shall include the philosophy, theory and/or principles of financial planning which will be utilized by the CFP Board designee; and

b. Resumes of principals and employees of a firm who are expected to provide financial planning services to the client and a description of those services. Such disclosures shall include educational background, professional/employment history, professional designations and licenses held, and areas of competence and specialization; and

c. A statement of compensation, which in reasonable detail discloses the source(s) and any contingencies or other aspects material to the fee and/or commission arrangement. Any estimates made shall be clearly identified as such and shall be based on reasonable assumptions. Referral fees, if any, shall be fully disclosed; and

d. A statement indicating whether the CFP Board designee's compensation arrangements involve fee-only, commission-only, or fee and commission. A CFP Board designee shall not hold out as a fee-only financial planning practitioner if the CFP Board designee receives commissions or other forms of economic benefit from related parties; and

e. A statement describing material agency or employment relationships a CFP Board designee (or firm) has with third parties and the fees or commissions resulting from such relationships; and

f. A statement identifying conflict(s) of interest(s).

Rule 403.

A CFP Board designee providing financial planning shall disclose in writing, prior to establishing a client relationship, relationships which reasonably may compromise the CFP Board designee's objectivity or independence.

Rule 404.

Should conflict(s) of interest(s) develop after a professional relationship has been commenced, but before the services contemplated by that relationship have been completed, a CFP Board designee shall promptly disclose the conflict(s) of interest(s) to the client or other necessary persons.

Rule 405.

In addition to the disclosure by financial planning practitioners regarding sources of compensation required under Rule 402, such disclosure shall be made annually thereafter for ongoing clients. The annual disclosure requirement may be satisfied by offering to provide clients with the current copy of SEC form ADV, Part II or the disclosure called for by Rule 402.

Rule 406.

A CFP Board designee's compensation shall be fair and reasonable.

Rule 407.

Prior to establishing a client relationship, and consistent with the confidentiality requirements of Rule 501, a CFP Board designee may provide references which may include recommendations from present and/or former clients.

Rule 408.

When acting as an agent for a principal, a CFP Board designee shall assure that the scope of his or her authority is clearly defined and properly documented.

Rule 409.

Whether a CFP Board designee is employed by a financial planning firm, an investment institution, or serves as an agent for such an organization, or is self-employed, all CFP Board designees shall adhere to the same standards of disclosure and service.

Rule 410.

A CFP Board designee who is an employee shall perform professional services with dedication to the lawful objectives of the employer and in accordance with this Code of Ethics.

Rule 411.

A CFP Board designee shall:

a. Advise the CFP Board designee's employer of outside affiliations which reasonably may compromise service to an employer; and
b. Provide timely notice to the employer and clients, unless precluded by contractual obligation, in the event of change of employment or CFP Board licensing status.

Rule 412.

A CFP Board designee doing business as a partner or principal of a financial services firm owes to the CFP Board designee's partners or co-owners a responsibility to act in good faith. This includes, but is not limited to, disclosure of relevant and material financial information while in business together.

Rule 413.

A CFP Board designee shall join a financial planning firm as a partner or principal only on the basis of mutual disclosure of relevant and material information regarding credentials, competence, experience, licensing and/or legal status, and financial stability of the parties involved.

Rule 414.

A CFP Board designee who is a partner or co-owner of a financial services firm who elects to withdraw from the firm shall do so in compliance with any applicable agreement, and shall deal with his or her business interest in a fair and equitable manner.

Rule 415.

A CFP Board designee shall inform his or her employer, partners or co-owners of compensation or other benefit arrangements in connection with his or her services to clients which are in addition to compensation from the employer, partners or co-owners for such services.

Rule 416.

If a CFP Board designee enters into a business transaction with a client, the transaction shall be on terms which are fair and reasonable to the client and the CFP Board designee shall disclose the risks of the transaction, conflict(s) of interest(s) of the CFP Board designee, and other relevant information, if any, necessary to make the transaction fair to the client.

Rules that Relate to the Principle of Confidentiality.

Rule 501.

A CFP Board designee shall not reveal - or use for his or her own benefit - without the client's consent, any personally identifiable information relating to the client relationship or the affairs of the client, except and to the extent disclosure or use is reasonably necessary:

a. To establish an advisory or brokerage account, to effect a transaction for the client, or as otherwise impliedly authorized in order to carry out the client engagement; or
b. To comply with legal requirements or legal process; or
c. To defend the CFP Board designee against charges of wrongdoing; or
d. In connection with a civil dispute between the CFP Board designee and the client.

For purposes of this rule, the proscribed use of client information is improper whether or not it actually causes harm to the client.

Rule 502.

A CFP Board designee shall maintain the same standards of confidentiality to employers as to clients.

Rule 503.

A CFP Board designee doing business as a partner or principal of a financial services firm owes to the CFP Board designee's partners or co-owners a responsibility to act in good faith. This includes, but is not limited to, adherence to reasonable expectations of confidentiality both while in business together and thereafter.

Rules that Relate to the Principle of Professionalism.

Rule 601.

A CFP Board designee shall use the marks in compliance with the rules and regulations of the CFP Board, as established and amended from time to time. (**Note from the authors:** To gain more information on the correct use of the CFP marks, see the CFP Board web site at www.CFP-Board.org and read the *Guide to Use of the CFP Certification Marks.*)

Rule 602.

A CFP Board designee shall show respect for other financial planning professionals, and related occupational groups, by engaging in fair and honorable competitive practices. Collegiality among CFP Board designees shall not, however, impede enforcement of this Code of Ethics.

Rule 603.

A CFP Board designee who has knowledge, which is not required to be kept confidential under this Code of Ethics, that another CFP Board designee has committed a violation of this Code of Ethics which raises substantial questions as to the designee's honesty, trustworthiness or fitness as a CFP Board designee in other respects, shall promptly inform the CFP Board. This rule does not require disclosure of information or reporting based on knowledge gained as a consultant or expert witness in anticipation of or related to litigation or other dispute resolution mechanisms. For purposes of this rule, knowledge means no substantial doubt.

Rule 604.

A CFP Board designee who has knowledge, which is not required under this Code of Ethics to be kept confidential, and which raises a substantial question of unprofessional, fraudulent or illegal conduct by a CFP Board designee or other financial professional, shall promptly inform the appropriate regulatory and/or professional disciplinary body. This rule does not require disclosure or reporting of information gained as a consultant or expert witness in anticipation of or related to litigation or other dispute resolution mechanisms. For purposes of this Rule, knowledge means no substantial doubt.

Rule 605.

A CFP Board designee who has reason to suspect illegal conduct within the CFP Board designee's organization shall make timely disclosure of the available evidence to the CFP Board designee's immediate supervisor and/or partners or co-owners. If the CFP Board designee is convinced that illegal conduct exists within the CFP Board designee's organization, and that appropriate measures are not taken to remedy the situation, the CFP Board designee shall, where appropriate, alert the appropriate regulatory authorities including the CFP Board in a timely manner.

Rule 606.

In all professional activities a CFP Board designee shall perform services in accordance with:

a. Applicable laws, rules, and regulations of governmental agencies and other applicable authorities; and
b. Applicable rules, regulations, and other established policies of the CFP Board.

Rule 607.

A CFP Board designee shall not engage in any conduct which reflects adversely on his or her integrity or fitness as a CFP Board designee, upon the marks, or upon the profession.

Rule 608.

The Investment Advisers Act of 1940 requires registration of investment advisers with the U.S. Securities and Exchange Commission and similar state statutes may require registration with state securities agencies. CFP Board designees shall disclose to clients their firm's status as registered investment advisers. Under present standards of acceptable business conduct, it is proper to use registered investment adviser if the CFP Board designee is registered individually. If the CFP Board designee is registered through his or her firm, then the CFP Board designee is not a registered investment adviser but a person associated with an investment adviser. The firm is the registered investment adviser. Moreover, RIA or R.I.A. following a CFP Board designee's name in advertising, letterhead stationery, and business cards may be misleading and is not permitted either by this Code of Ethics or by SEC regulations.

Rule 609.

A CFP Board designee shall not practice any other profession or offer to provide such services unless the CFP Board designee is qualified to practice in those fields and is licensed as required by state law.

Rule 610.

A CFP Board designee shall return the client's original records in a timely manner after their return has been requested by a client.

Rule 611.

A CFP Board designee shall not bring or threaten to bring a disciplinary proceeding under this Code of Ethics, or report or threaten to report information to the CFP Board pursuant to Rules 603 and/or 604, or make or threaten to make use of this Code of Ethics for no substantial purpose other than to harass, maliciously injure, embarrass and/or unfairly burden another CFP Board designee.

Rule 612.

A CFP Board designee shall comply with all applicable post-certification requirements established by the CFP Board including, but not limited to, payment of the annual CFP Board designee fee as well as signing and returning the Licensee's Statement annually in connection with the license renewal process.

Rules that Relate to the Principle of Diligence.

Rule 701.

A CFP Board designee shall provide services diligently.

Rule 702.

A financial planning practitioner shall enter into an engagement only after securing sufficient information to satisfy the CFP Board designee that:

a. The relationship is warranted by the individual's needs and objectives; and
b. The CFP Board designee has the ability to either provide requisite competent services or to involve other professionals who can provide such services.

Rule 703.

A financial planning practitioner shall make and/or implement only recommendations which are suitable for the client.

Rule 704.

Consistent with the nature and scope of the engagement, a CFP Board designee shall make a reasonable investigation regarding the financial products recommended to clients. Such an investigation may be made by the CFP Board designee or by others provided the CFP Board designee acts reasonably in relying upon such investigation.

Rule 705.

A CFP Board designee shall properly supervise subordinates with regard to their delivery of financial planning services, and shall not accept or condone conduct in violation of this Code of Ethics.

CFP BOARD'S FINANCIAL PLANNING PRACTICE STANDARDS

Statement of Purpose for Financial Planning Practice Standards.

Financial Planning Practice Standards (Practice Standards) are being developed and promulgated by the Certified Financial Planner Board of Standards, Inc. (CFP Board), for the practice of personal financial planning. These Practice Standards: (1) assure that the practice of financial planning by CFP Board designees is based on agreed upon norms of practice; (2) advance professionalism in financial planning; and (3) enhance the value of the personal financial planning process. The CFP Board has established the Board of Practice Standards, a subsidiary board comprised exclusively of CFP® practitioners, to draft these *Practice Standards.*

Practice Standards Defined.

A Practice Standard establishes the level of professional practice that is expected of CFP Board designees engaged in personal financial planning. The services provided depend on the facts and circumstances of a particular situation.

Practice Standards apply to CFP Board designees performing the tasks of personal financial planning regardless of the person's title, job position, type of employment or method of compensation. Practice Standards should be considered by all personal financial planning professionals when performing the financial planning task or activity addressed by the Practice Standards but are enforceable by the CFP Board only against CFP Board designees. Conduct inconsistent with a Practice Standard in and of itself is not intended to give rise to a cause of action nor to create any presumption that a legal duty has been breached. The Practice Standards are designed to provide CFP Board designees a structure for identifying and implementing expectations regarding the professional practice of personal financial planning. They are not designed to be a basis for legal liability.

Practice Standard 100-1

Establishing and Defining the Relationship with the Client.

Defining the Scope of the Engagement:

The scope of the engagement shall be mutually defined by the financial planning practitioner and the client prior to providing any financial planning service.

Explanation of this Practice Standard:

Prior to providing any financial planning service, a financial planning practitioner and the client shall mutually define the scope of the engagement. The process of "mutually-defining" is essential in determining what activities may be necessary to proceed with the client engagement.

This is accomplished by:

- Identifying the service(s) to be provided;
- Disclosing the practitioner's material conflict(s) of interest(s);
- Disclosing financial planning practitioner's compensation arrangement(s);
- Determining the client's and the financial planning practitioner's responsibilities;
- Establishing the duration of the engagement; and
- Providing any additional information necessary to define or limit the scope.

The scope of the engagement may include one or more financial planning subject areas. It is acceptable to mutually define engagements in which the scope is limited to specific activities. This serves to establish realistic expectations both for the client and the practitioner. This Practice Standard does not require the scope of the engagement to be in writing. However, as noted in Section 3, there may be certain disclosures that might be required to be in writing. As the relationship proceeds, the scope may change by mutual understanding. This Practice Standard shall not be considered alone, but in conjunction with all other Practice Standards.

Effective Date:

January 1, 1999.

Relationship of this Practice Standard to the CFP Board's Code of Ethics and Professional Responsibility:

This Practice Standard relates to the CFP Board's Code of Ethics and Professional Responsibility (Code of Ethics) through the Code of Ethics' Principle 4 - Fairness and Rule 402, and Principle 7-Diligence and Rule 702.

Principle 4 states that "a CFP Board designee shall perform professional services in a manner that is fair and reasonable to clients ...." Although, as stated earlier, there is no requirement that the scope of the engagement be in writing, Rule 402 in the Code of Ethics requires a financial planning practitioner to make "timely written disclosure of all material information relative to the professional relationship. In all circumstances such disclosure shall include...sources of compensation."

Principle 7 states that "a CFP Board designee shall act diligently in providing professional services." Rule 702 requires that financial planning practitioners enter into an engagement only after obtaining sufficient information to satisfy that "the relationship is warranted by the individual's needs and objectives; and the CFP Board designee has the ability to either provide requisite competent services or to involve other professionals who can provide such services."

Practice Standard 200-1

Gathering Client Data.

Determining a Client's Personal and Financial Goals, Needs and Priorities:

A client's personal and financial goals, needs and priorities that are relevant to the scope of the engagement and the service(s) being provided shall be mutually defined by the financial planning practitioner and the client prior to making and/or implementing any recommendations.

Explanation of this Practice Standard:

Prior to making recommendations to a client, a financial planning practitioner (practitioner) and the client shall mutually define the client's personal and financial goals, needs and priorities. In order to arrive at such a definition, the practitioner will need to explore the client's values, attitudes, expectations and time horizons as they affect the client's goals, needs and priorities. The process of "mutually-defining" is essential in determining what activities may be necessary to proceed with the client engagement. Personal values and attitudes shape a client's goals and objectives and the priority placed on them. Accordingly, these goals and objectives must be consistent with the client's values and attitudes in order for the client to make the commitment necessary to accomplish them.

Goals and objectives provide focus, purpose, vision and direction for the financial planning process. It is essential that objectives relative to the scope of the engagement are determined and that they are clear, precise, consistent and measurable. The role of the practitioner is to facilitate the goal-setting process in order to clarify, with the client, goals and objectives, and, when appropriate, the practitioner must try to assist clients in recognizing the implications of unrealistic goals and objectives.

This Practice Standard addresses only the tasks of determining a client's personal and financial goals, needs and priorities; assessing a client's values, attitudes and expectations; and determining a client's time horizons. These areas are subjective and the practitioner's interpretation is limited by what the client reveals. A practitioner performing the activity of "gathering client data" should consider together the various Practice Standards applicable to such activity. This Practice Standard shall not be considered alone, but in conjunction with all other Practice Standards.

Effective Date:

January 1, 1999.

Relationship of this Practice Standard to the CFP Board's Code of Ethics and Professional Responsibility:

This Practice Standard relates to the CFP Board's Code of Ethics and Professional Responsibility (Code of Ethics) through the Code of Ethics' Principle 7 - Diligence and Rules 701 through 703. Rule 701 states that "a CFP Board designee shall provide services diligently." Rule 702 requires a financial planning practitioner to "enter into an engagement only after securing sufficient information to satisfy the CFP Board designee that ... the relationship is warranted by the individual's needs and objectives...." In addition, Rule 703 requires a financial planning practitioner to "make and/or implement only recommendations which are suitable for the client."

Practice Standard 200-2

Gathering Client Data.

Information and Documents:

Obtaining Quantitative Information and Documents:

A financial planning practitioner shall obtain sufficient and relevant quantitative information and documents about a client applicable to the scope of the engagement and the services being provided prior to making and/or implementing any recommendations.

Explanation of this Practice Standard:

Prior to making recommendations to a client and depending upon the type of client engagement and its scope, a financial planning practitioner (practitioner) shall determine what quantitative information and documents are sufficient and relevant.

A practitioner shall obtain sufficient and relevant quantitative information and documents pertaining to the client's financial resources, obligations and personal situation. This information may be obtained directly from the client or other sources through interview, questionnaire, client records and documents.

A practitioner shall communicate to the client a reliance on the completeness and accuracy of the information provided and that incomplete or inaccurate information will impact conclusions and recommendations.

If a practitioner is unable to obtain sufficient and relevant quantitative information and documents to form a basis for recommendations, the practitioner shall either:

a. Restrict the scope of the engagement to those matters for which sufficient and relevant information is available; or

b. Terminate the engagement.

A practitioner shall communicate to the client any limitations on the scope of the engagement, as well as the fact that this limitation could affect the conclusions and recommendations. This Practice Standard shall not be considered alone, but in conjunction with all other Practice Standards.

Effective Date:

January 1, 1999.

Relationship of this Practice Standard to the CFP Board's Code of Ethics and Professional Responsibility:

This Practice Standard relates to the CFP Board's Code of Ethics and Professional Responsibility (Code of Ethics) through the Code of Ethics' Principle 7 - Diligence and Rules 701 through 703. Rule 701 states that "a CFP Board designee shall provide services diligently." Rule 702 requires a financial planning practitioner to "enter into an engagement only after securing sufficient information to satisfy the CFP Board designee that.... the relationship is warrant-ed by the individual's needs and objectives...." In addition, Rule 703 requires a financial planning practitioner to "make and/or implement only recommendations which are suit-able for the client."

Practice Standard 300-1

Analyzing and Evaluating the Client's Financial Status.

Analyzing and Evaluating the Client's Information:

A financial planning practitioner shall analyze the information to gain an understanding of the client's financial situation and then evaluate to what extent the client's goals, needs and priorities can be met by the client's resources and current course of action.

Explanation of this Practice Standard:

Prior to making recommendations to a client, it is necessary for the financial planning practitioner to assess the client's financial situation and to determine the likelihood of reaching the stated objectives by continuing present activities.

The practitioner will utilize client specified, mutually agreed upon, and/or other reasonable assumptions. Both personal and economic assumptions must be considered in this step of the process. These assumptions may include, but are not limited to, the following:

- Personal assumptions, such as: retirement age(s), life expectancy(ies), income needs, risk factors, time horizon and special needs; and
- Economic assumptions, such as: inflation rates, tax rates and investment returns.

Analysis and evaluation are critical to the financial planning process. These activities form the foundation for determining strengths and weaknesses of the client's financial situation and current course of action. These activities may also identify other issues that should be addressed. As a result, it may be appropriate to amend the scope of the engagement and/or to obtain additional information.

Effective Date:

January 1, 2000.

Relationship of this Practice Standard to the CFP Board's Code of Ethics and Professional Responsibility:

This Practice Standard relates to the CFP Board's Code of Ethics and Professional Responsibility (Code of Ethics) through the Code of Ethics' Principle 2 - Objectivity and Rules 201 and 202; Principle 3 - Competence and Rule 302, and Principle 7 - Diligence and Rule 701. Principle 2 states that "A CFP Board designee shall be objective in providing professional services to clients." Rule 201 states that "A CFP Board designee shall exercise reasonable and prudent professional judgment in providing professional services." And Rule 202 states that "A financial planning practitioner shall act in the interest of the client."

Principle 3 states that "A CFP Board designee shall provide services to clients competently and maintain the necessary knowledge and skill to continue to do so in those areas in which the designee is engaged." Rule 302 states that "A CFP Board designee shall offer advice only in those areas in which the CFP Board designee has competence. In areas where the CFP Board designee is not professionally competent, the CFP Board designee shall seek the counsel of qualified individuals and/or refer clients to such parties."

Under Principle 7, Rule 701 states that "A CFP Board designee shall provide services diligently."

Practice Standard 400-1

Developing and Presenting the Financial Planning Recommendation(s).

Identifying and Evaluating Financial Planning Alternative(s):

A financial planning practitioner shall consider sufficient and relevant alternatives to the client's current course of action in an effort to reasonably achieve the client's goals, needs and priorities.

Explanation of this Practice Standard:

After analyzing the client's current situation (Practice Standard 300-1) and prior to developing and presenting the recommendation(s) (Practice Standards 400-2 and 400-3), the financial planning practitioner shall identify alternative actions. The practitioner shall evaluate the effectiveness of such actions in reasonably achieving the client's goals, needs and priorities.

This evaluation may involve, but is not limited to, considering multiple assumptions, conducting research or consulting with other professionals. This process may result in a single alternative, multiple alternatives or no alternative to the client's current course of action.

In considering alternative actions, the practitioner also must recognize and, as appropriate, take into account his or her legal and/or regulatory limitations and level of competency in properly addressing each of the client's financial planning issues.

More than one alternative may reasonably achieve the client's goals, needs and priorities. Alternatives identified by the practitioner may differ from those of other practitioners or advisors, illustrating the subjective nature of exercising professional judgment.

This Practice Standard shall not be considered alone, but in conjunction with all other Practice Standards.

Effective Date:

January 1, 2001.

Relationship of this Practice Standard to the CFP Board's Code of Ethics and Professional Responsibility:

This Practice Standard relates to the CFP Board's Code of Ethics and Professional Responsibility (Code of Ethics) through the Code of Ethics' Principle 2 - Objectivity and Rules 201 and 202; Principle 3 - Competence and Rule 302; Principle 6 - Professionalism and Rule 609, and Principle 7 - Diligence and Rules 701 and 703.

Principle 2 states that "A CFP Board designee shall be objective in providing professional services to clients." Rule 201 states that "A CFP Board designee shall exercise reasonable and prudent professional judgment in providing professional services." Rule 202 states that "A financial planning practitioner shall act in the interest of the client."

Principle 3 states that "A CFP Board designee shall provide services to clients competently and maintain the necessary knowledge and skill to continue to do so in those areas in which the designee is engaged." Rule 302 states that "A CFP Board designee shall offer advice only in those areas in which the CFP Board designee has competence. In areas where the CFP Board designee is not professionally competent, the CFP Board designee shall seek the counsel of qualified individuals and/or refer clients to such parties."

Principle 6 states that "A CFP Board designee's conduct in all matters shall reflect credit upon the profession." Rule 609 states that "A CFP Board designee shall not practice any other profession or offer to provide such services unless the CFP Board designee is qualified ... and is licensed as required by state law."

Principle 7 states that "A CFP Board designee shall act diligently in providing professional services." Rule 701 states that "A CFP Board designee shall provide services diligently." Rule 703 states that "A financial planning practitioner shall make and/or implement only recommendations which are suitable for the client."

Practice Standard 400-2

Developing and Presenting the Financial Planning Recommendation(s).

Developing the Financial Planning Recommendation(s):

A financial planning practitioner shall develop the recommendation(s) based on the selected alternative(s) and the current course of action in an effort to reasonably achieve the client's goals, needs and priorities.

Explanation of this Practice Standard:

After identifying and evaluating the alternative(s) and the client's current course of action, the practitioner shall develop the recommendation(s) expected to reasonably achieve the client's goals, needs and priorities. A recommendation may be an independent action or a combination of actions which may need to be implemented collectively. The recommendation(s) shall be consistent with and will be directly affected by the following:

- Mutually defined scope of the engagement;
- Mutually defined client goals, needs and priorities;
- Quantitative data provided by the client;
- Personal and economic assumptions;
- Practitioner's analysis and evaluation of client's current situation; and
- Alternative(s) selected by the practitioner.

A recommendation may be to continue the current course of action. If a change is recommended, it may be specific and/or detailed or provide a general direction. In some instances, it may be necessary for the practitioner to recommend that the client modify a goal.

The recommendations developed by the practitioner may differ from those of other practitioners or advisors yet each may reasonably achieve the client's goals, needs and priorities.

This Practice Standard shall not be considered alone, but in conjunction with all other Practice Standards.

Effective Date:

January 1, 2001.

Relationship of this Practice Standard to the CFP Board's Code of Ethics and Professional Responsibility:

This Practice Standard relates to the CFP Board's Code of Ethics and Professional Responsibility (Code of Ethics) through the Code of Ethics' Principle 2 - Objectivity and Rules 201 and 202; Principle 3 - Competence and Rule 302; Principle 6 - Professionalism and Rule 609; and Principle 7 - Diligence and Rules 701, 703 and 704.

Principle 2 states that "A CFP Board designee shall be objective in providing professional services to clients." Rule 201 states that "A CFP Board designee shall exercise reasonable and prudent professional judgment in providing professional services." Rule 202 states that "A financial planning practitioner shall act in the interest of the client."

Principle 3 states that "A CFP Board designee shall provide services to clients competently and maintain the necessary knowledge and skill to continue to do so in those areas in which the designee is engaged." Rule 302 states that "A CFP Board designee shall offer advice only in those areas in which the CFP Board designee has competence. In areas where the CFP Board designee is not professionally competent, the CFP Board designee shall seek the counsel of qualified individuals and/or refer clients to such parties."

Principle 6 states that "A CFP Board designee's conduct in all matters shall reflect credit upon the profession." Rule 609 states that "A CFP Board designee shall not practice any other profession or offer to provide such services unless the CFP Board designee is qualified ... and is licensed as required by state law."

Principle 7 states that "A CFP Board designee shall act diligently in providing professional services." Rule 701 states that "A CFP Board designee shall provide services diligently." Rule 703 states that "A financial planning practitioner shall make and/or implement only recommendations which are suitable for the client." Rule 704 states that "... a CFP Board designee shall make a reasonable investigation regarding the financial products recommended to clients. Such an investigation may be made by the CFP Board designee or by others provided the CFP Board designee acts reasonably in relying upon such investigation."

Practice Standard 400-3

Developing and Presenting the Financial Planning Recommendation(s).

Presenting the Financial Planning Recommendation(s):

A financial planning practitioner shall communicate the recommendation(s) in a manner and to an extent reasonably necessary to assist the client in making an informed decision.

Explanation of this Practice Standard:

When presenting a recommendation, the practitioner shall make a reasonable effort to assist the client in understanding the client's current situation, the recommendation itself, and its impact on the ability to achieve the client's goals, needs and priorities. In doing so, the practitioner shall avoid presenting the practitioner's opinion as fact.

The practitioner shall communicate the factors critical to the client's understanding of the recommendations. These factors may include but are not limited to material:

- Personal and economic assumptions;
- Interdependence of recommendations;
- Advantages and disadvantages;
- Risks; and/or
- Time sensitivity.

The practitioner should indicate that even though the recommendations may achieve the client's goals, needs and priorities, changes in personal and economic conditions could alter the intended outcome. Changes may include, but are not limited to: legislative, family status, career, investment performance and/or health.

If there are conflicts of interest that have not been previously disclosed, such conflicts and how they may impact the recommendations should be addressed at this time.

Presenting recommendations provides the practitioner an opportunity to further assess whether the recommendations meet client expectations, whether the client is willing to act on the recommendations, and whether modifications are necessary.

This Practice Standard shall not be considered alone, but in conjunction with all other Practice Standards.

Effective Date:

January 1, 2001.

Relationship of this Practice Standard to the CFP Board's Code of Ethics and Professional Responsibility:

This Practice Standard relates to the CFP Board's Code of Ethics and Professional Responsibility (Code of Ethics) through the Code of Ethics' Principle 1 - Integrity and Rule 102; Principle 2 - Objectivity and Rule 201; and Principle 6 - Professionalism and Rule 607.

Principle 1 states that "A CFP Board designee shall offer and provide professional services with integrity." Rule 102 states that "... a CFP Board designee shall not ... knowingly make a false or misleading statement to a client ...."

Principle 2 states that "A CFP Board designee shall be objective in providing professional services to clients." Rule 201 states that "A CFP Board designee shall exercise reasonable and prudent professional judgment in providing professional services."

Principle 6 states that "A CFP Board designee's conduct in all matters shall reflect credit upon the profession." Rule 607 states that "A CFP Board designee shall not engage in any conduct which reflects adversely on his or her integrity or fitness as a CFP Board designee ...."

Practice Standard 500-1

Implementing the Financial Planning Recommendation(s).

Agreeing on Implementation Responsibilities:

A financial planning practitioner and the client shall mutually agree on the implementation responsibilities consistent with the scope of the engagement.

Explanation of this Practice Standard:

The client is responsible for accepting or rejecting recommendations and for retaining and/or delegating implementation responsibilities. The financial planning practitioner and the client shall mutually agree on the services, if any, to be provided by the practitioner. The scope of the engagement, as originally defined, may need to be modified. The practitioner's responsibilities may include, but are not limited to, the following:

- Identifying activities necessary for implementation;
- Determining division of activities between the practitioner and the client;
- Referring to other professionals;
- Coordinating with other professionals;
- Sharing of information as authorized; and
- Selecting and securing products and/or services.

If there are conflicts of interest, sources of compensation or material relationships with other professionals or advisors that have not been previously disclosed, such conflicts, sources or relationships must be disclosed at this time.

When referring the client to other professionals or advisors, the financial planning practitioner shall indicate the basis for the referral.

If the practitioner is engaged by the client to provide only implementation activities, the scope of the engagement shall be mutually defined, orally or in writing, in accordance with Practice Standard 100-1. This scope may include such matters as the extent to which the practitioner will rely on information, analysis or recommendations provided by others.

This Practice Standard shall not be considered alone, but in conjunction with all other Practice Standards.

Effective Date:

January 1, 2002.

Relationship of this Practice Standard to the CFP Board's Code of Ethics and Professional Responsibility:

This Practice Standard relates to the CFP Board's Code of Ethics and Professional Responsibility (Code of Ethics) through the Code of Ethics' Principle 3 - Competence and Rule 302; Principle 4 - Fairness and Rules 402 and 404; Principle 6 - Professionalism and Rules 606 and 609; and Principle 7 - Diligence and Rule 701.

Principle 3 states that "A CFP Board designee shall provide services to clients competently and maintain the necessary knowledge and skill to continue to do so in those areas in which the designee is engaged." Rule 302 states that "A CFP Board designee shall offer advice only in those areas in which the CFP Board designee has competence. In areas where the CFP Board designee is not professionally competent, the CFP Board designee shall seek the counsel of qualified individuals and/or refer clients to such parties."

Principle 4 states that "A CFP Board designee shall perform professional services in a manner that is fair and reasonable to clients ... and shall disclose conflict(s) of interest(s) in providing such services." Rule 402 states that "A financial planning practitioner shall make timely written disclosure of all material information relative to the professional relationship. In all circumstances such disclosure shall include conflict(s) of interest(s) and sources of compensation." Rule 404 states that "should conflict(s) of interest(s) develop after a professional relationship has been commenced, but before the services ... have been completed, a CFP Board designee shall promptly disclose the conflict(s) of interest(s) ...."

Principle 6 states that "A CFP Board designee's conduct in all matters shall reflect credit upon the profession." Rule 606 states that "... A CFP Board designee shall perform services in accordance with: (a) Applicable laws, rules, and regulations of governmental agencies and other applicable authorities ...." Rule 609 states that "A CFP Board designee shall not practice any other profession or offer to provide such services unless the CFP Board designee is qualified ... and is licensed as required by state law."

Under Principle 7, Rule 701 states that "A CFP Board designee shall provide services diligently."

Practice Standard 500-2

Implementing the Financial Planning Recommendation(s).

Selecting Products and Services for Implementation:

A financial planning practitioner shall select appropriate products and services that are consistent with the client's goals, needs and priorities.

Explanation of this Practice Standard:

A financial planning practitioner will use professional judgment in selecting the products and services that are in the client's interest. Professional judgment incorporates both qualitative and quantitative information. A financial planning practitioner shall reasonably investigate and evaluate products or services that address the client's needs. The financial planning practitioner shall have a reasonable basis for believing that the products or services selected are suitable for the client.

Products and services selected by the practitioner may differ from those selected by other practitioners or advisors. Alternative products or services may be suitable for the client and could reasonably achieve the client's goals, needs and priorities, illustrating the subjective nature of exercising professional judgment.

The practitioner must make all disclosures required to comply with applicable regulations.

This Practice Standard shall not be considered alone, but in conjunction with all other Practice Standards.

Effective Date:

January 1, 2002.

Relationship of this Practice Standard to the CFP Board's Code of Ethics and Professional Responsibility:

This Practice Standard relates to the CFP Board's Code of Ethics and Professional Responsibility (Code of Ethics) through the Code of Ethics' Principle 2 - Objectivity and Rule 202; Principle 4 - Fairness and Rules 402, 403, 404, 408, 409 and 416; Principle 6 - Professionalism and Rule 606; and Principle 7 - Diligence and Rules 701, 703 and 704.

Principle 2 states that "A CFP Board designee shall be objective in providing professional services to clients." Rule 202 states that "A financial planning practitioner shall act in the interest of the client."

Principle 4 states that "A CFP Board designee shall perform professional services in a manner that is fair and reasonable to clients ... and shall disclose conflict(s) or interest(s) in providing such services." Rule 402 states that "A financial planning practitioner shall make timely written disclosure of all material information relative to the professional relationship. In all circumstances such disclosure shall include conflict(s) of interest(s) and sources of compensation." Rule 403 states that "A CFP Board designee providing financial planning shall disclose in writing prior to establishing a client relationship, relations which reasonably may compromise the CFP Board designee's objectivity or independence." Rule 404 states that "Should conflict(s) of interest(s) develop after a professional relationship has been completed, a CFP Board designee shall promptly disclose conflict(s) of interest(s) to the client ...." Rule 408 states that "When acting as an agent for a principal, A CFP Board designee shall assure that the scope of his or her authority is clearly defined and properly documented." Rule 409 states that "Whether a CFP Board designee is employed by a financial planning firm, an investment institution, or serves as an agent for such an organization, or is self-employed, all CFP Board designees shall adhere to the same standards of disclosure and service." Rule 416 states that "If a CFP Board designee enters into a business transaction with a client ... the CFP Board designee shall disclose the risks of the transaction, conflict(s) of interest(s) of the CFP Board designee, and other relevant information ... necessary to make the transaction fair to the client."

Principle 6 states that "A CFP Board designee's conduct in all matters shall reflect credit upon the profession." Rule 606 states that "In all professional activities a CFP Board designee shall perform services in accordance with: (a) Applicable laws, rules, and regulations of governmental agencies and other applicable authorities; and (b) Applicable rules, regulations, and other established policies of the CFP Board."

Principle 7 states that "A CFP Board designee shall act diligently in providing professional services." Rule 701 states that "A CFP Board designee shall provide services diligently." Rule 703 states that "A financial planning practitioner shall make and/or implement only recommendations which are suitable for the client." Rule 704 states that "... A CFP Board designee shall make a reasonable investigation regarding the financial products recommended to clients."

Proposed Practice Standard 600-1

Monitoring the Financial Planning Recommendation(s).

Defining Monitoring Responsibilities:

The financial planning practitioner and client shall mutually define monitoring responsibilities.

Explanation of this Practice Standard:

The purpose of this Standard is to clarify the extent of the practitioner's role in the monitoring process. The practitioner and the client may have different perceptions about monitoring responsibilities.

When monitoring is included in the scope of the engagement, the financial planning practitioner shall identify which monitoring activities may be appropriate. The practitioner shall make a reasonable effort to define and communicate which monitoring activities the practitioner is able and willing to provide.

The practitioner and client shall mutually agree on the extent, frequency and duration of the monitoring activities, if any, to be provided by the practitioner. The scope of the engagement, as originally defined, may need to be modified.

Monitoring responsibilities may include but are not limited to:

- Identifying changes in conditions that would impact existing recommendations.
- Obtaining information from the client to determine changes in personal circumstances.
- Reviewing work done by other professionals or providers.
- Reviewing the client's progress toward financial goals.

The monitoring process may reveal the need to reinitiate any or all of the steps of the financial planning process.

Relationship of This Practice Standard to the CFP Board's Code of Ethics and Professional Responsibility:

This Practice Standard relates to the CFP Board's *Code of Ethics and Professional Responsibility* through the Code's Principle 7 – Diligence and Rule 702.

Principle 7 states that "a CFP designee shall act diligently in providing professional services." Rule 702 requires that financial planning practitioners enter into an engagement only after obtaining sufficient information to satisfy that "the relationship is warranted by the individual's goals and objectives; and the CFP designee has the ability to either provide requisite competent services or to involve other professionals who can provide such services."

Disciplinary Rules and Procedures

Article 1: Introduction.

Adherence to the Code of Ethics by CFP Board designees or to Practice Standards by CFP practitioners is required, with the potential for CFP Board sanctions against those who violate the regulations proscribed in these documents. The CFP Board will follow the disciplinary rules and procedures set forth below when enforcing the Code of Ethics and Practice Standards.

Article 2: Board of Professional Review.

The CFP Board's Board of Professional Review (referred to herein as the "Board"), formed pursuant to and governed by the bylaws of the CFP Board, is charged with the duty of investigating, reviewing and taking appropriate action with respect to alleged violations of the Code of Ethics and alleged noncompliance with the Financial Planning Practice Standards as promulgated by the Board of Governors and shall have original jurisdiction over all such disciplinary matters and procedures.

Article 3: Grounds for Discipline.

Misconduct by a CFP Board designee, individually or in concert with others, including the following acts or omissions, shall constitute grounds for discipline, whether or not the act or omission occurred in the course of a client relationship:

a. Any act or omission which violates the provisions of the Code of Ethics;

b. Any act or omission which fails to comply with the Practice Standards;

c. Any act or omission which violates the criminal laws of any State or of the United States or of any province, territory or jurisdiction of any other country, provided however, that conviction thereof in a criminal proceeding shall not be a prerequisite to the institution of disciplinary proceedings, and provided further, that acquittal in a criminal proceeding shall not bar a disciplinary action;

d. Any act which is the proper basis for professional suspension, as defined herein, provided professional suspension shall not be a prerequisite to the institution of disciplinary proceedings, and provided further, that dismissal of charges in a professional suspension proceeding shall not necessarily bar a disciplinary action;

e. Any act or omission which violates these Procedures or which violates an order of discipline;

f. Failure to respond to a request by the Board, without good cause shown, or obstruction of the Board, or any panel or board thereof, or CFP Board staff in the performance of its or their duties. Good cause includes, without limitation, an assertion that a response would violate a CFP Board designee's constitutional privilege against self-incrimination;

g. Any false or misleading statement made to the CFP Board.

The enumeration of the foregoing acts and omissions constituting grounds for discipline is not exclusive and other acts or omissions amounting to unprofessional conduct may constitute grounds for discipline.

Article 4: Forms of Discipline.

In cases where no grounds for discipline have been established, the Board may dismiss the matter as either without merit or with a cautionary letter. In all cases, the Board has the right to require CFP Board designees to complete additional continuing education or other remedial work. Such continuing education or remedial work may be ordered instead of, or in addition to, any discipline listed below. Where grounds for discipline have been established, any of the following forms of discipline may be imposed in these cases where grounds for discipline have been established.

4.1 Private Censure.

The Board may order private censure of a CFP Board designee which shall be an unpublished written reproach mailed by the Board to a censured CFP Board designee.

4.2 Public Letter of Admonition.

The Board may order that a Letter of Admonition be issued against a CFP Board designee, which shall be a publishable written reproach of the CFP Board designee's behavior. It shall be standard procedure to publish the Letter of Admonition in a press release or in such other form of publicity selected by the Board. In some cases when the Board determines that there are mitigating circumstances, it may decide to withhold public notification.

4.3 Suspension.

The Board may order suspension for a specified period of time, not to exceed five (5) years, for those individuals it deems can be rehabilitated. In the event of a suspension, it shall be standard procedure to publish the fact of the suspension together with identification of the CFP Board designee in a press release, or in such other form of publicity as is selected by the Board. In some cases when the Board determines that there are extreme mitigating circumstances it may decide to withhold public notification. CFP Board designees receiving a suspension may qualify for reinstatement to use the marks as provided in Article 15.

4.4 Revocation.

The Board may order permanent revocation of a CFP Board designee's right to use the marks. In the event of a permanent revocation it shall be standard procedure to publish the fact of the revocation together with identification of the CFP Board designee in a press release, or in such other form of publicity as is selected by the Board. In some cases when the Board determines that there are extreme mitigating circumstances it may decide to withhold public notification. Revocation shall be permanent.

4.5 Forms of Discipline Concerning Candidates.

Under certain circumstances, the Board may take action in matters involving the conduct of candidates for CFP certification. Action that may be taken in these cases, where grounds have been established, correspond in character and degree to the four forms of discipline described in Articles 4.1 through 4.4 above, and are correspondingly as follows:

a. Subject to the candidate's meeting all other requirements of certification, if any, of the candidate with a private censure in the candidate's record in the form stated;
b. Subject to the candidate's meeting all other requirements of certification, if any, of the candidate with issuance of a Letter of Admonition, published as applicable, and in the candidate's record in the form stated;
c. Certification, if any, suspended for a specified period, not to exceed five (5) years;
d. Certification, if any, denied.

In the event of either a suspension or a denial of certification, the fact of such suspension or denial shall be publishable at the discretion of the Board. A candidate for the CFP certification who has been the subject of an order to suspend certification may seek to reapply for certification according to the same procedures in 15.2. Such candidates, in addition, shall meet the requirements of original certification.

Article 5: Interim Suspension Status.

Interim suspension is the temporary suspension by the Board of a CFP Board designee's right to use the marks for a definite or indefinite period of time, while proceedings conducted pursuant to these procedures are pending against the CFP Board designee. Imposition of an interim suspension shall not preclude the imposition of any other form of discipline entered by the Board in final resolution of the disciplinary proceeding.

Article 6: Investigation.

Proceedings involving potential ethics violations shall be commenced upon a written request for investigation made by any person which shall be directed to the Board or commenced at the behest of CFP Board Staff Counsel. Proceedings involving Practice Standards nonconformance shall be commenced upon a written request for investigation made by any person(s) who have a contractual relationship with the CFP Board designee whose practices are being called into question. In either situation, the Board may, in making a determination of whether to proceed, make such inquiry regarding the underlying facts as they deem appropriate.

Article 7: Complaint - Answer – Default.

7.1 Inquiry Panel Decision.

If the Inquiry Panel determines that there is probable cause to believe grounds for discipline exists, the Inquiry Panel shall direct CFP Board Staff Counsel to issue a Complaint as set forth in Section 7.2 of this Article. The issuance of a Complaint for any other reason shall also be in accordance with Section 2 of this Article.

7.2 Complaint.

An original Complaint shall be prepared by CFP Board staff and forwarded to the CFP Board designee. Copies of the Complaint shall be included with the materials provided to the Hearing Panel in advance of the hearing. The Complaint shall reasonably set forth the grounds for discipline with which the CFP Board designee is charged and the conduct or omission which gave rise to those charges.

Article 8: Discovery and Evidence.

Discovery of a disciplinary case may be obtained only after a Complaint has been issued against a CFP Board designee. The CFP Board designee may obtain copies of all documents in the CFP Board designee's disciplinary file which are not privileged and which are relevant to the subject matter in the pending action before the Hearing Panel. Requests for copies of CFP Board documents must be made to CFP Board Staff Counsel in writing. Release of information contained in a CFP Board designee's disciplinary file is premised on the understanding that materials will be used only for purposes directly connected to the pending CFP Board action.

Article 9: Hearings.

Not less than thirty (30) calendar days before the date set for the hearing of a Complaint, notice of such hearing shall be given as provided in Article 17.2 to the CFP Board designee or to the CFP Board designee's counsel. The notice shall designate the date and place of the hearing and shall also advise the CFP Board designee that the CFP Board designee is entitled to be represented by counsel at the hearing, to cross-examine witnesses and to present evidence on behalf of the CFP Board designee.

Article 10: Report, Findings of Fact and Recommendation.

At the conclusion of the hearing, the Hearing Panel shall record its findings of fact and recommendations and submit the findings and recommendations to the Board for its consideration. In making its recommendation, the Hearing Panel may take into consideration the CFP Board designee's prior disciplinary record, if any.

Article 11: Appeals.

All appeals from orders of the Board shall be submitted to the Board of Appeals in accordance with the Rules and Procedures of the Board of Appeals. If an order of the Board is not appealed within thirty (30) calendar days after notice of the order is sent to the CFP Board designee, such order shall become final.

Article 12: Conviction of a Crime or Professional Suspension.

Every CFP Board designee, upon being convicted of a crime, except misdemeanor traffic offenses or traffic ordinance violations unless such offense involves the use of alcohol or drugs, or upon being the subject of professional suspension, shall notify the CFP Board in writing of such conviction or suspension within ten (10) calendar days after the date on which the CFP Board designee is notified of the conviction or suspension.

The term serious crime as used in these rules shall include: (1) any felony; (2) any lesser crime, a necessary element of which as determined by its statutory or common law definition involves misrepresentation, fraud, extortion, misappropriation or theft; and/or (3) an attempt or conspiracy to commit such crime, or solicitation of another to commit such crime.

Article 13: Settlement Procedure.

A CFP Board designee against whom proceedings are pending pursuant to these disciplinary rules and procedures may, after the issuance of a formal Complaint and prior to final action by the Board, tender an Offer of Settlement in exchange for a stipulated form of Board action. The Offer of Settlement shall be in writing and must be submitted to CFP Board Staff Counsel for its recommendation prior to being tendered to the Hearing Panel who will act upon such request. Submitting an Offer of Settlement shall suspend all proceedings conducted pursuant to these Disciplinary Rules and Procedures.

Article 14: Required Action After Revocation or Suspension.

After the entry of an order of revocation or suspension is final, the CFP Board designee shall promptly terminate any use of the marks and in particular shall not use them in any advertising, announcement, letterhead or business card.

Article 15: Reinstatement After Discipline.

15.1 Reinstatement After Revocation.

Revocation shall be permanent, and there shall be no opportunity for reinstatement.

15.2 Reinstatement After Suspension.

Unless otherwise provided by the Board in its order of suspension, a CFP Board designee who has been suspended for a period of one (l) year or less shall be automatically reinstated upon the expiration of the period of suspension, provided the CFP Board designee files with the CFP Board within thirty (30) calendar days of the expiration of the period of suspension an affidavit stating that the suspended CFP Board designee has fully complied with the order of suspension and with all applicable provisions of these Procedures, unless such condition is waived by the Board in its discretion. A CFP Board designee who has been suspended for a period longer than one (l) year must petition the Board for a reinstatement hearing within six months of the end of his/her suspension, or failure to do so will result in administrative relinquishment. Before any reinstatement hearing will be scheduled, the CFP Board designee must meet all administrative requirements for recertification, pay the reinstatement hearing costs and provide evidence, if necessary, that all prior hearing costs have been paid. At the reinstatement hearing, the CFP Board designee must prove by clear and convincing evidence that the CFP Board designee has been rehabilitated, has complied with all applicable disciplinary orders and provisions of these Procedures, and that the CFP Board designee is fit to use the marks.

Article 16: Confidentiality of Proceedings.

16.1 Confidentiality.

Except as otherwise provided in these Procedures, all proceedings conducted pursuant to these Procedures shall be confidential and the records of the Board, Hearing Panel, CFP Board Staff Counsel and the CFP Board staff shall remain confidential and shall not be made public.

16.2 Exceptions to Confidentiality.

The pendency, subject matter and status of proceedings conducted pursuant to these Procedures may be disclosed if (1) the proceeding is predicated on criminal conviction or professional suspension as defined herein; or (2) the CFP Board designee has waived confidentiality; or (3) such disclosure is required by legal process of a court of law or other governmental body or agency having appropriate jurisdiction.

Article 17: General Provisions.

In all disciplinary cases wherein a hearing is convened, the Board will assess against the CFP Board designee the costs of the proceedings. In addition, a CFP Board designee who desires an appearance, either telephonically or in person, will be required to submit hearing costs not less than thirty (30) days prior to the date of the scheduled hearing. In the event that the hearing results in a dismissal without merit, the Board shall have the discretion to refund the CFP Board designee's hearing fee; a CFP Board designee may specifically request that the Board consider refunding the hearing fee but such request must be made to the Hearing Panel in the CFP Board designee's Answer or at the hearing. A CFP Board designee who petitions for reinstatement from a suspension or revocation or who petitions for appeal shall bear the costs of such proceeding.

INDEX

E

F

G

H

I

J

L

M

N

O

P

Q

R

W

Insurance Planning

Outlines and Study Guides

TABLE OF CONTENTS

TABLE OF EXHIBITS

Insurance Planning

I. INTRODUCTION TO INSURANCE

A. Introduction to Insurance and Definition of Risk.

Insurance is a device for reducing risk by having a large pool of people share in the financial losses suffered by members of the pool. Another definition is the transference of risk to an insurance company.

B. The Various Definitions of Risk.

1. Risk is the chance of loss.
2. Risk is the possibility of loss.
3. Risk is uncertainty.
4. Risk is the variation of actual from expected results.
5. Risk is the probability of any outcome different from the one expected.
6. Risk is the expected variability of returns.

C. The Common Elements of Most Definitions of Risk.

1. The outcome is indeterminate.
2. There are at least two outcomes, and at least one of those is undesirable.

D. Usable Definition of Risk.

1. Risk is a condition where there is a possibility of an adverse deviation from an expected desired outcome.
2. Insurable risk is not subjective, but rather is a condition of the real world (objective).
3. The degree of risk may or may not be measurable.
4. The degree of risk is related to the likelihood of the occurrence.

E. Risk Distinguished from Peril, Hazard, and Loss.

1. Peril is the cause of a financial loss.
2. Hazard is a condition that increases the probability that a loss will occur.
3. Hazards are classified into three categories:
    a. Physical hazard - Physical characteristics of the person or property that increase the chance of loss (e.g., location of a house in a flood zone, high blood pressure).
    b. Moral hazard - The chance of loss from dishonesty (e.g., a person intentionally causes a loss or overstates the amount of the loss when a peril occurs).
    c. Morale hazard - Indifference to the loss (due to existence of insurance), which creates carelessness and increases the chance of loss (e.g., failure to take car keys or lock doors).
4. Loss is the disappearance or reduction in value (partially or completely).

F. CLASSIFICATION OF RISK.

1. Financial risk - The exposure to a risk that may cause financial loss.
2. Static and dynamic risks.
   a. Static risks are the losses that are caused by factors other than a change in the economy (e.g., natural disaster - earthquake/flood).
      i. Tend to occur with regularity.
      ii. Can be insured against.
   b. Dynamic risks are the result of the economy changing (e.g., changes in business cycle, inflation). Insurance does not cover these risks.
3. Fundamental and particular risk.
   a. Fundamental risk is impersonal and is usually a group risk (e.g., a recession or an earthquake).
   b. Particular risk is a personal and individual risk (e.g., a thief steals your car).
4. Pure and speculative risks.
   a. Pure risk involves only the chance of loss or no loss.
      i. Personal risk - Loss of income or asset resulting from the loss of ability to earn income through disability, death, or sickness.
      ii. Property risk - Direct or indirect loss from theft or destruction (e.g., fire or accident).
      iii. Liability risk - Intentional or unintentional injury to property or others (e.g., tort liability - loss of a civil suit).
      iv. Risk from the failure of others - Failure to meet or follow through on an obligation (e.g., breach of contract).
   b. Speculative risk involves both the chance of loss or gain (e.g., gambling). Speculative risk is not insurable.

G. MANAGING RISK.

1. Risk may be avoided if the person refuses to accept risk by not engaging in an action that creates a risk (removal of the peril - don't fly or drive).
2. Risk may be retained; therefore, no action is taken to avoid, transfer, or reduce risk. Risk may be voluntarily or involuntarily retained (failure to recognize exposure). Self insurance/coinsurance and use of deductibles are examples of ways in which risk is retained.
3. Risk may be transferred, either through an individual or a contract (insurance).
4. Risk may be shared (e.g., entity sharing using a limited partnership form/suborganization; health insurance with deductible and coinsurance – the small risks are borne by the insured).
5. Risk may be reduced through loss prevention methods and/or safety improvements (directed at reducing the frequency and the severity of the loss).
6. An example of risk reduction through loss prevention is incorporation, whereby the severity of the loss is limited to the investment in the corporation.

H. THE INSURANCE INSTRUMENT.

1. The nature and functions of insurance.

   a. Insurance deals with the transferring and sharing of risks to a group and sharing of losses by the members of such a group through increased premiums.

   b. Through the use of insurance, an individual gains protection against risk by substituting a small premium to insure against an unlikely but potentially catastrophic loss. If such a catastrophic loss were to occur, insurance would thereby reduce the probability of a major financial loss.

2. The following characteristics must be present to be considered an insurable risk:

   a. A large homogenous exposure to loss so as to adequately make a reasonable prediction of the loss.

   b. The loss must be measurable and definite (time, place, form, and monetarily measurable).

   c. The loss must be accidental (unexpected to the individual).

   d. The loss cannot be catastrophic to society (must be able to be spread).

3. Insurance seeks to avoid adverse selection. Adverse selection is the likelihood that parties with the greatest probability of loss are the ones who most desire the insurance (e.g., only persons with young children accept the orthodontic portion of dental insurance). Adverse selection also includes higher-risk persons seeking insurance coverage at standard rates.

I. RISK MANAGEMENT.

1. The nature of risk management.

   a. The objective of risk management is to choose efficiently among methods of handling risk so as to avoid catastrophic losses.

   b. Risk management is a scientific process that focuses on "pure risks" that can be identified and evaluated.

   c. Risk management includes, but is not limited to, insurance management. It manages both insurable and non-insurable risks.

   d. In risk management, insurance must be justified based on a cost/benefit analysis and only used as a last resort.

2. The risk management process has six distinct steps:

   a. Determine the objectives of the risk management program.

   b. Identify the risks to which the company is exposed.

   c. Evaluate the identified risks as to probability of occurrence and potential loss.

   d. Determine alternatives for managing risks and select the most appropriate alternative for each risk.

   e. Implement the alternative (program).

   f. Evaluate and review (control).

J. SOCIAL, PUBLIC, AND PRIVATE INSURANCE OVERVIEW.

1. Social insurance is mandatory insurance, of which benefits are determined by law. Social insurance seeks to protect individuals from large fundamental risks. Although administered by the government, it generally covers all individuals, not just government employees. Examples are:
   a. Old Age, Survivors, Disability, and Health Insurance (OASDHI).
   b. Medicare.
   c. Workers Compensation.
   d. Medicaid.
2. Public insurance seeks to enhance public trust in financial institutions. It is usually mandatory and government or quasi-government administered. Examples are:
   a. Federal Deposit Insurance Corporation (FDIC).
   b. Pension Benefit Guaranty Corporation (PBGC).
   c. Securities Investor Protection Corporation (SIPC).
3. Private insurance is voluntary insurance, of which benefits are related to premiums. Private insurance is protection against loss (marketed by private companies).
   a. Life insurance - protects against economic losses to survivor.
   b. Health insurance - protects against accidents and illness.
   c. Disability insurance - protects against loss of income.
   d. Property insurance - protects against theft and destruction.
   e. Liability insurance - protects against the negligence of the insured.

K. FINANCIAL PLANNING AND INSURANCE.

1. In general, financial planning attempts to minimize the impact of risks that could cause catastrophic loss through risk transfer or other risk management alternatives.
2. The risks usually addressed in personal financial planning include:
   a. Risks to the person.
      i. The risk of untimely death.
      ii. The risk of a shortened work life expectancy.
      iii. The risk of health-related problems, including long-term care.
   b. Risks to property.
      i. Home.
      ii. Automobile.
   c. Risks of liability due to negligence.
      i. Personal liability.
      ii. Professional liability.
3. Financial planning also has as an objective: the management of non-catastrophic risks utilizing cost benefit analysis (risk management).

II. THE LEGAL NATURE OF INSURANCE

A. GENERAL.

1. Insurance is dependent on law. The most applicable laws affecting insurance are the laws of agency, torts, and contracts.
2. Most insurance is sold by agents under an agency relationship, and all insurance is contractual.

B. INSURANCE AS A CONTRACT.

1. All insurance policies are contracts. An insurance policy is a contract derived from the general law of contracts. To be legally binding, an insurance contract must have the following five elements:
   a. Offer and acceptance.
      i. The offer must be unqualified and be accepted in the exact terms (contract of adhesion).
      ii. The contract (policy) does not have to be reduced to a written form to be binding, but most state insurance commissions require insurance contracts to be in writing.
      iii. Generally, the offeror is the insured. Generally, the acceptor is the insurance company.
   b. Consideration.
      i. The insurance contract requires the exchange of value to be legally binding.
      ii. The promise to pay the premium is usually sufficient consideration, for most insurance, to make the contract binding. However, for life insurance, the premium must be paid before the insurance contract is effective.
      iii. The submission of a completed insurance application (offer) plus the payment of the premium (consideration) to the insurance company will generally create a binding contract if the application would pass standard underwriting.
   c. Legal object - The subject of the insurance contract must be a legal business or for a legal purpose to make the contract enforceable. If the object of the contract is illegal, the contract is void.

Example

An illegal drug manufacturer cannot collect from an insurance policy written to cover business interruption. The contract of insurance is void because the object of the contract (illegal drug manufacture) is illegal.

   d. Competent parties - The individuals, groups, or businesses entering into the insurance contract must be capable of entering into a contract per the law (legal capacity). Minors and mentally incompetent people are not considered to have sufficient legal capacity to understand a contract; therefore, they are not bound by such contracts. If one of the parties is not competent, the contract is voidable by the incompetent party.
   e. Legal form - Although not required to be written, the form and content of insurance contracts are generally governed by state law; therefore, each contract must be filed and approved by a state regulatory agency before sales can proceed.
2. An insurance contract that lacks one of the five elements of a contract is an agreement that does not possess legal effect and cannot be enforced by either party.

Example

An insurance policy is written for a company that engages in counterfeiting (an illegal activity), and the premium for the policy is paid with counterfeit dollars the company made. The policy does not meet the five elements of a contract since the object of the contract was illegal and the consideration (counterfeit money) paid was of no value. Therefore, it is not enforceable by either party.

3. An insurance contract is a voidable contract, meaning that for reasons deemed satisfactory by a court, the contract can be set aside by one of the parties.

Example

If a 14-year-old minor purchases a life insurance contract on his own life, the contract is binding on the insurance company, but is voidable at the option of the insured until such time as the minor reaches the age of majority (unless excepted under state law).

C. TORT LIABILITY APPLIED TO INSURANCE (LIABILITY INSURANCE).

1. Acts or failures to act may cause liability or lawsuits against an individual or entity for real or imagined damage to persons or property.
2. Criminal acts (public wrongs) - Acts which are prosecuted by the state and are punishable by fine, imprisonment, or death. Insurance does not generally cover such liability. An umbrella policy may provide some coverage to specific wrongs.
3. Tort (private wrongs) - An infringement on the rights of another. The wrongdoer is a tortfeasor and creates a right in the damaged party to bring a civil action.
    a. Intentional torts - Battery (harmful touching), assault (threat causing apprehension), libel (written falsehood), slander (oral falsehood), false imprisonment (unlawfully holding against will), trespass to land, invasion of privacy, and intentional infliction of emotional distress. Most intentional torts are not covered by liability insurance.
    b. Unintentional torts (negligence) - An act or failure to act in a reasonably prudent manner, and such act or failure to act causes harm to another. Elements - duty, breach of duty, causation, and actual loss. Did the person exercise the proper degree of care to carry out his or her duty, and if not, was that the cause of the actual loss suffered by the other party? If so, the actor may be liable for negligence.
    c. Persons who may be liable other than normal adults.
        i. Children and minors may be liable depending on their mental capacity. Their parents or guardians may be vicariously liable for the acts of such persons.
        ii. Mental incompetents may, nonetheless, be required to exercise some duty of care, and if that level of care is not exercised, such incompetents may be liable.
        iii. Employers may be vicariously liable for the acts of employees.

d. Standards of care.

   i. Negligence - The failure to act in a way that a reasonably prudent person would have acted under the circumstances--in short, imprudent behavior.

   ii. Strict liability - Liability for damage resulting from some extraordinarily dangerous activity or other statutorily defined activities (e.g., product liability). Negligence does not have to be proved; however, defenses may be allowed to refute or lessen liability.

   iii. Absolute liability - Liability without regard to negligence or fault. Negligence does not have to be proved nor are defenses permitted to refute or lessen liability. Workers are indemnified for injuries regardless of who was at fault (example - workers compensation).

   iv. Negligence per se - The act itself constitutes negligence, thereby relieving the burden to prove negligence (drunk driving).

e. Burden of proof is initially borne by the injured party.

f. Standard of proof in most civil cases is the preponderance of the evidence (more than 50%).

g. Other concepts to consider include *res ipsa loquitur* ("The thing speaks for itself"). *Res ipsa loquitur* is a doctrine of the law of negligence that is concerned with the circumstances and the types of accidents, which afford reasonable evidence if a specific explanation of negligence is not available (e.g., a plane crash).

h. Damages.

   i. A tort can result in two forms of injury - bodily injury and property damage.

      A) Bodily injury may lead to medical expense, loss of income, pain and suffering, mental anguish, and loss of consortium.

      B) The damages for bodily injury can be:

         1) Special damages to compensate for measurable losses.

         2) General damages to compensate for intangible losses (pain and suffering).

         3) Punitive damages - amounts assessed against the negligent party as punishment.

      C) See the income tax planning section for a discussion of the taxation of damages.

      D) Property damage is usually measured by the actual monetary loss.

   ii. The collateral source rule holds that damages assessed against a negligent party should not be reduced simply because the injured party has other sources of recovery available such as insurance or employee benefits (health or disability insurance).

i. Vicarious liability - One person may become legally liable for the torts of another (e.g., parent/child, employer/employee acting in the scope of employment).

j. Joint and several liability - Negligence caused by two or more parties. Each party may be held fully liable. Obviously, any party paying more than its legal share can seek contribution from the other joint tortfeasors who have not paid their proportional share.

k. Defenses to negligence - There are various defenses available to alleged negligent parties that can relieve them of legal liability in spite of negligent behavior.

   i. Assumption of the risk - The injured party fully understood and recognized the dangers that were involved in an activity and voluntarily chose to proceed. This defense is not available in all states.

   ii. Negligence on the part of the injured party - This can be either contributory negligence, where there is evidence that the injured party did not look out for his own safety, or comparative negligence, where the amount of damage is adjusted to reflect the injured party's proportion of contribution to the cause of the injury (same with multiple defendants).

   iii. Contributory negligence theories usually cause the entire action to fail, thus effecting a harsh result.

   iv. Many states allow recovery for that portion of damage not caused by the injured party (comparative negligence).

   v. Last clear chance rule – A plaintiff who is endangered by his own negligence may, however, recover if the defendant had a last clear chance to avoid the accident and failed to do so.

   vi. Survival of tort actions - If the person who committed the injury dies, the action also dies, but there may be a claim against the estate. If the injured party dies, the tort survives in the estate of the injured party.

   vii. Bankruptcy will discharge a tort liability unless the liability is from a willful and malicious tort (or drunk driving).

D. THE LAW OF AGENCY - APPLIED TO INSURANCE.

1. An agent can legally bind a principal if the agent is within the scope of his authority. In the case of insurance, acts of an agent are deemed to be acts of the insurer.

2. The binding may be a result of express, implied, and sometimes, apparent authority.

   a. Express authority - The actual authority that an insurance company gives its representatives (agents). It may be in writing (i.e., agency agreement). The insurance company is responsible for the acts of its agents per the express authority.

   b. Implied authority - The authority that the public reasonably perceives the agent to possess, even without express authority. If implied authority exists, an insurer will be liable for the acts of its agent even if the agent knowingly or unknowingly misleads the insured.

   c. Apparent authority - When the agent leads or the insured is led to believe that the agent has authority, either express or implied, where no such authority actually exists. The insured is unaware that the agent has exceeded expressed or implied authority, and the insurer makes no attempt to stop the agent (a notice issue) from acting. Apparent authority may bind the insurer.

3. Nature of agency.

   a. By using a representative or agent, one person may conduct multiple business operations.

   b. A corporation can function by using agents exclusively.

4. Agency distinguished from other relationships.
   a. Principal--agent relationship.
      i. An agent acts on behalf of and instead of a principal in engaging in business transactions.
      ii. An agent may bind his or her principal in contract with a third person.
      iii. An agent has a degree of independent discretion.
   b. Employer (master) - employee (servant) relationship.
      i. In order to determine if a relationship is one of employment, examine the surrounding circumstances.
         A) The employer controls or has the right to control the employee in the performance of physical tasks.
         B) Employees have little or no independent discretion.
         C) Employees are paid for time rather than results.
      ii. The rights and duties of an employee differ from those of an agent. The distinction is important for purposes of applicability of legislation such as income tax, Social Security taxes, unemployment, workplace safety, and workers compensation statutes.
   c. Independent contractor.
      i. An independent contractor engages to bring about some specified result and is normally paid at the completion of performance.
      ii. The person employing an independent contractor does not exercise control over the details of the performance.
      iii. An independent contractor cannot bind the person employing him in a contract with a third party.
      iv. An independent contractor usually uses his own material, equipment, and employees.
      v. An independent contractor markets to the general public.
5. The formation of an agency relationship.
   a. In general.
      i. An agency may be formed for any legal purpose.
      ii. An agency is a consensual relationship but not necessarily a contractual one. Consideration need not be given by a principal.
      iii. Generally, no special formalities are required in order to create an agency.
         A) Unless required by the Statute of Frauds or other statute, a written document is not necessary.
         B) If the appointment of an agent is in writing, the writing is called a power of attorney.

iv. Capacity.

A) A principal must have legal (contractual) capacity because contracts, entered into by his or her agent, are treated as contracts of the principal. If a principal lacks capacity, such contracts are voidable by the principal but not the third party.

B) An agent need not have legal (contractual) capacity in order to act as agent, but the contract of agency may be voided by the agent who lacks capacity (but not the principal).

b. Agency created by agreement.

i. The agent and principal affirmatively indicate that they consent to the formation of the agency.

ii. The agreement may be express or implied from the conduct of the parties.

c. Agency may be created by ratification.

i. Ratification occurs after the principal's consent to the agency is given after the purported agent acts on behalf of the principal.

ii. Ratification may be either expressed or implied.

iii. Ratification relates back to the time that the agent acted without authorization.

d. Agency may be created by estoppel.

i. A principal may be estopped to deny the existence of an agency if the principal caused a third party to reasonably believe that a person was his agent because there was an appearance that an agency relationship existed (apparent authority).

6. Agent's duties to principal.

a. Duty to perform - An agent is required to follow instructions, use reasonable skill and diligence in carrying out agency obligations, and use special skills that the agent possesses, if applicable.

b. Duty to notify - An agent is required to notify the principal of material information that relates to the subject matter of the agency.

c. Duty of loyalty.

i. An agent may not compete with his principal or act for another principal unless full disclosure is made to the principal and the principal consents.

ii. After termination of an agency, the agent may not disclose trade secrets, confidential information (customer lists, etc., acquired in the course of the agent's employment).

iii. Conflicts of interest - Any secret profits or benefits received by an agent acting adversely to his principal belong to the principal who may recover them from the agent.

d. Duty to account - An agent must account to his or her principal for any monies or property rightfully belonging to the principal that have come into the agent's hands. An agent should not commingle such property with his or her own property or that of others.

e. Remedies available to principal for breach of duties by agent.

   i. Principal's right to indemnification - If a principal is required to pay damages to an injured party for an agent's tortious conduct or, as a result of an agent's violation of the principal's instructions, incurs a loss, the principal may recover the amount of resulting damages from the agent.

   ii. A principal may seek remedies based, in contract, upon breach of contractual duties, or in tort based upon a breach of the fiduciary duty.

   iii. Transactions engaged in by an agent, which violate the fiduciary duty, are voidable by the principal.

   iv. A court will impose a constructive trust on property received by an agent who has used his or her agency position in conflict with those of his principal so that the property (or the proceeds of its sale) is treated as held for the benefit of the principal.

7. Principal's duties to agent.

   a. A principal has an obligation to perform in accordance with his contract with an agent.

   b. A principal has a duty to compensate, indemnify, and reimburse an agent.

      i. A principal is required to pay any agreed compensation to the agent.

      ii. If no compensation is specified, a principal is required to pay expenses, losses, and reasonable compensation for services rendered by the agent unless the agency is a gratuitous one or there are circumstances, such as a family relationship, indicating that compensation had not been intended.

      iii. There is no duty to pay compensation to an agent who has failed to perform his or her duties.

   c. A principal has a duty of cooperation. A principal is required to assist an agent in performing the agent's duties and to do nothing to prevent such performance.

   d. A principal has a duty to provide safe working conditions.

   e. There are remedies available to an agent for breach of duties by a principal.

      i. Indemnification - A principal may be required to indemnify an agent for payments or liabilities incurred in executing the agent's obligations and for losses caused by the failure of the principal to perform the principal's duties.

      ii. An agent may obtain a lien against the principal's property.

      iii. An agent may sue for breach of contract or counterclaim if sued by his or her principal.

      iv. An agent may bring an action for an accounting.

      v. An agent may withhold further performance.

8. Termination of agency relationship.

   a. Termination by act of the parties.

      i. Lapse of time.

         A) Agency expires at the end of a specified time if a term is stated.

         B) Agency terminates after the expiration of a reasonable period of time if no term has been specified.

ii. Purpose accomplished.

Agency is terminated when the objective for which it was created has been achieved.

iii. Occurrence of specific event.

An agency ends upon the happening of a particular event, if its formation had been so conditioned.

iv. Mutual agreement.

The parties may mutually consent to the termination of an agency.

v. Termination by one party.

A) A principal may revoke the authority of an agent, or an agent may renounce the appointment as an agent.

B) Either party may have the power, but not necessarily the right, to terminate an agency.

1) If an agency is an agency at will (not for a stated term or for a particular purpose), either party has the power and the right to terminate the agency.

2) If an agency is not an agency at will, a party may not have the power or the right to terminate the agency and is, therefore, liable to the other party for the wrongful termination, which is a breach of contract.

C) An agency may be terminated for cause.

D) A principal has neither the power nor the right to terminate an agency coupled with an interest (which is also referred to as a power coupled with an interest or a power given as security).

1) The agency is said to be irrevocable.

2) The agency differs from situations in which an agent merely derives proceeds or profits from transactions.

b. Termination by operation of law.

i. Death or insanity terminates an agency.

A) Knowledge of the death or insanity is not required.

B) An agency coupled with an interest is not automatically terminated.

C) Statutory exceptions exist.

ii. Bankruptcy of the principal terminates the agency.

A) Insolvency does not terminate the relationship.

B) Bankruptcy of the agent does not necessarily terminate the agency relationship.

iii. Impossibility.

A) Destruction of the subject matter of the agency.

B) Outbreak of war.

C) Change in law making further conduct of the agency illegal.

iv. Unforeseen change in circumstances.

c. Notice required for termination.

i. If termination is by act of a party, the agency continues between the principal and agent until notice is given by the principal who is revoking or the agent who is renouncing authority.

ii. Notice must be given to third persons.

A) Actual notice must be given to third persons who have dealt with the agent.

B) Constructive notice must be given by publication in a newspaper, posting of a sign, etc., to those who knew of the agency.

iii. The party terminating the agency or another person may give the notice.

iv. Notice generally is not required if the agency is terminated by operation of law.

E. UNIQUE LEGAL CHARACTERISTICS OF INSURANCE CONTRACTS.

1. An insurance contract is one that requires indemnity (recovery of actual damages) to which the insured is entitled from the insurance company to the extent of the actual financial loss incurred. The indemnity principle is enforced through the following factors:

a. There must be an insurable interest. An insurable interest is a relationship where the person applying for the insurance has an expectation of benefits from the continuation of the subject of the insurance and will incur a loss from the destruction, damage, or death of the insured subject.

i. An insurable interest in property is created through a pecuniary relationship, such as ownership of property, or through holding a lien on collateralized property. However, to be valid for property, the insurable interest must exist both at issuance and at the time of the loss.

Example

If the insured owns a car and the car is destroyed, the insured will suffer a financial loss.

ii. An insurable interest must also exist for life insurance policies, but is based on sentimental interest as well as the risk of financial loss. The insurable interest must exist at the inception of the life insurance contract, but is not required at the time of loss (death).

Example

A family relationship, such as husband and wife, constitutes an insurable interest. In a business, the death of a partner may give rise to financial loss; therefore, an insurable interest exists between or among the partners to protect against the risk of financial loss from the death of such partners.

b. Actual cash value (ACV). The amount that can be recovered from a loss is the actual cash value of the loss, regardless of the amount of insurance purchased. This principle (indemnity) limits over-insurance and willful destruction of property. Life insurance policies are the exception to the indemnity principle, with the recovery amount being the face of the policy, not the actual value of the life insured. The underwriting process attempts to mitigate the risk of moral hazard (excessive insurance) in life insurance.

c. Other types of insurance contracts rather than cash value include:

   i. A valued policy sets an agreed value of the property at the inception of the contract. At the loss, the insurer must pay the face amount of the policy (not necessarily the actual cash value of the loss).

   ii. A cash payment policy is an agreement to pay a face amount of the policy in the event of death (life insurance).

   iii. Other insurance - Most insurance contracts prevent an insured from collecting more than ACV under two policies for the same loss. The exceptions are life and health insurance.

      A) The pro rata clause stating that each insurance company shares its proportion of the loss prevents an insured from profiting as a result of duplicate insurance.

      B) Exculpatory clauses identify specific articles that are covered by other insurance as being exempt from liability.

      C) Subrogation clause prevents profiting from insurance by granting the right to the insured's insurance company to collect from a negligent third party who caused the loss and for which an amount was paid to the insured.

2. The insurance contract is a personal contract in that it is owned generally by the insured entitling the insured to benefits or proceeds.

   a. Insurance contracts cannot be transferred (assigned) to another person without the written consent of the insurance company. This protects the insurance company from accepting as an insured risk a person or property that does not meet its underwriting standards. For example, if an insured sells his house, the homeowners policy will not transfer to the new owner. Life insurance is the exception and may be transferred to anyone without the consent of the insurer since the underlying risk does not change.

   b. The proceeds from any insurance policy may be assigned without the consent of the insurer.

3. An insurance contract is a contract of adhesion, meaning the insurance company prepares the entire contract. The insured can accept or reject the contract, but the insured cannot modify, alter, or negotiate the contract.

   a. Because the insurance company drafts the entire contract, any ambiguity in the contract will be decided in favor of the insured.

   b. The presumption of intent doctrine is important in an insurance contract. Courts assume that the insured has read the contract and agrees to its terms.

4. The insurance contract is a contract of the utmost good faith. The contract may be influenced by:

   a. Misrepresentation - An oral or written statement made by the applicant prior to, or simultaneously with, the formation of the contract that is false and is intended to defraud.

      i. It must be a material fact to render the contract voidable.

      ii. A material fact is one that would have caused the insurance company to not write the contract or to change the terms of the contract.

   b. Warranties - Promises made by the insured that are set forth in the policy. A breach of warranty may give grounds to void the policy and may do so without references to materiality. (Most statements in applications are representations not warranties.)

c. The failure to disclose material facts concerning the subject matter is concealment. Willful concealment of material facts is grounds for voiding the contract by the insurance company (e.g., previous heart attack).

d. Waiver is the intentional relinquishment of a known right by the insured.

e. Estoppel - prevents denying a fact that was previously admitted.

5. The insurance contract is a unilateral contract - only the insurer promises to do anything (i.e., no promise by the insured to pay the premium).

6. The insurance contract is a conditional contract; therefore, the payment of benefits by the insurance company is conditioned upon the insured paying the premium. The insurance company is the offeree. The insured is the offeror.

7. The insurance contract is an aleatory contract. If no loss occurs, the insurer will pay nothing. Alternatively, the insurer may, if a loss occurs, pay more than the premiums that it has collected. (The outcome is affected by chance, dollars collected by parties to the contract may be unequal).

EXHIBIT 1: SUMMARY OF UNIQUE CHARACTERISTICS OF INSURANCE CONTRACTS

- Contract of indemnity (only indemnified for actual loss).
- Personal contract (not transferable).
- Contract of adhesion (take it or leave it).
- Contract of utmost good faith.
- Unilateral contract (only one promise).
- Conditional (premium must be paid).
- Aleatory contract (outcome affected by chance, dollars collected may not be equal).

III. LIFE INSURANCE IN GENERAL

A. DESCRIPTION OF THE RISK.

1. The risk of untimely death of an income-earning individual is insured against with life insurance. There are four perils that affect the risk of loss of income-earning ability of an individual:
    a. Death.
    b. Disability.
    c. Unemployment.
    d. Superannuation (outliving income and accumulated assets).
2. An individual faces two mutually exclusive risks centering around the uncertainty of death:
    a. Premature death occurs at a point when others remain dependent on the individual's income.
    b. Superannuation.

B. FINANCIAL RISKS OF PREMATURE DEATH.

1. The expenses directly related to death, which include last medical expenses, funeral costs, and payment of outstanding debts and taxes, plus any adjustment period expenses.
2. The loss of income that could have been earned by the decedent if such decedent had lived.
3. Evaluation of risks associated with premature death:
    a. Who is financially affected by the death as a result of loss of income?
    b. Can those affected replace the lost income?
    c. If lost income cannot be replaced by other means, will adequate life insurance prevent a decline in the standard of living for the dependent's survivors?

C. CHARACTERISTICS OF LIFE INSURANCE.

1. Since a precise actual value cannot be determined for a human life, it is not possible to place the survivor in the exact financial position as before the loss. Therefore, life insurance is a modified indemnity contract rather than a pure contract of indemnity.
2. An insurable interest must exist at the inception of the policy.
3. The consent of the individual being insured is required if the insured is not the owner of the policy.

D. LIFE INSURANCE IS A CONTRACT.

1. Consideration, offer, and acceptance of the insurance contract.

    a. The payment of the premium, accompanied by the application, constitutes the consideration and offer from the insured to the insurer. The insurance company accepts first by conditional receipt and later by issuance of the policy.

    b. Acknowledgment of the receipt of the premium by the insurance company is made through a conditional binding receipt (relates back to date of application if applicant is determined to be insurable).

        i. The contract is effective as of the date of application, provided the applicant is insurable as determined by the insurance company underwriters.

        ii. In the event of death of an insurable applicant during the time of the binder, the insurance company must pay the benefits.

2. General provisions of all life insurance policies.

    a. There are no standard life insurance contracts; however, the final drafting of an insurance contract must be approved by the state commissioner of insurance in each state where the policy will be sold.

    b. In most states, the policy along with the attached application represents the entire contract between the insurance company and the insured.

        i. All statements in the application are considered to be representations and not warranties. If the statements are representations, the insurer will bear the burden of proving the materiality of any misrepresentation by the applicant. Alternatively, if statements are warranties, materiality will not be an issue because a warranty is a promise and may provide grounds for voiding the policy. A warranty need not be material to void a policy.

    c. A life insurance policy is property and may be owned at the inception by the insured, the beneficiary of the policy, or any other person with an insurable interest.

        i. The owner of the life insurance policy may assign or transfer the policy (usually without the approval of the insurer).

        ii. The owner may receive the cash value or dividends.

        iii. The owner may borrow against the policy if permitted.

    d. The person to whom the proceeds are payable is called the beneficiary. Beneficiaries may be primary or contingent, revocable or irrevocable.

        i. A primary beneficiary is the first person or party (could be the estate) entitled to the proceeds from the policy if death occurs.

        ii. A contingent beneficiary (secondary beneficiary) is a second person or party named to receive the proceeds should the primary beneficiary die before the insured.

        iii. A revocable beneficiary (normal) is one where the owner of the policy reserves the right to change the beneficiary designation at any time.

        iv. An irrevocable beneficiary is one where the policyowner has a restriction on the ability to change the beneficiary. The effect of naming an irrevocable beneficiary is that the policy becomes joint property with rights to both the owner and the irrevocable beneficiary. The owner can no longer borrow from the policy, etc., without the consent of the joint property owner (the irrevocable beneficiary).

v. Beneficiary designations.

A) Individuals (could be persons or entities, but at the inception the beneficiary must have had a sentimental or financial insurable interest, or the policy would not have been issued).

B) Trusts.

C) The estate of the insured (if so, the proceeds go through probate).

D) Minors (usually creates problems regarding legal capacity and judgment).

E) Charitable organizations.

vi. Beneficiaries should be clearly identified, avoiding the possibility of ambiguity (e.g., "my wife," when the owner has been married more than once, should be listed as Mary S. Black, residing at XYZ).

vii. All persons or entities will share equally if they are in the same category (primary or contingent) unless the beneficiary designation clearly indicates to the contrary (e.g., Tom and Karen, therefore 50/50. If what is desired is Tom 60% and Karen 40%, it must be stated unambiguously).

e. The incontestable clause of a life insurance contract is an unusual feature in that it states the policy is incontestable by the insurer after being in force for a period of generally two years. In some states, it may be only one year.

f. If an insured misstates his or her age at the time of application, the insurance company has the right to adjust the amount of the insurance that the premium paid would have purchased at the insured's correct age.

Example

Ms. Martin is 40 years old, but her youthful looks allow her to claim her age as 35. She has applied for a life insurance policy that has a premium of $25 per $1,000 for age 40 and $15 per $1,000 for age 35. On the application, Ms. Martin stated her age as 35 and purchased a $20,000 life insurance policy paying an annual premium of $300. Ms. Martin dies at the age of 41. The amount of the benefits to be paid to the beneficiary, assuming the insurance company discovers Ms. Martin misstated her age on the application is $12,000. The insurance company will adjust the face amount of the policy to reflect the amount of insurance that would have been purchased for the premiums that were actually paid, assuming the correct age.

Total premium paid	$300
Premium per $1,000 of insurance for insured (age 40)	$25
Face amount of policy [($300 ÷ 25) x $1,000]	$12,000

Note: The beneficiary will receive $12,000, not $20,000. The insurer probably discovered the correct age on the death certificate

---

g. All life insurance policies have a grace period of 31 days from the premium due date before the contract can lapse.

   i. The insured has 31 days from the due date to pay the premium in order to continue the policy as active.

   ii. If the insured dies during the grace period, the amount of premium due will be withheld from the benefits that are to be paid.

h. Most life insurance contracts permit reinstatement of a policy that has lapsed. However, the following conditions are common requirements by insurance companies before reinstatement:

   i. The lapse period cannot exceed three to five years as defined in the contract.

   ii. The policy has not been surrendered for the cash value.

   iii. Evidence of insurability of the insured, acceptable to the insurance company, is provided (proof of insurability).

   iv. All premiums due from the time of the lapse with interest must be paid.

   v. Any indebtedness must be repaid.

i. Generally, if the insured commits suicide within the first two years of the policy, the insurance company must only repay as benefits the premiums (without interest) that were paid on the policy. Some policies only have a one-year suicide clause.

   i. After the stipulated period (two years), suicide is considered the same as any other death, and full benefits are payable.

Example

Mr. Sanders bought a $250,000 whole life, double indemnity policy on August 1, 2002 (premiums were $200 per month). On September 30, 2003, Mr. Sanders committed suicide. The benefits payable to Mr. Sanders' beneficiary assuming the premiums were paid as agreed was $2,800*. The two-year suicide clause will prevent the payment of the face amount of the policy. However, the premiums paid through the date of the suicide will usually be returned without interest.

*(14 months x $200 = $2,800)

---

j. Most life insurance contracts contain a provision that allows a return of premiums plus interest as benefits if the insured is killed as a result of war (provided war is an exclusion).

3. Settlement options.

   a. Lump-sum option - The death benefit is paid in total at settlement.

   b. Interest option - The principal of the policy remains invested with the insurance company to be paid at a later date, and the interest earned on the principal is paid to the designated beneficiary.

   c. Fixed period installments option - The proceeds (principal and interest) are paid over a specified period or term.

   d. Fixed amount installments option - The proceeds are paid at a set dollar amount per month until all of the principal and interest are exhausted.

e. Life income options - Benefits are paid as an annuity.

   i. Single life annuity option - The beneficiary receives a specified amount for life and nothing more (this has the highest periodic payment of life income options).

   ii. Life annuity with term certain option - The beneficiary is paid a specified amount for life, but the payments are guaranteed for a certain number of periods. In the event of the beneficiary's death before the specified period ends, the payments continue through the term to the beneficiary's estate or to a contingent beneficiary.

   iii. Life annuity with refund option - The beneficiary is paid income for life. If the proceeds have not been exhausted at the time of the beneficiary's death, the remainder is paid to the contingent beneficiary.

   iv. Joint and survivor annuity option - Provides payment to two payees. At the death of the first payee, the payment may or may not be decreased to the second payee but will cease on the death of the second payee unless originally set up as a period-certain payoff.

f. When a beneficiary is paid in installments, the interest portion of the benefits is taxable as interest income, but the principal portion is not taxable (return of basis).

4. Other common provisions in life insurance policies.

   a. Loan provision.

      i. The insured may obtain a loan from the insurance company (usually equal to the cash surrender value) using the policy as collateral.

      ii. Automatic premium loan provision provides for the premium to be automatically charged against the cash value if not paid by the insured on the due date.

         A) Charges against cash value for premium payments are considered to be loans, and interest will be charged.

         B) Loans against cash value for premiums may continue as long as the cash value is sufficient to pay them (then the policy lapses).

         C) Outstanding loans reduce the death benefit payable at the time of death.

   b. Dividend provision.

      i. Dividends paid on participating policies represent the favorable difference between premiums paid and the actual cost of the policy based on the insurance company's mortality experience.

      ii. Dividends may be paid in cash, applied as payment to or reduction of premiums, used to purchase additional paid-up insurance, used to purchase one year term, or left with the insurance company to accumulate interest.

      iii. Dividends are not considered taxable income until distributed. A mutual company is owned by the policyholders, thus dividends received by mutual company policyholders are first considered a return of capital before being considered taxable income.

c. Nonforfeiture provisions.

i. The amount of cash value a life insurance policy has accumulated over a period of time (applies only to policies with a cash value).

ii. When an insured discontinues premium payments in a cash value policy, the insured is entitled to the cash value, or surrender value if less.

iii. The standard nonforfeiture clause requires the cash surrender value to be made available in cash to the owner. However, the insurance company may delay payment for a period of up to six months after surrender of the policy.

A) When an insured surrenders a policy for its cash value, the insurance contract is terminated.

B) At the time of surrender, excess cash received over the net paid premiums is considered income and is taxable to the insured.

iv. Instead of obtaining a complete termination through surrender in cash, an insured may elect to receive a reduced amount of paid-up insurance equivalent to what the cash value could purchase as a net single premium.

v. An insured may choose to surrender a cash value policy for a paid-up term insurance policy.

A) The term insurance is for the face amount of the original policy.

B) The period of the term insurance is determined by the net single premium the cash value can purchase.

5. Optional provisions.

a. A renewable term life policy contains a contractual provision that guarantees the renewal of the policy for a limited number of periods.

i. This option does not guarantee that the premium will not increase for the renewable term.

ii. An age limit is usually imposed, at or after which the policy is no longer renewable.

b. A conversion provision of term life insurance allows the insured to exchange the term policy for a permanent policy without evidence of insurability.

i. Conversion can take place even if the insured has become uninsurable.

ii. Most convertible policies have a time limit within which the conversion can take place.

c. A disability waiver of premium provision provides that the insurance company agrees to waive all premiums due on the policy should the insured become totally and permanently disabled.

i. The life insurance contract continues with the insurer paying the premiums during the period of disability.

ii. Cash value continues to increase and dividends will continue to be paid to the insured.

iii. Waiver of premium for disability is not an indemnity benefit nor is it incontestable.

iv. Waiver of premium provisions exclude self-inflicted disabilities that are results of war or occur during violation of laws.

d. The accidental death benefit provision is commonly known as double indemnity. The proceeds that are paid as a result of an accident-related death are twice the face amount of the life insurance policy.

   i. Death must occur within 90 days of the accident to qualify.

   ii. The cause of death must be related to the accident.

   iii. Accidental death benefits are usually subject to an age limit.

   iv. Accidental death benefits exclude suicide, death from disease, and acts of war.

e. A guaranteed insurability option permits the insured to purchase additional insurance at specific intervals without providing evidence of insurability.

   i. This option is generally applicable to permanent types of insurance.

   ii. The intervals for purchase are commonly every three years.

   iii. The age limitation is usually 40.

   iv. The purchase amount is usually limited to the face value of the original policy but can be less.

   v. Liberal insurance policies allow waiver of premium to accompany any insurance purchased through the guaranteed insurability option.

f. The common disaster clause stipulates that settlement of the policy is withheld for a specified (usually 30) number of days after the death of the insured. Furthermore, any surviving beneficiary that dies within this period is considered to have predeceased the insured.

g. A spendthrift clause provides protection against the beneficiary's dissipation of the policy proceeds by denying the beneficiary the right to convey, alienate, or assign his or her interest in the policy proceeds.

   i. Provides protection against creditors of the beneficiary.

   ii. Protects the proceeds only while the insurance company is holding them (not when in the hands of the beneficiary).

h. A cost of living rider offers additional insurance to the insured as inflation protection (usually indexed to CPI).

E. ACTUARIAL BASIS OF LIFE INSURANCE.

1. Life insurance premium computation - There are three elements in the computation of life insurance premiums: mortality, interest, and loading.

   a. Since the insurance company is assuming the risk of the individual's life, it is important that the company knows how many people are expected to die at each age; therefore, they use mortality tables. Large companies use their own experience to construct mortality tables to use in pricing. The computation of life insurance premiums is arithmetic once the mortality table is constructed or selected.

   b. The insurance company collects premiums in advance for payment of benefits at a future date and invests the excess to offset future premiums. Due to the advanced collection and interest, the present value concept must be applied to premiums to evaluate any policy.

c. There are net single premiums and level premiums for life insurance.

   i. A net single premium is a lump-sum payment at the date of issue of the policy that will pay the benefits of the policy as they come due.

   ii. A level premium is based on the net single premium converted into a series of annual payments utilizing the annuity due concept to age 100.

   iii. Level premiums may also be for a period shorter than full life expectancy duration (20-year pay).

2. Reserves on life insurance policies - Through level premiums, the insured pays more than the cost of protection in the early years of the contract, thus establishing a reserve.

   a. The reserve represents the prepayment of future premiums and the cash value of the insurance policy.

   b. The reserve equals the present value of future benefits minus the present value of future premiums.

3. Benefit certain and benefit uncertain contracts.

   a. Benefit certain contracts - If the insured is persistent in paying the premiums, the policy will eventually mature, and the benefits will be payable to the insured (age 100 for permanent insurance).

   b. Benefit uncertain contracts - If the insured is persistent in premium payments for the entire policy period, the insurer may or may not be obligated to make payments (e.g., term life insurance).

4. Premium calculation.

   a. The net level premium includes mortality and interest costs only and, therefore, assumes no expenses or profit to the insurer.

   b. The gross premium is the net premium plus a loading for the insurer's expenses and profitability.

5. Types of mortality tables used by the insurer.

   a. There are two different types of mortality tables:

      i. A valuation table is used to calculate cash surrender values and minimum reserves (balance sheet liabilities).

      ii. A basic table is used to calculate gross premiums and is reflective of the actual experience of the insured's population.

   b. Select, ultimate, and aggregate tables.

      i. A select table is based on newly insured lives (recently passed underwriting requirements, used in nonguaranteed element calculations).

      ii. An ultimate table excludes the mortality experience of the first 5, 10, or 15 years to eliminate the selection bias (used in calculation of premiums).

      iii. An aggregate table includes both select and ultimate mortality experience.

IV. TYPES OF LIFE INSURANCE

A. TERM LIFE INSURANCE.

1. Characteristics and description.

   a. Pure insurance protection that pays a predetermined sum if the insured dies during a specified period of time (e.g., the term, which may be 1, 5, 10, 20 years or longer).

   b. The protection ceases at the end of the term unless renewed.

   c. The premium pattern may be level or increasing on an annual or set period basis (e.g., five-year renewable term).

   d. The face amount may be level, decreasing, or increasing (e.g., there may be a cost of living provision that increases the face).

   e. There is generally no cash value, savings, or investment component.

   f. Term insurance is very inexpensive at young ages (substantially less than whole life).

   g. Provisions generally associated with term insurance:

      i. Renewable - Most term policies can be renewed without evidence of insurability (usually limited to age 70). Premiums increase exponentially as the insured ages.

      ii. Convertible - Most term policies have a provision to convert to a permanent insurance product without evidence of insurability for a particular period (may be less than the full term). Generally, the premium for the new convertible policy is the existing policy's rating for the age at conversion.

      iii. Waiver of Premium - If the insured becomes totally disabled, the premiums are waived during the period of disability.

   h. Term insurance allows for the transfer of mortality risk.

   i. Term insurance essentially states, "If you pay *x*, we will pay *y* if you die during the term."

2. Types of term insurance.

   a. Annual renewable term - level face, exponentially increasing premiums.

   b. Level term (3, 5, 7, 10, 15, 20, 30 year) - level face, premiums remain fixed for the term selected.

   c. Term to age 65 or 70. Exponentially increasing premiums.

   d. Decreasing term - level premiums, decreasing face (e.g., reverse exponential).

3. Applications.

   a. An excellent choice for a temporary insurance need.

   b. An excellent choice for a large death benefit with low cost.

   c. Cash flow driven.

4. Limitations.
    a. Exponentially increasing premiums for older age entry or renewal cause many policies to lapse.
    b. Most term policies lapse without collection of the death benefit by the insured.
    c. No savings component.
    d. May not meet permanent insurance needs.

B. ENDOWMENT LIFE INSURANCE (PURE AND REGULAR).

1. Pure endowment policies pay the face of the policy only if the insured survives the endowment period (not sold in U.S.).
2. Regular endowment policies pay the face of the policy if the insured dies within the endowment period or pay the face (usually in the form of an annuity) if the insured survives beyond the endowment period (e.g., a combination of death benefit and annuity).
3. The regular endowment policy combines term insurance with a savings component.

C. WHOLE LIFE INSURANCE POLICIES.

1. General characteristics and description.
    a. Whole life policy provides lifetime protection if the premiums are paid as agreed.
    b. All whole life policies prefund future higher mortality costs using present value analysis.
    c. Premium patterns may vary widely from a variety of level premiums to increasing premiums.
    d. Whole life policies have a savings or investment component with earnings accruing on the residual of the premium less the mortality and expense cost for the year plus any previous savings balance.
    e. Cash values may be used for loans or may be received if the policy is surrendered.
    f. Cash values usually have a minimum guaranteed rate of interest.
    g. Whole life policies may be participating (participating in the surplus or returns resulting from a block of policies) or non-participating (usually with a minimum guaranteed).
2. Types of whole life policies.
    a. Whole or ordinary life - Premiums are level for life; the face amount of insurance remains constant for life. (Premiums are paid to age 100, if still living.)
    b. Limited pay life - Premiums are level for a specific term; the face amount of insurance remains constant for life.
    c. Current assumption whole life (CAWL) - An interest-sensitive policy in which current investment experience (usually related to current interest rates) under non-participating policies is credited to cash values. Investment credits may be applied to particular groupings of policies depending on when they were issued as opposed to being applied to all policies that an insurer has. In effect, this is a pooling of policies by an insurer where each group has its own dedicated investment pool and mortality experience.
        i. The CAWL may either be a low initial but later increasing premium, or a high initial premium that is later reduced.
        ii. Premiums may be adjusted annually or periodically.

d. Variable life (similar to a variable annuity). The premium is fixed, but the face amount varies with no guarantee of cash values. Sometimes, the insured can choose from a wide variety of investment options (e.g., subaccounts similar to mutual funds). The death benefit cannot usually fall below a minimum amount and consists of two parts: the minimum and the excess amount created by favorable investment returns (death benefit has a guaranteed minimum). Insurance and securities licenses are required to sell variable life insurance.

e. Variations of whole life policies.

   i. Single premium whole life - May not be treated as insurance from a tax point of view (Modified Endowment Contract).

   ii. Graded premium whole life - Premiums usually start with pure term insurance and convert to whole life insurance over a 5-10-20 year term. It is yearly renewable term and then levels the premium at the advanced age where whole life begins.

   iii. Modified life - Similar to graded premium, but with a premium arrangement whereby the first five years of the premiums are slightly more than the convertible term life premium; then an increase occurs to a premium slightly more than what a whole life premium would have been at the age of inception, but slightly less than the level premium for ordinary life at the attained age of conversion.

f. Variable premium whole life.

   i. Universal life-A - A flexible premium, adjustable death benefit, unbundled life insurance contract. Policyholder may raise policy death benefits (subject to insurability). Policy cash values and pure insurance costs are unbundled (shown separately). The cash accumulation is determined by current interest rates, sometimes known as Option 1 or level death benefit.

   ii. Universal life-B - The same as Universal A except that death benefits vary directly with the cash values. Universal B is more expensive than Universal A because the death benefit is equal to a specified amount of insurance plus the cash value (Option 2).

g. Variable universal life - An interest-sensitive product with investment options (e.g., mutual funds) and no minimum guaranteed rate of return or interest. Death benefits are not guaranteed, and cash values can decline to zero, causing the policy to lapse unless additional premium payments are made. Insurance and securities licenses are required to sell variable universal life insurance.

h. General premium ranking of permanent insurance (initial premium from low to high).

   i. Graded premium.

   ii. Modified life.

   iii. Low CAWL.

   iv. Ordinary life.

   v. High CAWL.

   vi. Whole life, limited pay term.

   vii. Universal life-A (no minimum death benefit).

   viii. Variable life (due to minimum guarantee death benefit).

   ix. Universal life-B.

x. Variable Universal life-B.

> **Note:** The premium term of each of these would affect the rankings of the premiums.

D. OTHER TYPES OF LIFE INSURANCE.

1. Joint and survivor policies.
   a. First-to-die provides death benefits when the first insured dies. First-to-die life expectancy is less than either single life expectancy.
      i. May cost less than two separate policies for couples earning similar incomes who have specific dollar needs at death of first spouse (e.g., education, mortgage).
      ii. The policy can include an optional guaranteed insurability provision for the survivor without evidence of insurability but usually at current premium rates as of the death of the first insured.
      iii. Proceeds inclusion in the gross estate of the decedent is dependent on "incidents of ownership."
      iv. May be cost effective in a business application characterized by several key employees in contrast to purchasing multiple policies at the same face.
      v. May be any type of policy (term to variable life).
   b. Second-or-last-to-die policies provide death benefits when the second, or last, insured dies. Second-to-die life expectancy is greater than either individual life expectancy, therefore, lowering premiums.
      i. Usually applicable to spouses who intend to make substantial use of the marital deduction and need a cost-effective vehicle to provide estate liquidity at death of the second spouse where federal estate taxes are expected to be substantial.
      ii. May be used by businesses where the loss of one key employee would not be catastrophic but the loss of two or more would be catastrophic.
      iii. Usually, second-to-die policies are cost effective due to combined life expectancies that reduce premiums.
      iv. Sometimes used to offset the loss of assets to heirs or legatees that result from highly appreciated assets being placed in a Charitable Remainder Annuity Trust (CRAT) or a Charitable Remainder Unitrust (CRUT) with overall better estate and retirement results (referred to as Wealth Replacement Insurance).
      v. Premiums may increase significantly at the death of the first insured (second-to-die).

Example

John and Mary, both 65, with an estate of $5,000,000 consisting of a business with a zero taxable basis, need retirement income and have charitable objectives, but do not wish to disinherit their children who have no interest in the business. John and Mary transfer the business to a CRAT or CRUT and receive income for two lives with the remainder going to charity, reserving the right to change the name of the charitable remainder beneficiary. They receive a current income tax deduction. They use the value of such deduction to make gifts, utilizing the annual exclusion and/or lifetime exemption, to an irrevocable trust for the benefit of the children. The trust has the power to purchase life insurance on their lives (generally includes Crummey provision). The trustee, for the benefit of the children, then purchases life insurance of $5,000,000 (second-to-die).

- Could be any type of policy (usually permanent).
- Inclusion in the gross estate depends on the incidents of ownership. If properly arranged, the insurance proceeds will not be included in John or Mary's gross estate.
- The premiums may be blended or may increase dramatically at the death of the first insured.

2. Family income policies and riders.

   Family income policies are a combination of decreasing term and some form of whole life insurance where the term insurance provides for a specified payment per month from the insured's death to a specified date in the future.

3. Modified whole life.

   The distinguishing characteristic of a modified whole life policy is the premium arrangement. During the first five years, the premium is slightly more than a term life premium, then an increase occurs to the premium that is slightly more than a whole life premium would have been if taken at the time of the original purchase, but less than at the attained age.

4. Graded premium whole life.

   A graded premium whole life is a policy that begins with a low initial premium (usually pure term) and increases annually or at a point until it levels out (usually at about year 10).

5. Vanishing premium policy.

   A vanishing premium policy is usually a participating whole life policy where the dividends accumulated are expected to be sufficient to cover all future premiums. (The term "vanishing" is no longer used.)

6. Single premium life policy.

   A single premium life policy is one where a single premium is sufficiently large enough to create an immediate cash value and the income generated from the cash value pays the remaining cost of premiums.

   a. The rate of return may be guaranteed for a period of 1-5 years.
   b. Can be a traditional whole life insurance policy or a variable life policy.
   c. A single premium life insurance policy may have adverse federal income tax consequences if it does not meet the seven-pay test of the IRS. The result of such failure is classification as an MEC (modified endowment contract), thus making all loans (borrowing or pledging) from such a policy taxable income to the extent that the cash value of the policy exceeds the premiums paid. Also, MECs are subject to a 10% penalty for persons under 59½ years of age.

7. Credit life.

   a. Protects the lender and the borrower from financial loss in the event the borrower dies before completing payment of the debt.

   b. The face amount of the policy is usually the balance of the related loan. The terms provide for payment to be made to satisfy the debt from the proceeds should the debtor die. Since credit life policies usually have very high premiums relative to the amount of coverage, term is usually a better alternative.

8. Mixed life insurance - Some companies combine term and cash value into one policy. They use this mixture to provide a higher death benefit (the term portion) at a lower premium outlay so as to maintain competitiveness. This is attractive to the younger insured that has a substantial need for protection and a modest need for investment.

EXHIBIT 2: LIFE INSURANCE COMPARISON (BY TYPE AND ELEMENT)

Type	Description	Need	Death Benefit	Premium
Annual Renewable Term	"Pure" life insurance with no cash value element; initially, the highest death benefit for the lowest premium; premium exponentiates	Short to intermediate term need; largest death benefit for minimum initial premium	Fixed, level	Increasing, exponential
Whole Life	Known maximum cost and minimum death benefit levels; dividends may reduce premiums, pay-up policy, buy paid-up additions accumulated at interest, or be paid in cash; provides most guarantees	Anybody who needs lifetime coverage	Fixed, level	Fixed, level
Variable Life	Whole life contract; choice of investment assets; death benefits depend on investment results; but guaranteed minimum	Need for investment performance	Guaranteed minimum; can increase based on investment performance	Fixed, level
Universal Life A & B	Flexible premium current-assumption adjustable death benefit policy; policy elements unbundled; two death benefit options (A & B)	Flexibility in premiums and benefits	Adjustable; Option A like Ordinary Life; Option B like Ordinary Life plus term rider equal to cash value	Flexible option of policyowner
Variable Universal Life A & B	Features of universal and variable life	Need for performance and flexibility	Adjustable; Option A like Ordinary Life; Option B like Ordinary Life plus term rider equal to cash value	Flexible option of policyowner

LIFE INSURANCE COMPARISON (BY TYPE AND ELEMENT) (CONTINUED)

Type	CV and/or Dividend Use Current Interest	Cash Value (CV)	Advantages to Owner	Disadvantages to Owner
Annual Renewable Term	N/A	None	Low premium for coverage	Increasing premium; most term insurance is lapsed
Whole Life	Yes	Fixed	Predictable; forced savings and conservative investment	Higher premiums
Variable Life	N/A	Based on investment performance; not guaranteed	Combines life insurance and investments on excess premiums; tax shelter	All investment risk is to the owner
Universal Life A & B	Yes	Varies depending on face amount and premium; min. guaranteed interest; excess increases cash value	Flexibility	Some investment risk to owner
Variable Universal Life A & B	N/A	Varies depending on face amount, premium, and investment performance; not guaranteed	Flexibility and investments; tax shelter	All investment risk is to the owner; greater mortality risk to owner

V. RETIREMENT PROGRAMS AND BUSINESS USES OF LIFE AND HEALTH INSURANCE

A. GROUP LIFE AND HEALTH INSURANCE AS EMPLOYEE BENEFITS.

1. Group life and health insurance plans are used by many employers as a part of the compensation package for the employee.
2. Group term life insurance premiums up to the first $50,000 value of face paid by the employer are tax exempt for the employee.
   a. For any amount of group term coverage greater than $50,000, the scheduled premium per $1,000 from Section 79 is included in the employee's W-2.
   b. To qualify for favorable tax treatment, a group life and health plan must be nondiscriminatory. Nondiscriminatory means the plan must cover 70% or more of all eligible employees or benefit a group of at least 85% of the non-key employees.
3. The premiums paid by the employer for health insurance are tax exempt for the employee, and they are deductible by the employer.
4. If the employer provides ordinary life coverage and pays the entire premium, the employee is taxed on the non-term portion of the premium. This portion is deductible by the employer.
5. Group paid up life insurance premiums are paid by employee contributions.
6. Group universal life does not provide any tax advantage to the employer, and the premiums are usually paid by the employee.

B. SPLIT-DOLLAR LIFE INSURANCE.

1. Described.
   a. Split-dollar life insurance is an arrangement, typically between an employer and an employee, in which there is a sharing of the costs and benefits of the life insurance policy.
   b. The employer corporation may pay that part of the annual premium that equals the current year's increase in the cash surrender value of the policy.
   c. If the insured employee dies, the corporation recovers its premium outlay with the balance of the policy proceeds paid to the beneficiary chosen by the employee.
   d. The objective is to merge the employee's need for life insurance with the premium-paying ability of the employer.
2. Appropriate application of split dollar.
   a. When an employer wishes to provide an executive with a life insurance benefit at a low cost and low cash outlay to the executive. Split dollar is best suited for executives in their 30s, 40s, and early 50s since the plan requires a reasonable duration in order to build up adequate policy cash values and the cost to the executive at later ages (the Table 2001 costs approximate term mortality costs and may be excessive at later ages).
   b. When a preretirement death benefit for an employee is a major objective. Split dollar can be used as an alternative to an insurance financed non-qualified deferred compensation plan or in conjunction with a non-qualified, unfunded, deferred compensation plan.
   c. When an employer is seeking a totally selective executive fringe benefit.
   d. When an employer wants to make it easier for shareholder-employees to finance a buyout of stock under a cross purchase buy/sell agreement or make it possible for non-stockholding employees to effect a one-way stock purchase at an existing shareholder's death.

3. Advantages.
   a. A split-dollar plan allows an executive to receive a benefit of current value using employer funds with minimal or no tax cost to the executive.
   b. In most types of split-dollar plans, the employer's outlay is at all times fully secured. Upon the employee's death or termination of employment, the employer is reimbursed from policy proceeds for its premium outlays. The net cost to the employer for the plan is merely the loss of the net after-tax income the funds could have earned while the plan was in effect.
4. Disadvantages.
   a. The employer receives no tax deduction for its share of premium payments under the split-dollar plan.
   b. The employee must pay income taxes each year on the current Table 2001 cost.
   c. The plan must remain in effect for a reasonably long time, 10-20 years, in order for policy cash values to rise to a level sufficient to maximize plan benefits.
   d. The plan must generally be terminated at approximately age 65 since the employee's tax cost for the plan, the Table 2001 cost, rises sharply at later ages.
5. Design features.
   a. In a split-dollar arrangement between the employer and employee, at least three aspects of the policy can be subject to different types of split:
      i. The premium cost.
      ii. The cash value.
      iii. The policy ownership.
   b. Premium cost split categories.
      i. The classic, or standard, split-dollar plan under which the employer pays a portion of the premiums equal to the increase in cash surrender value of the policy.
      ii. The level premium plan under which the employee's premium share is leveled over an initial period of years, such as 5 - 10 years.
      iii. The employer pays all arrangements under which the employer pays the entire premium and the employee pays nothing.
      iv. The Table 2001 offset plan under which the employee pays an amount equal to the Table 2001 cost for the coverage.
6. Cash value and death proceeds split - The purpose of the split of cash value or death proceeds is to reimburse the employer, in whole or in part, for its share of the premium outlay in the event of the employee's death or termination of the plan.
7. Policy ownership methods.
   a. The endorsement method - The employer owns the policy and is primarily responsible to the insurance company for paying the entire premium. The split beneficiary designation provides for the employer to receive a portion of the death benefit equal to its premium outlay with the remainder of the death proceeds going to the employee's designated beneficiary. The employee's rights are protected by endorsement, giving the employee the right to name the residual beneficiary.

b. The collateral assignment method - The employee is the owner of the policy and is responsible for premium payments. The employer obligates itself and then makes interest-free loans in the amount of the premium the employee has agreed to pay under the split-dollar plan. To secure these loans, the policy is assigned as collateral to the employer. At the employee's death, the employer recovers its loan (aggregate premium payments) from the policy proceeds as the collateral assignee. The remainder of the policy proceeds is paid to the employee's designated beneficiary. Some states do not allow collateral assignment of life insurance contracts.

8. Income tax treatment. (Notice 2002-8)

a. Notice 2002-8 revoked Notice 2001-10 and provided some guidance regarding the taxation of split-dollar life insurance. However, the IRS intended to issue regulations addressing the tax treatment of split-dollar life insurance arrangements. At the time of publication of this material, the anticipated proposed regulations had not been issued. It is expected that the regulations will provide that any payment made by an employer under a split-dollar arrangement must be accounted for either as a loan to the employee under IRC Section 7872, or as compensation to the employee. This move closely reflects economic reality.

The IRS also issued new mortality tables reflecting increased life expectancy.

EXHIBIT 3: SPLIT-DOLLAR LIFE INSURANCE

Old Rules	New Rules (Expected)
Employee is taxed on the value of insurance received (Table 2001 costs or insurer's published premium rate if lower) or cash dividends or other benefits received reduced by employee premiums paid.	Alternatives: • Loans • Compensation

b. Death benefits from a split-dollar plan include both the employer's share and the employee beneficiary's share and are generally income tax free.

c. The tax-free nature of the death proceeds is lost if the policy has been transferred for value in certain situations. The transfer of an insurance policy is exempt from the transfer for value rules if it will not cause the loss of the death proceeds' tax-free nature. Examples of exemptions to the transfer for value rule:

i. A transfer of the policy to the insured.

ii. A transfer to a partner of the insured or to a partnership of which the insured is a partner.

iii. A transfer to a corporation of which the insured is a shareholder or officer.

iv. A transfer in which the transferee's basis is determined, in whole or in part, by reference to the transferor's basis (e.g., a substituted or carryover basis).

9. Estate tax treatment.

a. Incidents of ownership will cause inclusion in the gross estate if the decedent retained the ownership or had the right to name or change the beneficiary.

b. Inclusion in the gross estate could result from a policy transferred or assigned with the 3-year period prior to the insured/owner's death.

C. CROSS PURCHASE LIFE INSURANCE.

1. Death or disability of a proprietor, partner, or shareholder of a closely held business may cause serious business problems including liquidation and continuity of management problems. It may even cause dissolution of a partnership. It is appropriate to plan for the sale of the interests of any key person in advance of events such as death or disability.
2. It is possible to have a business buy-sell agreement without funding if the potential buyers have sufficient liquid assets. However, that is not usually the case.
3. A solid buy-sell agreement will have triggering events identified (e.g., death and disability), valuation methodology identified either by formula or process, and a funding mechanism in place. One such funding mechanism is cross purchase life insurance.
4. Under cross purchase life insurance, a partner or shareholder purchases a sufficient amount of life insurance on the lives of each other partner or shareholder to assure sufficient liquidity to buy out the deceased or disabled partner or shareholder.

Example

A and B are partners. They conclude that the partnership is worth $500,000. Each partner buys a $250,000 policy on the other and enters into an agreement binding on the respective heirs to sell the partnership interest to the surviving partner for $250,000 in the event of one of their deaths.

5. One problem with cross purchase life insurance is that when the number of partners or shareholders increases arithmetically, the number of policies increases geometrically. (Four partners equal twelve policies). The number of policies equals the number of partners times the number of partners minus one [n x (n - 1)]. (Example: 4 partners; 4 x 3 = 12 policies)
6. Another potential problem is the cost difference in funding a policy for older partners or shareholders (more expensive) versus that of funding a policy for younger partners or shareholders (less expensive).
7. Premiums are not tax deductible, and the proceeds are not includible in taxable income.
8. Allows increased tax basis for surviving owners.

D. ENTITY INSURANCE.

1. Entity insurance is also referred to as stock redemption if the entity is a corporation.
2. Entity insurance is an alternative to the cross purchase arrangement. The entity itself buys the insurance policies on each partner or shareholder. The advantage of entity insurance is that the number of policies is reduced to one per partner or shareholder.
3. Premiums are not tax deductible, and the proceeds are not includible in taxable income.
4. No increase in tax basis to surviving owners.

EXHIBIT 4: CROSS PURCHASE VS. ENTITY PURCHASE

CROSS PURCHASE		ENTITY	
Advantages	**Disadvantages**	**Advantages**	**Disadvantages**
• Basis adjustment	• Number of policies = n (n - 1) • Inequality in policy cost due to differing ages	• Fewer policies if 3 or more persons	• No basis adjustment • Potential corporate AMT • Possible dividend treatment by IRS

E. LIFE INSURANCE IN QUALIFIED PLANS.

1. Life insurance can be provided through a qualified plan or 403(b) plan as long as the incidental death benefit requirement is met. One of two tests must be passed to meet the incidental death benefit requirement.
   a. The cost of life insurance in a qualified plan is not deductible for self-employed individuals.
   b. IRAs and SEPs are not permitted to hold life insurance.
2. The 25 percent test (first test).
   a. Under this test, the aggregate premiums paid for a life insurance policy cannot exceed a certain percent of the employer contributions to the plan.
   b. No more than 50% of the employer contributions can be used to purchase whole life insurance.
   c. No more than 25% of the employer contributions can be used to purchase life insurance other than whole life insurance.
3. The 100 to 1 ratio rule (second test).
   a. For defined benefit plans, the life insurance limitation is based on a ratio compared with the expected monthly benefit of the employee.
   b. A death benefit cannot exceed 100 times the expected monthly benefit for the employee.
   c. For example, if the expected monthly benefit is $2,000, then no more than $200,000 of death benefit can be provided by life insurance.
4. Tax issues during participation.
   a. A participant must include into income the pure protection cost of life insurance provided in a qualified plan. This cost of life insurance is determined by way of the one-year premium term rate, which is called the Table 2001 cost. If the actual cost is lower, it may be used.
   b. The amount included in an employee's income is treated as basis for purposes of distributions from the plan.
5. Tax issues at death.
   a. The value of the life insurance will be included in the gross estate of the decedent employee for estate tax purposes.
   b. The proceeds paid to a beneficiary from a life insurance policy funded within a qualified plan may be subject to income tax. The portion that is taxable equals the cash surrender value of the policy. However, the beneficiary may offset this amount by the sum of the costs included in income by the decedent during the decedent's life. [Treas. Reg. 1.72-16(b)(6)]

VI. CALCULATING LIFE INSURANCE AMOUNT

A. PROGRAMMING LIFE INSURANCE.

1. Programming for life insurance is a method of evaluating a person's needs for capital resources.
    a. Programming involves evaluating the person's present financial position, forecasting future financial obligations, and determining the proper life insurance amount to meet future obligations.
    b. Programming establishes planning for the purchase of life insurance.
2. There are two primary approaches in determining the amount of life insurance that an individual should purchase to adequately provide for dependents.
    a. The human life value approach is an analysis based on the present value of the income earning ability of the individual lost to the survivor in the event of death of the provider.
    b. The needs approach attempts to determine the financial needs of the dependents over the dependency period should the provider die.

B. PROGRAMMING THE HUMAN LIFE VALUE APPROACH.

1. The human life value approach projects the income of the individual through the remaining work life expectancy, including raises. Then, utilizing a discount rate (either the riskless or the expected investment return rate), the present value of the life is determined.
2. Cash flows can be adjusted downward for what the individual would have personally consumed or paid in transfer costs (income and Social Security taxes). Alternatively, the percentage (%) of consumption and taxation can be applied to the present value to reflect the total present value of all income that would have been provided to the dependents of the deceased.

Example

Joe is 30 and expects to work to age 65. His remaining work life expectancy is 35 years. His salary is $30,000. He expects wage increases to be 5%. He expects inflation to be 5%. The riskless rate is 5%. The present value of Joe's life before consumption and taxes is ($30,000 x 35 years) = $1,050,000. Assume that Joe pays 15% in taxes (income) and 7.65% in Social Security taxes and personally consumes 20% of his after-tax net earnings.

Human Life Percentage Calculation

$100.00	Gross pay
(15.00)	Income tax
(7.65)	Social Security tax
$77.35	After tax net earnings
(15.47)	(20% of 77.35) consumption
$61.88	Net to survivors (as a % of gross income)

Therefore, Joe needs only to insure income to 0.6188 x $1,050,000 = $649,740. The value of a human life approach uses the income lost, not the projected needs of the surviving dependents to determine the amount of life insurance needed. It includes the build up of the estate over time.

C. THE NEEDS APPROACH TO CALCULATING LIFE INSURANCE AMOUNTS.

1. The needs approach examines all recurring expenses to dependent survivors and any unusual expenditures that may result from the death of the individual.
2. The factors that must be considered are marital status, roles of the spouses (employed or unemployed), size of the family, and whether the dependents are willing and able to work.
3. Lifestyles impact the analysis of needs.
   a. A person who is single and has no dependents has little need for life insurance. The life insurance need may only be to repay indebtedness and any expenses related to death.
   b. A single parent or a single person who supports dependents (children or parents) has a need for life insurance to continue the flow of income to these dependents should the individual die.
   c. Childless couples' need for life insurance (if both employed) is generally limited to the amount necessary to cover debts, death expenses, and maintain lifestyle.
   d. Children and other dependents increase the need for life insurance to guarantee the continuation of the current standard of living in the event of the death of the provider.
      i. If only one parent is employed, the primary insurance emphasis should be on the income-producing parent.
      ii. If both parents are employed, both should be insured to mitigate the risk of income lost through death.
      iii. If only one parent is employed, the value of the services of the non-income-producing parent should be considered to mitigate the risk that the non-income-producing parent may die and cause the survivor significant cost increases.
4. The needs of a family can be classified as follows:
   a. A fund for last expenses - Includes last medical costs and funeral costs.
   b. A fund for readjustment - Covers the period following death and may include nonrecurring costs as the family adjusts to the death of a provider, typically two years.
   c. The dependency period income - Is usually the period of the highest needs as the children and/or dependents are requiring income for current living and other routine costs to maintain a household.
   d. The mortgage payment fund - An effective way of reducing the amount of income that is needed during the dependency period is to be able to pay off the mortgage at the death of the income producer.
   e. The educational fund - Establishing a lump sum for education can eliminate some of the income strain during the dependency period.
   f. Life income for the surviving spouse - The need for this arises if the spouse is either not employed and does not have the necessary skills to become employed or cannot produce sufficient income. Life insurance also creates income for the blackout period when Social Security benefits cease for the spouse due to the child's age and such spouse has not reached age 60. It also includes any retirement income in excess of Social Security benefits.

> **Note:** This is most likely to be tested conceptually rather than quantitatively.

5. The needs of the family are listed on a month-by-month basis over a long period of time to reflect the amount of income that will be required to meet the needs (cash flow projections).
6. Each of the needs is inflated by the CPI, if appropriate, then each cash flow is discounted back to the present normally using a riskless rate of return for the term selected or an expected earnings rate depending on the asset allocation scheme of the survivor. (It would be inappropriate to inflate the cost of a fixed mortgage payment).
7. The needs of an individual change over time. Once a program has been developed, it should be periodically reviewed to adjust for changes that have occurred in the individual's life.

D. CALCULATING THE NEEDS APPROACH.

The needs approach may be calculated three ways:

1. An annuity approach - Expected to pay just enough to meet the needs of dependents through the life expectancy period of dependent survivors (problem: superannuation).
2. A capital preservation model - Provides for a lifetime annuity plus keeps the face value of the insurance intact (problem: the capital balance will have lost purchasing power).
3. A purchasing power preservation model - Provides for annuity income and capital preservation on an inflated basis so that there is no loss in purchasing power at the end of the life expectancy period of the surviving spouse.

VII. ANNUITIES

A. INTRODUCTION AND DEFINITION.

1. Annuities are a method of saving for retirement.
2. Annuities provide a periodic payment (usually fixed but could be variable) for a fixed period (term certain) or for someone's (could be more than one) lifetime (life annuity).
3. The only financial product that can guarantee protection for superannuation.

B. TYPES OF ANNUITIES - CLASSIFICATIONS.

1. When payments begin - immediately or deferred.
2. Form of annuity.
   a. Certain - Over a lifetime or over a lifetime with a minimum guaranteed term.
   b. Single life annuity - Payments continue until the death of the annuitant.
   c. Joint and survivor - Payments continue until the death of the last of two annuitants.
   d. Life annuity with guaranteed term - Payments continue to the annuitant(s) for the annuitant's lifetime. However, if that is less than the guaranteed term, then payments will continue to the designee for the term.
3. Premium method - May be single or periodic premium payments.
   a. Single premium deferred annuity (SPDA) - A lump-sum premium with a deferred payout period.
   b. Flexible premium deferred annuity (FPDA) - Allows periodic, non-fixed contributions where earnings accumulate free from current income tax and are then distributed later in one of the forms in Section VII, B2 above.
   c. Single premium immediate annuity - The annuity begins immediately following the premium payment. Typical examples include the structured settlement from a civil suit and the life insurance proceeds annuity.
   d. Variable annuity - The income will vary depending on the returns of the underlying investment accounts. A variable annuity benefit could result from a single premium or flexible premium and may be an immediate or deferred annuity.
   e. Annuities in retirement plans - Quite common as the preferred method of payout to both defined benefit plans and many 403(b) plans.

VIII.TAX TREATMENT OF LIFE INSURANCE AND ANNUITIES

A. LIFE INSURANCE RECEIVES FAVORABLE TAX TREATMENT.

1. Proceeds paid to ordinary beneficiaries are not usually included in taxable income.
2. Income that is earned (dividends) but not withdrawn on the cash surrender value of a cash value policy is not currently taxable to the owner of the policy. (Funds accumulate tax free). If the insured dies without surrendering the policy and withdrawing the cash value, the cash value accumulations are never taxed.
3. Partial withdrawals can be tax free (except modified endowment contracts (MECs) - see the tax planning section).
4. Loans can be tax free (except MECs).
5. Death benefits usually escape probate if there is a named beneficiary person or trust.

B. TAXATION OF LIFE INSURANCE - BENEFITS RECEIVED DURING LIFE (LIVING BENEFITS).

1. Dividends.
   a. Generally, dividends distributed are not taxable, but instead are considered a return of a portion of premium payments that reduce the policyowner's basis.
   b. There is an exception if dividends distributed exceed premiums, then the excess amount of dividends are taxed to the policyowner as ordinary income.
   c. The taxpayer has constructive receipt of living benefit interest paid on dividends in the year the policyowner has the right to withdraw the interest. The interest is then taxable as ordinary income.
2. Withdrawals.
   a. Withdrawals of living benefits within the first fifteen years of a life insurance policy that result in a reduction of death benefits are subject to LIFO (last in first out) treatment. Withdrawals made beyond the first fifteen years of the policy are subject to FIFO (first in first out) treatment.
   b. There is a higher taxable portion of a withdrawal during the first five years of the policy than during years six through fifteen of the life insurance policy.
   c. Modified endowment contracts (MECs) are life insurance policies that have excessively higher premiums within the first seven years of the policy or within seven years of a material change to a life insurance policy such that the policy acts more like an investment. Withdrawals and/or loans on MECs are subject to LIFO tax treatment. MECs are also subject to a 10% penalty on taxable gains withdrawn before age 59 ½.

3. Surrender.

   a. Lump-Sum Payments.

      i. The living benefits of a lump-sum payment of the cash value above the owner's cost basis is taxable to the owner as ordinary income.

   b. Interest Payments.

      i. Upon maturity or cash surrender, if the owner leaves living benefit proceeds with the insurer and selects the interest-only option, the interest is taxable as ordinary income when received or credited to payee.

      ii. If the interest option is selected prior to maturity or cash surrender and the right to withdraw proceeds is given up, then constructive receipt of the gain is avoided and the ultimate receiver of the proceeds will have the tax liability for the interest.

   c. Installment Payments.

      i. The portion of living benefit installment payments that are not a return of principal are taxed as ordinary income.

4. Transfer of Life Insurance Policy.

   a. If an existing policy is transferred for valuable consideration (transfer for value), the insurance proceeds are includible in the gross income of the transferee to the extent the proceeds exceed the basis (amount paid for policy plus any subsequent premiums paid), meaning the income tax exclusion is lost.

   b. There are five instances when transfer of a policy will not result in loss of exclusion treatment. These include transfers that involve the following:

      i. A transfer to the insured.

      ii. A partner of the insured.

      iii. A partnership in which the insured is a partner.

      iv. A corporation in which the insured is an officer or shareholder.

      v. A transferee whose basis in the policy is determined by reference to the transferor's basis (tax-free exchange or gift).

   c. Gift of Life Insurance.

      i. A gift of life insurance is treated the same as any other property gift and may be subject to the annual exclusion ($11,000 for 2003).

5. Premiums.

   a. Generally, premium payments for individual life insurance policies are not deductible. However, if a corporation pays the premium on a policy covering an employee and the corporation is not a beneficiary, then the premium is considered compensation and is deductible to the employer. Also, see below for information on life insurance premiums considered as alimony that are deductible when incident to a divorce settlement.

6. Divorce.

   a. A transfer of ownership of an existing life insurance policy that insures the life of one spouse to the other spouse, incident to a divorce, does not result in taxation for either spouse. Also, payment of subsequent death benefits remains tax free.

b. Premiums.

i. In the above transfer of ownership of an existing life insurance policy, if the spouse who transferred the policy is required by the divorce settlement to continue payment of premiums, then the payments are considered alimony and are therefore deductible to the payor and taxable to the payee as ordinary income.

ii. Conversely, if ownership of an existing life insurance policy is retained by the insured spouse and the premium payments are made by the ex-spouse, who is also the beneficiary, then the payments are not considered alimony and are not deductible. Subsequent payment of death benefits in this situation also remains tax free.

7. Summary - Taxation of Life Insurance on Living Benefits.

The following exhibit summarizes the taxation of living benefits for cash value life insurance policies.

EXHIBIT 5: TAXATION OF LIFE INSURANCE ON LIVING BENEFITS DURING LIFE

Type of Income	Situation	Taxation
Dividends	Dividends exceed premiums.	Ordinary income.
Withdrawals	Within first 15 years of policy.	LIFO tax treatment.
	After first 15 years of policy.	FIFO tax treatment.
	Modified Endowment Contract withdrawals and loans.	LIFO tax treatment regardless of the age of policy.
Lump-sum payments	Proceeds beyond cost basis.	Ordinary income.
Interest payments	Maturity or cash surrender and interest-only option selected.	Ordinary income.
Installment payments	Portion that is not a return of principal.	Ordinary income.
Transfer of life insurance policy	For valuable consideration to the extent proceeds exceed basis.	Ordinary income.
Premiums	On individual policies.	Generally not deductible.
	Corporation pays premiums and is not beneficiary.	Deductible to employer as compensation to employee.
Divorce and transfer of life insurance policy	Transfer of ownership of existing policy that insures one spouse, or the other spouse, as part of divorce settlement.	No tax consequences on transfer and death benefits remain tax exempt.
Premiums as part of divorce settlement	On transferred policy above as a result of divorce. Premiums still paid by original owner of policy.	Premiums are deductible as alimony to payor and taxable as income to payee.
Gift	Gift of a portion or all of life insurance policy.	Subject to gift tax. Annual exclusion of $11,000 may apply.

C. INCOME TAXATION OF LIFE INSURANCE - DEATH BENEFITS AND FEDERAL ESTATE TAXATION OF LIFE INSURANCE PROCEEDS.

1. Lump-Sum Death Benefits.
   a. Proceeds of death benefits as a result of an insured's death are excludable from gross income and are therefore tax exempt for income tax purposes.
2. Interest-Only Payments on Death Benefits.
   a. Insurer only pays death benefit interest proceeds to the beneficiary. The death benefit interest proceeds are taxable as ordinary income.
3. Installment Payments on Death Benefits.
   a. The principal portion of the death benefit installment payments is tax free to the beneficiary. The interest portion of installment payments, accruing after the date of insured's death, is taxable to the beneficiary as ordinary income.
   b. Life Insurance Proceeds Received as an Annuity.
      i. As previously stated, if the proceeds from a life insurance policy are received periodically in the form of an annuity (as a settlement option), then each payment has a return of basis component (exclusion ratio) and an ordinary income component (inclusion ratio).

Example

If Karen took an annuity settlement option for a $100,000 face policy that would pay her $644.30 per month for the rest of her life (life expectancy 25 years), how much of each monthly payment would be taxable?

Step 1:	Calculate the total to be received from the annuity $644.30 x 300 months = $193,290.00		
Step 2:	Determine her tax basis = $100,000 (face amount)		
Step 3:	Calculate the exclusion ratio 100,000/193,290.00	=	0.5174
Step 4:	Calculate the inclusion ratio 93,290.00/193,290.00	=	0.4826
Step 5:	Make sure the inclusion and exclusion ratios add to		1.0000
Step 6:	Multiply the monthly payment by the inclusion ratio $644.30 x 0.4826 = $310.94 taxable (monthly)		

Shortcut:

$\frac{100,000}{25 \times 12}$ = 333.33 tax free

333.33
(644.30)
310.97

---

4. What if the beneficiary dies prior to or survives beyond the exact life expectancy? The answer depends on whether the annuity is a purchased annuity or the result of a life insurance settlement.
   a. An annuity from life insurance retains its original inclusion/exclusion ratio even after the basis of the policy has been recovered, assuming that the beneficiary of a life annuity lives beyond the life expectancy.
   b. If the beneficiary of an annuity from a life insurance settlement dies earlier than the projected life expectancy, the beneficiary cannot recover any basis that remained. This rule is just the opposite from the purchased annuity rule. The purchased annuity rule states that once the basis is fully recovered (at life expectancy), any future payments received are fully taxable.
   c. If a beneficiary under the purchased annuity rule had not completely recovered his basis as a result of death prior to projected life expectancy, such beneficiary could deduct the remaining tax basis on his final income tax return. However, it is a miscellaneous itemized deduction not subject to the 2% floor.
5. Federal Estate Taxation.
   a. A life insurance policy is a contract and by its nature does not require the probate process for title transfer to occur if there is a named beneficiary. Furthermore, if the decedent of the policy has incidents of ownership in the life insurance policy the proceeds will be included in the gross estate and be subject to estate taxation. The following situations can lead to the life insurance policy being included in decedent-insured's estate:
      i. Proceeds are included in decedent-insured's gross estate if the policy was transferred within three years of decedent's death.
      ii. Proceeds are included in the decedent-insured's gross estate if the proceeds are payable to the estate or to the executor/executrix of the estate.
      iii. Proceeds are included in the decedent-insured's gross estate if incidents of ownership in the life insurance policy remain at decedent's death. Incidents of ownership can include the right to assign the policy, the right to change the beneficiary, and the right to change any of the provisions of the life insurance contract.
   b. If the decedent owns the policy and the proceeds are payable to the spouse, the proceeds are included in the gross estate of the decedent. In this situation, the federal estate unlimited marital deduction can be utilized and the proceeds can be deducted from the gross estate and thereby removed from estate taxation.

6. Summary - Taxation of Life Insurance on Death Benefits.

   The following exhibit summarizes the income taxation of death benefits for cash value life insurance policies.

EXHIBIT 6: INCOME TAXATION OF LIFE INSURANCE ON DEATH BENEFITS		
Type of Income	**Situation**	**Taxation**
Lump-sum payments	Proceeds payable as a result of insured's death	Tax exempt to beneficiary
Interest payments	Interest on proceeds payable to the beneficiary	Ordinary income
Installment payments	Principal plus earnings payable to beneficiary	Principal portion is tax free and earnings accrued since insured's death is taxable as ordinary income

D. VIATICAL AGREEMENTS (ACCELERATED DEATH BENEFITS).

1. Under a viatical agreement, the insured/beneficiary is expected to die within 24 months as certified by a doctor. The proceeds received of such a policy are not subject to income tax.
2. In addition, a chronically ill person can exclude gain if the proceeds are used for the long-term care of the insured. Chronically ill is certified by a doctor as being unable to perform, without assistance, certain activities of daily living.
3. Third parties who purchase life insurance policies on terminally or chronically ill insureds do not qualify for accelerated death benefits relief.

E. TAX TREATMENT OF ANNUITIES.

1. Withdrawals prior to the start of the annuity.
   a. For pre-August 14, 1982 annuities, a FIFO (first-in, first-out) method is used for withdrawals, such that withdrawals up to the owner's taxable basis are not included in taxable income but rather are a return of capital. Therefore, these may be an excellent source of non-taxed liquidity assuming there are no withdrawal penalties.
   b. For annuity contracts purchased after August 13, 1982, the withdrawal rule is LIFO (last-in, first-out). Withdrawals are presumed to come from earnings first and are taxed to the extent of earnings.
2. Each payment from a fixed annuity is considered a partial return of basis and partially taxable income using an inclusion/exclusion ratio. The numerator for the exclusion ratio is the cost basis in the annuity. The denominator is the total expected benefits. The numerator for the inclusion ratio is the total expected benefits less the cost basis. The denominator is the total expected benefits. Payments beyond projected life expectancy are fully taxable.
3. For a variable annuity, the exclusion ratio is determined by dividing the cost basis by the expected term of benefits. All payments in excess of the exclusion amount are taxable. Payments beyond projected life expectancy are fully taxable.
4. Ten-year forward averaging is not available for annuities.

5. Premature distributions (prior to 59½) are subject to 10% penalty, but see all of the exceptions to early withdrawal penalties (Retirement Planning section). There is no penalty for withdrawing basis on pre-August 14, 1982 contracts.

6. The Small Business Act (1996) allows a simplified method of recovery of basis from qualified plans (begins 1996, 90 days after enactment). This is an alternative to the life expectancy method.

Age	Recovery Period
≤ 55	360 payments
56-60	310 payments
61-65	260 payments
66-70	210 payments
> 70	160 payments

Example

Basis	$120,000
FMV at annuity start date	$380,660 at 65
Expected payments	192 (16 x 12)
Expected amount @ 6%	$3,073.45
Total expected to receive	192 x $3,073.45 = $590,102.40

a. Previous calculation.

$120,000 ÷ $590,103 = 20.34% exclusion, therefore, 79.66% inclusion.

Basis recovered $625.14 per month for 192 months (exclusion).

b. New alternative (not mandatory).

$120,000 ÷ 260 payments = $461.54 per month exclusion.

Takes 260 payments to recover the basis.

c. The alternative method is easier to calculate; however, the use of the simplified table may be disadvantageous to certain taxpayers because basis recovery is slower than using a life expectancy table.

IX. LIFE INSURANCE AND ESTATE AND GIFT PLANNING (INCLUDING GSTT)

A. GENERAL.

1. An objective of estate planning is to develop a plan of property transfer that reflects the person's wishes and objectives regarding property transfers, during life and at death, in such a manner as to minimize the overall tax liability (gift and estate) consistent with those objectives. Consideration should be given to tax strategies and their costs and benefits, including loss of control of any property transferred.

2. For estate planning purposes, life insurance is generally best owned by someone other than the insured. If the insured has any incidents of ownership in the policy, such incidents will cause inclusion of the proceeds in the insured's gross estate at death.

B. THE INCLUSION OF LIFE INSURANCE IN THE GROSS ESTATE.

1. Causes for inclusion of the entire proceeds of the policy.
   a. The transfer of ownership within three years of death.
   b. Incidents of ownership within three years of death (IRC Section 2035).
   c. Retained rights or reversionary rights.
   d. General Powers of Appointment over the policy (IRC Section 2043).
   e. Qualified Terminal Interest Property Trusts (QTIPs)(IRC Section 2044).

2. The inclusion of the lifetime value of a policy owned on the life of another person (IRC Section 2033). The value will generally be the replacement cost [permanent product - interpolated terminal reserve plus any unearned premium; if term – the unearned premium (note the following exceptions)].
   a. The election of the alternate valuation date when the insured has died within six months of the owner of a life insurance policy or a person with a General Power of Appointment over the policy could cause inclusion of the entire proceeds rather than the value of the interpolated terminal reserve (caution).
   b. Second-to-die policies are especially subject to the risk of using the alternate valuation date causing inclusion in the first estate.

C. OWNERSHIP OF LIFE INSURANCE POLICIES ON THE INSURED AND INCLUSION IN GROSS ESTATE OF DECEASED.

1. Ownership by the insured - The result is inclusion in the gross estate of the insured.

2. Joint ownership by insureds - Inclusion to the extent of the contribution rule (spouse deemed 50%) to the estate of the insured.

3. Ownership by someone other than the insured.
   a. If the policy was acquired outright by someone other than the insured and with an insurable interest, there is no inclusion in the estate of the decedent insured.
   b. If a policy is acquired by transfer or by assignment from the insured, the throwback rule (Section 2035) will cause inclusion in the insured's gross estate if such transfer was made within three years of the insured's death. If not made within three years, it is not pulled back into the estate.

c. If a second-to-die policy is transferred, the death benefit will be included in the gross estate of the second person to die, if the second person to die is deceased within three years of the transfer. If joint life (first-to-die) was transferred, then there is no inclusion (depends on ownership of policy).

D. LIFE INSURANCE AND GIFT TAXATION.

1. Outright transfers.
   a. A policy transferred from the original owner to another without adequate consideration is a gift.
   b. A policy purchased by one who designates another as owner at the inception has made a gift (if spouse, no consequence).
2. Transfer in trust - When the owner transfers a policy to a trustee, the owner has made a gift to the beneficiaries of the trust assuming that the gift is a completed gift.
3. Indirect gifts.
   a. Generally, the direct payment of premiums for a policy owned by another are indirect gifts.
   b. Indirect gifts may be avoided by gifting under the annual exclusion from payor to owner or, if in trust, using a Crummey provision.
4. Valuation (actual cost or replacement).
   a. Generally, the valuation of an insurance policy is the fair market value (at the date of the gift). This valuation applies to any paid up or newly issued policy.
   b. However, if the policy has been in force and premiums remain to be paid, the value is the interpolated terminal reserve plus any unearned premium plus dividend accumulations minus loans against the policy. This valuation applies to any policy in force with remaining premiums.
   c. Universal policies and whole life policies with vanishing premiums are valued using the terminal reserve method because there can be no absolute assurance that future premiums will not be necessary to keep the policy in force.
5. Crummey power (the power to lapse).
   a. A General Power of Appointment. If the power is lapsed, there has been a gift.
   b. Therefore, may cause application of the 5/5 lapse rule, if a multiple beneficiary trust exists and withdrawal powers are lapsed in excess of $5,000 or 5%. The lapsing beneficiary has made a future interest gift to the remaining beneficiaries for which the annual exclusion does not apply (careful drafting is critical).

E. THE MARITAL DEDUCTION.

1. If the entire ownership interest in a life insurance policy is gifted to the donor's spouse, the transaction will qualify for the unlimited marital deduction (IRC Section 2533(a)).
2. If a gift is in trust for the spouse, the transfer will qualify for the unlimited marital deduction only if it is made in a trust that qualifies under the terminable interest rules (e.g., POA trust, QTIP, etc.).

F. THE IRREVOCABLE LIFE INSURANCE TRUST.

1. The trust purchases life insurance directly on the life of the insured. It is not included in the insured's estate.
2. If the life insurance policy is assigned or transferred to the trust, the proceeds will be included in the transferor's estate if the transferor dies within three years of the transfer.

G. LIFE INSURANCE AND THE GSTT.

1. Payment of premiums - The use of the annual exclusion may reduce gift tax (in a trust, use a Crummey provision). Lifetime GSTT exemption ($1,100,000 for 2002) may reduce or eliminate GSTT.
2. Transfer of policies - When a life insurance policy is transferred to a skip person, such a transfer triggers GSTT.
3. When the grandparent is the owner of the policy, and the payment of insurance proceeds to a skip person (i.e., grandchild), it is a generation-skipping transfer.

H. SPECIAL ISSUES.

1. Joint life (first-to-die) policies may cost less and provide more for couples with similar income levels or for businesses with several key employees. A joint life policy usually costs less than two policies but has only one death benefit, thus actually costing more per dollar of death benefit. The base policy may include an option of guaranteed insurability for the survivor (insured under a subsequent policy without evidence of insurability, but at current rates).
2. Joint life (second-to-die) policies.
    a. Often used for a husband and wife to provide estate liquidity at the death of the second. Expectations are that the marital deduction will be used at the death of the first spouse.
    b. Inclusion in the gross estate of the decedent should be avoided by eliminating "incidents of ownership" on the part of the decedent.

X. CHOOSING LIFE INSURANCE COMPANIES

A. FINANCIAL STRENGTH OF INSURER-SAFETY.

1. Rating services (See exhibit "Summary of Various Company Ratings" on page 275).
2. Factors affecting financial strength.
   a. Adequate surplus reserves.
   b. Investment portfolio quality and diversification.
   c. Cash flows and liquidity.
   d. Recent earnings and historical earnings, earnings ability, and earnings stability.
   e. Management (quality and continuity).

B. EVALUATING PRODUCT PERFORMANCE AND CREDIBILITY OF ILLUSTRATIONS.

1. Risk factors in product performance.
   a. Mortality assumptions consistent with current performance.
      i. Non-guaranteed factors are based on assumptions regarding performance of mortality.
      ii. Mortality is the largest component of price and performance for term policies.
      iii. Mortality is a significant component of price and performance for whole life policies.
      iv. Mortality rates have improved at about 1% per year for the period 1970-1990.
      v. Future improved mortality expectations are built into the assumptions.

      (Any of the above factors, if not achieved, may cause the product to perform adversely to the illustrations.)
   b. Investment experience consistent with current performance.
      i. Largest component of price and performance for whole life policies dependent on interest rates.
      ii. Term has no investment component and is, therefore, not dependent on interest rates.
      iii. Variable and universal variable products pass all investment risk to the insured.
      iv. The investment risk in whole life is with the insurer for the guaranteed portion.
      v. With permanent insurance, the risk of guaranteed illustrations is with the insurer and the risk of non-guaranteed illustrations is to the insured.
   c. Lapse experience consistent with current performance.
      i. Pricing is generally better for companies with higher persistency (lower lapse) rates.
      ii. Are lapse assumptions consistent with current and historical actual experience?
      iii. Lapse and persistency statistics can be obtained from A.M. Best, Moody's, and S&P reports.
   d. Is expense experience consistent with current performance? Are expenses consistent with current and historical actual experience?

2. Illustrations and credibility.
    a. Comparability of illustrations (general and specific).
    b. Are assumptions consistent with current performance of insurer?
    c. "What if" illustrations (e.g., try dividends at 2% below current performance).
    d. Management commitment to the current policyholder and determination that this policy in the major market and the strategic positioning of the company.
    e. Forecasting results under alternative scenarios (e.g., dividends 2% less than current performance).

C. IMPORTANT FACTORS.

1. Safety of insurer - length of holding period.
2. Selection of appropriate type of life insurance - key objective.
3. Determination of face, death benefit needed or desired - key objective.
4. Settlement options.
5. Disclaimers.
6. Simultaneous death clauses.

D. ILLUSTRATIONS.

1. Guaranteed projection - The risk is to the insurer.
2. Nonguaranteed projection - The risk is to the insured.
    a. Improper selection.
    b. Unrealistic expectations.
    c. Failure to achieve overall financial goals.

E. GUARANTEED PERFORMANCE (WORST CASE SCENARIO).

1. Premiums.
2. Cash values.
3. Death benefits.

F. NONGUARANTEED PERFORMANCE-BASED ON CURRENT EXPERIENCE.

1. Dividends.
2. Lower premiums.
3. Improved accumulation benefits.

G. RISK DEFINED AS THE EXPECTED VARIABILITY OF RETURNS.

1. Projections using assumptions including improvements over current performance. Consider the following when evaluating policies:

    a. Risk to insurer.

    b. Risk to insured.

    c. Disclosure.

    d. Evaluate underwriting, investment performance, and management.

    e. Evaluate 5- to 10-year performance.

    f. Improved current performance may subsidize new product development rather than benefit current policyholder.

2. Analysis: Obtain past dividend and interest rate histories vs. original illustrations. Have new features been added to the current policyholder's policy when the tax laws changed? Is the product line a major business segment of the insurer? What is the average policy size vs. the sample related to the policy size in question? Set reasonable expectations based on historical experience. What were the objectives? React and adjust. Track performance.

XI. COST COMPARISON OF LIFE INSURANCE POLICIES

A. METHODS USED TO COMPARE LIFE INSURANCE POLICIES.

1. There are numerous methods used to compare life insurance policies. The relevant variables include the annual premiums, cash values, dividends, and the time value of money applied to each of the previous three. Each of the three methods described below has advantages and disadvantages such that no one method will be superior in all situations.

B. THE TRADITIONAL NET COST METHOD.

1. A time period is selected (10, 20, 30 years).
2. The total premiums are added for the selected time period.
3. Dividends for the selected time period are deducted.
4. The cash value at the end of the selected time period is deducted.
5. The net cost per year is calculated by dividing the cost by the term.
6. The net cost per $1,000 of insurance per year is calculated by dividing the net cost per year by the face of the policy in thousands.

Example

The Traditional Net Cost Method

Face of policy $100,000		
Total premiums for 30 years	$3,000	(2)
Dividends for 30 years	(800)	(3)
Net premiums for 30 years	$2,200	
Cash value at 30 years	(4,000)	(4)
Insurance cost for 30 years	($1,800)	
Cost per year	(60)	(5)
Cost per $1,000 per year	($0.06)	(6)

The method is weak in that:

- It does not consider the time value of money.
- It bases calculations on projected premiums, dividends, and cash values that may or may not be realized.
- The selected term is deterministic (given), and the likelihood that the insured will surrender the policy at exactly the selected term is remote.
- The method makes insurance appear to be a free good, which is not true, as illustrated by the negative cost per $1,000.
- The method allows the insurer preparing the illustration to alter the dividend and earnings rate in later years thus giving the appearance of being inexpensive because it ignores the cash flows in terms of time value of money.

C. THE INTEREST-ADJUSTED METHODS (THE SURRENDER COST INDEX AND THE NET PAYMENT COST INDEX).

1. The Surrender Cost Index measures the cost of insurance if surrendered for a selected term.
   a. Calculate the value of all premiums inflated at a selected fixed interest rate for the term selected.
   b. Calculate the value of all dividends inflated at a fixed interest rate (same one) for the term selected and subtract from the above.
   c. Subtract the cash value at the end of the selected term.
   d. Determine the face value cost.
   e. Calculate the annual PMT with N = selected term; i = interest rate.
   f. Calculate the cost per year.
   g. Calculate the cost per $1,000 per year.

Example

Surrender Cost Index

Policy face	$1,000,000	
Premiums each year	$100.00	
Total premiums for 30 years inflated at 6% (annuity due)	$8,380.17	(a)
Dividends per year inflated at 6% ($26.67 level dividends)	(2,108.22)	(b)
Net premiums (future value)	$6,271.95	(b)
Subtract cash value at 30 years	(4,000.00)	(c)
Insurance cost for 30 years (face value)	$2,271.95	(d)
Calculate PMT (annuity due) for N = 30; i = 6 cost per year	$27.11	(e)
Cost per $1,000 per year	$0.02711	(g)

2. The net payment cost index-interest adjusted.
   a. Measures the relative net payment of a policy for a given term assuming no surrender of the policy.
   b. Using the example above, just delete the cash value.

The Net Payment Cost Index	
Net premium (face value)	$6,271.95
Cost per year = PMT of annuity due	$74.84
Cost per $1,000 per year	$0.07484

3. Both interest-adjusted methods are more useful than the traditional net cost method, but comparison problems are created if the cash outlays are not equal. In such a case, a side investment fund can be created with earnings either projected at the same selected interest rate or at the client's after-tax opportunity cost for similar investments to improve the comparability.
4. The interest-adjusted methods have the same problems as the traditional net method regarding predictability of premiums, dividends, and cash values.
5. Insurers know that certain intervals are routinely selected for comparison (e.g., 10 years, 20 years, age 65), and thus, may manipulate the cash values to make favorable costs at these selected dates.
6. Both methods may give conflicting results when comparing two or more policies.
7. Comparison of different types of policies using these methods may be misleading and inappropriate.

Note: The whole life policy survey from A. M. Best Insurance is a very valuable reference.

D. THE IRR ON YIELD METHOD.

The method is used to determine the rate of return (implicit IRR) on the savings component of a cash value policy held for a particular term.

E. THE BELTH MODEL-RATE OF RETURN ON SAVINGS FOR CASH VALUE POLICY.

1. The formula:

$$i = \frac{(CV + D) + (YPT)(DB\text{-}CV)(0.001)}{(P + CVP)} - 1$$

Where: i = annual implicit interest rate on savings component.
CV = cash value at year-end.
D = annual dividend.
YPT = assumed benchmark price.
P = premium.
DB = death benefit.
CVP = cash value at beginning of year (end of last year).

Example

Bill purchased a $250,000 participating whole life policy at age 38. He is currently 44 and at the beginning of his seventh year of the policy. Calculate the yearly rate of return from the following facts: The annual premium is $3,000. The cash value of the policy is $14,000 and is expected to be $16,700 at year-end. The dividend this year is $800.

$$i = \frac{(16{,}700 + 800) + (4) + (250{,}000 - 16{,}700)(0.001)}{(3{,}000 + 14{,}000)} - 1$$

$i = 1.0843 - 1 = 8.43\%$

This rate can then be compared with the net after-tax rate of return for comparable investments.

The results may vary widely, depending upon which year is selected, but a calculation of the "i" for each and every year of the policy may prove insightful for comparative purposes of otherwise equal products.

F. RATING COMPANIES.

1. A. M. Best Company - Ratings are based on public information and interviews with management.
2. Duff & Phelps Credit Rating Company - Uses public information and management interviews. Public information alone may be used to assign ratings.
3. Moody's Investors Service - May assign ratings based on public information alone.
4. Standard & Poor's Corporation - Rates companies only upon request.
5. Weiss Research - Ratings are based on public information and proprietary methods of evaluation and are available only on a company-by-company basis.

EXHIBIT 7: SUMMARY OF VARIOUS COMPANY RATINGS

A. M. Best	Best's Description	D & P	Moody's	S & P	Weiss	Weiss' Description
A++	Superior	AAA	Aaa	AAA	A+	Excellent
A+	Superior	AA+	Aa1	AA+	A	Excellent
A	Excellent	AA	Aa2	AA	A-	Excellent
A-	Excellent	AA-	A1	AA-	B+	Good
B++	Very Good	A+	A2	A+	B	Good
B+	Very Good	A	A3	A	B-	Good
B	Good	A-	Baa1	A-	C+	Fair
B-	Good	BBB+	Baa2	BBB+	C	Fair
C++	Marginal	BBB	Baa3	BBB	C-	Fair
C+	Marginal	BBB-	Ba1	BBB-	D+	Weak
C	Weak	BB+	Ba2	BB+	D	Weak
C-	Weak	BB	Ba3	BB	D-	Weak
D	Poor	BB-	B1	BB-	E+	Very Weak
E	Under Regulatory Supervision	B+	B2	B+	E	Very Weak
F	In Liquidation	B	B3	B	E-	Very Weak
S	Rating Suspended				F	Failed

XII. LIFE INSURANCE POLICY REPLACEMENT - THE BASICS

A. THE DECISION TO REPLACE ONE POLICY WITH ANOTHER SHOULD BE MADE CAUTIOUSLY.

1. The methodology for such a decision includes fact gathering, calculations, and benchmark comparisons.

EXHIBIT 8: BELTH BENCHMARK

Age	Benchmark Price of Insurance per $1,000
<30	1.50
30-34	2.00
35-39	3.00
40-44	4.00
45-49	6.50
50-54	10.00
55-59	15.00
60-64	25.00
65-69	35.00
70-74	50.00
75-79	80.00
80-84	125.00

Table - (Joseph M. Belth, author)

2. The Belth price of protection model is:

$$CPT = \frac{(P + CV_0)(1 + i) - (CV_1 + D)}{(DB - CV_1)(0.001)}$$

CPT	=	Cost per thousand
P	=	Annual premium
CV_0	=	Cash value at beginning of year
i	=	Net after tax earning rate
CV_1	=	Cash value at year end
D	=	Current dividend
DB	=	Death benefit

Example

Assume i = 6%

Death benefit = $250,000

$$CPT = \frac{(3{,}000 + 14{,}000)(1.06) - (16{,}700 + 800)}{(250{,}000 - 16{,}700)(0.001)}$$

$$CPT = \frac{520.00}{233.30} = 2.23$$

Compare to benchmark table:

- If cost < benchmark price, then retain policy.
- If cost > benchmark but < 2 x benchmark, then retain policy.
- If cost > 2 x benchmark, consider replacement.

In the above example, the $2.23 was less than the $4.00 benchmark. The calculation should be made for each and every year to compare like policies. The policy with the best prices for the greatest number of years is probably the best one. Alternatively, calculate the discounted present value of the annual costs at an appropriate interest rate. The one with the lowest present value would be the best. The above analysis will place all policies on equal footing.

XIII. DISABILITY INSURANCE

A. DISABILITY INCOME INSURANCE.

1. Disability insurance provides benefits in the form of periodic payments for a person who is unable to work due to sickness or accidental injury.
2. Disability insurance is marketed as either group or individual coverage. Coverage under a group plan is sometimes broader than an individual plan and usually less expensive.
3. Disability insurance makes a distinction between short-term and long-term disability coverage.
   a. Short-term disability coverage provides coverage for up to two years. Most policies cover periods of weeks.
   b. Long-term disability coverage generally extends until age 62-65, for life, or for a term of years.

B. NEED FOR DISABILITY INSURANCE.

1. Disability insurance is important because the benefits are used to replace the loss of income that occurs when a person is disabled.
2. A disability may be more of a financial hardship than untimely death because increased expenses often accompany the loss of income.
3. The chance of disability loss is greater than the chance of untimely death (about 10 to 1).
4. If a disability arises in the course of employment, the benefits to the injured employee generally come from workers compensation (see "Section XVIII. Other Compulsory Social Insurance" on page 304).

C. DISABILITY CONTRACTS.

1. There are no standard disability insurance contracts, but there are provisions that are common to both group and individual policies.
2. Elements of a disability policy.
   a. The definition.
   b. The elimination period.
   c. The benefit amount or percentage.
   d. The benefit term.
   e. The coverage (perils insured against).
3. Insurance companies generally limit the amount of coverage to replace income.
   a. Short-term policies are limited to approximately 60% of weekly wages.
   b. Long-term policies can provide up to 75% to 80% of monthly gross wages (but usually provide only 50-60%).
   c. Many long-term disability policies provide for a dollar-for-dollar reduction in benefits for Social Security disability benefits received (so-called coordination of benefits provision).
4. The benefit period for disability policies varies. The length of time for benefits affects the premium of the policy.

5. Disability insurance is written to provide coverage for loss of income from an accident or sickness (accident only coverage is inadequate for most workers). The benefits payable under a policy that is written as accident or sickness will have differing intervals for benefit payments dependent on the cause of the disability.

6. The definition of disability affects the broadness of the coverage.

   a. The definition of disability used by most insurance companies is one or a combination of the following:

      i. Own occupation - The inability to engage in your own occupation (most expensive).

      ii. Modified own occupation - The inability to engage in any reasonable occupation for which you might be suited by education, experience training, or for which you could easily become qualified (hybrid).

      iii. Any occupation - The inability to engage in any occupation (very restrictive – Social Security definition).

      iv. A mental or physical impairment that prevents the worker from engaging in any substantial gainful employment. Such disability must have lasted for five months and be expected to last at least 12 months or result in the death of the worker (Social Security definition - very restrictive).

      v. Many hybrid forms of disability are sold today (e.g., two years own occupation, then, any occupation).

   b. The definition of injury includes one of the following:

      i. Accidental bodily injury (result must have been accidental).

      ii. Bodily injury by accidental means (result must have been accidental and the cause accidental).

   c. The definition of sickness is used to preclude preexisting conditions and addresses sickness as being contracted and beginning after the policy is in effect (sickness may have probationary period).

7. Disability policies have some exclusions depending on the insurance company, but the most common exclusion is disability resulting from war.

8. The waiting period (elimination period) that is part of a disability insurance contract acts as the deductible by making the insured cover part of the financial loss.

9. Disability policies may be written on a residual or partial basis. Residual means that if a disabled worker returns to work at lesser pay, the policy will pay the difference between the former pay and the current pay to the extent of available benefits.

D. TAXATION OF DISABILITY BENEFITS.

1. If disability benefits are received for an employer-provided disability policy, such benefits are totally includible in taxable income as "in lieu of wages."

2. If disability benefits are received from a personally paid disability policy, such benefits are excludable from taxable income.

3. If a disability policy is partially provided by the employer and partially by the employee, then benefits from such a policy will be includible in income to the extent of the employer pro rata share of premiums.

E. EVALUATING THE APPROPRIATENESS OF LONG-TERM DISABILITY COVERAGE.

When evaluating the appropriateness of long-term disability coverage for a particular client situation, consider these issues:

1. Disability insurance is income replacement insurance; therefore, the amount of the benefit must be appropriate (generally 60-70% of gross pay).
2. The term of the benefits should match the term of work-life expectancy.
3. The coverage should be appropriate including both sickness and accidents.
4. The elimination period should be appropriate to the situation (focus on the client's liquid assets).
5. If the benefits are taxable, the after-tax cash flows should be sufficient to replace the lost income.
6. The definition of disability should be appropriate to the worker (e.g., professor should have "own occupation").
7. The policy should be non-cancelable or guaranteed renewable.
8. The premium should be competitive.
9. If the policy has a coordination with Social Security disability benefits provision, that fact should be considered in the selection process.

Note: Retirees do not need disability coverage, as they have no earned income to replace. They do, however, need health insurance.

F. OTHER ISSUES.

1. Whether the policy is coordinated with any Social Security disability benefits (lowers premiums).
2. Whether the policy is coordinated with a workers compensation provision (lowers premiums).
3. An increase in the elimination period lowers the premium, but there is usually only a small marginal benefit for elimination periods in excess of 180 days.
4. Morbidity rate is the phrase used to describe the probability of a person becoming disabled as opposed to mortality rate which is used to describe the probability of death.

XIV.INDIVIDUAL HEALTH AND DISABILITY INSURANCE POLICY PROVISIONS

A. INDIVIDUAL HEALTH INSURANCE POLICIES.

1. Individual health insurance policies, both disability and medical, have several provisions regarding the insurance company's right to continue or discontinue the policy.
   a. Noncancellable policies are continuous, guaranteeing the insured the right to renew until a specific age or stated number of years at a nonchangeable premium.
   b. A guaranteed renewable policy is one where a right to renew is guaranteed, but the insurance company is allowed to adjust the premiums by policyholder class (normally on a group basis).
   c. Conditionally renewable policies are continuous-term policies that the insurance company may terminate if certain conditions stated in the contract are met.
   d. Policies that are renewable only at the insurance company's option are not guaranteed to the insured.
   e. A policy that does not contain renewable provisions is a single-term policy.
   f. A policy where the insurance company may terminate is a cancelable policy.

B. UNIFORMITY IN INSURANCE CONTRACTS.

1. To create uniformity in insurance contracts, there are 12 required provisions and several optional conditions that have been advanced by the National Association of Insurance Commissioners (NAIC).
2. Required provisions:
   a. Entire contract - The policy, endorsements, and attached papers constitute the entire contract.
   b. Time limit on certain defenses - The policy is incontestable after three years except for fraud.
   c. Grace period - A grace period applies to all policies.
   d. Reinstatement - A policy that has lapsed may be reinstated.
   e. Notice of claim - The policyholder must notify the insurance company of a claim within 20 days after the occurrence.
   f. Claim forms - The insurance company will furnish claim forms to the insured.
   g. Proof of loss - Insured must furnish written proof of loss within 90 days after termination of the plan year.
   h. Time of payment of claims - Benefits are payable by the insurance company immediately on proof of loss.
   i. Payment of claims - Indemnities are payable to the insured.
   j. Physical examination and autopsy - The insurance company can require physical examinations and autopsies.
   k. Legal action - No legal action can be brought to recover on a contract for 60 days following the loss.
   l. Change of beneficiary - The beneficiary may be changed unless the policyholder has denied this right.

3. Optional provisions.

   a. Change of occupation - The insurance company can adjust the premium to compensate for changes in occupation.

   b. Misstatement of age - The benefits are adjusted for misstatements of age.

   c. Other insurance with insurer - Insured may not recover more than the maximum loss not in excess of maximum (indemnity).

   d. Insurance with other insurers - Duplicate coverage with other companies will not yield payment of benefits in excess of maximum.

   e. Relation of earnings to insurance - Benefits under two or more policies will not exceed average earned income for a 2-year period.

   f. Unpaid premiums - The insurance company may deduct unpaid premiums from a claim if the premium is due.

   g. Cancellation clause - The company has the right to cancel a policy at any time with 5-days' notice.

   h. Conformity with state statutes - Policy must meet minimum requirements of state statutes.

   i. Illegal occupation - Insurance company is not liable if insured is engaged in an illegal occupation.

   j. Intoxicants and narcotics - Relieves the insurance company of liability if the insured is under the influence of alcohol or narcotics.

4. Additional options.

   a. Guaranteed insurability option – As the income of the insured increases, the insured may increase the amount of coverage.

   b. Cost of living adjustment benefit – Offsets the decline in the purchasing power resulting from inflation.

   c. Accidental death and dismemberment – A death benefit to be paid to the beneficiaries if the insured dies by accidental means. Benefits are paid to the insured for loss of limb or sight.

C. BUSINESS USES OF DISABILITY INCOME INSURANCE.

1. Disability overhead insurance is designed to cover the expenses that are usual and necessary expenses in the operation of a business should the owner or key employee insured become disabled.

   a. The premiums are deductible as a business expense.

   b. The benefits are taxable income to the entity.

2. Disability buyout policies are policies used to cover the value of the individual's interest in the business should that individual become disabled. (Disability buyouts are taxed as capital gains to the extent the amount paid is greater than the tax basis.)

D. COST OF DISABILITY INCOME INSURANCE.

The cost of disability insurance varies depending on occupation, age, sex of insured, length of benefits, extent of coverage, and the length of the waiting period (elimination period).

XV. HEALTH INSURANCE FOR MEDICAL EXPENSES

A. TYPES OF HEALTH INSURERS AND EXTENT OF COVERAGE.

1. Health insurance is available from the federal government in the form of Medicare and Medicaid.
   a. Medicare is a health insurance plan that covers people who are 65 or older, people who have been receiving Social Security disability benefits, and people who are on kidney dialysis treatment.
      i. Medicare consists of two parts, A and B.
         A) Part A is hospital insurance and provides coverage for hospitalization, skilled nursing care, home health care, and hospice.
         B) Part B is supplemental, voluntary medical insurance that covers doctors' services and other expenses not covered by Part A.
         C) Part A and Part B are subject to deductibles and coinsurance.
         D) Part A is financed by FICA payroll tax, but Part B is paid in part by the insureds who elect coverage.

> **Note:** See Section "Medicare Benefits" on page 302 for more detailed information.

   b. Medicaid is a federal and state medical insurance program for needy people.
      i. Medicaid is funded by both federal and state funds, but is administered by each state utilizing federal guidelines.
      ii. Each state sets its own indigence guidelines for eligibility and determines the health services to be covered.
         A) Federal law requires inpatient, outpatient, laboratory, X-ray, skilled nursing, and home health services be provided for people age 21 and older.
         B) For children under 21, federal guidelines also require that physicians' services be provided.
2. The private health insurance industry is comprised of commercial insurance companies, independent plans, and Blue Cross and Blue Shield organizations.
   a. Commercial insurance companies include Aetna, Metropolitan Life, Prudential, CNA, and others.
   b. Independent plans are prepayment organizations and include HMOs.
   c. Blue Cross and Blue Shield organizations provide health insurance to the insured and handle all administrative processes and claims processes.
   d. Self insurance is a fourth method of insurance where a company hires a third party administrator (TPA) to perform all the functions required in a self-insurance program.

B. TRADITIONAL FORMS OF MEDICAL EXPENSE INSURANCE.

1. Basic Coverage.

   a. Hospitalization insurance is sold as two alternative types of insurance contracts. One is an expense reimbursement contract and the other is a service contract.

      i. Expense reimbursement contracts are written to pay part or all of room and board costs during a hospital stay and other hospital expenses such as X-rays, operating room, and lab charges. Some contracts include maternity benefits.

      ii. A hospital service contract is where actual services of the hospital are provided to the insured for a stated number of days rather than a cash reimbursement to the insured for the use of the services.

      iii. As with all insurance, most hospitalization insurance contracts contain exclusions.

      iv. Hospital indemnity policies that provide a cash payment to the insured based on the number of days of hospital confinement are considered to be a type of hospitalization insurance.

   b. Surgical expense insurance is written through reimbursement contracts or service contracts.

      i. Surgical expense reimbursement contracts are based on a schedule that provides payment for different types of surgery.

      ii. Service contract surgical insurance provides an agreement with the physician to accept the compensation from the insurance company as payment for services based on usual, customary, and reasonable (UCR) charges.

   c. Physician expense insurance covers non-surgical physicians' fees.

2. Major Medical Coverage.

   a. A major medical policy is an insurance contract designed to eliminate the insurance contracts that are written on a first-dollar basis and provide protection from catastrophic losses. First-dollar coverage is hospital and surgical expense coverage that requires the insurance company to pay the first costs that are insured.

      i. Major medical policies usually contain high limits per loss and few exclusions.

      ii. Major medical policies contain deductibles for each member of the family for a stated dollar amount and period of time (usually calendar year) and are subject to a family maximum.

      iii. Major medical policies require the insured to share part of the loss through a co-payment (coinsurance) that is in excess of the deductible. However, some policies limit the co-pay to a maximum out-of-pocket amount (stop loss limit). A stop loss limit may be money out-of-pocket or where the coinsurance stops. The deductible may or may not be covered by the stop loss.

      iv. Major medical policies may be purchased as stand-alone major medical, supplementary major medical, or comprehensive major medical.

         A) A stand-alone major medical policy does not provide any first-dollar expense coverage.

         B) A supplementary major medical policy is usually written with a first-dollar insurance policy.

         C) A comprehensive major medical policy combines a first-dollar plan and a major medical plan into a single policy.

b. When two policies are in effect to cover an insured, insurance companies usually apply a coordination of benefits provision to prevent duplicate payment and to establish priority of coverage for the payment of a loss (usually depends on birth dates of spouses who are divorced covering same child).

c. Other medical expense insurance coverages exist.

   i. Medicare supplemental policies (Medigap) are designed to cover the deductibles and coinsurance associated with Medicare, and they cannot contain exclusions, limitations, or reductions that are not consistent with Medicare.

   ii. Long-term care policies cover the cost of nursing homes or extended care facilities.

   iii. A life contract living benefits provision is a rider to a life insurance policy that provides prepayment of a portion of death benefits, if the insured becomes confined to a nursing home or suffers a catastrophic illness.

   iv. Limited health insurance policies provide protection only for certain accidents or illnesses.

3. Dental insurance pays for normal dental care and covers damage caused by accidents.

Example

Ms. Jones has a comprehensive major medical insurance policy with a $500 deductible and an 80% coinsurance clause. She becomes ill and is admitted to the hospital for several days. When she is discharged, her hospital bill is $7,500, and her doctor bills are $3,250. Ms. Jones' insurance will pay $8,200.

Loss	$10,750
Deductible	(500)
Covered Loss	$10,250
Less 20%	(2,050)
Insurance Benefit	$8,200

C. HEALTH MAINTENANCE ORGANIZATIONS (HMO).

1. An HMO is an organization that provides a broad range of health services to its group of subscribers for a fixed periodic payment.

2. An HMO provides both the financing of health care and the delivery of the health care.

3. Operation of an HMO consists of comprehensive health care provided by contracted physicians and medical facilities for a prenegotiated payment.

4. A Preferred Provider Organization (PPO) is similar to an HMO, except it allows members to go outside of PPO providers. The insured, who goes outside, has a deductible similar to an indemnity plan.

5. Health care providers are employees of HMOs where the PPOs contract directly with the health care providers for a reduced price in exchange for increased patient volume and timely payment of fees.

D. PURCHASING HEALTH INSURANCE.

1. First-dollar coverage is hospital and surgical expense coverage that requires the insurance company to pay the first costs that are insured.
2. Payment of premiums by an employer through an employer-paid group plan is a deductible business expense to the employer. The benefits are not includible in taxable income to the employee.
3. For an individual, health insurance premiums only receive beneficial tax treatment if all medical expenditures exceed 7.5% of adjusted gross income, and the individual files a Schedule A (itemized deductions) with his/her tax return. Therefore, premiums paid for first-dollar coverage is not as attractive on an individual basis as on a business basis from a tax point of view.
4. Self-employed persons can deduct a portion of the cost of health insurance from their gross income for federal tax purposes; however, no corresponding itemized deduction is allowed. The deductions for health care premiums for the self-employed and spouse dependents are currently 100% for 2003.

Tax Year	Deduction %
2003	100%

5. Medical reimbursement plans and flexible spending accounts are useful alternatives to first-dollar coverage.

E. CONSOLIDATED OMNIBUS BUDGET RECONCILIATION ACT OF 1985 (COBRA).

1. Termination - Generally, group medical benefits for employees and dependents terminate on the earliest of:
   a. Employment termination.
   b. No longer eligible due to reduction in hours (part-time).
   c. Master contract termination.
   d. Insurer has paid lifetime limit on major medical.
   e. Dependent is no longer eligible to be covered as a dependent (age/divorce).
   f. Employee's death.
2. COBRA allows extended coverage.
   a. Applies to:
      i. Employers who have a plan and 20 or more employees in the plan anytime during the year.
      ii. Loss of coverage for the covered employee, employee's spouse, and/or dependent child.

b. Qualifying events.

   i. Death of the covered employee.

   ii. Termination of employment including retiring, voluntary resignation, being laid off, and being fired for anything except gross misconduct.

   iii. A change in status (example from full-time to part-time).

   iv. Divorce or legal separation causing spouse and/or dependent children to lose coverage.

   v. Child reaching an age where the child is no longer eligible to be covered.

   vi. Employee reaches Medicare age and spouse and/or dependent child loses coverage as a result.

c. Term of coverage.

   i. 18 months for employees and dependents for reduction in hours.

   ii. 18 months for employees and dependents for normal termination (except death).

   iii. 36 months for termination of master plan.

   iv. Up to 29 months if employee (or qualified beneficiary) meets Social Security definition of disabled.

   v. 36 months for divorce.

   vi. 36 months (from event) for Medicare.

   vii. 36 months for death.

d. Notice requirement from employee or spouse (60 days) to employer where employer has no knowledge (divorce). Eligible party must elect COBRA coverage and pay premium within 45 days.

e. Cost is borne by eligible beneficiary. Employer may charge up to 102% of normal group rates to cover administrative costs.

f. COBRA coverage definitely ends; therefore, it may be prudent to purchase an individual policy as soon as practical following a COBRA event.

F. ARCHER MEDICAL SAVINGS ACCOUNTS (MSAs).

1. The Health Insurance Portability and Accountability Act (The Health Act of 1996) established a tax-favored savings account for medical expenses called an Archer Medical Savings Account (Archer MSA) for tax years after 1996.

2. Contribution can be made by the employee or the employer.

   a. If contributions are made by the employee, they are deductible from income.

   b. If contributions are made by the employer, the contributions are deductible by the employer in the year for which they are made and are not subject to Social Security taxes and other payroll taxes. Employer contributions are not income to the employee.

3. Earnings on such Archer MSAs are tax deferred until distribution. If the distributions are for qualified medical expenses, they are not taxable. If the distributions are not for qualified medical expenses, the distributions are taxable. If non-medical expense distributions are made before age 65, they are additionally subject to a 15% excise penalty tax.

4. For an employer to qualify, the employer must have a high-deductible health plan with a maximum out-of-pocket cost. High deductible is defined as (2003):

	Deductible	+ Maximum Out of Pocket
For a single coverage	≥ $1,700; ≤ $2,500	$3,350
For family coverage	≥ $3,350; ≤ $5,050	$6,150

5. The maximum contribution to an Archer MSA is equal to:
   a. For a single coverage - 65% of the deductible.
   b. For family coverage - 75% of the deductible.
6. The person for whom an Archer MSA is established must not be covered by any other health plan.
7. There are various penalties, such as a 35% penalty, for discrimination on the part of an employer. There is also a 6% excise penalty for over-funding an account.
8. Employer contributions must be made by the due date for filing the tax return without extensions.
9. Tax treatment of distributions - For medical expenses, distributions are generally tax free. However, if a distribution is made in a year of contribution, the distribution is excludable from income only if the individual for whom the expenses were incurred was eligible to make the Archer MSA contribution.
10. At death.
    a. The account balance is included in the gross estate of the owner at death. If the surviving spouse is the named beneficiary, the property will qualify for the marital deduction. The balance will only be taxed if withdrawn for non-medical reasons.
    b. If the named beneficiary or legatee is someone other than the surviving spouse, it ceases to be an Archer MSA on the date of death, and the balance is taxable to the beneficiary at the date of death. The beneficiary has an itemized deduction equal to the estate tax attributable to the Archer MSA.
11. No Archer MSAs may be established after the year 2003.

XVI. THE BASIC ISSUES OF LONG-TERM CARE

A. THE BASIC ISSUES OF LONG-TERM CARE.

1. Recall that one of the goals of financial planning is financial independence.
2. As the population ages, there is an increased risk of need for long-term care and an increasing risk that for some parties, the only available solution other than Medicare and Medicaid will be long-term care insurance.
   a. Those who enter nursing homes after age 65 have a 40% chance of staying for greater than one year, but only a 15% chance of staying three years or longer.
   b. The growth rate of the U.S. population and the probability of needing long-term care is presented below.

EXHIBIT 9: U.S. POPULATION AND LONG-TERM CARE PROBABILITY

Aging Population (in Millions)			Nursing Home Residents	
Age	Year 2000	Year 2050*	Age	Year 2000*
≥ 65	27,000,000	164,000,000	65 – 74	1%
≥ 85	3,000,000	14,500,000	75 – 84	6%
			≥ 85	25%

**Estimated*

3. Individuals who require long-term care are generally not sick in the traditional sense. Instead, they are old and frail and unable to perform some of the basic activities of daily living.
4. A variety of chronic conditions, including Alzheimer's and emphysema, may also lead to the need for long-term care as afflicted individuals require assistance with day-to-day living.
5. The cost of long-term care is $30,000 - $100,000 per year, depending on region and level of care.
6. Families that traditionally provided care for the aged or infirmed are no longer willing or able to provide such care.
7. Many who are not aged, but infirmed (e.g., quadriplegic) are surviving for much longer periods, thus increasing long-term care needs.
8. Group and individual hospitalization plans and Medicare are inadequate to provide custodial care required.
9. Women, traditionally the caregivers, have longer life expectancies than their husbands. Many couples agree to care for each other at home. The healthy surviving spouse, typically the wife, is left without a caregiver.

B. SOLUTIONS TO THE LONG-TERM CARE PROBLEM.

1. Family.

   a. Traditionally, families had to bear the expense of taking care of older family members when they could no longer maintain their own daily activities.

   b. In the early stages of long-term care, family assistance may be a viable option as it only requires the family to minimally assist the older individual. This may involve the family helping with shopping, cooking, etc.

   c. Families may also opt to have the older individual move into the home of younger members to provide more assistance.

   d. In later stages of long-term care, the individual may need around-the-clock care. This is often costly and time prohibitive. With family members generally holding jobs outside of the home, no one is there to provide assistance, and the cost of hiring a qualified individual to replace the family member is often expensive. In addition, family members often live far away, causing uprooting of the older individual.

2. Personal assets.

   a. Many older individuals are uncomfortable relying on their children (or other family members) for support and may decide to use their own assets to pay for long-term care.

   b. One problem with this choice is that the assets may not be sufficiently liquid to provide the resources for the immediate or long-term needs.

   c. Many individuals will end up selling assets far below their market value in order to get the money available when they need it, thus significantly depleting assets that they intend to go to their children.

3. Medicare.

   a. Medicare provides some benefits relating to long-term care, but it is restrictive and limited.

   b. Medicare covers nursing home and home health care, but it is limited to skilled care.

   c. As mentioned, the individual may not be sufficiently ill to require skilled care. Therefore, if they are only receiving assistance with their daily activities, this aid will not be covered under Medicare.

   d. Medicare also requires that a physician certify the need for skilled care, and any nursing home must be certified by Medicare.

   e. Medicare will only cover up to 100 days of care, and only the first 20 days are covered at 100%.

4. Medicaid (welfare).

   a. Medicaid is designed to provide benefits for the indigent and impoverished.

   b. "Medicaid Planning" was previously used by planners to assist middle class clients in becoming artificially impoverished by transferring assets such that they became eligible for Medicaid. The Balanced Budget Act of 1997 made it a misdemeanor for planners to assist clients in participating in "Medicaid Planning."

   c. In any event, many individuals are not comfortable transferring their assets for fear that they will be forced to live below their standard of living (i.e., if the Medicaid benefits are not sufficient and the asset recipient refuses to assist them).

d. The Balanced Budget Act of 1997 contained a provision defining a look-back period for assets transferred for less than fair value. The period is 36 months for simple inter vivos transfers, and 60 months for transfers to or from a trust. If a transfer was made within the look-back period the individual will be ineligible for benefits for the length of time equal to the amount transferred divided by the average monthly cost of nursing home care for the region. (i.e., If the asset transferred is worth $10,000 and the monthly regional cost is $1,000, then the individual will be ineligible for 10 months.)

e. Long-term care insurance may be combined with Medicaid to provide coverage for the look-back period.

5. Lifetime care facilities provide continuing care for an entrance fee and monthly fee. These facilities move residents from independent living to assisted living to nursing care facilities with the fee structure somewhat dependent on the entrance fee (either increasing monthly fees with low entrance fees or level fees with larger entrance fees). For many, this is an expensive option.

6. Life insurance accelerated benefits.

   a. Some life insurance policies may provide a source of cash in the event that a person needs long-term care. This is generally termed as a living benefit rider where a part of the policy can be used to pay nursing home costs.

C. LONG-TERM CARE INSURANCE AND NAIC MODEL LEGISLATION.

1. Long-Term Care Insurance.

   a. Long-term care insurance is a recent innovation prompted by the increasing costs of health care associated with the extension of life provided by today's technology.

   b. Policies are not standardized but many contain, at a minimum, the standards set out by the NAIC model discussed below.

   c. Eligibility may be at any age but generally ranges from age 50 to age 85.

   d. Benefits.

      i. There are two benefit approaches used.

         A) The most popular is the defined period approach where coverage is for a defined period following an elimination period (i.e., 30, 60, 90, or 180 days). The maximum benefit period usually ranges from one to six years, but many policies have a feature that provides benefits for life.

         B) The second type is called a pool of money concept where the individual is entitled to coverage equal to a specific amount of dollars. Here the payments will last as long as the maximum amount of coverage has not been expended, regardless of time period.

      ii. Types of coverage include custodial care, intermediate care, and skilled nursing home care. Other types of coverage include home health care, assisted living, and adult day care and hospice.

e. After HIPAA (see below), most policies have two criteria for determining eligibility. The insured must usually meet one of the following:

   i. They must be chronically ill. Chronically ill is defined as unable to perform, without substantial assistance, two of six activities of daily living (ADLs) for at least 90 days. The ADLs include: eating, bathing, dressing, transferring from bed to chair, using the toilet, and continence (the ability to control one's bowel and bladder.)

   ii. Substantial services are required to protect the individual due to substantial cognitive impairment.

2. NAIC Model Legislation (National Association of Insurance Commissioners).

   a. The NAIC adopted model legislation for consideration by the states. Almost all states have adopted some aspect of the model legislation.

   b. Policy Provisions.

      i. Words must be defined.

      ii. The contract must be guaranteed renewable or noncancellable.

      iii. Limitations and exclusions are prohibited except: preexisting conditions (six months), mental and nervous disorders (except Alzheimer's), alcohol and drug addiction, war, felony, attempted suicide, and aviation if non-fare paying.

      iv. The contract cannot only provide skilled nursing care coverage.

      v. The contract cannot require prior hospital stay for benefits.

      vi. There must be a two-year incontestable clause for misrepresentation.

   c. Marketing Requirements.

      i. Provide applicant outline of coverage and shoppers guide.

      ii. 30-day free look.

      iii. Comparisons must be fair and accurate.

      iv. Expected loss ratio must be at least 60%.

      v. If the policy is a replacement policy, insurer must waive the time period regarding pre-existing conditions.

D. FEDERAL INCOME TAX ADVANTAGES OF QUALIFIED LONG-TERM CARE INSURANCE.

1. Health Insurance Portability and Accountability Act (HIPAA) legislated federal income tax deductions for "qualified" long-term care insurance.

2. The act allows favorable tax status to plans issued prior to January 1, 1997, if they complied with state standards.

3. For policies after January 1, 1997, the policy must meet all of the federal standards outlined in HIPAA to be "Qualified."

   a. Contract is limited to qualified long-term care services only.

   b. Contract cannot pay for expenses reimbursable under Medicare.

   c. Contract must be guaranteed renewable.

d. Contract may not provide for any surrender value, or other money that can be borrowed, paid, assigned, or pledged.

e. All refunds of premiums/dividends must reduce future premiums or increase future benefits (no payouts).

f. Contract must meet consumer protection provisions.

4. "Qualified" long-term care services are defined as "necessary diagnostic, preventative, therapeutic, caring, treating, rehabilitative services, and maintenance or personal care services required by a chronically ill person and provided by a plan prescribed by a licensed health care practitioner."

5. The act requires coverage to be triggered using the methods discussed above (i.e., person must be chronically ill or need to be protected due to a severe cognitive impairment.)

6. The act allows favorable tax treatment for premiums to and benefits from the plan for all qualified plans.

   a. Premiums paid by the individual are deductible as medical expenses for itemized deduction purposes depending on the individual's age. See the following exhibit for the annual deductible amount.

EXHIBIT 10: FEDERAL INCOME TAX DEDUCTION AS MEDICAL EXPENSES FOR LONG-TERM CARE PREMIUMS FOR YEAR 2003 (INDEXED)

Covered Persons (Age)	Annual Deductible per Covered Person
≤ 40	$250
41 – 50	$470
51 – 60	$940
61 – 70	$2,510
> 70	$3,130

   b. Employer payments for group premiums are tax deductible to the employer and not taxable income to the employee. Long-term care benefits cannot be included in a cafeteria plan or flexible spending account on a tax-advantaged basis.

   c. Benefits paid from the plan are generally excludable from income.

E. GROUP LONG-TERM CARE INSURANCE.

1. Group coverage is similar to high-end individual policies.
2. Eligibility usually requires full time employment and actively at work.
3. The cost of group coverage is usually a little less than individual coverage.
4. In group coverage, there may be restricted benefit levels and duration.
5. Usually, group coverage can be continued beyond termination on a direct-pay basis.
6. Typically allows coverage to extended family members (parents, in-laws, etc.).

XVII.THE OLD AGE, SURVIVORS, DISABILITY, AND HEALTH INSURANCE PROGRAM (OASDHI)

A. OLD AGE, SURVIVORS, DISABILITY, AND HEALTH INSURANCE (OASDHI).

1. OASDHI was created through the Social Security Act of 1935 and is designed to protect eligible workers and their dependents from financial loss resulting from death, illness, disability, and superannuation. Approximately 95% of all U.S. workers are covered by Social Security.
2. Full old age benefits currently begin at age 65 and provide a lifetime pension based on the worker's average earnings during the work years.
    a. Old age benefits are also available to certain dependents.
    b. Benefits are indexed annually based on the CPI.
3. Survivors' benefits were created to care for dependents of workers who died before (or after) retirement and are limited to dependent children and sometimes the surviving spouse and surviving dependent parents.
4. Disability benefits provide for a qualified worker who becomes totally and permanently disabled. Other dependents may be eligible for benefits.
5. The Medicare portion offers health care expense protection to persons over 65 and persons who qualify as disabled under Social Security.

B. ELIGIBILITY DEPENDS ON INSURED'S STATUS.

1. Fully insured (40 quarters of coverage) (Old Age and Survivors Benefits).
2. Currently insured (6 quarters during the 13-quarter period ending with the quarter of death) (Survivor Benefits only).
3. Disability insured (fully insured and has at least 20 quarters of coverage out of last 40 prior to disability) and meets Social Security definition of disability. If worker is between the ages of 24 and 30, they must have coverage for one-half of the quarters since age 21. If under age 24, they must have 6 out of the last 12 quarters ending with the quarter of disability.
4. A quarter of coverage in 2003 is given for each full $890 in annual earnings on which Social Security taxes are paid, up to a maximum of four quarters (indexed by CPI). (See www.ssa.gov for updates.)

C. SOCIAL SECURITY COVERAGE.

1. Who is covered?
    a. Employees of private companies.
    b. Federal civilian workers hired after 1983. Pre-1984 employees are covered for Medicare only.
    c. State and local government employees with some exceptions.
    d. Employees in not-for-profit organizations.
    e. The self-employed.
2. Who is not covered?
    a. Railroad workers subject to the Railroad Retirement Act.
    b. Federal civil service employees who are under Civil Service Retirement System (CSRS).

D. OASDHI PROGRAM FINANCING.

1. The OASDHI program is financed through FICA payroll tax at 7.65% paid by the employee and 7.65% paid by the employer. Self-employed people must pay 15.3%.
2. There is a maximum cap on the 6.2% that represents old age, survivors, and disability ($87,000 in 2003). (See www.ssa.gov for updates).
3. There is no cap on the 1.45% that represents the funding of Medicare (2.9% for self-employed).

E. OLD AGE BENEFITS.

1. Retirement.

   a. Normal retirement age is currently 65 (depending on date of birth).

Date of Birth	Normal Age Retirement	Early Retirement
1937 and earlier	65	62
1943 - 1954	66	63
1960	67	64

   Prorate 2 months for each year in between (i.e., 1958 = 66 and 8 months).

   b. Early Retirement is 62 (80%).

   (Reduction of 5/9 of 1% per month before normal retirement age (e.g., at age 62)

   36 months x 5/9 = 20% reduction), plus 5/12 of 1% for each month in excess of 36. So if an individual's NAR is 66 and they retire at 62, they will receive 75% of their PIA.

   c. Late retirement (for delayed retirement up to age 70 only).

Date of Birth	Yearly % Increase
1926 and earlier	3.5%
1931 – 1932	5.0%
1935 – 1936	6.0%
1939 – 1940	7.0%
1943 or later	8.0%

   Prorate ½ percent every 2 years between categories (i.e., 1941-1942 = 7.5%).

   d. Who is eligible to receive old age benefits (retirement)?

      i. Retired workers (62 or older).

      ii. Spouse of retired worker (62 or older).

      iii. Divorced spouse (married ten years) who is 62 or older, regardless of worker's actual retirement.

      iv. Unmarried children under age 18 who are dependents of retiree.

      v. Spouse with dependent child under 16 (any age).

      vi. Caretaker parent for a child disabled before age 22 (any age).

e. The amount of monthly benefits the worker receives is the primary insurance amount (PIA) and is computed as follows:

   i. For workers born before 1930, elapsed years are the years beginning with 1951 and ending with the year before the worker becomes 62, dies, or is disabled.

   ii. For workers born after 1930, elapsed years begin with the year the worker reaches age 22 and ends with the year before the worker becomes 62, dies, or is disabled.

   iii. The earnings are indexed to the average earnings in the 2nd year before the year of eligibility (approximately 4.5% IRR).

   iv. Five years are then eliminated to determine computation years (lowest indexed years are eliminated).

   v. The years with the highest earnings after 1950 are then used to find average earnings for benefits (sum of indexed earnings/420 months = AIME).

   vi. The PIA is then calculated by applying a 3-tiered formula to the AIME. In 2003 these portions are:

      A) 90% of the first $606 of AIME, plus

      B) 32% of AIME over $606 and through $3,653, plus

      C) 15% of AIME over $3,653.

      This amount is then rounded to the next lower multiple of $0.10.

Example

Assume AIME is $4,000. The PIA is:

90% x 606 = $545.40

32% x (3,653 - 606) = $975.04

15% x (4,000 - 3,653) = $52.05

Monthly benefit $1,572.49 (545.40 + 975.04 + 52.05) rounded down to $1,572.40

f. Earnings Test may result in loss of benefits.

Earnings Test (Maximum)*	
Worker/Beneficiary	**2003**
Under age 65	$11,520

*As of January 2000, the Retirement Earnings Test has been eliminated for individuals who have attained normal retirement age. It remains in effect for those ages under normal retirement age. A modified test applies for the year an individual reaches normal retirement age. (The Senior Citizens' Freedom To Work Act of 2000, signed into law by President Clinton on April 7, 2000.)

Note: One dollar in benefits will be withheld for every $2 in earnings above the limit.

2. Who is eligible to receive Survivors' Benefits?
    a. Unmarried children under age 18 (fully or currently).
    b. Unmarried disabled children if disabled before age 22 (fully or currently).
    c. Surviving spouse with children under age 16 (caretaker) (fully or currently).
    d. Surviving spouse (60 or over) (fully only).
    e. Disabled widow(er) (50-60) (fully only).
    f. Dependent parents of worker (62 or over) (fully only).
    g. $255 lump-sum benefit paid to widow(er) or child.
3. Disability benefits must be disability insured.
    a. Five-month waiting period.
    b. Must meet definition of disability (no gainful employment) expected to last 12 months or result in death.
    c. Receivers of benefits.
        i. Disabled worker (100% of PIA).
        ii. Spouse of disabled worker.
        iii. Unmarried child of disabled worker under age 18.
        iv. Unmarried child who is disabled before age 22.

EXHIBIT 11: SUMMARY OF COVERAGE REQUIRED AND BENEFIT % FOR SOCIAL SECURITY BENEFITS
WAGE REPLACEMENT % AND SOCIAL SECURITY BENEFITS

Recipient	Retirement Benefits	Survivor Benefits	Disability Benefits[1]
Nonretired worker	N/A	N/A	DI[2]
Retired worker age 62 or older	FI	N/A	N/A
Spouse of divorced spouse[3] 62 or older	FI	FI	DI
Spouse if caring for child . 16	FI	FI or CI	DI
Child < 18	FI	FI or CI	DI
Dependent Parent	N/A	FI only	N/A

FI = Fully Insured
CI = Currently Insured
DI = Disability Insured

[1]A blind person need only be FI.

[2]Disability insured:
Disabled before age 24 (6 quarters)
Disabled at 24-30 (50% of time since age 21 to disability)
Over 30 (FI and 20 of the last 40 quarters)

[3]A divorced spouse who had been married to worker over 10 years.

4. Other issues.
   a. Benefits cease upon death.
   b. All benefits except the $255 death benefit and Medicare are based on the PIA formula.
   c. If an individual is eligible to collect under more than one eligibility, he or she will be paid the highest benefit (e.g., divorce).
   d. Benefits are cost-of-living adjusted.
5. Loss of benefits.
   a. Benefits through OASDHI programs may be lost through disqualification. Disqualification may result from:
      i. Conviction of treason, sabotage, or subversive activity (note: not just <u>any</u> crime).
      ii. Deportation.
      iii. Working in foreign country.
      iv. Refusal of vocational rehabilitation by a disabled recipient.
      v. Divorce from the person receiving benefits.
      vi. Attainment of age 18.
      vii. Marriage, which causes eligibility to terminate (remarriage after divorce).
      viii. Adoption.
      ix. Disqualifying income.

F. TAXATION OF BENEFITS.

For people who earn significant income in addition to Social Security, a tax is levied on a portion of the Social Security benefit.

1. As much as 85% of Social Security benefits can be included in gross income for income tax purposes.
2. The amount subject to tax is based upon the taxpayer's income exceeding a specified base amount.
3. The taxable amounts can be determined by one of two formulas using the modified adjusted gross income (MAGI).
4. MAGI is AGI from all sources (minus Social Security) plus the foreign income exclusion and any tax-exempt interest income.
5. Two base amounts are established:
   a. First Base Amount.
      i. $32,000 for married individuals filing a joint return.
      ii. $0 for married taxpayers who do not live apart for the entire year, but file a separate return.
      iii. $25,000 for all other taxpayers.
   b. Second Base Amount.
      i. $44,000 for married individuals filing a joint return.

ii. $0 for married taxpayers who do not live apart for the entire year but file a separate return.

iii. $34,000 for all other taxpayers.

c. If MAGI plus one-half of Social Security exceeds the first set of base amounts, but not the second set, the taxable amount of Social Security is the lesser of the following:

i. 0.50 (Social Security Benefits).

ii. 0.50 (MAGI + 0.50 (Social Security) - base amount).

d. If MAGI plus one-half of Social Security exceeds the second set of base amounts, the taxable amount of Social Security is the lesser of the following:

i. 0.85 (Social Security Benefits)

ii. Sum of 0.85 (MAGI + 0.50 (Social Security) - base amount), and

Lesser of:

- Amount included through application of the first formula.
- $4,500 ($6,000 for married filing jointly).

Example

Matt and Andrea, a married couple who file jointly, have AGI of $35,000 with no tax-exempt interest. In addition, they receive $12,000 of Social Security benefits. How much of the Social Security benefits must they include in taxable income?

1st Set of Base Amounts

Step 1: 0.50 (12,000) = $6,000
Step 2: 0.50 [35,000 + 0.50 (12,000) - 32,000] = $4,500

Therefore, under the first test, they must include $4,500.

Example

Assume that the AGI above was $40,000, therefore MAGI + half of Social Security exceeds the second threshold.

2nd Set of Base Amounts

[40,000 + 0.50 (12,000)] . 44,000

Therefore,

1) 0.85 (12,000) = 10,200
2) Sum of:

0.85 [MAGI + 0.50 (Social Security benefits) - 44,000]		
0.85 [40,000 + 0.50 (12,000) - 44,000]	=	$1,700
Lesser of $10,200 or 6,000 (MFJ)	=	$6,000
Therefore,	=	$7,700

EXHIBIT 12: SUMMARY OF IMPORTANT SOCIAL SECURITY INFORMATION

	2003	
Cost of Living Adjustment (COLA)	1.4%	
Tax Rate		
Employee	7.65%	
Self-employed	15.30%	
Note: The 7.65% tax rate is the combined rate for Social Security and Medicare. The Social Security portion (OASDI) is 6.20% on earnings up to the applicable maximum taxable amount. The Medicare portion (HI) is 1.45% on all earnings.		
Maximum Earnings Taxable		
Social Security (OASDI only)	$87,000	
Medicare (HI only)	No limit	
Quarter of Coverage		
Retirement Earnings Test Exempt Amounts		
Age 65 - 69	Eliminated	
Under age 65	$11,520/yr. ($960/mo.)	
Maximum Social Security Benefit: Worker retiring at age 65 and 2 months in March 2003	$1,741/mo.	
SSI Federal Payment Standard		
Individual	$552/mo.	
Couple	$829/mo.	
SSI Resources Limits		
Individual	$2,000	
Couple	$3,000	
Estimated Average Monthly Social Security Benefits: Payable in January 2003	**BEFORE COLA**	**AFTER COLA**
All Retired Workers	$882	$895
Aged Couple, Both Receiving Benefits	$1,463	$1,483
Widowed Mother and Two Children	$1,812	$1,838
Aged Widow(er) Alone	$850	$862
Disabled Worker, Spouse, and One or More Children	$1,376	$1,395
All Disabled Workers	$822	$833

EXHIBIT 13: SUMMARY OF BASIC SOCIAL SECURITY COVERAGE AND BENEFITS (% OF PIA)
(ALL ARE SUBJECT TO FAMILY MAXIMUM DOLLAR BENEFITS AND ASSUME NORMAL RETIREMENT AGE)

Beneficiaries	Retirement Insurance	Disability Insurance[1]	Survivorship Insurance[2]	
Required Quarters to Earn Coverage FICA must be paid on $890 (for 2003) of earnings to receive a credit of one quarter	Required to be fully insured (40 quarters)	If < 24, 6 quarters. If < 31, half the quarters available since age 21. If ≥ 31, fully insured and 20 of the last 40 quarters.	Fully insured (40 quarters)	Currently insured (6 of last 13 quarters)
Covered Worker	100% at NRA[3]	100%	Deceased (none)	Deceased (none)
Non-Working Spouse Age 65 Age 62 Age 60	 50% 32 1/2 - 35 5/6% N/A	 50% 35 5/6% N/A	 100% 82.2% 71.5%	 0 0 0
Child < 18	50%	50%	75%	75%
Spouse if Caretaker of Child < 16	50%	50%	75%	75%
Dependent Parents ≥ Age 62	N/A	N/A	75 - 82 1/2%[4]	None
Divorced Spouse[5]	50%	N/A	N/A	N/A

1. A blind person need only be fully insured.
2. Plus a death benefit of $255 to spouse or dependent child, if fully or currently insured.
3. NRA = normal retirement age.
4. 75% each if 2 dependent parents; 82½% if 1 dependent parent.
5. A divorced spouse who has been married 10 years is eligible for retirement benefit (unless they have remarried before age 50) and may be eligible for widow(er)'s benefit.

G. NO HEALTH INSURANCE WAGE BASE CAP.

1. High-income taxpayers and their employers pay a higher Medicare tax than lower income taxpayers. The Medicare tax has no ceiling for earnings subject to the hospital insurance portion (HI) of the Social Security tax. The HI tax is 1.45 percent for both the employee and the employer and 2.9 percent for self-employed taxpayers. (See www.ssa.gov for updates.)

   a. Observations, illustrations, and planning tips.

      i. Observation - Although the OASDHI portion still has the wage cap of $87,000 (2003), this cap may well be raised or eliminated in health insurance reform or in future tax legislation.

      ii. Planning tip - Since S corporation earnings (other than salaries) are not considered self-employment income, they would not be subject to this tax. It may be possible in some cases to decrease salaries to avoid a portion of the HI tax. However, the salaries paid must be reasonable.

iii. Structured payments to reflect rental or interest income, which would not be subject to FICA. Note, however, that rental of personal property may be subject to FICA.

iv. A shareholder in a personal service S corporation may want to accumulate funds in the S corporation, instead of personally, to avoid the increased FICA tax.

H. MEDICARE BENEFITS

1. Medicare is comprised of two parts, Part A which covers hospital care, skilled nursing care, hospice care, and home health care, and Part B which is optional and covers physicians' fees and outpatient services.
   a. Almost everyone age 65 and older is eligible for Part A.
   b. If a person is receiving monthly Social Security or railroad retirement benefits, that person is automatically covered under Part A.
   c. People who are eligible for Medicare but are still working must be given an option to participate in their employer's group insurance.
   d. People who are eligible for Part A coverage are automatically enrolled in Part B coverage. If Part B is not wanted, persons may opt out.
2. Part A benefits.
   a. Hospital care benefits provide coverage for the cost of a hospital stay in excess of the deductible ($840 in 2003) during the first 60 days in the hospital. From day 61-90, the patient has a co-pay of $210 per day (2003). After 91 days, a lifetime reserve of up to 60 days is available, the patient co-pay for the lifetime reserve is $420 (2003) per day.
   b. Skilled nursing home benefits are limited to 100 days per benefit period. All expenses are paid for the first 20 days. The patient co-pay is $105 a day for the 21st to 100th day of each benefit period for 2003.
   c. Home health care is limited to 21 consecutive days per illness, and no hospital stay need precede the care. Must be set up by physician.
   d. There is a limit of 210 days of hospice care unless re-certified as terminal.
3. Part B benefits.
   a. There is a $100 deductible that the insured must pay, and then all covered services are paid at 80% with the insured responsible for the other 20%.
   b. Covered expenses include physician's services, home health services not requiring a hospital stay, diagnostic tests, medical equipment, and all outpatient services of a hospital.
   c. Part B pays 100% of X-ray and pathology services.

EXHIBIT 14: SUMMARY OF MEDICARE DEDUCTIBLE, COINSURANCE, AND PREMIUM AMOUNTS FOR 2003

Hospital Insurance (Part A)

- **Deductible** - $840 per each Benefit Period
- **Coinsurance**
  - $210 a day for the 61st through the 90th day, per Benefit Period
  - $420 a day for each "nonrenewable, lifetime reserve day"
- **Skilled Nursing Facility Coinsurance** - $105 a day for the 21st through the 100th day per Benefit Period
- Some people age 65 or older do not meet the Social Security Administration's requirements for premium-free Hospital Insurance (Part A). Individuals in this category can get Part A by paying a monthly premium. This is called "premium hospital insurance."

Medical Insurance (Part B)

- **Deductible** - $100 per year
- **Monthly Premium** - $58.70 (Note: A surcharge of 10% is assessed for each full 12 months (in the same continuous period of eligibility) in which a beneficiary could have been enrolled but was not.) The surcharge would not be assessed on months not enrolled in Part B while covered by an employer-sponsored group insurance plan.

Source: Office of the Actuary/HCFA
(See www.hcfa.gov or www.medicare.gov for updates)

XVIII.OTHER COMPULSORY SOCIAL INSURANCE

A. WORKERS COMPENSATION.

1. General.
   a. Workers compensation benefits compensate workers who are injured in the course of their employment.
   b. There are five basic principles upon which workers compensation laws are based.
      i. The workers compensation laws impose absolute liability (liability without fault) on the employer for any injury to the employee that occurs in the course of employment. Therefore, negligence by the employer or the employee is not a factor in determining liability.
      ii. The employee gives up the right to sue the employer for the benefits of workers compensation.
      iii. Benefits are paid periodically to protect the injured party from squandering a lump sum.
      iv. Employees cannot be required to contribute to workers compensation. The employer is responsible for providing the coverage.
      v. The employer must purchase and maintain workers compensation insurance.
   c. Not all employees are covered by workers compensation. Frequently, exempted employees are domestic and agriculture employees.
   d. Workers compensation is a compulsory law in all but three states.
   e. Covered injuries must arise out of and in the course of employment.
   f. Workers compensation covers occupational diseases and accidents.
2. The objectives of workers compensation laws are to:
   a. Provide broad coverage for employees for occupational injury and disease.
   b. Provide protection against income loss (income replacement) to the worker and/or the survivor dependents.
   c. Provide adequate medical care and rehabilitation services.
   d. Encourage employer/employee safety.
   e. Reduce litigation (especially between unequal litigants).
3. Workers compensation benefits.
   a. The benefits are payable to the injured worker or his dependents.
   b. Medical expenses resulting from a work-related injury are covered without limit.
   c. Disability income is classified into four types:
      i. Total temporary disability - When an employee is unable to work due to an injury but will recover and return to work. Benefits are a percentage of weekly earnings.
      ii. Partial temporary disability - For the worker who cannot pursue his or her own occupation but can pursue other work. Benefits are a percentage of weekly earnings.

iii. Total permanent disability - When an employee is unable to be gainfully employed due to an industrial injury. Benefits are payable for the entire period of disability.

iv. Partial permanent disability - An industrial injury resulting in a loss of limb. Benefits are based on a schedule.

d. Death benefits are available if an employee is killed while in the course of employment.

i. Payment for burial expenses is one type of death benefit.

ii. Survivors benefits are a second type of death benefit.

e. Rehabilitation benefits are paid during a period of training and rehabilitation subsequent to a work-related injury.

f. Second injury funds have been established in most states to encourage the employment of industrial physically handicapped workers by not requiring the employer to pay indemnity should a second accident occur.

g. Workers compensation benefits are excludable from income for federal income tax purposes (considered making the person whole).

B. UNEMPLOYMENT INSURANCE.

1. Unemployment insurance is designed to replace part of an employee's income when he or she is unemployed, although able and willing to work. It is funded by an employer payroll tax (FUTA/SUTA).

2. To be eligible for unemployment compensation, a person must have previous employment in a covered occupation and continued attachment to the labor force.

   a. Covered employment means that a tax must have been paid on behalf of the employee.

   b. The employee must have earned a certain minimum income during the preceding year.

   c. Unemployment must be involuntary.

3. Benefits to which the worker is entitled are related to previous earnings and are subject to a minimum and maximum determined by each state. All states impose a maximum period for which benefits can be received.

4. Unemployment benefits are includible in income for federal income tax purposes.

XIX.HOMEOWNERS INSURANCE - GENERAL PROVISIONS

A. HOMEOWNERS INSURANCE.

1. Homeowners insurance is a package policy (i.e., combines two or more separate coverages into one policy). Generally, homeowners insurance consists of a combination of fire, theft, and personal liability insurance as a package. Certain eligibility requirements exist with regard to homeowners insurance.

   a. The policy must be for an owner-occupied dwelling.

   b. No more than two families may be occupying the dwelling.

   c. Each family within the dwelling may only have a maximum of two boarders or roomers.

2. Levels of coverage for homeowners insurance (two basic types).

   a. Named-peril coverage.

      i. Named-peril coverage is coverage that provides protection from perils that are specifically mentioned (listed) in the policy.

      ii. This coverage applies to personal property under all forms and includes 18 perils that are basically indistinguishable among forms.

      iii. HO Forms 2 and 8 cover the dwelling and other structures against the same 18 perils that apply to personal property.

   b. Open-peril coverage.

      i. Open-peril coverage is designed to protect against all perils except those specifically excluded from coverage. This increased coverage results in a higher premium for the insured.

      ii. HO3 contains open peril coverage for dwelling and other structures.

3. Once a determination has been made that a loss is covered, the next step is to determine the amount of the loss. The property sustaining a loss will either be valued on an actual cash value (ACV) basis or on a replacement cost (RC) basis.

   a. Actual cash value.

      i. Actual cash value applies to personal property under all forms (unless an endorsement is added to insure the property on the basis of replacement cost).

      ii. ACV = Cost - Depreciation. (Replacement cost may be used instead of actual cost.)

         A) Cost is historical cost.

         B) Replacement cost is the expense of restoring the property or replacing the property to its previous condition.

         C) Depreciation is the deduction that reflects the condition of the property.

b. Replacement cost.

i. Dwellings and other building structures are covered from loss for replacement cost.

ii. As mentioned earlier, personal property may be valued on the basis of replacement cost if an endorsement is added.

iii. Generally, replacement or repair must actually occur before the insured can recover from the loss. The insurer will not pay more than actual cash value prior to the replacement or repair of the damaged property.

iv. Applies to HO1, HO2, HO3, HO6, and HO8 (replacement cost for HO8 is on a modified basis). The modified basis means replacement cost using currently available materials and workmanship.

4. There are five standard homeowners policy forms:

a. **HO2** - Broad form, residential. This named-peril form policy insures the dwelling, other structures, and personal property for specifically named perils (18).

b. **HO3** - Special form, residential. This special form insures the dwelling and other property against losses to the property for open perils (all except those specifically excluded). Personal property is subject to the same named-peril coverage as HO2 (unless an endorsement is added).

c. **HO4** - Contents broad form, residential, and tenant. HO4 provides protection from named perils (same as HO2) for a tenant's personal property.

d. **HO6** - Unit-owners form, condominium. HO6 insures the personal property of the insured (condominium owner) for named perils (same perils as HO2).

e. **HO8** - Modified coverage form, residential. This modified coverage provides protection for dwellings that have a fair market value (FMV) that is less than the replacement value of the dwelling (for example: a home, actual cash value of $150,000 with a replacement value of $400,000).

Note 1: The basic form (HO1) has been withdrawn from use in most states because the policy has such limited coverage.

Note 2: HO5, which provided comprehensive all-risk coverage for dwelling and personal property, has been withdrawn from use. This coverage can be replaced by adding a special personal property endorsement to the HO3 policy.

5. Each form contains two sections.

a. Section I: Coverage on the insured's owned property.

b. Section II: Coverage for liability and medical expenses.

6. Deductible.

a. Generally, any loss is subject to a $250 deductible. However, deductibles may be reduced to $100 or increased to $500, $1,000, or $2,500. Substantial rate reductions are available with higher deductibles.

b. The deductible does not apply to losses involving credit cards, counterfeit money, check forgery, or ATM cards.

7. The chance of using homeowners insurance is estimated to be 1 in 88.

B. HOMEOWNERS SECTION I COVERAGE.

Section I consists of 5 sections identified as A through D and Additional Coverages.

Section	Coverage
A	Dwelling
B	Other Structures
C	Personal Property
D	Loss of Use
Additional Coverage	Debris Removal, Damage to Trees, Credit Card Loss, etc.

1. Coverage A provides coverage on the dwelling.
   a. Dwelling includes:
      i. Structures attached to the dwelling, and
      ii. Materials and supplies intended for use in construction. This is an important element of the coverage because a homeowners policy will often be used to protect a dwelling under construction.
   b. Land is specifically excluded from Coverage A.
   c. Coverage on the dwelling is on a replacement cost basis provided that the amount of insurance coverage is 80% of the replacement cost of the building.
      i. If the insurance coverage is less than 80% of the replacement value, the insurance company will pay either actual cash value or the percentage of replacement cost the insurance company represents as a co-insurer.
      ii. Actual cash value is replacement cost less depreciation.
      iii. An inflation guard endorsement may be added to coverage and automatically increases the amount of insurance every quarter in response to inflation. This endorsement may guarantee that the insured never becomes a co-insurer.
2. Coverage B insures the garage and other structures on the premises that are detached from the dwelling.
   a. The amount of Coverage B is dependent upon the amount of coverage under Coverage A. Generally, 10% of the amount of insurance on the dwelling applies as insurance on detached structures. For example, if the home is insured for $150,000, the detached structures are insured for $15,000.
   b. There are three exclusions under Coverage B. These exclusions include:
      i. Coverage B, like Coverage A, does not extend to land.
      ii. Coverage B does not apply to any structure used for any business purpose (business exclusion).
      iii. Coverage B does not apply to any structure rented to someone who is not a tenant of the dwelling, except for a private garage, and then only if the garage is used for garage purposes (rental exclusion).

3. Coverage C covers personal property and/or contents.
   a. Personal property, either owned or used by the insured, will be covered. This coverage extends worldwide.
   b. While the coverage may be changed, generally, the amount of insurance on personal property will be 50% of the insurance on the dwelling. For example, if Bob's dwelling is insured for $150,000, his personal property is insured up to $75,000. An exception to this limit exists with respect to personal property generally located at another residence of the insured, such as a vacation home. In this instance, the amount of insurance for personal property is limited to the greater of $1,000 or 10% of the Coverage C insurance. Thus, Bob's personal property at his summer cottage would only be insured up to $7,500.
   c. Coverage C may be decreased to 40% of the value of the dwelling if the insured does not own personal property equal to 50% of the value of the dwelling. However, the coverage may not be reduced below 40%. This limitation applies to forms HO1, 2, and 3.
   d. Personal property exclusions and limitations.
      i. Personal property coverage is written to provide blanket coverage, meaning all personal property used or owned by the insured is covered under one policy.
      ii. Some personal property is covered by other types of insurance, and is excluded from the blanket coverage. Exclusions usually include:
         A) Personal articles that are specifically and separately insured under the homeowners policy or another insurance policy such as jewelry, furs, or boats.
         B) Animals, birds, or fish.
         C) Motorized land vehicles and the equipment, accessories, and apparatus that are operated solely by the electrical system of the vehicle. This includes cars, motorcycles, golf carts, and snowmobiles.
         D) Aircraft and their parts.
         E) Property of tenants not related to the insured.
         F) Property in an apartment or condominium that is rented or held for rental such as the refrigerator, stove, and furniture.
         G) Property held for rental such as bicycles or motor scooters.
         H) Business data such as papers, software, or drawings.
         I) Credit cards and ATM cards.
      iii. Personal property coverage also contains items that are subject to dollar limitations in the blanket policy. However, when the value of these items is higher than the limitations allowed, either a rider may be attached to the policy that specifically lists these items, or other insurance may be purchased for the specific items. These are to protect against loss due to moral hazard and loss adjustment issues.
         A) The items that are limited to $200 total, in most blanket policies, include cash and currency, bank notes, bullion, coins, and medals.
         B) The items that are limited to $500, in most blanket policies, include property away from the dwelling used for business purposes.

C) The items that are limited to $1,500, in most blanket policies, include securities, manuscripts, personal records, stamp collections, valuable papers, watercraft, trailers, jewelry, watches, furs, and electronic equipment (both business and personal, powered by the electrical system of a motor vehicle but capable of being operated by another source of power).

D) The items that are limited to $2,500 each, in most blanket policies, include:

1) Firearms,

2) Property at the dwelling used for business, and

3) Theft of silverware, silver-plated ware, gold-plated ware, and pewter ware.

E) If any of these items are insured separately or the limit is increased, they must be separately and particularly scheduled. The item is then no longer a part of the blanket coverage and thus not subject to the deductible.

4. Coverage D provides for living expenses or loss of income in the event of loss of use.

   a. Generally, Coverage D is limited to 20% of the amount of insurance on the dwelling for HO2 and HO3 policies (HO1 and HO8 policies are limited to 10% of the amount of insurance on the dwelling). The three types of benefits that are provided under Coverage D include: additional living expenses, fair rental value, and prohibited use.

   b. Additional living expense coverage pays for expenses incurred by the insured to continue to maintain the insured's standard of living in the event the house is deemed uninhabitable because of an insured peril. This benefit is only paid for the period of time reasonably required to repair or replace the damage or until the insured permanently relocates.

   c. If the insured does not incur additional living expenses, the insured will receive a benefit equal to the fair rental value of the property. In addition, fair rental value is also paid when a portion of the premises is rented to others but unusable.

   d. In the event that use of the property is prohibited because of some other event besides damage to the property, the insured may receive additional living expenses or fair rental value.

5. Additional coverage provides for such things as debris removal, damage to trees, shrubs, and plants, losses from credit cards, etc.

   a. Debris removal extension covers the expense incurred for the removal of debris from the insured's property that has been damaged by an insured peril.

   b. Tree, shrubs, plants, and lawn can be covered for perils including lightning, fire, explosion, aircraft, non-owned vehicle, theft, malicious mischief, riot, and vandalism.

   c. Fire department service charges.

   d. Credit cards, forgery, and counterfeit money coverage include credit card losses, unauthorized use of ATM cards, depositors' forgery, counterfeit money coverage, and defense coverage. The standard limits are $500 on most items; however, increased limits are available by endorsement up to $10,000.

   e. Collapse coverage is for the direct loss to covered property due to collapse caused by an insured peril, hidden decay, insect damage, weight of contents, equipment or people, weight of rain on roof, and defective material.

   f. Glass or safety glazing material.

   g. Landlord's furnishing covers appliances and carpet in an apartment on the premises of the residence that is rented or held for rent.

C. OTHER PROVISIONS.

There are separate conditions that relate to loss settlement which are applicable to Section I of the homeowners policy.

1. The insurance company is not liable for more than the insured's interest in the property or the limit of the liability in the policy (face).
2. The insured is required to notify the insurance company if a loss has occurred, prepare an inventory of damaged property and the extent of the damage, and submit a signed statement indicating the amount of loss, within 60 days of the request by the insurance company.
3. In the settlement of a loss, personal property will be settled at actual cash value, and buildings will be settled through replacement cost provisions (except HO8). Personal property may be settled on a replacement value basis if a personal property replacement value endorsement is attached.
4. If a single unit or item of a set (e.g., earrings) is damaged or lost, the insurance company may repair or replace the lost part to complete the set or restore the item to its value before the loss.
5. Glass will be settled on the basis of replacement.
6. If an appraisal is needed to determine an amount of loss, the party the appraiser represents will pay the fee associated with this service. (If there is an "appraisal provision" in policy, then three appraisals will be made.)
7. The insurance company agrees to pay the proportion of its liability when there is more than one insurance company.
8. A loss must be paid within 30 days after agreement on the amount of loss has been established.
9. A mortgagee listed in the policy becomes a party to the contract with distinct rights separate from the insured. The mortgagee has the right:
   a. To receive any loss or damage payments to the extent of its interest in the property, whether the insured has violated the policy provisions or a breach of contract has occurred.
   b. To receive notice of cancellation.
   c. To sue in his or her own name.

D. HOMEOWNERS SECTION II COVERAGE.

1. Each of the homeowners forms has identical liability coverage. This liability coverage takes two forms: Coverage E - Personal Liability and Coverage F - Medical Payments to Others. Section II liability coverage protects the insured, as well as other family members residing in the named insured's household, against most of the risks associated with personal activity, contracts, premises, etc., whether or not caused by negligence.
2. Coverage E - Personal Liability.
   a. This coverage protects the insured against claims arising out of both bodily injury and property damage. The insurer will cover both the damages and the costs of any defense of the claim or suit.
   b. The minimum amount of coverage is $100,000 per occurrence. Occurrence is defined as an accident, including continuous or repeated exposure to substantially the same general harmful conditions. Although an accident may meet the definition of occurrence, it may not be covered because certain situations are excluded, such as liability arising from an auto accident (see exclusions below and under the section: Liability Insurance for the Individual).

c. Liability coverage applies to the following individuals:

   i. The insured.

   ii. Family members residing in the household.

   iii. Any person under the age of twenty-one who is in the care of one of the above individuals.

d. Coverage E liability insurance is based on a legal liability to pay, which implies that the insurer will only pay when the insured is legally liable. It is important to note that the insurer will only pay to the lesser of the damage or the coverage. Therefore, if the insured has liability coverage of $100,000 and becomes legally liable for $125,000, then the insured will be responsible for the additional $25,000.

EXHIBIT 15: LIABILITY EXCLUSIONS APPLICABLE TO COVERAGES E AND F

Exclusion	Coverage E: Personal Liability	Coverage F: Medical Payments
Intentional Injury	☑	☑
Business and Professional Activities	☑	☑
Rental of Property	☑	☑
Professional Liability	☑	☑
Uninsured Premises	☑	☑
Motor Vehicles	☑	☑
Watercraft	☑	☑
Aircraft	☑	☑
War	☑	☑
Communicable Disease	☑	☑
Sexual Molestation or Abuse	☑	☑
Nuclear Exclusion	☑	☑
Workers Compensation	☑	☑
Controlled Substance	☑	☑
Contractual Liability	☑	
Property owned by or in custody of Insured	☑	
Injuries of Insured Person	☑	
Residence Employee Away from Premises		☑
Persons Residing on Premises		☑

3. Coverage F - Medical Payments to Others.

    a. The homeowners policy includes coverage for the medical payments to others for injuries that arise even where the insured is not liable for the injury. Medical expenses include reasonable charges for medical procedures, surgical procedures, hospital stays, ambulances, dental care, X-rays, professional nursing, prosthetic devices, and funeral services.

    b. This coverage does not apply to the insured or members of the insured's household. Medical payment coverage also excludes residence employees. An exception exists for residence employees who can receive medical payments under Coverage F if the residence employee is off the premises when injured and is in the course and scope of employment when injured unless the residence employee was or should have been covered by workers compensation.

    c. Medical payments coverage is not liability coverage and is not based on fault.

        i. Thus, it covers injuries that occur on the premises regardless of whether the injured was at fault.

        ii. Generally, Coverage F will pay up to $1,000 for medical payments to others.

        iii. Because medical payments are not based on fault, it allows the insurer to pay regardless of who is responsible. If the insured were liable, Coverage E would pay for the liability.

    d. One of the following conditions must be met for an individual to receive medical payments coverage from the insured's coverage:

        i. The injury occurs while the person has permission to be at the insured location.

        ii. The injury occurs while the person is away from the insured location and is caused by a condition at the insured location or on property immediately adjoining the insured location. For example, Bob is walking on a public sidewalk in front of Jack's house and trips over an extension cord extending from Jack's house to the street where Jack is vacuuming his car.

        iii. The insured injures another person while away from the insured location. For example, while playing basketball, Todd causes Scott to break his wrist when both reach for the basketball. Todd's Coverage F would cover Scott's medical cost (up to the limit, generally $1,000).

        iv. The injury occurs as a result of the actions of a residence employee of the insured away from the insured location while the employee is in the course of employment.

        v. An animal owned by or in the care of the insured injures an individual off the insured premises.

E. GENERAL PROVISIONS APPLICABLE TO SECTION I AND SECTION II.

1. The policy applies only to the losses incurred during the policy period.
2. The policy will be void if the insured willfully misrepresented or concealed any material fact concerning the insurance.
3. Any new form or endorsement made by the insurer during the term of the policy broadens the policy without additional premium.
4. No waiver is valid unless in writing.

5. Either party may cancel the contract. The insured may cancel immediately, but the insurance company may only cancel under certain conditions and must give advance written notice of cancellation.
   a. Conditions for cancellation by insurance company.
      i. Nonpayment of premium (requires 10-day written notice).
      ii. During the first 60 days, the insurance company can cancel a new policy for any reason, but after 60 days the insurance company can cancel only if there is a material misrepresentation by the insured or the risk has substantially changed. This type of cancellation requires 30-days written notice.
      iii. If the policy is written in excess of one year, it can be canceled on the anniversary date for any reason with 30-days written notice.
      iv. An insurance company may cancel a policy with a 5-day notice, if the building covered is vacant or unoccupied, if the building is damaged by an insured peril and repairs have not begun within 30 days, if the building has been condemned, if the building is salvageable and fixed items are being removed, or if utilities have been discontinued for 30 consecutive days.
6. If the insurance company is not renewing, a policy cancellation notice must be mailed 30 days before expiration.
7. Assignment of a homeowners policy is not valid without the insurance company's written consent.
8. The insured is required to assign his or her right of recovery against a third party to the insurer if the insurance company pays for a loss caused by the third party (subrogation).

F. CRITICAL PROVISIONS OF PROPERTY INSURANCE - BEYOND DECLARATION AND EXCLUSIONS.

1. Duties of the insured following a loss:
   a. Notify the insurer (usually in writing).
   b. Mitigate damages (take reasonable care of property).
   c. Provide evidence of the loss (affidavit).
   d. Assist and cooperate with insurer to investigate the loss.
2. Settlement options.
   a. Replacement - Insurer repairs or replaces damaged property of insured (insurer choice).
   b. Abandonment and salvage - Total loss (at option of either insured or insurer).
   c. Pairs and sets - Insurer indemnifies for decline in value (insurer has the right to repair/replace entire set or issue check for lost value).
   d. Coverage basis - May be either actual cash value (ACV) or replacement value.
   e. Insurable interest - There must be an insurable interest for life insurance at the inception and for property insurance at the time of loss (owners and creditors typically have an insurable interest).

3. Coinsurance.

   a. Property insurance - Usually 80% of replacement value. If the dwelling is insured for 80% of its replacement value, the insurer will pay all claims up to the face amount of the policy less the deductible. If less than 80%, insurer will pay according to the following formula.

      [(face amount divided by 80% of value) x (loss) – (deductible)] = insurer's portion

Note: The maximum benefit the insurer will pay is the face amount of the policy.

Example

Andrew owns a house with a replacement value of $280,000. The house is insured for $175,000 (80/20 coinsurance clause) with a $250 deductible. Andrew paid $175,000 for the house and suffers a loss of $40,250.

$$\frac{\text{Did carry}}{\text{Should have carried}} \quad \frac{\$175{,}000}{\$280{,}000 \times 0.80} = \frac{\$175{,}000}{\$224{,}000} = 78.125\%$$

Note: Not equal to 100%.

Insurer pays 78.125% of each loss (less the deductible)

Andrew pays 21.875% of each loss

		(21.875) Andrew	(78.125) Insurer	Total
Loss	$40,250	$8,805*	$31,445**	$40,250
Deductible	250	+ 250	- 250	0
		$9,055	$31,195	$40,250

*$40,250 x 0.21875 = $8,805 + $250 = $9,055

** $40,250 x 0.78125 = $31,445 - $250 = $31,195

If Andrew (insured) had carried $224,000 insurance, the insurer would have paid $40,250 - 250 = $40,000.

XX. PERILS

A. SECTION I - GENERAL EXCLUSIONS.

All homeowners policies have eight general exclusions that prevent coverage for a loss associated with these exclusions.

EXHIBIT 16: EIGHT GENERAL EXCLUSIONS	
• Ordinance or Law	• Neglect
• Earth Movement	• War
• Water Damage	• Nuclear Hazard
• Power Failure	• Intentional Loss

1. If the dwelling is deemed condemned, does not comply with the provisions of the local building code, the ordinance or law exclusion releases the insurance company of liability for the repairs or construction necessary to bring the building to local standards.
2. Earthquakes, including land shock waves or tremors before, during, or after a volcanic eruption, landslide, mudflow, earth sinking, rising or shifting, or any earth movement, are not covered in a homeowners policy.
3. Water damage.
   a. Flood, surface water, waves, tidal waves, and overflow of a body of water.
   b. Water that backs up through sewers or drains or overflows from a sump.
   c. Water below the surface of the ground that exerts pressure on, or seeps through, a building, sidewalk, driveway, foundation, swimming pool, or other structure.
4. Power failure exclusion prevents coverage for loss that relates directly to an interruption of power or other utility service. Coverage is provided for consequential loss when equipment on the premises is damaged by an insured peril such as lightning.
5. Loss resulting from neglect by the insured, to use a reasonable means at or after the loss to save the property, is excluded.
6. Losses caused by war are excluded.
7. Losses from a nuclear hazard are excluded.
8. Intentional damage is excluded.

> **Note:** Some of the above exclusions can be covered by special insurance policies (earthquake and flood).

B. PERILS INSURED AGAINST UNDER HOMEOWNERS INSURANCE.

1. An HO1 policy provides coverage for 12 named perils (see Exhibit 15 on page 312).
2. An HO2 policy is broad form coverage for damage to buildings and personal property for loss of use due to damage created by 18 named perils (see Exhibit 15 on page 312).
   a. The perils of fire and lightning are covered; however, the fire must be a hostile or unfriendly fire, meaning that the fire is not one that burns within the intended confines. The coverage from this peril is for the destruction caused by the actual fire and the damage that results from smoke, water, and the firefighter's attempts to extinguish the fire.
   b. Wind and hail peril coverage excludes interior damage that is caused by rain, sleet, sand, or dust, unless the exterior walls or roof are damaged first by the wind or hail. For example, a window that is left open and rain is blown into the dwelling that causes damage to the interior is not covered, but had the window been broken by the wind or hail and then the rain caused damage, the coverage would exist.
   c. Explosions are covered regardless of whether they are internal or external.
   d. Damages caused by riot and civil commotion, including pillage and looting that occur during and at the place of the riot or commotion are covered.
   e. Damages to the property caused by an aircraft, missile, or spacecraft are covered. This also includes objects falling from aircraft and sonic booms.
   f. Damages caused by vehicles are covered with the exceptions of damage to fences, driveways, or walkways by the insured's vehicle.
   g. Damages caused by smoke broaden the peril to include coverage for sudden and accidental smoke damage other than a hostile fire.
   h. Willful and malicious damages (i.e., vandalism) are covered if the building has not been vacant for more than 30 days or if the building is under construction.
   i. Theft, including attempted theft or loss of property from a known location when it is likely that the property has been stolen, is a peril.
      i. General theft exclusions are:
         A) Theft by the insured. For example, if one of the insured's children takes the family silver, there is no coverage.
         B) Theft in or from a building under construction.
         C) Theft from any part of a residence rented by an insured to anyone except another insured.
      ii. Off-premises exclusions are:
         A) Property at any other residence occupied by the insured except while the insured is actually residing at that location. For example, if the insured has a beach condo as a second home, the contents are covered for other perils; but theft coverage only applies when the insured is actually at the condo.
         B) Theft of watercraft, trailer, equipment, and outboard motor.
         C) Theft of campers or trailers when away from the premises.

j. Damages caused by falling objects, such as a tree, are covered. The interior of a building and the contents are not covered for loss due to falling objects unless the exterior of the building was damaged first.

k. Damage caused by the weight of ice, snow, and sleet is covered, but damage caused by melting snow such as leaks is not covered. The coverage excludes awnings, fences, patios, pavement, swimming pools, foundations, retaining walls, piers, and docks.

l. The accidental discharge, leakage, or overflow of water from plumbing, heating, air-conditioning, or automatic sprinkler system from within a domestic appliance is covered. Coverage includes the cost of tearing out and replacing part of the building to make the repairs, but excludes the loss to the appliance or system.

m. A wide range of losses to heating and air-conditioning systems are covered under the sudden and accidental tearing apart, cracking, burning, or bulging of heating or air-conditioning systems peril.

n. Loss that results from freezing of plumbing, heating, air-conditioning, or automatic sprinkler system is covered. If the building is vacant and the insured did not drain and shut the water off or if the insured did not use care in maintaining adequate heat, the coverage is excluded. This coverage applies for damage to a system or appliance.

o. Sudden and accidental injury to wiring and appliances from artificially generated electrical current is an insurance peril. This excludes damage to tubes, transistors, and electronic components (i.e., television sets and stereos are not covered).

p. Volcanic eruption coverage is for above-ground damage caused by lava and debris.

C. HO3: SPECIAL FORM (OPEN PERILS).

1. The special form homeowners policy provides coverage on dwellings and other structures on an open-perils basis resulting in coverage against all physical loss other than those specifically excluded.

   a. Under HO2 broad coverage, a loss is covered if it falls within the named 18 perils. Whereas with HO3 special form, losses are covered unless specifically excluded.

   b. The number of exclusions under a special form policy is usually extensive since all uninsurable perils are excluded.

   c. If a loss results from two causes, one excluded and one not, the loss is covered through the doctrine of concurrent causation.

2. The special form homeowners policy provides for loss of use on an open-perils basis. The personal property coverage is 50% of the coverage on the dwelling.

3. The special form homeowners policy contains exclusions that apply to all homeowners forms (which have been discussed earlier), but also excludes losses caused by weather conditions that contribute to an otherwise excluded peril. Examples include: a mudslide that is caused by excessive rain; losses caused by acts or decisions such as failure of a governmental agency to maintain flood control structures; and loss caused by faulty, inadequate, or defective activities such as the design, maintenance, or planning of a building.

4. The special form homeowners policy contains exclusions applicable to the open-perils coverage of the dwelling and other structures.
    a. Exclusion of collapse peril should be covered under additional insurance.
    b. Exclusions include the previously discussed exclusions in the named-peril forms.
    c. Standard open-peril exclusions are:
        i. Wear and tear, marring, or deterioration.
        ii. Inherent vice, latent defect, or mechanical breakdown.
        iii. Rust, mold, wet or dry rot.
        iv. Smog or smoke from agriculture smudging or industrial operations.
        v. Release, discharge, or dispersal of contaminants or pollutants unless caused by a named peril.
        vi. Settling, cracking, shrinking, building, or expansion of pavement, patios, foundations, walls, floors, or ceiling.
        vii. Birds, vermin, rodents, or insects.
        viii. Animals owned or kept by an insured.
5. The special form homeowners policy provides coverage on personal property for the same perils as HO2. However, an endorsement can be added to an HO3 policy so that personal property is covered on an all-risk (open-perils) basis.

D. HO4: CONTENTS BROAD FORM.

1. HO4 is designed for tenants and provides protection for furniture, clothes, and other personal property for the same perils as HO2 Broad Form.
2. Loss of use coverage is limited to 20% of the amount of Coverage C (personal property).
3. Tenant's improvements and betterments coverage protects the insured for the value for any additions, installations, or improvements made by the insured to the rented dwelling. This coverage is limited to 10% of the amount of personal property coverage.

E. HO6: CONDOMINIUM UNIT OWNERS.

1. The insurance responsibility in a condo arrangement is divided between the condo unit owner and the condo association.
    a. The condo association is responsible for the insurance policy to cover the common areas and the building.
    b. Condo unit owners are responsible for insurance for the additions to their own units and for contents within the condominium.
2. HO6 provides coverage for the personal property of the condo owner for the same named perils as HO2.
3. HO6 provides for loss of use coverage equal to 40% of the amount of Coverage C (personal property).

4. HO6 provides coverage for building alterations and additions, which include appliances, fixtures, real property that pertains exclusively to the insured's premises, property that is the insured's responsibility under the condo association agreement, and structures owned by the insured other than the condo unit. This coverage is generally $1,000.

5. Endorsements can be added to HO6 to provide open-peril coverage on the unit owner's building items, personal property, loss of unit rental, and assessment coverage.

6. HO6 and HO4 are similar type policies with minimal differences:

    a. HO6 has $1,000 of coverage for the condominium unit. HO4 does not have this type of coverage.

    b. HO6 provides Coverage D (loss of use) equal to 40% of the coverage for personal property. HO4 provides for 20% coverage for loss of use.

F. HO8: MODIFIED COVERAGE FORM (OLDER HOME COVERAGE).

1. Some homeowners are faced with the situation where their dwelling is not replaceable due to the type of construction. In this situation, the replacement cost for the home exceeds the fair market value of the home. HO8 is designed to cover losses to these types of structures based on the amount required to repair or replace the property based on current construction costs and materials.

> **Note:** This coverage differs from HO2 and HO3 in that it pays based on actual cash value and not replacement value.

2. An HO8 policy does not include a standard replacement cost provision, but utilizes a functional replacement cost provision for loss.

    a. Under the functional replacement cost, the insurance company agrees to pay the amount necessary to repair damage, but the coverage cannot be more than the materials and labor that are functionally equivalent to the original style of the dwelling.

    b. HO8 is appropriate for a home that had a current market price of $100,000 and a replacement cost (due to the methods and materials of construction) of $175,000.

3. Theft coverage applies to the premises only and is limited to $1,000 per occurrence.

G. HOMEOWNERS SECTION I OPTIONAL COVERAGES.

1. Coverage is available through optional endorsements for sinkhole collapse peril and earthquake peril.

2. Personal property coverage can be written on a replacement cost basis through an optional endorsement. The replacement cost coverage agrees to pay losses without the deduction for depreciation.

3. Four classes of property are not eligible for replacement cost coverage.

    a. Antiques, fine art, and similar property.

    b. Memorabilia, souvenirs, and collectors items.

    c. Property not kept in good working condition.

    d. Obsolete articles that are stored or not being used.

EXHIBIT 17: SUMMARY OF HOMEOWNERS INSURANCE POLICIES						
	HO1 (Basic Form)	HO2 (Broad Form)	HO3 (Special Form)	HO8 (For Older Homes)	HO4 (Renter's Contents Broad Form)	HO6 (For Condominium Owners)
Perils covered (descriptions are given below)	Perils 1 - 12	Perils 1 - 18	All perils except those specifically excluded from buildings; perils 1-18 on personal property.	Perils 1 - 12	Perils 1 - 18	Perils 1 - 18
Property coverages/ limits						
House and any other attached buildings	Amount based on replacement cost, minimum $15,000	Amount based on replacement cost, minimum $15,000	Amount based on replacement cost, minimum $20,000	Amount based on actual cash value of the home, minimum $15,000	Not Applicable	$1,000 on owner's additions and alterations to the unit
Detached buildings	10% of insurance on the home	10% of insurance on the home	10% of insurance on the home	10% of insurance on the home	Not covered	Included in coverage of Part A
Trees, shrubs, plants, etc.	5% of insurance on the home, $500 maximum per item	5% of insurance on the home, $500 maximum per item	5% of insurance on the home, $500 maximum per item	5% of insurance on the home, $500 maximum per item	10% of personal property insurance, $500 maximum per item	10% of personal property insurance, $500 maximum per item
Personal property	50% of insurance on the home	50% of insurance on the home	50% of insurance on the home	50% of insurance on the home	Chosen by the tenant to reflect the value of the items, minimum $6,000	Chosen by home owner to reflect the value of the items, minimum $6,000
Loss of use and/or additional living expense	10% of insurance on the home	20% of insurance on the home	20% of insurance on the home	10% of insurance on the home	20% of personal property insurance	40% of personal property insurance
Credit card, forgery, counterfeit money	$500	$500	$500	$500	$500	$500
Liability coverages/ limits						
Comprehensive personal liability	$25,000 - $100,000	$25,000 - $100,000	$25,000 - $100,000	$25,000 - $100,000	$25,000 - $100,000	$25,000 - $100,000
Damage to property of others	$250 - $500	$250 - $500	$250 - $500	$250 - $500	$250 - $500	$250 - $500
Medical payments	$500 - $1,000	$500 - $1,000	$500 - $1,000	$500 - $1,000	$500 - $1,000	$500 - $1,000
Special limits of liability*						

*Special limits apply on a per-occurrence basis (e.g., per fire or theft): money, coins, bank notes, precious metals (gold, silver, etc.), securities, deeds, stocks, bonds, tickets, stamps; watercraft and trailers, including furnishings, equipment, and outboard motors; trailers other than for watercraft; jewelry, watches, furs; silverware, goldware, etc.; guns.

EXHIBIT 18: LIST OF COVERED PERILS

BASIC NAMED PERILS		
1. Fire	5. Riot or civil commotion	9. Vandalism or malicious mischief
2. Lightning	6. Aircraft	10. Explosion
3. Windstorm	7. Vehicles	11. Theft
4. Hail	8. Smoke	12. Volcanic eruption

BROAD NAMED PERILS

Basic Named Perils 1 - 12, plus 13 – 18:

13. Falling objects
14. Weight of ice, snow, sleet
15. Accidental discharge or overflow of water or steam
16. Sudden and accidental tearing apart, cracking, burning, or bulging of a steam, hot water, air conditioning, or automatic fire protective sprinkler system, or from within a household appliance
17. Freezing of a plumbing, heating, air conditioning, or automatic fire sprinkler system, or of a household appliance
18. Sudden and accidental damage from artificially generated electrical current

	HO1*	HO2	HO3	HO4	HO6	HO8
Coverage A - Dwelling	Basic	Broad	Open Peril	N/A	Broad	Basic
Coverage B - Other Structures	Basic	Broad	Open Peril	N/A	N/A	Basic
Coverage C - Personal Property	Basic	Broad	Broad	Broad	Broad	Basic
Coverage D - Loss of Use	Basic	Broad	Open Peril/ Broad	Broad	Broad	Basic

* HO1 is no longer commonly sold.

XXI.OTHER PERSONAL FORMS OF PROPERTY INSURANCE

A. MONOLINE FIRE DWELLING PROGRAM.

1. There are many dwellings that are not eligible for coverage under a homeowners policy. These dwellings are insured through monoline fire forms, referred to as dwelling policies, which do not provide personal liability insurance or personal theft coverage. Recall that the homeowners policies are package policies combined with several types of coverage that are joined with a basic fire policy.
2. There are three forms of dwelling policies:
    a. Dwelling property 1 basic form.
    b. Dwelling property 2 broad form.
    c. Dwelling property 3 special form.

    The basic difference in the forms is the covered causes of loss.
3. Dwelling property, including dwellings in the process of construction, whether or not occupied, are eligible for coverage, with the exception of farm dwellings.

B. DWELLING PROPERTY 1 BASIC FORM (DP01).

1. This form is the most limited form of coverage available on dwelling and contents.
2. Coverage A - Dwelling Coverage.
    a. The dwelling is defined to include the described dwelling and any additions in contact with the dwelling. Also included in this coverage are materials and supplies for use in construction, alteration or repair of the dwelling and building equipment, and outdoor equipment used for the service of and located on the premises.
    b. This coverage is based on actual cash value, not replacement value as with homeowners policies.
3. Coverage B - Other Structures.
    a. This coverage applies to structures on the premises other than the dwelling.
    b. Examples would include such structures as a garage or swimming pool.
4. Coverage C - Personal Property.
    a. Coverage C applies to personal property owned or used by the insured or family members and includes a special provision for automatic transfer of coverage for 30 days at a new location.
    b. Up to 10% of the insurance can be applied to property located anywhere in the world.
5. Coverage D - Rental Value.
    a. This coverage provides payment for the amount of rental income the dwelling could have generated had a covered loss not occurred.
    b. This coverage is limited to 10% of the policy value for the loss of rent for a year and $1/12^{th}$ of 10% for each month of lost rents.

6. Additional coverages under the DP01 policies are:
    a. Other structure extension allows for supplementary coverage of 10% of the insurance on the dwelling to the other structures.
    b. Debris removal covers the expense of removing debris from the insured property that is damaged by an insured peril.
    c. If the insured is a tenant and installs fixtures and makes improvements or betterments at the insured's expense, an insurable interest has been created in these expenditures. Improvements, alterations, and additions coverage provides 10% of the amount of coverage to improvements.
    d. Coverage is worldwide on personal property.
    e. Rental value extension provides up to 10% of the amount of insurance on the dwelling for rent value.
    f. The cost of reasonable repairs to protect property from further damage is covered.
    g. Property-removed coverage provides open-peril coverage for property being removed from a building when threatened by an insured peril.
7. Dwelling basic form DP01 provides for coverage against fire, lightning, and inherent explosion that are internal, vandalism, and malicious mischief.
8. Exclusions are identical to the basic form homeowners policy.
9. Basic form is subject to a deductible.

C. DWELLING PROPERTY 2 BROAD FORM (DP02).

1. Coverage under DP02 is broader than the basic form. The number of perils covered is greater, and the coverage is on replacement value.
    a. Perils include those in the HO2 basic form with the exception of theft. The DP02 covers the damage that is created by burglars, but not the loss of property.
    b. Explosion peril does not include explosion from a steam boiler. Vehicle damage is broadened to cover the insured's vehicle.
2. The insured is required to carry insurance equal to 80% of the replacement cost of the building.
3. Coverage E - Additional Living Expense.
    a. This coverage is included to cover expenses related to relocation or rental in the event of a loss.
    b. This coverage is limited to 10% of the amount of insurance on the dwelling.
4. Broad form is subject to a deductible.

D. DWELLING PROPERTY 3 SPECIAL FORM (DP03 AND ENDORSEMENTS).

1. Special form dwelling DP03, other structure, rental value, and additional living expense coverage are provided for open-peril coverage subject to the exclusions in HO3 coverage.
2. Dwelling property can be covered through a modified coverage, like HO8, that provides settlement on a functional cost basis.
3. A theft endorsement can be added to provide coverage on the loss of personal property from theft.
4. A personal liability supplement can be purchased as an endorsement to dwelling coverage.

E. MOBILE HOME PROGRAM.

1. Coverage for a mobile home is provided through an endorsement to a homeowners policy with similar coverage as a conventional home tailored to meet the needs of mobile home owners.
2. To meet eligibility under mobile home coverage, the unit must be a portable trailer not less than 10 feet wide and 40 feet long that can be towed on its own chassis and designed for year-round living.
3. A mobile home policy defines dwelling to include utility tanks attached to the mobile home and permanently attached floor covering, dressers, cabinets, and other built-in items as part of the dwelling.
4. Coverage is for a maximum of 80% of replacement cost, but the policy can be endorsed to provide coverage on an actual cost basis.
5. Personal property coverage is limited to 40% based on the built-in contents covered by the dwelling definition.
6. Additional living expense coverage will provide up to 20% of the mobile home's insured value.
7. Property removal coverage will provide payment to move the mobile home when required to escape damage from an insured peril.
8. Transportation/moving endorsements cover collision upset, stranding, or sinking while the mobile home is being moved to a new location.

F. FLOOD INSURANCE.

1. The National Flood Insurance Program provides subsidized flood insurance to property owners in qualified areas. The coverage uses two forms:
   a. Coverage on dwellings and contents.
   b. Coverage on other types of eligible property.
2. Flood is defined as a general and temporary condition of partial or complete inundation of normally dry land areas from:
   a. The overflow of inland or tidal waters.
   b. The unusual and rapid accumulation or runoff of surface waters from any source.
   c. Mudslides or mudflows that are proximately caused by flooding.
3. Residential flood insurance provides coverage for physical loss by or from a flood. Flood is defined as a general and temporary condition of partial or complete inundation of normally dry areas resulting from overflow of inland or tidal waters or the unusual and rapid accumulation or runoff of surface waters from any source. It also includes mudslides that are caused by the flood.
4. The coverage is on an actual cash value basis, but replacement cost is available for any one-to-four-family dwelling that is occupied by the owner at least 80% of the year.
5. Contents coverage applies to household and personal property usual or incidental to the occupancy of the dwelling.
6. Coverage is subject to the standard exclusions and is subject to a deductible.
7. A flood policy is enforceable immediately during the first 30 days that coverage is available in a community. After the 30th day, there is a 5-day waiting period for coverage to be effective.
8. Property owners in special flood hazard areas are usually required to purchase flood insurance to satisfy mortgagees.

G. INLAND MARINE COVERAGE FOR THE INDIVIDUAL.

1. Insurance on specific items of personal property (including automobiles, motor vehicles, boats, and other personal property that is not covered under the homeowners policy) is provided under inland marine form insurance either as an endorsement to the homeowners policy or as a separate policy.
2. Coverage that is usually included on the homeowners policy as a scheduled endorsement (scheduled floater) are:
   a. Personal furs - each item must be scheduled with an amount of insurance that is applicable, additions are covered automatically with a limit of 25% of the scheduled insurance or $10,000. Acquisitions should be reported within 30 days and an additional premium paid. The coverage requires an appraisal, and the coverage is worldwide. Coverage is open peril. The coverage excludes loss caused by wear and tear, insect or gradual deterioration, loss by nuclear radiation, and loss from war.
   b. Jewelry - each item must be scheduled with an amount of insurance that is applicable; additions are covered automatically with a limit of 25% of the scheduled insurance or $10,000. Acquisitions should be reported within 30 days and an additional premium paid. The worldwide coverage requires an appraisal. Coverage is open peril. The contract has a clause for pairs or sets that prevents collecting on a total loss when only 1 item in a pair is lost.
   c. Silverware floater coverage is the same as jewelry.
   d. Golf equipment floater covers golf equipment kept in a locker at a clubhouse.
   e. Other endorsements are camera, fine art and antiques, stamp and coin collection, musical instrument, wedding presents, and personal property floaters.

Note: Endorsements remove items from blanket coverage.

H. INSURANCE ON WATERCRAFT.

1. Boat owner's policy covers liability, physical damage, medical payments, and uninsured watercraft.
2. Physical damage coverage is actual cash value coverage for the boat and permanently attached equipment, the motor including remote controls and batteries, and boat trailer, on an open-perils basis that is subject to wear and tear, gradual deterioration, and mechanical breakdown.
3. Liability coverage includes:
   a. Watercraft liability - Coverage for claims or suits against the insured for damages of bodily injury or property damage caused by watercraft. Liability coverage excludes intended bodily injury, liability of persons using watercraft without permission, damage to insured's property, injury to persons eligible for workers compensation, and liability of person in the business of selling, repairing, storing, or moving watercraft.
   b. Medical payments - Covers medical expense resulting from boating accidents.
   c. Uninsured boaters coverage - Covers bodily injury caused by an uninsured boater.

I. BUYING PROPERTY INSURANCE FOR THE INDIVIDUAL.

1. Premium cost is a function of rate, risk of loss and potential loss, locality, and the perils that are insured against.
2. For a dwelling, the premium is based on construction, the number of families, and the fire protection of the city.

XXII. LIABILITY INSURANCE FOR THE INDIVIDUAL

A. LIABILITY INSURANCE IN GENERAL.

1. Liability insurance is protection against legal obligations that arise from the negligent acts of an individual.
2. Liability insurance pays the costs, up to the face of the policy, for acts by the insured that result in liability.
3. Liability insurance usually provides defense for the insured in the event of a lawsuit arising from an act that is covered.

B. TYPES OF LIABILITY INSURANCE.

1. Liability insurance covers automobile liability, homeowners liability, employer liability, and general liability.
2. General liability is associated with any negligent act and does not have to be related to an automobile or work. General liability insurance is designed to protect business firms and individuals from acts of negligence and the associated legal liability.

C. COMPREHENSIVE PERSONAL LIABILITY COVERAGE.

1. Liability insurance that is designed to protect an individual is comprehensive because it insures against all types of liability hazards.
   a. The coverage is for the liability of the insured, the family members, or both.
   b. The coverage includes exposure at the residence or away from the residence.
2. Personal liability insurance provides coverage for the insured's legal obligation because of bodily injury or property damage.
3. Personal liability insurance also provides payment for reasonable medical expenses for the injured party.
4. Personal liability is included in Section II of the homeowners policy with a standard limit of $100,000. An insured can purchase additional coverage through an umbrella liability policy.
5. Under liability insurance, the definition of persons insured is important since it determines the coverage that is available for certain individuals other than the insured. In most policies, the insured includes you and residents of your household who are relatives, a person under 21 who is in the care of a relative, a person who has your permission to operate watercraft or tend to animals that belong to you, and any person engaged in your employment or using a vehicle on an insured location.

6. Liability insurance exclusions:
   a. There is no coverage for bodily injury or property damage if the act that created the injury or damage was intentional.
   b. Liability that is a result of business owned or conducted by the insured is not covered by the liability insurance.
   c. Liability that arises from rental operation conducted by the insured is not covered. However, there are exceptions for occasional rental of residence, rental of part the premises for residence, or rental of part of residence as an office.
   d. Professional liability is excluded and should be covered through a separate policy.
   e. Liability that occurs on an uninsured location that is owned by the insured and uninsured means there is no insurance coverage for the property or premises.
   f. Liability arising from the use of a registered motor vehicle is excluded. This liability is covered through automobile insurance.
   g. Liability that results from certain types of boats is excluded.
   h. Liability that results from aircraft is excluded.
   i. Other exclusions are liabilities related to war, communicable disease, sexual molestation or abuse, controlled substance usage, contracts, property owned by, rented to, or in the care of the insured, workers compensation, nuclear damage, and injuries to insured persons.

D. MEDICAL PAYMENTS TO OTHERS.

1. The homeowners policy includes coverage for medical payments to others for injuries that arise even if the insured is not liable for the injury.
   a. This coverage does not apply to the insured or members of their household.
   b. This coverage is not liability coverage.
   c. Covers injuries that occur on the premises even if the injured was at fault.
2. Medical payments coverage has the same exclusions as liability coverage previously discussed. Medical payment coverage also excludes domestic servants when they are away from the insured premise and not engaged in their employment.

E. DAMAGE TO THE PROPERTY OF OTHERS COVERAGE.

1. The coverage for damage to property of others is not liability coverage since it pays whether the insured is liable or not. Most coverage pays up to $500 for damage to property.
2. The exclusions for this coverage include losses that are covered under other parts of the homeowners policy: intentional damage, damage to property owned by or rented to any insured, damage that results from business pursuits, damage to uninsured locations, and damage to vehicles.

F. SECTION II CONDITIONS.

1. The limit of liability is the maximum payable.
2. The insurance applies separately to each insured.
3. The insured must cooperate with the insurance company in the event of a loss.
4. A person seeking coverage for medical payments must submit written proof of loss.
5. Bankruptcy by the insured does not relieve the insurance company of its obligation under the policy.

G. OPTIONAL PERSONAL LIABILITY ENDORSEMENTS.

1. Personal injury liability endorsement expands coverage for:
   a. False arrest, detention, imprisonment, or malicious prosecution.
   b. Libel, slander, defamation, or violation of the right of privacy.
   c. Wrongful entry, eviction, or other invasion of the right of private occupancy.

H. PROFESSIONAL LIABILITY INSURANCE.

1. Professional liability insurance covers the liability that may arise from a failure to use due care and possess a degree of skill that is expected of a person in a particular profession such as a physician, accountant, lawyer, or financial planner.
2. Medical malpractice insurance is professional liability coverage designed for physicians and hospitals and is not limited to bodily injury or property damage. Malpractice insurance also includes coverage for losses such as mental anguish. Intentional acts are not excluded from malpractice insurance.
3. Errors and omissions coverage is professional liability insurance designed to cover liability resulting from rendering, or failure to render, appropriate professional services.

I. UMBRELLA LIABILITY POLICY.

1. An umbrella policy provides protection against catastrophic liability by providing broader coverage and excess coverage in addition to liability insurance.
2. To qualify for an umbrella policy, the insurance company usually requires the insured to purchase certain underlying liability insurance. For example, the insured may need automobile liability insurance with limits of $50,000/$100,000/$25,000 for an insurance company to offer additional liability coverage through an umbrella policy.
3. Inexpensive - $1 million coverage covers items not covered in underlying policies (e.g., slander, libel, etc.).

XXIII. AUTOMOBILE INSURANCE

A. OVERVIEW OF AUTOMOBILE COVERAGES.

Automobile insurance is divided into four types of coverage.

1. Automobile liability insurance covers the loss resulting from legal liability when bodily injuries or property damages occur caused by a covered insured's automobile.
2. Automobile medical payment coverage provides reimbursement for medical expenses that arise from an automobile accident for the insured and family members.
3. Automobile physical damage coverage protects against the loss of the insured's automobile through comprehensive (also known as "other than collision") and collision agreements.
   a. Comprehensive coverage is open-peril coverage that provides for any insurable peril other than collision.
   b. Collision coverage provides for loss that results from collisions (with inanimate things).
4. Uninsured motorists coverage (includes under insured) is designed for the insurance company to pay the insured the amount that could have been collected from a negligent driver who did not have insurance or who committed a hit-and-run accident or who has an insolvent insurance company.
5. The chance of using automobile insurance is estimated to be 1 in 47.

B. LEGAL LIABILITY AND THE AUTOMOBILE.

1. Due to vicarious liability, where one party becomes liable for the negligence of another, an individual may be held liable in a situation where another person was the driver.
2. Many states have enacted laws requiring compulsory automobile liability insurance laws that require individuals involved in an accident that causes bodily injury or property damage to provide proof of the ability to pay any judgment resulting from the accident or face the loss of their license. This law is usually satisfied by an automobile liability policy.

C. INSURANCE FOR HIGH-RISK DRIVERS.

There are people that insurance companies are unwilling to insure due to the risk that is associated with their driving record. Coverage for such high-risk individuals can be purchased through several different avenues.

1. An automobile insurance plan is a risk-sharing pool that auto insurance companies utilize to write high-risk drivers.
   a. This pool makes auto liability insurance available for individuals who cannot obtain insurance in the normal channels.
   b. This pool provides equitable distribution of the risk among insurance companies.
2. Several states participate in reinsurance pools and joint underwriting associations to insure high-risk drivers.

D. THE COST OF AUTOMOBILE INSURANCE.

The Insurance Services Office (ISO) has established a rating system to determine auto insurance premiums based on a set of factors including the following:

EXHIBIT 19: AUTOMOBILE PREMIUM FACTORS

- Territory
- Age, sex, and marital status
- Use of automobile
- Driver education
- Good student discount
- Number and type of automobiles
- Driving record

1. Territory.
    a. Geographic location is an important element in determining the premium. Certain areas of the country have higher claim rates than other areas. These higher claim rates increase the cost of insurance for those areas.
    b. Cities generally have higher claim rates than rural areas, resulting in higher premiums.
2. Age, sex, and marital status.
    a. Young male drivers have the highest rates of automobile accidents. This results in young male drivers paying the highest insurance rates. This group is divided into 4 categories of drivers under the age of 30.
        i. Under 20.
        ii. 20 to 22.
        iii. 22 to 24.
        iv. 25 to 29.
    b. Young female drivers generally have lower accident rates than young male drivers.
    c. Young male drivers who are married have lower rates of accidents than unmarried young male drivers.
3. Use of automobile.
    a. Classifications.
        i. Farm use.
        ii. Pleasure use - not used for business or for work.
        iii. Drive to work (< 15 miles).
        iv. Drive to work (≥ 15 miles).
        v. Business use.
    b. The lowest rating factor is farm use followed by pleasure use. The highest rating factor is business use.

4. Driver education.
    a. Young drivers can receive a discount or credit for successfully completing a driver education course.
    b. This discount is generally about 10%.
5. Good student discount.
    a. This discount is based on the premise that good students tend to be better drivers.
    b. To qualify, the individual must be enrolled in high school or college on a full-time basis and meet one of the following:
        i. Top 20% of class.
        ii. B average or above.
        iii. 3.0 average or above.
        iv. Dean's list or honor roll.
6. Number and type of automobile.
    a. A multi-car discount is generally available for those who own more than one automobile.
    b. The age, type, damageability, and repairability of the automobiles are also important elements in determining the premium.
7. Driving record.
    a. Those drivers who do not have accidents or driving violations for three consecutive years often qualify for lower premiums.
    b. Insurers will impose a dollar premium or a surcharge for those drivers who do not have a clean driving record.

XXIV. THE PERSONAL AUTO POLICY

A. GENERAL NATURE OF THE PERSONAL AUTO POLICY (PAP).

1. The PAP is a package insurance policy that provides coverage for losses that result from legal liability, injury to the insured and/or members of the insured's family, and damage to or loss of the automobile.
2. The PAP only covers certain autos and people.
   a. The auto must be owned by an individual to be eligible for coverage. A partnership or corporation automobile is not eligible for PAP coverage.
   b. The auto must be a specific type such as a private passenger vehicle that weighs less than 10,000 pounds. Cars, pickups, and vans are included as long as they are not used for delivery purposes.
   c. Motorcycles, motor homes, golf carts, snowmobiles, and similar types of vehicles can be included in a PAP through an endorsement as long as owned by an individual.
3. The PAP is divided into six parts:

1. Part A - Liability coverage	4. Part D - Damage to your auto
2. Part B - Medical payments	5. Part E - Duties after an accident or loss
3. Part C - Uninsured motorists	6. Part F - General provisions

B. PART A - LIABILITY COVERAGE (MANDATORY).

1. Liability coverage is considered to be the most important part of a PAP policy.
2. Through the liability coverage, the insurance company is obligated to pay up to the policy limits the loss for which the insured is legally responsible due to an accident. The minimum limit of coverage in most states is $25,000 per accident, but this may be increased. In addition to the liability that the insured is legally responsible for paying, the insurance company also agrees to pay any legal costs for defense. Insurance company will stop paying for defense when liability amount is paid. Legal defense is additional to liability amount.
3. This coverage is usually written as $25/$50/$10, which means there is coverage up to $25,000 for bodily injury to one person, coverage up to $50,000 total for all persons injured, and coverage up to $10,000 for property damage, all based on a single accident.
4. This coverage may also be written as a single limit, which will apply to both property damage and bodily injury. For example, a single limit of $300,000 would apply to both bodily injury and property damage (total insurer exposure is $300,000, however applied).

5. The liability coverage is provided for the use of any auto or trailer by the insured and/or any family member, defined as any person related by blood, marriage, or adoption, who resides in the household of the insured.
   a. Persons other than the named insured and family members are covered while using the insured auto, provided they had the right to use the auto.
   b. Liability coverage extends to anyone vicariously liable for the operation of the owned auto, such as an employer of any person operating a covered auto.
   c. Liability coverage extends to anyone vicariously liable for the operation of a non-owned auto by the named insured.
6. The definition of covered auto is the vehicle listed in the policy and any vehicle on the date the insured becomes the owner, provided the vehicle meets the eligible vehicle description discussed earlier.
   a. A newly acquired auto is automatically covered for 30 days. However, the insurance company must be notified within the 30-day period to extend coverage.
   b. A newly acquired auto is covered based on the broadest coverage that applies under the written policy.
   c. A trailer, which is owned by the insured, is also considered to be a covered automobile. The liability section (Part A) would cover lesser losses resulting from a trailer.
   d. Any automobile that is being used as a temporary substitute automobile, such as a rental car, will be covered under the PAP. This coverage also includes a trailer not owned by the insured.
7. Liability exclusions.
   a. Intentional acts that cause bodily injury or property damage.
   b. Damage to property owned or being transported by an insured (generally, covered under a property insurance policy).
   c. Damage to borrowed or rented property (does not apply to immovable property).
   d. Injuries to employees in the course of employment where workers compensation applies.
   e. Liability while the auto is used as a delivery vehicle.
   f. Any person employed in the automobile business (this exclusion does not apply to the owned auto while being operated by the insured or family member).
   g. Business use of commercial vehicles.
   h. Liability resulting from any person using the vehicle without permission or a reasonable belief that they are entitled to use the vehicle.
   i. Nuclear liability.
   j. Liability arising out of motorcycles or other self-propelled vehicles with less than four wheels.
   k. Vehicles that are owned or furnished for the regular use of the insured other than the covered vehicle (e.g., a company car provided by the employer for use by the employee). The employer's policy must provide coverage in the event of an accident.
   l. Liability arising from autos owned or furnished for the regular use of family members.
   m. Liability does not apply to any automobile while it is being used in racing competition.

8. Other liability coverage provisions.

   a. Supplementary payments by the insurance company in addition to the legally obligated payments are:

      i. Cost of bail bonds up to $250.

      ii. Premium on appeal bonds.

      iii. Interest on a judgment.

      iv. Loss of earnings up to $50 a day while attending a hearing at the insurance company's request.

      v. Other expenses incurred at the request of the insurance company.

   b. Out-of-state coverage will adjust insurance coverage to meet the liability required by a state if an accident occurs in a state that has higher limits than the state of residence. This coverage also applies to compulsory insurance laws of states.

C. PART B - MEDICAL PAYMENTS COVERAGE (OPTIONAL).

1. Medical payments coverage has a basic limit of $1,000 per person with no maximum per accident and covers necessary medical expenses and funeral expenses for the insured and any family member who suffers bodily injury as a result of an accident. Coverage is available while the insured or family member is occupying any motor vehicle or is a pedestrian struck by any motor vehicle designed for use on a public road.

2. Exclusions for medical payments coverage include:

   a. Vehicles with less than four wheels.

   b. Autos used to carry persons or property for a fee.

   c. Autos owned (other than insured auto) or furnished for the regular use of the insured.

   d. Autos owned (other than insured auto) or furnished for the regular use of family members.

   e. Autos operated without a reasonable belief that the user is entitled to operate.

   f. Non-owned trucks being used in business.

3. Limitations to the medical payment recovery include:

   a. Payments made under the liability coverage reduce medical payments.

   b. Pro rata payments with other types of insurance.

   c. Subrogation.

D. PART C - UNINSURED MOTORISTS COVERAGE (OPTIONAL).

1. Uninsured motorists insurance is an agreement that pays the amount that an insured could have collected from an insurance company from a negligent uninsured driver if such a driver would have had auto insurance.

2. Uninsured motorists coverage applies when the insured is injured by a vehicle that is uninsured (i.e., a vehicle not covered for bodily injury liability, a hit-and-run vehicle, or a vehicle that was insured, but the insurance company is insolvent).

3. The insured persons under uninsured motorists are the named insured, any family member, and anyone occupying the insured vehicle.

4. Exclusions for uninsured motorists include the exclusion for liability previously discussed and the following other exclusions:
    a. The injured person settles with the negligent party without the insurance company's consent.
    b. Coverage for punitive or exemplary damages.

E. PART D - COVERAGE FROM DAMAGE TO YOUR AUTOMOBILE (OPTIONAL).

1. Physical damage coverage is an open-perils coverage and is implemented through two separate agreements: a) comprehensive, and b) collision.
2. Comprehensive coverage is for losses that result from something other than collision, such as breakage of glass, falling objects, fire, theft, storm damage, and damage from collision with flying and other animals (e.g., birds).
3. Collision coverage is the upset or collision with another inanimate object and applies regardless of who is at fault. Examples include:
    a. Insured's automobile hits another car, a fence, a telephone pole, a tree, or a building.
    b. Insured's automobile is dented while the insured is not in the automobile, such as in a parking lot.
    c. Damage occurs to the door from opening the door and hitting the automobile that is adjacent to the insured automobile.
4. Physical damage coverage also applies to non-owned vehicles, such as a rental cars.
5. Exclusions for physical damage are:
    a. Loss while the auto is used as a public or livery conveyance.
    b. Damage due to wear and tear, freezing, mechanical or electrical breakdown, and road damage to tires.
    c. Damage from radioactive contamination.
    d. Damage to non-owned autos being used by any insured while employed in the auto business.
    e. Damage to non-owned autos being used by any insured while employed in any business.
    f. Loss by destruction, or confiscation by government, due to illegal activities.
    g. Sound and communication systems installed in the auto.
    h. Coverage for camper bodies or trailers owned by the insured not listed in the policy.
    i. Coverage for awnings and equipment designed to create additional living space.
    j. Loss of radar detection devices.
    k. Loss of custom furnishings or equipment.
6. Other provisions available through physical damage coverage are:
    a. Losses are to be limited to the lesser of: the actual cash value of stolen or damaged property, or the amount required to repair or replace the property.
    b. Reimbursement for other modes of transportation in the event of a loss.
    c. Reimbursement for towing and labor in the event of a loss.

F. PART E - DUTIES AFTER AN ACCIDENT OR LOSS.

1. The insurance company should be promptly notified of how, when, and where the accident happened.
2. Cooperation with the insurance company in the investigation, settlement, or defense of any claim.
3. Send copies of all legal papers or notices relating to the accident to the insurance company.
4. Submit to insurance company a request for a physical examination.
5. Authorize the insurance company to obtain medical records.
6. Submit proof of loss.

G. PART F - GENERAL PROVISIONS.

1. Includes general provisions of the PAP that are similar to general provisions discussed in other automobile policies.
2. These provisions include the following:
   a. Bankruptcy.
   b. Changes.
   c. Legal action against the insurer.
   d. Right to recover payment.
   e. Policy period and territory.
   f. Termination.
   g. Transfer of your interest in the policy.
   h. Two or more automobile policies.
   i. Fraud.

H. MOTORCYCLES, MOTOR SCOOTERS, AND RECREATIONAL VEHICLES.

1. Coverage for motorcycles and motor scooters are written under a PAP with an endorsement called miscellaneous-type vehicle endorsement.
   a. The endorsement amends the definition of covered auto to include the motorcycle.
   b. The endorsement does not provide coverage for non-owned motorcycles.
2. Recreational vehicles are covered through the miscellaneous-type vehicle endorsement.

I. BUYING AUTOMOBILE INSURANCE.

1. If the vehicle is financed, the lender may require insurance to protect their financial interest. This is accomplished through comprehensive and collision insurance.
2. Liability insurance is essential for every driver.
3. If the insured has good health insurance, medical payment coverage in the auto policy may not be necessary for the insured but also covers others in an accident.

J. NO-FAULT INSURANCE.

1. Under this type of insurance, parties involved in an accident who sustain bodily injury would collect from their own policy regardless of who caused the accident.
2. There are many variations of no-fault insurance policies.

XXV.BUSINESS AND PROFESSIONAL USE OF PROPERTY AND LIABILITY INSURANCE

A. BUSINESS PROPERTY INSURANCE.

The Insurance Services Office (ISO) has developed a commercial insurance program including a package policy (meaning two or more coverages).

1. The Commercial Package Policy (CPP).
   a. If both property and liability coverage are combined into a single policy it is a multi-line policy (e.g., CPP). The advantages of such a policy include lower premiums and fewer gaps in overall coverage.
   b. Workers compensation coverage and surety coverages are not part of a CPP.
   c. A CPP policy format includes: (1) a declarations page, (2) a policy conditions page, and (3) two or more coverage parts or forms (property, general liability, crime, boiler and machinery, inland marine, commercial auto, farm).
   d. Each part or form of the CPP will specify covered property, additional coverages, extension of coverages, other provisions, deductibles, coinsurance, valuation provisions, optional coverages, and a cause of loss form. Coverages for causes of loss are basic, broad, special, or earthquake form. These forms are similar to the parallel homeowners forms. Business interruption insurance may be added. Also, a builders risk coverage form can be added to the CPP for buildings under construction.
2. Inland Marine Policies.
   a. Inland marine contracts cover domestic goods in transit, property held by bailees, mobile equipment and property, property of certain dealers and means of transportation and communication.
3. The Business Owner's Policy (BOP).
   a. The BOP is specifically designed for the needs of small to medium size businesses and covers buildings, business personal property (two forms: basic and special). Basic covers listed perils, as distinguished from special, which covers all perils not excluded. The policy has a standard $250 deductible and covers business liability for bodily injury and property damage.
4. Business Liability Insurance.
   a. General liability is the legal liability arising out of business activities excepting autos, motorized vehicles, aircraft, and employee (workers compensation) injuries. Liability issues, not including exceptions mentioned, are covered by commercial general liability policies (CGL).
   b. CGL can be written either as a stand-alone policy or as a part of a commercial package policy (CPP). The usual coverage, Coverage A, is for bodily injury, property damage and legal defense, but it has significant exclusions. Coverage B is for personal and advertising injury liability. Part C covers medical payments.
5. Workers Compensation.
   a. Most businesses are required to carry workers compensation insurance providing the following coverages: workers compensation insurance, employer liability insurance, and other state insurance. The workers compensation insurance covers benefits provided by the insurer (state). Part two covers lawsuits by employees injured in the course of employment, but not covered by state workers compensation law. Part three covers for other states listed (business trips, etc.).

6. Business Auto.
    a. Businesses also use commercial automobile insurance policies covering both physical damage to property and liability insurance.
7. Business Liability Umbrella.
    a. Business forms may also make use of commercial liability umbrella policies for excess coverage on liability, beyond the coverage provided by the firm's basic liability policy.
8. Professional Insurance.
    a. The professional liability policy provides coverage for malpractice causing harm or injury to the professional's client. The usual types of coverage included are broad coverage, liability not restricted to accidental acts, and negligent acts. There is a maximum per incident limit and an aggregate limit. The practitioner professional also needs general liability insurance.
9. Errors and Omissions.
    a. Errors and omissions coverage provides protection against loss from negligent acts, errors, or omissions by the insured. Many professionals (real estate agents, insurance agents, accountants, stockbrokers, attorneys, engineers) need errors and omissions coverage for negligent acts, or omissions, or failure to act within their own profession causing legal liability. Policies usually have large deductibles ($1,000).

EXHIBIT 20: INSURANCE CONCEPT SUMMARY FOR BUSINESSES AND PROFESSIONALS

	Businesses	Professionals
Property Insurance - Buildings	CPP*	CPP
Property Insurance - Personalty	CPP	CPP
General Liability Insurance	As needed	As needed
Inland Marine Coverage	If transporting goods	If transporting goods
Business Interruption Coverage	As needed	As needed
Build on Risk Insurance	If construction	If construction
Workers Compensation	If employees	If employees
Commercial Auto Insurance	If autos	If autos
Commercial Umbrella Policy	Excess liability coverage	Excess liability coverage
Malpractice	N/A	Yes
Errors and Omissions	N/A	Yes

* CPP (Commercial Package Policy)

INDEX

D

E

F

G

Q

R

S

T

U

V

W

Y

Investment Planning

Outlines and Study Guides

TABLE OF CONTENTS

TABLE OF EXHIBITS

TABLE OF APPENDICES

Investments

I. BASIC INVESTMENT CONCEPTS

A. The Investment Planning Process.

The six steps of the investment planning process are:

1. Means to invest - In order to begin the investment process, the investor must first make the choice to save rather than spend or consume.
2. Investment time horizon - The investor must then determine the time horizon for the investments based on financial objective(s). Thus, the investor must decide, based on the time horizon of the objectives, among short-term investments, long-term investments, or some combination of investment vehicles.
3. Risk and return - The investor must determine the acceptable level of risk for the portfolio based on the investor's risk tolerance. As the level of risk increases so does the potential for greater returns and greater losses.
4. Investment selection - Investments should be selected to meet the goals of the investor, based on Steps 2 and 3. These investments must be suitable to both the investor's time horizon and risk tolerance.
5. Evaluate performance - Once investments have been selected and expectations established, the performance of the investments should be determined by comparing the actual realized returns against the expected returns. The returns should also be compared to a benchmark, such as the S&P 500 Index. In addition, investments should be periodically reevaluated to determine if they continue to meet the investor's criteria.
6. Adjust portfolio - The portfolio should be monitored and adjusted to meet the changing goals and criteria of the investor.

B. Types of Investor Returns.

1. Expected return.
   a. The expected return is the anticipated growth, earnings, or income generated from an investment.
   b. The expected return is the return that is expected to occur for the amount of risk undertaken.
   c. The expected return will be calculated using different models, based on such variables as:
      i. Risk (beta or standard deviation).
      ii. Risk-free rate of return (such as T-bills).
      iii. Return for the overall market.

2. Required return.
   a. The required return is the return that is necessary to induce the investor to purchase the investment.
   b. Different investments will have different required returns depending on the amount of risk perceived. For instance, an investor requires a higher return for common stocks than for T-bills because the risk associated with equity investments is greater.
   c. The required rate of return is also used as a discount rate for valuation purposes. It is the rate at which the stream of cash flows is discounted for purposes of determining the security's value.
3. Realized (actual) return.

   The realized return is the return that is actually earned from an investment. It includes any interest or dividends collected plus any price appreciation less any price depreciation.

C. MEASURES OF RISK.

1. Investments are made for the purpose of yielding returns. However, the realized returns are indeterminable at inception due to uncertainty. This uncertainty is called risk.
2. Risk can be defined several ways.
   a. Risk can be thought of as the uncertainty of future outcomes.
   b. Alternatively, risk might be defined as the probability of an adverse result.
3. The total risk that an investor faces can be separated into two categories:
   a. Systematic risk.
   b. Unsystematic risk.

> **Note:** Total risk, the sum of systematic and unsystematic risk, is measured by the standard deviation of returns.

4. Exhibit 1: "Total Risk" illustrates that total risk is the sum of systematic and unsystematic risk. It also shows that, as more securities are added to a portfolio, the level of unsystematic risk declines due to diversification. Total risk cannot be reduced below systematic risk.

> **Note:** Systematic risk does not change as the number of securities in the portfolio increases.

EXHIBIT 1: TOTAL RISK

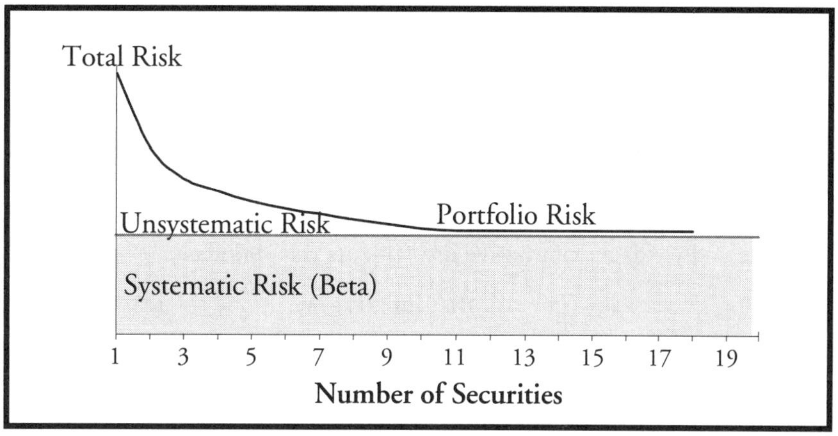

EXHIBIT 2: SYSTEMATIC AND UNSYSTEMATIC RISKS

Systematic Risks	Unsystematic Risks
Purchasing Power Risk	Business Risk
Reinvestment Risk	Financial Risk
Interest Rate Risk	Default Risk
Market Risk	Regulation Risk
Exchange Rate Risk	Country Risk

5. Systematic risks - Those risks that affect the entire market, such as market risk, interest rate risk, purchasing power risk, exchange rate risk, and reinvestment risk. Systematic risk cannot be eliminated through diversification because it affects the entire market. Beta is a measure by which systematic risk is determined. However, beta, as will be seen later, is only an accurate measure of systematic risk when calculated for a well-diversified portfolio. Beta does not measure unsystematic risk.

   a. Systematic risk may be estimated using regression analysis, which is used to determine the linear equation: $r_s = a + br_m$ where:

      r_s = The expected return of the stock.
      r_m = The expected return of the market.
      a = The Y intercept.
      b = The slope of the line (called beta).

   b. Systematic risk is also known as undiversifiable risk because it cannot be reduced through diversification.

   c. Market risk - The tendency for stocks to move with the market is referred to as market risk. When the market is increasing, most stocks have a tendency to increase in value. Conversely, most stocks tend to fall with declines in the market. Often, a move in the market is prefaced by some change in the economic environment. (About 85% of stocks are positively correlated to some degree with the market.)

d. Interest rate risk.

   i. The risk that changes in interest rates will affect the value of securities. There is a tendency for an inverse relationship to exist between the value of fixed investments and changes in interest rates (e.g., as interest rates increase, the value of bonds declines).

   ii. Rising interest rates generally have a negative effect on stocks as well. Reasons for this negative pressure include the increased discount rate utilized for valuation of cash flows, increased borrowing costs for corporations (thus, an expectancy of lower earnings), and increased yields on alternative investments (i.e., bonds).

e. Purchasing power risk - The risk that inflation will erode the real value of the investor's assets. As the price of goods increases, the purchasing power of assets decreases. The objective of investment planning is to generate returns in excess of inflation so that the real value of the assets is not eroded. Inflation is the main cause of purchasing power risk. Bonds held to maturity are likely to suffer from purchasing power risk because the maturity value (face value) remains constant regardless of price changes.

f. Exchange rate risk - The risk that a change in the relationship between the value of the dollar (or investor's currency) and the value of the foreign currency will occur where the investment is made.

Example

- John invests $1,000,000 in the Orval Corporation based in Mexico. Assuming that the conversion rate for pesos to dollars is 10 to 1, John would have to invest 10 million pesos in Orval Corporation. Orval Corporation does extremely well, and John is able to sell his interest for 15 million pesos. If John attempts to convert the pesos into dollars when the exchange rate has changed to 12 to 1, he will receive $1,250,000 ($15,000,000 ÷ 12).
  - This gain is comprised of a 50% (500,000 pesos) gain on the investment and a loss of 16.67% ($250,000 ÷ $1,500,000) or $250,000 from the change in the currency rate.
  - The net result is a 25% gain on the original investment; however, it is only half of the gain generated from the appreciation of Orval Corporation.

- Assume the same facts as in the previous example except that the exchange rate is now 8 to 1 instead of 12 to 1. In this case, John liquidates his interest in Orval Corporation and converts the pesos to $1,875,000. This $875,000 gain consists of $500,000 from the appreciation of Orval Corporation and $375,000 from the devaluation of the dollar relative to the peso.
  - In the first example, John's gain is reduced by 50%, and in the second example, John's gain is increased by 75%. Thus, changes in currency values can have a dramatic impact on the value of and returns from foreign investments.
  - Money managers often attempt to avoid such drastic changes in gains and losses by hedging against currency fluctuations. Forward or futures contracts tend to be used as hedging devices against currency risk.

g. Reinvestment risk - The risk that earnings (cash flows) distributed from current investments will be unable to be reinvested to yield a rate of return equal to the yields of the current investments. For example, if a bond is purchased today to yield 8% and the market interest rate subsequently declines, interest payments from the bond will be unable to be reinvested at 8%; thus, the overall yield to maturity will decline.

Note: Zero-coupon bonds are not subject to reinvestment rate risk during the term of the bond because payments are not made until maturity.

6. Unsystematic risks - Those risks that are unique to a single security, business, industry, or country. These risks include business risk, financial risk, default risk, regulation risk, and country risk. Unlike systematic risk, unsystematic risk can be eliminated through diversification. Several studies have found that unsystematic risk can be significantly reduced with portfolios of as little as 10 to 15 stocks. As more stocks are added to a portfolio, the less impact the losses of one company in the portfolio will have on the total performance of the portfolio of securities.

   a. Business risk.

      i. The riskiness of the specific business includes the speculative nature of the business, the management of the business, the philosophy of the business, etc. Different types of businesses will have different levels of risk.

      ii. For instance, searching for gold would generally be riskier than operating a gas station. However, both will have unique risk associated with that specific type of business. Business risk can also be thought of as the certainty or uncertainty of income.

      iii. Utility companies have relatively stable and steady income streams and, therefore, have lower business risk. Companies with unsteady or fluctuating income levels (cyclical companies) such as, auto manufacturers, are classified as having higher business risk. (Business risk is the asset side of the balance sheet.)

   b. Financial risk.

      i. The capital structure of a firm will affect the return on equity (ROE) for a company. The use of debt magnifies ROE and makes gains and losses more volatile.

Example

A firm that has 80% debt (20% equity) will have a ROE five times larger than a similar firm with the same net income and 100% equity. This financial leverage occurs because the return is based on a smaller amount of equity.

The equity of the leveraged company is one fifth that of the nonleveraged firm so that returns and losses for the leveraged firm will be five times larger on a percentage basis. (Financial risk is the liability side of the balance sheet.)

	Company A	Company B
Net Income	$50,000	$50,000
Debt	$0	$300,000
Equity	$400,000	$100,000
ROE (Return on Equity)	12.5%	50%

c. Default risk.

i. The risk that a business will be unable to service its debt to its creditors. Bonds issued by both corporations and municipalities are subject to default risk. Rating agencies, such as Moody's and Standard & Poor's, rate bonds issued from corporations and municipalities from the highest grade to default.

ii. Generally, obligations of the U.S. government (Treasuries and Ginnie Maes) are considered to be free from default risk.

iii. Default risk does not apply to stocks.

d. Regulation risk - The risk that changes in the law, such as zoning changes or changes in the tax rates, will have an adverse effect on an investment.

e. Country risk - The risk that international investments face which are unique to each country, including political and economic risks. The United States is generally thought to have the lowest country risk, since its political and economic systems are the most stable.

D. RISK AND RETURN.

1. There is a direct relationship between risk and return. As the level of risk increases, the expected return increases. Meanwhile as the level of risk declines the expected return declines. Thus, to receive higher returns, an investor must accept the trade-off of greater risk.
2. The risk and return concept is essential to the theories within investments and is essential when planning for clients.

E. LIQUIDITY AND MARKETABILITY.

1. Liquidity is the ability to sell an investment quickly and at a competitive price, with no loss of principal and little price concession.
2. Marketability refers to the ability of an investor to find a ready market where the investor may sell his or her investment.
3. There is a subtle difference between liquidity and marketability. For instance, real estate is marketable but may not be liquid. Treasury bills are both liquid and marketable.
4. Liquidity and marketability should be thought of as a spectrum with cash as the most liquid and marketable.
5. The term liquidity is a term that is often used to describe a market and the volume of transactions on the market. For example, the Treasury market is very liquid.

F. BASIC VALUATION OF SECURITIES.

1. Models for valuing securities are developed based on the concept of the present value of future cash flows.

a. Bonds - These cash flows include interest or coupon payments and the final return of principal or sale value.

b. Common stock - These cash flows include dividend payments and the final sales price.

c. Real estate - The cash flows include rents and interest from loan proceeds.

2. The basic model:

$$P_0 = \frac{CF_1}{(1+k)^1} + \frac{CF_2}{(1+k)^2} + \ldots + \frac{CF_t}{(1+k)^t}, \text{ where:}$$

P_0 = The value of the security today.
CF_t = The cash flow for period t.
k = The discount rate based on the type of security and the risk level of the investment.
t = The number of cash flows to be evaluated.

3. Other models, which will be discussed later, are based on this basic model for valuing securities. These other models include net present value, internal rate of return, yield to maturity, yield to call, geometric mean, time-weighted return, dollar-weighted return, constant growth dividend model, and the model for valuing perpetuities.

G. MARKET TRENDS.

1. Bull market - Market trends that are increasing are referred to as "Bull Markets."
2. Bear market - Market trends that are continuously downward are referred to as "Bear Markets."

H. MARKET POSITIONS.

1. Long position - The majority of investors take long positions (buy position). A long position is undertaken in the hopes that the security will appreciate over time.
2. Short position - A short position (sell position) will be taken by investors who believe that the market or a particular security will decline in the near future.

II. SECURITIES (TYPES & CHARACTERISTICS)

A. MONEY MARKET SECURITIES.

1. Treasury bills.

   a. The United States Treasury issues 13-week, 26-week, and 52-week Treasury bills (T-bills) in denominations of $1,000. The Treasury auctions 13-week and 26-week bills on a weekly basis, while 52-week bills are auctioned on a monthly basis. These Treasury instruments are considered to be default risk free and are often used as an estimate for the risk-free rate of return.

   b. T-bills are sold as pure discount bonds because coupon payments are not made. Instead, these bonds are sold at discounts with prices quoted as a percentage of the face value, such as 99.125, which translates into $99,125 for a $100,000 issue. At maturity, T-bills pay the face amount, such as $100,000. Thus, the investor would make $875 from such an investment.

   c. T-bills are not subject to the Original Issue Discount (OID) rules that other bonds are subject to because T-bills have maturities of 1 year or less. Therefore, the interest from T-bills is not taxable until the T-bill matures or is sold. For example, Bob buys a 52-week T-bill in August 2001. If he holds the bond until maturity, he will have interest income in 2002, but not in 2001.

   d. Treasury auction process.

      i. Treasury securities are auctioned off using a competitive bid process.

      ii. Competitive bids are submitted by bidding entities, such as large financial institutions.

      iii. Noncompetitive bids are submitted by bidding entities that are willing to purchase the securities being auctioned at the yield that is determined by the auction process. Individual investors typically purchase securities at auction by way of a noncompetitive bid. Noncompetitive bids only specify the quantity of securities desired, which may not exceed $1 million for Treasury bills or $5 million for Treasury coupon securities.

      iv. A competitive bid indicates both the quantity of securities desired and the yield at which the bidder is willing to purchase the security. Auction results are determined as follows:

         A) Subtract the total of all noncompetitive bids and nonpublic purchases (for example securities purchased by the Fed from itself) from the total amount of securities to be auctioned. The remaining amount is the amount that will be sold to competitive bidders.

         B) Competitive bids are ranked from lowest yield bid to highest yield bid, which in effect is ranking the bids from the highest dollar price offered to the lowest dollar price offered. Starting with the lowest yield, all competitive bids are then accepted until the amount to be sold to competitive bidders is exhausted. The stop yield is the highest yield accepted by the Treasury for a particular auction. Bidders at the stop yield are awarded a portion of the total amount of securities for which they have placed a bid.

      v. Every U.S. Treasury security is a single price auction. That is, all bidders (both competitive and noncompetitive) are awarded securities with the yield of the highest accepted competitive bid, the stop yield. This type of auction is known as a Dutch auction.

2. Commercial paper.

   a. Commercial paper consists of a private sector company's issue of short-term, unsecured promissory notes. This type of debt is issued in denominations of $100,000 or more and serves as a substitute for short-term bank financing.

   b. Maturities are 270 days or less (costly registration procedures are required for securities over 270 days) and are often backed by lines of credit from banks.

   c. In comparison to Treasury bills, these instruments have a slightly higher default risk, and are slightly less liquid. Therefore, commercial paper has slightly higher yields than T-bills of similar term structures.

3. Certificates of deposits (CDs).

   a. Negotiable CDs (also known as Jumbo CDs) are deposits of $100,000 or more placed with commercial banks at a specific stated rate of interest. These short-term securities can be bought and sold in the open market. These instruments usually yield slightly higher returns than T-bills because they have more default risk and less marketability.

   b. CDs with smaller denominations (as low as $500) are sold by some banks. However, these are not negotiable certificates of deposit and thus not traded on the open market.

4. Repurchase agreements.

   Securities dealers use repurchase agreements (known as repos) to finance large inventories of marketable securities from one to a few days. The issuer or seller agrees to repurchase the underlying security at a specific price and specific date. The repurchase price is higher than the selling price, creating the required return for the holder participating in the repo.

5. Bankers' acceptances.

   Bankers' acceptances are securities that act as a line of credit issued from a bank. Usually, the bank acts as an intermediary between a U.S. company and a foreign company. Companies that are too small to issue commercial paper will use bankers' acceptances to fund short-term debt needs. These securities usually have slightly higher interest rates than commercial paper.

6. Short-term municipal obligations.

   Municipalities (such as states, counties, parishes, cities, and towns) are politically incorporated bodies other than the federal government and its agencies. These municipalities issue debt instruments ranging in term from 30 days to 30 years. The shorter-term maturities are considered money market instruments.

7. Eurodollars.

   Deposits in foreign banks (originally developed in Europe) that are denominated in U.S. dollars are called Eurodollars. Essentially, Eurodollars are loans to credit-worthy foreign companies. The banks, acting as intermediaries, will often receive a fee of one tenth of one percent.

8. Federal funds.

   Commercial banks within the Federal Reserve System are required to maintain certain levels of cash either on hand or at the Federal Reserve System on a daily basis. This requirement frequently leaves banks with either too much cash or not enough cash. In order to meet the reserve requirements, banks with insufficient cash levels will borrow overnight at the federal funds rate from banks that have surplus cash.

B. BONDS.

1. Basic characteristics of bonds (U.S. Government, Municipal, and Corporate).

   a. Interest payments are usually paid semiannually or annually. Interest may be paid by check if the bond is registered or, with coupon bonds, when the coupon is presented to the bank.

   b. The coupon rate is the stated annual interest rate that will be paid each period for the term of the bond. It will be stated as a percentage of the face value of the bond. For instance, a 9% coupon bond will pay $90 per $1,000 bond (9% of $1,000) per year. If the bond pays semi-annually, then it will pay $45 two times during the year.

   c. Bonds can be registered bonds or bearer bonds. Registered bonds are registered with the corporation or organization, and any payments will be paid to the owner of record. Bearer bonds can be transferred like cash, and the debtor will pay the person who holds the bearer bond.

   d. Yield to maturity.

      i. The yield to maturity (YTM) for a bond is the internal rate of return for cash flows associated with the bond, including the purchase price, coupon payments, and maturity value. Bonds riskier than others of the same term structure will have higher yields to maturity.

      ii. When the market rate of interest for the same term and risk is higher than the coupon rate, the bond will be priced at a discount. The result is a YTM that is equal to the market rate. On the other hand, if the market rate of interest is below the coupon rate, the bond will be priced at a premium in order to yield a YTM equal to the market.

      iii. The YTM model assumes that coupon payments are reinvested at the YTM rate of return for the life of the security. If the coupon payments from the bond are reinvested at a rate less than the calculated YTM, then the actual yield will be less than the YTM. If the coupon payments are reinvested at a rate higher than the calculated YTM, then the actual yield will be greater from the calculated YTM.

   e. Call provisions may be included in the bond agreement. Such a provision allows the debtor to pay off the debt (call the bond) after a specific period of time and usually at a prestipulated price. This type of provision protects the issuer from declines in interest rates and causes the investor's required rate of return to be higher because of the call feature risk.

   f. Sinking funds are both established and funded by the bond issuer each year and accumulate over time to pay off debt upon maturity. These funds are usually held by a trustee to ensure the repayment of the bond proceeds.

   g. Secured bonds.

      i. Secured bonds are bonds that have a legal claim to specific assets in the event of missed interest or principal payments (default), insolvency, or liquidation.

      ii. A mortgage bond is secured by real property or buildings. Mortgage bonds may be open-ended, limited open-ended, or closed-ended, which indicates the degree to which additional debt may be issued against the same property.

      iii. Collateral trust bonds are usually secured by stocks and bonds of other companies held in trust.

h. Debenture bonds are unsecured bonds. Holders of debentures have the same rights as general creditors. To account for the larger default risk, debentures will have higher yields than secured bonds issued for the same term by the same issuer.

i. Convertible bonds contain a feature to convert the bonds to equity securities. This feature benefits the investor by allowing him or her to convert his or her debt to an equity interest and share in the fortunes of the company (convertible bonds are explained more fully in the section entitled "Security Analysis").

j. Zero-coupon bonds do not make any interest payments during the term of the bond. Instead, these bonds sell at a discount from face value and pay only the face amount at maturity. Zero-coupon bonds eliminate reinvestment risk because no payments are made until the bond matures. However, the bonds are still subject to interest rate risk and, if taxable, require taxes to be paid currently on the accrued interest earned each year (zero-coupon bonds fall within the Original Issue Discount (OID) rules). As will be discussed later, the duration of a zero-coupon bond is equal to its maturity.

2. Bond prices and interest rates.

   a. As interest rates increase, bond prices will decline. For example, a 10-year $1,000 bond (that pays interest semiannually) yields 10% and sells at par or 100% of face value ($1,000). If prevailing interest rates increase to 12%, buyers will pay less than par value for the bond so that the yield equals 12% (i.e., the prevailing market interest rate). Because of the increase in interest rates, investors will only be willing to pay $885.30 for the bond.

Prior to Interest Rate Changes		**After Interest Rates Change to 12%**		**After Interest Rates Change to 8%**	
N	= 20 (10 x 2)	N	= 20 (10 x 2)	N	= 20 (10 x 2)
i	= 5 (10 ÷ 2)	i	= 6 (12 ÷ 2)	i	= 4 (8 ÷ 2)
PMT_{OA}	= $50 (100 ÷ 2)	PMT_{OA}	= $50 (100 ÷ 2)	PMT_{OA}	= $50 (100 ÷ 2)
FV	= $1,000	FV	= $1,000	FV	= $1,000
PV	= ($1,000)	PV	= ($885.30)	PV	= ($1,135.90)

   b. Similarly, as interest rates decline, bond prices will increase. Considering the bond above, prevailing interest rates dropping to 8% would cause the price for a bond yielding 10% to increase above par ($1,135.90).

3. Types of bonds.

   a. United States Treasury Notes and Bonds.

      i. Treasury Notes and Bonds.

         A) United States Treasury Notes and Bonds are identical except for maturity; notes have maturities less than 10 years, while bonds have maturities of 10 years or greater.

         B) Both notes and bonds make semiannual coupon payments and are initially offered through Treasury auctions. These competitive auctions are similar to T-bill auctions except that bidders submit yields to maturity instead of discounted prices. These U.S. debt instruments are considered default risk free.

ii. Treasury Inflation Protection Securities (TIPS).

A) In 1997, the Treasury began issuing notes and bonds that are indexed with the consumer price index. The principal value of the bond is adjusted for changes in the CPI. The semiannual interest payments received by the investor are determined by multiplying the inflation-adjusted principal value by one-half of the stated coupon payment. The coupon rate remains the same for the life of the security, but the coupon payment will change based on the changing principal value.

B) At maturity, it is possible that the inflation-adjusted principal will be less than the initial par value (because of disinflation). However, the U.S. Treasury has structured TIPS so that the asset is redeemed at the greater of the inflation-adjusted principal or the initial par value.

Example

Assume a TIPS has a 4.5% coupon rate and the annual inflation rate is 4%. An investor purchases on January 1, $100,000 of par value of the issue. The semiannual inflation rate is 4% ÷ 2 = 2%.

The inflation-adjusted principal at the end of the six-month period is calculated by multiplying the original par value by the semiannual inflation rate as follows: $100,000 x 1.02 = $102,000.

This new inflation-adjusted principal is then used as the basis for computing the coupon interest rate for the first six months as follows: The six-month coupon rate is 4.5% ÷ 2 = 2.25% giving us a coupon payment of $2,295 ($102,000 x 2.25%)

Now, if the semiannual inflation rate for the next six months is 1.5%, the inflation-adjusted principal will be $103,530 ($102,000 x 1.015) and the coupon payment would then be $2,329.43 ($103,530 x 2.25%).

C) The indexed Treasuries provide protection from both interest rate risk and purchasing power risk making them an attractive security for those investors concerned about rising inflation and devaluation due to loss of purchasing power. Like the nonindexed Treasury notes and bonds, indexed Treasury securities are eligible for the STRIPS program discussed below.

iii. Treasury STRIPS.

A) The Treasury STRIPS program was introduced in February 1985. STRIPS is the acronym for Separate Trading of Registered Interest and Principal of Securities. The STRIPS program permits investors to hold and trade the individual interest and principal components of eligible Treasury notes and bonds as separate securities.

B) The Treasury does not issue or sell STRIPS directly to investors. STRIPS can be purchased and held only through financial institutions and government securities brokers and dealers who are the parties that separate the original security into its component parts.

C) When a Treasury-fixed principal or inflation-indexed note or bond is stripped, each interest payment and the principal payment becomes a separate zero-coupon security. Each component has its own identifying number and can be held or traded separately.

D) For example, a Treasury note with 10 years remaining to maturity consists of a single principal payment at maturity and 20 interest payments, one every six months for 10 years. When this note is converted to STRIPS form, each of the 20 interest payments and the principal payment become a separate security.

E) STRIPS are also called zero-coupon securities because the only time an investor receives a payment during the life of a STRIP is when it matures.

b. U.S. Savings Bonds.

i. Some of the most widely held forms of government debt include the Series E, H, EE, HH savings bonds, and the recently issued Series I savings bond.

EXHIBIT 3: U.S. SAVINGS BONDS

	Series E & EE	Series H & HH	Series I
Denominations	\$50, \$75, \$100, \$200, \$500, \$1,000, \$5,000, \$10,000	\$500, \$1,000, \$5,000, \$10,000	\$50, \$75, \$100, \$200, \$500, \$1,000, \$5,000, \$10,000
Purchased	With cash	By exchanging E or EE bonds	With cash
Annual Purchase Limit (per person)	\$15,000 issue price (\$30,000 face value)	No limit on conversion to HH bonds	\$30,000
Issued at	50% of face value	100% face value	100% face value
Maturity	30 years	20 years	30 years
Interest rate	90% of average 5-year Treasury	4% fixed rate	Combination of fixed and variable rates
Interest	Accrues	Paid semiannually	Accrues
Taxation of interest	Deferred	Taxable annually	Deferred
Interest can be completely excluded for qualified higher education costs	Yes	No	Yes

ii. Series E and EE bonds.

A) The Series E bond was designed to encourage more people to save money. Series E bonds were sold at a discount and paid no annual interest, similar to zero-coupon bonds.

B) The Treasury issued the new Series EE bond beginning July 1, 1980, in order to replace the Series E bond. The rate of interest changed from a fixed rate, as with the Series E bonds, to a variable rate equal to 90% of the five-year Treasury securities, updated semiannually. Although the formula for interest on Series EE bonds has changed, it is still a variable rate of interest based on market rates. This variable rate allows investors to benefit from increasing interest rates and will cause their yield to decline if interest rates fall.

C) EE bonds are purchased for one-half of its denomination (face value). For example, a $100 bond will cost $50. EE bonds are purchased with cash (can be through Payroll Savings Plans).

D) The interest earned for both E and EE bonds is not taxable until the bonds are redeemed or reach maturity. However, they do permit recognition of income in earlier years with a valid tax election. Recognizing the income from E and EE bonds may be a tax planning strategy for parents with young children who have no other taxable income and will thereby create tax basis in the bonds.

E) Interest earned on Series EE bonds that have been deferred, can be further deferred by exchanging the EE bonds for HH bonds. This deferral will continue until the HH bonds are sold or mature. However, the interest that is paid on the HH bond is not deferred.

F) The interest from Series EE U.S. government savings bonds may be completely excluded from gross income if the bond proceeds are used to pay qualified higher education expenses (tuition and fees for taxpayer, dependents, or spouse). However, the following criteria must be satisfied:

1) Savings bonds are issued after December 31, 1989.

2) The savings bonds are issued to an individual who is at least 24 years old at the time of issuance.

3) The exclusion is phased out at higher income levels (modified AGI threshold).

4) This exclusion is not available for married taxpayers filing separately.

G) Qualified higher education expenses include rolling over proceeds from the savings bonds into a Qualified Tuition Program (529 Plan) or a Coverdell Education Savings Account (formerly known as an Education IRA).

iii. Series H and HH bonds.

A) The Series HH bond is a new issue designed to replace the older Series H bonds. HH Bonds were introduced in January 1980.

B) Unlike EE bonds, HH bonds cannot be purchased with cash. They can only be obtained by exchanging Series E/EE bonds and savings notes that are at least six months old. Series H bonds can also be used to acquire Series HH bonds.

C) These H and HH bonds are sold at par in larger denominations (minimum of $500). The bonds have a maturity of 20 years. Interest is paid semiannually and is fully taxable in the year of payment. There is not an option to accumulate the interest or defer the taxes.

iv. Series I bonds.

A) The Treasury began selling Series I savings bonds on September 1, 1998, in an attempt to offer individuals a way to accrue income and to protect the purchasing power of their investment.

B) Series I bonds are issued at 100 percent of the face amount in denominations of $50, $75, $100, $200, $500, $1,000, $5,000, and $10,000. Series I bonds have a maturity period of 30 years, consisting of an original maturity period of 20 years and an automatic extension period of 10 years. The bonds have an interest-paying life of 30 years after the date of issue and cease to increase in value on that date. Like EE and HH bonds, Series I bonds are not transferable or marketable.

C) The Series I bond earnings rate is a combination of two separate rates: a fixed rate of return and a semiannual inflation rate. Each May and November, the Treasury announces a fixed rate of return that applies to all Series I bonds issued during the six-month period beginning with the effective date of the announcement, May 1 or November 1. The fixed rate for any given Series I bond remains the same for the life of the bond.

D) In addition, every May and November, the Treasury announces a semiannual inflation rate based on changes in the Consumer Price Index for all urban consumers (CPI-U). The semiannual inflation rate announced in May is a measure of inflation from the previous October through March; the rate announced in November is a measure of inflation from the previous April through September. The CPI-U is published monthly by the Department of Labor's Bureau of Labor Statistics. The semiannual inflation rate is then combined with the fixed rate of the Series I bond to determine the bond's earnings rate for the next six months.

E) Series I bonds can be redeemed anytime six months after the issue date to get the original investment plus the earnings. However, Series I bonds are meant to be longer-term investments. So, if a Series I bond is redeemed within the first five years, there is a 3-month earnings penalty. For example, if a Series I bond is redeemed after 18 months, only 15 months of earnings will be awarded.

F) Like EE bonds, Series I bonds accrue interest over time, and this interest is deferred for tax purposes. In addition, the interest can be completely excluded if its proceeds are used to pay qualified higher education costs.

v. It should be noted that interest earned from Series E, EE, H, HH and I bonds, like the interest from Treasury bills, bonds, and notes, is U.S. government interest and is not taxable by municipalities.

c. U.S. Government agency issues.

i. Various governmental agencies issue debt to finance activities. These agencies have very low default risk. In fact, some agencies are directly backed by the full faith and credit of the United States, and others have implied backing by the government. Because of lower liquidity, agency issues will have slightly higher yields than those of treasuries.

ii. These agencies include:

A) Federal Home Loan Bank.

B) The Farm Credit Assistance Corporation.

C) Federal Land Bank.

D) Resolution Funding Corporation.

d. Municipal bonds.

i. Municipalities include states, counties, parishes, cities, and towns. These governmental agencies issue debt instruments, referred to as municipal bonds. The two types of municipal bonds are general obligation bonds and revenue bonds.

A) General obligation bonds are backed by the full faith and credit of the government issuing the debt and are repaid through taxes collected by the government body.

B) Revenue bonds are issued by governmental bodies in order to finance specific projects (tollways, stadiums, etc.). These bonds are not backed by the full faith and credit of the issuing body. Instead, debts are repaid from revenue generated from the project that was financed. Therefore, these bonds are more risky than general obligation bonds and, thus, require higher yields for similar maturities.

ii. Term bonds or serial bonds may be used. The principal for term bonds is repaid in full upon maturity, whereas, serial bonds require that the municipality retire a certain amount of the bond issue each year.

iii. Tax issues of investing in municipal bonds.

A) Tax equivalent yield.

Municipal Bond Yield						
	4%	5%	6%	7%	8%	9%
Tax Rate						
15%	4.71%	5.88%	7.06%	8.24%	9.41%	10.59%
27%	5.48%	6.85%	8.22%	9.59%	10.96%	12.33%
30%	5.71%	7.14%	8.57%	10.00%	11.43%	12.86%
35%	6.15%	7.69%	9.23%	10.77%	12.31%	13.85%
38.6%	6.51%	8.14%	9.77%	11.40%	13.03%	14.66%

B) Interest earned from municipal bonds is not subject to federal income tax. Therefore, a 5% municipal bond will have an equivalent pretax yield of 7.14% [5% ÷ (1 - 30%)] assuming a 30% tax bracket. The formula for determining the taxable equivalent yield for a municipal bond is as follows:

$$\text{Pretax yield} = \frac{\text{Tax-exempt yield}}{1 - \text{marginal tax rate}}$$

C) Municipal bond interest may also be income tax exempt for various states. For example, Louisiana does not tax Louisiana municipal bond interest. However, they do tax all other states' municipal bond interest.

D) Private activity bonds.

1) Generally, a private activity bond is part of a state or local government bond issue that meets both of the following requirements:

a) More than 10% of the proceeds of the issue are to be used for a private business use.

b) More than 10% of the payment of the principal or interest is:

i) Secured by an interest in property to be used for a private business use (or payments for this property), or

ii) Derived from payments for property (or borrowed money) used for a private business use.

2) An example of private activity bonds would be bonds that are issued for a sports stadium or complex.

3) While municipal bond interest is not subject to regular tax, tax-exempt interest from private-activity bonds is a preference item for purposes of Alternative Minimum Tax (AMT). Therefore, large amounts of private activity bond interest may cause a taxpayer to be subject to AMT.

E) If a municipal bond is sold, any gain or loss is a capital gain or loss and, therefore, subject to federal income tax. However, under the Internal Revenue Code, a capital loss cannot occur when a municipal bond is called or matures. Any premium that is paid for a municipal bond is required to be amortized.

iv. Municipal bond insurance.

A) Some municipal bonds may be insured against default, thereby reducing the credit risk of the bond.

B) Common insurance companies that insure municipal bonds include:

1) AMBAC Financial Group (American Municipal Bond Assurance Corporation).

2) MBIA Insurance Corporation (a subsidiary of MBIA, Inc., formally known as Municipal Bond Insurance Association and Municipal Bond Investors Assurance).

3) Financial Guaranty Insurance Company (FGIC).

v. Obligations of territories.

A) The interest on the obligations of a territory or a possession of the United States, or any political subdivision of any of the foregoing, or of the District of Columbia is not includable in gross income.

Example

The interest on bonds issued by Puerto Rico would not be subject to federal or state income tax.

e. Bonds issued by corporations.

   i. Corporate debt issues are used to generate capital and are accompanied by a legal document between the corporation and the lender. This legal document is called an indenture and sets forth repayment schedules, restrictions, and promises. Bonds are senior securities of corporations (ahead of stockholders). Bonds are beneficial to corporations because they provide needed capital, and the interest payments are deductible for tax purposes, unlike dividends paid to shareholders that are not tax deductible.

   ii. Debentures are bonds that are unsecured, and creditors do not have a specific right to any assets. These creditors are general creditors of the corporation.

   iii. Special features of corporate bonds:

      A) Convertible bonds allow the creditor to exchange his or her bonds with the corporation for a given number of shares of stock. This benefit will cause the yield on the debt instrument to be lower than if the feature had not been offered.

      B) Warrants are often attached to bond issues. A warrant allows the holder to purchase a specific number of shares of stock at a specific price for a specific period of time. These warrants, like convertible bonds, allow the holder to participate in the growth of the company if the holder so chooses.

f. Mortgage-backed securities (MBSs) and collateralized mortgage obligations (CMOs).

   i. Description.

      A) Although relatively new, the market for mortgage-backed securities has seen tremendous growth since its inception in the 1970s. Mortgage-backed securities are ownership claims on a pool of mortgages. The originating mortgage lender will sell loans to investors in the secondary market. These investors pool mortgages together and sell interests in the pool to other investors.

      B) This process of transforming mortgages into securities that can be sold to the public is known as securitization.

   ii. Mortgage-backed securities.

      A) MBSs are often referred to as "pass-through" securities because the monthly mortgage payments are passed along to the holders of the MBSs, less a small servicing fee. These monthly mortgage payments consist of scheduled interest and principal payments, as well as unscheduled principal prepayments. These unscheduled principal prepayments result from borrowers making additional principal payments on their loans or from paying off loans, such as in the case of refinancing.

      B) Because MBSs are backed by mortgages, many of which are backed by the government and all of which are secured by real property, they have little credit risk. However, MBSs are subject to other risks. Just like other fixed-income obligations, these securities are subject to the fluctuation in interest rates. As interest rates increase, the value of the MBS decreases and as interest rates decrease, the value of the MBS increases.

      C) Since MBSs pass through payments on a monthly basis, the investor must reinvest these cash flows into some other investment. This reinvestment rate risk impacts MBSs in the same manner as other fixed-income securities that have cash flows occurring during the life of the security.

D) Unlike other fixed-income obligations, MBSs are subject to prepayment risk, which is the risk that homeowners will pay off their loans before the scheduled loan maturity date. Since the value of these securities is based on the schedule of cash flows, any mortgage prepayments will impact the return an investor receives on a mortgage-backed security. In addition to creating uncertainty as to the timing of the cash flows, these prepayments create a situation in which the investor must reinvest the additional principal payments perhaps at a lower interest rate, furthering the reinvestment risk.

E) The majority of the mortgage-backed securities have been issued by three government agencies. These include the Federal National Mortgage Association (FNMA or "Fannie Mae"), the Government National Mortgage Association (GNMA or "Ginnie Mae"), and the Federal Home Loan Mortgage Corporation (FHLMC or "Freddie Mac"). Only GNMAs are backed by the full faith and credit of the U.S. government and are, therefore, default-risk free.

iii. Collateralized mortgage obligations.

A) Due to the popularity of the mortgage-backed securities, private investment firms have created their own pass-through securities, which are referred to as collateralized mortgage obligations. CMBs are similar to MBSs in that they are backed by mortgages. They differ from MBSs, however, in that the cash flows associated with a pool of mortgages are divided into repayment periods called tranches. In the traditional MBS, each investor will receive a pro rata share of principal and interest each month. In effect, the note is being paid off every month.

B) The principal repayment method is different for collateralized mortgage obligations than for MBSs. As described above, tranches or repayment periods are established which dictate when an investor will receive principal repayments. Each of the tranches will receive regular interest payments with the investors of the first tranche receiving all principal payments until they are completely repaid their principal. Once the obligations of the first tranche are satisfied, all principal payments are made to the second tranche, and so on until all of the tranches are repaid. The holders of the CMOs of the first tranche have less interest rate risk than the holders of the CMOs for the last tranche since the maturity is longer for the securities of the last tranche.

C. PROMISSORY NOTES.

1. A promissory note is a promise to pay a certain sum of money or make a series of payments. Because the structure of a promissory note is similar, if not equivalent, to a bond, many of the same investment considerations that apply to bonds also apply to promissory notes.

2. The value of a promissory note can be determined by discounting the cash flows from the note at an appropriate discount rate. This approach is the same methodology that is used to value any fixed-income security.

3. Promissory notes are subject to the same risks as other fixed-income securities, including credit risk, interest rate risk, inflation risk, etc.

D. INSURANCE-BASED INVESTMENTS.

1. Guaranteed investment contracts (GICs).

    a. Guaranteed investment contracts (GICs), now called stable value funds, are securities sold primarily to pension plans by insurance companies. They are called guaranteed investment contracts because the rate of return is guaranteed for a fixed period of time (such as five years). Returns for GICs are generally low because the risk involved is low.

2. Annuities.

    a. Annuities are contracts issued by insurance companies that make regular periodic payments for a term certain or for the lifetime of an individual or individuals (joint life). Annuities may begin immediately or may be deferred to a future date.

    b. One of the benefits of deferred annuities is that the principal will accumulate over time on a tax-deferred basis. When annuity payments begin, they will consist of return of principal (nontaxable) and interest (taxable). This ratio will continue until such time as the tax basis in the annuity contract has been exhausted. All future payments will be fully taxable.

    c. Annuities may also be fixed or variable. Fixed annuities are generally tied to some fixed-income investment, such as Treasury bonds. Variable annuities often permit investments in a series of mutual funds. The value of a variable annuity will fluctuate as a result of the performance of the mutual funds or underlying security.

3. Cash value life insurance.

    a. Cash value life insurance products include ordinary whole life, universal life, and variable life insurance.

    b. Whole life (ordinary).

       This cash value policy will generally have level lifetime premiums. Level premiums prepay the later increasing cost of mortality.

    c. Universal life.

       i. Universal life allows the insured to alter the death benefit or premiums as financial need demands.

       ii. Cash value is credited with the earnings on the funds in the policy and deductions are made from the cash value for the cost of term insurance and for administrative expenses.

       iii. Universal life permits withdrawals to be made from the policy without terminating the policy.

    d. Variable life.

       i. Variable life policies have level premiums but variable cash value, and death benefits have a guaranteed minimum death benefit.

       ii. The death benefit and cash value are tied to the performance of the underlying investments. If the premiums are invested in low-yielding products, the policy amount will be lower than if the underlying investment had higher rates of return.

       iii. The NASD Series 6 licensing exam must be completed to sell variable products.

E. EQUITY SECURITIES.

1. Common stock.

   a. Types - There is a wide variety of types of stocks that are referred to below. Each of these types of stocks has particular characteristics that distinguish or differentiate them from other types of stocks. Investors often try to match their financial objectives with the particular characteristics of the stocks.

EXHIBIT 4: SUMMARY OF COMMON STOCKS

• Blue chip stocks	• Value stocks
• Growth stocks	• Defensive stocks
• Income stocks	• Interest-sensitive stocks
• Cyclical stocks	

i. Blue chip stocks.

A) Stocks issued by highly regarded, investment quality companies are called blue chip stocks. These companies tend to be older, well established companies that maintain the ability to pay dividends both in years the company has income and in years the company has losses.

B) Examples of blue chip stocks include:

1) American Telephone & Telegraph (AT&T).

2) General Motors.

3) ExxonMobil.

4) IBM.

C) The Dow Jones Industrial Average consists of 30 stocks that are primarily blue chip stocks.

ii. Growth stocks.

A) Growth stocks are stocks issued by companies that usually have sales, earnings, and market share growing at higher rates than average companies or the general economy. Many blue chip stocks can also be classified as growth stocks.

B) Because these companies are growing and expanding, they do not typically pay large dividends. Most of the earnings generated from these companies are reinvested back into the company. Therefore, these companies are expected to grow and appreciate more rapidly than ordinary companies.

C) Price appreciation is appealing to investors because it remains untaxed until the appreciation is recognized (i.e., there is no taxable gain until the stock is sold and the gain is recognized for tax purposes). This growth acts as an income tax deferral and allows for higher compounding returns. Since investors trying to accumulate wealth do not usually need current income, these stocks match their financial needs better than other investments due to smaller dividends and untaxed appreciation.

D) Long-term (stock is held for more than one year) capital gains currently receive favorable tax treatment. These gains are generally taxed at a significantly lower rate than ordinary income tax rates. This large difference in tax rates will cause investors to adjust their asset allocations to maximize after-tax returns at their level of risk tolerance.

E) There are also emerging growth stocks that are typically smaller and younger growth companies. These companies have survived the early years and are just beginning to grow and expand.

iii. Income stocks.

A) As people get older and stop working (specifically during the retirement years), their need for current income generally increases. Income stocks that pay regular and steady dividends can provide consistent current income for these investors.

B) Income stocks include well-established companies, such as utilities, telephone companies, and some blue chip stocks.

iv. Cyclical stocks.

A) Cyclical stocks tend to prosper in growing and expanding economies and tend to do poorly during down business cycles. When the economy is growing, demand usually strengthens. These companies are able to make large profits. When the economy is in a downturn, these companies are hurt by declines in demand and are less profitable. In recessions, they begin cost cutting measures to improve the bottom line so they will end up in good position for the next up cycle.

B) The companies regarded as cyclical usually have large investments in plant and equipment and, therefore, have high fixed costs. These stocks come from industries which include:

1) Automobiles.
2) Cement.
3) Paper.
4) Airlines.
5) Railroads.
6) Machinery.
7) Steel.

v. Value stocks.

A) Stocks trading at prices that are low given their historical earnings and current asset value are referred to as value stocks. Value stocks tend to have low price-to-earnings ratios and tend to be out of favor in the market.

B) Value managers attempt to find these high quality companies that are temporarily undervalued by the market in hopes that the market will recognize the true value of the companies resulting in stock appreciation.

vi. Defensive stocks.

A) Stocks that are relatively unaffected by general fluctuations in the economy are considered to be defensive stocks. These companies tend to have steady (although slow) growth and become more popular during economic recessions and less popular during economic booms.

B) Many of these companies provide products that are necessary for everyday life. Thus, the demand for the products will not be adversely affected by changing economic cycles. Defensive stocks are usually found in the following industries:

1) Utilities.

2) Soft drinks.

3) Groceries.

4) Candy.

5) Drug/Pharmaceuticals.

6) Tobacco.

vii. Interest-sensitive stocks.

A) The performance of some companies is largely affected by changes in interest rates. For example, the housing industry is more productive and has more demand when interest rates are low since it is cheaper for consumers to purchase homes. When interest rates increase, the cost of purchasing homes goes up causing the demand for new homes to typically decline. These trends also affect lumber, plumbing, furnishing, and household equipment companies.

B) Rising interest rates cause the cost of debt to increase; therefore, companies that have large amounts of debt will have increasing interest expense. These companies, like consumers, have the opportunity to refinance their debt during low interest rate periods.

C) Some companies that are affected by interest rates are:

1) Insurance companies.

2) Savings and loans.

3) Commercial banks.

4) Telephone companies.

5) Utility companies.

b. Characteristics of common stocks.

i. The common stockholders of the corporation are the owners of the corporation and, as such, are the largest risk takers of the company. In the event of bankruptcy, their stock will be the last security redeemed by the corporation, and they are unlikely to receive any consideration.

ii. Common stockholders elect a board of directors that oversees the operation of the organization. The common stockholders have two basic rights:

A) Control or voting rights - Voting rights can take one of two forms: noncumulative or cumulative.

1) Noncumulative - Usually, one share of common stock permits one vote for each member of the board of directors. This noncumulative voting allows a shareholder with 100 shares of common stock to cast 100 votes for each of the director's positions.

2) Cumulative - Alternatively, cumulative voting permits a shareholder to cast votes equal to the number of positions on the board of directors times the number of shares owned, allocated in any way the shareholder wishes. For example, a corporation that had cumulative voting and 3 positions on the board of directors would allow a shareholder with 100 shares to cast 300 votes for one position, 150 votes for two positions, 100 votes for each of 3 positions, or any combination that does not exceed the 300 allotted votes. Cumulative voting helps to protect minority shareholders' rights.

B) Preemptive right - The right to maintain ownership percentages.

1) When the corporation is issuing new stock, it is obligated to offer the existing shareholders the right to purchase the additional shares before offering to the general public. This right prevents dilution of an investor's ownership percentage when new shares are issued.

2) Rights offering is the term used to describe the offering of new securities to current shareholders.

3) Most large publicly traded stock does not include the preemptive right because the stock is readily available in the market.

iii. Common stock can be held in two different ways:

A) The company may directly issue the shareholder a certificate indicating the number of shares owned.

B) Alternatively, the stock may be held in street name. When brokers hold stock for investors (such as in a brokerage account), it is referred to as having the stock in street name.

iv. Par value refers to the face value of a share of stock. It is of little use when determining the value of a company and is merely a formality today. However, par value may be used to determine legal capital. Most companies have very low par valued stock.

v. Dividends - Common stockholders may receive cash dividends, stock dividends, or stock splits.

A) Cash dividends are payments to the owners of the corporation.

1) Companies that are growing tend to reinvest a larger portion of earnings back into the corporation and will pay small, if any, cash dividends. Larger, well-established companies will usually pay higher cash dividends.

2) When cash dividends are paid, the stock price will, in theory, adjust accordingly. For example, if the stock price is $50 and the company pays a $5 dividend, then the price of the stock will adjust to approximately $45. After the dividend is paid, the stockholder owns a stock worth $45 and has cash of $5, effectively maintaining the stockholders same economic position (without regard to tax effects or transaction costs).

3) There is a process that occurs from the time a company decides to pay a dividend and the time the shareholders actually receive the dividend. In this process, there are four important dates:

   a) The date of declaration - This is the date the board of directors approves and declares that a dividend will be paid. It is also the date on which the company obligates itself to pay the dividend.

   b) The X dividend date - This is the date that the market price adjusts for the dividend (i.e., market price is reduced approximately by the amount of the dividend).

   c) The date of record - This is the date that the company will determine who owns stock in the company and is entitled to a dividend. Shareholders who own stock as of this date will receive the dividend regardless of whether or not they own the stock as of the payment date. Shareholders who purchase the stock between the date of record and the date of payment are not entitled to the dividend.

   d) The date of payment - This is the date the company pays the dividend to the shareholders.

4) Investors should pay particular attention to these dates. Purchasing a stock just prior to it paying a dividend will dilute the investment and subject the investor to additional current taxable income.

Example

- John has $100,000 to invest. He purchases 2,000 shares of Davidson Company for $50 per share. If the company pays a dividend of $5 per share, John has $90,000 invested, $10,000 in cash, and owes additional taxes of $3,000 (assuming a 30% tax bracket). Investors in high tax brackets should attempt to avoid purchasing stocks just prior to dividend payments (this, of course, assumes that all other factors, such as value, are the same prior to and after the declaration and payment of the dividend).

- If the investor was in the unique position to be in a very low tax bracket, he could purposely generate current income and establish additional basis in the stock. Assume the same facts as above: John's basis in Davidson Corporation is $100,000 before and after the dividend. If he reinvests the $10,000 in Davidson, he will have $100,000 invested in Davidson Corporation and will have a basis of $110,000. The additional $10,000 of basis comes from paying tax on the dividend. If John was in a very low tax bracket or had no other current income, he could establish this additional basis with very little tax effect.

B) Stock dividends are dividends consisting of stock instead of cash. Besides an accounting entry on the corporation's books, stock dividends have little, if any, effect. The market price of the stock should decrease on a relative basis to the stock dividend. For example, if a company worth $11 million with 1 million shares outstanding issues a 10% stock dividend, the market price should adjust from $11 to $10 per share. The company's market value, theoretically, is unaffected by the payment of a stock dividend.

C) Stock splits are very similar to stock dividends except they are usually larger, in percentage terms. The New York Stock Exchange has defined stock splits to be any changes over 25% (25% or under is considered a stock dividend). Because the market price adjusts the same as with stock dividends, companies may issue a 2 for 1 stock split to reduce the market price per share of the stock. These splits allow smaller investors to purchase more shares than would be possible at higher stock prices.

2. Preferred stock.

   a. Preferred stock has characteristics of both fixed-income type investments and of common stock. Shareholders of preferred stock receive dividends each year equal to a stated percentage of the par value of the stock if the corporation declares them. For instance, a $100 par, 5.5% issue of preferred stock would pay a dividend of $5.50 each year for each share owned. The corporation must satisfy these dividends each year prior to paying a dividend to the common shareholders. If the corporation is required to pay any unpaid preferred dividends from prior years before paying a dividend to the common stockholders, the preferred stock is referred to as cumulative, otherwise it is noncumulative.

   b. Preferred stock can be participating. Participating preferred shareholders share in the profits of the corporation. Usually, the preferred shareholders receive dividend payments. Then, holders of common stock will receive their dividends equal to the amount paid to the preferred shareholders. If the preferred stock is participating, additional funds for dividends will then be allocated between the preferred and common shareholders according to stock agreements.

   c. Preferred stock has a preferential right to the assets of the corporation equal to the par value of the stock. This right must be satisfied prior to the common shareholders receiving any assets upon liquidation. However, creditors will be compensated prior to preferred shareholders receiving any assets of the corporation.

   d. Convertible preferred stock will have a conversion right that allows the holder to redeem or trade in the preferred stock for a specified number of common shares.

F. INVESTMENT COMPANIES.

1. Investment companies are financial services companies that sell shares of stock to the public and use the proceeds to invest in a portfolio of securities. Although each investor or shareholder may have a relatively small investment in total, the funds of all shareholders pooled together allow the investment company to create a widely diversified portfolio with certain economies of scale.

2. Investment companies are generally nontaxable entities. Investment companies act as flow-through entities or conduits whereby interest income, dividends, and capital gains all flow through from the investment company to the shareholders and are reported on the investor's individual tax returns. The income that flows through retains its character as to ordinary income or capital gain and is allocated to each shareholder based on the number of shares owned. The tax treatment of investment companies is similar in concept to the tax treatment of partnerships and S corporations.

3. To qualify for nontaxable treatment, investment companies, under Internal Revenue Code Section 851, must meet the following criteria:

   a. The investment company must earn at least 90 percent of its income from interest, dividends, and capital gains derived from investing in stocks, bonds, currencies or other securities.

   b. At least 90 percent of the investment company's taxable income must be distributed to its shareholders.

   c. For 50 percent of the portfolio, an investment in any one issuer is limited to an amount not greater than 5 percent of the total assets of the fund, and no more than 10 percent of the outstanding voting securities of such issuer.

   d. No more than 25 percent of the value of a fund's total assets can be invested in the securities of one issuer.

4. In addition to meeting specific requirements of the Internal Revenue Code, investment companies are also regulated by the Securities Exchange Commission (SEC) under the Investment Company Act of 1940. Investment companies are also regulated under the Securities Act of 1933, the Securities Exchange Act of 1934, and the Investment Advisers Act of 1940.

5. The three types of investment companies are unit investment trusts, closed-end funds, and open-end investment companies (mutual funds).

   a. A unit investment trust (UIT) is a registered investment company that is self-liquidating and passively managed and may invest in stocks, bonds or other securities.

      i. Investors generally purchase units, which are sold at net asset value plus a commission, with the idea that they will hold the units until they mature. As income is earned and securities mature, investors will receive both income (interest and/or dividends) and principal from the trust.

      ii. UITs are known as unmanaged or passively managed funds because professional managers initially select securities to be included in the portfolio and those securities are generally held until they mature.

   b. Closed-end investment companies.

      i. A closed-end fund is a type of investment company whose shares trade in the same manner that other publicly traded stocks trade in the secondary market. Shares of closed-end funds are listed on a stock exchange or trade in the over-the-counter market. Since the shares for closed-end funds are subject to supply and demand, the shares will generally sell at a premium or discount relative to the net asset value of the fund.

      ii. After the initial public offering, a closed-end fund will generally not issue additional shares in the market. Unlike an open-end fund, a closed-end fund's capitalization is considered to be fixed since it does not generally add assets to the fund after initial capitalization.

      iii. Since the pool of assets to be invested for a closed-end fund is fixed and shares are not redeemed, the manager of a closed-end fund has a great deal of flexibility in managing the assets within the fund. He does not have to worry about or plan for cash redemptions like a mutual fund (open-end investment company). This one characteristic of closed-end funds allows the manager to invest in less liquid securities that may have higher expected returns than more liquid securities.

c. Open-end investment companies (mutual funds).

i. Open-end investment companies are referred to as open-end because they are not limited in the number of shares that are sold. The total capitalization of these funds is constantly changing. Some investors are purchasing shares, while others are selling their shares. All shares are sold by the mutual fund family and redeemed by the mutual fund family or purchased and sold through a broker.

ii. The shares for open-end mutual funds are sold at Net Asset Value (NAV). NAV is the fair market value of securities within the portfolio, less any outstanding liabilities, divided by the shares outstanding. Thus, a fund with \$1,500,000 of stocks, \$750,000 of bonds, \$500,000 of cash, \$250,000 of liabilities, and 1,000,000 outstanding shares would have a net asset value per share equal to \$2.50. This would be the price per share to invest in the mutual fund.

Note: There may be a front-end load or a deferred sales charge associated with the purchase of mutual fund shares, especially when purchased through a broker.

6. There are a wide variety of investment objectives that mutual funds may provide. These objectives are important considerations when choosing a mutual fund in order to match the investment fund to the financial objective of the investor. The following is a summary of different mutual fund objectives (Exhibit 5).

EXHIBIT 5: SUMMARY OF FUND OBJECTIVES

Common Stock Funds	**Bond Funds**
• Aggressive Growth	• Municipal Bond
• Small Company	• High Yield
• Growth	• U.S. Government Bond
• Growth and Income	• Ginnie Mae
• International and Foreign	• Global and International
• Specialty	• Convertible Bond
• Sector	**Balanced Funds**
	Money Market Funds
	Index Funds
	Asset Allocation Funds

a. Common stock funds - These funds invest primarily in equities or common stocks, but, within this category, there are a wide variety of investment objectives. These objectives include the following:

i. Aggressive growth - These funds consist almost exclusively of equity investments, which stress capital appreciation. Risk level and turnover for these funds are usually high in comparison to the market.

ii. Small Company Funds - These funds invest in stocks of small domestic companies as determined by market capitalization (usually less than \$1 billion). Risk level is high in comparison with the market.

iii. Growth - Equity securities make up the majority of investments in this type of fund. As with aggressive growth funds the focus is on capital appreciation, but with less risk.

iv. Growth and income - A large portion of these funds' assets are invested in equities; however, some bonds may be held. These funds focus on both capital appreciation and current income sources.

v. International and foreign funds.

A) These types of funds invest in equities throughout the world. These funds often provide added diversification because the assets are invested in companies of numerous countries. Higher returns is an added potential because of the hopes for advancement of lesser-industrialized countries. These mutual funds may be worldwide or narrowed to a specific region of the globe.

B) International funds invest throughout the world (including the U.S.), while foreign funds invest outside the U.S.

C) Global and world are two other terms that are used to describe funds that invest in both U.S. and foreign securities.

vi. Specialty Funds - These funds invest in companies in related fields or specific industries. These fields may be narrower than sectors of the economy. These funds may also have special focuses, such as "green funds" that invest in only environmentally friendly companies.

vii. Sector funds - These funds generally have narrowly defined investment objectives. They invest in stocks related to a particular sector of the economy. For example, a sector fund might invest in science and technology companies or in companies that are related to the health care industry.

b. Bond funds - Generally, these funds are considered income funds and are less risky than equity or stock funds. Because they primarily invest in debt securities, these funds generate a significant amount of income. These funds may also have a variety of objectives:

i. Municipal bond funds - The primary objective is to generate nontaxable income and to obtain higher after-tax rates of return than other bond funds.

ii. High yield - These funds invest in higher yielding corporate bonds that generate higher income levels. These bonds are usually lower grade investment quality bonds (often referred to as junk bonds).

iii. U.S. Government bond funds - Primary investments are in U.S. Government bonds. May include short-term, intermediate, and long-term bonds. Income from these funds will not be subject to state income tax.

iv. Ginnie Mae - These funds have the potential for slightly higher returns than the U.S. Government funds because of additional risks.

v. Global and international - Managers of these funds purchase debt from companies and countries across the globe. These funds can generate higher returns than U.S. Government bond funds.

vi. Convertible Bond Funds - These funds invest in convertible securities, which have a relatively low correlation with bonds and only a moderate correlation to stocks, thus providing the opportunity for diversification within a portfolio.

c. Balanced funds - Similar portions of common stock and bonds are held together. The focus is on income rather than growth and has lower risk than the other common stock funds.

d. Money market funds - Money market funds invest in short-term fixed instruments in search of above-average, short-term yields.

e. Index funds - These funds are invested in the same securities (stocks or bonds) that make up a particular index and held in the same ratio. For instance, Vanguard's Index 500 fund has the same make up of stocks as the S&P 500. These index funds should have lower expenses than other actively managed funds because they require little management to build portfolios identical to indexes, such at the S&P 500. These funds also benefit because there is minimal turnover, which means that appreciation is not recognized for tax purposes and does not flow out to the shareholders. Thus, these funds have a tax advantage over other actively managed mutual funds.

f. Asset allocation funds - These funds invest in a mix of equities, fixed-income securities, and money market instruments. These funds generally maintain a specific weighting in each asset class in the portfolio.

7. A great disparity exists not only with financial objectives of mutual funds, but also with respect to the fees, loads, and charges. Mutual funds can be classified as no-load funds or load funds. They may have one or more of the following loads or expenses associated with the fund:

   a. Front-end load - This load is a sales charge that is deducted from the initial investment. For example, if Donna invests $1,000 in a mutual fund with a 7% front-end load, the initial value of her shares will be $930. Thus, Donna could sell her shares the same day and only receive $930. To increase the value of her investment back to $1,000, she would have to earn 7.53% over the next year (after other expenses, fees, and taxes).

   b. Back-end load or redemption fee.

      i. A back-end load is a sales charge that is imposed upon withdrawal from a fund. This back-end load is typically assessed on the lesser of the redemption value or the initial investment value.

      ii. For instance, Donna invests $1,000 into a fund with a 5% redemption fee, and it grows over five years to $2,000. She will receive $1,950 [$2,000 – ($1,000 x 5%)] from the sale of her shares. If Donna's account had grown to $500,000, a sales fee of $50 would still be deducted from the proceeds of her sale.

      iii. If the balance in Donna's account had fallen to $500, a sales fee of $25 (5% x $500) would be deducted from the proceeds of her sale. Many funds today have decreasing redemption fees where the fee is reduced by 1% each year. For example, a fund with a 5% back-end load may charge 5% to redeem shares in the first year, 4% in the second year, and so on, until finally no fee would be paid after the fifth year.

   c. 12b-1 plan - This plan allows an additional fee of up to 1.00% of the net asset value of the fund to be paid for advertising and marketing expenses. This annual fee is paid to the broker and is designed to attract more investors and increase the asset base of the fund. Joe invests $10,000 into XYZ Mutual Fund and earns 10% the first year. Assuming a 12b-1 expense of 1.00% and no other fees, Joe will have only earned 8.90% on his investment $[[[(1.10 \times 10{,}000) \times (1 - 0.01)] - 10{,}000] \div 10{,}000]$.

d. Administrative expenses or management fees - All funds have this type of operating expense. This expense pays for the overhead of the mutual fund, and the salaries of the fund manager and the employees of the fund. Expenses usually range from 1 to 2 percent of net asset value per year depending on the objective of the fund. However, some funds have administrative expenses as low as 0.18%, or 18 basis points.

e. Mutual funds that charge loads will often have different classes of shares for the same fund. While the funds invested will be managed the same way, each class of shares for the fund will have a different mix of sales charges and expenses. Common classifications include A, B, and C shares.

   i. Class A shares generally include a front-end load and often have a 12b-1 fee that is smaller than the 12b-1 fee for Class B shares. Class A shares do not, however, have a redemption fee.

   ii. Class B shares generally have a redemption fee plus the maximum 1 percent 12b-1 fee which is higher than for the Class A shares for the same fund. This class of shares does not have a front-end load, and the deferred charge often is in the form of a declining redemption fee. Class B shares generally convert to Class A shares after the expiration period of the contingent deferred sales charge. The benefit of converting to A shares is the reduced 12b-1 fee.

   iii. Class C shares are sold without initial sales charges, but often have a deferred sales charge if the shares are redeemed within one year. These shares have the maximum 1 percent 12b-1 fee and do not generally permit investors to convert to another class of shares.

Note: Each fund family determines the precise mix of sales charges and fees related to each class of shares. They may be slightly different for each fund family.

8. Benefits of mutual funds.

   a. Diversification - Mutual funds provide an easy way to diversify a portfolio at a low cost. Minimum initial investments for mutual funds are usually between $1,000 and $5,000 allowing investors to achieve broad diversification without requiring them to invest large sums of money into individual stocks and bonds. Trying to achieve the same level of diversification as a mutual fund would require a substantially greater investment than the usual minimum fund requirement.

   b. Easy access - Clearly defined investment objectives allow investors to choose the mutual funds that are most suitable to their needs. Purchasing shares of a fund does not necessitate a broker and can be accomplished directly through the mail.

   c. Professional management - While professional management is viewed as an advantage, approximately 70 percent of the mutual funds have not outperformed the market. Thus, if an investor had a portfolio that matched the market, he or she would have outperformed 70 percent of the mutual funds. However, in general, professional managers are more likely to have better performance than unsophisticated investors.

   d. Liquidity - Generally, shares of mutual funds can be redeemed very quickly.

   e. Services - Mutual funds provide a variety of services, such as checking, monthly statements, annual reports, reinvestment of interest and dividends, accumulation plans, and withdrawal plans.

9. Issues to look for when managing portfolios of mutual funds.
   a. Introduction.
      i. Once an investment strategy, including one that involves mutual funds, has been implemented, the portfolio must be monitored to be certain that it is performing in the way expected.
      ii. There are certain aspects of mutual funds that should be monitored to be certain that the fund is performing as anticipated. These characteristics include changing asset size, turnover, style shift, manager changes, and capital gain exposure.
   b. Changing asset size.
      i. When mutual funds have good performance for several years in a row, new assets flow to these funds making them bigger. This changing asset size can result in a change in the basic dynamics of the fund. This is especially true for funds that invest in small-cap and mid-cap asset classes (market capitalization under $5 billion).
      ii. There are only a limited number of small and mid-sized companies to invest in and, as we discussed above, mutual funds have restrictions on the amount that can be invested in any one particular company. Therefore, when a small-cap mutual fund dramatically increases its asset base, the fund may no longer be able to invest the additional assets as efficiently or effectively as it had in the past. If this occurs, returns suffer and assets may begin to leave the fund.
      iii. To prevent this problem, some funds will close temporarily to new investors, thus limiting the asset base of the fund to protect the dynamics of the fund. Therefore, it is important to monitor the asset size of small-cap and mid-cap equity funds to be sure they are not growing too fast.
   c. Turnover.
      i. The fund will generally have a specific investment style that leads to low, medium, or high portfolio turnover. Higher turnover involves buying and selling securities more often throughout the year resulting in higher transaction costs. Higher turnover can result in more short-term capital gains and can accelerate other taxable income. Such short-term capital gains that flow through from mutual funds are generally taxed as ordinary income, instead of the lower long-term capital gains tax rate.
      ii. Funds that have higher turnover will often cause the recognition of more frequent taxable gains through the selling of securities. Since the recognition of capital gains by the mutual fund requires shareholders to report these gains as income for federal income tax purposes, higher turnover funds accelerate the tax payments of the investor.
      iii. Since combined federal and state tax rates can range from 10 percent to 15 percent on the low side to over 50 percent on the high side, it is clear that taxes are the highest expense attributable to an investment.
      iv. For example, management fees average about 1 percent, significantly lower than the tax rates just mentioned. Therefore, it is extremely important to manage the taxation of mutual funds and be aware of the fund's portfolio turnover. Turnover is of minimal concern for tax-deferred accounts, such as pension plans, 401(k) plans, and IRAs since the gains are not taxed until distributed by such plan, usually at or during retirement.

d. Style shift.

i. As part of the asset allocation process, the large-cap equity allocation is often segregated into value, growth, and core styles. The purpose of this segregation is to have one growth fund, one value fund, and one core fund, for example. What happens, though, if the value fund begins using more of a growth style? All of a sudden, the diversified portfolio is now more heavily weighted toward growth.

ii. It may be that the portfolio is performing well at this time, but it is also likely that when the growth style goes out of favor the portfolio may decline significantly. Therefore, it is important to monitor that the fund's style remains consistent with the fund's stated objective.

e. Manager changes.

i. The reason managers of mutual funds are well compensated is that they are the ones making the buy-and-sell decisions, which causes the fund to have good or poor performance. Since the manager is responsible for the performance of the fund, it is important to watch for changes in the management structure of the fund.

ii. In most cases, one person manages the fund while in other cases a team manages the fund. A change in investment management means that there is increased risk that the fund will not be managed as before, and therefore, historical returns may have less significance to predicting future returns.

f. Capital gain exposure.

i. Mutual funds will generally have appreciated securities within the portfolio. A security's appreciation is considered a built-in gain inside the mutual fund. Selling these appreciated securities by the mutual fund causes income to be recognized for income tax purposes by the fund and then passed through to the investor. Taxable investors who purchase shares of mutual funds having these built-in gains subject themselves to potential taxable income without any associated economic gain.

ii. The built-in gain on mutual funds can range widely and depends on past performance of the fund. Investors should be cautious when purchasing mutual funds with large amounts of unrealized appreciation.

G. EXCHANGE-TRADED FUNDS.

1. Exchange-traded funds (ETFs) are portfolios or baskets of stocks that are traded on an exchange (offerings are generally traded on the American Stock Exchange). Common examples include QQQ (Nasdaq-100) and SPDR (Standard & Poor's Depository Receipts, tracking S&P 500 index, or sectors).

2. Unlike mutual funds, ETFs can be purchased and sold throughout the day. In addition, they can be bought on margin and can be sold short (and are not subject to the uptick rule). These ETFs typically have lower annual expenses compared to mutual funds. However, since ETFs are traded on exchanges, it is possible that in a market correction, investors may be unable to sell their shares. Recall that mutual funds must redeem investors' shares upon request.

3. ETFs are passively managed. They generally track a specific index, sector, or region.

4. Although ETFs are traded on exchanges, investors may be able to buy or redeem shares from the fund family in 50,000 share blocks. However, redemptions generally require the delivery of the underlying shares of stock. Generally, investors will buy and sell ETFs in the secondary market by using a broker.

5. The price of ETF shares is certainly based on the value of the underlying securities; however, it may not be equal to NAV due to supply and demand for the shares.

   a. Although the price of ETF shares may trade at a discount or premium, the difference should be minimal.

   b. If the shares were selling at a discount, then a large financial institution could purchase a large quantity (in blocks of 50,000 shares) of ETF shares and then redeem the shares for the underlying securities. These securities could then be sold in the market for a profit. A similar strategy can be employed by arbitrageurs in the event that shares are trading at a premium.

6. Generally, the annual expense ratio for ETF shares is lower than for the majority of mutual funds. For example, the annual expense ratio is 12 basis points (0.12%) for SPDRs, while Vanguard's 500 Index Fund charges 18 basis points (0.18%). However, ETF shares that are purchased using a broker will require a commission to be paid. Depending on the commission and the size of the investment, either alternative may be better.

7. ETFs have low turnover and, therefore, lower taxable distributions than most mutual funds. When there is a substantial amount of selling of mutual fund shares, the manager is forced to sell some of the underlying securities to generate enough cash for redemptions. This does not occur in an ETF. Shares are either sold, or redeemed in-kind.

8. Most mutual funds have cash that is not invested. This cash is a result of either investments or cash that is maintained for redemptions. ETFs do not have this cash management problem and may have better performance than similar mutual funds.

EXCHANGE TRADED FUNDS	INDEX	ANNUAL EXPENSES
Diamonds	DJIA	18 bp
HOLDRs (Holding Company Depository Receipts) Merrill Lynch	Various sectors	$2 per 100 shares
iShares*	Numerous sectors and regions	9 to 99 bp
SPDRs (Standard & Poor's Depository Receipts)	S&P 500	12 bp
Midcap SPDRs	S&P 400	25 bp
NASDAQ-100 Index Tracking Stock (QQQ)	Nasdaq-100	20 bp
Select Sector SPDRs	Sectors of S&P 500	28 bp
streetTRACKS	Various Dow Jones and MS indexes	20-50 bp
*iShares MSCI Series were formerly known as WEBS		

H. SHORT SELLING.

1. Normally, investors purchase stock with the hope that it will appreciate. The profit investors earn is the difference between the sales price and the purchase price plus dividends. However, investors can also make money when stocks decline if they sell short. Selling a stock short usually involves four basic steps:

    a. Use a stockbroker to borrow stock from another investor's account or from inventory. This requires that the short seller give a deposit, equal to the margin requirement times the FMV of the stock, to the broker. The purpose of the margin requirement is to reduce the broker's risk that the investor will be unable to cover any losses that occur.

    b. Sell the borrowed stock in the open market.

    c. Repurchase the stock in the open market.

    d. Replace the borrowed stock.

2. In addition to the above steps, the short seller must also have a margin account to sell short.

3. The following exhibit depicts the mechanics of a short sale.

EXHIBIT 6: THE MECHANICS OF A SHORT SALE

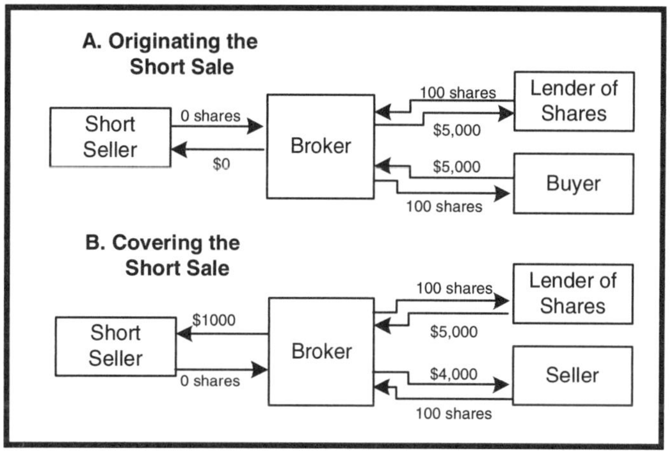

4. The short seller will make money if it is possible to repurchase the stock for less than the initial amount received on the sale of the stock (i.e., the stock price goes down). If the price of the stock increases, the short seller will lose money.

5. The person whose stock is borrowed and the person to whom the stock is sold both own the same security and are entitled to full rights associated with the stock.

    a. A problem arises since there is only one security with two people that effectively own it. The company will only pay one dividend. Therefore, the short seller is required to pay any dividends to the investor whose stock was borrowed. While this sounds like a reason not to sell short, this situation is, in fact, of little concern. When the dividend is paid by the company, the short seller must pay this amount to the owner of the stock. However, the stock price, as mentioned earlier, will theoretically adjust down by approximately the same amount as the dividend. The short seller is effectively left in the same economic position.

    b. Another problem that may arise is the right of the common stockholder to vote for the board of directors. Voting for a board of directors is usually a minor problem since most investors use proxies instead of actually casting their vote.

6. Benefits of short selling.

   a. Short selling allows investors to take advantage of falling stock prices. For example, a security that is overvalued by the market may be a likely target for a short. In addition, short selling gives investors the opportunity to benefit in both bull markets and bear markets. Short selling is widely used in hedge funds.

   b. "Shorting against the box."

      i. A phrase that refers to an investor taking a short position with the same market value as a long position that is held. For instance, if Larry owns 100 shares of IBM, he could "short against the box" by shorting 100 shares of IBM.

> **Note:** It may only be 50 shares if the 100 shares owned are not in a margin account because short sales are usually executed on margin.

      ii. The purpose of this strategy is to hedge against uncertainty. A "shorting-against-the-box" strategy may be appropriate for investments in which the market is waiting for an important piece of information (such as a merger or a court proceeding). The stock price is likely to go up if the news is positive, down if negative. The investor may wish to protect any gains, or protect against losses by implementing this strategy.

      iii. Another common use for this type of strategy was to defer the recognition of tax until the following tax year. If an investor believed that a stock had reached its high and wished to sell, the investor could have entered into a "short against the box" so that the gain would be frozen and recognized in the following year. However, the constructive sale rules have greatly limited the usefulness of the "short-against-the-box" technique for tax purposes.

      iv. Constructive sale rules.

         A) The constructive sale rules treat the "short-against-the-box" transaction as if the taxpayer had sold his long position for the price at which the short was entered into. For example, Rob owns ABC company stock and enters into an offsetting short position (i.e., short against the box) on July 5, 2002, at a price of $50. The constructive sale rules would require Rob to treat the transaction as though he had sold his long position in ABC for $50.

         B) However, the constructive sale rules will not apply and the "short against the box" will not be treated as a sale or exchange if the following conditions are met:

            1) The short sale must be closed on or before the 30th day following the tax year that the short sale was entered into, and

            2) The long position must be held (unhedged) for a period of at least 60 days after the close of the short position.

         C) For example, Rob's transaction would not be treated as a constructive sale if he closed the short position by January 30, 2003, and he maintained his long position (unhedged) for at least 60 days after he closes the short position.

         D) The "short-against-the-box" rules still allow an investor to defer gain until the following year. However, the rule requiring the investor to maintain the long position for a period of 60 days creates substantial uncertainty in the security.

v. The Uptick rule.

A) The Uptick rule requires that, before a short sale is executed, the stock must trade at an uptick, or increase.

Example

Given this set of stock prices ($45.00, $44.50, $44.50, $41.00, $41.50, $42.00), in chronological order, a short sale could not occur until the stock price moved from $41.00 to $41.50.

B) The SEC requires that all short sales be made on an uptick or zero-tick. A zero-tick is a trade that occurs at a price equal to the previous stock price that was an uptick. For example, the second trade at $44.50 would be considered a zero-tick if the first trade had been lower than $44.50 instead of $45.00. In this example, it is not a zero-tick because the previous trade was not an uptick.

I. DERIVATIVES.

1. A derivative is a security whose value is derived from the value of an underlying security. For example, the price of lumber futures will vary as the price of lumber changes. While derivatives have the potential for large gains or losses, they also provide benefits to investors, such as hedging and increased leveraging. Derivatives are limited only by the imagination of financial product designers. The most common derivatives include: 1) futures, 2) options, and 3) warrants.

2. Futures contracts.

a. A futures contract is an agreement between two parties to make or take delivery of a contract of a specific commodity of a specified quality at a future time, place, and unit price. One contract consists of one buyer and one seller, and the contract will specify all details, including:

i. Time of delivery (usually specified by a delivery month).

ii. Place of delivery.

iii. Quality and details of the commodity.

iv. Unit price.

b. To complete the contract, delivery can be made or taken, depending on if selling or buying. Another choice, which is most often selected, is to purchase the other side of a contract, thus, canceling the initial contract. Purchasing an opposite contract is called reversing out a position. Usually, delivery is not made with futures contracts; rather, the holder purchases an offsetting contract and cancels his or her original position.

c. Futures contracts, traded on exchanges such as the New York Mercantile Exchange, the Chicago Mercantile Exchange, and the Chicago Board of Trade, include commodities such as gold, tin, wool, lumber, cattle, sugar, copper, pork bellies, hogs, coffee, cotton, soybeans, oats, and wheat. In addition to commodities, futures contracts are written on financial assets, including Treasury bills and bonds, municipal bonds, and foreign currencies.

d. Purchasing futures contracts requires a margin account with an initial deposit (initial margin) and a required minimum balance (maintenance margin). Futures contracts require daily settlement or marking-to-market. Traders are required to realize losses in cash on a daily basis. If the value of the futures contract increases, the investor is permitted to withdraw the increase in the margin account. However, if the contract decreases in value below the maintenance margin, the investor may receive a margin call requiring a deposit of more money into the account so that the initial margin level is restored. Note that the margin requirement for stock accounts is different from that for futures accounts. Margin calls for equity accounts only require that the maintenance margin be restored, not the initial margin.

Example	
CONTRACT SPECIFICATIONS FOR A BRITISH POUND CURRENCY FUTURES CONTRACT	
Initial Margin Requirement	$1,500
Maintenance Margin	$1,100

On Monday morning, an investor takes a long position in a British Pound futures contract that matures in three weeks. At the close of trading on Monday, the account gains $200. At Tuesday close, the account has further gains of $100. At Wednesday close, the account loses $250. At Thursday close the account again falls, this time $900. At Friday close, the account loses $200.

Detail of the daily settlement process for the week:

TIME	CASH FLOW
Monday Morning	Investor deposits $1,500 as the initial margin.
Monday Close	Balance in account is $1,500 + $200 = $1,700.
Tuesday Close	Balance in account is $1,700 + $100 = $1,800.
Wednesday Close	Balance in account is $1,800 - $250 = $1,550.
Thursday Close	Balance in account is $1,550 - $900 = $650. This is below the maintenance margin, therefore, the investor receives a margin call and must deposit $850: $1,500 - $650 = $850. The account balance is $1,500.
Friday Close	Balance in account is $1,500 - $200 = $1,300.

Note: Commodity exchanges set margin requirements. If the investor does not increase his or her account after a margin call, the broker will close out his or her position by selling the contract. Investors are usually required to have strong balance sheets and deposited funds with a broker, in addition to sufficient knowledge of the risks, before they are permitted to trade futures.

e. As the delivery date draws closer, the futures price will converge with the spot price for that commodity. For example, if a futures contract was purchased on the final trade date for that contract, the price should be equal to the spot rate since today is the future price. If the futures contract was not purchased on the final trade day, you could purchase the lower of the two values, either the spot or the futures price, and then sell in the opposite market. This would be an arbitrage trade.

f. Terminology.

   i. Investors can take long or short positions in futures contracts. Purchasing a contract for future delivery is termed a long position (take delivery). Selling a contract for future delivery is called a short position (make delivery). Like stocks, a long position will increase in value if the underlying security increases in value; whereas, a short position will increase in value if the underlying security decreases in value.

   ii. The futures price is the price specified in the contract for future delivery of the commodity.

   iii. The spot rate is the current price of the commodity.

   iv. The daily limit is the maximum change in a commodity's price that is permitted during a day of trading.

   v. Open interest refers to the number of contracts that are outstanding for a particular futures contract.

g. Hedging is one of the primary uses of derivatives and involves purchasing a futures contract that is the opposite position that is currently held. The purpose of hedging is to reduce risk from fluctuating commodity prices. Two types of hedging will illustrate this point:

   i. The short hedge.

      A) If a farmer grows and sells wheat, he or she has a long position in wheat since the farmer will benefit when the price increases. If the price of the wheat declines, the farmer loses money. Therefore, the farmer is subject to the price changes in the commodity wheat. To eliminate his or her risk exposure to price fluctuations, the farmer can use a short hedge.

      B) To use a short hedge, the farmer must take a short position in wheat by selling a wheat contract. Once the farmer has a long position (his or her wheat crop) and a short position (the futures contract), the farmer has eliminated the risk of price fluctuations. If the price of wheat increases, the value of his or her crop increases. If the price of wheat declines, the value of the futures contract increases.

Example

Assume the following facts:

1. The cash or spot price for a bushel of wheat is $3.00.
2. The September futures price for wheat is $3.10.

Farmer Ted can currently sell his wheat for $3.00 and establish a futures price of $3.10. He will be able to freeze the price of his wheat at $3.00 and make a $0.10 profit per bushel from the futures contract regardless of what changes in the price of wheat occur. The cash price and the futures price will change over time. However, as September draws closer, the spot price and the futures price for September will converge. If the September price is $4.00, then Farmer Ted makes $1.00 from the crop and loses $0.90 from the futures contract. This $0.10 profit occurs because he sells his crop for $4.00 per bushel and reverses his futures position on the last trading day to $4.00 per bushel. Therefore, he loses $0.90 on the futures contract and yields a net $3.10 per bushel of wheat (as expected). The farmer's only problem is knowing how many bushels to sell and how many contracts to buy.

C) In the above example, if the September price for wheat fell to $1.00 per bushel, Farmer Ted would still make $3.10 per bushel of wheat. He would sell his wheat for $1.00 and would make an additional $2.10 per bushel on reversing his futures contract ($3.10 - $1.00). Thus, a short hedge permits a farmer to predict in advance the price per bushel of his crop with little risk of price fluctuations.

ii. The long hedge.

A) The long hedge works similarly to the short hedge with the exception that the long hedge involves a producer concerned about fluctuations in the prices of raw materials. Paper manufacturers and furniture makers both purchase and use wood as a raw material. If the price of wood or lumber increases, their cost of goods sold increases and their net income decreases. If the price declines, they benefit. Thus, they have a short position in lumber since they profit from its decline. To limit the risk of price fluctuations, these producers will need to take a long position that can be accomplished with a futures contract.

B) If the current price per 1,000 feet of lumber is $180.00 and the futures price is $185.00, the long hedge will allow the producer to lock in a price with a $5.00 loss. This assures that the price per thousand feet of lumber will be $185.00.

C) A long hedge allows a user of raw material to reduce the risk of price fluctuations by locking in a small, predetermined loss.

D) The alternative to a futures contract would be to purchase the lumber today at $180. However, there are carrying costs, such as interest and storage, that must be considered.

iii. Other hedging concerns.

A) Perfect hedge - Because contracts have predetermined quantities, it may be impossible to create a perfect hedge. For example, if a farmer produces 275,000 bushels of cotton and cotton futures contracts specify 50,000 bushels of cotton per contract, then it is impossible to perfectly hedge against price fluctuations. This farmer will have to either over-hedge or under-hedge. The farmer could sell 5 futures contracts to hedge 250,000 bushels of cotton or could sell 6 futures contracts to hedge against 300,000 bushels of cotton. Usually, the farmer will hedge in the direction that he or she feels price will most likely move (an imperfect hedge).

1) Additional concerns for a perfect hedge include the underlying asset and the maturity of the contract. If the underlying asset of the futures contract does not identically match the commodity that is being hedged, price fluctuations between the assets may not be exact. However, it is likely that they will be similar and highly correlated.

2) If the expiration date of the futures contract does not correspond with the date that the commodity is to be purchased or sold, a perfect hedge does not exist. The inability to match time horizons also subjects the hedger to the risks of price fluctuations.

B) Transaction costs have been disregarded in the above examples. A proper analysis requires that transaction costs be considered.

h. Leveraging is one of the reasons futures are risky investments. With a small investment in a futures contract comes the ability to control a large asset. For example, if the initial margin requirement to control $1 million of T-bills was $10,000, then any changes in the price of T-bills would be dramatically magnified in the price or value of the futures contract. If the price of the T-bill increased by 1%, then the value of the contract would increase by approximately $10,000 (a 100% return with a 1% change in the underlying security).

3. Options contracts.

a. Options consist of two primary types:

i. Call options - Give the holder the right (not the obligation) to purchase the underlying security for a specified price within a specified period of time.

ii. Put options - Give the holder the right (not the obligation) to sell the underlying security for a specified price within a specified period of time.

b. The value of an option fluctuates during the exercise period based on many factors (see Black-Scholes Option Valuation Model) including changes in the value of the underlying securities. Options contracts are in increments of 100 shares. One contract gives the holder the right to buy or sell 100 shares. Ten contracts allow the holder to buy or sell 1,000 shares.

c. These options are purchased for a price, called a premium, which gives the holder the right to buy or sell the underlying security. However, the investor is not obligated to invoke that right and may choose to let the option expire. Options expire at 11:59 PM Eastern Standard Time on the Saturday following the third Friday of the expiration month.

d. Option contracts will generally have one of three expiration cycles:
   i. January - April - July - October.
   ii. February - May - August - November.
   iii. March - June - September - December.

> **Note:** The premium for the call option with the lower exercise price will be higher because it is more likely that that option will be exercised.

e. Options for a company will be on one of the above cycles and within each expiration month will be a series of exercise prices. For instance, IBM may have the following contracts for the month of July:
   i. IBM July $100.
   ii. IBM July $105.
   iii. IBM July $110.

f. The premium for each option will vary depending on the time to expiration and the difference between the exercise price and the market price. See Black-Scholes Option Valuation Model below for more detail.
   i. Options can be purchased or sold (written).
   ii. There are four possible option positions.
      A) Purchasing a call.
      B) Writing a call (selling a call).
      C) Purchasing a put.
      D) Writing a put (selling a put).

EXHIBIT 7: REASONS FOR ENTERING INTO OPTION POSITIONS

	Call	Put
Purchase	An investor will purchase a call option in hopes that the stock will increase in value. Generally done to participate in the upward move of a security.	A put is generally purchased in expectation of a downward move in the underlying price of the security. In addition, puts are often purchased to provide downside protection for long positions.
Sell (Write)	A call option is often written on a stock that has recently hit a new high and is not expected to continue to rise in price. The investor hopes that the stock price will remain steady or decline. If the stock rises, then the seller may be required to deliver the stock to the option buyer. The seller would receive the exercise price as the sales price in addition to the premium for writing the option.	Puts are often written on stocks that have recently made new lows in price. The investor hopes that the stock price will rise. However, if the stock declines, the stock may be "put" to the seller of the option. The seller will have to buy the stock at the exercise price, but will also receive the premium for writing the option.

g. Option characteristics and definitions.

   i. Premium - The price to purchase an option contract, and the amount that the seller receives for writing the contract.

   ii. Expiration date - The date through which the option can be exercised or sold.

   iii. Exercise price - The specified price at which the option can be exercised. It is also called the contract price or the strike price.

   iv. Intrinsic value - The intrinsic value of an option is the minimum price at which an option will trade. It is the difference between the market price of the stock and the exercise price. The value of the option consists of two parts: the intrinsic value plus the time value of the option.

   v. Writing a covered option - Writing an option on a security that is already owned by the option's writer.

   vi. Writing a naked option - Writing an option where the underlying security is not owned by the option's writer (very risky).

   vii. Open interest - The number of contracts outstanding for a specific contract.

   viii. American vs. European options.

      A) American options can be exercised at any time during the contract period.

      B) European options can only be exercised on the day they expire.

   ix. In the money - This term refers to when the exercise price is below the market price for a call option (above the market price for a put option).

   x. At the money - This term refers to when the exercise price equals the market price for both calls and puts.

   xi. Out of the money - This term refers to when the exercise price is above the market price for a call option (below the market price for a put option).

EXHIBIT 8: OPTION TERMINOLOGY

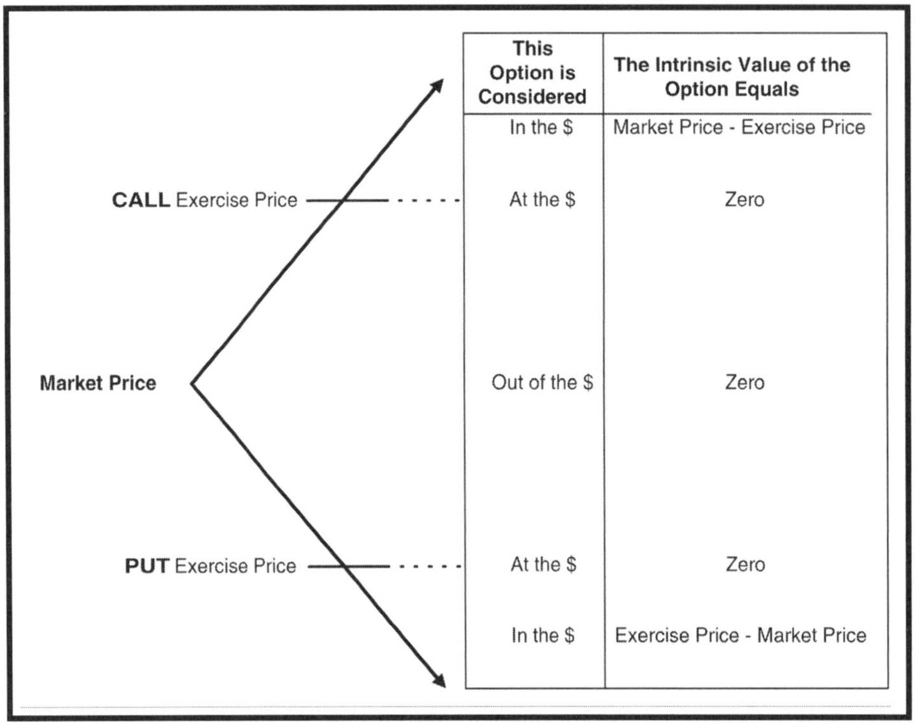

EXHIBIT 9: OPTION GAINS AND LOSSES

	Max Gain	Max Loss
Buy Call	Unlimited	Premium
Buy Put	Exercise Price – Premium	Premium
Sell Call	Premium	Unlimited
Sell Put	Premium	Exercise Price – Premium

h. Option gains and losses.

i. Notice in the above chart that options are considered a "zero-sum game" meaning that the amount that is gained by one party to the transaction is lost by the other party to the transaction.

ii. Gains.

A) The buyer has unlimited gain potential when purchasing a call option.

B) The buyer's gain when purchasing a put option is limited to the difference between the exercise price and the premium paid for the put option.

C) The seller's maximum gain is always limited to the premium received for writing the option – for both call options and put options.

iii. Losses.

A) The buyer's loss is always limited to the premium paid for the option – for both call options and put options.

B) The seller has unlimited loss potential when writing a call option.

C) The seller's loss when selling a put option is limited to the difference between the exercise price and the premium received for the put option.

i. The four exchanges that trade the majority of options are:

i. The Chicago Board of Options Exchange (CBOE).

ii. American Stock Exchange (AMEX).

iii. Philadelphia Stock Exchange (PHLX).

iv. Pacific Stock Exchange (PSE).

j. The Options Clearing Corporation (OCC) is owned by the four options exchanges and is the place where all options transactions are cleared. The OCC acts as a guarantor for the option contracts in the event that the option writer does not deliver. There is little risk of nondelivery on the part of the purchaser; therefore, options are very marketable securities.

k. Binomial option pricing.

i. The binomial option pricing model attempts to estimate the price of a European call option by determining the value of a separate portfolio with the same profits and losses as the call being priced. Consider the following example.

ii. Thc assumptions are as follows:

A) The call option being replicated has a strike price of $100.

B) The replicating portfolio consists of the following:

1) A long position in ½ share of stock, with a market price of $50 ($100 share price times ½), and

2) A short position in a risk-free bond that matures in one year with an initial price of $42.45 and matures at $45.00. The short position is equivalent to borrowing the $42.45 for one year at 6%.

3) The portfolio's value will depend on whether the value of the stock is $110 or $90 at the end of one year. The one half share will either be worth $55 or $45. Combined with the debt of $45, the outcome is either $10 or zero.

4) The option will either be worth $10 ($110 - $100) or zero at expiration. Both positions have the same payoffs.

iii. Because the portfolio and the option have the same payoffs at all times, they must have the same initial value. Otherwise, there would be an arbitrage opportunity that could be exploited.

EXHIBIT 10: BINOMIAL OPTION PRICING

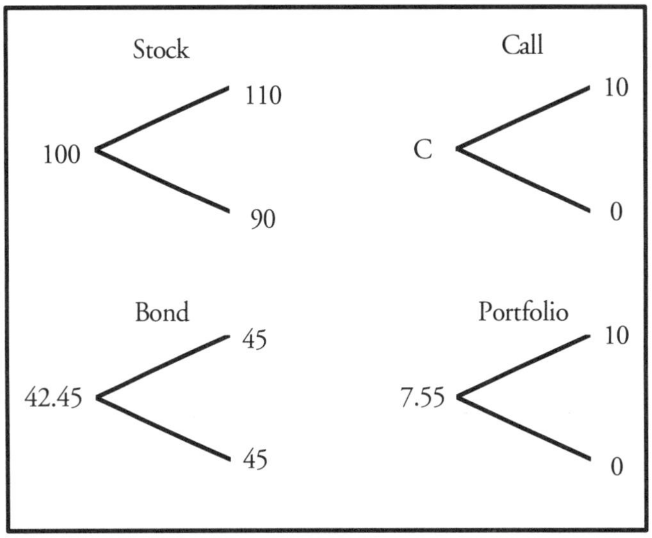

iv. Therefore, the option must equal $7.55 ($50.00 – $42.45). This equals the one-half share of stock minus the short bond.

v. The binomial option pricing model is further expanded for more than two possible outcomes and for multi-period analysis. Finally, this analysis leads to the Black-Scholes option valuation model.

l. Black-Scholes Option Valuation Model.

i. In 1973, the same year the Chicago Board of Options Exchange was established, Fischer Black and Myron Scholes developed the first options valuation model, which has since been named the Black-Scholes Option Valuation Model. Their model was designed to determine the value of a call option based on certain variables. These variables include the following:

A) Current market price - The call premium will be greater for higher priced stocks.

B) Exercise price - The call premium will be greater for lower exercise prices.

C) Time to expiration - The premium will increase as the time to expiration increases. More time is available for the stock price to trade above the exercise price.

D) Volatility (standard deviation) of returns - Stocks that are more volatile will cause the premium to increase because there is more potential for the stock to trade above the exercise price.

E) Risk-free rate of return - The call premium will increase as the risk-free rate increases.

ii. Assumptions of the Black-Scholes Option Valuation Model.

A) The Black-Scholes Option Valuation Model assumes that the option is a European Call option.

B) The Black-Scholes Option Valuation Model also assumes that there will be no cash dividends during the exercise period.

EXHIBIT 11: FACTORS THAT INFLUENCE THE PRICE OF A CALL OPTION

Variable	Call Option Price Increases if Variable
Market Price	↑
Exercise Price	↓
Time	↑
Volatility	↑
Risk-Free Rate	↑

m. Put/Call Parity Model.

  i. The Put/Call Parity Model is designed to determine the value of a put option from a corresponding call option. For example, an IBM put option would be valued using an IBM call option.

n. Index options.

  i. Stock index options.

    A) Options can be bought and sold on aggregate measures of the market, such as the S&P 500, S&P 100, Value Line Index, the NYSE Options Index, and the Dow Index.

    B) If an investor believes that the market is going to rise, the investor can purchase one of these options to take advantage of the potential increase in the market. Stock index options are especially beneficial when the overall market is going up. However, determining which sectors or companies will appreciate may be difficult or impossible. Index options provide for diversification because they are representative of the market.

    C) The investor has unlimited profit potential from the purchase of a call index option and is limited in the losses that can be sustained by the price of the premium paid.

  ii. Portfolio insurance.

    A) The majority of investors have a bullish outlook and take long positions in the majority of their portfolios. For those investors who are concerned about declines in the market, purchasing a put option on an index, such as the S&P 500, provides protection against such losses. A put option will protect the investor in the event that the market declines, because the put will increase in value as the stock portfolio declines in value. Thus, the portfolio is hedged against declines in the market. If the market increases, the premium will simply be the cost of insuring the portfolio.

    B) To be effective against losses from declines in the market, the put option must represent the market, such as the S&P 500, and the value that the option represents must coincide with the value of the stock portfolio hedged.

o. Examples of puts and calls.

EXHIBIT 12: THE CALL OPTION

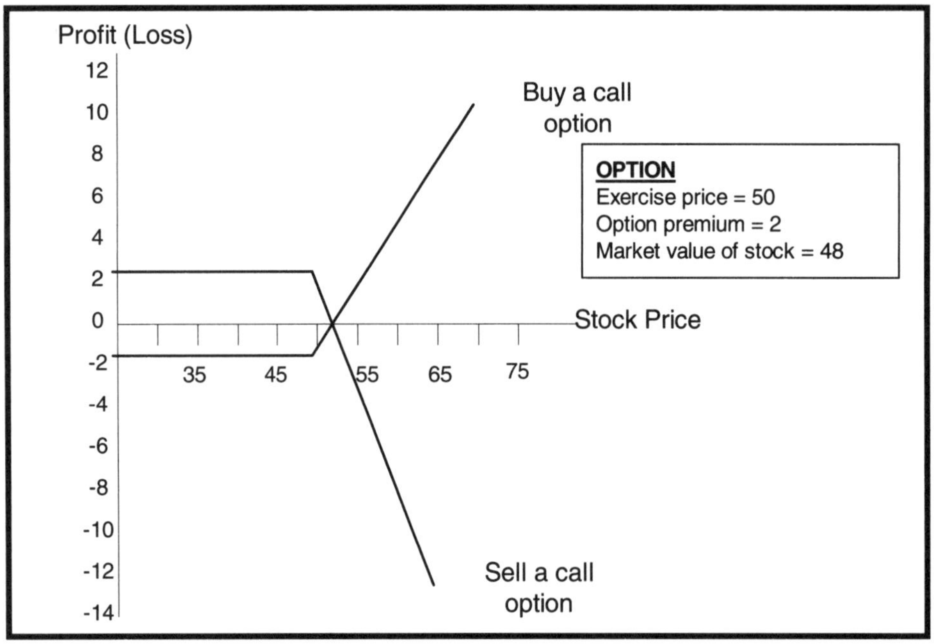

i. The exhibit above depicts the profit (loss) for both a buyer and seller of a call option. Notice that the buyer has unlimited profit potential while the seller has unlimited loss potential. Likewise, the buyer's loss and the seller's gain are limited to the premium paid.

EXHIBIT 13: THE PUT OPTION

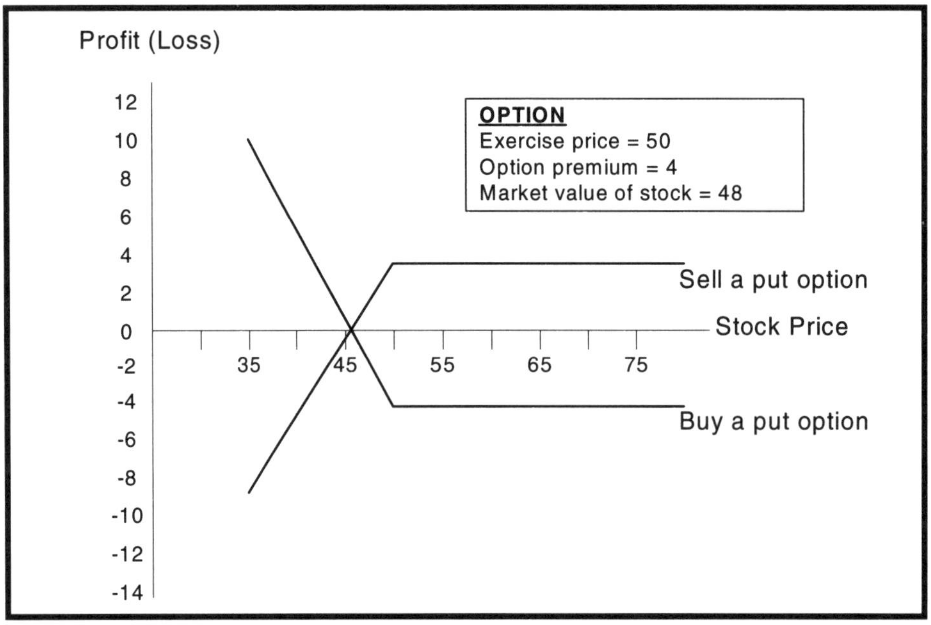

ii. The exhibit above depicts the profit (loss) for both a buyer and seller of a put option. Notice that the buyer has a large profit potential, while the seller has a large loss potential. Likewise, the buyer's loss and the seller's gain are limited to the premium paid.

p. Option strategies.

i. Combining different types of option contracts allows investors to create new risk return relationships for their option contracts. Different strategies are used under different market environments. For example, a long straddle is used if the investor believes that the stock price will make a large change, but is uncertain about the direction. Two more common option strategies include the straddle and zero-cost collar.

ii. Straddle.

A) A straddle is a combination of a put option and a call option in that each has the same exercise price and the same expiration date.

B) A straddle can be either long or short. A long straddle occurs when both options are purchased, whereas a short straddle occurs when both options are sold or written.

C) An investor can profit from a long straddle if the underlying stock price increases or decreases by an amount to cover the premiums paid for the two options. The most an investor can lose with a long straddle is the sum of the two premiums paid for the options.

D) An investor can profit from a short straddle if the underlying stock has minimal changes during the option period. The most an investor can make with writing a short straddle is the sum of the premiums for the two option contracts. However, a short straddle is subject to unlimited losses (the same as with writing a call option).

Example (Long Straddle)

1) Given:
   a) Put option premium is $5.
   b) Call option premium is $5.
   c) Exercise price for the put option and the call option is $60.

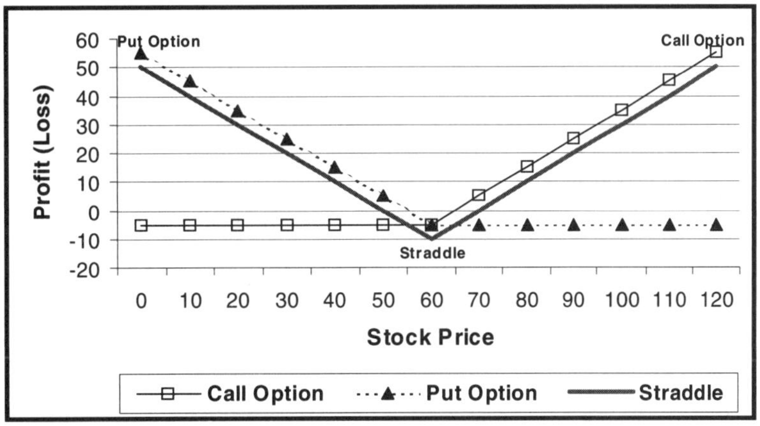

2) The buyer of the long straddle will break even if the stock increases to $70 [$10 (the sum of both option premiums) above the exercise price of $60] or if the stock decreases to $50 ($10 below the exercise price).
3) The buyer will lose a maximum of $10 (the sum of the two option premiums).

iii. Strips, Straps, and Strangles.

A) Strips, straps, and strangles are variations on the standard straddle.

B) A long strap combines two calls with one put, suggesting that the investor is more bullish than bearish.

C) A long strip combines two puts with one call, suggesting that the investor is more bearish than bullish.

D) A strangle is similar to a straddle, except that the options do not have the same exercise price. Rather, the options are purchased out of the money. Since the options are out of the money, the investor pays less in the way of premiums.

iv. Zero-cost collar.

A) A zero-cost collar is a strategy that is used to protect a gain in a long position of a stock. It consists of a long position in stock, a long put option, and a short call option. The investor purchases a put option to protect against downside risk and sells a call option to generate premium income to cover the cost of the premium for the put option.

B) The concept of a zero-cost collar is to protect a gain in stock without the cost of buying a put on the stock. This strategy pays for the premium on the put option by selling a call option.

C) The investor is protected from downside risk and only gives up the upside appreciation potential above the call exercise price.

Example

1) Given:

a) Stock price currently $100.

b) Put option premium is $5.

c) Exercise price for put option is $95.

d) Call option premium is $5.

e) Exercise price for call option is $105.

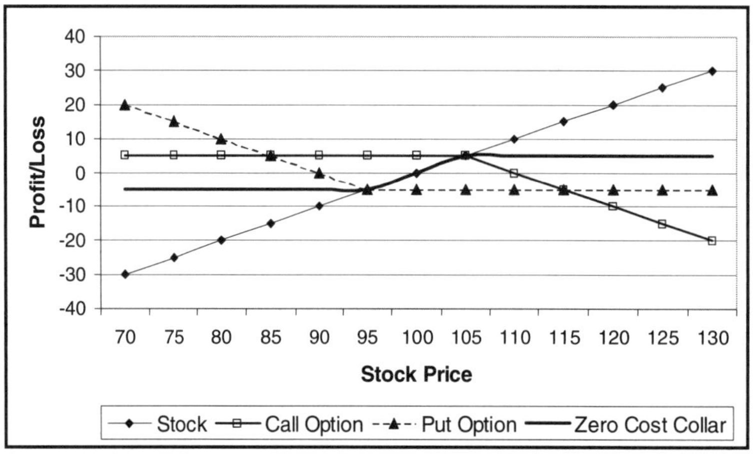

2) As depicted above, the investor will not lose money below $95 but will not participate in the appreciation above $105.

D) Tax issues.

1) The zero-cost collar strategy is subject to complex tax rules.

2) This strategy may also be subject to the constructive sale rules.

4. Warrants.

a. A warrant gives the holder the right to purchase a certain number of shares of a specified common stock at a predetermined price during the life of the warrant. Note that this definition is quite similar to the definition of a call option. However, two major differences exist between warrants and call options:

i. Warrants usually have longer lives. Options usually have lives of 3 to 9 months, while warrants have lives between 5 and 10 years.

ii. The second major difference is that options are written and exercised by investors, whereas warrants are issued by the company.

b. Warrants are issued by corporations for several reasons:

i. Warrants act as an incentive for creditors to purchase the bonds. If the company does well, the creditors either sell the warrants on the open market or purchase the stock to participate in the growth of the company.

ii. The cost of capital can be lowered by using warrants with bonds. Because the bond comes with a warrant (the warrant is an additional right), the interest rate for the bond can be lowered.

iii. Warrants also help the companies raise needed capital.

J. REAL ESTATE.

1. There are many types of real estate investments:

a. Home ownership.

i. Home ownership is an investment choice. Purchasing a home means that the investor has decided that ownership is more beneficial than renting.

ii. Home ownership provides certain tax benefits, such as deductible mortgage interest and deductible real estate taxes. These benefits, along with potential appreciation, should be factored in when deciding to invest in a home.

b. Developed land.

i. Developed land can include land with buildings, apartments, or other improvements, such as curbs, sewers, and roads.

ii. Developed land, such as apartments, can provide positive cash flows with little taxable income in early years due to depreciation (if the property meets specific tax requirements).

c. Undeveloped land.

i. Undeveloped land produces negative cash flows. This occurs because there is no positive cash flow from rents, but there are expenses. Negative cash flows result from the initial investment, interest on debt, maintenance, property taxes, other taxes, etc. Therefore, returns from undeveloped land come primarily from appreciation.

ii. There are certain risks associated with undeveloped land. These include:

A) The land may be adversely rezoned.

B) Building permits may not be attainable.

C) Access to land may not be developed.

D) The population may shift unexpectedly or not grow as expected.

iii. For all of these reasons, undeveloped land is an extremely risky investment.

d. Apartment buildings.

i. Apartment buildings may provide positive cash flows and have the potential for appreciation. Apartment buildings can also generate tax-deferred benefits through depreciation.

Note: Income and loss from apartments may be subject to the passive activity rules introduced in the 1986 Tax Reform Act.

e. Condominiums.

i. Condominiums can be developed and sold, or they can be purchased like a home and then sold. In addition to appreciation potential, condominiums can also generate rental income.

f. Partnerships and limited partnerships.

i. Real estate can be held in both partnerships and limited partnerships. The partnership form of business avoids the double taxation found with C corporations and allows the partners the freedom to structure compensation and earnings.

ii. A limited partnership differs from a general partnership in that it has both limited and general partners. A general partner is liable for all debts of the partnership, whereas a limited partner can only lose his or her initial investment. Limited partners have limited liability. Limited partners are limited in the control of the partnership. They are not permitted to participate in the management of the partnership.

g. Real estate investment trusts (REITs).

i. REITs are another way to invest indirectly in real estate. REITs are closed-end investment companies that fall under the Investment Company Act of 1940. REITs specialize in real estate and other mortgage securities. Like other closed-end investment companies, REITs are traded on exchanges and can sell at premiums or discounts to net asset value (NAV is the FMV of all assets less all liabilities).

ii. REITs can be classified as Equity Trusts, Mortgage Trusts, or Hybrid Trusts.

A) Equity Trusts generally acquire real estate for the purpose of renting the space to other companies. Income is generated from rental income and sales of appreciated real estate.

B) Mortgage Trusts are in the business of financing real estate ventures. They make loans to outside builders and make money from interest.

C) Hybrid Trusts have characteristics of both Equity and Mortgage Trusts.

2. Investing in real estate provides two primary benefits:

   a. Leverage - Real estate is usually purchased by financing a large portion of the original investment. Large debt ratios with real estate allow for magnified returns on equity. For example, if a $100,000 house is purchased with $10,000 down and a mortgage of $90,000, any appreciation will be magnified ten times. If the house is sold for $110,000, the investor will have realized a 100% return of invested capital [($110,000 - $100,000) ÷ $10,000].

   b. Tax deductions - Whether as a direct deduction for rental property or as an itemized deduction, interest and taxes both provide tax benefits to real estate investors. For example, a $100,000, 30-year mortgage at 8% will result in a monthly payment of $733.76. The first year will generate the following payments:

      - Total payments of $8,805.12 ($733.76 x 12).
      - Total principal of $835.36.
      - Total interest of $7,969.81.
      - Tax benefit of $2,151.85 (assuming a 27% tax bracket).

   Therefore, the net payments for the first year of this mortgage will be $6,653.27 ($8,805.12 - $2,151.85). The investor saves over 25% in tax deductions the first year. The interest portion of the payment will decline over time reducing the benefits of the tax deduction. This decline in the interest is illustrated in the chart below.

EXHIBIT 14: RELATIONSHIP BETWEEN INTEREST AND PRINCIPAL OVER TIME

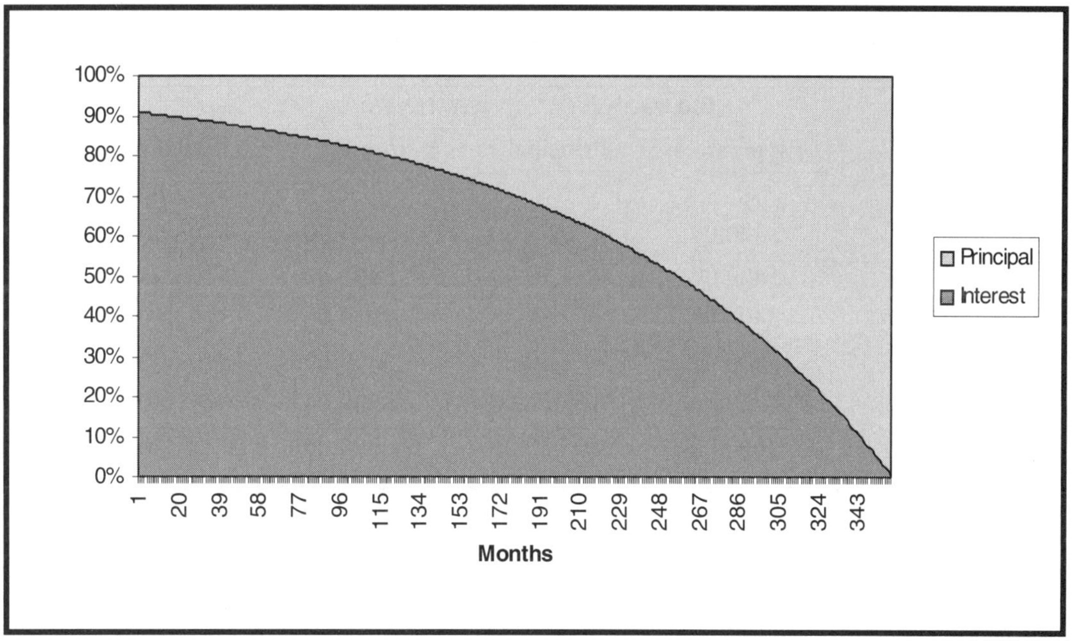

3. Loans can be structured in different ways:

   a. Conventional home mortgages are the most common way homes are purchased. A portion of the sale price is paid as a down payment with the remainder generally financed over 15 or 30 years. A portion of each payment will be interest and a portion will be principal. In the earlier years, the payment consists primarily of interest, whereas in later years principal is the majority of the payment. An example of an amortization schedule for a five-payment conventional mortgage is as follows:

CONVENTIONAL MORTGAGE (5 PAYMENTS)

Year	Payment	Principal	Interest	Balance
			8.00%	$10,000.00
1	$2,504.56	$1,704.56	$800.00	$8,295.44
2	$2,504.56	$1,840.92	$663.64	$6.454.52
3	$2,504.56	$1,988.20	$516.36	$4.466.32
4	$2,504.56	$2,147.25	$357.31	$2,319.07
5	$2,504.60	$2,319.07	$185.53	$0.00
Total	$12,522.84	$10,000.00	$2,522.84	$0.00

   b. A balloon note is structured such that payments throughout the term of the loan consist entirely of interest until the final payment. The final payment will consist of the original principal and an interest payment.

Example (Balloon Note)

BALLOON NOTE (5 PAYMENTS)

Year	Payment	Principal	Interest	Balance
			8.00%	$10,000.00
1	$800.00	$0.00	$800.00	$10,000.00
2	$800.00	$0.00	$800.00	$10,000.00
3	$800.00	$0.00	$800.00	$10,000.00
4	$800.00	$0.00	$800.00	$10,000.00
5	$10,800.00	$10,000.00	$800.00	$0.00
Total	$14,000.00	$10,000.00	$4,000.00	$0.00

   c. A fixed or variable rate of interest will be charged for mortgages. Variable interest rates change over time to reflect current interest rate movements. For mortgages, these variable rates are usually capped with annual amounts of increase commonly at 2% (or semiannual amounts at 1%) and life of loan increases capped at 6%. Therefore, a 6% variable rate mortgage with 2/6 caps will have a maximum interest rate of 12% over the life of the loan.

   d. Graduated payment mortgages are similar to conventional home mortgages except that the total monthly payments are initially low, then increase over time. In the early years, this results in negative amortization (i.e., principal is increasing because the monthly payments are not sufficiently servicing the debt). This arrangement can better match an individual's earning capacity that may increase over time. This will allow for a large initial mortgage because payments will increase in later years when earnings have increased.

4. Points - Points are an additional cost of obtaining a loan, that are charged by lending institutions and are stated as a percent of the mortgage loan. Thus, two points on a $150,000 loan would be $3,000. Tax deductibility of points:

   a. Points are fully deductible in the initial year of an original loan.

   b. Points on refinancing must be capitalized and amortized. However, if refinancing is incurred for home improvements and the points are paid from separate funds, the points are currently deductible.

K. PRIVATE PLACEMENTS & VENTURE CAPITAL AS AN ASSET CLASS.

1. Venture Capital – In General.

   a. Venture capital is financing for companies that are privately held and is one method of acquiring the capital needed for expansion. Companies in a variety of stages make use of venture capital.

   b. The most common type of investment by a venture capital firm is in the form of convertible preferred stock. However, other forms of investment may also be used, depending on the circumstances of the company.

   c. The various stages of financing are as follows:

      i. Early stages of financing.

         A) Seed financing – Funding for the purpose of research and development of an idea. Typically, funding does not exceed $50,000.

         B) Start-up financing – Funding for product development and marketing. Typically for companies that have not sold products or services commercially.

         C) First-stage financing – Funding for initial manufacturing and sales.

      ii. Expansion financing.

         A) Second-stage financing – Funding is for expansion of an existing company, whether profitable or not.

         B) Third-stage financing – Funding is for major expansion.

         C) Mezzanine or bridge financing – Funding for companies that expect to go "public" within approximately one year.

      iii. Venture capital may also be used in certain special cases, including:

         A) Turnarounds – Companies that are losing money and market share and are close to bankruptcy will often need a large capital infusement to "turnaround" the company from losing money to making money.

         B) Leveraged buyouts – A group of investors or a management group will use capital to purchase the company from the current owners. The company's assets are typically used as collateral for loans.

2. Venture Capital as an investment.

   a. Returns.

      i. Returns for venture capital are typically expected to average between 40% and 60% on an annual basis. However, long-term returns do vary depending on the types of companies that are invested in.

      ii. Just as a mutual fund portfolio will have numerous stocks, a venture capital portfolio will have numerous companies. Only 10% to 15% of the companies in the portfolio are expected to be extremely successful. Some of the other companies may be profitable with the remainder considered losers.

   b. Risk – Investing in companies with unproven track records is an obviously risky venture. In addition, investments must be made for long periods of time. The nature of these investments is illiquid.

   c. Correlation – Venture capital tends to be an effective method of diversification for a portfolio, since the correlation to other equity investments is relatively low.

   d. Portfolio diversification – Venture capital portfolios are often diversified four possible ways:

      i. Industrial sector.

      ii. Stage of company development.

      iii. Geographical region.

      iv. Vintage year.

L. INTERNATIONAL INVESTMENTS.

1. Investing overseas may provide substantial benefits to an existing portfolio of U.S. securities. These benefits include additional diversification and possibly increased returns.

   a. Diversification.

      i. Adding securities from different global markets provide added diversification to a portfolio because the United States market is not perfectly correlated with other global markets. Adding foreign securities is similar to adding securities from different sectors of the U.S. market. It provides less opportunity for losses from one portion of the portfolio to create drastic declines in the overall portfolio.

      ii. The reason that markets are not highly correlated is because each country has its own economic system with its various cycles. This low correlation provides the opportunity to benefit from economies that are prospering and to avoid those that are weak.

   b. Increased returns.

      The potential exists to capitalize on those foreign countries that have very large growth potential. These countries may be underdeveloped countries beginning their industrial revolution, or they may be countries undergoing significant economic and structural changes. Countries moving toward capitalist economies benefit those investors willing to take advantage of the new growth opportunity.

2. International investing does, however, subject investors to additional risks. These risks include foreign currency risk (such as devaluation of currency), and country risk, which is the risk that a foreign economy may go into a recession, or that foreign government regulation may adversely affect a foreign investment. Simply, the difficulties associated with dealing with the requirements of foreign countries can cause international investing to be risky.
3. There are four relatively easy ways to invest internationally: foreign mutual funds, American Depository Receipts, foreign closed-end funds, and purchasing foreign shares on a foreign stock exchange.
    a. Foreign mutual funds (including Exchange Traded Funds (ETFs)).
        i. There are many mutual funds that have international presence. Some funds may hold small amounts of foreign investments, while others specialize in regions of the world or even particular countries.
        ii. Examples of international funds include: global funds, Latin American funds, Pacific funds, Asian funds, etc.
        iii. There are ETFs that mimic a variety of foreign indexes allowing an investor to manage his exposure to his countries of interest.
    b. American Depository Receipts (ADRs).
        i. ADRs can be purchased on the New York Stock Exchange, the American Stock Exchange, and NASDAQ.
        ii. ADRs are trust receipts issued by a U.S. bank for shares of a foreign company purchased and held by a foreign branch of the bank. The ADRs are legal claims against the equity interest that the bank holds.
        iii. ADRs are an excellent alternative to direct investing in foreign companies that provide several benefits:
            A) ADRs are denominated and pay dividends in U.S. dollars, not in foreign currency. This saves the investor the transaction costs associated with converting the currency. (However, ADRs are still subject to exchange rate risks.)
            B) Information is often more attainable with ADRs because the bank which holds the equity security has access to such information.
            C) Because ADRs are traded on open exchanges, they are liquid and marketable investments.
            D) The foreign company is generally required to comply with the requirements of U.S. exchanges including compliance with U.S. GAAP (Generally Accepted Accounting Principles) and certain disclosure and reporting requirements.
    c. Foreign closed-end funds.
        i. Foreign closed-end funds provide the same basic benefits as foreign mutual funds. However, because closed-end funds trade on exchanges, they do not have the cash inflow and outflow that mutual funds frequently experience.
        ii. The fixed capitalization allows managers of closed-end funds to invest in less liquid securities without fear that investors will wish to liquidate their positions, forcing the manager to liquidate the illiquid securities in the portfolio.

d. Purchasing foreign shares on a foreign stock exchange.

i. Direct purchasing of foreign securities on foreign exchanges is more difficult than the other methods. However, with the benefits of technology, the process has become more simplified. Establishing a brokerage account in a foreign country or using a foreign branch of a U.S. broker can accomplish the purchase of foreign shares on foreign exchanges.

ii. The foreign transactions require completion in the local currency. Monitoring direct foreign investments is certainly more difficult than with the use of a mutual fund.

M. OTHER INVESTMENTS.

1. Precious metals.

a. Gold, silver, and platinum are precious metals that can be purchased as investments.

b. The price of gold often moves inversely with the price of the stock market (negative beta). It can be used as a hedge against bear markets.

c. These metals can be purchased directly through futures contracts or mutual funds.

d. Coin collections provide another medium to invest in metals. Coins have been collected for thousands of years and a few gold coins today sell for hundreds of times their face value.

e. Some U.S. coins may be held in IRA accounts.

2. Collectibles.

a. Collectibles can provide a dual benefit for investors: the pleasure from having a collection and the potential appreciation that collectors enjoy. Collectibles may take many forms:

i. Books and magazines.

ii. Oriental rugs.

iii. Furniture.

iv. Toy soldiers.

v. Barbie dolls.

vi. Cabbage Patch dolls.

vii. Postcards.

viii. Porcelain figurines.

ix. Art.

x. Coins.

xi. Wine.

xii. Diamonds and other precious stones.

xiii. Jewelry.

b. Unlike many other financial assets, collectibles do not have an efficient market. A certain level of expertise should be acquired before making a significant investment in collectibles. There may be marketability and liquidity problems associated with selling collectibles. Collectibles are, therefore, considered highly risky and illiquid.

N. RISK PYRAMID.

EXHIBIT 15: RISK PYRAMID

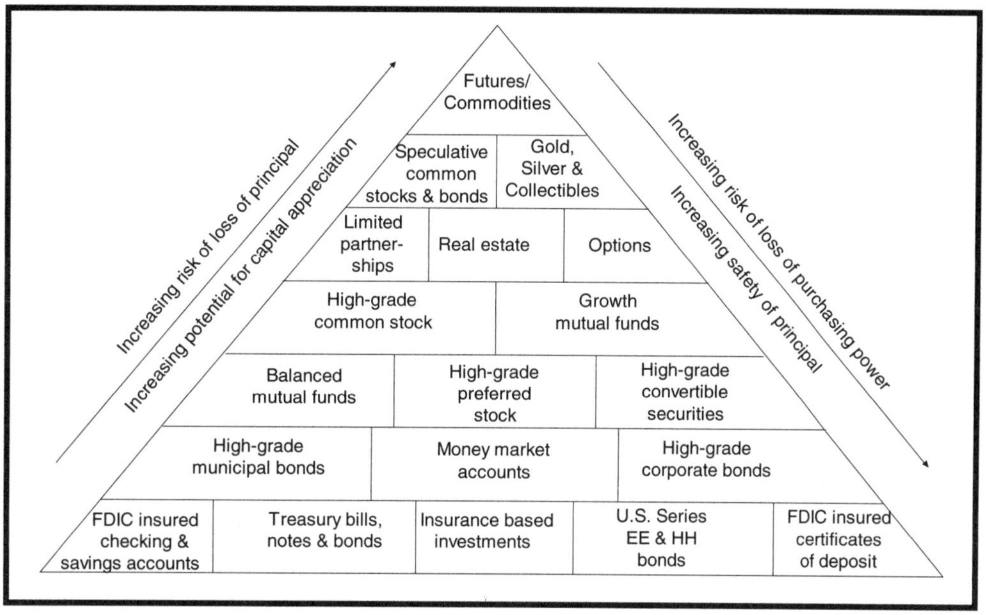

O. HISTORICAL PERFORMANCE OF INVESTMENT VEHICLES.

1. The table below depicts the approximate performance and risk level of various securities over the past 50 years (risk is measured by standard deviations).

EXHIBIT 16: SUMMARY OF RATES OF RETURN FOR VARIOUS SECURITIES

Type of Security	Rate of Return	Standard Deviation (σ)
Small Cap. Stocks	13%	30%
Large Cap. Stocks	11%	20%
Corporate Bonds	6%	9%
Intermediate Govt. Bonds	5%	9%
Long-Term Govt. Bonds	5%	8%
Treasury Bills	4%	3%
Inflation	3%	5%

2. Bonds have slightly outpaced the rate of inflation over this long period of time. Stocks have performed substantially better than bonds over the same period of time. However, stocks have sustained substantially more volatility than bonds. Investors with long-term perspectives and a willingness to sustain a higher level of volatility are more suited to equity-type investments.

III. SECURITY MARKETS

A. PRIMARY MARKET.

1. The purpose of the primary market is for initial sales of securities issued to the public. The primary market allows companies and entrepreneurs to acquire the needed funds and capital to expand and develop business.

2. Underwriting.

   a. Often, a company will seek the help of an investment banker to underwrite an issue of securities or to coordinate an initial public offering (IPO). An IPO is simply the first offering of stock to the general public.

   b. An underwriter may assume some of the risk associated with selling the securities to the public. For example, an investment banker might agree to purchase an issue for $12 per share and then resell the issue to the public for $13 per share. This $1 profit is referred to as an underwriter's spread. In addition, underwriters often help the issuing firm determine its financial needs and the best investment vehicle to achieve the needed funds. Underwriting can take one of four forms:

      i. Firm commitment.

      The underwriter purchases the entire issue of securities at a specific price then sells at a higher price. A firm commitment shifts all risk to the underwriter. If the issue cannot be resold at a price above the purchase price, the underwriter will lose money on the transaction. Often, a syndicate of underwriters will be set up to spread the potential risk.

      ii. Stand-by underwriting.

      The underwriter purchases the remaining securities left after an initial offering (usually to existing shareholders/owners) at a predetermined price.

      iii. Best-efforts.

      The underwriter sells as much of the issue as possible, and the remainder returns to the issuing company. No risk is shifted to the underwriter. Best-efforts occurs when the issuing company is confident that the issue will be sold or the underwriter is concerned about the risk because of the financial stability and risk of the company.

      iv. Private placement.

         A) A private placement must be sold to no more than 35 unaccredited investors. The attraction of a private placement is that it does not have the registration requirements of an IPO and is, therefore, less expensive and less time consuming. Generally, the issue can be placed in the market quickly and at a low cost. Underwriters help find investors and receive a finder's fee or commission of 0.25 percent to 1.5 percent. Bonds have been the most common of the privately placed issues.

         B) In addition to cost, private placements avoid all the registration requirements of the SEC and avoid the public access to information that occurs when conforming to SEC requirements. Although private placements are limited to 35 unaccredited investors, there is no limit as to the number of accredited investors that may purchase shares from the issuance of shares in a private placement.

         C) An accredited investor generally is an individual with over $200,000 of annual income, or a net worth of $1,000,000 or more.

3. Public placement – Generally, all issues of securities sold to more than 35 people (unaccredited investors) must be registered with the SEC.

B. ISSUING COSTS.

1. There are three primary costs associated with issuing securities. These costs include:
   a. Out-of-pocket costs - These expenses include actual costs spent to issue the securities, such as clerical costs, attorney fees, and accounting fees.
   b. Underwriter spread - The underwriter receives a spread, the difference between the purchase price and the sales price, for underwriting the issue.
   c. Price concession - Underwriters occasionally suggest that dropping the issue price will increase the demand for the issue and help facilitate placing the issue with investors. The difference between the equilibrium price, which is the price at which the stock would sell if not part of a new offering, and the concession price is termed the price concession.
2. It is difficult to quantify the expenses relating to issuing new securities. Information regarding out-of-pocket costs have not been studied or compiled. Underwriter spreads can range from 0.5% to 15%, depending on the size and risk of the issue. Finally, because it is difficult to measure the equilibrium price, it is difficult to determine the extent that price concessions are undertaken.

C. SHELF REGISTRATION.

This term refers to Rule 415 of the Securities and Exchange Commission (SEC) which permits a company to preregister a security sale. An issuing company can file all required registration documents and forms with the SEC then choose to issue securities or delay the offering. If the company chooses to delay offering securities and is approved by the SEC, it can at any future time execute a sale quickly without further registration requirements.

D. SECONDARY MARKETS.

1. The purpose of the secondary market is to provide investors with a method to buy and sell securities that have previously been issued in the primary markets. This market acts as a way to liquidate security investments. The secondary markets consist of exchanges, such as the New York Stock Exchange and the American Stock Exchange, and Over-the-Counter Trading. These exchanges house the buying and selling of securities that are listed on the particular exchange. This buying and selling represents the function of the secondary market.
2. New York Stock Exchange (NYSE).
   a. Formed in 1792, the NYSE is the oldest and largest organized exchange within the United States. Membership on the NYSE is in the form of a seat on the exchange. These seats, approximately 1,500 in total, are priced by supply and demand. The cost for a seat has ranged from about $35,000 to over $1,000,000. Members on the exchange will have one of four roles.
      i. Commission broker - Executes orders for the firm's clientele, often the large brokerage houses.
      ii. Floor broker - These brokers are not affiliated with serving the public. Instead, they fill the excess orders that the commission brokers do not handle.
      iii. Registered traders or floor traders - Unaffiliated traders who trade for their own benefit. They are speculators and trade without paying a commission because they have a seat on the exchange.

iv. Specialists - Specialists, who make up approximately 25% of the members of the exchange, are positioned on the floor of the exchange and make a market in one or more stocks. The specialist must maintain an orderly market for the individual stock and adjust the market price for the stock to accomplish this task. They make commissions from the other brokers by acting as a broker, and they are permitted to act as a dealer for their own accounts. However, the specialists must not place their own orders in front of orders already taken by other brokers or the public. The specialist buys at the bid price and sells at the ask price. He or she makes the difference that is referred to as the spread.

b. The NYSE has become highly automated in recent years. The computer process handling trading is referred to as Super DOT (designated order turnaround).

c. The NYSE has minimum requirements in order for a company to be listed on the exchange. These requirements, which are more stringent than other exchanges, include:

i. Earnings before taxes of at least $2.5 million in the most recent year.

ii. Earnings before taxes of at least $2.0 million during the two preceding years.

iii. Total market value of common stock of at least $100 million.

iv. Publicly held shares of at least 1.1 million.

v. More than 2,000 holders of 100 shares or more.

3. Nasdaq-Amex Market Group.

a. On November 2, 1998, the National Association of Securities Dealers, Inc. (NASD) and the American Stock Exchange (AMEX) completed their merger that will oversee the operation of the Nasdaq (National Association of Security Dealers Automated Quotation system) Stock Market and the Amex.

b. This combination creates the world's first major financial market that brings together a central auction specialist system (AMEX) and a multiple Market Maker system (Nasdaq). However, Nasdaq and AMEX continue to operate as separate markets.

c. The American Stock Exchange is the second largest floor-based securities exchange in the United States.

4. Discount brokers.

a. Discount brokerage houses are focused on providing efficient trading with lower commissions than the traditional brokerage companies.

b. To facilitate lower commission rates, these discount brokers will provide fewer services such as research and advisory services.

E. OVER THE COUNTER (OTC).

1. Unlike the New York Stock Exchange and the other exchanges, the OTC market does not have a physical location; rather it is a network of brokers communicating via telephones and computers. The term "over the counter" refers to the trading practices during the nineteenth century in which traders would present securities or cash at the counter of commercial banks.

2. The types of securities within the OTC market include stocks of various sizes, mutual fund shares, bank shares, and finance stocks. In addition, the majority of U.S. government, corporate, and municipal bonds are traded OTC.

3. Similar to the specialists on the established exchanges, market makers are brokers within the OTC market that specialize in particular stocks or securities and maintain an inventory of these stocks to trade with other brokers and the public. The market maker generates much of his or her income from the bid-ask spread.

   a. Bid price is the price at which the security will be purchased from the investor.

   b. Ask price is the price at which the security will be sold to the investor.

   c. The spread is the difference between the bid price and the ask price. The size of the spread will depend on several factors, such as:

      i. The number of market makers will affect the size of the bid-ask spread due to increased competition. With more competition, the size of the spread will tend to decrease.

      ii. The spread is inversely related to the volume of transactions. Securities that have large trading volume tend to have lower bid-ask spreads. When the number of securities traded is small, which is often referred to as a thin issue, the spread will tend to be larger.

4. The market maker also makes money from dividends paid on stock and interest paid on bonds for assets held in inventory. In addition, price appreciation or depreciation may occur from maintaining inventories of these securities.

5. These OTC brokers have formed the National Association of Security Dealers (NASD). This organization licenses brokers and regulates the trading practices of the OTC.

6. Pink Sheets.

   a. Named for the color of paper they have been historically printed on, pink sheets are the daily listings of price quotes for companies that trade in the over-the-counter market (OTC market).

   b. A vast majority of over-the-counter stocks are not eligible for trading on a national exchange, such as the NYSE or the Nasdaq, because these companies do not meet the minimum listing requirements. This could mean that the company does not meet the criteria for capitalization and number of shareholders, or if a company fails to file regular reports with the SEC and make information available to stockholders and potential investors.

   c. The companies quoted in the pink sheets tend to be extremely small and thinly traded. It can be very difficult for investors to find reliable, unbiased information about companies quoted in the pink sheets. Therefore, companies quoted in the pink sheets can be among the most risky investments.

F. THIRD AND FOURTH MARKETS.

1. The Third Market consists of stocks traded both on the organized exchanges and on the OTC market. Usually, the orders are large block trades (10,000 shares or more).

2. The Fourth Market is comprised of traders who trade without the help of the brokers. They trade directly with other interested parties. These traders can make use of the communication systems such as Instinet to allow them to find other interested parties. Most of these traders are institutional type investors with very large volumes.

EXHIBIT 17: SECOND, THIRD, AND FOURTH MARKETS

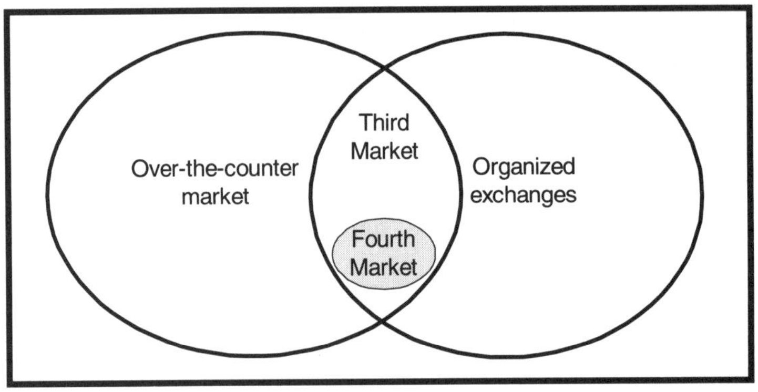

G. FOREIGN MARKETS.

1. International Stock Exchange (ISE).
   a. There were numerous exchanges in England, including the London Stock Exchange (LSE), until 1973 when all the British exchanges were merged into the International Stock Exchange.
   b. The ISE is attempting to become the primary securities exchange in the European Community.
   c. The exchange is fully computerized with the Stock Exchange Automated Quotations system (SEAQ).
   d. Holdings on the ISE include:
      i. 65% by pension plans.
      ii. 20% by individuals.
      iii. 15% by commercial companies, foreign investors, and banks.
2. Tokyo Stock Exchange (TSE).
   a. Prior to 1990, the TSE was the world's largest equity market in terms of value. However, 1990 saw a 40% decline followed by a 25% decline in 1992.
   b. Japanese exchanges have three defined sections.
      i. The first section consists of large companies and represents approximately 96% of the total market capitalization.
      ii. The second section consists of younger, smaller companies that might otherwise be traded OTC.
      iii. The third section is the OTC market.

H. TYPES OF ORDERS.

1. Investors can buy, sell, and short sell stocks on the securities markets. There are four basic types of orders that an investor might make:

   a. Market order.

      i. 75-80% of the orders are market orders, and these orders have the highest priority.

      ii. They must be filled prior to the other types of orders. However, while these are the fastest orders, they do not have limits or a specific price and, therefore, are subject to the fluctuations and timeliness of the market.

   b. Limit order.

      i. The objective of a limit order is to get a specific price, one that is better than the market at the time the order is placed. The price acts as a ceiling for purchases and a floor for sales, and the order will be held until filled or canceled.

      ii. The specialist keeps track of the orders and fills them in chronological order. Higher priced purchase limit orders take priority over lower priced limit orders. Even if the price for the stock is below (or above) the limit order, there is no guarantee that it will be filled.

Example

David, who is a shrewd investor, has analyzed all the relevant financial information and has determined that the Ashbey Corporation is worth $45 per share. If the stock is trading between $48 and $50, he can place a limit order at $45. This will assure that if the order is filled to purchase shares of Ashbey Corporation, David's price will be no higher than $45.

---

   c. Stop order.

      i. These orders, called stop-loss orders, are used to protect investors from large losses. If the market price reaches a certain point, the stop order will turn into a market order. For instance, an investor who is long in a security might place a stop order at 10 points below the market price to protect the appreciation of the stock against serious declines in the market price. Likewise, these orders can be used to limit losses in connection with short sales.

Example

Steve purchased Romig, Inc. for $29 per share, and it is now trading at $73 per share. He has an unrealized gain of $44. If Steve is concerned about the price declining, he can place a stop order at $70. If the stock price dropped to $70, a market order would be placed immediately. However, it may be filled at $69 or $68. The stop order protected his profit position.

---

d. Stop limit order.

i. These are similar to stop orders except they turn into limit orders when triggered. The stop order price and the limit order price are both specified. These are the least often used types of orders.

Example

If Dina owns 5,000 shares of Perez's Pretzels, which is selling at $35 per share, and is concerned about the price dropping, she may want to place a stop limit order. If she places a sell stop limit order at $30 and the stock subsequently falls below $30, the order will become a limit order to sell 5,000 shares at $30 or better.

Note: All orders are day orders unless otherwise specified. If they are not filled within the trading day, they will expire. Orders can be good for a specific period of time, or they can be "good-til-cancel." Time limits are normally used with limit and stop orders because they are not as likely to be filled during the day as market orders.

2. Stocks are traded in lots. Usually, stocks are traded in lots of 100 shares called round lots. Any variation from the 100-share lot is termed an odd lot. These odd lots require special attention by the broker or specialist and therefore command a larger commission per share. Thus, institutional investors rarely trade in odd lots, while individual investors are not always able to trade in round lots.

IV. SECURITIES LAW

A. GOVERNMENT REGULATION.

The purpose of government regulation is to protect investors. Both the federal and state governments require a substantial amount of regulation; however, most is from the federal government because the majority of trading is across state borders.

B. SECURITY REGISTRATION.

1. The Banking Act of 1933 (the Glass-Steagall Act).

   This was one of the first of many securities regulation laws that has impacted the investment markets. The Glass-Steagall Act prohibited commercial banks from acting as investment bankers, established the Federal Deposit Insurance Corporation (FDIC), and prohibited commercial banks from paying interest on demand deposits. However, this act was repealed by Congress in November 1999 by the Gramm-Leach-Bliley Act and eliminated many of the restrictions against affiliations among banks, securities firms, and insurance companies.

2. The Security Act of 1933.

   This securities act is primarily concerned with new issues of securities or issues in the primary market. It requires that all relevant information on new issues be fully disclosed, requires that new securities are registered with the SEC, requires audited financial statement information within the registration statements, and forbids fraud and deception. When sold, all securities must be accompanied by a prospectus. Small issues (under $1,500,000) and private issues are not required to comply with the Securities Act of 1933 requirements of full disclosure.

3. The Securities Exchange Act of 1934 (SEA).

   While the Securities Act of 1933 was limited to new issues, the 1934 Securities Act extended the regulation to securities sold in the secondary markets. The Act provided the following provisions:

   a. Establishment of the SEC - The SEC's primary function is to regulate the securities markets.

   b. Disclosure requirements for Secondary Market - Annual reports and other financial reports are required to be filed with the SEC prior to listing on the organized exchanges. These reports include the annual 10K Report, which must be audited, and the quarterly 10Q Report, which is not required to be audited.

   c. Registration of organized exchanges - All organized exchanges must register with the SEC and provide copies of their rules and bylaws.

   d. Credit regulation - Congress gave the Federal Reserve Board the power to set margin requirements for credit purchases of securities. Securities dealers' indebtedness was also limited to 20 times their owners' equity capital by this act.

   e. Proxy solicitation - Specific rules governing solicitation of proxies was established.

   f. Exemptions - Securities of federal, state, and local governments, securities that are not traded across state lines, and any other securities specified by the SEC are exempt from registering with the SEC. This includes Treasury bonds and municipal bonds.

g. Insider activities - A public report, called an insider report, must be filed with the SEC in every month that a change in the holding of a firm's securities occurs for an officer, director, or 10% or more shareholder. The 1934 SEA forbids insiders profiting from securities held less than 6 months and requires these profits be returned to the organization. In addition, short sales are not permitted by individuals considered to be insiders.

h. Price manipulation - The SEA of 1934 forbids price manipulation schemes such as wash sales, pools, circulation of manipulative information, and false and misleading statements about securities.

4. The Public Utility Holding Company Act of 1935 - The SEC was given authority to oversee the public utilities and to regulate the utility securities. All public utility holding companies must register with the SEC.

5. The Maloney Act of 1938 - Effectively, this act extended the SEA of 1934 to the OTC market. This act brought the OTC market under the regulation of the SEC and called for the self-regulation of the OTC securities dealers.

6. The Federal Bankruptcy Act of 1938, as Amended in 1978 - This act requires that a court-appointed trustee oversee the affairs of a firm for which bankruptcy charges have been filed, provides for liquidation of hopelessly troubled firms, provides for reorganization of troubled firms that might be able to survive, provides for arrangements for troubled firms that should be able to survive, and provides for repayment plans to govern moderately troubled firms that should be able to survive. This act also explained the downside risk of investing in bankrupt companies and explained that prices of these securities change due to anticipation of outcomes of court actions.

7. The Trust Indenture Act of 1939 - The purpose of this act is to protect the unwary bond investor from corrupt management. This act requires that every bond issue be governed by an indenture contract, that an objective third party trustee be provided to maintain the provisions of the contract, and that full disclosure be provided to the investors and the trustee.

C. REGISTRATION OF ADVISERS.

1. The Investment Advisers Act of 1940 - Any individual who provides investment advice to 15 or more interstate clients during a 12-month period is required to register with the SEC and file educational and background information (for all Registered Investment Advisers (RIAs)). The Investment Advisers Act of 1940 also forbids RIAs from assigning investment advisory contracts to other advisers without permission from the client, entering into profit-sharing agreements with clients, and prohibits advertising with selected testimonials.

2. An investment adviser is a person who:

   a. Provides advice, or issues reports or analyses, regarding securities.

   b. Is in the business of providing such services.

   c. Provides such services for compensation (compensation is "the receipt of any economic benefit" including commissions on the sale of products).

3. Certain organizations and individuals are excluded from being classified as an investment adviser:
    a. Lawyers, accountants, engineers, or teachers if their performance of advisory services is solely incidental to their professions;
    b. Brokers or dealers if their performance of advisory services is solely incidental to the conduct of their business as brokers or dealers, and they do not receive any special compensation for their advisory services;
    c. Publishers of bona fide newspapers, news magazines, or business or financial publications of general and regular circulation;
    d. Those persons whose advice is related only to securities that are direct obligations of or guaranteed by the United States.
    e. Incidental practice exception is not available to individuals who hold themselves out to the public as providing financial planning, pension consulting, or other financial advisory services.
4. Exceptions - The Act provides limited exemptions.

    Investment advisers who, during the course of the preceding twelve (12) months, had fewer than fifteen (15) clients and did not hold themselves out generally to the public as investment advisers.
5. Disclosure - The Act generally requires investment advisers entering into an advisory contract with a client to deliver a written disclosure statement on their background and business practices.
6. Inspections - The 1940 Adviser's Act and the SEC's rules require that advisers maintain and preserve specified books and records that are to be made available for inspection.
7. Restriction on the use of the term "Investment Counsel" - A registered investment adviser may not use the term "investment counsel" unless its principal business is acting as an investment adviser and a substantial portion of its business is providing "investment supervisory" services.
8. Anti-fraud provisions - Section 206 of the Act, Section 17 of the Securities Act of 1933, Section 10(b) of the Securities Exchange Act of 1934, and Rule 10b-5 prohibit misstatements or misleading omissions of material facts and fraudulent acts and practices in connection with the purchase or sale of securities or the conduct of an investment advisory business. An investment adviser owes his or her clients undivided loyalty and may not engage in activity in conflict with a client's interest.
9. Registration - Form ADV is kept current by filing periodic amendments.
10. Filing requirements.
    a. Forms - ADV and ADV-W can be obtained from the SEC's Office of Consumer Affairs and Information Services in Washington, DC or from the Commission office in your area.
    b. Copies - All adviser filings must be submitted in triplicate and typewritten. Copies can be filed, but each must be signed manually.
    c. Fees - Must include a registration fee of $150, by check or money order payable to the Securities and Exchange Commission, with your initial application of Form ADV. No part of this fee can be refunded.
    d. Name and signatures - Full names are required. Each copy of an execution page must contain an original manual signature.

11. Federal vs. State registration.

    a. Certain investment advisers must register with the Securities Exchange Commission, while other investment advisers must register with the state in which the adviser maintains his primary place of business.

    b. Advisers with assets under management less than $25 million are generally required to register at the state level.

    c. Advisers with assets under management of $25 million or more are generally required to register with the SEC.

D. DUE DILIGENCE.

1. Due diligence requires that investment advisers investigate any security prior to offering it for sale to a client. Additionally, the security must be "suited" to the client's needs and objectives.

2. Due diligence is addressed in the Securities Act of 1933.

E. INVESTMENT COMPANY ACT OF 1940.

1. The Investment Company Act of 1940 governs the management of investment companies. This act requires that investment companies register with the SEC, provide prospectuses to investors prior to the sale of shares, disclose the investment goals of the company, have outside members on the board of directors, use uniform accounting practices, and gain approval by shareholders for changes in management.

2. There are three types of investment companies: open-end funds, closed-end funds, and unit investment trusts. Open-end investment companies, or mutual funds, have unlimited shares and will continue to grow as investors send more money to the fund. Closed-end investment companies generally cannot accept additional investments once it is initially capitalized. Investment companies are not taxed at the corporate level. Instead, they pass any income, usually interest, dividends, or capital gains to the shareholders similar to S corporations and partnerships. A unit investment trust (UIT) is a registered investment company that is self-liquidating and passively managed and may invest in stocks, bonds, or other securities.

F. THE SECURITIES INVESTOR PROTECTION CORPORATION ACT OF 1970.

This act established the Securities Investor Protection Corporation (SIPC) to protect clients' accounts at failing brokerage firms. The SIPC Act requires that securities brokers pay dues to support the SIPC (similar to the dues required to be paid to the Pension Benefit Guarantee Corporation for defined benefit plans). The SIPC acts as an insurance company that pools money to cover the risks that occur in the brokerage industry.

G. THE EMPLOYEE RETIREMENT INCOME SECURITIES ACT OF 1974.

This act was designed to protect the retirement benefits of employees. It established the Pension Benefit Guarantee Corporation (PBGC), which is designed to insure benefits of insolvent defined benefit retirement plans. Plan sponsors are required to pay premiums to the PBGC each year to fund the pool of money. Many of the requirements of ERISA are synonymous with requirements of the Internal Revenue Code. Both provide for vesting rights, minimum coverage requirements, minimum participation requirements, and minimum benefits. ERISA also requires that employers make required payments for defined benefit plans; otherwise, the PBGC has the power to terminate the plan.

H. SECURITIES TRADING ABUSES.

1. Prior to federal regulation, abuse of securities trading was rampant. While some states had established securities laws, the laws were ineffective and were termed blue-sky laws. The phrase, "blue-sky laws," developed because some of the state laws were so poor, it was as if it was legal to sell someone a part of the blue sky.

2. Listed below are various abuses that occurred during the period of time prior to federal regulation.

   a. Fraud - Deception that is deliberately performed in attempts of obtaining unfair or illegal gains is called fraud. Examples of fraud include: insider trading, wash sales, misrepresentation, churning, and price manipulation.

   b. Unauthorized trading - Trading without the consent of the client is called unauthorized trading.

   c. Illegal solicitation - When brokers sell securities without first providing the investor a prospectus, which reveals all relevant information concerning the security.

   d. Unsuitability - It is the responsibility of brokers to sell securities that are not inappropriate to the risk tolerance, age, wealth, or other circumstances of their clients.

   e. Due diligence violation - This occurs when a dealer fails to learn all pertinent facts regarding every underwriting under their responsibility and fails to ensure that this information is provided to the investors.

   f. Wash sales - Selling a security at a loss and then repurchasing it within 30 days (before or after) is considered a wash sale. Generally, this is to establish a record of sale for tax purposes.

   g. Cornering the market - This technique involves purchasing all the available securities of a particular issue. Once the person owns all of a type of security, he or she is able to manipulate the price of the security because he or she controls the supply. Additionally, cornering the market may be done for the purpose of "squeezing" short sellers (a short squeeze causes the short seller to replace the stock that was borrowed and close out his or her position, usually at a loss).

   h. Churning - Churning involves brokers excessively buying and selling securities in a client's account for the sole purpose of generating sales commissions.

   i. Insider trading - This occurs whenever insiders make securities transactions based on information that was obtained by the position they held and this information was not available to the public. Insiders include corporate directors, 10% or more owners, and executives. Auditors, consultants, bankers, attorneys, photocopiers, and typists can be temporary insiders if they are exposed to information that is not available to the public.

V. SECURITY MARKET INDEXES & AVERAGES

A. TYPES.

1. Averages and indexes are constructed to inform investors about changes in the market. They also serve as benchmarks for the performance of investors' portfolios and the performance of money managers, such as mutual fund money managers. The most well known of these averages is the Dow Jones Industrial Average (DJIA).
2. Indexes give different weights to each security based on one of three methods.
    a. Share price - A \$50 stock has 5 times the impact of a \$10 stock.
    b. Market capitalization - A stock with a market value of \$25 million will have 10 times the impact of a \$2.5 million company.
    c. Security return - Returns of 20% will have 2 times the impact of a 10% return.

B. AVERAGES.

1. Averages are calculated by determining the average stock price for a group of stocks. For instance, the DJIA consists of 30 stocks. To determine the DJIA, the 30 stock prices are added and divided by an adjusted divisor. The divisor was originally 30, equaling the number of stocks for the average. However, the denominator for the DJIA, which is now less than 1.00, has changed dramatically since inception as a result of stock splits, stock dividends, and substitutions of stocks.
2. Problems with DJIA.
    a. The DJIA fails to reflect payment of cash dividends.
    b. It ignores stock dividends under 10%.
    c. It fails to account for the number of shares outstanding.
    d. It consists of a biased sample of stocks (mostly old blue-chip type companies).
3. While the DJIA does have fundamental problems, it is highly correlated to other broader market indexes, such as the S&P 500. The correlation coefficient between the DJIA and the S&P 500 is above 95 percent. A high correlation indicates that it is an adequate representation of the market in spite of its fundamental weaknesses.

Example

Assume Companies A, B, and C represent an average and have current market prices of \$25, \$80, and \$100, respectively. The following illustration will demonstrate the effect to the denominator when Company A's stock splits (2 to 1) and then Company B is replaced with Company D (market price of \$50).

SECURITY MARKET AVERAGE EXAMPLE			
Company	**Original**	**Company A's Stock Splits**	**Company B is Replaced with Company D**
A	25.00	12.50	12.50
B	80.00	80.00	-
C	100.00	100.00	100.00
D	-	-	50.00
Numerator	205.00	192.50	162.50
Denominator	3.00	2.82	2.38
Average	68.33	68.33	68.33

Notice that in each of the changes the average must remain the same. For this to happen, the denominator must change to make the average stay constant.

C. VALUE-WEIGHTED INDEXES.

1. S&P 500 Index.

   a. The S&P 500 is a value-weighted index. It is comprised of 500 different stocks from the NYSE and the NASDAQ and includes large and small companies. The S&P 500 is determined by summing the market value (which is the share price times the number of shares outstanding) of the 500 companies and dividing by the base year value then multiplying this amount by 10 (the initial index value). If the value of the S&P 500 increased from 100 to 200, this change would indicate that the value of the securities had doubled. This method automatically adjusts for stock splits and dividends by focusing on market value instead of price.

   b. The S&P 500 is the index used by most professionals as a benchmark for U.S. large-cap equity investments. It is comprised of industrial stocks, transportation stocks, utilities, and financial institutions.

2. Russell 2000 Index.

   a. The Russell 2000 Index is a well-known index that is used to benchmark small capitalization companies.

   b. The Russell Index is a market capitalization weighted index and is a subset of the Russell 3000 Index, which represents the majority of U.S. equities.

3. EAFE Index.

   a. In 1969, the Europe, Australia, and Far East (EAFE) index was created as a measure of the international securities markets.

   b. It provides an indication of how a portfolio consisting of companies outside the United States might perform over time. It is probably the most well-known measure of international markets.

4. Wilshire 5000 Index.
    a. The Wilshire 5000 Index is another well-known index that is used as a measure of the U.S. broad market.
    b. It consists of over 7,000 U.S. based companies, and is often used as a measure of the overall market within the United States.

D. OTHER INDEXES AND AVERAGES.

1. Geometric average.
    a. Geometric averages are more precise than normal indexes and averages; however, they are very rare.
    b. The Value Line Index is based on the geometric returns from 1,700 stocks.
2. Bonds.
    a. J.P. Morgan Indices track the performance of government bonds issued in various countries.
    b. Lehman Brothers Indices include publicly traded debt within the United States.

VI. INVESTMENT CONCEPTS

A. DIVERSIFICATION.

1. General.

   a. The goal of diversification is to reduce risk.

   b. The purpose of diversification is to reduce unsystematic risk (risks associated with a single industry or security) within a portfolio.

   c. An inverse relationship exists between the number of stocks and the amount of unsystematic risk within the portfolio. As the number of stocks increases, the level of unsystematic risk should decline. However, there is a point of diminishing returns with regard to adding securities to a portfolio. Adding an additional stock to a portfolio with only 5 stocks will have a greater impact on the level of diversification than adding an additional stock to a portfolio of 200 stocks.

2. Simple diversification.

   a. Random selections of securities can reduce unsystematic risk.

   b. Reduction of unsystematic risk remains the primary focus of simple diversification.

   c. Why does diversification reduce risk?

EXHIBIT 18: DIVERSIFICATION

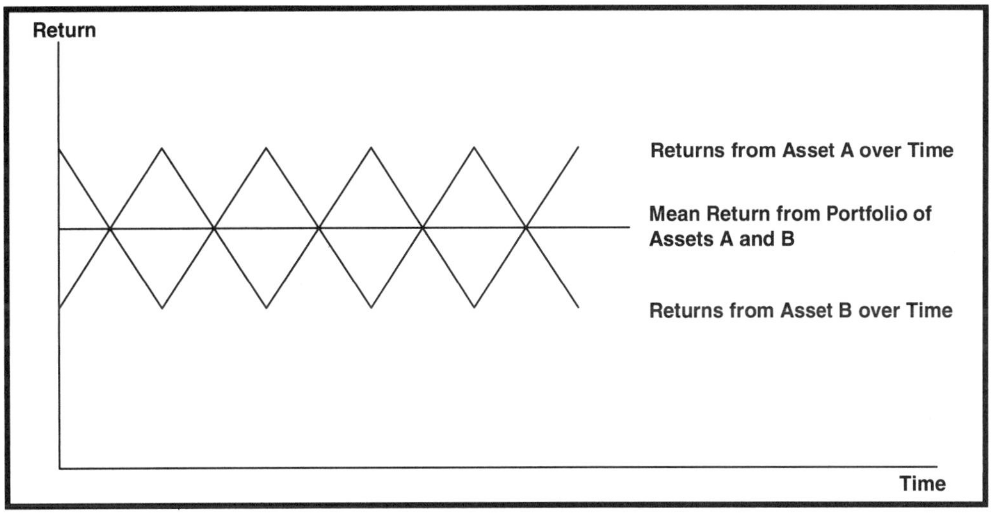

      i. The correlation coefficient (R) measures the movement between two securities. If the movement between the securities is identical, in rate and direction, the correlation coefficient equals +1. If the securities move in opposite directions at the same rate, the correlation coefficient equals -1 (see the above exhibit). The range for the correlation coefficient is from +1 to -1. This concept is illustrated in the exhibit below (R stands for the correlation coefficient).

EXHIBIT 19: CORRELATION COEFFICIENTS

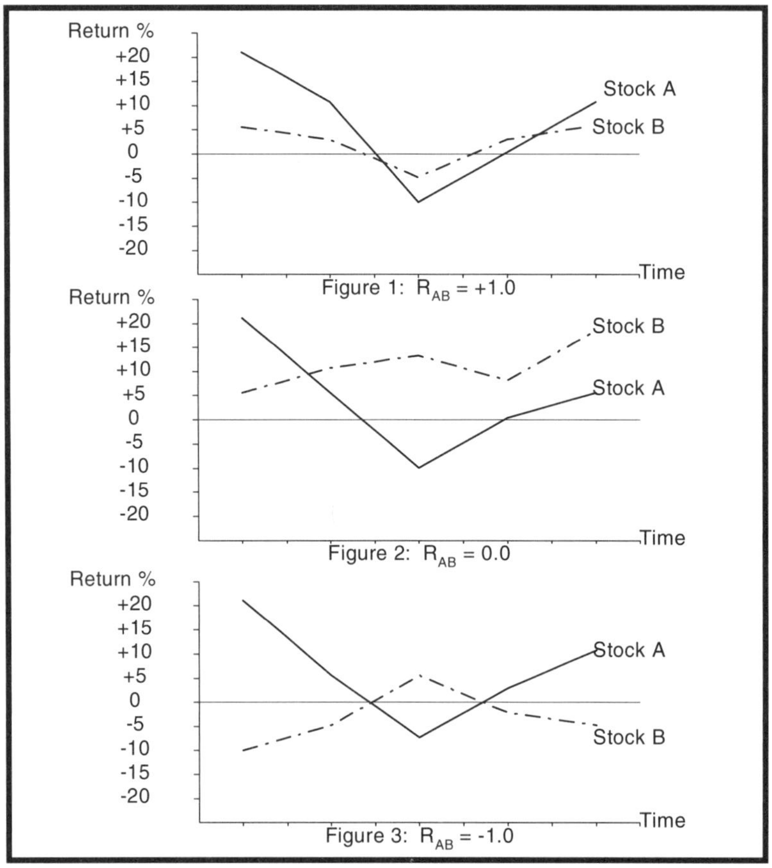

ii. The correlation coefficient between securities is rarely equal to 1. Therefore, the combination of securities, assuming the securities are not perfectly correlated, will reduce the overall portfolio risk by offsetting the risks of the individual securities.

iii. The standard deviation of a two-security portfolio is equal to:

$$\sigma = \sqrt{W_A^2\sigma_A^2 + W_B^2\sigma_B^2 + 2W_AW_B[\sigma_A\sigma_BR_{AB}]}\text{, where}$$

σ = Standard deviation of the two-asset portfolio.

W_A = The percent of the portfolio invested in security A.

W_B = The percent of the portfolio invested in security B.

$[\sigma_A\sigma_BR_{AB}]$ = Covariance between security A & B.

R_{AB} = Correlation coefficient.

Note: W_A plus W_B must sum to 100%.

iv. As the correlation coefficient $[R_{AB}]$ declines from +1 to -1, the variance and standard deviation of the portfolio also decline. If R_{AB} equals zero, the term $2W_AW_B[\sigma_A\sigma_BR_{AB}]$ drops out of the equation. Likewise, if R_{AB} is negative, the term $2W_AW_B[\sigma_A\sigma_BR_{AB}]$ is negative, which reduces the variance and standard deviation of the portfolio. As more securities that are not perfectly correlated (i.e., [R = +1]) are added to the portfolio, unsystematic risk will decline.

Example

Assume bond portfolio A and stock portfolio B have a mean return of 6% and 12.5%, respectively, and a standard deviation of 7.5% and 15.0%, respectively. Also assume that there is a correlation of 0.3 between portfolios A and B. The following chart illustrates the effects on the mean return and standard deviation of blending a portfolio with different proportions of A and B.

Percent A (Bonds)	Percent B (Stock)	Mean_{AB}	Std. Dev._{AB}
100%	0%	6.00%	7.50%
90%	10%	6.65%	7.34%
80%	20%	7.30%	7.47%
70%	30%	7.95%	7.87%
60%	40%	8.60%	8.51%
50%	50%	9.25%	9.34%
40%	60%	9.90%	10.31%
30%	70%	10.55%	11.38%
20%	80%	11.20%	12.53%
10%	90%	11.85%	13.74%
0%	100%	12.50%	15.00%

This chart illustrates that by adding a security that has a higher level of risk, such as B, to a portfolio consisting entirely of a security, such as A, the rate of return can be increased, while at the same time reducing the volatility of the portfolio. This example illustrates the concept of creating efficient portfolios.

Calculations of the mean and the standard deviation from the example above (80/20 Portfolio).

Mean = [(0.80) x (0.06)] + [(0.20) x (0.125)]

= 0.0480 + 0.0250

= 0.073 or 7.3%

$$\text{Standard Deviation} = \sqrt{W_A{}^2\sigma_A{}^2 + W_B{}^2\sigma_B{}^2 + 2W_AW_B[\sigma_A\sigma_BR_{AB}]}$$

$$= \sqrt{(.80)^2(.075)^2 + (.20)^2(.15)^2 + 2(.80)(.20)[(.075)(.15)(.3)]}$$

$$= \sqrt{.00360 + .00090 + .00108}$$

$$= \sqrt{.00558}$$

$$= .0747 \text{ or } 7.47\%$$

Notice that as the portfolio changes from 100% A to 90% A and 10% B, the average return increases and the standard deviation declines. This trend continues until 20% of the portfolio is invested in B.

When the portfolio is evenly divided between A and B, the average return increased by 54% (9.25 ÷ 6.0 = 154%), while the standard deviation or risk only increased by 24.5% (9.34 ÷ 7.5 = 124.5%). This relationship represents a significant increase in return with only a small increase in risk.

This example illustrates why creating a portfolio of different asset types is an effective method of diversification. Because of the low correlation between A and B (in this example), the blending of these asset types allows the investor to achieve higher returns with less volatility or risk. This concept can also be applied to diversifying with international investments because the correlation between U.S. markets and other markets is generally low.

Note: The mean of the portfolio was calculated using a weighted average and the standard deviation was calculated using the formula for standard deviation of a two-security portfolio.

3. Covariance.

   a. Covariance is a measure of how returns on assets move together. Covariance can be positive, negative, or zero. Positive covariance indicates that when one asset has a positive return, then the other asset has a positive return. Similarly, a negative covariance implies that when one asset has a positive return, the other asset has a negative return. If the returns between the assets are unrelated, the covariance will be zero.

   b. Covariance = $\sigma_A \sigma_B R_{AB}$.

Example

If the covariance between A and B is 0.0096 and the standard deviation for A and B are 40% and 12%, respectively, what is the correlation between A and B?

$0.0096 = (0.40)(0.12)(R_{AB})$; therefore, $R_{AB} = 0.20$.

4. Efficient diversification.

   a. The goal is to identify or create the portfolio with the highest expected return for a given level of risk.

   b. The Markowitz Model, developed by Harry Markowitz during the 1950s, is the first attempt at formulating this concept. Harry Markowitz is considered the father of modern portfolio theory.

B. RISK MEASUREMENTS.

1. Volatility.

   a. Risk can be thought of as the uncertainty of outcomes. Securities that tend to be more volatile have more uncertain outcomes. It follows that risk is often thought of and measured as volatility.

   b. The two most common measures of volatility are beta and standard deviation. Standard deviation is a measure of total risk (both systematic and unsystematic risk), whereas beta measures only systematic risk (beta must be used with diversified portfolios).

2. Beta.

   a. Beta is a relative measure of systematic risk. It can be used as a measure for the risk associated with a particular security; however, it is better used as a measure of the risk within a diversified portfolio because beta only measures systematic risk. A diversified portfolio is one that is void of unsystematic risk.

   b. If total risk is the combination of systematic and unsystematic risk and unsystematic risk is eliminated through diversification, beta will be an effective measure of total risk within this perfectly diversified portfolio.

   c. The market is defined to have a beta of 1. As a relative measure of risk, a security or portfolio with a beta of 1.25 would be considered 25% more volatile than the market. Securities with a beta less than 1 are less risky than the market.

d. Beta can be determined by using regression analysis and finding the linear equation that best represents the set of data points. The equation of the regression line is:

$r_s = a + br_m$, where:

r_s	=	The return on the stock.
r_m	=	The return on the market.
a	=	The Y intercept. (In theory, the y-intercept should approximate the risk-free rate of return.)
b	=	Beta. (The slope of the line.)

Note: This formula is the basis for the CAPM model (although it is not the CAPM).

Example

ABC stock has a beta of 1.25, the market return is expected to be 10%, and "a," or the Y intercept is 2%. Therefore, the expected return for ABC should be equal to 14.5% (0.02 + (1.25 x 0.10)).

e. To calculate beta, six steps must be performed:

   i. Select a historical time period.

   ii. Divide the time period into intervals (years, months, weeks, days, etc.).

   iii. Calculate the return on the stock for each interval.

   iv. Select a market index.

   v. Calculate the return on the index for each interval.

   vi. Perform the regression analysis between the two sets of data and develop the linear equation that best represents the set of data.

f. Portfolio beta.

   i. As mentioned, beta is best used within the context of a well-diversified portfolio. Studies show that betas for individual securities are not stable over time, but betas for portfolios are stable over time. The fluctuations in the beta for individual securities within a portfolio will tend to offset over time, thereby creating a reasonably stable portfolio beta.

   ii. To calculate the beta for a portfolio, consideration must be given to the value of the securities within the portfolio. This is accomplished by weighting the beta for a security by its relative portion of the value of the portfolio.

Example.

A $150,000 portfolio, which is assumed to be diversified, has the following 10 stocks with corresponding betas.

Security	Beta	FMV	Percent	Weighted Beta
1	0.90	$ 10,000	6.67%	0.0600
2	0.85	15,000	10.00%	0.0850
3	1.10	17,500	11.67%	0.1283
4	1.20	26,000	17.33%	0.2080
5	1.30	14,000	9.33%	0.1213
6	1.20	12,000	8.00%	0.0960
7	0.80	5,000	3.33%	0.0267
8	0.90	9,000	6.00%	0.0540
9	1.40	13,500	9.00%	0.1260
10	1.10	28,000	18.67%	0.2053
		$ 150,000	**100.00%**	**1.1107**

The weighted beta for this portfolio is 1.11. Assuming this portfolio is diversified, it is approximately 11 percent more volatile than the market.

Note: Even the most volatile stocks, such as Stock 9 with a beta of 1.40, do not unduly affect the volatility of the portfolio as long as its value is not a large portion of the portfolio.

iii. Another way to calculate the beta of a portfolio is to do so at the portfolio level. To find the amount of uncertainty within the portfolio relative to the market, divide the standard deviation of the portfolio by the standard deviation of the market. This value is multiplied by the correlation coefficient, representing the correlation between the portfolio and the market. This product represents the portfolio's beta.

β_p = $[\sigma_p \div \sigma_m] \times R_{pm}$, where:

β_p = Beta

σ_p = Standard deviation of the portfolio

σ_m = Standard deviation of the market

R_{pm} = Correlation coefficient between the portfolio and the market

g. Beta and correlation.

i. Beta should be used with diversified portfolios since it only measures systematic risk (diversified portfolios have theoretically eliminated unsystematic risk). A portfolio may be fully diversified or partially diversified. To ascertain the degree that the portfolio is diversified, it is important to determine the coefficient of determination.

ii. The correlation coefficient (R) describes the movement or relationship between two variables. The correlation coefficient ranges from -1 to +1. A positive one denotes perfect correlation between the two variables, while a negative one denotes opposite movement or correlation. A coefficient of zero indicates that the two variables are totally unrelated.

iii. The coefficient of determination (R^2) is calculated by squaring the correlation coefficient. The coefficient of determination describes the percentage of variability of the dependent variable that is explained by changes in the independent variable. For instance, if the coefficient of determination is 70% between ABC stock and the market, then 70% of ABC's movement in price can be explained by changes in the market. The remaining 30% of the movement in price is caused by other variables and is conceptually named unsystematic risk.

iv. The coefficient of determination is an important concept because unless it equals one, then beta will not measure total risk (total risk = systematic and unsystematic risk). Beta does not capture the unsystematic risk within the portfolio.

3. Standard deviation (historical).

a. Standard deviation is a measurement of risk or dispersion of outcomes (returns) around the mean or expected mean. Observations will tend to cluster around the expected mean, and standard deviation is the measure of this dispersion. There is a direct relationship between standard deviation and risk: as standard deviation increases, risk also increases. Standard deviation measures total risk, whereas beta measures systematic risk.

b. Because outcomes tend to cluster around the mean, the bell shaped curve is often used to represent the dispersion of outcomes, as illustrated below. The benefit of the bell shaped curve, or normal curve, is that the curve can be used to determine probabilities of outcomes.

EXHIBIT 20: AREA UNDER THE CURVE

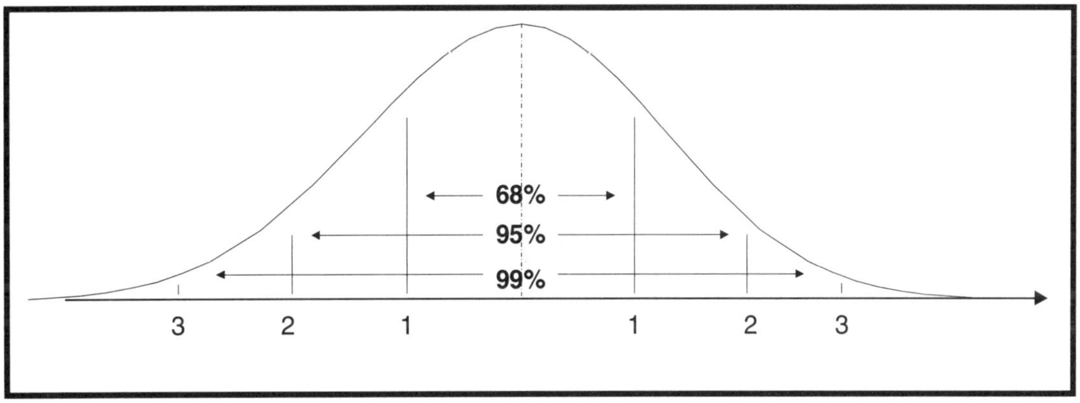

i. The curve represents 100% of possible outcomes. These outcomes tend to cluster around the mean; however, some occurrences will fall away from the mean (i.e., in the tails of the bell shaped curve).

ii. Approximately 68% of outcomes fall within one standard deviation (both above and below) of the mean.

Note: One standard deviation will be different for each individual security and may have a wide range.

iii. For example, if the mean return for Meyer, Inc. is 18% and the standard deviation is 6%, the area under the bell shaped curve that represents one standard deviation would range from 12% (18% - 6%) to 24% (18% + 6%). Therefore, 68% of the outcomes will fall between 12% and 24%.

iv. Approximately 95% of outcomes fall within two standard deviations (both above and below) of the mean. Therefore, 95% of the outcomes will fall between 6% and 30% (18% ± 2 x 6%) for Meyer, Inc.

v. Approximately 99% of outcomes fall within three standard deviations (both above and below) of the mean. Therefore, 99% of the outcomes will fall between 0% and 36% (18% ± 3 x 6%) for Meyer, Inc.

vi. This information about the normal curve allows investors to determine the probability of specific outcomes. For example, an investor might want to know the probability of a negative return from Meyer, Inc. stock. To determine the probability of a negative return, the first step is to determine how many standard deviations from the mean is zero. Zero is 3 standard deviations from the mean [(18% - 0%) ÷ 6%]. Within 3 standard deviations from the mean will occur 99% of outcomes. Therefore, 1% (100% - 99%) of outcomes will fall below 0% and above 36%. Since the investor is concerned only with the likelihood that the return will be negative, simply divide the 1% in half. Thus, there is a 0.5% chance that an investor will have a negative return with Meyer, Inc. stock.

A) The bell shaped curve is symmetrical around the mean.

B) One half (50%) of the outcomes occur to the left of the mean and one half (50%) of the outcomes occur to the right of the mean.

c. The exhibit below illustrates that two securities can have the same expected return with different levels of risk. Security B is more risky than Security A because its standard deviation is greater.

EXHIBIT 21: STANDARD DEVIATION OF TWO SECURITIES

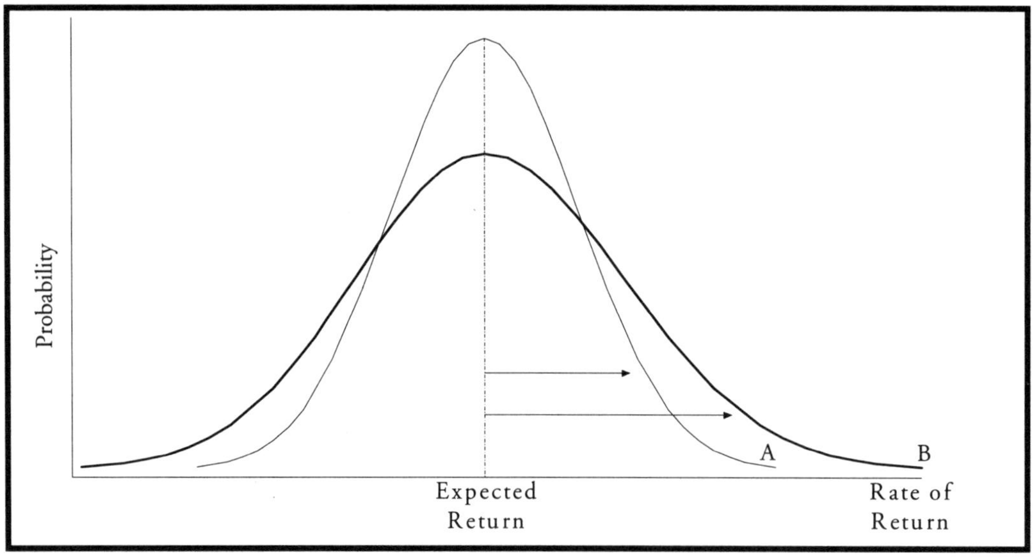

d. Standard deviation is calculated by taking the square root of the sum of the squared differences between the mean, which will remain constant, and the individual observations (or returns) divided by the number of observations minus one. This calculation can be done in five steps:

   i. For each observation, take the difference between the mean and the individual observations.

   ii. Square each difference.

   iii. Sum the squared differences.

   iv. Divide this sum by one less than the number of observations (if there are 10 observations, divide by 9).

   v. Take the square root of this division.

> **Note:** Certain requirements must be met to use this technique with accuracy.
>
> The standard deviation equals the square root of the variance. Thus, step iv. is equal to the variance and step v. is equal to the standard deviation.

Example

Assume Barco, Inc. has an average return of 12% and the following individual returns for the corresponding periods. What is the standard deviation for Barco, Inc.?

Year	Average Return	Actual Return	Difference	Difference Squared
1	12%	13.5%	-1.5%	0.0002250
2	12%	12.0%	0.0%	-
3	12%	5.0%	7.0%	0.0049000
4	12%	-2.0%	14.0%	0.0196000
5	12%	7.0%	5.0%	0.0025000
6	12%	23.0%	-11.0%	0.0121000
7	12%	6.0%	6.0%	0.0036000
8	12%	10.0%	2.0%	0.0004000
9	12%	45.0%	-33.0%	0.1089000
10	12%	10.0%	2.0%	0.0004000
11	12%	0.5%	11.5%	0.0132250
12	12%	14.0%	-2.0%	0.0004000
	The sum of the squared differences:			**0.1662500**

The standard deviation for Barco will be 12.29% $[(0.16625) \div (12 - 1)]^{\frac{1}{2}}$.

e. If the market is assumed to have a standard deviation of 17%, then any stocks with a standard deviation greater than 17% will be considered more risky than the market. Similarly, stocks with a standard deviation of less than 17%, such as Barco, will be considered less risky than the market.

f. The standard deviation for a set of actual investment returns can be calculated using a financial calculator, such as a HP 12C. Using the above information, the key strokes would be:

f	clx (clears registers)			
13.5	Σ+			
12.0	Σ+			
5.0	Σ+			
-2.0	Σ+			
7.0	Σ+			
23.0	Σ+			
6.0	Σ+			
10.0	Σ+			
45.0	Σ+			
10.0	Σ+			
0.5	Σ+			
14.0	Σ+			
To determine the mean:		g	0	[12]
To determine the standard deviation:		g	.(period)	[12.29375]

The result will be the same as calculating the standard deviation by longhand.

4. Standard deviation (projected).

a. Probability distribution of returns.

i. A probability distribution can be thought of as a set of outcomes with assigned probabilities. Within investments, a probability distribution often consists of possible rates of return (outcomes) with assigned probabilities.

A) The table below depicts an example of a probability distribution that lists the possible outcomes and assigned probabilities under different market conditions for a stock with a current market value of $100.

	Outcomes (Stock Price)	Probability	Single Period Rate of Return
Bull Market	$150	30%	50%
Slow Growth	$110	45%	10%
Bear Market	$85	25%	-15%

B) Probability distributions may be either objective or subjective.

1) Objective: The distributions are based on ex post (after the fact) returns and are called relative frequency distributions.

2) Subjective: The distributions are projections of future happenings based on an analyst's best information. Subjective distributions are used to help establish expectations about the future.

C) The probabilities must total 1.00 or 100%.

b. Expected rate of return - E(r).

i. The expected rate of return helps investors make decisions concerning where to invest their funds.

ii. The expected rate of return, which is the weighted-average rate of return, can be calculated easily.

A) Multiply each rate of return (percent) by the respective probability.

B) The expected rate of return is the total of the results.

C) As a formula, $E(r) = P_1(R_1) + P_2(R_2) + ... + P_t(R_{t.})$, where:

E(r) = The expected return.

P_1 = The probability assigned to the first rate of return.

R_1 = The first rate of return.

t = The number of events that are being examined.

Example

The expected rate of return for the probability distribution in the table above is 15.75% [(30% x 0.50) + (45% x 0.10) + (25% x -0.15)]. It is expected that an investment in this stock, priced at $100, would yield a rate of return of 15.75% or $15.75 per share.

c. Statistical risk analysis.

i. Risk, as mentioned above, is defined as the uncertainty of future outcomes. The distribution of returns (outcomes) for various assets is usually symmetrically distributed around the mean of the returns. This distribution forms what is referred to by statisticians as a normal distribution or bell shaped curve.

EXHIBIT 22: NORMAL DISTRIBUTION AND STANDARD DEVIATION

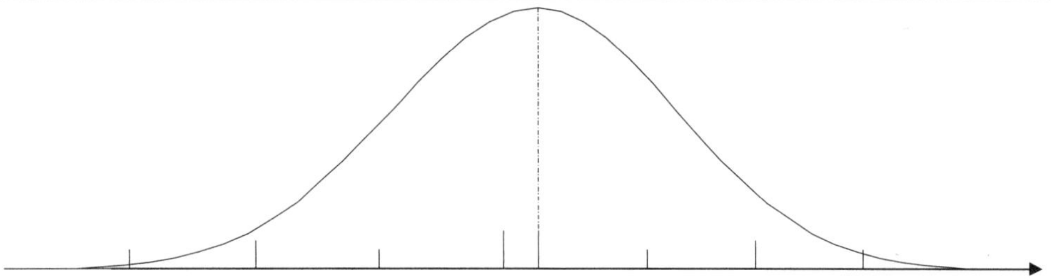

ii. Standard deviation (σ) is defined as the dispersion of outcomes around the mean. Standard deviation is used to measure risk for normal distributions: the greater the standard deviation, the greater the risk (volatility). Total risk (systematic and unsystematic) is measured by standard deviation.

A) The mean is simply the average return for the sample of data (such as the returns for a portfolio or for an asset class).

B) Variance is the standard deviation squared (σ^2).

$\sigma = \text{Var.}(r)^{1/2}$.

Note: ($\sqrt{x} = x^{1/2}$).

iii. Standard deviation equals the square root of the summation of products of the squared deviations of each possible rate of return from the expected rate of return multiplied by the corresponding probability factor.

σ = $\text{Var.}(r)^{1/2} = [P_1[r_1 - E(r)]^2 + P_2[r_2 - E(r)]^2 + \ldots + P_t[r_t - E(r)]^2]^{1/2}$, where:

$E(r)$ = Expected return (calculated).

r_t = Forecasted return for outcome t.

P_t = Probability of outcome t.

σ = Standard deviation.

Example

Using the information from the table above, the standard deviation is equal to 24.56%.

$\sigma^2 = P_1[r_1 - E(r)]^2 + P_2[r_2 - E(r)]^2 + P_3[r_3 - E(r)]^2$

$\sigma^2 = 0.3[0.5 - 0.1575]^2 + 0.45[0.1 - 0.1575]^2 + 0.25[-0.15 - 0.1575]^2$

$\sigma^2 = 0.03519 + 0.00149 + 0.02364$

$\sigma^2 = 0.06032$

Therefore, $\sigma = (0.06032)^{1/2} = 0.2456$ or 24.56%.

---

5. Semivariance.

   a. Semivariance is another statistical measure of risk. However, it differs from variance in that semivariance only considers the downside volatility of an investment. Specifically, semivariance measures the variability of returns below the average or expected return.

   b. Critics of variance and standard deviation state that investors do not complain, nor are concerned about volatility above the average return. Rather, investors are only concerned about volatility below the average return. Therefore, a portfolio manager with a large variance may be punished for having superior positive returns. Semivariance attempts to correct for this perceived flaw by only considering returns and volatility below the expected or average return.

C. PERFORMANCE MEASURES.

1. The Sharpe Performance Measure.

   a. The Sharpe Performance Index is stated as follows:

   $$S_p = \frac{R_p - R_f}{\sigma}, \text{ where:}$$

   S_p = Sharpe Performance Measure for portfolio p.

   R_p = The average rate of return for a given time period.

   R_f = The risk-free rate of return during the same time period.

   s = The standard deviation of rate of return for portfolio p during the same time interval.

   b. Sharpe based his index on the Capital Asset Pricing Model and the Capital Market Line. The index is a relative measure of the risk-adjusted performance of a portfolio based on total risk (systematic and unsystematic risk). Sharpe uses standard deviation as a measure of total risk. If a portfolio is fully diversified (void of unsystematic risk), this measure should yield the same results for a comparison of several investments as the Treynor Performance Measure.

   c. Since it is a relative performance measure, the Sharpe index must be used to compare alternative investments. These alternative investments should be ranked from highest Sharpe index to lowest Sharpe index. Ranking the alternative investments in this fashion produces a ranking of the highest risk-adjusted return on top to the lowest risk-adjusted return on the bottom of the ranking.

Example

Risk-free rate of return	=	3%		
		Portfolio A	**Portfolio B**	**Portfolio C**
Portfolio Return		18%	15%	12%
Standard Deviation		15%	9%	6%
Sharpe Index	=	$\frac{0.18 - 0.03}{0.15}$	$\frac{0.15 - 0.03}{0.09}$	$\frac{0.12 - 0.03}{0.06}$
Sharpe Index	=	1.0000	1.3333	1.5000

d. In this example, Portfolio A has the highest return (18%), but the lowest Sharpe index (1.0000), indicating that Portfolio A has the lowest risk-adjusted rate of return. Portfolio C, on the other hand, has the lowest return (12%), but the highest risk-adjusted return (1.5000), based on the Sharpe index. Portfolio B falls in the middle in terms of absolute return and risk-adjusted return.

2. The Treynor Performance Measure.

   a. The Treynor Performance Index is stated as follows:

   $$T_p = \frac{R_p - R_f}{B_p}, \text{ where:}$$

   T_p = Treynor Performance Measure for portfolio p.

   R_p = The average rate of return for a given time period.

   R_f = The risk-free rate of return during the same time period.

   B_p = Beta for the same period or slope of the portfolio's characteristic line during the period.

   b. Treynor's measure, like Sharpe's, is a relative measure of the risk-adjusted rate of return of a given portfolio. Treynor also relied on the CAPM in developing his model. However, Treynor used beta, which is a measure of systematic or market risk, while Sharpe used standard deviation, a measure of total risk. Therefore, if a portfolio is fully diversified, both models should yield the same result because diversification will eliminate all unsystematic risk from a portfolio.

   c. Since it is a relative performance measure, the Treynor index must be used to compare alternative investments. These alternative investments should be ranked from highest to lowest Treynor index to reflect the highest risk-adjusted returns.

Example

Risk-free rate of return	=	3%		
		Portfolio A	**Portfolio B**	**Portfolio C**
Portfolio Return		18%	15%	12%
Beta		1.5	1.0	0.6
Treynor Index	=	$\frac{0.18 - 0.03}{1.5}$	$\frac{0.15 - 0.03}{1.0}$	$\frac{0.12 - 0.03}{0.6}$
Treynor Index	=	0.1000	0.1200	0.1500

d. As with the Sharpe Index example, the ranking from highest to lowest for these portfolios is C, B, and A. Again, Portfolio C has the highest risk-adjusted return, but the lowest actual return. Portfolio A has the highest actual return, but the lowest risk-adjusted return.

> **Note:** In the Sharp index example and the Treynor index example, both indexes produced the same ranking, portfolios C, B, A, in terms of risk-adjusted return. However, in some cases, the Sharpe index and Treynor index may produce different rankings. This occurs because the two indexes use different measures of risk. Sharpe uses standard deviation, which measures total risk, while Treynor uses beta, which only measures systematic risk. Since standard deviation measures total risk, the Sharpe index is the better measure.
>
> The reason that the indexes produce different rankings is because beta is being used when the portfolio is not sufficiently diversified, which happens to be a prerequisite for using beta. When the portfolios are sufficiently diversified, beta will be an appropriate measure of risk and the two indexes should produce the same rankings.

3. The Jensen Performance Index.

a. The Jensen Model is stated as follows:

$(R_p - R_f)$ = $\alpha_p + \beta_p[R_m - R_f] + e$, where:

$(R_p - R_f)$ = The return that is earned solely for bearing risk.

α_p = Alpha, which represents the return that is able to be earned above or below an unmanaged portfolio with identical market risk.

β_p = Beta, which is the measure of systematic or market risk, of the portfolio.

R_m = The return on the market.

R_f = The risk-free rate of return.

e = The error term.

> **Note:** The values of α_p and β_p can be estimated using statistical regression analysis.

b. The Jensen Performance Index is similar to the Sharpe and Treynor performance measures in that all are based on the CAPM. However, the Sharpe and Treynor performance measures are relative measures while Jensen's alpha is an absolute measure of performance.

c. The Jensen Performance Index is determined by solving for alpha. Alpha, as mentioned above, denotes how well the managed portfolio performed relative to an unmanaged portfolio of equal risk. The formula is often presented as follows:

$\alpha_p = R_p - [R_f + \beta_p(R_m - R_f)]$

> **Note:** The last section of the equation, $[R_f + \beta_p(R_m - R_f)]$, is equivalent to the Capital Asset Pricing Model. Thus, alpha is equal to the difference between the actual return and the expected return, given the level of risk undertaken by the portfolio.

Example

Risk-free rate of return = 3%

Market return = 15%

		Portfolio A	Portfolio B	Portfolio C
Actual return of the portfolio		18%	15%	12%
Beta of the portfolio		1.5	1.0	0.6
Expected return (CAPM)	=	0.03+1.5(.15-0.03)	0.03+1.0(0.15-0.03)	0.03+0.6(0.15-0.03)
Expected return (CAPM)	=	21.00%	15.00%	10.20%
Alpha (actual – expected)	=	(3%)	0%	1.8%

d. As with Sharpe and Treynor, the Jensen method also concludes that the best portfolio on a risk-adjusted basis is Portfolio C, even though it has the lowest actual return. Portfolio B is the second best, while Portfolio A has the lowest risk-adjusted return, as indicated by it lowest alpha.

Note: A similar problem that occurs with the Treynor index can occur with the Jensen model because both models use beta as the measure of risk. In the Jensen model, beta is used to determine the expected return. If beta is too high (too low), then the expected return will be too high (too low). When this occurs, the alpha, which is the difference between the actual return and the expected return, will be undervalued (overvalued). Again, the Jensen model should produce the same ranking as Sharpe when beta is appropriate (the portfolio is sufficiently diversified).

D. PORTFOLIO THEORY.

1. Markowitz used risk and expected return as the basis for determining "efficient" combinations of assets. These combinations of assets were called portfolios and the spectrum of portfolios on the risk-return scale created what is known as the Efficient Frontier.

EXHIBIT 23: THE EFFICIENT FRONTIER

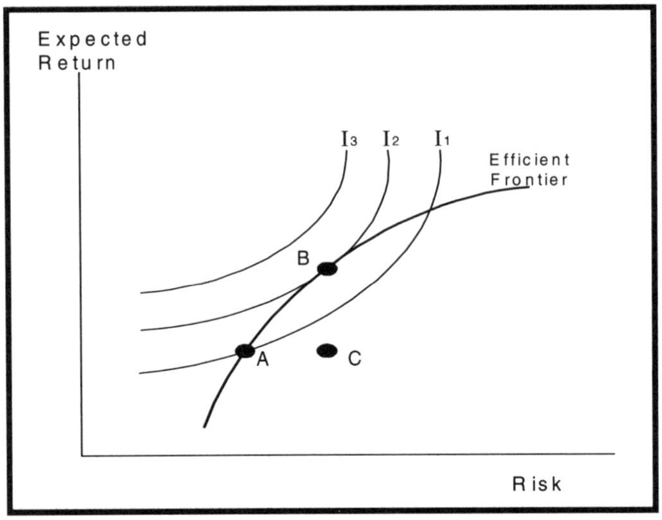

a. The Efficient Frontier consists of portfolios with the highest expected return for a given level of risk.

i. Notice in the previous exhibit that portfolios A and B are efficient portfolios. Portfolio C is not. Portfolio A is more efficient than portfolio C because it has the same expected return with much less risk. Portfolio B is more efficient than portfolio C because it has a much higher expected return for the same level of risk.

ii. Following are three rules for choosing efficient assets:

A) For any two risky assets with the same expected return, choose the one with the lowest risk.

B) For any two assets with the same risk, choose the one with the highest expected return.

C) Choose any asset that has a higher expected return and lower risk.

iii. Portfolios may exist below the efficient frontier.

iv. Portfolios may not exist above the efficient frontier since the efficient frontier consists of the most efficient portfolios (portfolios of assets with the highest expected return for a given level of risk). Therefore, any portfolio above the efficient frontier is unattainable.

v. The X-axis represents the level of risk that is measured by the standard deviation of the portfolio.

vi. The Y-axis measures the expected return from the portfolio.

b. Indifference curves (Exhibit 23: I_1, I_2, and I_3) that curve upward are used to measure the risk-reward tradeoffs that investors are willing to make. The indifference curve will cross the efficient frontier in two locations, unless it is tangent to the indifference curve that has only one intersection point.

c. Using indifference curves in conjunction with the efficient frontier allows investors to choose the best portfolio for the given level of risk. The portfolio that lies at the tangent between the indifference curve and the efficient frontier is the optimum portfolio for the investor. Remember, each investor may have varying indifference curves.

E. CAPITAL ASSET PRICING MODEL.

1. The Capital Asset Pricing Model (CAPM), developed largely by William F. Sharpe, relied and expanded on the concepts developed by Harry Markowitz.

2. Two key assumptions are used in developing this model:

a. All informed investors have uniform expectations about the risk-return relationship of risky assets.

b. Investors can both borrow and lend at a specific positive risk-free rate of return (R_f).

c. Other assumptions include:

i. Transaction costs are equal to zero.

ii. Taxes are equal to zero.

3. Using these assumptions, Sharpe said it was possible to identify a portfolio on the efficient frontier that would be considered the market portfolio (M). This market portfolio consists of all risky assets.

4. A line can be drawn from R_f, which is the risk-free rate of return (located on the Y-axis), through portfolio M. This line becomes the new efficient frontier and consists of some combination of the market portfolio and the risk-free asset, R_f.

EXHIBIT 24: THE CAPITAL MARKET LINE

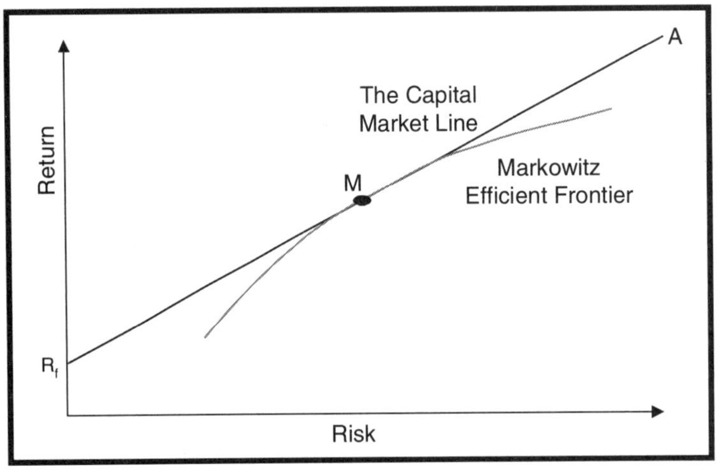

a. This new efficient frontier is called the Capital Market Line (CML). The CML, like Markowitz's efficient frontier, uses standard deviation as a risk measure.

b. Lending portfolio - The CML to the left of portfolio M. This consists of some combination of the market portfolio and risk-free assets, R_f. Effectively, some portion of the portfolio is invested in the market portfolio, and the remainder is loaned to outside investors at the risk-free rate R_f.

c. Borrowing portfolio - The CML to the right of portfolio M. In this situation, the investor has invested 100% of his or her assets into the M portfolio and has borrowed funds at the risk-free rate to invest in the M portfolio. This investor has effectively leveraged his or her investment.

d. The formula for the CML is based on the equation of a straight line:

Y	=	a + bX , where
Y	=	The return on the portfolio.
a	=	The Y intercept and is the risk-free rate of return R_f.
b	=	The slope of the line.
X	=	The risk premium.

e. The equation for the CML is:

$$R_p = R_f + \left(\frac{R_m - R_f}{\sigma_m}\right) \sigma_p \text{, where}$$

R_p	=	The return of the portfolio.
R_f	=	The risk-free rate of return.
R_m	=	The return on the market.
$(R_m\text{-}R_f)$	=	The risk premium (the return from the market that exceeds the risk-free rate of return).
σ_m	=	The standard deviation of the market.
σ_p	=	The standard deviation of the portfolio.

f. The CML is a representation of the relationship of risk and return for efficient portfolios. The CML is a broad or macro perspective of the risk return relationship, while the more common SML (Security Market Line) has the versatility to be used with portfolios and individual securities.

5. The Security Market Line (SML) depicts the risk-return relationship for efficient portfolios of securities. The SML uses Beta (β) as a risk measure, whereas the CML uses standard deviation (σ).

   a. The equation for the SML is:

   R_s = $R_f + \beta\,(R_m - R_f)$, where:

R_s	=	The return for a portfolio.
R_f	=	The risk-free rate of return.
β	=	Beta, which is a measure of the systematic risk associated with a particular portfolio.
$(R_m - R_f)$	=	The risk premium, which is the additional return of the market over the risk-free rate of return.

Note: The SML may also be used with individual securities. The equation for the SML is the equation that is generally thought of as the Capital Asset Pricing Model.

   b. The SML, like the CML, can be used to compare actual results to expected results on a risk-adjusted basis.

Example

Assume Michael has a diversified portfolio that had an actual return of 16% last year. During the same time, the market yielded 12%. The risk-free rate of return for this period was 7%, and the beta for Michael's portfolio was 1.25 (or 25% more volatile than the market). Michael wants to know whether or not his portfolio performed well on a risk-adjusted basis.

The expected return for this portfolio is $E(R) = R_f + B(R_m - R_f)$,

$E(R) = 0.07 + 1.25 \times (0.12 - 0.07)$. $E(R) = 13.25\%$.

Because the actual return exceeded the expected return, adjusted for risk, it is clear that Michael's portfolio outperformed the market on a risk-adjusted basis.

6. The Characteristic Line (CL) is the line that best fits a set of points representing the rate of return for the security against the rate of return for the market for a specified period of time. This line is determined using regression analysis. The intercept and slope for the line are unique and characteristic of the particular asset being analyzed.

    a. The equation for the CL is:

    $R_j = \alpha_j + \beta_j R_m + e$, where

    R_j = Return for asset j.
    α_j = Y intercept or constant term.
    β_j = The slope of the line (beta).
    R_m = Rate of return for the market.
    e = Error term from the analysis.

    b. The characteristic line can be used to explain both the systematic and unsystematic risk for an asset or portfolio.

        i. Systematic risk is measured by the term: $\beta_j \times R_m$.

        ii. Unsystematic risk is measured by the terms: $\alpha_j + e$.

F. ARBITRAGE PRICING THEORY.

1. The CAPM explains the returns for a stock as two variables: 1) volatility of the stock relative to the market, and 2) the market return. Arbitrage Pricing Theory (APT) attempts to explain the return in terms of multiple factors or variables.

2. Arbitrage is profiting from a distortion in the price of a security. Arbitrage transactions have the following characteristics:

    a. They require no risk.

    b. They require no capital expenditure since profits are earned by trading on imbalances in the market price.

Example

Assume Store 1 sells six-packs of soda for \$1.00, and Store 2 sells six-packs of soda for \$2.00. In this case, there is an imbalance in price for substitute or identical goods. This imbalance provides the opportunity to make money without taking risk or having capital. Someone could take orders outside store 2 for \$1.50 and immediately buy for \$1.00 from Store 1. An arbitrage profit of \$0.50 would be made on each transaction. This would continue until the price for a six-pack of soda was identical for Store 1 and Store 2.

c. Stated in terms of economics, the above example demonstrates the Law of One Price. This economic theory states that prices for goods that are perfect substitutes for each other must be priced identically. If they are not priced identically, then arbitrage transactions will occur until such time as the prices are identical.

d. Supporters of APT believe that returns for securities are based on a variety of factors that affect different groups of investments. Some factors will affect all securities such as inflation, interest rates, and population growth. Other factors may only affect a specific industry; thereby affecting only a subset of securities. Finally, certain events or factors, such as a factory burning down, may only affect a single company.

e. The formula for APT encompasses the belief that multiple factors will affect the return from a security:

$R = a_0 + b_1F_1 + b_2F_2 + \ldots + b_nF_n + e$, where:

R = The return from the security.

a_0 = The return that is expected for all securities when the value of all factors is zero. In some cases, this is called the expected return.

b_n = The sensitivity of the security to factor F_n.

F_n = The factor that affects the security, such as GNP of 3%.

e = The return that is unique to the security. It is also called an error term in some cases. This error term should drop out if all relevant factors are captured by the equation.

Note: The APT is a linear equation developed from the output of a multiple regression.

f. Example of multiple regression/APT.

Examples of multiple regression include the economic models used to forecast the economy or interest rates. Each of these models has numerous variables or factors that are considered in determining the direction of the economy or interest rates.

Example

Howie has used the concept of multiple regression to determine the sensitivity of a certain stock to various factors. Howie has found that the following factors are the most indicative of this stock's returns:

Factor	Factor Beta	Factor Risk Premium
Inflation	1.1	5%
Unemployment	0.8	7%
Industrial production	0.5	6%

If the rates on current T-bills is 4 percent, then the expected return for this stock equals 18.1%:

$$\text{Return} = a_0 + b_1F_1 + b_2F_2 + b_3F_3$$

$$\text{Return} = 0.04 + 1.1(0.05) + 0.8(0.07) + 0.5(0.06)$$

$$\text{Return} = 0.04 + 0.055 + 0.0560 + 0.03 = 18.1\%$$

G. THE EFFICIENT MARKET HYPOTHESIS (EMH).

1. This theory suggests that investors are unable to outperform the market on a consistent basis. The market's efficiency in valuing securities is extremely quick and accurate, and it does not permit investors to find undervalued stocks on a consistent basis. The basic assumption of this theory is that current stock prices reflect all available information for a company and that the prices rapidly adjust to reflect any new information.

2. Day-to-day price changes follow a random walk pattern. This pattern occurs because future events cannot be predicted from past information since current stock prices fully reflect all known information. Therefore, price changes are unpredictable and random. If prices move in a random fashion, any trading rules or techniques will be useless. New information must be unexpected, otherwise it would be reflected in the current stock price. Therefore, if new information is unexpected and random, changes in the stock price will also be random.

3. The EMH has three distinct forms:

   a. The weak form.

      i. Holds that current stock prices have already incorporated all historic market data, such as prices, trading volume and published financial information.

      ii. Technical analysis is founded on the concept of analyzing past security prices and levels of trading volume in an attempt to predict demand and, therefore, future prices. The EMH and technical analysis are in direct contradiction.

      iii. Fundamental analysis and insider information may produce above-market returns under the weak form.

b. The semi-strong form.

   i. The current stock price not only reflects all past historical price data but also data from analyzing financial statements, industry, or current economic outlook. Stock prices will adjust quickly to reflect any new information (including market, economic, social, political, and global).

   ii. This form suggests that many analysts follow the same stock and that any new information will be quickly incorporated into the current price. Thus, even fundamental analysis is not likely to yield above-market returns.

c. The strong form.

   i. Holds that stock prices reflect all public information and most private (insider) information. Therefore, even inside traders are unlikely to consistently outperform the market.

   ii. Neither technical analysis, fundamental analysis, nor insider information will allow investors to achieve consistently superior market performance under the strong form.

EXHIBIT 25: THE THREE FORMS OF THE EMH

Form		Type of Information
Weak	⟷	Technical Analysis
Semi-Strong	⟷	Fundamental Analysis
Strong	⟷	Insider Information

d. Empirical evidence.

   Numerous studies have been conducted to determine the validity, if any, of the three forms of the Efficient Market Hypothesis. These studies have produced evidence supporting all three forms of market efficiency. However, exceptions to efficient markets do exist. These exceptions are called anomalies.

4. Anomalies are situations that occur unexpectedly if the EMH was completely true for all markets. Following are various anomalies that contradict the efficient market hypothesis:

   a. The P/E (price earnings ratio) effect suggests that higher returns are attainable with portfolios consisting of securities with low P/E ratios. There has been much research and evidence to support the validity of this anomaly. Considering the evidence, it seems firms that generally trade at low price-to-earnings multiples have higher returns than other firms.

   b. The small-firm effect (also known as the "neglected-firm" effect) relates to the number of analysts that follow smaller sized companies. With fewer analysts following a stock, the value of the security may not be efficiently priced and result in undervalued (and overvalued) stocks. These small-cap stocks are not followed as closely as the large-cap stocks that make up the Dow 30. This neglect permits investors to find bargain priced stocks and ultimately earn superior returns.

   c. The January effect has been observed for decades. Stocks have a tendency to decline in value during the month of December and to move up significantly in January. Some have theorized that this anomaly is caused by tax-related sales in December and subsequent reinvestment in January. However, no isolated causes have been scientifically proven.

   d. Value Line Enigma relates to the stocks rated 1 on Value Line's scale (1 to 5, with 1 being the highest) having a historical tendency to outperform the stock market averages.

VII. SECURITY ANALYSIS

A. FUNDAMENTAL ANALYSIS.

1. Fundamental analysis is the process of determining the FMV or intrinsic value of a security. This value is then compared to the current market value to determine what course of action will be undertaken: buy, sell, or hold.

2. Intrinsic value.

   a. Variables, such as current and future earnings, interest rates, and risk levels, are examined by fundamentalists in an attempt to determine the intrinsic value of a security. Fundamental analysis also involves market analysis, industry analysis, company analysis, and portfolio management.

   b. The intrinsic value of a security is the present value of expected future cash flows discounted at an appropriate discount rate, taking the risk of the investment into consideration. Intrinsic value can also be thought of as the FMV (FMV does not necessarily mean the market value).

3. Factors considered by fundamental analysts.

EXHIBIT 26: FACTORS CONSIDERED BY FUNDAMENTAL ANALYSTS

• Economic Environment	• Monetary Policy
• Stock Market Tendencies	• Fiscal Policy
• Interest Rates and Business Cycles	• Industry Analysis
• Money Supply	

   a. The economic environment.

      i. The stages of the economy are called business cycles. The economy will expand to reach a peak and then decline until it reaches a trough. This is the basic cycle of the economy that continues to repeat over time.

      ii. Recession - Declines in economic activity often accompanied by rising unemployment and declining national production.

      iii. Expansion - Rises in economic activity often accompanied by inflation if the supply of money exceeds productivity.

      iv. Analyzing and forecasting the economic environment is vitally important in determining the value of a security. Some stocks, such as cyclical stocks, are drastically affected by changes in the economy. Other stocks, such as defensive stocks, are relatively unaffected by changes in economic conditions.

   b. Stock market tendencies.

EXHIBIT 27: ECONOMIC ENVIRONMENT - EXPANSION VS. CONTRACTION

General Economic Factors	Expansion	Contraction
Income	↑	↓
Demand	↑	↓
Sentiment	↑	↓
Consumer Credit	↑	↓
Retail Sales	↑	↓
Auto Sales	↑	↓
Mortgage Debt	↑	↓
Housing Starts	↑	↓
Inflation	↓	↑
Unemployment	↓	↑
Consumer Price Index	↓	↑

EXHIBIT 28: ECONOMIC ENVIRONMENT - PEAK VS. TROUGH

Economic Variables	Peak	Trough
GNP	↑	↓
Producer Price Index	↑	↓
Inflation	↑	↓
Output	↑	↓
Industrial Production	↑	↓
Capacity Utilization	↑	↓
Labor Productivity	↓	↑
Efficiency	↓	↑

EXHIBIT 29: THE ECONOMY AND THE MARKET

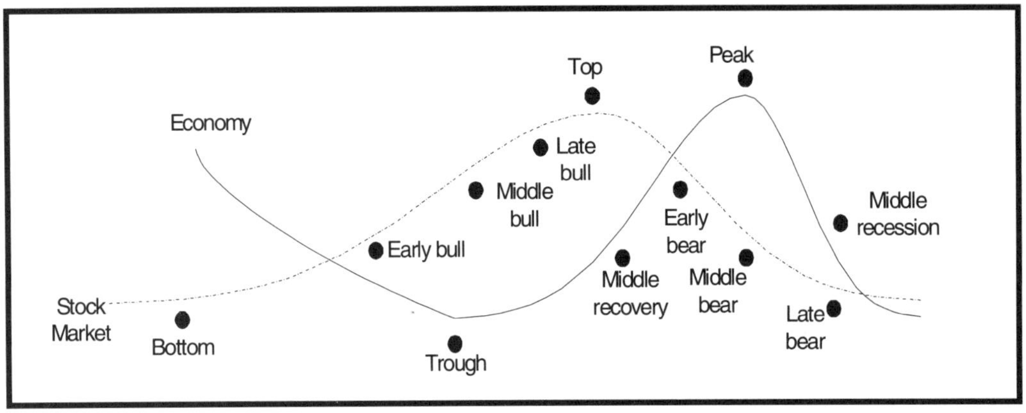

i. Stock prices and the stock market in general have a tendency to decline months in advance of an economic recession or slowdown. This provides investors with a signal to sell securities or take short positions in the market.

ii. The market has had a tendency to reach the bottom of a bear market several months prior to a trough in economic activity. This provides a signal for investors to buy.

c. Interest rates and business cycles.

i. Increases in real interest rates have preceded the majority of recessionary periods.

ii. Similarly, declines in real interest rates have preceded the majority of economic recoveries.

iii. Thus, interest rates and business cycles have a distinct pattern that fundamental analysts consider when analyzing securities.

d. Money supply.

i. M-1 is the sum of demand deposits, coins, and currency.

ii. M-2 is the sum of demand deposits, coins, currency and savings accounts at banks.

e. Monetary policy.

i. The Federal Reserve Bank (Fed) controls the supply of money that enables it to significantly impact interest rates. The Fed will follow a loose, or easy, monetary policy when it wants to increase the money supply and expand the level of income and employment. In times of inflation and when it wants to constrict the supply of money, the Fed will follow a tight monetary policy.

A) Easy monetary policy - The supply of money increases resulting in the circulation of more money. This increases the availability of funds for banks to lend and ultimately leads to a decline in interest rates.

B) Tight monetary policy - The supply of money is restricted resulting in less money available for banks to lend. This leads to an increase in interest rates.

EXHIBIT 30: MONETARY POLICY

Monetary Policy	Easy	Restrictive
Reserve Requirements	Decrease	Increase
Discount Rate	Decrease	Increase
Open Market Operation	Buy	Sell

ii. The Fed has several methods of controlling the money supply.

A) Reserve requirements.

1) The reserve requirement for a bank is the percent of deposit liabilities that must be held in reserve.

2) As this requirement is increased, less money is available to be loaned to customers resulting in a restriction of the money supply.

B) Federal Reserve discount rate.

1) This is the rate at which commercial member banks can borrow funds from the federal reserve to meet reserve requirements.

2) When the Fed raises the discount rate, it increases the borrowing cost to discourage banks from borrowing funds. Raising the discount rates will result in the money supply contracting.

3) The Fed will lower the discount rate when it wants to increase the money supply. Since banks are able to borrow funds at lower rates, they lend more money, and that increases the supply.

4) The discount rate is the borrowing rate from the Fed, while the Fed Funds Rate is the overnight lending rate between commercial banks.

C) Open market operations.

1) This is the process of the Federal Reserve purchasing and selling government securities in the open market.

2) Buying government securities will cause more money to be in circulation.

3) The Fed will sell government securities to restrict the money supply. As investors purchase government securities, more money leaves circulation.

f. Fiscal policy.

i. Taxation, expenditures, and debt management of the federal government is called fiscal policy. The goals of economic growth, price stability, and full employment may also be pursued by changes in fiscal policy.

ii. Changes in taxation will affect corporate earnings, disposable earnings, and the overall economy.

A) As tax rates increase, a corporation's after-tax income will decline reducing the availability to pay dividends. This may cause the price of equities to decrease.

B) Taxation increases reduce an individual's disposable income and limit the amount of money entering the economy.

C) The demand for tax-free investments is affected by changes in taxation levels. As increases in taxes occur, the attractiveness of tax-free instruments also increases.

iii. Deficit spending.

Deficit spending occurs when expenditures exceed revenues of the government. By selling securities to the public to finance deficits, Treasuries will be competing with other securities driving the prices down. This decrease in price will cause the yields to rise.

iv. Government expenditures.

Corporate earnings will benefit from increases in government expenditures.

EXHIBIT 31: FISCAL POLICY

Fiscal Policy	Easy	Restrictive
Taxation	Decrease	Increase
Deficit Spending	Buy	Sell
Government Spending	Increase*	N/A

*Depends on where the increase is directed as to which sector benefits.

g. Industry analysis.

i. Industries, like companies, go through phases of development. These phases are called the industry life cycle and include the following:

EXHIBIT 32: INDUSTRY LIFE CYCLE

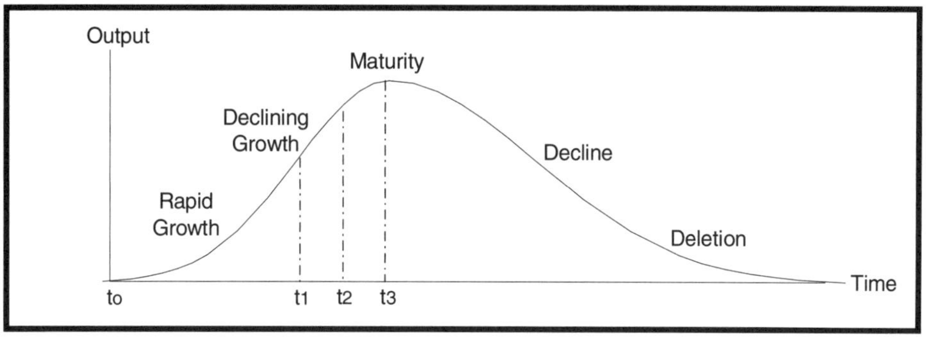

A) Rapid growth - Many firms enter the market during this period when the industry is rapidly expanding. Nearing the end of this stage, the industry becomes or begins to become saturated. The companies that are able to be competitive and make it to the stage of maturity provide the investors who took the high risks with substantial returns. Examples of these companies include McDonald's, Wendy's, Coca-Cola, Ford, etc. However, for every one of the companies that is able to be successful, numerous others fall by the wayside.

B) Decline in growth rate - This stage is evidenced primarily by stronger firms taking market share from smaller firms (the process of consolidation begins). Market leaders begin to take shape during this stage providing investors with significant growth opportunity with less risk than in the rapid growth stage.

C) Maturity - When the industry is in its maturity stage, there usually is a small group of dominant market leaders with minimal industry growth. These companies are often blue-chip type companies that are financially strong.

D) Decline - Competition is fierce in the declining market as participants attempt to maintain their current market share.

ii. The various stages of the industry life cycle provide different investment opportunities and different levels of risk for the investor.

4. Ratio analysis.

a. Ratios are one of the most frequently used tools of the fundamental analyst. They are easy to calculate and understand. Many services, such as Dun & Bradstreet, provide industry data for comparison purposes.

b. Ratio analysis is usually performed in one of two ways.

i. Time series analysis is the analysis of a company from one year to the next for several years. This type of analysis attempts to find a pattern or trend in the performance of the company.

ii. Cross sectional analysis is used to compare the target company to other companies in the same industry. Several services provide industry analysis of companies based on size of assets, size of revenue, etc.

c. Liquidity ratios.

   i. Liquidity ratios provide insight into a company's ability to convert assets into cash without sustaining a loss on the transaction. High degrees of liquidity mean that a company will likely be in a position to meet its debt obligations.

   ii. Current ratio.

$$\text{Current ratio} = \frac{\text{current assets}}{\text{current liabilities}}$$

      A) The current ratio indicates the ability to meet current liabilities with current assets.

   iii. Acid test or quick ratio.

$$\text{Quick ratio} = \frac{\text{current assets - inventory}}{\text{current liabilities}}$$

      A) This ratio provides another view of the liquidity of the company.

      B) The company may have sufficient current assets to cover current liabilities, but the assets may consist largely of obsolete inventory. The quick ratio depicts the company's ability to pay its current debts with cash and highly liquid assets.

d. Activity ratios.

   i. Activity ratios provide insight into a company's ability to turn inventory and receivables into cash.

   ii. Inventory turnover ratio.

$$\text{Inventory turnover ratio} = \frac{\text{annual sales}}{\text{average inventory}}$$

      A) This ratio indicates the speed with which inventory is turned into cash.

      B) Companies that have low inventory turnover may have growing levels of obsolete inventory and high inventory costs.

   iii. Average collection period.

$$\text{Average collection period} = \frac{\text{receivables}}{\text{sales per day}}$$

      A) The average collection period is the time it takes to turn receivables into cash.

      B) Companies may have substantial receivables but may be unable to collect timely from customers.

iv. Fixed asset turnover.

$$\text{Fixed asset turnover} = \frac{\text{annual sales}}{\text{fixed assets}}$$

A) This ratio indicates the sales per dollar investment of fixed assets.

B) Through investments in new plant, property, and equipment (PP&E), some companies will have the ability to generate more sales per dollar investment in PP&E.

e. Profitability ratios.

i. These ratios provide different measures of a company's earning capacity.

ii. Operating profit margin = earnings before interest and taxes ÷ sales.

iii. Net profit margin = earnings after taxes ÷ sales.

iv. Return on assets = earnings after taxes ÷ total assets.

Return on assets indicates the earnings, as opposed to sales with the fixed asset turnover ratio, generated from the assets of a firm.

v. Return on equity (ROE) = earnings after tax ÷ equity.

ROE is an important ratio for investors. It is an indication of the earnings generated per dollar of investment in the company.

Note: ROE will be affected by the level of debt a company maintains.

f. Leverage ratios.

i. The use of debt will magnify ROE and make gains and losses more volatile. This is the concept of financial risk. It is not only important to know if a company can service its debt, but also whether earnings and losses have been magnified.

ii. Debt Ratio = debt ÷ equity or total assets.

g. Ratios for bond analysis.

i. The primary concern for bondholders is a company's ability to service its debt obligations. Inventory turnover and receivable turnover are both important ratios for bondholders because they give some indication as to the company's ability to generate cash to service its interest and principal payments. Another ratio that is useful in analyzing bonds is the times interest earned ratio.

ii. Times interest earned = earnings before interest and taxes ÷ annual interest charges.

A) This ratio indicates the number of times a company can service its debt.

B) Earnings before interest and taxes are used because interest is a deductible expense for tax purposes. Thus, if a company consumed its net income with interest payments, the company would not have an income tax liability.

h. Ratios for stock analysis.

i. Stockholders are interested in returns from dividends and from price appreciation. The ratios that are needed for stock analysis include return on equity, return on assets, gross profit margin, etc. In addition, stockholders are interested in the payout ratio and the price earnings ratio.

ii. Payout ratio.

A) Payout ratio = dividends ÷ earnings.

B) The payout ratio indicates what portion of earnings has been paid to stockholders in the form of dividends.

Example

XYZ earns $4 per share in the current year and makes a dividend payment of $1. Therefore, the payout ratio equals 25% ($1 ÷ $4).

---

iii. Price/earnings ratio (P/E).

A) Price earnings ratio = market price per share ÷ earnings per share.

B) $$P/E = \frac{D/E}{k - g}$$

Where:

D/E = dividend payout ratio

k = required rate of return

g = expected dividend growth rate

Example

Chard stock had an expected dividend payout of 40 percent, a required return of 14 percent, and an expected dividend growth rate of 8 percent. Based on these factors, the P/E ratio equals 6.67, as follows:

$$P/E = \frac{0.40}{0.14 - 0.08} = 6.67$$

C) Small changes in either k or g can make a significant difference in the result.

D) The price earnings ratio indicates what the market is willing to pay for a dollar of earnings from this company.

E) The P/E ratio can be used as a method of valuation by forecasting future earnings and then multiplying the earnings forecast by the P/E ratio. This will give the value of the stock if the forecasted earnings are realized and if the P/E ratio remains constant.

iv. Price to free cash flow.

A) The price to cash flow ratio is another measure of relative value. In valuation, cash flow is generally preferred over accounting earnings. This ratio captures the cash flow impact, instead of accounting earnings, which can be manipulated or may be different from industry to industry.

B) The price to book and price to cash flow are considered good substitutes or compliments of the P/E ratio.

v. Price to sales.

A) This ratio is an indication of how much an investor is paying for a specific revenue stream.

B) One problem with this ratio is that it does not take into consideration the net income. For example, a company may have significant sales, but negative earnings.

vi. Price to earnings/growth (PEG).

A) The PEG ratio is calculated by dividing a firm's PE ratio by the firm's expected growth rate of earnings. The PEG ratio is a measure of relative valuation that can be used to compare companies with different growth rates.

B) Proponents of the PEG ratio believe that companies with a low PEG ratio will have higher rates of return.

C) As a general rule, stocks with PEGs less than 1.0 are considered a possible value company.

EXHIBIT 33: SUMMARY OF FINANCIAL RATIOS

Liquidity Ratios	
Current Ratio	Current Assets / Current Liabilities
Acid Test or Quick Ratio	(Current Assets - Inventory) / Current Liabilities
Activity Ratios	
Inventory Turnover Ratio	Annual Sales / Average Inventory
Average Collection Period	Receivables / Sales per Day
Fixed Asset Turnover	Annual Sales / Fixed Assets
Profitability Ratios	
Operating Profit Margin	EBIT / Sales
Net Profit Margin	Earnings after Taxes / Sales
Return on Assets (ROA)	Earnings after Taxes / Total Assets
Return on Equity (ROE)	Earnings after Taxes / Equity
Leverage Ratios	
Debt Ratio	Debt / Equity or Total Assets
Ratios for Bond Analysis*	
Times Interest Earned	EBIT / Annual Interest Charges
*Also see Inventory Turnover and Receivables Turnover	
Ratios for Stock Analysis**	
Payout Ratio	Dividends / Earnings
Price Earnings Ratio	Market Price per Share / Earnings per Share
**Also see ROE, ROA, and Gross Profit Margin	

B. TECHNICAL ANALYSIS.

1. Technical analysis is an attempt to determine the demand side of the supply/demand equation for a particular stock or set of stocks. It is based on the belief that studying the history of security trades will help predict movements in the future. These technical analysts (or chartists, referring to their reliance on charts), believe that the history of the stock price will tell the whole story of the security and that there is no need to be concerned with earnings, financial leverage, product mix, management philosophy, etc. Recall that technical analysis is in direct contradiction to the efficient market hypothesis which, at all levels, states that the current price already reflects all historical price data.
2. Technical analysts believe there are basic economic assumptions that support the theories of technical analysis. These assumptions include the following:
    a. The interaction between supply and demand is the foundation for the value of any good or service.
    b. Both rational and irrational factors control supply and demand. The market weighs each of these factors.
    c. Generally, both the market and individual securities tend to move in similar trends that endure for substantial periods of time.
    d. Variations in the relationship between supply and demand cause changes in the prevailing trends.
    e. Shifts or variations in supply and demand can always be detected in the movement of the market.
3. Definitions (see exhibit below).
    a. Peak - A peak marks the end of a bull market and the beginning of a bear market.
    b. Trough - A trough marks the end of a bear market and the beginning of a bull market.

EXHIBIT 34: PEAKS AND TROUGHS

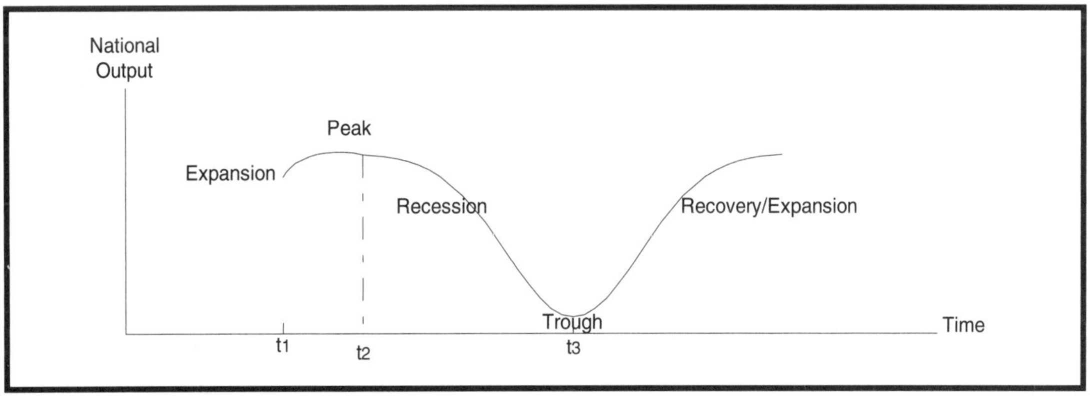

4. Technical analysts use a variety of techniques to predict the trend of the market.

5. Stock price and volume techniques.

   a. Dow Theory.

      i. Dow Theory was developed initially by Charles H. Dow and later expanded by William Hamilton. It is the basis for many of the theories of technical analysis. The Dow Theory suggests three types of price movements.

         A) Primary moves are the first type of movement and represent large trends that last anywhere from one to four years. These moves are considered bull or bear markets for up or down moves, respectively.

         B) The second type of movement is called an intermediate move that is a temporary change in movement called a technical correction. The time frame for these corrections is generally less than two months.

         C) The final type of movement is referred to as a ripple that occurs during both primary and secondary movements and represents a small change in comparison to the first two movements.

      ii. It is believed that all three of these movements are occurring at the same time.

      iii. The Dow Theory uses the Dow Jones Industrial Average (DJIA) and the Dow Jones Transportation Average (DJTA) as indicators of the market. This theory is based on the concept that measures of stock prices, such as averages and indexes, should move coincidentally. Thus, if the DJIA is moving upwards, the DJTA should also be increasing. Support from both market indicators would suggest a strong bull market. Likewise, if both averages are declining, there is considerable support for a strong bear market. When the averages are moving in opposite directions, then the future direction of stock prices is unclear.

   b. Moving averages.

      i. Moving averages are used as indicators of trends in the market. One of the more common moving averages is the 200-day moving average. A moving average can be developed as follows:

         A) Select a stock or index to measure, such as the S&P 500.

         B) Choose a time frame, such as January 1, 1990 to the present.

         C) Choose the number of days for the average, such as 200 days.

         D) Sum the closing prices of the S&P 500 for the 200 days preceding the beginning date (in this case, January 1, 1990) and divide by 200. This result will be the 200-day average price for the S&P 500 for January 1, 1990.

         E) The next step is to replace the earliest date with the next day's information, which in this case would be the closing price for January 1, 1990. Once the process of replacing the earlier day's closes with the later day's results of the market is complete, a 200-day moving average is formed.

      ii. Technicians believe that when prices cross the moving average it is an indication of a change in the market. For example, if the stock price for IBM fell through its 200-day moving average, technicians would view this move as a signal to sell the security. Likewise, a stock increasing above the moving average would indicate a buy signal.

c. Relative strength analysis.

i. Supporters of relative strength analysis believe that a trend will generally continue until a major event occurs to change the direction of the market. Technical analysts will search for stocks or industries that have strong trends relative to the market. It is believed that such stocks or industries will produce better than average results.

ii. To determine which stocks should be selected, technicians calculate ratios for industries or stocks and compare them to other industries or stocks.

6. Contrary opinion rules.

a. The thought behind contrary opinion rules is that the majority of investors are generally wrong about investment decisions. Therefore, analysts who believe in this theory act in a manner opposite of that of the majority of investors. If most investors believe that the market is going to increase, contrarians will trade as if the market is going to decline.

b. The odd-lot short-sales theory.

i. Short selling is considered to be risky and will only be undertaken when investors are adamant about a market's bearish trend. Technical analysts see an increased sign of short selling as an indicator that the market is near a trough and will soon turn around. As a result, these analysts will invest as if the market was about to change from a bear to a bull market.

ii. Smaller investors are more likely to trade in odd lots than larger institutional investors. Institutional investors will not trade in odd lots because commissions associated with odd lots are more costly than commissions for round lots (multiples of 100). Technical analysts believe that when a large portion (3% or more) of odd-lot sales is odd-lot short sales, then there is a heavy bearish attitude among the majority of investors. Technical analysts consider this a signal to buy stocks. Likewise, when the percentage of odd lot short sales is very small (less than 1%), technical analysts believe that it is a signal to sell stocks.

c. Mutual fund cash position.

i. Mutual funds maintain cash for several reasons.

A) Cash is needed for redeeming investors who liquidate holdings.

B) Funds continuously receive cash for new purchases of shares that are not currently invested.

C) If the fund manager has a bearish outlook for the market, he or she may liquidate some of his or her positions resulting in increases in cash balances.

ii. Technical analysts believe that mutual funds are incompetent at predicting changes in market direction. Since large cash balances would indicate that mutual funds believed that the market was bearish, technicians use this information to conclude that the market should be near its trough or bottom. Based on this conclusion, technical analysts who believe in the contrary opinion rules will purchase stocks. Likewise, extremely low cash balances would indicate that mutual funds were fully invested in the market and that they had a bullish outlook for the market. Technicians then conclude that the market is near its peak and, therefore, begin liquidating their positions in the market. The cash balances of mutual funds are reported in various financial newspapers.

d. Credit balances in brokerage accounts.

i. Using the credit balances in brokerage accounts is a similar trading rule to the Mutual Fund Cash Balances trading rule. Investors typically have cash balances resulting from sales of stocks. Technicians believe that very low credit or cash balances indicate that investors have a bullish outlook, while increasing credit balances indicate a bearish outlook. Using this thought process, technicians watch these credit balances and trade in the opposite direction from most investors.

7. Following sophisticated investors.

a. The Confidence Index is a relative measure of the strength of the economy.

i. The Confidence Index is calculated by dividing the average yield of high-grade bonds by the average yield of low-grade bonds. Bondholders have a tendency to shift their bond holdings to high-grade bonds when the economy is weak and to shift to lower-grade bonds when the economy is strong.

ii. As investors purchase more low-grade bonds generally yielding higher returns than high-grade bonds, the average yield on lower-grade bonds should decline. However, the yields of low-grade bonds will never be as low as high-grade bonds, which means that the Confidence Index will never exceed 1.00. If the index increases towards 1.00, it indicates that investors are demanding more low-grade bonds, and, thus, the economy must be strengthening. A strengthening economy is interpreted as a buy signal or as a signal of a bull market. On the other hand, a falling Confidence Index is a sign that investors are shifting from low-grade to high-grade bonds and that the economy must be weakening. Technicians consider this declining index as a sign of a bear market.

b. Debt balances in brokerage accounts.

i. Investors who engage in trading securities on margin are considered to be more sophisticated than the average investor. By analyzing the balances in brokerage accounts, technical analysts are able to determine when debt levels in margin accounts are increasing or decreasing. Increasing levels of debt are considered to signal a bull market since investors believe that yields in the market are higher than the cost to borrow funds. Similarly, declining levels of debt in brokerage accounts indicate that investors have a bearish outlook on the market.

8. Other market environment indicators.

a. Breadth of the market.

i. Breadth of the market is used to determine the strength of market advances and declines. By comparing the number of stocks that increased to the number of stocks that declined, investors are able to gauge the strength, or breadth, of the market. It is possible that an index could rise while the majority of stocks declined for a trading day.

ii. Technicians often analyze the daily breadth of the market with a cumulative measure of the breadth of the market.

C. BOND VALUATION.

1. Miscellaneous.

   a. Basis point.

      i. A basis point represents one hundredth of a percent (0.01% or 0.0001).

      ii. For example, if a yield declines from 6.35% to 6.22%, 13 basis points have been lost.

   b. Bond rating agencies.

      i. Bond rating agencies analyze the financial information of thousands of companies attempting to determine a credit rating for the various debt issues of a particular company. The two largest and most popular rating agencies are Standard & Poor's and Moody's.

	Standard & Poor's	**Moody's**
Investment Grade:		
High Grade	AAA - AA	Aaa - Aa
Medium Grade	A - BBB	A - Baa
Noninvestment Grade:		
Speculative	BB - B	Ba - B
Default	CCC - D	Caa - C
Overall Range	AAA - D	Aaa - C

      ii. Investment grade bonds have a high probability of payment of interest and repayment of principal.

      iii. Noninvestment grade bonds are those where a significant risk exists to either interest or principal payments, or both.

iv. Definitions of ratings.

AAA/Aaa	The highest rating and indicates very high ability to service debt.
AA/Aa	Only slightly lower than AAA/Aaa, this rating indicates a very high rating, but not as much protection as AAA/Aaa.
A/A	These companies are strong and possess favorable characteristics, but may not be able to sustain adverse economic conditions.
BBB/Baa	These issuers currently have the capacity to service debt, but do not possess the financial strength to withstand weakened economic conditions.
BB	This rating and below is considered junk bonds. There is little protection for payment of principal and interest.
B	There is little assurance that principal and interest will be paid for these bonds.
CCC/Caa	These issues are in default or may soon be in default
CC/Ca	Very poor quality issue that is likely in default or extremely close to default.
C/C	No interest is being paid on these bonds. This is Moody's lowest rating, indicating that the company may be in bankruptcy soon.
D	These bonds are in default and interest and principal payments are in arrears.

v. Two other large rating agencies are Duff and Phelps, and Fitch.

vi. The rating agencies generally rate bonds the same. In some cases, there may be a slight difference between the ratings of the different agencies. This difference is referred to as a split rating.

vii. The first four ratings are considered investment grade bonds. Anything below BBB or Baa should be considered junk bonds.

2. Basic concepts.

a. Yield to maturity.

i. The general valuation model is the same model discussed earlier regarding the PV of cash flows. It can be used to determine the securities value, the purchase price, or the earnings rate. The general valuation model is stated as follows:

$$P_0 = \frac{CF_1}{(1+k)^1} + \frac{CF_2}{(1+k)^2} + \ldots + \frac{CF_t}{(1+k)^t}, \text{ where:}$$

P_0 = The value of the security today.

CF = The cash flow for a particular period.

k = The discount rate per period.

t = The number of cash flows to be evaluated.

Example

- A 3-year bond has a coupon rate of 8% (paid semiannually). If the yield for this type of bond is 10% annually, what should the bond sell for?

$$P_0 = \frac{CF_1}{(1+k)^1} + \frac{CF_2}{(1+k)^2} + \frac{CF_3}{(1+k)^3} + \frac{CF_4}{(1+k)^4} + \frac{CF_5}{(1+k)^5} + \frac{CF_6}{(1+k)^6}$$

$$P_0 = \frac{40}{(1.05)^1} + \frac{40}{(1.05)^2} + \frac{40}{(1.05)^3} + \frac{40}{(1.05)^4} + \frac{40}{(1.05)^5} + \frac{1{,}040}{(1.05)^6}$$

$$P_0 = 38.10 + 36.28 + 34.55 + 32.91 + 31.34 + 776.06$$

P_0 = \$949.24 (The bond should sell for \$949.24)

The YTM in this example is 10% (5% per period). In general, the YTM is the annualized interest rate that the bond earns over the term of the bond.

- A 3-year bond with a coupon of 6% paid annually is selling for \$750. What is the YTM?

$$P_0 = \frac{CF_1}{(1+k)^1} + \frac{CF_2}{(1+k)^2} + \frac{CF_3}{(1+k)^3}$$

$$750 = \frac{60}{(1+k)^1} + \frac{60}{(1+k)^2} + \frac{1{,}060}{(1+k)^3}$$

$$[750 \times (1+k)^3] = [60 \times (1+k)^2] + [60 \times (1+k)] + 1{,}060$$

$$k = 17.38\%$$

Note: It is much easier to use a financial calculator than trying to solve such an equation.

The keystrokes are:

PV = (\$750)

N = 3

PMT = 60

FV = \$1,000

Solve for i

Result is 17.38498 (17.38%). This is the yield to maturity.

ii. Assumptions of YTM.

A) A major assumption when calculating the YTM is that all interest payments are reinvested at the calculated YTM. Therefore, if the calculated YTM is 12%, any interest payments generated from the bond are assumed to be reinvested at 12%.

B) If the interest payments are not reinvested at the YTM rate, the realized or actual return will be different from the calculated or expected return or YTM.

b. Yield to call.

i. Bonds will often be issued with a call feature permitting the issuer to pay off the debt obligation at a predetermined price and time. This feature is a benefit to the issuer because it permits the issuer to refinance its debt in the event that interest rates decline. It, therefore, causes the required yield to increase for investors because the investment horizon is no longer certain.

ii. The yield to call (YTC) should be calculated to determine how the call feature will affect the bond's return.

Example

Davis Company issues a 25-year bond paying a 12% coupon paid annually and selling at par ($1,000). If Davis Co. has the option to call the bonds in 5 years for 105% of face, what is the yield to call?

FV = $1,050
PV = ($1,000)
PMT = 120
n = 5
Press i
Result is 12.775 - This is the yield to call.

Note: The YTM is 12% (this is evident because the bond is selling at par).

c. Bond prices and interest rates.

i. Bond prices move inversely with changes in interest rates. If interest rates increase, the price of bonds decreases. This occurs because the bond is yielding a lower rate than is currently available in the market. Investors are unwilling to purchase the lower yielding bond for the same price as a current, higher yielding bond. Thus, the price of the lower yielding bond will decline accordingly.

ii. Similarly, bond prices will increase if interest rates decline. This occurs because the bond is yielding a higher rate than is currently available in the market. Therefore, investors are willing to pay a premium for this higher yielding bond because the market is offering lower yields.

d. Time & volatility.

Bond prices move inversely with changes in interest rates. However, the term of the bond will affect the degree to which the price of the bond fluctuates. Bonds with longer terms are subject to more volatility with changing interest rates than bonds with shorter terms. A 30-year Treasury bond will be more volatile than a 5-year Treasury note.

e. Coupon rate & volatility.

The volatility of a bond to interest rate change is dependent on the bond's coupon rate. Bonds with higher coupon rates are more stable to interest rate change than bonds with lower coupon rates. A zero-coupon bond will have a tendency to be more volatile in value than a bond with a 10% coupon.

f. Evaluating bonds with regard to interest rate risk requires consideration of both term and coupon rate of the bond. It stands to reason that bonds with low coupon rates and long maturities will be the most sensitive to interest rate changes. These bonds will have much higher price fluctuations than bonds of shorter maturities and larger coupon rates. Therefore, the most volatile bond will be a long-term zero-coupon bond.

3. Yield curve.

a. A yield curve is a graph of interest rate yields for bonds ranging from 31 days to 30 years. Typically, yield curves include Treasury instruments for these various maturities. Yield curves have a tendency to slope upward and outward denoting that as the maturity of bonds increase, the corresponding interest rate yields increase (see exhibit below). Occasionally yield curves may be flat (denoting no difference in the yield relative to the maturity) or inverted (denoting that current short-term borrowing costs are higher than long-term borrowing costs).

EXHIBIT 35: POSITIVELY SLOPED YIELD CURVE

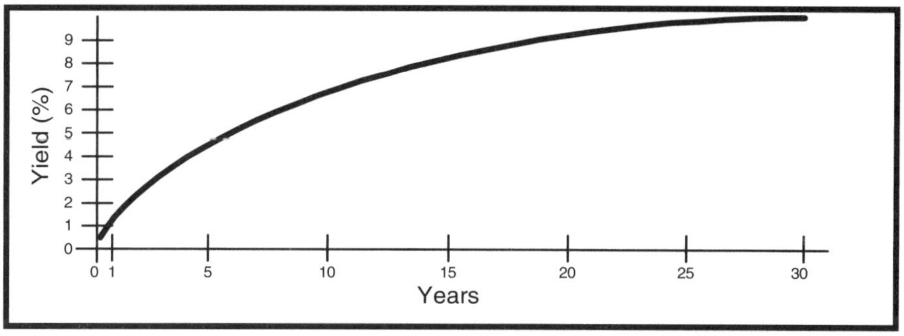

b. Three theories about yield curves:

i. Expectations Theory.

A) Expectations Theory is based on the concept that long-term rates consist of many short-term rates and that long-term rates will be the average (or geometric mean) of short-term rates.

1) For example: If the current 1-year rate is 8% and the 1-year rate is expected to be 10% the following year, the 2-year rate will be approximately the average of the two 1-year rates or 9%. If the expected 1-year rate for the third year is 15%, then the current 3-year rate will be approximately 11% [(8% + 10% + 15%)÷ 3 years].

2) The current rate is known as the spot rate.

3) The rate that is expected in the future is called the forward rate.

ii. Liquidity Premium Theory (also known as Liquidity Preference Theory).

A) The Liquidity Premium Theory is based on the expectations theory, but goes on to incorporate a liquidity premium into the model.

B) The Liquidity Premium Theory is based on the concept that longer-term bonds are more price sensitive to interest rate changes than shorter-term bonds.

C) The Liquidity Premium Theory also implies that investors pay a premium (i.e., lower yields) for shorter maturity bonds to avoid the high interest rate risk associated with long-term bonds.

iii. Market Segmentation Theory.

A) Market Segmentation Theory relies on the concepts of supply and demand for various maturities of borrowing and lending. These different maturities of borrowing and lending make up different markets. The markets for borrowing and lending can be broken into three categories:

1) Short term - Usually a maturity of one year or less. Commercial banks tend to lend short term, while consumer finance firms borrow short term.

2) Intermediate term - Usually one to five years. Savings and loan institutions typically lend for the intermediate term. Similarly, manufacturers borrow for working capital needs.

3) Long term - Greater than five years. Life insurance companies tend to lend for longer terms to match their liabilities. Expansion of plant, property, and equipment is usually financed with long-term debt.

B) Lenders in each market need to match their assets, or lending, with their liabilities, or debts. For example, commercial banks have many demand deposit accounts that are shorter-term maturities. Therefore, they need to match their lending term with their demand term.

C) Borrowers attempt to match the term of indebtedness with the period of time they need to borrow the funds.

D) Supply and demand in the various markets is thought to be independent, which allows for the shape of the yield curve to change over time.

4. Macaulay Duration.

a. Macaulay Duration can be thought of as a weighted-average number of years until principal and interest payments are received.

Example

Consider a three-year bond selling for \$974.23, paying interest annually, with a face value of \$1,000, a coupon rate of 7%, and a YTM of 8%.

Year	Cash Flow	PV of CF	PV x Year
1	\$70.00	\$64.81	\$64.81
2	\$70.00	\$60.01	\$120.03
3	\$1,070.00	\$849.40	\$2,548.20
		\$974.23	\$2,733.04

Duration is then determined by dividing this sum by the market price for the bond.

i. To calculate duration for a bond requires the following steps:

A) List the years.

B) List the cash flows.

C) Determine the present value of the cash flows using the year and the YTM for the bond, 8%.

D) Multiply the digit associated with the year by the present value (e.g., 2 x 60.01 = 120.03).

E) Sum the last column and divide by the current market price.

ii. The duration of this bond is determined by dividing the sum in the last column by the purchase price of the bond, yielding 2.8 years (\$2,733.04 ÷ \$974.23).

iii. The previous problem can also be solved using the following formula:

$$D = \frac{1+y}{y} - \frac{(1+y)+T(c-y)}{c[(1+y)^T - 1]+y}, \text{ where}$$

y = yield to maturity

c = coupon rate

T = years until maturity

$$D = \frac{1+0.08}{0.08} - \frac{(1+0.08)+3(0.07-0.08)}{0.07[(1+0.08)^3 - 1]+0.08}, \text{ where}$$

D = 2.8 years

b. Concepts of duration.

i. There is an inverse relationship between the coupon rate of a bond and the duration of a bond.

A) Zero-coupon bonds will always have a duration equal to maturity. This occurs because all cash flows are at maturity.

B) A bond with coupon payments will always have a duration less than its maturity because its cash flows occur before maturity.

ii. There is an inverse relationship between the duration and YTM of a bond. As the YTM increases, the duration will decline.

iii. Call provisions can cause the duration to decline due to early maturity of the bond.

c. Convexity.

i. Convexity refers to the degree to which duration changes as a result of changes in the YTM. Large convexity implies a large change in duration. Convexity is likely to be the greatest with the following types of bonds:

A) Low-coupon bonds.

B) Long-maturity bonds.

C) Low-YTM bonds.

	Duration	Convexity
Coupon Rate	Inverse	Inverse
Maturity	Direct	Direct
Yield to Maturity	Inverse	Inverse

ii. In the formula below, duration can be used to estimate the change in the price of a bond based on changes in interest rates. However, the formula is only an approximation of the change in the price of a bond and is more accurate for small changes in interest rates. Convexity is a measure that can refine the calculation of this estimate of the price change.

iii. Bonds and bond portfolios have different convexity measures, as well as different duration measures. Just as fixed-income portfolio managers will structure a bond portfolio with a specific duration, they will also structure it to have a certain level of convexity.

d. Estimating bond price changes using duration.

i. The following equation is used to estimate the percentage change in the price of a bond, based on the duration (D) of the bond:

$$\frac{\Delta P}{P} = \frac{-D}{1 + k} \times \Delta k, \quad \text{where:}$$

D = Duration of the bond.
k = Yield to maturity for the bond.
Δk = Percentage point change in k.

ii. Consider the example above. What would happen to the price of the bond if the YTM changed from 8% to 7.5%? You should instantly recognize that the price of the bond will increase. The question is, by how much.

$$\frac{\Delta P}{P} = \frac{-2.8}{1 + 0.08} \times (0.075 - 0.080)$$

$$\frac{\Delta P}{P} = 0.01296$$

Thus, the price of the bond should increase by 0.01296 or 1.3%. This would result in a new price of $986.89 (1.013 x $974.23). Using a financial calculator to test what the price will be with a YTM of 7.5% will result in a bond price of $986.99.

FV = 1,000
N = 3
i = 7.5
PMT = 70
PV = 986.99

Notice the estimate of the bond price was close; however, it was off by $0.10. The formula for estimating the change in the price of a bond based on duration is more precise for small yield changes than for large changes in the YTM. Consider the following chart:

EXHIBIT 36: BOND CONVEXITY

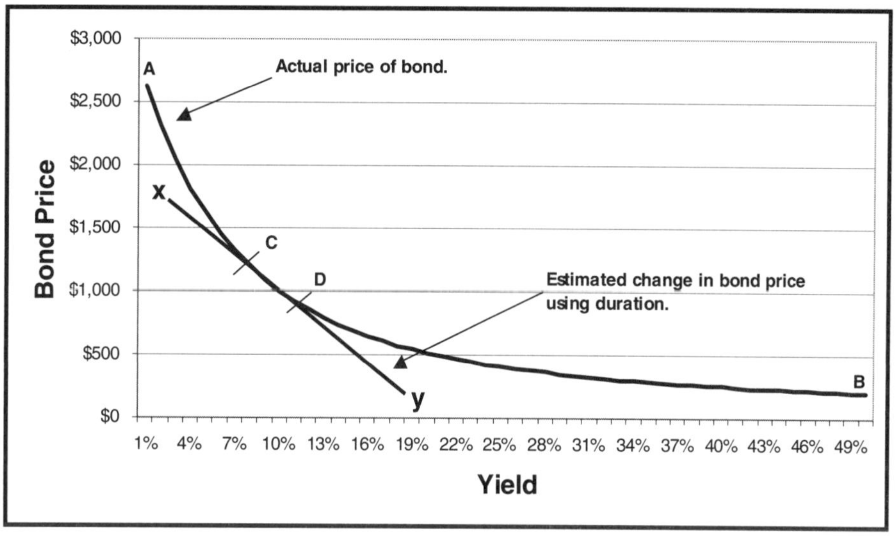

Line 'x – y' represents the estimate of the change in the price of a bond when interest rates change. This line is based on the formula:

Notice that the line 'x – y' is effective at estimating the price change in a bond (line 'A – B') based on changes in interest rates from point C to point D. This reaffirms the concept that the formula for estimating price changes for a bond based on duration is effective for small changes in interest rates. However, the formula will not be effective for large changes in interest rates.

e. Modified Duration $= \dfrac{\text{Macaulay Duration}}{(1 + \text{YTM})}$

Modified duration is used as an estimate of the change in the price of a bond given a 100 basis point change in interest rates. For example, if the duration of a bond equals 5.5 years when the YTM is 10 percent, then the modified duration equals 5.0 (5.5 / 1.10).

Therefore, if interest rates were to increase by 1 percent (100 basis points), then the bond should decrease in value by approximately 5 percent. If interest rates were to decrease by 1 percent (100 basis points), then the bond should increase in value by approximately 5 percent. If interest rates were to increase by 50 basis points, then the bond should decrease in value by approximately 2.5 percent.

f. Other duration measures.

i. Fisher-Well Duration.

ii. CIR Duration (Cox, Ingersoll, and Ross).

iii. Babbel Duration.

g. Duration for bond portfolios.

i. The duration for a bond portfolio is equal to the weighted average of the duration for each of the individual bonds in the portfolio.

The following bonds (coupon payments made annually) are held in a portfolio with the given information:

# Owned		Yield	Term	Coupon	PV	Duration
100	Bond 1	10%	10	8%	$877.11	7.04395
500	Bond 2	12%	20	9%	$775.92	8.75438
1,000	Bond 3	8%	15	10%	$1,171.19	8.85693
400	Bond 4	11%	12	10%	$935.08	7.33973

To find the duration of the portfolio, simply find the percentage that each bond represents in the portfolio and multiply it by the duration of each bond.

<1> Number of Bonds	<2> Bond PV	<3> Portfolio Value	<4> Portfolio Percentage	<5> Bond Duration	<4>x<5> Portfolio Duration
100	$877.11	$87,710.87	4.34%	7.0439	0.30572
500	$775.92	$387,958.35	19.20%	8.7544	1.68062
1,000	$1,171.19	$1,171,189.57	57.95%	8.8569	5.13294
400	$935.08	$374,030.58	18.51%	7.3397	1.35845
2,000	$3,759.29	$2,020,889.36	100.00%	-	8.47773

5. Immunization.

   a. The goal of immunization is to protect the bond portfolio from interest rate fluctuations and reinvestment rate risk. Immunization should provide a stable compound rate of return that equals the YTM, despite interest rate fluctuations. The portfolio is immunized if the realized rate of return is at least the computed YTM calculated at inception. Another way to think of immunization is that a bond portfolio is immunized when the actual future value is at least as great as it had been expected at inception.

   b. One concern that bondholders have is that the interest payments will be reinvested at a rate that is lower than their original investment (reinvestment risk).

   c. A bond portfolio will be initially immunized at the point of duration. Therefore, if an investor were to match the duration of a bond portfolio to his time horizon for his goal, then his portfolio would be initially immunized. For example, the duration of a zero-coupon bond equals its maturity. Thus, the bond is considered immunized at its point of maturity. Coupon bonds also work in this manner.

Example

Bond Characteristics	
Yield	15%
Coupon	6% (annual)
Term	6 years
Duration	5.000 years

		Initial Change in Interest Rates			
		15%	15.5%	16.0%	14.5%
PMT	=	60	60	60	60
N	=	5	5	5	5
i	=	15%	15.5%	16.0%	14.5%
$FV_{5.0}$	=	404.5429	408.5668	412.6281	400.5561
FV	=	1,060	1,060	1,060	1,060
N	=	1.0	1.0	1.0	1.0
i	=	15%	15.5%	16.0%	14.5%
$PV_{5.0}$	=	921.7391	917.7489	913.7931	925.7642
$FV_{5.0}$	=	1,326.2820	1,326.3157	1,326.4212	1,326.3203

The example above illustrates the concept of immunization. This bond will be considered immunized if the future value at other rates of return is at least as great as $1,326.28. Although the interest rate changes from 15%, the future value at the point of duration (5 years) for these other points is at least as great as the future value if the interest rates had remained at 15%. (This is the definition of immunization.)

d. The following steps should be taken to immunize a portfolio:

   i. Choose a time horizon that matches that of the investor, such as 10 years.

   ii. Purchase bonds with varying maturities, both less than 10 years and greater than 10 years. The duration of the portfolio should be equal to 10 years. An alternative would be to buy all zero-coupon bonds with maturities equal to the time horizon.

   iii. The portfolio should be rebalanced every six months to a year. As six months passes, the portfolio should be rebalanced so that the duration equals 9.5 years instead of 10 years. This process continues until the time the funds are needed (10 years) or until the portfolio should be rebalanced for a new time horizon.

e. Approaches.

   i. Laddered portfolio (also known as staggered maturities).

      A) The laddered approach is accomplished by establishing a portfolio of bonds with staggered maturities. For example, $20,000 of bonds could be purchased with maturities ranging from one to ten years for a total portfolio of $200,000. The shorter maturity bonds would be less subject to price fluctuation and, therefore, would reduce the overall portfolio interest rate risk.

      B) This approach provides two advantages:

         1) Since there is a combination of long-term and short-term bonds in the portfolio, the laddered portfolio will provide higher yields than a portfolio consisting entirely of short-term bonds.

         2) Because one bond matures each year, cash is available to the investor. Furthermore, the funds may be used to purchase another bond with a 10-year maturity that will maintain the original structure of the bond portfolio and minimize the risk of increasing interest rates.

      C) One important disadvantage of the laddered approach is that it reduces flexibility of the portfolio because all bonds may need to be liquidated in the event that the investor wishes to restructure the portfolio.

   ii. Dumbbell strategy.

      A) With this approach, the available funds are invested in short-term and long-term bonds. For example, $200,000 would be invested with $100,000 in short-term bonds and $100,000 in long-term bonds. The dumbbell strategy provides the advantage of only selling one group of bonds in the event that the structure of the portfolio needs to be changed due to changing interest rates.

      B) The dumbbell strategy will not maintain its original structure because each year the short-term bonds mature and need to be reinvested. Thus, the maturity of the long-term bonds is reduced. This means that the portfolio requires active management to periodically rebalance the portfolio.

   iii. Bullet strategy.

      A) When investors purchase a series of bonds with similar maturities that are focused around one point in time, it is considered a bullet strategy.

      B) The bullet strategy is one in which the average maturity declines by one each year and may be effective in matching duration to the cash needs of an investor. Like the dumbbell strategy, to maintain the original structure, the entire portfolio must be liquidated, resulting in significant transaction costs.

6. Bond swaps.

   a. Bond swapping is the process of selling one debt instrument and replacing it with another. The goal of this technique is to increase the overall rate of return.

   b. Types of bond swaps.

      i. Substitution swap.

         A) Substitution swap involves exchanging bonds with identical characteristics (including credit rating, maturity, coupon interest payment, call feature, etc.) selling for different prices. This price difference is an arbitrage opportunity and will only last until the lower-priced bond is bid upward. These opportunities arise when there are temporary market imperfections.

         B) Several risks associated with substitution swaps should be considered:

            1) The bonds may not be perfect substitutes for each other.

            2) The gain may not be sufficient to cover any required transaction costs.

            3) The workout time, which is the time it takes for the bonds' prices to equal each other, may be longer than originally expected. This will reduce the realized yield for the swap.

      ii. Intermarket spread swap.

         A) Intermarket spread swap involves the exchange of similar bonds with different coupon rates. The goal of this type of swap is to capitalize on the spread between two similar bonds.

            1) Consider two bonds:

               Bond A: Ten-year bond yielding 8% (coupon 8%) selling at par.

               Bond B: Ten-year bond yielding 7.5% (coupon 5%) selling at a discount.

            2) If the 50-basis point spread (0.08 - 0.075) between A and B is historically small, then there is an opportunity to benefit from a spread swap. Three possibilities are possible for the spread to increase from 50 basis points to 70 basis points (historical spread):

               a) Bond A's yield could rise from 8% to 8.2%.

               b) Bond B's yield could decrease from 7.5% to 7.3%.

               c) A combination of both (Bond A could increase and Bond B decrease).

            3) If any of the three options occur, the swap benefits the investor:

               a) If Bond A's yield does increase 20 basis points, selling it before the change avoids a potential capital loss (note the price would have to decline for Bond A for the yield to increase - this is the capital loss exposure that is avoided).

               b) If Bond B's yield does decline 20 basis points, then purchasing it before the change will provide the potential for a capital gain (note the price would need to increase for the yield of Bond B to decline).

B) If the yield on the bonds moves in the opposite direction than the one anticipated, losses will occur.

iii. Rate anticipation swap.

A) If rates are expected to increase, long-term bonds should be swapped for short-term bonds. With rising interest rates, the price for long-term bonds will decline (recall that long-term bonds are more sensitive to interest rate changes than short-term bonds). These rate increases would be consistent with a booming economy and hints of inflation.

B) If rates are expected to decline, long-term bonds should be purchased to capitalize on the price increases for these bonds.

iv. Pure yield pickup swap.

This swap involves exchanging a lower YTM bond with a higher YTM bond. However, the new bond that replaces the old bond will have to be either a longer-term bond or a lower quality bond to make this swap effective.

v. Tax swap.

A) These swaps are motivated by current tax law.

B) One such swap involves gaining from a capital loss. Take a bond that was purchased for $1,000 and now trades for $800. Selling the bond provides $800 to invest and a capital loss of $200 (worth approximately $60 assuming a 30% tax bracket). The investor can then use the proceeds to repurchase the same bond for $800 and have use of the $60 until maturity (note that there will be a capital gain upon maturity or the discount may be required to be amortized over the maturity of the bond).

C) Careful consideration should be given to the current tax laws. For example, the wash sale rule will disallow the capital loss that the tax swap generated if the identical security is purchased within thirty days before or after the sale. This rule is designed to prevent taxpayers from maintaining their current positions and simultaneously recognizing a capital loss. The wash sale rules are easily avoided in the case of fixed-income securities by substituting a bond with similar or the same characteristics (i.e., coupon, term, quality, etc.) as long as it is issued by a different company (IRC Section 1091).

7. Riding the yield curve.

a. This is a "buy and hold" strategy applicable when long-term rates are higher than short-term rates.

b. The investor or money manager will purchase long-term bonds and hold them until the maturity of the bonds shorten and the bonds begin to travel down the yield curve.

c. As the bond travels down the yield curve, the bond will increase in value compared with newly issued bonds with the same maturity because the long-term bond was yielding a higher rate of return when originally purchased.

d. The risk associated with this strategy is that interest rates will increase, instead of decrease, thus causing the value of the bond to decline.

8. Convertible securities.

   a. Convertible securities are a type of hybrid security that allow the holder to acquire shares of common stock from the issuing company by exchanging the currently held security under a specific formula. Similar to an option contract, the holder's ability to convert the current security into common stock is a right that the holder has, not an obligation. The conversion will hinge on the value of the stock upon conversion.

   b. Benefits to the issuing company.

      i. Convertible securities allow the issuer to reduce the cost of interest for a bond issue by paying a lower yield. The lower yield is a result of the buyer purchasing not only a steady stream of cash flow, but also an option to convert the bond to common stock.

      ii. In some cases, a company may be able to issue common stock at a higher price through convertible bonds in comparison to directly selling common stock.

   c. Advantages and disadvantages to the holder of convertible securities.

      i. Advantages.

         A) Convertible securities provide the holder a steady stream of cash flow with the ability to participate in the growth of the underlying company, assuming that it is prospering.

         B) Convertible securities have a relatively low correlation with bonds and moderate correlation to stocks, thus providing the opportunity to diversify within a portfolio.

         C) Convertible securities are a senior security in terms of liquidation when compared to common stock.

         D) Convertible stocks are also very marketable.

      ii. Disadvantages.

         A) The flexibility of maintaining a steady steam of cash flow or participating in the growth of the company comes with a price. This price is in the form of a lower yield compared to yields on nonconvertible bonds.

         B) If the value of the common stock does not increase, then the investor has given up the possibility of higher yields.

   d. Analysis.

      i. Conversion price is the price that is paid for each share of common stock that is acquired through the conversion of the convertible security.

      ii. Conversion ratio is the number of shares of common stock of the issuing company that can be acquired by exchanging the convertible security.

$$\text{Conversion Ratio} = \frac{\text{Par Value of Convertible Security}}{\text{Conversion Price}}$$

         A) For example: The owner would receive 100 shares if a bond with a face value of \$1,000 was converted and the conversion price was \$10.

         B) The higher the conversion price, the fewer the shares that are received upon conversion.

iii. Market conversion price represents the cost of each share of stock obtained through the conversion. This market conversion price is found by dividing the market value of the convertible security by the conversion ratio (number of shares that can be obtained through conversion).

A) For example: If the market price of the convertible security is $1,200 and 50 shares of common stock can be obtained, then the market conversion price is $24 per share.

B) If the market price of the stock is $20, then the bond is selling at a conversion premium, because the market conversion price exceeds the market price.

iv. Conversion Value.

A) The conversion value of a convertible bond represents the value of the bond if it were converted based on current market conditions.

Conversion value = conversion ratio x market price of common stock.

B) For example, if ABC Company stock was trading at $75 per share and its convertible bond had a conversion ratio of 15, then the conversion value of the convertible bond equals $1,125 ($75 × 15).

D. EQUITY VALUATION.

1. Intrinsic value of stock.

a. The intrinsic value of a stock is the present value of future cash flows discounted at a risk-adjusted interest rate.

2. Equity returns.

a. Holding period return.

i. The holding period return is equal to the return on the investment (ROI) for the time the asset has been held.

ii. The formula for the holding period return is:

$$HPR = \frac{\text{Ending Value of Investment - Beginning Value of Investment +/- Cashflows}}{\text{Beginning Value of Investment}}$$

b. Internal Rate of Return (IRR).

i. From a mathematical point of view, IRR is the interest rate (or k, or yield, or return) that will satisfy the following formula:

$$P_0 = \frac{CF_1}{(1+k)^1} + \frac{CF_2}{(1+k)^2} + \ldots + \frac{CF_t}{(1+k)^t}\text{, where:}$$

P_0 = The value of the security today.
CF_t = The cash flow for period t.
k = The discount rate based on the security type.
t = The number of cash flows to be evaluated.

ii. The IRR is also equivalent to the YTM, the compound average rate of return, and the geometric mean. All have been developed to determine the exact earnings rate that occurs over the life of the investment.

3. Valuation models.

   a. General.

      i. The general valuation model for stocks is the same model discussed earlier regarding the PV of cash flows. It can be used to determine the security's value, the purchase price, or the earnings rate.

$$P_0 = \frac{CF_1}{(1+k)^1} + \frac{CF_2}{(1+k)^2} + \ldots + \frac{CF_t}{(1+k)^t}, \text{ where:}$$

P_0 = The value of the security today.

CF_t = The cash flow for period t.

k = The discount rate based on the security type.

t = The number of cash flows to be evaluated.

Example

Assume McGuffin Company will pay a dividend of $1 this year and increase the dividend $1 each year for 3 years, and that the stock will be able to be sold for $40 at the end of the 4th year. How much would an investor pay for this stock if the investor's required rate of return was 12%?

$$P_0 = \frac{CF_1}{(1+k)^1} + \frac{CF_2}{(1+k)^2} + \ldots + \frac{CF_t}{(1+k)^t}$$

$$P_0 = \frac{1}{(1+0.12)^1} + \frac{2}{(1+0.12)^2} + \frac{3}{(1+0.12)^3} + \frac{4+40}{(1+0.12)^4}$$

$$P_0 = 0.89 + 1.59 + 2.14 + 27.96$$

$$P_0 = 32.58$$

An investor, who had a required rate or return of 12%, would not pay more than $32.58 for a share of McGuffin Company stock.

---

      ii. This model allows the investor to evaluate the market price for securities and determine which ones are undervalued and which ones are overvalued.

b. Constant Dividend Growth Model.

i. This model is used to determine the price for a security in which dividends are growing at a constant rate.

ii. The formula for this model is:

$$P_0 = \frac{D_1}{k - g} \quad \text{where:}$$

P_0 = Price for the security.

D_1 = The dividend paid at period 1.

k = The investor's required rate of return.

g = The growth rate of the dividends. The growth rate can be negative, positive, or zero. See perpetuities for a zero growth rate.

Note: Problems involving this formula will often provide the current dividend, which is D_0. The dividend one period from today (D_1) can be determined by multiplying D_0 by $(1 + g)$.

The model does not allow for the growth rate (g) to be greater than or equal to the required rate of return (k).

Example

Assume Francis Corporation stock is currently paying a dividend of $2.00, and the dividend will grow at a constant rate of 7%. What should the value of the security be if the investor's required rate of return is 11%?

$$P_0 = \frac{D_1}{k-g}$$

$$P_0 = \frac{[2 \times (1 + 0.07)]}{0.11 - 0.07}$$

$$P_0 = \frac{2.14}{0.04}$$

$$P_0 = \$53.50$$

Therefore, the investor should not pay more than $53.50 per share for Francis Corporation stock.

---

iii. Assumptions of the model.

A) The Constant Dividend Growth Model assumes the growth rate of dividends is constant; it is inapplicable for companies that do not have dividends growing at a constant rate. In practice, it is generally uncommon for companies to sustain constantly growing dividends. However, the model is often used as a terminal value in the calculation of the values of a company.

B) The growth rate cannot be equal to or greater than the required rate of return. As the growth rate (g) approaches (k), the value of the security will approach infinity.

C) The model assumes that the investor's required rate of return is known and remains constant. It does not allow for changes in (k) as a result of changes in the risk associated with the security.

iv. Adjustments to the Constant Growth Dividend Model.

A) The constant growth dividend model can be modified for the purpose of evaluating the P/E ratio of the firm in terms of dividends, growth of the dividends and required return.

4. Perpetuities.

a. If the growth of the dividend is zero, then the dividend will continue to be the same amount. To determine the value of this type of dividend stream, simply substitute zero for (g) in the previous model.

$$P_0 = \frac{D_1}{k - g}$$

$$P_0 = \frac{D_1}{k - 0}$$

$$P_0 = \frac{D_1}{k}$$

The new formula is the dividend for the first period divided by the required rate of return. However, since the dividend is constant, it could be the dividend for any period..

Example

Assume Francis Corporation always pays a $2.00 dividend, and the investor's required rate of return is 11%. The value of the security would be $18.18 ($2/.11).

---

b. A good example of a perpetuity is preferred stock. Preferred stock generally pays a set dividend each year.

c. This is the same formula that is used for the capitalized earnings valuation method.

5. Capitalized earnings.

   i. Capitalized earnings are a simplistic method for valuing a firm. The formula for capitalizing earnings is:

   $$V = \frac{E}{R_d}\text{, where:}$$

   V = The value of the company or firm.

   E = The earnings used to value the firm.

   R_d = The discount rate.

   ii. This is the same formula used for valuing perpetuities.

   iii. Several problems exist with regard to the Capitalized Earnings Method for valuing companies.

   A) Earnings, as determined by Generally Accepted Accounting Principals (GAAP), do not necessarily represent cash flows. One of the problems is determining what earnings should be capitalized and if any adjustments should be made to the earnings figure. These adjustments include adding back to earnings any excessive salary bonuses paid to owners and adjusting for noncash outflows such as depreciation and amortization.

   B) An appropriate discount rate must be determined when using this formula. The discount rate should have a risk factor, an inflation factor, and various other adjustments to reflect the true cost of capital on a risk-adjusted basis.

   C) The method also fails to consider the residual value of the assets at the term end.

6. Other values.

   a. Par value - The specified value on the stock certificate or corporate charter is called the par value. It has no economic meaning in terms of value. Par value, or stated value, is simply a formality and is usually very low. In fact, companies may have stock without par value. Par value may represent legal capital in some states.

   b. Book value - Book value refers to the amount of equity within a company. It is determined by subtracting liabilities from assets. This result is the net assets or book value of the company. Generally, book value does not depict an accurate measure of the value of the company.

   i. Since accounting for financial purposes is done on a historical basis, the assets listed on the balance sheet may have appreciated or depreciated from the historical cost.

   ii. Different inventory accounting methods, such as FIFO vs. LIFO, often yield a different value for assets on the balance sheet.

   c. Liquidation value - The liquidation value of a security is the cash received if the company discontinues business, sells all assets, and distributes the funds to the shareholders. Liquidation value generally represents the minimum value of the company. However, liquidation value is difficult to determine because the value of all assets needs to be determined and transaction costs, associated with liquidation, have to be considered.

7. Equity leveraging.

   a. Margin accounts allow investors the ability to use leverage with their investments. The initial margin, set by the Federal Reserve, is 50%. The initial margin represents the amount that the investor is required to fund in the margin account.

Note: Exchanges and brokers may have more stringent requirements.

   b. When an investment is purchased on margin, one-half of the funds are put up by the investor and one-half is borrowed from the broker (assumes a 50% initial margin).

   c. Key terms.

      i. Initial margin - The percent of the original purchase prior that must be provided by the investor (currently 50%).

      ii. Maintenance margin - This is the level at which an investor will be required to add additional funds to the margin account. Maintenance margins are usually set at 35% but may differ from broker to broker.

      iii. Debit balance - The amount owed to the broker. This amount will include the original amount borrowed plus any interest.

      iv. Equity - This is the value of the security less the debit or margin balance.

      v. Margin - The ratio of equity over collateral (FMV of the security) is called the margin.

   d. Formula for determining when a margin call will occur:

$$\text{Margin call occurs when stock price} = \frac{\text{Loan Amount}}{1 - \text{Maintenance Margin}}$$

Example

Hardy pays \$20,000 to purchase shares of Solvent Company (trading at \$25 per share). If Hardy uses a margin account (50% initial margin) to purchase this stock, he can buy 1,600 [(20,000 x 2) ÷ 25] shares. \$20,000 is borrowed from the broker. Hardy is concerned about receiving a margin call. At what point will Hardy receive a margin call (assume a maintenance margin of 35%)?

Answer: Hardy will receive a margin call when the stock price reaches \$19.23.

$$35\% = \frac{x - \$12.50}{x} \quad (x = \text{FMV of stock; } \$12.50 = \text{loan per share})$$

$$65\%(x) = \$12.50$$

$$x = \$19.23$$

OR:

$$\frac{\text{Loan Amount}}{1 - \text{Maintenance Margin}} = \frac{\$12.50}{1 - 0.35} = \$19.23$$

Note: Margin call can be determined on a per share basis or on a total market value basis.

Example

Assume the same facts as the previous example. If the stock price dropped to $15, how much money would Hardy be required to put up for the margin call?

Required Equity		**Current Equity Position**	
Stock	$15.00	Stock	$15.00
Equity %	35%	Loan Amount	(12.50)
Required Equity	$5.25	Equity	$2.50

$2.75 Difference

Hardy will be required by the broker to put up $2.75 per share to maintain the equity position of 35%. To determine this, the current equity position must be compared to the required equity position.

8. Strategies.

   a. Passive.

      i. Passive strategies are based on the concept that the markets are efficient in pricing securities, and that it is unlikely that an investor will be able to outperform the market on a consistent basis (similar to the Efficient Market Hypothesis).

      ii. Passive portfolios generally are well diversified and have low turnover rates.

      iii. Another consideration for these passive portfolios is the risk and asset allocation of the investments. By adjusting the asset mix or allocation, the risk level can be matched with the needs of the investor.

      iv. Index funds are an example of a passively managed portfolio. These funds match an index, such as the S&P 500, and require little maintenance.

      v. Another option to passively managed portfolios is the buy and hold strategy. Transactions costs, including capital gains tax, are kept to a minimum with this type of a strategy.

   b. Active.

      i. Active portfolio management is based on the concept that above-market returns can be achieved through security selection, market timing, or both. Those that believe that active management can outperform the market do not believe that the market is perfectly efficient.

      ii. Security selection and market timing work in concert with each other. It is not sufficient to determine which security should be selected; the investors must determine when and under what conditions the investment should be purchased (or sold). The real question is what should be invested in today? Two methods that investors use to make security selections are Fundamental Analysis and Technical Analysis.

E. REAL ESTATE VALUATION.

1. Real estate is an important asset class to investors that may provide further diversification to one's investment portfolio due to the low correlation coefficient between real estate and other asset classes, specifically to stocks and bonds. Investments in real estate take many forms, including:
   a. Home ownership.
   b. Developed land.
   c. Undeveloped land.
   d. Apartment buildings.
   e. Condominiums.
   f. Partnerships and limited partnerships.
   g. Real estate investment trusts (REITs).
2. There are three traditional methods for valuing real estate. An appraiser of real estate will always use one of the three methods and will generally try to use two or all three methods to confirm the results of the other methods used. However, not all methods are appropriate for every type of real estate. The three traditional methods of valuing real estate are:
   a. The Sales Comparison Approach.
   b. The Cost Approach.
   c. The Income Capitalization Approach.
3. The Sales Comparison Approach.
   a. The sales comparison approach is most appropriate when there are several properties in a market that have recently been sold that have similar characteristics as the property that is being valued.
   b. By looking at similar properties in the same market an appraiser can reasonably estimate what the market is willing to pay for similarly situated property located in the particular area. With this market information an appraiser can estimate the value of the specific property.
   c. The appraiser generally looks at the characteristics of comparable properties and the property he is valuing so that he can make adjustments, either up or down, to what he thinks the value of the property should be in comparison to the recently sold properties.
   d. The most common application of the use of this method is the valuation of personal residences.
4. The Cost Approach.
   a. The cost approach is designed to estimate the value of a property by determining how much it would cost to replace the property and then making any adjustments for depreciation or deterioration of the property.
   b. The first step is to separate the value of the land from the building. The value of the land can be estimated by looking at comparable properties. The next step is to estimate the current cost of constructing such a building. To this value, any adjustments should be made to reflect deterioration of the property.
   c. The cost approach is appropriate when valuing special use buildings (e.g., a church) and also newly constructed property because the value of the property should not have changed dramatically in a short period of time and there should be little depreciation or deterioration to consider.

5. The Income Capitalization Approach.
   a. The income capitalization approach takes the position that the value of the property is based on the income that can be generated from the property. This income stream is approximated and then discounted to determine an estimated value of the property.
   b. There are two methods for applying this approach:
      i. Direct capitalization.
      ii. Discounted cash flow analysis.
   c. Direct capitalization.
      i. This is the most basic method of income capitalization.
      ii. The formula for this method is:

$$\text{Value of the Property} = \frac{\text{Income}}{\text{Discount Rate}}, \text{ where:}$$

- Income is the income that is generated from the property. However, it should generally be Net Operating Income (Net operating income is defined below).
- The Discount Rate is the rate at which the cash flows will be discounted. This rate could be the cost of capital, an opportunity cost, or a required rate of return. It may also be a rate that is based on the sales of other properties. For example, a property that recently sold for $12 million and generated income of $2.16 million per year has an implied capitalization rate of 18 percent ($2.16 million divided by $12 million).

A) The assumption generally inherent in this model is that the income will remain constant into the future.

B) You should recall that this model is identical to the model used to value perpetuities and the capitalized earnings valuation method.

Example

Assume that XYZ property generated NOI of $75,000 per year and that an appropriate capitalization rate for this type of property in this market was 12%.

The value of XYZ should be $625,000 ($75,000 ÷ 12%) based on the direct capitalization method.

---

   d. Discounted cash flow analysis.
      i. The discounted cash flow analysis is appropriate when the assumption that income will remain constant into the future is not reasonable. In such a case, the valuation of the property would begin by forecasting net operating income (in many cases this is done by forecasting income and then forecasting operating expenses) for several years out. At the point at which it is no longer reasonable to forecast net operating income, the assumption would be made that the income level would remain constant from that point into the future. The direct capitalization method would be used to value the income stream at the point net operating income is assumed to remain constant. This value is often referred to as a terminal value. These cash flows would then be discounted at an appropriate capitalization rate to determine the value of the property.

Example

Assume that you forecast NOI for ABC property as is indicated in the table below. The value of the property is found by discounting all of the cash flows at an assumed discount rate of 15 percent. These cash flows include the assumed value that you could sell the property for at the end of year five, known as the terminal value.

	Cash Flow (NOI)	i	N	Present Value
Year 1	$50,000	15%	1	$43,478
Year 2	55,000	15%	2	41,588
Year 3	58,000	15%	3	38,136
Year 4	64,000	15%	4	36,592
Year 5	70,000	15%	5	34,802
Years 6 and beyond	77,000			
Subtotal				$194,596
Terminal Value*	770,000	15%	5	382,826
Total PV				$577,422

*The terminal value is calculated by dividing the forecasted NOI for year 6 of $77,000 by an assumed discount rate of 10 percent. It is estimated that NOI for years 6 and beyond will remain constant.

Based on the above analysis and the forecasted stream of income, ABC property is worth approximately $577,422.

It is worth noting that the calculation of the terminal value in year 5 was based on the forecasted income of $77,000 in year 6. You should immediately think of this technique as being the same as the constant growth dividend model, which based the value today (t=0) on the dividend (D_1) one period from today.

6. Net Operating Income (NOI).
    a. Net operating income is defined as net income (income less fixed and variable operating expenses) before depreciation and mortgage debt service (interest and principal).
    b. NOI is generally used as the measure of income because it is does not consider mortgage payments or depreciation.
    c. The value of a property should not be impacted by the method the current owner has used to finance the property. Therefore, the impact of mortgage interest and principal should be eliminated from the measure of income.
    d. Since depreciation is a noncash expense, it should be added back to net income before determining the level of income used to value the property.

Example

Operating Statement for XYZ Apartments

Income		
Rental income:		
15 units @ $9,600 per year	$144,000	
10 units @ $12,000 per year	120,000	
5 units @ $15,000 per year	75,000	
3 units @ $18,000 per year	54,000	
Income at 100% occupancy	$393,000	
Less vacancy and collection costs @ 6%	(23,580)	
Gross Income		$369,420
Operating Expenses		
Fixed Expenses		
Depreciation	$ 50,000	
Insurance	20,000	
Interest (mortgage)	40,000	
Management fee	15,000	
Property taxes	15,000	
Total Fixed Expenses	$140,000	
Variable Expenses		
Advertising	$ 5,000	
Utilities	4,000	
Payroll	8,500	
Repairs and maintenance	18,000	
Other	7,000	
Total Variable Expenses	$ 42,500	
Total Operating Expenses		**($182,500)**
Net Income		**$186,920**
Plus:		
Depreciation	$ 50,000	
Mortgage Interest	$ 40,000	
Total Additions		**+$90,000**
Net Operating Income		**$276,920**

i. As depicted above, the NOI for this apartment complex is $276,920. It is not the net income of $186,500.

ii. Based on the NOI and a capitalization rate of 12 percent, the XYZ Apartment complex is worth approximately $2,307,667 ($276,920 ÷ 12%) using the direct capitalization method.

7. Capitalization rates.

   a. Since the value of property is equal to Net Operating Income divided by the capitalization rate, it is easy to estimate the capitalization rate of similar properties from the value and net operating income from the similar properties.

   b. For example: If a property has sold for $1 million and it generates NOI of $100,000 per year, then the implicit capitalization rate is 10 percent ($1 million ÷ $100,000).

   c. Applying this method to several similar properties helps to determine the appropriate discount rate or cap rate that should be used to value a property.

8. Reconciliation of the methods.

   a. The appraiser will often use as many of the three methods as possible.

   b. However, before the appraisal is completed, he will reconcile the different methods used and determine if all of the methods have concluded the same or a similar value for the property.

   c. In theory, all of the methods should provide for the same conclusion regarding the value of a property. However, with certain properties, it is impossible to obtain the proper data to evaluate a property using all three methods. For example, it is very difficult to use the income approach when valuing a residential home because these types of real estate do not generally generate income.

VIII. PERFORMANCE MEASUREMENTS

A. HOLDING PERIOD RETURN.

1. The holding period return (also known as the single period return) is the basic method to evaluate the speed at which an investment grows or declines. The holding period return is determined by dividing the change in wealth by the initial investment.

2. The formula for the holding period return is:

$$\text{HPR} = \frac{\text{Ending Value of Investment - Beginning Value of Investment +/- Cashflows}}{\text{Beginning Value of Investment}}$$

Example

Bob purchases 100 shares of Disney stock for \$40 per share. Two years later, Bob sells the 100 shares for \$52 per share. In addition, Bob received a dividend of \$2 per share in the first year and a dividend of \$3 per share in the second year. His single period rate of return is calculated as follows:

Sales Price (ending value) = \$5,200 (100 x \$52).

Purchase Price (beginning value) = \$4,000 (100 x \$40).

Cash flow = \$500 = (100 x \$2) + (100 x \$3).

Therefore, the holding period return is 42.5%.

$$\frac{\$5{,}200 - \$4{,}000 + \$500}{\$4{,}000} = 42.5\%$$

Example

Harold purchases a Treasury bond for \$1,050, receives interest of \$160, and sells the bond for \$980. His holding period return is 8.57%.

$$\frac{\$980 - \$1{,}050 + \$160}{\$1{,}050} = 8.57\%$$

The holding period return (single period rate of return) refers to the overall percentage gain the investor has received. The holding period return is not often used as a measure of performance because it ignores the time value of money, and it does not address the time over which the investment has grown.

B. ARITHMETIC MEAN.

1. The arithmetic mean is calculated by dividing the sum of the returns for each period by the total number of periods (*n*) being evaluated. The formula is written as follows:

$$\text{AM} = \frac{\sum_{t=1}^{n} \text{HPR}_t}{n}$$

2. For example, the arithmetic mean for the following set of data is 13.18%.

1999	2000	2001	2002	2003
15.2%	9.1%	6.5%	18.3%	16.8%

$$AM = \frac{15.2\% + 9.1\% + 6.5\% + 18.3\% + 16.8\%}{5} = 13.18\%$$

3. The arithmetic mean is an approximation of the earnings rate for an investment over time. However, large fluctuations in returns from year to year, especially negative returns, will have a tendency to cause the arithmetic mean to be incorrect.

C. GEOMETRIC MEAN.

1. Geometric mean is the average compounded return or the internal rate of return (annualized return). The geometric mean is calculated using the following formula:

$$GM = \sqrt[n]{(1 + R_1)(1 + R_2)\ldots(1 + R_n)} - 1$$

Therefore, the geometric mean for the previous data is equal to 13.09%.

$$GM = \sqrt[5]{(1 + .152)(1 + .091)(1 + .065)(1 + .183)(1 + .168)} - 1$$

$$GM = \sqrt[5]{1.8495} - 1$$

$$GM = 13.09\%$$

2. The reason the arithmetic and geometric means differ is that the arithmetic mean does not take into consideration the compounding effect of the returns.
   a. For example, if $1,000 is invested and earns 50% the first year and loses 50% the second year, the arithmetic mean equals 0% [(0.5 - 0.5)÷2]. However, the geometric mean equals -13.39% $[(1 + 0.5) \times (1 + -0.5)]^{1/2} - 1$.
   b. This large discrepancy is because the first year yielded a 50%, or $500 return. The second year yielded a 50% loss; however, this loss was 50% of the $1,500, or $750. The arithmetic mean does not take this compounding effect into consideration and will, therefore, be subject to inaccuracy. Conceptually, the geometric mean is more accurate.
3. The geometric mean will always be less than the arithmetic mean, except when the returns for each period are equal, in which case the geometric and arithmetic means will be equal.
4. The geometric mean is the same as the IRR or annual compound return. For example, if $1,000 is invested and earns the rates of returns illustrated above, the IRR will be equal to the geometric mean. The first year 15.2% is earned, 9.1% in the second year, and so on. After the fifth year, the initial investment of $1,000 has grown to be $1,849.50. The internal rate of return can be calculated as follows:

PV = (1,000)
N = 5
PMT = 0
FV = 1,849.50
Solve for i
i = 13.09%
Recall that the geometric mean also equals 13.09%.

D. REAL RETURN (INFLATION ADJUSTED).

1. The loss of purchasing power is one of the risks that investors face in achieving their financial goals. Real returns reflect the excess earnings from an investment that are above the inflation rate. However, simply subtracting the rate of inflation from the investment rate of return will not yield the real return.

Example

Assume that \$1,000 is invested at the beginning of the year and earns 10%, resulting in \$1,100. Also assume that over the same period inflation is 4%. Thus, \$1,040 at the end of the year is equal to the initial investment of \$1,000 at the beginning of the year. The real return is equal to the difference between the earnings (\$100) and the increase as a result of inflation (\$40), which is \$60, divided by the initial investment adjusted for inflation (\$1,040). This results in a real return of 5.77%.

   a. Conceptually, the real return of 5.77% makes sense, in that the absolute return was 10% and the inflation was 4%, the difference was 6%.

   b. The real earnings for this investment are \$60.

2. The real return can be calculated using the formula:

$$\left[\frac{1 + \text{Nominal return}}{1 + \text{Inflation rate}}\right] - 1 \times 100, \text{ where}$$

Nominal rate = The absolute return (in the example above, it was 10%).

Inflation rate = The rate of inflation for the period.

Example

a. Nominal rate = 10%

b. Inflation rate = 4%

c. Inflation-adjusted discount rate = [(1.10 ÷ 1.04) – 1] x 100 = 5.76923%.

3. Many financial calculators will have an easy method for calculating the real rate of return.

E. TOTAL RETURN.

The total return for any investment can be thought of as the sum of the appreciation and the earnings from that investment. For stocks, this would be the appreciation in stock price plus dividends received. Similarly, the total return for bonds includes appreciation and interest payments. These two components are taken into consideration in the basic present value model discussed earlier.

F. INTERNAL RATE OF RETURN (IRR).

1. The IRR is the earnings rate at which the present value of a series of cash flows will equal its cost. Recall the basic model for determining the present value of a series of cash flows.

2. The Basic Model:

$$P_0 = \frac{CF_1}{(1+k)^1} + \frac{CF_2}{(1+k)^2} + \ldots + \frac{CF_t}{(1+k)^t}\text{, where:}$$

P_0 = The value of the security today.
CF_t = The cash flow for period t.
k = The discount rate or internal rate of return.
t = The number of cash flows to be evaluated.

3. The underlying assumption of this equation is that the cash flows that occur during the life of the investment will be reinvested at the investment's internal rate of return. This is the same assumption found in computing the yield to maturity.

G. TIME WEIGHTED VS. DOLLAR WEIGHTED.

The internal rate of return is a dollar-weighted return since it takes into consideration the different cash flows of the investor. A time-weighted return is determined without regard to the cash flows of the investor. It is a measure of the performance of an investment over a period of time, without regard to specific cash flows. It can be used to determine how well an investment has done over a period of time. For example, most returns reported on mutual funds are time-weighted returns.

Example

Connie purchased one share of XYZ stock for $50. One year later the stock paid a dividend of $4, and Connie purchased an additional share for $65. At the end of the second year, Connie sold XYZ stock for $75 per share.

Time-Weighted Question.

What is the annualized time-weighted return for XYZ stock for the two-year period?

Solution:

Period	Cash Flow
0	($50.00)
1	$4.00
2	$75.00
IRR	26.54%

Dollar-Weighted Question.

What is Connie's annualized dollar-weighted return over the two-year period for XYZ stock?

Solution:

Period	Cash Flow
0	($50.00)
1	($61.00) [$4.00 - $65.00]
2	$150.00 [75.00 x 2]
IRR	22.63%

The time-weighted calculation only uses the cash flows associated with the initial share. This occurs because the time-weighted return is the return for a specific security over a specific period of time. It does not reflect the purchases and sales of stock that an investor might make over the evaluation period. Unlike the time-weighted return, the dollar-weighted return considers the subsequent purchases and sales of stock of the investor. This occurs because the dollar-weighted return focuses on the return that the investor actually received, instead of the return on the stock, assuming that the stock had simply been purchased and held over the evaluation period (which is the time-weighted return).

H. TAX-ADJUSTED RETURNS.

1. A tax-adjusted return is the realized return multiplied by (1 - tax rate). It is important to factor in taxes when comparing one investment alternative to another. For example, the after-tax yield on a municipal bond may be higher than for a corporate bond, even though the corporate bond carries a higher stated rate of return or has a higher yield to maturity.

Example

If Jeannine earns 12% (10% from appreciation and 2% from capital gains and dividends) from her equity portfolio and her marginal tax bracket is 36%, then the after-tax return for Jeannine is 11.28% (10% + (2% x (1 - 0.36))).

Note: Any portion of the 2% return that represented capital gains would have been taxed at a maximum rate of 20%, assuming that they were long-term capital gains held longer than 12 months.

---

2. The after-tax return should reflect both federal and local taxes.
3. Nontaxable income.
   a. Federal - The interest from municipal bonds is not taxable by the federal government. In addition, unrealized appreciation is not taxable by the federal government.
   b. Municipalities - The interest from Treasury bills, bonds, and notes, as well as savings bonds, is not taxable by states and municipalities. Additionally, most municipalities do not tax interest from municipal bonds issued by its own government.

I. RISK-ADJUSTED RETURNS.

1. It is important to compare, or benchmark, returns with some standard, such as the S&P 500 Index. As mentioned above, it is also important to compare after-tax returns of different investments. Another equally important comparison is the risk-adjusted return. It is important to know that the return from an investment is not only better than a more conservative investment, but is also better on a risk-adjusted basis. This permits the investor to determine whether or not the return was worth the risk that was undertaken.

2. Treynor, Sharpe, and Jensen performance measures are possible methods of comparing risk-adjusted returns.

J. WEIGHTED-AVERAGE RETURN.

1. The weighted-average return represents the return for a set of securities, such as a portfolio, where each return is weighted by the proportion of the security to the entire group or portfolio.

Example.

Company	Market Price	% of Total	Return	Weighted Return
A	$80.00	64%	5%	3.20%
B	$35.00	28%	25%	7.00%
C	$10.00	8%	50%	4.00%
	$125.00	100%	80%	14.20%

The simple average for the portfolio above is 26.67% (80 ÷ 3). Notice, however, that 64% of the portfolio had a return of only 5%. The weighted-average return reflects the return that was received by the portfolio on a dollar-adjusted basis. The weighted-average return is equal to 14.20% as illustrated above.

Example (alternative method).

Company	Market Price	Return (%)	Return ($)
A	$80.00	5%	$4.00
B	$35.00	25%	$8.75
C	$10.00	50%	$5.00
	$125.00		$17.75

Weighted Return = $17.75 ÷125.00 = 14.20%

The alternative method saves time because it avoids the step of calculating the percentage each security is to the total portfolio.

Note: Many of the financial calculators can automatically calculate the weighted-average return for a portfolio.

2. The same approach, as illustrated in the above two examples, can be used to calculate the weighed beta of a portfolio or the duration of a portfolio.

K. SEC YIELD.

1. The SEC yield calculation is a standardized calculation that the SEC requires mutual funds to report. It allows for investors to compare yields with consistency.

2. The SEC yield uses the fund's net investment income over the preceding 30 days to project the annualized yield. It is calculated as follows:

$$\text{SEC Yield} = 2\left[\frac{(I - E)}{(N \times P)} + 1\right]^6 - 1\text{, where}$$

I = the dividends and interest during the period.

E = the expenses accrued for the period.

N = the average daily number of shares outstanding during the period, that were entitled to receive dividends.

P = the maximum price per share on the last day of the period.

IX. INVESTMENT STRATEGIES

A. INVESTMENT POLICY STATEMENTS.

1. An investment policy statement is a written document that sets forth a client's objectives and sets forth certain limitations for the investment manager. The investment policy statement gives guidance to the investment manager and provides a means for evaluating investment performance.
2. The investment policy statement is generally structured as follows:

	DESCRIPTION
OBJECTIVES	
Return Requirements	There are certain return requirements of any portfolio. These issues and objectives are discussed in this section. The required return may be for an individual relating to a retirement objective, or an institution.
Risk Tolerance	All investors have unique tolerances for risk. These issues are discussed in this section.
CONSTRAINTS	
Time Horizon	The time horizon may be infinite as with the goals of many institutions, or finite, as with goals of most individuals.
Liquidity	Cash may or may not be needed from the portfolio. If the portfolio, such as a defined benefit plan, must distribute cash each year, the manager must accommodate this need. With many individual investors' goals, cash and liquidity may not be needed for some time.
Taxes	The tax status of the account is discussed in this section. May be taxable, or nontaxable, as in an IRA or a nontaxable entity.
Laws and Regulations	Foundations, trusts, and other entities may have certain restrictions on the types of investments.
Unique Circumstances and/or Preferences	Any unique circumstance of the investor is discussed in this section.

3. The policy statement is a document that can be given to the portfolio manager as a guide to the characteristics of the portfolio.
4. The manager's performance should be measured against the constraints and objectives of the policy statement.

B. DOLLAR-COST AVERAGING.

Dollar-cost averaging is the process of purchasing securities over a period of time by investing a predetermined amount at regular intervals. The goal of dollar-cost averaging is to reduce the effects of market price fluctuations. When the market is rising, shares benefit from the price increases. When the market is declining, the additional shares purchased are purchased at lower prices and will yield more shares per dollar invested.

C. DIVIDEND REINVESTMENT.

1. Dividends are basically returns from an investment. Investors must choose to consume (spend) the dividend payment or to invest it in the same investment or some other investment. The term dividend reinvestment refers to dividends being invested back into the investment from which they were earned.
2. The benefits that are derived from this strategy can be impressive. If an investor chooses to consume dividends, the principal will grow only from appreciation.

Example

Assume a stock sells for $30, pays a dividend of $2.00 at the end of each year, and appreciates over time at a compound rate of 10%. The following table illustrates the results of consuming or reinvesting the dividends after 10 years.

Reinvesting the dividends will result in a 41% larger asset at the end of a 10-year period.

Consuming Dividends			Reinvesting Dividends		
PV	=	$30.00	PV	=	$30.00
N	=	10 years	N	=	10 years
i	=	10%	i	=	10%
PMT	=	$0.00	PMT	=	$2.00
FV	=	$77.81	FV	=	$109.69

3. Mutual funds.

   One option offered by mutual funds is to reinvest dividends back into the mutual fund.
4. Dividend reinvestment plans (DRIPs).

   DRIPs are offered by many companies as a service to their shareholders. Participation is usually permitted to shareholders of one or more shares of stock. These plans provide several benefits.
   a. Dividends are automatically reinvested into the company's stock.
   b. Additional purchases of shares can be made without a broker and/or for minimal commissions.
5. Dividends reinvested are treated the same for tax purposes as dividends received in the form of cash. These dividends, like other dividends, will be reported to the IRS on Form 1099-Div and are subject to income tax in the year distributed.

D. ASSET ALLOCATION.

1. Asset allocation refers to the process of apportioning assets available for investment among various investment classes. These investment classes include the various investment types discussed earlier.
   a. Money market securities.
   b. Fixed-income securities.
   c. Common stock.
   d. International investments.
   e. Real estate.
   f. Collectibles (generally small or nonexistent).
2. Asset allocation is important because approximately 90 percent of long-term performance is determined by the asset allocation of the portfolio.
3. The objective in building an asset allocation model is to determine which investment categories will be used and the appropriate percentages for each asset class. The asset allocation model may encompass any one of many different strategies, but each should be built with the following considerations:
   a. The client's level of risk tolerance.
   b. The client's level of sophistication with regard to investment alternatives.
   c. The required rate of return necessary to meet the objectives of the client.
   d. The financial position and tax situation of the client.
4. Buy and hold.
   a. A buy and hold strategy begins with a set percentage of assets in each class. Over time this ratio will change as the value of each asset class changes.
   b. The major benefit of a buy and hold strategy is that transaction costs and taxes are minimized.
   c. The use of index funds is an example of a buy and hold strategy. Index funds attempt to match the make up of an index, such as the S&P 500. Because indexes are relatively stable, with regard to the stocks that make up the index, transaction costs and taxes are minimized and research costs are eliminated.
5. Passive.
   a. A passive asset allocation scheme begins by setting specific percentages for each asset class. These percentages should be maintained over time. To achieve percentage maintenance, the portfolio will require periodic rebalancing.
   b. For example, an investor may decide on a portfolio allocation consisting of 50% equities and 50% fixed-income securities. Over time, the ratio of equities and fixed-income securities will deviate from the original allocation percentage because of gains, losses, and income. To maintain the original asset allocation percentage, assets from one class will have to be liquidated and reinvested in the other asset class. This process is called rebalancing.
   c. Rebalancing causes transaction costs and taxes to incur.
   d. A passive strategy should not be confused with a buy and hold strategy.

6. Strategic.

   a. The purpose of strategic asset allocation is to choose an appropriate asset allocation based on forecasts of the economy, expectations of selected asset classes, and the risk tolerance of the client. Once these factors are considered, an asset allocation is chosen that represents the long-run strategic asset mix. This mix will remain constant until another analysis is conducted. As such, this strategy may also be called a constant mix strategy. Because the performance of asset classes is different, rebalancing must take place to bring the portfolio back in line with the strategic mix. Rebalancing typically occurs once or twice per year. Rebalancing more frequently than twice per year is likely to incur transaction costs that outweigh any benefit resulting from the rebalancing.

   b. Factors considered:

      i. Client.

         A) The risk tolerance of the client must be assessed in conjunction with their current phase in the client lifecycle. As you may recall, there are four phases in the lifecycle:

            1) Asset accumulation.

            2) Consolidation.

            3) Spending.

            4) Gifting.

         B) Clients who are younger are typically more able to tolerate risk than those who are older, however, many other issues must also be addressed.

      ii. Asset classes.

         A) The asset classes that are being considered must be chosen for inclusion. For some planners, the available asset classes may be limited to stocks, bonds, and cash. For other planners, ten to twenty asset classes may be considered.

         B) For each asset class that is to be included in the analysis, the planner must have the following information: expected return, expected standard deviation (or variance), and correlation with all other asset classes.

      iii. Based on the risk tolerance of the client and the potential portfolios that exist, a strategic mix is selected for the client.

7. Active.

   a. Active asset allocation refers to changing the mix of investment classes based on changing market conditions. This strategy is often referred to as market timing and is based on the belief that investors can increase returns over time by switching among asset classes. Market timers analyze the different asset classes to determine which ones are thought to be undervalued or overvalued. Securities in overvalued asset classes are sold in expectations of falling prices. Securities in undervalued asset classes are purchased in anticipation of rising prices.

   b. Tactical asset allocation (TAA) is similar to market timing. This strategy involves evaluating asset classes or industries as to their value. In general, undervalued classes should be purchased, and overvalued classes should be sold.

   c. Active asset allocation may generate high transaction costs from constantly changing the mix between asset classes.

8. Asset allocation in practice.

   a. The purpose of investment planning is to build an investment portfolio that is capable of accomplishing the goals of the client while matching the level of risk in the portfolio to the investor's tolerance for risk.

   b. Mean variance optimization software.

      i. Most financial planners who provide investment counseling use some type of mean-variance optimization software to determine an optimum portfolio or asset allocation based on a client's goals, risk tolerance, time horizon, tax situation, and economic forecasts.

      ii. The goal in using these software packages is to build an efficient portfolio for the client. Remember that an efficient portfolio is one that has the highest level return (in practice, the return should be an after-tax return) for the given level of risk.

      iii. Software inputs.

         A) Economic variables.

            1) Asset classes considered.

            2) Expected returns for each asset class.

            3) Standard deviation of each asset class.

            4) Correlation of each asset class to every other asset class.

         B) Client variables.

            1) Risk tolerance.

            2) Time horizon.

            3) Marginal tax rates.

      iv. Software outputs.

         A) Asset allocation (percentage of portfolio to be invested in each asset class).

         B) Expected before-tax return of the portfolio.

         C) Expected after-tax return of the portfolio.

         D) Expected standard deviation of the portfolio.

         E) Where on the efficient frontier the portfolio will fall.

   c. Sample portfolios – Exhibit 37 illustrates three possible asset allocations: one for a conservative investor, one for a moderate investor, and one for an aggressive investor.

EXHIBIT 37: SAMPLE ASSET ALLOCATIONS

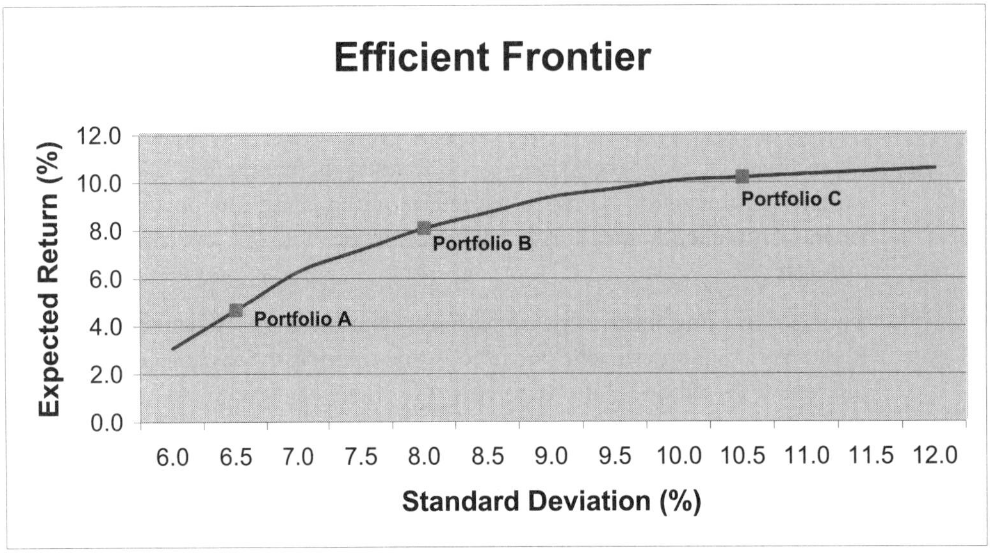

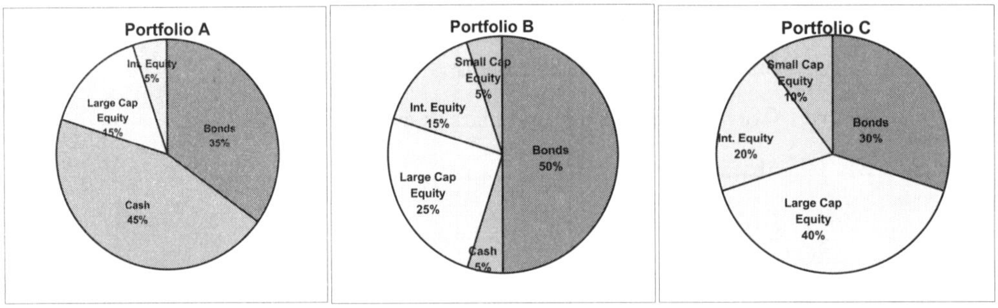

Type of Investor:	"Conservative"	"Moderate"	"Aggressive"
	Portfolio A	**Portfolio B**	**Portfolio C**
Bonds	35%	50%	30%
Cash	45%	5%	0%
Large Cap Equity	15%	25%	40%
Int. Equity	5%	15%	20%
Small Cap Equity	0%	5%	10%
Total	100%	100%	100%

i. Portfolio A – Conservative.

A) This portfolio consists of 45% cash, 35% fixed income, 15% large-cap equity, and 5% international equity.

B) The expected returns for a conservative portfolio are generally low when compared to equity returns, but will have a minimal level of risk, as measured by the standard deviation.

C) This type of portfolio might be appropriate for:

1) An investor who has little experience investing in stocks and bonds and/or has little tolerance for volatility in his or her portfolio; or

2) A retired investor who has a significant investment portfolio capable of generating enough income and cash flow to maintain the investor's standard of living.

ii. Portfolio B – Moderate.

A) This portfolio consists of 5% cash, 50% fixed income, 25% large-cap equity, 15% international equity, and 5% small-cap equity.

B) The expected returns for a moderate portfolio will be greater than a conservative portfolio, but will have a higher level of risk.

C) This type of portfolio might be appropriate for:

1) An investor who has at least some experience investing in stocks and bonds and is willing to accept additional risk for the possibility of higher expected returns; or

2) An investor who has a relatively high level of tolerance for risk, but is retiring and needs to adjust his portfolio in such a way as to generate higher yields and less capital appreciation.

iii. Portfolio C – Aggressive.

A) This portfolio consists of 0% cash, 30% fixed income, 40% large-cap equity, 20% international equity, and 10% small-cap equity.

B) The expected returns for an aggressive portfolio will be greater than a moderate portfolio, but will have a higher level of risk.

C) This type of portfolio might be appropriate for:

1) A young investor who has a very long time horizon; or

2) An investor who has substantial experience investing in stocks and bonds and is willing to accept a significantly higher level of additional risk for the possibility of higher expected returns; or

3) A retired investor who has a significant net worth and a significant investment portfolio capable of generating enough income and cash flow from the bond portion of the portfolio to maintain the investor's standard of living. The remainder of the portfolio is invested for purposes of future growth.

E. BENCHMARKING PORTFOLIO PERFORMANCE.

1. It is important to determine not only the rate of return that a portfolio has earned, but also how this rate of return compares to an appropriate benchmark such as the S&P 500. Benchmarking is the process of comparing the performance of an investor's portfolio to the relevant market's performance over the same period of time.

2. Although many investors use comparisons to other managers as a measure of performance, benchmarks should contain certain characteristics. The primary characteristics of a good benchmark include the following:

   a. Unambiguous. The composition and weighting of the components of the benchmark must be clearly delineated.

   b. Investable. The option to invest in the benchmark is available.

   c. Measurable. It should be possible to calculate the benchmark's return on a relatively frequent basis.

   d. Appropriate. The benchmark must be consistent with the manager's investment philosophy and style.

e. Reflective of current investment opinions. The manager has current investment knowledge of the securities that make up the benchmark.

f. Specified in advance. The benchmark should be constructed before the beginning of the evaluation period.

These six properties improve the usefulness of a benchmark as an investment management tool and allow for a better measure of a portfolio manager's performance.

3. In addition to meeting the above six properties, a benchmark should also be highly correlated to the portfolio. Generally, this is measured by the statistic R^2, which is called the coefficient of determination.

4. The comparison between a portfolio and the market may take several forms:

   a. Absolute returns.

   b. Risk-adjusted returns.

   c. After-tax return.

5. Generally, comparisons are made on a risk-adjusted basis. This allows the investor to determine the portfolio performance when adjusted for the level of risk.

   a. The S&P 500 is the most common estimate of the U.S. large-cap market.

   b. International portfolios are generally compared to the EAFE (Europe, Australia, Far East) index.

6. Three methods previously discussed to evaluate the performance of a portfolio include:

   a. The Sharpe Performance Measure.

   b. The Treynor Performance Measure.

   c. The Jensen Performance Index.

7. The Sharpe and Treynor Performance Measures are relative measures of performance. A relative performance measure does not give a measure of absolute performance. It must be compared to other measures, such as the measure for the market or other alternative portfolios in order to be meaningful. The Jensen Performance Index is an absolute measure of the performance of a managed portfolio above an unmanaged portfolio for a similar level of risk.

8. Once the risk-adjusted performance of the portfolio is determined, the investor will then be in a position to evaluate whether the portfolio needs to be adjusted.

F. STRATEGIES FOR DEALING WITH CONCENTRATED PORTFOLIOS.

1. A common problem that clients face is that a substantial portion of their wealth is concentrated in a single security. This type of situation is found with small business owners, executives with substantial stock options, and others.

2. Clearly, a concentrated portfolio faces substantial unsystematic risk. From an investment perspective, it is important to eliminate or reduce the exposure to this unsystematic risk. The obvious solution to this problem is to sell the security and reinvest the proceeds into a diversified portfolio. However, there are a variety of problems that may occur:

   a. There may not be a market for the security.

   b. The basis in the security is low relative to its value.

   c. The client has a desire to keep the asset.

3. Strategies for dealing with concentrated portfolios:

   a. Sale.

      i. Outright sale – assuming there is a market for the stock, an outright sale is an effective method of eliminating the concentrated portfolio and allowing the proceeds to be reinvested into a diversified portfolio. However, if the security has a low tax-adjusted basis, there will be significant tax attributable to the sale. The high tax cost is usually a deterrent to an outright sale.

      ii. Installment sale – an installment sale is another method of selling the security, however, on a deferred basis. The installment sale introduces other risks, such as default risk.

      iii. Private annuity and self canceling installment note (SCINs) – Similar to an installment sale, but generally done with related parties. These techniques are discussed in the Estates Section.

      iv. ESOP – an ESOP may solve many of the problems associated with concentrated portfolios. For example, an ESOP creates a market for a security that could not be sold outside the firm. In addition, the creation of an ESOP may allow the owners of the company to sell their ownership to the ESOP, receive proceeds, and pay no tax on the transaction. There are certain requirements for this nonrecognition of gain treatment that are discussed in the retirement section.

   b. Charitable Remainder Trusts (CRT).

      i. Charitable remainder trusts have a variety of advantages in dealing with concentrated portfolios. When a CRT is established and assets are transferred to the CRT, a charitable deduction is generally created and can be used to offset current income.

      ii. In addition to the charitable deduction that is created, the asset transferred to the CRT can be sold without tax impact to the CRT since it is a nontaxable entity. The proceeds can then be reinvested into a diversified portfolio to generate income. Payments from the CRT, either in the form of an annuity or a unitrust payment, are distributed to the donor.

      iii. In addition, the transfer to the CRT provides creditor protection, since the assets no longer belong to the donor. These techniques are discussed in the Estates Section.

   c. Option strategies.

      i. Put option.

         A) Put options are a great method of minimizing or eliminating downside risk for a security or a portfolio. However, put options are generally only written on publicly traded securities. In addition, put options are generally not inexpensive and, they expire.

         B) Put options are very effective for minimizing downside risk for limited periods of time. For example, publicly traded stock that is received in a buyout of a private company will often be restricted stock. This stock generally cannot be sold for a period of time. A put option could protect the value of the security in the event that the stock decreased in price.

ii. Collar.

A) Options can be used to create a collar around the value of the stock. For example, a call option can be written on a stock that will generate premium to pay for the premium on a put option.

B) The call option creates a ceiling on the value of the security, while the put establishes a floor for the value of the security.

Example

If the value of the security was $80, a call option written at a strike price of $100 might generate enough premium to pay for a put option with a strike price of $60. In this example, there are three possible outcomes:

1. The stock may end up between the two strike prices (between $60 and $100). In this case, both options will expire worthless and unexercised.
2. The stock may end up at a market price less than the put strike price (below $60). In this case, the stock could be sold for $60.
3. Finally, the stock price may end up at a price in excess of the strike price of the call option. In this case, the security could be delivered for a price of $100.

C) This type of arrangement is generally referred to as a zero-cost collar since there is no cost to the investor. However, the option contracts will expire and the collar would have to be put back in place after expiration.

d. Exchange Fund.

i. Many financial institutions sponsor exchange funds that allow investors with concentrated portfolios of publicly traded stock to contribute the stock to the fund. In exchange, the investor will receive an interest in the overall fund. Since the fund holds numerous securities, the investor receives an interest in a fund that is diversified.

ii. Once again, the stock generally must be publicly traded with an established market value.

iii. The benefits of the exchange fund is that an undiversified portfolio is exchanged for an interest in a diversified portfolio without it being a taxable transaction.

G. PROBABILITY ANALYSIS.

1. Monte Carlo Analysis.

a. Monte Carlo Analysis (MCA) is a technique used to model uncertainty. It allows the user to substitute uncertainty into their models.

b. Consider the uncertainty in retirement planning. Small changes in the projected rate of return will make a dramatic difference in the outcome. The life expectancy is also another important variable that may be incorrectly approximated.

c. MCA uses a random number generator to provide an output with specific probabilities of outcomes. It provides insight into the most likely outcome, but with other possible outcomes. With the analysis, the user also gets a best-case scenario and a worst-case scenario.

X. CLIENT ASSESSMENT

A. INTRODUCTION.

Investment planning requires that the financial situation of the client be examined so that the goals of the client can be met while meeting the investment needs and requirements of the investor. To do an effective job of investment counseling, the following areas should be examined and reviewed:

1. Financial goals.
2. Risk tolerance and risk exposure.
3. Client tax situation.
4. Liquidity and marketability needs.
5. Analysis and evaluation of client financial statements.
6. Client preferences, investment understanding, and experience.

B. FINANCIAL GOALS.

1. The financial goals of the client are the driving force behind an investment plan. These goals help to establish the time horizon, the level of risk to be undertaken, and the specific asset classes that should be used to meet objectives. Effective investment plans require that clients establish clear, realistic, quantifiable goals. These goals should specify the time horizon and the dollar amount. Because of limited resources, the goals must be prioritized.
2. In many cases, the financial planner needs to assist the client in developing and prioritizing the financial goals. The financial planner may determine that the goals are either too aggressive (unrealistic) or too conservative. In either case, the goals may be modified. Examples of possible goals that a client may strive for include:
   a. Establishing an emergency fund.
   b. Becoming financially independent.
   c. Retiring at age 55.
   d. Provide funding for child or grandchild's college education.
   e. Purchasing a retirement home.
   f. Taking a trip around the world at retirement.
3. Once the goals have been clearly defined with time horizons and dollar requirements, the planning can begin. Both the time horizon and the dollar amounts affect the choice of investment vehicles.
   a. Time horizon.
      i. The time horizon of each investment goal is an important factor in determining the investment vehicles used to meet that goal.
      ii. Generally, long-term horizons, such as retirement for a 30 year old, permit more risk to be taken than shorter-term goals, such as a retirement plan for a 64 year old.
      iii. Risk is the variability or volatility of expected outcomes. Investments that are more risky, such as equities, have more volatile returns than investments such as Treasury bills. However, over a long period of time, the volatility of returns even out and the compound returns should be higher for riskier types of investments (equities). Short-term goals cannot tolerate wide fluctuations in value and, therefore, require less risky investment vehicles.
   b. Dollar requirements.

The dollar amount of the goal can be a decisive factor in choosing the investment vehicle. Each goal requires a specific compound return over the time horizon for the goal to be achieved. If this required rate of return is high, the client must either accept additional risk or adjust the goal to require a lower rate of return. Accepting additional risk provides the possibility for higher rates of return. However, this consideration cannot be decided in isolation. Other factors, such as the time horizon and risk tolerance of the investor, must be considered when choosing the type of investment vehicle.

C. RISK TOLERANCE AND RISK EXPOSURE.

The risk tolerance of an investor is vital in determining which investments are chosen. Risk tolerance is the level of risk that an investor is willing to assume regardless of the potential returns. Some investors are only willing to invest in assets that are no more risky than Treasuries. The potential returns for these types of investors will be less than for investors who are willing to accept more risk. However, the level of risk tolerance must be considered in the analysis.

D. CLIENT TAX SITUATION.

1. Another important consideration in the investment planning process is the client's tax situation. All investment alternatives should be analyzed on an after-tax basis so that the returns from tax-exempt investments is comparable to taxable investments. With combined federal and state rates in excess of 40% for high-income individuals, yields on tax-exempt securities can be quite attractive.
2. Alternatives to tax-exempt securities (i.e., municipal bonds) include tax-deferred investments, such as qualified plans, IRAs, insurance-based investments, and growth stocks (nondividend paying common stock). Tax-deferred investments can have dramatic differences in wealth accumulation over long periods of time as depicted in the following table:

Tax-Deferred Investment			Taxable Investment (Tax Rate = 30%)		
PV	=	0	PV	=	0
PMT	=	$2,000	PMT	=	$2,000
N	=	35	N	=	35
i	=	10%	i	=	7% [10% x (1 - 0.30)]
FV	=	$542,048.74	FV	=	$276,473.76

3. Over a 35-year horizon (for example, a 30-year-old investing for retirement at age 65), the difference in the two accounts is substantial. The tax-deferred account increased over 96% more than the taxable investment account during the 30-year period. For the taxable investment to be equal to the tax-deferred account at the end of 35 years, a payment of $3,921 (instead of $2,000) must be made each year.

E. INVESTMENT STRATEGIES IN TAX-ADVANTAGED ACCOUNTS.

1. Net Unrealized Appreciation (NUA).
   a. As discussed more fully in the retirement section of this text, NUA represents the appreciation of employer securities within a qualified plan from the date the stock was contributed to the plan. A qualifying lump-sum distribution of employer securities permits special tax treatment (long-term capital gain instead of ordinary income) for the portion that represents NUA, if the distribution is from a qualified plan (does not apply to assets held in an IRA).

b. If employer stock is rolled into an IRA, then the special tax treatment no longer is available, and any distribution from the IRA will be taxed as ordinary income.

2. Appropriate assets for tax-advantaged vs. taxable accounts.

a. Taxable accounts.

i. Because income that is earned in a taxable account results in current income tax, it is generally better to invest in either appreciating assets or assets that are not subject to income tax.

ii. Appreciating assets have the advantage of being taxed at lower capital gains rates, which are currently significantly lower than ordinary income tax rates.

iii. Municipal securities have the advantage of being exempt from federal and, possibly, state income tax. Therefore, if a client is in a high enough marginal tax bracket, any fixed income should likely be invested in municipal securities, which may have a short or long duration.

b. Tax-advantaged accounts.

i. Generally, distributions from tax-advantaged accounts consist of income that is subject to ordinary income tax rates. Therefore, any fixed-income securities held in a tax-advantaged account would consist of taxable and not municipal (assuming that taxable returns are greater than municipal) securities.

ii. In addition, it seems reasonable that much of the fixed-income portion of an individual's portfolio be allocated to tax-deferred accounts, while much of the portfolio that consists of appreciating assets is held outside of tax-deferred accounts. However, there certainly must be a balance between the two.

F. LIQUIDITY AND MARKETABILITY NEEDS.

1. One of the first considerations for a financial plan is the need for an emergency fund. This fund should consist of liquid assets so as to be easily accessible in the event of an emergency (loss of job, disability, etc.).

2. If a client does not have an emergency fund or access to funds in case of an emergency, investments that have the potential for large price fluctuations, such as common stock, should be a smaller portion of the overall portfolio. Likewise, investments that do not have efficient markets, such as real estate, should be limited from an investment portfolio.

G. ANALYSIS AND EVALUATION OF CLIENT FINANCIAL STATEMENTS.

1. The financial planner uses the financial information as a basis for creating a plan to achieve the goals of the client. The client's financial statements should contain a balance sheet and cash flow statement. These statements provide the planner with the resources available for accomplishing the client's goals. Recall that it is possible that the planner, after reviewing the financial information, will determine that the client's goals are unrealistic based on the current financial position and earning capacity. In such a case, the goals should be revised to reflect more realistic objectives.

2. The balance sheet provides the planner with a list of assets stated at FMV and any corresponding debt. An analysis of the balance sheet allows the planner to determine which assets are income producing and which assets are use assets. Subsequently, the planner can analyze income-producing assets to determine if they are generating income or growth at optimum levels or if there might be better alternatives for these assets.

3. The cash flow statement details the client's sources of funds and the allocation of funds.
   a. The inflows will include salary, rents, interest, dividends, guaranteed payments from partnerships, etc.
   b. The outflows will include taxes, monthly expenses (such as, loan payments for home and automobile, rent, groceries, utilities, insurance, student loans, credit card bills, phone bills, etc.) and savings.
   c. The difference between the inflows and the outflows is called discretionary income. In many cases, the client may be able to reduce or eliminate certain expenses. For example, assuming comparable interest rates, mortgage interest is better than other types of interest because it is deductible as an itemized deduction for income tax purposes. Therefore, shifting debt to increase the level of mortgage interest may be a way to reduce yearly taxes, and thus increase cash flow.
4. Expected resources may also be included in this analysis if they are relatively certain. These resources might include bonuses, promotions, or inheritances. In some cases, such as a large inheritance, the expected resource may make it possible for the client to accomplish all of his or her objectives.

H. CLIENT PREFERENCES AND INVESTMENT UNDERSTANDING AND EXPERIENCE.

Preferences and understanding of investments may initially limit the possible investment vehicles. Clients, who are unfamiliar with a type of investment, such as equities, will naturally be somewhat hesitant about investing in it simply out of fear of the unknown. Once the client has a better understanding of the basic investment types, he or she will be in a better position to determine which vehicles are acceptable alternatives in achieving his or her objectives.

I. MATCHING INVESTMENT VEHICLES TO CLIENT NEEDS.

1. The purpose of investment planning is to match appropriate investment vehicles to the needs of the client. After the planner has examined the needs of the client, investment vehicles must be chosen. These vehicles will be chosen based on the same criteria as previously discussed:
   a. Financial goals.
   b. Risk tolerance and risk exposure.
   c. Client tax situation.
   d. Liquidity and marketability needs.
   e. Analysis and evaluation of client financial statements.
   f. Client preferences and investment understanding and experience.

APPENDIX 1: FORMULAS

✔Denotes formula that will likely be provided on exam, without the variable definitions. (See Appendix 2 for actual formulas provided on the exam.)

CAPITAL ASSET PRICING MODEL (CAPM)

Capital Market Line (CML)

✔ $R_p = R_f + \left(\frac{R_m - R_f}{\sigma_m}\right)\sigma_p$

R_p	=	The return of the portfolio.
R_f	=	The risk-free rate of return.
R_m	=	The return on the market.
$(R_m\text{-}R_f)$	=	The return from the market that exceeds the risk-free rate of return.
σ_m	=	The standard deviation of the market.
σ_p	=	The standard deviation of the portfolio.

Security Market Line (SML)

✔ $R_s = R_f + \beta(R_m - R_f)$

R_s	=	The return for a stock.
R_f	=	The risk-free rate of return.
β	=	Beta, which is a measure of the systematic risk associated with a particular stock.
$(R_m\text{-}R_f)$	=	The risk premium, which is the additional return of the market over the risk-free rate of return.

Characteristic Line (CL)

$R_j = \alpha_j + \beta_j R_m + e$

R_j	=	Return for asset j.
α_j	=	Y intercept or constant term.
β_j	=	The slope of the line (beta).
R_m	=	Rate of return for the market.
e	=	Error term from the analysis.

ARBITRAGE PRICING THEORY (APT)

Arbitrage Pricing Theory (APT)

✔ $R = a_0 + b_1F_1 + b_2F_2 + \ldots + b_nF_n + e$

R	=	The return from the security.
a_0	=	The return that is expected for all securities when the value of all factors is zero. In some cases, this is called the expected return.
b_n	=	The sensitivity of the security to factor F_n.
F_2	=	The factor that affects the security, such as GNP of 3%.
e	=	The return that is unique to the security. It is also called an error term in some cases. **Note:** This error term should drop out if all relevant factors are captured by the equation.

MEASURES OF RISK

Beta

$$\beta_p = \left(\frac{\sigma_p}{\sigma_m}\right)(R_{pm})$$

β_p	=	Beta.
σ_p	=	Standard deviation of the portfolio.
σ_m	=	Standard deviation of the market.
R_{pm}	=	Correlation coefficient between the portfolio and the market.

Weighted-Average Beta

$$\bar{\beta}_w = \sum_{i=1}^{N}(\beta_i \times \%_i)$$

β_w	=	Weighted average.
β_i	=	Return for security i.
$\%_i$	=	Portion of security i to total portfolio.
N	=	Number of securities.

Expected Rate of Return

$$E(r) = P_1(R_1) + P_2(R_2) + \ldots + P_t(R_t)$$

$E(r)$	=	The expected return.
P_1	=	The probability assigned to the first rate of return.
R_1	=	The first rate of return.
t	=	The number of events that are being examined.

Standard Deviation of Forecasted Returns

$$✔\ \sigma = \text{Var.}(r)^{1/2} = [P_1[r_1 - E(r)]^2 + P_2[r_2 - E(r)]^2 + \ldots + P_t[r_t - E(r)]^2]^{1/2}$$

$E(r)$	=	Expected return (calculated).
r_t	=	Forecasted return for outcome t.
P_t	=	Probability of outcome t.
σ	=	Standard deviation.

Standard Deviation of Historical Returns

$$✔\ \sigma = \sqrt{\frac{\sum_{i=1}^{n} (r_i - \bar{r})^2}{(n-1)}}$$

σ	=	Standard deviation.
n	=	Number of observations.
r_i	=	Actual return for period i.
$\bar{r}$	=	Average return.

Standard Deviation of a Two-Security Portfolio

$$✔\ \sigma = \sqrt{W_A^2\sigma_A^2 + W_B^2\sigma_B^2 + 2W_AW_B[\sigma_A\sigma_BR_{AB}]}$$

σ^2	=	Variance.
σ	=	Standard deviation.
W_A	=	The percent of the portfolio invested in security A.
W_B	=	The percent of the portfolio invested in security B.
$[\sigma_A\sigma_BR_{AB}]$	=	Covariance between security A & B.
R_{AB}	=	Correlation coefficient.

Note: W_A plus W_B must sum to 100%.

Duration (Example)

Bond:

PV	=	$974.23
N	=	3
i	=	8%
PMT	=	70
FV	=	$1,000.00

Duration Calculation			
Year	**Cash Flow**	**Year x Cash Flow**	**PV @ 8%**
1	70	70	64.81
2	70	140	120.03
3	1,070	3,210	2,548.20
	1,210	N/A	2,733.04

Duration = 2,733.04 ÷ 974.23 = 2.8 years

Change in Price Using Duration

✔ $$\frac{\Delta P}{P} = \frac{-D}{1 + YTM} \times \Delta YTM$$

$\frac{\Delta P}{P}$	=	Percent change in price of a bond.
D	=	Duration.
YTM	=	Yield to Maturity.

PERFORMANCE MEASURES

The Sharpe Performance Index

✔ $S(p) = \dfrac{(R_p - R_f)}{\sigma}$

$S(p)$	=	Sharpe Performance Measure for portfolio p.
R_p	=	The average rate of return for a given time period.
R_f	=	The risk-free rate of return during the same time period.
σ	=	The standard deviation of the rate of return for portfolio p during the same time interval.

The Treynor Performance Measure

✔ $T_p = \dfrac{(R_p - R_f)}{B_p}$

T_p	=	Treynor Performance Measure for portfolio p.
R_p	=	The average rate of return for a given time period.
R_f	=	The risk-free rate of return during the same time period.
B_p	=	Beta for the same period or the slope of the portfolio's characteristic line during the period.

The Jensen Model

$(R_p - R_f) = \alpha_p + \beta_p[R_m - R_f] + e$

$(R_p\text{-}R_f)$	=	The return that is earned solely for bearing risk.
α_p	=	Alpha, which represents the return that is able to be earned above or below an unmanaged portfolio with identical market risk.
β_p	=	Beta, which is the measure of systematic or market risk.
R_m	=	The return on the market.
R_f	=	The risk-free rate of return.
e	=	The error term.

The Jensen Performance Index

✔ $\alpha_p = R_p - [R_f + \beta_p(R_m - R_f)]$

RATES OF RETURN

Holding Period Return (HPR)

$$HPR = \frac{\text{Ending Value of Investment - Beginning Value of Investment +/- Cashflows}}{\text{Beginning Value of Investment}}$$

Internal Rate of Return (IRR)

$$P_0 = \frac{CF_1}{(1+k)^1} + \frac{CF_2}{(1+k)^2} + \ldots + \frac{CF_t}{(1+k)^t}$$

P_0 = The value of the security today.
CF_t = The cash flow for period t.
k = The discount rate based on the security type.
t = The number of cash flows to be evaluated.

Yield To Maturity (YTM)

$$P_0 = \frac{CF_1}{(1+k)^1} + \frac{CF_2}{(1+k)^2} + \ldots + \frac{Par}{(1+k)^t}$$

P_0 = The value of the security today.
CF_t = The cash flow for period t.
k = The discount rate based on the security type.
t = The number of cash flows to be evaluated.

Yield to Call (YTC)

$$P_0 = \frac{CF_1}{(1+k)^1} + \frac{CF_2}{(1+k)^2} + \ldots + \frac{\text{Call Price}}{(1+k)^t}$$

P_0 = The value of the security today.
CF_t = The cash flow for period t.
k = The discount rate based on the security type.
t = The number of cash flows to be evaluated.

Arithmetic Mean

$$AM = \frac{\sum_{t-1}^{n} HPR_t}{n}$$

Time Weighted

$$P_0 = \frac{CF_1}{(1+k)^1} + \frac{CF_2}{(1+k)^2} + \ldots + \frac{CF_t}{(1+k)^t}$$

P_0	=	The value of the security today.
CF_t	=	The cash flow for period t.
k	=	The discount rate based on the security type.
t	=	The number of cash flows to be evaluated.

> **Note:** Time-weighted return considers cash flows of investment only. It does not consider cash flows of the investor.

Geometric Mean

$$GM = \sqrt[n]{(1+R_1)(1+R_2)\ldots(1+R_n)} - 1$$

R_n	=	Return for each period.
n	=	Number of periods.

After-Tax Rate of Return

Tax-Adjusted Return = R(1 - TR)

R	=	Real return.
TR	=	Tax rate.

Inflation-Adjusted Rate of Return

$$R_i = \left[\frac{(1+R)}{(1+IR)} - 1\right](100)$$

R_i	=	Inflation-adjusted return.
R	=	Earnings rate.
IR	=	Inflation rate.

Weighted-Average Return

$$\bar{x}_w = \sum_{i-1}^{N} [(R_i)(\%_i)]$$

$\bar{x}_w$ = Weighted average.
R_i = Return for security i.
$\%_i$ = Portion of security i to total portfolio.
N = Number of securities.

VALUATION MODELS

The Basic Present Value (Valuation) Model

$$P_0 = \frac{CF_1}{(1+k)^1} + \frac{CF_2}{(1+k)^2} + \ldots + \frac{CF_t}{(1+k)^t}$$

P_0 = The value of the security today.
CF_t = The cash flow for period t.
k = The discount rate based on the type of security and risk level of the investment.
t = The number of cash flows to be evaluated.

Constant Dividend Growth Model

✔ $$P_0 = \frac{D_1}{k - g}$$

P_0 = Price for the security.
D_1 = The dividend paid at period 1.
k = The investor's required rate of return.
g = The growth rate of the dividends. The growth rate can be negative, positive or zero. See perpetuities for a zero growth rate.

Capitalized Earnings

$$V = \frac{E}{R_d}$$

V = The value of the company or firm.
E = The earnings used to value the firm.
R_d = The discount rate.

Perpetuity

$$P_0 = \frac{D_1}{k}$$

P_0	=	Price of the security.
D	=	The dividend paid per period.
k	=	Investor's required rate of return.

Conversion Factor

✔ $$CV = \left(\frac{1{,}000}{CP}\right)(P_s)$$

CV	=	Conversion value.
CP	=	Conversion price of stock.
P_s	=	Current price of stock.

Note: Bond face = $1,000.

APPENDIX 2: FORMULA PAGE PROVIDED ON CFP® CERTIFICATION EXAMINATION

$$V = \frac{D_1}{r - g}$$

$$T_i = \frac{r_p - r_f}{B_p}$$

$$r = \frac{D_1}{P} + g$$

$$Si = \frac{r_p - r_f}{\sigma_p}$$

$$r_p = r_f + \sigma_p\left(\frac{r_m - r_f}{\sigma_m}\right)$$

$$a_p = r_p - [r_f + (r_m - r_f)B_p]$$

$$r_i = r_f + (r_m - r_f)B_i$$

$$Dur = \frac{\sum_{t=1}^{n} \frac{C_t(t)}{(1+i)^t}}{\sum_{t=1}^{n} \frac{C_t}{(1+i)^t}}$$

$$r_i = a_i + b_1F_1 + b_2F_2 + b_3F_3 + e_i$$

-OR-

$$Dur = \frac{1+y}{y} - \frac{(1+y) + T(c-y)}{c[(1+y)^T - 1] + y}$$

$$\sigma = \sqrt{\frac{\sum_{t=1}^{n}(r_t - \bar{r})^2}{n-1}}$$

$$\frac{\Delta P}{P} = -D\left[\frac{\Delta(1+y)}{1+y}\right]$$

$$COV_{ij} = \sigma_i \times \sigma_j \times corr.coeff._{ij}$$

$$CV = \left(\frac{1{,}000}{CP}\right)P_s$$

$$\sigma_p = \sqrt{\sum_{i=1}^{N} W_i^2\sigma_i^2 + \sum_{\substack{i=1 \\ i \neq j}}^{N}\sum_{j=1}^{N} W_iW_jCov_{ij}}$$

Reprinted, with permission, from the CFP Board of Standards Guide to CFP® Certification booklet.

INDEX

D

E

F

G

H

I

J

L

M

N

O

P

R

S

T

U

V

W

Y

Income Tax Planning

Outlines and Study Guides

TABLE OF CONTENTS

TABLE OF EXHIBITS

Income Tax

I. BECOMING TAX SAVVY

A. REALIZE THAT TAX SAVINGS ARE ONLY PART OF THE STORY!

1. Focus on wealth maximization, not just tax savings. The objective of tax planning is to balance the net present value of the tax consequences of various alternatives with the objectives of the client.
2. The economic costs can be greater than the tax benefits of a transaction. Don't abandon good business sense just to decrease tax liability.
3. The risk of some investment opportunities may be unsuitable regardless of the tax benefits.

B. DISTINGUISH BETWEEN TAX AVOIDANCE VS. TAX EVASION.

1. Avoidance is working within the law to arrange financial affairs in order to minimize tax liability. Effective tax planning uses tax avoidance tools.
2. Evasion is the reduction of taxes through illegal means such as fraud. Tax evasion can result in fines and imprisonment.
3. Sometimes the line between avoidance and evasion becomes blurred. A taxpayer who is both ill informed and very aggressive sometimes loses sight of the line entirely!

C. DISTINGUISH BETWEEN TAX-FREE VS. TAX-DEFERRED INCOME.

1. Tax-free income - Taxes are never levied on the income (e.g., interest income from tax-exempt municipal bonds or limited exclusion of gain from the sale of a personal residence).
2. Tax-deferred income - Taxes will eventually be paid, but no tax liability is due in the current year. Because of the time value of money, tax deferral is often considered good tax planning. However, future marginal income tax rates need to be considered to fully evaluate the desirability of tax deferral. One example of tax deferral is the deductible Traditional IRA. Tax is not currently paid on the contribution, but is due when distributed to the recipient.

D. DEVELOP A TAX ATTITUDE.

1. Maintaining good records on all transactions is essential. Examples:
   a. Sale of investments - A taxpayer has a choice when selling investments whether to use specific identification or assume first-in first-out (FIFO).
   b. Mutual funds - If capital gains or ordinary income are reinvested by the fund, the taxpayer needs to add the amount included in taxable income to the adjusted taxable basis each year or risk paying double taxes.
2. Maximize deductions and make sure proper documentation as prescribed by law is in place. For example, there are very specific documentation rules for business use of automobiles and for charitable contributions.
3. Think tax all year. Be continually aware of tax objectives, approximate tax liability, and required estimated payments.

4. Use a multi-year approach to planning. Projections of income, future events, and marginal tax brackets must be considered to optimize tax planning over multiple years.
5. Use available IRS publications, particularly Publication 17, "Your Federal Income Tax," and Publication 334, "Tax Guide for Small Business." These are now available on the Internet at www.irs.gov.
6. Consider year-end tax planning. Optimizing the timing of capital gains and losses, accelerating deductions and deferring income are examples of year-end tax planning for a client.
7. Consider the tax impact in all transactions, but remember not to let the tax tail wag the economic dog.

E. THE ROLE OF THE FINANCIAL ADVISER IN TAX MATTERS

1. Review the projected tax liability situation at year-end.
2. Review the prior years' tax returns and amend the returns where advantageous.
3. Develop plans for tax minimization consistent with other personal financial planning goals.

II. TAX LAW – LEGISLATIVE, ADMINISTRATIVE, AND JUDICIAL

A. STATUTORY SOURCES OF THE TAX LAW.

1. The Internal Revenue Code (IRC).
    a. The Internal Revenue Code is the highest source of authority.
    b. In 1939, Congress codified (separated and organized) the federal tax laws. The IRC was recodified in 1954. The Tax Reform Act of 1986 (TRA) renamed the 1954 code the Internal Revenue Code of 1986.
    c. The IRC is located in Title 26, with income taxes located in Subtitle A. IRC is normally quoted by code sections, which are typically broken down in sub-parts. For example, Section 150(e)(1)(A) cites Section 150, subsection (e), paragraph (1), and subparagraph (A).
    d. Because of cross-references, exception upon exception, and verbose language, the Code can sometimes be very difficult to interpret. Treasury Regulations (described below) can help taxpayers decipher the intent of the law.
2. Tax legislative process - Federal tax legislation usually originates in the House Ways and Means Committee and is submitted to the House of Representatives for approval or disapproval. Sometimes, a tax bill originates in the Senate as a rider to a nontax bill. The House-approved bills are submitted to the Senate Finance Committee and then to the entire Senate for approval. If approved with no changes, the bill is sent to the President for approval or veto. If the House and Senate versions differ, the Joint Conference Committee will iron out the differences and send the bill back to the House and Senate for approval before forwarding to the President for signature.
3. Each committee involved in the passage of a bill will prepare a Committee Report, which explains proposed changes and the rationale behind the changes. These reports are an important source of information where the tax law is ambiguous.
4. The Joint Committee on Taxation sometimes prepares a general explanation of tax legislation, referred to as the Blue Book.
5. Objective of treaties - The U.S. is a partner to over 40 income tax treaties with other countries. The primary purpose of these treaties is to establish primary taxing authority. When treaties conflict with the IRC, the Technical and Miscellaneous Revenue Act of 1988 provides that the most recent prevails. Anytime a taxpayer takes a position where treaty overrides law, the return must disclose the conflict or a penalty may apply.

B. ADMINISTRATIVE SOURCES OF THE TAX LAW.

1. Treasury Department Regulations - The U.S. Treasury Department interprets the Code and issues Regulations that are the highest source of authority next to the Code. Regulations have the full force and effect of the law. Income tax regulations are cited by the number 1, followed by the applicable code section. For example, a regulation dealing with Code Section 72 would be cited as Reg 1.72.
2. Revenue Rulings - Revenue Rulings provide interpretations of the tax law with regard to taxable income, deductions, and credits. They are issued by the National Office of the IRS to deal with problems more specific than Regulations. Rulings do **not** have the full force of law and do not carry the force and effect of Regulations but can be cited as precedent. They are published by the government to give guidance to IRS personnel and taxpayers.

a. Rulings are identified by the year released and the ruling number for the year. For example, Rev. Rul. 99-28 was the 28th ruling released in 1999. This Revenue Ruling reversed an IRS long-standing position that "stop smoking" programs were not deductible medical expenses. Now these programs, along with drugs prescribed to alleviate the symptoms of nicotine withdrawal, are considered deductible medical expenses by the IRS.

b. Before relying on a Revenue Ruling as support, care should be taken that the ruling has not been affected by subsequent law changes, administrative rulings, or judicial decisions.

3. Revenue Procedures - Revenue Procedures explain the internal management practices and procedures of the IRS.

   a. Often, the IRS uses Revenue Procedures to distribute information to the general public. For example, tax tables and inflation-indexed amounts are released to the public in the form of a Revenue Procedure.

   b. Like Revenue Rulings, Revenue Procedures are identified by year issued and number of issue (e.g., Rev. Proc. 2000-01 which gives user fees for letter rulings).

4. Letter Rulings - three types.

   a. Private Letter Ruling (PLR) - At the request of the taxpayer, the IRS will describe its position on a specific tax issue (typically a proposed transaction). Although a PLR applies only to the taxpayer who requested it, PLRs are considered substantial authority for the purpose of avoiding accuracy-related penalties. The IRS does not officially publish PLRs. They do purge the PLRs of any identifying taxpayer information and make them available to commercial sources who, in turn, make them available to the general public. PLR cannot be cited as precedent by anyone other than the taxpayer who requested the ruling, but can provide guidance to the IRS's position on specific topics.

   b. Determination Letters - Similar to PLRs, Determination Letters are issued by District Directors. They usually involve completed transactions rather than proposed transactions. They are not published by the IRS but may be available from other sources.

   c. Technical Advice Memorandum (TAMs) – This is a ruling from the IRS National Office usually prompted by a request from an agent performing an audit when there is need for clarification that cannot be provided by the local office. The ruling concerns a completed transaction and only applies to the taxpayer whose audit prompted the ruling.

EXHIBIT 1: ADMINISTRATIVE SOURCES OF TAX LAW

Type	Issued By	Description
Regulation	U. S. Treasury	Full force and effect of law.
Revenue Ruling	National Office of the IRS	Addresses questions of income, deductions, and credits in the context of a specific set of facts.
Revenue Procedure	National Office of the IRS	Explains IRS practices and procedures. Used to distribute information to taxpayers.
Letter Ruling	National Office of the IRS	Issued in response and applies only to a taxpayer request about a proposed transaction.
Determination Letter	District Director	Issued in response to a taxpayer request about a completed transaction.
Technical Advice Memorandum	National Office of the IRS	Requested by agent to clarify issue encountered in an audit in progress.

Note: All of the administrative sources of law listed above are considered to be sources of substantial authority for the purposes of the requirements of IRC Section 6662. This code section imposes a penalty on the substantial underpayment of tax except where the taxpayer has substantial authority for the position taken on the return.

C. JUDICIAL SOURCES OF TAX LAW.

1. The judicial process.
   a. Any tax-related dispute that cannot be resolved by the taxpayer and the IRS or by using the administrative review process may be taken to the Federal Courts. If not resolved by a court of original jurisdiction (trial court), an appeal may be made and taken to the appropriate appellate court.
2. The federal judicial system has three trial courts:
   a. The U.S. District Court.
      i. Hears cases on legal matters involving tax and nontax issues. Has one judge per court (typically a generalist), and is located in the taxpayer's jurisdiction. A jury trial is available in this court.
      ii. The taxpayer must first pay any deficiency assessed and then sue for a refund. The taxpayer is the plaintiff in such a civil matter.
      iii. This is usually where a taxpayer would take an emotional issue rather than a technical issue.
      iv. Decisions can vary significantly among the different districts.

b. The U.S. Court of Federal Claims.

   i. Decides monetary claims against the United States, has 16 judges, and has a nationwide jurisdiction. A jury trial is not available in this court.

   ii. The taxpayer must first pay any deficiency assessed and then sue for a refund. The taxpayer is the plaintiff in such a civil matter.

   iii. Must follow only appeals decisions rendered by the Federal District of the Court of Appeals, not the Circuit Court of Appeals.

c. The U.S. Tax Court.

   i. Decides tax cases only, has 19 judges, and has nationwide jurisdiction. A jury trial is not available in this court.

   ii. The taxpayer does not have to pay the deficiency prior to trial. Payment will only become due if there is an adverse judgment.

   iii. The Small Cases Division of the U.S. Tax Court decides cases where the amount in dispute does not exceed $50,000. There is no appeal from the Small Cases Division of the U.S. Tax Court. Decisions of the Small Cases Division have no precedential value.

3. Appellate courts.

   a. There are 11 geographical circuit courts of appeals (usually referred to by circuit number and hearing cases originating in specified states), the Washington, D.C. Court of Appeals, and the Court of Appeals for the Federal Circuit.

   b. The location of an appeal will depend on where the litigation originated.

   c. District Courts, the Tax Court and the Court of Federal Claims must follow the precedents set by the Court of Appeals of their jurisdiction. In other words, the Tax Court and the U.S. District Court follow the precedents set in the appeals court in the taxpayer's home circuit. The Court of Federal Claims must follow decisions of the Court of Appeals for the Federal Circuit.

   d. A Court of Appeals in one jurisdiction is not required to follow the decisions of a Court of Appeals in another jurisdiction.

   e. All courts must follow the decisions of the U.S. Supreme Court. The Supreme Court infrequently hears tax cases, as most major cases are settled in the appellate or lower courts.

EXHIBIT 2: THE JUDICIAL PROCESS

	U.S. District Court	U.S. Court of Federal Claims	U.S. Tax Court	U.S. Tax Court, Small Claims Division
Number of Courts	95	1	1	1
Number of Judges	1 (per court)	16	19	19
Jurisdiction	District	National	National	National
Subject Matter	Criminal and Civil	Claims against Government	Tax only	Tax only
When to Use?	Emotional issue	District court has ruled unfavorably on the issue	Technical tax issue	Deficiency is less than $50,000
Pay Deficiency First?	Yes	Yes	No	No
Jury Available?	Yes	No	No	No
Appeal	U.S. Court of Appeals	U.S. Court of Appeals - Federal Circuit	U.S. Court of Appeals	None

Example

If John lost his tax case in the U.S. District Court he would appeal to the U.S. Court of Appeals. Appeals from the U.S. District Court go to the taxpayer's home circuit of the U.S. Court of Appeals.

III. TAX RATES AND BRACKETS

A. RATES AND BRACKETS.

1. The following exhibit represents the 2003 tax rates and brackets.

EXHIBIT 3: 2003 TAX RATES AND BRACKETS

Single – Schedule X

If taxable income is: Over --	But not over --	The tax is:	Of the amount over --
$0	$6,000	--------------- 10%	$0
6,000	28,400	$600.00 + 15%	6,000
28,400	68,800	3,960.00 + 27%	28,400
68,800	143,500	14,868.00 + 30%	68,800
143,500	311,950	37,278.00 + 35%	143,500
311,950	------------	96,235.50 + 38.6%	311,950

Head of Household – Schedule Z

If taxable income is: Over --	But not over --	The tax is:	Of the amount over --
$0	$10,000	--------------- 10%	$0
10,000	38,050	$1,000.00 + 15%	10,000
38,050	98,250	5,207.50 + 27%	38,050
98,250	159,100	21,461.50 + 30%	98,250
159,100	311,950	39,716.50 + 35%	159,100
311,950	------------	93,214.00 + 38.6%	311,950

Married Filing Jointly or Qualifying Widow(er) – Schedule Y-1

If taxable income is: Over --	But not over --	The tax is:	Of the amount over --
$0	$12,000	--------------- 10%	$0
12,000	47,450	$1,200.00 + 15%	12,000
47,450	114,650	6,517.50 + 27%	47,450
114,650	174,700	24,661.50 + 30%	114,650
174,700	311,950	42,676.50 + 35%	174,700
311,950	------------	90,714.00 + 38.6%	311,950

Married Filing Separately – Schedule Y-2

If taxable income is: Over --	But not over --	The tax is:	Of the amount over --
$0	$6,000	--------------- 10%	$0
6,000	23,725	$600.00 + 15%	6,000
23,725	57,325	3,258.75 + 27%	23,725
57,325	87,350	12,330.75 + 30%	57,325
87,350	155,975	21,338.25 + 35%	87,350
155,975	------------	45,357.00 + 38.6%	155,975

2. Taxpayers with taxable income less than $100,000 will use the tax tables provided by the IRS. All others use the tax schedules presented previously in Exhibit 3.

3. EGTRRA 2001.

   a. The regular income tax rates are reduced over a six-year period. The following table details the regular income tax rate reductions:

Calendar Year	28% Rate Reduced to:	31% Rate Reduced to:	36% Rate Reduced to:	39.6% Rate Reduced to:
2002 - 2003	27%	30%	35%	38.6%
2004 - 2005	26%	29%	34%	37.6%
2006 and later	25%	28%	33%	35%

   b. A ten percent rate applies to the first $6,000 of taxable income for single individuals and married couples filing separate returns ($7,000 for 2008 and thereafter), $10,000 of taxable income for heads of households, and $12,000 for married couples filing joint returns ($14,000 for 2008 and thereafter).

IV. BASIC TAX FORMULA AND INFLATION-ADJUSTED AMOUNTS

A. THE TAX FORMULA.

Income (broadly conceived)	$xx,xxx	
Less: Exclusions from Gross Income	(x,xxx)	*Section VI. Gross Income - Exclusions*
Gross Income	$xx,xxx	*Section V. Gross Income - Inclusions*
Less: Deductions for Adjusted Gross Income	(x,xxx)	*Section VII. Deductions for Adjusted Gross Income*
Adjusted Gross Income (AGI)	$xx,xxx	
Less: The Greater of--		
Total itemized deductions or standard deduction	(x,xxx)	*Section VIII. Basic Standard Deduction and Additional Standard Deductions*
Less: Personal and Dependency Exemptions	(x,xxx)	*Section IX. Personal and Dependency Exemptions*
Taxable Income	$xx,xxx	

B. REQUIRED PAYMENTS.

1. Employer must withhold income taxes and FICA (Social Security) taxes from an employee's paycheck.
2. Taxpayers who receive income that is not subject to withholding must make quarterly estimated payments.
   a. For calendar-year taxpayers, estimated payment due dates are 4/15, 6/15, 9/15 and 1/15 of the following year. If the 15th falls on a Saturday or Sunday, the due date will be the following Monday.
   b. To avoid an underpayment penalty, taxpayers must make estimated payments that are the lesser of:
      - 90% of the tax liability shown on the current year return.
      - 100% of tax liability shown on prior year return if AGI is $150,000 or less.
      - If AGI is > $150,000, then required payment based on prior year return is based on the following table:

Current Tax Year	% of Prior Year Tax
2003 and later	110%

3. No penalty is imposed if the taxpayer did not have a tax liability for the previous year.

EXHIBIT 4: EXEMPTIONS

Item	2003	Text Reference
Personal and Dependency Exemptions	$3,050	IX.A.
Exemption Phaseout begins at – Married/Joint	$209,250	IX.D.
Exemption Phaseout begins at – Single	$139,500	IX.D.
Exemption Phaseout begins at – Head of Household	$174,400	IX.D.
Exemption Phaseout begins at – Married/Separate	$104,625	IX.D.

EXHIBIT 5: STANDARD DEDUCTIONS/ADDITIONAL AMOUNT FOR OVER 65 AND BLIND

Item	2003 Basic Standard Deduction	2003 Additional Standard Deduction	Text Reference
Married/Joint	$7,950	$950	VIII.
Single	$4,750	$1,150	VIII.
Head of Household	$7,000	$1,150	VIII.
Married/Separate	$3,975	$950	VIII.
Standard Deduction for an Individual Claimed as a Dependent	$750	$1,150	X.D.

EXHIBIT 6: OTHER INFLATION-ADJUSTED AMOUNTS

Item	2003	Text Reference
Itemized Deduction Phaseout AGI threshold – Married/Joint, Single, and Head of Household	$139,500	XVII.H.
Itemized Deduction Phaseout AGI threshold – Married/Separate	$69,750	XVII.H.

V. GROSS INCOME - INCLUSIONS

A. DEFINITION.

1. Gross income is broadly defined as "all income from whatever source derived" (Code Section 61(a)). The following is a partial list of gross income:

EXHIBIT 7: ITEMS INCLUDED IN GROSS INCOME

- Alimony
- Annuities (partial)
- Awards
- Back pay
- Bargain purchase by employee
- Bonuses
- Breach of contract damages
- Business income
- Certain compensatory damages
- Clergy fees
- Commissions
- Compensation for services
- Death benefits from employer
- Debts forgiven
- Director fees
- Dividends
- Embezzled funds
- Employee awards
- Employee benefits - limited
- Estate and trust income
- Farm income
- Fees
- Gains from illegal activities
- Gains from sale of property
- Gambling winnings
- Cost of group term life insurance for coverage over $50,000
- Hobby income
- Interest
- Jury duty fees
- Living quarters, meals
- Mileage allowance
- Military pay
- Notary fees
- Partnership income
- Pensions
- Prizes
- Professional fees
- Punitive damages
- Rent
- Rewards
- Royalties
- Salaries
- Severance pay
- Strike and lockout benefits
- Supplemental unemployment
- Tips and gratuities
- Travel allowance
- Unemployment compensation
- Wages

2. An economic view of income is the change in the taxpayer's net worth, in terms of market value, plus the value of assets consumed during the period. It is not used for tax purposes. Rather, an accounting method is used that includes cash basis and accrual-basis concepts of income.
3. Gross income is not limited to cash received. It may be realized in any form, whether in money, property, or services.
4. When a taxable sale or exchange occurs, the seller is permitted to recover his or her investment (or other adjusted basis) in the property before gain or loss is recognized.

B. ACCOUNTING PERIODS.

1. In General:

   a. Taxable income is generally computed based on an annual accounting period, known as a taxable year.

   b. A taxable year is the annual period over which income is measured for income tax purposes.

   c. A calendar year is a 12-month period ending on December 31. Most individuals and many businesses use a calendar year.

   d. A fiscal year is a 12-month period ending on the last day of any month other than December. Many businesses use a fiscal year based on the natural business year (i.e., schools).

2. Requirements.

   a. All taxpayers may use a calendar year. A fiscal year may be adopted only by taxpayers who maintain adequate records.

   b. The accounting period is initially established when an individual or business files its initial income tax return. Once the accounting period has been established, the taxpayer cannot change it without IRS consent.

3. Tax year for business entities.

   a. Partnerships – must generally use the same tax year as the tax year of the partners, unless the partnership can establish a business purpose for having a different tax year.

   b. S corporations – must generally use the calendar year, unless the S corporation can establish a business purpose for having a different tax year.

   c. If a partner or S corporation shareholder has a different tax year than the partnership or S corporation, the partner or shareholder must report their share of the entity's income in their taxable year within which the entity's tax year ends.

Example

Orentlich Partners is a partnership with a fiscal year ending on September 30. Bethany, a 20% partner in the partnership, is a calendar year individual taxpayer. For the taxable year ending September 30, 2003, Orentlich had operating income of $100,000. Orentlich also had operating income of $30,000 for the period of October 1, 2003, through December 31, 2003. Bethany must report $20,000 (20% partnership interest x $100,000 partnership income) on her year 2003 income tax return. Any income earned by the partnership from October 2003 through December 2003 will be reported on Bethany's 2004 tax return.

C. ACCOUNTING METHODS.

1. Cash method.

   a. Taxpayer generally reports income when cash is collected (or taxpayer has constructive receipt) and reports expenses when cash payments are made.

   b. For fixed assets, the cash-basis taxpayer claims a deduction through depreciation in the same manner as an accrual-basis taxpayer.

c. Prepaid expenses must be capitalized and amortized if the life of the asset extends "substantially beyond" the end of the tax year.

d. The cash method can be used by:

   i. Individuals.

   ii. Partnerships that do not have C corporations as partners.

   iii. Corporations or partnerships, if annual gross receipts for all prior years do not exceed $5 million.

   iv. Certain farming businesses.

   v. Qualified personal services corporations in the fields of accounting, law, engineering, health, consulting, architecture, actuarial science, or performing arts.

e. Exceptions for Cash-Method Taxpayers.

   i. Constructive receipt - If income is available, it is subject to income tax even though it is not physically in the taxpayer's possession. An example of this is accrued interest on a savings account. Under the constructive receipt of income concept, the interest is taxed to the depositor in the year it is available rather than the year actually withdrawn.

   ii. Series E and Series EE bonds - The income on these savings bonds can be tax deferred. A cash-basis taxpayer has the choice to either (1) defer income recognition until maturity or redemption, or (2) elect to include in gross income the annual increment in redemption value.

      A) When a taxpayer elects to report the income from the bonds on an annual basis, the election applies to all such bonds the taxpayer owns at the time of the election.

      B) If a cash-basis taxpayer has not made the election to report interest currently on Series E or EE bonds held, he may exchange these bonds within one month of their maturity date for HH bonds, and defer interest recognition until the HH bonds mature.

   iii. Original issue discount - Under the general rules, the cash-basis taxpayer would not report the original issue discount (the difference between the original loan and the amount due at maturity) as interest income until the year the amount is collected, although an accrual-basis taxpayer would claim the interest as it is earned. However, the Code treats cash-basis and accrual-basis taxpayers the same by requiring that the original issue discount be reported when it is earned regardless of the accounting method.

   iv. Amounts received under an obligation to repay - No income is realized in receipt of borrowed funds. Receipt of funds is not necessarily a taxable event. For example, a deposit on equipment rental is not taxable until forfeited.

Example

Peggy, a cash-basis taxpayer, has the following items of income for 2003:

- Salary $40,000.
- $5,000 Bonus check issued and available at payroll office (but not picked up until 1/5/04).
- Borrowed $10,000 on a home equity line.
- Original Issue Discount corporate bond, accrual amount of $2,000.
- A U.S. savings bond that increased in redemption value by $200. Last year she elected to include the annual increment in redemption value in income.

Her gross income for the year is:

Salary	$40,000	
Bonus	5,000	(included because it was available)
OID	2,000	(although not received in cash, this is an exception for cash-basis taxpayer)
Savings bond	200	(she must be consistent in her election on this bond)
Total gross income	$47,200	

The proceeds on the home equity line are not included in gross income because Peggy is obligated to repay.

2. Accrual Method.

   a. This method reports expenses when incurred and income when earned for any single tax year.

   b. Expenses do not have to be paid to be deductible, nor does income have to be received to be taxable. The controlling factor for the accrual method is when the income was earned or the expenses incurred.

   c. Exceptions for Accrual-Basis Taxpayers.

      i. Prepaid income - For tax purposes, prepaid income is taxed in the year of receipt. Prepaid rents and prepaid interest may not be deferred by the accrual-basis taxpayer.

      ii. Deferral of advance payments for goods - A taxpayer can elect to defer recognition of income for advance payments for goods if the method of accounting for the sale is the same for tax and financial reporting.

      iii. Deferral of advance payments for services - Taxpayers can defer recognition of income for advance payments for services to be performed by the end of the tax year following the year of receipt. No deferral is allowed if the taxpayer might be required to perform any services after the tax year following the receipt of the advance payment.

Examples

- Julia, an accrual-basis taxpayer, owns an office building. On December 1, 2003, she rented the unit to a tenant that had a rather shaky credit history. As a result, she asked him for a year's rent in advance that amounted to $18,000. Julia must claim the entire $18,000 rent in 2003.

- Johnny Rocket, an accrual-basis taxpayer, runs a pool maintenance business. In December 2003, he signed an 18-month contract with a customer and received full payment of $9,000. Since services will be performed after 2004 (the tax year following year of receipt), the entire $9,000 is taxable in 2003. If instead, Johnny had signed a 12-month contract for $6,000, then $500 would be taxable in 2003 and $5,500 in 2004.

3. Long-Term Contracts.

   a. In General.

      i. A long-term contract is any contract for the manufacture, building, installation, or construction of property.

      ii. To be considered a long-term contract, the contract must not be completed within the same year it was entered into.

      iii. If the contract is a manufacturing contract, it will only be considered a long-term contract if it involves the manufacture of a unique item not normally carried in inventory (such as machinery) and normally requires more than 12 months to manufacture.

      iv. Generally, long-term contracts must be accounted for using the percentage-of-completion method. However, home construction contracts and contracts of small businesses can be accounted for using the completed contract method.

   b. Percentage-of-Completion Method.

      i. Requires the taxpayer to recognize a portion of the gross profit on the contract based on the estimated percentage of the contract completed.

      ii. The portion of the contract price reportable in a given year is based on the following ratio:

$$\text{Total contract price} \times \frac{\text{Costs incurred during the current period}}{\text{Total estimated costs for the contract}}$$

Example

In September 2003, Johnson Corporation entered into a contract to build a hotel that will be completed by December 2004. The contract price was $2,000,000, and the estimated costs of construction were $1,000,000. During 2003, actual costs incurred were $600,000. In 2003,4 the hotel was completed at a total cost of $1,100,000. Johnson Corporation will report the following income in 2003 and 2004:

	2003	2004
Revenue reported on tax return	$1,200,000 *	$800,000
(Costs)	(600,000)	(500,000)
Net income	$600,000	$300,000

*($600,000 ÷ $1,000,000) = 60% x $2,000,000 = $1,200,000

iii. If less than 10% of the total estimated contract costs have been incurred, the taxpayer may choose to defer reporting of the revenue until the year in which the 10% threshold has been reached.

iv. If the percentage-of-completion method is used for a contract, special "look-back" provisions apply in the tax year the contract is completed.

A) Annual income must be recomputed based on actual final costs rather than estimated costs.

B) Interest will be owed by or payable to the taxpayer if there was an underpayment or overpayment for any tax year.

Example

Assuming the same facts in the previous example, Johnson Corporation's income should have been $490,000 in 2003, as calculated below. Johnson overstated income by $110,000 ($600,000 reported - $490,000). As a result, the IRS is required to pay Johnson interest on the overpayment of the related tax.

	2003
Revenue based on actual costs	$1,090,000*
(Costs)	(600,000)
Net income	$490,000

*($600,000 ÷ $1,100,000) = 54.5% x $2,000,000 = $1,090,000

c. Completed Contract Method.

i. The completed contract method allows the taxpayer to defer revenue recognition until the contract is completed.

ii. The completed contract method can only be used in two situations:

A) Home construction contracts - at least 80% of the costs are related to buildings containing no more than four dwelling units.

B) Small contractors - contracts completed within two years by contractors with average annual gross receipts (for the last three years) of $10,000,000 or less.

d. Alternative Minimum Tax (AMT) Consequences.

i. The percentage-of-completion method must be used for AMT purposes, except for home construction contracts, which can use the completed contract method for AMT purposes.

ii. If a small contractor uses the completed contract method for regular tax purposes, there will be an AMT adjustment required each year of the contract.

iii. There is no AMT adjustment required for home construction contracts, since they can be accounted for using the completed contract method for both regular tax and AMT purposes.

4. Installment Sales.

a. See Section XX. Property Transactions - Topic L - "Installment Sales" on page 685 for details on the installment method of accounting.

5. Hybrid method.

a. A combination of the accrual and the cash method of accounting.

b. The taxpayer may account for some items of income on the accrual method (e.g., sales) and other items on the cash method (e.g., interest income).

6. Accounting method changes.

a. Once an accounting method has been adopted, it cannot be changed without approval from the IRS.

b. Taxpayers requesting a change in accounting method must file Form 3115.

c. Changes in accounting methods may include:

i. A change from the cash to accrual method.

ii. A change in inventory valuation (FIFO to LIFO, etc.).

iii. A change from the completed contract method to the percentage-of-completion method for long-term contracts.

d. Taxpayers who change their method of accounting must make certain adjustments to income in the year of the change (or over a longer period, if certain conditions are met). The adjustments are necessary to prevent the omission or duplication of income or deductions.

Example

Kalfoglou Enterprises is a corporation that switched from the cash method of accounting to the accrual method of accounting this year. At the end of last year, the company's outstanding receivables were $40,000. If Kalfoglou Enterprises were allowed to switch to the accrual method of accounting without any income adjustment, $40,000 would completely escape taxation. Therefore, the company must report $40,000 in income in this year as a result of the change in accounting method.

e. A change in accounting method is different from a correction of an error on a tax return. An error, such as a mathematical mistake, can be corrected on an amended return without IRS approval.

D. INCOME SOURCES.

1. Personal services.

   a. When an employee renders services to his employer's customer, the employer is taxed on the income received from the customer. The employer then pays deductible compensation to the employee who has taxable compensation.

   b. Assignment of income.

      i. Under the assignment of income concept, a taxpayer cannot avoid income tax by assigning income earned to some other person or entity.

Example

Jill, who is in the highest income tax bracket, directs her employer to pay $18,000 of her salary to her son, who is a college student in the lowest income tax bracket. Jill cannot assign the income to her son because Jill earned it. Her W-2 will include the $18,000 and she may have to file a gift tax return.

2. Income from property - Income from property (such as stocks, bonds, and rental property) must be included in the gross income of the owner of the property. This discourages, for example, owners giving away coupons from bearer bonds prior to the payment date.

   a. Interest is accrued daily.

   b. Dividends are paid at the discretion of the corporation and, unlike interest, do not accrue daily. They accrue after declaration and date of record.

   c. Dividends are taxed to the person who is entitled to receive them. If a taxpayer sells stock after a dividend has been declared but before the record date, the dividend will be taxed to the purchaser, instead of the seller (date of record is controlling).

   d. The income-producing property must also be assigned for the income to be taxed to the assignee.

Examples

- Joe, a taxpayer in the highest income tax bracket, owns a rental property that generates \$2,000 of rental income per month. Joe instructs the tenant of his rental property to pay the rent to Joe's daughter, Mary, who is in the 15% income tax bracket.

  Since Joe owns the rental property, the payment of rent to his daughter will be an assignment of income. Joe will be taxed on the rental income, even though his daughter received the actual payments.

- Cornelius owns 20 shares of Qualco stock. Qualco declares a dividend on September 1, for shareholders of record September 15, payable October 15. If Cornelius sells his shares on September 16, he will still have dividend income, even though he did not own the stock at the dividend payment date, because he held it on the date of record.

3. Income from partnerships, S corporations, trusts and estates.
   a. Partnerships and S corporations are pass-through entities.
   b. Income from partnerships is taxed to the partners at their own individual rates. The partnership must file an informational return (Form 1065).
   c. The shareholders, rather than the corporation, pay the tax on an S corporation's income. An S corporation files Form 1120S.
   d. The beneficiaries of estates and trusts generally are taxed on income that is distributed from the trust. Any income not distributed is taxed to the estate or trust, according to the trust tax schedule.

Example

Carla is a calendar-year taxpayer. She receives a K-1 on March 1, 2003, from a partnership that has a January 31 year end. The income will be included on her 2003 tax return, since she must report partnership distributive share for the partnership tax year ending in her tax year.

4. Income in community property states.
   a. Arizona, California, Idaho, Louisiana, Nevada, New Mexico, Texas, Washington, and Wisconsin are community property states. All other states are common law states.
   b. In a community property state, one-half of the earnings of each spouse is considered owned by the other spouse (a one-half undivided individual interest).

c. Community property spouses living apart - A spouse (or former spouse) will be taxed only on actual earnings from personal services if all of the following conditions are met:

i. The spouses live apart for the entire year.

ii. They do not file a joint return.

iii. No portion of the earned income was transferred between the spouses.

E. ALIMONY AND SEPARATE MAINTENANCE PAYMENTS.

1. Alimony and separate maintenance payments are deductible by the payor and are includible in the gross income of the payee.

2. Post-1984 divorce agreements and decrees.

a. To avoid confusing alimony (a taxable event) and property settlements (a nontaxable event), Congress developed rules to classify the payments. Payments are classified as alimony only if all of the following conditions are satisfied:

i. The payments are made in cash.

ii. The agreement or decree does not specify that the payments are not alimony for federal income tax purposes.

iii. The payee and payor are not members of the same household at the time the payments are made.

iv. There is no liability to make the payments for any period after the death of the payee.

v. Paid directly to payee spouse or to third party for direct benefit of payee spouse (e.g., making the mortgage payment).

3. Front-loading (also referred to as alimony recapture).

a. A measure to discourage disguising property settlements as alimony.

b. If there is more than a $15,000 decrease in alimony payments between any of the first 3 years, there may be alimony recapture.

c. The formula to calculate alimony recapture is as follows (this formula is the same as the one in the Code but uses different variable names). *Note: R_2 cannot be less than zero. If you get a negative number, then you set equal to zero*

$$R_3 = R_1 + R_2$$

$$R_2 = P_2 - (P_3 + 15{,}000)$$

$$R_1 = P_1 - \left[\frac{(P_2 - R_2 + P_3)}{2} + \$15{,}000\right]$$

R_1 = Recapture Year 1 P_1 = Payments Year 1

R_2 = Recapture Year 2 P_2 - Payments Year 2

R_3 = Recapture Year 3 P_3 = Payments Year 3

d. Alimony recapture affects the third year of alimony payments only. R_3 will be claimed as income by the original payor and claimed as a deduction from income by the payee. In other words, the effect of the original transaction is reversed.

Example

Ann and Mark divorce in 2002. Mark will make the following alimony payments:

2002	$60,000
2003	$40,000
2004	$20,000
2005	$40,000

Recapture is calculated as follows:

$$R_2 = \$40{,}000 - (\$20{,}000 + \$15{,}000) = \$5{,}000$$

$$R_1 = \$60{,}000 - \left[\frac{(\$40{,}000 - \$5{,}000 + \$20{,}000)}{2} + \$15{,}000\right] = \$17{,}500$$

$$R_3 = \$5{,}000 + \$17{,}500 = \$22{,}500$$

In 2004, Mark will include $22,500 in gross income, and Ann will have a $22,500 deduction for AGI.

Shortcut Method (the easy way):*

$R_3 = P_1 + P_2 - 2P_3 - \$37{,}500$

$R_3 = \$60{,}000 + \$40{,}000 - (2 \times \$20{,}000) - \$37{,}500$

$R_3 = \$22{,}500$

*The shortcut method will not always work, but may be used to help estimate recapture when there are three payments. For example, if there is not a full $15,000 decrease each year, then the formula will not work

e. Divorcing taxpayers may purposely create alimony recapture where the payer's income tax bracket in the third year is expected to be less than the bracket in the first year, and where the payee's bracket in the third year is expected to be greater than in the first year.

Example

Dave and Sue's divorce became final on January 2nd of the current year. Dave is an executive for a Fortune 500 company, and Sue is starting her own business this year. In the current year (Year 1 of the divorce agreement), Dave expects his marginal income tax rate to be 35%, while Sue's marginal income tax rate will be 27%, due to some initial expenses of her new business. Two years from now (Year 3 of the divorce agreement), Dave will retire, and will be in the 15% tax bracket, while Sue's business, a sole proprietorship, will cause her to be in the 37.6% tax bracket. Dave intentionally front-loaded his alimony payments to Sue ($60,000 in Year 1, $40,000 in Year 2, and $20,000 in Year 3), resulting in alimony recapture for Dave of $22,500 (see previous example for calculation of recapture amount) in Year 3.

In Year 1, Dave will get a deduction of $60,000, when his tax rate is 35%. Sue will include the alimony received in her gross income, when her tax rate is only 27%.

In Year 3, Dave must report (in his gross income) the alimony recapture of $22,500, when his tax rate will be only 15%. Sue would get a deduction of $22,500, when her tax rate is 37.6%.

F. CHILD SUPPORT.

1. Money received for child support is not includible in income by the payee and is not deductible by the payor.
2. Distinguishing alimony from child support is not always obvious! If payments are reduced when the child reaches a certain age, marries, or dies, the amount of the reduction is presumed to be child support, and the remainder is considered alimony if it meets the alimony criteria.

Example

As part of their divorce agreement, David must pay Michelle $4,000 per month. In five years, when their daughter attains age 18, the payments are reduced to $2,800 per month.

The reduction of $1,200 ($4,000 - $2,800) will be considered child support and will not be deductible by David.

G. INTEREST ON BELOW-MARKET LOANS.

1. Generally income is not recognized unless it is realized. However, in instances where a lender has issued a below-market-rate loan, the taxpayer may be required to recognize interest income (lender) and interest expense (borrower) when, in fact, none has been received or paid.
    a. Imputed interest is calculated using the federal government's borrowing rate, compounded semiannually and adjusted monthly.
    b. If the interest charged on the loan is less than the federal rate, the imputed interest is the amount of difference.
2. The imputed interest rules apply to the following types of below-market-rate loans:
    a. Gift loans - Made out of love, affection, or generosity. The lender has interest income and the borrower has interest expense to the extent of imputed interest. In addition, a gift has been made to the borrower in the amount of imputed interest.
    b. Compensation-related loans - Employer loans to employees. The corporation has interest income and compensation expense for the amount of the imputed interest. The borrower will have compensation income and interest expense (may or may not be deductible) for the same amount.
    c. Corporation-shareholder loans - A loan to a nonemployee shareholder by the corporation. The corporation will have interest income and a dividend distribution for the amount of the imputed interest. The shareholder/borrower will have dividend income and interest expense (may or may not be deductible) for the same amount.
    d. Tax avoidance loans - Loans that significantly affect the borrower or lender's federal tax liability.
3. There are exceptions and limitations to the imputed interest rules.
    a. No interest is imputed on total outstanding gift loans in the aggregate of $10,000 or less between individuals, unless the proceeds are used to purchase income-producing property.

b. On loans greater than or equal to $10,000 and less than or equal to $100,000 between individuals, the imputed interest cannot exceed the borrower's net investment income (from all sources) for the year. A further exception is carved out by law stating that if the borrower's net investment income for the year does not exceed $1,000, no interest is imputed on loans of $100,000 or less.

c. If the principal purpose of the loan is tax avoidance, none of the exceptions apply.

Example

On January 1, Richie loaned his daughter, Lori Beth, $90,000 to purchase a new personal residence. There were no other loans outstanding between Richie and Lori Beth. Lori Beth's only income was $30,000 salary and $4,000 interest income. Richie had investment income of $200,000. Richie did not charge Lori Beth interest. The relevant federal rate was 9%.

Richie must recognize imputed interest income of $4,000. The $100,000 exemption applies and, thus, Richie's imputed interest income (and Lori Beth's imputed interest expense) is limited to Lori Beth's net investment income. In addition, Richie is deemed to have made a gift to Lori Beth of $4,000. The gift will be eligible for the annual exclusion.

H. PRIZES AND AWARDS.

1. Cash and the fair market value of property of prizes and awards are included in gross income. Yes, if you win a dream vacation on a game show, the fair market value of your prize is income to you.
2. When the winner has an option of taking a lump sum or an annuity, if the annuity is chosen, current inclusion of the full value of the prize is not required.
3. If the winner receives the award for religious, charitable, scientific, educational, artistic, literary, or civic achievement <u>and</u> turns the proceeds over to a governmental unit or qualifying charity, the award may be excluded from income.

I. INCOME FROM ANNUITIES.

1. An annuitant pays a fixed sum to an insurance company to receive a stream of payments in the future.
2. As the value of the annuity increases, the annuitant does not report any income because it hasn't been constructively received.
3. Tax treatment of withdrawals before the scheduled annuity starting date.
   a. Withdrawals (including loans) on contracts issued after August 13, 1982, are included in gross income up to the total interest earned (LIFO basis recovery). Amounts received in excess of post-August 13, 1982 increases in cash value are treated as a recovery of capital until the taxpayer's cost has been entirely recovered. The taxpayer may also be subject to a 10% penalty for early withdrawals if under 59 1/2 years of age. This penalty would apply only to the taxable portion of the withdrawal.
   b. Collections before the annuity start date on contracts issued on 8/13/82 or earlier, are subject to FIFO tax treatment, so that adjusted taxable basis is received first and is not taxable.

4. Tax treatment of annuity payments received on and after the annuity starting date.
   a. The annuitant can exclude (as a recovery of capital) the proportion of each payment that the investment (cost) in the contract bears to the expected return under the contract. The exclusion amount is calculated as follows:

$$\frac{\text{Investment}}{\text{Expected Return}} \text{ x Annuity Payment = Exclusion Amount}$$

   b. To determine the amount taxable, subtract the exclusion amount from the total annuity payment received. For retirement plan distributions, the IRS provides a simplified method for calculating exclusions.

Example

Wendy, a 55-year-old woman, has begun receiving an annuity over her life expectancy of 25.5 years. She receives $1,500 per month. Her contributions to the annuity were after tax and amounted to $91,800. Payments began April 1st of this year. Wendy can exclude $2,700 of the annuity payments received this year.

Exclusion ratio is $91,800 ÷ ($1,500 x 12 x 25.5) = 20%.

20% x $1,500 x 9 months = $2,700.

J. GROUP TERM LIFE INSURANCE.

1. An employee can exclude premiums paid by the employee's employer on the first $50,000 of group term life insurance.
2. Only employees are eligible for this benefit (partners and proprietors and 72% S corporation owners are not employees).
3. If the group term life insurance amount exceeds $50,000, the taxable amount of the benefit is computed by applying the premium from the Uniform Premium Table to the excess coverage (see Exhibit 8: "Cost per $1,000 of Protection for One Month (Section 79)").
4. If the plan is discriminatory, key employees lose the $50,000 exclusion. They must include in income the greater of the actual cost of the insurance or the premium calculated using the Uniform Premium Table.

EXHIBIT 8: COST PER $1,000 OF PROTECTION FOR ONE MONTH (SECTION 79)

Age	Cost
Under 25	$0.05
25 through 29	$0.06
30 through 34	$0.08
35 through 39	$0.09
40 through 44	$0.10
45 through 49	$0.15
50 through 54	$0.23
55 through 59	$0.43
60 through 64	$0.66
65 through 69	$1.27
70 or older	$2.06

See Reg. 1.79-3(d)(2)

Example

Taxpayer is 51 years old and works for Employer A. Taxpayer's coverage with Employer A is $80,000. Taxpayer pays premiums of $50 a year under the Employer A group plan.

Figure the amount to include in the taxpayer's income as follows:

Employer A coverage (in thousands)	$80
Less: Exclusion (in thousands)	(50)
Excess amount (in thousands)	$30
Multiply by cost per $1,000 per month, age 51 (from table)	0.23
Cost of excess insurance for 1 month (0.23 x 30)	$6.90
Multiply by number of full months coverage at this cost	12
Cost of excess insurance for tax year	$82.80
Less: Premiums paid	(50.00)
Cost to include in income as wages (W-2)	**$32.80**

K. UNEMPLOYMENT COMPENSATION.

1. Unemployment compensation benefits are included in gross income (in lieu of wages).

L. SOCIAL SECURITY BENEFITS.

1. As much as 85% of Social Security benefits can be included in gross income.
2. The amount subject to tax is based upon the taxpayer's income exceeding a specified base amount.
3. The taxable amounts can be determined by one of two formulas using the modified adjusted gross income (MAGI).
4. MAGI is AGI from all sources (minus Social Security) plus the foreign income exclusion and any tax-exempt interest income.
5. Calculation of the taxable amount.
    a. Two base amounts are established:
        i. First base amount.
            A) $32,000 for married filing joint.
            B) $0 for married taxpayers who do not live apart for the entire year but file a separate return.
            C) $25,000 for all other taxpayers.
        ii. Second base amount.
            A) $44,000 for married individuals filing joint.
            B) $0 for married taxpayers who do not live apart for the entire year but file a separate return.
            C) $34,000 for all other taxpayers.
    b. If MAGI plus one-half of Social Security exceeds the first set of base amounts, but not the second set, the taxable amount of Social Security is the lesser of the following:
        i. 0.50 (Social Security Benefits), or
        ii. 0.50 (MAGI + 0.50 (Social Security) - base amount).
    c. If MAGI plus one-half of Social Security exceeds the second set of base amounts, the taxable amount of Social Security is the lesser of the following:
        i. 0.85 (Social Security Benefits), or
        ii. Sum of 0.85 (MAGI + 0.50 (Social Security) - second base amount), plus lesser of:
            - Amount included through application of the first formula.
            - $4,500 ($6,000 for married filing jointly).

M. FICA TAX.

1. FICA tax consists of the Social Security tax (OASDI) and the Medicare tax (HI).
2. For OASDI, a rate of 6.2% is applied to wages, with a base cap of $87,000 in 2003 (indexed to changes in average wages). Employers must match this rate for employees. Self employed pay a total OASDI rate of 12.4% on net income.
3. The Medicare tax has no ceiling for earnings subject to the hospital insurance portion (HI) of the Social Security tax. The HI tax is 1.45% for both the employee and the employer. Self-employed taxpayers pay 2.9% on net income.
4. Observations, illustrations, and planning tips.
   a. Although the OASDI portion still has the wage cap of $87,000 (2003), this cap may well be raised or eliminated by future legislation. This can significantly affect a taxpayer's take-home pay.
   b. When calculating self-employment tax, the taxpayer reduces net earnings from self-employment by 50% of the self-employment rate. In addition, the self-employed taxpayer gets to deduct one-half of the self-employment tax paid as a deduction for AGI.

PLANNING TIPS

1. Since S corporation earnings (other than salaries) are not considered self-employment income, they are not subject to FICA tax. It may be possible, in some cases, to decrease salaries to avoid a portion of the HI tax. However, the salaries paid must be reasonable.
2. Structure payments to reflect rental or interest income that is not subject to FICA. Note, however, that rental of personal property may be subject to FICA.
3. A shareholder in a personal service S corporation may want to accumulate funds in the S corporation, instead of personally, to avoid the increased FICA tax.

VI. GROSS INCOME - EXCLUSIONS

A. INTRODUCTION.

Only those items that are specifically excluded by statute are excludable from income. Generally, items excluded are those that are donative in nature, a return of capital, or that make you whole again, socially desirable, or are simply a matter of legislative grace, usually resulting from the lobbying efforts of a special interest group. Exhibit 9: "Exclusions from Gross Income" lists the exclusions from gross income.

EXHIBIT 9: EXCLUSIONS FROM GROSS INCOME

Items Characterized by Love, Affection, or Assistance
Gifts, bequests, and inheritances (Section 102) Scholarships (Section 117) Life insurance proceeds paid by reason of death (Section 101) Accelerated Death Benefits, including sale of policy to a viatical settlement provider (Section 101)
Personal and Welfare Items
Injury or sickness payments (Section 104) Amounts received under insurance contracts for certain living expenses (Section 123) Reimbursement for the costs of caring for a foster child (Section 131)
Employer-Provided Benefits
a. **Fringe Benefits** Accident and health benefits (Sections 105 and 106) Archer Medical Savings Accounts (Section 106) Long-term care insurance (Section 7702) Lodging and meals furnished for the convenience of the employer (Section 119) Employee achievement awards (Section 74(c)) Employer contributions to employee group term life insurance (Section 79) Cafeteria plans (Section 125) Educational assistance payments (Section 127) Child or dependent care (Section 129) Services provided to employees at no additional cost to the employer (Section 132) Employee discounts (Section 132) Working condition and de minimis fringes (Section 132) Athletic facilities provided to employees (Section 132) Qualified transportation fringe (Section 132) Tuition reductions granted to employees of educational institutions (Section 117) Adoption assistance (Section 137)
b. **Military Benefits** Combat pay (Section 112) Housing, uniforms, and other benefits (Section 134)
c. **Foreign Earned Income** Choice between foreign earned income exclusion and foreign income credit (Section 911)
Investments
Interest on state and local government obligations (Section 103) Gain exclusion (50%) for Small Business Stock (Section 1202)
Benefits for the Elderly
Social Security benefits (partial, see Section V.- Section L. Social Security Benefits. (Section 86)
Other Benefits
Income from discharge of indebtedness (Section 108) Recovery of a prior year's deduction that yielded no tax benefit (Section 111) Educational savings bonds (Section 135) Gain from sale of personal residence-$250,000 single exclusion; $500,000 for married filing joint (Sec. 121)

B. GIFTS, BEQUESTS, AND INHERITANCES.

1. A gift is defined by the courts as a voluntary transfer of property by one to another without adequate (valuable) consideration.
2. The recipient (donee) of a gift or inheritance is allowed to exclude the value of the property from gross income. However, the recipient of a gift of income-producing property is subject to tax on any income subsequently earned from the property.

C. SCHOLARSHIPS.

1. Scholarship recipients (must be a candidate for a degree) may exclude from gross income amounts used for tuition and related expenses (books, fees, but not room and board), provided the conditions of the grant do not require that the funds be used for other purposes.
2. If the scholarship is received in one year and spent in the subsequent year, the student does not have to include in income the amount in excess of qualified expenses until all expenditures have been made. The amount would be taken into income in the year resolution occurs.
3. Employees of nonprofit educational institutions are allowed to exclude a tuition waiver from gross income (generally undergraduate only), if the waiver is pursuant to a qualified tuition reduction plan.
4. Payments by a donor made directly to an educational institution are qualified payments, are not includible in the student's income, and are not subject to gift tax.

Example

- On June 1, 2003, Mark was awarded a full tuition scholarship for his freshman year at Dalton University. He began his freshman year in August 2003 and completed it in May 2004. One half of the tuition is due 8/1/2003 and one-half due 1/1/2004. Since the scholarship was for tuition only, nothing will be included in Mark's gross income in 2003 or 2004.

- On January 1, 2003, David was awarded a post-graduate fellowship grant of $6,000 by a tax-exempt educational organization. David is not a candidate for a degree and was awarded the grant to continue his research. The grant was awarded for the period August 1, 2003, through July 31, 2004. On August 1, 2003, David elected to receive the full amount of the grant.

  Since David is not a candidate for a degree, he must include all of the grant received on his 2003 tax return. The issue of proration between years is not relevant in this case, Prop. Reg. 1.117 - 6(b)(2).

D. LIFE INSURANCE PROCEEDS (PRESUMED GIFT).

1. In General.
   a. Proceeds paid to a beneficiary because of death of the insured are generally exempt from income tax.
   b. If the proceeds are received in installment payments, any interest income will be taxable.

Example

Susan, a widow, elected to receive the proceeds of a $200,000 face value insurance policy on the life of her deceased husband in ten annual installments of $22,000 each (beginning last year). In the current year, she received $22,000, which included $2,000 interest. Susan must include the $2,000 interest in her gross income.

2. Cashing in the policy before insured's death.
   a. If the owner cancels the policy and receives any cash surrender value, the owner must recognize the gain to the extent of the excess of the amount received over the cost basis of the policy.
   b. Losses are not deductible.
3. Transfer for valuable consideration.
   a. If an existing policy is transferred for valuable consideration, the insurance proceeds are includible in the gross income of the transferee to the extent the proceeds exceed their basis (amount paid for policy plus any subsequent premiums paid).
   b. There are five instances when the transfer of a policy will not result in loss of exclusion treatment. These include transfers to:
      i. The insured.
      ii. A partner of the insured.
      iii. A partnership in which the insured is a partner.
      iv. A corporation in which the insured is an officer or shareholder.
      v. A transferee (such as a child) whose basis in the policy is determined by reference to the transferor's basis (tax-free exchange or gift).
4. Viatical agreements (accelerated death benefits).
   a. Amounts received under a life insurance contract on the life of a terminally ill or chronically ill individual are excluded from gross income. The exclusion also applies to sale/assignment of a contract to a qualified "viatical" settlement provider.
   b. A terminally ill individual is an individual that has been certified by a physician as having an illness or condition that can reasonably be expected to result in death within 24 months of the date of certification.
   c. A chronically ill individual is generally a person who is unable to perform at least two activities of daily living (e.g., eating, bathing) for a period of at least 90 days. If the individual is chronically ill, the benefits will only be excluded from income to the extent they are used for long-term care services.

Example

Erwin Scott was recently diagnosed with a rare liver disorder and has been certified by his physician, on July 15 of the current year, as terminally ill. Erwin immediately resigned from his sales position with ABC Company and sold his life insurance policy with a face value of $500,000 to a viatical settlement provider (VSP) for $340,000. Erwin paid $30,000 in premiums over the last few years.

Since Erwin was certified as terminally ill, none of the proceeds he received from the VSP will be taxable to him. If instead he was certified as chronically ill, the proceeds would be excluded from his gross income only if the proceeds were used for long-term care services.

5. Modified endowment contract (MEC).
    a. An MEC is an insurance policy issued after June 21, 1988, that fails the seven-pay test.
        i. Seven-pay test - contract is an MEC if the premiums paid during the first 7 years of the contract exceed the total of the net level premiums that would have been paid if the policy provided for paid-up benefits after the 7th year.
    b. In the case of withdrawals or loans from the MEC, basis is recovered last (LIFO). As a result, withdrawals (including loans) to the extent of earnings are currently taxed. This is different from a traditional life insurance policy, which features FIFO basis recovery.
    c. If the intent of the purchase is to never borrow money against the MEC, it may be an effective estate planning tool because the classification as a MEC does not affect the taxation of the death benefit.

E. COMPENSATION FOR INJURIES AND ILLNESS.

1. Taxability of damages received.
    a. Compensatory damages.
        i. If the damages are awarded for physical injury or sickness, the damages are excludable from gross income (special damages).
        ii. Personal, nonphysical, damages (e.g., emotional distress, business reputation damages, breach of contract, age discrimination, sexual harassment, slander and libel, pain and suffering) must be included in gross income (general damages).
    b. Punitive damages are generally included in gross income.
2. Workers compensation amounts received are excluded by statute from gross income.
3. Taxation of accident and health insurance benefits (for accidents and illness) depends on whether the premiums were paid by the employer or the employee. Benefits collected under an accident and health insurance policy purchased by the taxpayer are excludable. For example, a taxpayer collects payments under a disability policy. If the taxpayer purchased the policy, the payments are not included in income. If the taxpayer's employer purchased the policy, the payments are included in income.

F. EMPLOYER-PROVIDED BENEFITS.

1. Accident and health plans.

   a. Premiums - Premiums paid by the employer for accident, health, and disability insurance policies are deductible for the employer and excludable from the employee's income.

   b. Benefits paid under employer-sponsored health and accident plans.

      i. If the payments are received for the medical care of the employee, spouse, or dependents, the payments are not included in the taxpayer's income.

      ii. Payments for permanent loss or the loss of the use of a member or function of the body or permanent disfigurement of the employee, spouse, or dependent are not included in the taxpayer's income.

      iii. Other insurance benefits collected are included in gross income.

      iv. If a taxpayer pays the cost of a disability policy with after-tax dollars, any subsequent benefits are not taxable. If the employer pays the premiums, the benefits are taxable. If the employer and taxpayer each pay a portion of the premium, there will be a fractional allocation to the nontaxed benefits based on contributions to the plan.

   c. Employees are not taxed on the value of coverage under a long-term care plan provided by their employer. This exclusion does not apply if coverage is reimbursed under a tax-free flexible spending plan or provided through a cafeteria plan.

   d. Contributions made by an employer to a medical savings plan are not included in the employee's income.

2. Meals and lodging.

   a. Excludable by employee if furnished by the employer on the business premises for the employer's convenience.

   b. If free lodging is an employee benefit, the employee must be required to accept it as a condition of employment in order to exclude it from his income.

Example

Tom is the manager of a hotel. To be available in emergency situations, Tom's employer requires that he live in one of the hotel rooms without charge. The value of the room is $1,500 per month if occupied each night. The hotel is ordinarily 70% occupied. If Tom did not live there, he would live in an apartment that would rent for $900 per month. The room is furnished for the convenience of the employer on the employer's premises. Therefore, Tom will not be required to report income.

---

3. Group term life insurance - See Section V.J. Group Term Life Insurance. on page 569.

4. Child and dependent care services - Employees can exclude up to $5,000 in child care expenses paid by their employer to enable the employee to work. If the taxpayer is married, the exclusion is limited to the income of the lesser-paid spouse. In addition, child care provided under a cafeteria plan is not eligible for the dependent care credit.

5. Athletic facility provided to employees - The value of a health facility or gymnasium provided by the employer on the premises solely for the use of employees is excluded from the employee's gross income. If the employer pays the health club dues of an employee, the dues are taxable to the employee.
6. Educational assistance.
   a. Qualified employer-provided educational assistance is excluded from gross income.
   b. The exclusion is subject to an annual ceiling of $5,250.
   c. The exclusion applies to both undergraduate and graduate education (TRA 2001).
   d. Cannot discriminate in favor of highly compensated employees.
7. Cafeteria plans.
   a. Under a cafeteria plan, an employer offers his employee the choice between cash or selected nontaxable benefits. If the employee chooses the benefit, it remains nontaxable. If the employee chooses cash equal to the cost of the benefit, the cash is included in income. A cafeteria plan can also provide employees an opportunity to buy certain benefits with after-tax contributions.
8. No additional cost services - Excluded from income under the following conditions:
   a. The employee receives services, not property.
   b. The employer does not incur substantial additional cost, including forgone revenue, in providing the services to the employee.
   c. The services are offered to customers in the ordinary course of the business in which the employee works (e.g., travel privileges for employees of an airline).
   d. Nondiscrimination provision - If the plan is discriminatory in favor of highly compensated employees, then the highly compensated are denied exclusion treatment.
9. Qualified employee discounts - When an employer offers goods or services to an employee at a discount, the discount can be excluded from income if:
   a. In the case of property, it is not real property or investment-type personal property.
   b. The property or services are offered in the same line of business in which the employee works.
   c. In the case of property, the exclusion is limited to the gross profit component of the price to customers.
   d. In the case of services, the exclusion is limited to 20% of the customer price.
   e. Nondiscrimination provision - If the plan is discriminatory in favor of highly compensated employees, then the highly compensated are denied exclusion treatment.
10. Working condition fringes - When an employer provides property or services to an employee that an employee could have deducted had she paid for them herself, the value of the property or services is a nontaxable fringe. Discrimination does not affect the exclusion status.

Example

Frances is a member of her state CPA society. Her employer pays the annual dues. This is a nontaxable fringe since Frances could have deducted it as an employee business expense had she paid them herself.

11. De minimis fringes - The benefits are so small that accounting for them is impractical. They are, therefore, excludable. For example, the personal use of a company-owned computer or copy machine is considered a nontaxable de minimis fringe benefit. Discrimination does not affect the exclusion status.
12. Qualified transportation fringes - To encourage mass transit for commuting to and from work, this fringe benefit is nontaxable and includes:
    a. Transportation in a commuter highway vehicle between the employee's residence and the place of work.
    b. A transit pass within limits.
    c. Qualified parking within limits.
    d. The dollar limits are adjusted annually for inflation.
13. Employer-Provided Adoption Assistance.
    a. Employer-provided adoption assistance can be excluded from an employee's income. The maximum exclusion is $10,000 per eligible child, including special needs children.
    b. Phaseout of adoption assistance. The adoption assistance exclusion is phased out beginning at modified AGI of $150,000 with complete phaseout at $190,000.
14. Employer-provided auto - Personal use of an employer-provided car is usually a taxable fringe benefit. The taxable amount is determined by the employer and included on the employee's W-2.
15. See Exhibit 10: "Summary of Fringe Benefits" for a summary of fringe benefit exclusions, along with the effect of discriminatory application.

EXHIBIT 10: SUMMARY OF FRINGE BENEFITS

Fringe Benefit	Exclusion	Effect of Discrimination in Favor of Highly Compensated
Premiums on employer-provided health insurance	Employee excludes from gross income	Highly compensated must include excess benefits in income
Employer-paid premiums on Group Term Life	Premiums paid on coverage up to $50,000 excluded	Key employees must include greater of actual cost or table cost in income
No additional cost services	Excluded as long as in line of business and no additional cost incurred	No exclusion for highly compensated employees if plan is discriminatory
Qualified employee discounts for goods	Excluded to extent discount does not exceed gross profit	No exclusion for highly compensated employees if plan is discriminatory
Qualified employee discounts for services	Exclusion limited to 20% of customer price	No exclusion for highly compensated employees if plan is discriminatory
Meals and lodging	Excluded if furnished by the employer on the business premises for employer's convenience Lodging must be a condition of employment	N/A
Employer-provided child and dependent care services	Exclude up to $5,000, limited to the income of the lesser-paid spouse	No exclusion for highly compensated employees if plan is discriminatory
Athletic facility provided to employees	Excluded if provided on employer's premises solely for use of employees	N/A
Educational assistance	Undergraduate and graduate, excluded up to $5,250/year	No exclusion for highly compensated employees if plan is discriminatory
Working condition fringes	Excluded if the expenses would have been deductible by the employee	No effect
De minimis fringes	Excluded if immaterial	No effect
Qualified transportation	Excluded with limit for transit passes, commuter van, and parking	No effect
Adoption assistance	Limit of $10,000 (2003) per child with AGI phaseout $150,000 - $190,000	No exclusion for highly compensated employees if plan is discriminatory

G. INVESTMENT RELATED.

1. Interest on certain state and local government obligations - The interest on state and local government obligations is exempt from federal income taxation. However, the exemption does not apply to gains on the sale of tax-exempt securities.
2. Educational savings bonds.
   a. A taxpayer may elect to exclude interest on Series EE U.S. government savings bonds from gross income if the bond proceeds are used to pay qualified higher education expenses.
   b. The following requirements must be met:
      i. The savings bonds are issued after December 31, 1989.
      ii. The savings bonds are issued to an individual who is at least 24 years old before the time of issuance.
      iii. The savings bonds are issued at a discount.
   c. It should also be noted that the exclusion does not apply for married couples filing separate returns.
   d. The exclusion is limited by a Modified AGI (MAGI) threshold. For 2003, the threshold begins at $87,750 on a joint return ($58,500 on others) and is completely phased out at $117,750 ($73,500 others).
3. Life insurance - The annual increase in the cash surrender value of the policy is not taxable. By borrowing on the policy's cash surrender value, the owner can actually receive the policy's increase in value in cash, without recognizing income.
4. Noncorporate investors can exclude up to 50% of the gain they realize on qualified small business stock (Section 1202). Any remaining gain is taxed at the 28% capital gains rate.
   a. The stock must be issued after 8/10/93.
   b. The stock must be held more than five years.
   c. Exclusion limited to greater of $10 million or ten times the taxpayer's basis in the stock.
   d. 42% of excluded amount of gain (21% of total gain) is a tax preference item for Alternative Minimum Tax (AMT) purposes. The preference percentage drops to 28% in the case of stock with a holding period that begins after 2000.

H. OTHER BENEFITS.

1. Tax benefit rule.
   a. A rule that limits the recognition of income from the recovery of an expense or loss properly deducted in a prior year to the amount of the deduction that generated the tax benefit. For example, a taxpayer who claims the standard deduction in 2002 receives a $500 state income tax refund in 2003. The refund is not taxable because the taxpayer did not deduct the state income taxes paid. If the taxpayer had claimed $12,000 of itemized deductions in 2002, the $500 refund would have been taxable in 2003.
   b. In other words, if a taxpayer obtains a deduction for an item in one year and in a later year recovers all or a portion of the prior deduction, the recovery is included in gross income in the year received (such as a state tax refund on taxes deducted in the prior year).

2. Income from discharge of indebtedness.
   a. Generally, if a lender forgives a borrower's debt, the borrower must report the forgiven debt as income.
   b. Bankrupt and insolvent taxpayers may exclude the income.
   c. If a taxpayer transfers appreciated property to satisfy a debt, income is realized. The transaction is treated as a sale of the appreciated property followed by payment of a debt.
   d. When a creditor forecloses on a piece of property, it is treated as a sale or exchange.
   e. In some special instances, the taxpayer is allowed to reduce the basis of the asset by the realized gain from discharge of debt. Included are discharge of qualified real property business indebtedness, a seller's cancellation of the buyer's indebtedness and forgiveness of student loans.
   f. Students who are granted loans which are forgiven in return for working in the state after graduation, do not have to include the debt forgiveness in their income.
3. Foreign earned income.
   a. The U.S. taxes all income of its citizens regardless of where it is earned. Without special provisions, U.S. taxpayers could be in danger of having non-U.S. income taxed twice, once by the U.S. and again by the foreign country.
   b. The following options are available to mitigate double taxation:
      i. Include the foreign income in taxable income and then claim a credit for foreign taxes paid, or
      ii. Exclude the foreign earnings from U.S. gross income, limited as follows:

Year	Maximum Exclusion
2002-2007	$80,000

   c. Foreign earned income is the earnings from the taxpayer's personal services in a foreign country.
   d. To qualify for the exclusion, the taxpayer must be either:
      i. A bona fide resident of the foreign country.
      ii. Present in a foreign country for at least 330 days during any 12 consecutive months.
   e. The exclusion is limited to an indexed amount per year. A taxpayer who is present in the country for less than the entire year must prorate the exclusion using the following formula:

$$\text{Maximum Exclusion x } \frac{\text{Number of days present in foreign country}}{\text{Number of days in entire year}}$$

   f. Taxpayers who live and work abroad may elect to exclude amounts for employer-provided foreign housing costs.

I. EDUCATIONAL INCENTIVES.

The TRA of '97 included several educational incentives that involve gross income exclusions for certain types of income and benefits.

1. Coverdell Education Savings Accounts (formerly Education IRA).

   a. Contributions.

      i. Up to $2,000 per beneficiary (under 18) may be contributed to a Coverdell Education Savings Account.

      ii. The contribution is phased out at certain Modified Adjusted Gross Income (MAGI) levels. MAGI is defined as AGI increased by any amounts excluded due to foreign earned income.

         A) The $2,000 contribution is phased out at the following MAGI levels:

Taxpayer Filing Status	MAGI Phaseout
Single	$95,000 – 110,000
Married Filing Jointly	$190,000 – 220,000

   b. Distributions and Rollovers.

      i. Distributions from such accounts used to pay qualified education expenses of an eligible student are excluded from income.

      ii. The amounts must be distributed to the beneficiary by age 30 if unused. Then, distributions are taxable and subject to 10% penalty.

      iii. A Coverdell Education Savings Account may be rolled over to the account of a new beneficiary who is a member of the same family free of taxation and the penalty.

      iv. A taxpayer may claim a HOPE credit or lifetime learning credit for a taxable year and also exclude from gross income amounts distributed from a Coverdell Education Savings Account on behalf of the same student, as long as the distribution is not used for the same educational expenses for which a credit is claimed.

   c. Qualified Education Expenses.

      i. Qualified education expenses include tuition, fees, books, supplies, and equipment required for the enrollment or attendance of the designated beneficiary at an eligible education institution.

      ii. Eligible education institutions generally include accredited post-secondary educational institutions offering credit toward a bachelor's degree, an associate's degree, a graduate-level or professional degree, or another recognized post-secondary credential.

      iii. EGTRRA expands the definition of qualified education expenses to include qualified elementary and secondary school expenses (kindergarten through grade 12).

2. Prepaid state tuition plans.

   a. Earnings on qualified tuition plans accumulate free from income tax.

   b. Distributions from qualified tuition programs are excluded from gross income to the extent that the distribution is used to pay for qualified higher education expenses.

   c. A taxpayer can claim a HOPE credit or lifetime learning credit for a taxable year and also exclude from gross income amounts distributed from a qualified tuition program on behalf of the same student (as long as the distribution is not used for the same expenses for which a credit is claimed).

   d. A transfer from one qualified tuition program for the benefit of a designated beneficiary to another qualified tuition program for the benefit of the same beneficiary (rollover) is not considered a distribution.

   e. See Retirement Planning outline for a discussion of tax incentives available through regular IRAs and Roth IRAs.

   f. See Section VII.K. Interest on Educational Loans on page 588 for a discussion of the deduction for student loan interest.

   g. See Section VI.F.7. Cafeteria Plans on page 579 for a discussion of employer-provided educational assistance.

VII. DEDUCTIONS FOR ADJUSTED GROSS INCOME

These deductions are subtracted from a taxpayer's gross income to arrive at adjusted gross income. Deductions for adjusted gross income (AGI) include:

A. ORDINARY AND NECESSARY EXPENSES INCURRED IN A TRADE OR BUSINESS.

1. Expenses related to a taxpayer's trade or business are deductions for AGI.
2. These expenses, along with the revenue from the business, are reported on Schedule C of an individual's Form 1040 if the individual is a sole proprietor.
3. Unreimbursed business expenses of an employee are deductible as miscellaneous itemized deductions, subject to the 2% of AGI floor.

B. ONE-HALF OF SELF-EMPLOYMENT TAX PAID.

1. To help mitigate the burden of paying both halves of FICA, self-employed individuals are allowed a deduction for AGI of one-half of self-employment tax paid.
2. For self-employed individuals, the self-employment tax is based on net income.

C. ALIMONY PAID TO TAXPAYER'S EX-SPOUSE.

1. Alimony paid to an ex-spouse is a deduction for AGI.
2. A spouse who receives alimony must include the alimony in taxable income.

D. PAYMENTS TO KEOGH AND SELF-EMPLOYED SEPS AND SIMPLE PLANS.

1. See the Retirement Planning Section for details of contribution limits, deductions, and distribution rules.
2. Keoghs must be established by year-end and funded by the extension due date. The maximum contribution is dependent on the type of plan.
3. SEPs must be established and funded by the extended due date of the employer. SEP contribution limits are covered in the Retirement Planning Section.

E. IRA CONTRIBUTIONS.

1. For 2003, taxpayers can contribute a maximum of $3,000 for themselves and $3,000 for their spouse (working or nonworking). If the contribution is made to a Traditional IRA, the contribution may be deductible. See the Retirement Planning Section for rules regarding the deductibility of contributions to a Traditional IRA.
2. Roth IRA contributions are never deductible.

F. MOVING EXPENSES.

1. General.
   a. Allowed with commencement of work at a new place.
   b. A new job must be at least 50 miles farther from the old residence than the old job.
      i. The location of the new residence is irrelevant.

Example

Davin moved to a new home less than 50 miles from his former home because he changed job locations. His old job was 3 miles from his former home. Davin's new job is 60 miles from the former home. Because Davin's new job is 57 miles farther from his former home than the distance from his former home to his old job, he meets the 50-mile distance test.

c. Must be employed full-time at the new job for 39 weeks during the next 52 weeks.

d. If self-employed, the requirement is 78 weeks of full-time work in the next 104 weeks.

2. Moving expenses include:

a. Moving of household goods and personal effects.

b. Travel to the new location (including lodging) and out-of-pocket travel of 12 cents per mile (for 2003).

i. No meal deduction is allowed.

ii. No house-hunting expenses are deductible.

iii. No temporary living expenses are deductible.

c. Tax treatment.

i. Qualified expenditures reimbursed/paid by the employer are not reported on the employee's Form W-2 (and employer payment is not included in income).

ii. Qualified, unreimbursed expenditures are deductible by the taxpayer for AGI.

iii. Unqualified expenditures paid by or reimbursed by the employer are included in the employee's gross income and deducted by the employer as compensation.

Example

Karen is transferred by her employer from New Orleans to Houston. Her expenses are not reimbursed and are as follows:

Cost of moving household furnishings	$1,600
Transportation costs	300
Meals en route	400
Lodging en route	250
	$2,550

Her qualified moving expenses are $2,150.

($1,600 + $300 + $250) = $2,150. Meals are not deductible while moving.

G. FORFEITED INTEREST PENALTY FOR PREMATURE WITHDRAWAL OF TIME DEPOSITS.

1. Any forfeited interest on withdrawals from CD's is deductible for AGI.

Example

Dan has immediate need for a large amount of cash and his most liquid asset is a 3-year CD that does not mature for 18 more months. When he redeems the CD early, the bank charges him 3 months interest as a penalty. The 3 months interest is reportable as income, but it is also a deduction for AGI.

H. CAPITAL LOSSES.

1. Capital losses can offset capital gains without limit.
2. Capital losses can offset ordinary income up to a maximum of $3,000 per year.
3. Unused capital losses are carried forward indefinitely. Capital losses cannot be carried back.

I. SELF-EMPLOYED HEALTH INSURANCE PREMIUMS.

1. Self-employed taxpayers and wage earners who are more-than-2% shareholders of an S corporation can take a limited deduction (not to exceed net earnings from self-employment) for amounts paid for health insurance for taxpayers, spouses, and dependents.

Year	Percentage of Expense Deductible
2002	70%
2003 and later	100%

J. CONTRIBUTIONS TO ARCHER MEDICAL SAVINGS ACCOUNT (ARCHER MSAS).

1. Employees of small employers and self-employed individuals with high deductible health insurance plans can make tax-deductible contributions to an Archer MSA and use the funds accumulated in the Archer MSA to pay medical expenses. If the employer makes the contributions, they are excluded from the employee's income.
2. Earnings generated by the plan are not taxable, and distributions from an Archer MSA used to pay medical expenses are not taxable.
3. Distributions not used for medical expenses are taxable and subject to a 15% penalty tax, unless made after age 65 or upon death or disability.

K. INTEREST ON EDUCATIONAL LOANS

1. In General.
   a. Interest paid on qualified education loans is deductible in arriving at adjusted gross income (above-the-line deduction).
   b. Loan proceeds must have been used for higher education tuition, fees, room, board, and other necessary expenses (e.g., transportation).
   c. The taxpayer may not be claimed as a dependent of another and deduct interest on education loans.

2. Limitations:

   a. The maximum allowable annual deduction is $2,500. The deduction is phased out at certain modified adjusted gross income (MAGI) levels.

   b. MAGI phaseout levels by filing status:

Filing Status	MAGI Phaseout
Single	$50,000 - $65,000
Married Filing Jointly	$100,000 - $130,000

L. DEDUCTION FOR QUALIFIED HIGHER EDUCATION EXPENSES.

1. In General.

   a. For tax years between 2002 and 2005, an above-the-line deduction is permitted for qualified higher education expenses paid by the taxpayer.

   b. Qualified higher education expenses are defined in the same manner as for purposes of the HOPE credit.

   c. Taxpayers are not eligible to claim the deduction and a HOPE credit or lifetime learning credit in the same year with respect to the same student.

   d. A taxpayer may not claim a deduction for amounts taken into account in determining the amount excludable due to a distribution from a Coverdell Education Savings Account (formerly Education IRA) or the amount of interest excludable with respect to education savings bonds.

   e. A taxpayer may not claim a deduction for the amount of a distribution from a qualified tuition plan that is excludable from income.

2. Deduction Limits.

   a. In general, the maximum deduction is $3,000 for years 2002-2003, and $4,000 for years 2004-2005.

   b. The deduction is based on the taxpayer's filing status and AGI.

MAXIMUM DEDUCTION FOR UNMARRIED TAXPAYERS

AGI	Max Deduction 2003-2004	Max Deduction 2004-2005
\$0-\$65,000	\$3,000	\$4,000
\$65,001-\$80,000	\$0	\$2,000
> \$80,000	\$0	\$0

MAXIMUM DEDUCTION FOR MARRIED FILING JOINTLY TAXPAYERS

AGI	Max Deduction 2003-2004	Max Deduction 2004-2005
\$0-\$130,000	\$3,000	\$4,000
\$130,001-\$160,000	\$0	\$2,000
> \$160,000	\$0	\$0

M. EDUCATOR'S DEDUCTION FOR CLASSROOM EXPENSES

1. For 2002 and 2003, educators are permitted an above-the-line deduction of up to \$250 for unreimbursed expenses incurred in connection with books, supplies, computer equipment and software, and other materials used in the classroom.
2. Educators must work at least 900 hours in grades K-12 as a teacher, counselor, principal, or aide.

N. ADJUSTED GROSS INCOME (AGI).

1. This subtotal serves as the basis (amount) for computing percentage limitations on certain itemized deductions such as charitable (≤ 50% of AGI), medical (> 7.5% of AGI), casualty losses (> 10% of AGI) and miscellaneous itemized deductions (> 2% of AGI). AGI also serves as a benchmark for limiting total itemized deductions, personal and dependency exemptions, and passive rental real estate losses. Many states start their calculation of taxable income with federal AGI.

VIII. BASIC STANDARD DEDUCTION AND ADDITIONAL STANDARD DEDUCTIONS

A. BASIC STANDARD DEDUCTION.

1. Basic standard deduction amounts are based on filing status.

EXHIBIT 11: STANDARD DEDUCTION AMOUNT

Filing Status	2003
Single	4,750
Married filing jointly	7,950
Qualifying widow(er)	7,950
Head of household	7,000
Married filing separately	3,975

2. Beginning in 2005, the basic standard deduction for married filing joint taxpayers will be increased. By 2009, the basic standard deduction for married filing joint will be double the basic standard deduction for single taxpayers (TRA 2001). The deduction will be increased based on the following schedule:

EXHIBIT 12: INCREASE OF STANDARD DEDUCTION FOR MARRIED FILING JOINTLY

Calendar Year	Standard Deduction for Joint Filers as % of Standard Deduction for Single Filers
2005	174%
2006	184%
2007	187%
2008	190%
2009 and later	200%

B. ADDITIONAL STANDARD DEDUCTION.

1. A taxpayer who is age 65 or blind qualifies for an additional standard deduction depending on the filing status. Two additional standard deductions are allowed for a taxpayer who is age 65 and blind.

EXHIBIT 13: AMOUNT OF EACH ADDITIONAL STANDARD DEDUCTION

Filing Status	2003
Single	1,150
Married, filing jointly	950
Qualifying widow(er)	950
Head of household	1,150
Married filing separately	950

Example

The 2003 standard deduction for a taxpayer who is age 55, single, and blind is $5,900 ($4,750 + $1,150).

The 2003 standard deduction for a married couple where both are 68 years old and both are blind is $11,750 [$7,950 + (4 x 950)].

IX. PERSONAL AND DEPENDENCY EXEMPTIONS

A. PERSONAL EXEMPTIONS.

1. One for the taxpayer and one for the spouse if a joint return is filed ($3,050 each for 2003).

B. DEPENDENCY EXEMPTIONS.

1. There are five tests.
    a. Support (over 50%, except multiple support agreement).
    b. Relationship or member of your household (relationship extends to but does not include cousins). Stepfather/mother/son/daughter are considered relatives, as are father/mother/son/daughter-in-law. A foster child is considered a relative if the taxpayer's household is the child's principal place of residence.
    c. Gross income must be less than the exemption amount, except if a child of the taxpayer is under 19 or if the child is a full-time student and under the age of 24, in which case the gross income test is waived.
    d. No joint return (if married) except to receive a refund of all tax withheld (not required to file).
    e. Citizenship (either a U.S. citizen, or a resident of the U.S., Canada, or Mexico).
2. As long as all the tests are met, a dependency exemption can be taken for a person who is born or dies during the year, without any reduction.

EXHIBIT 14: DEPENDENCY EXEMPTION FLOW DIAGRAM

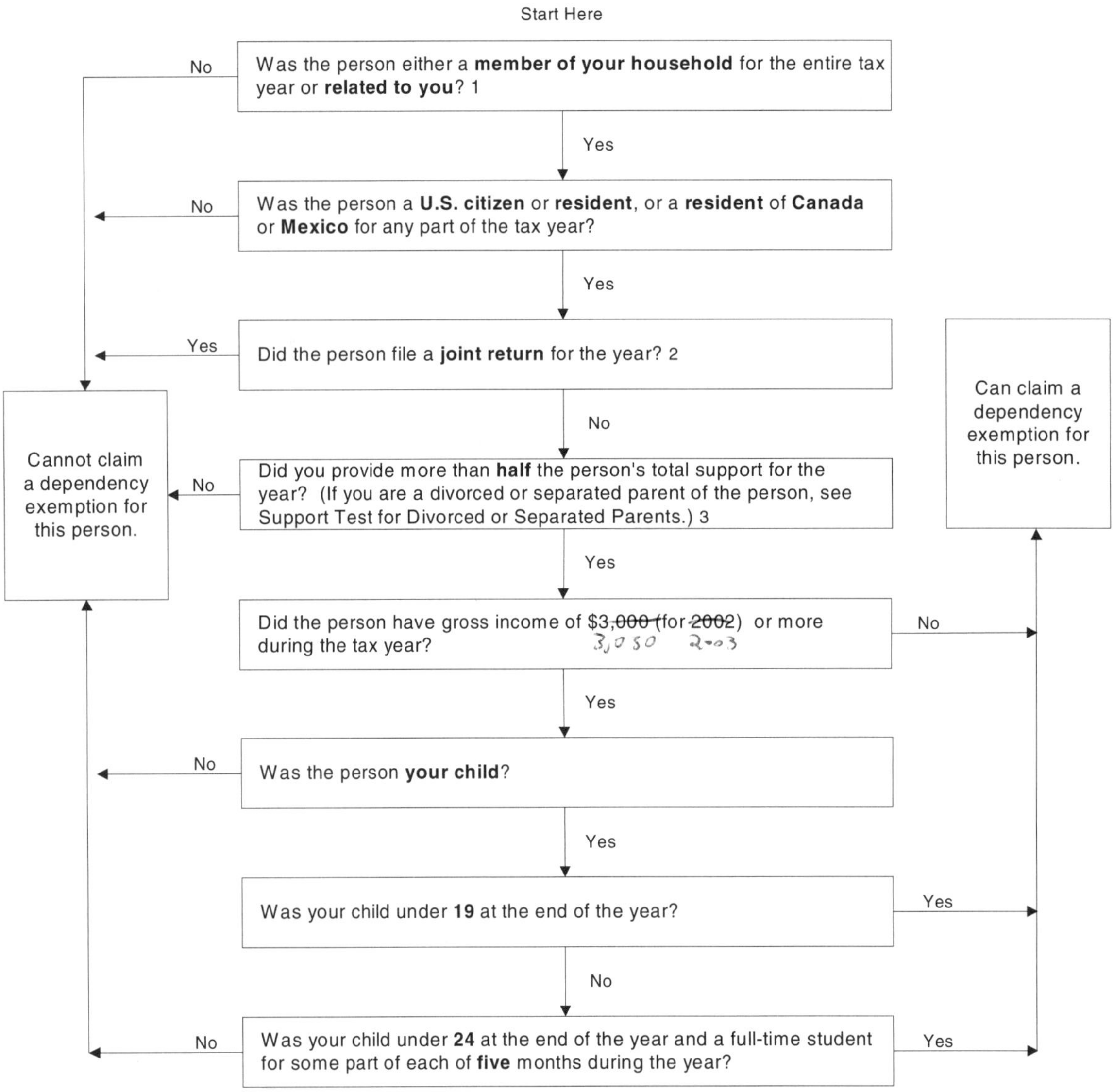

1 If the person was your legally adopted child and lived in your home as a member of your household for the entire tax year, answer "yes" to this question.

2 If neither the person nor the person's spouse is required to file a return but they file a joint return to claim a refund of tax withheld, you may answer "no" to this question.

3 Answer "yes" to this question if you meet the multiple support requirements under *Multiple Support Agreement*.

IRS Publication 17

Example

- Erin and Brian, both age 50, filed a joint return for the current year. They provided all the support for their 19-year-old daughter who had no income. Their 23-year-old son, a full-time student at a university, had $5,000 of income and provided 70% of his own support.

  Three exemptions are allowed: two personal exemptions for Erin and Brian, and one dependency exemption for their daughter. No exemption is allowed for their son. Although the gross income test is waived, they did not meet the support test for him.

- Dennis, age 50, filed a joint return with his wife, Kelly, age 24. Their son, Derek, was born December 16 of the taxable year. Dennis provided 60% of the support for his 73-year-old widowed mother until May 1, when she died. His mother's only income was from Social Security benefits totaling $3,500.

  The couple is entitled to four exemptions - Dennis, Kelly, their son Derek, and Dennis' mother. An exemption is allowed for a dependent who was alive during any part of the taxable year. Dennis' mother's Social Security income is excluded from gross income; thus, it is not considered in applying the gross income test.

- Andre provided more than one-half of the support for his cousin, his niece and his foster parent. None of them were members of Andre's household. None of these relatives had any income, nor did any of them file an individual or joint return. All of the relatives are U.S. citizens. Of the potential dependents listed, only the niece is a qualifying relative.

C. STANDARD DEDUCTION WHEN CLAIMED AS A DEPENDENT.

1. The standard deduction of a person who may be claimed as a dependent of another is limited to the greater of (a) $750 (for 2003), or (b) earned income plus $250. However, in no event can a dependent's standard deduction be greater than the regular standard deduction. No personal exemption is allowed.

Example

Andrea is claimed as a dependent on her parents' return. During 2003, she earned $2,900 as a runner for her Dad's law firm. She also has $2,000 in dividend and interest income. Andrea's standard deduction is $3,150 ($2,900 + 250). She receives no personal exemption since she is claimed as a dependent on someone else's return.

D. PHASEOUT OF EXEMPTIONS.

1. The amount you can claim as a deduction for exemptions is phased out when your adjusted gross income (AGI) exceeds a certain level based on your filing status. These levels are as follows:

EXHIBIT 15: PHASEOUT OF EXEMPTIONS

Filing Status	2003 AGI Phaseout
Married filing separately	$104,625 - 165,875
Single	$139,500 - 262,000
Head of household	$174,400 - 296,900
Married filing jointly	$209,250 - 331,750
Qualifying widow(er)	$209,250 - 331,750

2. Reduce the dollar amount of exemptions by 2% for each $2,500, or part of $2,500 ($1,250 if married filing separately), that AGI exceeds the threshold amount.

Example

Taxpayers (MFJ) have AGI of $275,000 in 2003. These taxpayers have a total of 5 personal and dependency exemptions. Determine their actual deductible personal and dependency exemption.

5 exemptions x $3,050		$15,250	
AGI Income	$275,000		
Threshold	(209,250)		
Difference	$65,750		
Divide by 2,500	26.3		
Round up to next integer	27		
Multiply by 2%	54%		
Apply personal & dependency exemption (54% x $15,250 = $8,235)		(8,235)	Loss due to threshold
		$7,015	Exemption amt. after phaseout

Note: It is unlikely that the exam will test this type of calculation, but it has been provided for your convenience.

3. Beginning in 2006, the phaseout of personal exemptions is reduced. The phaseout is completely eliminated for tax years after 2009 (TRA 2001).

X. TAX DETERMINATION

A. TAX TABLE METHOD.

Most taxpayers can determine their tax liability by utilizing the tax tables. Exceptions include individuals who file a short period return, individuals whose taxable income exceeds the maximum amounts on the tax table, estates, and trusts.

B. TAX RATE SCHEDULE.

The rate schedules are different for single, married, married filing separately, and heads of household. However, all schedules are progressive with graduated rates of 10%, 15%, 27%, 30%, 35%, and 38.6% for the 2003 tax year.

C. COMPUTATION OF NET TAXES PAYABLE/REFUND DUE.

1. Estimated taxes, taxes previously withheld, and tax credits are subtracted from tax liability to reduce the tax due dollar-for-dollar. Tax credits include earned income credit, credit for child and dependent care expenses, credit for the elderly, and foreign tax credit.
2. An underpayment penalty will apply if an insufficient amount has been paid. See Section "Required Payments" on page 554 for ways to avoid the penalty.
3. Prior year's tax that must be paid by high-income (high income is defined as exceeding $150,000 AGI) taxpayers to avoid the estimated tax penalty is 110% of prior year's tax for 2003.

D. KIDDIE TAX.

1. The kiddie tax applies to any unearned income of a minor under age 14. This income is taxed at the parents' highest marginal rate. The net unearned income is the amount taxed at the parents' rate, computed as follows:

   Total Unearned Income

   Less: $750 for 2003.

   Less: The greater of:

   - $750 for 2003, or
   - The amount of the allowable itemized deductions directly connected with the production of the unearned income.

   Equals: Net unearned income.

Example

Ann is 11 years old and earned $5,200 from baby sitting in 2003. She also had interest from her savings account of $2,000. Ann's net unearned income is:

$2,000	Gross unearned income
(1,500)	
$500	Net unearned income taxed at parents' rate

Ann's taxable income is:

$5,200	Baby sitting
2,000	Savings account interest
$7,200	Gross income
(4,750)	Standard deduction (Earned Income plus $250 but limited to $4,750)
(0)	Personal exemption
$2,450	Taxable income

Of the $2,450 in taxable income, $500 ($2,000 - $1,500) is taxed at her parents' highest rate and $1,950 is taxed at Ann's rate.

E. EXAMPLE OF THE TAX FORMULA.

Example

Mary is single, 45 years old, and has no dependents. She has a salary of $60,000, earned $1,200 interest on her checking account, won $800 in the state lottery, and earned $2,000 from interest on municipal bonds. Her deductions for AGI were $3,000, and total itemized deductions were $7,100. Mary's taxable income for 2003 is computed as follows:

Income (broadly conceived) ($60,000 + 1,200 + 800 + 2,000 = $64,000)	$64,000
LESS: Exclusions (municipal bonds interest)	(2,000)
Gross Income	$62,000
LESS: Deductions for Adjusted Gross Income	(3,000)
Adjusted Gross Income	$59,000
LESS: The greater of:	
Total itemized deduction	($7,100)
The standard deduction	0
Personal and dependency exemptions (1 x $3,050)	(3,050)
Taxable Income (Loss)	$48,850
Tax on $48,850:	
on $6,000 @ 10%	$600
on $22,400 ($28,400 - $6,000) @ 15%	$3,360
on $20,450 ($48,850 - $28,400) at 27%	5,522
Total Tax:	**$9,482**

Note: The CFP® Certification Examination does not regularly test the actual calculation of tax due to annual bracket changes. However, the exam may test the determination of taxable income or AGI.

Examples

- Bryan and Susan, both age 35, are married and have 2 dependent children. They file a joint federal income tax return. Their combined salaries total $75,000. They had deductions for AGI of $6,000 and total itemized deductions of $8,100. Their 2003 tax liability is calculated as follows:

Gross Income	$75,000
LESS: Deductions for Adjusted Gross Income	(6,000)
Adjusted Gross Income	$69,000
LESS: The greater of:	
Total Itemized Deduction	($8,100)
The Standard Deduction	0
Personal and Dependency Exemptions (4 x $3,050)	(12,200)
Taxable Income (Loss)	$48,700
Tax on $48,700:	
on $12,000 @ 10%	$1,200
on $35,450 ($47,450 - $12,000) @ 15%	5,318
on $1,250 ($48,700 - $47,450) at 27%	337
Total Tax	**$6,855**

- Taxpayer earned a salary of $50,000 and incurred a long-term capital loss of $4,000. He also paid alimony of $6,000, made a deductible contribution of $3,000 to his IRA, and paid $2,000 of investment interest expense. The taxpayer's adjusted gross income is:

$50,000	- Salary
($3,000)	- LTCL (limited to $3,000 with $1,000 carryover)
($6,000)	- Alimony
($3,000)	- Deductible IRA contribution
$38,000	= Adjusted Gross Income (AGI)

Investment interest expense is a deduction FROM AGI (itemized deduction) and only deductible to the extent of investment income.

XI. FILING CONSIDERATIONS

A. FILING STATUS.

1. There are five filing status categories:
   a. Single.
   b. Married Filing Jointly.
   c. Married Filing Separately.
   d. Head of Household.
   e. Qualifying Widow(er) with dependent child.
2. Single.
   a. An unmarried, separated, or divorced individual who does not qualify for another status must file as a Single taxpayer.
   b. There are exceptions. For example, abandoned spouses who live apart may be able to use the more advantageous Head of Household rate schedule.
   c. Marital status is determined as of the last day of the tax year, except when a spouse dies during the year in which case the survivor may file Married Filing Jointly.
3. Married Filing Jointly or Separately.
   a. Married individuals are allowed to file joint returns or separate returns.
   b. When filing separate returns, each spouse reports only his or her own income, exemptions, deductions, and credits. In addition, each spouse must use the tax rate for married persons filing separately.
   c. The tax law places limits on married taxpayers filing separately. For example, they cannot take the credit for child and dependent care expenses, the earned income credit, or the education credits. In addition, if one spouse itemizes, then the other should generally itemize because the standard deduction would be reduced to zero (some exceptions apply.)
   d. It is usually advantageous for married persons to file a joint return since the combined amount of tax is generally lower.
   e. Special situations may exist which result in a lower married filing separate tax liability (e.g., spouse with low income has high medical expenses). It is wise to compute the tax under both assumptions to determine the most advantageous filing status.
4. Head of Household.
   a. Unmarried individuals who maintain a household for a qualifying person are entitled to use the Head of Household rates.
   b. This rate schedule ranks between the Joint and the Single return tax rate schedules.
   c. To qualify for Head of Household rates, a taxpayer must pay more than half the cost of maintaining a household for a qualifying person, and the household must be the qualifying person's principal home.

d. Qualifying persons.

i. Child, grandchild, stepchild, or adopted child. A single child does not have to be a dependent. A married child must qualify as a dependent unless the child is claimed by the noncustodial parent under a written court agreement.

ii. Other relatives that the taxpayer claims as dependents. Qualifying relatives are limited to parents, grandparents, siblings, half-siblings and stepsiblings, stepparents, in-laws, and, if related by blood, uncles, aunts, nephews and nieces.

iii. Parents may be claimed as the qualifying person for Head of Household even when not a member of the household. If the taxpayer maintains a separate home for parents and pays more than half the cost of upkeep on that home, or pays more than half the cost of a rest home or home for the elderly, then the taxpayer may claim Head of Household filing status.

EXHIBIT 16: QUALIFYING PERSONS

Qualifying Person	Must Claim as a Dependent	Must Live in Taxpayer's Home > Half of the Year
Single Child	No	Yes
Married Child	Yes[1]	Yes
Other Relative	Yes	Yes
Parents	Yes	No[2]

[1] Must qualify as dependent unless noncustodial spouse claims the exemption.
[2] Taxpayer pays more than half of the cost of separate home or elder care home.

5. Qualifying Widow(er) with dependent child.

a. The taxpayer with deceased spouse will file Married Filing Jointly with two personal exemptions in the year of the death of the spouse.

b. Taxpayer may be eligible to use Qualifying Widow(er) with dependent child as the filing status for two years following the year of death of a spouse. For example, if taxpayer's spouse died in 2003 and taxpayer has not remarried, the taxpayer may be able to use this filing status for 2004 and 2005. The taxpayer would file Married Filing Jointly in 2003.

c. This filing status entitles the taxpayer to use joint return tax rates with one personal exemption and the highest standard deduction amounts (if taxpayer does not itemize deductions). This status does not authorize the taxpayer to file a joint return or claim an exemption for the deceased spouse.

d. Eligibility rules for filing as a Qualifying Widow(er) with dependent child.

i. A taxpayer is eligible to file as a Qualifying Widow(er) with dependent child if taxpayer meets all of the following tests:

A) Taxpayer was entitled to file a joint return with spouse for the year spouse died (it does not matter whether the taxpayer actually filed a joint return).

B) The taxpayer did not remarry before the end of the tax year in question.

C) The taxpayer has a child, stepchild, adopted child, or foster child who qualifies as a dependent for that year.

D) The taxpayer paid more than half the cost of upkeep of the home that is the main home for the taxpayer and the child for the entire year except for temporary absences.

Example

John Reed's wife died in 2003. John has not remarried. He continued during 2004 and 2005 to maintain a home for himself and his dependent child. In 2003, he was entitled to file a joint return. In 2004 and 2005, he may file as a Qualifying Widower with a dependent child. After 2005, he may file as Head of Household if he qualifies (otherwise Single).

B. Filing Requirements.

1. The following individuals are not required to file unless their income is equal to or exceeds their exemption amount plus the applicable standard deductions:
   a. Single Individuals.
   b. Head of Households.
   c. Surviving Spouses.
2. Married Filing Jointly individuals are not required to file unless their combined gross income equals or exceeds the basic standard deduction, plus twice the exemption amount. Married Filing Separately must file if income equals or exceeds the exemption amount.
3. See Section XII. Filing Levels on page 606 for 2003 required filing levels.
4. Filing requirements for dependents - If someone claims the taxpayer as a dependent, filing requirements for the dependent are controlled by the amount and type of income of the dependent. See Section IX.B. on page 593 for Dependent Standard Deduction rules.

Type of Income	Filing Required If Income Equals or Exceeds
Earned income only	Standard deduction amount including additional standard deduction amounts for age and blindness.
Unearned income only	Standard deduction[1] including additional standard deduction amounts for age and blindness.
Earned income and unearned income	Standard deduction[2] including additional standard deduction for age and blindness.

[1] With no earned income, the standard deduction would be $750 (2002) plus any additional amounts.
[2] Greater of $750 (2003) or earned income plus $250 plus any additional amounts.

Example

- In 2003, a single individual, who is claimed by a parent as a dependent, has earned income of only $3,800. No return would be required since the income is less than the standard deduction amount ($4,750).
- In 2003, a single, blind individual, who is claimed by a parent as a dependent, has unearned income only amounting to $1,200. The dependent does not need to file since gross income does not exceed $1,900 ($750 + 1,150 (additional for blindness)).
- In 2003, a single individual, claimed as a dependent by a parent, has earned income of $2,000 and unearned income of $1,800 (total income-$3,800). This taxpayer must file since the earned and unearned income total is more than the standard deduction of $2,250 (earned income plus $250).

5. Selecting the proper form - Depending on the level of complexity, an individual taxpayer may file a Form 1040, Form 1040A, or Form 1040EZ.

C. RETURN DUE DATE.

1. Return is due on the 15th day of the fourth month after the end of the tax year. If this date falls on a weekend/holiday, return is due the next business day.
2. A four-month extension of time to file can be requested on Form 4868.
3. If taxpayer overpays taxes and wants a refund, a claim must be filed by the later of three years from the date the return was filed (if filed early, return is counted as filed on the due date) or two years from the date tax was last paid.
4. The '98 Act suspends the limitation period on refund claims if the taxpayer is seriously incapacitated (condition either is expected to result in death or to last at least 12 months).

D. DECEDENT'S FINAL INCOME TAX RETURN.

1. A final income tax return must be filed for a decedent for the portion of the tax year that ends on the date of the decedent's death.
2. The return is due on the filing date that would have applied if death had not occurred. This would be April 15th for a calendar-year individual. Typically, the final income tax return will be filed by the executor or the administrator of the estate.
3. The surviving spouse may file a joint return with the decedent if the following conditions are met:
   a. An executor or administrator has not been appointed by the time the joint return is prepared.
   b. An executor or administrator has not been appointed before the extended due date of the tax return for the surviving spouse.
   c. The decedent did not previously file a tax return for the tax year.
4. Income inclusion.
   a. Cash-basis taxpayer – only income actually or constructively received up to the date of death is included in the decedent's final income tax return. This could include any uncashed payroll or dividend checks.

   b. Accrual-basis taxpayer – generally, only income accrued up to the date of death is included in the decedent's final income tax return.

5. Deductions.

   a. Cash-basis taxpayer – the expenses the decedent paid before death are deductible on the final income tax return.

   b. Accrual-basis taxpayer – the expenses for which the decedent was liable before death, regardless of whether the expenses were paid, are deductible on the final income tax return.

   c. Even though the return is for a short period, the standard deduction and personal exemption amounts are allowed in full.

XII. FILING LEVELS

EXHIBIT 17: FILING LEVELS (REQUIRED TO FILE)

Filing Status	2003 Gross Income
Single	
Under 65	$7,800
65 or older	$8,950
Married Filing Joint Return	
Both spouses under 65	$14,050
One spouse 65 or older	$15,000
Both spouses 65 or older	$15,950
Married Filing Separate Return	
All - whether or not 65 or older	$3,050
Head of Household	
Under 65	$10,050
65 or older	$11,200
Qualifying Widow(er)	
Under 65	$11,000
65 or older	$11,950

Note: The additional standard deduction for age is taken into account, but the one for blindness is not.

XIII. DEDUCTIONS AND LOSSES

A. CLASSIFICATION OF DEDUCTIBLE EXPENSES – FOR OR FROM AGI.

1. Deductions for Adjusted Gross Income (AGI) are identified in Section 62 of the Code. Deductions for AGI, which are often referred to as "above-the-line" deductions, include expenses relating to a trade or business, alimony paid, 50% of self-employment tax paid, capital loss deduction, interest penalty for early withdrawal of savings, IRA contributions, student loan interest, and moving expenses (see Section VII.)
2. Itemized deductions are deductions from AGI. Itemized deductions, which are often referred to as "below-the-line" deductions, include charitable contributions, medical expenses, mortgage interest, taxes paid, casualty losses, and unreimbursed employee business expenses.
3. Section 162 allows deductions for expenses incurred in a trade or business while Section 212 allows deductions for expenses incurred in connection with investment activities.
   a. Most expenses incurred in a trade or business are deductions for AGI (above-the-line) while investments expenses are deductions from AGI (with the exception of expenses incurred to produce rents and royalties).
   b. Both Section 162 and Section 212 expenses must have a profit motive.
4. Reporting procedures - Deductions for AGI are reported on the front of Form 1040. Deductions from AGI are itemized deductions reported on Schedule A.

B. ORDINARY, NECESSARY, AND REASONABLE REQUIREMENTS.

1. Ordinary and necessary requirement - Expenses are necessary if a "prudent" person would make the same expenditure in the same situation. Expenses are ordinary if it is normal or customary to make the expenditure (not capital).
2. Reasonableness requirement - In addition to ordinary and necessary, there is a reasonableness requirement typically associated with compensation amounts and particularly with closely held corporations.

C. DEDUCTIONS AND LOSSES - TIMING OF EXPENSE RECOGNITION.

See also Sections V.B., C., and D.

1. Taxpayer method of accounting.
   a. The two most common methods of accounting are the cash method and the accrual method.
   b. A cash-basis taxpayer generally gets a deduction when the expense has been paid.
   c. An accrual-basis taxpayer generally gets a deduction when the expense is incurred.
2. Cash method requirements.
   a. Deduction is allowed only when paid. Income is not recognized until cash is constructively received.
   b. Capital outlays (even if made in cash) are not current deductions except as depreciation, amortization, or depletion.
   c. Prepaid expenses are required to be capitalized and amortized only if the life of the asset extends more than one taxable year after the year of payment.

3. Accrual method requirements.
    a. Taxpayer takes a deduction/claims income when all the events have occurred to create the taxpayer's liability/right to receive income and the amount of the liability/income can be determined with reasonable accuracy (all events test).
    b. Economic performance test must also be satisfied for deductions.

D. DISALLOWED DEDUCTIONS.

1. Code and courts deny deductions for activities that are contrary to public policy.
    a. Fines and bribes are not deductible.
    b. Bribes, kickbacks, and other illegal payments are disallowed.
    c. Expenses relating to the trafficking of controlled substances (i.e., drugs) are disallowed (Section 280E).
2. Political contributions - Political contributions are not deductible whether paid to PACs or directly to political candidates.
3. Lobbying activities.
    a. No deduction allowed.
    b. Exceptions allowed for local, monitoring, and de minimis (< $2,000 annual).
4. Disallowance of deductions for capital expenditures - No current deduction is available for buildings, betterments, or permanent improvements made to property. The taxpayer must capitalize and depreciate these expenditures over an appropriate period.
    a. Capital expenditures are depreciated by ACRS or MACRS. The asset must have an ascertainable life (e.g., land has none and, therefore, is not depreciable).
    b. Intangible assets are amortized over 15 years (including goodwill).
5. Personal expenditures - Deductions of this nature are only deductible if a section of the Code specifically allows it (Section 262).
6. Expenditures made on behalf of others.
    a. No deduction is allowed for expenditures that benefit another taxpayer, but an exception is allowed for payment of medical expenses. Medical expenditures for a spouse and dependents are deductible by a taxpayer.

Example

Fred paid the following expenses for his dependent son during the current year:

Payment of son's automobile loan	$15,000
Payments of interest on above loan	1,500
Payment of son's medical expenses	4,000
Payment of son's property taxes (ad valorem)	1,000

The $4,000 medical expenses are deductible by Fred. The other items are not incurred for the taxpayer's benefit or as a result of the taxpayer's legal obligation.

7. Tax-exempt income related expenses and interest - If income is tax exempt, taxpayer cannot take any expenses/interest related to that income as a deduction.

E. LIMITED DEDUCTIONS (COMPENSATION, INVESTIGATION OF A NEW BUSINESS, HOBBY LOSSES, AND VACATION RENTAL HOMES).

1. Executive compensation - Maximum of $1,000,000 on the deductibility of executive compensation of big, publicly held corporations. Excluded from this cap are commissions, performance based bonuses, tax-qualified retirement contributions, and payments excluded from gross income.
2. Investigation expenses related to a new business.
   a. If a taxpayer investigates a business that is similar to the one he is already in, the expenses are deductible whether or not he acquires the business.
   b. If a taxpayer investigates a business that is a new line of business and acquires the business, the expenses should be capitalized and amortized over 60 months. If he does not acquire the business, the expenses are nondeductible.

	TP Already in a Similar Business	**TP Not Already in Similar Business**
TP acquires the business	Expenses currently deductible	Capitalize costs and can elect to amortize over 60-month period
TP does not acquire business	Expenses currently deductible	Not deductible

Example

Kristin, a calendar-year, cash-basis taxpayer, owns and operates furniture rental outlets in Georgia. She wants to expand to other states. During the current year, she spends $20,000 investigating furniture stores in Alabama and $12,000 investigating stores in Florida. She acquires the Alabama stores, but not the stores in Florida. Since she is already in the business, the expenses in both Alabama and Florida are deductible.

3. Losses incurred in hobby activities.

    a. Classification as a hobby or business is important because it affects the deductibility of losses. If an activity is deemed to be a hobby, any losses incurred may not be fully deductible. If an activity is a trade or business, the losses are deductible and can offset other taxpayer income.

    b. Is an activity a hobby or a trade/business? The answer depends on whether there was intent to earn a profit. IRS Regulations and court cases specify the factors to be considered as follows:

        i. Whether the activity is conducted in business-like manner.

        ii. Expertise of the taxpayers or their advisers.

        iii. Time and effort expended.

        iv. Expectation that the assets of the activity will appreciate in value.

        v. Previous success of the taxpayer in the conduct of similar activities.

        vi. History of income or losses from the activity.

        vii. Relationship of profits earned to losses incurred.

        viii. Financial status of the taxpayer (is there other income?)

        ix. Elements of personal pleasure or recreation in the activity.

        x. Conducting business professionally, time spent, regular hours, etc.

    c. Presumptive Rule of Section 183 - If profits have been generated for 3 out of 5 years, the burden of proof is on the IRS, rather than the taxpayer, to prove that the activity is NOT a business.

    d. Hobby income is reduced first by taxes and interest, then by other noncapital-related expenses, then by expenses that affect basis.

    e. Gross hobby income is reported on page 1, line 21 of Form 1040 (other income), and hobby expenses are reported on Schedule A (itemized deductions) as miscellaneous itemized deductions subject to the 2% of AGI floor.

Example

Sara pursued a hobby of selling antique furniture in her spare time. During the year, she sold furniture for $3,000. She incurred expenses as follows:

Cost of goods sold	$2,000
Supplies	1,200
Interest on loan to get business started	800
Advertising	750

Assuming that the activity is a hobby, and that she cannot itemize this year, she should include $3,000 in income and deduct nothing for AGI since hobby expenses must be itemized, and she cannot itemize.

---

4. Vacation home rentals.

   a. Restrictions are designed to prevent taxpayers from holding personal-use vacation homes and generating deductible rental losses. Restrictions limit the deductions to total income. Tax treatment depends on the relative time rented vs. personal use.

EXHIBIT 18: VACATION HOMES

Type	Description	Treatment
Personal Use	Property rented less than 15 days a year	• Exclude rental income from gross income • Expenses nondeductible except mortgage interest and taxes (Schedule A)
Rental	If the rental property is rented at least 15 days a year and is not used for personal use more than the greater of 14 days per year or 10% of rental days, it is classified as primarily rental use.	• Allocate expenses between business and personal • Can deduct loss up to \$25,000 (phased out at AGI between \$100,000-\$150,000) • Report income and expenses on Schedule E
Mixed Use (vacation status)	Rented more than 14 days and personal use exceeds the standard for rental (see above)	• Deduct expenses (in order of interest/taxes, operating, and then depreciation, up to amount of income) • Cannot deduct loss • Report income and expenses and Schedule E (apply hobby rules)

   b. Primarily personal use - If property is rented <15 days per year, it is a personal residence.

      i. Rent is excluded from gross income and normal personal residence deductions apply (i.e., mortgage interest and taxes).

      ii. Income is not claimed.

   c. Primarily rental use - If the rental property is rented at least 15 days a year and is not used for personal use more than the greater of 14 days per year or 10% of rental days, it is classified as primarily rental use.

      i. A loss can be used to offset other taxpayer income.

      ii. The expenses must be allocated between personal and rental days.

      iii. Passive activity loss rules may apply.

      iv. Reported on Schedule E, with income/loss carried to front of 1040.

   d. Personal/rental use (mixed use).

      i. If the property is rented too much for b (above) and used personally too much for c (above), expenses can be deducted only to extent of income (i.e., there can be no deductible loss. This is the same as the hobby loss rules – deemed to be not-for-profit).

      ii. The order that expenses are deducted is the same as for hobby losses (interest and taxes, operating expenses, expenses that affect basis).

      iii. Income and allowable expenses are reported on Schedule E.

Example

Doug and Cathy own a house at the beach. The house was rented to unrelated parties for 8 full weeks during the current year. Doug and Cathy used the house 16 days for their vacation during the year. After properly dividing the expenses between rental and personal use, it was determined that a loss was incurred as follows:

Gross rental income ($800 per week)		$6,400
Less: allocable mortgage interest and property taxes	$5,000	
Other allocated expenses	3,000	(8,000)
Net rental loss		**($1,600)**

The deductible rental expenses are limited to the gross rental income. They cannot take a net loss - similar to the hobby loss rule. This is a mixed-use property. The interest and taxes allocated to personal use may be deductible on Schedule A as itemized deductions.

5. Related-party transactions (Code Section 267 applies to losses only).
   a. These transactions are restricted to prevent transactions with paper losses but no real economic loss suffered by either party.
   b. Losses between related parties are disallowed but can be recovered at the eventual sale to an unrelated party. If the deduction is not recovered at a subsequent sale, it is lost forever.
   c. Related parties include the immediate family (brothers, sisters, spouse, ancestors, and lineal descendants), closely held corporations (owned > 50%), sister corporations, etc.

Note: This section does not relate to gains.

Example

On January 10, 2002, Billy sold stock with a cost of $6,000 to his son, Patrick, for $4,000 (its fair market value). On July 31, 2003, Patrick sold the same stock for $5,000 in a bona fide arms length transaction.

Neither Billy nor Patrick has a recognized gain or loss in either 2002 or 2003. Billy has a $2,000 realized loss in 2002 but cannot recognize it due to Section 267. Billy forever loses the ability to take a deduction for the loss. Patrick has a realized gain of $1,000 in 2003. He can reduce his gain by Billy's loss (up to the amount of gain). Patrick has no gain or loss in 2003. The remaining $1,000 loss is no longer available to any taxpayer.

F. OTHER DEDUCTIONS AND LOSSES.

1. Legal and Accounting Fees.

   a. When legal/accounting fees are incurred in connection with trade or business or for the production of rents and royalties, they are deductible FOR AGI. If these fees are incurred in the determination of any tax, they are deductible FROM AGI.

   b. Legal fees incurred for personal purposes are nondeductible.

   c. Legal fees related to the acquisition of an asset are added to the basis of the property.

2. Worthless Securities.

   a. Securities must be completely worthless to be deducted (Section 165). Losses are deemed to be capital losses occurring on the last day of the year in which they become worthless, thereby creating increased long-term capital loss treatment (net capital loss deduction remains limited to $3,000 per year).

3. Small business stock (Section 1244 – applies to losses only).

   a. Generally any security loss is capital in nature, but Section 1244 allows ordinary loss treatment if the loss is sustained by an individual who acquires the securities directly from the corporation (which must meet certain requirements).

   b. Section 1244 losses are limited to $50,000 annually ($100,000 for joint filers).

   c. In order to qualify for Section 1244 treatment, the corporation must receive less than $1,000,000 in capital for stock at time of issue.

   d. Section 1244 applies only to losses on the investment, not to gains.

Examples

- Tom, a single taxpayer, owns Section 1244 stock he purchased three years ago for $80,000. This year, he sold all of the Section 1244 stock for $10,000, incurring a loss of $70,000. He had no other investment transactions for the year.

  Since Tom is single, the first $50,000 of the loss on the Section 1244 stock will be treated as ordinary loss. The remaining $20,000 ($70,000 - $50,000) loss will be treated as a capital loss, of which Tom can currently deduct $3,000. The remaining capital loss of $17,000 can be carried forward.

- On October 15, 2002, Kurt purchased stock in Tech Corporation (the stock is not small business stock) for $2,000. On June 15, 2003, the stock became worthless.

  Kurt will have a $2,000 long-term capital loss. Worthless securities are treated as becoming worthless on the last day of the tax year; therefore, it is a long-term capital loss even though his actual holding period was only eight months. If the stock had been Section 1244 stock, Kurt would have had a $2,000 ordinary loss.

---

4. Bad Debts.
   a. Specific charge-off method.
      i. Specific charge-off method is usually required.
      ii. Deductions are only allowed in year of worthlessness.
      iii. If a previously deducted bad debt is later collected, income is recognized only if a tax benefit was received.
   b. Business bad debts.
      i. Bad debts are sales or revenues (accounts receivable) on credit that later become worthless. A deduction is only allowed if the income from the receivable was previously included in income (i.e., if accrual basis, because income was reported at time of service; not for cash basis because no payment means income was never reported).
      ii. There must be an identifiable relationship between the creation of the debt and the trade/business.
      iii. Deduction is allowed when business debts become partially or wholly worthless.
      iv. Business bad debts are deductible as an ordinary loss in year incurred.
   c. Nonbusiness bad debts.
      i. Some nonbusiness debts can be written off, but they must be wholly worthless.
      ii. Nonbusiness bad debt is debt not related to the taxpayer's trade or business.
      iii. Nonbusiness bad debts are always considered short-term capital losses.
      iv. It does not matter what the borrowed funds are used for (because the deduction relates to the lender not the borrower).

Type of Debt	Deduction
Business - Partial or whole	Ordinary loss in year incurred
Nonbusiness - Wholly worthless	Short-term capital loss in year incurred
Nonbusiness - Partially worthless	None

Examples

- XYZ, Inc. is an accrual-basis taxpayer. XYZ uses the accounts receivable aging approach to calculate their accounting allowance for bad debts. The following information is available for the current year related to bad debts.

Credit sales	$450,000
Collections on credit sales	$375,000
Amount added to the allowance account	$60,000
Beginning balance in the allowance account	$25,000
Bad debts written off in the current year	$32,000

  The tax deduction for bad-debt expense for XYZ, Inc. for the current year is $32,000. Only the specific charge-off method can be used. Allowances for estimated expenses are not allowed for tax purposes.

- Bob Doll, CPA, files his tax return using the cash method. In April 2002, Bob billed a client $4,500 for the following professional services:

Estate planning	$3,000
Personal tax return preparation	$1,000
Compilation of business financial statements	$500

  No part of the $4,500 was ever paid. In April 2003, the client declared bankruptcy, and the $4,500 obligation became totally uncollectible. No loss is allowed for Bob because the indebtedness was never taken into income since Bob was a cash-basis taxpayer.

5. Loans between related parties.
   a. The question is whether there exists a bona fide loan or a gift.
   b. To be a loan, there must be an enforceable obligation to pay a specific amount of money.
   c. Other considerations are collateral, collection efforts, intent, interest paid, etc.
6. Loss of deposits in insolvent financial institutions.
   a. Loss of deposits may be deducted as personal casualty losses instead of nonbusiness bad debts, but they are then subject to 10% AGI limit and $100 floor.
   b. This may be elected only by qualified individuals (i.e., not >1% owners, relatives or officers).
   c. Amount of loss equals basis less amount to be received.

7. Business or Held for Production of Income Casualty Losses.
   a. The identifiable event must be sudden, unexpected, or unusual.
   b. Losses related to business/trade property are deductible for AGI. They are not subject to the $100 or 10% AGI floors that individuals are held to.
   c. Losses relating to property held for profit are not subject to the $100 and 10% floors and are deductible for AGI only if the property is held for rent or royalty. Other for-profit property losses are deductible from AGI (included in other miscellaneous itemized deductions) and are subject to a 2% AGI floor.
   d. If completely destroyed, the loss is the adjusted basis of the property. If partially destroyed, the loss is the lesser of the adjusted basis or the decline in the FMV of the property (preevent and postevent).
   e. See Section XVII, Itemized Deductions, for a discussion of personal casualty losses.

G. NET OPERATING LOSSES (NOL).

1. The purpose of allowing NOLs is to create an equitable situation for cyclical businesses that might otherwise lose substantial money without receiving any tax benefit. The inequality would cause excessive average taxes for a business with irregular income and/or expenses when compared to a business with the same average income but with uniform income and expenses.
2. Carryback and carryover periods. (IRS Section 172)
   a. General rules - Net operating losses can be carried back to the two years preceding the loss year and then forward to the 20 years following the loss year. For net operating losses in tax years beginning before August 6, 1997, taxpayers can carry back an NOL to the three years preceding the loss year and then forward to 15 years following the loss year. No deduction is allowed in the year the loss is incurred. The three-year carryback period is retained for the portion of the NOL that relates to casualty and theft losses of individual taxpayers and to NOLs that are attributable to Presidentially declared disasters and are incurred by taxpayers engaged in farming or by a small business.
      i. NOLs arising in 2001 and 2002 may be carried back 5 years and forward 20 years. This provision was added as part of the government's response to the 9/11/01 terrorist attacks.
   b. Sequence of use of NOLs - The oldest is completely written off prior to using any of the more recent NOLs. Each loss is computed and maintains its own integrity.
   c. Election to forgo carryback - This election is irrevocable. The election produces a tax advantage if the taxpayer was in a low tax bracket in earlier years and expects to be in a higher bracket in the carryforward years.

XIV.DEPRECIATION, COST RECOVERY, AMORTIZATION, AND DEPLETION

A. INTRODUCTION.

1. Taxpayers may recover the cost of certain assets used in trade/business through depreciation, amortization, or depletion. The amount of annual recovery depends on the type of property, when it was acquired, and the elected method of recovery.
2. Property eligible for capital recovery includes personalty, realty, and intangibles. The property must have a determinable useful life and be subject to wear and tear, decay or decline from natural causes, or obsolescence.
3. The basis of an asset must be reduced by the cost recovery taken and by not less than the amount the taxpayer could have taken. In other words, if you don't take the depreciation allowed, you still have to reduce the basis by the allowable depreciation.

B. MODIFIED ACCELERATED COST RECOVERY SYSTEM (MACRS).

1. Under MACRS, tangible personalty is either 3-year, 5-year, 7-year, 10-year, 15-year, or 20-year property. The percentages are based on 200% declining balance for 10-year-and-less property, and 150% declining balance for 15-year and 20-year property.
   a. Both 200% declining balance and 150% declining balance switch over to straight-line depreciation when it results in a larger deduction.
   b. A half-year convention is used (half-year depreciation is allowed during the year placed in service and a half-year depreciation in the year of disposition). However, the mid-quarter convention may apply (see discussion below).
2. Under MACRS, residential real estate has a 27.5-year life; nonresidential has a 39-year life.
   a. Cost recovery percentages are calculated using straight line.
   b. Mid-month convention is used (a half-month depreciation allowed for month placed in service and a half-month for month of disposition).
3. IRS tables provide the statutory percentages.
   a. The statutory percentage is applied against the asset cost (no reduction for salvage value).
   b. The tables incorporate the conventions for the year/month placed in service.
4. Mid-quarter convention.
   a. In order to reduce the benefits of the half-year convention for property placed in service late in the year, the mid-quarter convention was developed. If more than 40% of the personal property is placed in service during the last quarter of the year, the mid-quarter convention applies to all personal property assets placed in service that year.
   b. In the first year of service, first-quarter assets get 10.5 months of depreciation, second-quarter assets get 7.5 months, third-quarter assets get 4.5 months, and fourth-quarter assets get 1.5 months.
   c. The mid-quarter convention does not apply to real property.
5. For <u>new</u> property placed in service after 9/11/01 and before 9/11/04, additional (bonus) depreciation of 30% of the adjusted basis of the property (after subtracting any Section 179 expense) is allowed. This provision was added as part of the government's response to the 9/11/01 terrorist attacks.

C. ELECTION TO EXPENSE ASSETS.

1. Section 179 allows an annual write-off of up to $25,000 (for 2003) of the cost of tangible personal property used in trade/business and placed in service during 2003.
2. Annual limitations.
   a. If the total amount of property placed in service for a given year is above $200,000, the allowance is reduced dollar-for-dollar for any amount over $200,000. No carryover is allowed.
   b. The amount of the deduction cannot exceed the taxable income from total trade/business of the taxpayer (carryforward is available).

Example

- In 2003, Roth Corporation purchased and placed in service a piece of machinery costing $40,000. Assuming Roth had taxable income of $5,000 (without regard to Section 179 expense), the maximum Section 179 expense that can be taken is $5,000. $25,000 is eligible, but the amount is limited to the taxable income. $20,000 ($25,000 - $5,000) will be carried forward to 2004.

- In 2004, Roth Corporation purchased $2,000 in new equipment and had taxable income (without regard to Section 179 expense) of $100,000. Section 179 expense of $2,000 can be taken in 2003 (2004 purchases) + 20,000 (carried from 2003) = $22,000. Neither of the annual limitations apply.

---

3. Effect on adjusted taxable basis.
   a. The adjusted taxable basis of the property is reduced by the amount of the Section 179 deduction taken and is adjusted for the property placed in service limitation. It is not adjusted for the income limitation.

Example

The adjusted taxable basis of the property acquired by Roth in 2003 and 2004 before additional depreciation for equipment purchased in 2004 is:

Year 2003 = $40,000 – 25,000 = $15,000 for equipment purchased in 2003.

Year 2004 = $2,000 - 2,000 = $0 for equipment purchases in 2004.

Example

In 2003, Babe Corp. purchased and placed in service a machine to be used in its manufacturing operations. This machine cost $207,000. What portion of the cost may Babe elect to treat as an expense rather than as a capital expenditure assuming net taxable income of $400,000?

Max §179 expense for 2003	$25,000
Reduction ($207,000 - $200,000)	(7,000)
Allowed §179 expense	18,000
Cost of property	207,000
§179 expense	(18,000)
Adjusted taxable basis of property	189,000

D. REPAIRS VS. CAPITAL EXPENDITURES.

1. The cost of repairing business property is currently deductible as a business expense. A repair could include:
   a. An incidental expense that does not materially add to the value of the property.
   b. An incidental expense that does not appreciably prolong the life of the property.
   c. An expense that maintains the property in its normal operating state.
2. If a cash outlay is considered a capital expenditure, the cash outlay is not currently deductible. Instead, the cost must be capitalized and depreciated over the property's useful life. A capital expenditure could include:
   a. Expenditures that materially add to the value of the property.
   b. Expenditures that substantially prolong the property's useful life.
   c. Expenditures as part of a general plan of renovating, improving, or altering the property.

Example

Tom Hall operates Hall's Limo, a limousine service. Tom occasionally incurs expenses for the upkeep of his limos. These expenses, which include items such as spark plugs, oil changes, and labor, would be considered repair and maintenance expenses since the expenses do not significantly prolong the limo's useful life. However, if Tom replaced the transmission at a cost of $800, the expense would be considered a capital improvement.

E. BUSINESS USE OF LISTED PROPERTY.

Listed property includes passenger automobiles, entertainment assets, computers, and phones. If the business usage of listed assets is > 50%, then the taxpayer may use the statutory percentages for depreciation. If business usage is ≤ 50%, then the taxpayer is limited to straight line.

1. Autos and other listed property used predominantly in business.
   a. The percentage of business use must be above 50%. The 50% test is based on business use only and not on production of income. However, if the test is met, then the cost recovery amount is based on both the business and production of income usage.
   b. The amount of cost recovery available is based on the percentage of the total use that is business related.
   c. There is a limit on annual depreciation. This limit is applied prior to the adjustment for business use percentage. The caps are adjusted for inflation each year.

Placed in Service	1st Year Depreciation	2nd Year Depreciation	3rd Year Depreciation	4th Year and Later
2002/2003	$7,660*	$4,900	$2,950	$1,775

*The Job Creation and Worker Assistance Act of 2002 added $4,600 to the first year depreciation limit for automobiles placed in service after 9/10/01 and before 9/11/04.

   i. The depreciation caps are much higher for electric vehicles.

2. Autos and other listed property not used predominantly in business.
   a. The depreciation for this property must be based on the straight-line method and the alternative depreciation system (ADS) which require a 5-year period for autos.
   b. The dollar limits previously described are still applicable.
   c. If the property fails the 50% test, it must be depreciated using the straight-line method even if it later could pass the 50% test.
3. Change from predominantly business use - If property initially passes the 50% test but later fails the test, the property is subject to cost recovery recapture. The amount of recapture is the amount of cost recovery claimed less the amount that could have been claimed if the straight-line method had been used from the beginning.
4. Leased automobiles - In order to prevent circumvention of the cost recovery rules by leasing, an annual inclusion amount *(*figured from IRS tables) is required to be reported as gross income. The amount reported is based on the fair market value, the number of days of use during the year, and the percentage of business vs. personal use. The effect is to reduce the deduction of the lease payments by the inclusion amount.
5. Substantiation requirements - Records must substantiate the taxpayer's claims pertaining to amount of expenditures, business purpose, and percentage use for business purposes.

Example

Catherine purchased an automobile in 2002 for $20,000. During 2002, she uses the car 40% for personal and 60% for business reasons. The MACRS statutory percentage for 5-year property, year 1 is 20%. Catherine's depreciation deduction for 2002 is $1,836. Catherine's depreciation deduction using the MACRS percentage is $4,000 (20% x $20,000). This is limited to $3,060. The business percentage is then applied to $3,060. $3,060 x 60% = $1,836.

F. ALTERNATIVE DEPRECIATION SYSTEM (ADS).

1. ADS must be used for alternative minimum tax adjustments, international asset use, tax-exempt entities, tax-exempt bond financed assets, and assets from certain discriminating countries for earnings and profit purposes.
2. For personal property, taxpayers may use 150% declining balance instead of 200% declining balance and compute the ordinary tax instead of adjusting for the AMT. However, the period must be based on ADS, not the usual asset-class periods.

G. AMORTIZATION.

1. Certain intangible assets are amortizable over 15 years.
2. Section 197 assets include goodwill, trademarks, covenants not to compete, copyrights, and patents if they are used in a trade or business or for the production of income. Self-created intangibles are not considered amortizable assets under Section 197.

Example

Maria acquired a business on July 1 of the current year. The purchase price included a copyright valued at $30,000. Maria can claim $1,000 of amortization in the current year. The annual amortization will be $30,000 ÷ 15 = $2,000. Maria held it only six months during the current year.

H. DEPLETION.

1. Natural resources (except land) are subject to depletion. An owner of the resource is someone who acquires economic interest and receives income from the resource. The owner is entitled to a deduction for AGI to recover his costs. There are four types of expenditures: cost of natural resources, cost of intangible development, tangible asset costs, and operating costs.
2. Intangible drilling and development costs.
   a. There are two options for the taxpayer:
      i. Expense in year incurred.
      ii. Capitalize and deplete.
   b. After the election is made, all future expenditures of a similar nature are handled the same way. Generally, the expense option is more advantageous.

3. Depletion methods.
   a. There are two depletion methods:
      i. Cost.
      ii. Percentage.
   b. This is an annual election and usually the method yielding the larger deduction is chosen.
   c. Cost depletion - The asset basis is divided by the estimated total number of recoverable units of the asset and then multiplied by the number of units sold (not produced) to determine the amount of the deduction for the year. If the estimated total number of recoverable units is inaccurate, future calculations are based on a revised estimate.
   d. Percentage depletion - A statutory percentage is applied to the gross income from the property (limited to 50% of the gross income). This method is unrelated to the cost or basis of the asset.
   e. Effect of intangible drilling costs on depletion - If the costs are capitalized, the basis of the property is increased and the cost depletion increases. If the costs are expensed, the 50% depletion limits may apply.

Example

Mr. Coleman owns a sulfur mine that had 100,000 total estimated tons when he purchased it for $2,000,000. In the current year, 20,000 tons were extracted and 18,000 tons were sold. The statutory percentage for sulfur is 22%. Gross income for the year was $1,000,000. His depletion deduction for the current year is $360,000.

Cost Method: $\frac{\$2{,}000{,}000}{100{,}000} \times 18{,}000 = \$360{,}000$

Percentage Method: 22% x 1,000,000 = $220,000.

Mr. Coleman's depletion deduction will be $360,000 (the higher of the two methods).

XV. PASSIVE ACTIVITY LOSSES.

A. TAX SHELTER INVESTMENTS.

1. Primarily, tax shelter investments defer or eliminate taxes for the investor. Before Congress curbed tax shelter abuse, the shelters allowed paper losses in excess of the amount of capital the investor provided due to the high expenses (depreciation, interest, development, etc.) and low revenues in the early years of a project.
2. Two major changes in the IRC have significantly reduced the benefit of tax shelters:
   a. At-risk limits.
   b. Passive activity loss limits.
3. At-risk limits are applied before the passive activity loss limits.

B. AT-RISK LIMITS (SECTION 465).

1. The maximum deductible loss for an activity is limited to the amount that the investor has at risk at the end of the current tax year (i.e., the potential economic loss).
2. The amount at risk is the total of the cash and property invested and the debt for which the investor is personally liable (typically referred to as "recourse" debt). The amount is adjusted annually based on the taxpayer's share of profit or loss from the venture.
3. If a loss is disallowed because of at-risk rules, the loss can be carried forward and taken in the first year that the at-risk amount becomes a positive amount (enough to absorb the loss) or when the investment is sold.

Example

In 2003, Bob invested $50,000 for a 20% interest in a partnership in which he was a material participant during the year. The partnership incurred a loss, and Bob's share was $75,000.

Since Bob has only $50,000 of capital at risk, he cannot deduct more than $50,000 against his other income. Bob's nondeductible loss of $25,000 can be carried over and used when the at-risk provisions allow. If Bob has taxable income of $45,000 from the partnership in 2004 and no other transactions that affect his at-risk amount, he can use all of the $25,000 loss carried over from 2003.

C. PASSIVE ACTIVITY LOSS LIMITS.

1. Apply to:
   a. Individuals.
   b. Estates.
   c. Trusts.
   d. Closely Held C Corporations.
   e. Personal Service Corporations (PSCs).

2. In general, the passive activity loss rules divide all income into active, passive, and portfolio. The rules then limit the deduction for passive losses to the amount of passive income only (with exceptions for real estate activities).
3. The limits are applied to closely held corporations to prevent an individual or business from incorporating solely to take advantage of passive losses. Closely held corporations may offset passive losses against active income, but not portfolio income.
4. The limits are applied to Personal Service Corporations (PSCs) to prevent professionals from forming a PSC and using it to acquire investments that produce passive losses to deduct against active corporate profits. A PSC is a corporation where the primary economic activity is the performance of personal services by the owners of the corporation.

D. CLASSIFICATION OF INCOME AND LOSSES.

1. Taxpayer must classify income and losses into active, passive, or portfolio. Passive loss limitations prevent the taxpayer from deducting passive losses against active or portfolio income.
2. Active income examples are:
   a. Wages, salaries, and other employee compensation.
   b. Trade/business income when taxpayer is a material participant.
   c. Intangible property income when taxpayer significantly contributed to the creation.
   d. Qualified low-income housing project income.
3. Portfolio income examples are:
   a. Interest, dividends, annuities, and royalties.
   b. Gain/loss from disposition of property that produces portfolio income or is held for investment.

E. PASSIVE ACTIVITIES DEFINED.

1. Either of the following conditions creates a passive activity (Section 469).
   a. The taxpayer does not materially participate (except oil and gas partnerships).
   b. The activity is a rental activity (even if the taxpayer does materially participate).
2. If any of the following conditions are met, the taxpayer is a material participant:
   a. Does taxpayer complete more than 500 hours of participation during the year?
   b. Does the individual's participation in the activity constitute substantially all of the participation in the activity of all individuals (including individuals who are not owners) for the year?
   c. Does taxpayer participate for more than 100 hours, and is this amount equal to or more than any other participant in the activity?
   d. Is the activity a significant participation activity (i.e., >100 hours of participation), and does total participation in all such activities exceed 500 hours?
   e. Did the taxpayer materially participate in the activity in at least five of the last ten years?
   f. Is the activity a personal service activity, and did the taxpayer materially participate in the activity in any of the three previous years?
   g. Using the existing facts and circumstances, did the taxpayer participate on a regular, continuous, and substantial basis during the year?

3. An oil or gas activity that involves a working interest in any oil or gas property that a taxpayer owns directly or through an entity that does not limit the taxpayer's liability interest is not a passive activity (Section 469(c)(3)(A)). Therefore, losses can be applied against active and portfolio income. This exception is applied on a well-by-well basis.
4. Limited partners are not material participants because they are not allowed to participate in the management of the business.
5. Rental Activities.
   a. Unless excepted by the Code, all rental activities are deemed passive. Rental activities occur when payments are received for the use of tangible property. If an activity is excepted by the Code, it must still pass the material participation test to be considered active.
   b. An activity is not rental under any of the following 6 conditions:
      i. The average customer use is 7 days or less.
      ii. The average customer use is 30 days or less, and the owner provides significant personal services.
      iii. The owner also provides extraordinary services (rental period is irrelevant).
      iv. The rental activity is incidental to a nonrental activity of taxpayer (investment or trade/ business).
      v. The property is customarily made available during business hours for nonexclusive use by customers (e.g., golf course).
      vi. The property is used in a partnership, S corporation, or joint venture where the owner has an interest.

F. EXCEPTION FOR REAL ESTATE ACTIVITIES.

1. Real estate trade/business.
   a. Post-1993 losses are not considered passive for certain real estate professionals provided that:
      i. Real estate is >50% of their personal services for the year, and
      ii. The taxpayer performs >750 hours of service in real property trades or business in which the taxpayer materially participates.
   b. Real estate professionals that meet the participation test above will treat losses from real estate rental activities as nonpassive and can offset those losses against active and portfolio income.
2. Real estate rental activities for non-real estate professionals.
   a. Individuals can deduct up to $25,000 of rental real estate losses against active and portfolio income.
   b. Two tests must be met to qualify for this exception:
      i. Active participation in the activity (participates in management decisions, an easier hurdle to clear than material participation), and
      ii. Ownership of 10% or more (in value) of all interests in the activity during the taxable year.

c. The $25,000 offset allowance is reduced by 50% of AGI in excess of $100,000 (complete phaseout at $150,000 AGI). Therefore, there is a loss of $1 for every $2 of AGI greater than $100,000. The loss is deducted from the $25,000 maximum available. Note: If you are required to calculate this, there are two steps:

1. Determine the maximum allowable after phaseout.
2. Limit #1 by actual rental real estate losses incurred.

G. SUSPENDED LOSSES/CARRYOVERS.

The at-risk rules are applied before the passive loss rules. If a loss is not allowed because of the at-risk limitations, it is not a suspended loss under the passive loss rules. Rather, it is suspended under the at-risk rules.

Examples

- Ronnie, who earned a salary of $180,000, invested $30,000 for a 15% interest in a passive activity in the current year. Operations of the activity resulted in a loss of $300,000, of which Ronnie's share was $45,000. $15,000 of Ronnie's loss is suspended under the at-risk rules, which leaves a potential deduction of $30,000. The $30,000 loss is suspended under the passive loss rules.

- Larry has the following income and losses for the current year:

Salary for managing an S corporation	$50,000
Dividend income from ABC Company stock	$1,000
Loss from a 20% limited partnership interest in Realty Capital Partners, a limited partnership	$4,000
Loss from a 10% interest in an S corporation, in which he works full time managing one of the branches	$3,000

His AGI is calculated as follows:

Salary	$50,000
Dividend Income	1,000
Limited partnership interest (passive loss cannot be deducted because limited partners are not material participants)	0
S corporation interest (works full time, and is therefore a material participant)	(3,000)
Adjusted Gross Income	$48,000

XVI.EMPLOYEE EXPENSES

A. TYPE OF DEDUCTION.

1. Section 162 allows employees who incur expenses while performing their job duties a deduction for these amounts.
2. Most unreimbursed employee expenses are miscellaneous itemized deductions subject to the 2% of AGI floor. Exceptions include impairment-related work expenses of handicapped individuals (miscellaneous itemized deductions not subject to the 2% floor) and moving expenses (deduction for AGI).
3. For a self-employed taxpayer, job-related expenses are deductions <u>for</u> AGI (typically reported on Schedule C).

B. TRANSPORTATION.

1. Expenditures Allowed.
   a. Taxpayer may deduct unreimbursed expenditures related to transportation from one place to another while on company business as deductions from AGI (2% miscellaneous itemized deduction).
   b. Employee cannot be in travel status.
   c. Examples are automobile expenses, parking, and taxi fares.
2. Commuting.
   a. Normally disallowed (personal expense).
   b. Exceptions that allow a deduction.
      i. Transporting heavy tools (incremental cost only).
      ii. A commute to a second job (based on distance between jobs; location of taxpayer home is irrelevant).
      iii. Employer requires employee to travel between work stations (expenses between work stations only are deductible).
      iv. Taxpayer commutes to a temporary work location (generally defined as less than one year).

EXHIBIT 19: WHEN ARE LOCAL TRANSPORTATION EXPENSES DEDUCTIBLE?

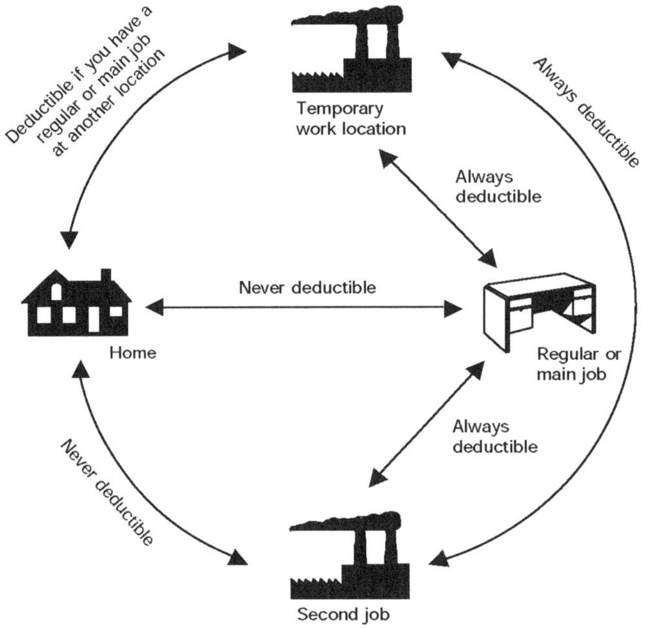

Publication 17; Figure 28-B

3. Computation of auto expenses.
   a. Actual operating cost method.
      i. Include depreciation, gas, licenses, maintenance, insurance, etc.
      ii. Must be prorated between business and personal use.
   b. Automatic mileage method - A fixed amount of money per business mile plus tolls, parking, etc. The mileage rate for 2003 is 36 cents per mile.
   c. General rules - Either method is acceptable with the following constraints:
      i. Vehicle must be owned by the taxpayer claiming the deduction.
      ii. Only one vehicle can be used at any given time.
      iii. If standard mileage rate is used in Year 1, then MACRS cannot be used later.
      iv. If election to expense under Section 179 or MACRS is used in Year 1, then no change to the automatic mileage method is allowed.

C. TRAVEL.

1. Must be away from tax home.
   a. To deduct travel expenses, the taxpayer must determine the location of the tax home. Generally, the taxpayer's tax home is the regular place of business or post of duty regardless of where the taxpayer maintains the family home.
   b. If the taxpayer does not maintain a residence or have a regular place of business, the taxpayer is considered a transient (an itinerant). The tax home is wherever the taxpayer is currently working. As a transient, the taxpayer cannot claim a travel expense deduction because the taxpayer is never considered away from home.

Example

Tiffany lives in Cincinnati where she has a seasonal job for 8 months and earns $15,000. She works the remaining 4 months in Miami, also at a seasonal job, and earns $4,000. Cincinnati is her main place of work because she spends most of her time there and earns most of her income there.

2. Description of deduction.
   a. Transportation, meals, lodging, and incidentals while away from home on business.
   b. Expenditures are unreimbursed expenses and are miscellaneous itemized deductions subject to the 2% of AGI floor.
   c. An overnight stay is required. Overnight is defined as substantially longer than a work day.
   d. Meals and lodging are not deductible if the travel is a single day trip. Meals are limited to a 50% deduction.
3. The employee's absence from home must be temporary in nature.
   a. A temporary assignment must be 1 year or less. If assignment is more than 1 year, the tax home changes, and the away-from-home requirement is not met.
   b. The taxpayer's household cannot be moved to the new location.
4. Restrictions on certain types of business travel.
   a. Conventions must be related to the trade or business to be classified as deductible travel.
   b. Spousal travel is disallowed unless it is for a bona fide business purpose.
   c. Deductions for travel on cruise ships are limited to twice the highest per diem amount allowed for a day of domestic travel by employees in the executive branch of the federal government.
   d. While expenses related to attending a meeting or seminar related to income-producing activities are not allowed, they are deductible if connected with the taxpayer's trade or business. If the meeting is on a U.S. cruise ship, the maximum deductible amount is $2,000.
5. Combined business and pleasure travel.
   a. Domestic travel.
      i. A domestic trip must be primarily for business purposes in order to deduct transportation expenses. If primarily business, taxpayer can deduct 100% of transportation expenses. If not primarily business, taxpayer cannot deduct any transportation expenses.
      ii. Other expenses must be allocated between business and personal.

Example

Marleen works in Atlanta, and takes a business trip to New Orleans. On her way home, she stops in Mobile to visit her parents. She spends $630 for the 9 days she was away from home for travel, meals, lodging, and other travel expenses. If she had not stopped in Mobile, she would have been gone only 6 days and her total cost would have been $580. She can deduct $580 for her trip, including the cost of round-trip transportation to and from New Orleans. The cost of her meals is subject to the 50% limit on meal expenses.

b. Foreign travel.

   i. An allocation of transportation expenses is required between business and personal travel unless:

      A) The total time is 7 days or less, or

      B) Less than 25% of the time was spent on personal travel, or

      C) The taxpayer has no control over the schedule, or

      D) The desire for vacation is not a major factor in deciding to take the trip.

   ii. This differs from domestic travel in that an allocation is required rather than an all-or-nothing consequence.

Examples

- Victor traveled to Paris primarily for business. He left Denver on Tuesday and flew to New York. On Wednesday, he flew from New York to Paris, arriving the next morning. On Thursday and Friday, he had business discussions, and from Saturday until Tuesday, he was sightseeing. He flew back to New York, arriving Wednesday afternoon. On Thursday, he flew back to Denver. Although Victor was away from his home in Denver for more than a week, he was not outside the United States for more than a week because the day of departure does not count as a day outside the United States. He can deduct his cost of the round-trip flight between Denver and Paris. He can also deduct the cost of his stay in Paris for Thursday and Friday while he conducted business. However, he cannot deduct the cost of his stay in Paris from Saturday through Tuesday because those days were spent on nonbusiness activities. (He should have worked on Monday).

- Jody flew from Seattle to Tokyo. She spent 14 days on business and 5 days on personal matters and then flew back to Seattle. She spent one day flying in each direction. Because only 5/21 (less than 25%) of her total time abroad was for nonbusiness activities, she can deduct as travel expenses what it would have cost her to make the trip if she had not engaged in any nonbusiness activity. The amount she can deduct is the cost of the round-trip plane fare and 16 days (14 days plus the 2 days of travel) of meals (subject to the 50% limit), lodging, and other related expenses.

Example

Allison took a trip from Montgomery, Alabama to London, England. She was away from home for 10 days. She spent 2 days vacationing and 8 days on business (including the 2 travel days). Her expenses are as follows:

Airfare	$1,200
Lodging (10 days x $150)	$1,500
Meals (10 days x $90)	$900

Allison's deduction is $2,760. [$1,200 + (8 x 150) + 1/2 (8 x 90) = $2,760]. Less than 25% of the time was personal so no allocation of transportation expenses is required.

EXHIBIT 20: DEDUCTIBLE TRAVEL EXPENSES

Expense	Description
Transportation	The cost of travel by airplane, train, or bus between your home and your business destination. If you were provided with a ticket or you are riding free as the result of a frequent traveler or similar program, your cost is zero.
Taxi, Commuter Bus, and Limousine	Fares for these and other types of transportation between the airport or station and your hotel, or between the hotel and your work location away from home.
Baggage and Shipping	The cost of sending baggage and sample or display material between your regular and temporary work location.
Car	The costs of operating and maintaining your car when traveling away from home on business. You may deduct actual expenses or the standard mileage rate, including business-related tolls and parking. If you lease a car while away from home on business, you can deduct business-related expenses only.
Lodging	The cost of lodging if your business trip is overnight or long enough to require you to get substantial sleep or rest to properly perform your duties.
Meals	The cost of meals only if your business trip is overnight or long enough to require you to stop to get substantial sleep or rest. Includes amounts spent for food, beverages, taxes, and related tips. Only 50% of meal expenses are allowed as a deduction.
Cleaning	Cleaning and laundry expenses while away from home overnight.
Telephone	The cost of business calls while on your business trip, including business communication by fax machine or other communication devices.
Tips	Tips you pay for any expenses in this chart.
Other	Other similar ordinary and necessary expenses related to your business travel such as public stenographer's fees and computer rental fees.

IRS Publication 334

D. EDUCATION EXPENSES.

1. General requirements for deductibility.
   a. To maintain or improve existing skills in the present job - Nondegree classes are allowed as long as they maintain or improve existing skills.
   b. To meet legally imposed or employer requirements to retain current job, such as continuing education requirements.
2. Nondeductible expenses.
   a. To meet minimum requirements of the current job (education degree to become a teacher).
   b. To qualify the taxpayer for a new job (law degree).
   c. For review classes or exams for items such as the CPA or bar exams.
3. Allowable expenditures.
   a. Direct expenses.
      i. Books.
      ii. Tuition.
      iii. Typing, photocopying, etc.
   b. Indirect expenses.
      i. Transportation (i.e., from office to school).
      ii. Travel.
         A) Meals subject to 50% reduction.
         B) Lodging.
      iii. Laundry while in travel status.

Example Question

Dawn, who holds a Bachelors degree in Art History, is a middle school teacher in New Orleans. The school board recently changed its minimum education requirement by prescribing five years of college training. Existing teachers, such as Dawn, are allowed 10 years to acquire the additional year of education. Pursuant to this requirement, Dawn spends her summer break attending the University of Hawaii taking art history courses. Her expenses are as follows:

Books and tuition	$2,000
Meals	1,000
Lodging	700
Laundry while in travel status	200
Transportation	700
Total	**$4,600**

What is Dawn's deductible education expense deduction?

Answer: $4,100. [2,000 + 0.5 (1,000) + (700 + 200 + 700)] = 4,100. The shortcut would be to take the total and deduct 50% of the meals. Before taking this approach, it would be wise to check each category and make sure each category is deductible.

EXHIBIT 21: DEDUCTIBLE EDUCATIONAL EXPENSES FLOW DIAGRAM

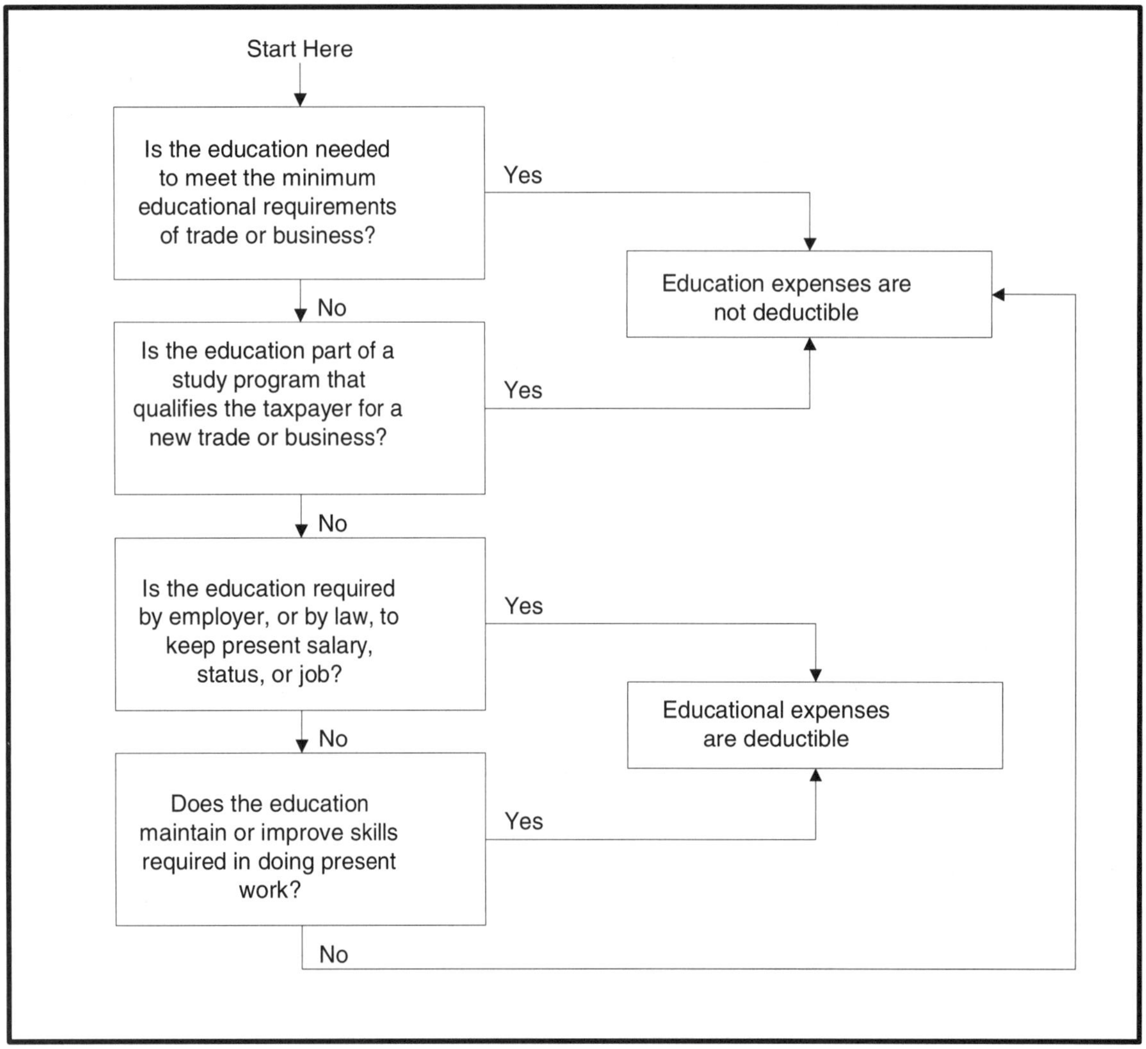

IRS Publication 17

E. MEALS AND ENTERTAINMENT (ONLY 50% DEDUCTIBLE).

1. Entertainment expenses are subject to the 50% reduction.
   a. Meals - Including taxes and tips.
   b. Entertainment - Including cover charges, parking, and entertainment room rentals.
2. There are exceptions to the 50% reduction.
   a. Transportation (e.g., cab fare).
   b. If the full value of expenditure is included in employee's compensation.
   c. If the value is de minimis.
   d. If it is a company event (e.g., parties or picnics).

3. Classification of expenses.
    a. Directly related to business.
        i. Entertainment precedes or follows an actual business meeting.
        ii. Not necessary for actual benefit to occur but must have expectation of benefit.
        iii. The expenditure should be in a clear business setting.
    b. Associated with business.
        i. Promoting goodwill and maintaining customer relations.
        ii. There must be intent to obtain new business or to continue existing business.
4. Restrictions.
    a. Business meals.
        i. Directly related to or associated with a business meeting.
        ii. Must be reasonable cost.
        iii. Taxpayer must be present at the meal.
    b. Club dues.
        i. No deduction allowed.
        ii. Entertainment costs at club may still qualify (subject to 50% deductibility).
    c. Tickets for entertainment.
        i. Eligible amount is limited to face value of the tickets plus tax (but not fees).
        ii. Skybox amount limited to number of seats available (even if all are not used) times price of regular seats.
        iii. Subject to 50% deductibility.
    d. Business gifts.
        i. Limited to $25 per donee per year.
        ii. Gifts less than $4 and promotional items (e.g., pens with business name) are excluded from limits.
        iii. Additional deductions allowed for incidental costs (e.g., engraving, delivery, gift wrapping).
        iv. No deduction allowed for gifts to superiors or employers.
        v. Employee achievement awards based on length of service or safety under $400 are excluded.

Example

- Kay entertains one of her clients and incurs the following:

Taxi	$30
Door cover fee	25
Dinner	128
Tips to waitress	25
Total	**$208**

Assuming proper substantiation, Kay's deduction is $119. [30 + 1/2 (25 + 128 + 25)] = 119.

- Chelsea, the sales director for a software company, pays $2,000 to obtain a skybox for an evening production of "Cats." The skybox holds 15 seats and Chelsea invites 14 clients. Nonluxury seats sell for $25 each. The refreshments served to Chelsea and her clients cost $455. A substantial business discussion was held before and after the show and Chelsea has all necessary substantiation. Chelsea's deduction is $415. 50% [(15 seats x $25) + 455] = $415.

- Elizabeth made the following gifts during the current year:

To Candace, a key client ($4 of the amount listed was for gift wrapping)	$104
To Kathy, Elizabeth's secretary, on Kathy's birthday	24
To Jan, Elizabeth's boss, at Christmas	28
Total Gifts	**$156**

Assuming proper substantiation, Elizabeth's deduction is $53. $29 + $24 = $53. The cost of gift wrapping is allowed. No deduction is available for a gift to a superior. $25 per person limit.

F. HOME OFFICE.

1. Must be exclusively and regularly used for business, and also be one of the following:
   a. Must be principal place of business.
      i. For tax years beginning after 1998, a home office will be considered a principal place of business if it is used exclusively and regularly by the taxpayer for administrative or management activities of a trade or business, and there is no other fixed location where these activities are performed to a substantial extent.
   b. Place of business used by clients, patients, or customers.
2. Deductions and limits.
   a. Requires allocation of total household expenses.

b. Cannot exceed net income of business (i.e., cannot create a loss).

c. Must first deduct expenses that would be allowed anyway (i.e., taxes, mortgage interest).

d. For self-employed individuals, the deduction is for AGI.

e. For employees, the deduction is from AGI (2% miscellaneous itemized deduction).

f. Disallowed expenses can be carried forward.

3. Coordination with personal residence gain exclusion.

a. Taxpayers who claim a home office deduction, even for five out of five years, may still exclude $250,000 (if single; $500,000 if filing jointly) when they sell their homes. Any depreciation claimed after May 6, 1997, must be reported as income to the extent of gain.

G. JOB HUNTING EXPENSES.

1. Seeking new employment in the same trade or business--deductible whether taxpayer gets job or not.
2. Seeking employment in different trade or business--not deductible.
3. Deductible expenses include travel, printing, postage, and employment agency fees.
4. No deduction is allowed if you are seeking employment for the first time.

H. OTHER EMPLOYEE EXPENSES.

1. Classified as Miscellaneous Itemized Deductions, subject to the 2% of AGI floor.

a. Professional dues and subscriptions.

b. Union dues and work uniforms.

c. Malpractice insurance premiums.

2. Miscellaneous expenses not subject to 2% floor.

a. Impairment-related work expenses of handicapped individuals.

b. Gambling losses to the extent of gambling winnings.

I. WHEN EMPLOYEE EXPENSES ARE REIMBURSED.

1. Accountable plans.

a. Requires adequate accounting of all expenditures.

b. Employee must return any unused allowance.

c. Requires substantiation.
    i. Amount of expenditure.
    ii. Time and place of expenditure.
    iii. Business purpose.
    iv. Relationship to person entertained.
    v. Itemized receipts for all lodging.
    vi. Itemized receipts for all expenditures $75 or more.
    vii. Not required if a per diem method is used.
d. Reimbursements are excluded from employee's gross income and expenses are not deductible from gross income.
e. If employee does not comply, the nonaccountable plan rules are used.

2. Nonaccountable plans.
    a. If you are not in an accountable plan, then you are in a nonaccountable plan.
    b. All reimbursements are income to the employee.
        i. Expenses related to the reimbursement are deductible as miscellaneous itemized deductions subject to the 2% of AGI floor.
    c. Unreimbursed employee expenditures.
        i. 50% deductibility applies for meals and entertainment.
        ii. Expenses are deductible as miscellaneous itemized deductions subject to the 2% floor.
        iii. If reimbursement is available and not sought, no deduction is allowed.
3. Per diem allowances for meals and lodging.
    a. Simplifies record keeping.
    b. The IRS publishes tables that provide per diem amounts for lodging and for meals and incidental expenses (based on city location).

EXHIBIT 22: HOW TO PROVE CERTAIN BUSINESS EXPENSES

<table>
<tr><th></th><th colspan="4">THEN you must keep records that show details of the following elements.</th></tr>
<tr><th>If you have expenses for:</th><th>Amount</th><th>Time</th><th>Place or Description</th><th>Business Purpose and Business Relationship</th></tr>
<tr><td>Travel</td><td>Cost of each separate expense for travel, lodging, and meals. Incidental expenses may be totaled in reasonable categories such as taxis, daily meals for traveler, etc.</td><td>Dates you left and returned for each trip and number of days spent on business.</td><td>Destination or area of your travel (name of city, town, or other designation).</td><td>Purpose: Business purpose for the expense or the business benefit gained or expected to be gained.
Relationship: N/A</td></tr>
<tr><td>Entertainment</td><td>Cost of each separate expense. Incidental expenses such as taxis, telephones, etc., may be totaled on a daily basis.</td><td>Date of entertainment. (Also see Business Purpose).</td><td>Name and address or location of place of entertainment. Type of entertainment if not otherwise apparent. (Also see Business Purpose.)</td><td rowspan="2">Purpose: Business purpose for the expense or the business benefit gained or expected to be gained. For entertainment, the nature of the business discussion or activity. If the entertainment was directly before or after a business discussion; the date, place, nature, and duration of the business discussion, and the identities of the persons who took part in both the business discussion and the entertainment activity.
Relationship: Occupations or other information (such as names, titles, or other designations) about the recipients that shows their business relationship to you. For entertainment, you must also prove that you or your employee was present if the entertainment was a business meal.</td></tr>
<tr><td>Gifts</td><td>Cost of the gift.</td><td>Date of the gift.</td><td>Description of the gift.</td></tr>
<tr><td>Transportation (cars)</td><td>Cost of each separate expense. For car expenses, the cost of the car and any improvements, the date you started using it for business, the mileage for each business use, and the total miles for the year.</td><td>Date of the expense. For car expenses, the date of the use of the car.</td><td>Your business destination (name of city, town, or other designation).</td><td>Purpose: Business purpose for the expense.

Relationship: N/A</td></tr>
</table>

IRS Publication 17; Table 28-2

Note: While it is unlikely that the exam will test substantiation requirements in this detail, the chart is provided for your convenience.

EXHIBIT 23: TRAVEL, ENTERTAINMENT, AND GIFT EXPENSES AND REIMBURSEMENTS

Type of Reimbursement (or Other Expense Allowance) Arrangement	Employer Reports on Form W-2	Employee Shows on Form 2106[1]
Accountable		
Actual expense reimbursement. Adequate accounting and excess returned.	Not reported.	Not shown if expenses do not exceed reimbursement.
Actual expense reimbursement. Adequate accounting and return of excess both required but excess not returned.	Excess reported as wages in box 1.[2] Amount adequately accounted for is reported only in box 13 -- it is not reported in box 1.	All expenses (and reimbursements reported on Form W-2, box 13) only if some or all of the excess expenses are claimed.[3] Otherwise, the form is not filed.
Per diem or mileage allowance (up to federal rate). Adequate accounting and excess returned.	Not reported.	All expenses and reimbursements only if excess expenses are claimed.[3] Otherwise, form is not filed.
Per diem or mileage allowance (exceeds federal rate). Adequate accounting up to the federal rate only and excess not returned.	Excess reported as wages in box 1.[2] Amount up to the federal rate is reported only in box 13 -- it is not reported in box 1.	All expenses (and reimbursements equal to the federal rate) only if expenses in excess of the federal rate are claimed.[3] Otherwise, form is not filed.
Nonaccountable Either adequate accounting or return of excess, or both, not required by plan.	Entire amount is reported as wages in box 1.	All expenses.[3]
No Reimbursement	Normal reporting of wages, etc.	All expenses.[3]

IRS Publication 334

[1] Employees may be able to use Form 2106-EZ. The qualifications are listed on the form.

[2] Excess is also reported in boxes 3 and 5, if applicable.

[3] Any allowable business expense is carried to line 20 of Schedule A (Form 1040) and deducted as a miscellaneous itemized deduction.

XVII. ITEMIZED DEDUCTIONS

A. ITEMIZED DEDUCTIONS - IN GENERAL.

1. Major itemized deductions.
   a. Medical expenses.
   b. Taxes.
   c. Interest.
   d. Charitable contributions.
   e. Casualty losses.
2. Miscellaneous itemized deductions.
   a. Deductions not subject to the 2% floor.
      i. Impairment related work expenses.
      ii. Gambling losses.
      iii. Annuity contract basis recovery.
      iv. Pro rata portion of estate taxes paid with respect to income in respect of decedent.
   b. Deductions subject to the 2% floor.
      i. Employee business expenses.
      ii. Home office expenses.
      iii. Investment expenses.
      iv. Tax return preparation fees.
      v. All other miscellaneous itemized deductions.

B. MEDICAL EXPENSES.

1. In general.
   a. Includes expenditures for taxpayer, spouse, and any dependents.
   b. Must not be reimbursed expenditures.
   c. Subject to 7.5% of AGI floor.
   d. Must be paid on behalf of taxpayer, spouse, or dependent.
2. What is covered.
   a. Diagnosis, cure, mitigation, treatment, or prevention of disease.
   b. Transportation primarily for and essential to the medical expenses in (a) above.
   c. Qualified long-term care services.
   d. Insurance premiums covering all of the above.

3. What is not covered.
    a. Unnecessary cosmetic surgery.
    b. Funerals.
4. Diagnosis, cure, mitigation, treatment, or prevention of disease.
    a. Examples: hospital charges, doctor's fees, glasses, insurance premiums, stop-smoking programs, surgery to correct vision, legal abortion, and weight loss programs.
    b. Prescription medicines and insulin.
    c. Nursing home expenditures (including meals) may be allowed if medical care is primary reason for admittance.
    d. Cost of lead-based paint removal.
    e. Surgery to correct a congenital deformity or disfiguring disease.
    f. Tuition for a special school may be allowed if the school has special facilities or medical care related to the infirmity is received.
    g. Capital expenditures - allowable with some restrictions.
        i. Expenditures are of a medical nature.
        ii. Expenditures are on the advice of a physician.
        iii. Facilities are used primarily by patient alone.
        iv. Facilities are built at a reasonable expense.
        v. Operating and maintenance expenditures are also allowable.
        vi. Appraisal costs for determining the change in value are also allowable (miscellaneous itemized deduction subject to 2% of AGI floor).
        vii. Capital expenditure deduction is allowed in the year incurred, not in the year paid.
        viii. Limited to the amount that the expenditures exceed any increase in the value of the property.
        ix. Deduction is only allowed while the medical condition exists.
        x. The 7.5% AGI floor applies to capital expenditures
5. Transportation and lodging.
    a. These expenditures are allowed as medical expenses (subject to 7.5% AGI floor).
    b. Includes: fares, ambulance, personal car, tolls, parking, etc. Personal car allowance can be actual expenses or standard rate ($0.12/mile plus parking and tolls for 2003).
    c. Includes the travel costs of parent with a minor child.
    d. Includes the travel costs of any person necessary to travel with the patient.

e. Lodging also included with some restrictions.
   i. Must be primary and essential for medical care.
   ii. Must be in a licensed medical care facility.
   iii. Accommodations must be reasonable.
   iv. No significant element of personal pleasure can be involved.
   v. Limited to $50 per night for each person.
f. No meal deduction is allowed with one exception.
   i. If meals are provided on site and are part of the medical care.
   ii. The 50% meal deductibility does not apply to this exception.

6. Qualified long-term care expenses.
   a. Medical services for a chronically ill person which are provided under a prescribed plan of care.
      i. Chronically ill is defined as being unable to perform (without substantial assistance from another individual) at least 2 activities of daily living (e.g., eating, dressing, bathing) for a period of at least 90 days due to a loss of functional capacity.
   b. Includes expenditures for diagnostic, therapeutic, preventive, rehabilitative and personal care services.

7. Health Insurance premiums.
   a. Expenditures for accident and health insurance premiums are deductible (subject to 7.5% AGI floor).
      i. Individual and group policies are covered.
      ii. Any premiums paid by the employer are not deductible.
      iii. Special rules for self-employed persons.
         A) 70% of the health insurance premiums can be deducted for AGI. This portion increases to 100% in 2003.

Tax Year	% Eligible Costs Deductible for AGI
2002	70%
2003 and thereafter	100%

         B) The remainder of health insurance premiums can be deducted from AGI as an itemized deduction subject to a 7.5% floor.
         C) No deduction is allowed for premiums paid by an employee if an employer-paid plan is available.
   b. The premiums paid for long-term care are qualifying medical expenses subject to the 7.5% floor. The maximum deductible premium depends on the taxpayer's age.

EXHIBIT 24: 2003 MAXIMUM DEDUCTIBLE LONG-TERM CARE PREMIUMS
(SUBJECT TO 7.5% OF AGI FLOOR)

Attained Age Before Close of Taxable Year	Annual Maximum Deductible Premiums
40 or less	$250
More than 40 but not more than 50	$470
More than 50 but not more than 60	$940
More than 60 but not more than 70	$2,510
More than 70	$3,130

8. Year of deduction.
   a. A deduction is available in the year paid for both cash-basis and accrual-basis taxpayers.
   b. A deduction is available in the year incurred for deceased taxpayers.
   c. If a payment is made on a credit card, the payment is deemed to have been made at the time of the charge.
   d. A current deduction is not allowed for prepayment of future medical care unless the taxpayer is under an obligation to make the payment.
9. Reimbursements.
   a. Expected reimbursements are disregarded in determining the amount of deduction.
   b. Tax benefit rule applies if a reimbursement occurs in a future year.
   c. Reimbursement is considered part of gross income if a tax benefit resulted.

Example

Mae, an employee of XYZ Company, has AGI of $20,000. She incurred the following medical expenses (she itemizes her deductions):

Health insurance premiums	$850
Dental expenses	$500
Unreimbursed medical	$450 ($1,000 medical expenses less $550 reimbursement)

Her total medical expenses are $1,800 ($850 + $500 + $450). She must reduce this amount by 7.5% of her AGI. Therefore, deductible medical expenses are $300 ($1,800 - $1,500).

C. TAXES.

1. General.
   a. Taxes defined.
      i. An enforced contribution.
      ii. Purpose is to raise revenue (i.e., not payment for special use or privilege).
      iii. Certain taxes are deductible as an itemized deduction.

   b. Fees defined.
      i. Purpose is to collect payment for a special use or privilege.
      ii. Only deductible as a business expense (ordinary and necessary).
2. Summary of deductible taxes.
   a. State, local, and foreign real property taxes.
   b. State and local personal property taxes (if tax is based on value of property).
   c. State, local, and foreign income taxes.
3. Property taxes, assessments, and apportionment of taxes.
   a. Property taxes.
      i. Deductible for the person the taxes are imposed on regardless of who pays them.
      ii. Must be based on the value of the property (ad valorem).
   b. Assessments.
      i. Imposed for purposes of local benefit (e.g., roads, schools, etc.), actions that typically increase the value of the property.
      ii. Usually not deductible but added to the basis of the property.
   c. Apportionment for real estate transfers.
      i. Based on the number of days each held the property during the tax year.
      ii. Apportionment rules govern the deduction - not the purchase agreement.
      iii. Based on the date of the transfer.
      iv. If purchase agreement does not apportion, then basis adjustment is required.
         A) If buyer pays all the tax:
            1) Seller's portion is added to the amount realized by the seller.
            2) Buyer's basis is increased by the same amount.
         B) If seller pays all the tax:
            1) Buyer's portion is deducted from the amount realized by seller.
            2) Buyer's basis is reduced by the same amount.
4. State and local income taxes.
   a. These taxes paid are itemized deductions only.
   b. For cash-basis taxpayers the amount included is the withheld amount.
   c. Estimated tax payments are also allowed as deductions.
   d. Refunds occurring in future years are included in Gross Income at that time, to the extent a tax benefit was received.
   e. Any state income taxes that are paid, whether for the previous, current, or future year, are deducted in the year paid.
5. Remember that property taxes and state/local income taxes incurred in a trade or business or on production of income property are deductions for AGI.

Examples

- Robin withheld $4,200 in state income taxes in 2003, and she paid an additional $1,200 in estimated state income tax payments. She filed her 2002 state income tax return in April 2003, and received a state tax refund of $700 in 2003. She claimed the standard deduction on her federal return for 2002. If she itemizes, she can deduct $5,400 ($4,200 + $1,200) in state income tax on her 2003 federal income tax return. The $700 refund is not offset against the itemized deduction and is not taxable income because Robin claimed the standard deduction for 2002.

- During 2003, Irma paid the following taxes:

Taxes on residence (for the period from January 1 through August 31, 2003)	$2,000
State motor vehicle tax (based on the value of the automobile)	120

  Irma sold the residence on June 30, 2003. The real estate taxes were not prorated between the buyer and the seller. The amount that qualifies as a deduction from AGI for 2003 for taxes (rounded to nearest $) is $1,601. [(180 days ÷ 243 days x $2,000) + $120]

- Sherry generally itemizes deductions and is a resident of a state that imposes income tax. Information regarding Sherry's state income tax transactions for 2003 is as follows:

State taxes withheld in 2003	$7,200
Refund received in 2003 from overpayment of 2002 state tax liability	1,500
Deficiency assessed as paid for 2001 (as a result of audit by the state)	3,000
Interest paid on the tax deficiency	500

  The 2001 deficiency and interest thereon were paid by Sherry in 2003. If she elects to itemize deductions for 2003, she can deduct $10,200. (7,200 + 3,000) = 10,200. The interest on the deficiency is personal interest and is not deductible. The refund is reported as income under the tax benefit rule. It does not affect the amount deductible.

EXHIBIT 25: WHICH TAXES CAN YOU DEDUCT?

	You Can Deduct	You Cannot Deduct
Income Taxes	State and local income taxes. Foreign income taxes (may be taken as a credit instead).	Federal income taxes. Employee contributions to private or voluntary disability plans.
Real Estate Taxes	State and local real estate taxes. Foreign real estate taxes. Tenant's share of real estate taxes paid by cooperative housing corporation.	Taxes for local benefits. Trash and garbage pickup fees. Rent increase due to higher real estate taxes. Homeowners' association charges.
Personal Property Taxes	State and local personal property taxes.	
Other Taxes	Taxes that are expenses of your trade or business or producing income. One-half of self-employment tax paid. Taxes on property producing rent or royalty income. Occupational taxes.	Many taxes, such as state and local sales taxes and federal excise taxes, generally are not deductible.
Fees and Charges		Fees and charges, such as fees for driver's licenses or charges for water bills, generally are not deductible.

Publication 17; Table 24-1

D. INTEREST.

1. Investment interest.
   a. Interest on funds borrowed to acquire investment assets.
   b. Deduction for investment interest is limited to net taxable investment income.
      i. Investment income.
         A) Gross income from interest, dividends, annuities, royalties, etc.
         B) Cannot be derived in the ordinary course of business.
         C) Does not include tax-exempt interest income.
      ii. Investment expenses.
         A) Must be directly connected with the production of income.
         B) Do not include interest expense in investment expenses for this calculation.
         C) Includes subscriptions to professional newsletters, safe deposit box rentals, etc.
   c. Net investment income = investment income - investment expenses.
   d. Carryover of disallowed investment interest allowed indefinitely.

Example

Mario had the following items of income and expense for the current year:

Dividend income from Crow Company stock	\$2,000
Interest income from Inron Company bonds	\$3,000
Interest income from State of Louisiana bonds	\$1,000
Margin interest expense (investment interest)	(\$7,000)

If he itemizes, Mario can only deduct \$5,000 of the investment interest expense. His taxable investment income is \$5,000 (\$2,000 dividends + \$3,000 TAXABLE interest). The State of Louisiana bonds are municipal bonds, and the interest is tax exempt.

2. Qualified residence interest.
   a. Interest paid or incurred on debt for a qualified residence of the taxpayer is deductible.
      i. Qualified residence includes a primary residence and one other residence.
      ii. May include a condo, trailer, boat with living quarters, and mobile homes.
      iii. The debt must be secured by the property.
      iv. Maximum allowable acquisition indebtedness is \$1,000,000 (\$500,000 for married filing separately).
      v. Acquisition indebtedness also includes construction and substantial improvements.
   b. Home equity loans are also covered.
      i. Home equity loan debt cannot exceed FMV less acquisition indebtedness.
      ii. Home equity loan debt cannot exceed \$100,000.
      iii. Interest is deductible up to these limits of indebtedness.

Example

Mary owned a home with a FMV of \$400,000. The first mortgage had a balance of \$320,000. Mary takes out a home equity loan of \$90,000. How much of the debt will be qualified residence interest? All of Mary's first mortgage (acquisition indebtedness) will qualify, but only \$80,000 (\$400,000-\$320,000) will qualify on the home equity loan since total indebtedness cannot exceed FMV.

3. Interest paid for services.
   a. Points on a home loan are deductible in the year paid (principal residence loans only).
      i. Borrower is treated as paying any points seller paid for borrower's mortgage.
      ii. Can deduct points up to funds provided plus seller-paid points.
      iii. Buyer must reduce basis in home by points paid by seller. Seller reduces amount realized by this amount.

b. Points on other loans must be capitalized and amortized.

c. Must be compensation for use of money.

d. Points on refinancing must be capitalized and amortized over the life of the loan. However, if refinancing is incurred for home improvements, and the points are paid from separate funds, the points are currently deductible.

Examples

- When Gary took out a $100,000 mortgage loan to buy his home in the current year, he was charged one percentage point ($1,000). He met all the tests for deducting points except the only funds he provided was a $750 down payment. Of the $1,000 charged for points, he can deduct $750 in the current year.

- When Stephanie took out a $100,000 mortgage loan to buy her home in the current year, she was charged one percentage point ($1,000). Tim, who sold her the home also paid one point ($1,000) to help her get her mortgage. Stephanie met all the tests for deducting points, except the only funds she provided was a $750 down payment. In the current year, Stephanie can deduct $1,750 ($750 of the amount she was charged plus the $1,000 paid by Tim). She must reduce the basis of her home by the $1,000 paid by Tim.

EXHIBIT 26: ARE MY POINTS FULLY DEDUCTIBLE THIS YEAR?

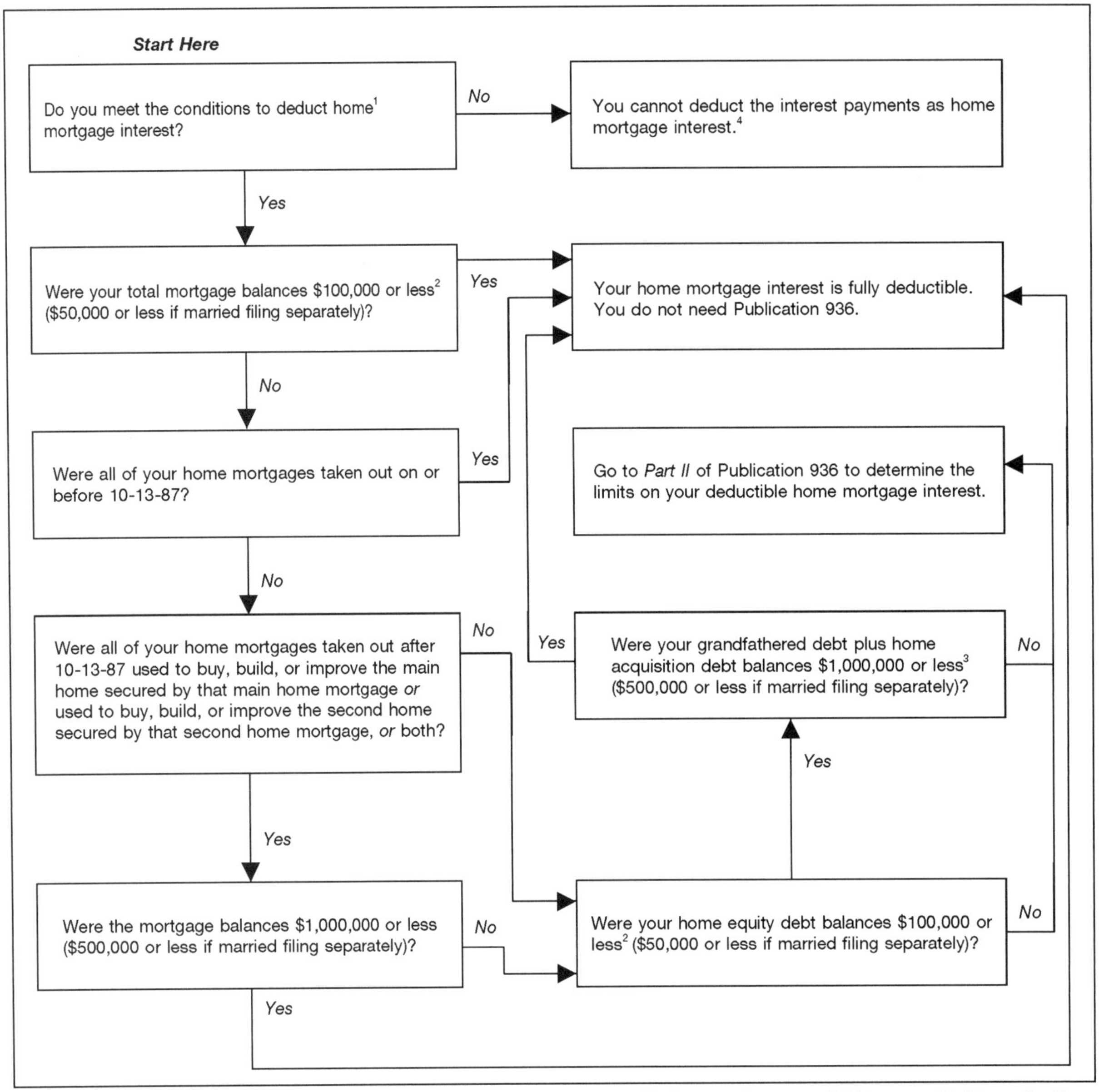

[1]You must itemize deductions on Schedule A (Form 1040) and be legally liable for the loan. The loan must be a secured debt on a qualified home. See *Home Mortgage Interest.*

[2]If all mortgages on your main or second home exceed the home's fair market value, a lower limit may apply. See *Home equity debt limit* under *Home Equity Debt* in *Part II* of Publication 936.

[3]Amounts over the $1,000,000 limit ($500,000 if married filing separately) qualify as home equity debt if they are not more than the total home equity debt limit. See Publication 936 for more information about grandfathered debt, home acquisition debt, and home equity debt.

[4]See *Table 25-1* for where to deduct other types of interest payments.

Publication 17; Figure 25-B

Note: While this is unlikely to be tested in this detail on the exam, the chart is provided for your convenience.

4. Prepayment penalty - Considered to be interest paid and is deductible (if the interest itself is eligible).
5. Interest paid to related parties.
   a. Deductible according to normal interest rules.
   b. Refer to rules on loans to related parties.
6. Other restrictions.
   a. Cannot deduct interest paid on behalf of another (e.g., child, parent).
   b. Prepaid interest deduction is based on accrual-basis rules for all taxpayers.
7. Classification.
   a. If interest is paid for a business use or the production of income, then it is deductible for AGI.
   b. If interest is paid for personal use (investment interest and qualified residence interest), then it is deductible from AGI.
8. Personal Interest - Personal interest is not deductible (e.g., bank cards, consumer loans).

Example

During the current year, Albert paid the following interest charges:

Home mortgage	$9,000
On loan to purchase household furniture (personal)	800
On loan to purchase State of Louisiana general obligation bonds (tax exempt)	750

If Albert itemizes his deductions for the current year, the amount deductible as interest expense is $9,000. The interest on the loan to purchase household furniture is nondeductible consumer interest. The interest on the loan to purchase State of Louisiana bonds is not deductible under Section 265.

Example

Rowena, a single taxpayer, purchased an airplane for $130,000. In order to obtain financing for the purchase, Rowena issued a lien on her personal residence in the amount of $130,000. At the time, the residence had a fair market value of $400,000 and a first mortgage of $320,000. For the plane loan, Rowena may claim the interest on $80,000 as qualified residence interest. Home equity loans are limited to the lesser of:

- The fair market value of the residence, reduced by acquisition indebtedness, or
- $100,000.

Thus, $400,000 (fair market value) - $320,000 (first mortgage) provides a limit of $80,000. Interest on the remaining $50,000 of the loan will be treated under the consumer interest rules (i.e., not deductible).

---

9. Certain taxpayers may deduct up to $2,500 (for 2003) of interest paid on a higher education loan.
   a. AGI phaseout for 2003:
      - Joint return $100,000 - 130,000
      - All others $50,000 - 65,000

EXHIBIT 27: WHERE TO DEDUCT INTEREST

Type of Interest	Where to Deduct	Where to Find Information
Student loan interest	Form 1040; line 24 or Form 1040A, line 16	Publication 970
Deductible home mortgage interest and points reported on Form 1098	Schedule A (Form 1040), line 10	Publication 936
Deductible home mortgage interest *not* reported on Form 1098	Schedule A (Form 1040), line 11	Publication 936
Points not reported on Form 1098	Schedule A (Form 1040), line 12	Publication 936
Investment interest (other than interest incurred to produce rents or royalties)	Schedule A (Form 1040), line 13	Publication 550
Business interest (nonfarm)	Schedule C or C-EZ (Form 1040)	Publication 535
Farm business interest	Schedule F (Form 1040)	Publication 225 and 535
Interest incurred to produce rents or royalties	Schedule E (Form 1040), line 10	Publication 527 and 535
Personal interest	Not Deductible	

Publication 17; Table 25-1

E. CHARITABLE CONTRIBUTIONS.

1. Criteria for a gift
   a. Donative intent.
   b. Lack of consideration from donee.
   c. Acceptance by donee.
2. Donations to what kind of organizations qualify for a deduction?
   a. Must be made to a qualified organization.
      i. U.S. District of Columbia, a state or possession of the U.S., or a political subdivision of a state or possession.
      ii. Organizations located in U.S. that are organized and operated exclusively for religious, charitable, scientific, literary, or educational purposes or for the prevention of cruelty to children or animals.
      iii. Veterans' organizations.
      iv. Cemetery companies.
      v. IRS Publication 78 lists qualified charitable organizations. This information can also be obtained from www.irs.ustreas.gov.

EXHIBIT 28: EXAMPLES OF CHARITABLE CONTRIBUTIONS – A QUICK CHECK

Use the following lists for a quick check of contributions you can or cannot deduct. See the rest of Publication 17; Section 26 for more information and additional rules and limits that may apply.

Deductible as Charitable Contributions	**Not Deductible as Charitable Contributions**
Money or property you give to: • Churches, synagogues, temples, mosques, and other religious organizations • Federal, state, and local governments, if your contribution is solely for public purposes (for example, a gift to reduce the public debt) • Nonprofit schools and hospitals • Public parks and recreation facilities • Salvation Army, Red Cross, CARE, Goodwill Industries, United Way, Boy Scouts, Girl Scouts, Boys and Girls Clubs of America, etc. • War veterans' groups Costs you pay for a student living with you, sponsored by a qualified organization Out-of-pocket expenses when you serve a qualified organization as a volunteer	Money or property you give to: • Civic leagues, social sports clubs, labor unions, and chambers of commerce • Foreign organizations (except certain Canadian, Israeli, and Mexican charities) • Groups that are run for personal profit • Groups whose purpose is to lobby for law changes • Homeowners' associations • Individuals • Political groups or candidates for public office Cost of raffle, bingo, or lottery tickets Dues, fees, or bills paid to country clubs, lodges, fraternal orders, or similar groups Tuition Value of your time or services Value of blood given to a blood bank

Publication 17; Table 26-1

3. Qualifying organizations are also classified as:
   a. Public charities.
      i. Receive broad public support.
      ii. General examples – churches, educational institutions, hospitals, medical research organizations.
      iii. Specific examples – American Red Cross, Girl Scouts, United Way, Goodwill, Mercer University.
   b. Private foundations.
      i. Not defined directly in the Code but, rather, by reference to a list of the types of organizations that are not private foundations.
      ii. Typically funded by large contributions from a small number of contributors and income from investments and businesses unrelated to the foundation's charitable purposes.
      iii. Usually functions as a charity by making grants to organizations that conduct charitable activities, instead of performing the activities itself.
4. Deduction is allowed in year paid for both cash and accrual-basis taxpayers.

5. Consequences of a benefit received by donor.
   a. If benefit is inconsequential, may deduct in full.
   b. If a consequential benefit is received, the contribution deduction must be reduced by the fair market value of the benefit.
   c. There is a special rule for contribution related to the right to buy athletic tickets from universities - 80% of donation qualifies as deductible charitable contribution (Section 170(l)).
6. No deductions allowed for volunteering of services, but related personal expenses are deductible.
   a. Mileage for charitable use of an automobile is 14 cents per mile (for 2003) or actual unreimbursed expenses for oil and gas.
   b. Rental value of property used by a qualified charity is not deductible.
   c. Cost of child care while performing charity-related activities is nondeductible.
   d. Donating blood is considered to be a nondeductible personal service.
7. Record keeping.
   a. Must have written receipt for gifts over $250.
      i. Receipt must have amount of cash or description of property.
      ii. Taxpayer must have receipt by due date of return or when return is filed.
   b. Noncash property over $500 and less than or equal to $5,000.
      i. Noncash contributions with a value of $500-$5,000 must be reported on Section A of Form 8283.
      ii. An appraisal is not required. However, taxpayers may wish to get an independent appraisal to support the deduction claimed.
   c. Noncash property over $5,000 ($10,000 for nonpublic stock).
      i. Noncash contributions with a value over $5,000 must be substantiated by a qualified appraisal of the property. A summary of the appraisal must be attached to the donor's income tax return (on Form 8283) for the year in which the deduction is first claimed.
      ii. The appraisal requirement will also apply if a taxpayer donates, to one or more charities, a number of similar items (such as coins) with a total value exceeding $5,000.
      iii. An appraisal is not required for contributions of publicly traded securities for which market quotes are readily available on an established securities market.
      iv. The costs of an appraisal are not deductible as a charitable contribution. However, these costs are deductible by individuals as miscellaneous itemized deductions, subject to the 2% of AGI floor.
   d. Valuation.
      i. Generally, fair market value at the date of gift.
      ii. Taxpayer must keep records of terms of agreement, basis, appraisals, etc.

8. Limits.
   a. General.
      i. Depending on the type of property and the type of charity, there is a limit on the amount of deductible contribution.
      ii. There is a general overall 50% limit for <u>all</u> charitable contributions during a year.
      iii. Carryover up to five years is available for disallowed amounts.
   b. Ordinary income property - property that, if sold, gives rise to ordinary income.
      i. Includes inventory, taxpayer-created art, and short-term capital assets.
      ii. Deduction is the lesser of the FMV or adjusted basis.
   c. Capital gain property - Property that, if sold, gives rise to long-term capital gain or Sec. 1231 gain.
      i. Stocks, bonds, real estate, etc.
      ii. Deduction amount equals FMV.
         A) Exception for capital gain portion of property given to some private foundations (do not receive funding from the general public, e.g., Ford Foundation).
            1) If operating foundation (spends its income on charitable purpose) - fully deductible.
            2) If nonoperating foundation - only adjusted basis is deductible.
         B) Exception for capital gain portion of tangible personalty (to any organization).
            1) If the donee puts property to unrelated use - adjusted basis only.
            2) Fully deductible if donor believes that property will be put to a related use.
   d. Contributions made to the following organizations cannot exceed 50% of AGI.
      i. Religious, public, education, governmental institutions.
      ii. Private operating foundations.
      iii. Some private nonoperating foundations.
         A) If they distribute within 2½ months of the beginning of the following year to public charities and private operating foundations.
         B) If they pool donations and distribute.
   e. The following contributions are limited to 30% of AGI.
      i. Cash and ordinary income property to private nonoperating foundations (that do not qualify as 50% organizations).
      ii. Applies to LTCG property donated to 50% organizations.
         A) If donor elects to forego deduction of capital gain, property moves to 50%.
         B) If donor elects to forego capital gain, deduction is lost - not carried over.
      iii. Donations to 50% organizations are applied to limits before 30% gifts.
   f. 20% Ceiling - Applies to LTCG property given to nonoperating foundations (not 50% organizations).

EXHIBIT 29: CHARITABLE CONTRIBUTION DEDUCTIONS

Types of Property	Amount of Deduction	Limit for Public Charities, Private Operating Foundations and Certain Private Nonoperating Foundations	Limit for Other Private Nonoperating Foundations
Cash	FMV	50% of AGI	30% of AGI
Ordinary Income Property and ST Capital Gain Property	Lesser of the adjusted basis or the FMV	50%	30%
Long-Term CG Property:			
• Intangibles	FMV Basis election	30% 50%	20% 20%
• Tangible Property (related use)	FMV Basis election	30% 50%	20% 20%
• Tangible Property (unrelated use)	Basis	50%	20%
• Real Property	FMV Basis election	30% 50%	20% 20%

Example

Gina graduated from Mumford University. She donated $2,000 to the athletic department of the University to guarantee priority to purchase two premium season tickets to home football games. In addition, Gina purchased two season tickets for the regular price of $500 ($250 each). Gina's charitable contribution for the current year is $1,600. 80% of $2,000 is deductible since Gina is paying for the right to purchase tickets. The $500 expenditure for the tickets cannot be claimed since it provided Gina with a benefit.

Example

- Clarence makes the following charitable donations:

	Basis	Fair Market Value
Inventory held for resale in Clarence's business (a sole proprietorship)	$8,000	$6,000
Stock in Roth Corp. held as an investment (acquired 2 years ago)	10,000	40,000
Coin collection held as an investment (acquired 10 years ago)	1,000	7,000

The inventory was given to a local public school. The Roth Corp. stock was given to Clarence's church, and the coin collection was given to the Boy Scouts. Both donees promptly sold the property for the stated fair market value. Ignoring percentage limitations, Clarence's charitable contribution for the current year is $47,000.

Inventory is ordinary income property, but the fair market value ($6,000) must be used if lower than the basis ($8,000). Stock is intangible property and is not subject to the tangible personalty rules. Since a sale of the Roth Corp. stock would have yielded a long-term capital gain, the full fair market value qualified for the deduction ($40,000). The coin collection comes under the tangible personalty exception (unrelated use), and the adjusted basis ($1,000) must be used. ($6,000 + 40,000 + 1,000) = $47,000.

- Colleen, a calendar-year taxpayer, made the following charitable contributions:

	Basis	Fair Market Value
Cash to church	$5,000	$5,000
Unimproved land to the city of Violet, Louisiana	40,000	70,000

The land had been held as an investment and was acquired 5 years ago. Shortly after receipt, the city of Violet sold the land for $90,000. Colleen's AGI is $120,000. She has two options with respect to the contribution deduction. First she can deduct the FMV of the land limited to 30% of her AGI. In this case the total deduction would be $41,000 ($5,000 (cash) + $36,000 ($70,000 FMV limited to 30% x $120,000)). The carryover for the next five years is $34,000 ($70,000 FMV - $36,000 current year deduction). Alternatively, she can deduct the adjusted basis, limited to 50% of AGI. In this case, the total deduction would be $40,000 for the land plus $5,000 cash for a total of $45,000.

g. Charitable contributions by business entities.

   i. Partnerships and S corporations – the charitable contributions are deducted by the partners and shareholders on their individual income tax returns. The amount of the deduction is reported to the partners and S corporation shareholders on Schedule K-1.

   ii. C corporations – the charitable deduction is reported on the corporation's income tax return (Form 1120). The deduction is based on the type of property donated, the type of organization to which the property is donated, and the corporation's taxable income before taking into account the charitable deduction.

      A) Ordinary income property (inventory, etc.) - generally, a corporation may deduct the basis of ordinary income property donated to charity. However, the corporation will receive a deduction equal to basis plus half of the unrealized appreciation (not to exceed twice the basis) in the following situations:

         1) The property is used by the charitable organization to care for the ill or infants.

         2) The property is scientific equipment that will be donated to a college or university for research or experimentation.

         3) The property is computer equipment that will be donated to a primary or secondary school (grades K - 12).

      B) Capital-gain property – generally, the corporation may deduct the fair market value of the capital-gain property donated to charity. However, the deduction will be limited to the property's adjusted basis in the following situations:

         1) The property is tangible personal property that is use-unrelated. Use-unrelated means that the property is put to a use that is not related to the charity's exempt purpose.

         2) The property is donated to certain private foundations.

      C) Limit on charitable deduction.

         1) The maximum charitable deduction a corporation can take in a taxable year is limited to 10% of the corporation's taxable income before certain deductions.

            a) The deductions that are not taken into account include the charitable-contribution deduction, the dividends-received deduction, and net operating loss and capital loss carrybacks.

Example

<u>In the current year</u>, XYZ Corporation had net income from operations of $60,000 and received a dividend of $4,000, which is eligible for the 70% dividends-received deduction. During the year, the corporation donated $8,000 in cash to the University of New Jersey.

The maximum charitable contribution deduction that XYZ is entitled to is $6,400 ($60,000 + $4,000 = $64,000 x 10% = $6,400).

XYZ will have taxable income of $54,800 ($60,000 + $4,000 - $2,800 dividends-received deduction - $6,400 charitable-contribution deduction).

---

         2) Any disallowed deduction may be carried forward for up to five years.

Example

Assume the same facts as the previous example. XYZ Corporation may carry forward the disallowed deduction of $1,600 ($8,000 donation - $6,400 deduction) for up to five years.

F. CASUALTY LOSSES FOR INDIVIDUALS.

1. Section 165.
   a. Losses of nonbusiness property are limited to losses from fire, storm, shipwreck, or other casualty or theft.
   b. Casualties refer to losses meeting three criteria:
      i. Identifiable event.
      ii. Property damage results.
      iii. Event is sudden, unusual, and unexpected.

Examples

- Car accident (unless willful negligence or willful act caused it).
- Fires (unless taxpayers set it or paid someone else to).
- Earthquake.
- Flood.
- Tornado.
- Vandalism.

2. Events that are not casualties.
   a. Termite damage is an example of something that is not expected and is identifiable but is not considered "sudden" by the IRS. However, the courts did allow casualty loss treatment for a sudden Southern Pine Beetle attack since these insects can destroy a tree in 5-10 days.
   b. Also not allowed are property devaluations caused by storm damage to neighboring houses, but not to the taxpayer's property.
   c. The Tax Court denied neighbors of O.J. Simpson a casualty loss deduction resulting from a 30% decline in the market value of their house as a result of the murder trial. The ruling centered on the fact that there was no physical damage (Chamales v. Commr., TC Memo 2000-33). Similarly, taxpayers were denied a casualty loss deduction for buyer resistance to the sale of their house due to an earthquake in the area (Palos v Commr).
   d. Most drought-related losses are considered progressive deterioration and are not casualties.
3. Theft losses.
   a. Includes larceny, embezzlement and robbery, but excludes misplaced items.
   b. Theft losses are deducted in the year of discovery not the year of theft. The deduction is only allowed to the extent that the loss exceeds the expected recovery from any insurance.

c. If the insurance claim is greater than the adjusted basis, a gain is recognized.

4. When to deduct casualty losses.

   a. General rule - Loss is deductible in the year the loss occurs (except theft losses). If a reasonable chance of recovery from insurance exists, no loss is allowed.

   b. Disaster area losses.

      i. When the President declares a disaster area, the losses are allowed to be deducted in the year preceding the actual loss.

      ii. If previous year's taxes have already been filed, the taxpayer may file an amended return.

      iii. Disaster loss rules also apply to a personal residence if the disaster causes the residence to be unsafe, and, within 120 days of the President's declaration, local authorities order the structure demolished.

5. Measuring the amount of loss.

   a. Amount of loss.

      i. The amount of the loss is the lesser of:

         A) The adjusted basis, or

         B) The FMV before the event less the FMV after the event.

      ii. Losses from property held for partial business and partial personal use is determined separately for each portion.

      iii. Losses are reduced by any insurance recovery.

      iv. Appraisal or cost of repairs is generally required to determine the extent of the loss.

   b. Reduction for $100 and 10% of AGI floor - The deduction for casualty losses on personal use property is reduced by both the $100 floor and by 10% of AGI. The $100 floor applies to each incident, but the 10% floor is applied to the aggregate casualty loss amount for the year.

   c. Personal use property losses are itemized deductions.

Example

Larry had art worth $10,000 (basis of $15,000) stolen from his apartment. During the year, he had a salary of $30,000 and no other deductions. Larry's itemized deduction from the theft of the art.

Loss	$10,000	(lesser of basis or reduction in FMV)
Less: 10% AGI (10% x $30,000)	(3,000)	
$100 floor	(100)	
Itemized deduction	$6,900	

---

6. Personal casualty gains and losses - If the taxpayer has both losses and gains, they are netted. If gains exceed losses, both gains and losses are treated as gains and losses from sale of capital assets and may be short term or long term. The different types of property are not netted together. If losses exceed gains, all items are ordinary income and losses.

G. MISCELLANEOUS ITEMIZED DEDUCTIONS.

1. Subject to 2% of AGI floor (some of these were discussed in Employee Business Expense section).
   a. Job search costs.
      i. Only deductible if looking for job in present occupation.
      ii. Not necessary to get the job in order to get the tax deduction.
      iii. Includes employment agency fees, travel, resume expenses.
   b. Work clothes and uniforms.
      i. Wearing must be condition of employment.
      ii. Must not be suitable for everyday wear.
      iii. Full-time military uniforms are usually not deductible.
   c. Professional organization dues.
   d. Hobby expenses (to extent of hobby income).
   e. Work tools if expected to last ≤ 1 year.
   f. Expenses to produce or collect income (e.g., safe deposit box used to store securities).
   g. Expenses related to paying any tax (e.g., appraisal fees, tax preparation fees).
   h. Other unreimbursed employee expenses.
2. Not subject to 2% AGI floor.
   a. Federal estate tax on income in respect of decedent (IRD).
   b. Gambling losses to extent of gambling winnings.
   c. Unrecovered investment in annuity contract when annuity ceases because taxpayer died.
   d. Amortizable premium on taxable bonds (does not apply to bonds acquired after 12/31/87).
   e. Impairment-related work expenses of handicapped taxpayer.

H. OVERALL LIMITATION ON CERTAIN ITEMIZED DEDUCTIONS.

1. When AGI exceeds $139,500 for 2003 ($69,750 for Married Filing Separate), a taxpayer will begin to lose the benefit of some itemized deductions.
   a. Does not apply to medical, investment interest, casualty losses, or gambling losses.
   b. Adjustment is 3% of AGI above the threshold.
   c. Maximum reduction is 80% of covered itemized deductions.
   d. Reduction is made after other code provisions (e.g., 2% AGI floor for miscellaneous items).
2. Beginning in 2006, the overall limitation on itemized deductions is reduced. The overall limitation is eliminated for tax years after 2009 (TRA 2001).

XVIII. ALTERNATIVE MINIMUM TAX.

A. GENERAL.

1. This tax is a backup to the income tax to ensure that no taxpayer with substantial economic income can avoid significant tax liability using deductions and exclusions.

B. INDIVIDUAL ALTERNATIVE MINIMUM TAX.

1. This tax parallels the federal income tax in many ways. For example, both allow depreciation deductions, but the amount used in the calculation will be different.
2. A taxpayer may have to pay the AMT (Form 6251) if their taxable income for regular tax purposes, combined with any adjustments and preference items, exceeds:
   a. $49,000 (for 2001-2004) if married filing a joint return or a qualifying widower with dependent child.
   b. $35,750 (for 2001-2004) if filing status is single or head of household.
   c. The exemptions are phased out at upper income levels (see table below for phaseout levels).
3. Calculating Alternative Minimum Taxable Income (AMTI):

	Regular taxable income
+	Positive AMT adjustments
-	Negative AMT adjustments
+	Tax preferences
=	Alternative Minimum Taxable Income

4. Calculating Alternative Minimum Tax (AMT):

	AMTI
-	AMT exemption
=	Minimum tax base
X	AMT rate
=	Tentative AMT
-	Regular income tax on taxable income
=	AMT

5. Adjustments.
   a. Adjustments made to taxable income in the formula can be either positive or negative.
   b. Most adjustments relate to timing differences because of separate income tax and AMT calculation procedures/rules. A positive adjustment is made when the deduction allowed for income tax purposes exceeds the deduction allowed for AMT purposes. The opposite is true for a negative adjustment.
   c. If the income received for AMT purposes exceeds the income reported for regular income tax, the adjustment is positive. A negative adjustment is made when the income for regular tax is more than for AMT.

EXHIBIT 30: ALTERNATIVE MINIMUM TAX

Adjustment	Regular Tax	AMT	Positive/ Negative
Personal and Dependency Exemptions	Allowed	Disallowed	Positive
Standard Deduction	Allowed	Disallowed	Positive
Itemized Deduction – Medical	> 7.5% of AGI	>10% of AGI	Positive
Itemized Deduction – Taxes (income taxes and property taxes)	Allowed	Disallowed	Positive
Miscellaneous Itemized Deductions	Allowed >2%	Disallowed	Positive
Interest on Student Loans	Allowed	Disallowed	Positive
Difference between qualified-housing interest and qualified-residence interest	Allowed	Disallowed	Positive
Investment Interest Expense as limited for AMT purposes (related to qualified-residence interest and private-activity-bond interest)	Allowed	Disallowed	Positive
Exercise of Incentive Stock Options	Not taxed	Bargain element is an addback	Positive
Tax benefit rule for state income tax refund	Included in income	Not included in income	Negative
Reduction of itemized deductions	Some deductions disallowed	No cutback	Negative
Depreciation of post-86 property	MACRS allowed	ADS allowed	Both*
Mining Exploration and development costs			Both*
Pollution control facilities			Both
Research and experimental expenses			Both
Completed contract method	Small businesses can use the completed contract method	Small businesses must use the percentage-of-completion method	Both
Passive activity losses			Both
Adjusted gain/loss			Both

*Both means the adjustment could be positive or negative depending upon circumstances.

6. Tax preferences are always positive.
   a. The AMT is designed to take back all or part of the tax benefits derived through the use of these tax preferences (remember that all tax preferences are positive). These items include:
      i. The part of deduction for certain depletion that is more than the adjusted basis of the property.
      ii. Tax-exempt interest on certain private activity bonds (e.g., stadiums).
      iii. 50% exclusion of gain on sale of certain small business stock (Section 1202).
         A) Tax years ending after May 6, 1997, preference is 42% of excluded amount.
         B) For qualified stock acquired after 2000, the AMT preference will be 28% of excluded amount.
      iv. Accelerated depreciation on certain property placed in service before 1987.
7. Other components of the AMT formula (exemption amount) - Different exemption amounts are used depending on the status of the taxpayer. The exemption is phased out across the board at a rate of $0.25 for each dollar over the threshold amount.

Filing Status	Exemption Amount	Phaseout Range
Married, Joint	$49,000	$150,000 - $346,000
Single	$35,750	$112,500 - $255,500
Head of Household	$35,750	$112,500 - $255,500
Married, Separate	$24,500	$75,000 - $173,000

8. AMT credit - An alternative minimum tax credit may be generated when AMT is paid. It may be carried over indefinitely. It is applicable only from the AMT that occurs due to timing differences (i.e., it is not applicable to exclusions such as the standard deduction, personal exemptions, etc.).

C. MINIMUM TAX CREDIT FOR INDIVIDUALS.

a. In General.
   i. Generally, the alternative minimum tax paid in one year may be used as a credit against regular tax in a future year.
   ii. The credit may be carried forward (not back) indefinitely.
   iii. For individual taxpayers, the credit is claimed on Form 8801.
b. Exclusion vs. deferral items.
   i. For noncorporate taxpayers, the credit is only available to the extent the alternative minimum tax was attributable to deferral items, which are timing differences. The alternative minimum tax attributable to exclusion items is not available as a credit.
   ii. The minimum tax credit is determined by calculating the adjusted net minimum tax. The adjusted net minimum tax is the difference between the actual alternative minimum tax paid and the alternative minimum tax that would have been paid taking into account only exclusion items.

iii. The following AMT adjustments/preferences are considered exclusion items:

A) Standard deduction.

B) Itemized deduction.

C) Personal exemption.

D) Exclusion of gain from qualified small business stock.

E) Tax-exempt interest treated as a tax preference for AMT.

F) Percentage depletion treated as a tax preference for AMT.

iv. Any adjustment/preference that is not an exclusion item is a deferral item.

Example

Dave Myers, a single taxpayer, just filed his income tax return for the year 2002. With the return, Dave had to pay $35,000 of alternative minimum tax, resulting from the exercise of incentive stock options (deferral item) and some tax-exempt interest from private-activity bonds (exclusion item). If Dave had taken into account only the exclusion items (tax-exempt interest), his AMT liability would have only been $20,000. Therefore, his minimum tax credit is $15,000, calculated as follows:

Alternative Minimum Tax (AMT) paid with return	$35,000
Less: AMT based on exclusion items only	(20,000)
AMT based on deferral items (minimum tax credit)	$15,000

D. CORPORATE ALTERNATIVE MINIMUM TAX.

1. Corporations may have to pay the AMT (Form 4626) if taxable income for regular tax purposes, combined with any adjustments and preference items, exceeds $40,000. The exemption is phased out at a rate of $0.25 for each dollar of AMTI in excess of $150,000.

2. Exemption from AMT for small businesses.

   a. The Taxpayer Relief Act of 1998 exempts certain small businesses from the AMT.

   b. In their first year of existence, all corporations are exempt.

   c. In the second year of existence, the corporation will be exempt if its gross receipts were less than $5,000,000 in the prior year.

   d. In the third year (and going forward), the corporation will be exempt if its average annual gross receipts for all prior three-year periods are less than $7,500,000.

   e. Once the corporation fails the gross receipts test, the corporation becomes subject to AMT prospectively.

3. Adjustments.

   a. AMT adjustment applicable only to corporations.

      i. The Adjusted Current Earnings (ACE) adjustment applies only to corporate taxpayers. This adjustment was designed to ensure that all corporations pay some minimum tax on economic income.

      ii. The ACE adjustment is equal to 75% of the difference between adjusted current earnings (ACE) and alternative minimum taxable income (AMTI). Adjusted current earnings is essentially economic income.

Example

XBA Corp has AMTI of $200,000 before any ACE adjustment. The corporation has adjusted current earnings of $300,000. Therefore, the ACE adjustment is $75,000 [($300,000 - $200,000) x 75%]. The $75,000 would be added to the AMTI before the ACE adjustment in arriving at Alternative Minimum Taxable Income.

---

   b. Some AMT adjustments are not applicable to corporations (only applicable to individuals).

      i. Adjustments for itemized deductions, standard deductions, and personal exemptions of individuals are not applicable to corporations.

      ii. Adjustments for Incentive Stock Options (ISOs) are not applicable to corporations.

      iii. Adjustments for circulation and research expenditures are not applicable to corporations.

      iv. Adjustments for qualified small business (Section 1202) stock are not applicable to corporations.

4. Calculation of Alternative Minimum Taxable Income (AMTI):

	Taxable Income
+	Positive AMT adjustments
-	Negative AMT adjustments
+	Tax preferences
=	Alternative Minimum Taxable Income before ACE Adjustment
+	ACE Adjustment
=	Alternative Minimum Taxable Income

5. Calculation of Alternative Minimum Tax (AMT):

	AMTI
-	AMT exemption ($40,000)
=	Minimum tax base
x	AMT rate (20%)
=	Tentative AMT
-	Regular income tax on taxable income
=	AMT

E. THE TICKET TO WORK AND WORK INCENTIVES ACT OF 1999.

1. The Ticket to Work and Work Incentives Act of 1999 permits personal nonrefundable credits (e.g., dependent care credit, adoption expense credit, HOPE credit) to offset both the regular tax and the AMT.
2. This is done by limiting the amount of nonrefundable credits by the sum of the taxpayer's regular tax liability less any allowable foreign tax credit plus the amount of AMT liability.

XIX. TAX CREDITS

A. TAX CREDITS.

Provide benefits on a more equitable basis than tax deductions; credits are not affected by the tax rate of the taxpayer.

B. OVERVIEW AND PRIORITY OF CREDITS.

1. Refundable tax credits - These are paid to the taxpayer even if the amount exceeds the taxpayer's tax liability.
2. Nonrefundable tax credits - At best, your tax liability can be reduced to zero. If the taxpayer has multiple nonrefundable tax credits, they must be offset using the priority list defined in the Code. Some credits are subject to carryover provisions (e.g., foreign tax credit).
3. General business credits - Comprised of a group of credits.

C. GENERAL BUSINESS CREDITS.

1. Rehabilitation expenditures credit.
   a. Tax credit allowed to rehabilitate industrial and commercial buildings and certified historic sites. It is set up to discourage businesses from moving to newer locations.
   b. To qualify for the rehabilitation credit, the expenditures must exceed either the adjusted basis of the property or $5,000.
   c. The basis of the building is reduced by the full rehabilitation credit. The residual investment amount is added to the basis of the property.
2. Energy credit -- 10% credit on qualified energy property (generates energy from a solar or geothermal source).
3. Reforestation credit -- 10% of basis of qualified timber property.
4. Work Opportunity Tax Credit allows a credit of 40% of the first $6,000 paid during the first year of work to each targeted group employee hired after September 30, 1997, and before January 1, 2002. For summer youth employees, the amount is $3,000 for any 90-day period between May 1 and September 15. The maximum credit is $2,400 per employee ($1,200 for summer youth).
5. Research activity credit.
   a. This credit is the sum of the incremental research credit and the basic research credit.
   b. Incremental research credit - The Code does not specifically list what research activities qualify. However, it does state what is not allowed.
   c. Basic research credit - This credit applies to C corporations but not S corporations or Personal Service Corporations. It allows qualifying corporations to take an additional 20% credit for basic research payments.
6. Low-income housing credit.
   a. This credit is available to qualified low-income housing projects. One requirement for qualification is to have the property certified under such a title.
   b. If the property continues to qualify, the credit has a 10-year life.

7. Disabled access credit.

   a. This credit is 50% of the "eligible access" expenditures over $250 but not more than $10,250 [maximum credit equals ($10,250 – 250) x 50% or $5,000].

   b. Only eligible small businesses can claim the disabled access credit. An eligible small business is a business with $1 million or less in gross receipts and 30 or fewer full-time employees.

   c. The credit applies to any qualifying project (installation of ramps, raised markings on routine usage items, etc.).

   d. If the credit is used, the adjusted basis for that piece of property is reduced by that same amount.

D. PERSONAL CREDITS.

1. Earned income credit (EIC).

   a. The credit is designed to encourage economically disadvantaged individuals to join the work force.

   b. Earned income equals the summation of employee compensation and/or self-employment earnings less one-half of self-employment tax. It excludes from income such things as interest, dividends, and alimony.

   c. The earned income credit is calculated by multiplying a maximum income by a credit percentage.

EXHIBIT 31: EARNED INCOME CREDIT FOR TAX YEARS BEGINNING IN 2003

Qualified Individuals with	Credit Percentage (A)	Earned Income Level (B)	Phaseout Percentage	Phaseout Level Range*	Max Credit (A x B)
No qualifying children	7.65%	$4,990	7.65%	$6,240-11,230 (MFJ $7,240-12,230)	$382
1 qualifying child	34%	$7,490	15.98%	$13,730-29,666 (MFJ $14,730-30,666)	$2,547
2 or more qualifying children	40%	$10,510	21.06%	$13,730-33,692 (MFJ $14,730-34,692)	$4,204

**Greater of modified adjusted gross income or earned income.*

   d. The beginning and ending amounts of the phaseout are increased for married taxpayers filing a joint return. As reflected in the table above, the phaseout amount is increased as follows:

Calendar Year	Increase in Phaseout Range
2002-2004	$1,000
2005-2007	$2,000
2008 or later	$3,000

e. Two types of nontaxable income are included in the AGI phaseout amount. They are tax-exempt interest and amounts received from a pension or annuity, and any distributions or payments received from an individual retirement plan to the extent not included in income.

f. In addition, each child must meet all 3 of the following tests: relationship, residency, and age.

g. The earned income credit is also available to certain workers without children.

Examples

- Jim and Helen have one child, Bo, who turns 18 in 2003 and has been living with them since his birth. In 2003, their combined income was $15,000 and Bo did not work. Jim and Helen plan to file a joint income tax return for 2003. Their earned income credit for 2003 is: ($7,490 x 34% = $2,546), $2,546 - (($15,000 - $14,730) x 15.98%) = $2,463.

- Ann and her daughter, Stephanie, lived with her mother, Joy, in 2003. Ann is 25 years old. Her only income was $9,100 from a part-time job. Joy's only income was $35,000 from her job.

  Stephanie is a qualifying child of both Ann and Joy. Since Ann and Joy both have the same qualifying child, only one can take the credit. Only Joy can take the credit because her adjusted gross income is higher than Ann's. However, Joy cannot take the earned income credit because her adjusted gross income is above the phaseout level. Even though Joy cannot take the earned income credit, Ann cannot take the credit either, because her mother's adjusted gross income is more than Ann's.

- Diane and Suzanne are sisters. They shared a house for all of 2003. Diane has 3 young children who lived in the household all year. Suzanne does not have any children. However, she cares for Diane's children as if they were her own. Diane earns $12,000 and Suzanne earns $13,000.

  The children meet the age and residency test for both Diane and Suzanne. They meet the relationship test for Diane because they are her children. They also meet the relationship test for Suzanne because they lived with her in the same household for the whole year. She cared for them as if they were her own children. Therefore, they qualify as her eligible foster children.

  Diane's children are qualifying children for both Diane and Suzanne. However, because Suzanne's adjusted gross income is higher than Diane's, she is the only one who can take the credit.

2. Credit for the elderly or disabled.

   a. This limited, nonrefundable credit applies to taxpayers 65 and older or those under 65 who are retired and permanently or totally disabled. If married, the couple must file a joint return.

   b. The maximum credit is 15% of $5,000 for all filers except MFJ ($7,500 for MFJ).

   c. The $5,000/$7,500 amounts are reduced by Social Security not included in gross income and one-half of AGI in excess of $7,500 ($10,000 for married/joint).

Example

Ricky and Regina are husband and wife, both age 69. During the current year, they receive Social Security benefits of $4,000, have adjusted gross income of $12,000, and file a joint return. Their credit for the elderly is $375 ($7,500 (base amount) - $4,000 (Social Security benefits) - $1,000 (one-half of adjusted gross income in excess of $10,000) = $2,500 x 15% = $375).

---

3. Foreign tax credit.

   a. The foreign tax credit is a means of avoiding double taxation by granting a tax credit for taxes paid or accrued to a foreign country or a U.S. possession.

   b. A taxpayer may not take advantage of both the foreign tax credit and the foreign earned income exclusion.

   c. If the tax in the foreign jurisdiction is more than the U.S. tax, it is generally more advantageous to take the tax credit rather than the income exclusion.

4. Child and Dependent Care Credit.

   a. The credit is allowed for a portion of child or dependent care expenses paid for the purpose of allowing the taxpayer to be gainfully employed.

   b. For eligibility, the taxpayer must have earned income, must be paying the expenses in order to work or look for work, and must keep a home for a qualifying individual. A qualifying individual is:

      i. A dependent under age 13 for whom a dependency exemption may be claimed.

      ii. Any other person who is physically or mentally incapable of caring for himself or herself. In this case, the taxpayer must either (1) be able to claim the person as a dependent, or (2) be able to claim the person as a dependent except for the fact that the person had income exceeding the exemption amount.

      iii. The taxpayer's spouse who is physically or mentally incapable of self-care.

      iv. Certain dependent children of divorced parents.

   c. Household services, in addition to expenses for the care of the children, can be included to determine the credit amount.

   d. For 2003, the employment-related expenses eligible for the credit are limited to $3,000 for one qualifying child and $6,000 for two or more qualifying children.

   e. To calculate the credit, multiply the work-related expenses by a percentage (which depends upon gross income).

EXHIBIT 32: CHILD AND DEPENDENT CARE CREDIT FOR 2003

Adjusted Gross Income		Applicable Percentage
Over	**But not over**	
$0	$15,000	35%
15,000	17,000	34%
17,000	19,000	33%
19,000	21,000	32%
21,000	23,000	31%
23,000	25,000	30%
25,000	27,000	29%
27,000	29,000	28%
29,000	31,000	27%
31,000	33,000	26%
33,000	35,000	25%
35,000	37,000	24%
37,000	39,000	23%
39,000	41,000	22%
41,000	43,000	21%
43,000	No Limit	20%

Example

Billy and Jo have two preschool children, ages 3 and 5. They claim their children as dependents and file a joint income tax return. Billy earned $10,000 and Jo earned $28,000. During the current year, they paid $7,500 for child care expenses at Elmwood Street Nursery.

They figure their credit as follows:

AGI	$38,000
Applicable % for credit	23%
Total work-related expenses	$7,500
Maximum expenses that can be taken into account in calculating credit	$6,000
Amount of credit ($6,000 x 23%)	**$1,380**

This credit level is reduced dollar-for-dollar by the amount of reimbursement from a dependent care assistance plan.

5. Adoption credit.

   a. The adoption credit is a nonrefundable credit for qualified adoption expenses. The maximum credit is $10,160 (for 2003) per eligible child, including special needs children.

   b. The credit is taken in the year the adoption becomes final. Any unused credit may be carried forward up to five years.

   c. The credit is phased out beginning at modified AGI of $152,390 with complete phaseout at $192,390.

6. Child tax credit.

   a. For 2003, a $600 credit is given for each qualifying child of taxpayer under the age of 17. The credit will increase in future years based on the following schedule:

Year	Credit Per Child
2002-2004	$600
2005-2008	$700
2009	$800
2010 and later	$1,000

   b. Qualifying child includes child, stepchild, grandchild, or eligible foster child.

   c. Credit is reduced $50 for each $1,000 above threshold.

Status	AGI Threshold
Married filing joint	$110,000
Single or head of household	$75,000
Married filing separately	$55,000

   d. The child tax credit is a refundable credit.

      i. The child tax credit is refundable to the extent of 10% (for 2002-2004) of the taxpayer's earned income in excess of $10,500 (for 2003).

7. Tax Credit for Employer-Provided Child Care Facilities

   a. In General.

      i. Taxpayers are eligible to receive a tax credit for certain qualified employee child care expenses.

ii. Qualified child care expenses include costs paid or incurred:

A) To acquire, construct, rehabilitate or expand property that is to be used as part of the taxpayer's qualified child care facility.

B) For the operation of the taxpayer's qualified child care facility, including the costs of training and certain compensation for employees of the child care facility, and scholarship programs.

C) Under a contract with a qualified child care facility to provide child care services to employees of the taxpayer.

iii. To be a qualified child care facility, the principal use of the facility must be for child care (unless it is the principal residence of the taxpayer), and the facility must meet all applicable state and local laws and regulations, including any licensing laws.

b. Amount of Credit.

i. The credit is equal to 25% of qualified expenses for employee child care and 10% of qualified expenses for child care resource and referral services.

ii. The maximum total credit that may be claimed by a taxpayer cannot exceed $150,000 per taxable year.

iii. Any amounts for which the taxpayer may otherwise claim a tax deduction are reduced by the amount of these credits.

8. HOPE Scholarship Credit.

a. Available for tuition and fees incurred and paid in the first two years of postsecondary education for taxpayer, spouse, or dependent.

i. Books, room and board are not qualifying expenses.

ii. Qualifying expenses must be reduced by any tax-free income, and taxpayers cannot use the same educational expense for figuring more than one benefit.

b. The credit is 100% of first $1,000 of qualified expenses paid in the tax year plus 50% of the next $1,000. Maximum of $1,500 (indexed) for the tax year. Calculated on a per student basis.

c. Student must carry at least half of normal load during one term.

d. See Exhibit 33 on page 675 for AGI phaseout.

9. Lifetime Learning Credit.

a. Available for tuition and fees (undergraduate, graduate, or professional degree programs).

b. May claim 20% of qualified expenses up to $10,000 for 2003. Maximum of $2,000 credit per year per family. Note that maximum is family not student based like the HOPE credit.

c. Student must be enrolled at least half time in a degree/certificate program.

d. If courses are taken to acquire or improve job skills, student can be enrolled less than half time.

e. Credit can be claimed an unlimited number of years.

f. Cannot claim both the HOPE credit and lifetime learning credit for the same individual in one year.

g. TRA 2001 allows a taxpayer to claim a HOPE scholarship credit or lifetime learning credit for a taxable year and to exclude from gross income amounts distributed (both the contributions and the earnings portions) from a Coverdell Education Savings Account on behalf of the same student as long as the distribution is not used for the same educational expenses for which a credit was claimed for years after 2001.

EXHIBIT 33: MAGI* PHASEOUT FOR HOPE AND LIFETIME LEARNING CREDITS FOR 2003

Married filing joint	$83,000 - $103,000
All other taxpayers	$41,000 - $51,000

*MAGI - AGI and foreign earned income exclusion and U.S. possessions and Puerto Rico income exclusions.

EXHIBIT 34: HIGHLIGHTS OF TAX BENEFITS FOR HIGHER EDUCATION FOR 2003

	Hope Credit	Lifetime Learning Credit	Coverdell Education Savings Account[1]	Traditional, Roth, SEP & SIMPLE IRAs[1]	Student Loan Interest	State Tuition Programs[2] (Section 529 Plans)	Education Savings Bond Program[1]	Employer's Educational Assistance Program[1]	Qualified Higher Education Expenses[4]
What is your benefit?	Credits can reduce the amount of tax you must pay		Earnings are not taxed	No 10% additional tax on early withdrawal	You can deduct the interest	Earnings are not taxed	Interest is not taxed	Employer benefits are not taxed	Deduction of expenses "for AGI"
What is the annual limit?	Up to $1,500 per student	Up to $2,000 per family	$2,000 contribution per beneficiary	Amount of qualifying expenses	$2,500	None	Amount of qualifying expenses	$5,250	Maximum: 2002-2003 $3,000 2004-2005 $4,000
What expenses qualify besides tuition and required enrollment fees?	None		Books Supplies Equipment Room & board if at least a half-time student Payments to state tuition program	Books Supplies Equipment Room & board if at least a half-time student	Books Supplies Equipment Room & board Trans-portation Other necessary expenses	Books Supplies Equipment Room & board if at least a half-time student	Payments to Coverdell ESAs Payments to state tuition program	Books Supplies Equipment	None
What education qualifies?	1st 2 years of under-graduate	All undergraduate and graduate[3]							Qualified higher education expenses
What are some of the other conditions that apply?	Can be claimed only for 2 years Must be enrolled at least half-time in a degree program		Can contribute to Coverdell Education Savings Accounts and state tuition program in the same year Must withdraw assets by age 30		No longer a 60 month limit Must have been at least half-time student in a degree program	Distribution is excluded from gross income Hope and Lifetime Learning Credit are permitted in the same year but not for the same expenses	Applies only to qualified series EE bonds issued after 1989 or series I bonds	Does not expire after December 31, 2001	Cannot claim Hope or Lifetime Learning Credit in same year for the same student
In what income range do benefits phase out?	2003: $41,000 - $51,000; $83,000 - $103,000 for joint returns		$95,000 - $110,000; $190,000 - $220,000 for joint returns	No phaseout	$50,000 – $65,000 $100,000 – $130,000 for joint returns	No phaseout	2003: $58,500 - $73,500; $87,750 - $117,750 for joint returns	No phaseout	2002-2003 Single < $65,000 MFJ < $130,000 2004-2005 Single $65,000-80,000 MFJ $130,000 – 160,000

[1] Any nontaxable withdrawal is limited to the amount that does not exceed qualifying educational expenses.
[2] Exclusion is extended to distributions from Qualified Tuition programs established by an entity other than a State after December 31, 2003.
[3] For Coverdell Education Savings Accounts, qualified elementary and secondary school expenses are also permitted (Grades K-12).
[4] For years 2004 – 2005 AGI less than $65,000 ($130,000 married) can take a maximum deduction of $4,000 and taxpayers with AGI between $65,000 and $80,000 ($130,000 and $160,000 married) can take a maximum deduction of $2,000. This deduction expires for years after 2005.

XX. PROPERTY TRANSACTIONS - CAPITAL GAINS AND LOSSES

A. TYPES OF ASSETS.

1. Capital Assets.
   a. Capital assets are personal use assets and most investment assets. Losses from personal use assets are not deductible but losses from investment assets are.
   b. Section 1221 in the Code defines what is not a capital asset as follows (the Code does not have a list defining capital assets, only those that are not capital assets).
      i. Accounts and notes receivable - This refers to receivables acquired from the sale of inventory or services associated with a business.
      ii. Copyrights and creative works - These types of assets are usually considered ordinary assets and not capital assets.
      iii. Inventory - This refers to inventory held for sale to customers - mainly for business use.
      iv. Depreciable property or real estate - If these assets are used by a business, they are not considered capital assets.

      Note: Remember A-C-I-D.
2. Ordinary Assets.
   a. Property which, if sold, results in the recognition of ordinary income.
   b. Examples.
      i. Inventory.
      ii. Accounts and notes receivable.
      iii. Works of art in the hands of the creator.
      iv. Copyright for the person who applied for and received it.
3. Section 1231 Assets.
   a. Depreciable or real property used in business or for the production of income.
   b. By statute, specifically includes:
      i. Timber, coal or iron ore.
      ii. Livestock.
      iii. Unharvested crops.
      iv. Goodwill, intangibles.

B. RATES.

1. Long-term capital gains generally receive preferential tax treatment.
2. Taxpayers use the capital gains rate only when it is advantageous to do so.
3. Assets held more than one year are long term. Assets held one year or less are considered short term. The day of disposition (but not the day of acquisition) is included in the holding period.

EXHIBIT 35: CAPITAL GAINS RATES

Type	Holding Period	Tax Rate
Long-term capital gains	More than one year	20%/10%*
Short-term capital gains	One year or less	Ordinary Income
Unrecaptured Section 1250 Gain (depreciable real property)	More than one year	25%
Collectibles	More than one year	28%
Section 1202 Qualifying Small Business Stock	N/A	28%

* The 10% rate applies to a taxpayer in the 15% ordinary income tax bracket. In addition, see below for new 8/18% rates.

4. Two additional rates are available for capital gains if the asset is held for more than five years.
   a. An 18% rate will replace the 20% rate if the asset is held for more than five years and the holding period began after 2000.
      i. If the asset was purchased before 2001, the taxpayer could have elected to treat the asset as being sold and repurchased at the beginning of 2001.
      ii. Making the "deemed-sale" election started a new post-2000 holding period running without requiring the taxpayer to go through the administrative hassle (and expense) of actually selling and repurchasing the shares.
      iii. The election triggered capital-gain taxation based on the fair market value as of January 1, 2001 (or the next business day). If the individual would realize a loss from the deemed sale, the loss is not recognized.

Example

John Nugent is in the highest ordinary income tax bracket. In 1998, he purchased 100 shares of WasCo stock for $1,000. He plans on holding the shares for a long time, and would like to take advantage of the 18% rate when he sells the stock. The stock had a fair market value of $1,200 on January 2, 2001. If John made the deemed-sale election, he reported capital gain of $200 ($1,200 - $1,000 basis) on his 2001 income tax return. His five-year holding period began on January 2, 2001, and his new basis in the shares would be $1,200 ($1,000 original cost + $200 capital gain recognized).

   b. An 8% rate will replace the 10% rate if the asset is held for more than five years regardless of when the holding period began. This rate will apply to taxpayers who are in the 15% bracket.

C. CAPITAL GAINS NETTING PROCEDURE.

1. Net STCG and STCL. If there is a NSTCL, it reduces any net LTCG from the 28% group, then 25% group, and then 20% group.
2. Net gains and losses from the 28% group. If there is a net loss, use first to reduce gain from 25% group, then the 20%.
3. Net gains and losses from 20% group. If there is a net loss, use first to reduce gain from 28% group, then 25% group.
4. If there exists a net STCG and any LTCL, net them first against 28%, then 25%, then 20% LTCLs.

Examples.

		Example 1		Example 2		Example 3	
ST	STCG	$4,000		$3,000		$1,000	
	STCL	2,000		9,000		5,000	
		$2,000	Gain (STCG)	$6,000	Loss (STCL)	$4,000	Loss (STCL)
28% LT	Gain	$3,000		$4,000		$2,000	
	Loss	9,000		1,000		1,000	
		$6,000	Loss (LT)	$3,000	Gain (LT)	$1,000	Gain (LT)
25% LT		$0		$1,000	Gain (LT)	$2,000	Gain (LT)
20% LT	Gain	$13,000		$4,000		$2,000	
	Loss	9,000		1,000		1,000	
		$4,000	Gain (LT)	$3,000	Gain (LT)	$1,000	Gain (LT)
Net Net	Net	$2,000	STCG	$6,000	STCL	$4,000	STCL
		$2,000	LTCL (28%)	$7,000	LTCG	$4,000	LTCG
Final Net	These are then net to 0 in this case			$1,000	LTCG (20%)	$0	Gain or loss

Note: It is not possible to end up with both gains and losses.

D. DETERMINING GAIN OR LOSS – SUMMARY.

1. The realized gain or loss is the economic result of the transaction. It is calculated by reducing the amount realized by the adjusted basis of the property.
   a. Amount realized.
   b. Adjusted basis.
   c. If the amount realized exceeds the adjusted basis, then gain results. If the amount realized is less than the adjusted basis, then loss occurs.
2. The recognized gain/loss is the gain/loss that is reported on the tax return.
   a. Any gain or loss that is not currently recognized, is either deferred or tax free (disallowed).

E. DETERMINING GAIN OR LOSS.

1. Realized gain or loss.

   a. The difference between the amount realized from the sale or other disposition of property and the property's adjusted basis - A realized gain indicates the amount realized exceeded the property's adjusted basis and a realized loss indicates the excess of the adjusted basis over the amount realized.

   b. Sale or other distribution - One must determine whether a sale or distribution occurred as opposed to a fluctuation in property value. Trade-ins, casualties, condemnations, thefts, and bond retirements are treated as dispositions of property.

   c. Amount realized.

      i. This is the sum of any money received, plus the FMV of other property received, plus real property taxes owed by the seller but paid by the buyer, plus any liability on the property assumed by the buyer (e.g., mortgage or some other liability - 2nd mortgage, lien, etc.).

      ii. The fair market value of property received in a sale or other disposition has been defined by the courts as the price at which property will change hands between a willing seller and a willing buyer, both with knowledge of relevant facts, when neither is compelled to buy or sell.

2. Adjusted basis.

   a. This is the property's original basis adjusted to the date of disposition (cost + capital additions - capital recoveries) = adjusted basis.

Example

Harold bought a building for $20,000 cash and assumed a mortgage of $80,000. Harold's basis in the building is $100,000.

---

3. Capital recoveries.

   a. There are many forms of capital recoveries but the most widely known are depreciation, casualties, and theft.

4. Capital additions - Cost of capital improvements made to the property by the taxpayer (this does not include ordinary repair and maintenance).

5. Sales, exchange, or condemnation of personal use assets. Realized losses associated with personal-use assets are not recognized. Exception: casualty or theft losses. In contrast, realized gains may be fully taxable.

F. RECOVERY OF CAPITAL DOCTRINE.

1. This doctrine allows taxpayers to recover the cost or other original basis of property acquired, free from tax on that amount. For example, the cost or other basis of depreciable property is recovered through annual depreciation deductions.

2. Rule 1 - A realized gain that is never recognized results in the permanent recovery of more than the taxpayer's cost or other basis for tax purposes. For example, under Section 121, up to $500,000 of realized gain on the sale of a personal residence may be excluded from income.

3. Rule 2 - A realized gain where recognition is postponed results in the temporary recovery of more than the taxpayer's cost or other basis for tax purposes. For example, a like-kind exchange under Section 1031 or an involuntary conversion under Section 1033 are all eligible for postponement treatment.
4. Rule 3 - A realized loss that is never recognized results in the permanent recovery of less than the taxpayer's cost or other basis for tax purposes. For example, a loss on the sale of a personal use asset is not deductible.
5. Rule 4 - A realized loss where recognition is postponed results in the temporary recovery of less than the taxpayer's cost or other basis for tax purposes.

G. DETERMINATION OF BASIS OF PROPERTY RECEIVED FROM A SALE.

This is generally the property's cost - the amount paid for in cash or other property. Exception: A bargain purchase has a cost basis equal to its FMV (Logic: bargain purchase element would have been included in income).

1. Lump-sum property purchases - The lump-sum cost is allocated between the properties based on their respective fair market values.

Example

Scott bought a tract of land for $20,000 and subdivided the land into 10 building lots of equal size. If Scott sells all 10 lots individually his basis in each would be $2,000.

H. DETERMINATION OF BASIS WHEN PROPERTY IS RECEIVED BY GIFT.

1. A gift indicates that there is no cost to the recipient. However, a basis to the gifted property is still assigned and depends on the following:
   a. The date of the gift.
   b. The basis of the property to the donor.
   c. The amount of the gift tax paid.
   d. The fair market value of the property.
2. Gift basis if no gift tax paid.
   a. Generally, the basis of a gift to the donee is the carryover basis of the donor. If the basis is carried over, the donor's holding period is added ("tacked on to") the donee's holding period. The exception is when the FMV at the date of the gift is less than the donor's basis. In this case, the donee's basis upon acquisition is the FMV for losses and the donor's basis for gains (the double-basis rule).
   b. A realized gain occurs if the donee subsequently sells the property at a higher price than the property's adjusted basis. The opposite occurs for a realized loss. However, a zero gain/loss situation can arise when the property sells for a cost between the adjusted basis and FMV.

      Bill received an acre of land as a gift. At the time of gift the land had a FMV of $7,000. The donor's adjusted basis was $11,000. If Bill subsequently sells the property at a price between $7,000 and $11,000, he will not have a gain or loss.

Examples

- Nicole, a single taxpayer, made the following gift in the current year to her son, Scott:

  Securities costing $50,000, FMV at date of gift is $90,000.

  Which statement is correct?

  a. Scott has taxable income of $40,000.
  b. Scott's basis in the securities is $50,000.
  c. Scott's basis in the securities is $90,000.
  d. None of the above.

  Answer: b. The basis to Scott is carryover basis of $50,000. No taxable income would result from the gift.

- Gift property (no gift tax was paid by the donor):

  a. Has a zero basis to the donee because the donee did not pay anything for the property.
  b. Has the same basis to the donee as the donor's adjusted basis if the donee disposes of the property at a gain.
  c. Has the same basis to the donee as the donor's adjusted basis if the donee disposes of the property at a loss, and the fair market value on the date of gift was less than the donor's adjusted basis.
  d. Has a zero basis to the donee if the fair market value on the date of gift is less than the donor's adjusted basis.
  e. None of the above.

  Answer: b. Assuming no gift tax paid by the donor, the donee's gain basis for the property received is the same as that of the donor. The donee's loss basis is the lower of the donor's adjusted basis or fair market value on the date of the gift.

3. Gift basis if gift taxes are paid.

   a. This applies only if the FMV of the property at the date of disposition exceeds the donor's adjusted basis. This allows the donee to calculate a new gain basis using the following equation:

$$\text{Donee's basis} = \text{Donor's adjusted basis} + \left[\frac{(\text{unrealized appreciation}) \cancel{\times \text{gift tax paid})}}{\text{FMV}} \times \text{gift taxes paid}\right]$$

Example

Chelsea gave Virginia stock with a FMV of $60,000, and paid gift tax of $15,000. Chelsea had originally acquired the stock for $20,000. Virginia's basis in the gift is $30,000.

$$\$20{,}000 + \left[\frac{40{,}000}{60{,}000} \times \$15{,}000\right] = \$30{,}000 \text{ basis}$$

Basis includes $20,000 carryover basis, plus $10,000 of the gift tax paid.

I. BASIS OF PROPERTY RECEIVED FROM A DECEDENT.

1. When receiving property from a decedent, the basis of such property is the FMV at the date of death or, if the alternate valuation date is properly elected, the FMV up to six months after the date of death. However, there are restrictions on electing the alternate valuation date.
2. Alternate valuation date limitations.
   a. An estate tax return must be filed.
   b. Both the value of the gross estate and the estate tax liability must be reduced below what the primary valuation date would have yielded.
   c. The alternate valuation date is six months after the date of death.
3. Deathbed gifts.
   a. If appreciated property is given to a donee who then dies within one year and wills it back to the donor, the basis of the inherited property will be the donor's adjusted basis at the time of the gift. No stepped-up basis is received.

Example

Joey gives property to his father in 2003 that on the date of the gift has a FMV of $7,000. No gift taxes were paid. Joey has an adjusted basis in the property of $2,300. Joey's father dies at the end of 2003 and wills the property back to Joey, within one year of the date of the gift. Hence, Joey's basis in the property is $2,300 (donor's basis).

4. Survivor's share of property (JTWROS).
   a. The basis of such property is the FMV at the date of the decedent's death for the portion related to decedent. This is added to the basis of survivor.

Example

Martin and Mary owned, as joint tenants, land that they purchased for $60,000. At the date of Mary's death, the property had a FMV of $100,000. Local law states that joint tenants each have a half-interest in the income for jointly held property. Martin figures his basis in the property as follows:

Interest Martin bought up front	$30,000
Interest Martin received @ Mary's death	$50,000
Martin's basis @ Mary's death	$80,000

Common law states don't allow an adjustment to the surviving owner's interest in the property.

5. The holding period of property acquired from a decedent - The holding period of property acquired from a decedent is deemed to be long term. This provision applies regardless of whether the property is disposed of at a gain or loss.
6. Community property - Community property receives an adjustment in basis to FMV on both halves at the death of the first spouse.

J. HOLDING PERIOD EXCEPTIONS.

1. Generally, property must be owned over a year to be treated as long-term property.
2. Gift property - If the donor's basis carries over to the donee, then the donor's holding period is added (tacked on) to the donee's holding period.
3. Inherited property - The property is treated as long term no matter the actual original holding period.
4. Capital asset or Section 1231 asset - In a like-kind exchange between a capital asset or Section 1231 asset, the newly acquired property includes the holding period of the former property.
5. Mark to market rules.
    a. Apply to Section 1256 contracts.
        i. Regulated futures contracts.
        ii. Foreign currency contracts.
        iii. Nonequity options, such as S&P 500 Index Option.
        iv. Dealer equity options.
    b. Any Section 1256 contracts must be marked to market at year-end and gain/loss must be reported. The effect is to treat the contract as if it were sold on the last day of the taxable year.
    c. Capital gain/loss is treated as if 40% short term and 60% long term. Gain is adjusted by any amounts considered in previous years and is reflected in adjustment to basis.

K. DISALLOWED LOSSES.

1. Related taxpayers - Losses from sales to related parties are disallowed.
    a. Related parties include brothers, sisters, and lineal descendants (it stops at and does not include cousins); corporations in which the taxpayer has a 50% or greater interest; and several other complex relationships.
    b. However, if the subsequent sale of the property by the recipient results in a gain, this gain can be reduced by the previously disallowed loss.
2. Wash sales.
    a. A wash sale occurs if the taxpayer sells or exchanges stock/securities for a loss and, within 30 days <u>before or after</u> the date of the sale or exchange, acquires relatively identical/similar stock/securities.
    b. If such an event occurs, the basis of the new stock/securities will include the unrecovered portion of the basis of the formerly held stock/securities.

Example

Tiffany purchased 100 shares of Ace Corporation stock for $28,000 on January 1, 2002. In the current tax year, she sells 30 shares of the 100 shares purchased on January 1, 2002, for $8,000. Twenty-nine days earlier, she purchased 30 shares for $7,500.

Tiffany's recognized loss is $0, calculated as follows:

Amount realized	$8,000
Adjusted basis (30 x $280)	(8,400)
Realized loss	(400)
Recognized loss	$0

Her basis in the new shares is $7,900:

Basis in old shares	$7,500
Add: postponed loss	400
Basis in new shares	$7,900

3. Conversion of personal property to business property or income-producing property.
   a. If converted, the basis for loss is the lower of the property's FMV on the date of conversion or the adjusted basis.
   b. The basis for gain is the property's adjusted basis.
   c. The basis for depreciation is the same as the basis for loss, explained above.

L. INSTALLMENT SALES

1. In General.
   a. The general rule of taxation is that all gains are recognized in the year of sale or exchange. An exception to this rule applies to the installment sale method of accounting.
   b. An installment sale is any sale of property (see exceptions below) in which the seller will receive at least one payment after the close of the tax year in which the sale occurs.
   c. The installment-sale method allows the taxpayer to spread out the gain as the payments are received.
   d. The installment method is automatic for sales that qualify. However, the taxpayer is allowed to elect out of the installment method by reporting the entire gain in the year of sale.
2. Installment treatment is not available for:
   a. Property held for sale in ordinary course of business (inventory).
   b. Gains on stocks/securities traded in an established market.

3. Tax ramifications of installment sales.

   a. The gain is reported based on the amount of cash received and the gross-profit percentage resulting from the sale.

      i. The gross-profit percentage is calculated by subtracting the seller's adjusted tax basis from the total contract price, and dividing that by the contract price.

Example

Mike Orentlich sold a 40-acre tract of land for $500,000 on January 1, 2003. The land had an adjusted basis of $300,000. The agreement specified a down payment of $100,000, with the remaining $400,000 sales price paid over a 5-year-note term at 10% interest. The gross profit from the sale is $200,000 ($500,000 - $300,000), and the gross-profit percentage is 40% ($200,000 profit ÷ $500,000 sales price).

---

      ii. Down payment – the down payment received from an installment sale is partially a capital gain and partially a return of capital. The capital gain portion is based on the amount of cash received and the gross-profit percentage calculated above.

Example

Assume the same facts as above. The down payment of $100,000 received by Mike is reported as a $40,000 capital gain and a $60,000 return of capital. The capital-gain portion is calculated by multiplying the down payment by the gross-profit percentage ($40,000 = $100,000 down payment x 40% gross-profit percentage). The remaining $60,000 of the down payment will be considered a nontaxable return of capital.

---

      iii. Note payments – the note payments received from the buyer are partially ordinary income, partially capital gain, and partially a return of capital.

Example

Assume the same facts as above. Mike received a note payment of $120,000 in the first year, of which $40,000 represented accrued interest. Therefore, the note payment represented $40,000 of interest and $80,000 of principal repayment. The note payment would be reported as $40,000 ordinary income, $32,000 capital gain ($80,000 principal payment x 40% gross-profit percentage), and $48,000 nontaxable return of capital ($120,000 note payment - $40,000 interest - $32,000 capital gain).

---

4. Other provisions of installment sales.

   a. Gains recaptured as ordinary income under Sections 1245 and 1250 (depreciable property) are not eligible for installment-sale treatment. These amounts are fully recognized in the year of the sale.

   b. If the selling price is more than $3,000 and the contract does not have a reasonable rate of interest, interest will be imputed.

c. If property is sold to a related party and the related party sells the property to a third party within two years, the deferred gain must be recognized in full by the original seller.

d. If an installment obligation is sold or otherwise disposed of, any unreported gain must be reported in the year the note was transferred.

e. Installment sales must be reported on Form 6252 for the year of sale and each subsequent year in which a payment is collected.

M. CONSTRUCTIVE OWNERSHIP (IRC SECTION 318).

1. The Code provides for deemed or constructive ownership in some stock-related transactions.
2. The family attribution rules for an individual dictate that for specific situations, usually dealing with stock redemptions, shares owned by certain related parties will be deemed owned by the taxpayer.
3. Related parties include:
   a. Spouse.
   b. Children.
   c. Grandchildren.
   d. Parents.
4. Siblings and grandparents are generally not included in the attribution rules.

N. SALES OR EXCHANGES – SPECIAL ISSUES.

1. Worthless securities - If the securities are capital assets, they will be treated as being disposed of/ sold on the last day of the tax year.
2. Options - If the option is a capital asset, the grantee will realize a capital gain or loss upon sale/ exchange. If the grantee fails to exercise the option, the sale/exchange will be considered to have occurred on the expiration date.
3. Patents.
   a. When all substantial rights to a patent are transferred by the holder, it is treated as a sale/ exchange of a long-term capital asset.
      i. Substantial rights - This means that no contingencies or limitations exist. For example, the holder cannot put restrictions on the transfers to certain geographic locations.
      ii. Definition of holder – Must be an individual (usually the creator of the patent).
   b. Exception: Authors, artists, and composers cannot obtain capital gain treatment when transferring their works (usually treated as ordinary gain or loss).
4. Franchises, trademarks, trade names.
   a. When transferring a franchise, trademark, or trade name, if the transferor retains significant power, the transferred asset is not considered to be a capital asset under Section 1253. A franchise transfer is not considered the sale/exchange of a capital asset.
   b. Relinquish significant power - This means that the transferor will not have control over assignments, advertisings, product quality, and supply and equipment purchases, to name a few.

c. Noncontingent payments - If the transferor retains a significant power, the periodic noncontingent transfer payments will be considered ordinary income. The franchisee must capitalize and amortize the payments over 15 years.

5. Contingent payments - These are treated as an ordinary deduction for the franchisee and ordinary income for the franchiser.

6. Short sales.

   a. Taxpayer anticipates a decline in the price of stock and sells it short.

   b. Taxpayer sells stock she has borrowed and repays it with substantially identical property (either already owned or purchased after the sale).

Example

Ginna has been watching the market carefully and decides that Pear Computer is not going to make its target quarterly income. In anticipation that the stock price will decline, Ginna sells 100 shares of Pear (borrowed from her broker) for $10,000. In 60 days, Ginna purchases 100 shares for $8,000 and repays her broker, closing the short sale. Ginna made $2,000 on the transaction.

---

   c. The term "short sale against the box" refers to a short sale where the seller borrows stock but actually already owns the same stock.

Example

Ginna already owned 100 shares of Pear but borrowed 100 shares from her broker. To close the short sale, she delivers the shares she already owns. The advantage is that she has more flexibility in reporting when the sale occurs (limited after TRA '97).

---

   d. The nature of the gain. If the stock is a capital asset to the taxpayer, then the gain/loss is capital.

      i. If the taxpayer has not held substantially identical securities for the required long-term holding period at the date of the short sale or the substantially identical property is acquired between the short-sale date and the closing date, any gain/loss is short term.

      ii. If substantially identical property has been held for the long-term holding period on the short-sale date and it is used to close the sale, the gain is long term.

      iii. If substantially identical property has been held for the long-term holding period on the short-sale date and a loss occurs, it is considered long term whether the substantially identical property was used to close the sale or not.

   e. TRA '97 introduced constructive sale rules to reduce the reporting flexibility for short sales against the box. If a taxpayer does not close a short position by January 31st in the year following the short sale, a constructive sale is deemed to have been made on the earlier of (1) the short-sale date (if the taxpayer owned substantially identical securities then) or (2) when the taxpayer acquired substantially identical securities during the year of the short sale.

XXI.PROPERTY TRANSACTIONS: NONTAXABLE EXCHANGES

A. GENERAL.

1. The tax law recognizes that nontaxable exchanges result in a change in the form but not in the substance of the taxpayer's relative economic position. The replacement property received in the exchange is viewed as substantially a continuation of the old investment.
2. In a nontaxable exchange, realized gains or losses are not recognized. However, the nonrecognition is usually temporary because the gain or loss is postponed. This is accomplished by assigning a carryover basis to the replacement property.

B. LIKE-KIND EXCHANGES - SECTION 1031.

1. In General.
   a. Section 1031 provides for nontaxable exchange treatment if the following requirements are satisfied:
      i. The form of the transaction is an exchange.
      ii. Both the property transferred and the property received are held either for productive use in a trade or business or for investment.
      iii. The property is like-kind property.
2. Like-kind property.
   a. The words "like-kind" refer to the nature or character of the property and not to its grade or quality. One kind or class of property may not be exchanged for property of a different kind or class.
   b. The following properties/exchanges are NOT considered like-kind:
      i. Personal use assets (personal auto).
      ii. Ordinary assets (inventory).
      iii. Securities.
      iv. Personalty exchanged for realty. Depreciable tangible personal property must be within the same general business asset class or the same product class (e.g., office furniture, information systems, automobiles, and trucks).
      v. Livestock of different sexes.
      vi. Foreign real estate for domestic real estate.
3. Exchange requirement - The transaction must actually involve an exchange of property to qualify as a like-kind exchange.
4. Boot.
   a. Property exchanged in a like-kind transaction that is not "like-kind" is referred to as boot, including cash.
   b. The receipt of boot will:
      i. Result in the recognition of gain if there is a realized gain.
      ii. Result in no recognition if there is a realized loss.

5. Basis and holding period of property received.

   a. The basis of like-kind property received in the exchange is the property's FMV less postponed gain or plus postponed loss. If the exchange partially qualifies for nonrecognition (if recognition is associated with boot), the basis of like-kind property is the property's FMV less postponed gain or plus postponed loss. The basis of any boot received is the boot's FMV.

   b. The Code provides an alternative approach for determining the basis of like-kind property received:

      Adjusted basis of like-kind property surrendered

      \+ Adjusted basis of boot given

      \+ Gain recognized

      \- FMV of boot received

      \- Loss recognized

      = Basis of like-kind property received

Example (Like-Kind Exchange)

Pat exchanges real estate (adjusted basis $50,000, FMV $80,000) held for investment for other real estate (FMV $80,000) held for investment. Pat's basis in the new property is $50,000.

Example (Partially Nontaxable Exchange)

Craig trades in a truck (adjusted basis $6,000) for a new truck (FMV $5,200) and receives $1,000. Craig's basis in the new truck is:

Adjusted basis of old truck	$6,000
Cash received	($1,000)
Gain recognized ($6,200-$6,000)	$200
Basis of new truck	$5,200

---

   c. The holding period of the property surrendered in the exchange carries over and tacks on to the holding period of the like-kind property received.

   d. The boot's holding period starts from the date of exchange rather than a carryover holding period.

6. Other requirements.

   a. If like-kind property is exchanged with a related party, the taxpayer and related party must not dispose of the like-kind property received in the exchange within a 2-year time period following the exchange. Exception: death and involuntary conversions.

   b. The property to be received in an exchange must be identified in a written agreement within 45 days after the transferred property is surrendered.

c. Property in the exchange must be received on or before the earlier of:

   i. 180 days after the transfer of the property given up, or

   ii. The due date of the tax return (including extensions) for the year the property was given up.

C. INVOLUNTARY CONVERSIONS - SECTION 1033.

1. An involuntary conversion results from the destruction (complete or partial), theft, seizure, requisition, condemnation, or sale or exchange under threat or imminence of requisition or condemnation of the taxpayer's property.

2. Section 1033 allows a taxpayer who incurs an involuntary conversion to postpone recognition of gain realized from the conversion (remember: this is the exception to the two-year holding period under like-kind exchanges). The rules for nonrecognition are as follows:

   a. If the amount reinvested in replacement property equals or exceeds the amount realized, realized gain is not recognized.

   b. If the amount reinvested in replacement property is less than the amount realized, realized gain is recognized to the extent of proceeds not reinvested.

3. Computing the amount realized - Typically the amount realized from the condemnation of property is equal to the amount received as compensation for the property. Severance damages are usually not included in the amount realized.

4. Replacement property.

   a. The general requirement is that the replacement property is similar in service or use to the involuntarily converted property. For an owner-user, the functional use test applies, and for an owner-investor, the taxpayer use test applies.

      i. Functional use test - The taxpayer's use of the replacement property and of the involuntarily converted property must be the same.

      ii. Taxpayer use test - The owner-investor's properties must be used in similar endeavors as the previously held properties. There is more flexibility with this test than the functional use test.

5. Time limitation on replacement.

   a. Normally the taxpayer has a 2-year time period at the end of the taxable year in which any gain is realized from the involuntary conversion to replace the property. Exception: Condemnation of real property used in a trade or business or held for investment has a 3-year period.

   b. The earliest date for replacement is typically the date the involuntary conversion took place.

6. Nonrecognition of gain - This can be either mandatory or elective depending upon the disposition/conversion of the replacement property (was it money or similar property).

   a. Direct conversion - If converting to replacement property, nonrecognition of realized gain is mandatory. The basis of the converted property is the same as the replacement property. Direct conversion is rare in practice.

b. Conversion into money - If the conversion is into money, nonrecognition is elective. The basis of the replacement property is the property's cost less postponed (deferred) gain. If postponement is elected, the holding period of the replacement property includes the holding period of the converted property.

c. Section 1033 applies only to gains, not losses.

Example

Bill had some property condemned by the State of Louisiana. The property had an adjusted basis of $26,000. Bill received $31,000 from the state for the property. Bill just realized a gain of $5,000 ($31,000 - $26,000) and bought new property that was similar in use to his old property for $29,000. He must recognize a gain of $2,000 ($31,000 - $29,000). Bill's basis in his new property is as follows:

Cost of new property	$29,000
Gain not recognized (deferred gain)	($3,000)
Bill's basis in the new property	$26,000

7. Involuntary conversion of a personal residence.

   a. The tax consequences depend on whether a casualty or condemnation occurred, and if it produced a realized loss or gain.

   b. Loss circumstances.

      i. If the conversion is a condemnation, the realized loss is not recognized.

      ii. If the conversion is a casualty, the realized loss is recognized subject to the personal casualty loss limitations.

   c. Gain circumstances.

      i. If the conversion is a condemnation, the gain may be postponed under either Section 1033 or 1034.

      ii. If the conversion is casualty, the gain is only postponed under the involuntary conversion provisions.

D. SALE OF A PERSONAL RESIDENCE - SECTION 121.

1. Effective for sales after May 6, 1997, Section 121 gives a universal exclusion of up to $250,000 (married filing joint, $500,000) to any taxpayer who meets certain use tests.

   a. Home must have been owned and used as a principal residence for at least 2 of the 5 years before the sale (do not have to be consecutive years).

   b. Either spouse can meet the ownership requirement, but both must meet the use requirement. Neither spouse can be ineligible because of the once-every-two-year limit in (c).

   c. Exclusion can be used once every two years.

   d. If taxpayer fails to meet (a) and (b) because of a change in employment or health, taxpayer may be entitled to a partial exclusion based on the shorter of either the use or ownership.

e. If one spouse can take a full exclusion and one cannot, then the exclusion is the sum of the amounts calculated on a separate basis as if they had not been married.

f. The exclusion does not apply to gain attributable to post May 6, 1997, depreciation for business/rental use of the house.

g. Taxpayers who deferred gain under the older Section 1034 provisions may tack on the old residence's use and ownership period to the new residence.

Example

- Gloria, a single taxpayer, sold her condominium in Seattle because she has a new job in Detroit. On the sale date, she had owned the condo for only 18 months. Since Gloria failed to meet both the use and ownership tests due to a change in employment, she can get a partial exclusion: 18 months/24 months x $250,000 = $187,500.

  If Gloria had lived in the condo for two years, but had only owned it for one year (she rented for a year before she purchased it), proposed Regs specify that the shorter of the two periods should be used. Her partial exclusion would then be: 12 months/24 months x $250,000 = $125,000.

- Merrily and Wallace get married and Wallace moves into the house that Merrily has been using as her principal residence for six years. Nine months later, Wallace gets a big promotion and the newlyweds move to another city. They realized a $700,000 gain on the sale of their residence. Merrily meets the ownership and use tests and so she gets a full exclusion of $250,000. Wallace does not need to meet the ownership test (since his wife did), but he is held to the use test. He has only been there 9 months, so his exclusion is 9/24 x $250,000 = $93,750. Their total exclusion is $250,000 + $93,750 = $343,750. If Wallace and Merrily just moved to a larger house in the same city, Merrily gets her $250,000 exclusion (she has met all tests, and it has been at least two years since she claimed an exclusion), but Wallace gets no exclusion. Remember that the partial exclusion is only allowed if the sale is necessitated by a change in employment, health, or to the extent provided by the IRS, unforeseen circumstances.

2. When selling a personal residence, like any other personal asset, losses are not recognized.

XXII.SECTION 1231 AND RECAPTURE PROVISIONS

A. SECTION 1231 ASSETS.

1. Relationship to capital assets - If a business is disposing of depreciable and/or real property, any loss is treated, as per Section 1231, as an ordinary loss (deductible for AGI). Gains are given capital gain treatment.
2. Section 1231 property.
   a. Included.
      i. Depreciable personal or real property used in business (see below) or for the production of income (e.g., machinery, equipment, and buildings).
      ii. Timber, coal, or domestic ore.
      iii. Livestock held for breeding, dairy, or sport.
      iv. Unharvested crops on land used in a business.
      v. Certain nonpersonal-use assets.
   b. Excluded.
      i. Property not held for the long-term holding period (12 months or less).
      ii. Property where casualty losses exceed casualty gains.
      iii. Inventory/property held for sale to customers.
      iv. Intangible assets.
      v. Capital assets.
3. Special rules for certain Section 1231 assets.
   a. Timber - If the taxpayer elects to treat cut timber as being held for sale or business, the transaction qualifies under Section 1231.
   b. Livestock - There is a 24-month holding period for cattle and horses and a 12-month holding period for other livestock to qualify for Section 1231 treatment.
   c. Select nonpersonal use capital assets - These are assets held for the production of income (land, investment painting, etc.). If disposed of by casualty or theft, they may fall under Section 1231.
4. Section 1231 netting procedure.
   a. Step 1 - Net all long-term gains and losses from casualties or theft of nonpersonal use property.
   b. Step 2 - Net all Section 1231 gains and losses.
   c. Step 3 - Any net Section 1231 gain from Step 2 is offset by the nonrecaptured net Section 1231 losses from the five preceding years.

B. SECTION 1245 RECAPTURE.

1. Requires any recognized gain to be treated as ordinary income to the extent of depreciation taken on the property disposed of up to the gain recognized. It does not apply if the property is disposed of at a loss. Any remaining gain will usually be Section 1231 gain.

2. Section 1245 property.
   a. Includes all depreciable personal property, patents, copyrights, and leaseholds.

Example

Blaine bought a depreciable business asset for $75,000. Before selling it for $60,000, he was able to write off $45,000 in depreciation. Following Section 1245, Blaine has to treat the entire gain on the sale of the business asset as ordinary income.

Purchase price	$75,000
Depreciation written off	(45,000)
Basis in asset before sale (adjusted basis)	$30,000
Selling price	$60,000
Basis in asset (adjusted basis)	(30,000)
Gain on sale (ordinary income)	$30,000
Recapture depreciation to extent of gain realized	($30,000)
Net 1231 Gain	$0

3. This section does not apply to losses - Section 1231 rules are used, resulting in ordinary loss treatment.

C. SECTION 1250 RECAPTURE.

1. This provision prevents taxpayers from receiving benefits of both accelerated depreciation and long-term capital gain treatment. It requires the recapture of the depreciation deducted by the taxpayer over what it would have been using straight line.
2. Section 1250 property is depreciable real property (typically buildings and structural components).
3. Losses do not have any depreciation recapture and are usually treated as Section 1231 losses (i.e., if a business loss, then deducted for AGI, other losses are deducted from AGI).
4. Gain attributable to straight-line depreciation is taxed at 25% maximum capital-gains rate.
5. Any gain not attributable to depreciation is subject to 20% rate.

Example

Mark sold a building on June 15, 2002 for $100,000. He had originally acquired the building in 1998 for $75,000. Straight-line depreciation taken was $30,000. Mark is in a 38.6% marginal tax bracket. The character of his gain is $30,000 at 25% rate; $25,000 at 20% rate. The unrecaptured Section 1250 gain (i.e., depreciation) is taxed at 25% while the remaining long-term capital gain receives a 20% tax rate.

D. CONSIDERATIONS TO SECTIONS 1245 AND 1250.

1. Exceptions - Recapture under Sections 1245 and 1250 do not apply to the following:
    a. Gifts - The recapture potential carries over to the donee.
    b. Death - When owner of asset dies, asset receives step to fair market value in basis; therefore, no recapture to heir.
    c. Charitable transfers - Recapture potential reduces the amount of charitable contribution deduction (under Section 170).
    d. Certain nontaxable transactions - Recapture potential carries over to the transferee.
    e. Like-kind exchanges - Any remaining recapture potential carries over to the property received.
    f. Involuntary conversions - Any remaining recapture potential carries over to the property received.
2. Other applications (installment sales) - Recapture gain is recognized in the year of sale and is treated as ordinary income until the recapture potential is fully netted out.

E. SPECIAL RECAPTURE PROVISIONS.

1. When sale/exchange of depreciable property between certain related parties, any gain recognized is ordinary income.

XXIII. TAXATION OF INVESTMENT TRANSACTIONS

EXHIBIT 36: SUMMARY OF TAXATION OF INVESTMENT TRANSACTIONS

		Income	Sale at Gain	Sale at Loss	Adjusted Taxable Basis
A	Stocks	Taxable	Capital Gain	Capital Loss	Generally Cost
B	Bonds - Corp. or Treasury	Taxable	Capital Gain	Capital Loss	Generally Cost
C	Municipal Bonds	Not Taxable	Capital Gain	Capital Loss	Generally Cost
D	OID Bonds - Corp. or Treasury	Taxable	Capital Gain	Capital Loss	Generally Cost
E	Options on Stocks	See NQSOs & ISOs			Cost + Income Recognized
F	Exchanges (Tax-free)	N/A	Capital Gain to extent of boot	Postponed	Generally Carryover
G	Installment Sales	Taxable Interest	Capital Gain	N/A	Cost
H	Property Inherited	Taxable	Long-Term Capital Gain	Long-Term Capital Loss	FMV @ Death or Alternate Value
I	Mutual Funds	Taxable	Capital Gain	Capital Loss	Cost + Income Reinvested
J	Gifts	Taxable	Capital Gain	Capital Loss	Double-Basis Rule
K	Personal Residence	N/A	Exempt to $250,000 or $500,000	Disallowed	Cost
L	Personal Use Property	N/A	Capital Gain	Disallowed	Cost
M	1244 Stock	Taxable	Capital Gain	Ordinary Loss (limited)	Cost
N	Exchange of Series E/EE bonds	Not Taxable	Capital Gain	Capital Loss	Generally Cost
O	1202 Stock	Taxable	Capital Gain (exclude 50% of gain, gain recognized is taxed at 28%)	Capital Loss	Cost

Note 1: Income refers to proceeds from the investment after acquisition.
Note 2: Capital gains are long term or short term depending on the holding period.
Note 3: Basis depends on how acquired.
Note 4: Cost includes purchase price and transaction costs.

A. SALES OF STOCK.

1. The basis will be the purchase price of the stock plus any commissions or fees associated with the purchase. Basis may be subsequently adjusted for nontaxable stock dividends, stock splits, or nontaxable distributions that are a return of capital.
2. Basis options when selling.
   a. FIFO.
   b. Specific identification.
3. Gain will be calculated as net sales proceeds less adjusted basis.
4. Follow capital-gain rules explained in Section XXD on page 679.
5. Cash dividends are includible in taxable income.
6. A sale will result in capital gain or loss unless sold for basis.
7. Reinvested dividends are currently taxed and taxpayers will add dividends reinvested to the basis of stock.

B. BONDS - CORPORATE OR TREASURY.

1. Income (interest) is taxable.
2. The sale of a bond creates a capital gain or loss if disposed of at an amount different from basis.
3. If a corporate bond is bought at a premium, then the taxpayer will reduce the basis by the amount of amortization taken (if elected).
4. Treasury bond interest is not subject to state income tax.

C. MUNICIPAL BONDS.

1. The interest on municipal bonds is tax exempt for federal tax purposes.
2. The sale of a municipal bond creates a capital gain or loss if disposed of at an amount different from basis.
3. Premiums on municipal bonds must be amortized and the basis must be reduced by the amortized amount. No deduction is taken for the amortization on municipal bonds.

D. ORIGINAL ISSUE DISCOUNT (OID) BONDS – CORPORATE OR TREASURY.

1. OID typically applies to zero-coupon or deep-discount bonds.
2. Interest is usually accrued and includible in income in spite of an absence of cash flow.
3. The sale of an OID will result in capital gain or loss if the sale proceeds are different from the adjusted tax basis.
4. The accrued interest reported each year by the taxpayer is added to the basis.

E. STOCK OPTIONS.

1. Usually given by employer as a form of compensation.
2. Gives taxpayer right to buy company's stock at a certain price within a specific time frame.
3. Generally, no income is recognized when the option is granted.

4. The amount and timing of income recognition depends upon the type of stock option awarded.
   a. Nonqualified stock options (NQSOs).
      i. Not given any preferred tax treatment.
      ii. Individual will recognize income when NQSO is granted, only if the option is traded on an exchange and there is not a substantial risk of forfeiture, such as cannot exercise for a year.
      iii. Individual taxed when option is exercised on the difference between FMV of the stock on the date of exercise and the option price.
      iv. Taxed at ordinary income rates and included in employee's W-2.
      v. Any appreciation that occurs after exercise is taxed as capital gain (basis is the FMV at date of exercise, holding period determines if long term or short term).
   b. Incentive stock options (ISOs).
      i. No income recognized when option is granted.
      ii. No tax due when option is exercised.
      iii. Tax is due when stock is sold. If taxpayer does not dispose of stock within two years after option grant and holds the stock more than one year (after exercise), any gain will be capital gain. If taxpayer sells stock within one year after exercise date, gain is treated as ordinary income. If within the calendar year, then it is W-2 income and there is no AMT positive adjustment.
      iv. AMT may require earlier recognition of income and so the difference between the option price and the FMV at date of exercise is an addback for AMT purposes.

Example

- John's employer grants him a nonqualified stock option (NQSO) with an exercise price of $25. John exercises the NQSO when the market value is $40. The $15 difference is included in John's W-2 income and is subject to FICA and FUTA. If John sells the stock two years later for $60, his basis in the stock is $40 and he has a long-term capital gain of $20. The gain will be taxed at 20%.

- George's employer grants him an incentive stock option (ISO) on January 1, 2002, with an exercise price of $25. George exercises the ISO on January 1, 2003, when the market price is $40. No ordinary income recognition is triggered (but $15 will be an AMT adjustment). George sells the stock two years later for $60, his basis is $25 and he has a $35 long-term capital gain (20%) for regular tax.

  Note: His AMT basis is $40, and AMT gain is $20.

F. MUTUAL FUNDS.

1. Mutual funds usually distribute income and capital gains on an annual basis.
2. If income and gains are distributed in cash, the taxpayer includes them in taxable income and makes no adjustment to the basis.
3. If, however, the taxpayer (as most do) reinvests all dividend and capital gains, the taxpayer must still include the income and capital gains reported in taxable income and must add these same amounts to the taxpayer's adjusted taxable basis.
4. Basis options when selling:
   a. FIFO.
   b. Average cost.
   c. Specific identification. Note: To use, must identify shares before the sale.

G. PERSONAL USE PROPERTY.

1. The sale of personal use property at a gain will generally be a capital gain.
2. The loss on a sale of personal use property is nondeductible.

H. SECTION 1244 STOCK.

1. Gains from the sale of Section 1244 stock are capital gains.
2. Losses on Section 1244 stock are ordinary losses up to $50,000 per year for single taxpayers and up to $100,000 for married filing jointly taxpayers.
3. Any excess losses beyond the $50,000 or $100,000 as applicable in the year are capital losses.

I. EXCHANGE OF E OR EE BONDS FOR HH BONDS.

1. If a cash-basis taxpayer has not made the election to report interest currently on Series E or EE bonds held, he may exchange these bonds for Series HH bonds without recognizing any of the deferred interest on the E/EE bonds.
2. The basis of the E/EE bonds carries over, and when the HH bonds are redeemed, the deferred interest is then recognized.

XXIV. BUSINESS ENTITIES

Type of Business Organization						
	Sole Proprietor	Partnership*	LLP	LLC**	S-Corp	Corporation
What type of liability do the owners have?	Unlimited	General partnership – unlimited; Limited partnership – limited	Limited	Limited	Limited	Limited
What federal tax form is required to be filed for the organization?	Form 1040, Schedule C	Form 1065 (information return)	Form 1065 (information return)	Form 1040, Schedule C or Form 1065 or Form 1120 or Form 1120S	Form 1120S (information return)	Form 1120
Under what concept is the organization taxed?	Individual Level	Flow-through	Flow-through	LLCs can be taxed as sole proprietorships, partnerships, corporations, or S corporations	Flow-through	Entity Level
On what tax form is the owner's compensation reported?	Form 1040, Schedule C	Schedule K-1	Schedule K-1	Form 1040, Schedule C, or Schedule K-1, or Form W-2 and Schedule K-1, or W-2	W-2 and Schedule K-1	W-2 (dividends are reported on Form 1099-DIV)
What is the nature of the owner's income from the organization?	Self-employment income	Self-employment income*	Self-employment income	Self-employment income, or W-2 income and ordinary income, W-2 income	W-2 income and ordinary income	W-2 income and dividend income
What is the basis for determining tax- advantaged retirement plan contributions?	Net Schedule C income (less 1/2 SE tax)	Self-employment income* (less 1/2 SE tax)	Self-employment income (less 1/2 SE tax)	Self-employment income (less 1/2 SE tax) or W-2 income	W-2 income	W-2 income

Flow-through: All items of income will flow from the entity to the individual partners/owners/members return while retaining the character of the income at the entity level.
*Limited Partners will generally not have self-employment income.
**The LLC will have the same tax characteristics and attributes as the type of entity it has elected to be taxed as.

Note: Family Limited Partnerships (FLPs) have the same treatment for general partners as general partnerships and for limited partners the same treatment as limited partnerships.

XXV. TAXATION OF TRUSTS AND ESTATES

A. IN GENERAL.

1. A trust is a legal arrangement whereby an individual transfers legal ownership of property to a trustee.
2. Trusts are generally treated as separate taxable entities subject to taxation under Subchapter J of the Internal Revenue Code.
3. An estate is a legal entity that comes into existence upon the death of an individual and remains in existence until the decedent's assets pass to the heirs.
   a. The estate consists of the probate estate.
   b. The estate holds and protects the assets, collects income from those assets, and satisfies obligations of the estate until all the assets are distributed.
4. Trusts and estates are referred to as fiduciaries.
5. Trust income can be taxed to:
   a. Trust - if income is accumulated in the trust.
   b. Beneficiary - if income is distributed from the trust.
   c. Grantor - if the trust is a grantor trust (discussed below).

B. TYPES OF TRUSTS.

1. Simple trust.
   a. Required to distribute all income to beneficiaries each year.
   b. Charitable donations are prohibited.
   c. Principal distributions are prohibited.
   d. Allowed a personal exemption of $300.
2. Complex trust.
   a. A trust in which income can be accumulated.
   b. Principal can be distributed.
   c. The trust pays tax on accumulated income.
   d. Allowed a personal exemption of $100.
3. Grantor trust.
   a. If a trust is a grantor trust, the grantor pays tax on all trust income.
   b. Trust is ignored for income tax purposes.
   c. A trust will be a grantor trust if the grantor retains the power to control enjoyment. These powers include the power to:
      i. Add or remove beneficiaries.
      ii. Determine the timing of distributions.
      iii. Alter the beneficiary's share of principal or income.

C. FIDUCIARY ACCOUNTING INCOME.

1. The accounting income of a fiduciary is determined by the decedent's will (in the case of an estate), or the trust instrument (in the case of a trust).
2. Every fiduciary may have its own unique set of rules for the computation of accounting income.
3. A common difference between fiduciary accounting income and fiduciary taxable income is the treatment of capital gains.
   a. For accounting purposes, capital gains generally represent an increase in the value of the principal and are not available for distribution to the income beneficiaries.
   b. For tax purposes, the capital gains represent taxable income.
4. Trustee fees are generally deductible for tax purposes, but may be treated as either income or principal for trust accounting purposes.

D. FIDUCIARY TAXABLE INCOME AND DISTRIBUTION DEDUCTION.

1. The taxable income of a trust is similar to the calculation of taxable income for an individual taxpayer.
2. Major differences between trust taxable income and individual taxable income:
   a. A trust is entitled to a deduction for distributions made to beneficiaries.
   b. A trust is not entitled to a standard deduction.
   c. A trust is entitled to a personal exemption of $300 for a simple trust and $100 for a complex trust.
3. If an administrative expense is claimed as a deduction on the estate tax return of a decedent, it may not also be claimed as a deduction on the income tax return of the decedent's estate. However, the deduction can be prorated between the two returns.
4. Medical expenses paid for the care of the decedent before his or her death:
   a. If paid within one year after death, the medical expenses can be deducted either on the final income tax return (Form 1040) of the decedent or the estate tax return of the decedent (Form 706), but not both.
   b. If paid more than one year after death, the expenses can only be deducted on the estate tax return.
5. Deduction for distributions made to beneficiaries.
   a. The fiduciary is allowed a deduction for the amount of distributions made to beneficiaries during the year. The amount deductible by the fiduciary is the same amount that is taxable to the beneficiaries.
   b. The distribution deduction is calculated as the lesser of Distributable Net Income (DNI) or the amount actually distributed to the beneficiaries.
   c. Distributable Net Income (DNI).
      i. DNI is similar to fiduciary accounting income.
      ii. Includes most normal income/expense items.
      iii. Excludes items relating to corpus such as capital gains, stock splits, and depreciation of business assets.

E. FIDUCIARY TAX RATES AND FILING REQUIREMENTS.

1. Fiduciaries file Form 1041 on or before the 15th day of the fourth month after the close of the tax year. Grantor trusts may also file a Form 1041.
2. A trust must adopt a calendar year.
3. Estates may adopt either a calendar year or fiscal year. The first taxable year begins on the day following the decedent's death.
4. Estates and trusts are subject to the following rate schedule (a very highly progressive structure).

Trust and Estate Tax Rates (Year 2003)

If taxable income is: Over --	But not over --	The tax is:	Of the amount over --
$0	$1,900	---------------15%	$0
$1,900	$4,500	$285 + 27%	$1,900
$4,500	$6,850	$987 + 30%	$4,500
$6,850	$9,350	$1,692 + 35%	$6,850
$9,350	------------	$2,567 + 38.6%	$9,350

5. Any component of fiduciary taxable income consisting of long-term capital gain is taxed at a maximum rate of 20%.
6. Trusts may be subject to alternative minimum tax.

F. TAX TREATMENT OF DISTRIBUTIONS TO BENEFICIARIES.

1. Beneficiary is taxed on an amount equal to the distribution deduction.
2. The fiduciary receives a deduction for the distribution.
3. Income distributed to the beneficiary maintains its character (capital gain, ordinary income, etc.).
4. A beneficiary who receives a distribution from a fiduciary will receive a Schedule K-1 each year. The K-1 summarizes the amounts and character of the various items of income that constitute the taxable portion of the distribution.
5. A beneficiary who receives a distribution from a fiduciary with both taxable and nontaxable DNI will only be taxed on a portion of the distribution received.

Example

ABC Trust has DNI of $100,000, of which $40,000 is nontaxable. The beneficiary received a distribution of $20,000 during the year. The distribution received will be taxable in the amount of $12,000 [$20,000 distribution x ($60,000 taxable DNI divided by $100,000 total DNI)] and nontaxable for the remaining $8,000.

6. Because a simple trust is required to distribute all trust income to its beneficiaries, the entire amount of taxable DNI will be taxed to the beneficiaries each year.

XXVI.AUDIT, PENALTIES, AND TAXPAYER'S RIGHTS

A. IN GENERAL.

1. A Taxpayer Compliance Measurement Program (TCMP) randomly selected returns used for statistical purposes of the IRS to develop discriminate analysis standards (presently indefinitely suspended).
2. Audit probability varies with income level and type of income.
3. Situations that might trigger an audit.
   a. Significant investment losses.
   b. Business expenses that produce significant losses.
   c. Operating a cash business.
   d. Deductions that are larger than the average deduction taken by taxpayers at a similar income level.

B. TYPES OF AUDITS.

1. A correspondence audit is one in which the issue is generally minor and is performed through the mail.
2. An office audit is usually restricted in scope to specific item(s) and is performed at the IRS office.
3. A field audit is an examination of numerous items and is performed on the premises of the taxpayer.

C. STATUTE OF LIMITATIONS.

1. Three years from the filing date of the return or due date if later.
2. Six years if 25% of gross income is unreported.
3. No statute of limitations for failure to file or if a fraudulent return is filed.

D. INTEREST AND PENALTIES.

1. Interest - Interest runs from unextended due date.
2. Penalties.
   a. Failure to file: 5.0% per month up to 25%. If failure-to-file penalty is fraudulent, the penalty is increased to 15% per month up to a 75% maximum.
   b. Failure to pay: 0.5% per month up to 25%. If both a failure-to-file penalty and a failure-to-pay penalty apply, the failure-to-file penalty is reduced by the failure-to-pay penalty.
   c. Accuracy-related penalty: 20% of underpayment for intentional disregard of rules and regulations without intent to defraud.

Example

Taxpayer files a timely tax return but fails to pay an amount of $15,000 in additional tax. $6,000 is attributable to the taxpayer's negligence. The negligence penalty will be $1,200. A 20% penalty is applied to the $6,000.

d. There are various fraud penalties for deliberate actions (deceit, misrepresentation, and concealment).

Example

Taxpayer files tax return 39 days after the due date. Along with the return he remits a check for $6,000, which is the balance of the tax owed. Disregarding any interest element, the total failure-to-file and failure-to-pay penalties are $600.

Calculated as follows:

Failure-to-pay penalty:		
[1/2% x $6,000 x 2 (two months, any fraction counts as a full month)]	$60	
Plus: Failure-to-file penalty [5% x $6,000 x 2 months]	600	
Less: Failure-to-pay penalty (they run concurrently)	(60)	540
Total penalties (failure-to-file and failure-to-pay)		$600

The failure-to-file penalty of $600 is reduced by the failure-to-pay penalty of $60 making the adjusted failure-to-file penalty $540. Adding the failure-to-pay penalty of $60 (it reduced the failure-to-file, but it did not go away) makes a total penalty of $600.

E. BURDEN OF PROOF.

1. The IRS has the burden of proof on factual matters if the taxpayer has creditable evidence supporting his or her position.
   a. The taxpayer must have records and must cooperate with IRS.
   b. Corporations, trusts, and estates must have a net worth of $7 million or less to qualify.

F. INNOCENT SPOUSE RELIEF.

1. Spouses can obtain apportioned relief for the part of the understatement that they had no knowledge of.
2. An election exists for taxpayers who are no longer married or legally separated (or living apart for at least 12 months) that establishes a separate tax liability for items attributable to each taxpayer.

G. REPRESENTING CLIENTS BEFORE THE IRS.

1. In General.
   a. Only a recognized representative can represent a client before the Internal Revenue Service.
   b. A representative can act on the client's behalf at conferences, hearings, or meetings with the IRS.
   c. The representative must be granted authority to act on behalf of the client. Authority is granted through a Power of Attorney.
2. Recognized Representative.
   a. A recognized representative must file a written declaration with the IRS that states he or she is qualified and authorized to represent the client.
   b. Recognized representatives can include:
      i. Attorneys.
      ii. CPAs.
      iii. Enrolled agents or enrolled actuaries.
      iv. Certain unenrolled individuals, such as an unenrolled tax return preparer.
         A) Unenrolled individuals typically have limited authority to represent the client.
         B) Unenrolled individuals must present satisfactory identification and proof of authority to represent the client.
   c. Recognized representatives do not include:
      i. Individuals convicted of a criminal offense.
      ii. Individuals under disbarment or suspension from practicing as attorneys, CPAs, or actuaries.
      iii. Individuals who are suspended from practice before the IRS.
      iv. Officers or employees of the U.S. government or of the District of Columbia.
      v. Members of Congress, if receiving compensation regarding the IRS issue.
      vi. CFPs.
3. Power of Attorney.
   a. A power of attorney is a written authorization for an individual to act on one's behalf.
   b. With a power of attorney, any representative (other than an unenrolled preparer) can usually perform the following acts:
      i. Represent the client before the IRS.
      ii. Record the interview.
      iii. Sign on the client's behalf:
         A) Waiver of restriction on assessment or collection of a tax deficiency.
         B) Consent to extend the statutory time period for assessment or collection of a tax.
         C) Closing agreement.
      iv. Receive (but not cash) a refund check.
   c. A representative generally cannot sign a client's income tax return, except as preparer.

H. REFORM OF IRS'S PROCEDURES.

1. Extensive reform of the IRS's procedures relating to audit:
    a. There must be a reasonable notice on third-party summons.
    b. The Act limits use of financial status and economic reality techniques.
    c. The criteria for audit selection must be disclosed.
    d. The attorney-client privilege is extended to tax advisers who are authorized to practice before the IRS.
    e. Due process must be followed for tax collection levies.

INDEX

J

K

L

M

N

O

P

Q

R

S

Retirement Planning

Outlines and Study Guides

TABLE OF CONTENTS

TABLE OF EXHIBITS

TABLE OF APPENDICES

Retirement Planning

I. INTRODUCTION TO RETIREMENT PLANS, PENSION PLANS, AND PENSION LEGISLATION

A. DEMOGRAPHICS.

1. The average retiree can expect a retirement period of 20-25 years.
2. 50% of U.S. workers will retire by age 60.
3. Average workers do not begin saving for retirement until they are in their late thirties or later.
4. Work life expectancy is contracting.
5. Retirement life expectancy is expanding due to an increase in life expectancy and early retirement.
6. The average savings rate for the U.S. is less than 3% of gross income.

B. RETIREMENT NEEDS ANALYSIS.

1. Retirement needs tend to be 60-80% of preretirement income in order to maintain the person's lifestyle. This percentage is called the wage replacement ratio (WRR).
2. The savings rate required beginning at age 25 to achieve a 60-80% wage replacement ratio is about 10% of gross income. This is approximately three times the current U.S. savings rate. In addition, age 25 is 10 to 15 years earlier than most people begin to think about saving for retirement. The U.S. savings rate appears to be improving for younger employees as they begin to save through employer-provided 401(k) plans.
3. The process of analyzing the accumulation of sufficient resources for retirement is referred to as capital needs analysis and/or retirement needs analysis. An example will serve to identify the issues and risks related to capital needs analysis.

Example (Capital Needs Analysis-Annuity Model)

Stuart, single and age 52, is currently earning $70,000 per year. He wants to retire at age 62 and maintain his current lifestyle. He expects salary increases to equal the Consumer Price Index (CPI). Stuart's financial planner gathers the following facts and opinions from Stuart:

Stuart believes that he could retire comfortably with 80% of his current taxable income (Wage Replacement Ratio (WRR)). He determined this from the following analysis:

Current Income %	100.00%
Less: FICA Contribution % (no FICA on Retirement Income)	(7.65%)
Less: Current Savings as a % of Gross Pay	(10.00%)
Less: Expected Savings from Deduction of Work Related Expenses %	(2.35%)
Wage Replacement Ratio	80.00%

Observation: Since Stuart is 52 and expects to retire at age 62, a pro forma retirement budget in today's dollars may be more appropriate to use than the wage replacement percent method. Such a budget is likely to be more precise than the above percentage wage replacement ratio method and can incorporate some of the following issues:

- Will debts or mortgages be eliminated by the time he retires? (If so, this will reduce his income needs.)
- Significant lifestyle changes (e.g., extensive travel) could cause an increase in expenses.
- Work-related expenses could be eliminated.
- Medical expenses may increase.

Conclusion: After careful budgeting, Stuart determined his wage replacement ratio to be 82%. (This is assumed for the example.)

a. Determine Stuart's life expectancy.

Fact: The IRS mortality tables indicate the life expectancy of a 52-year-old male to be:

Life expectancy of:

Both Sexes	Male	Female
26.1	23.3	28.8

Observation: Since traditional life expectancy tables are prepared for the 50th percentile, there is a risk that Stuart will outlive the 50th percentile and, therefore, possibly outlive his retirement money. To mitigate against this risk (superannuation), the planner should inquire how long Stuart's parents and grandparents have lived. It would be wise to construct or obtain a probabilistic life expectancy table and plan at the 90th percentile rather than the 50th.

Conclusion: While the basic table indicates a life expectancy of 75.3, the planner should plan for a life expectancy of 90 and a retirement life expectancy of 28 years.

b. Stuart expects inflation to average 5% as measured by the Consumer Price Index (CPI).

Observation: The best estimate of future inflation is the historical long-run inflation rate compared with the recent inflation rate. The CPI overstates inflation by about ½ to 1%, according to some leading economists. Furthermore, the market basket of goods represented by the CPI does not necessarily represent the market basket of goods and services that Stuart is expected to purchase during retirement. Some of Stuart's expenditures, like his mortgage, may be fixed, thus unaffected by inflation.

Conclusion: An expected inflation rate of 3.5% is chosen for the retirement projections in this example.

c. After repositioning his investment portfolio to a diversified investment portfolio consisting of 60% stocks and 40% bonds, Stuart's pretax rate of return is expected to be 10.5%.

Fact: All of Stuart's savings are in tax-advantaged accounts.

Conclusion: For projection purposes, use the pretax rate of return and prepare the capital needs analysis on a pretax rather than a post-tax basis.

d. Stuart has received the results from completion of Social Security Form SSA 7004. The results indicate that he will receive $14,000 per year at age 66 (normal retirement age) in today's dollars.

Fact: If Stuart retires at age 62, and immediately begins receiving Social Security benefits, he will receive 75% of what he would have received were he age 66.

Observation: An analysis of Social Security benefits at varying ages 62 to 66 indicates that, regardless of when they are received, a recipient's benefits are approximately actuarially equivalent.

Conclusion: Stuart decides to plan to take Social Security retirement benefits at age 62.

Capital Needs Analysis:

Current Salary	$70,000	
Wage Replacement (82%)	$57,400	($70,000 x 0.82)
Social Security Benefits (today's dollars)	(10,500)	($14,000 x 0.75)
Retirement Needs (today's dollars)	$46,900	for each year of retirement
Future Value of Retirement Needs at Age 62	$66,157	(N = 10, i = 3.5, PV = $46,900)

Retirement Term (90 - 62) = 28 years x 12 = 336 months

Monthly Payment ($66,157 ÷ 12) = $5,513.08 PMT_{AD} (This is an annuity due.)

Interest Rate [[(1.105 ÷ 1.035) -1] x 100] ÷ 12 = 0.563607

Calculated Value of the Capital Balance needed at age 62 = $834,846

At age 62, $834,846 is needed to provide a projected retirement benefit of $5,513.08 per month exclusive of Social Security benefits. Social Security benefits are indexed and not included in this analysis. The following alternatives demonstrate the effect of different starting balance amounts and the savings amounts needed to meet Stuart's objectives.

Alternative Assumptions 1, 2, 3, 4, and 5 are as follows:

	1	2	3	4	5
Beginning balance of savings at age 52	$0	$100,000	$200,000	$300,000	$400,000
*Savings per month spread through year	$9,100	$9,100	$9,100	$9,100	$9,100
Earnings rate on portfolio (annual)	10.5	10.5	10.5	10.5	10.5
N =	120	120	120	120	120
i = 10.5 ÷ 12	0.875	0.875	0.875	0.875	0.875
PMT_{OA} ($9,100 ÷ 12)	$758.33	$758.33	$758.33	$758.33	$758.33
Account balance at 62 (retirement age)	$159,868	$444,331	$728,794	$1,013,257	$1,297,720
Additional monthly savings needed	$3,201.76	$1,852.41	$503.06	$0	$0

** Stuart's employer matches Stuart's 10% contribution with 3% in his 401(k), and Stuart expects the total savings to remain fixed at $7,000 (10%) plus $2,100 (the employer match) for a total of $9,100 per year.*

Conclusion: If Stuart is to accomplish his goal, his current investment account balance must be:

PMT_{OA} = $758.33
i = 0.875
FV = $834,846
N = 120
PV = $237,281.79

Observation: If Stuart is unable to meet his goal, he has at least five alternatives:

1. Retire one year later (a year less of retirement, and an additional year of savings and compounding).
2. Save more (makes the goal easier but may be unrealistic).
3. Reduce his retirement needs (makes the goal easier but may be unrealistic).
4. Reposition the investment portfolio to accept additional investment risk to increase the expected portfolio returns (not recommended).
5. Some combination of the above.

e. Risks to Stuart's plan:

1. Inflation may be greater than expected.
2. Portfolio returns may be less than expected.
3. Stuart's retirement needs may increase.
4. Stuart may still outlive the plan.
5. Stuart's ability to save may decline.
6. Marriage and children.
7. Job loss (downsizing).
8. Some combination of the above.

f. Ways to mitigate the risks:

1. Increase the projected inflation rate to 4% or 4.5% (more conservative).
2. Reduce the expected portfolio rate of return to 9.5% or 10% (more conservative) or lower depending on the client's transaction tolerance for risk.
3. Some combination of 1 and 2.
4. Use a capital preservation model.
5. Use a purchasing power preservation model.

Example (Capital needs analysis using a Capital Preservation Model)

(Refer to Stuart example). A Capital Preservation Model is one in which an account balance remains at life expectancy in an amount equal to the account balance calculated as required at retirement age (e.g., $834,846).

Assumptions:

N	=	336 months of retirement
PMT_{AD}	=	$5,513.08 per month (amount needed in real terms)
i	=	0.563607
PV	=	$834,846

Determine the present value of $834,846 for 28 years.

N	=	28 = Age 90 - 62
FV of capital	=	$834,846
i	=	10.5 investment rate
PV	=	$50,987.37

Add this to the capital needs required under the annuity approach.

$834,846.00	The account balance of $885,833.37 at age 62 would allow for the
50,987.37	principal balance of $834,846.00 to remain at life expectancy (age 90)
$885,833.37	assuming all projection assumptions materialize as expected.

Example (Capital needs analysis using a Purchasing Power Preservation Model)

(Refer to Stuart example). In the Purchasing Power Preservation Model, an account balance exists at life expectancy equal to the amount calculated as needed at retirement as adjusted for inflation. This account balance at life expectancy has the same purchasing power at life expectancy as at retirement.

PV = \$834,846
i = 3.5
N = 28 (90 - 62)
FV = \$2,187,440 (FV of \$834,946 at life expectancy of 90)
N = 28, i = 10.5 (the earnings rate)
PV = \$133,596 (the amount needed to add to the capital balance required under the annuity model at age 62)

\$834,846	Annuity method
133,596	Additional amount for Purchasing Power Method
\$968,442	Capital needed at 62

Utilizing a Purchasing Power Preservation Model, \$968,442 is the amount needed that will leave Stuart with \$2,187,440 in his capital balance at age 90, with a purchasing power equal to \$834,846 at retirement (age 62).

Observation: Funding either a Capital Preservation Model or a Purchasing Preservation Model is more expensive than the straight Annuity Model, but doing so reduces some of the risks inherent in the annuity model.

C. SOCIAL SECURITY BENEFITS.

1. Social Security retirement benefits are the foundation of retirement income for some workers.
   a. Social Security provides up to 45% of the Wage Replacement Ratio (WRR) for the single low-income worker (e.g., \$20,000) at normal retirement age (65).
   b. Social Security provides up to 67.5% of the WRR for the married low-income worker with same age nonworking spouse.
   c. Social Security provides only 13.5% of the WRR for the single high-income worker (e.g., \$100,000).
   d. Social Security provides only 20.25% of the WRR for the married worker making \$100,000 with same age nonworking spouse.
2. Social Security will not meet the total retirement needs of most workers.

II. TYPES OF RETIREMENT PLANS

EXHIBIT 1: RETIREMENT PLANS

QUALIFIED PLANS[A]		OTHER TAX-ADVANTAGED PLANS	NONQUALIFIED PLANS
Pension Plans[B]	*Profit-Sharing Plans[C]*		
• Defined-Benefit Plans[D] • Cash-Balance Plans • Target-Benefit Plans[D] • Money-Purchase Plans	• Profit-Sharing Plans • Stock Bonus Plans • ESOPs • 401(k) Plans[E] • Thrift Plans • SIMPLE 401(k) • Age-Based Profit-Sharing Plans[D] • New Comparability Plans[D]	• SEPs • SARSEPs • Traditional IRA • Roth IRA • SIMPLE (IRA) • 403(b)	• Deferred Compensation Plans • Nonqualified Stock Option Plans • Incentive Stock Option Plans • Phantom Stock Plans • Split-Dollar Life Insurance • 457 Plans • ESPPs

A Distribution from qualified plans may qualify for ten-year forward averaging. Other plans and nonqualified plans do not.

B Pension plans promise either a benefit or contributions; therefore, mandatory annual funding and no in-service withdrawals.

C Profit-sharing plans promise tax deferral; therefore, no mandatory annual funding and in-service withdrawals are allowed if the plan so provides.

D Tested for discrimination based on benefits as opposed to contributions.

E Tested for discrimination regarding employee elective deferrals and employer matching contributions.

A. QUALIFIED PLANS.

1. They must meet ERISA requirements including:
    a. Coverage.
    b. Participation.
    c. Vesting.
    d. Reporting and disclosure.
    e. Fiduciary requirements.
2. Employer and employee receive tax advantages.

B. OTHER TAX-ADVANTAGED RETIREMENT PLANS.

> **Note:** These are not qualified plans but have many similarities to qualified plans, especially regarding distributions.

1. Types.
   a. SEPs (Simplified Employee Pension).
   b. Traditional IRAs (Individual Retirement Annuities and Accounts).
   c. Roth IRAs.
   d. SIMPLE IRAs (Savings Incentive Match Plan for Employees).
   e. 403(b)s (Supplementary Retirement Annuities, TSAs, TDAs).
2. Promise - pay what is in the individual account at retirement.
3. Distribution rules are essentially the same as those for qualified plans.

C. NONQUALIFIED PLANS.

> **Note:** Essentially nontax-advantaged deferred compensation plans.

1. Nonqualified plans are not subject to the same ERISA rules as qualified plans.
2. Nonqualified plans do not benefit from tax advantages that apply to qualified plans or other tax-advantaged plans.
3. Nonqualified plans generally are provided to key employees only.
4. Nonqualified plans usually supplement qualified plans and may defer taxes, thereby changing ordinary income into capital gains income.
5. Types of nonqualified plans (Top Hat Plans).
   a. Deferred compensation.
   b. Excess benefit plans - Provides salary continuation through excess benefits or contributions that exceed IRC Section 415 limits.
   c. Supplemental executive retirement plan (SERP) - May be used below IRC Section 415 limits for key executives.
   d. Phantom stock plans - An accounting entry without actual stock ownership.
   e. Stock options - Incentive stock options (ISOs) and nonqualified stock options (NQSOs).
   f. Employee Stock Purchase Plans (ESPPs).

III. OVERVIEW OF QUALIFIED PLANS

A. ADVANTAGES OF QUALIFIED PLANS.

1. Qualified plans receive tax benefits not available to nonqualified plans.
   a. Employer contributions (and employee salary reduction contributions) are deductible by the employer (and excluded from the employee's gross income) in the year the contributions are made.
   b. Employees are not taxed on employer contributions in the year that the employer contributes to the plan.
   c. For taxpayers born prior to January 1, 1936, certain lump-sum distributions are eligible for reduced tax rates using ten-year forward averaging, pre-1974 capital gain treatment, and NUA.
   d. The plan itself is a tax-exempt fund. Earnings on plan investments are not currently taxed to the employer or employee, but rather accumulate tax deferred until distributed.
   e. Funds are only taxed when withdrawn as distributions. Rollovers to IRAs are permitted. If loans are permitted, they are not considered distributions.
2. Qualified plans are protected from creditors by ERISA (federal law).

B. TYPES OF QUALIFIED RETIREMENT PLANS.

1. Qualified retirement plans are either pension or profit-sharing plans.
   a. Characteristics of a pension plan.
      i. The promise to pay a pension.
      ii. Mandatory annual funding.
      iii. No in-service withdrawals.
   b. There are four types of pension plans: defined-benefit, cash-balance, money-purchase pension plans, and target-benefit money-purchase pension plans.
   c. Characteristics of profit-sharing plans.
      i. The promise to defer taxes. There is no particular term for such deferral.
      ii. In-service withdrawals are allowed if the plan document permits.
      iii. Do not require mandatory annual funding, although, to remain qualified, the plans must make substantial and recurring contributions.

	Pension Plan	Profit-Sharing Plan
Legal Promise	To pay a pension	To defer tax
In-Service Withdrawals	Not permitted	Permitted after two years
Mandatory Funding	Yes	No
Employer Securities Limit	10%	100%
Deductible Contribution Limit by Employer	25%	25%

EXHIBIT 2: DEFINED-BENEFIT VS. DEFINED-CONTRIBUTION GENERAL CHARACTERISTICS

Defined-Benefit	Defined-Contribution
• Commingled accounts	• Individual accounts
• Investment risk is borne by the employer	• Investment risk is borne by the employee
• Identifies the benefit for which the employer is responsible	• Identifies the contributions for which the employer is responsible
• Benefit limit (2003 - $160,000)	• Contribution limit for employees (2003 - 100% or $40,000)

2. Defined-benefit plans.
   a. Defined-benefit plans provide a specific amount of benefit to the employee at normal retirement age (usually age 65).
      i. Plans are funded actuarially and require annual actuarial work (may be costly).
      ii. The annual funding amount is greater for employees who are older at plan-entry age. This makes defined-benefit plans attractive to professionals and closely held business owners who may be the older employees in the plan.
   b. Retirement eligibility:
      i. Early retirement provisions may cause a reduced periodic benefit amount due to the extended retirement life expectancy.
      ii. Eligibility can be a service-only requirement, an age-only requirement, an age-and-service requirement, or the sum-of-age-and-service requirement.
   c. Determination of benefits.
      i. Benefits may be determined by an earnings-based formula to terminal earnings or to career earnings.
      ii. Defined-benefit plans specify time and percent of benefits in the plan document.
3. Defined-contribution plans.
   a. In a defined-contribution plan, the employer establishes and maintains an individual account for each plan participant. When the participant becomes eligible to receive benefit payments, usually at retirement or termination of employment, the benefit is based on the total amount in the participant's account. The account balance includes employer contributions, employee contributions, and earnings on the account for the years of deferral.
   b. The employer does not guarantee the amount of benefit a participant will ultimately receive, but the employer must make contributions under a formula specified in the plan.

c. The employer must specify the rules in the plan document for:
   i. Eligibility.
   ii. Participation.
   iii. Vesting.
   iv. Retirement eligibility.
   v. Determining contributions.
   vi. Investment decisions.
   vii. Withdrawals.
   viii. Loans (if any).
   ix. Distribution of benefits.

d. Defined-contribution plans.
   i. Pension plans.
      A) The employer must make mandatory annual contributions to each participant's account under a formula based on compensation established at inception.
      B) The employee bears the risk of varying investment results.
      C) Types of defined-contribution pension plans.
         1) Money-purchase plans.
         2) Target-benefit plans.
   ii. Profit-sharing plans.
      A) A profit-sharing plan is a defined-contribution plan where the employer determines the amount of the contribution each year with no stated contribution obligation (discretionary funding).
      B) Types of profit-sharing plans.
         1) Profit-sharing plans.
         2) Stock bonus plans.
         3) ESOP.
         4) 401(k) plans.
         5) Thrift plans.
         6) SIMPLE 401(k) plans.
         7) Age-based profit-sharing plans.
         8) New comparability plans.

C. MATCHING EMPLOYER OBJECTIVES TO THE RIGHT PLAN DESIGN.

1. Proper plan design consists of getting the right match between employer objectives and the available qualified plans.

   a. The usual objective: Maximize the proportion of plan contributions that benefit the highly compensated employees (usually owners and top management).

   b. Many employers, particularly small closely held companies, view retirement plans as beneficial only when they provide substantial tax-sheltered retirement benefits for key employees (those in a position to decide to implement a plan).

   c. Commonly used techniques for accomplishing objectives:

      i. Defined-benefit plans are widely used with large employee groups.

      ii. Service-based contribution or benefit formulas can be based on an employee's years of service with the employer.

      iii. Use of a target-benefit plan that utilizes age and compensation weighting.

      iv. Use of any age-based profit-sharing plans.

      v. The nondiscrimination rules applicable to 401(k) plans, allow a higher rate of contribution for highly compensated employees than for other employees.

      vi. Employers are allowed to integrate (permitted disparity) their plan with Social Security benefits (with some exceptions).

      vii. Various objectives and the types of plans that accomplish that objective follow:

         A) **Objective**: To provide a savings medium that employees perceive as valuable, defined-contribution plans include:

            1) ESOP/Stock bonus plan.

            2) Money-purchase pension plan.

            3) Profit-sharing plan.

            4) Savings plan.

            5) Section 401(k) plan.

            6) Simplified employee pension (SEP).

            7) Target-benefit pension plan.

            8) Tax-deferred annuity.

         B) **Objective**: To provide adequate replacement income for each employee's retirement, the defined-benefit plan is the best vehicle because:

            1) A defined-benefit plan can provide a benefit based on final average compensation, regardless of the employee's years of service.

            2) There is no investment risk assumed by the employee.

            3) Employer funding of the benefit is mandatory, subject to under-funding penalties, even if the employer's profits decline.

C) **Objective:** To create an incentive for employees to maximize performance of the company, some options include:

   1) Profit-sharing plan.

   2) ESOP/Stock bonus plan.

   3) Any other defined-contribution plan or cash-balance plan.

D) **Objective:** To minimize turnover, defined-benefit plans that use a graduated vesting schedule are the best option.

E) **Objective:** To encourage early retirement, a defined-benefit plan can:

   1) Allow benefits to fully accrue after a specified period of time (e.g., 25 years).

   2) Relatively easy to design, a subsidized early retirement benefit provides a benefit at age 62 that is more than the actuarial equivalent of what the retiree would get at age 65.

F) **Objective:** To provide employer with maximum contribution flexibility, the most flexible plans from a contribution standpoint are qualified profit-sharing plans and SEPs. Amounts contributed each year can be entirely at the employer's discretion.

IV. QUALIFIED PLAN REQUIREMENTS

A. INTRODUCTION.

1. Plan requirements.
   a. The plan must be in writing.
   b. The plan must be communicated to employees.
   c. The plan must be permanent.
   d. The plan must not allow or have prohibited transactions (exclusive benefit rule).
2. There is an established procedure where a plan can be submitted to the IRS for a ruling on whether the terms of the plan meet the requirements of Internal Revenue Code Section 401 (Letter of Determination).
3. A qualified plan has four elements:
   a. The plan document provides the terms and benefit amounts provided by the plan. Once adopted, the plan is recognized as a separate legal entity (must be in writing).
   b. The trust holds the plan assets. The trustee is usually selected by the employer.
   c. The funds, once contributed, become the plan funds and, except in unusual circumstances, cannot be returned to the employer.
   d. The employer and the participants.
      i. The employer has the right to control the plan subject to the terms of the plan document, and usually retains the right to amend the terms of the plan or terminate the plan.
      ii. The participants are usually the passive beneficiaries of the plan.
4. A qualified plan must cover a broad group of employees, not just key employees and business owners. The plan must meet age and service requirements, overall coverage, and participation requirements.
5. ERISA requirements for qualified plans.
   a. Eligibility.
   b. Coverage.
   c. Vesting.
   d. Reporting and disclosure.
   e. Fiduciary.

B. ELIGIBILITY.

1. The plan cannot require more than 1 year of service for eligibility, and any employee who has attained the age of 21 must be allowed to enter the plan upon meeting the plan's waiting period requirements (21 and 1 rule).
   a. As an alternative to the 21 and 1 rule, the waiting period can be increased to 2 years if the plan provides immediate 100% vesting upon entry. However, a 401(k) plan may <u>not</u> use the 2-year waiting period.
   b. For eligibility purposes, a year of service means a 12-month period during which the employee has worked at least 1,000 hours.

2. Plan entrance dates.

    a. Once an employee has met the eligibility requirements, he will enter the plan on the next available entrance date. Qualified plans may have a variety of entrance dates: monthly, quarterly, semiannual, etc.

    b. A plan cannot make an employee wait more than six months to enter the plan after meeting the eligibility requirements. Therefore, qualified plans must have at least two entrance dates.

Example

ABC Company maintains a qualified plan that has 2 plan entrance dates, January 1 and July 1. The plan maintains the standard eligibility requirements of age 21 and one year of service. If Arnold is hired on 2/2/02, the first time he could enter the plan is 7/1/03

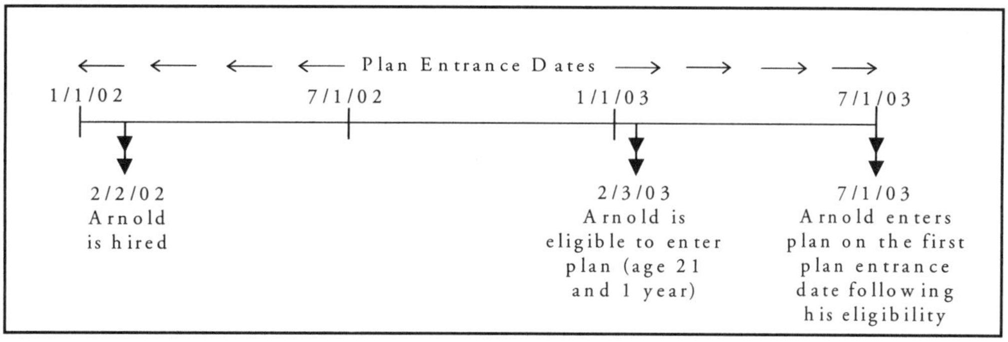

C. COVERAGE TESTS.

1. General Rule: The employer must cover 70% of all nonhighly compensated employees (Safe Harbor Test).

2. Plans that do not meet the safe harbor test must satisfy one of the following two exceptions: The ratio percentage test or the average benefits percentage test. The plan must meet only one of these three tests to pass the coverage requirement of ERISA.

    a. The ratio percentage test - the plan must cover a percentage of nonhighly compensated (NHC) employees that is at least 70% of the percentage of highly compensated (HC) employees covered.

    $$\text{Ratio Percentage Test} \Rightarrow \frac{\%\ \text{NHC Covered}}{\%\ \text{HC Covered}} \geq 70\%$$

    b. The average benefits percentage test has two components to satisfy annually:

        i. The nondiscriminatory component.

            A) Classification is reasonable and based on objective business criteria (e.g., job categories, location, hours, weeks);

            B) The ratio percentage of the plan can be either ≥ 70% or be nondiscriminatory based on facts and circumstances.

        ii. The average benefits percentage test. The average benefits percentage accrued for nonhighly compensated employees as a group must be ≥ 70% of the average benefits percentage accrued for the highly compensated employees as a group.

        $$\text{Average Benefits Percentage Test} \Rightarrow \frac{\text{Average Benefits \% NHC}}{\text{Average Benefits \% HC}} \geq 70\%$$

Example

Employer employs 200 nonexcludable employees of whom 10 are highly compensated. Nine of the 10 highly compensated, and 120 of the 190 nonhighly compensated employees benefit from the plan. The average benefit for the highly compensated is 8% and the average benefit for the nonhighly compensated is 6%.

Safe Harbor Test $\Rightarrow \frac{120}{190} = 63\%$

Ratio Percentage Test $\Rightarrow \frac{120/190}{9/10} = 70\%$

Average Benefits Percentage Test $\Rightarrow \frac{6\%}{8\%} = 75\%$

- Even though this plan fails the safe harbor test, it meets the coverage test either using the ratio percentage test or the average benefits percentage test.
- If only 119 of the nonhighly compensated were covered, the plan would fail the ratio percentage test. However, it would still pass the average benefits percentage test; therefore, the plan would meet the coverage requirement.

What about the 71 people?

- If there are 120 NHC and 9 HC employees that are covered out of a total of 200 employees, then why are the remaining 71 employees not covered? These 71 people may belong to an excluded class. Recall that the 200 employees all meet the eligibility tests of age 21 and one year of service. Therefore, the only way these employees are not covered is if they belong to an excluded class.
- Employers are permitted to design qualified plans to exclude certain classes of employees from coverage, as long as the plan meets the coverage rules. Recall that by definition, a plan must only cover 70% of NHC employees. For example, an employer may exclude salaried employees, commissioned employees, hourly employees, etc. However, employers may not exclude classes of employees based on age and service because there are rules (eligibility rules) related to age and service.

3. Coverage defined.
   a. For purposes of the coverage test, being covered means an employee is benefiting under the plan. For 401(k) plans, an employee is considered covered as long as he is eligible to defer.
   b. This is a different definition than being an active participant or being covered for purposes of determining deductibility of IRA contributions (discussed under the IRA section).

D. THE 50/40 TEST.

Note: Additional Coverage Test for Defined-Benefit Plans.

1. All defined-benefit plans require coverage on each day of the plan year for the lesser of:
   a. 50 employees.
   b. 40% or more of all employees.
      i. For purposes of the 40% test, the plan does not have to consider employees who are not eligible for the plan. Noneligible employees include the following:
         A) Those employees who do not meet age and service requirements (typically, age 21 and one year of service).
         B) Excluded employees, such as union employees, certain airline pilots, and nonresident aliens.

Note: If the employer has five or fewer employees, then two employees must be covered. In the case of a single employee, that person is required to be covered.

2. In addition, defined-benefit plans must also meet one of the safe harbor, ratio percentage, or average benefits percentage tests.

E. HIGHLY COMPENSATED: DEFINITION FOR EMPLOYEE BENEFIT PURPOSES.

1. A highly compensated employee is an employee that:
   a. Was, at any time, a GREATER THAN 5% owner of the employer any time during the current year or preceding year, OR
   b. For the preceding year, had compensation GREATER THAN $90,000 (for 2003).
      i. If the employer makes an election, only those persons in the top 20% of compensation greater than $90,000 (for 2003) are included as highly compensated. This exception is generally for large employers and helps the plan pass coverage and/or the ADP test for 401(k) plans.

F. NONDISCRIMINATION IN BENEFITS AND CONTRIBUTIONS.

1. Qualified plans may not discriminate in favor of highly compensated employees either in terms of benefits or in terms of employer contributions to the plan.
2. Either the contributions or the benefits must be nondiscriminating in amount.
   a. Benefits, rights, and features provided under the plan must be available to participants in a nondiscriminatory manner (distribution options, loans, etc.).
   b. Plan amendments must be nondiscriminating.

G. INTEGRATION WITH SOCIAL SECURITY (PERMITTED DISPARITY).

1. Qualified plan benefit or contribution formulas can be integrated (permitted disparity) with Social Security (there are exceptions).
2. Retirement benefits are one of the major benefits under the Social Security system. Both employees and employers contribute to Social Security through FICA payments. FICA consists of two parts: 1) OASDI (Old Age Survivor Disability Insurance), and 2) Medicare. The tax for OASDI is 6.2% of wages up to the Social Security wage base, which is increased each year. The Medicare portion equals 1.45% of wages with no limit.
3. Earnings above the wage base are effectively not counted for purposes of retirement benefits under the Social Security system. For example, employee A earns $50,000 per year while employee B earns $160,000 per year. If the wage base was $80,000, then the employer would be paying 6.2% on all of employee A's salary and only half of employee B's salary. Because there is this disparity in the Social Security system, qualified plans are generally allowed to integrate with Social Security.
4. Defined-benefit plans.

   There are two methods for integrating defined-benefit formulas with Social Security: the excess method and the offset method. Either method can be used by a defined-benefit plan.

   a. Under the excess method of integration with Social Security, the plan defines a level of compensation called the integration level, then provides a higher rate of contribution and benefits for compensation above the integration level.
   b. Under the offset method of integration, a fixed amount or a formula amount that is designed to represent the existence of Social Security benefits reduces the plan formula.
   c. The maximum difference (maximum permitted disparity) between the benefit percentage below and above the covered compensation level is 3/4 of 1% times years of service, up to 35 years. This applies for both the excess and offset methods of integration. Therefore, the maximum increase in benefits for earnings above covered compensation level is 26.25%.
5. Defined-contribution plans.

   Defined-contribution plans can only be integrated with Social Security using an excess method (there is no benefit formula to affect).
6. Excess method (defined-contribution plans).

   a. The excess method provides higher contributions above the integration level than below the integration level. The benefit level below the integration level is called the base percentage; the benefit level above the integration level is called the excess percentage. The excess percentage can be no greater than twice the base percentage, limited to a total difference of 5.7 percent. This difference between the base percentage and the excess percentage, which is referred to as the maximum permitted disparity, can be illustrated with the following chart:

Base Percentage	Maximum Permitted Disparity	Excess Percentage
1%	1%	2%
3%	3%	6%
5%	5%	10%
6%	5.7%	11.7%
10%	5.7%	15.7%
15%	5.7%	20.7%

Example

Assume Wiess Company sponsors a money-purchase pension plan that provides a base contribution of 10 percent and an excess percentage of 15.7 percent. Assume the integration level and the Social Security wage base for this example equals $80,000 (generally, the integration level will equal the Social Security wage base). What will the contribution to the money-purchase pension plan equal for employees A, B, and C if their compensation is $50,000, $100,000, and $250,000, respectively?

	Employee A	Employee B	Employee C
Compensation	$50,000	$100,000	$200,000 *
Base contribution (10%)	$5,000	$8,000	$8,000
Excess contribution (15.7%)	$0	$3,140	$18,840
Total contribution	$5,000	$11,140	$26,840
Additional contribution due to integration	$0	$1,140	$6,840

**Covered compensation is limited to $200,000 (for 2003)*

The base contribution is calculated by multiplying the base percentage (10 percent) by the amount of income below the integration level ($80,000 in this example). The excess contribution is calculated by multiplying the excess percentage (15.7 percent) by the amount of income above the integration level.

Employees B and C have received contributions to the money-purchase pension plan at a higher rate for income earned above the integration level than for income earned below the integration level. By integrating the plan, employees B and C were able to receive an additional $1,140 and $6,840 contribution, respectively.

b. Integration level.

i. The integration level is generally equal to the Social Security wage base, which is $87,000 for 2003. The integration level can be lower than the Social Security wage base, which allows more income to be considered for the excess contribution level. However, as the integration level is lowered, so is the maximum difference between the base percentage and the excess percentage. The following table illustrates the different integration levels:

If the integration level is more than:	But not more than:	Then the 5.7 percent factor in the maximum excess is reduced to:
Zero	20% of taxable wage base	Not reduced
20% of taxable wage base	80% of taxable wage base	4.3%
80% of taxable wage base	Amount less than taxable wage base	5.4%

ii. It may be beneficial for employers to adjust the integration level to something other than the Social Security wage base. By lowering the integration level, more income receives the excess percentage.

iii. Generally, the integration level will be set based on the employee census.

7. Generally, all qualified plans and Simplified Employee Pensions (SEPs) are permitted to integrate with Social Security.

8. Plans that may not integrate with Social Security.

   a. ESOPs, SIMPLEs, and SARSEPs (ones that are still in existence) are not permitted to integrate with Social Security. In addition, employee elective deferrals and employer matching contributions to 401(k) plans cannot be integrated with Social Security. However, the profit-sharing contribution by the employer to a 401(k) plan can be integrated.

H. VESTING.

1. The portion of the benefit attributable to employer contributions (other than matching contributions) must vest at least as rapidly as one of the following two schedules (assuming the plan is not top heavy):

   a. 5-year cliff vesting - No vesting is required before 5 years of service. 100% vesting is required after 5 years of service (referred to as 5-year cliff).

   b. 3-7 year graduated (or graded) vesting - The plan must provide vesting that is at least as fast as the following schedule:

Years of Service	Vested Percentage
3	20%
4	40%
5	60%
6	80%
7 or more	100%

   c. Employer <u>matching</u> contributions (such as 401(k) matching contributions) must vest at least as rapidly as one of the following two schedules:

      i. 3-year cliff vesting - No vesting is required before 3 years of service. 100% vesting is required upon the completion of 3 years of service.

      ii. 2-6 year graduated (or graded) vesting - The plan must provide vesting that is at least as fast as the following schedule.

Note: These are the same vesting schedules used with top-heavy plans.

Years of Service	Vested Percentage
2	20%
3	40%
4	60%
5	80%
6 or more	100%

d. The employer may choose a vesting schedule that is more favorable to the employee, but not less favorable than the cliff.

Example

ABC Company offers a 401(k) plan that has an employer match. The company has the following vesting schedule with respect to matching contributions: 25% vested after one year, 50% vested after two years, and 100% vested after three years. Although this vesting schedule does not exactly match the vesting schedules listed above, it is acceptable because it is more favorable to the employee than the vesting schedules listed above. Note: If the plan was a money-purchase plan, or a noncontributory profit-sharing plan, the employer can use the slower 5-year cliff or 3-7 year graded vesting schedules because the contributions to these plans are not matching contributions.

---

2. If a qualified plan provides for employee contributions, the portion of the benefit or account balance attributable to employee contributions must at all times be 100% vested (nonforfeitable).
3. Years of service for purposes of vesting.
   a. A year of service for purposes of vesting is considered 1,000 hours within a 12-month period. All years of service must be counted with few exceptions. Two of the more common exceptions are:
      i. Years prior to the implementation of the plan, and
      ii. Years prior to age 18.
   b. Both years prior to the implementation of the plan and years prior to age 18 may be considered at the choice of the employer (must be in the plan document).
4. Situations in which employer contributions are 100% vested:
   a. Plan termination: Benefits become 100% vested in the event of a plan termination.
   b. SEPs, SARSEPs, and SIMPLEs: All contributions to these are fully vested.
   c. Attainment of normal retirement age: In the event of an employee attaining normal retirement age, the employee will be automatically fully vested.
   d. Under a 401(k) plan, elective deferrals, qualified nonelective contributions and qualified matching contributions are 100 percent vested at all times.
   e. Safe harbor contributions to a safe harbor 401(k) plan.

I. LIMITATIONS ON BENEFITS AND CONTRIBUTIONS.

1. To prevent a qualified plan from being used primarily as a tax shelter for highly compensated employees, there is a limitation on plan benefits and employer contributions.
2. Defined-benefit limits.
   a. The benefit paid from a defined-benefit plan at age 65 or the Social Security retirement age, if later, cannot exceed the lesser of:
      i. 100% of the participant's compensation averaged over the three highest consecutive years of compensation, or
      ii. For 2003, the maximum benefit amount is $160,000.
3. Defined-contribution plan limits.
   a. The "annual additions" limit for all defined-contribution plans sponsored by one employer cannot exceed the lesser of:
      i. 100% (for 2003) of the participant's annual compensation, or
      ii. $40,000 (for 2003).
   b. Annual additions include:
      i. Employer contributions.
      ii. Employee contributions (both pretax and after-tax), and
      iii. Forfeitures allocated to the employees plan.
   c. Multiple annual additions limits.
      i. If a taxpayer has two separate sources of income (but not from a controlled group) then he or she may be eligible to have two annual additions limits, one for each source of income.

Example

In 2003, Joe worked for both ABC Company and DEF Company, which are not part of a controlled group. He earned $100,000 from ABC Company and $100,000 from DEF Company. Since the two companies are not part of a controlled group, each company can contribute up to $40,000 (the maximum annual additions limit) to their respective qualified plan on Joe's behalf. In this case, total contributions could be as high as $80,000.

---

4. Compensation limit.
   a. For purposes of qualified plans, compensation is capped at $200,000 for the year 2003.
   b. Thus, only the first $200,000 of each employee's compensation (for 2003) may be used to calculate contributions for any qualified plan.

J. TOP-HEAVY REQUIREMENTS.

1. A top-heavy plan is one that provides more than 60% of its aggregate accrued benefits or account balances to "key" employees (see definition below). Top-heavy plans must meet certain additional qualification rules. A defined-benefit plan is top heavy if the present value of accrued benefits for key employees is greater than 60% of the present value of accrued benefits for all employees. A defined-contribution plan is top heavy if the account balances of key employees is greater than 60% of the account balances of all employees.

2. Vesting.

   a. If a plan is top heavy for a given year, it must provide more rapid vesting than generally required. Such a plan can either provide 100% vesting after 3 years of service (3-year cliff vesting replaces 5-year cliff vesting) or 2-6 year graduated vesting (2-6 year graded vesting replaces 3-7 graded vesting) as follows:

Years of Service	Vested Percentage
2	20%
3	40%
4	60%
5	80%
6 or more	100%

3. Funding.

   a. A top-heavy defined-benefit plan must provide minimum benefit accrual of 2% times the number of years of service up to 20%.

Example

For example, assume the normal benefit formula of a defined-benefit plan provides for a benefit of 1.5 percent times the employees number of years of service times the final salary.

Years of Service	Normal Benefit	Top-Heavy Benefit
5 Years	7.5%	10%
10 Years	15%	20%
20 Years	30%	N/A

In the above example, the top-heavy rules provide for higher benefits to those employees who have not accrued a benefit of at least 20%.

For employees who have already accrued a benefit of at least 20%, the top-heavy rules are irrelevant.

4. For a defined-contribution plan that is top heavy, the minimum contribution is 3% of total compensation. If the contribution for key employees is less than 3%, the contribution to nonkey employees can be equal to key employees (Section 416(c)).

5. Key employee defined.
   a. A key employee is an employee who at any time during the plan year or prior year met one of the following definitions:
      i. An officer with compensation in excess of $130,000 (adjusted for inflation).
      ii. A greater than 5% owner.
      iii. A greater than 1% owner with compensation > $150,000 (not indexed).

EXHIBIT 3: INDEXED LIMITS FOR RETIREMENT PLANS (2002-2003)

Type of Limit	2002	2003
Defined-benefit plan maximum limit	$160,000	$160,000
Defined-contribution plan maximum limit	40,000	40,000
401(k) elective deferral limit (under age 50)	11,000	12,000
401(k) elective deferral limit (age 50 or older)	12,000	14,000
Highly compensated employee – 414(q)		
- 5% owner (owns more than 5%)	Any	Any
- compensation	90,000	90,000
SIMPLE elective deferral limit (under age 50)	7,000	8,000
SIMPLE elective deferral limit (age 50 or older)	7,500	9,000
SEP plans		
- minimum required earnings for employee eligibility	450	450
- maximum compensation that can be taken into account when determining contributions	200,000	200,000
457 plans elective deferral limit (under age 50)	11,000	12,000
457 plans elective deferral limit (age 50 or older)	12,000	14,000
Maximum compensation that can be taken into account when determining contributions	200,000	200,000

K. LIFE INSURANCE IN QUALIFIED PLANS.

1. Life insurance can be provided through a qualified plan or 403(b) plan as long as the incidental death benefit requirement is met.
   a. The cost of life insurance in a qualified plan is not deductible for self-employed individuals.
   b. Because IRAs and SEPs are not qualified plans, they are not permitted to hold life insurance.
2. The 25 percent test (first test).
   a. Under this test, the aggregate premiums paid for a life insurance policy cannot exceed a certain percent of the employer contributions to the plan.
   b. No more than 50% of the employer contributions can be used to purchase whole life insurance.
   c. No more than 25% of the employer contributions can be used to purchase life insurance other than whole life insurance.

3. The 100 to 1 ratio rule (second test).
   a. For defined-benefit plans, the life insurance limitation is based on a ratio compared with the expected monthly benefit of the employee.
   b. A death benefit cannot exceed 100 times the expected monthly benefit for the employee.
   c. For example, if the expected monthly benefit is $2,000, then no more than $200,000 of death benefit can be provided by life insurance.
4. Tax issues during participation.
   a. A participant must include in income the pure protection cost of life insurance provided in a qualified plan. This cost of life insurance is determined by way of the one-year premium term rate, which is called the Table 2001 cost (formerly PS 58 cost). If the actual cost is lower, it may be used.
   b. The amount included in an employee's income is treated as basis for purposes of distributions from the plan.
5. Tax issues at death.
   a. The value of the life insurance will be included in the gross estate of the decedent employee for estate tax purposes.
   b. The proceeds paid to a beneficiary from a life insurance policy funded within a qualified plan may be subject to income tax. The portion that is taxable equals the cash surrender value of the policy. However, the beneficiary may offset this amount by the sum of the costs included in income by the decedent during the decedent's life [Treas. Reg. 1.72-16(b)(6)]. These costs include the PS 58 costs and costs under Table 2001.

L. RELATED EMPLOYERS TREATED AS A SINGLE EMPLOYER.

1. Controlled groups.
   a. Under IRC Section 414(b) and (c), employers that have a significant degree of common ownership will be treated as a single employer for purposes of qualification under IRC Section 401, employer deduction, participation (coverage), vesting, limits on contributions or benefits, top-heavy rules, and limits of simplified employee pensions.
   b. Types of controlled groups.
      i. Brother – sister.
      ii. Parent – subsidiary.
2. Affiliated service groups.
   a. The purpose of the affiliated service group rules is to prevent discrimination of rank-and-file employees through the use of separate entities.
   b. Under these rules (IRC Section 414(m)), any organization which is a member of an affiliated service group is treated as belonging to a single employer.

3. Leased employees (IRC Section 414(n)).
    a. In many cases, a leased employee must be covered by the plan of the employer who is leasing the "leased employee."
    b. Generally, to fall within these rules, the services of the leased employee must be pursuant to an agreement with a leasing organization, be on a substantially full-time basis and extend for at least one year, and be at the direction of the employer (lessor).
    c. When these rules apply, the employer (lessor) must treat the leased employee as if he were an employee and therefore, cover him under the plan (or at least consider him as an employee for purposes of coverage, nondiscrimination of benefits, etc.). However, any contributions or benefits provided by the leasing organization are considered to be contributions of the employer (lessor).

M. LOANS.

1. Because of the 10% penalty tax on early withdrawals from qualified plans, a plan provision allowing loans to employees may be attractive. However, loan provisions increase administrative costs for the plan.
2. Any type of qualified plan or Section 403(b) annuity plan may permit loans. However, usually only 401(k) and 403(b) plans have loans.
3. Loans from qualified plans to sole proprietors, more-than-10% partners, and more-than-5% shareholders in an S corporation are permitted (loans to these parties were not permitted before 2002).

> **Note:** IRA participants are still not allowed to take loans from their IRAs.

4. All loans must be repaid within five years with interest (except mortgage loans). Loans for the purpose of buying a residence must be repaid over a "reasonable period of time." The plan document will generally set forth the repayment for these loans.
5. Generally, loans are limited to one-half the vested account balance and cannot exceed $50,000. However, when account balances are less than $20,000, loans up to $10,000 are available. The following table summarizes the maximum loan that may be taken:

Vested Loan Balance	Maximum Loan Amount
$10,000 or Less	Vested Account Balance
$10,001 - $20,000	$10,000
$20,001 - $100,000	50% of Vested Account Balance
Greater than $100,000	$50,000

6. The maximum loan amount may be further reduced by any loan balance the participant had in the one-year period preceding the loan. If it weren't for this reduction, participants could abuse the five-year repayment rule by repaying the loan on the last possible date and then immediately taking out the loan again.

Example

Five years ago, Cory borrowed $50,000 from her qualified plan. Last year, she made the final payment of $10,000 to satisfy the loan obligation. Cory has a current plan balance of $300,000, and she would like to borrow another $50,000 from the plan. However, Cory can only borrow $40,000, because the $50,000 maximum loan amount must be reduced by $10,000, the outstanding loan balance in the prior year.

7. Loans are advantageous to participants because they are not subject to the 10% pre-59½ penalty, unless somehow recharacterized as distributions.
8. Nondeductible (after tax) employee contributions, such as in a thrift plan, are not available for loans.

N. PENALTIES FOR DISTRIBUTIONS FROM QUALIFIED PLANS.

1. Early distribution penalty (Too Early) - 10%.
   a. See Section XVI.A "Distributions From Qualified Plans" on page 806 for a summary of the early distribution penalty and exceptions to the penalty.
2. Minimum distribution requirements and penalty (Too Little) - 50%.
   a. See Section XVI.C "Minimum Distributions" on page 814 for a summary of the minimum distribution penalty and calculations.

O. TERMINATIONS.

1. Upon termination of a qualified plan, all employees of the plan become fully vested in their benefits as of the date of termination. Sponsors that terminate a qualified plan must discontinue all contributions and benefit accruals and must distribute all plan assets within a reasonable period of time after the termination of the plan. [Treas. Reg. 1.401-6(b)] There are differences in terminating defined-benefit plans and defined-contribution plans.
2. Defined-benefit plan terminations.
   a. Title IV of ERISA requires that a defined-benefit plan terminate under a standard, distress, or involuntary termination.
      i. A standard termination is one in which the employer has sufficient assets to pay all benefits (liabilities) at the time of final distribution.
      ii. A distress termination occurs when the plan fails as a standard termination and each of the sponsors fall under the distress criteria. These criteria include liquidation in bankruptcy, reorganization, inability to pay debts, or unreasonably burdensome pension costs.
      iii. An involuntary termination may be initiated by the PBGC for a plan that is unable to pay benefits from the plan.
   b. Because the PBGC is responsible for under-funded defined-benefit plans, there are more requirements for terminating a defined-benefit plan than for a defined-contribution plan.
   c. Under ERISA Section 204(h), sponsors of pension plans are required to provide employees with a 15-day notice of any change in the benefits under the plan that significantly reduces the future rate or amounts of future benefits.

3. Defined-contribution plan terminations.
   a. Relative to defined-benefit plans, terminating defined-contribution plans is relatively easy.
   b. Final contributions must be made and assets must be distributed from the plan.

P. FIDUCIARIES AND THEIR OBLIGATIONS

1. Named fiduciary.

   The plan document must specifically designate a named fiduciary or fiduciaries that will be responsible for the administration and management of the plan. The fiduciary must manage plan assets solely in the interests of the plan participants and beneficiaries.

2. Other fiduciaries.
   a. Other individuals beyond the named fiduciary may acquire fiduciary obligations with respect to the plan. A fiduciary is defined as a person who controls plan management, assets, or administration or who renders investment advice for a fee or other compensation.
   b. Generally, corporate officers and directors, plan administrators, bank trustees, members of a plan sponsor's investment committee, investment advisers, and any persons who select the fiduciaries take on fiduciary obligations.

3. ERISA imposed obligations of fiduciaries.
   a. The fiduciary must exercise the care, skill, and diligence of a prudent person acting solely in the interest of plan participants and beneficiaries.
   b. The fiduciary has an obligation to diversify the plan's assets to reduce the risk of loss.
   c. The fiduciary must also act in accordance with the plan's provisions and must refrain from acts forbidden under the law.
   d. A fiduciary may not:
      i. Be paid for services if already receiving full-time pay from an employer or union whose employees or members are participants.
      ii. Act in any transaction involving the plan on behalf of a party whose interests are adverse to those of the plan or its participants or beneficiaries.
      iii. Receive any consideration for his or her own personal account from any party dealing with the plan in connection with a transaction involving the assets of the plan.
      iv. Cause a plan to engage in certain transactions with parties in interest.
      v. Permit more than 10% of plan assets to be invested in employer securities or real property except in the case of certain defined-contribution plans (such as ESOPs or stock bonus plans).

4. Parties in interest.
   a. Parties in interest are limited in or excluded from transactions with qualified plans. These parties include: any administrator, officer, trustee, custodian, counsel, or employee of a plan; a fiduciary; a person providing services to the plan; the employer or employee union; a 50% or greater owner of the company; certain relatives of parties of interest; and certain other related corporations, employees, officers, directors, partners, and joint ventures.

b. Prohibited transactions.

  i. Sale, exchange, or lease of any property between the plan and a party in interest.

  ii. Loan between plan and any party in interest.

  iii. Transfer of plan assets to or use of plan assets for the benefit of a party in interest.

  iv. Acquisition of employer securities or real property in excess of legal limits.

5. Scope of fiduciary's responsibilities.

  a. One fiduciary may become responsible for the acts or omissions of another if the fiduciary participated in the breach of duty, knowingly concealed it, or imprudently allowed it to occur.

  b. ERISA provides a procedural, not a performance, standard for assessing the behavior of fiduciaries. A fiduciary is not required to be successful in managing the plan's assets.

  c. In smaller firms, the firm's owner may also be the plan's administrator and principal decision-maker and, as a result, the only fiduciary.

V. DEFINED-BENEFIT PENSION PLANS

A. GENERAL OBJECTIVES.

1. The plan objective is to provide an adequate level of retirement income to each employee regardless of his or her age at plan entry.
2. The employer wants to allocate plan costs to the maximum extent to older employees.
3. The older controlling employees in a small business want to maximize tax-deferred retirement savings for key employees.
4. The organization must be able to tolerate mandatory funding and bear the risk of investment returns.

B. ADVANTAGES.

1. In defined-benefit plans, employees obtain a tax-deferred retirement savings.
2. Retirement benefits, at adequate levels, can be provided to all employees regardless of age at plan entry.
3. The benefit levels are guaranteed, both by the employer and by the Pension Benefit Guaranty Corporation (PBGC)(limited).
4. For older, highly compensated employees, a defined-benefit plan generally allows the maximum amount of tax-deferred retirement savings.
5. Defined-benefit plans may encourage early retirement.

C. DISADVANTAGES.

1. Actuarial and PBGC aspects of defined-benefit plans result in higher installation and administration costs than costs for defined-contribution plans.
2. Defined-benefit plans are complex to design.
3. Employees who leave before retirement may receive relatively little benefit from the plan.
4. The employer is subject to a recurring annual mandatory funding obligation, regardless of profit or loss.
5. The employer assumes the risk of bad investment results in the plan.
6. Requires annual actuarial work (costly).

D. DESIGN CHARACTERISTICS AND PROVISIONS.

1. Accrual Requirements – All qualified defined-benefit plans must meet one of three benefit accrual tests: the 3% method, the 133% rule, or the fractional rule. Each of these rules under IRC 411(b) is designed to protect the benefits of employees.
    a. The 3% Method.
        i. A participant's benefit upon separation from service must not be less than 3 percent of the normal retirement benefit to which he would be entitled if he commenced participation at the earliest possible entry age under the plan and served continuously until the earlier of age 65 or the normal retirement age specified under the plan, multiplied by the number of years (not in excess of 33 1/3) of his participation in the plan.

b. The 133% Rule.

   i. The accrued benefit payable at normal retirement is equal to the normal retirement benefit, and

   ii. The annual rate at which any individual who is, or could be, a participant can accrue the retirement benefits payable at the normal retirement age under the plan for any later plan year is not more than 133 1/3 percent of the annual rate at which he can accrue benefits for any year beginning on or after such particular plan year and before such later plan year.

Example

Visual Company sponsors a plan that provides a benefit equal to 3% of compensation for the first ten years of participation, 4% for the next ten years of participation and 5% for the following ten years of participation.

The change from 3% to 4% meets the 133 1/3% test, because 4% is exactly 133 1/3% of 3%. However, 5% is more than 133 1/3% of 3%. Therefore, the rule is not satisfied.

---

c. The Fractional Rule.

   i. The accrued benefit to which any participant is entitled upon his separation from service must not be less than a fraction of the annual benefit commencing at normal retirement age to which he would be entitled under the plan.

      A) The calculation assumes that the employee earns the same rate of compensation annually (upon which his normal retirement benefit would be computed under the plan) until normal retirement age.

      B) The fraction is determined as if the employee had attained normal retirement age on the date on which such determination is made (but taking into account no more than the 10 years of service immediately preceding his separation from service).

   ii. Such fraction shall not exceed 1 and equals:

$$\frac{\text{Total years of participation in the plan (at separation)}}{\text{Total years of participation if separation occurred at normal retirement}}$$

Example

Scott leaves Cap Company at age 55 with ten years of service. If the benefit he were to receive at normal retirement equaled $10,000, then the employee must be entitled to an annual benefit of at least $5,000 under the fractional rule.

$$\text{Annual Benefit} = \$10{,}000 \times \frac{\text{10 years of participation}}{\text{20 years of potential participation}}$$

---

2. Formulas and benefit determination.

   a. Flat amount formula.

Example

Pension of $800 per month for life, beginning at age 65; such a plan might require some minimum service such as 15 to 20 years with the benefit scaled back for fewer years of service.

      i. A flat amount formula does not differentiate among employees with different compensation.

      ii. A flat benefit formula does not use an accrued benefit actuarial cost method.

   b. Flat percentage formula.

      i. Quite common.

      ii. Provides a retirement benefit that is a percentage of the employee's average earnings (average earnings can be calculated numerous ways).

      iii. Typically, the plan will require certain minimum service, such as 25 years, to obtain the full percentage benefit with the percentage scaled back for fewer years of service.

   c. Unit credit formula (unit benefit formula).

      i. Employee's service with the employer - The formula might provide 1.5% of earnings for each of the employee's years of service.

   d. Two methods are generally used to compute average earnings for these formulas:

      i. Career average method uses earnings averaged over the employee's entire career with the employer (risk: loss of purchasing power).

      ii. Final average method - (Terminal earnings method) earnings are averaged over a number of years - usually 3 to 5 years immediately prior to retirement. (The results may be as much as double the benefits of the career average method. Generally, larger benefit when compared to career average.)

   e. These formulas are further modified by integration with Social Security benefits (offset cannot reduce pension benefit by more than 50%).

   f. Vesting tends to be a 5-year cliff vesting schedule.

   g. A unit benefit method must use an accrued benefit cost actuarial method.

3. Contribution limits (see Exhibit 3: "Indexed Limits for Retirement Plans (2002-2003)" on page 746).

4. Funding is mandatory.

5. Earnings and forfeitures affect funding.

   a. Earnings in excess of projected earnings lower annual fund costs.

   b. Terminations lower annual fund cost to the extent of forfeiture.

   c. Poor earnings increase annual plan costs by requiring increased funding.

EXHIBIT 4: ANALYSIS OF DEFINED-BENEFIT VARIABLE AND IMPACT ON PLAN COSTS

	Direction Compared to Expected	Impact on Plan Costs	Relationship of Variable to Plan Costs
Investment Returns	↑ ↓	↓ ↑	Inverse
Turnover of Employees	↑ ↓	↓ ↑	Inverse
Mortality	↑ ↓	↓ ↑	Inverse
Life Expectancies	↑ ↓	↑ ↓	Direct
Wages	↑ ↓	↑ ↓	Direct
Average Age of New Employee	↑ ↓	↑ ↓	Direct
Cost of Living Adjustments	↑ ↓	↑ ↓	Direct
Inflation Impact on Plan Costs	↑ ↓	↑ ↓	Direct

E. TAX AND OTHER IMPLICATIONS.

1. Employer contributions to the plan are deductible for income tax when made.
2. Taxation to the employee on employer contributions is deferred until distribution.
3. Under Code Section 415, there is a maximum limit on the projected annual benefit that the plan can provide beginning at age 65; the maximum life annuity or joint and survivor benefits are the lesser of:
   a. $160,000 (for 2003); or
   b. 100% of the participant's compensation averaged over 3 consecutive highest earning years.
4. Distribution from the plan must follow the rules for qualified plan distributions.
5. The plan is subject to the minimum funding rules of Section 412 of the Internal Revenue Code.
6. A defined-benefit plan is subject to mandatory insurance coverage by the Pension Benefit Guaranty Corporation(PBGC). However, a defined-benefit plan that is maintained by a professional service employer with 25 or fewer employees does not have to be covered by the PBGC. These professional individuals include among others:
   a. Attorneys.
   b. Accountants.
   c. Architects.
   d. Actuaries.
   e. Engineers.
   f. Doctors.
   g. Dentists.

F. ERISA REQUIREMENTS.

The plan is subject to all the ERISA requirements for qualified plans (participation, funding, vesting, etc.).

G. TERMINATIONS.

1. A standard termination requires that the plan has sufficient assets to cover benefits accrued to the date of termination.
2. A distress termination requires either that the employer be liquidated or that the termination is necessary for the company's survival. If a defined-benefit plan is terminated without sufficient assets to pay accrued benefits, the PBGC is liable for the balance (limited).

H. PBGC PREMIUMS.

1. Benefit payments by the PBGC are financed by premiums paid by the sponsors of defined-benefit plans.
2. The PBGC premium consists of two components:
   a. A base premium paid by all employers; plus
   b. A variable premium with no overall maximum.

I. PBGC-INSURED BENEFITS.

1. PBGC insurance may not cover all plan benefits.
2. PBGC insurance does not cover benefits added to a plan less than five years before a distress termination.

J. CASH-BALANCE PENSION PLAN.

1. Description.
   a. A cash-balance pension plan is a defined-benefit, qualified employer pension plan that looks like a defined-contribution plan to employees.
      i. The plan provides for annual employer contributions at a specified rate to hypothetical individual accounts that are set up for each plan participant.
      ii. The employer guarantees not only the contribution level, but also a minimum rate of return on each participant's account.
      iii. The rate of return may be fixed or tied to some market rate, such as a Treasury rate.
   b. A cash-balance plan looks like a money-purchase pension plan with an employer guaranteed rate of return. However, there are certain important differences.
      i. The funds that are contributed to the plan are generally invested more aggressively than is reflected by the guaranteed interest rate. This allows plan sponsors to contribute less than would be necessary in a money-purchase pension plan, assuming investment performance is reasonable.
      ii. Although participants receive an account statement reflecting contributions and earnings, this amount may not be the amount received in the event of a lump-sum distribution. Cash-balance and other defined-benefit plans have a method for converting the normal defined-benefit (such as a joint and survivor annuity) into a current lump-sum value. Sometimes the amount paid will be higher than the hypothetical account balance and other times it will be lower.

2. Application.
   a. A cash-balance pension plan is appropriate when the employee group is relatively young.
   b. A cash-balance pension plan is appropriate when the employees are concerned with security of retirement income.
   c. A cash-balance pension plan is appropriate when the work force is large and the employees are primarily middle-income wage earners.
   d. A cash-balance pension plan is appropriate when the employer is able to spread administrative costs over a relatively large group of plan participants.
3. Advantages.
   a. A tax-deferred savings medium for employees.
   b. Plan distributions are eligible for the special ten-year forward averaging tax computation.
   c. Employer guarantee removes investment risk from employee.
   d. Plan benefits are guaranteed by the Federal Pension Benefit Guaranty Corporation (PBGC).
   e. The advantages and benefits of a cash-balance pension plan are easily communicated.
   f. Benefits methods are flexible. Employers may provide the same benefit to all employees, as in the case of a fixed percentage of compensation. Alternatively, contribution percentages can be higher for employees with longer service.
4. Disadvantages.
   a. Retirement benefits may be inadequate for older plan entrants.
   b. Because of the annual actuarial work and PBGC insurance, the plan is more complex administratively than qualified defined-contribution plans.
   c. The investment risk is to the employer and increases employer costs. The guaranteed investment return is usually low (3%–4%). The participant is not credited with actual returns where the return exceeds the guarantee.

Example

CASH-BALANCE PLAN ACCUMULATIONS
PAY CREDIT: 10 PERCENT OF COMPENSATION
INTEREST CREDIT: 8 PERCENT ANNUALLY GUARANTEED RATE

Age at Plan Entry	Annual Compensation*	Annual Contribution	Account Balance at Age 65
25	$30,000	$3,000	$777,170
30	30,000	3,000	516,950
40	30,000	3,000	219,318
50	30,000	3,000	81,456
60	30,000	3,000	17,600

* No salary increases nor earnings in excess of guarantees are considered in this example.

5. Tax Implications.
   a. Employer contributions to the plan are deductible when made.
   b. Code Section 415(b) limits the benefits provided under the plan to the lesser of $160,000 (for 2003) or 100% of the participant's highest consecutive three-year average compensation. This is the defined-benefit plan limit.
   c. Taxation to the employee on employer contributions is deferred.
   d. Distributions from the plan must follow the rules for qualified plan distributions.
   e. Qualifying lump-sum distributions may be eligible for a special ten-year forward averaging tax calculation (only for those who were born prior to 1936).
   f. The plan is subject to the minimum funding rules of Section 412 of the Internal Revenue Code.
   g. A cash-balance plan is a defined-benefit plan and is subject to mandatory insurance coverage by the PBGC and annual actuarial work.
   h. The plan is subject to ERISA reporting and disclosure rules.

EXHIBIT 5: DEFINED-BENEFIT AND CASH-BALANCE PLANS - COMPARISON

	Typical Defined-Benefit Plan (DB)	**Cash-Balance Plan**
Contribution	Actuarially determined	Percentage of salary (actuarially determined)
Investment Risk	Employer	Employer
Size of Work Force	Any Size	Large
Investment Earnings	Employer Responsible	Employer Responsible
Social Security Integration	Yes	Yes
Pension Benefit Guarantee Corporation Insurance	Yes	Yes
Employee Contribution Feature	No	No
Favors Older Entrants	Yes	No
Administrative Cost	Generally higher than DC Plans due to actuary and insurance	Generally higher than DC Plans due to actuary and insurance

VI. DEFINED-CONTRIBUTION PLANS

A. CHARACTERISTICS OF DEFINED-CONTRIBUTION PLANS.

1. Each employee has an individual account in the plan.
2. Plan benefit consists of the amount accumulated in the account at retirement or termination.
3. Tax-deferred retirement plan.
4. Annual additions to each employee's account in a money-purchase plan is limited to:
   a. 100% (for 2003) of compensation; or
   b. $40,000 (for 2003).
5. Employee bears investment risk.

B. MONEY-PURCHASE PENSION PLANS.

1. Characteristics.
   a. A money-purchase plan is a qualified employer "pension" retirement plan.
      i. The employer makes annual mandatory contributions to each employee's account under a nondiscriminatory contribution formula (either a fixed percentage or a flat dollar amount).
         A) The formula requires a contribution by the employer of a specified percentage (up to 25%) of each employee's annual compensation.
         B) Simplicity of administration:
            1) A money-purchase plan is a relatively simple pension plan to administer as compared to a defined-benefit plan.
            2) The accounting is straightforward.
            3) The plan does not require any services of an actuary.
            4) The employer cannot purchase plan benefit insurance from the Pension Benefit Guaranty Corporation (PBGC).
            5) The costs of administering a money-purchase pension plan are lower than those of all other pension plans (no actuary, no insurance).
         C) There are known funding costs.
         D) There is a lack of funding flexibility (mandatory funding).
         E) Money-purchase plans favor younger employees due to the long compounding periods.
         F) There is no mechanism to influence employee retirement and turnover decisions.
         G) Money-purchase plans severely limit the ability to use plan contributions to finance the company (maximum 10% of stock).
   b. A money-purchase pension plan can accept employee contributions (voluntary or mandatory) (not usual).
   c. The failure to make mandatory employer contributions results in penalty (excise tax).

2. Appropriate uses.
    a. When an employer wants to install a qualified retirement plan that is simple to administer and easy to explain to employees and employer does not mind mandatory funding.
    b. When the employees to be benefited are relatively young.
    c. When a self-employed person has no employees and does not mind mandatory funding.
    d. When employees are willing to accept the investment risk in their plan accounts.
    e. When some degree of retirement income security in the plan is desired.
    f. Fit best with mature labor intensive businesses with predictable cash flows. Funding certainty allows and requires cash flow planning.
3. Advantages.
    a. A money-purchase plan is relatively simple and inexpensive to design, administer, and explain.
    b. A money-purchase plan formula can provide a deductible, annual employer contribution of up to 25% of each employee's compensation.
    c. A money-purchase plan account balance can be distributed as lump-sum, single or joint annuity, or rolled over into an IRA.
4. Disadvantages - general.
    a. Money-purchase plan retirement benefits may be inadequate for employees who enter the plan at older ages.
    b. There is no funding flexibility with money-purchase plans.
    c. Money-purchase plans cannot use plan contributions to finance company (except 10% in company securities).
    d. The plan is subject to the ERISA's minimum funding requirements.
5. Disadvantages - employer perspective.
    a. Money-purchase pension plan retirement benefits may be inadequate and not very enticing for employees entering the plan at older ages.
    b. Money-purchase pension plans have mandatory funding (inflexible).
    c. Money-purchase pension plans cannot have more than 10% of plan assets invested in qualifying employer securities.
6. Disadvantages - employee perspective.
    a. Retirement benefits are uncertain and hard to project (depends on time, contributions, and investment expense).
    b. Money-purchase plans do not permit withdrawals prior to retirement, death, disability, or termination of plan.
    c. Loan provisions are unusual in money-purchase plans.
    d. Employee contributions are not tax deductible in money-purchase plans.

7. Design features.

   a. Money-purchase plans have a benefit formula requiring a mandatory employer contribution that is a flat percentage of each employee's compensation.

   b. Up to a 25% contribution may be made and deducted by the employer.

   c. Only the first $200,000 (for 2003) of each employee's compensation can be taken into account.

   d. The plan benefit formula can be integrated with Social Security; however, permitted disparity requirements must be met.

8. Tax implications.

   a. Employer contributions to the plan are immediately deductible as long as the plan remains qualified. Any employee contributions are not deductible.

   b. Assuming the plan remains qualified, taxation of employer contributions to the plan is deferred until distribution.

   c. The plan is subject to the minimum funding standards of Section 412 of the Code.

   d. The plan is subject to the ERISA reporting and disclosure rules.

9. Nondiscrimination requirements.

   a. The plan may not, in general, discriminate in favor of highly compensated employees.

   b. The plan must meet the nondiscrimination requirements.

   c. Uniform contributions are defined as the same percentage of pay or the same dollar amount for every covered employee.

   d. If the plan is integrated with Social Security so that there is a higher contribution rate for pay above a specified level, the plan must meet a permitted disparity requirement.

   e. TRA 2001 impact on money-purchase plans.

      i. The TRA 2001 increased the profit-sharing plan's deductible employer contribution percentage to 25% (from 15%). This increase will most likely cause a substantial decline in the use of money-purchase plans going forward.

      ii. In the past, money-purchase plans were primarily used in tandem with a profit-sharing plan to increase the employer's deduction percentage to 25% (profit-sharing plans were limited to 15% employer deduction; therefore, 10% money-purchase plans were implemented in addition to the profit-sharing plan). Now that the profit-sharing plan deduction limit has been increased to 25%, money-purchase plans no longer help employers increase their deduction. Therefore, employers are more likely to exclusively adopt a profit-sharing plan because of the profit-sharing plan's discretionary contributions.

      iii. Going forward, many employers with tandem plans will most likely choose to merge the money-purchase plan into the profit-sharing plan.

10. Forfeitures.
    a. Forfeitures are created when nonvested or partially vested employees terminate employment.
    b. The unvested portion of the account reverts back to the plan.
    c. In money-purchase plans, as in all defined-contribution plans, employers can use these forfeitures alternatively:
        i. To reduce future employer contributions. Forfeitures will reduce the amount of contributions that can be deducted or;
        ii. To allocate among the remaining participants.
            A) Thus increasing remaining participant's account balances (annual additions limits apply).
            B) Reducing future employer contributions can have a disruptive effect on a company's financial planning, since it can result in having more cash on hand than planned (not usually a big problem).
    d. Forfeitures must be allocated in a nondiscriminatory way.
        i. By using a weight equal to the participant's share of payroll rather than a weight equal to the participant's share of all account balances.

C. PROFIT-SHARING PLANS.

1. Description and characteristics.

   The legal promise of a profit-sharing plan is to defer taxes. Thus, there are no mandatory funding requirements, and if the plan document permits (most don't), there may be in-service withdrawals.

    a. A profit-sharing plan is a qualified, defined-contribution plan featuring a flexible employer contribution provision.
    b. The employer's contribution to the plan each year can be either a purely discretionary amount (or nothing at all if the employer wishes) or can be based on some type of formula usually relating to the employer's annual profits.
    c. Contributions are generally allocated on the basis of a nondiscriminatory formula. Age-weighted formulas can be used to determine contributions.
    d. Contributions are generally pooled for investment purposes and then allocated to each individual participant's account.
    e. Employees can contribute to a profit-sharing plan (voluntary or mandatory), and the contributions can be before tax or after tax.
    f. Profit-sharing plans permit in-service distributions (withdrawals) for a variety of reasons (e.g., medical, home purchase).
    g. For a profit-sharing plan to remain viable, contributions must be substantial and recurring (IRS standard).

2. Distributions.
   a. Benefits can be distributed in installments as a life annuity or as a lump sum.
   b. Profit-sharing plans may permit preretirement distributions under a variety of other circumstances (e.g., buying a home) as long as clearly stated in the plan.
3. Tax deductibility.
   a. There is an explicit limit on the amount of profit-sharing plan contribution an employer can deduct from taxes.
   b. The employer can deduct a maximum of 25% of all participants' compensation.

Note: Some individual plan participants may have contributions in excess of 25%, as long as total company contributions do not exceed 25% and contributions do not violate the rules of discrimination.

   c. Excess contributions are subject to a 10% excise tax.
4. Employer contributions.
   a. Discretionary contributions give the employer maximum flexibility to adjust contributions to match financial position and the employer's need for cash flow.
   b. Formula-based contributions.
      i. Formula approach plans specify a method for determining contributions--generally, a percent of profits, but can be a percent of compensation.
      ii. A profit-based formula can define profits as either before tax or after tax and can be a flat percentage of profits or a sliding percentage.
      iii. A compensation-based formula can define compensation as base pay or as base pay plus overtime and bonuses, or it can determine contributions based on profit levels.
      iv. The formula-based approach offers much less flexibility to the employer, but may provide incentives for employees if contributions are tied to profits.
5. Forfeitures.
   a. Forfeitures can be used to reduce employer contributions.
   b. Alternatively, forfeitures can be allocated to the accounts of remaining participants.
      i. If allocated, forfeitures in a profit-sharing plan must be allocated in a nondiscriminatory manner. Forfeitures are usually allocated in the same way contributions are allocated (e.g., relative compensation).
      ii. They are viewed as an addition to an employee's individual account.
6. Withdrawals.

   It is possible to design a profit-sharing plan allowing employees to withdraw all or part of their vested account balance prior to retirement.
7. Participant-directed investments.
   a. The employer (or plan trustee) can either invest the plan's assets in a single fund without any input from plan participants, or the employer can allow participants to choose from among several different investment options.
   b. The advantage of allowing participant-directed investments is that it limits the employer's fiduciary responsibility. However, Internal Revenue Code Section 404(c) does require that the plan have at least three choices (money market fund, bond fund, and stock fund) and that the employer provide education to the participants.

8. Application.

   a. A profit-sharing plan is appropriate when an employer's profits, or financial ability to contribute to the plan, vary from year to year. A profit-sharing plan is particularly useful as an alternative to a qualified pension plan where the employer anticipates that there may be years in which no contribution can be made.

   b. A profit-sharing plan is appropriate when the employer wants to adopt a qualified plan with an incentive feature by which employee accounts increase with the employer's profits.

   c. A profit-sharing plan is appropriate when the employee group has the following characteristics:

      i. Many of the employees are relatively young and have substantial time to accumulate retirement.

      ii. The employees can and are willing to accept a degree of investment risk in their accounts.

   d. A profit-sharing plan is appropriate when the employer wants to supplement an existing defined-benefit plan.

   e. TRA 2001 impact on profit-sharing plans.

      i. TRA 2001 increased the employer deduction percentage from 15% to 25% for profit-sharing plans.

      ii. The increase in this deduction percentage is likely to cause an increase in the popularity of profit-sharing plans among employers. The flexibility of profit-sharing plans, combined with the increased deduction allowed, will allow the profit-sharing plan to satisfy the retirement plan needs of more employers.

      iii. Employers who currently maintain money-purchase plans will most likely decide a profit-sharing plan is more suited for the company, and may choose to merge their money-purchase plan into an existing profit-sharing plan.

D. STOCK BONUS PLAN.

1. Description and characteristics.

   a. The major difference between a stock bonus plan and a profit-sharing plan is that benefits are generally distributed in the form of employer stock, not cash.

   b. In a stock bonus plan, the employer contributes either cash or employer securities to the plan. The contributions are determined in a variety of ways (a percentage of either profits or covered payroll).

   c. A stock bonus plan can permit employee contributions, but usually does not.

   d. Contributions to a stock bonus plan must be allocated (for accounting purposes) to individual participant accounts. Stock bonus plans are subject to the same nondiscrimination requirements as a profit-sharing plan.

   e. The assets of a stock bonus plan can be invested primarily in employer stock or securities. Dividends from this stock can be either reinvested or distributed directly to participants.

2. Distributions.
   a. Generally, distributions are in the form of employer stock.
   b. For securities that cannot be easily traded on an established market, participants can request that the employer repurchase the securities at a fair price (the "put" option), and the employer must comply.
   c. Distributions of account balances must occur in a timely fashion. If funds are distributed because of retirement, disability, or death, the distribution must begin within one year. Other types of separation distributions must begin within six years.
   d. Distributions must be paid out over a period of five years or less in essentially equal periodic payments.
3. Voting rights.
   a. Participants must be given the right to vote the shares of stock that have been allocated to their account.
   b. If the employer is closely held, plan participants need only be given the right to vote on issues requiring more than a majority of outstanding common shares for passage. Typically, major issues include mergers, consolidations, recapitalizations, liquidation, and corporate dissolution.
4. Valuation of stock.

   If the stock of the employer is not publicly traded, an employer must hire an independent appraiser to value the stock as of each contribution (costly).
5. Deducting noncash contributions.

   For stock bonus plans that invest in employer stock, the employer can claim a tax deduction for noncash contributions to the plan. The deduction is the FMV of the asset contributed (may require a formal valuation).
6. Employee tax advantages.
   a. Participants can defer the net unrealized appreciation on their share of employer securities if they receive the distribution in stock as a lump sum.
   b. Participant retirees are not taxed on the current market value. Instead, the net unrealized appreciation is taxed as capital gains when the participant or beneficiary sells the stock.
   c. At the distribution, the participant recognizes ordinary income equal to the sum of the deductions that the employer took at the time of contributions. The ordinary income recognition establishes a basis in the stock for the participant equal to the employer's tax deduction. Any further appreciation is subject to capital gains if stock is taken as the distribution. If the distribution is in cash, the entire distribution is subject to ordinary income tax. Normal rollover rules and withholding rules apply.
7. Disadvantages of investing in employer stock.

   There are three major disadvantages to investing in employer stock:
   a. The employee has a nondiversified portfolio.
   b. Plans that invest in employer securities generally have higher costs (due to appraisals).
   c. Employers with plans that invest in employer securities must worry about dilution of existing ownership (e.g., loss of control).

E. EMPLOYEE STOCK OWNERSHIP PLAN (ESOP).

1. Description.

   An employee stock ownership plan (ESOP) is a qualified employer plan similar to a profit-sharing plan in which participant accounts are invested in stock of the employer's company.

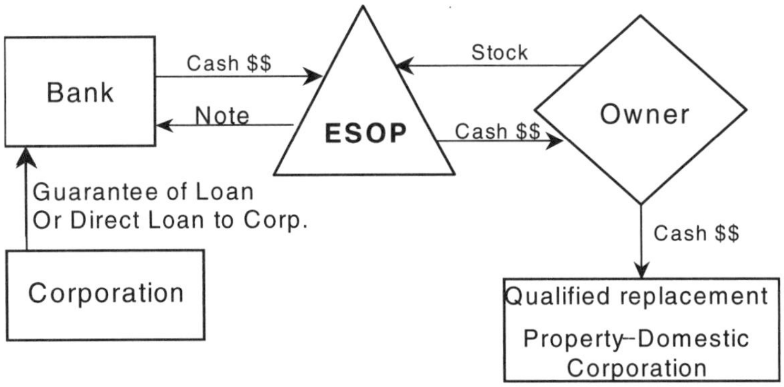

2. Application.

   a. An ESOP is appropriate to provide a tax-advantaged means for employees to acquire company stock at low costs to the employer.

   b. An ESOP is appropriate when estate and financial planning for principal shareholders would benefit from the additional market for company stock. The ESOP not only creates a market, but also provides estate tax benefits for the sale of the stock to the ESOP. (The Internal Revenue Code requires that ESOPs be for the benefit of the employees of the company).

   c. An ESOP is appropriate to provide an advantageous vehicle for the company to borrow money for business needs (may be leveraged).

   d. An ESOP is appropriate when a company wants to broaden its ownership to help prevent a hostile takeover of the company.

   e. An ESOP is appropriate when the business is a C corporation. Partnerships do not have stock. S corporations are now permitted to issue stock to an ESOP.

3. Advantages of an ESOP.

   a. Employees receive an ownership interest in the employer company that may provide a performance incentive.

   b. A market is created for employer stock that helps improve liquidity for existing shareholders.

   c. Employees are not taxed until shares are distributed. Unrealized appreciation of stock held in the plan is not taxable to the employees until receipt of a distribution from the plan and may be deferred until shares are sold by the employee.

   d. The employer receives a deduction either for a cash contribution to the plan or a noncash plan contribution in the form of shares of stock.

e. A shareholder can obtain tax benefits by selling stock to the plan. The shareholder that reinvests the proceeds received from the ESOP sale in domestic securities pays no current capital gains. This allows the shareholder to create a diversified retirement portfolio from a previously nondiversified investment without tax consequences. This nonrecognition of gain treatment on the sale of stock by a shareholder to an ESOP occurs if the following three requirements are met:

   i. The ESOP must own at least 30% of the stock (either of each class or of total value);

   ii. The owner must have held the stock for at least three years prior to the sale; and

   iii. Qualified replacement property must be purchased within one year after the sale (or three months prior to the sale). Qualified replacement property includes publicly traded domestic stock, as well as privately owned stock.

4. Disadvantages.

   a. Since an ESOP is a qualified plan, all the qualified plan requirements apply (coverage, vesting, funding, reporting and disclosure, and others).

   b. In an ESOP, issuing shares of stock to employees dilutes (reduces the relative value of) existing shareholders' stock and their control.

   c. The employer stock may be a very speculative investment. Such risk can create employee ill will, because the plan is either not considered valuable by employees or employees expect too much from the plan.

5. Design.

   a. ESOPs and stock bonus plans are qualified defined-contribution plans similar to profit-sharing; however, participants' accounts are stated in terms of shares of employer stock.

   b. An ESOP is distinguished from a regular stock bonus plan primarily by the leveraging feature of an ESOP that enables the employer company to borrow money on a favorable basis.

      i. The ESOP trustee borrows money from a lending institution such as a bank.

      ii. The trustee uses the loan proceeds to purchase stock of the employer from the employer corporation or from principal shareholders of the corporation.

      iii. The employer makes tax-deductible contributions to the ESOP in amounts sufficient to enable the trustee to pay off the principal and interest of the loan to the bank or other lender.

6. Tax implications.

   a. Employer contributions to the plan are deductible when made, up to an annual limit.

      i. For a stock bonus plan and an ESOP, the limit is 25% of compensation of employees covered under the plan.

   b. The regular annual additions limit for defined-contribution plans applies to both ESOPs and stock bonus plans.

   c. Within certain limitations, a corporation can deduct dividends paid on stock acquired with an ESOP loan.

   d. Taxation to the employee on employer contributions is deferred, as with any qualified plan. Additional tax benefit to employees with a stock bonus plan or ESOP plan is the deferral of tax on unrealized appreciation of stock received in a lump-sum distribution.

   e. An ESOP plan is subject to eligibility and vesting rules applicable to all qualified plans.

7. ERISA and other regulatory requirements.
   a. An ESOP plan is subject to the usual ERISA eligibility, vesting, and funding requirements for qualified plans.
   b. Certain directors and policy-making officers with ESOP or stock bonus accounts may be subject to "insider trading" restrictions under federal securities laws.

F. SAVINGS/THRIFT PLAN.

1. Description.
   a. A savings plan (or thrift plan) is a qualified defined-contribution plan that is similar to a profit-sharing plan with features that provide for and encourage after-tax employee contributions to the plan.
   b. A typical savings plan provides after-tax employee contributions with matching employer contributions.
   c. Pure savings plans, featuring only after-tax employee contributions, have generally been replaced by the 401(k) type of plan. However, a savings plan with after-tax employee contributions is often added to a Section 401(k) plan.
   d. The sponsor must set up the plan as a money-purchase plan, profit-sharing plan, or stock bonus plan to be qualified (usually profit-sharing plan).
2. Application.
   a. A savings/thrift plan is used as an add-on feature to a Section 401(k) plan to allow employees to increase contributions beyond the annual limit on salary reductions under Section 401(k) plans.
   b. The usual employee group has the following characteristics:
      i. The employees are relatively young and have substantial time to accumulate retirement savings.
      ii. The employees are willing to accept a degree of investment risk.
      iii. There is a wide variation among employees in the need or desire for retirement savings.
   c. A savings/thrift plan is used when the employer wants to supplement the company's defined-benefit pension plan with a plan that features individual participant accounts and the opportunity for participants to save on a tax-deferred basis.
3. Advantages.
   a. As with all qualified plans, a savings plan provides a tax-deferred retirement savings medium for employees. Employee contributions to the plan are not tax deferred and must be on an after-tax basis. Subsequent investment earnings on after-tax employee contributions are generally not subject to tax until distributions are made.
   b. The plan allows employees to control the amount of their savings (voluntary).
   c. Thrift plans are not subject to the ADP testing of 401(k) plans.

4. Disadvantages.
   a. Employees cannot rely on the plan to provide an adequate retirement benefit.
      i. Benefits will not be significant unless employees make substantial contributions to the plan on a regular basis and the investments appreciate over time.
      ii. Employees who enter the plan at older ages may not be able to make sufficient contributions to the plan due to:
         A) The limits on annual contributions.
         B) The limited number of years remaining for plan contributions prior to retirement.
   b. Since employee accounts and matching amounts must be individually accounted for in the plan, the administrative costs for a savings plan are greater than those for a money-purchase or simple profit-sharing plan without employee contributions.
5. Design features.
   a. Typical savings plans provide after-tax employee contributions with employer-matching contributions.
      i. Participation in the plan is voluntary.
      ii. Each employee elects to contribute a chosen percentage of compensation up to a maximum percentage specified in the plan.
      iii. The employee receives no tax deduction for this contribution, and the contribution is fully subject to income tax.
      iv. The employer may make a matching contribution to the savings plan based on a predefined formula (such as $0.50 to each $1.00 up to 6% of compensation).
   b. Higher-paid employees are in a position to contribute considerably more to this type of plan than lower-paid employees.
   c. Employers often adopt a plan that combines all the features of a regular profit-sharing plan, a savings plan, and Section 401(k) salary reductions. Combined plans can have one or more of the following features:
      i. Employee after-tax contributions.
      ii. Employer matching of employee after-tax contributions.
      iii. Employee pretax salary reductions (Section 401(k) amounts).
      iv. Employer matching of Section 401(k) amounts.
      v. Employer contribution based on a formula.
      vi. Discretionary employer contribution.
   d. These plans must meet the actual contribution percentage test (ACP).

6. Tax implications.
   a. Employer contributions to the plan are deductible, as long as the plan remains qualified and separate accounts are maintained for all participants in the plan.
   b. Employee contributions to the plan, whether or not matched, are not tax deductible.
   c. Assuming a plan remains qualified, taxation of the employee is deferred with respect to:
      i. Employer contributions to the plan (not employee contributions).
      ii. Investment earnings on both employer and employee contributions.
   d. Distributions from the plan must follow the rules for qualified plan distributions.
   e. The plan is subject to the ERISA reporting and disclosure rules.

G. SECTION 401(K) PLAN (CODA).

1. Description.

   A Section 401(k) plan (also known as a qualified cash or deferred plan or CODA) is a qualified profit-sharing or stock bonus plan under which plan participants have an option to put money in the plan (as indexed for inflation – see table below for maximum contribution amounts) or receive taxable cash compensation. Amounts contributed are not taxable to the participants until withdrawn.

2. Application.
   a. A 401(k) plan is appropriate when an employer wants to provide a qualified retirement plan for employees, but can afford only minimal extra expense beyond existing salary and benefit costs. A 401(k) plan can be funded entirely from employee salary reductions, except for installation and administration costs.
   b. A 401(k) plan is appropriate when the employee group has one or more of the following characteristics:
      i. Employees would like some choice as to the level of savings, that is, a choice between various levels of current cash compensation and tax-deferred savings. A younger, more mobile work force often prefers this choice.
      ii. Employees are relatively young and have substantial time to accumulate retirement savings.
      iii. Employees are willing to accept a degree of investment risk in their plan accounts.
   c. A 401(k) plan is appropriate when an employer wants an attractive, savings-type supplement to its existing qualified retirement plan.

3. Advantages.
   a. Section 401(k) plans allow employees a degree of choice in the amount they wish to save under the plan.
   b. Section 401(k) plans can be funded entirely through salary reductions by employees.
   c. In-service withdrawals by employees for hardship are permitted; these are not available in qualified pension plans.
   d. Loans may also be permitted by the plan.

4. Disadvantages.

    a. As with all defined-contribution plans, account balances at retirement age may not provide adequate retirement savings for employees who entered the plan at later ages.

    b. The maximum salary reduction contribution is:

Year	Maximum Contribution Before Age 50	Maximum Contribution Age 50 or Older
2003	$12,000	$14,000
2004	$13,000	$16,000
2005	$14,000	$18,000
2006	$15,000	$20,000
2007	Indexed	Indexed

    c. Employer deductions for plan contributions cannot exceed 25% of the total compensation of employees covered under the plan.

Example

David Martinez (age 37) earns a salary of $100,000 working for MADCO, a manufacturing company. The maximum amount that can be contributed to David's 401(k) plan in 2003 is $37,000, calculated as follows:

David's salary	$100,000
Employer maximum deduction %	25%
Employer contribution	$25,000
David's maximum elective deferral	12,000
Total contribution	$37,000

If David was age 50 or older, he could defer an additional $2,000 for the year 2003.

5. Design features.

    a. Coverage.

        i. A 401(k) plan must satisfy the ratio percentage test or the average benefits percentage test under IRC Section 410(b).

        ii. The plan must also satisfy both the ACP and ADP tests.

        iii. Because of the actual deferral percentage (ADP) nondiscrimination tests, a 401(k) plan can be relatively costly and complex to administer.

b. Salary reduction.

   i. Virtually all Section 401(k) plans are funded entirely or in part through salary reductions elected by employees.

   ii. Salary reductions must be elected by employees before the compensation is earned.

   iii. The participant in a 401(k) is always 100% vested in any salary reductions contributed to the plan and any plan earnings on those salary reductions.

c. Employer contributions.

   i. Some Section 401(k) plans provide direct employer contributions in order to encourage employee participation and make the plan more valuable to employees. Typically, one or more of the following are types of employer contributions:

      A) Formula matching contributions.

      B) Discretionary matching contributions.

      C) Pure discretionary or profit-sharing contribution.

      D) Direct formula contribution (nonelective).

   ii. Direct (nonelective) employer contributions, which are nonforfeitable provisions in Section 401(k)plans, are used to help the plan meet the ADP tests.

   iii. A forfeiture from a partially vested participant that is used to allocate to other participants is included in the ACP test as a matching contribution.

d. Plan distributions.

   i. Distributions from Section 401(k) plans are subject to the qualified plan distribution rules.

   ii. Section 401(k) plans often allow participants to make in-service withdrawals (withdrawals before termination of employment). Section 401(k) accounts based on elective deferrals cannot be distributed prior to occurrence of one of the following events:

      A) Retirement.

      B) Death.

      C) Disability.

      D) Separation from service with the employer.

      E) Attainment of age 59½ by the participant.

      F) Plan termination (if the employer has no other defined-contribution plan other than an ESOP).

      G) Hardship.

   iii. Many preretirement distributions will not only be taxable, but will also be subject to the 10% early withdrawal penalty tax.

6. Tax implications.

   a. Employee elective contributions (deferrals) are not currently taxable income to the employee. However, such elective deferrals are subject to FICA (Social Security tax and Medicare).

   b. Nonelective employer contributions to the plan and employer elective contributions are deductible by the employer for federal income tax purposes up to a limit of 25% of the total covered compensation of all employees covered under the plan.

   c. Income tax credit for elective deferral contributions.

      i. In general.

         A) For years after 2001 and before 2007, a nonrefundable income tax credit is available for elective contributions made to a 401(k) plan, 403(b) plan, 457 plan, SIMPLE, SEP, Traditional IRA, or Roth IRA.

         B) The credit is in addition to any deduction or exclusion that would otherwise apply with respect to the contribution.

         C) The credit is available to individuals who are 18 or over, other than full-time students or individuals claimed as a dependent by another taxpayer.

      ii. Amount of credit.

         A) The maximum annual contribution eligible for the credit is $2,000.

         B) The credit rate depends on the taxpayer's adjusted gross income for the year. The following table details the credit rate based on AGI and filing status:

Married Filing Joint	Head of Household	Other Filing Status	Credit Rate
$0 - $30,000	$0 - $22,500	$0 - $15,000	50%
$30,000 - $32,500	$22,500 - $24,375	$15,000 - $16,250	20%
$32,500 - $50,000	$24,375 - $37,500	$16,250 - $25,000	10%
Over $50,000	Over $37,500	Over $25,000	0%

         C) The amount of any contribution eligible for the credit is reduced by taxable distributions from 401(k) plans, 403(b) plans, 457 plans, SIMPLEs, SEPs, Traditional IRAs, or Roth IRAs.

   d. Actual Deferral Percentage (ADP) test.

      i. Employee elective contributions must meet a special test for nondiscrimination called the actual deferral percentage (ADP) test. The plan must meet one of the following two tests in actual operation:

         A) Test 1 - The ADP for eligible highly compensated employees must not be more than the ADP of all other eligible employees multiplied by 1.25.

         B) Test 2 - The ADP for eligible highly compensated employees must not exceed the ADP for other eligible employees by more than 2%, and the ADP for eligible highly compensated employees must not be more than the ADP of all other eligible employees multiplied by 2.

EXHIBIT 6: ADP GENERAL RULES (SIMPLIFIED)

If ADP for NHC:	Maximum ADP for HC is:
≤ 2%	2 x ADP of NHC
≥ 2%, but ≤ 8%	2% + ADP of NHC
> 8%	1.25 x ADP of NHC

* Same rules as ACP tests

NHC = Nonhighly compensated
HC = Highly compensated

	ADP of NHC	ADP Limit for HC
2 Times	1%	2.00%
	2%	4.00%
Plus 2 Percentage Points	3%	5.00%
	4%	6.00%
	5%	7.00%
	6%	8.00%
	7%	9.00%
	8%	10.00%
1.25 Times	9%	11.25%
	10%	12.50%
	11%	13.75%
	12%	15.00%
	13%	16.25%
	14%	17.50%
	15%	18.75%

ii. The result of the ADP test is that deferrals of highly compensated employees are limited based on deferrals of nonhighly compensated employees. Thus, matching contributions and loan provisions are often incorporated into 401(k) plans to entice the nonhighly compensated employees to increase their deferrals and increase the ADP for nonhighly compensated employees.

iii. If the ADP test is failed, the employer has two options.

A) A corrective distribution can be made which will decrease the ADP of the highly compensated employees. This distribution is made in the following tax year and will be included in gross income for the taxpayer (highly compensated employee). The excess contribution must be corrected within 2½ months after the end of the year or the employer will be required to pay a 10 percent penalty (excise tax) on the amount not corrected; or

B) An additional contribution can be made for nonhighly compensated employees. This additional contribution can take one of two forms, both of which are considered to be 100% vested:

1) Qualified matching contribution – additional contribution for only those NHC who deferred for the plan year; or

2) Qualified nonelective contribution – additional contribution for all eligible NHC (even if they had not been participating).

e. Actual Contribution Percentage (ACP) test.

i. The ACP test applies to employer-matching contributions and employee after-tax contributions.

ii. Employer-matching contributions must meet a special test for nondiscrimination called the actual contribution percentage (ACP) test. The plan must meet one of the following two tests in actual operation:

A) Test 1 - The ACP for eligible highly compensated employees must not be more than the ACP of all other eligible employees multiplied by 1.25.

B) Test 2 - The ACP for eligible highly compensated employees must not exceed the ACP for other eligible employees by more than 2%, and the ACP for eligible highly compensated employees must not be more than the ACP of all other eligible employees multiplied by 2.

C) The ACP interpreted is the same as the ADP, and can be summarized with the following table:

EXHIBIT 7: ACP GENERAL RULES (SIMPLIFIED)

If ACP for NHC:	Maximum ACP for HC is:
≤ 2%	2 x ADP of NHC
≥ 2%, but ≤ 8%	2% + ADP of NHC
> 8%	1.25 x ADP of NHC

NHC = Nonhighly compensated
HC = Highly compensated

f. Safe Harbor Rule (Alternative methods of meeting nondiscrimination testing requirements).

i. Employers can avoid ADP and ACP testing if the plan meets one of the safe harbor provisions under IRC Section 401(k)(12). The following contributions made by the employer must be 100 percent vested at all times.

ii. Alternative methods.

A) Matching contributions for NHC employees.

1) 100 percent match up to 3% of compensation plus 50% match for contributions between 3% and 5% of compensation. In addition, the matching contribution percentages for the HC employees cannot exceed those for NHC employees.

2) As an alternative, the employer may elect to match 100% up to 4% of compensation.

EXHIBIT 8: SAFE HARBOR BASIC MATCHING FORMULA

Employee Contribution as a % of Compensation	Employer-Matching Contribution as a % of Compensation
0%	0%
1%	1%
2%	2%
3%	3%
4%	3.5%
5% or greater	4%

B) Nonelective contributions.

1) The employer may choose to make contributions of 3% or more of compensation for all employees who are eligible to participate in the plan, regardless of whether or not the employee chooses to participate.

iii. Other requirements.

A) As mentioned, to meet the safe harbor requirements, the matching and nonelective contributions must be 100% vested.

B) The above contributions may not be considered for purpose of permitted disparity.

C) The employer must provide notice to each eligible employee about rights and obligations under the plan.

Example

The ADP for highly compensated and nonhighly compensated employees is the average of the individual actual deferral percentage for each participant of that group. The ADP is the total elective contribution divided by the participants' covered compensation. Qualified matching contributions (QMC) and qualified nonelective contributions (QNC), which are nonforfeitable, are included in the deferral amount used in the numerator.

	ADP	
Employee	**HC**	**NHC**
1	6%	
2	6%	
3	6%	
4		3%
5		5%
6		4%
7		3%
	18%	15%
Average	6%	3.75%

NHC = 3.75%
HC = 6.00%

The plan facts*

* Company could add qualified nonelective deferral of 0.25% to each NHC participant and satisfy the ADP test.

The ACP test operates the same way as the ADP test except, rather than being applied to employee deferrals, it applies to matching contributions & after-tax employee contributions.

EXHIBIT 9: DEFINED-BENEFIT, DEFINED-CONTRIBUTION, AND CASH-BALANCE PLANS - COMPARISON

	Typical Defined-Benefit Plan (DB)	Typical Defined-Contribution Plan (DC)	Cash-Balance Plan
Contribution	Actuarially determined	Percentage of salary (could be age weighted)	Percentage of salary (actuarially determined)
Investment Risk	Employer	Employee	Employer
Size of Work Force	Any Size	Any Size	Large
Investment Earnings	Employer Responsible	Variable	Employer Responsible
Social Security Integration	Yes	Yes*	Yes
Pension Benefit Guarantee Corporation Insurance	Yes	No	Yes
Employee Contribution Feature	No	Available in profit-sharing plan	No
Favors Older Entrants	Yes	No	No
Administrative Cost	Generally higher than DC plans due to actuary and insurance costs	Generally lower than DB plans	Generally higher than DC plans due to actuary and insurance costs

VII. HYBRID PLANS

A. TARGET/AGE-WEIGHTED PLAN.

1. Description.

   a. A target or other age-weighted plan and formula, for a defined-contribution plan, allows higher contribution levels (as a percentage of compensation) for older plan entrants.

   b. Broad types of age-weighted plans include:

      i. The traditional target plan is an age-weighted money-purchase pension plan. A traditional target plan is a hybrid between a defined-contribution pension plan and a defined-benefit plan.

         A) Similarity with defined-benefit plan - The funding of each participant's account is aimed at producing a target amount, or benefit, at retirement, like a defined-benefit plan.

         B) Similarity with defined-contribution plan - The actual benefit the employee is entitled to is the amount of the employee's account at retirement. Like a defined-contribution plan, the plan participant assumes the investment risk.

      ii. The age-based profit-sharing plan is a profit-sharing plan with an age-weighted factor in the allocation formula. Since the plan allocations are age-weighted, older plan entrants are favored.

      iii. The new comparability plan represents an attempt to push age weighting to its maximum limit under the cross-testing provisions of the proposed nondiscrimination regulations under Code Section 401(a)(4).

2. Application.

   a. Age-weighted plans are appropriate when there are older employees whose retirement benefits would be inadequate under a traditional defined-contribution plan because of the relatively few years remaining for participation in the plan.

   b. Age-weighted plans are appropriate when an alternative to a defined-benefit plan is needed to provide older employees adequate retirement benefits, but has the lower cost and simplicity of a defined-contribution plan.

   c. Age-weighted plans are appropriate when the employer wants to terminate an existing defined-benefit plan in order to avoid the increasing cost and regulatory burdens associated with these plans.

   d. Age-weighted plans are appropriate when a closely held business or professional corporation has a relatively large number of key employees who are approximately age 50 or older.

3. Advantages.
   a. Retirement benefits can be made adequate for employees who enter the plan at older ages.
   b. More of the total employer contributions in the age-weighted plan will likely be allocated to owners and key employees who are probably older.
   c. An age-weighted plan provides a tax-deferred retirement savings medium.
   d. The age-weighted plan is relatively simple and inexpensive to design, administer, and explain to employees.
   e. Qualifying lump-sum distributions may be eligible for the special ten-year forward averaging tax computation available for certain qualified plans.
   f. Individual accounts for participants allow participants to benefit from good investment results.
4. Disadvantages.
   a. A target-benefit plan is a pension plan and is, therefore, subject to the minimum funding standards applicable to all pension plans. Employers are obligated to make minimum contributions each year under the plan's contribution formula or be subject to minimum funding penalties. An age-weighted profit-sharing plan is not subject to the minimum funding requirements but requires recurring and substantial contributions.

> **Note:** For older employees, a defined-benefit plan may allow a much higher level of employer contributions to the plan than defined-contribution plans.

5. Design features.
   a. The concept of age weighting is not new. The design of current age-weighted plans is dictated by the need to meet the proposed nondiscrimination requirements under Code Section 401(a)(4).
      i. Target pension plan.
         A) The employer chooses a target level of retirement benefits as a percentage of annual compensation.
         B) The plan designer chooses actuarial assumptions to determine how much must be contributed for each participant in order to provide the targeted level of benefit.
            1) Unlike a defined-benefit plan, there are no periodic actuarial valuations.
            2) The participant gets the benefit of good investment results and bears the risk of poor investment results.
            3) Target pension plans must take the following into account:
               a) The life expectancy table must be a unisex table.
               b) Actuarial assumptions must be reasonable.
               c) The investment return assumption must be no less than 7.5% and no greater than 8.5%.

4) Benefit payments.

   a) The target in a target plan is a retirement benefit similar to that provided in a defined-benefit plan. A target plan provides benefits similar to other types of defined-contribution plans, particularly money-purchase plans:

      i) Employer contributions.

      ii) After-tax employee contributions (rare in target plans).

      iii) Forfeitures from other employee's accounts.

      iv) Interest, capital gains, and other investment returns realized over the years.

      v) Benefits actually determined by account balance.

   b) As a condition of qualification, a target-benefit plan must provide for a qualified joint and survivor annuity as its automatic benefit, unless waived by the participant with the consent of spouse.

5) Nondiscrimination regulations.

   a) Under proposed nondiscrimination regulations, target plans generally must apply the rules for defined-benefit plans to the target formula.

   b) A defined-contribution plan can be tested on the basis of its projected benefits at retirement, and a defined-benefit plan can be tested on the basis of annual employer contributions. This is cross testing.

   c) Cross testing makes age-weighted defined-contribution plans permissible. Such plans are discriminatory on the basis of their annual contribution levels, but are designed through cross testing to be nondiscriminatory regarding benefits.

   d) If projected benefit levels in an age-weighted plan are not discriminatory, the plan meets nondiscrimination tests of proposed regulations.

   e) Cross testing can be used to design a defined-contribution plan that has the maximum permissible level of discrimination. The planner works backward from the projected benefit levels that minimally meet cross testing requirements and then computes those projected benefits levels.

   f) Age-weighted plans permit low contribution levels for younger, lower-paid participants and extremely high contributions for older employees.

6) Other provisions.

   a) Vesting and investment features of target plans are similar to those for money-purchase plans.

   b) Target-benefit contribution formulas can be integrated with Social Security.

6. Alternatives.

   a. Defined-benefit plans provide more benefit security because of the employer and government guarantee of benefit levels. They also allow greater tax-deductible employer contributions for older plan entrants who are highly compensated because the defined-contribution plan annual additions limit does not apply. However, defined-benefit plans are more complex and costly to design and administer.

   b. Money-purchase plans offer an alternative similar to target plans, but without the age-related contribution feature.

   c. Nonqualified deferred compensation plans can be provided exclusively for selected executives. Employer's tax deduction is generally deferred.

   d. Individual retirement savings is available as an alternative or supplement to an employer plan.

B. TARGET-BENEFIT PLANS.

1. Description.

   a. A target-benefit plan is a money-purchase pension plan under which contributions are made for each participant in level annual contributions to fund the participant's target benefit at the plan's normal retirement age.

   b. The plan must specify a target-benefit formula and define the funding assumptions to accumulate the necessary cash at retirement.

   c. The result is that contributions on behalf of older participants will be much higher than for younger participants.

   d. Since business owners tend to be older and more highly compensated than other employees, a target plan will substantially direct contributions in favor of owners, officers, and management.

C. AGE-BASED PROFIT-SHARING PLAN.

1. Description.

   a. An age-based profit-sharing plan is a defined-contribution profit-sharing plan.

   b. Allocations to participants are made in proportion to each participant's age-adjusted compensation.

   c. A participant's compensation is age adjusted by multiplying the participant's actual compensation by a discount factor based on the participant's age and interest rate elected by the employer. The interest rate allowed by the IRS is from 7.5% to 8.5% and may be selected by the plan.

   d. Under an age-based allocation formula, each participant's equivalent accrual rates will, in theory, be the same.

   e. Equivalent accrual rates will be the basis of nondiscrimination testing.

   f. Other issues.

      i. If allocation to a nonhighly compensated employee is limited due to Internal Revenue Code Sec. 415, his accrual rate is reduced and may cause the allocation to be discriminatory.

      ii. If the plan is top heavy, allocations to all nonkey employees must satisfy a top-heavy minimum.

Example

Illustration of age-based profit-sharing plan:

Assume that a business owner is age 50, earns $200,000 per year, and elects to make a contribution of $40,540 to a discretionary age-based profit-sharing plan. The plan will also benefit one employee, age 25, earning $18,000 per year.

	Business Owner	Employee	Total
Age	50	25	
Compensation	$200,000	$18,000	$218,000
Adjustment Factor @ 8.5%	0.294139	0.038265	
Age-Adjusted Compensation	$58,828	$689	$59,517
Allocation	$40,071	$469	$40,540
Annual additions limit (100% or $40,000)	$40,000	$18,000	
Top-Heavy Minimum (3% of compensation)	$0	$540	
Actual Allocation	$40,000	$540	$40,540
Contribution Rate	20.00%	3.00%	
Percent of Contribution	98.67%	1.33%	

Although the maximum deductible limit for a profit-sharing plan is 25% of eligible compensation (25% x $218,000 = $54,500) the employer would only fund the plan so that he reached the $40,000 limit.

$$\frac{\$58,828}{\$59,517} \times \$40,540 = \$40,071$$

$$\frac{\$689}{\$59,517} \times \$40,540 = \$469$$

D. NEW COMPARABILITY PLAN - DESCRIPTION.

1. A new comparability plan is a defined-contribution plan that is either a money-purchase pension plan or a discretionary profit-sharing plan.
2. The common design factor is that new comparability plans have an allocation or contribution formula which result in one group or class of employee receiving a given contribution level while another group receives a different level.
3. This type of plan works well where owners are different ages, thus, precluding an aged-based plan.
4. The plan can define particular classifications of employees in a number of ways:
    a. Service with the employer.
    b. Job title, such as officer or partner.
    c. Employment at a particular division or subsidiary.
    d. Compensation level.
    e. Age.
    f. Class of employee, such as salaried or hourly.
    g. Any combination of the above.

5. For example, a plan may be written to provide officers a contribution of 20% of pay and all other employees a contribution of 3%.
6. Allocations are restricted in that the employer must design the contribution structure in such a way that the plan passes the nondiscrimination tests.
7. In the event the plan fails the nondiscrimination tests, the plan should have provisions to reallocate or shift contributions from highly compensated employees to selected nonhighly compensated employees to satisfy the nondiscrimination rules. It should be designed to increase accrual rates for nonhighly compensated employees one at a time until the nondiscrimination test is passed.
8. These reallocation provisions must be precise in that the allocation formula must be definitely determinable and preclude employer discretion.

E. COMBINED NEW COMPARABILITY PLAN WITH 401(K) FEATURE.

1. All features of the plan are aggregated and must pass the nondiscrimination test.
2. The Section 401(k) feature will allow for younger, highly compensated employees to achieve full contributions through elective deferrals rather than employer contributions.
3. Older, highly compensated employees can receive an employer contribution of up to $40,000 and will not defer under the 401(k) feature. No elective deferrals by certain highly compensated employees will improve results of the ADP test for the 401(k) plan.
4. The employer contribution is subject to an overall deduction limitation equal to 25% (for 2003) of eligible compensation.

F. SMALL BUSINESS TAX CREDIT FOR NEW RETIREMENT PLAN EXPENSES

1. In General.
    a. A nonrefundable income tax credit is available for certain administrative and retirement-education expenses for any small business that adopts a new qualified plan, SIMPLE plan, or SEP.
    b. The credit is available to any employer that did not employ more than 100 employees in the prior year. Only employees with compensation over $5,000 are counted in the 100 employee test.
    c. To be eligible for the credit, the plan must cover at least one nonhighly compensated employee.
    d. The credit is a general business credit.
2. Amount of credit.
    a. The credit is available for 50% of the first $1,000 in administrative and retirement-education expenses for the plan for each of the first three years of the plan.
    b. The 50% of qualifying expenses that are used in calculating the credit are not deductible. The other 50% of the qualifying expenses are deductible to the extent permitted by law.
    c. The credit cannot be carried back to tax years before 2002.

VIII.HR 10 (KEOGH) PLAN

A. DESCRIPTION.

1. A Keogh plan, sometimes referred to as an HR 10 plan, is a qualified retirement plan that covers one or more self-employed individuals.
2. Under current law, Keogh plans are basically like any other qualified plan. The word "Keogh" should be thought of as meaning that someone in the firm is self-employed. There are only two primary differences that result for a Keogh plan:
   a. First, self-employed individuals must calculate their retirement plan contribution based on "earned income" instead of W-2 income.
   b. Second, self-employed individuals must use a "net contribution rate" in determining their allowable contribution to a Keogh defined-contribution plan.

B. APPLICATION.

1. When long-term capital accumulation, particularly for retirement purposes, is an important objective of a self-employed business owner.
2. When an owner of an unincorporated business wishes to adopt a plan providing retirement benefits for regular employees as an incentive and employee benefit as well as retirement savings for the business owner. The types of entities that have Keogh plans include:
   a. Sole proprietorships.
   b. Partnerships.
   c. LLPs.
   d. LLCs taxed as sole proprietorships or partnerships.
   e. S corporations do not have self-employed owners and, therefore, do not have Keogh plans. Their contributions are based on W-2 earnings.
3. When a self-employed person has a need to shelter some current earnings from federal income tax.
4. When an employee has self-employment income as well as income from other employment and wishes to invest as much of the self-employment income as possible and defer taxes on it.

C. ADVANTAGES.

1. Keogh contributions are deducted from taxable income. The tax is deferred until funds are withdrawn from the plan at a later date.
2. Income generated by the investments in a Keogh plan is free of income taxes until it is withdrawn from the plan.
3. Certain lump-sum distributions from Keogh plans may be eligible for favorable ten-year forward averaging income tax treatment.
4. From the viewpoint of an employee of an unincorporated business, Keogh plans are advantageous because employees of the business must be permitted to participate in the plan if certain conditions are met.

D. DISADVANTAGES.

1. Keogh plans involve all the costs and complexity associated with qualified plans. However, for a small plan, it is relatively easy to minimize these costs by using prototype plans offered by insurance companies, mutual funds, banks, and other financial institutions.
2. They require nondiscriminatory plan coverage requirements.
3. Life insurance in a qualified plan for a self-employed person, described below, is treated less favorably than for regular employees.

E. TYPES OF KEOGH PLANS.

1. In general, any type of qualified plan can be designed to cover self-employed persons. A Keogh plan is usually designed as either:
   a. A profit-sharing plan.
   b. A money-purchase plan.
   c. A target plan.

F. HOW ARE KEOGHS DIFFERENT FROM OTHER QUALIFIED PLANS?

1. Keogh plans cover self-employed individuals who are not technically considered employees.
2. Earned income.
   a. The most important special rule is the definition of earned income. Earned income takes the place of compensation in applying the qualified plan rules.
      i. Income is defined as the self-employed individual's net income from the business after all deductions including the deduction for any Keogh plan contributions.
      ii. In addition, the IRS has ruled that the self-employment tax must be computed and a deduction of one-half of the self-employment tax must be taken before determining the Keogh deduction.
   b. Steps in determining the Keogh deduction:
      i. Determine net income from Schedule C (or Schedule K-1).
      ii. Subtract one-half of the actual amount of the self-employment tax (applicable to that income).
      iii. Multiply the result by the net contribution rate from the rate table (See Appendix 3: Self-Employed Person's Rate Table).

Example

Kim earns $70,000 of Schedule C Income in 2003. Her 25% profit-sharing (P/S) plan maximum contribution is calculated as follows:

Schedule C Income	$70,000.00	
Less: ½ of Self Employment tax paid	(4,902.40)	(assumed amount)
Equals	$65,097.60	
Multiply by Table Factor *	x 0.20	
Maximum P/S Contribution	$13,019.52	

* The table factor can be determined by (0.25 ÷ 1.25 = 0.20)

Proof

Salary	$70,000.00
Less: ½ FICA	(4,902.40)
Net Salary	$65,097.60
- P/S Contribution	(13,019.52)
Earned Income	$52,078.08
Contribution %	x 25%
P/S Contribution	$13,019.52

3. Life insurance.

   a. Life insurance can be used as an incidental benefit in a qualified plan covering self-employed individuals, but the tax treatment for the self-employed individuals is different from that applicable to regular employees in a qualified plan.

   b. The entire cost of life insurance for regular employees is deductible as a plan contribution. Employees then pick up the value of the pure life insurance element as extra taxable compensation.

   c. For a self-employed individual:

      i. The pure life insurance element of an insurance premium is not deductible.

      ii. Only the portion of the premium that exceeds the pure protection value of the insurance is deductible.

      iii. The pure protection value of the insurance is determined using Table 2001(formerly, the P.S. 58 table was used).

   d. For regular employees:

      i. They have a cost basis (a nontaxable recovery element) in a plan equal to any Table 2001 costs if the plan distribution is made from the same life insurance contract on which the Table 2001 costs were paid.

      ii. For a self-employed individual, however, the Table 2001 costs, although effectively included in income since they were nondeductible, are not includible in their cost basis.

4. Alternatives.

   a. The disadvantages, if any, of Keogh status of any qualified plan can be eliminated if the business owner incorporates as a C corporation and adopts a corporate plan.

   b. A simplified employee pension (SEP) may be even easier to adopt than a Keogh plan particularly if only one self-employed individual is covered. SEPs can be adopted as late as the individual's tax return filing date. SEP contributions are limited to 25% of earned income (which is effectively 20% due to the deduction of the self-employment contribution).

   c. Tax deductible Traditional IRAs are available if the individual (or his spouse) is not an active participant in a qualified plan. (See limitations and rules for higher income taxpayers.)

G. BENEFIT PLANS FOR PROPRIETORSHIPS, PARTNERSHIPS, AND S CORPORATIONS

1. General Characteristics.

   a. Owners of these businesses are not technically employees of the business.

   b. Proprietorships, partnerships, and S corporations can have benefit plans for their employees that are exactly the same as those of regular C corporations.

   c. The deductibility of benefit costs is the same, and tax treatment to the regular employees is also the same as to C corporations.

   d. When the plan attempts to cover business owners, some differences arise.

   e. The benefit packages for proprietorships, partnerships, and S corporations involve less favorable benefits for owners.

2. Partnerships and Proprietorships.

   a. With the exception of health insurance premiums and contributions to qualified plans, most benefits and compensation paid to a proprietor are not deductible business expenses.

   b. Employee benefits for partners with qualified retirement plans: (1) contributions are deductible by the partnership along with those for regular employees, (2) partners are taxed on qualified plan contributions and benefits much the same as regular employees.

   c. The effective percentage limits for contributions to qualified plans are lower for self-employed business owners than for other employees due to the definition of "compensation" for these parties.

IX. SIMPLIFIED EMPLOYEE PENSION (SEP)

A. DESCRIPTION.

1. A simplified employee pension (SEP) is an employer-sponsored individual retirement account or individual retirement annuity arrangement that is similar to a qualified profit-sharing plan (requires a written plan).
2. A SEP combines simplicity of design with a high degree of flexibility from the employer's perspective.
3. A SEP is an employer agreement to contribute on a noncontributory and nondiscriminatory basis to IRAs opened and maintained by employees.
4. The limits for SEP contributions are much higher than those for Traditional or Roth IRAs, up to the lesser of:
   a. 25% of compensation (compensation is limited to $200,000 for 2003).
   b. $40,000 (for 2003).
5. SEP contributions are discretionary.
6. There are no vesting schedules with a SEP. All contributions are owned by the employees immediately (i.e., 100% vested).

B. APPLICATION.

1. A SEP is appropriate when the employer is seeking an alternative to a qualified profit-sharing plan that is easier and less expensive to install and administer (usually for small employers).
2. A SEP is appropriate when an employer wants to install a tax-deferred plan and it is too late to adopt a qualified plan for the year in question (after December 31). SEPs can be adopted and funded as late as the tax return filing date, including extensions, for the year in which they are to be effective.
3. SARSEPs (salary reduction SEPs) can no longer be established, but existing SARSEPs can be maintained.

C. CHARACTERISTICS.

1. A SEP can be adopted by completing a simple IRS form.
2. The monetary benefits of a SEP are totally portable by employees, for funding consists entirely of IRAs for each employee.
3. Employer contributions are always fully vested and are not forfeitable.
4. A SEP provides as much, or more, flexibility in the amount and timing of contributions as a qualified profit-sharing plan. The employer is free to make no contribution to the plan in any given year.
5. Individual IRA accounts allow participants to benefit from wisely selected investments.

6. The SARSEP salary reduction contribution limit for 2003 is $12,000. In addition, individuals who have attained age 50 may make additional catch-up contributions. The additional catch-up amount is $2,000 for 2003, $3,000 for 2004, $4,000 for 2005, and $5,000 for 2006 (indexed after 2006). The following table summarizes the allowed salary reduction contributions to a SARSEP plan in future years:

Year	Maximum Contribution Before Age 50	Maximum Contribution Age 50 or Older
2003	$12,000	$14,000
2004	$13,000	$16,000
2005	$14,000	$18,000
2006	$15,000	$20,000
2007	Indexed	Indexed

7. An income tax credit is allowed for certain taxpayers with respect to elective contributions to a SEP. See section, "Income tax credit for elective deferral contributions." on page 773.
8. A SEP, but not a SARSEP, can be integrated (permitted disparity) with Social Security.
9. SEPs may be established by C corporations, S corporations, partnerships, and sole proprietorships.

D. DISADVANTAGES.

1. Employees cannot rely upon a SEP to provide an adequate retirement benefit.
2. The benefits are not significant unless the employer makes substantial, regular contributions to the SEP. The employer has no obligation to do this under the plan.
3. The employee bears the investment risk under the plan.

E. TAX IMPLICATIONS.

1. An employer may deduct contributions to a SEP up to the contribution limit. The major SEP requirements are:
   a. A SEP must cover all employees who are at least 21 years of age and who have worked for the employer during three out of the preceding five calendar years. Part-time employment counts in determining service.
   b. Contributions need not be made on behalf of employees whose compensation for the calendar year was less than $450 (for 2003).
   c. The plan can exclude employees who are members of collective bargaining units if retirement benefits have been the subject of good faith bargaining.
2. If an employer maintains a SEP and also maintains a regular qualified plan, contributions to the SEP reduce the amount that can be deducted for contributions to the regular plan.
3. In a SEP, each participating employee maintains an IRA.
4. Salary reductions, but not direct employer contributions, are subject to Social Security (FICA) and federal unemployment (FUTA) taxes.
5. Distributions to employees from the plan are treated as distributions from an IRA.
6. Investments are limited to investments in an IRA (no collectibles and no insurance).
7. A 10% excise tax is assessed on excess contributions (IRC Section 4979).
8. Participation in a SEP counts as "active participant status" for purposes of determining the deductibility of separate IRA contributions.

X. TRADITIONAL IRA

A. DESCRIPTION.

1. There are two kinds of Traditional IRAs:
    a. Individual Retirement Accounts.
    b. Individual Retirement Annuities (Insurance Companies).

B. APPROPRIATE APPLICATION.

1. When there is a need to shelter current compensation or earned income from taxation.
2. When it is desirable to defer taxes on investment income.
3. When long-term accumulation, especially for retirement purposes, is an important financial objective.
4. When a supplement or alternative to a qualified pension or profit-sharing plan is needed.

C. ADVANTAGES.

1. For 2003, eligible individuals may contribute up to $3,000 to an IRA ($6,000 if a spousal IRA is available) and deduct this amount from their current taxable income. (See rules/limitations for certain higher-income taxpayers.)
2. Individuals who have attained age 50 may make additional catch-up contributions. The additional catch-up amount is $500 for years 2003-2005 and $1,000 for years after 2005. The following table summarizes the allowed contributions to an IRA in future years:

Year	Maximum Contribution Before Age 50	Maximum Contribution Age 50 or Older
2003	$3,000	$3,500
2004	$3,000	$3,500
2005	$4,000	$4,500
2006	$4,000	$5,000
2007	$4,000	$5,000
2008	$5,000	$6,000
2009	Indexed	Base contribution (as indexed) plus $1,000

3. An income tax credit is allowed for certain taxpayers with respect to contributions to a Traditional or Roth IRA. See section, "Income tax credit for elective deferral contributions." on page 773.
4. Investment income earned on the assets held in an IRA is not subject to federal income tax until it is withdrawn from the account.

> **Note:** The Small Business Act of 1996 permits Spousal IRA (SPIRA) of up to $3,000 (i.e., $6,000 combined total) if the compensation limit is met by one spouse for tax years after 1996.

D. DISADVANTAGES.

1. IRA withdrawals are subject to a 10% penalty on premature withdrawals (pre-59½).
2. IRA distributions are not eligible for ten-year forward averaging that applies to certain lump-sum distributions from qualified plans.
3. IRAs cannot be established once an individual reaches age 70½ (except in the case of a rollover IRA or Roth IRA) and, withdrawals from the account are required by April 1 of the year following the year that the individual reaches age 70½ (except in the case of a Roth IRA).
4. All distributions from IRAs are ordinary income to the extent taxable (see exceptions for Roth IRA under Section "Roth IRAs" on page 793)

E. TAX IMPLICATIONS.

1. Deductibility rules.
   a. For taxpayers who are not active participants in a qualified plan, SEP, SARSEP, SIMPLE, or 403(b) plan, contributions to a traditional IRA are fully deductible, regardless of the taxpayer's AGI.
   b. For taxpayers who are active participants in a qualified plan, SEP, SARSEP, SIMPLE, or 403(b) plan, the deduction for Traditional IRA contributions is limited (or eliminated) when a taxpayer's adjusted income reaches certain levels. These phaseout levels are listed in Exhibit 10.

EXHIBIT 10: IRA CURRENT PHASEOUT LIMITS

Tax Year	Taxpayer Filing Status	
	Phaseout Range Single	Phaseout Range Married Filing Jointly
2003	$40,000 – 50,000	$60,000 – 70,000
2004	$45,000 – 55,000	$65,000 – 75,000
2005	$50,000 – 60,000	$70,000 – 80,000
2006	$50,000 – 60,000	$75,000 – 85,000
2007 and after	$50,000 – 60,000	$80,000 – 100,000

   c. An individual will not be considered an "active participant" in an employer-sponsored retirement plan solely because his or her spouse is an active participant. However, when only one spouse is an active participant, the nonparticipant spouse will have his or her deduction phased out at AGI levels between $150,000-$160,000.

Example

Scott and Anne are married and have a combined AGI of $100,000. Anne is an active participant in her company's 401(k) plan. Scott's employer does not offer a retirement plan. Both Scott and Anne make $3,000 contributions to their traditional IRAs. Since Anne is an active participant, and the combined AGI exceeds $70,000 (the upper end of the Married Filing Joint phaseout range for 2003), her entire contribution is nondeductible. Scott is not an active participant, however, and, therefore his deduction will be phased out starting at AGI of $150,000. Since the combined AGI is $100,000, Scott will get a full $3,000 deduction for his contribution.

d. An individual participating only in a Section 457 plan will not be considered an active participant.

Example

Steve, a 45-year-old single taxpayer with AGI of $90,000 this year, participates in his employer's Section 457 plan. Since he is not considered an active participant, Steve can make a fully deductible $3,000 contribution (for 2003) to a Traditional IRA. If Steve were an active participant in a qualified plan, SEP, SARSEP, SIMPLE, or 403(b) plan, his deduction would be fully phased out at his AGI level.

2. Active participant.

   a. The plans that are considered for purposes of deducting IRA contributions include qualified plans, 403(b) plans, SEPs, and SIMPLEs. In addition, federal, state and local government plans are also taken into account.

   b. The test for active participant is testing whether a taxpayer is benefiting under one of the above-mentioned plans. However, there are different rules for defined-benefit-type plans and defined-contribution-type plans.

   c. Defined-benefit plans.

      i. Unless an employee is excluded from participation, he is considered an active participant in a defined-benefit plan.

      ii. If an employee is not eligible or is excluded from the plan, then he is not considered an active participant.

   d. Defined-contribution plans.

      i. An employee is considered an active participant for the year if an annual addition is made to the plan during the year. An annual addition is any of the following:

         A) An employee contribution to the plan, such as an elective deferral to a 401(k) plan.

         B) An employer contribution to the plan.

         C) A forfeiture allocation.

      ii. Employees who are participants in a defined-contribution pension plan are considered active participants because pension plans require mandatory funding. However, employees who are participants of a profit-sharing plan may not be an active participant for a particular year if there is no employer contribution, employee contribution, or forfeiture allocation.

e. It should be noted that if a taxpayer is an active participant for any part of the year, then the taxpayer is considered an active participant for the entire year. Vesting has no impact on this status.

f. Contributions to a Roth IRA may preclude contributions to a Traditional IRA. The total contributions in aggregate, for Roth and Traditional IRAs, cannot exceed $3,000 (for 2002 per individual per year), plus any catch-up adjustment.

g. Individuals who are not covered as active participants can contribute to a deductible IRA without consideration of income limits.

h. Earned income does not include:

   i. Earnings and profits from property such as rental income, interest income, dividend income, and investment income.

   ii. Pension or annuity income.

   iii. Any deferred compensation received (compensation payments postponed from a prior year).

   iv. Foreign earned income and/or housing cost amounts that are excluded from income.

   v. Any other amounts that are excluded from income.

i. Earned income <u>does</u> include alimony received.

3. Excess contribution penalty - 6% excise tax (each year) if excess contribution is not withdrawn.

4. Contribution due date is the due date of the tax return without extension (generally April 15).

F. ROTH IRAS

1. In general.

   a. Roth IRAs are treated like Traditional IRAs except where the Internal Revenue Code specifies different treatment.

   b. The treatment of Traditional IRAs and Roth IRAs is the same for the following:

      i. Prohibited transactions.

      ii. Permitted investments.

      iii. Maximum allowable contribution.

      iv. Spousal IRA limits.

      v. Definition of earned income.

2. Contributions.

   a. For 2003, the Roth IRA allows for nondeductible contributions up to $3,000 per individual.

b. Individuals who have attained age 50 may make additional catch-up contributions. The additional catch-up amount is $500 for years 2002-2005 and $1,000 for years after 2005. The following table summarizes the allowed contributions to a Roth IRA in future years:

Year	Maximum Contribution Before Age 50	Maximum Contribution Age 50 or Older
2003	$3,000	$3,500
2004	$3,000	$3,500
2005	$4,000	$4,500
2006	$4,000	$5,000
2007	$4,000	$5,000
2008	$5,000	$6,000
2009	Indexed	Base contribution (as indexed) plus $1,000

c. Like Traditional IRAs, contributions to Roth IRAs cannot exceed earned income. Earned income for Roth IRAs, as with Traditional IRAs, includes alimony.

d. Contributions can be made as late as the due date of the individual's return (April 15th) for the previous year.

e. Phaseouts for contributions – Only taxpayers with income below certain limits are permitted to make contributions to a Roth IRA. Contributions are phased out between modified AGI of:

   i. Married filing jointly: $150,000 - $160,000

   ii. Single: $95,000 - $110,000

   iii. Married filing separately: $0 - $10,000

f. Modified AGI does not include income that is attributable to the conversion of a Traditional IRA to a Roth IRA.

g. Contributions to a Roth IRA can be made for years beyond the age of 70½. This is an important distinction from Traditional IRAs in which contributions cannot be made after the attainment of age 70½.

3. Converting Traditional IRAs to Roth IRAs.

   a. An amount in a Traditional IRA may be converted to an amount in a Roth IRA if two requirements are satisfied:

      i. First, the IRA owner must have modified AGI of $100,000 or less (Modified AGI does not include income that is attributable to a conversion of a Traditional IRA to a Roth IRA); and

Note: Taxpayers using the "Married Filing Separate" filing status cannot convert.

ii. The amount converted must satisfy the definition of a qualified rollover contribution which includes any of the following three methods:

A) An amount distributed from a Traditional IRA is contributed (rolled over) to a Roth IRA within 60 days after the distribution;

B) An amount in a Traditional IRA is transferred in a trustee-to-trustee transfer from the trustee of the Traditional IRA to the trustee of the Roth IRA; or

C) An amount in a Traditional IRA is transferred to a Roth IRA maintained by the same trustee.

b. Distributions from a qualified plan cannot be converted directly to a Roth IRA, nor can amounts in an Coverdell Education Savings Account be converted to a Roth IRA.

c. Any converted amount is treated as a distribution from a Traditional IRA and is included in gross income for the year in which the distribution occurs. Any amount converted that is a return of basis is not included in income. The 10% early withdrawal penalty under IRC Section 72(t) does not apply to the taxable conversion amount.

4. Distributions.

a. A distribution from a Roth IRA is not includible in the owner's gross income if it is a "qualified distribution" or to the extent that it is a return of the owner's contributions to the Roth IRA.

b. A qualified distribution is a distribution from a Roth IRA that satisfies both of the following tests:

i. The distribution must be made after a five-taxable-year period (which begins January 1st of the taxable year for which the first regular contribution is made to any Roth IRA of the individual or, if earlier, January 1st of the taxable year in which the first conversion contribution is made to any Roth IRA of the individual).

Example

- On July 5, 2003, Tom Hall established a Roth IRA with a $1,200 contribution. Since this was his first contribution to a Roth IRA, his five-year period begins on January 1, 2003.
- On February 16, 2003, Mary made an initial contribution of $900 to a Roth IRA. She made the contribution for the 2002 tax year (remember, a taxpayer has until April 15th of the current year to make contributions to a Traditional or Roth IRA for the prior tax year). Therefore, her five-year period begins on January 1, 2002, even though she made her initial contribution in 2003.

ii. In addition to the five-year test, the distribution must satisfy one of the following requirements:

A) Made on or after the date on which the owner attains the age 59½, or

B) Made to a beneficiary or estate of the owner on or after the date of owner's death, or

C) Is attributable to the owner being disabled, or

D) For first-time home purchase (lifetime cap of $10,000 for first-time home buyers includes taxpayer, spouse, child, or grandchild who has not owned a house for at least 2 years).

c. The five-taxable-year period is not redetermined when the owner of a Roth IRA dies. Thus, the beneficiary of the Roth IRA would only have to wait until the end of the original five-taxable-year period for the distribution to be a qualified distribution.

d. Distributions used for educational expenses are taxable but not subject to the 10% early withdrawal penalty (see section, "Distributions From Qualified Plans" on page 806), and the HOPE and lifetime learning credits are available to offset the expenses.

e. Any amount distributed from an individual's Roth IRA is treated as made in the following order (determined as of the end of a taxable year and exhausting each category before moving to the following category):

   i. From regular contributions [i.e., the $3,000 (for 2003) annual contributions];

   ii. From conversion contributions, on a first-in-first-out basis; and then

   iii. From earnings.

f. The significance of the distribution ordering is for distributions that are not qualified distributions. In the event of a distribution that is not a qualified distribution, the first layer will be return of basis (or contribution) followed by conversion contributions that have also been included in income (because of the conversion).

g. Taxation of nonqualified distributions from Roth IRAs.

   i. A distribution that is not a qualified distribution, and is neither contributed to another Roth IRA in a qualified rollover contribution nor constitutes a corrective distribution, is includible in the owner's gross income to the extent that the amount of the distribution, when added to the amount of all previous distributions from the owner's Roth IRAs (whether or not they were qualified distributions), exceeds the owner's contributions (both regular contributions and conversion contributions) to all his or her Roth IRAs. Thus, distributions will generally not be taxable to the extent that total distributions do not exceed total contributions and conversions.

   ii. The 10 percent early withdrawal penalty will generally apply to any distribution from a Roth IRA that is includible in gross income. The penalty also applies to a nonqualified distribution, even if it is not includible in gross income, to the extent it is allocable to a conversion contribution, if the distribution is made within the five-taxable-year period beginning with the first day of the individual's taxable year in which the conversion contribution was made. For purposes of applying the penalty, only the amount of the conversion includible for gross income as a result of the conversion is taken into account.

      A) It is important to note that although a nonqualified distribution may be subject to the 10 percent penalty based on the Roth IRA rules, the penalty may be avoided if the distribution falls within one of the exceptions under IRC Section 72(t).

SUMMARY OF NONQUALIFIED ROTH IRA DISTRIBUTIONS		
	Subject to Taxation?	**Subject to 10% Penalty?**
Contributions	No	No
Conversions	No	Yes - within 5 years of conversion*
Earnings	Yes	Yes*

**Penalty does not apply if taxpayer's distribution falls within the standard exceptions to the 10% penalty.*

Example

- Bunny, age 45, converts $20,000 to a Roth IRA in 1998 and $15,000 (in which amount Bunny had a basis of $2,000) to another Roth IRA in 1999. No other contributions are made. In 2003, a $30,000 distribution, that is not a qualified distribution, is made to Bunny. The distribution is treated as made from $20,000 of the 1998 conversion contribution and $10,000 of the 1999 conversion contribution that was includible in gross income. As a result, for 2003, no amount is includible in gross income; however, because $10,000 is allocable to a conversion contribution made within the previous 5 taxable years, that amount is subject to the 10% additional tax under Section 72(t) as if the amount were includible in gross income for 2003, unless an exception applies. The result would be the same whichever of Bunny's Roth IRAs made the distribution.
- Assume the same facts as the previous example, except Bunny is age 60 (instead of age 45). The distribution allocable to the conversion contribution made within the previous 5 taxable years ($10,000) is <u>not</u> subject to the 10% additional tax under Section 72(t). Since Bunny is over age 59 1/2, she will be exempt from the 10% penalty.

h. Minimum distributions do not apply to Roth IRAs while the Roth IRA owner is alive. This is another important distinction from Traditional IRAs.

5. Inherited Roth IRAs.

a. The Roth IRA owner is treated as dying prior to his required beginning date. (See section "Death before required beginning date." on page 817 for a discussion of the distribution requirements after a Roth IRA owner dies).

6. Impact.

a. Young people should definitely maximize contributions to Roth IRAs.

b. Many people should consider the rollover if eligible, especially younger people currently in low tax brackets and expecting to be in higher income tax brackets later.

7. Educational IRAs (Coverdell Education Savings Accounts).

a. General comments.

i. Educational IRAs were renamed to Coverdell Education Savings Accounts (CESAs) in July 2001.

ii. Nondeductible amounts up to $2,000 per beneficiary (under 18) may be contributed to a Coverdell Education Savings Account. Earnings on this account are tax free if distributions from such accounts are used to pay qualified education expenses of an eligible student. Certain higher income taxpayers cannot use these accounts:

Taxpayer Filing Status	AGI Phaseout
Single	$95,000 - 110,000
Married Filing Jointly	$190,000 - 220,000

iii. Balances must be distributed to beneficiary by age 30, if unused. Then, distributions are taxable and subject to 10% penalty. Alternatively, the Coverdell Education Savings Account may be rolled over to a new Coverdell Education Savings Account beneficiary who is a member of the same family.

G. PROHIBITED TRANSACTIONS.

1. Generally, a prohibited transaction is any improper use of an IRA account or annuity by the individual or any disqualified person.
2. Some examples of disqualified persons for this purpose are:
   a. The account fiduciary.
   b. Members of the individual's family (spouse, ancestor, lineal descendant, and any spouse of a lineal descendant).
3. Some examples of prohibited transactions with an IRA are:
   a. Borrowing money from it.
   b. Selling property to it.
   c. Receiving unreasonable compensation for managing it.
   d. Using it as security for a loan.
   e. Buying property for personal use (present or future) with IRA funds.
4. The effect on an IRA account.

   Generally, if an individual or the individual's beneficiary engages in a prohibited transaction with the individual's IRA account at any time during the year, it will not be treated as an IRA as of the first day of the year.
5. The effect on the individual (or beneficiary).
   a. If the individual (or beneficiary) engages in a prohibited transaction in connection with the IRA account at any time during the year, the individual (or beneficiary) must include the fair market value of all (or part, in certain cases) of the IRA assets in gross income for that year. The fair market value is the price at which the IRA assets would change hands between a willing buyer and a willing seller, when neither has any need to buy or sell, and both have reasonable knowledge of the relevant facts.
   b. The individual must use the fair market value of the assets as of the first day of the year engaged in the prohibited transaction. The individual may also have to pay the 10% tax on premature distributions.
6. Borrowing on an annuity contract.

   If an individual borrows money against an IRA annuity contract, the individual must include in gross income the fair market value of the annuity contract as of the first day of the tax year. The individual may also have to pay the 10% additional tax on premature distributions.
7. Pledging an account as security.

   If an individual uses a part of his/her IRA account as security for a loan, that part is treated as a distribution and is included in gross income. The individual may have to pay the 10% additional tax on premature distributions.

H. PROHIBITED INVESTMENTS.

1. Investment in collectibles.

   a. If an individual's IRA invests in collectibles, the amount invested is considered distributed to the individual in the year invested. The individual may also have to pay the 10% tax on premature distributions.

   b. Collectibles include artworks, rugs, antiques, metals, gems, stamps, coins, alcoholic beverages, and certain other tangible personal property.

   c. An exception exists for IRA investments in one, one-half, one-quarter, or one-tenth ounce U.S. gold coins, or one-ounce silver coins minted by the Treasury Department. Starting in 1998, an IRA could also hold certain platinum coins, as well as gold, silver, platinum, and palladium bullion.

I. TRANSFERS INCIDENT TO DIVORCE.

If an interest in an IRA is transferred from a spouse or former spouse (transferor) to an individual (transferee) by reason of divorce or separate maintenance decree or a written document related to such a decree, starting from the date of the transfer, the interest in the IRA is treated as the individual's (transferee's) IRA. The transfer is tax free under IRS Section 1041.

J. SUBJECT TO JUDGMENT CREDITORS.

Whether an IRA account or annuity is subject to alienation by creditors depends on state law; ERISA protection does not apply to IRAs. Therefore, there is not an automatic alienation clause. IRA's may or may not be exempt from seizure under state law. IRAs are not exempt from liens by the IRS.

XI. SIMPLE RETIREMENT PLANS

A. ELIGIBILITY.

1. Employers with 100 or fewer employees on any day during the year who earned at least $5,000 during the preceding year and who do not maintain another employer-sponsored retirement plan (two-year grace period to continue to maintain plan when employees > 100).
2. Employees who earned $5,000 during any two preceding years and are reasonably expected to receive at least $5,000 during the current year are participants.
3. Self-employed person can participate.
4. Employer does not maintain another qualified plan, SEP, SARSEP, or 403(b) plan. However, the employer can maintain a Section 457 plan and still have a SIMPLE.

B. CHARACTERISTICS.

1. Either an IRA or part of a 401(k) CODA.
2. SIMPLE IRAs are not subject to nondiscrimination rules generally applicable to qualified plans (including top-heavy rules).
3. SIMPLE 401(k) plans do not have to meet special ADP tests and are not subject to top-heavy rules. Other qualified plan rules apply.

C. CONTRIBUTIONS.

1. SIMPLE IRA allows employees to make elective contributions as a percentage of compensation up to $8,000 (for 2003).
2. In addition, individuals who have attained age 50 may make additional catch-up contributions. The additional catch-up amount is $1,000 for 2003, $1,500 for 2004, $2,000 for 2005, and $2,500 for 2006 (indexed after 2006). The following table summarizes the allowed salary reduction contributions to a SIMPLE plan in future years:

Year	Maximum Contribution Before Age 50	Maximum Contribution Age 50 or Older
2003	$8,000	$9,000
2004	$9,000	$10,500
2005	$10,000	$12,000
2006	Indexed	Indexed amount plus $2,500

3. An income tax credit is allowed for certain taxpayers with respect to elective contributions to a SIMPLE plan. See section "Income tax credit for elective deferral contributions." on page 773.
4. Employer must make contributions to the SIMPLE based on one of the following options:
   a. Match dollar-for-dollar up to 3% of employee's compensation. Alternatively, employer can match as little as 1% of compensation in no more than 2 out of 5 years; or
   b. Make a 2% of compensation nonelective contribution for each eligible employee.

5. All contributions are fully vested.
6. No more than $200,000 of compensation (for 2003) can be taken into account for purposes of the 2% nonelective contribution.
7. An employee (under age 50) who earns $8,000 in 2003 could have contributions to the SIMPLE of up to $8,240 [$8,000 + (0.03 x $8,000)], more than a SEP or qualified plan.

D. TAX DEDUCTIBILITY.

1. Contributions by employer are deductible if made by due date of tax return (including extensions).
   a. Employee contributions are not subject to payroll tax.
2. Contributions made by employees are excludable from the employee's gross income for income tax purposes.
   a. Employee contributions are subject to payroll tax.

E. SPECIAL RULES FOR SIMPLE PLANS.

1. Withdrawals made within two years of initial participation are subject to a 25% premature distribution penalty tax (rather than 10%). However, certain exceptions to the penalty apply under IRC Section 72(t). See section, ""Distributions From Qualified Plans" on page 806" for a list of exceptions to the early withdrawal penalty.
2. A SIMPLE plan cannot be rolled over into another plan within two years of initial participation.
3. After-tax contributions are not allowed in a SIMPLE plan.

F. 401(k) PLANS (SIMPLE).

1. Employee elective deferrals are limited to $8,000 (for 2003).
2. Employer matches elective deferrals up to 3% of compensation, or alternatively makes a 2% of compensation nonelective contribution on behalf of all eligible employees.
3. Employer contributions are 100% vested.
4. Employer cannot (unlike IRA) reduce matching percentage to below 3%.

XII. TAX-DEFERRED ANNUITY - 403(b) PLANS

A. DESCRIPTION.

1. A tax-deferred annuity plan (also called a TDA plan or Section 403(b) plan) is a tax-deferred employee retirement plan that is adopted only by certain tax-exempt organizations and certain public schools and colleges. Employees have individual accounts in a TDA plan to which employers contribute (or employees contribute through salary reductions).
   a. TDA contributions are not currently taxable to employees.
   b. Account balances accumulate tax free until distribution.
2. TDA plans are very similar to Section 401(k) plans for a tax-exempt organization or public school. In the past, these organizations could not adopt 401(k) plans, so the TDAs provided similar benefits. Today, these organizations are generally permitted to adopt either a 401(k) or 403(b) plan.

B. APPLICATION.

1. The employer organization must be one of the following:
   a. A tax-exempt employer described in Section 501(c)(3) of the Code.
      i. The employer must be organized and operated exclusively for religious, charitable, scientific, testing for public safety, literary, or educational purposes, or to foster national or international amateur sport competition, or for the prevention of cruelty to children or animals.
      ii. The organization must benefit the public rather than a private shareholder or individual.
      iii. The organization must refrain from political campaigning or propaganda intended to influence legislation. Most familiar nonprofit institutions such as churches, hospitals, private schools and colleges, and charitable institutions are eligible to adopt a TDA.
   b. An educational organization with:
      i. A regular faculty and curriculum.
      ii. A resident student body operated by a state or municipal agency. Most public schools and colleges may adopt a TDA plan.
2. A TDA plan is appropriate when:
   a. The employer wants to provide a self-reliant or tax-deferred retirement plan for employees, but can afford only minimal extra expense beyond existing salary and benefit costs. A TDA plan can be funded entirely from employee salary reductions (elective deferrals).
   b. The employee group has one or more of the following characteristics:
      i. Employees want a choice as to the amount or rate of savings (i.e., a choice between various levels of current cash compensation and tax-deferred savings).
      ii. A younger work force often prefers this type of plan because it is similar to a defined-contribution plan.
      iii. Employees are willing to accept the investment risk in their plan accounts.
   c. A qualifying employer wants a savings-type supplement to its existing retirement plans.

C. ADVANTAGES.

1. Provides for a tax-deferred retirement savings opportunity for employees.
2. Salary reduction TDAs allow employees a choice in the amount, or rate of savings that is equal to that of 401(k) plans.
3. In-service withdrawals are generally permitted.

D. DISADVANTAGES.

1. Account balances at retirement age may be insufficient to provide adequate retirement amounts for employees who entered the plan at later ages.
2. Due to nondiscrimination testing, a TDA plan can be relatively costly and complex to administer. Although the ADP test does not apply, 403(b) plans must comply with the ACP test for matching contributions.
3. Employees bear the risk for investments in their individual accounts.
4. Individual stocks and bonds are not permitted as investments in 403(b) plans.

E. FEATURES.

1. The maximum salary reduction contribution is $12,000 for 2003. For tax years after 2001, individuals who have attained age 50 may make additional catch-up contributions. The additional catch-up amount is $2,000 for 2003, $3,000 for 2004, $4,000 for 2005, and $5,000 for 2006 (indexed after 2006). The following table summarizes the allowed salary reduction contributions to a 403(b) plan in years after 2001:

Year	Maximum Contribution Before Age 50	Maximum Contribution Age 50 or Older
2003	$12,000	$14,000
2004	$13,000	$16,000
2005	$14,000	$18,000
2006	$15,000	$20,000
2007	Indexed	Indexed

2. For tax years after 2001, an income tax credit is allowed for certain taxpayers with respect to elective contributions to a 403(b) plan. (See section, "Income tax credit for elective deferral contributions." on page 773.)
3. Plan investments for 403(b) plans are limited to:
   a. Annuity contracts, or
   b. Custodial accounts invested in mutual funds.

4. Catch-up provisions.
   a. There are two provisions that permit employees to increase contributions to a TDA.
   b. One of the two catch-up provisions applies when an employee has completed 15 years of service for the employer and the employer is an eligible organization. Eligible organizations include the following:
      - Educational institutions,
      - Hospitals,
      - Home health service agencies,
      - Churches, and
      - Other religious organizations.
   c. If the above requirements are met, the employee may increase their contribution limit by an amount equal to the lesser of the following:
      - $3,000;
      - $15,000 reduced by amounts previously excluded under this catch-up provision; or
      - $5,000 multiplied by the employee's years of service with the employer minus the sum of all prior salary deferrals.
   d. The second catch-up provision applies to those who have attained the age of 50 by the end of the taxable year as follows:

Year	Catch-up Contribution (for participants age 50 or older)
2003	$2,000
2004	$3,000
2005	$4,000
2006	$5,000
After 2006	Indexed in $500 increments

5. Employer contributions must not discriminate in favor of highly compensated employees. Highly compensated is defined the same as for qualified plans.
6. Only the first $200,000 (for 2003) of each employee's compensation can be used to calculate any contribution formula.
7. A TDA plan is subject to the annual additions limit of IRC Section 415. Annual additions to each participant's account are limited to the lesser of:
   - 100% for 2003.
   - $40,000 for 2003.

8. Salary reductions, but not employer contributions, are subject to FICA (Social Security and Medicare) and federal unemployment (FUTA) payroll taxes.

   a. Plan distributions.

      i. Distributions from TDA plans are subject to the qualified plan distribution rules. Many plans provide for distributions in a lump sum at termination of employment. However, a plan subject to ERISA must either provide for a qualified joint and survivor annuity as its automatic benefit or provide that, if the participant dies, 100% of the participant's nonforfeitable benefit will be paid to the surviving spouse unless the spouse is deceased or has consented to another beneficiary.

      ii. TDA plans can allow participants to make in-service withdrawals, however, in-service withdrawals are not permitted from a TDA custodial account (mutual funds) before:

         A) Attainment of age 59½.

         B) Death, disability, or separation from service.

      iii. All distributions from TDAs are subject to ordinary income tax. In-service distributions from TDAs may also be subject to the 10% early withdrawal penalty tax. See section "Distributions From Qualified Plans" on page 806 for a list of exceptions to the early withdrawal penalty.

      iv. Many TDA plans have loan provisions for participants.

XIII. DISTRIBUTIONS FROM QUALIFIED PLANS AND IRAs

A. DISTRIBUTIONS FROM QUALIFIED PLANS

1. Plan provisions - Required spousal benefits.
2. All qualified plans must provide two forms of survivorship benefits for spouses (except certain profit-sharing plans).
   a. The qualified preretirement survivor annuity.
   b. The qualified joint and survivor annuity.
3. Preretirement survivor annuity - Once a participant is vested, the nonparticipant spouse acquires the right to a preretirement survivor annuity payable to the spouse in the event of the participant's death before retirement. This right is an actual property right created by federal law that can be transferred at death. This is the equivalent of a term life insurance policy with an annuity as the preselected settlement option.
   a. Qualified joint and survivor annuity - A qualified joint and survivor annuity is a post-retirement death benefit for the plan participant's spouse.
   b. Waiver of either joint and survivor annuity (before or at retirement) requires consent in writing by spouse witnessed by notary or official of the plan and is irrevocable.
   c. Most profit-sharing plans, stock bonus plans, ESOPs, and 401(k)s (plans not subject to minimum funding requirements under IRC Section 412) are not required to provide qualified preretirement survivor annuities or qualified joint and survivor annuities if certain requirements are met. These requirements include:
      i. The plan does not pay the participant a life annuity benefit, and
      ii. The participant's nonforfeitable accrued benefit is payable to the surviving spouse upon the participant's death.
4. Plan provisions - Other benefit options.
   a. A qualified plan can offer a wide range of distribution options.
   b. A qualified plan must provide for direct rollovers of certain distributions. Failure to elect a direct rollover (trustee to trustee) will subject the distribution to a mandatory 20% withholding for federal income tax. (Includes lump-sum distributions.)
      i. This rule does not relate to distributions from IRA accounts.
5. Defined-benefit plan distribution provisions.
   a. Defined-benefit plans must provide a married participant with a joint and survivorship annuity as the automatic form of benefit. For an unmarried participant, the plan's automatic form of benefit is usually a single-life annuity.
   b. To elect any option that eliminates the benefit for a married participant's spouse, the spouse must consent on a notarized written form to waive the spousal right to the joint and survivor annuity.

6. Defined-contribution plan distribution provisions.

   Defined-contribution plans include such plans as profit-sharing plans, 401(k), and money-purchase plans. Section 403(b) tax-deferred annuity (TDA) plans also have distribution provisions similar to defined-contribution plans. Some defined-contribution plans provide annuity benefits like those in defined-benefit plans. Money-purchase plans, target-benefit plans, and Section 403(b) tax-deferred annuity plans subject to ERISA must meet the preretirement and joint and survivor annuity rules. (For these purposes, these plans are pension plans as opposed to profit-sharing plans.)

7. Nontaxable and taxable amounts/cost basis.

   Qualified plans may contain after-tax employee contributions (that is, contributions that have already been taxed; e.g., thrift plan). The first step in determining the amount subject to income tax for any plan distribution is to determine the participant's cost basis in the plan benefit. The participant's adjusted taxable cost basis includes:

   a. The total after-tax contributions made by the employee to a contributory plan.

   b. The total cost of life insurance actually reported as taxable income on federal income tax returns by the participant if the plan distributions are received under the same contract that provides the life insurance protection.

8. Taxation of annuity payments.

   a. Amounts distributed, as or from an annuity, are taxable in the year received, except for a proportionate recovery of the adjusted taxable cost basis. The cost basis is recovered as a part of each benefit payment through the calculation of an exclusion ratio and an inclusion ratio applied to each payment to determine the nontaxable and taxable amounts.

> **Note:** The taxation of annuity payments is covered more extensively in the Tax Planning section of this book.

B. LUMP-SUM DISTRIBUTIONS.

1. Lump-sum distributions from a qualified plan may receive special tax treatment. Generally, any distribution from a qualified plan will be taxed as ordinary income (with the exception of basis within the plan) and subject to ordinary income tax rates. However, there are several important exceptions to the standard ordinary income treatment for lump-sum distributions. These exceptions include:

   a. Ten-year forward averaging.

   b. Pre-1974 capital gain treatment.

   c. Treatment of distributions of employer securities (net unrealized appreciation treatment).

2. Lump-sum distribution defined. A lump-sum distribution is a payment or distribution that occurs within one taxable year of the balance of the account or benefit of the participant from a qualified plan. The distribution or payment must meet the following four requirements:

   a. The distribution represents the entire amount of the employee's benefit in the plan.

   b. An election must be made by the participant or, in the case of the participant's death, by his estate within one year of receipt of the distribution. The election is made by attaching Form 4972 to the taxpayer's federal income tax return for the year in which the distribution occurred.

c. The distribution must be due to one of the following:
   - The employee dies,
   - Attains the age of 59½,
   - Separates from service (does not apply to self-employed individuals in the plan), or
   - Becomes disabled.

d. The employee participated in the plan for at least five taxable years prior to the tax year of distribution (a death benefit is exempted from this requirement).

3. Aggregation of plans.
   a. In determining the total distribution, all pension plans maintained by the same employer are treated as a single plan. A profit-sharing plan maintained by the same employer as the pension plan would not be counted as part of the pension plan.
   b. All profit-sharing plans maintained by the employer shall be treated as a single plan.
   c. Similarly, all stock bonus plans maintained by the employer shall be treated as a single plan.

4. Ten-year forward averaging.
   a. A plan participant is eligible to elect the ten-year forward averaging if he or she attained age 50 before January 1, 1986 (i.e., was born before January 1, 1936).
   b. Using the ten-year forward averaging method, the tax on the lump-sum distribution <u>may</u> be lower than the tax would be if the distribution were included in current taxable income and taxed at current ordinary income tax rates.
      i. The concept of averaging is that the income tax for the qualified plan distribution is calculated by determining the tax attributable to an amount equal to one tenth (the distribution is divided by ten) of the total distribution. This amount is then multiplied by ten to determine the total tax due on the distribution.
      ii. The entire amount of the tax on the lump-sum distribution must be paid in the year of the distribution. Ten-year forward averaging does not allow the taxpayer to spread the tax payments over a ten-year period.
      iii. The benefit of ten-year forward averaging is that the taxpayer will avoid the distribution being taxed at higher income tax brackets.
      iv. Ten-year forward averaging is based on 1986 tax rates, not current tax rates.
      v. The tax on the lump-sum distribution may not be lower under the 1986 rates. Consideration must be given to current rates, and the method creating the lowest total tax should be utilized.

c. Ten-year forward averaging calculation:

Calculation of Ten-Year Forward Averaging		
Step 1	**Lump-Sum Distribution**	
Step 2	Less employee's contribution	This includes participant's after-tax contributions to a qualified plan, PS-58 costs (resulting from life insurance within a qualified plan), and certain loans from qualified plans that are treated as taxable distributions.
Step 3	Less minimum distribution allowance	The minimum distribution allowance is an amount equal to the lesser of $10,000 or one-half of the total taxable amount, reduced (not below zero) by 20% of the amount, if any, by which the total taxable amount exceeds $20,000.
Step 4	**Equals taxable amount of distribution**	
Step 5	Divide taxable amount by 10	
Step 6	Determine tax on result of Step 5	Tax is calculated by using 1986 income tax rates.
Step 7	Multiply result of Step 6 by 10	Result is tax attributable to distribution.

Example

Ann has received a distribution of $50,000 from her qualified plan (she had not made contributions to the plan). If she elected ten-year forward averaging, the tax would be calculated as follows:

Lump-sum distribution	$50,000	
Less minimum distribution allowance	(4,000)	[$10,000 - 6,000 [($50,000 - 20,000) x 20%]]
Taxable portion of distribution	$46,000	
One tenth of taxable portion	$4,600	
Tax on one tenth	$690	Assumed 15% 1986 tax bracket
Tax due on distribution ($690 x 10)	$6,900	Ten times the amount previously calculated

5. Pre-1974 capital gain treatment.

   a. Participants born prior to January 1, 1936, are also eligible to treat the portion of a lump-sum distribution attributable to pre-1974 participation in a qualified plan as a capital gain, subject to tax at a 20% capital gain rate. If a lump-sum distribution is received by a taxpayer who ceased participating in a qualified plan before 1974, then the entire distribution will be eligible for capital gains treatment. However, if participation continued beyond 1973, there will be an ordinary income portion and a capital gains portion.

b. The capital gains portion is determined as follows:

$$\text{Capital gains portion} = \frac{\text{Months of pre-1974 participation}}{\text{Total months of participation}} \times \text{Taxable distribution}$$

c. The portion remaining is eligible for ten-year forward averaging.

6. Net Unrealized Appreciation (NUA).

a. Lump-sum distributions that consist entirely, or in part, as employer securities receive special tax treatment. The portion of the distribution that is considered NUA is not taxed upon distribution and will only be taxed upon the disposition of the securities. The disposition of the securities will result in capital gain, as opposed to ordinary income.

b. Net unrealized appreciation defined.

i. Net unrealized appreciation is defined as the excess of the market value of the employer securities distributed over the cost or basis of the securities to the trust. The cost or basis of the securities to the trust is generally the total value of the securities at the time of the contribution.

ii. The cost or basis of the securities is taxed as ordinary income in the year of distribution. However, this amount is eligible for ten-year forward averaging if the participant was born prior to January 1, 1936.

iii. The NUA will be treated as long-term capital gain. Any subsequent appreciation after the distribution of employer securities will be treated as long-term or short-term capital gain, depending on holding period since distribution.

Example

- Brisco received a lump-sum distribution of stock (10,000 shares) from his employer's qualified plan valued at $1,000,000. The value of the stock contributed over the years was $250,000 (basis to the trust).
- In this example, $750,000 is treated as net unrealized appreciation and is not taxed upon distribution. $250,000 will be taxable as ordinary income in the year of the lump-sum distribution.
- Because $250,000 was treated as ordinary income, Brisco's adjusted taxable basis in the 10,000 shares equals $250,000. If Brisco sells shares of stock, his adjusted taxable basis for tax purposes will equal $25 per share and any gain will be subject to capital gains tax.

c. Employer securities generally include stock of the employer corporation, but may also include bonds or debentures of the employer. Securities of a parent or subsidiary may also qualify as employer securities for NUA treatment.

d. Inherited stock distributed from a qualified plan.

i. In the event that stock that is attributable to a distribution from a qualified plan is inherited, the portion that is treated as NUA will be treated as income in respect of a decedent (i.e., the beneficiary will not receive a step up in basis with respect to the NUA). As a result, the basis of the stock to the beneficiary will be equal to the value at the date of death less the amount that is treated as NUA.

Example

- Brisco received a lump-sum distribution of stock (10,000 shares) from his employer's qualified plan valued at $1,000,000. The value of the stock contributed over the years totaled to $250,000 (basis to the trust). Brisco dies with the value of the stock equal to $2,000,000.
- The adjusted taxable basis to his beneficiary will equal $1,250,000 ($2,000,000 less the NUA of $750,000).

C. QUALIFIED DOMESTIC RELATIONS ORDERS (QDROs).

1. In general, a qualified plan benefit cannot be assigned or alienated by a participant, voluntarily or involuntarily. This rule protects the participant's retirement fund from attachment by creditors. An exception to this rule applies to claims of spouses and dependents in domestic relations situations.
2. The exception permits an assignment of a qualified plan benefit under a Qualified Domestic Relations Order (QDRO) as defined in Code Section 414(p). A QDRO is a decree, order, or property settlement under state law relating to child support, alimony, or marital property rights that assigns part or all of a participant's plan benefits to a spouse, former spouse, child, or other dependent of the participant.
3. Distributions made to an alternate payee pursuant to a QDRO will not be subject to the 10 percent early withdrawal penalty.
4. Other taxed-advantaged plans.
   i. IRAs, SEPs, and 403(b) plans are not qualified plans and, therefore, do not have the same protection from creditors. Only qualified plan assets are protected from creditors because they are protected under ERISA. However, some states now protect IRAs and SEPs from creditor alienation.

D. RETIREMENT PLAN ROLLOVERS.

1. Tax-free rollovers of distributions from qualified plans, IRAs and SEPs, and Section 403(b) tax-deferred annuity plans are specifically allowed by the Internal Revenue Code.
2. If the rollover is made within 60 days of receipt of the distribution and follows IRS rules, the tax on the distribution is deferred. However, eligible rollover distributions from qualified plans and Section 403(b)tax-deferred annuities are subject to mandatory withholding at 20%, unless the rollover is effected by means of a direct (trustee to trustee) rollover. (The 20% mandatory withholding is not applicable to IRAs or SEPs.)

E. IRA ROLLOVERS.

1. Rollovers in general.
   a. As an alternative to paying tax on a qualified plan distribution, individuals are able to defer taxation by rolling all or a portion of the distribution into an IRA or another qualified plan within 60 days of the receipt of the distribution. Once in the IRA, the benefits are not subject to income tax until they are withdrawn from the account. They do, however, lose ERISA alienation protection and the ability to elect ten-year forward averaging, pre-1974 capital gain treatment, and net unrealized appreciation treatment.

b. The opportunity for ten-year forward averaging, pre-1974 capital gain treatment, and net unrealized appreciation does not exist for a distribution from an IRA.

c. Recipients of a qualifying distribution can generally roll the benefit into another qualified plan. Distributions rolled into an IRA Rollover Account can subsequently be rolled into another qualified plan. An IRA Rollover Account maintains the integrity or character of the qualified plan distribution. If qualified funds and nonqualified funds are commingled, rollover into another qualified plan is generally not permitted.

d. Eligible rollover distributions from qualified retirement plans, section 403(b) plans, and governmental Section 457 plans generally can be rolled over to any of such plans or arrangements. Similarly, distributions from an IRA are generally permitted to be rolled over into a qualified plan, Section 403(b) plans, or governmental Section 457 plan.

2. Eligible rollover distributions.

a. Generally, eligible rollover distributions are all distributions from qualified plans or tax-sheltered annuities, except:

i. Any distribution that is one of a series of substantially equal periodic payments (not less frequently than annually) made for the life of the employee, or the joint lives of the employee and the employee's designated beneficiary, or for a period of 10 years or more, and

ii. Required distributions at age 70½.

b. Plans are required to provide participants with the option to have eligible rollover distributions transferred directly to another plan or IRA. Plans are not required to accept rollover contributions. Direct transfers of distributions are distributions for purposes of the Retirement Protection Act (RPA). The necessary spousal waivers must be secured in advance of the distribution. Distributions not transferred directly to another qualified plan or IRA are subject to a mandatory 20% withholding requirement. Plans are required to provide participants with a written explanation of the direct transfer option, the mandatory withholding rule, and other rules relating to the taxation of the distribution.

F. EARLY DISTRIBUTION PENALTY

1. Description.

a. Generally, distributions taken from qualified plans, 403(b) plans, and IRAs before the owner attains age 59½ are subject to an early distribution penalty.

b. The early distributions penalty is applied to the taxable portion of the distribution. If the distribution includes after-tax (nondeductible) contributions, the after-tax portion will not be subject to the penalty.

Example

Elaine, age 40, withdrew the entire balance of $10,000 from her Traditional IRA to fund a vacation. Three years ago, she opened the IRA with a nondeductible contribution of $2,000, which represents the only contribution she made to the IRA. Her taxable distribution is $8,000 ($10,000 - $2,000 basis), resulting in an early distribution penalty of $800 ($8,000 x 10%). Elaine would also be required to pay ordinary income tax on the distribution.

c. For SIMPLE plans, the penalty is 25% for distributions occurring within the first two years of initial participation in the plan. After the first two years, the penalty for a SIMPLE reverts to a 10% penalty.

2. Exceptions to the early distribution penalty - the penalty must be paid unless the plan owner qualifies for one of the exceptions.

   a. Exceptions for all qualified plans, 403(b) plans, and IRAs – The early withdrawal penalty will not apply to distributions:

      i. Made on or after the attainment of age 59½.

      ii. Made to the owner's beneficiary or estate on or after the owner's death.

      iii. Attributable to the owner's disability.

      iv. That are part of a series of substantially equal periodic payments (SEPP) made at least annually over the life or life expectancy of the owner, or the owner and a designated beneficiary.

         A) In the case of a qualified plan or 403(b) plan, the participant must separate from service before taking substantially equal periodic payments.

         B) Substantially equal payments must continue for the greater of five years or until age 59½.

         C) There are three methods for calculating substantially equal payments. These include:

            1) IRC Section 401(a)(9) method – distributions are made over remaining life expectancy.

            2) Amortization method – amortize the participant's account balance over a period of time equal to the life expectancy of the participant (or joint life expectancy with beneficiary). Interest rate must be a reasonable rate of interest on the date the payments begin.

            3) Annuity method – the participant's account can be divided by an annuity factor to determine a payment. A reasonable interest rate and a reasonable mortality table must be used in the calculation of the payment.

      v. Made for medical expenses exceeding 7.5% of the owner's adjusted gross income. The owner is not required to itemize deductions on his or her tax return to take advantage of the exception.

   b. Exceptions for all qualified plans and 403(b) plans (these exceptions do not apply to IRAs). The early withdrawal penalty will not apply to distributions:

      i. Made after separation from service after attainment of age 55.

      ii. Made to a qualifying family member under a Qualified Domestic Relations Order (QDRO).

   c. Exceptions for IRAs only (these exceptions do not apply to qualified plans or 403(b) plans). The early withdrawal penalty will not apply to:

      i. Distributions for higher education costs for the taxpayer, spouse, child, or grandchild.

      ii. Distributions to pay certain acquisition costs of a first-time home buyer, up to a $10,000 lifetime maximum. A first-time home buyer is someone who has had no interest in a principal residence during the two years ending on the date of purchase of the new home. The home buyer can be the IRA owner, spouse, child, or grandchild.

      iii. Distributions to pay health insurance premiums for unemployed individuals.

G. ROLLOVERS.

1. IRAs can be used to receive a rollover of certain distributions from employer-sponsored retirement plans.
2. Eligible rollover distributions must be either transferred to the IRA via a direct rollover or a transfer by the participant.
   a. A direct rollover is an eligible rollover distribution that is paid directly to a rollover IRA for the benefit of the participant. A direct rollover usually involves a wire transfer or a check that is negotiable only by the custodian of the IRA. Transfers to an IRA through a direct rollover are not subject to a mandatory withholding of 20%.
   b. If the participant receives a distribution check payable to the participant, this is not considered a direct rollover. In this situation, the participant must complete the rollover within 60 days after the check is received. Also, the check received may be subject to a mandatory withholding of 20%.
3. Loans from a rollover IRA are not permitted.
4. Distributions from a rollover IRA do not qualify for ten-year forward averaging on lump-sum distributions.
5. An IRA can be used as a conduit between two 403(b) plans.
6. For distributions after 2001, the following rules will apply to rollovers:
   a. Rollovers are allowed among qualified plans, 403(b) plans, and Section 457 plans.
   b. Distributions from an IRA generally are permitted to be rolled over into qualified plans, 403(b) plans, and Section 457 plans.
   c. Employee after-tax contributions may be rolled over into another qualified plan or Traditional IRA.
      i. In the case of a rollover of after-tax contributions from one qualified plan to another qualified plan, the rollover can only be accomplished through a direct rollover.
      ii. A qualified plan is not permitted to accept rollovers of after-tax contributions unless the plan provides separate accounting for such contributions and earnings.
      iii. After-tax contributions are not permitted to be rolled over from an IRA into a qualified plan, 403(b) plan, or Section 457 plan.

H. MINIMUM DISTRIBUTIONS

1. Minimum Required Distributions.
   a. Participants in qualified plans, 403(b) plans, and owners of IRAs are required to take distributions from their plans.
   b. After distributions are required to begin (Required Beginning Date), if sufficient amounts are not withdrawn, a 50% excise tax will apply to any shortfall.

Example

Anne Smith, age 75, began taking required minimum distributions from her IRA several years ago. In the current year, her required minimum distribution is $5,000. If Anne only withdraws $4,000 from the IRA this year, she will have a minimum distribution penalty of $500 ($5,000 - $4,000 = $1,000 shortfall x 50% = $500 penalty).

c. Minimum required distributions do not apply to Roth IRAs while the Roth IRA owner is alive.

2. Required beginning date.
   a. Generally, the first distribution must be made by April 1 of the year after the year age 70½ is attained. In subsequent years, the distribution must be made by December 31.
   b. The participant must determine the minimum amount required to be distributed each year. The participant can always withdraw more than the required minimum distribution.
   c. If the first distribution is delayed to April 1 following the year that the person reaches age 70½, there must be two distributions in that calendar year (the second distribution must occur before 12/31).
   d. Participants in qualified plans and 403(b) plans can defer the required beginning date until April 1 following the year of retirement, if the participant continues to work after attaining age 70½. This deferral option is:
      i. Not available for IRAs.
      ii. Not available if the participant owns 5% or more of the business sponsoring the retirement plan. Therefore, not available for self-employed individuals.
      iii. Only available for the employer's plan.

Example

If an employee is working for XYZ company, but has a 401(k) from ABC company, a former employer, the deferral of the required beginning date is only available for the 401(k) of XYZ company.

3. Determining the minimum distribution amount.
   a. The minimum required distribution (MRD) is determined each year by dividing the account balance (as of the close of business on December 31st of the preceding year) by the distribution period.
   b. The distribution period is determined by looking up the participant's age, as of December 31st of the distribution year, in the uniform distribution table. (See Appendix 2: Uniform Distribution Table). The beneficiary's age is ignored when determining the distribution period (see exception below).

Example

Joe attained the age of 70½ in March 2003. Since Joe will be 71 years old on December 31, 2003, his distribution period is 26.5 years. If his IRA balance is $500,000 on December 31, 2002, (remember, use prior year's account balance), his required minimum distribution will be $18,868 ($500,000 ÷ 26.5). He must take this distribution from his IRA by April 1, 2004.

c. The uniform distribution table is always used to calculate the minimum distribution, with one exception. If the participant's designated beneficiary is the participant's spouse, and the spouse is more than 10 years younger than the participant, then actual joint life expectancies are used to calculate minimum distributions. This will result in a longer life expectancy and a smaller minimum distribution.

Example

Scott has an IRA with a balance of $300,000, and he has named his spouse, Shania, as the beneficiary. On December 31, 2003, Scott will be 71 years old and Shania will be 51 years old. Since the beneficiary is the spouse and she is more than 10 years younger, Scott will use actual joint life expectancy to determine the required minimum distribution for 2003. Their joint life expectancy is 34.2 years, resulting in a required minimum distribution of $8,772 ($300,000 ÷ 34.2). This amount must be withdrawn from the account by April 1, 2004.

Note: Under the uniform distribution table, the distribution period would have been 26.5, resulting in a required minimum distribution of $11,321.

4. Subsequent Year Distributions.

   a. To determine the required minimum distribution after the first distribution year (the year the owner attains age 70½), reduce the account balance as of December 31 of the first year by any distribution for the first year made after December 31 of the current year.

   b. No adjustment is necessary if the final distribution is received by December 31 of the year in which the participant attains the age of 70½.

Example

Joe attains the age of 70½ in March 2002. His wife, the designated beneficiary of his IRA, turned age 63 in September of 2002. Joe's IRA account balance was $30,000 on December 31, 2001. Since Joe's spouse is less than 10 years younger than Joe, the uniform distribution table is used to determine the distribution period of 25.3 years. The required minimum distribution for 2002, the first distribution year, is $1,186 ($30,000 divided by 25.3).

   c. This amount must be distributed to Joe by April 1, 2003.

   d. Assume Joe's account balance as of December 31, 2002 is $32,000. To figure the minimum amount that must be distributed for 2003, the IRA account balance of $32,000 must be reduced by the $1,186 required minimum distribution for 2002 that was made on April 1, 2003. Therefore, the account balance used to determine the required distribution for 2003 is $30,814 ($32,000 - $1,186), resulting in a required minimum distribution of $1,263 ($30,814 divided by 24.4, the distribution period for a 72-year old). This distribution must be made by December 31, 2003. Therefore, under this scenario, Joe will be taking two distributions in the 2003 calendar year (April 1 and December 31).

   e. The reduction of the account balance by the first year's minimum distribution only occurs in the second year and will occur only if the first distribution is deferred until after December 31 of the year in which the participant attained age 70½.

I. DISTRIBUTIONS AFTER DEATH.

1. Determination of designated beneficiary.
   a. The designated beneficiary is determined as of the end of the year (December 31) following the year of the participant's death.
   b. Plans may disregard any beneficiary eliminated by disclaimer or distribution of the benefit during the period between the participant's death and December 31 of the following year.
   c. If there is more than one designated beneficiary, the beneficiary with the shortest life expectancy is used as the measuring life. However, the plan may be divided into separate accounts, with each account using the life expectancy of the respective beneficiary.
   d. If a trust is named as beneficiary, the beneficiaries of the trust will be treated as designated beneficiaries as long as:
      i. The trust is valid under state law,
      ii. The trust is irrevocable or will become so upon the participant's death,
      iii. The beneficiaries of the trust are identifiable from the trust instrument, and
      iv. Appropriate documentation has been provided to the plan administrator.
2. Death before required beginning date.
   a. Spouse beneficiary – If the surviving spouse is the beneficiary of the plan:
      i. The surviving spouse can receive distributions over his or her remaining single-life expectancy, recalculated each year. Distributions must begin in the year in which the owner would have attained age 70½.
      ii. The surviving spouse can roll the plan balance over, and wait until he or she attains age 70½ to begin taking minimum distributions. This election may only be made if the surviving spouse is the sole beneficiary.
      iii. The surviving spouse can elect to distribute the entire account balance within five years after the year of the owner's death (5-year rule). This election can only be made if the plan provisions allow the 5-year rule.
   b. Nonspouse beneficiary – If the beneficiary is someone other than the surviving spouse:
      i. The distribution period is the remaining life expectancy of the designated beneficiary. Life expectancy is calculated using the age of the designated beneficiary in the year following the year of the employee's death, reduced by one for each subsequent year.
      ii. The beneficiary can elect to distribute the entire account balance within five years after the year of the owner's death (5-year rule). This election can only be made if the plan provisions allow the 5-year rule.
   c. No beneficiary – If no beneficiary has been named by December 31 of the year following the owner's death (or the beneficiary is the decedent's estate or charity):
      i. The account must be fully distributed before the end of the fifth year following the year of death.

3. Death after required beginning date.

   a. Spouse beneficiary – If the surviving spouse is the beneficiary of the plan:

      i. The surviving spouse can receive distributions over his or her remaining single-life expectancy, recalculated each year. Distributions must begin in the year following the year of death.

      ii. The surviving spouse can rollover the plan balance, and wait until he or she attains age 70½ to begin taking minimum distributions. This election may only be made if the surviving spouse is the sole beneficiary.

   b. Nonspouse beneficiary – If the beneficiary is someone other than the surviving spouse:

      i. The distribution period is the remaining life expectancy of the designated beneficiary. Life expectancy is calculated using the age of the designated beneficiary in the year following the year of the employee's death, reduced by one for each subsequent year.

   c. No beneficiary – If no beneficiary has been named by December 31 of the year following the owner's death (or the beneficiary is the decedent's estate or charity):

      i. Distributions must continue over the remaining distribution period of the deceased owner. The distribution period is reduced by one each year (do not use the uniform distribution table).

4. Summary of distributions after death.

Beneficiary	Death Before Required Beginning Date	Death After Required Beginning Date
No designated beneficiary (includes charity, decedent's estate, and trusts with no designated beneficiary)	5-Year Rule	Remaining distribution period of decedent, reduced by one each year.
Nonspouse beneficiary	1) Remaining life expectancy of the beneficiary in the year following the year of death, reduced by one for each subsequent year, or 2) Elect 5-Year Rule, if plan provisions allow.	Remaining life expectancy of the beneficiary in the year following the year of death, reduced by one for each subsequent year.
Spouse beneficiary	1) Distributions over spouse's remaining single life expectancy, beginning in the year the decedent would have attained age 70½, or 2) Roll over and treat as spouse's own, or 3) Elect 5-Year Rule, if plan provisions allow.	1) Distributions over spouse's remaining single life expectancy, beginning in the year following the year of death, or 2) Roll over and treat as spouse's own.

XIV. CHOOSING A RETIREMENT PLAN

A. ESTABLISH OBJECTIVES FOR THE PLAN.

Example objectives.

1. To benefit all employees.
2. To benefit select employees (consider nonqualified plans).
3. To attract, retain, or retire workers.
4. As a tax-advantage tool.

B. IDENTIFY THE TYPES OF PLANS THAT CAN MEET THE OBJECTIVES.

1. Prepare an employee census to forecast the financial impact of alternative plans.
2. Assess each plan's financial characteristics:
    a. Contribution costs.
    b. Costs of administration.
    c. Flexibility of contribution.
    d. Burden of investment risk.
    e. Risk of benefit amounts.
    f. Company profits and stability of cash flows.

C. EVALUATE INITIAL LIST OF PLANS FOR FINANCIAL FEASIBILITY.

D. FORECAST COSTS AND BENEFITS FOR THE FORESEEABLE FUTURE FOR EACH DIFFERENT PLAN.

E. SELECT THE APPROPRIATE PLAN.

Example 1

Assume Brewster owns a small company with the following census information:

Employee	Age	Total Compensation	Covered Compensation
Brewster	30	$180,000	$180,000
Jack	30	$20,000	$20,000
Patty	35	$20,000	$20,000
John	30	$20,000	$20,000
Totals		**$240,000**	**$240,000**

What type of retirement plan would you recommend assuming Brewster has the ability to fund?

A SEP or profit-sharing plan would certainly be appropriate, depending on other objectives, such as vesting, participation, etc. Either plan could be integrated with Social Security.

Either a pension plan or a profit-sharing plan would allow a contribution of up to 25% of covered compensation.

How would your recommendation change if Brewster were age 55?

Because Brewster is significantly older than the rest of the employees, an age-weighted (cross-tested) type plan may be appropriate. Alternatively, a defined-benefit plan would allow higher contributions for Brewster compared with the remaining employees.

How would the inclusion of a 401(k) feature impact the plan recommendation?

In the case of a 401(k), Brewster would need to have a profit-sharing or stock bonus plan. The 401(k) would allow the employee deferrals on top of the 25% plan limit.

Example 2

Assume Brewster and Jack own a small company with the following census information:

Employee	Age	Compensation
Brewster	55	$180,000
Jack	30	$160,000
Patty	35	$20,000
John	30	$20,000

How does the age difference between the owners of the business impact the retirement plan selection?

Because one owner is older and one owner is younger, an age-weighted plan will provide greater benefits to Brewster over Jack.

However, using a profit-sharing plan or a money-purchase pension plan, both owners could contribute up to $40,000 (limitation for 2003). In addition, a defined-benefit plan could also be added to provide higher benefits.

They could also use a new comparability plan with one of the classes as "owners."

Example 3

ABC company would like to start a retirement plan with the following objectives:

- Attract and retain employees.
- Allow the employer to make all initial contributions to the plan using company stock.
- Allow integration with Social Security.

What plan would be appropriate for ABC Company?

A profit-sharing or stock bonus plan would be an appropriate plan.

A profit-sharing plan or stock bonus plan will allow contributions of company stock and allows integration of Social Security.

What plans would not be appropriate for the company?

A pension plan would not be appropriate because it does not permit more than 10% of plan assets to be invested in employer securities.

An ESOP would not be appropriate because it cannot be integrated with Social Security.

SEPs and SIMPLEs would not be appropriate because contributions must be made in cash.

Example 4

Charlie Clines is a 30-year-old CPA with his own tax practice. For most of the year, he works by himself, preparing and reviewing income tax returns. For the last four years, he has hired three part-time employees to assist him during busy season. Each of these employees works approximately 200 hours, earning an average salary of $3,000. Charlie would like to establish a retirement plan that would allow him to save for his retirement without the administrative costs of a qualified plan.

What would be an appropriate retirement plan for Charlie?

A SIMPLE IRA would be an appropriate plan because it involves very little administrative costs, and would allow Charlie to exclude the part-time employees. To be eligible for a SIMPLE, an employee must have earned at least $5,000 in compensation from the employer in any two prior years and expect to earn at least $5,000 in compensation in the current year.

What plans would not be appropriate for Charlie?

A SEP would not be appropriate because all of Charlie's part-time employees would be eligible to receive a contribution to the SEP. An employee is eligible for a SEP if he or she has attained age 21 and has worked at least one hour for the employer for three of the last five years. Charlie could not exclude any of his part-time employees from the SEP.

A qualified plan would be inappropriate because Charlie does not want to incur the costs of a qualified plan.

Example 5

Lauren Falke, age 36, is the sole shareholder of Old Economy, an S corporation. She earns a salary of $45,000 from her company, and she has two employees with average compensation of $20,000. She wants to establish a retirement plan that will accomplish the following objectives:

- Allow the employees to save for their retirement (self-reliance).
- Allow the employees to borrow from the plan in case of financial hardship (loans).
- Allow the employees to withdraw funds from the plan while still with the company (in-service withdrawals).
- Allow for flexible employer contributions to the plan (discretionary contributions).

What would be an appropriate plan for Lauren?

A 401(k) plan would probably be the most appropriate plan.

The 401(k) plan would meet all of her objectives, especially self-reliance.

What would not be an appropriate plan for Lauren?

A pension plan would not be appropriate because pensions are generally completely employer-funded plans and because pension plans have mandatory funding. The pension plan would also not allow loans or in-service withdrawals.

A SEP or SIMPLE IRA would not be appropriate because these plans do not allow loans.

XV. SECTION 457 PLANS

A. DESCRIPTION.

1. A Section 457 plan is a deferred compensation plan of governmental units, governmental agencies, and nonchurch controlled, tax-exempt organizations.
2. A Section 457 plan is not a qualified plan.

B. CHARACTERISTICS - CONTRIBUTIONS.

1. The amount deferred annually by an employee under a Section 457 plan cannot exceed the lesser of $12,000 (for 2003) or 100% (for 2003) of the employee's compensation currently includible in gross income.
2. In addition, individuals who have attained age 50 may make additional catch-up contributions. The additional catch-up amount is $2,000 for 2003, $3,000 for 2004, $4,000 for 2005, and $5,000 for 2006 (indexed after 2006). The following table summarizes the maximum contributions to a 457 plan:

Year	Maximum Contribution Before Age 50	Maximum Contribution Age 50 or Older
2003	$12,000	$14,000
2004	$13,000	$16,000
2005	$14,000	$18,000
2006	$15,000	$20,000
2007	Indexed	Indexed

3. The contribution limit is doubled in the three years prior to an individual's retirement. During this three-year period (before retirement), the catch-up rule does not apply.
4. An income tax credit is allowed for certain taxpayers with respect to elective contributions to a Section 457 plan. See section, "Income tax credit for elective deferral contributions." on page 773.

C. SALARY REDUCTION ELECTIONS.

1. Employee elections to defer compensation monthly under Section 457 must be made under an agreement entered into prior to earning the compensation.

D. DISTRIBUTION REQUIREMENTS.

1. Plan distributions cannot be made before one of the following:
   a. The calendar year in which the participant attains age 70½.
   b. Separation from service.
   c. An unforeseeable emergency as defined in regulations.
   d. In-service withdrawals are allowed for accounts ≤ $3,500.
2. Distributions must begin no later than April 1st of the calendar year after the year in which the plan participant attains age 70½. Minimum distributions must be made under the rules of Code Section 401(a)(9).

XVI.NONQUALIFED PLANS

A. GENERAL.

1. Nonqualified plans are deferred compensation arrangements not meeting IRC Section 401 requirements. They are used to benefit key employees beyond the qualified plan 415 limit.
2. Types of nonqualified plans.
   a. Nonqualified deferred compensation plans.
   b. Supplemental Executive Retirement Plans (SERPs).
   c. Insurance – split-dollar plans.
   d. Stock options – NQSOs and ISOs.
   e. Employee Stock Purchase Plans (ESPPs).
   f. Phantom stock.
   g. Loans.
3. Advantages of nonqualified plans.
   a. They do not have to meet nondiscrimination requirements of qualified plans.
   b. The benefits and contributions can exceed IRS Section 415 limits.
   c. They are not subject to the same ERISA requirements as qualified plans.
4. Taxation and economic arrangement.
   a. Generally, just a promise to pay from the employer.
   b. There must be a substantial risk of forfeiture (i.e., subject to the classes of general creditors); otherwise, there will be constructive receipt and, therefore, taxable income to the participant.
   c. Not deductible by the employer until paid.
   d. Includible by the employee at the time of receipt.
   e. Generally, there are no deferrals, rollovers, or averaging.

B. NONQUALIFIED DEFERRED COMPENSATION PLANS.

1. A nonqualified deferred compensation plan is any employer retirement, savings, or deferred compensation plan for employees that does not meet the tax and labor law (ERISA) requirements applicable to qualified pension and profit-sharing plans.
2. Application.
   a. A nonqualified deferred compensation plan is appropriate when an employer wants to provide a deferred compensation benefit to an executive or group of executives, but the cost of a qualified plan would be prohibitive because of the large number of nonexecutive employees who would need to be covered.
   b. A nonqualified deferred compensation plan is appropriate when an employer wants to provide additional deferred compensation benefits to an executive who is already receiving the maximum benefits or contributions under the company's qualified retirement plan.

c. A nonqualified deferred compensation plan is appropriate when the business wants to provide certain key employees with tax-deferred compensation under terms or conditions different from those applicable to other employees.

d. A nonqualified deferred compensation plan is appropriate when an executive or key employee wants to use the employer to, in essence, create a forced, automatic investment program that uses the employer's tax savings to leverage the future benefits.

e. A nonqualified deferred compensation plan is appropriate when an employer needs to recruit, retain, reward, or retire.

f. A nonqualified, deferred compensation plan is appropriate when a closely held corporation wants something to attract and hold nonshareholder employees.

3. Advantages.

   a. The design of nonqualified plans is much more flexible than that of qualified plans:

      i. Allows coverage of any group of employees or even a single employee, without any nondiscrimination requirements. Generally, nonqualified plans benefit key executives.

      ii. Can provide an unlimited benefit to any one employee (subject to the reasonable compensation requirement for deductibility).

      iii. Allows the employer to provide different benefit amounts for different employees, on different terms and conditions.

   b. A nonqualified plan involves minimal IRS, ERISA, and other governmental regulatory requirements, such as reporting and disclosure, fiduciary, and funding requirements.

   c. A nonqualified plan can provide deferral of taxes to employees (but the employer's deduction is also deferred).

   d. A nonqualified plan can be used by an employer as a form of golden handcuffs that help to bind the employee to the company.

   e. Although the plan generally involves only the employer's unsecured promise to pay benefits, security to the executive can be provided through informal financing arrangements such as a corporate-owned life insurance policy or a rabbi trust arrangement.

4. Disadvantages.

   a. The company's tax deduction is generally not available for the year that compensation is earned. It is deferred until the year that the income is taxable to the employee.

   b. From the executive's point of view, the principal problem with deferred compensation plans is the lack of security as a result of depending solely on the company's unsecured promise to pay.

   c. Disclosure of executive nonqualified plans in financial statements may be required.

   d. Not all employers are equally well suited to take advantage of nonqualified plans.

      i. S corporations and partnerships cannot take full advantage of nonqualified plans.

      ii. The employer must be one that is likely to continue in existence long enough to make the payments promised under the plan.

5. Tax issues.

   a. Constructive receipt and substantial risk of forfeiture.

      i. Constructive receipt.

         A) Occurs within a nonqualified plan if the executive has access to funds or if the funds are securely set aside for the executive.

         B) The funds that are deemed to be constructively received are required to be reported as taxable income by the executive, defeating the primary tax advantage of nonqualified deferred compensation, which is tax deferral.

      ii. Substantial risk of forfeiture.

         A) If there exists a substantial risk of forfeiture, then the deferred compensation will not be treated as constructively received. Thus, no current taxable income.

         B) What qualifies as substantial risk of forfeiture?

            1) An unsecured promise to pay qualifies since there is no certainty that the executive will receive the deferred compensation.

            2) A rabbi trust qualifies because the funds set aside for the executive may be used for the purpose of satisfying creditors of the employer in the event of bankruptcy/liquidation.

            3) A secular trust will ***not*** qualify because the funds are secured for the benefit of the employee – there is no risk.

   b. Plan funding.

      i. Nonqualified plans may be funded or unfunded.

      ii. If the plan is funded, then the executive is taxed on the funds in the plan at the time the funds are contributed or at the time the executive becomes vested. Because the tax implications of a funded plan are inconsistent with the objective of nonqualified plans, most are unfunded.

      iii. Since an unfunded promise to pay has an element of risk, there is no current taxation to the executive. Similarly, there is risk involved in a rabbi trust, resulting in it not being taxable.

   c. Employer's deduction for deferred compensation.

      i. The deductibility of contributions, payments, or funding for deferred compensation plans is relatively straightforward.

      ii. The deduction for the employer will follow the inclusion of income by the executive. Therefore, when the funds are constructively received and included in taxable income for the executive, the employer will then receive a deduction.

6. Plan design.

   a. Types of benefit and contribution formulas.

      i. Nonqualified deferred compensation plans generally use either a salary continuation or salary reduction approach:

         A) The salary continuation approach provides a specified deferred amount payable in the future without any stated reduction of current salary.

         B) The salary reduction design provides for the deferral of a specified amount of the employee's compensation, otherwise currently payable.

      ii. Corporate-owned life insurance.

         Insurance policies can be purchased on the employee's life, owned by and payable to the employer to fund the obligation under nonqualified deferred compensation plans. These funds provide for benefits in the event of death before retirement (see Split-Dollar Life Insurance).

      iii. Rabbi trust.

         A) A trust set up to hold property used for financing a deferred compensation plan where the funds set aside are subject to the claims of the employer's general creditors.

         B) Other than general creditor claims, the funds are secure.

         C) As discussed above, the risk of forfeiture is considered "substantial." Thus, there is no current taxation for the executive. Taxation occurs when payments are received from the rabbi trust.

SUMMARY OF DEFERRED COMPENSATION FUNDING METHODS			
	Promise to Pay	**Rabbi Trust**	**Secular Trust**
Funds are set aside?	No	Yes	Yes
Security against employer's unwillingness to pay?	No	Yes	Yes
Security against employer bankruptcy?	No	No	Yes
Provides tax deferral for employee?	Yes	Yes	No
Provides employer with current tax deduction?	No	No	Yes

C. SUPPLEMENTAL EXECUTIVE RETIREMENT PLAN (SERP).

1. Description.

   a. A SERP is a nonqualified deferred compensation plan that focuses on providing adequate retirement income to executives.

   b. Can complement existing retirement plans to bring executive benefits up to desired levels.

   c. SERPs are sometimes referred to as salary continuation plans.

2. Application.
   a. SERPs are appropriate for employers:
      i. Who want to provide additional retirement benefits for executives over those benefits provided for other employees.
      ii. Looking to cut back benefits under a qualified plan due to the higher costs of qualified plans.
      iii. Who want to avoid the limit on compensation that can be considered in determining benefits from qualified plans.
      iv. Attempting to recruit mid-career executives who otherwise would be entitled to modest retirement benefits due to relatively few years of service.
3. Advantages.
   a. Provides benefits to executives over and above the benefits available with a qualified plan.
   b. Can reward continued employment or encourage early retirement.
   c. Can be completely unfunded, paying benefits only as needed from the company's assets.
   d. Subject only to ERISA Reporting and Disclosure requirements. Not subject to nondiscrimination testing.
   e. Can be integrated with Social Security, without being subject to the complex integration (permitted disparity) rules applicable to qualified plans.
   f. A SERP can be set up to protect executives from involuntary termination if the company changes ownership. This could be accomplished by providing the executive with increased benefits from the SERP if the company is taken over.
4. Disadvantages.
   a. If the SERP is unfunded, it may be an ineffective recruiting tool, since there is no guarantee of benefits.
   b. From the executive's point of view, the principal problem with deferred compensation plans is the lack of security as a result of depending solely on the company's unsecured promise to pay.
   c. Disclosure of executive nonqualified plans in financial statements may be required.
5. Plan Design.
   a. A salary continuation design, which provides a specified deferred amount payable in the future without any stated reduction of current salary.
   b. Benefit formulas and other plan provisions are similar to those for qualified defined-benefit plans, without the limits of defined-benefit plans.

Example

Joe is an executive with a company that offers him a SERP benefit of 60% of final average compensation. If Joe's final average compensation is $400,000, his annual SERP benefit would be $240,000, which is much higher than the maximum benefit allowed with a qualified defined-benefit plan.

---

c. Typically set up with forfeiture provisions, which can accomplish several employer objectives. Qualified plan vesting schedules do not apply to SERPs.

d. SERPs must be maintained primarily for a select group of management or highly compensated employees. The executive's title or position typically determines whether or not the executive will be included in the SERP.

e. An "Offset" SERP is a special type of SERP that provides a desired benefit to an executive, taking into account the benefits the executive will receive under a qualified plan.

6. Tax Ramifications.

   a. The employer gets a deduction only when benefits are paid to executive.

   b. The executive is subject to ordinary income tax upon the receipt of the benefit from the SERP.

D. SPLIT-DOLLAR LIFE INSURANCE.

1. Description.

   a. Split-dollar life insurance is an arrangement, typically between an employer and an employee, in which there is a sharing of both the costs and the benefits of the life insurance policy.

   b. Usually, the employer corporation pays that part of the annual premium that equals the current year's increase in the cash surrender value of the policy.

   c. If the insured employee dies, the corporation recovers its premium outlay. The balance of the policy proceeds is paid to the beneficiary chosen by the employee.

2. Appropriate application when:

   a. An employer wishes to provide an executive with a life insurance benefit at a low cost and a low cash outlay to the executive.

      i. It is best suited for executives in their 30's, 40's, and early 50's since the plan requires a reasonable duration in order to build up adequate policy cash values.

      ii. The cost to the executive can be excessive at later ages.

   b. A preretirement death benefit for an employee is a major objective. Split dollar can be used as an alternative to an insurance-financed nonqualified deferred compensation plan.

   c. An employer is seeking a totally selective executive fringe benefit.

   d. An employer wants to make it easier for shareholder-employees to finance a buyout of stock under a cross purchase buy-sell agreement or make it possible for nonstockholding employees to effect a one-way stock purchase at an existing shareholder's death.

3. Advantages.

   a. A split-dollar plan allows an executive to receive a benefit of current value using employer funds, with minimal or no tax cost to the executive.

   b. In most types of split-dollar plans, the employer's outlay is, at all times, fully secured. Upon the employee's death or termination of employment, the employer is reimbursed from policy proceeds for its premium outlay. The net cost to the employer for the plan is merely the loss of the net after-tax income the funds could have earned while the plan was in effect.

4. Disadvantages.
   a. The employer receives no tax deduction for its share of premium payments under the split-dollar plan.
   b. The employee must pay income taxes each year on the current Table 2001 cost (Table 2001 replaces the P.S. 58 table).
   c. The plan must remain in effect for a reasonably long time (10-20 years) in order for policy cash values to rise to a level sufficient to maximize plan benefits.
   d. The plan must generally be terminated at approximately age 65 since the employee's tax cost for the plan rises sharply at later ages.
   e. Interest on policy loans is generally nondeductible.
5. Design features.
   a. In a split-dollar arrangement between the employer and employee, at least three aspects of the policy can be subject to different types of splits:
      i. The premium cost.
      ii. The cash value.
      iii. The policy ownership.
   b. Premium cost split categories:
      i. The classic or standard split-dollar plan under which the employer pays a portion of the premiums equal to the increase in cash surrender value of the policy.
      ii. The level premium plan under which the employee's premium share is leveled over an initial period of years, such as 5 or 10.
      iii. The employer pays all arrangements, with the employer paying the entire premium and the employee paying nothing.
      iv. The offset plan under which the employee pays an amount equal to the cost for the coverage.
   c. Cash value and death proceeds split. The purpose of the split of cash value or death proceeds is to reimburse the employer, in whole or in part, for its share of the premium outlay, in the event of the employee's death or termination of the plan.
   d. Policy ownership methods.
      i. The endorsement method - The employer owns the policy and is primarily responsible to the insurance company for paying the entire premium. The beneficiary designation provides for the employer to receive a portion of the death benefit equal to its premium outlay, with the remainder of the death proceeds going to the employee's designated beneficiary.
      ii. The collateral assignment method - The employee is the owner of the policy and is responsible for premium payments. The employer makes what are, in effect, interest-free loans of the amount of the premium the employer has agreed to pay under the split-dollar plan. To secure these loans, the policy is assigned as collateral to the employer.
      iii. At the employee's death, the employer recovers its aggregate premium payments from the policy proceeds, as collateral assignee. The remainder of the policy proceeds is paid to the employee's designated beneficiary.

6. Income tax treatment (Notice 2002-8).

   a. Notice 2002-8 revoked Notice 2001-10 and provided some guidance regarding the taxation of split-dollar life insurance. However, the IRS intends to issue regulations addressing the tax treatment of split-dollar life insurance arrangements. At the time of publication of this material, the anticipated proposed regulations had not been issued.

   b. It is expected that the regulations will provide that any payment made by an employer under a split-dollar arrangement must be accounted for either as a loan to the employee under IRC §7872 or as compensation to the employee. This move closely reflects economic reality.

   c. The IRS also issued new mortality tables (Table 2001) reflecting increased life expectancy.

   d. Death benefits from a split-dollar plan, both the employer's share and the employee's beneficiary's share, are generally free from income tax.

      i. The tax-free nature of the death proceeds is lost if the policy has been transferred for value in certain situations.

      ii. Transfers of insurance policies that are exempt from the transfer for value rules will not cause the loss of the death proceeds' tax-free nature. Examples:

         A) A transfer of the policy to the insured.

         B) A transfer to a partner of the insured or to a partnership of which the insured is a partner.

         C) A transfer to a corporation of which the insured is a shareholder or officer.

         D) A transfer in which the transferee's basis is determined in whole or in part by reference to the transferor's basis (i.e., a substituted or carryover basis).

E. STOCK OPTIONS (NQSOS AND ISOS).

1. In general.

   a. Stock options give the employee the right to purchase a fixed number of shares of employer stock at a fixed price, over a stated period of time.

   b. The grant of a stock option is generally a nontaxable event, because the option price is usually made equal to the stock's market price on the grant date. The option will therefore have no ascertainable value and the grant will not be a taxable event.

   c. Types.

      i. Nonqualified Stock Options (NQSOs) – a NQSO is any option that is not an Incentive Stock Option.

      ii. Incentive Stock Options (ISOs) – an ISO is an option that meets the requirements of Internal Revenue Code Section 422.

2. Nonqualified Stock Options (NQSO).

   a. Requirements.

      i. There are no special requirements under the Internal Revenue Code for NQSOs.

      ii. The employer may grant the employee an NQSO on any terms, exercisable over any period of years.

      iii. The option may be granted to an employee, an independent contractor, a family member, or any other beneficiary of the employee or independent contractor.

b. Taxation.

i. At exercise.

A) W-2 income and subject to payroll taxes for the difference between the option exercise price and the current fair market value.

B) Taxable basis – after the exercise, the basis in the stock for capital gains or losses is the exercise price plus the ordinary income recognized (i.e., approximately equal to the FMV on the date of exercise).

ii. Sale of shares acquired through the exercise of NQSOs.

A) Results in either a capital gain or loss.

B) Long term or short term depends on the holding period.

Example

Brewster receives 10,000 NQSOs to purchase ABC stock at $10 per share. Once vested, he exercises the options when the market price of ABC is $25 per share. Several years later, Brewster sells the 10,000 shares of ABC stock for $100 per share.

Treatment of each transaction.

- No taxable event on the grant of the options.
- Brewster will have $150,000 [($25 - $10) x 10,000] of additional W-2 income in the year that he exercises the options. He will have to pay $100,000 to exercise the 10,000 NQSOs.
- Brewster will have a capital gain of $750,000 when he sells the shares of stock at $100 per share. His adjusted taxable basis equals $25 per share ($10 from the exercise price and $15 of W-2 income).

---

c. Transfer and gifting of NQSOs.

i. Transfers to family members and other persons.

A) Income tax consequences.

1) The employee does not recognize gain on the transfer date.

2) The employee (or employee's estate, if the employee is deceased) will have compensation income when the transferee exercises the option.

3) The transferee will have an adjusted taxable basis in the stock equal to the fair market value of the stock at the time of exercise.

B) Gift and estate tax consequences.

1) The transfer of an NQSO is a completed gift on the date of transfer (or date of vesting, if later).

2) The options must be valued at the date of the gift. In some cases, the Black-Scholes option valuation model may be used.

3) The options and shares of stock acquired upon exercise are not included in the employee's gross estate upon death.

ii. Transfers to charity.

A) Income tax consequences.

1) The employee does not recognize gain on the transfer date.

2) The employee will have compensation income when the charity exercises the option, if the employee is still living when the options are exercised. There is no compensation income if the charity exercises the option after the death of the employee.

3) The employee will be allowed a charitable income tax deduction on the date of transfer (or date of vesting, if later).

B) Gift and estate tax consequences.

1) The transfer of an NQSO is a completed gift on the date of transfer (or date of vesting, if later).

2) The value of any unexercised option is included in the employee's gross estate upon death.

3) If the employee dies within three years after the option is exercised by charity, the employee's gross estate must include the value the options would have had at the date of death.

4) The employee's estate is eligible for the estate tax charitable deduction for the transfer of the options to charity.

	Transferred to Noncharitable Recipient	Transferred to Charity
Income Tax	1) No gain recognized at transfer. 2) Employee or employee's estate will have compensation income when option exercised. 3) Transferee basis in stock equal to FMV at exercise.	1) No gain recognized at transfer. 2) Employee (if still living) has compensation income when charity exercises option. 3) No compensation income if exercised after death. 4) Employee allowed a tax deduction on date of transfer (or vesting, if later).
Gift Tax	1) Transfer is a completed gift on the date of transfer (or date of vesting, if later). 2) The options must be valued at the date of the gift.	1) Transfer is a completed gift on the date of transfer (or date of vesting, if later). 2) The options must be valued at the date of the gift.
Estate Tax	1) Option and shares of stock acquired upon exercise are not included in employee's gross estate.	1) Value of unexercised option is included in gross estate. 2) If employee dies within three years after exercise, the gross estate must include the value the options would have had at the date of death. 3) Estate eligible charitable deduction.

3. Incentive Stock Options (ISOs) (IRC Section 422).

   a. Requirements.

      i. ISOs must be part of a written plan approved by the stockholders.

      ii. The exercise period cannot exceed 10 years from the date of grant.

      iii. The option (strike) price cannot be less than the market price of the stock at the time of grant.

      iv. There is an annual limit of $100,000 on the value of the ISOs granted during one year to a single employee.

      v. ISOs may only be granted to employees of the company.

      vi. ISOs are not transferable by the employee during life, but may be transferred at death by will.

      vii. ISOs must be exercised within three months from the date of retirement or termination.

      viii. The shares received through the exercise of ISOs cannot be sold within two years from the date of grant or one year from the date of exercise. Otherwise, the favorable tax treatment of the ISO will be lost.

   b. ISO exercise of option – taxation and taxable basis.

      i. Taxation – upon exercise there is no regular taxable income. However, there is an AMT adjustment to the extent the FMV exceeds the option exercise price (the excess of the fair market value of the stock over the exercise price is sometimes referred to as the "bargain element"). The AMT adjustment can be large enough for executives who exercise a large number of ISOs to cause them to pay AMT.

      ii. Taxable basis – the taxable basis for the regular tax is the option exercise price. For AMT purposes, the basis equals the option price plus appreciation at the exercise date (equivalent to the market price of the stock on the date of exercise).

      iii. Effect on company - the employer does not receive an income tax deduction when an employee exercises an ISO. However, if the employee disposes of the ISO shares in a disqualifying disposition, then the employee will generally have ordinary income and the employer will receive a tax deduction.

   c. Sale of shares acquired through the exercise of ISOs.

      i. If shares are sold within the calendar year of exercise, it is considered W-2 income equal to the difference between the exercise price and the market price of the stock on the date of exercise. This is the same tax treatment as a NQSO.

      ii. If the stock is sold within 1 year from the date of exercise or 2 years from the date of grant, but not in the calendar year of exercise, the gain is considered ordinary income, but not W-2 income.

      iii. If sold after 1 year from the date of exercise and 2 years from the date of grant, it is considered a long-term capital gain.

Example

Brewster receives 10,000 ISOs to purchase ABC stock at $10 per share. Once vested, he exercises the options when the market price of ABC is $25 per share. Several years later (beyond 2 years from the date of grant and 1 year from the date of exercise), Brewster sells the 10,000 shares of ABC stock for $100 per share.

Treatment of each transaction.

- No taxable event on the grant of the options.
- Brewster will have no additional income for regular tax purposes upon exercise.
- Brewster will have an AMT adjustment of $150,000 [($25 - $10) x 10,000] upon exercise of the ISOs. This will most likely result in him paying AMT.
- Brewster will have a long-term capital gain of $900,000 ($1,000,000 - $100,000). His adjusted taxable basis equals $10 per share ($10 from the exercise price).
- Brewster will have a capital gain for purposes of AMT of $750,000 when he sells the shares of stock at $100 per share. His adjusted taxable basis equals $25 per share ($10 from the exercise price and $15 from the AMT adjustment). This results in a negative AMT adjustment of $150,000 in the year of sale.
- If he had sold the ISO shares within the same year of exercise, then the treatment would be the same as if the shares were from the exercise of NQSOs.

d. Tax benefits of ISOs.

   i. The gain (bargain element) from the exercise of the ISO is not included in the employee's gross income, whereas the gain is taxable as W-2 income for a NQSO.

   ii. The gain for ISOs will be taxed at capital gains rates (20%) instead of ordinary income tax rates (38.6%). The gains for NQSOs are taxed as W-2.

e. Disqualifying dispositions of ISOs.

   i. A "disqualifying disposition" occurs when an employee disposes of ISO stock before the statutory holding period expires. If a disqualifying disposition occurs, then the employee will generally recognize as ordinary income the difference between the fair market value of the stock at exercise and the exercise price of the option.

   ii. The employee recognizes the income in the tax year during which the disqualifying disposition occurs. The recognized ordinary income will be added to the ISO stock's basis to determine the capital gain that must be recognized because of the disqualifying disposition.

   iii. If the FMV of the stock on the date of sale is less than the FMV on the date of exercise, there will be no capital gain or loss at sale. Instead, the employee will recognize ordinary income based on the excess of the proceeds received from the sale over the exercise price of the option.

Example

- On January 1, 2002, Stan, an employee of Decline Corp, was granted 1,000 ISOs to purchase shares of Decline Corp at the fair market value of the stock on the date of grant ($20). On June 30, 2003, he exercises all of the ISOs when the fair market value is $40. On December 30, 2003 he sells 500 of the shares for $50 per share.

Date	Event	Fair Market Value
January 1, 2002	Date of Grant – Exercise Price	$20 per share
June 30, 2003	Date of Exercise	$40 per share
December 30, 2003	Date of Sale of ISO shares	$50 per share

  Since this is a disqualifying disposition, Stan will recognize ordinary income of $10,000 [($40 exercise price less $20 option price) x 500 shares]. He will also recognize short-term capital gain of $5,000 [($50 sale price less $40 adjusted tax basis) x 500 shares].

- Assume the same facts as the previous example, except the FMV of the ISO shares dropped to $35 on the date of sale (December 30, 2003). This is a disqualifying disposition, and Stan will recognize ordinary income of $7,500 [($35 - $20) x 500 shares]. He will have no capital gain or loss upon the sale.

4. Cashless exercise of options.

   a. In general.

      i. A cashless exercise involves the exercise of options, without any cash outlay by the employee.

      ii. The arrangement typically works as follows:

         A) The stock option is exercised by the employee.

         B) After exercise, a sufficient amount of the employer stock is sold to satisfy the exercise price and any other costs associated with the exercise, such as income taxes.

         C) The employee receives the net amount of the stock (the stock remaining after the sale of shares), or all cash.

      iii. A cashless exercise is typically suitable for employees who do not have the liquid assets sufficient to satisfy the exercise price of the option.

Example

Three years ago, Tina was granted a nonqualified stock option to purchase 100 shares of employer stock at $20 per share. She exercised the option when the fair market value of the stock was $30. Assume Tina's marginal income tax rate is 27%. If Tina opts for a cashless exercise, she will receive 24 shares of the employer stock, calculated as follows.

- The exercise cost of the option is $2,000 (100 shares x $20 per share). In addition, since the option is a NQSO, Tina will have to pay ordinary income tax of $270 on the bargain element [($30 FMV less $20 exercise price) x 100 shares x 27% tax rate]. Therefore, the total cost of the option is $2,270.
- With a cashless exercise, enough shares must be sold to cover the total cost of the option. In order to cover the total cost of the option, 76 shares of the stock must be sold ($2,270 total cost divided by $30 fair market value per share).
- When Tina sells the remaining 24 shares, she will have a capital gain or loss.
- Alternatively, she will have $1,000 of W-2 income and have $270 of withholding.

b. Cashless exercise of incentive stock options.

   i. To receive the favorable tax treatment of incentive stock options, the shares must be held at least one year from the date of exercise and two years from the date of grant.

   ii. A cashless exercise will result in a disqualifying disposition with respect to the shares sold because the holding requirements are not met. As a result, the employee will recognize ordinary income equal to the excess of the fair market value of the stock sold over the exercise price (the bargain element).

EXHIBIT 11: SUMMARY OF REGULAR TAX AND AMT TREATMENT OF ISOS AND NQSOS

<table>
<tr><th rowspan="2"></th><th rowspan="2">NQSOs</th><th colspan="4">ISOs</th></tr>
<tr><th colspan="3">Regular Tax</th><th>AMT</th></tr>
<tr><td>At Exercise</td><td>W-2 Income to extent of FMV > Exercise Price</td><td colspan="3">No Income</td><td>AMT income to extent FMV > Exercise Price</td></tr>
<tr><td>Adjusted Taxable Basis at Exercise</td><td>Fair Market Value (Exercise price plus W-2 Income)</td><td colspan="3">Exercise Price</td><td>Fair Market Value (Exercise price plus AMT income)</td></tr>
<tr><td rowspan="2">At Sale</td><td rowspan="2">Capital Gain or Loss (Sale Price less Adjusted Taxable Basis)</td><td>Within calendar year of exercise</td><td>Within one year of exercise or within two years of grant</td><td>After one year from exercise and two years from grant</td><td>AMT deduction (negative AMT adjust) equal to the FMV at Exercise Less Exercise Price</td></tr>
<tr><td>W-2 Income to extent sales price > adjusted taxable basis</td><td>Ordinary Income to extent sales price > adjusted taxable basis</td><td>Long-term Capital Gain</td><td></td></tr>
</table>

F. EMPLOYEE STOCK PURCHASE PLANS (ESPPS).

1. Characteristics.
   a. ESPPs are options that give the employees the right to purchase employer stock.
   b. The employee generally pays no income tax on the option or the stock until the shares are disposed of.
   c. The plan must be nondiscriminatory (see exceptions below).
   d. The plan can limit the amount of stock an employee can buy. Often, the amount of stock available to an employee is tied to the employee's compensation.
2. Requirements.
   a. Must be a written plan that is approved by the shareholders.
   b. The option price must be at least 85% of the fair market value of the stock at the time of grant.
   c. The shares acquired must be held by the employee for at least two years from the grant of the option and one year after the exercise. Note: A similar rule applies to incentive stock options.
   d. If the employee does not remain employed by the company, any outstanding stock options must be exercised within three months after leaving the company.
   e. Employees owning more than 5% of the corporation cannot participate in the ESPP.

f. The plan must be nondiscriminatory. All employees must be included in the plan, except:

   i. Employees with less than two years of employment.

   ii. Highly compensated employees.

   iii. Part-time employees and seasonal workers.

g. No employee can acquire the right to buy more than $25,000 of stock per year, valued at the time the option is granted.

3. Tax treatment of ESPPs.

   a. No tax ramifications at date of grant or date of exercise.

   b. No alternative minimum tax consequences.

   c. At the date of disposition of the shares:

      i. The employee will recognize ordinary income based on the lesser of:

         A) The FMV of the stock at the grant date less the option price, or

         B) The FMV of the stock on the disposition date (or date of death, if sooner) less the option price.

      ii. The balance of any gain is treated as capital gain.

Note: If the option price is equal to the FMV of the stock at the date of grant, all gain at disposition will be capital gain (if the shares are held by the employee for at least two years from the grant of the option and one year after the exercise).

Example

Through his company's ESPP, David receives an option to purchase 1,000 shares of XYZ stock at $20 per share, when the fair market value of the stock was $22 per share. He exercises the options when the market price of XYZ is $25 per share. Several years later (beyond 2 years from the date of grant and 1 year from the date of exercise), David sells the 1,000 shares of XYZ stock for $100 per share.

Treatment of each transaction.

- No taxable event on the grant or exercise of the options.
- When David sells the shares, he will have a total gain of $80,000 ($100,000 FMV less the option price of $20,000). The $80,000 gain will be considered $2,000 ordinary income and $78,000 capital gain, calculated as follows:
- Ordinary income is $2,000, which is the lesser of:
  - $2,000, the FMV of the stock at the grant date less the option price ($22,000 FMV at grant less $20,000 exercise price), OR
  - $80,000, the FMV of the stock on the disposition date less the option price ($100,000 FMV at sale less $20,000 exercise price).
- Capital gain is $78,000, which is the remaining gain ($80,000 total gain less $2,000 ordinary income).

G. PHANTOM STOCKS (SHADOW STOCKS).

1. Characteristics.

   a. A fictional deferred compensation units account is created as an accounting entry. The assigned base value is equal to the current value of the company's common stock.

   b. When dividends are declared an equivalent credit is made to the account.

   c. The plan may provide for adjustments to the account for appreciation of the common stock.

   d. Upon retirement or some other termination event, the participant receives the value of the account either as a lump sum or in installments. The payment will be in the form of cash.

   e. No actual common stock is ever issued to the participant (avoids dilution if a closely held company).

2. Tax treatment.

   a. Employee taxed (at ordinary rates) when payment is received.

   b. The employer receives a tax deduction at the time of payment to the participant.

H. RESTRICTED STOCK.

1. In general.

   a. Restricted stock is employer stock that is forfeited if the executive's performance is subpar or if the executive terminates employment before a stated period of time (substantial risk of forfeiture).

   b. The value of the stock will not be subject to income tax as long as the stock is subject to a substantial risk of forfeiture. Any of the following could be considered a substantial risk of forfeiture:

      i. A forfeiture if the employee doesn't remain with the employer for a specified period of time.

      ii. A forfeiture if the employee doesn't meet certain sales or performance goals.

      iii. A forfeiture if the employee goes to work for a competitor.

   c. When the stock is no longer subject to a substantial risk of forfeiture, the value of the stock (less any amounts paid for the stock by the employee) will be taxed as W-2 income to the employee.

2. Section 83(b) election.

   a. An employee who receives restricted stock may elect to recognize the income immediately rather than waiting until there is no longer a substantial risk of forfeiture. This election not to defer the income is called a Section 83(b) election (Code Section 83(b)(1)).

   b. The election must be made within 30 days of receiving the restricted stock.

   c. If the election is made, the employee will include (in W-2 gross income) the fair market value of the stock at receipt, less any amount paid for the property. Any subsequent appreciation in the value of the stock will be treated as capital gain and may be taxed at lower capital-gain rates when the stock is sold.

Example

- Maria's employer, DEF Company, granted her 1,000 shares of restricted stock, worth $10 per share at the time of grant. Maria will forfeit the shares unless she continues to be employed by DEF Company for five more years. Assume at the end of five years, the stock is worth $40 per share, and at the end of seven years, she sells the stock for $45 per share. Maria's ordinary income tax rate is 36% and her capital gain rate is 20%.
- If Maria does not make the Section 83(b) election, she will have no income tax consequences until the end of the five-year period, when the shares are no longer subject to a substantial risk of forfeiture. At that time, she will report W-2 income of $40,000 ($40 FMV x 1,000 shares), resulting in tax of $14,400 ($40,000 x 36%). Her adjusted taxable basis in the stock will also be $40,000. Two years later, when she sells the stock, she will have capital gain of $5,000 ($45,000 FMV less $40,000 basis), resulting in tax of $1,000. The total tax paid on the restricted stock is $15,400 ($14,400 ordinary income tax plus $1,000 capital gain tax).
- If Maria makes the Section 83(b) election, she will immediately report ordinary income of $10,000 ($10 FMV at receipt x 1,000 shares), resulting in tax of $3,600 ($10,000 x 36%). Her adjusted taxable basis in the stock will also be $10,000. Seven years later when she sells the stock, she will have capital gain of $35,000 ($45,000 FMV less $10,000 basis), resulting in tax of $7,000. The total tax paid on the restricted stock is $10,600 ($3,600 ordinary income tax plus $7,000 capital gain tax). Therefore, making the Section 83(b) election will result in tax savings of $4,800 ($15,400 tax with no election, less $10,600 tax with election).

d. If the employee makes the Section 83(b) election and then forfeits the stock, the employee is not allowed a deduction or refund of tax previously paid on income reported. However, the employee will have a capital loss at the time of forfeiture.

I. LOANS TO KEY EXECUTIVES.

1. See the tax section on gift loans; loans between shareholders and corporations (dividends); and loans to employees (compensation).

XVII. EMPLOYEE BENEFITS AND BUSINESS INSURANCE

A. GROUP LIFE AND HEALTH INSURANCE AS EMPLOYEE BENEFITS.

1. Group life and health insurance are used by many employers as a part of the compensation package for their employees.
2. Group term life insurance premiums paid by the employer are tax exempt to the employee for the first $50,000 of face amount of insurance.
   a. The premium per $1,000 must appear on the employee's W-2 for any amount of coverage greater than $50,000.
   b. To qualify for the tax treatment, a group plan must be nondiscriminatory - the plan must cover 70% or more of all employees and at least 85% that are not key employees.
3. The premiums paid by the employer for health insurance are tax exempt to the employee and they are a deductible business expense for the employer.
4. If the employer provides ordinary life coverage and pays the entire premium, the employee is taxed on any nonterm portion of the premium. This portion is deductible by the employer as wages.
5. Group paid up life insurance is paid by employee contributions.
6. Group universal life does not provide any tax advantage to the employer and the premiums are usually paid by the employee.

B. SPECIALIZED USES OF LIFE INSURANCE IN BUSINESS.

1. Business continuation insurance is designed to provide the funding for the other parties in a business to continue operation in the event of death of a key employee by purchasing the interest of the decedent.
   a. Premiums are paid by the partners, partnership, stockholders, or corporation who would receive the benefits. Premiums are not tax deductible.
   b. Under an entity plan, the firm is the owner and beneficiary of the policy, but the premiums paid are not tax deductible.
2. Key person insurance covers employees who are considered critical to the success of a business and whose death might cause financial loss to the company. The company has an insurable interest in the person. Therefore, the company pays the premiums and is the beneficiary. Premiums are not deductible.
3. Split-dollar insurance is a plan where an employer and employee share the cost of a life policy on the employee (usually permanent insurance such as whole life or variable universal).
   a. The employer pays the portion of premium equal to the increase in the cash value and is owner of the policy and beneficiary to the extent of cash value.
   b. The employee's spouse or other person designated by the employee is the beneficiary of the death proceeds in excess of the employer's premiums.

4. Deferred compensation is an arrangement between the employer and the employee where the employer will make payments to an employee after retirement or the employee's spouse if the employee should die prior to retiring.
   a. It provides the benefit of shifting the income to the employee to a period when the tax burden is not as heavy (i.e., retirement).
   b. Some employers fund deferred compensation through a permanent life insurance policy on the employee.
   c. Premiums for this type of insurance are not deductible by the employer, but amounts paid to the employee or to the employee's dependents are deductible by the employer when paid.

C. BUSINESS USES OF DISABILITY INCOME INSURANCE.

1. Disability overhead insurance is designed to cover the expenses that are usual and necessary expenses in the operation of a business should the owner become disabled.
   a. Premiums are deductible as a business expense.
   b. Benefits are taxable income to the entity.
2. Disability buyout policies are policies to cover the value of the individual's interest in the business should they become disabled.

XVIII. CAFETERIA PLANS

A. DESCRIPTION.

A cafeteria plan is a plan in which employees may, within limits, choose the form of employee benefits from a selection of benefits provided by their employer. Cafeteria plans must include a cash option. A cash option is an option to receive cash in lieu of noncash benefits of equal value.

B. APPLICATION.

1. A cafeteria plan is appropriate when employee benefit needs vary within the employee group; the employee mix includes young, unmarried people with minimal life insurance and medical benefits needs, as well as older employees with families who need maximum medical and life insurance benefits.
2. A cafeteria plan is appropriate when employees want to choose the benefit package most suited to their individual needs.
3. A cafeteria plan is appropriate when an employer seeks to maximize employee satisfaction with the benefit package thereby maximizing the employer's benefit from its compensation expenditures.
4. A cafeteria plan is appropriate when the employer is large enough to afford the expense of such a plan.
5. A cafeteria plan is a way of managing fringe benefit costs to the employer by individually pricing each benefit and providing a total dollar equivalency to each employee to effectively shop for the best mix of benefits for that person.

C. ADVANTAGES.

1. Cafeteria plans help give employees an appreciation of the value of their benefit package.
2. The flexibility of a cafeteria benefit package helps meet varied employee needs.
3. Cafeteria plans can help control employer costs for the benefit package because the cost of provisions for benefits that employees do not need is minimized.

D. DISADVANTAGES.

1. Cafeteria plans are more complex and expensive to design and administer.
2. Benefit packages usually include some insured benefits.
3. Medical and life insurance benefits are usually included.
4. Complex tax requirements apply to the plan under Section 125 of the Internal Revenue Code.
5. Highly compensated employees may lose the tax benefits of the plan if it is discriminatory.

E. TAX IMPLICATIONS.

1. A cafeteria plan must comply with the provisions of IRC Section 125 that provides an exception for cafeteria plans from the constructive receipt doctrine.
   a. If the terms of Section 125 are not met in a cafeteria plan, an employee is taxed on the value of any taxable benefits available from the plan, even if the participant chooses nontaxable benefits such as medical insurance.

b. Limitation on nontaxable benefits to key employees.

i. The nontaxable benefits provided to key employees must not be greater than 25% of the total nontaxable benefits provided under the plan to all employees.

ii. See Top Heavy for definition of key employee.

2. Under Section 125 and its regulations, only certain qualified benefits can be made available in the cafeteria plan.

a. Qualifying benefits include cash and most tax-free benefits provided under the Code, except:

i. Scholarships and fellowships.

ii. Educational assistance.

iii. Employee discounts - no additional cost services and other fringe benefits provided under Code Section 132.

iv. Retirement benefits such as qualified or nonqualified deferred compensation; however, a 401(k) arrangement can be included.

3. A cafeteria plan must meet certain nondiscrimination requirements.

a. Participation - the plan must be made available to a group of employees in a manner that does not discriminate in favor of highly compensated employees.

b. Benefits - the plan must not discriminate in favor of highly compensated employees as to contributions and benefits.

F. ALTERNATIVES.

1. The flexible spending account (FSA) is a cafeteria plan funded through salary reductions. An FSA is a special type of cafeteria plan that should be considered whenever cafeteria benefits are reviewed. FSAs are discussed in detail in the next section.

2. Fixed benefit programs without employee choice may be adequate where most employees have the same benefit needs or where the employer cannot administer a more complex program.

3. Cash compensation, as an alternative to benefits, forfeits tax advantages in favor of maximum employee choice, and assumes that employees will have adequate income to provide benefits on their own.

XIX.FLEXIBLE SPENDING ACCOUNT

A. DESCRIBED.

1. A flexible spending account (FSA) is a cafeteria plan under which employees can choose among cash and specified benefits that are funded through salary reductions elected by employees each year.

B. APPLICATION.

1. A flexible spending account is appropriate when an employer wants to expand employee benefit choices without significant employer extra out-of-pocket costs (or possibly realize some actual dollar savings).
   a. Where many employees have employed spouses with duplicate medical coverage.
   b. Where employees contribute to health insurance costs.
   c. Where the employer's medical plans have large deductibles or coinsurance (co-pay) provisions.
   d. Where employees are nonunion.
   e. Where there is a need for benefits that are difficult to provide on a group basis, such as dependent care.
2. A flexible spending account is appropriate when costs of employee benefit plans, such as health insurance, have increased and the employer must impose additional employee cost sharing in the form of:
   a. Increased employee contributions.
   b. Deductibles.
   c. Coinsurance: The FSA approach minimizes employee outlay since the FSA converts after-tax employee expenditures to before-tax expenditures.
3. The FSA provides a tax benefit for employees not available through any other plan.
4. Because of administrative costs, FSAs are usually impractical for businesses with only a few employees.
5. FSA benefits cannot be provided to self-employed persons or partners.

C. ADVANTAGES.

1. The plan provides employees some degree of choice as to whether to receive compensation in cash or benefits.
2. The FSA is funded entirely through employee salary reductions requiring no extra outlay by the employer, except for administrative costs.
3. The plan may result in a reduction in some employment taxes (FICA, FUTA, SUTA) paid by the employee and employer since taxable payroll is reduced.
4. Salary reductions elected by employees to fund nontaxable benefits under the plan are not subject to federal income taxes or payroll tax.
5. There are many nontaxable benefits available from such a plan which include many benefits that employers might not otherwise provide to employees (e.g., dependent care, group legal, dental).
6. Using a flexible spending account to pay for dependent care expenses (if allowed) may provide more tax savings than utilization of the Child and Dependent Care Credit.

Example

Marjorie, a mother of two young children, earns an $80,000 salary working for ABC Widgets, Inc. Marjorie is in the 30% income tax bracket. This year, she chose to contribute $4,800 to her company's flexible spending account. The contributions will be used to pay for child care expenses, such as the cost of a baby-sitter. Since Marjorie is in the 30% income tax bracket, the pretax contributions to the flexible spending account will reduce her tax liability by $1,440 ($4,800 x 30%). If Marjorie had chosen to pay the child care expenses with after-tax dollars, she would be eligible for a Child and Dependent Care Credit of $960 ($4,800 x 20% Child and Dependent Care Credit percentage; see Tax Planning section for details of the calculation). Therefore, using her flexible spending account contributions to fund her child care costs will result in a tax savings of $480 ($1,440 - $960) over utilizing the credit.

D. DISADVANTAGES.

1. An FSA must meet all complex nondiscrimination requirements for cafeteria plans.
2. FSAs require employees to evaluate their personal and family benefit situations and file a timely election form every year estimating their benefit needs.
3. The plan could result in adverse selection that would ultimately raise benefit costs.
4. Administrative costs are greater than those incurred in a fixed benefit plan.
5. IRS proposed regulations require an employer to be at risk regarding the total annual amount an employee elects to allocate to health benefits under his or her FSA.
6. If the employee fails to use all contributed amounts within a certain time period, these dollars are forfeited (use it or lose it).

E. TAX IMPLICATIONS.

1. Employee salary reductions applied to nontaxable benefits are not subject to income tax or payroll tax.
2. The employer gets a tax deduction for the amounts it pays.
3. The employer's payroll subject to payroll taxes is reduced by the amount of any employee salary reductions under an FSA.
   a. FICA is not paid.
   b. FUTA is not paid.
   c. State unemployment taxes are not paid.
   d. Workers compensation is not paid.

F. ERISA REQUIREMENTS.

The ERISA requirements are those applicable to the various individual plans (health insurance, dependent care, etc.) that are part of the FSA arrangement.

Note: The Health Act of 1996 - Long-term care services cannot be reimbursed tax free under a flexible spending account.

XX. OTHER EMPLOYEE FRINGE BENEFITS

A. ACCIDENT AND HEALTH PLAN.

1. Premiums paid by the employer for accident, health and disability insurance policies are deductible to the employer and excluded from the employee's income.
2. When the insurance benefits are paid they are includible in income with the exception of:
   a. Payments received for medical care of the employee, spouse, and dependents.
   b. Payments for permanent loss or the loss of the use of a member or function of the body or permanent disfigurement of the employee, spouse, or dependent.

B. MEALS AND LODGING.

1. Furnished for the convenience of the employer. The value of meals and lodging provided by the employer is excluded from income providing:
   a. They are furnished by the employer, on the employer's premises, and for the employer's convenience.
   b. The employee is required to accept the lodging as a condition of employment.

Example

Tom is the manager of a hotel. To be available in emergency situations, Tom's employer requires that he live in one of the hotel rooms. Tom lives there without charge. The value of the room is $1,500 per month if occupied each night. The hotel is ordinarily 70% occupied. If Tom did not live there, he would live in an apartment that he would rent for $900 per month. Tom's inclusive monthly gross income from living in the hotel room is $0. The room is furnished for the convenience of the employer.

C. GROUP TERM LIFE INSURANCE.

1. Life insurance premiums on group term life insurance of $50,000 or less paid by an employer are excluded from the employee's gross income. Any amount in excess of $50,000 is taxed using an IRS table (see Appendix 11: "Cost Per $1,000 of Protection for One Month (Section 79)" on page 865).

Example

- Taxpayer is 56 years old and works for Employers A and B. Both employers provide group term life insurance coverage for Taxpayer. Taxpayer's coverage with Employer A is $35,000, and coverage with Employer B is $45,000. Taxpayer pays premiums of $50 per year under the Employer B group plan. Figure the amount to include in the taxpayer's income as follows:

Employer A coverage (in thousands)	$35
Employer B coverage (in thousands)	45
Total coverage (in thousands)	80
Less: Exclusion (in thousands)	(50)
Excess amount (in thousands)	30
Multiply by cost per $1,000 per month, age 56 (from table)	x 0.43
Cost of excess insurance for 1 month	$12.90
Multiply by number of full months coverage at this cost	x 12
Cost of excess insurance for tax year	$154.80
Less: Premiums paid by employee	(50.00)
Cost to include in your income as wages	**$104.80**

- Keri Hill, age 55, is covered by a $180,000 group term life insurance policy of which her daughter is the beneficiary. Keri's employer pays the entire cost of the policy, for which the uniform annual premium is $9 per $1,000 of coverage. $1,170 of this premium is taxable to Keri.

  $50,000 of group term is nontaxable.
  $180,000 - 50,000 = $130,000 x $9/thousand = $1,170 taxable
  (reported on W-2 by employer).

D. CHILD AND DEPENDENT SERVICES.

1. The employee does not have to include in gross income the value of child and dependent care services paid for by the employer and incurred to enable an employee to work. The exclusion, however, cannot exceed $5,000 per year.
2. To qualify, nondiscrimination and other requirements must be met.

E. ATHLETIC FACILITY PROVIDED TO EMPLOYEES.

The value of a health facility or gymnasium provided by the employer on the employer's premises (or on a premises leased by the employer) is excluded from gross income by the employee (benefits may be provided to both the employee and dependents). However, dues paid to a private health club by the employer are taxable to the employee as wage compensation.

F. EDUCATIONAL ASSISTANCE.

Qualified employer-provided educational assistance at undergraduate and graduate levels is excluded from gross income. The exclusion is subject to an annual ceiling of $5,250.

G. NO ADDITIONAL COST SERVICES.

1. Excluded from gross income if:
   a. The employee receives services, as opposed to property, that are offered by the employer to customers in the course of business.
   b. The employer does not incur substantial additional cost, including forgone revenue, in providing the services to the employee.
   c. The services are offered to customers in the ordinary course of the business in which the employee works (e.g., travel privileges for employees of an airline).
2. Nondiscrimination provision.
   a. If the plan is discriminatory in favor of highly compensated employees, these key employees are denied exclusion treatment.
3. Qualified employee discounts.
   a. Employee discounts can be excluded if:
      i. The exclusion is not available for real property or for personal property of the type commonly held for investments.
      ii. The property or services must be in the same line of business in which the employee works.
      iii. In the case of property, the exclusion is limited to the gross profit component of the price to customers.
      iv. In the case of services, the exclusion is limited to 20% of the regular customer price.
4. Nondiscrimination provision.

   If the plan is discriminatory in favor of highly compensated employees, these key employees are denied exclusion treatment.

H. DE MINIMIS FRINGES.

De minimis fringe benefits are benefits so small that accounting for them would be impractical. Therefore, they are excludable from the employee's gross income. For example, the personal use of a company-owned computer or copy machine would be de minimis.

I. QUALIFIED TRANSPORTATION FRINGES.

To encourage mass transit for commuting to and from work, this fringe benefit is nontaxable and includes:

1. Transportation in a commuter highway vehicle between the employer's residence and the place of employment and a transit pass (exclusion is limited).
2. Qualified parking (exclusion is limited).

EXHIBIT 12: FRINGE BENEFITS BY ENTITY TYPE

Benefit	Proprietorship	Partnership	S Corp	LLC	C Corp
Qualified plan	✓	✓	✓	✓	✓
Group life	×	×	×	×	✓
Group health	✓	✓	✓	✓	✓
Group disability	×	×	×	×	✓
Medical reimb. plans	×	×	×	×	✓
Accidental death	×	×	×	×	✓
Disability income plan	×	×	×	×	✓
Employee death benefit					
- Employer provided	×	×	×	×	✓
- Qualified plan	✓	✓	✓	✓	✓
Cafeteria plan	×	×	×	×	✓
Deferred compensation	×	×	×	×	✓

LLC=Limited Liability Company

✓ = Yes; × = No

XXI. VOLUNTARY EMPLOYEES' BENEFICIARY ASSOCIATION (VEBA)

A. DESCRIPTION.

1. A Voluntary Employees' Beneficiary Association (VEBA) is not a retirement plan.
2. VEBAs are types of welfare benefit plans into which employers make deposits that will be used to provide specified employee benefits in the future.
3. Either a trust or a corporation is set up by an employer or through collective bargaining to hold funds used to pay benefits under an employee benefit plan. The income of the VEBA is exempt from regular income tax if the VEBA meets the requirements of Code Section 501(c)(9).

B. APPLICATION.

1. VEBAs are appropriate when an owner of a professional corporation or closely held business wants to increase the level of prefunded, tax-deferred benefits beyond the levels allowed under qualified plans. The VEBA approach allows additional benefits to be prefunded on a tax-deductible basis.
2. VEBAs are appropriate when an employer wants to provide benefit security for all covered employees by placing amounts in trust for the exclusive benefit of employees and beyond the reach of corporate creditors.

C. ADVANTAGES.

1. A VEBA can permit the employer's tax deduction for welfare benefits to be accelerated.
2. Individual employee risk is reduced using a VEBA, as the VEBA is an irrevocable trust for the exclusive benefit of employees and protected against funds reverting to the employer.

D. DISADVANTAGES.

1. A VEBA is complex and costly to install and administer.

E. FUNDING.

1. The level of annual contributions to the VEBA in order to fund benefits is determined actuarially. This amount is paid annually, or in more frequent installments if the employer desires, and is fully deductible to the employer in the year in which each contribution is made.

F. BENEFITS THAT CAN BE PROVIDED BY A VEBA.

1. Life insurance before and after retirement.
2. Other survivor benefits.
3. Sickness and accident benefits.
4. Other benefits including vacation and recreation benefits, severance benefits paid through a severance pay plan, unemployment and job training benefits, disaster benefits, and legal service payment for credits.

G. BENEFITS THAT CANNOT BE PROVIDED BY A VEBA.

1. Savings, retirement, or deferred compensation.
2. Coverage of expenses such as commuting expenses.
3. Accident or homeowners insurance covering damage to property.
4. Other items unrelated to maintenance of the employee's earning power.

APPENDIX 1: TABLE V - ORDINARY LIFE ANNUITIES; ONE LIFE - EXPECTED RETURN MULTIPLES (REG. SECTION 1.72-9)

Age	Multiple	Age	Multiple	Age	Multiple
5	77.7	42	41.7	79	10.8
6	76.7	43	40.7	80	10.2
7	75.8	44	39.8	81	9.7
8	74.8	45	38.8	82	9.1
9	73.8	46	37.9	83	8.6
10	72.8	47	37.0	84	8.1
11	71.8	48	36.0	85	7.6
12	70.8	49	35.1	86	7.1
13	69.9	50	34.2	87	6.7
14	68.9	51	33.3	88	6.3
15	67.9	52	32.3	89	5.9
16	66.9	53	31.4	90	5.5
17	66.0	54	30.5	91	5.2
18	65.0	55	29.6	92	4.9
19	64.0	56	28.7	93	4.6
20	63.0	57	27.9	94	4.3
21	62.1	58	27.0	95	4.1
22	61.1	59	26.1	96	3.8
23	60.1	60	25.2	97	3.6
24	59.1	61	24.4	98	3.4
25	58.2	62	23.5	99	3.1
26	57.2	63	22.7	100	2.9
27	56.2	64	21.8	101	2.7
28	55.3	65	21.0	102	2.5
29	54.3	66	20.2	103	2.3
30	53.3	67	19.4	104	2.1
31	52.4	68	18.6	105	1.9
32	51.4	69	17.8	106	1.7
33	50.4	70	17.0	107	1.5
34	49.4	71	16.3	108	1.4
35	48.5	72	15.5	109	1.2
36	47.5	73	14.8	110	1.1
37	46.5	74	14.1	111	0.9
38	45.6	75	13.4	112	0.8
39	44.6	76	12.7	113	0.7
40	43.6	77	12.1	114	0.6
41	42.7	78	11.4	115	0.5

APPENDIX 2: TABLE FOR DETERMINING APPLICABLE DIVISOR FOR MINIMUM DISTRIBUTIONS (MINIMUM DISTRIBUTION APPLICABLE DIVISOR)*

Age	Applicable Divisor	Age	Applicable Divisor
70	27.4	93	9.6
71	26.5	94	9.1
72	25.6	95	8.6
73	24.7	96	8.1
74	23.8	97	7.6
75	22.9	98	7.1
76	22.0	99	6.7
77	21.2	100	6.3
78	20.3	101	5.9
79	19.5	102	5.5
80	18.7	103	5.2
81	17.9	104	4.9
82	17.1	105	4.5
83	16.3	106	4.2
84	15.5	107	3.9
85	14.8	108	3.7
86	14.1	109	3.4
87	13.4	110	3.1
88	12.7	111	2.9
89	12.0	112	2.6
90	11.4	113	2.4
91	10.8	114	2.1
92	10.2	115	1.9

* Use this table if the beneficiary is 1) someone other than spouse, or 2) a spouse that is no more than 10 years younger than the participant.

APPENDIX 3: SELF-EMPLOYED PERSON'S RETIREMENT PLAN CONTRIBUTION RATE TABLE

Column A	Column B
If the plan contribution rate is: (shown as a %)	The self-employed person's rate is: (shown as a decimal)
1	.009901
2	.019608
3	.029126
4	.038462
5	.047619
6	.056604
7	.065421
8	.074074
9	.082569
10	.090909
11	.099099
12	.107143
13	.115044
14	.122807
15	.130435
16	.137931
17	.145299
18	.152542
19	.159664
20	.166667
21	.173554
22	.180328
23	.186992
24	.193548
25*	.200000 * ←

* The deduction for annual employer contributions to a SEP cannot exceed 25% of the common-law employee participant's compensation, or 20% of the self-employed compensation (figured without deducting contributions) from the business that has the plan. Factor is calculated as follows: (0.25 ÷ 1.25 = 0.20).

Note: The deduction for annual employer contributions to a profit-sharing or money-purchase plan is also limited to 25% of the employee's compensation, or 20% of the self-employed compensation.

APPENDIX 4: SUMMARY OF PLANS

	Money-Purchase Plan	Profit-Sharing Plan	Stock Bonus Plan	Savings or Thrift Plan	401(k) Plan	ESOP	SEP/ SARSEP	Cash-Balance Pension Plan	Target-Benefit Plans (not profit-sharing)
Employer Contributions									
Fixed	✓				✓	✓		✓	✓
Discretionary		✓	✓	✓	✓	✓	✓		
Employee Contributions									
Pretax		✓			✓				
After tax	✓	✓		✓ (usually)					
Investment in Co. Stock									
Restricted	✓				✓		✓	✓	
Not restricted		✓	✓	✓		✓			
Guaranteed Investment Return								✓	
Right to Vote	N/A	No	Yes	No	N/A	On some matters	N/A	N/A	N/A
Leverage Borrowing to Purchase Co. Stock	N/A	N/A	N/A	N/A	N/A	✓	N/A	N/A	N/A
In-Service Withdrawals, Timing & Form of Distribution Prior to Retirement	No	Yes	Yes	Yes	Yes	Yes	Yes	No	No
At Retirement In Cash	✓	✓	Perhaps	✓	✓	Perhaps	✓	Possible	Possible
Company Stock	N/A	Possible	✓	N/A	N/A	✓	Perhaps	Possible	Possible
Integration	Yes	Yes	Yes	Yes	Yes	No	Yes/No	Yes	Yes
Forfeitures Reduce Plan Coverage	Can	Can	Can	Can	Can	Can	N/A	Must	Must

SUMMARY OF PLANS (CONTINUED)

	Money-Purchase Plan	Profit-Sharing Plan	Stock Bonus Plan	Savings or Thrift Plan	401(k) Plan	ESOP	SEP/ SARSEP	Cash-Balance Pension Plan	Target-Benefit Plans (not profit-sharing)
Loans	Possible	Possible	Possible	Possible	Possible	Possible	No	Possible	Possible
Ten-Year Forward Averaging	Yes	Yes	Yes	Yes	Yes	Yes	No	Yes	Yes
Investment Risk									
Employee	✓	✓	✓	✓	✓	✓	✓		✓
Employer								✓	
PBGC Insurance	No	No	No	No	No	No	No	Yes	No
Actuarial Costs	No	No	No	No	No	No	No	Yes	Yes
Vesting									
Immediate (100%)	No	No	No	No	No	No	Yes	No	No
5-year cliff or 3-7 graduated	Yes	Yes	Yes	Yes	No	Yes	No	Yes	Yes
3-year cliff or 2-6 graduated	If Top Heavy	If Top Heavy	If Top Heavy	If Top Heavy	Yes	If Top Heavy	No	If Top Heavy	If Top Heavy
Favors Older (O) or Younger (Y) Employees	Y	Y	Y	Y	Y	Y	Y	Y	O

APPENDIX 5: CAPITAL NEEDS ANALYSIS

Client Age	45	WLE = 21
Retirement Age	66	
Current Income	\$80,000	
Needs (in %)/Wage Replacement Ratio	80%	
Expected Social Security (today's dollars)	\$15,000	RLE = 24
Inflation Rate	4%	
Investment Return	10.2%	
Life Expectancy	90	

Step 1:

Current Income	\$80,000
Wage Replacement Ratio	0.80
	\$64,000
Expected Social Security	15,000
PV of capital needs	\$49,000

Step 2:

PV of capital needs	\$49,000
i (inflation rate)	4
N (retirement age - current age) or (66-45)	21
FV	\$111,660

Step 3:

PMT_{AD}	\$111,660
i	[(1.102 ÷ 1.04) - 1] x 100
$N_{\text{(Retirement Life Expectancy)}}$	24
FV	0
$P.V._{A.D.}$@ 66	\$1,490,204

Note: Numbers are rounded.

APPENDIX 6: KEOGH CONTRIBUTION CALCULATION

OWNER IS SELF-EMPLOYED

		$106,000	Sch. C net income
Self Employment Tax (Assumed)	$12,000	- 6,000	½ SE Tax
		$100,000	Basis for contribution
SEP	$\frac{0.25}{1 + 0.25} = 0.20000$	$20,000 [100,000 x 0.20000]	SEP contribution
Profit Sharing (PS)	$\frac{0.25}{1 + 0.25} = 0.20000$	$20,000 [100,000 x 0.20000]	PS contribution
Money Purchase (MP)	$\frac{0.25}{1 + 0.25} = 0.20000$	$20,000 [100,000 x 0.20000]	MP contribution

APPENDIX 7: SOCIAL SECURITY FACT SHEET
KENNETH S. APFEL, COMMISSIONER
2003 SOCIAL SECURITY CHANGES

Cost-of-Living Adjustment (COLA):

Based on the increase in the Consumer Price Index (CPI-W) from the third quarter of 2001 through the third quarter of 2002, Social Security beneficiaries and Supplemental Security Income (SSI) recipients received a 1.4 percent COLA for 2003. Other important 2003 Social Security information is as follows:

Tax Rate:

	2002	2003
Employee	7.65%	7.65%
Self-Employed	15.30%	15.30%

Note: The 7.65% tax rate is the combined rate for Social Security and Medicare. The Social Security portion (OASDI) is 6.20% on earnings up to the applicable maximum taxable amount (see below). The Medicare portion (HI) is 1.45% on all earnings.

Maximum Earnings Taxable:

	2002	2003
Social Security (OASDI only)	$84,900	$87,000
Medicare (HI only)	No Limit	No Limit

Quarter of Coverage:

2002	2003
$870	$890

Retirement Earnings Test Exempt Amounts*

As of January 2000, the Retirement Earnings Test has been eliminated for individuals age 65-69. It remains in effect for those ages 62-64. A modified test applies for the year an individual reaches age 65.

	2002	2003
Year individual reaches 65*	$30,000/yr.	$30,720/yr.
	$2,500/mo.	$2,560/mo.
Under age 65	$11,280/yr.	$11,520/yr.
	$940/mo.	$960/mo.

***Note:** Applies only to earnings for months prior to attaining age 65. One dollar in benefits will be withheld for every $3 in earnings above the limit. There is no limit on earnings beginning the month an individual attains age 65.

One dollar in benefits will be withheld for every $2 in earnings above the limit.

Maximum Social Security Benefit: Worker Retiring at Age 65 in January of 2002 and 2003:

2002	2003
$1,660/mo.	$1,741/mo.

SSI Federal Payment Standard:

	2002	2003
Individual	$545/mo.	$552/mo.
Couple	$817/mo.	$829/mo.

SSI Resources Limits:

	2002	2003
Individual	$2,000	$2,000
Couple	$3,000	$3,000

Estimated Average Monthly Social Security Benefits: Before and After the December 2002 COLA:

	Before 1.4% COLA	After 1.4% COLA
All Retired Workers	$882	$895
Aged Couple, Both Receiving Benefits	$1,463	$1,483
Widowed Mother and Two Children	$1,812	$1,838
Aged Widow(er) Alone	$850	$862
Disabled Worker, Spouse and One or More Children	$1,376	$1,395
All Disabled Workers	$822	$833

APPENDIX 8: MEDICARE DEDUCTIBLE, COINSURANCE AND PREMIUM AMOUNTS 2003

Hospital Insurance (Part A)

- **Deductible** - $840 per each Benefit Period
- **Coinsurance**
  - $210 a day for the 61st through the 90th day, per Benefit Period
  - $420 a day for each "nonrenewable, lifetime reserve day"
- **Skilled Nursing Facility coinsurance** - $105 a day for the 21st through the 100th day per Benefit Period

* Some people age 65 or older do not meet the Social Security Administration's requirements for premium free Hospital Insurance (Part A). Individuals in this category can get Part A by paying a monthly premium. This is called "premium hospital insurance."

Medical Insurance (Part B)

- **Deductible** - $100 per year
- **Monthly Premium** - $58.70 (Note: A surcharge of 10% is assessed for each full 12 months (in the same continuous period of eligibility) in which a beneficiary could have been enrolled but was not.)

Source: Office of the Actuary/HCFA (See www.hcfa.gov or www.medicare.gov for updates)

APPENDIX 9: TABLE VI - ORDINARY JOINT LIFE AND LAST SURVIVOR ANNUITIES; TWO LIVES - EXPECTED RETURN MULTIPLES

Ages	65	66	67	68	69	70	71	72	73	74
65	26.2	25.8	25.4	25.0	24.6	24.3	23.9	23.7	23.4	23.1
66	25.8	25.3	24.9	24.5	24.1	23.7	23.4	23.1	22.8	22.5
67	25.4	24.9	24.4	24.0	23.6	23.2	22.8	22.5	22.2	21.9
68	25.0	24.5	24.0	23.5	23.1	22.7	22.3	22.0	21.6	21.3
69	24.6	24.1	23.6	23.1	22.6	22.2	21.8	21.4	21.1	20.8
70	24.3	23.7	23.2	22.7	22.2	21.8	21.3	20.9	20.6	20.2
71	23.9	23.4	22.8	22.3	21.8	21.3	20.9	20.5	20.1	19.7
72	23.7	23.1	22.5	22.0	21.4	20.9	20.5	20.0	19.6	19.3
73	23.4	22.8	22.2	21.6	21.1	20.6	20.1	19.6	19.2	18.8
74	23.1	22.5	21.9	21.3	20.8	20.2	19.7	19.3	18.8	18.4
75	22.9	22.3	21.6	21.0	20.5	19.9	19.4	18.9	18.4	18.0
76	22.7	22.0	21.4	20.8	20.2	19.6	19.1	18.6	18.1	17.6
77	22.5	21.8	21.2	20.6	19.9	19.4	18.8	18.3	17.8	17.3
78	22.4	21.7	21.0	20.3	19.7	19.1	18.5	18.0	17.5	17.0
79	22.2	21.5	20.8	20.1	19.5	18.9	18.3	17.7	17.2	16.7
80	22.1	21.3	20.6	20.0	19.3	18.7	18.1	17.5	16.9	16.4
81	21.9	21.2	20.5	19.8	19.1	18.5	17.9	17.3	16.7	16.2
82	21.8	21.1	20.4	19.7	19.0	18.3	17.7	17.1	16.5	15.9
83	21.7	21.0	20.2	19.5	18.8	18.2	17.5	16.9	16.3	15.7
84	21.6	20.9	20.1	19.4	18.7	18.0	17.4	16.7	16.1	15.5
85	21.6	20.8	20.1	19.3	18.6	17.9	17.3	16.6	16.0	15.4
86	21.5	20.7	20.0	19.2	18.5	17.8	17.1	16.5	15.8	15.2
87	21.4	20.7	19.9	19.2	18.4	17.7	17.0	16.4	15.7	15.1
88	21.4	20.6	19.8	19.1	18.3	17.6	16.9	16.3	15.6	15.0
89	21.3	20.5	19.8	19.0	18.3	17.6	16.9	16.2	15.5	14.9
90	21.3	20.5	19.7	19.0	18.2	17.5	16.8	16.1	15.4	14.8
91	21.3	20.5	19.7	18.9	18.2	17.4	16.7	16.0	15.4	14.7
92	21.2	20.4	19.6	18.9	18.1	17.4	16.7	16.0	15.3	14.6
93	21.2	20.4	19.6	18.8	18.1	17.3	16.6	15.9	15.2	14.6
94	21.2	20.4	19.6	18.8	18.0	17.3	16.6	15.9	15.2	14.5
95	21.1	20.3	19.6	18.8	18.0	17.3	16.5	15.8	15.1	14.5
96	21.1	20.3	19.5	18.8	18.0	17.2	16.5	15.8	15.1	14.4
97	21.1	20.3	19.5	18.7	18.0	17.2	16.5	15.8	15.1	14.4
98	21.1	20.3	19.5	18.7	17.9	17.2	16.4	15.7	15.0	14.3
99	21.1	20.3	19.5	18.7	17.9	17.2	16.4	15.7	15.0	14.3
100	21.1	20.3	19.5	18.7	17.9	17.1	16.4	15.7	15.0	14.3
101	21.1	20.2	19.4	18.7	17.9	17.1	16.4	15.6	14.9	14.2
102	21.1	20.2	19.4	18.6	17.9	17.1	16.4	15.6	14.9	14.2
103	21.0	20.2	19.4	18.6	17.9	17.1	16.3	15.6	14.9	14.2
104	21.0	20.2	19.4	18.6	17.8	17.1	16.3	15.6	14.9	14.2
105	21.0	20.2	19.4	18.6	17.8	17.1	16.3	15.6	14.9	14.2
106	21.0	20.2	19.4	18.6	17.8	17.1	16.3	15.6	14.8	14.1
107	21.0	20.2	19.4	18.6	17.8	17.0	16.3	15.6	14.8	14.1
108	21.0	20.2	19.4	18.6	17.8	17.0	16.3	15.5	14.8	14.1
109	21.0	20.2	19.4	18.6	17.8	17.0	16.3	15.5	14.8	14.1
110	21.0	20.2	19.4	18.6	17.8	17.0	16.3	15.5	14.8	14.1
111	21.0	20.2	19.4	18.6	17.8	17.0	16.3	15.5	14.8	14.1
112	21.0	20.2	19.4	18.6	17.8	17.0	16.3	15.5	14.8	14.1
113	21.0	20.2	19.4	18.6	17.8	17.0	16.3	15.5	14.8	14.1
114	21.0	20.2	19.4	18.6	17.8	17.0	16.3	15.5	14.8	14.1
115	21.0	20.2	19.4	18.6	17.8	17.0	16.3	15.5	14.8	14.1

APPENDIX 10: TABLE 2001 COSTS

Age	Annual Rates	Age	Annual Rates	Age	Annual Rates
0	0.70	34	0.98	68	16.92
1	0.41	35	0.99	69	18.70
2	0.27	36	1.01	70	20.62
3	0.19	37	1.04	71	22.72
4	0.13	38	1.06	72	25.07
5	0.13	39	1.07	73	27.57
6	0.14	40	1.10	74	30.18
7	0.15	41	1.13	75	33.05
8	0.16	42	1.20	76	36.33
9	0.16	43	1.29	77	40.17
10	0.16	44	1.40	78	44.33
11	0.19	45	1.53	79	49.23
12	0.24	46	1.67	80	54.56
13	0.28	47	1.83	81	60.51
14	0.33	48	1.98	82	66.74
15	0.38	49	2.13	83	73.07
16	0.52	50	2.30	84	80.35
17	0.57	51	2.52	85	88.76
18	0.59	52	2.81	86	99.16
19	0.61	53	3.20	87	110.40
20	0.62	54	3.65	88	121.85
21	0.62	55	4.15	89	133.40
22	0.64	56	4.68	90	144.30
23	0.66	57	5.20	91	155.80
24	0.68	58	5.66	92	168.75
25	0.71	59	6.06	93	186.44
26	0.73	60	6.51	94	206.70
27	0.76	61	7.11	95	228.35
28	0.80	62	7.96	96	250.01
29	0.83	63	9.08	97	265.09
30	0.87	64	10.41	98	270.11
31	0.90	65	11.90	99	281.05
32	0.93	66	13.51		
33	0.96	67	15.20		

APPENDIX 11: COST PER $1,000 OF PROTECTION FOR ONE MONTH (SECTION 79)

Age	Monthly Cost Per $1,000
Under 25	5 cents
25 through 29	6 cents
30 through 34	8 cents
35 through 39	9 cents
40 through 44	10 cents
45 through 49	15 cents
50 through 54	23 cents
55 through 59	43 cents
60 through 64	66 cents
65 through 69	$1.27
70 or older	$2.06

INDEX

#

A

B

C

D

E

F

R

S

T

U

V

W

ESTATE PLANNING

Outlines and Study Guides

TABLE OF CONTENTS

TABLE OF EXHIBITS

TABLE OF APPENDICES

Estate Planning

I. BASIC CONCEPTS

A. What is Estate Planning?

1. Estate planning is the process of accumulation, management, conservation, and transfer of wealth, considering legal, tax, and personal objectives. In short, it is financial planning for death.

> **Note:** If a person dies without a will, the state of domicile has a plan for the decedent; it is called intestacy.

2. Estate planning choices are not always clear-cut since emotional issues such as control and affection must be considered.
3. Estate planning objectives should include the efficient transfer of assets (minimize costs).
   a. Costs include opportunity costs, costs of transfer taxes (up to 49% for 2003), costs of documents, costs of probate.
4. Estate planning objectives should include the effective transfer of assets (the assets go to the desired beneficiary).
   a. Eliminate conflicts between will and property titling with survivorship rights.
   b. Eliminate conflicts between will and named beneficiaries in contracts.

B. Who Needs Estate Planning?

Persons who have . . .

1. Spouses.
2. Minor children.
3. Dependents (parents, handicapped, and children).
4. Substantial assets.
5. Specific items of personal property that they want to go to someone in particular (e.g., jewelry, collections, and art).
6. Charitable objectives.
7. Issues that need to be dealt with after their death, including:
   a. Unrelated persons who need to be provided for (e.g., life partners).
   b. Pets.
   c. Businesses.
   d. Problem family members (e.g., those who may contest the will or who cannot handle money).

C. WHY PEOPLE DON'T PLAN FOR ESTATE TRANSFERS.

1. They procrastinate due to an unwillingness to face the reality of mortality and an unwillingness to make transfer choices.
2. They are unaware of the present or future value of their estate. Therefore, they think there is no need to plan.
3. They are unaware of estate tax rates and transfer costs.
4. They are aware of the need and are willing to make choices, but simply consider themselves too busy to take the time to plan.

Note: Failure to plan could cost the decedent's estate up to 49% in federal estate taxes.

D. BENEFITS FROM ESTATE PLANNING (OBJECTIVES).

1. The client can reduce or eliminate the estate tax. This is relatively simple for estates less than 3-4 million dollars.
2. The client can make effective transfers during life and at death. Gifts of assets may include assets that are expected to appreciate greatly in the future.
3. Allows the client to arrange for efficient business succession.
4. A plan for health care and treatment can be created for decisions that may need to be made when the client is unable to do so.
5. The client can avoid the probate process including costs and delays (in certain instances).
6. The client has the ability to pass property to the individuals of the client's choice.
7. The client has peace of mind.

E. COSTS AND RISKS ASSOCIATED WITH FAILURE TO EFFECTIVELY PLAN FOR ESTATE TRANSFERS.

1. Assets are not transferred to appropriate heir (intestacy).
2. Costs and delays associated with probate are incurred due to the failure to optimize the use of assets that pass outside of probate (e.g., joint property with survivorship features, contracts with named beneficiaries, and trusts).
3. Excessive estate taxes may be incurred. Heirs would receive a smaller portion of the estate than would be possible with estate planning (see Common Estate Planning Mistakes - Section XVII).

F. COLLECTING CLIENT INFORMATION AND DEFINING TRANSFER OBJECTIVES.

1. Information to be collected:
   a. Family information (parents, children, ages, health, etc.).
   b. Detailed list of assets, ownership, and liabilities.
   c. Medical and disability insurance.
   d. Life insurance in force, ownership, insured, and beneficiaries.
   e. Annuities.
   f. Wills, trusts, or gifts previously made.
   g. Powers of appointment held by the client.
   h. Value of assets at fair market value and the determination of the expected growth rate.
   i. Tax returns and mortgages.
2. Examples of transfer objectives:
   a. Minimizing estate and transfer taxes (this will maximize the assets received by heirs).
   b. Avoiding probate.
   c. Using lifetime transfers – applicable exclusion amount (credit equivalent).
   d. Meeting liquidity needs.
   e. Planning for children from all marriages of the client.
   f. Planning for possible incapacity.
   g. Providing for the needs of the surviving spouse.
   h. Fulfilling charitable intentions.

G. THE ESTATE PLANNING PROCESS.

1. Gather client information.
   a. Current balance sheet (list all assets, including FMV, basis, date acquired, how title is held).
   b. Cash flow statement.
   c. Family information.
2. Establish client objectives.
3. Define problem areas which may include:
   a. Disposition of assets.
   b. Liquidity issues.
   c. Excessive taxes or costs.
   d. Other situational needs (e.g., disability).

4. Determine liquidity needs now and at every five-year interval for remaining life expectancy including estate transfer costs.
5. Establish priorities for objectives.
6. Develop a comprehensive plan with all information and objectives.
7. Implement the plan.
8. Review the plan periodically and update when necessary.

H. THE ESTATE PLANNING TEAM.

1. May consist of a number of professionals.
    a. Attorney.
    b. Accountant.
    c. Life insurance underwriter.
    d. Financial planner.
    e. Trust officers.
2. The financial planner helps to integrate the work of the team in developing the plan.

Example

While a financial planner would usually ask a client for a current cash flow statement, recommend a specified type of disability policy, and discuss tax-planning opportunities with the client's accountant, he cannot draft a trust document, or any other legal document unless he is also a practicing attorney.

II. BASIC DOCUMENTS INCLUDED IN AN ESTATE PLAN

A. WILL.

1. A will is a legal document that enables the testator to transfer the property in the manner the testator desires.
2. Advantages of a will include:
   a. Executor can be named.
   b. Can transfer property to anyone desired.
   c. Assures the maximum marital deduction if decedent wants property to pass to spouse.
   d. Can specify how estate taxes are apportioned.
   e. Can designate guardians for minors.
   f. Can contain provisions to establish trusts.
   g. Charitable beneficiaries can be named.
3. Intestacy.
   a. To die "intestate" is to die without a valid will. In this case, the probate court directs how the decedent's property will be distributed according to the state's intestacy laws. Just as one suit size will not fit everyone, the intestacy laws are not likely to distribute property the way you would have if you had written your own will.
   b. There are some possible adverse consequences of intestacy.
      i. In some states, a spouse's share of the decedent's estate will be equal to a child's. For example, the surviving spouse's share with one child might be one-half, with nine children it will be one-tenth.
      ii. Some states provide that a spouse's share is only a life estate with the true owner being the children.
      iii. The surviving spouse may share with the deceased spouse's parents or brothers and sisters when there are no children.
      iv. Children may be treated equally, but not necessarily equitably. Each child's needs may be quite different.
      v. Intestacy may require the administrator to furnish a surety bond and obtain probate court approval of the administrator's actions, thereby raising the cost of administration.
      vi. The court will select the administrator of the estate.
4. General rules for making a valid will.
   a. The will-maker must be 18 years old (unless emancipated minor).
   b. The will-maker must be of sound mind (testamentary capacity). The sound mind rules are not as stringent as those that are required to contract.
      i. Must understand the nature of the act.
      ii. Must understand the general nature of the property.
      iii. Must have the ability to remember and understand the nature of the relationship to the persons affected.

c. Absence of undue influence.

   i. Undue influence is present when the testator's free will has been substituted by someone else's free will.

Example

University official visits dying alum and convinces alum that building a new business school will give alum immortality. This is considered undue influence.

---

d. Absence of fraud.

   i. Fraud is the intentional misstatement of fact with the intent of deceiving the testator, which results in amending the will.

   ii. Must ask if fraud was the sole motive of the bequest.

5. Types of wills.

   a. Holographic (handwritten) will.

      i. Allowed by about 50% of the states.

      ii. Material provisions are in the testator's handwriting.

      iii. Must be signed and dated.

      iv. Need not be witnessed.

   b. Nuncupative (oral) will - dying declaration before sufficient witnesses.

      i. Recognized by less than half of all states.

      ii. May only be able to pass personal property (and not real) in some states.

      iii. Use is fairly restricted.

   c. Statutory (formal) will.

      i. Should be drawn by an attorney.

      ii. Must comply with the laws of the domiciliary state.

      iii. Usually signed in the presence of two witnesses (beneficiary usually can't be a witness).

6. The general provisions of a will.

   a. An introductory clause to identify the testator.

   b. Establishment of the domicile. This is important because each jurisdiction has its own Probate Code. Any property outside the domicile will be subject to ancillary probate.

   c. A declaration that this is the last will and testament.

   d. A revocation of all prior wills and codicils.

   e. Identification of executor/executrix and successor executor/executrix.

   f. A payments of debts clause.

   g. A payments of taxes clause.

h. A disposition of tangible personal property clause.

i. A disposition of real estate clause (residence).

j. Specific bequests of intangibles and cash.

k. A residuary clause (the transfer of the balance of any other assets to someone or something).

> **Note:** Failure to have a residuary clause will result in the risk of having intestate assets (e.g., from assets being accumulated after the will was prepared) that will pass through probate. Also, taxes will be paid from the residuary unless specifically directed otherwise.

l. An appointment and powers clause that names fiduciaries, guardians, tutors, etc.

m. A testator's signature clause.

n. An attestation clause (witness clause).

7. Other clauses in a will.

   a. Simultaneous death clause - in the event that both spouses die simultaneously; it provides that one spouse (predetermined) predeceased the other spouse.

   b. Survivorship clause - a beneficiary must survive a specified period beyond the testator's death in order to receive the inheritance or bequest. Such a clause will prevent property from being included in two estates in rapid succession. In order to qualify for the marital deduction, the will cannot require the spouse to survive for more than six months to receive the bequest.

   c. Spendthrift clause - bars transfer of beneficiary's interest and stipulates that it is not subject to claims of beneficiary's creditors. The spendthrift clause is not usually effective in a will.

   d. Clauses regarding disclaimers - while unnecessary to include, a disclaimer clause reminds the reader that disclaiming may be an effective tool in estate planning (see Section V.I.6. on page 912 for more information on disclaimers).

   e. No contest clause - discourages heirs from contesting the will by substantially decreasing or eliminating their bequest if they file a formal contest.

   f. A Codicil - a separate document that amends a will.

8. Ways property can be distributed in a will:

   a. Per stirpes distribution.

      i. Per stirpes means "by the roots."

      ii. With a per stirpes distribution, members of a designated class inherit property as members of the class.

         A) This election is usually used by the courts in the absence of a selection in the will.

Example

Stephen has 3 children (Jay, Tawnee, and Laura). Tawnee is deceased and is survived by 2 children (Paul and Damien). Laura is alive and has 1 child (Marie). If Stephen had a $300,000 asset, and his will had a per stirpes distribution:

- Jay would receive $100,000 (1/3).
- Paul and Damien would each receive $50,000 (half of Tawnee's 1/3).
- Laura would receive $100,000 (1/3).

b. Per capital distribution.

i. Per capital means "by the head."

ii. Members of a class, including heirs of a deceased member, share in the inheritance as individuals.

Example

Stephen has 3 children (Jay, Tawnee, and Laura). Tawnee is deceased and is survived by 2 children (Paul and Damien). Laura is alive and has 1 child (Marie). If Stephen had a $300,000 asset, and his will had a per capita distribution:

- Jay would receive $75,000 (1/4).
- Paul would receive $75,000 (1/4).
- Damien would receive $75,000 (1/4).
- Laura would receive $75,000 (1/4).

Most people want to transfer an equal portion to each of their children, and barring abnormal circumstances, will leave grandchildren of deceased parents the portion the deceased child would have received to equally divide among them. Notice the difference in distributions received by each child/grandchild. Close attention must be used in referring to the type of distribution as it will greatly affect the wealth transfer to each beneficiary.

B. LIVING WILLS AND MEDICAL DIRECTIVES (ADVANCED MEDICAL DIRECTIVES).

1. A living will establishes the medical situations in which the testator no longer wants life-sustaining treatment.

   a. Must generally meet the requirements of a formally drafted state statute. A durable power of attorney for health care may or may not substitute (usually not).

   b. Only covers a narrow range of situations, usually applies only to terminal patients.

   c. Does not appoint a surrogate decision maker.

   d. May create problems that arise from vagueness or ambiguities in drafting.

2. An alternative to the living will is a durable power of attorney for health care.
    a. Appoints person to make health care decisions.
    b. Always springs (becomes effective) on incapacity.
    c. Recognized in most states.
    d. May not be sufficient to terminate life support.

C. DURABLE POWER OF ATTORNEY FOR PROPERTY.

1. A written document enabling one individual (principal) to designate another person or persons to act as his "attorney-in-fact" (agent) is termed a durable power of attorney. The principal:
    a. Must be 18.
    b. Must be competent.
2. The power survives disability and/or incapacity, but not death (a nondurable power of attorney does not survive client's incapacity).
3. The power may be limited (e.g., to pay any bills) or unlimited (e.g., all of the legal powers I have myself).
    a. A limited power is a special power.
        i. Held to an ascertainable standard (health/education/maintenance/support).
        ii. May be almost as broad as a general power except no appointing to self/creditors/heirs/ heirs' creditors.
    b. An unlimited power is a general power that gives the appointee the power to do anything the principal could do.
        i. The unlimited power to appoint to oneself or one's creditors may result in gift tax or inclusion in the estate of the one who has the power.

> **Note:** A person possessing an unlimited durable power of attorney, in most cases, is not permitted to make gifts to himself or other family members (usually in conjunction with estate planning). If the power to gift is a desirable feature of the Power of Attorney, it should be separately and explicitly stated.

4. Such a device may negate the necessity to petition a local court to appoint a guardian ad litem or conservator.
5. Such a device provides for continuity in the management of affairs in the event of disability and/or incapacity.
6. The power may be springing or immediately effective (nonspringing). Generally, if springing, the device must indicate that the power springs upon disability or incapacity and is not affected by subsequent disability or incapacity (not authorized by all states).
7. The power is revocable by the principal.
8. Usually less expensive to set up and administer than a living trust or conservatorship.
9. Durable powers of attorney can be abused so the principal should give serious consideration to naming the attorney-in-fact.

Example

- Sam, a small business owner in poor health, is concerned about who will make not only business decisions should he become incapacitated, but also who would manage his personal affairs. Sam could execute two durable powers, each naming an attorney-in-fact to make decisions. A relative could be named to manage personal affairs, while a business associate could be named to manage the business. The powers would only spring upon Sam's incapacity.
- Durable powers of attorney are particularly important for nontraditional couples (heterosexual couples who have decided not to marry or same-sex couples). Without this document in place (for both property and health care), the ability to make crucial decisions may fall to family members rather than a partner in the relationship.

D. A SIDE OR PERSONAL INSTRUCTION LETTER.

1. Details and wishes regarding tangible possessions and disposition of body of decedent, including funeral arrangements, etc.
2. Avoids cluttering the will with small details.

III. OWNERSHIP OF PROPERTY AND HOW IT IS TRANSFERRED

A. PROPERTY INTERESTS (TITLE AND OWNERSHIP).

1. Types.

   a. Fee simple - Complete ownership with all rights (sell, gift, alienate, convey, etc.). Property will pass through probate process (fee simple absolute). Fee simple property is also referred to as "sole ownership" property.

   b. Life estate - Income interest in property ceases upon the death of the owner of the life estate.

   c. Usufruct - A Louisiana concept similar to life estate that will cease on the death of the usufructuary (or remarriage if legal usufruct). If a legal usufruct, the property passing to a spouse will not qualify for the unlimited marital deduction due to the terminable interest rule. (The right to use and the right to fruits, e.g., income).

   d. Interest for term - Another version of life estate or usufruct, but for a definite term as opposed to a life term.

2. Forms.

   a. Tenancy in common - Two or more persons holding an undivided interest in the whole property (relative ownership percentage may differ). The property is treated as owned outright and one's interest can be sold, donated, willed, or passed intestate. When one owner dies, the other owner does not automatically receive the decedent's interest. The property usually passes through probate. There is a right of partition.

Example

Richard and Robert own a piece of land in southern Alabama. Richard is a 2/3 owner and Robert owns 1/3. Since the percent interests differ, the property must be held as tenants in common. Joint tenants must be equal owners.

   b. Joint tenancy - Two or more persons holding the same fractional interest (equal owners). Normally implied is the right of survivorship (JTWROS). Joint tenants have right to sever interest in property without the consent of the joint tenant (and destroy the survivorship right). Property held JTWROS passes to the surviving owners outside of probate according to operation of law.

   c. Tenancy by the entirety - A JTWROS between husband and wife. Generally will not be able to sever interest without the consent of the spouse. This form of ownership is only recognized in certain states and gives greater creditor protection than a regular JTWROS.

   d. Community property.

      i. In general.

         A) Married individuals own an equal undivided interest in all wealth accumulated during the marriage.

         B) Community property states include: Arizona, California, Idaho, Louisiana, Nevada, New Mexico, Texas, Washington, and Wisconsin.

ii. Characteristics.

A) There is no automatic right of succession of ownership of community property.

B) One half of the value of all community property is included in the gross estate of the first to die.

C) There is a step-up in both halves of community property in the hands of the heir at the death of the first spouse.

D) Quasi-community property – property acquired by residents of noncommunity property states that would be considered community property if acquired in a community property state.

EXHIBIT 1: KEY PROPERTY INTEREST

	Gross Estate Inclusion	Inclusion in Probate Estate	Rights of Survivorship	Unlimited Marital Deduction	Partitionable without Consent
Fee Simple (outright ownership)	100%	Yes	No	If spouse	N/A
Tenants in Common (2 or more holding different interests)	Percent ownership	Yes	No	If spouse	Yes
Joint Tenancy (WROS)	Non-spouses - rule of contribution; spouses - 50%	No	Yes	If spouse	Yes
Tenancy by Entirety (between spouses)	50%	No	Yes	Yes	No
Community Property (between spouses)	50%	Yes	No	If spouse	No

iii. Exceptions to community property (separate property).

A) Property acquired prior to marriage.

B) Property acquired by gift.

C) Property inherited by one spouse.

D) Property acquired by court award.

E) It is possible to create separate property out of community property by donating a spouse's interest to the other spouse (and vice versa). Individuals in community property states can usually opt out of the community property scheme by filing a declaration with the state (partition of community property).

iv. Migratory couples.

A) Moving from a community property state to a common law (separate property) state.

1) In general, the character of property is not changed, and therefore will remain community property.

2) The spouses may choose to divide the property upon arrival in a common law state. If the property is divided, when one spouse dies, the benefits of a stepped-up basis of both halves of the property will be lost.

B) Moving from a common law state to a community property state.

1) In general, separate property owned while in a common law state remains separate property after a move to a community property state.

2) Upon death, a surviving spouse typically has no claim against the separate property. However, several states have elective share statutes that prevent a spouse from being disinherited.

B. TYPES OF INTERESTS TRANSFERRED.

1. Outright - Transferee receives both legal title and beneficial (economic) ownership.
2. Legal - Transferee receives only legal title (e.g., trustee of trust).
3. Beneficial - Transferee receives economic or beneficial ownership but not legal title (beneficiary of trust).

C. TRANSFERS DURING LIFE.

1. Arms-length transactions.
   a. Sales and exchanges.
   b. Installment sales.
2. Transfers to loved ones.
   a. Sales/exchanges – include:
      i. Sales and installment sales.
      ii. Private annuities.
      iii. Self-canceling installment notes.
   b. Partial gift/sales.
      i. Grantor Retained Trusts (i.e., GRATs and GRUTs).
      ii. Qualified Personal Residence Trust (QPRTs).
   c. Transfers not subject to gift tax.
      i. Legal support.
      ii. Qualified transfer (educational and medical expenses paid directly to institutions).
      iii. Gifts to spouses.
      iv. Annual exclusion.
      v. Gift loans.
      vi. Disclaimers.

d. Transfer subject to gift tax.
   i. Use of applicable exclusion amount ($1,000,000 for 2003).
   ii. Gifts beyond applicable exclusion amount will create a gift tax liability.
e. Common order of transfers to loved ones (precise order depends on facts and circumstances).
   i. Legal support.
   ii. Annual exclusion gifts ($11,000/yr. per donee).
   iii. Gift loans.
   iv. Qualified transfers (generally for benefit of grandchildren).
   v. Gifts to spouses.
   vi. Use of applicable credit amount.
   vii. Taxable gifts.
   viii. Private annuities.
   ix. Use of disclaimers.

3. Transfers to charities.
   a. Completed gifts.
   b. Direct gifts.
   c. Partial gifts/exchanges.
   d. Charitable gift annuity.
   e. Pooled income fund.
   f. Charitable Remainder Trust (CRATs and CRUTs).
   g. Charitable Lead Trust (CLATs and CLUTs).
4. Advantage of lifetime gifts.
   a. Qualified transfers reduce gross estate.
   b. Using the annual exclusion reduces the gross estate.
   c. Can give unlimited gifts to spouse without transfer tax consequences (provided spouse is a U.S. citizen).
   d. Can give up to $1,000,000 (for 2003) without incurring transfer tax.
   e. After completion of the gift, appreciation on the gifted property is not subject to transfer tax.
   f. Gift tax paid on gifts prior to three years before death is not subject to transfer tax.
   g. Income shifting on gifts can be accomplished.

D. TRANSFERS AT DEATH.

1. By will.
2. By laws of intestacy.
3. By other laws (e.g., jointly held property - JTWROS).
4. By contract (named beneficiary – other than estate). Such as:
   a. Insurance policies.
   b. IRAs.
   c. Retirement plan assets (e.g., 401(k) plans).
   d. Marriage contracts.
   e. Annuities.
   f. Pay on Death (PODs) account – bank account that has a named beneficiary and passes outside of probate (similar to Totten Trust).
   g. Transfer on Death (TODs) account – investment account that has a named beneficiary and passes outside of probate.
5. By trust.
   a. Revocable trusts (revocable prior to death, irrevocable at death).
   b. Irrevocable trusts (usually treated as a gift or transfer during life).

E. CONSEQUENCES OF TRANSFERS.

a. Loss of control if sale or gift.

b. Taxes may have to be paid. Gift taxes may be due for inter vivos (lifetime) transfers and are paid by the donor (unless net gift).

> **Note:** Gifts of a future interest generally do not qualify for the annual exclusion. A remainder interest in a trust is an example of a future interest gift.

c. Costs and delays may occur in probate for assets transferred by will or intestacy (see Exhibit 2).

F. NONTRADITIONAL RELATIONSHIPS.

1. In general.
   a. Nontraditional relationships include same-sex relationships, communal relationships, and cohabitation.
   b. Nontraditional relationships can have many gift and estate tax disadvantages.
   c. Certain planning opportunities available to married couples are not available to unmarried couples.

2. Disadvantages.
   a. No gift tax marital deduction is available to unmarried couples.
      i. In some cases, a common law husband and wife may be eligible for the marital deduction.
      ii. An unmarried donor will only be able to use the annual exclusion to reduce the amount of the taxable gift. (In addition, gift splitting is not available.)
   b. No estate tax marital deduction is available to unmarried couples.
      i. The estate of an unmarried person is more likely to pay federal estate tax than the estate of a married individual.
   c. Surviving cohabitants have no intestacy rights to the decedent's property.
      i. If decedent dies without a will, the intestacy laws determine who will receive the decedent's property.
      ii. Unmarried couples should generally have a will, legal titling, or trusts to prevent undesired consequences.
3. Planning for nontraditional relationships (generally avoid probate).
   a. Create a will leaving specific bequests to the partner.
   b. Make lifetime gifts to partner.
   c. Convert property owned outright into Joint Tenancy With Right of Survivorship (JTWROS) or Tenancy in Common.
      i. JTWROS property will avoid probate, but the entire date-of-death value must be included in the gross estate of the decedent who purchased the property initially.
      ii. Tenancy in Common property will not avoid probate, but it is possible that only the decedent's share of the property will be included in his or her estate at death.
   d. Name the other cohabitant as the beneficiary of qualified plans and IRAs.
   e. Obtain life insurance policy with the other cohabitant as beneficiary.
   f. Make charitable bequests at death to take advantage of the estate tax charitable deduction.
   g. Use P.O.D. (Pay on Death) and T.O.D. (Transfer on Death) beneficiary designations for bank and investment accounts.

IV. THE PROBATE PROCESS

A. DEFINITION.

Property must change title when transferred from one person to another. When someone dies, probate is the legal process that performs the function of transferring title to those properties that do not transfer title some other way (See IV.B. below). Probate also proves the validity of any will, supervises the orderly distribution of assets to the heirs, and protects creditors by insuring that debts of the estate are paid.

EXHIBIT 2: DUTIES OF EXECUTOR AND/OR ADMINISTRATOR

Decedent Dies Testate (with will)	Decedent Dies Intestate (without will)
Executor:	Administrator:
1. Locates and proves will.	1. Petitions court for his or her own appointment.
2. Locates witnesses to will.	2. Receives letters of administration.
3. Receives letters testamentary from court.	3. Posts required bond.

Duties of the Executor or Administrator
1. Locates and assembles property.
2. Safeguards, manages, and invests property.
3. Advertises in newspapers.
4. Locates and communicates with potential beneficiaries.
5. Pays expenses of decedent.
6. Pays debts and taxes (files tax returns, such as Forms 1040, 1041, and 706).
7. Distributes assets to beneficiaries according to will or laws of intestacy.

B. PROPERTY PASSING OUTSIDE OF PROBATE.

1. Contracts.
   a. Life insurance proceeds with a named beneficiary.
   b. All pension plans and IRAs with named beneficiaries.
   c. All annuities with named joint annuitants.
2. By operation law.
   a. Property held by joint tenants with survivorship rights (JTWROS or Tenants by Entirety).
   b. All trust property - by trust terms. Both revocable and irrevocable trusts avoid probate.

EXHIBIT 3: ASSETS PASSING THROUGH AND AROUND THE PROBATE PROCESS

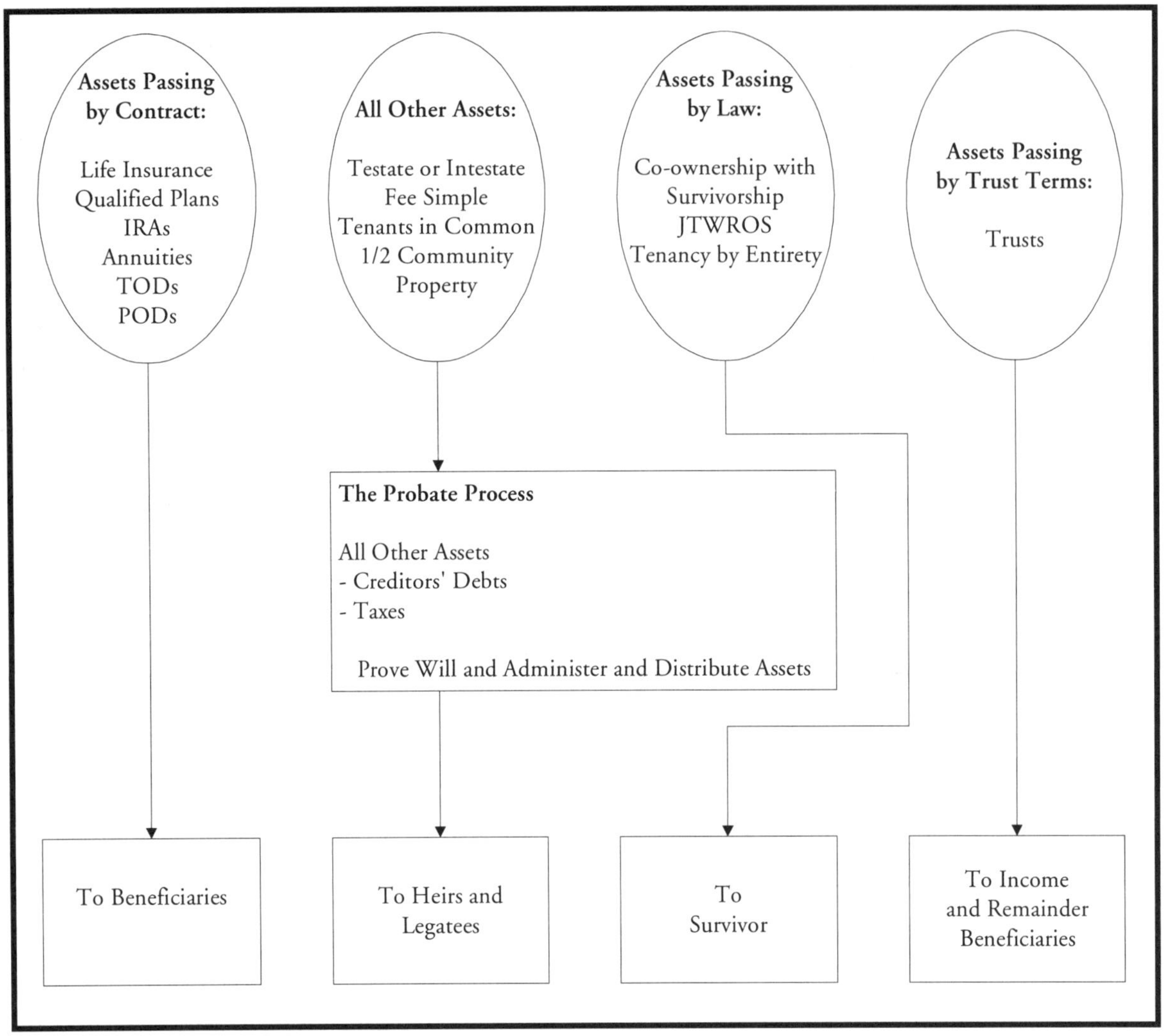

C. PROPERTY PASSING THROUGH PROBATE.

1. Property disposed of by will.
    a. Fee simple (title).
    b. Tenancy in common.
    c. All other willed property.
2. Property owned but not transferred by will (intestate property, including that resulting from the failure to provide a residuary clause).

D. ADVANTAGES OF THE PROBATE PROCESS.

1. Protects creditors by insuring that debts of the estate are paid.
2. Implements disposition objectives of the testator of a valid will.
3. Provides clean title to heirs or legatees.
4. Increases the chance that all parties in interest have notice of proceedings and, therefore, have a right to be heard.
5. Provides for an orderly administration of decedent's assets.

E. DISADVANTAGES OF THE PROBATE PROCESS.

1. Probate can be costly and complex. Real property located in a state outside the testator's domicile will trigger a separate probate in that state.
2. Probate can create delays.
3. The probate process is open to public scrutiny.

F. ALTERNATIVES TO PROBATE.

1. Joint tenancy with survivorship.
2. Tenancy by the entirety.
3. Living trust (revocable inter vivos, irrevocable at death).
4. Other trusts (See section titled, "Trusts").
5. Holding property that passes outside of probate by law or contract.

V. FEDERAL GIFT AND ESTATE TAXATION

A. HISTORY.

1. Prior to the Tax Reform Act of 1976:

   a. A separate federal estate tax and a separate federal gift tax existed. The gift tax rates were lower than those applicable to the federal estate tax. For gifts in excess of the annual exclusion, a specific lifetime exemption of $30,000 was allowed per donor.

   b. Every estate was allowed an exemption of $60,000. Decedents with modest amounts of wealth would not be subject to the federal estate tax.

   c. Lifetime giving had no effect on the determination of the federal estate tax except in the case of certain gifts made within three years of the donor's death.

2. The Tax Reform Act of 1976 made sweeping changes to the existing structure of the federal gift and estate taxes. For transfers after 1976:

   a. The separate sets of gift and estate tax rates were replaced with a unified transfer tax rate schedule, progressive in nature with the top marginal rate of 55%.

   b. Both gift and estate tax exemptions were replaced by a unified tax credit. The unified credit is now referred to as the applicable credit amount. For 2003, the applicable credit amount for gift and estate taxes is $345,800, which effectively shelters up to $1,000,000 of assets from estate and gift tax.

   c. Taxable gifts made after December 31, 1976, must be added to the taxable estate in arriving at the tax base for applying the estate tax at death.

3. The Economic Growth and Tax Relief Reconciliation Act of 2001 (TRA 2001) effectively creates different gift and estate applicable exclusion amounts and applicable credit amounts in future years. (See table below.)

   a. Estate tax - the estate tax applicable exclusion amount is increased in future years, and the highest estate tax rate will be decreased based on the following schedule. The estate tax will be repealed completely after 2009.

   b. Gift tax - the gift tax applicable exclusion amount is $1,000,000 ($345,800 gift tax applicable credit amount) for 2003. This applicable exclusion amount will remain at $1,000,000 for all future years. The gift tax is not repealed after 2009.

   c. Generation-skipping transfer taxes are repealed after 2009.

   d. Sunset provisions – under the new law, the estate, gift, and transfer tax provisions provided for in EGTRA 2001 will sunset in 2010. Thus, rates, laws, and exclusions will return to 2001 rates after 2010.

Year of Death	Maximum Gift Tax Rate	Gift Tax Applicable Exclusion Amount	Gift Tax Applicable Credit Amount	Maximum Estate Tax Rate	Estate Tax Applicable Exclusion Amount	Estate Tax Applicable Credit Amount
2003	49%	$1,000,000	$345,800	49%	$1,000,000	$345,800
2004	48%	$1,000,000	$345,800	48%	$1,500,000	$555,800
2005	47%	$1,000,000	$345,800	47%	$1,500,000	$555,800
2006	46%	$1,000,000	$345,800	46%	$2,000,000	$780,800
2007	45%	$1,000,000	$345,800	45%	$2,000,000	$780,800
2008	45%	$1,000,000	$345,800	45%	$2,000,000	$780,800
2009	45%	$1,000,000	$345,800	45%	$3,500,000	$1,455,800
2010	35%	$1,000,000	$330,800	Repealed	Repealed	Repealed

B. TRANSFER TAXES - OVERVIEW.

1. The unified transfer tax, which is an excise tax, covers all taxable gratuitous transfers after December 31, 1976.
   a. The gift tax is a tax on transfers during the donor's lifetime (including gifts prior to 1977 and after 1976).
   b. The estate tax is a tax on transfers at or after death.
2. Persons subject to the tax:
   a. The gift tax applies to all completed transfers of property during the donor's lifetime, wherever situated, by individuals who, at the time of the gift, are citizens or residents of the United States. For those who are neither residents nor citizens of the United States, the federal gift tax is applicable to only those gifts of property located within the United States.
   b. The federal estate tax applies to U.S. citizens, residents, and nonresidents owning U.S. property. However, the application may be different in cases involving nonresident property owners depending on individual treaties.

3. Tax formula (See Exhibit 5).

   a. The computation of the federal gift tax is as follows:

	Current Transfers/Gifts
-	Split gifts
-	Annual exclusion
=	Taxable transfer
-	Less deductions:
	Charitable deduction
	Marital deduction
=	Taxable gifts made in current year
+	Taxable gifts from prior years
=	Total Taxable Gifts
	Unified transfer tax on total taxable gifts
-	Tax paid or deemed paid on prior taxable gifts*
-	The unified tax credit
=	**Tax due on gifts made in current year**

   b. The federal estate tax is computed as follows (See Exhibit 7).

	Gross estate	
	Less:	Funeral expenses
		Administrative costs
		Debts
		Unpaid taxes
		Losses
=	Adjusted gross estate	
	Less:	Marital deduction
		Charitable deduction
=	Taxable estate	
+	Post-1976 taxable gifts	
=	Tax base	
	Tentative tax on total transfers	
-	Tax paid or deemed paid on prior taxable gifts*	
-	Tax credits (including unified tax credit)	
=	Federal estate tax due	

* *Credit on prior gifts is calculated at current unified transfer tax rates (See Section VI.M. "Deemed Paid Adjustment.")*

4. The fair market value of property on the date transferred generally determines the amount subject to gift or estate tax. An estate may elect the alternate valuation date. (See page 975 for "Alternate Valuation Date.")

EXHIBIT 4: 2003 UNIFIED TAX RATE SCHEDULE (FOR GIFTS AND ESTATES)

Over $0 but not over $10,000	**18%** of such amount
Over $10,000 but not over $20,000	$1,800 plus **20%** of the excess of such amount over $10,000
Over $20,000 but not over $40,000	$3,800 plus **22%** of the excess of such amount over $20,000
Over $40,000 but not over $60,000	$8,200 plus **24%** of the excess of such amount over $40,000
Over $60,000 but not over $80,000	$13,000 plus **26%** of the excess of such amount over $60,000
Over $80,000 but not over $100,000	$18,200 plus **28%** of the excess of such amount over $80,000
Over $100,000 but not over $150,000	$23,800 plus **30%** of the excess of such amount over $100,000
Over $150,000 but not over $250,000	$38,800 plus **32%** of the excess of such amount over $150,000
Over $250,000 but not over $500,000	$70,800 plus **34%** of the excess of such amount over $250,000
Over $500,000 but not over $750,000	$155,800 plus **37%** of the excess of such amount over $500,000
Over $750,000 but not over $1,000,000	$248,300 plus **39%** of the excess of such amount over $750,000
Over $1,000,000 but not over $1,250,000	$345,800 plus **41%** of the excess of such amount over $1,000,000
Over $1,250,000 but not over $1,500,000	$448,300 plus **43%** of the excess of such amount over $1,250,000
Over $1,500,000 but not over $2,000,000	$555,800 plus **45%** of the excess of such amount over $1,500,000
Over $2,000,000	$780,800 plus **49%** of the excess of such amount over $2,000,000

VI. THE FEDERAL GIFT TAX

A. INTRODUCTION.

1. A gift is a completed transfer of an interest in property by an individual in exchange for less than full and adequate consideration. Gifts, for gift tax purposes, generally fall under the category of love and affection. Gifts by businesses are generally not considered to be for love and affection and, subject to de minimis exceptions, may be included in the income of the recipient.
2. Gift tax applies to completed lifetime gifts (inter vivos).
3. Gifts at death are called bequests and are subject to federal estate tax.

B. COMPLETED INTER VIVOS TRANSFERS (COMPLETED LIFETIME GIFTS).

1. Under state law, for a gift to be complete, all of the following conditions must be present:
   a. The donor must be competent to make the gift.
   b. There must be donative intent on behalf of the donor.
   c. There must be actual or constructive delivery of the property (gift) to the donee or to the donee's representative.
   d. There must be valid acceptance of the gift by the donee.

Note: As with bequests, the donee may refuse to accept the gift.

2. Completed gifts are subject to gift tax unless de minimis or a particular exclusion applies.
3. For federal gift tax purposes, donative intent is not required to fall within the statutes but is presumptive evidence that a gift has occurred.
4. Outright transfers where the donor has completely given up dominion and control over the property are completed. Donations in trust may be complete, partially complete, or totally incomplete. Recalls (contingent gifts) and gifts that are incomplete are not subject to gift tax until they become complete.

Example

Pedro gave his girlfriend an antique box that he paid $15 for at a flea market. When the girlfriend opened the present, she was so excited that she dropped the box and a diamond rolled out of a secret compartment. The diamond was appraised for $15,000. Pedro made a gift of $15. There was no donative intent on the diamond since he didn't know it existed, therefore, there was no gift of the diamond.

C. PERSONS SUBJECT TO GIFT TAX.

The federal gift tax applies to all individual U.S. citizens or residents, regardless of where the property is located and whether the transfer is direct or indirect, tangible or intangible, personal or real property. The federal gift tax also applies to nonresident aliens with regard to transfers of real and tangible personal property located within the United States.

D. INCOMPLETE TRANSFERS.

1. The federal gift tax does not apply to incomplete transfers.
2. Examples of incomplete transfers include those where the donor retained a right to reclaim the interest donated, or where the donor had not completely given up dominion and control over the property (revocable trusts).
3. An incomplete transfer may subsequently become complete and would, at that time, be subject to gift tax (i.e., when a revocable trust becomes irrevocable).
4. The creation of a joint bank account does not result in a gift until the noncontributing party withdraws funds for their own benefit.

Example

Patrick created a joint bank account for himself and his friend Kristie. There is no gift until Kristie (the donee) draws on the account for her own benefit.

E. THE ANNUAL EXCLUSION AND GIFT SPLITTING.

1. Under IRC Section 2503(b), a donor may exclude from taxable gifts the first $11,000 (for 2003) of gifts each year to each donee.
   a. The gifts must be of a present interest, meaning that the donee has the immediate right to the use and enjoyment of the transferred property.
   b. Gifts of a future interest, where the donee's interest is vested at a future time or based on some contingency, are not eligible for the annual exclusion.
   c. For gifts in trust, the annual exclusion applies to each beneficiary or contingent beneficiary of the trust (Estate of Maria Christofani, 97 TC 74 (1991)) assuming the trust has a Crummey Power (See Crummey Powers, Crummey v. Comm., 397 F2d 82 (9th Cir. 1961)).

Example

Jennifer, who is single, gave an outright gift of $60,000 to a friend, Tiffany, who needed the money to pay her medical expenses. The gift is outright to Tiffany and, therefore, qualifies for the $11,000 annual exclusion. This is not a qualified transfer for educational or medical purposes because the payee is not an institution.

---

2. The annual exclusion can be doubled to $22,000 (for 2003) per donee by gift splitting with a spouse.
   a. The gift is made by the donor but the spouse must consent to gift splitting.
   b. A gift tax return (Form 709) is required for all split gifts and both spouses must sign the return.
   c. Gifts of community property do not require gift splitting since, by nature, each spouse is deemed to own one-half of the community property.
   d. Gift splitting was enacted as a way to equalize community and noncommunity property states.

> **Note:** If an election to split gifts is made, it applies to all gifts made during that year. In addition, a gift may only be split with a spouse, and the donor must have been married at the time of the gift.

Example

Kelly (single) made the following gifts in the current year:

Gift	Donee	Value
Cash	Nephew	$12,000
6-month CD	Niece	8,000
Antique rifle	Friend	20,000
Bonds in irrevocable trust: Life estate to:	Father	60,000
Remainder to:	Niece	18,000

Kelly's total taxable gifts for the current year $77,000.

Donee	FMV	Annual Exclusion	Taxable Gifts
Nephew	$12,000	$11,000	$1,000
Niece	8,000	8,000	0
Friend	20,000	11,000	9,000
Father	60,000	11,000	49,000
Niece	18,000	- -	18,000
Total	$118,000	$41,000	$77,000

Possible mistakes:

1. Not knowing the difference between gross gifts and taxable gifts - wrong answer: Gross gifts = $118,000.
2. Not knowing remainder interest does not qualify for gift of present interest: $18,000 - $3,000 = $15,000. Therefore, $74,000.
3. Taking the annual exclusion of $11,000 from remainder interest, therefore, calculating total taxable gifts of $66,000.
4. Five donees x $11,000 = $55,000 ($118,000 - $55,000 = $63,000).

Example

John and Mary made the following gifts during the current year (assume all gifts are present interests):

	From John	From Mary	Total
To son, Paul	$40,000	$16,000	$56,000
To daughter, Virginia	40,000	6,000	46,000
To granddaughter, Terry	20,000	4,000	24,000
	$100,000	$26,000	$126,000

John and Mary's taxable gifts if gift splitting is elected and if it is not elected:

Gift Splitting Elected (Must split all gifts made during year)

	From John	From Mary	Total
To Paul	$28,000	$28,000	$56,000
To Virginia	23,000	23,000	46,000
To Terry	12,000	12,000	24,000
Total Gross Gifts	$63,000	$63,000	$126,000
Less Exclusions			
For Paul	$11,000	$11,000	$22,000
For Virginia	$11,000	$11,000	$22,000
For Terry	$11,000	$11,000	$22,000
Total Exclusions	$33,000	$33,000	$66,000
Current Taxable Gifts	$30,000	$30,000	$60,000

No Gift Splitting

	From John	From Mary	Total
To Paul	$40,000	$16,000	$56,000
To Virginia	40,000	6,000	46,000
To Terry	20,000	4,000	24,000
Total Gross Gifts	$100,000	$26,000	$126,000
Less Annual Exclusions			
For Paul	$11,000	$11,000	$22,000
For Virginia	$11,000	$6,000	$17,000
For Terry	$11,000	$4,000	$15,000
Total Exclusions	$33,000	$21,000	$54,000
Current Taxable Gifts	$67,000	$5,000	$72,000

The gift-splitting election decreased the current taxable gifts from $72,000 to $60,000.

F. EXCEPTION TO THE FUTURE INTEREST RULE.

An exception to the future interest rule concerns gifts to minors. Provided the following conditions are met, the gift will be considered a gift of a present interest (2503(c) trust):

1. Both the property and the income from the property may be expended by or for the benefit of the minor donee before he attains the age of 21.
2. If the property is not expended, it will pass to the minor upon the attainment of age 21.
3. If the donee dies before reaching the age of 21, the property will pass to his estate or to another entity as he may appoint under a general power of appointment.

G. EXCLUSION VS. EXEMPTION.

1. Exclusion - The annual exclusion of $11,000 per donee or $22,000 per donee if gift splitting is elected. If a gift is $11,000 or less and the annual exclusion applies, then there is no taxable gift.
2. Exemption - The applicable credit amount of $345,800 (for 2003 and later years) is the equivalent of $1,000,000 of gifts and must be utilized prior to paying gift tax. In other words, for gifts over and above the annual exclusion, an individual can make another $1,000,000 in aggregate taxable gifts to all donees before he or she has to pay any gift tax.

H. OTHER TRANSFERS WHICH MAY BE SUBJECT TO THE GIFT TAX.

1. Creation of joint ownership (joint tenancy).
   a. Generally, when an individual transfers a partial interest in property, a gift has been made.

Example

Mom buys a condo at the beach for $200,000 and takes title in her name and the names of her three daughters equally. Mom has made a gift of $50,000 to each of the three daughters. The gifts are eligible for the annual exclusion. $200,000 ÷ 4 owners = $50,000/owner

   b. Exceptions – There are two exceptions to the general rule.
      i. Joint tenancy bank account – gift not made until funds are withdrawn.
      ii. Joint tenancy savings bond – gift not made until redeemed by donee.
2. Transfers of life insurance policies.
   a. Transfer of ownership during life will trigger a gift in the amount of cash value of the policy plus any unexpired premiums.
      i. Not a completed gift unless all incidents of ownership are relinquished.
      ii. Premium payment on a policy owned by someone else is considered a gift to the owner of the policy.

Example

Rue transfers ownership of her $100,000 life insurance policy to her niece, Carol. The cash value of the policy on the date of the gift was $12,000. In addition, Rue intends to continue making the $800 annual premium each year. Rue has made a gift of $12,000 and will make a gift each year of $800 when she pays the premium.

b. Gift tax can arise at death of insured if a non-insured owner and beneficiary of the policy are different. For example, wife buys policy on husband and names her boyfriend as beneficiary. When husband dies she has made a gift to her boyfriend for the amount of proceeds.

3. Exercise of a general power of appointment.

   a. Power of appointment – the power to name someone to receive a beneficial interest in property.

   b. Events that trigger gift tax to holder of Power of Appointment:

      i. Holder exercises general Power of Appointment.

      ii. Holder releases general Power of Appointment.

      iii. Lapse of holder's right to exercise (See Section, "Crummey Powers Crummey v. Comm., 397 F2d 82 (9th Cir. 1961)" for discussion of Crummey Powers).

Example

Jim transfers property into a revocable trust, with the income benefiting his wife, Carol, for her life. Jim has made a gift to Carol. Carol also has the power to direct the principal or income to anyone she wishes either during life or at death. If Carol does not direct the remainder in her will, the principal goes to Jim's personal secretary, Sue. Carol has been given a general power of appointment.

- If Carol directs any part of the assets to someone else during her life, she has exercised her power of appointment and has made a gift.
- If Carol dies and leaves the trust assets to her children, the assets are included in her gross estate.
- If Carol dies and fails to exercise her power of appointment, the assets are still included in Carol's estate and the assets pass to Sue.

4. Gift loans (between family or related parties).

   a. Imputed interest on gift loans will be considered a gift from the lender to the borrower. (See Section I.1.3, "Interest on Gift Loans" for exceptions to the below market rate loan rule.")

I. TRANSFERS NOT SUBJECT TO GIFT TAX.

1. Qualified transfers (IRC Section 2503(e)) - Medical payments and tuition paid directly to the provider.
   a. A transfer of any amount (note: unlimited) to an educational institution for the payment of tuition is not subject to gift tax.
   b. A payment of any amount to a provider of medical care is not subject to gift tax.
   c. The payment must be made directly to the educational or medical institution to qualify for this exclusion.
2. Property settlements between divorcing spouses - As part of a written divorce agreement are deemed to be for full and adequate consideration and, therefore, not subject to gift tax (IRC Section 2516). Applies to transfers up to three years after divorce.
3. Interest on gift loans.
   a. Interest on gift loans of less than $10,000 is not subject to gift tax unless the loan proceeds are used by the donee to purchase income-producing property (in which case, apply the rules of (b) below).
   b. Interest on gift loans of less than $100,000 where donee's net investment income does not exceed $1,000 is not subject to gift tax.
      i. Net investment income is gross income from all investments less related expenses.
   c. If the loan is less than or equal to $100,000 and the unearned income of the borrower is greater than $1,000, the imputed interest is the difference between the interest at the federal rate less the interest charged, not to exceed the borrower's net investment income.
   d. If there is no imputed interest, there is no gift. If there is a gift, the lender is deemed to have given a gift of the imputed interest and the borrower as having received a gift of the imputed interest.
   e. These limitations for loans of $100,000 or less do not apply if the principal purpose of a loan is tax avoidance.
   f. On below-market interest rate loans between employer and employee, the imputed interest is deemed to be compensation. On loans between corporation and shareholder, the imputed interest is characterized as a dividend.

Example

In the current year, Marilyn, who is single, made the following gifts:

- Paid $16,000 in medical bills for her friend, Lisa. The payments were paid directly to her friend's hospital.
- $18,000 to her mother to pay for her apartment rent, utilities, and food.
- $14,000 to her nephew, Skip, to get him started in business.
- Marilyn also had made a $30,000 interest-free demand loan to her nephew, Skip, during the previous year. The loan is still outstanding at the end of the current year. The applicable federal interest rate during the year remained constant at 8%. Skip had no investment income.

Marilyn's taxable gifts in the current year are $10,000:

Payment directly to hospital is a qualified transfer, not a gift	$0
$18,000 to mother is reduced by $11,000, therefore, taxable gift	$7,000
$14,000 to Skip is reduced by $11,000, therefore, taxable gift	$3,000
Loan is less than $100,000 and donee's net investment income is less than $1,000, therefore, imputed interest is not a gift	$0
Total Taxable Gifts	**$10,000**

Examples

- Grace made an interest-free loan to her daughter of $9,000. The daughter had no investment income. There is no imputed interest since the loan is less than $10,000 and the borrower had no investment income.
- Grace made an interest-free loan to her daughter of $50,000. Based on applicable federal rates, the interest would be $4,000. The daughter had net investment income of $500. There is no imputed interest since the loan was not more than $100,000 and the borrower's net investment income is less than $1,000.
- Grace made an interest-free loan to her daughter of $90,000. Based on applicable federal rates, the interest would be $7,200. The daughter's net investment income is $3,000. The imputed interest is $3,000. Since the borrower's net investment income is more than $1,000, interest is imputed as the difference between the federal rate ($7,200) and the actual rate ($0), capped by the net investment income ($3,000). Grace has also made a gift of $3,000 to her daughter.
- Grace made an interest free loan to her daughter of $150,000. The applicable federal interest is $12,000. The borrower's net investment income is $0. Since the loan is more than $100,000, it does not meet any exception. Grace will have interest income of $12,000. Her daughter will have interest expense of $12,000 (deductibility determined by use of loan proceeds). Grace has given a gift of $12,000. Her daughter has received a gift of $12,000. The annual exclusion will apply to the first $11,000.

4. Payments made under an obligation of support (usually determined by state law).
5. Donations to political organizations.
6. Disclaimer.
   a. A disclaimer is a refusal by a person to accept property that is designated to be transferred or passed to him or her. The effect of the disclaimer is to pass the property to someone else, thereby possibly avoiding the payment of a transfer tax.
   b. An effective disclaimer for federal transfer tax purposes:
      i. Must be in writing and must be irrevocable.
      ii. Must be issued within the later of 9 months after (1) interest came into being, or (2) the person named to receive the property reaches age 21.
      iii. The disclaiming party cannot have previously benefited from the interest disclaimed.
      iv. Must pass the interest without the direction of disclaimant.
   c. When to use disclaimers.
      i. Property is left to a spouse who does not need it. Spouse can disclaim and let it pass to the contingent beneficiary (usually children).
      ii. Individual wants to make a tax-free gift to the contingent beneficiary.
      iii. Parent receives a large bequest from a relative and would like the assets to pass to the next beneficiary in line.

Example

- John dies on July 1. He leaves his entire estate to his wife, Jessie (or to his children if she predeceases him), thus over-qualifying the estate. If Jessie does not need the assets, she can disclaim an amount equal to the exemption equivalent, and let it pass to the children. By disclaiming in a timely manner, Jessie has not made a gift to the children.
- Theodore leaves his son, Teddy, $500,000 with the stipulation that if Teddy disclaims, the amount goes to a charity. Teddy has three options: 1) take the $500,000 and keep it, 2) take the $500,000, donate it and receive the related income tax deduction, or 3) disclaim it and let the estate take the charitable deduction.

J. TRANSFERS THAT ARE DEDUCTIBLE FOR DETERMINING TAXABLE GIFTS.

1. Gifts to qualified charities are deductible from gross gifts for donors who are U.S. citizens or residents.
2. Gifts and transfers between spouses, provided the transfer is not a terminable interest unless the transfer meets the exception to terminable interest rules (e.g., QTIP).
3. For a noncitizen spouse, only the first $112,000 (for 2003) per year of gifts of a present interest are not subject to gift tax (in effect, a special annual exclusion).
4. For a noncitizen spouse, all gifts of a future interest are subject to gift tax.

Example

When Stacey and James became engaged in August 2003, James gave Stacey a ring that had a fair market value of $68,000. After their wedding in October 2003, James gave Stacey $45,000 in cash so Stacey could have her own bank account. James and Stacey are U.S. citizens. James' marital deduction is $45,000. The engagement ring does not qualify because they were not married at the time of the gift. The $68,000 gift is first reduced by the $11,000 annual exclusion, and when the gift tax return is filed, James has utilized $57,000 of his lifetime exemption equivalency.

Note: In some states (e.g., Minnesota), unless an engagement ring is clearly intended to be a gift, it is conditioned on marriage. No marriage - no gift. The example says it was a gift, so we can assume it was so.

K. VALUATION OF A GIFT.

1. The value of a gift for gift tax purposes is the fair market value on the date of the gift.
2. Any consideration received by the donor reduces the value of the gift.
3. For securities, the value is the average of the high and low price on date of gift.
   a. Value of stocks for Form 706 will be the average of the high and low trading values for the stock on the date of death or alternate valuation date.
   b. If the stock is not traded on the date of death or gift, the value of the stock, according to the IRS Regulations, should be the stock price following the death multiplied by the number of days from the date of death to the previous stock trade before the date of death. Added to this is the stock price directly preceding the death, multiplied by the number of days (trading days) between the death and the next trading day. This sum should be divided by the sum of the days before and after the death.

Example

On July 11, Lisa gave her sister, Michelle, one share of XYZ stock that was traded on an exchange. July 11 was a Thursday. Below are the quoted prices on Monday the 8th and Friday the 12th. No sales occurred any other day that week.

SALES PRICE

Date	High	Low	Closing
7/08	$60	$56	$58.50
7/12	$62	$58	$59.00

The fair market value of Lisa's gift is $59.50. It is calculated as follows:

$$\frac{\left[\left(\frac{60+56}{2}\right)\times 1\right]+\left[\left(\frac{62+58}{2}\right)\times 3\right]}{4} = \$59.50$$

Note: The value is not determined by the closing price.

4. Life Estate and Remainder Interests.

   a. A life estate is the right to possession, enjoyment, and profit from property during the individual's lifetime.

   b. A remainder interest is an interest in property that begins in the future.

      i. Gift tax value of a remainder interest is the present value of the remainder interest on the date of the gift.

      ii. Use IRS Table S to determine present value factor.

Example

John places $500,000 in an irrevocable trust at First National Bank. The trust instrument specifies that John's brother, Ned, (age 65) will receive income for life, and that Sally, John's niece, will receive the assets upon Ned's death. Using Table S, Single Life Remainder Factors, and assuming an interest rate of 8%, the value of Sally's remainder interest is $500,000 x 0.33208 = $166,040. The life interest transferred to Ned will be $500,000 - $166,040 = $333,960.

L. LIABILITY FOR GIFT TAX.

1. The donor is liable for any gift tax due.

2. The donee is not subject to gift tax or income tax on the gift. However, if the donor fails to pay, the donee may become liable.

3. Net gifts occur where the donor and donee agree, prior to the gift, that the donee will pay any gift tax due.

   a. This transaction is considered to be part sale and part gift causing the donor to realize taxable income to the extent that the gift tax paid exceeds the donor's adjusted basis.

   b. Net gifts are an appropriate technique when the donor does not have sufficient liquid investments (cash) to pay the gift tax liability.

Example

In 2002, Bill gives his friend, Susan, a parcel of land, FMV $3,000,000, basis $50,000. Susan agrees to pay gift tax of $1,275,800. Bill has taxable income of $1,225,800 ($1,275,800 - $50,000).

M. DEEMED PAID ADJUSTMENT.

1. All prior taxable gifts are added back in the gift tax calculation formula and credit is given for the gift tax on the prior taxable gifts.

2. Since taxable gifts in the past may have been subject to a lower rate, it would be unfair to give credit for actual taxes paid.

3. A donor will be allowed a deemed paid credit on prior gifts, which means the credit is calculated using current tax rates.

N. FILING REQUIREMENTS.

1. Form 709 (U.S. Gift Tax Return) must be filed for each calendar year in which any of the following occur:
   a. The gifts to one donee for one calendar year exceed the annual exclusion of \$11,000 (for 2003).
   b. Gift of a future interest has been given.
   c. To elect gift splitting between spouses:
      i. Form 709 must be filed and signed by the consenting spouse.
      ii. This does not apply to community property donors.
2. The due date of Form 709 is April 15 of the year following the gift, but may be extended to the income tax return extended due date.

O. GIFT BASIS OF DONEE.

1. A gift indicates that there is no cost to the recipient. However, a basis to the gifted property is still assigned and depends on the following:
   a. The date of the gift.
   b. The donor's basis.
   c. The amount of the gift tax paid.
   d. The fair market value of the property.
2. Basis when appreciated property is gifted.
   a. If the fair market value of the property gifted exceeds the donor's adjusted basis on the date of the gift (appreciated property), the basis to the donee is the adjusted basis of the donor (carryover basis).
   b. If the donor paid gift taxes on the gift, the donee can further increase their basis in the gift received. The basis is calculated using the following formula:

$$\text{Donor's adjusted basis} + \left(\frac{\text{Unrealized appreciation}}{\text{FMV}} \times \text{Gift tax paid}\right) = \text{Donee's gain basis}$$

3. Basis when loss property is gifted.
   a. When the FMV at the date of gift is less than the donor's adjusted basis, the double-basis rule applies.
   b. Under the double-basis rule, the donee's basis upon acquisition is the FMV for losses and the donor's carryover basis for gains.
      i. A realized gain occurs if the donee subsequently sells the property at a higher price than the property's carryover basis (gain basis).
      ii. A realized loss will occur if the sales price is less than the FMV (loss basis).
      iii. If the sales price is between the adjusted basis (gain basis) and FMV (loss basis), then no gain or loss is recognized.

Examples

- Bill received an acre of land as a gift. At the time of the gift, the land had a FMV of $7,000. The donor's adjusted basis was $11,000. If Bill sells the land for $13,000, he will have a $2,000 gain. If Bill sells the land for $6,000, he will have a $1,000 loss. If Bill sells the land at a price between $7,000 and $11,000, he will not have a gain or loss.

- Last year, Melissa gave her daughter, Melanie, stock with a fair market value of $20,000. Melissa paid gift tax of $5,000. Melissa purchased the stock several years ago and her adjusted taxable basis on the date of the gift was $12,000. In the current year, Melanie sold the stock for $24,000. Melanie's basis on the date of sale is $14,000.

Melissa's basis	$12,000	
FMV at date of gift	$20,000	
Donee's basis before gift tax	$12,000	(Donor's basis)
Gift tax paid	$5,000	
(8,000 ÷ 20,000) x 5,000	$2,000	Gift tax paid adjustment

Donor's basis of $12,000 + $2,000 gift tax paid adjustment = donee's basis of $14,000

- Jack gave Emily stock in four different companies. The fair market value and adjusted taxable basis for Jack for each of the stocks was:

	(No gift tax paid on 1 & 2)		(Gift tax paid on 3 & 4 - $34)	
	Stock 1	Stock 2	Stock 3	Stock 4
Fair market value	$68	$3	$68	$68
Adjusted taxable basis	$40	$50	$40	$78
Realized gain/(loss)	$28	($47)	$28	($10)

Emily's adjusted taxable basis for each stock is:

Stock 1: $40 – the carryover basis.

Stock 2: $50 for gains and $3 for losses (double basis).

Stock 3: $54 – carryover $40 plus $14 gift tax on appreciation.

Stock 4: $78 for gains and $68 for losses (double basis). Do not add gift tax back since FMV was less than basis at the date of gift.

Gift Basis Example

The following three examples illustrate the general rule, the gift tax paid rule, the double basis rule, and the double basis with gift tax rule at three different sales prices.

EXAMPLE 1

	General Rule	Gift Tax Paid	Double Basis	DB with Gift Tax
Sales Price $150				
Donor's basis	20	20	100	100
Current FMV	100	100	20	20
Gift tax paid	-	30	-	30
Donee Sells:				
Proceeds	150	150	150	150
Less: Basis	(20)	(44)*	(100)	(100)
Gain/(Loss)	130	106	50	50

EXAMPLE 2

	General Rule	Gift Tax Paid	Double Basis	DB with Gift Tax
Sales Price $80				
Donor's basis	20	20	100	100
Current FMV	100	100	20	20
Gift tax paid	-	30	-	30
Donee Sells:				
Proceeds	80	80	80	80
Less: Basis	(20)	(44)*	(80)	(80)
Gain/(Loss)	60	36	-	-

EXAMPLE 3

	General Rule	Gift Tax Paid	Double Basis	DB with Gift Tax
Sales Price $10				
Donor's basis	20	20	100	100
Current FMV	100	100	20	20
Gift tax paid	-	30	-	30
Donee Sells:				
Proceeds	10	10	10	10
Less: Basis	(20)	(44)*	(20)	(20)
Gain/(Loss)	(10)	(34)	(10)	(10)

$$* \left(\frac{\$100 - \$20}{\$100}\right) \times \$30 = \$24 \text{ (allocated gift tax)} + \$20 \text{ (carryover basis)} = \$44$$

4. Holding period.
    a. For gain basis - Starts on the date the donor acquired the property.
    b. For loss basis - Starts on the date of the gift.
5. Basis for depreciation.
    a. The basis for depreciation is the donee's carryover basis.
    b. The life for depreciation is the same as if the donee purchased it.

P. INCOMPLETE TRANSFERS (A REMINDER).

1. A transfer is not considered a gift if it is incomplete. An incomplete transfer, however, may become a gift upon the later occurrence of some event that makes the transfer complete.
2. A revocable trust becomes a gift when the grantor releases the power of revocation, and the trust becomes irrevocable.

Example

Lauren sets up a revocable trust and names the bank as trustee. The trust instrument directs the trustee to pay the income to Lauren's friend Emily as long as Emily lives, and then the remainder goes to Emily's daughter. Until the first income payment has been made to Emily, Lauren has not made a gift because she could revoke the trust. If five years later Lauren decides to make the trust irrevocable, then she has made a gift of the remaining income interest to Emily, and a gift of the remainder to Emily's daughter.

Q. CRUMMEY POWERS <u>CRUMMEY V. COMM.</u>, 397 F2D 82 (9TH CIR. 1961).

1. Issue #1 - Getting the annual exclusion - Gifts of a future interest do not qualify for the $11,000 (for 2003) annual exclusion. For example, if you put $11,000 into an irrevocable trust for your child where the child gets the income and principal at some later date, then there is not a present interest, and the gift does not qualify for the annual exclusion. By placing a lapsing power to withdraw (referred to as a Crummey Power) in an irrevocable trust, however, a future interest can be converted to a present interest, which qualifies for the annual exclusion. The present interest gift is usually the lesser of the annual exclusion or the amount contributed to the trust.
2. The beneficiary must be given notice that he has the power to withdraw the funds for a limited period of time (generally noncumulative). This power gives him the ability to currently enjoy the interest, thus qualifying the gift as a present interest.
3. Issue #2 - Does lapsing the power create a gift tax problem? A potential problem in a trust with multiple beneficiaries with Crummey Powers is that if a holder of a general power of appointment releases or lets the power lapse, then the holder may be deemed to have made a gift. In other words, if the beneficiary lets his power to withdraw lapse, he may be deemed to have made a gift to the other beneficiaries of the trust.
4. To avoid gift tax consequences of a lapsed power, the annual right to withdraw must be limited to the greater of 5% of the value of the property out of which the withdrawal can be made, or $5,000. Another alternative is to set up multiple trusts where each trust has only one beneficiary. The separate trusts can often be treated as one trust for administrative purposes.

Example - Trust with Crummey provision, one beneficiary.

John set up a trust for his only child, Jaimie. The trust is funded with $20,000. Jaimie is given the power to withdraw the lesser of $11,000 or the annual contribution. Jaimie lets his power to withdraw the $11,000 lapse.

Tax consequences: John (father) gets a $11,000 annual exclusion. Since there are no other trust beneficiaries, Jaimie has not made any gifts as a result of letting his power lapse.

Example - Trust with Crummey provision, two beneficiaries, lapse < 5/5 lapse rule.

Charles sets up an irrevocable trust for his two children, Katty and Passie. The trust is initially funded with $10,000. Each year for a period of 30 days, Katty and Passie have the right to withdraw the lesser of 50% of the amount of property contributed that year or the annual exclusion. Katty and Passie do not exercise their right to withdraw during the current year.

Tax consequences: Charles has included a power to withdraw and, therefore, he gets a $10,000 annual exclusion ($5,000 per child). There are multiple beneficiaries, so Charles needs to address the 5/5 lapse rule to see if there are any gift tax consequences from the lapse. Since the withdrawal was limited to $5,000, and this does not exceed the 5/5 benchmark of $5,000 (the greater of 5% or $5,000), then no gift between Katty and Passie has been triggered by the lapse of power.

Example - Trust with Crummey provision, two beneficiaries, lapse > 5/5 lapse rule.

In the current year, George and his wife, Helen, contribute $120,000 to a trust established for the benefit of his two children, both equal income and remainder beneficiaries. Each child has the right to withdraw the lesser of the annual exclusion ($22,000) or 25% of the annual contribution (25% x $120,000 = $30,000). The children do not exercise their right of withdrawal during the year, thus causing a lapse and a gift of one-half of the lapse to the other child.

Tax consequences: George and Helen included a Crummey provision so they get an annual exclusion of $44,000 ($22,000 per child). There are two beneficiaries, so they need to check the 5/5 lapse rule and see if there are any gift tax consequences resulting from the lapse. Withdrawal was limited to $22,000 which exceeds the 5/5 benchmark of $6,000 (the greater of $6,000 (5% x $120,000) or $5,000). Each of the children made a gift to the other child to the extent that ½ of their lapsed amount exceeded the 5/5 amount ($22,000/2) ($11,000 - $6,000 = $5,000). The $5,000 gift is a gift of a contingent future interest and is not eligible for the annual exclusion. The gift is between the two children and will require the filing of a gift tax return for each of the two children to the extent of $5,000 each.

5. Contingent beneficiaries.

   a. Estate of Maria Cristofani, 97 TC 74 (1991).

      In Cristofani, the taxpayer established a trust where her grandchildren were contingent beneficiaries of the trust in the event that their parents (the primary beneficiaries) died before the trust terminated. The IRS's position was that there was no reason that the contingent beneficiaries would not be highly motivated to exercise their right to withdraw since the probability of their ever receiving benefit from the trust was quite small. If the contingent beneficiaries let the power lapse, it must have been due to an "understanding" that they would do so, therefore, no present interest existed. The Court ruled that the controlling factor was the legal right of a contingent beneficiary to withdraw, not the probability that they would do so. Therefore, the annual exclusion is available for primary and contingent beneficiaries. However, the IRS acquiesced in result only, meaning that they may continue to challenge contingent beneficiaries.

   b. Kohlsaat v. Commissioner, T.C. memo 1997-212.

      The use of Cristofani trusts was reinforced in the Kohlsaat case. Taxpayer set up an irrevocable trust during 1990. Taxpayer's two children were primary beneficiaries. Crummey powers were given to the children and to grandchildren and great-grandchildren, (total of 18 Crummey powers). The IRS claimed that the contingent beneficiaries did not qualify for the annual exclusion. The Tax Court cited Cristofani and granted the annual gift tax exclusion for all 18 beneficiaries.

R. ESTATE FREEZING.

1. Revenue Ruling 93-12 (1993-7 IRB 13).

   A minority share interest discount will not be disallowed solely because a transferred interest, if combined with interests held by family members, would constitute a controlling interest.

Example

Father owns 100% of the stock of a closely held corporation, FMV \$300,000. He gives 1/3 to each of three daughters. Since each daughter was given a minority interest, a 25% discount is taken on each transfer. On Form 709, Father reports three gross gifts of \$75,000 (total gifts of \$225,000). If the stock had been passed at death, 100% of the stock value would have been subject to the estate tax.

---

2. Rev. Rul. 93-12 launched the popularity of family limited partnerships (FLPs) as a planning tool. Taxpayer forms an FLP to hold a closely held business. Taxpayer becomes the general partner and gives limited partnership interests to children/grandchildren. When the limited partnerships are valued for gift tax purposes, they are given discounts for minority interest and lack of marketability. This is an effective way of saving estate and gift taxes and maintaining family control over assets.

3. IRS has begun to aggressively challenge FLPs as shams created to avoid taxes.

4. Recapitalization is an estate freezing technique for corporations where the common stock is traded for both common and preferred stock. The owner retains the preferred stock and gives the common stock to the children. The idea is to limit the amount included in the owner's estate to the value of the preferred stock. Any appreciation that occurs after the recapitalization and gifting of common stock, is attributed to the common stock, thereby keeping the appreciation out of the owner's estate.
   a. Section 2701 allows some estate freezing, but generally the preferred stock is valued at zero, and so the gift becomes the full value of the business.
   b. Under certain conditions (e.g., preferred stock is cumulative), some value may be assigned to the preferred stock.

S. GIFT TAX FORMULA.

EXHIBIT 5: GIFT TAX FORMULA

(1) Total gifts in current year (fair market value of all gifts)		$
(2) Less:		
(a) One-half of value of gifts split with spouse	$	
(b) Annual exclusions ($11,000 per donee for present interests)		
(c) Marital deduction (can be unlimited if spouse is a U.S. citizen)		
(d) Charitable deduction (can be unlimited)		
(e) Total subtractions		
(3) Equals: Taxable gifts in current year		$
(4) Add: Post-1976 taxable gifts made in prior years		
(5) Equals: Total taxable gifts to date		
(6) Tentative tax on total taxable gifts to date		
(7) Less: Tax paid or deemed paid on prior taxable gifts		( )
(8) Equals: Gift tax on current year taxable gifts before applicable credit amount		
(9) Less: Applicable credit amount		( )
(10) Equals: Gift tax due on current year taxable gifts		$

Example

Susan and Mike Brown, a happily married couple, made the following gifts during 2003:

Susan's gifts:

- $100,000 to each of their three children.
- Leroy Neiman painting FMV $120,000 to her niece.
- Paid $14,000 private school tuition for her college roommate's daughter.
- Paid hospital bill related to co-worker's hospitalization due to food poisoning $2,000.
- Placed $650,000 in an irrevocable trust with Mike as the income and remainder beneficiary. The trust is funded with 6% coupon bonds. Susan wants to elect to take the marital deduction.

Mike's gifts:

- Federal Express stock, held long term, FMV $40,000, basis $10,000 to the University of Georgia.
- $50,000 cash to his high school's homecoming queen.

Susan made $750,000 of taxable gifts in 1988 and paid $55,500 in gift tax. Calculate Susan's gift tax liability assuming the gift-splitting election is made.

Description	Value of Gift	Gift Split	Annual Exclusion	Marital/ Charitable	Taxable Gift
Child One	$100,000	($50,000)	($11,000)		$39,000
Child Two	100,000	(50,000)	(11,000)		39,000
Child Three	100,000	(50,000)	(11,000)		39,000
Painting	120,000	(60,000)	(11,000)		49,000
Irrevocable Trust	650,000	(325,000)	(11,000)	($314,000)	0
Stock (Mike's gift)	40,000	(20,000)	(11,000)	(9,000)	0
Cash (Mike's gift)	50,000	(25,000)	(11,000)		14,000
Total	$1,160,000	($580,000)	($77,000)	($323,000)	$180,000

(1)	Total gifts in current year (fair market value of all gifts)		$1,160,000
(2)	Less:		
	(a) One-half of value of gifts split with spouse	$580,000	
	(b) Annual exclusions ($11,000 per donee for present interests)	77,000	
	(c) Marital deduction (can be unlimited if spouse is a U.S. citizen)	314,000	
	(d) Charitable deduction (can be unlimited)	9,000	
	(e) Total subtractions		(980,000)
(3)	Equals: Taxable gifts in current year		$180,000
(4)	Add: All taxable gifts made in prior years		750,000
(5)	Equals: Total taxable gifts to date		$930,000
(6)	Tentative tax on total taxable gifts to date		318,500
(7)	Less: Tax paid or deemed paid on prior taxable gifts		(55,500)
(8)	Equals: Gift tax on current year taxable gifts before applicable credit amt		$263,000
(9)	Less: Applicable credit amount		(263,000)
(10)	Equals: Gift tax due on current year taxable gifts		$0

Note: The hospital bill and the school tuition were paid directly to providers and, therefore, are excluded. Mike's gift of Federal Express stock is a charitable contribution and is eligible for the charitable deduction.

T. BASIC STRATEGIES FOR TRANSFERRING WEALTH THROUGH GIFTING.

1. Generally, if the objective of the transferor is to reduce the size of the transferor's gross estate, the transferor can use the following lifetime gifting techniques to achieve a lower gross estate at death:
   a. Make optimal use of qualified educational transfers (pay tuition for children and grandchildren from private school through professional education directly to provider institutions).
   b. Pay medical costs for children, grandchildren, and heirs directly to provider institutions (not limited to heirs).
   c. Make optimal use of the $11,000 annual gift exclusion ($22,000 if the gift is made jointly with the spouse).

Example

John is married to Joan and has 3 adult children who all have stable marriages and there are 7 grandchildren. John and Joan can gift $286,000 per year without being subject to gift tax. ($22,000 x 13 transferees – 3 children, 3 spouses, 7 grandchildren.)

   d. A spouse may make unlimited lifetime gifts to their spouse, if the recipient spouse is a U.S. citizen. Gifts to noncitizen spouses are limited to $110,000 annually.
2. If the above four (a-d) are completely exhausted, the transferor can begin using his/her applicable exclusion amount ($1,000,000 in 2003) to avoid gift tax until the summation of lifetime taxable gifts exceeds the applicable exclusion amount.

VII. THE FEDERAL ESTATE TAX

A. WHAT IS INCLUDED IN THE GROSS ESTATE?

EXHIBIT 6: WHAT IS INCLUDED IN THE GROSS ESTATE?

Code Section	Property Description
2033	Property owned by decedent or in which decedent had an interest.
2034	Dower and curtesy interests.
2035	Gift tax on gifts made within three years of death. Gifts made within three years of death that would have been included under 2036, 2037, 2038, 2042.
2036	Transfers with a retained life interest.
2037	Transfers taking effect at death.
2038	Revocable transfers.
2039	Annuities.
2040	Jointly owned property.
2041	Powers of appointment.
2042	Proceeds of life insurance.

1. Section 2033 - Property owned by the decedent.
   a. The gross estate is composed of the value of all property in which the decedent has an interest at his death. It includes the value of certain properties he might have transferred during his life, in which he retained some rights, powers, use, or possession after the transfers (strings).
   b. Property in which the decedent had an interest (such as automobile, house, clothes, savings, etc.) will account for most of the property included in the gross estate. Other items also included in the gross estate are:
      i. Medical insurance reimbursements due to a decedent on account of hospital and doctor bills paid.
      ii. State income tax refunds received after death but relating to tax decedent paid prior to death.
      iii. Court award for pain and suffering the decedent experienced as a result of a fatal automobile accident caused by another. The award was paid to decedent's surviving spouse. Because the cause of action was personal to the decedent, it is includible in the gross estate.
      iv. Rental income on rental property of $3,000 ($1,000 of which accrued after the deceased-landlord's death) paid to the estate. Whether or not the decedent was on a cash basis or accrual basis of accounting, $2,000 of this amount would be includible in the gross estate.
      v. Property excluded - Court award for wrongful death paid to decedent's family. Since a wrongful death suit is based on the wrongdoer's depriving the family of future earnings due to the death of the breadwinner, it is an interest that arises after death. Therefore, it is not included in the decedent's gross estate.

2. Section 2034 - Dower and curtesy interest - Generally, the common law concepts of dower and curtesy have been created by state statutes that give the surviving spouse a statutory share of the deceased spouse's estate. The value of this property will be included in the gross estate. Dower and curtesy interests are fully deductible under the marital deduction.
3. Section 2035 - Gifts made within 3 years of death.
   a. Any gift tax paid on gifts made within three years of death must be added to the gross estate. Called the gross-up approach, the procedure prevents the amount of the gift tax from escaping the estate tax.
   b. Gifts made within three years of death are NOT included in the gross estate of the donor. They are, instead, treated the same way as any other post-1976 taxable gift (i.e., added to taxable estate; see Exhibit 7). Exceptions to this general rule include property which was given away within three years but otherwise would have been included under Sections 2036 (transfers with life estate), 2037 (transfers taking effect at death), 2038 (revocable transfers), and 2042 (proceeds of life insurance). These sections deal with gifting of life insurance or severance of a retained interest. Premiums paid within three years by the insured on a policy the insured doesn't own won't be pulled back into the estate under Section 2035. These premiums may constitute a taxable gift if they exceed the annual exclusion.
4. Section 2036 - Transfers with a retained life estate. Sections 2036, 2037, and 2038 are premised on the notion that the decedent has made a gift of property, but, because he or she has retained a certain degree of control and enjoyment over such property, the property will be included in the gross estate.
5. Section 2037 - Transfers taking effect at death.
   a. Possession or enjoyment of the property can, through ownership of such interest, be obtained only by surviving the decedent and
   b. The decedent has retained a reversionary interest in the property and the value of such reversionary interest immediately before the death of the decedent exceeds 5% of the value of such property.
6. Section 2038 - Revocable transfers. Transfers where decedent, at time of death, had power to alter, amend, or revoke the transfer.
7. Section 2042 - Proceeds of life insurance.
   a. Proceeds of a life insurance policy on the life of the decedent will be includible in the decedent's gross estate if, at the insured's death, either the proceeds were receivable by the decedent's executor, or the decedent possessed an incidence of ownership in the policy.

> **Note:** The entire proceeds under split dollar arrangements will still be includible, even though a part of the proceeds is payable to a third party, usually the employer.

   b. Under Section 2033 (property owned at death), the terminal value (cash surrender value) of a life insurance policy on the life of someone other than the decedent will be includible in the decedent's gross estate to the extent, at the decedent's date of death, that the decedent had an ownership interest in the policy.

> **Note:** These policies are not included under Section 2042.

c. Under Section 2035, the proceeds of a life insurance policy on the life of the decedent will be includible in the decedent's gross estate if, within three years of death, the nonowning decedent made a completed transfer of all incidence of ownership in the policy.

d. Finally, under Section 2001, the decedent's adjusted taxable gifts (not gross estate) will include the taxable terminal value of the gift of any life insurance policy (as of the date of the gift) for which the decedent made a completed transfer more than three years before death.

8. Section 2039 - Annuities.

a. Straight life annuities – This type of annuity pays the annuitant until their death. In this case, nothing is included in the gross estate since the annuitant's interest in the contract terminates at death.

b. Survivorship annuities – This type of annuity provides payments to one person, and then provides payments to a second person upon the death of the first. When the first annuitant dies, the value of a comparable policy on the second annuitant is included in the first to die's estate. If the second to die has contributed to the purchase of the policy, then only a proportional amount will go into the first to die's estate.

Example

Consider these three different scenarios:

1. Jeff purchases a straight life annuity. When he dies, the annuity is not included in the gross estate because the annuity extinguishes at Jeff's death.
2. Jeff purchases a survivorship annuity. Jeff dies and his companion, Nancy, becomes the annuitant. The cost of a comparable policy, based on Nancy's age, will be included in Jeff's estate.
3. Jeff and Nancy purchase a survivorship annuity together. They each pay half of the premium. When Jeff dies, only half of the value of Nancy's survivor annuity will be included in his estate since he contributed only half of the premiums.

---

9. Sections 2040 - Joint interests.

a. As a general rule, the gross estate will include the entire value of property held jointly with others.

b. Exception - If the only surviving joint owner is the decedent's spouse, the property is a qualified joint interest. In this case, one half of the total value will always be includible, regardless of that spouse's original contribution and regardless of whether or not that contribution can be proven.

c. Exception - For jointly owned property held by the decedent and at least one person who is not the decedent's surviving spouse, the decedent's gross estate will include the entire value of the property, reduced only by an amount attributable to that portion of the consideration in money or money's worth which can clearly be shown to have been furnished by the survivors. This is called the consideration furnished test (Contribution Rule).

Note: It is the responsibility of the executor to prove if other contributions were made to the property.

d. Funds received as a gift from the deceased co-owner and applied to the cost of the property cannot be counted as funds provided by the co-owner.

e. If the owners received the property as a gift from a third party, each owner is considered to have contributed the value of their interest.

Example

Martha and Raymond are married and hold title as joint tenants to a beach-front lot in Gulf Shores, Alabama. Raymond dies. One half of the property will be included in his estate.

Suppose now that Martha and Raymond are lifelong companions, but not legally married. When Raymond dies, all of the beach property will go into his estate unless Martha can prove that she furnished part of the funds to purchase the property. If Martha can prove she furnished 30% of the funds, then only 70% goes into Raymond's estate. However, if Raymond had gifted her the 30%, her contribution would not count, and Raymond must include 100% of the value of the lot.

10. Section 2041 and 2514 - Powers of Appointment.

a. Recall from a previous section, "Other Transfers Which May Be Subject to the Gift Tax," that a Power of Appointment is the power to name who will enjoy or own property. The players are:

i. The donor – grants power.

ii. The holder – receives power.

iii. The appointee – person whom the holder appoints to enjoy the property.

b. Powers can be general or limited.

i. A general power is a power in which the holder can appoint to the holder, to the holder's estate, to the holder's creditors, or to the creditors of the holder's estate to enjoy the property subject to the power. A general power should only be given to a spouse.

ii. A limited power is any power that is not a general power. A limited power is also called a "special" power.

c. Estate tax ramifications.

i. General Power of Appointment – the gross estate of a decedent will include any assets under a general power of appointment held by a decedent at the time of death (whether exercised or not). However, there are several exceptions:

A) If the right to exercise is held to an ascertainable standard (health, education, maintenance, or support), then the power is not included in the decedent's gross estate.

B) If the right to exercise requires approval of the holder or someone else (who is termed an adverse party – someone who has an interest in the property), then the power of appointment is not included in the decedent's gross estate.

C) If the right to exercise is limited to the greater of $5,000 or 5% of the aggregate value of the property each year, then the power of appointment is generally not included in the decedent's gross estate.

1) This right to withdraw is referred to as a "5-and-5" power.

2) The 5-and-5 power must be noncumulative. If the withdrawal is not made during the year, that year's right to withdraw is lost.

Example

Mary Sue is the beneficiary of a trust established by her deceased husband, Dennis. The trust includes a 5-and-5 power, allowing Mary Sue to withdraw the greater of $5,000 or 5% of the trust principal each year. If Mary Sue doesn't exercise her right to withdraw this year, she cannot take an extra $5,000 or 5% out of the trust principal next year.

3) The value of the 5-and-5 power is includible in the decedent's gross estate in the year of death. Generally, the value of the 5-and-5 power will be 5% of the trust value at death.

Example

Mary Sue is the beneficiary of a trust established by her deceased husband, Dennis. The trust includes a 5-and-5 power, allowing Mary Sue to withdraw the greater of $5,000 or 5% of the trust principal each year. Before exercising the 5-and-5 power for the current year, Mary Sue died. The trust balance at the time of her death was $500,000. Mary must include $25,000 (5% x $500,000) in her gross estate.

4) The lapse of a power that exceeds the $5,000/5% limit will be included in the decedent's gross estate.

Example

Mary Sue is the beneficiary of a trust established in the year 2002 by her deceased husband, Dennis. The trust allows Mary Sue to withdraw 8% of the trust principal each year. Mary Sue made no withdrawals from the trust. In 2003, Mary Sue died. The trust balance in the year 2002 and 2003 was $1,000,000. Mary must include 11% of the trust balance ($110,000) in her gross estate.

How is this calculated? She must include 3% (8% withdrawal right exceeds the 5-and-5 power by 3%) of the trust balance in her gross estate due to the lapse of the general power in 2002, and must include another 8% due to the 2003 (year of death) unexercised general power.

ii. Limited Power of Appointment – The assets under a limited power of appointment are not included in the holder's gross estate at death.

B. DEDUCTIONS FROM THE GROSS ESTATE.

The taxable estate is the gross estate reduced by various deductions. The deductions include:

1. Funeral expenses.
2. Administrative expenses such as:
   a. Commissions paid to executors.
   b. Attorney fees.
   c. Accountant fees.
   d. Court costs.
   e. Selling expenses for asset dispositions.
   f. Appraisal fees.
3. Unpaid mortgages.
4. Claims against the estate (debts and unpaid taxes).
5. Losses incurred in administering the estate (such as casualty losses).
6. Charitable contributions (unlimited).
7. Transfers to the surviving spouse (unlimited).

C. TAXABLE ESTATE AND ESTATE TAX LIABILITY.

The tentative estate tax is determined by applying the rate from the estate tax table to the combined value of the taxable estate and post-1976 taxable gifts.

1. Tax paid or deemed paid on prior taxable gifts - The tentative tax is then reduced by any gift tax paid or payable on gifts included in the tax base.

Note: Gift tax paid or payable is a reduction of estate tax and not a credit.

2. Estate tax credits - Having determined the tentative estate tax, the next step is to deduct the allowable credits for:
   a. The applicable credit amount (see section titled, "Federal Gift and Estate Taxation").
   b. State death taxes - Limited to lesser of amount paid or Section 2011 table value.
      i. The state death tax credit will be reduced beginning in 2002.
      ii. In 2005, the state death credit is repealed, and will be replaced with a deduction (not a credit) for death taxes actually paid to any state.
   c. Federal estate taxes on prior transfers - Credit is given for estate taxes paid 2 years prior to and 10 years after death for property included in the gross estate of the decedent. The credit is subject to a percentage limitation that depends upon how long the decedent survived the transferor.

Years Between Deaths	Credit Percentage
More than 2, not more than 4	80%
More than 4, not more than 6	60%
More than 6, not more than 8	40%
More than 8, not more than 10	20%
More than 10	0%

d. Foreign death taxes - Estate taxes paid to other countries.

3. Estate tax liability - The result of these deductions from the tentative estate tax is the net estate tax due.

D. DUE DATE OF THE FEDERAL ESTATE TAX RETURN.

The federal estate tax return, Form 706, when required, is due nine months after the date of the decedent's death. An extension of time to file can be requested.

E. INCLUSION OF AN ITEM IN THE GROSS ESTATE VERSUS ADDING ITEM TO TAXABLE ESTATE.

It is difficult to appreciate the difference between the inclusion of an item in the gross estate or adding it to the taxable estate as a prior taxable gift.

1. If the gift has to be added to the gross estate, the value of the property must be redetermined. The value of the property included in the gross estate is the fair market value of the property as of the date of death (or alternate valuation date, if elected). The result of this treatment is that all appreciation from the date of the gift will be included and taxed in the estate. If the gift is included in the gross estate, the value of the gift at the time the gift was made must be removed from the category of post-1976 gifts.

2. If, on the other hand, the taxable gift is added to the taxable estate, the value at the date of the gift applies. Usually the amount is net of the annual exclusion and net of post-gift appreciation, since only the taxable gift is added.

EXHIBIT 7: ESTATE TAX FORMULA

(1) Total gross estate		$
(2) Less: Expenses, debts, and losses:		
(a) Funeral and administrative expenses		
(b) Debts of decedent, mortgages, losses		
(3) Equals: Adjusted gross estate (AGE)*		
(4) Less: Total allowable deductions:		
(c) Charitable deduction		
(d) Marital deduction		
Total allowable deductions		($)
(5) Equals: Taxable estate		$
(6) Add: Adjusted taxable gifts (post-1976)		
(7) Compute: Tentative tax base		
(8) Compute: Tentative tax		
(9) Less: Tax paid or deemed paid on prior taxable gifts		($)
(10) Equals: Estate tax before reduction for allowable credits		
(11) Less:		
Applicable credit amount		
Other credits		
(12) Equals: Estate tax liability		$

*The term "Adjusted Gross Estate" is not on Form 706, however this concept comes up in Section 6166 and may be tested on the exam. Therefore, we have inserted it for your convenience.

F. BASIS OF PROPERTY ACQUIRED FROM A DECEDENT.

1. When receiving property from a decedent, the basis of such property is the FMV at the date of death or, if the alternate valuation date is selected, the FMV 6 months after the date of death. However, there are restrictions on electing the alternate valuation date.

2. Alternate valuation date limitations.

   a. An estate tax return must be filed.

   b. Both the value of the gross estate and the estate tax liability must be reduced below what the primary valuation date would have yielded.

   c. The election is made on Form 706, but will not be valid if the return is filed one year after the time prescribed by law (including extension) for filing the Form 706.

Example

Ben died recently and left the following assets shown below at their value at the date of death (DOD) and at six months after the DOD:

Item	Value at DOD	Value Six Months after DOD
Land	$5,000,000	$4,500,000
Stock	$300,000	$310,000
Annuity	$100,000	$95,000
Condominium	$300,000	Sold 2 months after DOD for $295,000

If Ben's executor elects the alternate valuation date, Ben's total estate will be $4,500,000 + $310,000 + $100,000 + $295,000 = $5,205,000. The land and stock will use the six-month valuation, the annuity (a wasting asset) must be valued at the DOD, and the condominium will be valued as of the sale date.

3. Deathbed gifts.
   a. If a beneficiary receives property from a decedent that the decedent acquired by gift from the beneficiary within one year of the decedent's death, the donor/beneficiary takes the decedent's basis (which will be the donor's basis). No stepped-up basis is received.

Example

Joey gives property to his son that at the date of gift has a FMV of $7,000. No gift taxes were paid. Joey has an adjusted basis in the property of $2,300. Joey's son dies within one year of the date of the gift. The property was bequeathed to Joey. Hence, Joey's basis in the property is $2,300 (donor's basis).

4. Survivor's share of property (JTWROS).
   a. The basis of such property is the FMV at the date of the decedent's death for the portion related to the decedent. This is added to the basis of survivor.

Example

Michael and Jeff owned, as joint tenants with survivorship, land that they purchased for $60,000. Jeff furnished two-thirds of the purchase price and Michael one-third. At the date of Jeff's death, the property had a FMV of $100,000. Michael figures his basis in the property as follows:

Interest Michael bought initially	$20,000
Interest Michael received @ Jeff's death ($^2/_3$ of 100,000)(Step to FMV)	<u>$66,000</u>
Michael's basis @ Jeff's death	$86,000

Common law states do not allow an adjustment to the property's basis for excluded property interests (e.g., a spouse's share of jointly held property).

5. Community property.

    a. Receives an adjustment in basis to the FMV on both spouses halves at the death of the first spouse.

Example

Ted and his wife, Alice, jointly own a mountain retreat. Ted dies and leaves the property, which has a basis of $200,000 and a FMV at DOD of $1,000,000, to Alice. If Ted and Alice live in a community property state, Alice's new basis is $1,000,000. If Ted and Alice do not live in a community property state, Alice's new basis is $600,000 (her basis of $100,000 plus his ½ at FMV $500,000).

---

6. Holding period of property acquired from a decedent. Is deemed to be long term (i.e., held for the required long-term holding period). This provision applies regardless of whether the property is disposed of at a gain or loss and regardless of decedent's holding period.

7. Basis rules for years beginning after 2009 (TRA 2001).

    a. Beginning in 2010, after the estate and generation-skipping transfer taxes have been repealed, the rules providing for a fair market value basis for property acquired from a decedent are repealed.

    b. Recipients of property transferred at the decedent's death will receive a basis equal to the lesser of the adjusted basis of the decedent or the fair market value of the property on the date of the decedent's death. In other words, the recipient will receive a carryover basis, unless the FMV is lower.

    c. An executor can increase (i.e., step up) the basis in assets owned by the decedent and acquired by the beneficiaries at death.

        i. In general, each decedent's estate is permitted to increase (i.e., step up) the basis of assets transferred by up to a total of $1.3 million.

        ii. The basis of property transferred to a surviving spouse can be increased by an additional $3 million. Thus, the basis of property transferred to surviving spouses can be increased by a total of $4.3 million.

        iii. The basis of the property received from the decedent can never be increased above the FMV at the decedent's date of death.

VIII. VALUATION OF ASSETS

A. REAL ESTATE.

1. Appraisal required.
2. Special Use Valuation (Section 2032A) may be available. (See section titled, "Special Use Valuation Section 2032A.")
3. If land is sold within a short period of time after decedent's death to an unrelated party, the sales price will usually be accepted as its value.

B. STOCKS.

1. Stocks on Form 706:

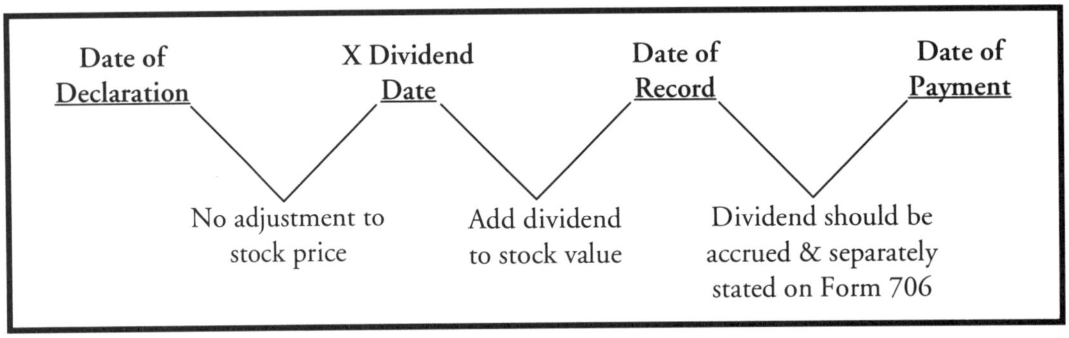

   a. Date of declaration - This is the date the board of directors approves and declares that a dividend will be paid to the shareholders.

   b. X dividend date - This is the date that the market price of the stock adjusts for the dividend (i.e., the market price is reduced approximately by the amount of the dividend).

   c. Date of record - This is the date that the company determines who owns stock in the company and is entitled to a dividend regardless of whether or not they own the stock as of the payment date. Shareholders who purchase stock between the date of record and the date of payment are not entitled to the dividend.

   d. Date of payment - This is the date the company pays the dividend to its shareholders.

2. Value of stocks for Form 706 - The value of the stocks will be the average of the high and low trading values for the stock on the date of death or alternative valuation date. If the stock is not traded on the date of death, the value of the stock according to the IRS Regulations should be the stock price following the death multiplied by the number of days from the stock trade before the date of death. Added to this is the stock price directly preceding the death multiplied by the number of days (trading days) between the death and the next trading day. This sum should be divided by the sum of the days before and after the death. (This is the same calculation discussed for gift tax in the section titled, Valuation of a Gift.)

Examples

- Bill Cole died on August 29. At that time he owned stock in XYZ Corporation. The stock traded on both August 28 and August 29. Given the following excerpt from the *Wall Street Journal* for both days, the reported value of XYZ stock on Form 706 will be $59.

August 28	August 29
High - 63	High - 60
Low - 52	Low - 58
Close - 57	Close - 59.5

The value of the stock reported on Form 706 will be the mean of the high and the low stock price for the date of death. It is not the closing price for stock on the trading day.

- ABC stock does not trade on a regular basis. If John Smith dies on Thursday, June 5 and the most recent trades for ABC stock are:

Monday	6/2	27
Wednesday	6/4	25
Monday	6/9	28
Tuesday	6/10	29

The date of death value that should be used for the federal estate return is $26.

$$\frac{(1 \times 28) + (2 \times 25)}{3} = \frac{78}{3} = \$26$$

According to the IRS Regulations, the stock price following the death should be multiplied by the number of days from the stock trade before the date of death (in this case, 1 day). Added to this is the stock price directly preceding the death, multiplied by the number of days (trading days) between the death and the next trading day (in this case, 2 days, Friday and Monday). This sum should be divided by the sum of the days before and after the death (2 + 1 = 3 days).

C. LIFE INSURANCE.

1. The value of life insurance for gift tax purposes will be the terminal value (cash surrender value) of the policy.
2. The value of life insurance included in the gross estate will be the proceeds received. If settlement option is chosen by the beneficiary, the amount includible in the gross estate will be the amount that would have been payable as a lump sum.

D. GOVERNMENT BONDS.

1. Series E – valued at redemption price at date of death.

E. THE CLOSELY HELD BUSINESS.

1. Factors to be considered in closely held company valuation (Rev. Ruling 59-60):
   a. Nature of the business.
   b. Economic outlook.
   c. Book value of stock.
   d. Financial condition of business.
   e. Goodwill.
   f. Earning capacity and ability to pay dividends.
   g. Shares that have been sold previously.
2. Estate freezing techniques – see Estate Freezing.

F. BUY-SELL AGREEMENTS

1. Benefits of a buy-sell agreement.
   a. Can establish estate value of the business.
   b. Provides cash to the decedent's estate.
   c. Provides for business continuation.
   d. Guarantees that there will be a buyer for the business at the decedent's death.
   e. Reduces a business' credit risk because of continuation.
2. Provisions in a buy-sell agreement.
   a. Parties to and purpose of the agreement.
   b. Description of the business interest.
   c. Restrictions on transfers before death.
   d. Method used to determine purchase price.
   e. Funding of the purchase price.
   f. Whether agreement can be modified or terminated.
3. Two types of buy-sell agreements:
   a. Cross-purchase agreement.
      i. In a cross-purchase agreement, partners/shareholders purchase deceased partner's/shareholder's business interest from the estate.
      ii. Partners/shareholders provide the funds.
      iii. If the agreement is funded with life insurance, each partner/shareholder purchases insurance policies on the other partners/shareholders.

iv. Tax ramifications.

A) Under the cross-purchase method, the estate will have a capital gain on the sale of the decedent's interest.

B) Since the interest has a step to fair market value at the business owner's death, there will be very little capital gain.

C) The purchaser(s) in a cross-purchase agreement will have a basis in the purchased interest equal to the price paid for the interest.

b. Entity redemption agreement.

i. Under an entity redemption agreement, the partnership/corporation purchases the decedent's interest in the business from the decedent's estate.

ii. If entity is a corporation, shares are typically held by the corporation as treasury stock.

iii. Tax ramifications.

A) Under the entity method, the entity will not receive a deduction for the amounts paid to the deceased owner's estate.

B) Since the owners are not purchasing the business interest, they do not receive any increase in their basis.

4. Choosing the type of buy-sell agreement.

a. The following factors must be considered when choosing a type of agreement:

i. Number of partners/shareholders.

ii. Flexibility.

iii. Funding.

iv. Valuation.

b. Number of partners/shareholders.

i. The entity approach is typically favored if there are a lot of partners/shareholders.

ii. Entity approach is easier, and the funding is easier to obtain.

iii. Cross purchase will most likely require more policies [N x (N-1)].

c. Flexibility.

i. A cross purchase agreement can be more flexible, because survivors can change their ownership percentage disproportionately when a partner/shareholder dies.

ii. Under the entity agreement, there is no change in the ratio of ownership after a partner's death.

d. Funding.

i. A cross purchase agreement can cause problems when the owner's ages differ.

A) Younger owners will pay high premiums on the lives of older owners.

ii. The business entity pays the premiums under the entity approach.

A) With a partnership, older partners may get a lower distributive share from the partnership.

B) More equitable than cross purchase.

e. Valuation.

   i. Cross purchase - each surviving owner receives insurance proceeds when a partner/ shareholder dies.

      A) Surviving owners buy decedent's interest from the estate.

   ii. Entity redemption - entity owns policies and receives distribution when a partner dies.

G. VALUATION DISCOUNTS

1. In General.

   a. The transfer tax value of closely held businesses, real estate, and other assets may be significantly reduced by the utilization of various valuation discounts.

   b. These discounts are often used in conjunction with a family limited partnership (See XI.A. Family Limited Partnership) or a family limited liability company.

2. Minority Discount.

   a. A reduction in value of an asset transferred is often allowed if the asset transferred represents a minority interest in a business.

   b. A minority interest is any interest that, in terms of voting, is not a controlling interest.

   c. Minority owners cannot manage the business or compel its sale or liquidation. Therefore, outside buyers would not be willing to pay the same amount for a minority interest as they would for a majority or controlling interest.

   d. For transfer tax purposes, minority discounts (when available) often range from 15%-50%.

3. Lack of Marketability Discount.

   a. A reduction in value of an asset transferred is often allowed if the asset transferred has an inherent lack of marketability.

   b. Interests in a closely held business and partnership interests are more difficult to sell than interests in other assets such as publicly traded stock. Therefore, a discount is often allowed for the lack of marketability.

   c. Lack of marketability discounts typically range from 15%-50%, and can be utilized for both minority and majority interests.

   d. A lack of marketability discount can be used in conjunction with a minority discount to produce a larger overall discount.

Example

Tom gave his son a 3% interest in his closely held business. The business is valued at $500,000, and Tom applied a lack of marketability discount and a minority discount that totaled 40%. For gift tax purposes, the value of the gift is only $9,000 [$500,000 x 3% x (1 - 40%)]. The $9,000 gift is eligible for the annual exclusion, resulting in a taxable gift of zero.

---

4. Blockage Discount.

   a. A blockage discount is a discount attributable to the value of large blocks of corporate stock that are listed on a public exchange.

   b. A discount may be available because a large block of stock is often less marketable than smaller amounts of stock.

   c. The theory behind a blockage discount is that a large amount of stock included in the decedent's gross estate cannot be liquidated at one time without a decrease in the stock's market price.

   d. The discount would be based on the decrease in the realizable price below the current market price of the stock.

5. Key Person Discount.

   a. A discount may be allowed for a business in which a key person has died or becomes disabled.

   b. The discount is based on the premise that the stock of a closely held business will decline if a key person, such as the founder, dies or becomes disabled.

   c. The discount may be reduced by the value of key person life insurance proceeds payable to the corporation on the death of the key person.

IX. THE MARITAL DEDUCTION

A. DEFINITION.

The decedent's estate can claim as a deduction an unlimited qualifying bequest or transfer of property to a surviving spouse.

1. This treatment parallels the marital deduction for gift tax.
2. This does not apply to surviving spouses who are not U.S. citizens. They have their own separate rules described in the section titled "Alien Surviving Spouses" on page 942.

B. QUALIFICATIONS FOR DEDUCTION.

1. The property must be included in the decedent's gross estate.
2. The property must be passed to the decedent's spouse.
3. The interest in the property must not be a terminable interest.
   a. A terminable interest is defined as an interest that ends upon an event or contingency. In other words, the spouse initially gets the interest in the property. This interest will terminate upon some event (usually death) and then the interest will pass to someone else.
   b. There are some exceptions to the terminable interest rule:
      i. When the only condition of bequest is that the survivor live for a period not exceeding six months, the marital deduction is allowed if the surviving spouse actually lives for the period specified.
      ii. When there is a right-to-life annuity coupled with a power of appointment, the marital deduction is allowed.
      iii. When there is a bequest to spouse of income from a Charitable Remainder Annuity Trust or a Charitable Remainder Unitrust and the spouse is the only noncharitable beneficiary, the marital deduction is allowed.
      iv. Certain marital trusts.

C. STRAIGHT BEQUESTS.

1. The first spouse dies and leaves everything to the surviving spouse.
2. Estate of the decedent spouse gets 100% marital deduction. The property will be taxed in estate of second spouse.
3. Advantages.
   a. Simple and inexpensive.
   b. Surviving spouse gets unfettered control over the assets.
4. Disadvantages.
   a. May overqualify estate since the first spouse to die does not take advantage of the applicable credit amount ($345,800 for 2003).
   b. Total estate tax between the two spouses may be higher if all property is bequeathed to the surviving spouse.

D. QUALIFIED TERMINABLE INTEREST PROPERTY TRUST (QTIP).

1. Allows a terminable interest to be passed to a surviving spouse and the property still qualify for the marital deduction.
2. Election is made on Form 706.
3. Income from the trust must be payable to the surviving spouse at least annually for life.
4. The value of the trust assets must be included in the estate of the surviving spouse when he or she dies.
5. Surviving spouse is not usually given a general power of appointment.
6. Usually the first spouse to die has specified in the trust provisions the ultimate disposition of the property.
7. Sometimes called a "C" Trust or a "Q" Trust.

E. POWER OF APPOINTMENT TRUST.

1. Allows a terminable interest to be passed to the surviving spouse and the property still qualify for the marital deduction.
2. No election required as with QTIP.
3. Income from the trust must be payable to the surviving spouse at least annually for life.
4. The trust will be included in the estate of the surviving spouse when they die.
5. Surviving spouse is given a general power of appointment over the property during life or at death.
6. The first spouse to die does not control the ultimate disposition of the property.
7. Sometimes called an "A" Trust.

F. BYPASS TRUST.

1. The purpose of a bypass trust is to take advantage of the applicable credit amount ($345,800 for 2003).
2. The property does not qualify for the marital deduction and is taxed in the estate of the first spouse to die.
3. A common scenario is for the first spouse to leave everything to the surviving spouse except for the applicable exclusion amount ($1,000,000 for 2003), which is transferred into a bypass trust. The surviving spouse can invade the trust for health, education, maintenance, and support. When wife dies, it does not go into her estate, and the property passes to children.
4. A bypass trust can be used instead of an outright bypass bequest to heirs who are not sophisticated or mature enough to handle the property. The choice of the trust over the bequest does not save any tax dollars; it simply provides the transferor with some peace of mind.
5. Often, highly appreciating assets are placed in a bypass trust to freeze the value for estate tax purposes at the death of the first spouse.
6. Also called a Credit Equivalency Trust, a Credit Shelter Trust, a Family Trust, or a "B" Trust.

G. USE OF DISCLAIMERS.

1. Allows spouse to disclaim part of estate, which would then go to the bypass share.
2. A specific direction to disclaim is not necessary in the will.
3. Allows more flexibility in the estate.
4. If spouse disclaims the property, her control over the property is minimized.
5. Since disclaimer has to be made within nine months of the spouse's death, the surviving spouse may find it difficult to give up property at a time when they may not be feeling very secure.

H. ALIEN SURVIVING SPOUSES.

1. Section 2056(d) disallows the unlimited marital deduction if the surviving spouse is not a U.S. citizen.
2. If the spouse becomes a citizen before the federal estate tax return is filed (Form 706 within nine months), Section 2056(d) does not apply. The spouse must have been a U.S. resident at the time of the decedent's death.
3. Marital deduction is allowed for property placed in a Qualified Domestic Trust (QDOT) that passes to a non-U.S. surviving spouse.
   a. Trust document requires at least one trustee to be U.S. citizen or U.S. corporation.
   b. Trustee has a right to withhold estate tax on distribution.
   c. Must meet requirements of the Treasury.
   d. Executor must make irrevocable election.

X. TRUSTS

A. GENERAL.

1. A trust is a legal arrangement that involves three parties.

   a. Grantor (settlor) transfers the property (called the principal or corpus) into the trust.

   b. Trustee – Holds the legal title to the assets and has a fiduciary responsibility to safeguard the property and distribute corpus and trust income as directed by the trust instrument.

   c. Beneficiary – The person or persons the trust benefits is said to have a beneficial interest.

   d. It is not always the case that three different individuals are involved. There are some cases where an individual may serve two or even more functions.

      i. Grantor names himself trustee.

      ii. Grantor names himself beneficiary.

      iii. Grantor is both trustee and beneficiary. This is called a grantor trust and is not recognized for tax purposes.

2. Types of trust interests.

   a. Income interest – The beneficiary receives the accounting income (income earned from trust assets) of the trust.

   b. Remainder interest – Beneficiary receives the trust principal upon termination of the trust. A vested remainder is one that is nonforfeitable. A contingent remainder is where the interest depends on whether a certain future event happens.

   c. Reversionary interest – A grantor who retains the remainder interest is said to have a reversionary interest.

3. Duration.

   a. The terms of the trust will dictate the length of the trust life.

   b. Rule against perpetuities (certain states do not have a rule against perpetuities).

      i. The rule against perpetuities prevents trusts from having an infinite life.

      ii. The rule aims to prevent a transferor of property from controlling the disposition of property for an unreasonably long period after making the transfer.

      iii. This rule, which has its roots in English common law, states that an interest cannot last longer than 21 years after the death of someone who was alive on the date the interest was created.

      iv. The date on which the interest is created is different for revocable and irrevocable trusts. If the trust is an irrevocable trust, the interest is created on the date the trust is created. If the trust is a revocable trust, the interest is created on the date in which the trust becomes irrevocable (usually at the date of death of the settlor).

      v. To avoid application of the rule against perpetuities, most trusts and wills contain a perpetuities savings clause requiring that the trust terminate no later than the outer limits of the rule (21 years).

      vi. Charitable trusts are exempt from the rule against perpetuities.

B. Reasons for Creating a Trust.

1. To avoid probate.
2. To avoid or reduce taxes.
3. Asset management for an individual who is the grantor and the beneficiary in the case he becomes incapacitated.
4. Asset management for beneficiaries who are not grantors. (The grantor may not have confidence in the beneficiaries abilities to invest assets.)
5. To make a charitable contribution while retaining some interest.

C. Trust Characteristics.

1. When created.
    a. Inter vivos – created during life.
    b. Testamentary – created by will and included in estate. Gift tax does not apply since transfer occurs at death.
2. Permanency.
    a. Revocable – A trust that is able to be rescinded or amended by the grantor.
    b. Irrevocable – A trust where the grantor has given up all control over the property. The trust cannot be changed by the grantor.
3. Funding.
    a. Funded – Trust has property placed in it. There is a principal or corpus amount.
    b. Unfunded – A trust that is legally ready to receive property but has not done so yet.
4. Income payout requirements.
    a. Simple trust – required to pay out all income to beneficiaries annually.
    b. Complex trust – any trust that isn't a simple trust.

D. Types of Trusts.

1. Living trust.
    a. Grantor creates an inter vivos trust that is funded with part or all of the grantor's property.
    b. This property does not pass through probate at death and so transfer is accomplished with a minimum of publicity, expense, and delays.
    c. Revocable living trust – revocable during the grantor's life, and becomes irrevocable at grantor's death.
        i. Includible in estate.
        ii. No gift tax at time of creation since there is no completed gift.
    d. Irrevocable living trust – Grantor places property into a trust that he cannot rescind or amend.
        i. Transfers constitute completed gifts and so gift tax may apply at the time the trust is created.
        ii. Has income and estate tax benefits (freeze value of estate assets).

2. Grantor trusts.
   a. Grantor trust rules rest on the idea that if a grantor has control over the trust then a completed gift has not been made, the grantor still has ownership of the assets, and the trust is not a separate taxable entity. Therefore, any income is taxed to the grantor.
   b. Sections 671-677 state that if a trust is a grantor trust, then the grantor is treated as the owner of the assets. Consequently, all the income, deductions, and credits of the trust are attributable to the grantor.
   c. Circumstances when the grantor is deemed owner of the trust:
      i. Reversionary interest in the corpus or income of the trust.
      ii. Power to control the beneficial enjoyment of the property or income (withdraw funds and change beneficiaries).
      iii. Certain administrative powers, such as borrowing.
      iv. Power to revoke a portion of the trust.
      v. Income for the benefit of the grantor, such as purchasing life insurance on the grantor or paying for support obligations of the grantor.
3. Standby trust – A trust (usually revocable) that has been legally created but will not actually function until some event occurs. For example, a trust that will spring upon incapacity to manage the assets when the grantor becomes unable.
4. Pourover trust – Assets are poured from another source (e.g., from a will, IRA, insurance contract, etc.) into the trust. May be revocable or irrevocable.
5. Charitable transfers.
   a. General – In general, a charitable income tax deduction is available for transfers to charities during life. Such transfers may take a variety of forms.
      i. To receive a current income tax deduction, charitable remainder trusts must be in the precise form of one of the following:
         A) Direct outright gift – charitable deduction equal to the gift if cash, basis, or value of appreciated property (see income tax rules).
         B) Charitable gift annuity – an irrevocable transfer of assets for a charitable annuity. Transfer is for less than a commercial annuity, therefore, a charitable income tax deduction is available for the difference using the IRS method.
         C) Pooled income fund – an irrevocable transfer of assets to a charity for an income stream from the charity's commingled asset management. A charitable deduction is available.
            1) Pooled income fund - public charity.
               a) Created and maintained by the charity.
               b) Donor transfers property including irrevocable remainder interest to charity (must be a 50% type charity and managed by the charitable remainderman).
               c) Property commingled with property of other donors.
               d) Retains income interest for one or more beneficiaries for life (no term trusts).
               e) Investments cannot include tax-free municipal bonds.
               f) Payment to donor is determined by earnings of trust annually.
               g) Sprinkling is not allowed.

D) Charitable Remainder Trusts (CRT).

1) Overview.

a) A CRT is an irrevocable trust in which the remainder beneficiary is a qualified charity.

b) A CRT can take the form of a Charitable Remainder Annuity Trust (CRAT) or a Charitable Remainder Unitrust (CRUT).

2) Common features of both a CRAT and a CRUT.

a) Trust is irrevocable.

b) Remainder interest is paid to charity.

c) Trust can last for life of grantor, or for a term of up to 20 years.

d) The present value of the remainder interest at the inception of the trust must be at least 10% of the initial fair market value of the property transferred to the trust.

e) The charity does not have to know they were named as the remainder beneficiary.

f) Annuity/unitrust payout rate must be at least 5%, and less than or equal to 50%.

3) Unique features of a Charitable Remainder Annuity Trust (CRAT).

a) Grantor receives either a fixed percentage of the <u>initial fair market value</u> of the property transferred to the trust or a fixed dollar amount annually.

b) Annuity must be paid in spite of necessity to invade principal due to income deficiency.

c) No additional contributions are permitted after inception.

d) Very inflexible.

4) Unique features of a Charitable Remainder Unitrust (CRUT).

a) Grantor receives a fixed percentage of the trust assets, <u>valued annually</u>.

i) Unitrust amount may be limited to income earned.

ii) Trust may provide for catch-up provisions when income does not meet the percentage requirement and then later exceeds the current percentage payout.

iii) Annual valuation may be expensive if property in trust is not easily valued (e.g., closely held businesses, real estate).

b) Additional contributions to the trust are permitted after inception.

c) Very flexible.

Example

Virginia, a 70-year-old widow, has charitable inclinations, but needs the income from all her assets during her retirement years. She decides to establish a Charitable Remainder Annuity Trust with $500,000 cash. Virginia will get a payment of 5% of the principal each year for the rest of her life. Assuming a rate of 10%, Virginia would go to Table S (Single Life PV of Annuity, Life Estate and Remainder Interests) to determine the value of her retained interest [6.4093 x $25,000 (500,000 x 5%) = 160,233]. Virginia then receives a charitable contribution deduction for the remainder interest of 339,767 (500,000 - 160,233).

E) Charitable Lead Trust (CLT).

1) Income from property transferred to trust is distributed to charity. Remainder reverts to noncharitable beneficiary (often a family member).

2) If set up as a grantor trust, a charitable income tax deduction for the income interest is available at the inception. However, the trust income is taxable to the grantor.

3) If set up as a nongrantor trust, no charitable income tax contribution deduction is available; however, the gift is valued at FMV less the charitable income interest.

4) Used by high wealth individuals who have no need for the current income from the assets. Advantageous to fund with high appreciation assets since it will remove appreciation from the estate (if nongrantor type trust is used).

Example

John sets up a CLT with $500,000 that pays a charity a 10% fixed annuity with the remainder going to his children at the end of the trust term. If John uses a grantor trust, John will calculate the present value of the annuity, and he will be able to take a current income tax deduction for the present value of the annuity stream as a charitable contribution. However, John will have to treat the entire annual income of the trust as income during the trust term. John will also have made a taxable gift equal to the present value of the remainder interests. This is a gift of a future interest not subject to the annual exclusion. If John uses a nongrantor trust, he will not get a current charitable deduction, but he will remove the entire asset ($500,000) from his estate at the discounted amount of the taxable gift.

EXHIBIT 8: CHARITABLE REMAINDER TRUSTS

	CRAT	CRUT	Pooled Income Fund
Income Tax Deduction	Total value of property - PV of retained income interest	Total value of property - PV of retained income interest	Total value of property - PV of retained income interest
Income Recipient	Noncharitable beneficiary (usually donor)	Noncharitable beneficiary (usually donor)	Noncharitable beneficiary (usually donor)
Payment	At least 5% of initial FMV of assets paid at least annually for life or term ≤ 20 years (similar to fixed annuity). Cannot exceed 50% of value of trust.	At least 5% of current FMV of assets (revalued annually) paid at least annually for life or term ≤ 20 years (similar to variable annuity). Cannot exceed 50% of value of trust.	Trust rate of return for year
Remainder Beneficiary	Charity	Charity	Charity
Additional Contributions	No	Yes	Yes
Sprinkling	Yes	Yes	No
When Income is Insufficient for Payout	Must invade corpus	Can pay up to income and make up deficiency in subsequent year	N/A
Can Hold Tax-Exempt Securities	Yes	Yes	No

6. Gifts to minors.

   a. Uniform Gifts to Minors Act (UGMA).

      i. Adopted in all states.

      ii. Gifts can include cash, securities, life insurance, but usually not real property.

      iii. No bonding or accounting usually required.

      iv. Donees usually must receive property by age 21.

      v. If donor is custodian and predeceases the beneficiary, then custodial property would be included in donor's estate.

   b. Uniform Transfers to Minors Act (UTMA).

      i. More flexible than Uniform Gifts to Minors Act (UGMA).

      ii. Less than half of the states have adopted it.

      iii. Allows any property interests to be a fiduciary gift.

c. Guardianship.

   i. Very restrictive - requires bonding and accounting.

   ii. Court must supervise.

   iii. Donee must receive property at age 18.

d. Irrevocable minor's trusts.

   i. Section 2503(b) trust (Mandatory Income Trust - MIT).

      A) Mandatory income distribution.

      B) Trust controls use of principal for minors.

      C) May meet the requirements of annual gift tax exclusion.

      D) May be excluded from donor's estate.

   ii. Section 2503(c) trust.

      A) Income distribution is discretionary.

      B) Principal distribution is discretionary until minor reaches adulthood (usually age 21).

      C) While not meeting the requirements of a present interest, the Internal Revenue Code provides an exception in Section 2503(c) whereby gifts to such trusts are deemed to be gifts of a present interest.

      D) If the donee dies before age 21, property must go to the donee's estate or the donee must hold a general power of appointment.

      E) Trust pays income tax on the undistributed income.

   iii. Crummey Minor's Trust.

      A) Advantageous over Section 2503(b) and Section 2503(c) trusts since income distribution and corpus distribution at age 21 are not mandatory.

      B) See section, "Crummey Powers Crummey v. Comm., 397 F2d 82 (9th Cir. 1961)" regarding Crummey powers.

7. Grantor retained trust.

   a. In a grantor retained trust, a grantor transfers property into a trust but retains some right of enjoyment of the property, usually income. If transferor survives the income period, all beneficial interest in the trust ceases, and the asset is out of the transferor's estate.

   b. The value of the taxable gift is calculated by taking the FMV of the property and reducing it by the retained interest. This equals the remainder interest that is considered a gift.

   c. Section 2702 severely limits the advantage of a grantor retained trust by valuing the income interest at zero when the transfer is made for the benefit of a member of the transferor's family and an interest is retained by the transferor or an applicable family member.

      i. Member of transferor's family - Ancestors, descendants, spouse, and siblings; ancestors and descendants of spouse; and, spouses of transferor's ancestors, descendants, and siblings.

      ii. Applicable family member - Transferor's spouse, ancestors of the transferor or the transferor's spouse, and any spouse of such ancestor.

d. When the retained interest is valued at zero, the remainder interest will be valued at FMV as if an outright gift had occurred.

e. Section 2702 carves out exceptions from the zero value rule for qualified personal residence trusts (QPRT), grantor retained annuity trusts (GRAT), grantor retained unitrusts (GRUT), and tangible personal property trusts. Remainder interests can be given to family members for these types of trusts and will escape the zero valuation rules in Section 2702.

f. Grantor Retained Interest Trust (GRIT) - The GRIT is only effective when used for a personal residence and is sometimes known as a Residence GRIT or Qualified Personal Residence Trust (QPRT). The grantor transfers a personal residence to a trust and retains the right to live in the residence during the trust term.

   i. An interest in only one residence.

   ii. The benefit is that the value of the gift will be equal to the fair market value of the house discounted for the number of years of the term of its trust at the applicable Section 7520 rate. Used most effectively when residence is expected to rapidly appreciate.

   iii. Cannot be occupied by someone other than termholder and family.

   iv. May be subject to mortgage.

   v. Prohibits distribution of trust income to anyone but termholder.

   vi. At the option of the termholder, may convert to qualified annuity interest.

   vii. The house can be rented or repurchased by grantor after trust term.

   viii. A QPRT may be an appropriate estate planning technique for a vacation home.

   ix. Grantor may be trustee.

QUALIFIED PERSONAL RESIDENCE TRUST (QPRT)
Key Features • This transaction results in a taxable gift. • No limit on trust term. • If transferor lives beyond term of trust there is no inclusion of the asset in the gross estate. • If the transferor dies before the expiration of the trust term the property is included in the gross estate at the fair value at the date of death. • This transaction may commonly result in the asset being leased back to the transferor at the end of the term if the transferor is still living. The lease payments will further the transferor's estate, but the beneficiaries will have taxable lease income. • The gift is a future interest (no annual exclusion). • The trust assets can only consist of a personal residence (maybe a small amount of cash). • This transaction does not make use of minority discounts. • This is an irrevocable trust. • Purchasing power risk to transferor. • Interest rate risk to transferor. • Reinvestment risk to transferor. • This transaction makes use of the applicable credit amount. • This transaction may require sophisticated valuation at the time of the initial transaction.

Example

Virginia, a 70-year-old widow, is in the 49% estate tax bracket. She places her $100,000 personal residence into a QPRT that provides for her to live there 10 years, and then the property passes to her children. Virginia will calculate the present value of her right to live in the house and subtract it from the FMV of her house to calculate the remainder gift to her children. If Virginia dies before 10 years, the FMV of the property at her death will be included in her estate. After 10 years, Virginia could be permitted to remain in the residence provided the agreement is arms' length, and the market rent is charged.

g. Grantor Retained Annuity Trust (GRAT).

i. Income taxed to grantor during lifetime for income taxes.

ii. Not taxable in grantor's estate unless grantor dies within income period (term of trust).

iii. Gift to the extent that the value of the property exceeds income interest calculated at time of creation (this is the remainder interest).

iv. Remainder passes to family members at end of income term.

v. Designed to produce estate tax savings for grantor. (Freezes value at trust creation if grantor outlives trust term.)

vi. Makes fixed payments to grantor at least annually.

vii. Fixed annuity does not have to be the same for each year. However, annuity payment in any year cannot exceed 120% of previous year.

viii. Qualified retained interest is not valued at zero for purposes of Section 2702.

ix. A GRAT is usually used with a family member and where the transferor has a better than average probability to outlive the term of the trust.

GRANTOR RETAINED ANNUITY TRUST (GRAT)
Key Features • Used only between loved ones. • For any specific term (usually < 5 years). • Grantor receives an annual payment from the trust of either a fixed amount or a fixed percentage of the initial FMV of the trust assets. • If transferor lives beyond term of trust, there is no inclusion of the asset in the gross estate. • If the transferor dies before the expiration of the trust term, the property is included in the grantor's gross estate at the FMV at the date of death. • The gift is a future interest (no annual exclusion). • The trust cannot be used as a personal residence trust. • This transaction does not make use of minority discounts. • This trust is an irrevocable trust. • Purchasing power risk to transferor. • Interest rate risk to transferor. • Reinvestment risk to transferor. • This transaction makes use of the applicable exclusion amount. • This transaction may require sophisticated valuation at the time of the initial transaction.

h. Grantor Retained Unitrust (GRUT).

  i. Makes payments at least annually of a fixed percentage of the net fair market value of the trust assets as determined annually.

  ii. All other characteristics are like a GRAT.

i. Tangible personal property trusts.

  i. Tangible personal property is transferred to the trust, with the grantor retaining a term certain interest in the trust (retained interest). At the end of the trust term, the beneficiaries receive the remainder interest in the trust.

  ii. Depreciable property cannot be used. Artwork can be used because it is not depreciable.

  iii. The zero valuation rule of Section 2702 does not apply to tangible personal property trusts. The value of the retained interest in the trust will be equal to the amount the interest could be sold for to an unrelated third party.

  iv. The grantor has the burden of establishing the value of the retained interest. Because of the difficulty in valuing the retained interest, tangible personal property trusts are not common.

Example

Kevin established a tangible personal property trust by transferring a $500,000 painting to the trust. Kevin gave his son a remainder interest in the trust, and Kevin retained a 15-year term certain interest. The value of the gift would be $500,000 less the value of the retained interest. Kevin has the burden of establishing the value of the retained interest.

8. Credit equivalency trust.

  a. Usually testamentary.

  b. Does not ordinarily qualify for the unlimited marital deduction.

  c. Ensures that the estate makes use of the applicable exclusion amount ($1,000,000 for 2003). Otherwise, property would automatically be taxed in second spouse's estate if marital deduction was used.

  d. Spouse may be income beneficiary.

9. Dynasty trust.

  a. Passes a life insurance policy to grandchildren.

  b. Avoids GSTT.

  c. Transfers substantial wealth.

10. Totten trust (similar to POD/TOD).

  a. A trust created by New York statute.

  b. When an individual who opens an account "in trust for" another it is not a completed transfer. The income is taxed to the grantor until the trust is made irrevocable.

11. Blind trust.

    a. A blind trust can be used to hold assets where ownership of the assets may give rise to conflict of interest issues.

    b. These trusts are commonly used by government officials.

    c. The official, his/her spouse, or dependent child has a beneficial interest, which is certified by the Director of the Office of Government Ethics.

    d. The official has no knowledge or control of the management of the trust assets and only receives the income from the assets.

EXHIBIT 9: TRUSTS - SUMMARY OF TRUST CLASSIFICATION AND USE

TRUST	PURPOSE	CHARACTERISTICS	PLANNING OPPORTUNITIES	INCOME / ESTATE / GIFT TAX CONSEQUENCES
QTIP Trust known as "C" Trust or "Q" Trust	Marital trust that creates a terminable interest for spouse but that DOES qualify for the unlimited marital deduction and gives power to settlor to name remainderman.	All income must be payable to surviving spouse at least annually for life. Surviving spouse is usually <u>not</u> given power of appointment. QTIP election made on Form 706 by executor.	Place assets in QTIP, income to spouse for life, remainder to children.	Assets of the trust are not included in the first decedent's estate but rather in the surviving spouse's estate. Trust pays its pro rata share of estate tax for surviving spouse.
Power of Appointment Trust known as "A" Trust or Marital Trust	Marital trust that creates a terminable interest for spouse but that DOES qualify for the unlimited marital deduction and gives general power to appoint to surviving spouse to name remainderman.	All income must be payable to surviving spouse at least annually for life. Surviving spouse has general POA. No election required.	Place assets in POA Trust, income to spouse. Spouse is given POA over property exercisable during life or at death. Has to be general POA, not limited power to qualify for unlimited marital deduction.	Not included in taxable estate of decedent spouse but included in the taxable estate of the surviving spouse (as long as he or she has not gifted or consumed it during life). If surviving spouse gives the property away (exercises her unlimited POA during life), then surviving spouse has made a taxable gift.
Bypass Trust known as "B" Trust or Credit Shelter Trust	Purpose is to take advantage of the applicable credit amount afforded 1st decedent spouse. A trust that is sometimes used to pass property to surviving spouse, but can be used to give any beneficiary an income interest, with a different remainderman. Does NOT qualify for the marital deduction.	An alternative to an outright transfer. Takes advantage of the unified credit of decedent. Useful when a split investment exists between income and remainder.	Instead of leaving an outright bequest to children, decedent spouse puts property into a bypass trust, income to surviving spouse for life, and remainder to children upon surviving spouse's death.	Taxed in first decedent spouse's estate.
Charitable Remainder Annuity Trust (CRAT)	Split interest gift where part of an interest is given to charity. Donor receives a fixed annuity and remainder goes to charity. Usually created during life.	Contributions at setup only. Must receive an annuity income of at least 5% of the original value of assets transferred into trust. Can be for life or term ≤ 20 years PV of RI ≥10 at inception.	Good for clients who desire certainty of fixed income. As government interest rates go up, the deductible charitable remainder interest goes up.	Donor receives an immediate charitable contribution deduction for income tax purposes if created during life. The value of the property is included in the gross estate but an equivalent charitable deduction reduces the taxable estate amount to zero.
Charitable Remainder Unitrust (CRUT)	Split interest gift where part of an interest is given to charity. Donor receives a variable annuity and remainder goes to charity.	Contributions after initial setup are permitted. Must receive an annuity income of at least 5% of the current fair market value of assets. Can be for life or term ≤ 20 years. PV of RI ≥10 at inception.	Appeals to clients who want hedge against inflation. Can provide for income on lesser of unitrust amount or amount actually earned on property, with makeup, but net income with makeup CRUTS (NIMCRUTS) are risky.	Donor receives an immediate charitable contribution deduction for income tax purposes if created during life. The value of the property is included in the gross estate but an equivalent charitable deduction reduces the taxable estate amount to zero.

TRUSTS – SUMMARY OF TRUST CLASSIFICATION AND USE (CONTINUED)

TRUST	PURPOSE	CHARACTERISTICS	PLANNING OPPORTUNITIES	INCOME/ ESTATE / GIFT TAX CONSEQUENCES
Pooled Income Fund	Investment fund created and maintained by target charity. Pools property from all contributors and pays a return based on earnings of fund.	No tax free securities may be held by PIF. Sometimes limit donations to cash and cash equivalents.	Preferred by those who want to avoid having to establish and maintain a trust. Frequently maintained by colleges and universities.	Donor receives an immediate charitable contribution deduction for income tax purposes if created during life. The value of the property is included in the gross estate but an equivalent charitable deduction reduces the taxable estate amount to zero.
Charitable Lead Trust (CLAT or CLUT)	Property is transferred to a trust that distributes income to a charitable beneficiary for a specific term with the remainder reverting to a noncharitable beneficiary (may be grantor or other remainderman).	Noncharitable beneficiary can be grantor, spouse, child or other.	Good for clients who have a large amount of highly appreciating assets and can forego the income from these assets. When interest rates are low, this increases the valuation of the deductible interest donation because of the lower valuation of the remainder.	If it is a grantor trust, then the grantor claims the income and receives the charitable deduction equal to the amount the trust pays to the charity. However, if the trust is a nongrantor trust where the remainderman is someone other than the grantor, then the grantor does not claim the income and cannot receive an income tax charitable deduction but the value of the asset is out of the estate.
2503(b) Trust or Mandatory Income Trust	Trust set up for a beneficiary composed of an income interest and a remainder interest. Mandatory distribution of income entitles donor to annual exclusion.	Annual exclusion is available for the income interest. Income must be distributed.	Less attractive since Crummey decision. Often used for gifts to minors.	Income is taxable to beneficiary.
2503(c) Trust	Trust set up for minor that is a gift of a future interest but qualifies for the annual exclusion.	Property and income for benefit of minor. Income distribution is discretionary. Property must be available to beneficiary at age 21. If minor dies before age 21, property goes to minor's estate.	Less attractive since Crummey decision. Created to discourage income payout to immature minors solely to take advantage of annual exclusion.	If minor dies before age 21, property goes to minor's estate.
Crummey Trust	Trust that allows a right to withdraw for a brief period thus creating a present interest that qualifies for the annual exclusion.	Beneficiary usually allowed to withdraw the lesser of the amount of the available annual exclusion or the value of the gift property transferred. Beneficiary must be given notice of right to withdraw.	Demand right should not exceed greater of $5,000 or 5% of value of property to avoid taxable gift to remainderman. Cristofani decision extended annual exclusion treatment to contingent beneficiaries.	Present interest is created by the right to withdraw.
Irrevocable Life Insurance Trust	Enables donor to control the disposition of life insurance proceeds. To purchase insurance, the trust may be created, or to receive insurance, assigned by the grantor to it.	Excludes insurance proceeds from taxable estate of both spouses. Excludes proceeds from probate.	Transferor must surrender all interest in policy. Can be used as source of funds to pay estate taxes by beneficiaries. Grantor can make annual gifts to trust (qualify for annual exclusion) that will cover policy premiums if Crummey provision is used.	Excluded from transferor's estate if no incidence of ownership. May have gift tax on cash value of policy assigned transferred into trust. Will be included in transferor's estate if he does not live three years after transfer if policy assigned.

E. SPECIAL TRUST PROVISIONS.

1. Sprinkling - The power to direct income at the discretion of the trustee for the benefit of the beneficiary. (The trustee can choose when/how much to distribute to the beneficiary.)
2. Beneficiary power to withdraw to limited extent.
3. Crummey power - Limited power to withdraw (usually 30 to 60 days).
4. Special or limited power (for example, the power to invade the principal for the health, education, maintenance, or support of the income beneficiary).
5. General powers (e.g., the power to appoint income or corpus to the trustee by the trustee).

F. OVERVIEW OF TRUST AND ESTATE TAXATION.

1. Trusts are generally treated as separate taxable entities. Remember that grantor trusts are not recognized for tax purposes.
2. A simple trust is one that:
   a. Is required to distribute all of its income currently (each year).
   b. Has no charitable beneficiaries.
   c. Does not distribute any corpus.
3. A complex trust is any trust that cannot be classified as a simple trust.
4. An estate is created when a decedent dies.
   a. The estate consists of the probate estate.
   b. The estate holds and protects the assets, collects income from those assets, and satisfies obligations of the estate until all the assets are distributed.
5. Estates and trusts are subject to the same rate schedule, a very highly progressive structure where the top rate of 38.6% begins at $9,350 (for 2003).
6. Fiduciaries file Form 1041 on or before the 15th day of the fourth month after the close of the tax year. Grantor trusts may also file a Form 1041.

G. CALCULATING THE TAX.

1. Similar to calculating tax for individuals.
   a. Gross Income – Deductions = Taxable Income.
   b. Deductions include a distribution deduction.
   c. Deductions include an exemption.
      i. Exemption for most simple trusts is $300.
      ii. Exemption for most complex trusts is $100.
2. Fiduciary long-term capital gains rate is no more than 20%.
3. Fiduciaries may be subject to AMT.

H. How Income is Taxable.

1. Beneficiary is taxed on an amount equal to the distribution deduction.
2. Trust is not taxed on this amount since the trust gets a deduction for it.
3. The distribution deduction is the lesser of DNI or the amount actually distributed to the beneficiaries.
4. Income distributed maintains its character (ordinary, tax exempt, capital).

I. Distributable Net Income (DNI).

1. Important and complicated concept in fiduciary taxation.
2. Equals maximum distribution deduction.
3. Equals maximum amount beneficiaries can be taxed on.
4. DNI is similar to fiduciary accounting income.
   a. Includes most normal income/expense items.
   b. Excludes items relating to corpus such as capital gains, stock splits, and depreciation of business assets.

XI. OTHER LIFETIME TRANSFERS (OTHER THAN STRAIGHT SALES AND GIFTS)

A. FAMILY LIMITED PARTNERSHIP

1. In General.

   a. A family limited partnership is a partnership that is created to transfer assets to younger generations at a reduced gift tax valuation and cost.

   b. A major objective is to generate valuation discounts (for estate and gift tax purposes) on the transfer of a limited interest in the partnership. The discounts are available because a limited partner cannot easily sell his or her partnership interest (lack of marketability discount) and cannot manage the partnership's operations (minority discount). (See Section VIII.G. "Valuation Discounts" for a discussion of minority and lack of marketability discounts.)

   c. Typically, a senior family member transfers an asset (such as a closely held business) to a partnership in exchange for a 1% general partnership interest and a 99% limited partnership interest.

   d. The senior family member then makes gifts (over time) of the limited partnership interests to junior family members.

   e. The transfer of the limited partnership interests constitute a gift, eligible for the annual exclusion.

2. Advantages.

   a. The senior family member can retain control of the business, since the senior family member is the only family member with a general partnership interest (limited partners are not allowed to participate in management of the business).

   b. Restrictions can be placed on transfers of limited partnership interests by junior family members.

   c. Some creditor protection may be afforded.

   d. Transfers can be made at substantial discounts as compared to the value of underlying assets.

   e. Gifts of limited partnership interests are eligible for the annual exclusion.

3. Disadvantages.

   a. Attorney fees will be incurred when the partnership is established.

   b. Appraisal fees may be required to support underlying asset valuation and discounts taken.

FAMILY LIMITED PARTNERSHIP
Key Features • Used only between loved ones. • Makes use of minority discounts. • Makes use of lack of control discounts. • Can allow the transferor to maintain control of the asset with little ownership interest. • Makes use of the annual exclusion. • Makes use of the credit equivalency. • The minority interest usually has transfer restrictions. • The gift is of a present interest. • This transaction requires sophisticated and perhaps repeated valuation.

B. BARGAIN SALES.

1. In General.
   a. Sale of an asset for less than full consideration, usually made to related parties or family members.
   b. Considered part sale and part gift.
2. Income and estate tax ramifications.
   a. The difference between the sales price of the asset and the seller's basis in the asset will be a taxable gain to the seller for income tax purposes.
   b. The difference between the fair market value of the asset and the consideration received is considered a gift.
   c. The buyer's tax basis is equal to the price paid plus the carryover basis from the donor of the gifted portion.
   d. The gift portion will qualify for the annual exclusion if it is a completed gift.
   e. The property sold will not be included in the seller's gross estate upon death. However, the portion of the property that is considered a taxable gift will be added back to the seller's taxable estate (as a prior taxable gift) in arriving at the estate tax base.

Example

Steve owns property with a basis of $50,000 and a current value of $140,000, which he sells to his son, Murray, for $90,000. Steve will have a taxable gain of $40,000 ($90,000 sales price less $50,000 basis). Steve has also made a gift of $50,000 ($140,000 value less $90,000 sales price). The gift will be eligible for the annual exclusion.

C. INSTALLMENT SALES & SCINS.

1. Sale for a single or series of installment notes. An installment sale can defer income tax, but because the present value of the notes will be included in seller's estate, no estate tax relief is obtained.

2. An exception - arm's length. Therefore, the present value of the notes canceled at death of the seller are not included in the seller's estate, but any payments due, but not yet paid, at the death of the seller are included as an asset in the gross estate. The gain inherent in these notes payable is income in respect of decedent and the estate's income tax return will be allowed the appropriate deduction for income in respect of decedent (Sec. 691). SCINs are usually made to family members.

SELF-CANCELLING INSTALLMENT NOTE (SCIN)
Key Features • Used only between loved ones. • Transaction is a sale - seller will have capital gain, ordinary income (if depreciable property), and return of capital. • The sale is for the full fair market value of the property (buyer pays a risk premium). • Removes asset from gross estate. • Used when seller is in ill health relative to table life expectancy. • For a specific term. • No step to fair market value at death of seller. (Buyer's basis is sum of payments to seller.) • Risk to transferee of paying more than fair value (if seller lives the full term). • Purchasing power risk to seller. • Interest rate risk to seller. • Reinvestment risk to seller. • Indebtedness may be collateralized. • Does not use minority discounts. • Does not use the annual exclusion (not a gift). • Does not use the applicable credit amount. • Requires sophisticated valuation only at the time of sale.

Example

A.C., age 65, has some land (FMV $200,000, Basis $80,000) he wants to sell to his son. A.C. and son enter into a 15-year, self-canceling installment agreement. To avoid gift treatment, A.C. will charge his son either a higher interest rate, a higher payment, or more than $200,000. If A.C. were 75 instead of 65, the SCIN premium would be more than it would be at 65. If A.C. dies before the son pays off the note, the value of the note is not included in A.C.'s gross estate.

D. PRIVATE ANNUITIES.

1. The sale of an asset (usually to a related party) in exchange for an unsecured promise to pay a lifetime annuity to transferor.
2. Consequences.
    a. There will be no gift and, therefore, no gift tax as long as value of property transferred equals the value of property received (PV of annuity).
    b. No immediate income tax implications, but gain is reported like payments received from an installment sale. The gain is recognized using an exclusion/inclusion ratio (like an annuity) after recognizing interest income to the extent of market rate.
        i. Income is the interest component.
        ii. Return of basis - based on exclusion ratio.

        $$\frac{\text{Investment in contract}}{\text{Total expected return}} = \text{Exclusion ratio}$$

        iii. Capital gain - based on inclusion ratio.
    c. Since a private annuity is for life, it is not included in transferor's (decedent) gross estate.
    d. May not have security or be collateralized.
    e. If annuitant outlives life expectancy, the payor will have made a bad bargain and the annuitant will include all the annuity payments not consumed in his estate. However, the transferor could use his annual exclusion and forgive up to $11,000 ($22,000 for split gift) of the payment without incurring any gift tax consequences.
    f. Ordinarily used when transferor is not expected to live the full table life expectancy.

Example

Using the example under SCINs above, let's change the scenario. Suppose that A.C. decides to transfer the land under a private annuity arrangement. Using the applicable federal rate (say 8%), A.C. would go to Table S to calculate his annuity payment ($200,000/8.1360) of $24,582. There is no gift and the asset is removed from A.C.'s estate. Each payment made to A.C. will be taxed as part return of basis, part gain, and part ordinary income. If A.C. lives less than his life expectancy, the son has paid less than FMV for the asset. Any unrecovered basis will be a loss deduction on A.C.'s final tax return. If A.C. lives longer than his life expectancy, the son has paid more than the FMV and would probably think he had not made a good deal!

PRIVATE ANNUITY
Key Features • Used only between loved ones. • This transaction is a sale. • The sale is for the full fair market value of the property. • Removes asset from gross estate. • Used when seller is in ill health relative to table life expectancy. • For a full life term. • No basis step to fair market value at death of seller. • Risk to buyer of paying more than fair value. (Buyer's basis is sum of payment made until death of seller and payments forgiven (gifted) by seller.) • Purchasing power risk to seller. • Interest rate risk to seller. • Reinvestment risk to seller. • Indebtedness may not be collateralized. • Does not use minority discounts. • Does not use control discounts. • Does not use the annual exclusion. • Does not use the credit equivalency. • This transaction requires sophisticated valuation only at the time of sale.

XII. LIFE INSURANCE IN ESTATE PLANNING

A. NEED.

Death usually creates a need for liquidity - often that need is satisfied by using life insurance.

B. USE IN ESTATE PLANNING.

It is impossible for the insured in a life insurance policy to collect the death benefits. However, if the decedent is the owner or has incidents of ownership in any insurance policy where the decedent is also the insured, then the face amount of the policy will be included in the decedent's gross estate. This increases the decedent's estate tax and creates a need for additional liquidity (a very bad result). Therefore, it is fundamental in estate planning to consider moving life insurance from the insured's ownership either to the hands of the beneficiaries as owners or a trustee of an irrevocable insurance trust.

C. INCOME TAX.

Life insurance proceeds are not subject to income tax to an ordinary beneficiary (nontransferred for value).

D. GIFT TAX.

1. Insurance transferred may be subject to gift tax if it has a cash value and if that cash value is assigned. However, such a transfer will qualify for the annual exclusion. An exception is made when a policy is transferred to an irrevocable trust, but may still qualify if a Crummey provision is utilized. Term insurance may be considered a gift of a future interest because donee is unable to enjoy any immediate benefits.
2. Unholy trinity - Owner, insured, and beneficiary are three different individuals. Upon death of insured, owner of the policy is deemed to have made gift of proceeds to the beneficiary. If owner and beneficiary are the same person, this result is avoided.

E. DECEDENT'S ESTATE.

Life insurance proceeds will be included in decedent's estate if:

1. The decedent's estate was the beneficiary of the policy.
2. Decedent owned or had incidents of ownership in the policy at death.
3. The decedent made a complete transfer of all incidents of ownership in the policy within three years of death.
4. If decedent made a completed transfer more than three years before death, then the taxable terminal value, as of the date of the gift, will be included in the decedent's adjusted taxable gifts (if greater than the annual exclusion).
5. Any ownership of a policy on the life of another will be included at terminal value.

F. BENEFICIARIES.

The selection of owners and beneficiaries of life insurance is of great importance due to the possible inclusion in the decedent's estate.

1. Generally, it is wise to make either the beneficiaries or an irrevocable trust the owner of the policy.
2. Assignment may be effective, but the three-year throwback rule may defeat the objective of removing the proceeds from the estate.

G. INSURANCE TRUSTS.

1. Advantages.
   a. Avoids probate.
   b. Can restrict use of funds by beneficiaries.
   c. Greater flexibility in distributions.
   d. Trustee has more investment policy discretion.
2. Revocable - no income tax advantage but still has nontax advantages listed above.
3. Irrevocable.
   a. Unfunded - Grantor contributes the cash to pay premiums at a later time.
   b. Funded - Cash/property contributed to trust to pay premiums.

XIII.THE GENERATION-SKIPPING TRANSFER TAX (GSTT)

A. DESIGN.

The GSTT is designed to tax large transfers between skipped generations (e.g., grandfather to grandson). It is a separate tax from the unified gift and estate tax and is in addition to these taxes. It applies to both inter vivos and testamentary transfers. For years beginning after 2009, the GSTT is repealed (TRA 2001).

B. THREE TYPES OF TRANSFERS SUBJECT TO TAX.

1. Direct skips - Transferee is at least two (2) generations younger than transferor. Transferor is liable for tax (or transferor's estate).

Example

Grandfather leaves in his will $100,000 each to his grandson and granddaughter. Both legatees are direct skips.

2. Taxable termination - The termination (by death, lapse of time, release of power or otherwise) of an interest in property held in trust that passes to a skip person will be subject to GSTT, for which the trustee is liable.
3. Taxable distribution - Any distribution of property from a trust to a skip person. The transferee is liable for any tax.

C. GENERATION ASSIGNMENT.

1. A nonlineal descendant is placed in their generation based on age. A person within 12.5 years of the transferor is considered the same generation. After the first 12.5 years, every 25 years is considered a new generation. Therefore, a transfer to a nonlineal descendant ≥ 37.5 years younger than the transferor is subject to GSTT.
2. A lineal descendant of the transferor is assigned to the generation that results from comparing the number of generations between the transferor and the transferee.
3. An individual who has been married at any time to the transferor shall be assigned to the transferor's generation.
4. A married individual is assigned to the same generation as their spouse for purposes of gifts from the spouse's lineal ancestors.
5. A relationship by legal adoption is treated as a relationship by blood.

D. GSTT RATE.

1. Any GSTT paid by the donor will be added to the value of the gift to determine the value at which to apply the federal gift tax.

EXHIBIT 10: GSTT RATES AND EXEMPTIONS

Calendar Year	GSTT Rate	GSTT Exemption
2003	49%	$1,120,000
2004	48%	$1,500,000
2005	47%	$1,500,000
2006	46%	$2,000,000
2007	45%	$2,000,000
2008	45%	$2,000,000
2009	45%	$3,500,000
2010	GSTT Repealed	GSTT Repealed

E. REPORTING.

Reported on Form 709 for lifetime generation-skipping transfers and on Form 706 for testamentary generation-skipping transfers.

F. EXCEPTIONS TO GSTT.

1. GSTT annual exclusion is $11,000 (for 2003) per donee per donor for direct skip transfers (gift splitting is available if both spouses elect).
2. The predeceased parent direct skip - If a parent has died, the grandparent may donate or bequest to the grandchild without the grandchild being considered a skip person ("moves up" one generation). Parent may be transferor's child or spouse's child. Grandchild may be any grandchild. This exception extends to collateral heirs if a decedent has no living lineal descendents. In other words, grandparent who has no grandchildren can make a gift to a grand nephew or grand niece without incurring GSTT.

> **Note:** There is no additional penalty for skipping more than one generation.

3. GSTT Exemption.
   a. For 2003, the GSTT lifetime exemption is $1,120,000.
4. For purposes of GSTT, gift splitting is available to married individuals if the election to gift split was made with regard to the underlying gift. Thus, if a married couple made the election to split gifts for gift tax purposes, they automatically get to split gifts for GSTT.
5. Qualified transfers (e.g., medical, tuition) are excluded from GSTT.

G. EXEMPTIONS FROM GSTT.

1. Trusts that were irrevocable prior to September 25, 1985.
2. Wills that could not be changed after 1987 (capacity).

H. APPLICABLE RATE.

1. GSTT = Taxable amount x GSTT rate x inclusion ratio.
2. Inclusion ratio = (1 - AF).
3. Applicable fraction (AF) = (remaining exemption ÷ value of property transferred).

Example

Grandfather makes a gift to grandson of $5,000,000 in year 2003. Grandfather has made no other generation-skipping transfers. After the annual exclusion ($11,000) and the lifetime exclusion ($1,120,000 for 2003), Grandfather has GSTT of 49% x $3,869,000 = $1,895,810 (which is in addition to the gift tax levied). The GSTT will be added back to the $5,000,000 to determine the gift tax liability.

XIV.SPECIAL PROVISIONS FOR SMALL BUSINESSES, FARMS, ILLIQUID ESTATES

A. SPECIAL USE VALUATION (SECTION 2032A).

1. If a decedent owned real property that was used as a farm or in connection with a closely held business, then a reduced valuation may be available for the property.
2. The reduced valuation is made on the basis of the current actual use rather than its highest and best use. The aggregate reduction in value cannot exceed $840,000 (for 2003).
3. Several conditions must be met:
   a. Value of the property (real or personal) must be at least 50% of the adjusted gross estate.
   b. Value of the real property alone must be at least 25% of the adjusted gross estate.
   c. Decedent or family member must have been a material participant in the business for at least 5 of the last 8 years.
4. Executor makes election.
5. If the special-use property is disposed of to a nonfamily member or if the property discontinues its qualified use within ten years of the decedent's death, then all or part of the estate tax savings may be recaptured.

B. DEFERRED PAYMENT OF ESTATE TAX (SECTION 6166).

1. This is an election available to owners of farms or closely held businesses.
   a. Value of the closely held business exceeds 35% of the value of the adjusted gross estate.
   b. Applies to proprietorships, partnerships, and corporations.
2. Executor may elect to defer for five years, any estate tax payment relating to the closely held business. The estate tax can then be paid in ten annual installments beginning after the five-year deferral period. Interest is paid during the deferral period.
3. A 2% interest rate applies to the taxes attributable to the first $1,120,000 (for 2003) of taxable value. Any value over that has a rate equal to 45% of the regular underpayment interest rate.
4. Unpaid installments will be accelerated if the total dispositions of property from the business is equal to or more than 50% of the estate tax valuation.

C. STOCK REDEMPTION (SECTION 303).

1. Permits the estate of a decedent shareholder to redeem the decedent's shares with favorable income tax treatment.
2. The transaction will be treated as a disposition of an asset rather than receipt of a dividend.
3. Conditions to be met:
   a. Stock must be included in the decedent's estate.
   b. The value of the stock must be more than 35% of the gross estate less taxes, expenses, debts and losses.
   c. Redemption proceeds eligible for capital gain treatment can't exceed death taxes plus deductible funeral and administrative expenses.

D. FAMILY-OWNED BUSINESS DEDUCTION (SECTION 2057).

1. A limited deduction is available for a family-owned business (for 1997, this deduction was an exclusion).
2. This deduction is in addition to special-use valuation (Section 2032A) and installment payments of estate tax (Section 6166).
3. Calculation of the deduction.
   a. The estate tax is calculated as if the estate is given a deduction of up to $675,000 and a unified credit exemption equivalent of $625,000 for a total of $1.3 million. However, if the qualified family-owned business (QFOBI) deduction amount is less than $675,000, the excess is added to the unified credit exemption of $625,000 up to the maximum allowed for the year.
   b. If the value of the family-owned business is less than $675,000, then the regular estate exclusion amount increases dollar-for-dollar up to the exemption equivalent for the year.
4. Conditions to be met:
   a. Must meet the 50% liquidity test. All interests passed at death plus certain inter vivos gifts to family members must be greater than 50% of the adjusted gross estate.
   b. Recapture may occur if:
      i. Heir ceases material participation.
      ii. Heir sells interest or ceases to be U.S. citizen.
      iii. Principal place of business ceases to be in U.S.

Example

In 2003, the QFOBI deduction for Sarah's estate is $200,000. Since this is less than the $675,000 maximum deduction allowed, the excess $475,000 is added back to the $625,000 applicable credit amount allowed ($475,000 + $625,000 = $1,100,000). However, the maximum applicable credit amount for 2003 is $1,000,000 so that is all that is allowed. If she has $1,000,000 of nonqualified family-owned business assets, her total deduction and applicable credit amount is $200,000 + $1,000,000 = $1,200,000. If the QFOBI deduction had been $650,000, then only $25,000 would have been added back to the $625,000 and the applicable credit equivalency exclusion amount would be $650,000.

5. Beginning in 2004, the family-owned business deduction is repealed (TRA 2001).

XV. POSTMORTEM PLANNING

A. JOINT INCOME TAX RETURN.

Joint income tax return with a surviving spouse is generally advantageous due to rate schedule and closing period of the surviving spouse. A possible disadvantage may be to subject the estate and the surviving spouse to additional tax liability due to joint and several liability.

B. WAIVER OF COMMISSIONS.

Waiver of commissions for executor spouse is generally preferred if the estate is taxable and the unlimited marital deduction is used. However, the waiver may not be beneficial if the marginal tax bracket is lower than the applicable estate tax rate.

C. MEDICAL EXPENSES.

Medical expenses paid within one year of death are deductible on decedent's final tax return (Form 1040) or as an estate tax deduction (Form 706). If the medical expenses are deducted on the final income tax return, the expenses will be subject to a 7.5% of AGI floor. If the expenses are deducted on the estate tax return, there is no limit on the deduction. The estate would not claim this deduction on the estate tax return if no tax is otherwise due.

D. INCOME IN RESPECT OF A DECEDENT.

1. In General.

   a. Income in respect of a decedent (IRD) is income at death which the decedent had earned and was entitled to but which had not been received as of the date of death.

   b. IRD will be considered an asset for estate tax purposes (Form 706) and income for federal income tax purposes (Form 1040 or 1041).

   c. Examples of IRD.

      i. Distributions from a qualified plan or IRA made after the date of death. The beneficiary receiving the distribution must report the taxable portion of the distribution in his or her taxable income.

      ii. Forgiveness of debt at death of an installment note. The entire amount of any remaining unrecognized gain will be IRD to the estate.

      iii. Salary earned by the decedent that is paid after the date of death. The party receiving the salary has IRD in the year of receipt.

      iv. Rental income and interest income accrued but unpaid at death.

      v. Annuity payments received after death.

2. Estate tax ramifications.

   a. IRD items represent assets of the decedent and, therefore, will be included in the decedent's gross estate.

   b. The decedent's basis of the IRD asset carries over to the new owner of the asset. In other words, no step to fair market value in basis occurs at death.

3. Income tax ramifications.

   a. IRD will be included in the gross income of the recipient of the IRD. Typically, the recipient would be the decedent's estate or a beneficiary of the estate.

   b. The character of the IRD income (ordinary, tax-exempt, capital gain, etc.) is the same to the recipient as it would have been in the hands of the decedent. For example, a distribution from an IRA received by the decedent's beneficiary will be taxed as ordinary income to the beneficiary.

   c. Whoever receives the IRD is entitled to any deductions associated with the IRD.

   d. An income tax deduction will be allowed for the portion of estate tax attributable to the IRD. The deduction is allowed each year IRD is included in income.

      i. The deduction is calculated in two steps.

         A) Determine the estate tax that is attributable to IRD.

Example

When Mike Orentlich died, his gross estate included a qualified plan (IRD asset) worth $700,000. The total estate tax liability for Mike's estate was $2,000,000. The estate tax liability would have been $1,600,000 if the qualified plan was excluded from his gross estate. Therefore, the estate tax attributable to the IRD (qualified plan) is $400,000 ($2,000,000 - $1,600,000).

B) Calculate the deduction based on the recipient's proportionate amount of IRD.

Example

Assume the same facts as the previous example. Mike's son, George, the beneficiary of Mike's qualified plan, received a taxable distribution from the plan in the amount of $350,000. The entire $350,000 will be included in George's taxable income, but George will also be entitled to an income tax deduction of $200,000 ($350,000 ÷ $700,000 x $400,000).

---

ii. The deduction is available on Form 1041 or may flow to the beneficiary of the property, which generated the IRD, by way of the Form K-1 from Form 1041.

iii. If the deduction is claimed by an individual, it will be an itemized deduction not subject to the 2% of AGI floor.

E. SERIES E AND EE BONDS.

It is generally advisable to report accrued interest on Form 1040 by making the election. Failure to make the election results in income in respect of a decedent (IRD). The associated tax liability is deductible on the estate return.

F. QUALIFYING WIDOW(ER).

Does survivor qualify as surviving spouse? If so, then the surviving spouse is eligible for Qualifying Widow(er) filing status on Form 1040 for two years after the close of the year in which the decedent died. There must be a dependent child residing in the household.

G. ADMINISTRATIVE EXPENSES AND CASUALTY LOSSES.

There is usually a choice of deducting these on the estate return (Form 706) or fiduciary return (Form 1041). The choice depends on relative brackets.

H. INTEREST DEDUCTIONS.

1. Personal interest is nondeductible.
2. Trade or business interest is deductible.
3. Investment interest is deductible to the extent of investment income.
4. Qualified residence interest is deductible in a limited manner.

I. SELECTING VALUATION DATE FOR ESTATE ACCOUNTS.

1. Date of death.
2. Alternate valuation date (6 months after date of death) will be permitted when:
    a. There is a decrease in the value of gross estate, and
    b. There is a decrease in the sum of the estate and GSTT tax.
3. Consider partial QTIP election. The executor can make a QTIP election on an asset-by-asset basis.

J. DISCLAIMERS.

1. By spouse to children - Reduces overqualification.
2. By children to spouse - Increases use of marital deduction.
3. May disclaim general power of appointment.
4. Must be irrevocable, in writing, and made within 9 months. The disclaiming person must have no direction to passing. The beneficiary disclaiming the property must not have accepted benefits from the property (such as rental income from a rental property) prior to disclaiming the transfer.

K. QUALIFYING TERMINABLE INTEREST PROPERTY.

1. In General.
    a. Generally, a terminable interest to the spouse does not qualify for the marital deduction.
    b. Qualified Terminable Interest Property (QTIP) allows a terminable interest transferred to the spouse to qualify for the unlimited marital deduction.
    c. QTIP is an alternative to the life income interest plus general power of appointment. However, life income interest plus general power of appointment can result in the risk of loss of control of ultimate disposition.
    d. The primary benefit of a QTIP is that the spouse receives the income from the property for life, and the property is able to pass to the beneficiary designated by the decedent.
    e. The QTIP property is usually placed in a QTIP trust.

2. Requirements.
    a. The spouse must receive all income from the property at least annually for life.
    b. The right to the income cannot be contingent.
    c. The executor must make a QTIP election when the estate tax return (Form 706) is filed.
    d. The property must be included in the surviving spouse's gross estate at his or her death.
    e. During the surviving spouse's lifetime, the property cannot be appointed to anyone other than the surviving spouse.
3. Reverse QTIP.
    a. Under GSTT rules, QTIP property included in the surviving spouse's estate is considered transferred by the surviving spouse, not by the decedent. Therefore, if a decedent transfers property into a QTIP trust, and the trust beneficiaries are grandchildren, the decedent will not be allowed to use his or her GSTT exemption. The surviving spouse would be required to use his or her exemption at death.
    b. The Reverse QTIP election is a special election available for GSTT purposes. The election treats the QTIP property as if the QTIP election was not made for GSTT purposes.
    c. The marital deduction will be available for estate tax purposes, but not for GSTT purposes.
    d. The Reverse QTIP election is often made to utilize a decedent's GSTT exemption ($1,120,000 for 2003).

Example

John died in 2003, owning $1,120,000 of property. Upon his death, $1,000,000 of John's assets were transferred to a credit shelter trust, with his grandchildren as the beneficiaries. The remaining $120,000 of John's assets were transferred to a QTIP trust, which qualifies for the marital deduction. The beneficiaries of the QTIP trust are also John's grandchildren. Without a reverse QTIP election, only the assets in the credit shelter trust would be eligible for the GSTT exemption. Therefore, John will have wasted $120,000 of his GSTT exemption.

If a reverse QTIP election is made, the $120,000 of assets transferred to the QTIP trust will still qualify for the marital deduction for estate tax purposes. These assets will not qualify for the marital deduction for GSTT purposes, but John could use his remaining GSTT exemption to avoid any GSTT. Therefore, with a reverse QTIP election, John could fully utilize the GSTT exemption in the year of death.

L. ALTERNATE VALUATION DATE.

1. Executor can make election to value estate six months after date of death, if such election will decrease both the value of the gross estate and the estate tax liability. Under this election, all assets are valued six months after date of death or on their date of disposition if earlier. Alternate valuation applies to all assets, not to specific assets. Three key points:
   a. Executor must make the election to use alternate valuation date.
   b. Election must lower both the gross estate and the estate tax.
   c. Election applies to all assets. There are exceptions for:
      i. Wasting assets, (e.g., annuities, patents, and installment notes) which will be valued at date of death (DOD); and,
      ii. Assets disposed of between the date of death and the alternate valuation date that will be valued at the date of disposal.
2. Since a lower valuation will result in a lower income tax basis to the beneficiary, consideration should be given to the marginal estate tax rate vs. the beneficiary's marginal income tax rate. Further complicating the picture, an assessment should be made on whether the beneficiary intends to sell the asset.
3. All assets disposed of between the date of death and the alternate valuation date are valued on the date of disposition if the alternative valuation date is properly elected.
4. All wasting assets (examples include: annuities that have been annuitized, leases, patents, installment sales, and cash accounts) are valued as of the date of death regardless of selecting the alternate valuation date.

XVI.ESTATE TAX REDUCTION TECHNIQUES

A. DO NOT OVERQUALIFY ESTATE.

Use credit equivalency (See Appendix 1, 2, and 3 for examples).

B. DO NOT UNDERQUALIFY ESTATE.

Use appropriate marital deduction (See Appendix 1, 2, and 3 for examples).

C. REMOVE LIFE INSURANCE FROM ESTATE.

Change ownership or use irrevocable life insurance trust (must remove all incidents of ownership).

D. USE LIFETIME GIFTS.

Annual exclusion with gift splitting.

E. USE BASIC TRUSTS WITH CRUMMEY PROVISIONS.

Remember the 5-and-5 rule and the availability of the annual exclusion for contingent beneficiaries.

F. USE CHARITABLE CONTRIBUTIONS AND TRANSFERS.

CRATs, CRUTs, CLTs, Pooled Income Funds, Private Foundations.

XVII.COMMON ESTATE PLANNING MISTAKES

A. INVALID, OUT-OF-DATE, OR POORLY DRAFTED WILL.

1. Will does not meet statutory requirements. Invalid will makes estate subject to intestacy laws.
2. Will does not contemplate changes in tax laws. Fails to minimize estate taxes because will is out of date.
3. Decedent has moved to another state of residence and domicile. Possibility that the will does not conform to probate laws of new state making estate subject to intestacy laws of new state.
4. Will has no residuary clause or lacks drafting specificities.

B. SIMPLE WILLS ("SWEETHEART" OR "I LOVE YOU" WILLS).

Leaving everything to your spouse. (See Appendix 1, 2, and 3 for examples.)

1. Causes an overqualification of the estate. Fails to take advantage of the applicable exclusion amount for the first spouse who dies. The second spouse to die may pay estate taxes that could have been avoided with a Bypass Trust or bequest.
2. Mismanagement of assets may occur. Assets may be put in the hands of a spouse who does not have the education, experience, training, or desire to manage them efficiently and effectively.

C. IMPROPERLY ARRANGED OR INADEQUATE LIFE INSURANCE.

1. Failure to remove proceeds from estate.
   a. If the insurance policy is owned by the decedent, the proceeds will be included in the estate.
   b. Regardless of ownership, if the decedent has any incidence of ownership in the policy or if the beneficiary is the estate, the proceeds will be included in the estate.
   c. Any transfer within three years of death will be included in the estate.
2. Leaving proceeds directly to beneficiary.
   a. Proceeds left directly to a beneficiary may create a problem if the beneficiary is ill equipped (e.g., emotionally, legal capacity, minor) to receive and manage those assets. A trust may provide the needed management of the insurance proceeds.
   b. If the insurance policy fails to name a successor contingent beneficiary, the proceeds may end up back in the estate where it may be subject to creditor claims, state inheritance laws, or federal estate taxes (or all three).
3. Inadequate life insurance coverage.
   a. The proceeds are inadequate to cover the needs of the insured (survivor needs and estate liquidity needs). Generally, the survivor needs are calculated as the present value of the lost income (net of taxes and decedents consumption) over the remaining work life expectancy. An industry heuristic is to use 10 times salary to offset inflation. However, either or both of these may be inadequate with regards to providing sufficient estate liquidity where the majority of the other assets in the estate are both large in value and illiquid (real estate or a closely held business).
   b. Another approach is to calculate the present value of the lost future earnings.

D. POSSIBLE ADVERSE CONSEQUENCES OF JOINTLY HELD PROPERTY.

1. Joint title may result in state and federal gift and estate tax. If joint title results in a completed gift, consequences may be federal and state gift tax liability.
2. Double estate taxation. For jointly owned property (not by spouses), property value may be included in first decedent's estate, then included in survivor's estate (recall, credit for tax on prior transfer).
3. Property passed by law but not by will, (JTWROS) can thwart the intentions of decedent because property will pass automatically by law.
4. Jointly held property allows survivor to name ultimate remainderman. Decedent may not be able to direct property to person or entity to whom he/she wishes.

E. ESTATE LIQUIDITY PROBLEMS.

1. Insufficient cash assets.
   a. Estate may be forced to liquidate assets at a time when they are not fully valued or have not reached their potential value.
   b. Assets may have to be sold at less than full value.
   c. Closely held businesses may have to be sold to an "outsider" in order to generate the cash to pay the estate tax.
2. Inadequate planning.

   Estate may be forced to liquidate assets at a time when they are not fully valued or have not reached their potential value.

F. WRONG EXECUTOR/TRUSTEE/MANAGER.

Poor estate management always increases costs.

1. Potential conflicts of interest.
2. Proximity problems/family conflict.
3. Named executor/trustee is incapable of administering estate efficiently and effectively.
4. Being an executor is work and the person chosen should be capable and willing.

APPENDIX 1: EXAMPLE 1

(ESTATE TAX CALCULATION)

Kurt Smith has the following assets at his death in 2003:

Boat	$50,000	Owned in his name only.
Note Receivable (present value)	$650,000	Owned in his name only.
Insurance (policy on Kurt at face value)	$125,000	Owned in his name only/spouse beneficiary.
Ranch	$400,000	Owned in his name only.
House	$120,000	Owned jointly with his spouse (JTWROS) FMV = $120,000 (50% = $60,000).
Annuity	$80,000	Payable to his spouse.

* All assets (except the life insurance) are stated at fair market value.

At his death, Kurt also had $60,000 in debts and a $100,000 mortgage on his ranch. His insurance was payable to his spouse. His will gave everything to his daughter and son equally and provided that all debts, expenses, and taxes were to be paid out of his probate residue. The expenses of administering his estate were $40,000. He made no taxable gifts during his life. His estate has no credits against the tax except the applicable credit amount and the state death tax credit. Calculate the net federal estate tax, if any, due on Kurt's estate. Kurt lives in a separate property state.

EXAMPLE 1 - SOLUTION/COMMENT

Estate Tax Formula

(1)	Total gross estate		$1,365,000 **
(2)	Less: Expenses, debts, and losses:		
	(a) Funeral and administrative expenses	$40,000	
	(b) Debts of decedent, mortgages, losses	160,000	$(200,000)
(3)	Equals: Adjusted gross estate (AGE)*		$1,165,000
(4)	Less: Total allowable deductions:		
	(c) Charitable deduction	0	
	(d) Marital deduction	$265,000	
	Total allowable deductions		(265,000)***
(5)	Equals: Taxable estate		$900,000
(6)	Add: Adjusted taxable gifts (post-1976)		0
(7)	Compute: Tentative tax base		$900,000
(8)	Compute: Tentative tax		$306,800
(9)	Subtract: Gift taxes paid on prior transfers		(0)
(10)	Equals: Estate tax before reduction for allowable credits		$306,800
(11)	Subtract:		
	Allowable applicable credit amount (max $345,800)	$306,800	
	Other credits	0	$306,800
(12)	Equals: Estate Tax Liability		$0

COMMENT

No estate tax due, however, nonmarital amount was not maximized.
State inheritance or estate tax may be due, regardless of the federal estate tax liability.

ASSETS

Probate		Nonprobate			
Boat	$ 50,000	Insurance	$125,000	Total Probate	$1,100,000
Note	650,000	House (1/2)	60,000	Total Nonprobate	265,000
Ranch	400,000	Annuity	80,000		
	$1,100,000		$265,000	**Total Estate**	**$1,365,000** **

** Note the $1,365,000 is reconciled to the gross estate.

*** $265,000 qualifies for the marital deduction.

APPENDIX 2: EXAMPLE 2

Kurt Smith has the following assets at his death in 2003*:

Boat	$50,000	Owned in his name only.
Note Receivable (present value)	$650,000	Owned in his name only.
Insurance (policy on Kurt at face value)	$125,000	Owned in his name only/ spouse beneficiary.
Ranch	$400,000	Owned in his name only.
House	$120,000	Owned jointly with his spouse (JTWROS) FMV = $120,000 (50% = $60,000).
Annuity	$80,000	Payable to his spouse.

* All assets (except the life insurance) are stated at fair market value.

At his death, he also had $60,000 in debts and a $100,000 mortgage on his ranch. His insurance was payable to his spouse. His will gave everything to his spouse and provided that all debts, expenses, and taxes were to be paid out of his probate residue. The expenses of administering his estate were $40,000. He made no taxable gifts during his life. His estate has no credits against the tax except the applicable credit amount and the state death tax credit. Calculate the net federal estate tax, if any, due on Kurt's estate. Kurt lives in a separate property state.

EXAMPLE 2 - SOLUTION/COMMENT

Estate Tax Formula

(1)	Total gross estate		$1,365,000**
(2)	Less: Expenses, debts, and losses:		
	(a) Funeral and administrative expenses	$40,000	
	(b) Debts of decedent, mortgages, losses	160,000	(200,000)
(3)	Equals: Adjusted gross estate (AGE)*		$1,165,000
(4)	Less: Total allowable deductions:		
	(c) Charitable deduction	0	
	(d) Marital deduction	$1,165,000***	
	Total allowable deductions		$(1,165,000)
(5)	Equals: Taxable estate		0
(6)	Add: Adjusted taxable gifts (post-1976)		0
(7)	Compute: Tentative tax base		0
(8)	Compute: Tentative tax		0
(9)	Subtract: Gift taxes paid on prior transfers		0
(10)	Equals: Estate tax before reduction for allowable credits		0
(11)	Subtract:		
	Allowable applicable credit amount (max $345,800)	0	
	Other credits	0	0
(12)	Equals: Estate Tax Liability		$0

COMMENT

He has overqualified the estate by $1,000,000, the lesser of the adjusted gross estate or the applicable exclusion amount.

State inheritance or estate tax may be due, regardless of the federal estate tax liability.

ASSETS

Probate		Nonprobate			
Boat	$50,000	Insurance	$125,000	Total Probate	$1,100,000
Note	650,000	House (1/2)	60,000	Total Nonprobate	265,000
Ranch	400,000	Annuity	80,000		
	$1,100,000		$265,000	**Total Estate**	**$1,365,000****

** Note the $1,365,000 is reconciled to the gross estate.

*** While $1,365,000 qualifies for the marital deduction, only $1,165,000 can be used. This is due to the fact that the spouse will only receive $1,165,000 in assets because the assets have been reduced by the expenses, debts, and losses.

APPENDIX 3: EXAMPLE 3

Kurt Smith has the following assets at his death in 2003:

Boat	$50,000	Owned in his name only.
Note Receivable (present value)	$650,000	Owned in his name only.
Insurance (policy on Kurt at face value)	$125,000	Owned in his name only/son and daughter beneficiary.
Ranch	$400,000	Owned in his name only.
House	$120,000	Owned jointly with his spouse but spouse has no right of survivorship. FMV = $120,000 (50% = $60,000).
Annuity	$80,000	Payable to his son and daughter.

At his death, he also had $60,000 in debts and a $100,000 mortgage on his ranch. His insurance was payable to his children. His will gave everything to his son and daughter and provided that all debts, expenses, and taxes were to be paid out of his probate residue. The expenses of administering his estate were $40,000. He made no taxable gifts during his life. His estate has no credits against the tax except the applicable credit amount and the state death tax credit. Calculate the net federal estate tax, if any, due on Kurt's estate. Kurt lives in a separate property state.

EXAMPLE 3 - SOLUTION/COMMENT

Estate Tax Formula

(1)	Total gross estate		$1,365,000**
(2)	Less: Expenses, debts, and losses:		
	(a) Funeral and administrative expenses	$40,000	
	(b) Debts of decedent, mortgages, losses	160,000	(200,000)
(3)	Equals: Adjusted gross estate (AGE)*		$1,165,000
(4)	Less: Total allowable deductions:		
	(c) Charitable deduction	0	
	(d) Marital deduction	0	
	Total allowable deductions		0
(5)	Equals: Taxable estate		$1,165,000
(6)	Add: Adjusted taxable gifts (post-1976)		0
(7)	Compute: Tentative tax base		$1,165,000
(8)	Compute: Tentative tax		$413,450
(9)	Subtract: Gift taxes paid on prior transfers		0
(10)	Equals: Estate tax before reduction for allowable credits		$413,450
(11)	Subtract:		
	Allowable applicable credit amount	$345,800	
	State death tax credit	21,480***	
	Total credits		$(367,280)
(12)	Equals: Federal Estate Tax Liability		$46,170

** See next page.

*** See next page.

COMMENT

The federal estate tax liability of $46,170 was due to the failure to use marital deduction. In addition, a state death tax of $21,480 will be required to be paid, making the total estate tax $67,650.

The state must be paid to receive the credit.

EXAMPLE 3 - SOLUTION/COMMENT (CONTINUED)

ASSETS

Probate		Nonprobate			
Boat	$50,000	Insurance	$125,000	Total Probate	$1,160,000
Note	650,000	Annuity	80,000	Total Nonprobate	205,000
Ranch	400,000	Total	$205,000	**Total Estate**	**$1,365,000** **
House (1/2)	60,000				
Total	$1,160,000				

** Note the $1,365,000 is reconciled to the gross estate.

State Death Tax Credit Section 2011(b)***	
Taxable Estate	$1,165,000
Exemption	(60,000)
Adj. Taxable Income	$1,105,000
State Death Tax Credit =	**$21,480**
[$38,800 + 6.4% (1,105,000 - 1,040,000)] x 50% (for 2003)	

See Table in Section 2011(b) Appendix 6.

APPENDIX 4: EXAMPLE 4 (2003)

Additional assumption added to Example 1.

Kurt Smith had made $1,000,000 of previously taxable gifts in 1996 and paid gift tax of $153,000. Kurt died in 2003.

	Gross estate	$1,365,000	
-	Funeral and admin. exp.	(200,000)	
=	AGE	$1,165,000	
-	Marital deduction	(265,000)	
=	Taxable estate	$900,000	
+	Plus post-76 gifts	1,000,000	
=	Tentative tax base	$1,900,000	
	Tentative tax	$735,800	
-	Previous gift tax paid	(153,000)	= ($345,800 - 192,800; tax at the time of the gift)
=	Estate tax before credit	$582,800	
-	Applicable credit amount	(345,800)	
=	Estate tax liability	$237,000	

APPENDIX 5: EXAMPLE 5 (2003)

Example 5 – same as Example 4 except 1,000,000 gift made in 2001, and gift tax of $125,250 was paid on the gift.

	Gross estate*	$1,490,250	= ($1,365,000 + $125,250)
-	Funeral and admin. exp.	(200,000)	
=	AGE	$1,290,250	
-	Marital deduction	(265,000)	
=	Taxable estate	$1,025,250	
+	Plus post-76 gifts	1,000,000	
=	Tentative tax base	$2,025,250	
	Tentative tax	$793,173	
-	Gift tax paid	(125,250)	= ($345,800 – $220,550)
=	Estate tax before credits	$667,923	
-	Applicable credit amount	(345,800)	
=	Estate tax liability	$322,123	

Note: Difference in tax liability between Example 4 and Example 5 is $85,123. (See reconciliation.)

* Includes $125,250 of the prior gift tax paid.
This is an application of the gross-up rule for gift tax paid on gifts made within three years of death.

APPENDIX 6: MAXIMUM CREDIT AGAINST FEDERAL ESTATE TAX FOR STATE DEATH TAXES PAID (FOR 2003)

If the adjusted * taxable estate is:		The maximum tax credit will be:	
Over (1)	**But not over** (2)	**Tax on** (1)	**Rate on Excess**
$0	$90,000	$0	8/10 of 1% (over $40,000)
$90,000	$140,000	$400	1.6%
$140,000	$240,000	$1,200	2.4%
$240,000	$440,000	$3,600	3.2%
$440,000	$640,000	$10,000	4.0%
$640,000	$840,000	$18,000	4.8%
$840,000	$1,040,000	$27,600	5.6%
$1,040,000	$1,540,000	$38,800	6.4%
$1,540,000	$2,040,000	$70,800	7.2%
$2,040,000	$2,540,000	$106,800	8.0%
$2,540,000	$3,040,000	$146,800	8.8%
$3,040,000	$3,540,000	$190,800	9.6%
$3,540,000	$4,040,000	$238,800	10.4%
$4,040,000	$5,040,000	$290,800	11.2%
$5,040,000	$6,040,000	$402,800	12.0%
$6,040,000	$7,040,000	$522,800	12.8%
$7,040,000	$8,040,000	$650,800	13.6%
$8,040,000	$9,040,000	$786,800	14.4%
$9,040,000	$10,040,000	$930,800	15.2%
Over $10,040,000		$1,082,800	16.0%

* Taxable estate reduced by $60,000. Note: The state death tax credit was reduced in 2002. In 2003, the credit is 50% of the table amount. In 2005, the state death credit will be repealed and replaced with a deduction for death taxes actually paid to any state.

APPENDIX 7: IRS FORM 706

Form **706**

(Rev. August 2002)

Department of the Treasury
Internal Revenue Service

United States Estate (and Generation-Skipping Transfer) Tax Return

Estate of a citizen or resident of the United States (see separate instructions).
To be filed for decedents dying after December 31, 2001, and before January 1, 2003.
For Paperwork Reduction Act Notice, see the separate instructions.

OMB No. 1545-0015

Part 1.—Decedent and Executor

1a Decedent's first name and middle initial (and maiden name, if any)	1b Decedent's last name		2 Decedent's Social Security No.
3a Legal residence (domicile) at time of death (county, state, and ZIP code, or foreign country)	3b Year domicile established	4 Date of birth	5 Date of death
6a Name of executor (see page 3 of the instructions)	6b Executor's address (number and street including apartment or suite no. or rural route; city, town, or post office; state; and ZIP code)		
6c Executor's social security number (see page 3 of the instructions)			
7a Name and location of court where will was probated or estate administered			7b Case number
8 If decedent died testate, check here ▶ ☐ and attach a certified copy of the will.	9 If Form 4768 is attached, check here ▶ ☐		
10 If Schedule R-1 is attached, check here ▶ ☐			

Part 2.—Tax Computation

1	Total gross estate less exclusion (from Part 5, Recapitulation, page 3, item 12)		1
2	Total allowable deductions (from Part 5, Recapitulation, page 3, item 23)		2
3	Taxable estate (subtract line 2 from line 1)		3
4	Adjusted taxable gifts (total taxable gifts (within the meaning of section 2503) made by the decedent after December 31, 1976, other than gifts that are includible in decedent's gross estate (section 2001(b)))		4
5	Add lines 3 and 4		5
6	Tentative tax on the amount on line 5 from Table A on page 4 of the instructions		6
7	Total gift tax payable with respect to gifts made by the decedent after December 31, 1976. Include gift taxes by the decedent's spouse for such spouse's share of split gifts (section 2513) only if the decedent was the donor of these gifts and they are includible in the decedent's gross estate (see instructions)		7
8	Gross estate tax (subtract line 7 from line 6)		8
9	Maximum unified credit (applicable credit amount) against estate tax	9	
10	Adjustment to unified credit (applicable credit amount). (This adjustment may not exceed $6,000. See page 5 of the instructions.)	10	
11	Allowable unified credit (applicable credit amount) (subtract line 10 from line 9)		11
12	Subtract line 11 from line 8 (but do not enter less than zero)		12
13	Credit for state death taxes (cannot exceed line 12). Attach credit evidence (see instructions). Figure the credit by using the amount on line 3 less $60,000. See Table B in the instructions. Enter the amount here from Table B ▶ .... x .75 ▶		13
14	Subtract line 13 from line 12		14
15	Credit for Federal gift taxes on pre-1977 gifts (section 2012) (attach computation)	15	
16	Credit for foreign death taxes (from Schedule(s) P). (Attach Form(s) 706-CE.)	16	
17	Credit for tax on prior transfers (from Schedule Q)	17	
18	Total (add lines 15, 16, and 17)		18
19	Net estate tax (subtract line 18 from line 14)		19
20	Generation-skipping transfer taxes (from Schedule R, Part 2, line 10)		20
21	Total transfer taxes (add lines 19 and 20)		21
22	Prior payments. Explain in an attached statement	22	
23	United States Treasury bonds redeemed in payment of estate tax	23	
24	Total (add lines 22 and 23)		24
25	Balance due (or overpayment) (subtract line 24 from line 21)		25

Under penalties of perjury, I declare that I have examined this return, including accompanying schedules and statements, and to the best of my knowledge and belief, it is true, correct, and complete. Declaration of preparer other than the executor is based on all information of which prepare r has any knowledge.

Signature(s) of executor(s)   Date

Signature of preparer other than executor   Address (and ZIP code)   Date

Cat. No. 20548R

Form 706 (Rev. 8-02)

Estate of:

Part 3—Elections by the Executor

Please check the "Yes" or "No" box for each question. (See instructions beginning on page 6.)		Yes	No
1 Do you elect alternate valuation?	1		
2 Do you elect special use valuation? If "Yes," you must complete and attach Schedule A–1.	2		
3 Do you elect to pay the taxes in installments as described in section 6166? If "Yes," you must attach the additional information described on page 9 of the instructions.	3		
4 Do you elect to postpone the part of the taxes attributable to a reversionary or remainder interest as described in section 6163?	4		

Part 4—General Information

(Note: Please attach the necessary supplemental documents. You must attach the death certificate.) (See instructions on page 10.)

Authorization to receive confidential tax information under Regs. sec. 601.504(b)(2)(i); to act as the estate's representative before the IRS; and to make written or oral presentations on behalf of the estate if return prepared by an attorney, accountant, or enrolled agent for the executor :

Name of representative (print or type)	State	Address (number, street, and room or suite no., city, state, and ZIP code)

I declare that I am the ☐ attorney/ ☐ certified public accountant/ ☐ enrolled agent (you must check the applicable box) for the executor and prepared this return for the executor. I am not under suspension or disbarment from practice before the Internal Revenue Service and am qualified to practice in the state shown above.

Signature	CAF number	Date	Telephone number

1 Death certificate number and issuing authority (attach a copy of the death certificate to this return).

2 Decedent's business or occupation. If retired, check here ▶ ☐ and state decedent's former business or occupation.

3 Marital status of the decedent at time of death:

☐ Married

☐ Widow or widower—Name, SSN, and date of death of deceased spouse ▶

☐ Single

☐ Legally separated

☐ Divorced—Date divorce decree became final ▶

4a Surviving spouse's name	4b Social security number	4c Amount received (see page 10 of the instructions)

5 Individuals (other than the surviving spouse), trusts, or other estates who receive benefits from the estate (do not include charitable beneficiaries shown in Schedule O) (see instructions). For Privacy Act Notice (applicable to individual beneficiaries only), see the Instructions for Form 1040.

Name of individual, trust, or estate receiving $5,000 or more	Identifying number	Relationship to decedent	Amount (see instructions)
All unascertainable beneficiaries and those who receive less than $5,000 ▶			
Total			

Please check the "Yes" or "No" box for each question.	Yes	No
6 Does the gross estate contain any section 2044 property (qualified terminable interest property (QTIP) from a prior gift or estate) (see page 10 of the instructions)?		

(continued on next page)

Page 2

Form 706 (Rev. 8-02)

Part 4—General Information (continued)

Please check the "Yes" or "No" box for each question.	Yes	No
7a Have Federal gift tax returns ever been filed? If "Yes," please attach copies of the returns, if available, and furnish the following information:		
7b Period(s) covered / 7c Internal Revenue office(s) where filed		
If you answer "Yes" to any of questions 8 –16, you must attach additional information as described in the instructions.		
8a Was there any insurance on the decedent's life that is not included on the return as part of the gross estate?		
b Did the decedent own any insurance on the life of another that is not included in the gross estate?		
9 Did the decedent at the time of death own any property as a joint tenant with right of survivorship in which (a) one or more of the other joint tenants was someone other than the decedent 's spouse, and (b) less than the full value of the property is included on the return as part of the gross estate? If "Yes," you must complete and attach Schedule E		
10 Did the decedent, at the time of death, own any interest in a partnership or unincorporated business or any stock in an inactiv e or closely held corporation?		
11 Did the decedent make any transfer described in section 2035, 2036, 2037, or 2038 (see the instructions for Schedule G beginning on page 12 of the separate instructions)? If "Yes," you must complete and attach Schedule G		
12 Were there in existence at the time of the decedent 's death:		
a Any trusts created by the decedent during his or her lifetime?		
b Any trusts not created by the decedent under which the decedent possessed any power, beneficial interest, or trusteeship?		
13 Did the decedent ever possess, exercise, or release any general power of appointment? If "Yes," you must complete and attach Sched		
14 Was the marital deduction computed under the transitional rule of Public Law 97-34, section 403(e)(3) (Economic Recovery Tax Act of 1981)? If "Yes," attach a separate computation of the marital deduction, enter the amount on item 20 of the Recapitulation, and note on item 20 "computation attached."		
15 Was the decedent, immediately before death, receiving an annuity described in the "General" paragraph of the instructions for Schedule I? If "Yes," you must complete and attach Schedule I		
16 Was the decedent ever the beneficiary of a trust for which a deduction was claimed by the estate of a pre-deceased spouse under section 2056(b)(7) and which is not reported on this return? If "Yes," attach an explanation		

Part 5—Recapitulation

Item number	Gross estate		Alternate value	Value at date of death
1	Schedule A—Real Estate	1		
2	Schedule B—Stocks and Bonds	2		
3	Schedule C—Mortgages, Notes, and Cash	3		
4	Schedule D—Insurance on the Decedent's Life (attach Form(s) 712)	4		
5	Schedule E—Jointly Owned Property (attach Form(s) 712 for life insurance)	5		
6	Schedule F—Other Miscellaneous Property (attach Form(s) 712 for life insurance)	6		
7	Schedule G—Transfers During Decedent's Life (att. Form(s) 712 for life insurance)	7		
8	Schedule H—Powers of Appointment	8		
9	Schedule I—Annuities	9		
10	Total gross estate (add items 1 through 9)	10		
11	Schedule U—Qualified Conservation Easement Exclusion	11		
12	Total gross estate less exclusion (subtract item 11 from item 10). Enter here and on line 1 of Part 2—Tax Computation	12		

Item number	Deductions		Amount
13	Schedule J—Funeral Expenses and Expenses Incurred in Administering Property Subject to Claims	13	
14	Schedule K—Debts of the Decedent	14	
15	Schedule K—Mortgages and Liens	15	
16	Total of items 13 through 15	16	
17	Allowable amount of deductions from item 16 (see the instructions for item 17 of the Recapitulation)	17	
18	Schedule L—Net Losses During Administration	18	
19	Schedule L—Expenses Incurred in Administering Property Not Subject to Claims	19	
20	Schedule M—Bequests, etc., to Surviving Spouse	20	
21	Schedule O—Charitable, Public, and Similar Gifts and Bequests	21	
22	Schedule T—Qualified Family-Owned Business Interest Deduction	22	
23	Total allowable deductions (add items 17 through 22). Enter here and on line 2 of the Tax Computation	23	

Page 3

APPENDIX 8: IRS FORM 709

Form **709** — Department of the Treasury, Internal Revenue Service

United States Gift (and Generation-Skipping Transfer) Tax Return

(Section 6019 of the Internal Revenue Code) (For gifts made during calendar year 2002)

▶ See separate instructions.

OMB No. 1545-0020 — **2002**

Part 1—General Information

1 Donor's first name and middle initial	2 Donor's last name	3 Donor's social security number
4 Address (number, street, and apartment number)		5 Legal residence (domicile) (county and state)
6 City, state, and ZIP code		7 Citizenship

		Yes	No
8	If the donor died during the year, check here ▶ ☐ and enter date of death .... , ...		
9	If you received an extension of time to file this Form 709, check here ▶ ☐ and attach the Form 4868, 2688, 2350, or extension letter		
10	Enter the total number of donees listed on Schedule A—count each person only once. ▶		
11a	Have you (the donor) previously filed a Form 709 (or 709-A) for any other year? If the answer is "No," do not complete line 11b		
11b	If the answer to line 11a is "Yes," has your address changed since you last filed Form 709 (or 709-A)?		
12	Gifts by husband or wife to third parties.—Do you consent to have the gifts (including generation-skipping transfers) made by you and by your spouse to third parties during the calendar year considered as made one-half by each of you? (See instructions.) (If the answer is "Yes," the following information must be furnished and your spouse must sign the consent shown below. If the answer is "No," skip lines 13–18 and go to Schedule A.)		
13	Name of consenting spouse — 14 SSN		
15	Were you married to one another during the entire calendar year? (see instructions)		
16	If the answer to 15 is "No," check whether ☐ married ☐ divorced or ☐ widowed, and give date (see instructions) ▶		
17	Will a gift tax return for this calendar year be filed by your spouse?		

18 Consent of Spouse— I consent to have the gifts (and generation-skipping transfers) made by me and by my spouse to third parties during the calendar year considered as made one-half by each of us. We are both aware of the joint and several liability for tax created by the execution of this consent.

Consenting spouse's signature ▶ Date ▶

Part 2—Tax Computation

1	Enter the amount from Schedule A, Part 3, line 15	1		
2	Enter the amount from Schedule B, line 3	2		
3	Total taxable gifts (add lines 1 and 2)	3		
4	Tax computed on amount on line 3 (see Table for Computing Tax in separate instructions)	4		
5	Tax computed on amount on line 2 (see Table for Computing Tax in separate instructions)	5		
6	Balance (subtract line 5 from line 4)	6		
7	Maximum unified credit (nonresident aliens, see instructions)	7	345,800	00
8	Enter the unified credit against tax allowable for all prior periods (from Sch. B, line 1, col. C)	8		
9	Balance (subtract line 8 from line 7)	9		
10	Enter 20% (.20) of the amount allowed as a specific exemption for gifts made after September 8, 1976, and before January 1, 1977 (see instructions)	10		
11	Balance (subtract line 10 from line 9)	11		
12	Unified credit (enter the smaller of line 6 or line 11)	12		
13	Credit for foreign gift taxes (see instructions)	13		
14	Total credits (add lines 12 and 13)	14		
15	Balance (subtract line 14 from line 6) (do not enter less than zero)	15		
16	Generation-skipping transfer taxes (from Schedule C, Part 3, col. H, Total)	16		
17	Total tax (add lines 15 and 16)	17		
18	Gift and generation-skipping transfer taxes prepaid with extension of time to file	18		
19	If line 18 is less than line 17, enter balance due (see instructions)	19		
20	If line 18 is greater than line 17, enter amount to be refunded	20		

Attach check or money order here.

Sign Here — Under penalties of perjury, I declare that I have examined this return, including any accompanying schedules and statements, and to the best of my knowledge and belief, it is true, correct, and complete. Declaration of preparer (other than donor) is based on all information of which preparer has any knowledge.

▶ Signature of donor — Date

Paid Preparer's Use Only — Preparer's signature ▶ — Date — Check if self-employed ▶ ☐

Firm's name (or yours if self-employed), address, and ZIP code ▶ — Phone no. ▶ ( )

For Disclosure, Privacy Act, and Paperwork Reduction Act Notice, see page 12 of the separate instructions for this form. Cat. No. 16783M Form 709 (2002)

Form 709 (2002) Page 2

SCHEDULE A Computation of Taxable Gifts (Including Transfers in Trust)

A Does the value of any item listed on Schedule A reflect any valuation discount? If the answer is "Yes," see instructions. . Yes ☐ No ☐

B ☐ ◄ Check here if you elect under section 529(c)(2)(B) to treat any transfers made this year to a qualified state tuition program as made ratably over a 5-year period beginning this year. See instructions. Attach explanation.

Part 1—Gifts Subject Only to Gift Tax. Gifts less political organization, medical, and educational exclusions—see instructions

A Item number	B • Donee's name and address • Relationship to donor (if any) • Description of gift • If the gift was made by means of a trust, enter trust 's EIN and attach a description or copy of the trust instrument (see instructions) • If the gift was of securities, give CUSIP number	C Donor's adjusted basis of gift	D Date of gift	E Value at date of gift
1				

Total of Part 1 (add amounts from Part 1, column E) . . . . ▶

Part 2—Gifts That are Direct Skips and are Subject to Both Gift Tax and Generation-Skipping Transfer Tax. You must list the gifts in chronological order. Gifts less political organization, medical, and educational exclusions—see instructions. (Also list here direct skips that are subject only to the GST tax at this time as the result of the termination of an "estate tax inclusion period." See ins tructions.)

A Item number	B • Donee's name and address • Relationship to donor (if any) • Description of gift • If the gift was made by means of a trust, enter trust 's EIN and attach a description or copy of the trust instrument (see instructions) • If the gift was of securities, give CUSIP number	C Donor's adjusted basis of gift	D Date of gift	E Value at date of gift
1				

Total of Part 2 (add amounts from Part 2, column E) . . . . ▶

Part 3—Taxable Gift Reconciliation

1	Total value of gifts of donor (add totals from column E of Parts 1 and 2)	1	
2	One-half of items .... attributable to spouse (see instructions)	2	
3	Balance (subtract line 2 from line 1)	3	
4	Gifts of spouse to be included (from Schedule A, Part 3, line 2 of spouse 's return—see instructions) . .	4	
	If any of the gifts included on this line are also subject to the generation-skipping transfer tax, check here ▶ ☐ and enter those gifts also on Schedule C, Part 1.		
5	Total gifts (add lines 3 and 4)	5	
6	Total annual exclusions for gifts listed on Schedule A (including line 4, above) (see instructions) . . .	6	
7	Total included amount of gifts (subtract line 6 from line 5)	7	
	Deductions (see instructions)		
8	Gifts of interests to spouse for which a marital deduction will be claimed, based on items .... of Schedule A 8		
9	Exclusions attributable to gifts on line 8 9		
10	Marital deduction—subtract line 9 from line 8 10		
11	Charitable deduction, based on items ....less exclusions . . 11		
12	Total deductions—add lines 10 and 11	12	
13	Subtract line 12 from line 7	13	
14	Generation-skipping transfer taxes payable with this Form 709 (from Schedule C, Part 3, col. H, Total) .	14	
15	Taxable gifts (add lines 13 and 14). Enter here and on line 1 of the Tax Computation on page 1 . . .	15	

(If more space is needed, attach additional sheets of same size.) Form 709 (2002)

Form 709 (2002) Page 3

SCHEDULE A Computation of Taxable Gifts (continued)

16 Terminable Interest (QTIP) Marital Deduction. (See instructions for line 8 of Schedule A.)

If a trust (or other property) meets the requirements of qualified terminable interest property under section 2523(f), and

a. The trust (or other property) is listed on Schedule A, and

b. The value of the trust (or other property) is entered in whole or in part as a deduction on line 8, Part 3 of Schedule A,

then the donor shall be deemed to have made an election to have such trust (or other property) treated as qualified terminable interest property under section 2523(f).

If less than the entire value of the trust (or other property) that the donor has included in Part 1 of Schedule A is entered as a deduction on line 8, the donor shall be considered to have made an election only as to a fraction of the trust (or other property). The numerator of this fraction is equal to the amount of the trust (or other property) deducted on line 10 of Part 3, Schedule A. The denominator is equal to the total value of the trust (or other property) listed in Part 1 of Schedule A.

If you make the QTIP election (see instructions for line 8 of Schedule A), the terminable interest property involved will be included in your spouse's gross estate upon his or her death (section 2044). If your spouse disposes (by gift or otherwise) of all or part of the qualifying life income interest, he or she will be considered to have made a transfer of the entire property that is subject to the gift tax (see Transfer of Certain Life Estates on page 4 of the instructions).

17 Election Out of QTIP Treatment of Annuities

☐ ◄ Check here if you elect under section 2523(f)(6) NOT to treat as qualified terminable interest property any joint and survivor annuities that are reported on Schedule A and would otherwise be treated as qualified terminable interest property under section 2523(f). (See instructions.) Enter the item numbers (from Schedule A) for the annuities for which you are making this election ►

SCHEDULE B Gifts From Prior Periods

If you answered "Yes" on line 11a of page 1, Part 1, see the instructions for completing Schedule B. If you answered "No," skip to the Tax Computation on page 1 (or Schedule C, if applicable).

A Calendar year or calendar quarter (see instructions)	B Internal Revenue office where prior return was filed	C Amount of unified credit against gift tax for periods after December 31, 1976	D Amount of specific exemption for prior periods ending before January 1, 1977	E Amount of taxable gifts
1 Totals for prior periods	1			
2 Amount, if any, by which total specific exemption, line 1, column D, is more than $30,000			2	
3 Total amount of taxable gifts for prior periods (add amount, column E, line 1, and amount, if any, on line 2). (Enter here and on line 2 of the Tax Computation on page 1.)			3	

(If more space is needed, attach additional sheets of same size.) Form 709 (2002)

Form 709 (2002) Page 4

SCHEDULE C Computation of Generation-Skipping Transfer Tax

Note: Inter vivos direct skips that are completely excluded by the GST exemption must still be fully reported (including value and exemptions claimed) on Schedule C.

Part 1—Generation-Skipping Transfers

A Item No. (from Schedule A, Part 2, col. A)	B Value (from Schedule A, Part 2, col. E)	C Split Gifts (enter ½ of col. B) (see instructions)	D Subtract col. C from col. B	E Nontaxable portion of transfer	F Net Transfer (subtract col. E from col. D)
1					
2					
3					
4					
5					
6					

If you elected gift splitting and your spouse was required to file a separate Form 709 (see the instructions for "Split Gifts"), you must enter all of the gifts shown on Schedule A, Part 2, of your spouse's Form 709 here.

In column C, enter the item number of each gift in the order it appears in column A of your spouse's Schedule A, Part 2. We have preprinted the prefix "S-" to distinguish your spouse's item numbers from your own when you complete column A of Schedule C, Part 3.

In column D, for each gift, enter the amount reported in column C, Schedule C, Part 1, of your spouse's Form 709.

Split gifts from spouse's Form 709 (enter item number)	Value included from spouse's Form 709	Nontaxable portion of transfer	Net transfer (subtract col. E from col. D)
S-			
S-			
S-			
S-			
S-			
S-			
S-			
S-			

Part 2—GST Exemption Reconciliation (Section 2631) and Section 2652(a)(3) Election

Check box ▶ ☐ if you are making a section 2652(a)(3) (special QTIP) election (see instructions)

Enter the item numbers (from Schedule A) of the gifts for which you are making this election ▶ ....

1	Maximum allowable exemption (see instructions)	1	
2	Total exemption used for periods before filing this return	2	
3	Exemption available for this return (subtract line 2 from line 1)	3	
4	Exemption claimed on this return (from Part 3, col. C total, below)	4	
5	Exemption allocated to transfers not shown on Part 3, below. You must attach a Notice of Allocation. (See instructions.)	5	
6	Add lines 4 and 5	6	
7	Exemption available for future transfers (subtract line 6 from line 3)	7	

Part 3—Tax Computation

A Item No. (from Schedule C, Part 1)	B Net transfer (from Schedule C, Part 1, col. F)	C GST Exemption Allocated	D Divide col. C by col. B	E Inclusion Ratio (subtract col. D from 1.000)	F Maximum Estate Tax Rate	G Applicable Rate (multiply col. E by col. F)	H Generation-Skipping Transfer Tax (multiply col. B by col. G)
1					50% (.50)		
2					50% (.50)		
3					50% (.50)		
4					50% (.50)		
5					50% (.50)		
6					50% (.50)		
					50% (.50)		
					50% (.50)		
					50% (.50)		
					50% (.50)		
Total exemption claimed. Enter here and on line 4, Part 2, above. May not exceed line 3, Part 2, above			Total generation-skipping transfer tax. Enter here, on line 14 of Schedule A, Part 3, and on line 16 of the Tax Computation on page 1				

(If more space is needed, attach additional sheets of same size.) Form 709 (2002)

INDEX

M

N

O

P

Q

R

S

T

U

V

W

X

NOTES

NOTES

NOTES

NOTES

NOTES

NOTES

NOTES

NOTES

NOTES

NOTES

NOTES

NOTES

NOTES

NOTES